CANADA

Lake Superior

MAINE
1820

VT.
1791

N.H.

MASS.

CONN.

R.I.

NNESOTA
1858

WISCONSIN
1848

Lake Michigan

Lake Huron

MICHIGAN
1837

Lake Ontario

Lake Erie

NEW YORK

St. Lawrence R.

IOWA
1846

PENNSYLVANIA

THIRTEEN COLONIES

NEW
JERSEY

1790

ILLINOIS
1818

INDIANA
1816

OHIO
1803

MASON-DIXON LINE

DELAWARE

MARYLAND

MISSOURI
1821

KENTUCKY
1792

WEST
VIRGINIA
1863

VIRGINIA

ATLANTIC

2010

THE ORIGINAL UNITED STATES
(By Treaty with Britain, 1783)

THE ORIGINAL

OCEAN

36°30'N
MISSOURI
COMPROMISE
LINE

TENNESSEE
1796

NORTH
CAROLINA

ARKANSAS
1836

Mississippi R.

MISSISSIPPI
1817

ALABAMA
1819

SOUTH
CAROLINA

GEORGIA

Territorial Growth
of the
United States

LOUISIANA
1812

1820 Date of states admission to the Union
● Geographic center of population by decade

(Seized from Spain,
1810, 1813)

FLORIDA
(By Treaty with
Spain, 1819)

0   150   300 Km.

0   150   300 Mi.

FLORIDA
1845

Gulf of Mexico

BAHAMAS

PUERTO RICO
(Acquired from
Spain, 1898)

VIRGIN IS.
(Acquired from
Denmark, 1916–1917)

19°N

68°W

PUERTO RICO

VIRGIN
ISLANDS

18°N

0   25   50 Km.

0   25   50 Mi.

67°W

66°W

65°W

CUBA

DOMINICAN
REPUBLIC

HAITI

90°W   80°W   70°W

D0782609

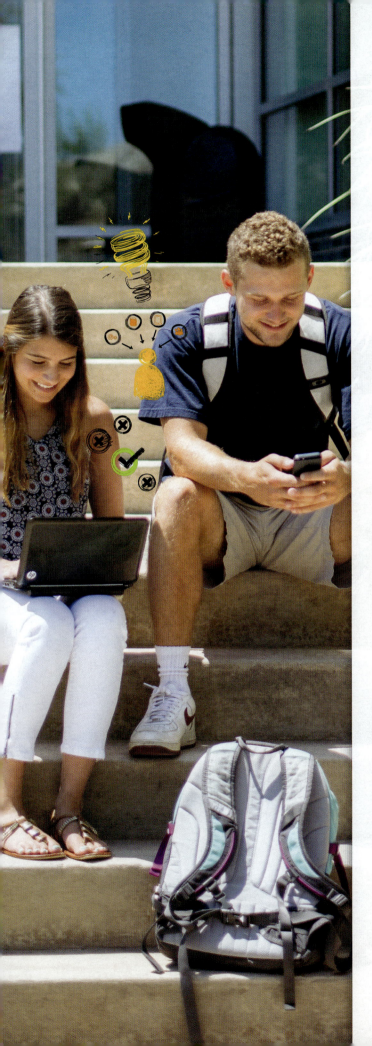

CENGAGE brain.com

CengageBrain.com is the smart move when it comes to getting the right stuff on time, every time. Whether you rent or buy, we'll save you time, money, and frustration.

- **You've Got Options:** Convenient digital solutions and textbooks the way you want them — to buy or rent.

- **You Get Access:** Anytime, anywhere access of digital products, eBooks, and eChapters, on your desktop, laptop, or phone.

- **You Get Free Stuff:** Free 14-day eBook access, free shipping on orders of $25 or more, free study tools like flashcards and quizzes, and a free trial period for most digital products.

Look, we get it. You've got a full schedule — we've got your back(pack). Get what you need to get the grades at CengageBrain.com

Want to turn C's into A's?

Obviously, right?

But the right way to go about it isn't always so obvious. Go digital to get the grades. MindTap's customizable study tools and eTextbook give you everything you need all in one place.

Engage with your course content, enjoy the flexibility of studying anytime and anywhere, stay connected to assignment due dates and instructor notifications with the MindTap Mobile app...

and most of all... **EARN BETTER GRADES.**

TO GET STARTED VISIT
WWW.CENGAGE.COM/STUDENTS/MINDTAP

CENGAGE Learning® | MindTap®

GLOBAL AMERICANS

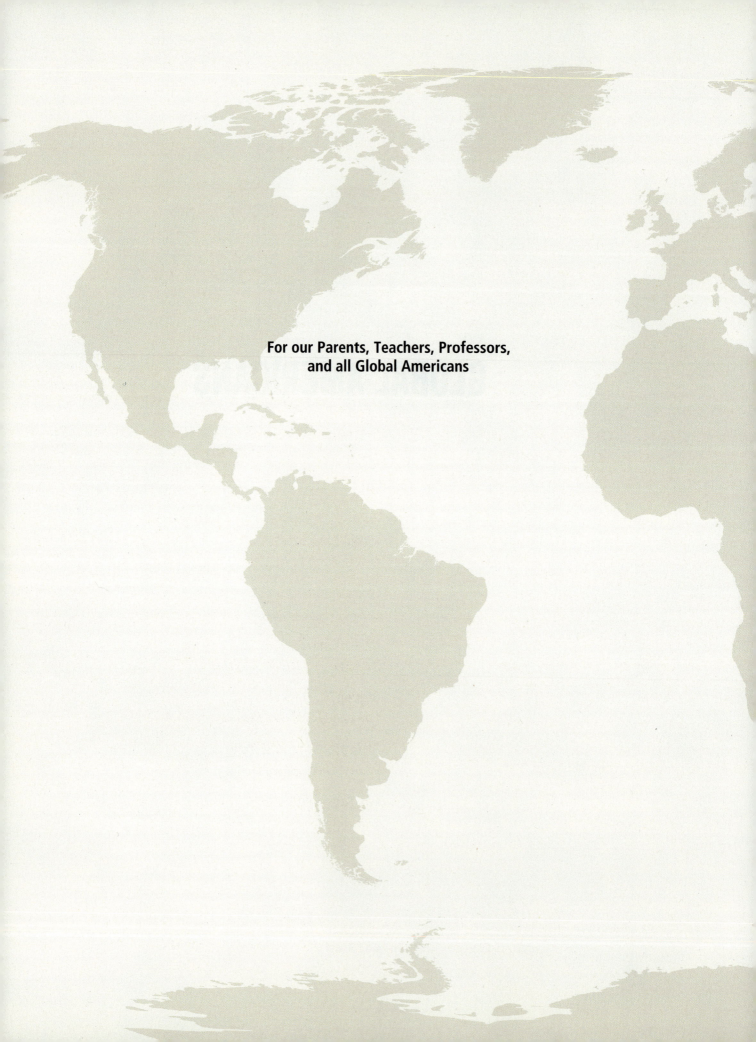

For our Parents, Teachers, Professors,
and all Global Americans

GLOBAL
AMERICANS

A History of the United States

Maria E. Montoya
New York University

Laura A. Belmonte
Oklahoma State University

Carl J. Guarneri
Saint Mary's College of Californina

Steven W. Hackel
University of California, Riverside

Ellen Hartigan-O'Connor
University of California, Davis

Lon Kurashige
University of Southern California

Australia • Brazil • Mexico • Singapore • United Kingdom • United States

Global Americans: A History of the United States

Maria E. Montoya / Laura A. Belmonte /
Carl J. Guarneri / Steven W. Hackel /
Ellen Hartigan-O'Connor / Lon Kurashige

Product Director: Paul Banks

Product Manager: Joseph Potvin

Managing Content Developer:
Anais Wheeler

Content Developer: Erika Hayden

Associate Content Developer:
Andrew Newton

Product Assistant: Emma Guiton

Senior Marketing Manager:
Valerie Hartman

Senior Content Project Manager:
Carol Newman

Senior Art Director: Cate Barr

Manufacturing Planner: Fola Orekoya

IP Analyst: Alexandra Ricciardi

IP Project Manager: Erika Mugavin

Production Service / Compositor:
SPi Global

Text Designer: Jeanne Calabrese

Cover Designer: Nilou Moochhala /
NYM Design

Cover Image: (left to right) Milton
Friedman (Keystone/Hulton Archive/
Getty Images), Hedy Lamarr (Silver Screen
Collection/Hulton Archive/Moviepix/
Getty Images), Sarah Mar'gru (William
H. Townsend, Sketches of the Amistad
Captives. General Collection, Beinecke
Rare Book and Manuscript Library,
Yale University), Samson Occam (The
Reverend Mr Samson Occom, engraved
by Jonathan Spilsbury, 1768 (mezzotint),
Chamberlin, Mason (1727-87) (after) /
Private Collection / © Michael Graham-
Stewart / Bridgeman Images), Florence
Kelly ("Underwood & Underwood/
Corbis), James Baldwin (Library of
Congress Prints and Photographs
Division[LC-USZ62-42481])

© 2018 Cengage Learning

WCN: 01-100-101

ALL RIGHTS RESERVED. No part of this work covered by the copyright
herein may be reproduced, transmitted, stored, or used in any form
or by any means graphic, electronic, or mechanical, including but
not limited to photocopying, recording, scanning, digitizing, taping,
web distribution, information networks, or information storage
and retrieval systems, except as permitted under Section 107 or 108
of the 1976 United States Copyright Act, without the prior written
permission of the publisher.

For product information and technology assistance, contact us at
Cengage Learning Customer & Sales Support, 1-800-354-9706
For permission to use material from this text or product,
submit all requests online at **www.cengage.com/permissions**.
Further permissions questions can be emailed to
permissionrequest@cengage.com.

Library of Congress Control Number: 2016951291

Student Edition:
ISBN: 978-0-618-83310-8

Cengage Learning
20 Channel Center Street
Boston, MA 02210
USA

Cengage Learning is a leading provider of customized learning
solutions with employees residing in nearly 40 different countries
and sales in more than 125 countries around the world. Find your
local representative at **www.cengage.com**.

Cengage Learning products are represented in Canada by Nelson
Education, Ltd.

To learn more about Cengage Learning Solutions, visit
www.cengage.com.

Purchase any of our products at your local college store or at our
preferred online store **www.cengagebrain.com**.

Printed in the United States of America
Print Number: 01 Print Year: 2016

Brief Contents

Contents

Maps & Features

History Without Borders

Global Americans

Timelines

Preface

Global Americans embodies a new, internationalized approach to American history. In their form and content, most textbooks portray the United States as a national enterprise that developed largely in isolation from the main currents of world history. In contrast, this textbook speaks to an increasingly diverse population of students and instructors who seek to understand the nation's place in a constantly changing global, social, and political landscape. It incorporates a growing body of scholarship that documents how for five centuries North America's history has been subject to transnational forces and enmeshed in overseas activities and developments.

American history was global in the beginning, and it has been ever since. We therefore present a history of the United States and its Native American and colonial antecedents in which world events and processes are central features, not just colorful but peripheral sidelights. Our narrative is meant to show how at each stage of its unfolding, the American story was shaped by exchanges of goods, people, and ideas with others, and in turn how Americans exerted growing influence abroad. This enlarged American history is intended to break down curricular walls that discourage connections between U.S. and world history. Its globally informed narrative also aims to capture more accurately how Americans have actually experienced their lives in the past as well as the present.

Students today face a world that is rapidly changing with stepped-up exchanges of ideas and goods that reshape the economy; new technologies that transform work and communication; global conflicts over ideologies and religions; and political and economic developments that challenge the United States' role in the world. We believe that history students need a narrative that recovers the global contexts of America's past and helps them understand the origins of the interconnected world in which we live. *Global Americans* weaves together stories, analysis, interpretation, and visual imagery from across time and place to craft a new American history that develops in relation to events and peoples across this continent and beyond. While integrating this enlarged geographic coverage into our narrative, we have taken care not to sacrifice the detailed coverage of domestic events that are keys to the nation's history and to include consideration of the distinctive features and ideas that have shaped that history.

World history narratives sometimes neglect the human element in favor of describing economic systems and impersonal forces. *Global Americans* instead focuses on people. Our narrative is committed to integrating the experiences of Americans whose stories are often omitted from U.S. history courses because they are somehow deemed foreign or because they represented minority voices. We also cast new light on familiar figures and events by placing them in a global or transnational context. *Global Americans* reflects our belief that different groups of people have had, and still have, claims to being American and part of U.S. history. The narrative of American history is enriched by exploring the world of Native Americans prior to their contact with Europeans and Africans, as well as examining the full range of Spanish, French, Dutch, and English colonial projects for trade and settlement. Just as we do not see global contexts as incidental to this history, we do not portray the period prior to the founding of the United States as simply a prelude to nationhood. The colonial history of North America is the story of a place laid claim to by various peoples and governments. Including its diversity of actors and aspirations adds contingency to a national story that is often told as if destined or preordained. After the United States achieved independence, its history similarly underwent a process of conflict and experiment in the context of international and local events and people. The nation's territorial spread, its mix of peoples, and its global position were forged in the crucible of powerful domestic and international influences. Today's Americans experience the effects of both the local and the global as they work, play, worship, consume, travel, and wage war or peace. We have aimed to construct a historical narrative that does justice to the dramatic conflicts, diverse peoples, and myriad connections that have created our American world.

What's New About This Textbook?

A global perspective informs the presentation of the essential social, economic, religious, and political themes of American history.

Global Context

U.S. history textbooks have traditionally conceptualized American history as distinct and standing apart from the rest of the world, with events beyond its borders acknowledged almost solely through U.S. foreign policy and wars. Yet recent scholarship has emphasized how the United States has considered global social, economic, and cultural factors, and historians have highlighted the role of the United States in the world. Engaging this expanded notion of U.S. history requires a new look at the United States as a nation with a web of worldwide connections.

We build on this scholarship by suggesting that borders have historically been porous and fluid and that demographics have constantly shifted from the precolonial era to the present. We show that the early history of North America was created by the intersections of Atlantic, Pacific, Indian, and African history, as well as one element in Europe's expansion during the early modern era. Thus, the experiences of Indians, the Spanish, the French, the Dutch, and the English all figure prominently in the early chapters. We consider transatlantic slavery and the diaspora of African peoples as part of a thousand-year saga that is not limited to the history of North America or the United States. We continue the focus on migration and diverse populations throughout the nineteenth- and twentieth-century chapters, and we give special attention to commerce and trade and the ways in which technology, culture, and ideas are transmitted across national boundaries. With a global perspective, the narrative of U.S. history connects to the rest of the world not only through the actions of presidents, generals, and diplomats, but also through the experiences of business leaders, social activists, missionaries, workers, immigrants, refugees, athletes, musicians, artists, tourists, and consumers.

At the same time, the core narrative of American political, economic, and social history constitutes the spine of *Global Americans*. Our work covers all the major domestic trends and events and highlights all the familiar players. Presidents and presidential elections serve to mark eras and change over time. Students will always know that they are situated in the broadly familiar terrain of U.S. history. But the traditional narrative looks different within a global context, and this informs the other themes that run through the book.

A Continental Nation

Global context necessitates a continental orientation. Our work takes seriously that the history of all parts of the nation and its territories matters, not just the regions formally incorporated into the United States during the Revolutionary War. What happened before the United States became a nation had important consequences for the society that would later develop. For example, we want our students to understand how California Indians experienced the Franciscan missions, how Spanish soldiers and settlers reacted to life in this distant frontier, and how North American regions settled by Spain differed from New France or British North America. We also want our students to understand how the peoples and lands of the trans-Mississippi West were and were not incorporated into the United States during the nineteenth and twentieth centuries. Our focus on the American West, on the nation's continental borderlands, and on its territories, including Alaska and Hawai'i, provides new perspectives on westward migration, the slavery controversy, railroads and industrialization, and the centrality of California to modern American culture.

One of the most important recent intellectual developments in history has been the move to view the Atlantic World as a loosely integrated region with connections that transcend nation-states and national boundaries. Just as we chronicle the integration of the Americas into an Atlantic system of politics, commerce, and culture during the Age of European Expansion, we similarly treat the Pacific Ocean and the lands adjacent to it as an integrated region that has long affected American history. Seeing the U.S. East and West coasts as elements within their respective oceanic communities reinforces our global integration framework.

Diversity in Global and Continental Contexts

Global integration and a continental orientation allow a fresh look at issues of race, class, and gender. In recent decades, historians and their textbooks have given much consideration to racial and ethnic minorities, the lives of working people, and the roles of women, yet they have been slower to advance an interpretive framework that presents U.S. history from their varying points of view and acknowledges multiple perspectives within these groups. In contrast, we examine what it looked like to live through events in U.S. history from different perspectives; we explore diversity *within* the categories of race, ethnicity, and class; and we situate movements for women's rights and LGBT rights within national and transnational contexts. For example, we discuss the very different impact the diffusion of European consumer goods in the eighteenth century had on the lives and politicization of free women, enslaved women, and Cherokee women. In an example from the nineteenth century, we describe the roles played by the *Californio*, *Tejano*, and New Mexican *Hispano* elite in the economic and political conquest of the Southwest by the United States during the 1830s and 1840s, and we examine the ways colonialism affected women and families in this region. During the twentieth century, we place World War II in the context of worldwide, concurrent racial ideologies and situate the U.S. civil rights movement in the context of global struggles for human rights. We also look at the rise of politically conservative Christian activity in light of rising religious fundamentalism worldwide.

Format for Each Chapter

Global Perspective

Each chapter deliberately embeds a global framework in the text and in the features. The opening vignette sets the focus by making global connections, and the chapter introduction deliberately surveys the global context of the chapter's time frame. This global context is reinforced in presentation of events and people throughout the chapter text and reiterated at the end of the chapter in a summary and globalized timeline. The strategy for achieving a global perspective derives from what we have come to call, during the book's development, the Five Cs: comparisons, connections, concepts, contexts, and consequences. Different national experiences are *compared. Connections* among international social movements are examined as are theories and models concerning, for example, revolutions, nation building, industrialization, imperialism, feminism, and racism. We look at the broad international *contexts* for what seem to be internal developments, such as the American Revolution and Progressivism. We track worldwide *consequences* for what seem to be American events—plantation slavery and commercial cotton, for example, or Henry Ford's moving assembly line—as well as the impacts of international ideas and events on America's history.

Opening Vignette

Each chapter opens with a story of an individual who has crossed borders—in geography, national boundaries, culture, or identity—and whose experience exemplifies the book's global integration framework.

Visual Headings

Each section within a chapter opens with an image that signals the content that follows. These photos, cartoons, paintings, and objects of material culture prompt students to connect, understand, and remember major points and ideas. An informative caption directs interpretation of the image and promotes visual learning. For example, in the book's first chapter, the "Open Hand" symbol of the Eastern Woodlands peoples can be read as either a welcome or a warning. In the chapter on the American Revolution, an eyewitness watercolor depicting four different soldiers in the Continental forces at Yorktown—a black soldier, a New England militiaman, a backcountry rifleman, and a French officer—demonstrates not only the diversity among fighting men but also the different motives for fighting the American War for Independence. Furthermore, in the chapter on the New Deal, we use an image of Franklin Roosevelt broadcasting a "fireside chat" to signal his innovations in connecting the presidency to the people through technology and his efforts to explain his administration's policies in everyday language.

Focus Questions and Subheading Clues

At the end of each visual heading is a focus question that guides students in absorbing and interpreting the information in the subsections that follow. For example, the major section on the U.S. Constitution asks:

- As you read, focus on the ways in which the relationship between local and federal power was central to the framing of the Constitution and the debates over its ratification. Which side won the debate initially? Ultimately?

Each subheading in that section is then annotated with a brief statement of core content intended both to cue understanding and aid in review.

- The Constitutional Convention rethinks the new nation's political structure.
- The new Constitution creates a stronger central government.
- The debates over ratifying the Constitution center on federal powers and the nature of a republic.
- The continuing importance of protecting individual rights against a powerful central government reflects the Revolution's legacy.

Together, these clues build toward an informed, comprehensive answer to the focus question that opened the section. In conjunction with the focus question, the clues are designed to support departmental and campuswide learning objectives and assessment programs.

Key Terms

Within each chapter, approximately forty specialized terms are boldfaced for students' attention with brief definitions appearing on the same page. Terms highlighted include concepts, laws, treaties, movements and organizations, legal cases, and battles. Unlike other textbooks, *Global Americans* also includes specialized terms relating to world events that affected Americans, such as *Revolutions of 1848* and *blitzkrieg*. The key terms thus highlight the connections between U.S. history and developments around the globe.

Global Americans Portraits

Each chapter features three portraits—brief biographies and often an image—of individuals whose lives or careers cross borders or were affected by international events. These portraits also highlight the various ways people experienced the social, economic, and political turmoil discussed in the chapter narrative. The familiar (e.g., Harriet Tubman) and less familiar (e.g., Medicine Snake Woman and Dith Pran) are both represented. Collectively, the portraits aim to challenge preconceptions and offer surprising new insights into people as diverse as Daniel Boone, who joined both sides of the American Revolution and ended up a local official in Spanish North America, and Hedy Lamarr, who is best-known as a Hollywood starlet, but who was also a self-taught inventor who made a major contribution to the wireless communication revolution.

History Without Borders

Each chapter includes a global feature highlighting an issue, idea, product, or material object that was not constrained by political borders. A brief essay, images, and a world or hemisphere map trace the global path of ideas and goods. Often this feature reveals something not well known by Americans on a topic not typically included in a U.S. history textbook, such as the Iroquois' adoption of Chinese vermilion as body paint, Japan's antinuclear movement in the 1950s, and the impact of artificially created nitrogen fertilizer on world food production. Critical thinking questions help students place American events or trends in a larger, global context. This feature is not merely global decoration but rather an extension of an already globalized text.

Summary and "Thinking Back, Looking Forward"

The core text of each chapter ends with a summary that revisits the focus questions to establish large-scale generalizations and promote a synthetic understanding of U.S. history and its connections to the world. The "Thinking Back, Looking Forward" element directs students to see long-term trends and recurring themes that appear across chapters.

Timeline

A timeline at the end of each chapter is intended to help students review by visualizing chronology and events' cause and effect. Timelines conventionally list the most important events covered in the chapter. In our chapters, timelines incorporate international events to reinforce the book's global framework and use maps to correlate the regions of the world with events in the timeline.

Resources

A list of secondary and Internet sources appears in each chapter. These are the resources that we believe are useful to both students and instructors who want to dig deeper into the content of the chapter. They are not meant to be comprehensive but rather to suggest the richness of the field.

Note on Terminology

As authors we have grappled with the challenge of finding the appropriate term for a specific ethnic or racial group during a particular period in history. These terms are not fixed, but in fact shift over historical periods, adding even more complexity. The terms we have chosen to use in each of the chapters are deliberate and reflect our understanding of both the historiography and contemporary uses. Our intention is not to make a final determination about the use of specific ethnic and racial labels, but rather to help teachers suggest that these terms can be used as a basis for discussion regarding the importance of names and who gets to decides various labels.

Note on Images

The images in *Global Americans* have been thoughtfully chosen to help students engage with the text on a visual level as well as a reading comprehension level. We encourage instructors to have their students "read" the images carefully and ask questions about each of them. We have also selected some images that are quite disturbing, such as an image of the lynching of Will Brown in Chapter 18 and the liberation of Jews from a World War II concentration camp in Chapter 21. We debated the pros and cons of using these images, deciding to do so because we believe that they reflect important historical moments with which we want students to engage and interpret.

MindTap

MindTap Instant Access Code: ISBN – 9781337114677
MindTap Printed Access Card: ISBN – 9781337116107

MindTap for *Global Americans* is a personalized, online learning platform that provides students with an immersive learning experience to build and foster critical thinking skills. Through a carefully designed chapter-based learning path, MindTap allows students to easily identify learning objectives; draw connections and improve writing skills by completing unit-level essay assignments; read short, manageable sections from the e-book; and test their content knowledge with map- and timeline-based critical thinking questions.

MindTap allows instructors to customize their content, providing tools that seamlessly integrate YouTube clips, outside Websites, and personal content directly into the learning path. Instructors can assign additional primary source content through the Instructor Resource Center and Questia primary and secondary source databases that house thousands of peer-reviewed journals, newspapers, magazines, and full-length books.

The additional content available in MindTap mirrors and complements the authors' narrative, emphasizing the global forces and dynamics that have been central to the history of the United States. It also includes primary source content and assessments not found in the printed text. To learn more, ask your Cengage Learning sales representative to demonstrate it for you—or go to www.Cengage.com/MindTap.

Instructor Resources

The Instructor's Companion Website, accessed through the Instructor Resource Center (login.cengage .com), houses all of the supplemental materials you can use for your course. This includes a Test Bank, Instructor's Manual, and PowerPoint Lecture Presentations. The Test Bank, offered in Microsoft® Word® and Cognero® formats, contains multiple-choice, identification, true or false, and essay questions for each chapter. Cognero® is a flexible, online system that allows you to author, edit, and manage test bank content for Western Civilization, 10e. Create multiple test versions instantly and deliver through your LMS from your classroom, or wherever you may be, with no special installs or downloads required. The Instructor's Resource Manual includes chapter summaries, suggested lecture topics, map exercises, discussion questions for the primary sources, topics for student research, relevant websites, suggestions for additional videos, and online resources for information on historical sites. Finally, the PowerPoint Lectures are ADA-compliant slides collate the key takeaways from the chapter in concise visual formats perfect for in-class presentations or for student review.

Acknowledgements

The development and writing of *Global Americans* has taken almost a decade. Along the way, we have indebted ourselves to some very fine editors and scholars who helped us find our collective voice as well as the will to continue on what has been an enormous project. We would like to thank Irene Beiber and Sally Constable who first approached us about writing such a textbook. Along the way, we had the great fortune to work with Ann West and Jean Woy who both helped shape the book in the early stages. We were also lucky enough to have Clint Attebery guide the team through a critical juncture. Our biggest debt, however, goes to Ann Grogg, an exceptional editor, who worked closely with each of us to translate our knowledge into a readable and usable text for college students. We are all better writers from having her skillful touch on our prose.

We also owe a debt of gratitude to each other for the years of hard work as we each read and edited chapters that were often far afield from our own special area of expertise. Throughout the long process of writing and editing, we coauthors have held lively biweekly conference calls in which every stage of every chapter was discussed in detail. *Global Americans*, therefore, is the outcome of countless hours of shared discussions about American history and how it should be presented to a new generation of students.

We are also indebted to many colleagues who voiced their encouragement, read draft chapters, and provided helpful suggestions for improvement.

Alexander Haskell, *University of California, Riverside*
James Huston, *Oklahoma State University*
Ann M. Little, *Colorado State University*
Peter Mancall, *University of Southern California*
Lisa Materson, *University of California, Davis*
Andrew Needham, *New York University*
Marcy Norton, *George Washington University*
Gregory E. O'Malley, *University of California, Santa Cruz*
Lorena Oropeza, *University of California, Davis*

Thomas J. Osborne, *Santa Ana College (emeritus)*
Robert C. Ritchie, *Henry E. Huntington Library*
Susanah Shaw Romney, *New York University.*
Virginia Scharff, *University of New Mexico*
Carole Shammas, *University of Southern California*
Terri Snyder, *California State University, Fullerton*
Michael Witgen, *University of Michigan*

We want to thank all the scholars who were contracted by Cengage as expert reviewers of the text at various stages. Their critiques were thoughtful and much appreciated.

Thomas Adam, *The University of Texas at Arlington*
Ian Aebel, *University of Iowa*
Brian Alnutt, *Northampton Community College*
Rick Ascheman, *Rochester Community and Technical College*
Shelby Balik, *Metropolitan State University of Denver*
Evan Bennett, *Florida Atlantic University*
Katherine Benton-Cohen, *Georgetown University*
Angela Boswell, *Henderson State University*
Blanche Brick, *Blinn College*
Rachel Buff, *University of Wisconsin*
Brian Casserly, *Bellevue College*
Tonia Compton, *Columbia College*
Cynthia Counsil, *Florida State College at Jacksonville*
David Dalton, *College of the Ozarks*
Bruce Daniels, *The University of Texas at San Antonio*
Wendy Davis, *Campbellsville University*
Rodney Dillon, *Palm Beach State College*
Shaughnessy Doyel, *Saint Charles Community College*
Shannon Duffy, *Texas State University*
Mark Elliott, *University of North Carolina at Greensboro*
Richard Filipink, *Western Illinois University*
Kristen Foster, *Marquette University*
Jennifer Fry, *Moravian College*
Joshua Fulton, *Moraine Valley Community College*
Bryan Garrett, *The University of Texas at Arlington*
Matthew Garrett, *Bakersfield College*
Diane Gill, *North Lake College*
Aram Goudsouzian, *University of Memphis*
Larry Grubbs, *Georgia State University*
Elisa Guernsey, *Monroe Community College*
David Hamilton, *University of Kentucky*
Kristin Hargrove, *Grossmont College*
Aimee Harris-Johnson, *El Paso Community College*
Justin Hart, *Texas Tech University*
Mary Ann Heiss, *Kent State University*
Robin Henry, *Wichita State University*
Warren Hofstra, *Shenandoah University*
Thomas Humphrey, *Cleveland State University*
Matthew Hutchinson, *Kennesaw State University*
Sheyda Jahanbani, *University of Kansas*
Ely Janis, *Massachusetts College of Liberal Arts*
Volker Janssen, *California State University, Fullerton*
Patricia Knol, *Triton College*

Tim Lehman, *Rocky Mountain College*
Carmen Lopez, *Miami Dade College*
Frances M. Jacobson, *Tidewater Community College*
Eric Mayer, *Victor Valley College*
Suzanne McFadden, *Austin Community College*
Mark Mengerink, *Lamar University*
Robert O'Brien, *Lone Star College-CyFair*
Deirdre O'Shea, *University of Central Florida*
Stephen Patnode, *Farmingdale State College*
Darren Pierson, *Blinn College*
David Raley, *El Paso Community College*
Monica Rankin, *The University of Texas at Dallas*
Nik Ribianszky, *Georgia Gwinnett College*
Ayesha Shariff, *Saint Paul College*
John Smolenski, *University of California, Davis*
Diane Vecchio, *Furman University*
Felicia Viator, *University of California, Berkeley*
Elwood Watson, *East Tennessee State University*
William Whisenhunt, *College of DuPage*
Vibert White, *Bethune Cookman University*
Scott Williams, *Weatherford College*
Mary Wolf, *University of Georgia*

We are indebted to the following for creating the instructor and student resources for *Global Americans*: Elizabeth Bischof, University of Southern Maine; Christopher Jillson, New York University; Carmen Lopez, Miami Dade College; Sarah Nytroe, DeSales University; Jacqueline Shine, University of California, Berkeley; and Mary Montgomery Wolf, University of Georgia.

We are also happy to have this opportunity to express our gratitude to the great folks at Cengage who have shepherded this project through the process that took words on a manuscript page and made them into the vibrant text and on-line resources that you see here, especially Paul Banks, product director; Joe Potvin, product manager; Carolyn Lewis, executive director of development; Anais Wheeler, content development manager; Lauren MacLachlan, production manager; Carol Newman, senior content project manager; Cate Barr, senior art director; Valerie Hartman, senior marketing manager; Erika Hayden, content developer; Andrew Newton, associate content developer; Rob Alper, senior learning design author/consultant; Charlotte Miller, art editor; Emma Guiton, product assistant; Erika Mugavin, intellectual property project manager; and Alexandra Ricciardi, intellectual property analyst.

Finally, we are so appreciative of our families who have hung in there with us as we drafted chapters, slogged through rewrites, sat through too many conference calls while on vacation, and rejoiced as it all came together. It does not go without saying that we could not have done this without all of their support. Thank you.

About the Authors

Maria E. Montoya earned her B.A at Yale University in 1986 and Ph.D. at Yale in 1993. She is Associate Professor of History at New York University as well as the Dean of Arts and Science at New York University, Shanghai. She was previously Associate Professor of History at the University of Michigan where she also served as the Director of Latina/o Studies. Her articles include works on western, labor, Latina/o, and environmental history, and they have appeared in the *Western Historical Quarterly, The Journal of Women's History*, and *American Quarterly*. She is the author of *Translating Property: The Maxwell Land Grant and the Conflict over Land in the American West, 1840-1900* (University of California Press, 2002). She has taught the U.S. History survey for more than twenty years and has worked on the AP U.S. History Development Committee and consulted with the College Board.

Laura A. Belmonte earned her B.A. at the University of Georgia and her Ph.D. at the University of Virginia in 1996. She is Department Head and Professor of History at Oklahoma State University. A specialist in the history of U.S. foreign relations, she is the author of *Selling the American Way: U.S. Propaganda and the Cold War* (University of Pennsylvania Press, 2008) and numerous articles on cultural diplomacy. Belmonte is editor of *Speaking of America: Readings in U.S. History* (Cengage, 2nd edition, 2006), and she is concurrently working on books on U.S. global policy on HIV/AIDS and the history of the international LGBT rights movement (Bloomsbury, forthcoming 2017). She is a member of the U.S. Department of State's Historical Advisory Committee on Diplomatic Documentation. After participating in the 2005 National Endowment for the Humanities summer institute "Rethinking America in Global Perspective," she began teaching undergraduate and graduate courses with a transnational focus, including "America in International Perspective" and "HIV/AIDS in Transnational Perspective."

Carl J. Guarneri earned his B.A. at the University of Pennsylvania, M.A. at the University of Michigan, and his Ph.D. at Johns Hopkins University in 1979, and he is Professor of History at Saint Mary's College of California, where he has taught since then. He has also been a visiting professor at Colgate University and the University of Paris. A historian of nineteenth-century America, Guarneri has won national fellowships for his research and published books and articles on reform movements, utopian socialism, the Civil War, and American cultural history, which include *The Utopian Alternative: Fourierism in Nineteenth-Century America* (Cornell University Press, 1991) and two edited collections: *Religion and Society in the American West* (University Press of America,

1987), and *Hanging Together: Unity and Diversity in American Culture* (Yale University Press, 2001). He is currently writing a book on the Civil War career of Charles A. Dana, an influential New York journalist and Assistant Secretary of War. Through his publications and presentations, Guarneri has also been a leading voice in the movement to globalize the study and teaching of U.S. history. He has codirected institutes for the National Endowment for the Humanities on "Rethinking America in Global Perspective." His survey-course reader, *America Compared: American History in International Perspective* (Cengage, 2nd ed., 2005), and his brief textbook, *America in the World: United States History in Global Context* (McGraw-Hill, 2007) are seminal undergraduate texts, and his anthology, *Teaching American History in a Global Context* (M.E. Sharpe, 2008), offers a globalizing "toolkit" for U.S. history instructors.

Steven W. Hackel earned his B.A. at Stanford University and his Ph.D. at Cornell University in 1994. From 1994 to 1996, he was a postdoctoral fellow at the Omohundro Institute of Early American History and Culture and a visiting Assistant Professor at the College of William and Mary. He taught at Oregon State University from 1996 to 2007 and is now Professor of History at the University of California, Riverside. Within the larger field of early American history, Hackel's research focuses on the Spanish Borderlands, colonial California, and California Indians. Hackel is especially interested in Indian responses to Spanish colonialism, the effects of disease on colonial encounters, and new ways of visualizing these processes through digital history. His first book, *Children of Coyote, Missionaries of Saint Francis: Indian-Spanish Relations in Colonial California, 1769-1850*, was published by the Omohundro Institute of Early American History and Culture (2005) and garnered numerous national prizes. His most recent book, *Junípero Serra: California's Founding Father* (Hill and Wang, a division of Farrar, Straus and Giroux, 2013), was named a top-ten book for 2013 by Zócalo Public Square and the best book of the year on early California by the Historical Society of Southern California. He has edited two volumes of essays and published nearly two dozen scholarly essays and has been awarded fellowships from the National Endowment for the Humanities and many other agencies.

Ellen Hartigan-O'Connor earned her B.A. at Yale University and Ph.D. at the University of Michigan in 2003. She is Associate Professor of History at the University of California, Davis, where she teaches courses on gender, American social and cultural history, and the histories of colonialism and capitalism. She is the author of *The Ties That Buy: Women and Commerce in Revolutionary America*

(University of Pennsylvania Press, 2009) as well as articles and book chapters on gender and economy in the eighteenth and nineteenth centuries. With support from the National Endowment for the Humanities, she is currently completing a project on auctions and market culture in early America, tracing the economic and cultural power of a widespread but little-studied institution. She became interested in globalizing U.S. history through her expertise in Atlantic world and transnational women's and gender histories. She is coeditor of the *Oxford Handbook of American Women's and Gender History* (Oxford University Press, forthcoming), and a board member of Women and Social Movements. A founding and Standing Editor of *Oxford Bibliographies—Atlantic History*, Hartigan-O'Connor is also a speaker with the Organization of American Historians' Distinguished Lectureship Program.

Lon Kurashige earned his B.A. from the University of California, Santa Barbara and his Ph.D. from the University of Wisconsin-Madison in 1994. Since 1995, he has taught at the University of Southern California, where he is Associate Professor of History. He is author of *Two Faces of Exclusion: The Untold History of Anti-Asian Racism in the United States* (Chapel Hill: University of North Carolina Press, 2016) and *Japanese American Celebration and Conflict: A History of Ethnic Identity and Festival, 1934-1990* (University of California Press, 2002). He was the winner of the History Book Award from the Association for Asian American Studies in 2004. He coedited "Conversations in Transpacific History," a special edition of *Pacific Historical Review* (2014) and *Major Problems in Asian American History*, 2nd ed. (Cengage Learning, forthcoming 2017). His article "Rethinking Anti-Immigrant Racism: Lessons from the Los Angeles Vote on the 1920 Alien Land Law" won the Carl I. Wheat prize for best publication to appear in the *Southern California Quarterly* between 2012 and 2014. His other publications include articles published in the *Journal of American History*, *Pacific Historical Review*, and *Reviews in American History*. Kurashige has been awarded fellowships from the Fulbright Program, Social Science Research Council, Rockefeller Foundation, the National Endowment for the Humanities, and other funding agencies.

The Tewa's Mole story tells of how they came to their homeland in the Rio Grande Valley in New Mexico, emerging from a dark world into the light.

1

The First American Peoples: Migration, Settlement, and Adaptation

In the beginning, according to a Native American creation story, the whole world was dark. The people lived underground in blackness. They did not know that their world was dark because they had no knowledge of anything else; no one had taught them about the blue sky world. After a long time in darkness, the people began to get restless. Some asked, "Is this all the world there is? Will there never be another world?"

Then Mole came to visit, digging his way through the darkness with his little paws and sharp-pointed nails. The old men asked Mole, "Is there more to the world than this, friend? You travel far and fast underground. What have you discovered? Is there anything else?"

"Follow me," said Mole. The people lined up behind Mole, and he began to dig his way upward. As Mole clawed away the earth, the people took it from his little paw-hands and passed it back along their line, from one person to the next, to get it out of their way. That is why the tunnel that Mole dug upward for the people was closed behind them. That is why they could never find their way back to their old dark world.

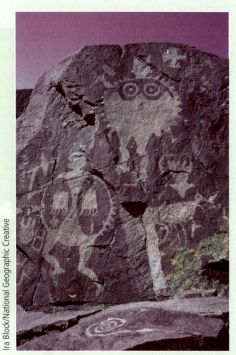

Ira Block/National Geographic Creative

When at last Mole stopped digging and the people came out into their new world, light shone all round them and washed them like a blessing. The people, like Mole, were blinded by the light. They were frightened and hid their eyes with their hands to protect their sight.

While all the people were standing there, arguing about what to do, they heard a woman speaking to them. "Be patient, my children" she said, "and I will help you. . . . Take your hands away from your eyes, but do it slowly, slowly. Now wait a minute. Move them a little bit farther away. Now, do it again. And again."

Four times the people moved their hands away from their eyes. At last their eyes were freed and opened, and they could see little old Spider Woman, grandmother of the Earth and of all living things.

She showed them corn and told them to weed it and hoe it and water it. She told them to go live near the great Turtle Mountain in the south. But they were not sure where it was.

Old Spider Woman then told them, "When you find the signs of your two friends again—Mole and me—you will have found your place."

For a very long time the people wandered here and there. They endured hardships and quarreled about what they should do. Finally, only two were left, man and woman. They journeyed southward over a hard road. Then they saw a strange animal crawling along.

"Look what a strange track this thing leaves in the sand," they said, and they remembered that they had seen these tracks before. "They look like Mole's tracks," he said. She said, "Its back is as hard as stone, but it has a design carved and painted on it. Look, that design is Grandmother Spider's web!"

And at that moment, they knew they had found their home.

How is the Tewa's origin story reflective of the experiences shared among the first American peoples?

Go to MindTap® to watch a video on the Tewa's Mole story and learn how this creation myth illustrates the themes of this chapter.

This is how the Tewa—a group of Pueblo Indians of the Rio Grande Valley in New Mexico—understand how they came to their homeland. Their story, like those of so many other Indians and others who settled in America, speaks of a migration from a distant land, an uncertain fate, the importance of family, a dependence on animals, and the eventual adaptation of people to their environment with a growing sense of rootedness and history. These themes—migration, settlement, and adaptation—have been central to human history since time immemorial. In more recent times, humans across the globe have increasingly innovated, using fire, irrigation, and metallurgy to modify their homelands and create labor-saving tools while developing complex and novel social structures to organize their societies. All of these developments unfolded at different rates in different societies as diverse peoples responded to changes in their environment or envisioned new opportunities for development and advancement. The challenge for the people of ancient America—and all of those who came later—was, as they saw it, to find their proper place within nature and the larger world. For them, it is a story that unfolded over more than 15,000 years. In some places, people established empires; elsewhere they lived in smaller groups. Everywhere human society developed as people exchanged commodities and ideas across networks that fostered regionally specific cultures that together supported millions of inhabitants. By 1500 CE (in the common era), a tapestry of peoples with distinctive economic, social, political, and religious systems called America their home.

1-1
First Peoples of the Americas

This artistic representation depicts an extended family, probably like the ones who came to the land of Beringia more than 12,000 years ago. Small groups like this were among the first inhabitants of North America, and their descendants peopled much of the Americas.

As you look at this image, what sort of technologies do you see displayed? How might they have these allowed people to survive in frigid Beringia? ▶

Go to MindTap® to practice history with the Chapter 1 **Primary Source Writing Activity: Adaptation and America's First Peoples.** Read and view primary sources and respond to a writing prompt.

Canadian Museum of Civilization

Modern science offers its own story about human origins in the Americas, one that is not necessarily at odds with Indian origin stories. This chapter of human history unfolded long before there were written records and in places where the archaeological record is scant or gone. But scientific evidence has enabled scholars to describe human origins and migrations across the globe and into the Americas. The work of physical anthropologists suggests that humans first came to the Americas at least thirteen thousand years ago from the places that we know today as Siberia, Alaska, and the Yukon Territory. As the first American peoples moved south, they splintered and evolved into different groups. Over millennia, the peoples developed different cultures as they settled in different environments with different resources and challenges. Societies came and went in response to environmental changes and their own internal logic. The most prominent societies endured for centuries if not longer. Others vanished quickly, leaving no trace in the archaeological record.

☞ **As you read, focus on the different understandings of Native American origins. To what degree do you think that science and Native American origin stories can be reconciled?**

1-1a Scientific Evidence

Until about 2 million years ago, **Homo erectus**, the distant ancestors of modern humans, lived only in Africa. Their dispersal was slow and probably caused

Aided by modern science, scholars map the earliest migrations to the Americas.

by a change in the earth's climate and a drying out of the Sahara region. By 1.8 million years ago, these early humans had spread to western Asia and the island of Java in Indonesia, which was connected at that time to the mainland. By 500,000 years ago *Homo erectus* lived in China. About 400,000 years ago *Homo erectus* evolved into **Homo sapiens** and sometime around 150,000 to 100,000 years ago, anatomically modern humans known to us as **Homo sapiens sapiens** evolved in East Africa. Again, climate change drove humans to settle new lands. During the last worldwide glacial advance, 50,000 years ago, sea levels fell when much of the earth's moisture became trapped in the ice caps, exposing more of the earth's land to settlement by these creative and adaptive humans. The new lands and connections among them allowed humans to settle another 60 percent of the earth. People migrated into northeastern Asia; some went by boat to Australia. Later, a group ventured overland from Siberia to Alaska and ultimately southward in the Americas (see Map 1.1).

Specifically, most archaeologists believe that the earliest immigrants to the Americas came from Asia across a land bridge about 12,500 to 10,000 BCE (before the common era), but perhaps as long ago as 23,000 BCE. Nearly all ancient human skulls found in the Americas have a dental pattern that matches those of ancient human remains found in northeastern Asia. Moreover, most Native Americans today have blood type O or A as opposed to type B, which evolved after humans migrated to the Americas.

To understand events and migrations that occurred so many thousands of years ago among peoples who left no written records, scholars rely on material evidence, such as stone tools and fired pottery, burial remains, and food scraps. Stone and clay tools used to kill and cook animals predominate in the archaeological record. Organic matter, such as clothes, shelters, or foods, has only occasionally survived. Thus, scholars know something about how early humans hunted, prepared their food, and what they ate but only a little about what they wore, the homes they built, and the thoughts and behaviors that animated their lives.

Given these limits, the scientific technique known as carbon 14 (C14) dating has been extremely helpful for the study of early human history across the globe. Carbon 14, a radioactive atom produced in the upper atmosphere, is incorporated into carbon dioxide and absorbed from the air by green plants. When animals eat plants, carbon dioxide is absorbed into the animals' tissue. When a plant or animal dies, the C14 atoms within it break down at a constant rate. Therefore, by measuring the amount of C14 in anything that was once alive—seeds, cotton, bone, or wood—scientists can measure the length of time that has passed since the organism died. Carbon 14 dating has allowed archaeologists to determine with precision the antiquity of the organic matter in tools, bones, clothing, and even feces left behind by the first human inhabitants of the Americas. This has allowed scholars to map the geographic distribution and cultural evolution of ancient Americans with some authority. In the future, the study of DNA—the basic inherited genetic material that determines the makeup of human bodies—taken from ancient human, plant, and animal remains promises to increase our understanding of people who came to inhabit America long ago.

1-1b Beringia during the Pleistocene

Although Alaska, Canada's Yukon Territory, and northeast Siberia are divided today by political boundaries, rugged mountains, and frigid ocean

People from Siberia move across Beringia, an arid and frigid land.

waters, they share a common history related to the Pacific Ocean and its periodic changes from dramatic fluctuations in the earth's climate. During the geologic period known as the **Pleistocene**, which stretched from roughly 2.6 million to 11,700 years ago, nearly all the northern regions of the Northern Hemisphere were covered by enormous ice sheets. Yet the lowlands of Alaska, the Yukon, and northeast Siberia remained mostly ice free because they were so **arid**. As the climate cooled, much of the earth's water was trapped in ice, lowering the level of the Pacific Ocean as much as 360 feet. During the final phase of the Pleistocene, **Beringia**, the land mass between Siberia and Alaska, was exposed (see Map 1.2), and a continuous thousand-mile wide land bridge, the **Bering land bridge**, connected Asia to North America.

Beringia was frigid. It was cold enough to grow glaciers but too dry to do so. As the earth became steadily colder, its grasslands became a refuge for large mammals, such as wooly mammoths, horses, saber-toothed cats, rhinoceros, antelope, **bison**, musk-ox, caribou, grizzly bears, wolverines, wolves, and lions. Beringia was home to such an abundance and diversity of animals that it can be likened to today's East African Savannah.

Homo erectus Meaning "upright human." Extinct species of early humans that emerged in Africa 1.9 million years ago and lived throughout much of the Pleistocene.

Homo sapiens Meaning "wise human." Human ancestor with greater intelligence and adaptability than *Homo erectus.*

Homo sapiens sapiens Anatomically modern humans. Evolved from *homo sapiens* 150,000 years ago.

Pleistocene Geological epoch that lasted from 2.6 million to 11,700 years ago covering the latest period of repeated glaciation.

arid Absence or scarcity of water to the extent that animal and plant life is hindered or prevented.

Beringia Frigid grassland that emerged between Siberia and Alaska during the Pleistocene when more of the earth's water was trapped in the polar ice caps.

Bering land bridge Thousand-mile wide bridge of land in eastern Beringia that connected Asia and North America during the Pleistocene.

bison Large grass-eating animal that inhabited much of the Northern Great Plains. Referred to as the *American Buffalo*, but buffalo and bison are not the same species.

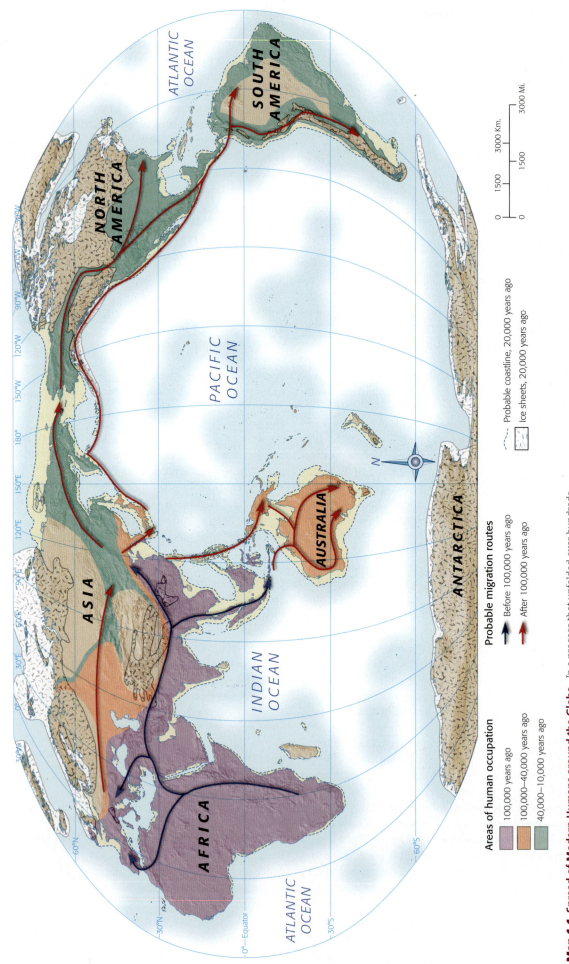

Map 1.1 Spread of Modern Humans around the Globe. In a process that unfolded over hundreds of thousands of years, human occupation of the globe spread from East Africa to the Americas. Humans took two routes from Asia to the Americas: Some traversed a land bridge across Beringia while others ventured down the Pacific Coast in small watercraft. ▲

Areas of human occupation

■ 100,000 years ago

■ 100,000–40,000 years ago

■ 40,000–10,000 years ago

Probable migration routes

→ Before 100,000 years ago

→ After 100,000 years ago

- - - Probable coastline, 20,000 years ago

▨ Ice sheets, 20,000 years ago

Humans of the late Pleistocene—known to us as **Paleoindians**—probably first came to Beringia more than twelve thousand five hundred years ago. They had mastered the use of fire to survive the cold and learned to hunt large mammals for food and to make clothing of their fur or hides. Paleoindians did not completely depend upon big game. They also relied on plants and smaller animals. Women and men together gathered and prepared the daily foods.

Once Paleoindians had moved beyond the southern reaches of Beringia (south and east as far as Alaska and central Canada), they encountered ice sheets a mile high that blocked passage southward. An Arikara creation story tells of the First People encountering "wide, thick ice and deep water" on their original great journey. Other Native American oral traditions recount perilous travels through frigid or dark lands. Many describe ancestral origins in an underworld or a place of darkness, perhaps metaphorical renderings of memories of life above the Arctic Circle in the winter.

The first settlers of the Americas came from Beringia, but they took more than one route. It seems certain that about 10,500 BCE, as the climate warmed, Paleoindians moved south through an ice-free corridor east of the northern Rocky Mountains in present-day western Canada. But the discovery of human artifacts in Monte Verde, Chile, that date to the same time period suggest that by then, some groups had already come down the Pacific coast in watercraft. Rafts or boats were used at the time; fifty thousand years ago, people from Southeast Asia had used them to reach Australia. Human remains ten thousand years old have been found on an island off the California coast.

Scholars debate why Paleoindians moved south. One theory holds that as hunters, they were following large mammals. Another suggests that seasonal waterfowl migrations inspired their move. Notably, in some Native American myths, birds are often the discoverers of lands unseen to humans. In the biblical story of Noah and the great flood, a dove sent out to see whether the waters had receded returns with a fresh olive leaf to prove that they had done so. An ancient story among the Paiutes tells how humans overcame an insuperable ice barrier with the help of ravens and eventually migrated to the American West. According to the Paiutes, long ago, "Ice had formed ahead of them and it reached all the way to the sky. The people could not cross it. . . . A Raven flew up and struck the ice and cracked it. Yet the people still could not cross. Another Raven flew up again and cracked the ice again. Again Raven flew up again and broke the ice, this time allowing the people to cross."

1-1c Clovis Peoples

Although the exact date when humans came to Beringia or when they headed south is not known, they were in North America by 11,000 BCE, thereby initiating one of the final chapters in the global advance of humans that began in Africa millions of years

Clovis people make beautifully distinctive fluted projectile points.

ago. These first migrants entered a hunter's paradise—animals were abundant and not afraid of humans. The settlers would have been well nourished and increased in numbers rapidly, possibly doubling or tripling with each generation. Thus, a small band of just twenty-five Beringian Paleoindians could have initiated a population of one million across the Americas within three hundred fifty years.

In 1932 in Clovis, New Mexico, archaeologists unearthed a fluted stone spear tip from these early Americans determined to be about thirteen thousand years old. These points—known as **Clovis Points**—have been found throughout much of North and South America and date to roughly the same time, suggesting that these peoples settled the Americas within about two hundred years.

At the peak of Clovis culture, most large mammals in the Americas died off. These extinctions coincided with a dramatic and sudden global warming after the Late Pleistocene. Around 8000 BCE, the enormous ice sheets that had covered much of northern North America began to melt. The runoff raised sea levels and flooded coastal regions, including much of Beringia. The melting ice sheets also led to changes in weather patterns. The cold grasslands of the Americas warmed and dried, large lakes disappeared, and forests grew in regions that had been tundra. As habitats changed, **megafauna**, large grazing animals, such as mammoths and mastodons, died out. Human hunting accelerated their extinction. As Clovis peoples overhunted large predators, such as lions and cats, populations of smaller **herbivores** that fed on plants increased, and as these herbivores overgrazed dwindling grasslands, they destroyed the habitats of megafauna, horses, and camels.

Paleoindians Earliest peoples to settle the Americas during the late Pleistocene, probably about 12,500 years ago.

Clovis Points Distinctive fluted-projectile points, typically 3 to 6 inches long, manufactured by the Paleoindians (Clovis peoples) between 13,000 to 10,000 years ago and found across North America.

megafauna Large animals, such as mastodons.

herbivores Animals that subsist by eating plant material.

Clovis Point, Arizona, Thirteen Thousand Years Before Present (BP) Clovis points are finely worked, typically three to six inches long, and sharp enough to penetrate and kill large animals. Markings indicate that the points were bound to shafts or straight sticks. These points were exceptionally well-designed pieces of weaponry and were more advanced than any projectile produced in the world at that time. This point and others like it were most likely made by descendants of Paleoindians who came from Beringia. ▲ Brian Brockman/Getty Images

Map 1.2 The Peopling of the Americas About thirteen thousand years ago, America's earliest human inhabitants began to arrive from Beringia, a now submerged land mass that connected Siberia and Alaska. Some came over land and, in a separate migration, others came by sea, hugging the Pacific Coast all the way to the southern tip of South America. ▲

Map labels: SIBERIA, ASIA, BERINGIA, ARCTIC OCEAN, ALASKA, YUKON, NORTH AMERICA, Kennewick, Clovis, Poverty Point, Beothuk I., ATLANTIC OCEAN, MESOAMERICA, PACIFIC OCEAN, SOUTH AMERICA, Monte Verde, Tropic of Cancer, Equator—0°, Tropic of Capricorn, Arctic Circle

Legend:
- 0 500 1000 Km.
- 0 500 1000 Mi.
- Extent of land, ca. 33,000–10,500 B.C.E.
- Glaciers, ca. 15,000 B.C.E.
- Probable ancient shoreline
- Probable migratory route
- Selected Paleo-Indian site

With these extinctions, Clovis peoples began to hunt bison and smaller mammals, and they made smaller projectile points. More important, they dispersed and separated, forming distinct cultures. The megafaunal extinctions also limited the ways their cultures could develop as horses and camels died out. The Clovis peoples, therefore, did not have an opportunity to domesticate these animals or to gain immunity to diseases that come from living with domesticated animals. Thus, in the distant future, they and the myriad peoples of the Americas who descended from them would be vulnerable to epidemics that originated in some domesticated animals.

1-2

From the Archaic Period to the Dawn of Agriculture

Depicted here is *Chicomecoatl*, an Aztec goddess of agriculture. She holds in her hands cobs of corn, a crop planted in Mexico more than 3,890 years before the present. Its cultivation marked a period of transition for many peoples of the Americas toward an agricultural existence.

As you look at this image of an ancient corn cob, think about how it differs from those of today. What does it suggest about plant adaptations in the wake of human settlement across North America? ▶

Carver Mostardi/Alamy Stock Photo

In the absence of megafauna and in the wake of retreating ice sheets, the first peoples of the Americas continued to disperse and form distinct cultures. As people adapted to environmental shifts after the Late Pleistocene, they depended less on migrating animals, lived more in families, and moved locally to be near seasonal food sources. Some took up agriculture, and their societies grew large and complex. Others sustained themselves in a variety of ways as hunter-gatherers.

☞ As you read, focus on the diversity of peoples and cultures across the Americas. How did this diversity come to be? In what ways was it expressed? What, if anything, did the diverse peoples of the Americas have in common?

1-2a The Archaic Period

With global warming, the Paleoindian world gave way to the **Archaic period**, an epoch that began about 8000 BCE and lasted some seven thousand years. The Archaic period describes in general terms an Indian culture markedly different from that of the Paleoindian. Each group left the Paleoindian period and entered the Archaic at its own rate, at a different time, and on its own terms.

{ Indians' technological advances lead to new ways of hunting and subsistence.

In the final millennia of the Archaic, many groups established year-round settlements, some of which were inhabited for decades and even centuries. This **sedentism** was in part a response to the increasing population of the Americas, which made it impossible for peoples to obtain new resources by simply moving into unoccupied regions. During the Archaic period, Indians domesticated the dog, a descendant from wild ancestors in the Eastern hemisphere. In **Mesoamerica**, dogs became a source of food, just as chickens would become later. Farther north, Indians bred dogs to carry or pull loads. In Mesoamerica, Indians raised turkeys for food, and other birds, such as macaws and parrots were raised for their plumage.

Most Archaic peoples were **hunter-gatherers**, pursuing diversified food sources. They caught fish, gathered nuts and berries, or hunted small animals, such as ducks and squirrels, and large ones such as deer, moose, and caribou. In the Late Archaic, about 3000 BCE to 1000 BCE, Indians in coastal New England built fish traps in shallow tidal backwaters. They cut small trees for stakes and drove them into the ground parallel to the shore, then heaped low brush among them. High tide brought fish and water across the traps, and when the tide receded, fish could be caught in nets and baskets.

In the plains of central North America, some hunting groups pursued bison, which they killed in great numbers either with spears or by driving them off cliffs. The primary weapon of the Archaic hunter was the spear thrower, or **atlatl**, a flexible shaft with a handle at one end and a hook at the other into which a spear was fitted.

Archaic period Stage of cultural development following the Paleoindian period and marked by sedentism. Commonly began around 8000 BCE but varied from group to group.

sedentism Society or people that remain in one place year round.

Mesoamerica Cultural region in the Americas stretching from Mexico to northern Costa Rica. Site of numerous ancient civilizations.

hunter-gatherers Society in which most food is obtained from wild plants and animals.

Brittney Tatchell, Smithsonian Institution

Global Americans In 1996, two college students in Kennewick, Washington, found a human skull along the Columbia River. Scientists who eventually unearthed a complete skeleton recently determined that it was from a man, known as **Kennewick Man**, who lived 9,000 years ago. He was a descendant of maritime hunters who worked their way along the shoreline of Beringia and eventually ventured down the Pacific coast to the tip of South America. Stocky and muscular when he died at age forty, Kennewick Man's right arm was overdeveloped—like a baseball pitcher's—from a lifetime of spear throwing. His hands and forearms suggest that he often pinched his fingers together, perhaps as he made spear points. The food and water that he consumed left a chemical signature in his bones that reveals an adventurous life on the road. He died 300 miles inland, yet for twenty years he had lived on marine animals, such as seals, sea lions, and fish. And the water he drank was Alaskan in origin. Thus, Kennewick Man was a traveler who died far from his home. He very well might have been a trader of projectile points, perhaps crafted from stone quarried in the north. His life speaks to the mobility of America's earliest inhabitants as they made a living across regions that were sparsely settled and rich with opportunity. Most humans are forgotten within three generations of their lives. Remarkably, Kennewick Man speaks to us 360 generations after he lived.

Modern recreation of the facial features of Kennewick Man

The weapon essentially lengthened the arm of the hunter and allowed the snap of the hand and wrist to add speed and make the spear more deadly. Some Late Archaic hunters added stone weights to atlatls to increase their force. Archaic peoples of the Upper Midwest and the Great Lakes region also made axes, harpoons, and smaller tools of copper so pure they did not need smelting, the extraction of base metal from ore.

In addition to using these advanced tools and hunting technologies, Archaic peoples modified the environment in ways unimagined by Clovis peoples. By deliberately setting fires, they created and maintained meadows favored by deer, which they then herded or killed according to their needs. As they became more sedentary, they developed heavy stone tools, food storage sites, and large-scale trade networks. Indians also began to deposit exotic stones and other items as grave goods.

1-2b **Daily Life**

Like the Clovis peoples, Archaic peoples lived across the Americas. Most left only tools, bones, and garbage as indications of their lives. Some, however, left clues to their diet in desiccated feces. Those found in caves in Kentucky reveal that Archaic peoples drank a beverage brewed from now-extinct grasses.

{ *Archaic peoples build enormous earthen mounds.*

One of the most enduring innovations of the Archaic period in northeastern North America was the construction of large earthen mounds. Around 5000 BCE, peoples in Beothuk Island, Newfoundland, buried an adolescent under a mound. Around the youth's neck was a whistle, and next to the body were a harpoon, knives, weapon points, and an antler used to crush minerals into paint. Around 4000 BCE, people in northeast Louisiana at a site known today as Poverty Point, began constructing a circular complex of eleven mounds, the tallest of which

atlatl Tool used by Indians to accelerate the throwing velocity of a spear.

Poverty Point Earthworks Peoples at Poverty Point, Louisiana, created a complex of nested octagonal earthworks, the largest of which is more than three-quarters of a mile across. The size and intricacy of these structures suggest a labor-intensive construction program and a complex social and political organization not possible during the nomadic days of the Clovis peoples. ▼ Richard A. Cooke/Documentary Value/Corbis is twenty-five feet high. These mounds must have been used for food preparation, for they contain remains of mussels, snails, fish, deer, and turkeys as well as many plants. But they also presumably were important centers of rituals.

Nearly everywhere in ancient America, shamans or priests served as intermediaries between people and the gods. But individuals frequently believed that they, too, received messages from the gods or the deceased through dreams or in times of solitude with the use of hallucinogenic drugs. Sacred power was everywhere—in plants and animals, in the oceans and heavens, and in all of creation. Time passed in cycles of decades or centuries and then repeated itself. The world was thus by and large a predictable place according to the most learned leaders of these ancient societies.

1-2c Development of Agriculture and Declines in Health

Agriculture—the methodical cultivation of food crops—developed gradually in the Americas as it did elsewhere in the world. Rather than a

> Agriculture leads to increased concentrations of people and declines in their health.

conscious choice by Indians to put down their atlatls and take up hoes, the dawn of agriculture in the Americas came about through the coevolution of humans and plants. In the earliest phases of this process, plants that humans ate were dispersed—by excretion or spillage—and underwent genetic changes that made them more attractive to and more dependent on humans for dispersal and reproduction. This incidental domestication began with **maize** (also known as *corn* today) in Mesoamerica about 3500 BCE, although Mesoamericans did not cultivate it until about 2700 BCE. In the American Southwest, maize, squash, and beans were first domesticated about 1500 BCE, although maize did not become a staple crop for another two thousand years. Indians first began to eat sunflower, squash, and march elder in eastern North America about 5000 BCE. The incidental domestication of these plants began to occur in river floodplains around 2000 BCE. But it was another five hundred years before people cultivated these crops.

Almost certainly, maize, squash, and beans were carried north from Mesoamerica. One simple fact—the north-south orientation of the western hemisphere—dictated the pace of agricultural diffusion. As people move north or south over hundreds of miles, they pass through different climate zones. This is not so much the case when they move along an east-west axis. Thus, a crop that prospered in one region of the Americas might require generations of modification before it could survive in a region to the north or south that had a slightly different climate.

The gradual shift to agriculture involved more than simply farming crops and herding animals. It entailed major changes in residential patterns, the organization of work, and the creation of material culture. Typically, agriculture is associated with the development and use of ceramic pots for cooking or fiber baskets for gathering, and it involves clearing brush or forest and the cultivation of cereals that can be stored through the seasons.

In Western culture, agriculture is associated with progress toward more complex political, social, and economic organization and is usually associated with large populations. But analysis of ancient human bones suggests that human health and nutrition declined with the advent of agriculture. The healthiest Native Americans were the earliest who lived in small, mobile groups. They wasted no time or energy building large monuments but consumed a nutritious and varied diet. Moreover, their relative isolation from others protected them from infectious diseases, and mobility reduced their contact with germs and parasites associated with waste. As people became more agricultural and lived in larger urban settlements, they lost the health advantages of the Paleoindian and Archaic lifestyle. They spent more time acquiring food and lived fewer years.

The greatest brake on population growth in ancient America was not a shortage of food or high mortality but low **fertility** (live births per woman). Most Paleoindian and Archaic people lived into their thirties; on average, women produced only two to three children. Although estimates of the population of the Americas in 1500 range from below 10 million to above 100 million, probably about 50 million people lived in the Americas in the year 1500. The most densely populated regions were associated with the Indian empires of Mesoamerica and Central and South America. Most people lived south of Mexico; between 7 and 10 million people lived north of Mexico in 1500.

1-2d Diversity, Commonalities, and Gender

As people dispersed throughout the Americas, they splintered into hundreds and then thousands of separate groups, each distinct from the other, in what

> Diverse cultures understand gender in their own ways.

is known as **cultural differentiation**. These societies were built on different systems of labor, political organization, religious beliefs, and material resources. Native American peoples spoke thousands of different languages, and their economies were shaped to local environments. Some remained primarily hunter-gatherers; others turned mainly to agriculture. Some lived in brush huts; others crafted large apartment-style homes out of rock and adobe. Some lived in large towns of thousands and thousands of people, and others lived in hamlets of only a few families. Some lived in the same place year round. Others followed game across large territories throughout the year.

agriculture Cultivating the soil, producing crops, and raising livestock to enhance human life. Requires labor organization and allows food surpluses that support sedentism.

maize Grain known as *corn* in English-speaking countries, domesticated by Mesoamericans more than 5,000 years ago. An important staple and commodity in ancient America.

fertility Production of offspring as opposed to the capability to do so.

cultural differentiation Process through which cultures evolve separately and differentiate from one another.

kinship Social relationship determined by blood, marriage, or residence. Kinship categories and relationships often differ across cultures.

gender Culturally constructed category of people that varies across societies and over time and relates to nearly all aspects of social organization.

sex Category rooted in biology suggesting that one is male or female based on reproductive anatomy and other physical attributes.

Thousands of years of human experience also resulted in commonalities among people of the Americas. Nearly everywhere, people drew their identity from their family, community, or village. **Kinship**—the extended family ties that bind humans together—was basic to human society in the Americas. In fact, people were likely to have their most enduring ties with their kin, not with their spouses. Marriage was a respected institution but one that was not always lifelong. Male leaders might have more than one wife or marry sisters. Such arrangements ensured that leadership would be centralized and passed to the offspring of ruling elites and families. In most societies, men held the political power, but women held society together through their economic activities, their contributions to the household and family, and their family lineages. Indian societies were marked by inequalities, and slavery was common. Most slaves were war captives or criminals. They were more than menial laborers and on occasion played important and valued roles in village society, especially if they were adopted into a family.

Throughout human history, societies have assigned tasks and responsibilities to individuals based upon their sex and gender. But they have not always done so in the same way. **Gender** is a culturally constructed category that varies across societies and over time and relates to nearly all aspects of social organization. **Sex**, however, is rooted in biology and suggests that one is male or female based on biological characteristics. Native American societies of the past usually assigned gender roles based on sex. Typically, men hunted and held political power and women farmed and gathered fruits, nuts, and other edible vegetation that they prepared for their families. But most Indian societies also had at least one other category beyond male and female. Some individuals had within themselves both male and female spirits. As such, they occupied a third gender and were referred to as *two-spirits*.

The creation stories of some Indian groups reveal a wide spectrum of gender categories beyond the simple binary of male/female. For example, in Southern California, among the Kumeyaay, *Warharmi*, a man-woman spirit, provided seeds and culture. Among the Zunis, who lived in the Southwest, such individuals were the *two-spirit Ko'lhamana* who brought together and reconciled the warring and often incompatible lifestyles of male hunters and female farmers, thereby bringing greater harmony to society. Thus, within native society itself at the time of creation and beyond, people and beings who occupied what can be termed a third gender transcended the expectations of their biological sex and played a meaningful role in society.

1-3

Mesoamerica and Peru

The Maya book known as the *Dresden Codex* is a twelfth century copy of a text that was created three or four centuries earlier. It is the oldest surviving manuscript written in the Americas and is one of fifteen surviving pre-Columbian manuscripts. Not all of the seventy eight pages of the Codex have been deciphered, but it is known to contain almanacs, astronomical and astrological tables, and ritual schedules as well as instructions concerning New Year's ceremonies as well as descriptions of the Aztec Rain God's locations.

As you study this image, look for the dramas and emotions being played out. Can you decipher any of the codes or symbols or tools? ▶

Throughout the Americas, as people moved from one region to another and traded and interacted with neighbors near and far, they created diverse cultures and sophisticated civilizations. Local environments and different belief systems led to a stunning array of cultures across the Americas. Some followed big game; others were agricultural or used fire to manage their environment. As trade networks evolved, diverse peoples became integrated into regional economies (see Map 1.3). Four broad cultural regions suggest the diversity of Native America in the year 1500 CE: Mesoamerica and Peru, the Agricultural Southwest and the Arid Interior, the Pacific West, and the Woodlands.

Universal History Archive/Universal Images Group/Getty Images

☞ As you read, think about the common characteristics that marked the cultures of the Americas. What roles do ritual, ceremony, and gender play in the early civilizations of the Americas?

1-3a The Maya and Teotihuacán

Central America and the Mexican Highlands were to Ancient America what Mesopotamia and Egypt were to Eurasia—densely populated areas from

{ *Two monumental civilizations rise and decline.*

which political, economic, and social change emanated. The Mayans created a grand, urbanized civilization that lasted from 150 BCE to 800 CE (see Map 1.4). At its peak, it had a population of 3 to 5 million. Its kings and occasional queens held religious, political, and military authority over a vast expanse of people and lands. Nobles helped control the subject peoples who, practicing intensive agriculture, produced a surplus of corn that supported urban elites and artisans.

The Mayans had an advanced understanding of the movement of the stars and planets. Their calendar was based on the solar year, and they conceived of time as cyclical. Learned men looked to the stars to understand the distant past, and they carved accounts of the events on slabs that adorned their palaces, temples, and pyramids. The Mayans built large pyramids with distinctively steep slopes that were often topped with temples. They were dedicated to their gods who, they believed, required sacrifices. In time, they began to practice human sacrifice.

Tikal was one of the most important Mayan cities. By 100 BCE, it was an important center for trade and the production of artisan goods involving flint, jade, granite, shells, and **obsidian**—a naturally occurring glass that can be fashioned into blades, arrowheads, and ornaments. Tikal's population was probably fifty thousand in 200 CE, and grew until 400 CE, when it came under the domination of its rival Teotihuacán.

obsidian Naturally occurring volcanic glass widely traded throughout ancient America and processed into projectile points and artifacts.

Map 1.3 North American Indian Peoples, ca. 1500 CE. Nearly every corner of North America was occupied by native peoples, who practiced an incredible range of diverse cultures. This map shows only the largest, most populous peoples, omitting scores of other groups and the thousands of individual villages that characterized native North America. ▼

Map 1.4 South America and Mesoamerica, ca. 900–1500 CE. Mesoamerica and South America were the sites of Ancient America's most populous, wealthy, and dominant Indian empires. Their political, cultural, and economic influence stretched well beyond the territories they controlled. ▲

In conquering Tikal, the Teotihuacanos were likely attempting to control sources of obsidian and gain a monopoly over cutting tools and weaponry in Mesoamerica, but they also may have been trying to secure a reliable source of cacao, a tree that produced edible seeds. Cacao seeds were not just the main currency of Mesoamerica; they were also the basis for *Chocolatl*, a drink favored by the ruling elite.

North and west of the Mayas, near today's Mexico City, the ancient city of Teotihuacán flourished from 150 BCE to 650 CE. By 100 CE, it had a population of about eighty thousand people and was marked by grand avenues and monuments. At its peak five hundred years later, it covered twenty square miles and had two hundred thousand residents. This growth depended on good land, abundant water, intensive agriculture, and the control of important resources, such as obsidian. The city was also a center for north-south commerce and highland-lowland trade. Until about 300 CE, most of Teotihuacán's inhabitants lived in adobe structures. After that time, most lived in more permanent stone buildings with multiple apartments.

Teotihuacán controlled Mesoamerica's most important sources of obsidian. Ten percent of the city's laborers worked in the city's six hundred obsidian workshops. Teotihuacán also had a least one hundred ceramic workshops and exported clay pottery and figurines in addition to textiles, wood, and leather products. To support these nonagricultural workers, the city extracted a large surplus of food from the countryside.

Hugo Brizard/Shutterstock.com

Teotihuacán Teotihuacán was a sacred community, much like Mecca today. The construction of the huge Sun Pyramid, which would eventually be 245 feet high, began around 1 CE; at the same time, most of the population from around Teotihuacán moved into the city itself. The pyramid, one of the largest structures of ancient America, required at least three million cubic feet of earth. Twenty other pyramid complexes, as well as numerous wide avenues, were constructed in Teotihuacán. ▲

In addition to its wide trade networks and vibrant economy, the city was held together by devotion to Tlaloc, a fertility god, and to Quetzalcóatl, the "Feathered Serpent." Priests performed religious rituals that attracted thousands. The priests also governed the city, serving as clerks and administrators. Like the Maya, the priests of Teotihuacán had an advanced knowledge of astronomy and mathematics, and they kept careful records of the seasons as well as of tribute from the countryside.

For reasons that remain obscure, Teotihuacán collapsed in about 650 CE. Most likely, problems in trade and subsistence reinforced a sense that the city was no longer favored by the gods, and the ruling priests lost their authority. By 750 CE, the city was in ruins, home to only three thousand people. Most Teotihuacanos returned to the countryside from which their ancestors had come. The city's collapse dealt a devastating blow to the Maya. By 900 CE, Mayan civilization had declined, but even now it remains a vibrant and distinctive culture.

1-3b The Mexica and Tenochtitlán

After the fall of the Maya and Teotihuacán, the Toltec, who migrated into Mexico's central valley from the north, achieved brief dominance in Mesoamerica through their adoption of the cult of Quetzalcóatl and the formation of a loose military alliance of many Mexican peoples. But drought, war, and famine undermined the Toltec state, which collapsed in 1168 CE. In its wake rose the Mexica, or Aztecs, a Mesoamerican society famed

> The Mexica create a society based on conquest, violence, and literacy.

for its militarism. The Mexica came to central Mexico from the north in the mid-1200s, and their culture and society were shaped by perpetual war and their belief that they were a chosen people. They believed their war god Huitzilopochtli had told them to build a city where they saw an eagle perched on a cactus eating a snake. When they saw such a sight in a lagoon near the ruins of Teotihuacán, they founded Tenochtitlán, "the place of the cactus." To them, the eagle represented Huitzilopochtli, and the snake it consumed their drive for conquest. The cactus on which the eagle landed was full of symbolism: Its red fruit calls to mind the human heart, the organ that would become so central to the Mexica rite of human sacrifice.

Through wars and political struggles, the Mexicas dominated Mesoamerica by 1428 CE. As their power and conquests increased, a cult arose around Huitzilopochtli. The war god became the center of a vigorously enforced state religion that was promoted through a form of centralized education. Mexica priests, like those of Teotihuacán, were clerks and administrators, but they also were responsible for the cult and for mediating between people and the gods. Mexica society was intensively militaristic; children of the elite were trained as warriors. Its laws, pronounced by kings but validated by priests and considered to be divinely inspired, were strict and feared. Drunkards were enslaved and then killed if they repeated their crime. Thieves and adulterers were executed.

Mexica society was hierarchical: At the top stood the emperor and his officials; next were the warrior-nobles, whose men, if captured by enemies, were expected to die with honor. Priests kept and prepared the sacred books. Commoners might work as artisans or farmers on land owned by nobles. The elite dined on meat, tortillas, and tamales and enjoyed drinking chocolate. Commoners rarely ate meat and subsisted on ground maize, beans, and vegetables. Elite men served the state. Elite women stayed at home until marriage and then were charged with producing children and woven goods. Women commoners often worked outside the home as vendors or midwives. Their boys went to school to learn religion and the arts of war; girls learned religion and domestic skills in preparation for marriage, which usually occurred around age sixteen.

The cult of Huitzilopochtli cannot be separated from the Mexica interest in human sacrifice. Previous Mesoamerican peoples had practiced human sacrifice on occasion, but the Mexica brought this bloody ritual to a new level. They believed it was necessary to appease an angry god and to maintain the cycle of existence. Human sacrifice kept the sun rising, the rain falling, and the seasons passing. The sacrifice itself was incidental to the central rite: the excision of the living human heart.

Humans sacrificed for Huitzilopochtli were held down over a stone slab. The priest slashed the victim's chest with an obsidian knife, removed the palpating heart, and threw it into a caldron of fire. Then the body was tossed down the temple steps, where it tumbled past victims ascending to similar deaths. The corpses were eaten or traded, and

History without Borders

Obsidian—A Mirror on the Past

Selected source of obsidian

Trade route

Culture areas of North America
- Northwest Coast
- California
- Plateau
- Great Basin
- Southwest
- Great Plains
- Woodlands
- Subarctic
- Arctic

Major civilizations and culture areas of Mesoamerica and South America
- Aztec empire
- Inca empire
- Maya civilization
- Other militaristic chiefdoms
- Tropical farming peoples
- Desert farming peoples
- Nomadic hunter/fisher/gatherer peoples

Major Sources of Obsidian and Routes of Diffusion through 1520. Throughout the Americas, obsidian was among the most valued commodities. Mined in specific areas, and prized for its translucence, strength, and razor-sharpness, it was widely traded and worked into a host of items that ranged from everyday carving instruments and jewelry to spectacular mirrors used by Mesoamerican leaders as a window into the future. ▲

The Granger Collection, New York

Aztec Warriors with Obsidian Swords In a world without steel, Mesoamerican warriors fashioned swords and clubs out of wood into which they embedded razor-sharp blades of obsidian. These weapons, known as *macuahuitl*, were deadly in close combat. Here three warriors are shown armed with *macuahuitl*; they also carry shields and regalia. ▲

Werner Forman/UIG/AGE Fotostock

Aztec Mirror, 1400–1520 In Mesoamerica, mirrors were not used to study one's own appearance but rather as divinatory aids that could provide a portal to otherworld entities and the distant future. Created by master artisans of finely worked obsidian, obsidian mirrors were prized by the elite as important symbols of their status. ▲

Before 1500, the Americas were largely without metal tools. In a world without steel, obsidian—a dark volcanic glass—was among the commodities most valued by native peoples. For thousands of years, people across the Americas used it to make cutting tools as well as ritual artifacts and everyday trinkets. Its value derived from its relative scarcity, its luminosity, and its workability. Notably, obsidian does not have a crystalline structure, so in the hands of a skilled artisan, it can be carved or knapped into deadly blades, projectile points, brilliant jewelry, and other items for domestic and ritual use. Because obsidian points can be made microscopically thin, even today the sharpest scalpels are made of obsidian rather than metal.

The molecular content of each obsidian flow is unique and thus all obsidian objects can be traced to a specific site and source. This allows scientists to determine the precise origin of the obsidian used across the Americas. As a result of their studies of how the first inhabitants of America used obsidian, scholars can glimpse the extensive trade networks that tied together the distant and disparate peoples of the Americas. It is now clear that obsidian was among the most widely circulated commodities in the Americas. Obsidian originally mined in the American West has been found by archaeologists in the Northeast, and obsidian from Mesoamerica has been found in many regions of North America, such as Oklahoma and the Southeast.

Because obsidian was often mined near active or extinct volcanoes—places Indians often associated with gods, sacred animals, and revered ancestors—many peoples believed that it was imbued with special characteristics that gave it unusual power. Some held that as a substance, it was nearer to the gods than people. Among the Aztec, the trade and veneration of obsidian reached epic proportions. It seems entirely possible that had the Aztec not had adequate sources of obsidian, its culture might not have placed such a premium on human sacrifice. Its warriors prayed for success in their wars with these words: "May he savor the fragrance, the sweetness of death by the obsidian knife. . . . May he desire the flowery death by the obsidian knife. May he savor the scent . . . the sweetness of the darkness, the din of battle."

The Aztecs believed that *Tezcatlipoca*, the Master of Fate, saw the world reflected in a magical obsidian mirror. In a sense, scholars today play a similar role. They study this beautiful, mysterious glass for insight into the ways and beliefs of the ancient peoples of the Americas who, because of the passage of hundreds and even thousands of years, can be glimpsed darkly by the scant traces of their lives that survive today.

Critical Thinking Questions

▶ What role did obsidian play in Mesoamerican society?

▶ Can you think of other goods and commodities that were similarly central to Mesoamerican society?

Johan Reinhard/National Geographic Creative

Global Americans In 1999, the frozen bodies of three children sacrificed more than 500 years ago were found enshrined near the 20,000-foot summit of Volcán Llullaillaco, the highest volcano in the Andes. Child sacrifice was important to the expansionist imperial Inca state and performed at pivotal moments, such as a ruler's death or a natural disaster. The eldest of the three children, likely a 13-year-old girl, known to us as the "**Llullaillaco Maiden**," was probably a peasant from the countryside selected for her beauty; the younger two were probably her attendants. A year before her death, the Maiden was taken to Cuzco where her life was transformed. She lived as an elite under the direction of priestesses and practiced the exalted feminine arts of weaving textiles and brewing *chicha*, a beer made of fermented corn. In the weeks before her death—according to a chemical analysis of her long, tightly-braided hair—she consumed increasing amounts of coca and *chicha* as she participated in sacred ceremonies along the hundreds of miles to the Volcán Llullaillaco. Heavily sedated and clenching a small clump of coca between her teeth, she succumbed to the frigid high altitude at the appointed time on Llullaillaco. She was surrounded by items from across the empire: seashells, feathers, coca, corn, and dried meat. She was far from her home and her upbringing, but the coca and the *chicha* and her tomb atop the Andes placed her in proximity to the Inca gods and perhaps even eternity.

their skulls were stored on racks in the temple. During the inauguration of the Great Temple in 1487 CE, more than twenty thousand people were sacrificed over four days. Most were conquered peoples. Some were drugged; others went calmly to their deaths as they, too, believed in the rituals that consumed them. Although the exact number of victims will never be known, it is clear that as the empire expanded, so did the practice of human sacrifice. In addition to its brutality, the empire was also noted for its literate priesthood, its monumental architecture, its finely worked gold and silver artifacts, and its unparalleled feather works.

Under Mexica rule, the Valley of Mexico had a population of at least 1 million. With 300,000 residents, the city of Tenochtitlán was the most populous in the world outside of Asia. Although the Mexica created a complex system of gardens and canals in their capital city, Tenochtitlán could supply only about 5 percent of the food it needed. The Mexica state successfully managed the redistribution of food and labor from countryside to city, but it was an unwieldy empire with thirty-eight subject provinces rendering tribute, diverse peoples and languages, and a territory half the size of Mexico today. By 1500, the empire had stalled. Its wars against rival nations had become quagmires. Soon, the empire began to collapse. It seemed the gods could no longer be appeased and the cycle of life was imperiled. Moctezuma, the ruler, became depressed, berated his troops, and worried aloud at the approach of the Mexica year *Ce Acatl* (in Europe, 1519), for it was believed that in that year, the man-god Quetzalcoatl would return.

1-3c The Inca of Peru

The last and most extensive American Indian empire emerged in central Peru around 1200 CE. Like the Mexica, the Inca built an empire through

> The Inca establish ancient America's most expansive empire.

con-quest and the subjugation of productive farming societies. By 1525, from their capital of Cuzco, home to tens of thousands of people, the Inca dominated nearly all of the Andes, a mountain chain running the length of South America. Each Inca king was believed to be divine, and after his death, his wealth maintained his cult and his mummified body. Thus, to secure his own legacy, every Inca king launched new wars of conquest.

The Inca conquest could be brutal—nearly all men captured in war were forced into the Inca army—but the Inca state tolerated conquered peoples' religions and brought their elites into the state. In fact, many of the Inca's greatest cultural achievements—unique stone masonry, exquisite textiles and ceramics and gold work, precise astronomical observations—were derived from earlier or conquered Andean civilizations. The Inca excelled in organizing and centralizing their sprawling empire.

Unlike in Mesoamerica where Mayan and Mexica merchants dealt independently with one another, the Inca state controlled the economy. It built a system of regional warehouses and maintained more than fourteen thousand miles of roads. An elaborate system of runners and pack trains allowed supplies and messages to reach all corners within days. The Inca were skilled in agriculture. With the development of a vast system of irrigation, they grew potatoes, maize, peanuts, and cotton. They were also skilled surgeons and unparalleled weavers. Although they had no formal writing system, they recorded trade and census data with colored and knotted strings called *quipus*. All the cords in a Quipu hung from a single string. Their positions and colors signaled what was being counted, and the type of knot indicated a number. Typically, the knot's placement signified units of 1, 10, 100, or more. Altogether, the Inca created the most efficient, integrated empire in the Americas, incorporating millions of people into their economy and culture.

1-4

The Agricultural Southwest and the Arid Interior

The Hohokam created extensive canals to irrigate their fields in the area that is now Phoenix, Arizona. These massive canals not only moved huge amounts of water but are also monuments to Hohokam engineering skill and social organization.

What does this image, which shows the size of an ancient irrigation canal from the American Southwest, tell you about how and why some early societies built such canals while others did not? ▶

Peter V. Bianchi/National Geographic Stock

A thousand miles north of the Valley of Mexico in the arid region that became the American Southwest, complex but far less populous civilizations emerged. The Hohokams and the Anasazis adopted agriculture, sedentism, and pottery making. Further east, the Numa moved into the arid Great Basin. In the prairie-grasslands of the Great Plains, where there were few streams for irrigation but vast expanses of sturdy grasses, Indian life and culture formed around vast herds of bison.

☞ As you read, think about how climate and resources shaped the cultures of the Southwest and the Great Plains. What set the cultures of the Southwest apart from others in ancient America?

1-4a The Hohokam Peoples

Central to the development of Hohokam communities in the Gila and Salt River valley of present-day southern Arizona was the creation of a dependable system for allocating water (see Map 1.5). Unlike Mesoamerican farmers, who had reliable water sources, the Hohokam of the arid desert dug irrigation canals that were ten feet deep, thirty feet wide, miles long, and lined in plaster to capture and divert scarce water. In the Salt River Valley, fourteen major canals distributed water through a thousand miles of smaller canals and channels. With this water, the Hohokam raised corn, beans, and squash, which they harvested twice a year. They also grew agave, cotton, tobacco, and other plants. To supplement their diet, they gathered wild plants from the desert and hunted rabbits, deer, and antelope. Befitting their desert environment, the Hohokam lived in brush-covered semisubterranean homes in towns situated beyond river floodplains to ensure their survival. They constructed large earthen mounds, produced fine pottery, and created ornaments from shells they obtained from peoples of the Pacific coast and the Gulf of California. The most important export of the Hohokam

> The Hohokam trade across great distances and create elaborate irrigation systems.

was turquoise, which Mesoamericans prized for its color and the ease with which it could be worked into jewelry. In return, the Hohokam imported copper bells and tropical macaws, which they bred in pens.

Altogether, the Hohokam numbered about fifty thousand, and Snaketown, their largest town, had several thousand inhabitants at its peak. It was sustained by canals that irrigated huge fields of maize, squash, and cotton. Among the Hohokam, ball games brought communities together. They played with a small rubber ball on slightly oval ball courts up to sixty-five yards long with large hoops or rings through which contestants sought to kick goals. The Hohokam constructed more that two hundred of these ball courts. Fans sat in earthen bleachers to watch their team play.

After the fall of the Toltec in 1168, Mesoamerican influences in the north declined. The Hohokam stopped building ball courts and abandoned their semisubterranean homes for adobe dwellings built above ground. Soon thereafter, the Hohokam abandoned their small, dispersed settlements and congregated into fewer and larger towns. At this time, the Hohokam began to construct their Great Houses, such as Casa Grande. At the center of this large walled complex was a building that was several stories high; most likely it was used for celestial observations and to survey canals. A flood, not invaders, devastated these desert-dwelling people by sweeping away most of their communities and irrigation canals in the second half of the fourteenth century. The Sonoran desert would not be inhabited again until the modern city of Phoenix was established six centuries later.

1-4b The Anasazi

At the same time that the Hohokam emerged as an agricultural and sedentary people, the Anasazi developed a similar culture in the high desert plateau of the Southwest. The Anasazi were skilled stonemasons, and in this exceptionally arid climate, many of

> The Anasazi build extensive roads and communities.

Map 1.5 The Peoples of the Great Plains and Southwest, ca. 1450. In the largely arid interior of the North American West, the Great Basin and the Great Plains were thinly settled, but in the Southwest tens of thousands of people lived in scores of permanent settlements adjacent to rivers or on the tops of highly defensible mesas. In the Southwest, irrigation and the manipulation of water were central to agriculture. ▲

their buildings survive. A thousand years ago, some five thousand Anasazi lived in Chaco Canyon in the San Juan Basin of New Mexico. Pueblo Bonito, their largest town, was at the center of a sprawling network of Anasazi communities and housed several hundred people, who worshiped their deities in semisubterranean **kivas**. To collect and transport water to their fields, the residents of Chaco Canyon built an extensive system of dams, ditches, canals, and reservoirs. The Anasazi also built cliff dwellings, and at Mesa Verde in southwestern Colorado, they built a nearly impregnable two hundred-room complex into the cliffs.

By about 1150, roads linked Pueblo Bonito to one hundred fifty smaller communities. These roads radiated out from Chaco Canyon straight as an arrow for hundreds of miles. Some were narrow; others were nearly thirty feet wide; some paralleled each other for miles. They were built by a people who had neither wheeled vehicles nor pack animals, and their use remains somewhat of a mystery. Clearly, though, the roads enabled the Anasazi to more easily transport over great distances food and the hundreds of thousands of timbers required to build their towns in Chaco Canyon and elsewhere.

If too much water in the form of a flood destroyed the Hohokam, not

enough water doomed the Anasazi. Tree-ring studies indicate a terrible drought between 1150 and 1180 CE, forcing people to move from Chaco Canyon and related sites as food systems failed. Perhaps the people went 60 miles north, for at this time the community known today as *Aztec Ruins* emerged. When it, too, collapsed a century later, another community, Paquimé (or Casas Grandes), 390 miles south of Pueblo Bonito, became a regional center. Here Katsinas—supernatural beings associated with rain and fertility—were first depicted on walls and murals. In all likelihood, the Paquimé are the ancestors of today's Pueblo Indians of Arizona and New Mexico because Zuni and Hopi traditions tell of Chaco Canyon as a place where their ancestors lived. By 1500, around two hundred fifty thousand Puebloans lived in some 134 communities across Arizona and New Mexico.

1-4c The Great Basin

About a thousand years ago, the Numas, ancestors of the Utes and Shoshones, moved from California and Nevada into the arid Great Basin, bringing

{ The Numa move seasonally, skillfully taking advantage of resources.

kivas Semisubterranean rooms used by Puebloan and the Hohokam peoples for spiritual ceremonies.

Pueblo Bonito, Chaco Canyon Pueblo Bonito had six hundred rooms, a central plaza, and forty "kivas," or half-underground rooms with wood roofs that were important ceremonial centers. The community's crescent shape allowed the sun to light and warm each of the town's structures. ▲

Martin Gray/Getty Images

with them their techniques of food production. They set up small encampments alongside lakes, streams, and springs. Few Numa practiced agriculture but most relied on **camas**, potato-like lily bulbs, and pine nuts. These two sources of food could be processed and stored for later use. The peoples moved seasonally from encampment to encampment to be near their sources of food. Men fished and hunted, and in late spring, women dug up camas, which they pounded into meal. In the fall, family groups harvested pine nuts. The Numas were skilled basket weavers, and they wove containers that other societies might have produced out of ceramics.

Almost alone among peoples of the Great Basin, the Northern Paiutes of the Owens Valley of southeastern California practiced agriculture. They irrigated root plants that, with the region's seeds and nuts, allowed them to establish small, permanent villages. To the north, the Northern Paiutes of southern Utah and Nevada grew maize, beans, squash, and sunflowers near streams and springs; elsewhere they used irrigation to grow their crops.

1-4d The Great Plains

Over millennia, humans and bison developed together on the Great Plains. In bison, humans had a dependable source of a lean, flavorful

{ Indians of the Great Plains develop their culture based on bison.

meat; a sweet supply of fat; thick hides for robes and covers for their homes; horns and bones to make into tools and weapons; and wool for garments and rugs. As the extent of the Great Plains shifted with the climate, so did bison ranges, and humans migrated accordingly. Bison increased in numbers when humans burned the prairie grasslands annually, an intervention into the plains ecology that stimulated the growth of the tender grasses on which bison fed.

The societies that developed alongside the bison were among the most stable in the Americas. About 2500 BCE,

the plains became less arid, and bison herds increased, supporting small bands of nomadic hunter-gatherers for the next two thousand years. Around 250 CE, Plains Indians adopted the bow and arrow, which they used to kill bison at close range.

The rhythms of Plains Indian society followed those of the bison. For most of the year, bison lived in small herds composed of calves and a mature cow while bulls grazed in small numbers on their own. In late summer, bison cows and bulls came together to mate and to feed on tender grasses. As winter approached, cows with their calves separated from bulls. Similarly, plains peoples lived in small groups most of the year and came together in the summer in groups that ranged from twenty-five to one hundred individuals, the numbers required to hunt bison most efficiently. In the winter, when food was scarce, bands contracted to the size of a few families to survive. They carried their tipis, clothes, and food on their backs, or they bred dogs as beasts of burden.

In a typical hunt, Plains Indians constructed a corral at the base of a bluff or the end of a ravine. To call the bison, a young man sang a song that sounded like a distressed bison. This call attracted cows, who led the herd over the embankment or up into the ravine, where armed men slaughtered dozens of the confused and injured animals. Men and women butchered the bison and spent days celebrating the successful hunt. The meat not consumed immediately was cut into long thin strips and dried into strips or pounded and mixed with fat and berries to form **pemmican** for later use. For thousands of years, and long after 1500, peoples of the Central Plains lived in this manner.

But other Plains Indians were sedentary. About 1 CE, some began to live in villages, and some around modern Kansas City began to cultivate small amounts of maize. Others constructed burial mounds. Around 850 CE, some peoples settled as far north as central South Dakota, building homes of wooden posts and earthen roofs, which provided excellent protection from frigid winters. Although they still relied on bison, these peoples also grew maize, beans, squash, and sunflowers. For centuries, they expanded up the Missouri Valley. As their numbers grew, so did the size of their villages. Known today as the *Oneotas*, these people improved the soil with ash and planted maize in ridge-and-ditch fields, an agricultural practice that was as labor intensive as it was productive.

About the same time that the Oneotas were settling the Upper Midwest, the Wichitas, the Pawnees, and the Arikaras moved onto the Central Plains. They shared a common culture, although they developed separate polities and languages. They lived in square earth lodges in villages next to fields where they grew maize, beans, squash, and sunflowers. Their villages lasted until about 1450 when drought or a colder climate caused them to disperse.

camas Plant in the lily family with an edible bulb.

pemmican Concentrated food used by Indians consisting of lean meat dried, pounded fine, and mixed with melted fat.

The Pacific West

Some Native Americans made pots, but most in the Far West were expert basket weavers and created baskets that varied widely in shape, size, and function. California Indian basketry reveals the diversity and creativity of Native American culture.

As you look at this image, can you discover some of the uses for these baskets? Why did California Indians make baskets of such a wide range of shapes and sizes? ▶

The Granger Collection, New York

The peoples of the Pacific West, encompassing Alaska, the Northwest Coast and Columbia Plateau, California, and Hawai'i, did not adopt formal agriculture, but they did consistently modify the land to maximize food production. They had no large urban centers and lived in thousands of decentralized villages. Nowhere else in the Americas were there so many languages and different cultures.

☞ As you read, focus on the diversity of the peoples of the Pacific West. Can you discern how the peoples of the Pacific West used the sea?

1-5a Alaska

Although it is widely accepted that North America was settled by Paleoindians who came south from what is now Alaska, very little is known about the peoples who took their place in Alaska. It seems that by about 3000 BCE, a new wave of immigrants—the Aleuts and the Inuits, also known as *Eskimos*—came to the area from Siberia (see Map 1.6). These people had begun to develop separate cultures before they crossed the Bering Sea by canoe, and they spoke their own languages. The Aleuts settled the Aleutian Islands, and the Inuits settled on the Alaska mainland.

{ Aleuts and Eskimos build a rich culture.

Over thousands of years, the Aleuts became highly skilled maritime peoples ingenious in making watercraft and tools and in using animal hides, intestines, and bladders. They even used whale skins for clothing. With canoes, spears, and nets, Aleutian men ventured into icy waters to hunt fish, whales, porpoises, seals, sea lions, and sea otters. They built homes of drift logs and whalebone; most were about twenty feet across and oval shaped with walls sunk several feet into the ground. Mats of skin and grass provided a place for people to eat and sleep. Scholars have found evidence of permanent villages on high bluffs. Aleutian society, like that of Northwest Coast peoples, was stratified into the rich, the ordinary, and slaves, usually war captives or orphans who performed hard labor.

Alaska's remoteness and heavy forest cover complicate archaeological work, but it is known that the Eskimos ate game and wildfowl and hunted whales. They often concentrated in large villages and spent summers along the coast where they harvested and dried salmon for later use. In other seasons, they lived in semisubterranean homes covered with sod to keep out the cold. They insulated their clothes with fur. They made blades and projectile points out of slate and pottery of local earth, and they carved ivory from walrus tusks into exquisite animal- and humanlike figures.

1-5b Northwest Coast and Columbia Plateau

From Northern California through Southeast Alaska, along what is now called the *Northwest Coast*, scores of different groups developed an economy and society dependent on rivers, forests, and the sea. Persistent fogs make this area unsuited for maize agriculture, but tobacco and camas can grow. The northwestern coastal peoples also ate sea mammals, fish, deer, berries, and roots. They built multifamily houses out of enormous planks hewed from cedar trees and wore distinctive, beautiful basketry hats.

{ The Chinook and others trade extensively and depend on salmon for their subsistence.

Among these Pacific Northwest peoples, the most important ceremony was the **potlatch**. Elite families held this feast to commemorate significant moments in the lives of their children, such as a naming or a marriage. The potlatch began with speeches, continued through feasting and socializing, and culminated in the giving of beads, food, artwork, and other items of great value to the guests. This generosity redistributed wealth and cemented power relationships by creating reciprocal obligations across the community.

The Chinook of the lower Columbia River were the most prominent of the Pacific Northwest peoples. Class divisions structured their daily life, and slavery was common. Those born into freedom had their foreheads cradled and shaped to be long and sloping. Slaves, by contrast, had natural, rounded heads. They performed basic labor and suffered abuse from their masters. Some were captives seized in war; others had lost everything, including their own freedom, through gambling or other misadventures.

The Chinook lived at the center of a crucial trading zone, and their language became the language of commerce across the Pacific Northwest. Salmon was the mainstay of the economy, even for those who lived far inland

potlatch Ceremonial feast of Northwest Coast Indians marked by the host's distribution of gifts to demonstrate wealth and generosity with the expectation of eventual reciprocation.

On the map labels:
INUIT — ARCTIC — INUIT
YUPIK
ALEUT
Aleutian Is.
Yukon R.
Arctic Circle
ATHAPASKAN
SUBARCTIC
TLINGIT
HAIDA
NORTHWEST COAST
KWAKWAKA'WAKW
NOOTKA
MAKAH
CHINOOK
TILLAMOOK
PACIFIC OCEAN
PLATEAU
SPOKANE
COEUR D'ALENE — FLATHEAD
CAYUSE
NEZ PERCE
Columbia R.

Additional peoples of California not shown on map
Awaswas
Barbareño
Bear River
Chilula
Chimariko
Cupeño
Esselen
Ineseño
Juaneño
Karkin
Karuk
Kashaya
Kato
Kitanemuk
Konomihu
Lassik
Maricopa
Mattole
New River Shasta
Nomlaki
Nongati
Obispeño
Okwanuchu
Purisimeño
Ramaytush
Sinkyone
Tataviam
Ventureño
Wailaki
Wappo
Whilkut
Wiyot

TOLOWA
SHASTA
YUROK
HUPA — MODOC
WINTU — ACHUMAWI
YUKI — ATSUGEWI
YANA
MAIDU
KONKOW
POMO — PATWIN — NISENAN
COAST MIWOK — WASHO
CHOCHENYO — MIWOK — NORTHERN PAIUTE
TAMYEN
MUTSUN — MONO
RUMSEN — YOKUTS
CHALON
SALINAN — PANAMINT
TUBATULABAL
KAWAIISU
CHUMASH — CHEMEHUEVI
SERRANO — MOJAVE
TONGVA
LUISEÑO — CAHUILLA
KUMEYAAY — TIPAI QUECHAN

CALIFORNIA
Colorado R.
Channel Is.

CHINOOK Peoples
Modern boundaries, for reference
0   200   400 Km.
0   200   400 Mi.

PAIPAI
KILIWA
COCHIMÍ
GUAYCURA

Kauai
Oahu
Molokai
Lanai — Maui
Hawai'i
PACIFIC OCEAN
LAPITA
160°W — 20°N — 155°W
0 50 100 Km.
0 50 100 Mi.

Map 1.6 The Peoples of Alaska, the Pacific Northwest, and California, ca. 1450. The tremendously rich natural environments along the coast and interior river valleys of the Pacific Northwest and California contributed to a tremendous range of Indian groups and extremely dense settlements across enormous regions. In California, Indians often used fire to modify their natural environment, promoting the growth of plants and animals they valued for food and the production of cultural items. ▲

on the Columbia Plateau. The Chinook caught and processed enormous amounts of salmon, which they dried and pounded into a flour for later use. Through these and other activities, such as gathering berries, men and women contributed protein to the diet.

1-5c California

Around 2000 BCE, when sea levels stabilized and the Pacific Coast climate became predictable, the people in what

> California is among the most diverse and densely settled regions in the Americas.

is now California began to thrive as they learned to use a marvelous variety of plants and animals. Nowhere in North America were there more local variations in climate—even within narrow valleys, environments vary from one side to another—and people adapted to them, creating regional cultures along the wet coastal regions of the north, the desert of the southeast, the moderate climate of central California, and the Sierra Nevada mountain range.

A hallmark of ancient Native California is the seeming paradox of a very large population that was dense, diverse, and decentralized. Recent estimates suggest that some three hundred to three hundred fifty thousand people lived in California in the year 1500. Collectively, they spoke more than one hundred different languages—20 percent of all of the languages spoken in North America. Each language group was composed of an even larger number of independent peoples. The basic political unit was a central village and one or more affiliated hamlets. In some regions, groups were as small as two hundred fifty people; in others, as large as fifteen thousand people. The relatively small territories that Indian groups controlled initially led scholars to believe they were unsophisticated, but research has shown that they were as worldly as any ancient American people. They manufactured baskets of great utility and beauty. They studied the heavens as skilled astronomers and mathematicians. They relied on trade to obtain goods such as obsidian that were not locally available. And because of their small villages, they looked to their neighbors for marriage partners.

As hunter-gatherers, California peoples managed their environment and practiced intensive plant and animal husbandry. They used fire to clear fields and encourage the growth of grasses, which would provide food for deer. Coastal people tended oyster beds. Rather than developing a single crop, such as maize, California Indians profited from the diversity of edible plants that grew naturally.

California Indians relied most of all on acorns produced by the abundant oaks. Women gathered the acorns in huge baskets and crushed, soaked, and dried them several times to remove a poisonous acid. The dried meal was used year-round to make porridge or thin cakes. Protein-rich acorns supported large and dense populations; men supplemented the diet by hunting deer and other game and fish.

For gathering acorns and other purposes, California Indians made a stunning variety of baskets. Some were large for gathering grains; some were small for keeping precious items; others were so tightly woven that they could carry water. Just

tomols Plank-built boats constructed by the Chumash and other California groups to ply the coast and travel between the mainland and coastal islands.

aquaculture Cultivation of fish for food.

about every group had its own style. Some wove the fibers clockwise, others counterclockwise; some embroidered baskets with bird feathers, and others enhanced them with small shells. More than just containers, baskets were an expression of a local aesthetic that used natural resources in a way to suggest the unity of the earthly world with the supernatural.

Most of California was characterized by small semiautonomous villages. Warfare among California Indians was uncommon but erupted sporadically, prompted by competition over food sources. Unlike most California Indians, the Chumash of the Santa Barbara region, numbering about fifteen thousand people, lived in scores of related villages. The Chumash of the coast and the Channel Islands had **tomols**, seaworthy canoes about thirty feet long. They were constructed of planks cut from driftwood or redwood and held together by a sort of glue and then reinforced by hemp cords passed through small holes. The canoes were sealed with pine tar and dried asphalt and then sanded with shark skin and painted.

Like most peoples, the Chumash had a clear division of labor. Women gathered acorns and shellfish, and men hunted seals and sea lions. The Chumash who lived in the interior drew geometric shapes and mysterious human animal figures in local caves that continue to inspire even as they confound. Like most coastal people in California, the Chumash converted local olivella shells into beads, which became a medium of exchange across California. In fact, the name *Chumash* means "bead money makers."

1-5d Hawai'i

Sixteen or seventeen hundred years ago, thousands of years after most of the Americas had been settled, perhaps a single large ocean-going canoe sewn together by cords and propelled by a woven sail, set forth from the Marquesa Islands in the South Pacific. The canoe was double hulled and contained a rich cargo: edible plants as well as breeding pairs of dogs, pigs, and fowl and stowaway

> The Hawaiian islands are among the most recently settled regions of the Pacific.

rats and weeds. The crew was composed of twenty or so Lapita Polynesians, a people who for centuries had been settling the islands of the Pacific east of Samoa. They were well prepared to establish a permanent presence wherever they made landfall.

What led these Lapita explorers to sail out into the ocean is not known, but it was an epic voyage. A reconstruction of ocean currents and wind patterns reveals that the canoe sailed, rather than drifted, some two thousand miles northwest. After weeks at sea, they reached a chain of uninhabited volcanic islands ideally suited for the Polynesian lifestyles and economy. The migrants named them Hawaiki, or Hawai'i, after their homeland. For fifteen centuries, the Hawaiian islands supported a rich and flourishing society that evolved from the descendants of that single canoe.

The Lapita were wise to bring plants and animals with them, for Hawai'i had only one native mammal, a small bat, and few edible plants. Soon after their arrival, the Lapita began to cultivate taro, sweet potato, banana, breadfruit, yam, and coconut. Rainfall was adequate to support their crops, and vegetation provided cordage and thatching. They ate seabirds and native geese and derived much of their subsistence from the tropical waters, which contained hundreds of species of fish and crabs and more than 1,000 types of mollusks.

Archaeologists have discovered a great variety of hooks, sinkers, and nets used by the islands' early dwellers. They have also found that by the 1300s, Hawaiians had initiated **aquaculture**, building hundreds of shore and inland ponds that they stocked with fish to harvest. The harvest yielded more than 2 million pounds of fish per year. For their rich bounty, the Lapita thanked Lono, the god of fertility and production, to whom they dedicated an annual festival.

Early Hawaiians did not live in major population centers; rather, like most farmers, they were dispersed across the land. They built temples and shrines out of stone and adorned them with carved sculptures. They possessed no draft animals or wheeled vehicles. They used canoes to travel along the coast and walked overland on a network of trails.

In the first centuries after the Lapita arrived, the population of the islands doubled with each generation. By around 1100, it had reached about twenty thousand inhabitants. Over the next four centuries, the population increased steadily, probably exceeding two hundred thousand. Hawaiian society was hierarchical with a chief and a ruling class on top and a base of laborers at the bottom. As the population increased, so did competition for land, and by 1100, territorial boundaries were well marked and defended by local chiefs who paid tribute to a paramount chief.

Rock Art, Chumash, Painted Cave Like many Native Americans in the West, the Chumash of California adorned some of the caves in their homelands with mysteriously complex and beautiful images that most likely were the creation of their religious and spiritual leaders. It is believed that some of these drawings represented celestial bodies and others concerned themes of reproduction and animal life. ◄

Witold Skrypczak/Getty Images

1-6
The Woodlands

This open hand is an iconic image from the Eastern Woodlands peoples who lived east of the Mississippi River nearly two thousand years ago. Cut skillfully from a piece of Mica, a sheet mineral that cleaves nearly perfectly, this hand may have been worn or carried. It is just one example of the artistic accomplishments of the Woodlands peoples, who often created beautiful jewelry and decorated their everyday items with images and geometric designs.

In looking at this graceful form, do you think it draws us into Hopewell culture, or does it warn us away? ▶

Heritage Images/Fine Art/Corbis

The Woodlands refers to both the forested eastern half of North America and the common culture of Native Americans who lived there beginning thousands of years ago. The Woodlands can be very cold in winter and very humid in the summer. The forests of the Woodlands have an abundance of streams and rivers with varied food sources, including deer in the south, caribou in the north, and fish and sea mammals along the coast. Woodlands peoples developed agriculture, extensive trade networks, and social and political systems that supported some of the largest urban centers in ancient North America.

☞ As you read, focus on the unique cultures of the peoples of the Woodlands. Can you identify the cultural characteristics shared by Woodlands peoples?

1-6a The Adenas and Hopewell

Two thousand years ago, the Adenas and then the Hopewell of the Ohio River Valley (see Map 1.7), who lived in small agricultural settlements, built some of the largest, most exact, and numerous geometric earthen constructions ever. Remains of these huge earthworks, some of which were miles long, can still be seen in aerial photographs, although most were destroyed by twentieth-century urban development. Their purposes are uncertain but they may have functioned as burial mounds or calendrical or astronomical devices. The Adenas and Hopewell were exceptionally skilled in producing textiles and ceramics and in crafting objects of aesthetic and symbolic value—wondrous copper ear spools, breast plates, mirrors, figurines, and pipes for tobacco.

> The Adena and Hopewell build earthen structures of unparalleled size.

The metals, shells, and woods of which these objects were made came from great distances. The Hopewell used grizzly bear teeth from the Rockies, obsidian from Yellowstone in Wyoming, iron from Kansas, mica from North Carolina, shells and shark and alligator teeth from the Gulf of Mexico, copper from the Great Lakes, and silver from Ontario. In turn, the goods they created were carried far across eastern North America and have been recovered in burial sites throughout the Southeast. For reasons that are still unclear, the Hopewell went into decline around 400 CE and had disappeared by 800 CE, but elements of their culture had already spread through trade over much of eastern North America.

1-6b Cahokia and the Mississippians

In the region of the Mississippi Valley known as the **American Bottom**, elements of the Adena and Hopewell tradition survived among a people known as the *Mississippians*. The American Bottom is a broad floodplain of the Mississippi River in southwestern Illinois about twenty-five miles long and at most a dozen miles wide. Its swamps and small lakes were rich in game, plants, and waterfowl, and Mississippian peoples found its soil ideally suited for agriculture. By around 900 CE, its fertile lands were increasingly and intensively planted, and over the next five centuries the region experienced a remarkable cycle of rise and decline. The building of Cahokia, its largest town, coincided with the onset of a global warming trend that increased summer rainfall and improved the corn harvest. By 1050–1150 CE, the American Bottom held one of the largest populations north of Mexico—at least ten thousand people, and perhaps as many as thirty thousand.

> Cahokia emerges as one of the great urban centers of ancient America.

Mississippians were like the Hopewell in that they were at the center of a wide trade network, produced beautiful artifacts, and built large mounds. But the Mississippians outstripped their predecessors in the production of maize, in their mound building, and in their social and town organization. They grew maize on raised ridge-and-ditch fields, and maize production became the key to the increasing population of the Mississippians.

Mississippian towns were marked by large mounds and plazas, and they dominated the flat river valleys of the American Bottom. Just outside modern

American Bottom Flood plain of Mississippi River near modern-day St. Louis where indigenous culture flourished a thousand years ago.

Map 1.7 The Peoples of the North American Woodlands, ca. 1450. Across much of the eastern half of North America, native peoples combined hunting and agriculture. They developed complex and hierarchical cultures rooted in trade, agriculture, and often, through systems of coerced labor, large public monuments, such as pyramids and mounds. ▲

St. Louis, Cahokia flourished from 800 to 1200 CE. It was a sacred place, just as Teotihuacán was for Mesoamerica, and it drew people from small, semi-independent communities across the area. Its urban design, monumental mounds, dependence on maize, and overall layout seem to reflect Mesoamerican influences.

Building Cahokia's mounds required a complex and coercive labor system. The greatest construction, Monks Mound, is among the largest ancient structures in the Americas. At its base, it is 330 yards by 250 yards, and it is more than 30 yards high. This massive mound composed of 22 million cubic feet of soil was built one basket of earth at a time. To prevent its erosion, Cahokian engineers used four different types of soils and installed a complicated system of drains. Monks Mound was crowned with a large wooden structure that faced south, toward the sun. It was

but one of some 100 mounds the Cahokians constructed. Smaller mounds were often used as burial sites for rulers and men and women who were sacrificed at the time of their ruler's burial. In one tomb, archaeologists unearthed 260 victims, who seem to have been killed so that they could accompany their leader in the afterlife.

During its height in 1000 CE, Cahokia's residents built neighborhoods of small, rectangular houses and numerous wood buildings most likely used for rituals and astronomical observations. By 1200 CE, the central plazas and mounds were ringed with a wooden palisade. Cahokia became fragmented and declined during the 1300s. Its abandonment likely coincided with the onset of a cooler climate that reduced maize harvests and undermined its society. Nonetheless, elements of Mississippian culture survived in the American Southeast into the early eighteenth century.

1-6c Southeastern Societies

In the centuries after Cahokia collapsed, other Mississippian societies flourished. Major cities, such as Cofitachequi in present-day South Carolina,

> Many Southeastern societies are hierarchical and have religious leaders as rulers.

and Moundville, south of Tuscaloosa, Alabama, were, like Cahokia, agriculturally based and relied on forced labor. These hierarchical societies with a total population of about ten thousand were organized as **chiefdoms** and overseen by a class of priests. Like other Mississippian societies, they produced many items for export and trade. They drew on Mesoamerican and Cahokian cultural traits.

Some Mississippians shared a Southeastern Ceremonial Complex centered on a trio of gods or individuals who were variously represented in stone, ceramic, shell, and copper objects. An important symbol was a man-god with hawk wings and a tobacco-moth proboscis. For the Mississippians, hawks were symbols of power, and tobacco moths were valued for pollinating tobacco, an important crop. Southeastern Ceremonial Complex personages were often depicted wearing the spiraling shell of a conch, a symbol that for Mesoamericans indicated legitimate leadership.

The Pensacola on the Gulf Coast, the Calusas in Florida, and the Guales—Southeastern Woodlands peoples who lived farther east along the Atlantic Coast—were not associated with this complex, although they were also organized into chiefdoms and had some cultural resemblance to Mississippian peoples. These peoples lived in settlements that were smaller than Cahokia and did little farming because they were surrounded by bountiful food sources. The historic peoples of the Southeast—the Caddos, Choctaws, Chickasaws, Cherokees, and the Creeks—would not emerge until the sixteenth century in the wake of collapse of the chiefdoms of the South.

1-6d Iroquoian Speakers

Iroquoian Woodlands people lived east of the Great Lakes and in what is today upstate New York. Sometime after 500 CE, many of the people of

> Iroquoian-speaking peoples form one of North America's most important political confederacies.

the Northeast began to cultivate corn, which they most likely received from peoples to their west. By 1300 CE Iroquoian peoples depended on corn. As the climate cooled and became drier, competition and warfare broke out among the peoples of the Northeast. As a result, Iroquoians began to consolidate and fortify their towns against raids from their enemies, most likely the Wendat (Huron), an agricultural and hunting people who lived in the northern Great Lakes region. Iroquoians had extensive trade relations with peoples farther north. Eventually, Iroquois villages were configured into five related entities—the Mohawk, Oneida, Onondaga, Cayuga, and Seneca—and they formed the **Haudenosaunee** (whole house), **Iroquois Confederacy**, or **League of the Five Nations**.

Through their league, the Five Nations would ultimately emerge as the most powerful Indians in the Northeast.

The Haudenosaunee lived in towns of about fifty residences, each occupied by several families. Most towns were made up of clans descended from a common female ancestor, and people of these **matrilineal** clans, who traced their descent through the maternal line, shared a **longhouse**. These impressive wooden structures—some more than one hundred yards long—had a central hallway, semiprivate rooms, and rooftop openings to allow smoke to escape. The Iroquois typically inhabited their town sites for about three generations and then built a new town about ten miles away where soil and timber had not been depleted.

Among the Haudenosaunee and Wendat, various forms of labor were divided according to gender, which in turn shaped social organization and family relations. Women cared for the longhouses; planted and harvested village fields of corn, beans, squash, and tobacco; crafted clothes and pottery; and watched over children. Men prepared the cornfields for planting, caught fish, and hunted deer, beaver, elk, rabbit, turkeys, geese, and pigeons. Men were also responsible for external relations, namely war, trade, and diplomacy. By the nature of their work, women spent more time in and around villages than men, who were often absent fishing, hunting, and trading. This gendered division of labor led to **matrilocal** residential patterns within Iroquoian peoples. This meant that a married couple would reside with the wife's parents, not the groom's. It would have been logical for women rather than men to have lived together and formed the basis of households. Furthermore, descent, inheritance, and family ties were matrilineal in that children did not inherit their father's property but that of their mother's brother,

Effigy Smoking Pipe, Second Century BCE to First Century CE This stone pipe fragment is carved in the shape of a tattooed warrior head. The surviving ear bears a large piercing. ▲ The Ohio Historical Society; Photographer

chiefdoms Form of social, political, and economic organization in which power is exercised by a single person, the paramount chief, over many communities.

Haudenosaunee, Iroquois Confederacy, or League of the Five Nations "Whole House," confederacy, or league formed by the five Iroquois nations: the Mohawk, Oneida, Onondaga, Cayuga, and Seneca.

matrilineal Kinship system in which ancestral descent is traced through the maternal line.

longhouse Long narrow residential building favored by Iroquoian-speaking Indians in northeastern North America.

matrilocal System in which a married couple resides with or near the wife's parents.

The Granger Collection, New York

Global Americans Iroquoian-speaking communities before 1500 were often bathed in blood as villagers fell upon one another and their neighbors in a cycle of violence and revenge. In the later decades of the 1400s, Hiawatha, a leader from Onondaga, embodied the suffering caused by these conflicts. Through the words of a stranger, **Deganawidah**, a Huron (Wendat) prophet from the north, who came to be known as the Peacemaker, Hiawatha led his people toward peace, power, and unity. Hiawatha had lost three daughters to violence. With words of condolence and gifts of beads, the Peacemaker eased Hiawatha's grief and articulated rituals that became the basis for unity among all five Iroquois Nations. Words and beads (wampum) were to replace war and weapons. Tribes were to retain control over their own villages, but a Grand Council of fifty leaders would oversee common concerns. Deganawidah charged the leaders of each of the Nations to show patience "that your skin be of a thickness of seven spreads of the hands." The words of Deganawidah preserved peace among the Haudenosaunee, but in a bitter irony, the Haudenosaunee, then freed from their own internecine conflict, turned on their enemies, in particular Deganawidah's Huron. As the life of Deganawidah suggests, Indian communities in early America were independent yet integrated into larger networks of contact and exchange. Villages might very well be ringed with palisades, but individuals and ideas moved across borders.

and in old age, individuals often counted on their nieces and nephews for support rather than their own children.

1-6e Algonquian Speakers

The Haudenosaunees warred and traded with a range of Algonquian-speaking peoples who lived around them and occupied most of the Northeast from Beothuk Island south along the coast to the Chesapeake Bay. To the north were the Ottawas, Algonquins, and Montagnais; to the east were the Mahicans, Abenakis, and Wampanoags. To the south were the Delawares and Susquehannocks, and in the west were the Shawnees, Potawatomis, Anishinaabegs, Illinois, and Fox. Like the Haudenosaunees, Algonquian-speaking peoples had a vast knowledge of plants and animal behaviors that enabled them to subsist in a demanding and variable seasonal climate. They did not

> Autonomous Algonquian-speaking peoples inhabit much of the Northeast Woodlands.

organize themselves into large polities like the southern Mississippians or into confederacies like the Haudenosaunee. Algonquian communities were generally small, and most people lived in dome-shaped houses made of bent saplings covered with mats of hides. Those who lived close to the sea had more food options than other peoples of the Eastern Woodlands, so Algonquians relied less on cultivated agriculture than did the Haudenosaunees or the Wendats. North of Maine the growing season was too short for agriculture.

In New England and the mid-Atlantic, the Massachusetts, Wampanoags, Narragansetts, and Lenapes built few permanent towns, relying more on more seasonal camps. In summer, coastal Algonquians hunted seals and whales, gathered shellfish, and caught fish. In the winter, northern family groups moved into the interior to hunt deer, elk, moose, bear, and beaver for food and for the raw materials for clothing and tools. This varied economy served them well for centuries, but limited food sources and harsh winters kept their numbers low.

Summary

The peopling of the Americas was a relatively recent development in a global process that has been ongoing since the emergence of humanity in Africa millions of years ago. Human migration to the Americas was the result of technological advance and changes in the earth's climate. When the earth's ocean levels fell as the earth cooled, Beringia emerged from the ocean, and skilled hunters who had harnessed fire were able to push the human frontier of settlement across this land bridge into the Americas. Others ventured down coastal waters all the way to the tip of South America.

The first peoples who settled across the Americas quickly made their homes in habitable regions, and beginning about thirteen thousand years ago, a common culture known as *Clovis* dominated much of North America. Soon after the rise of Clovis, the earth's climate changed again. This gradual global warming—the result of a slight change in the earth's axis—and the skill of Clovis hunters led to the extinction of the large mammals that had been the prey and cultural foundation of the first peoples who settled across the Americas. Predictably, humans adjusted to these changes, and as they did, they developed agriculture and other skills that allowed them to make a living just about everywhere in the Americas.

As humans came to inhabit more of the regions of the Americas, they developed diverse cultures, all in response to their needs, desires, and local environmental conditions. In South America and Mesoamerica, vast agricultural empires emerged, peopled by millions. They were united by complex cosmologies and religious beliefs and were supported by agricultural surpluses that flowed into capital cities, such as Tenochtitlán. Further north, across North America, the locus of daily life was the village, and Indians developed an enormous range of cultures and languages. Some relied on animals, such as bison, for food and clothing. Others depended on acorns or salmon for sustenance. Nearly all the peoples of the Americas traded with neighbors for commodities they could not produce. But even as they consumed goods from beyond their own region, peoples remained distinctly diverse. This diversity was the essence of America in 1500 and the product of millennia of migration, settlement, and adaptation.

‹Thinking Back, *Looking Forward*›

As you review this chapter, think about universals in human experience. What prompted the migrations of the first American peoples before 1500? In the next chapters, look for what prompts later migrations to the Americas. Look, too, for the mechanisms of empire—how do conquests and absorptions of diverse people change across time? In what ways are family structures in Native American, European, and African societies related to economies? How does gender correlate to work? How do religious beliefs shape communities and the roles of individuals in them?

These are just some of the themes from Chapter 1 that subsequent chapters will explore. To make your study concrete, review the timeline and reflect on the entries there. Think about their causes, consequences, and connections. How do they fit with global trends?

Additional Resources

Books

Calloway, Colin G. *One Vast Winter Count: The Native American West before Lewis and Clark.* **Lincoln: University of Nebraska Press, 2003.** ▶ Synthesis of Native American history and life in the western half of North America.

Clendinnen, Inga. *Aztecs: An Interpretation.* **Cambridge, England: Cambridge University Press, 1991.** ▶ Wonderfully written cultural history of the Aztecs and the rite of human sacrifice.

Fagan, Brian M. *Chaco Canyon: Archaeologists Explore the Lives of an Ancient Society.* **Oxford, England: Oxford University Press, 2005.** ▶ Accessible and illustrated discussion of one of the most important archaeological sites in North America.

Mann, Charles C. *1491: New Revelations of the Americas before Columbus.* **New York: Vintage Books, 2006.** ▶ Highly readable account of Native North America through 1491.

Richter, Daniel K. *Before the Revolution: America's Ancient Pasts.* **Cambridge, MA: Harvard University Press, 2011.** ▶ Masterful overview of North American Indians before contact and through the colonial period.

Snow, Dean R. *The Iroquois.* **Oxford, England: Blackwell, 1994.** ▶ Concise account of Iroquois history and culture through the eighteenth century.

Sturtevant, William C., ed. *Handbook of North American Indians.* **Washington, D.C.: Smithsonian Institution, 1978–2008.** ▶ Comprehensive multivolume work covering the history and anthropology of Native North America in totality.

Trigger, Bruce G. *North America. Cambridge History of the Native Peoples of the Americas.* **Cambridge, England: Cambridge University Press, 1996.** ▶ Comprehensive synthesis of discussion of American Indians before contact with Europeans.

——— *The Huron Farmers of the North.* **2nd Ed. Belmont, California: Wadsworth/Thomson Learning, 2002.** ▶ Opening chapters provide best historical account of Huron culture and life.

> Go to the MindTap® for **Global Americans** to access the full version of select books from this Additional Resources section.

Websites

Infinity of Nations. (http://nmai.si.edu/exhibitions/ infinityofnations/california-greatbasin/134512.html). ▶ Descriptions and images of material culture from across all regions of the Americas. National Museum of the American Indian.

Chaco Canyon: History and Culture. (http://www.nps .gov/chcu/learn/historyculture/index.htm). ▶ National Park Service Website discussing the center of Chacoan culture.

Continue exploring online through MindTap®, **where you can:**
- **Assess your knowledge with the Chapter Test**
- **Watch historical videos related to the chapter**
- **Further your understanding with interactive maps and timelines**

The First American Peoples

2,600,000–50,000 BCE	50,001–25,000 BCE	25,001–10,000 BCE	10,001–5000 BCE	5001–2500 BCE
Glaciers advance often covering much of the northern portions of the northern hemisphere as far south as the 40th parallel during the Pleistocene epoch.	Climate cools and glaciers advance, exposing more land along coastal areas.	Paleoindians move across Beringia overland to North America and down coastal waters of the Pacific all the way to southern South America.	Climate warms, melting ice sheets, submerging Beringia and the ancient coastline of Pacific Ocean. Clovis peoples disperse across much of the Americas.	**3000 BCE** Inuits settle Alaska mainland.
150,000–100,000 BCE	Humans travel to Australia in watercraft and settle.	**11,500 BCE** Clovis culture emerges.		**2500 BCE** Aleuts settle Aleutian Islands.
Homo sapiens sapiens emerges in East Africa.				Bronze metallurgy emerges in Asia.

Largest mammals in North America go extinct, including the horse.

Agriculture emerges in the Middle East (9000 BCE), the Sahara (8000 BCE), Asia (7000 BCE), and Mesoamerica (5000 BCE).

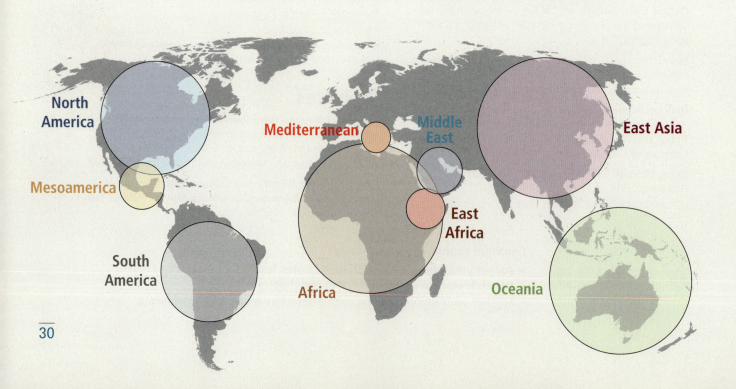

North America

Mesoamerica

South America

Mediterranean

Middle East

East Africa

Africa

East Asia

Oceania

2501 BCE–1 CE	2–500 CE	501–1000 CE	1001–1275 CE	1276–1500 CE
2000 BCE Indians settle most of California and use fire to manage the environment.	Plains Indians adopt bow and arrow and develop culture around bison hunting.	**650 CE** Teotihuacán declines.	**1000 CE** Numa move to Great Basin. Mississippian chiefdoms emerge.	**1300 CE** Cahokia is abandoned.
1000 BCE Iron metallurgy emerges in the Mediterranean. Rome is founded.	**300 CE** Pacific Islanders settle Hawaiian Islands.	**800 CE** Hopewell culture disappears. Cahokia emerges as an urban center.	**1100 CE** Emergence of Iroquois Confederacy.	**1325 CE** Mexicas establish capital of Tenochtitlán.
600 BCE Iron metallurgy emerges in China.		**800–900 CE** Mayan civilization declines.	**1168–1350 CE** Hohokam peoples build Casa Grande.	**1350 CE** Flooding destroys Hohokam fields.
200 BCE Adena culture declines.			**1168 CE** Toltec civilization declines.	
150 BCE Mayan and Teotihuacán civilizations flourish.			**1180 CE** Drought undermines Anasazi.	
			1200 CE Incan empire emerges in Peru.	**1428 CE** Mexicas achieve dominance over Mesoamerica.
			1230s CE Mali empire begins in Africa.	**1438 CE** The Incan empire comes to dominance in South America.
			1300 CE Cahokia is abandoned.	**1500 CE** Mississippian cultures decline.

Go to MindTap® to engage with an interactive version of the timeline. Analyze events and themes with clickable content, view related videos, and respond to critical thinking questions.

2

Joining the Hemispheres: Europe, Africa, and the Americas to 1585

Born in North Africa in 1508, Estebanico's travels to the New World heralded the coming of Europeans and Africans to North America.

Among the most important events and themes in the related histories of Europe and the Americas are the encounters between different civilizations. For thousands of years, Indians in the Americas traded and shared ideas and commodities among themselves as did the peoples of Asia, Africa, and Europe. Beginning in the late fifteenth century, Europeans crossed the Atlantic Ocean and brought the two worlds into permanent contact. Few individuals from this period more fully embody these encounters than Estebanico, a black man born in Africa, enslaved and taken to Spain, and transported to the Americas. There he embarked on a transcontinental journey—from Florida to Texas to Mexico—in one of the great odysseys in American history.

Print Collector/Getty Images

Estebanico was probably born in the early 1500s in Azemmour, a Muslim city in the province of Doukkala in the North African kingdom of Morocco. This region boasted expansive plains ideal for wheat cultivation. In the late fifteenth and early sixteenth centuries, gold and slaves attracted the Portuguese to coastal Africa. They conquered Azemmour in 1508.

Estebanico was baptized as a Christian and was given the name Stephen to honor the first Christian martyr, who in 35 CE (or common era) had been stoned to death for his beliefs. At some point early in his life, Estebanico was enslaved and most likely was taken to Spain in the early 1520s. There Andrés Dorantes de Carranza, a Spanish nobleman, purchased him. A few years later, Dorantes requested permission from the Spanish monarch to join an expedition to Florida led by the Spanish nobleman Pánfilo de Narváez. The king approved his request and appointed him a captain. In 1527, Dorantes sailed to the Caribbean, bringing Estebanico with him.

The expedition was a fiasco. Narváez disembarked with 400 men and 80 horses near present-day Tampa Bay. A local people, the Timucua, hoping to encourage the newcomers to leave their lands, assured Narváez that "gold and plenty of everything" lay just to the northwest in the Apalachee province. Before long, Narváez's overland party, which included Dorantes and Estebanico, became separated from ships trailing them along the coast. Soon, the ships returned to Spain, leaving more than 240 men on land to fend for themselves. Many became ill and died; others were cut down by Apalachee bowmen. Survivors ate their horses, made rafts from the horses' skins and sails from their own clothes, and tried to sail to Mexico. Off what is now Galveston Island, a storm destroyed their rafts and killed most of them, including Narváez. Eighty made it ashore.

For the next six years, Narváez's second in command, Álvar Núñez Cabeza de Vaca, and three others, including Estebanico, lived among the Karankawa and their neighbors, first as slaves and then as emissaries and healers. In 1534, the four set out for Mexico on foot. According to Cabeza de Vaca's narrative of the journey, "The black man always spoke to [Indians along the way] and informed himself about the roads we wished to travel and the villages that there were and about other things that we wanted to know." The four moved from one local people to another, presenting themselves as healers, using Catholic

How does Estebanico's story herald the coming of Europeans and Africans to the Americas?

Go to MindTap® to watch a video on Estebanico and learn how his odyssey relates to the themes of this chapter.

rituals, rudimentary medical knowledge, and a bit of theater. Two years later, escorted by 600 Pima Indians, the four men stumbled on a group of Spanish slave raiders several hundred miles north of central Mexico.

In 1537, after hearing the survivors' tales, Antonio Mendoza, the viceroy of New Spain—as Spain called the colony of Mexico—launched an exploration of the north. When he could not persuade any other survivors to join him, he turned to Estebanico, whose skill as both scout and mediator was well known. On his return journey to what would become the American Southwest in April 1539, Estebanico's earthly adventures ended. An Indian leader, perhaps the leader of the Zuni town of Cíbola, asked Estebanico if he had brothers. Sensing that the man was speaking metaphorically, Estebanico replied that he had an infinite number and that they were armed and nearby. Hearing that, the Indians killed him.

Estebanico's journeys heralded the coming of Europeans and Africans to the Americas: Waves of men and women would cross the Atlantic carrying with them ideas, beliefs, technologies, plants, animals, and germs that would remake the Western Hemisphere. But Estebanico's story also harkened back to the integration of Europe and Africa that had begun more than a thousand years before. His enslavement, his religion, his great travels, and his death—all were emblematic of the brutal inequalities, religious conflicts, and clashes of culture that marked the interactions of Europe, Asia, Africa and then America through the late sixteenth century.

2-1

Europe, the Mediterranean World, and Africa to 1500

Known as a T-O map, this stylized rendering of Europe, Africa, and Asia was popular in Europe in the early Middle Ages. The T represents the Mediterranean Sea; it separates the three known continents of Asia, Europe, and Africa. All are surrounded by an O, which represents the outer sea that was believed to surround the habitable portions of the earth. Typically, T-O maps had Jerusalem at their center, suggesting the close relationship between science and religion in the Middle Ages. As people mapped, settled, and conquered the Greater Mediterranean, they believed they had conquered the world.

What does this map reveal about how Europeans understood the world and its peoples? ▶

Royal 12 F.IV, f.135v Diagrammatic world map, c.1175 (vellum), ./British Library, London, UK/© British Library Board. All Rights Reserved/Bridgeman Images

From ancient times, the Mediterranean was a hub of trade linking Europe, Africa, and Asia. People, commodities, ideas, and disease all moved along the established trade routes. One of the oldest and most important routes carried millions of West Africans into slavery among Muslims in the east. Trade was not the only force bringing disparate peoples into close contact. In Europe at various times and in various regions, religion produced unity, polarization, and conflict. But European Christians also engaged in wars with Muslims to the east. Both trade and religion divided the Greater Mediterranean world and established patterns of conquest and dominion that would persist for centuries. During the Middle Ages and continuing through the early modern period, Europeans transformed their economic, political, and religious institutions in ways that led them to look far beyond their own borders.

☞ As you read, consider how war and conquest, religion, trade, and disease affected the Greater Mediterranean world over the course of centuries. How did these factors variously unite and divide people?

2-1a The Greater Mediterranean and Overland Empires

The peoples of Europe, Asia, the Middle East, and Africa first came into contact with one another via overland trade networks and the

> Expanding overland trade networks link the Mediterranean to Asia and Africa.

relatively calm waters of the Mediterranean. As peoples of the Greater Mediterranean encountered one another and traded technologies, ideologies, and even people, they created an integrated world just as Indians had done across North America. As early as 3000 BCE (before the common era), the eastern Mediterranean witnessed the emergence of some of the world's first agricultural societies. By 1500 BCE (see Map 2.1 on page 37) as a result of an emphasis on farming, which allowed for food production on a mass scale, the population of Egypt reached into the millions, and its influence extended as far as Syria to the east and Nubia, a gold-rich African province to the south. Nubians themselves established overland caravans that linked their own trade networks—and by extension, Egypt's—to the Niger and Congo basins of western Africa as well as those of Ethiopia. Traders moved goods from central and southern Africa to the Mediterranean, the Red Sea, and even to India and China.

Across the Mediterranean from Egypt, the Minoans on the isle of Crete emerged as the Mediterranean's first maritime power. By 2000 BCE, they were trading regularly with Egypt, Sicily, Greece, and the Aegean islands. The Mycenaeans of southern Greece, meanwhile, eventually conquered much of the Mediterranean, sending ships as far as the Iberian Peninsula and the Black Sea. Around 1000 BCE, the Phoenicians of the Middle East began to dominate Mediterranean trade with western Asia. To cement their presence in distant lands, they founded the city of Carthage in North Africa in 750 BCE. After the decline of the Phoenicians, the empires of Persia and Greece rose to power, leading to a fierce rivalry between them during the fifth and fourth centuries BCE.

The integration of the Mediterranean world accelerated under Alexander of Macedonia, better known today as Alexander the Great. Between 334 and 323 BCE, he defeated the Persian Empire and conquered lands stretching from Greece to India. Greek dominance lasted until the rise of Rome. By 117 CE, the Romans controlled the entire Mediterranean, binding together between 50 and 60 million people in Europe, western Asia, and North Africa by granting all conquered peoples the full privileges of Roman citizenship. During the *Pax Romana* (31 BCE to 180 CE), large fleets of ships moved enormous quantities of goods across the Mediterranean. Roman overland routes reached into east Asia and sub-Saharan Africa where merchants traded for gold and other commodities. A portion of this gold was then shipped along the **Silk Road** to East Asia in exchange for spices, jewelry, and silk.

During the erosion of Roman authority by 476 CE, the eastern portion of the empire developed into Byzantium, which included the Balkans, Greece, Anatolia (modern-day Turkey), Syria, Palestine, and Egypt.

As Europeans, Asians, North Africans, and the people of the Middle East came into sustained contact, devastating epidemics started to occur more frequently. The most severe—known as a **virgin soil epidemic**—struck when a population was exposed to a disease for the first time without having been able to build up immunity. In this era, virgin soil epidemics of smallpox, measles, influenza, typhus, or bubonic plague typically claimed up to one-third of an affected population within a few months of first exposure. Epidemics coincided not only with trade but also with urbanization. Growing cities produced enormous amounts of waste and filth, attracting rats and fleas that carried disease and spread parasitic infections.

In 1260, the Mongols—a pastoral nomadic Asian people led by Genghis Khan (1206–1227) and his descendants—reached Egypt. Over the next century, they established the largest land empire in human history, ruling more than 200 million people from the Black Sea to the Pacific coasts of China and Korea. Although the Mongol Empire was relatively short lived, it represented a pivotal time in the increasing integration of East and West. People, not just goods, moved between them. Asian technologies, such as gunpowder, movable type, and the compass, flowed into Europe. The Italian explorer Marco Polo traveled the Silk Road to China, reaching the seat of the Mongol Empire in 1275. His account of his travels, the riches of the Mongols, and their innovations, such as the use of coal as a heating fuel, excited Europeans and whetted the appetites of merchants who imagined huge markets in the East.

Soon after the collapse of the Mongol Empire in the fourteenth century due to disputes among the descendants of Genghis Kahn, the Silk Road was taken over by the Ottoman Turks, a Muslim people who became, by the sixteenth century, the great rival to Christian Europe. By 1500, Istanbul, the capital of the Ottoman Empire situated on the southwestern coast of the Black Sea, had become Europe's largest city. The Ottomans conquered Greece and the Balkans, southeastern Europe, much of western Asia, and North Africa from Egypt to Persia. Although the Empire, which encompassed as many as 50 million people, was Muslim, it tolerated Christians and Jews. Under Sultan Suleiman the Magnificent (1520–1566), the Turks gained control of overland routes that linked Europe to the Indian Ocean. With the improvement of maritime technologies during the fourteenth century, European merchants and rulers began to dream about ocean routes that could bypass the Turks and link them directly with the Chinese and the Indies.

Silk Road Ancient 4,000-mile trade route from China to the Mediterranean Sea. Opened around 100 BCE and closed in 1453 when the Ottoman Turks took Constantinople.

virgin soil epidemic Virulent and often lethal epidemic caused by the introduction of a disease into a society to which the group has had no exposure and is therefore largely immunologically defenseless.

2-1b Religion and the Greater Mediterranean

Increasingly united through trade and conquest, the Greater Mediterranean was also united through religion, but sometimes not without coercion. The ancient Hebrews, a Semitic people, played a crucial role in the acceptance throughout the Greater Mediterranean of **monotheism**, the belief that there is only one god. Around 3000 BCE, the Hebrews wrote what we know today as the Torah and the Hebrew Bible (or to Christians, the Old Testament), which became foundational not only for Judaism but also for Christianity and Islam.

> Monotheistic religion expands cross the Mediterranean.

Christianity emerged in ancient Palestine at the same time that the Roman Empire was expanding its reach in the region. The life and death of Jesus of Nazareth, a Jewish man who lived in Roman-ruled Palestine in the first century, inspired a group of Jews to start a new sect. These followers of Jesus considered him the divine son of God and believed that their religion should be spread to all peoples. They won converts to Christianity throughout the Mediterranean, and in 313 CE, the Roman Emperor Constantine ended the persecution of Christians in his empire. By 400, Christianity had become the official Roman religion.

Islam, the third major religion to emerge in the Greater Mediterranean, was founded by Muhammad Ibn Abdullah about two hundred years later. Muhammad was born in Mecca, a remote trading city in the Arabian desert west of the Red Sea, around 570 CE. In 610, he experienced a series of visions in which he was visited by the angel Gabriel who revealed to him a new faith and named Muhammad the last of God's messengers, the final prophet in a line that included Abraham, Moses, and Jesus. His followers compiled the Quran, a poetic account of his revelations. Like Christianity, Islam sought to convert unbelievers to the faith.

After Muhammad's death, Muslim Arab armies conquered much of the Greater Mediterranean. By 750, the Islamic world extended from Iberia and Morocco in the west to Central Asia in the east. Nonbelievers had to submit to Muslim rule. One result was that many Christians longed for the reconquest of Spain, a process that would not be completed until the late fifteenth century.

Connected to this and other struggles against Islam, Christians sponsored their own military expeditions, the **Crusades**, to take what they saw as the "Judeo-Christian" Holy Land—or Palestine—back from the Muslims. A single Crusade could be composed of as many as sixty thousand soldiers. The first Crusade, launched in 1095, succeeded in conquering Jerusalem and much of the rest of the Holy Land for a while, offering Europeans more direct access to trade routes that brought exotic textiles and spices from the East.

2-1c Africa and Slavery in the Ancient World

Even before the expansion of Islam into North Africa and sub-Saharan Africa, the continent had become part of the Mediterranean world through a sprawling slave trade. By the seventh century, Africa had been connected to Eurasia through trade routes that ran across sub-Saharan Africa and into the East African coast. The Mali and Songhai Empires of the sub-Saharan Sudan had long shipped gold and salt to the east of Africa and increasingly sent enormous numbers of slaves across the continent. The Sudanese benefited most from this trade and created powerful regional empires. By the 1460s, Gao, the capital city of the Songhai Empire, had as many as 100,000 people and a large merchant class that worked closely with Mediterranean traders. The Songhai sent gold and slaves north to Mediterranean societies, and in return, they received glass, copperware, cloth, perfumes, and horses.

> Sprawling trade including grain, precious metals, salt, and slaves links Africa to Europe and the Middle East.

In many African societies, slavery was common simply because there was no other private, revenue-producing property recognized in African law. In the Sudan, some slaves were manual laborers while others were valued for their intellectual abilities. Typically, however, slaves in Africa were considered members of the household, enjoying basic rights. Notably, there was no unifying sense of Africanness across the continent, and many African peoples seem to have thought little about enslaving those who lived in neighboring kingdoms.

The ancient Mediterranean world had embraced slavery. Classical Greece and ancient Rome were both slave societies: Well over 20 percent of their populations were enslaved. Later, beginning in the seventh century, Mediterranean merchants and their leaders, as well as Arabs and their Muslim allies, promoted a slave trade that over centuries ensnared 10 to 15 million individuals from sub-Saharan Africa and delivered them as bondsmen to the Greater Mediterranean, North Africa, and the Persian Gulf states. Unlike in classical Greece and ancient Rome, where just about anyone could be enslaved, in this new system, the least respected slaves were those who were black. Thus, Europeans, Africans, and Arabs developed complex trade systems that moved African slaves across Africa and linked their enslavement with the color of their skin. The subtleties of African slave ownership were rarely recognized in the societies of the Greater Mediterranean.

---

monotheism Belief in the existence of one transcendent god.

Crusades Medieval period military campaigns sanctioned by the Catholic Church to push Muslims out of the Holy Land and restore Christian access to sacred sites.

Map 2.1 Trade Routes Connecting Europe, Africa, and Asia, Fifteenth Century Beginning in 1420, Portuguese mariners explored the coast of West Africa to create direct trade with Africans. Once they had traveled south of the Sahara they began to establish more direct relationships with people of the interior. Eventually Portuguese mariners sailed all the way around Africa and into the Indian Ocean. ▲

2-1d Medieval Europe: Capitalism, War, and Disease

Medieval Europe was at once dynamic and rigid. Its dynamism lay in its growing population and its expanding commerce throughout the

> Medieval Europe is characterized by extensive trade and a rigid social structure.

Greater Mediterranean; its rigidity lay in its static social structures. During the Middle Ages, the cities of northern and western Europe were small backwaters. In the year 1000, Paris and London had only about 20,000 and 10,000 residents, respectively. By comparison, Cordoba in Spain had 500,000 inhabitants and Baghdad was home to nearly 1 million people. However, between 700 and 1300, the population of Europe increased from 25 million to 70 million as a result of the general peace that prevailed and improvements in agricultural technologies. In the eleventh and twelfth centuries, cities such as Paris and Milan expanded to nearly 100,000 residents, and with this growth came other changes.

One change was that the urban poor increased in number. As a result, the Roman Catholic Church, towns, and private individuals founded **almshouses**, places where the poor could get food and shelter. The rise of cities was also accompanied by the growth of an increasingly influential merchant class that sought commodities and luxuries in distant and exotic trading centers. Between 1100 and 1350, European trade with Asia in luxury goods hit new peaks. Europeans shipped flax, wines, olive oil, woolen textiles, timber, fruit, and hemp to China. In return, they received such luxuries as perfumes, silk, gems, and spices. By the early 1200s, commerce centered on the Mediterranean began to replace agriculture as the central focus of the economy of western Europe. In the following centuries, as commerce and trade accelerated, **capitalism**—a dynamic system oriented toward economic growth and private control of resources and profits—emerged first in Venice, Genoa, Bruges, and Antwerp. But capitalism was at this time constrained by the Catholic Church's condemnation of usury—the practice of charging interest on borrowed money—and complicated by cumbersome business practices.

Merchants, nobles, and the clergy were the most outward-looking members of European society, but they constituted only about 10 percent of the population. The overwhelming majority—80 percent—of Europe's residents were peasants, trapped in a social system known as **manorialism**, in which peasants payed dues to a lord on whose land they lived in return for the lord's military protection. Also at the very bottom of society were laborers, farmhands, and shepherds who had no land and whose work and wages were less secure.

Religion also determined one's place in society. The vast majority of Europeans were Christian, and they considered local religious minorities, including Jews and Muslims, to be pagans or infidels. Non-Christians, most notably Jews, were often relegated—if not confined—to their own neighborhoods. Some countries expelled Jews altogether as did France in 1182 and Spain in 1492.

The Roman Catholic Church itself dominated medieval Europe. Priests were presumed to have enormous influence over whether an individual's soul would go to heaven after death. During the Middle Ages, the power of the Pope, the head of the Catholic Church and the ultimate authority within it, greatly increased. In some areas, the power of the papacy rivaled or exceeded that of secular rulers. Two religious orders, or formally organized communities of faith, recognized by the church and lay governments, arose at this time: the Franciscans and the Dominicans. Both espoused poverty, chastity, and obedience, and both relied on the donations of laymen. The men in these orders did not retreat from the world but ventured out to spread Catholicism through Europe and the Greater Mediterranean.

In response to increased papal power and growing national rivalries, European rulers tried to exercise more control over their lands and people. The increase in royal power was not uncontested from below. King John of England was compelled to sign the **Magna Carta** in 1215, thereby agreeing to not levy taxes without the approval of his nobles and granting all men immunity from illegal imprisonment. Yet during the Hundred Years War (1337–1453) between England and France, monarchical power in both countries increased as kings increased taxes on their constituents in order to fund their armies. The consolidation of power was most dramatic in Spain. In 1469, Queen Isabella and King Ferdinand subordinated the nobility and towns to their rule. They introduced the Inquisition in 1478 to investigate and punish religious dissidents and conquered Granada in 1492, expelling 150,000 Jews and 300,000 Muslims from Spain. After these monarchs defeated Granada, they never fully deactivated the army, forming the core of a standing army that supported their increasingly powerful state. Isabella and Ferdinand also began to regulate the domestic economy and foreign trade. For instance, they blocked the import of any commodities that might weaken home industries, promoted the export of Spanish goods, and restricted Spanish merchants' use of foreign flagged ships. By the end of the fifteenth century, Ferdinand and Isabella of Spain, Henry VII of England, and Louis XII of France presided over powerful political structures that controlled the resources necessary to put large armies in the field and ensure that their nations' economies supported the state.

Increasingly powerful monarchies could do nothing to stop the onset of climate change, which, in a phenomenon known as the **Little Ice Age**, led to a drop in temperatures in Europe and elsewhere between the fourteenth and nineteenth centuries. The coldest years were the first third of the fourteenth century. The resulting crop failures and famine killed 10 percent of Europe's population, and survivors were ravaged by epidemics. The plague that arrived in Europe in 1347 from the Black Sea on a ship carrying grain and infected rats quickly spread through crowded cities and their sewage-strewn streets. Within a few years, the Black Death killed nearly 1 in 3 Europeans; in crowded cities, 7 in 10 died during the height of the epidemic. As a result of the Black Death and other epidemics, Europe's population fell from 70 million in 1200 to 45 million in 1400. The plague was even more devastating in Egypt and other parts of Africa, and in Asia (see Map 2.2). In Egypt, it ended centuries of prosperity and stability, killing up to one-third of Egypt's population in less than two years. In North Africa, where the Black Death had the greatest impact, it led to nearly five centuries of decline.

almshouses Buildings in which poor people are allowed to live for free; originated in Europe in the Middle Ages.

capitalism Economic system in which the things that are used to make and transport products (such as land, factories, ships) are privately owned.

manorialism Social system in which people known as serfs worked and fought for and rendered tribute to nobles who gave them protection and the use of land in return.

Magna Carta Latin for *Great Charter*, which English barons forced King John of England to accept in 1215, guaranteeing English subjects fundamental rights and privileges.

Little Ice Age Period of declining global temperatures from the early fourteenth to mid-nineteenth centuries in Europe and North America.

Map 2.2 The Spread of the Plague across Asia, North Africa, and Asia, Mid-Fourteenth Century
As trade networks increasingly tied together the economies of Asia, North Africa, and Asia, diseases, such as the plague, spread with devastating effect, killing millions and undermining commerce and trade. ▲

2-1e The Emergence of Early Modern Europe

In 1500, at the dawn of what we now call the *Early Modern Period*, western Europeans were still dominated by the Roman Catholic Church, centered on the Greater Mediterranean, and were only dimly aware of the world beyond the Mediterranean. But dramatic changes would soon reshape not only Europe but distant lands as well. A central event in western European history was the unification in 1492 of Spain under a single monarchy and the *Reconquista*—the reconquest, or the ultimately successful war to drive

{ European religious and national rivalries deepen.

Muslims from the Iberian Peninsula. The Spanish conquerors won fame, wealth, and honor. Soon they would turn their sights across the Atlantic.

While the *Reconquista* transformed the Iberian Peninsula, the **Renaissance**, a century-long efflorescence of the arts, literature, and science, redirected much of European thought and culture. The Renaissance coincided with the population rebound after the Black Death and was spurred by the patronage of great artists and scientists by the leading monarchs of Europe. By 1600, Europe's population numbered 80 million. Paris had

Reconquista Period of conflict with Muslims in Iberia for 781 years from 711 (Muslim conquest) to 1492 (their expulsion by Spanish Catholics after the fall of Granada).

Renaissance Period of European history (fourteenth and seventeenth centuries) bridging Medieval and Early Modern periods; characterized by new interest in science and ancient art and literature.

500,000 residents, London had 200,000, and Seville had 150,000. Human knowledge expanded, spurred by the movement of inventions and ideas among Europe, China, and Asia.

The Renaissance was also marked by a return to the classical texts of ancient Greece and Rome, a growing belief in the power and worth of the individual, the expansion of secularism, and the development of ideas of scientific inquiry. The foundation of many of these changes was Johannes Gutenberg's invention of movable type in 1454 (it had actually been invented by the Chinese centuries before, but Gutenberg was not aware of Chinese techniques), allowing books to be printed easily and cheaply in Europe for the first time, which led to the spread of knowledge geographically and to the lower levels of society.

At the same time that the Renaissance led many to question European institutions, the Christian Church split. Until 1517, all the followers of Christ were united under the Roman Catholic Church or the Greek Orthodox Church. That changed when the German monk-turned-professor Martin Luther (1483–1546) claimed that everyone, not just priests, was entitled to hear and interpret the word of God. He broke further from Catholicism when he argued that only faith, not specific acts, could absolve a person of sin and ensure salvation. Excommunicated from the Catholic Church, Luther led a religious revolution known as the **Protestant Reformation**. The Roman Catholic Church responded with the **Counter-Reformation**. The Pope summoned the Council of Trent (1543–1563) to affirm Catholic doctrine and expanded the Inquisition to persecute dissidents. But ultimately the Church turned from confronting Protestants to attempting to convert people outside of Europe.

Library of Congress Prints and Photographs Division Washington, D.C. 20540 USA

Portrait of John Calvin (1509–1564) A follower of Luther, John Calvin even more forcefully rejected Catholicism by arguing for predestination, the belief that God chooses people before their birth for either heaven or hell. Both Lutherans and Calvinists disavowed the celibacy of priesthood, changed the form and content of the Mass, rejected Catholic saints and church hierarchies, and focused on the life of Christ and his teachings rather than on the Virgin Mary and the belief that one could obtain divine favors through her intercession. ▲

Beginning in the sixteenth century, this religious conflict between Protestants and Catholics heightened national rivalries. England, long a rival of Spain, became Protestant under Henry VIII (1509–1547), who left the Roman Catholic Church and became head of an independent Church of England when the Pope refused to annul his current marriage so that he could marry his mistress, Anne Boleyn. France remained divided between Catholics and French Protestants, known as *Huguenots*, and religious conflicts convulsed France from the 1560s through the 1580s, especially after Huguenot rioting in Paris in 1572 that was followed by Catholics massacring some 30,000 Huguenots.

Throughout this era, Phillip II of Spain (1556–1598) remained resolutely Catholic and saw himself as the great defender of the faith. He confronted one of his greatest challenges in what were known as the Low Countries of northern Europe—a region consisting largely of today's Netherlands and Belgium and ruled by his family, the Spanish Habsburgs. There, his attacks on Protestants angered businessmen and nobles, who increasingly demanded freedom of worship and political autonomy from Spain. These tensions led to a general revolt in the Low Countries against Spain in 1566 and Spain's sack of Antwerp in 1576. In 1581, in the **Union of Utrecht**, the seven northern Dutch provinces united to form the United Provinces of the Netherlands. In 1588, the northern provinces of the Low Countries finally separated from Spain. They became fully independent in 1609 when they formed the country known today as the Netherlands or Holland.

Amid these upheavals, a new form of capitalism rose to prominence in north and northwest Europe. Under **commercial capitalism**, money was typically invested in

Protestant Reformation
Religious movement initiated by Martin Luther, John Calvin, and others in 1517 that caused a split within Christianity, dividing Catholics and Protestants.

Counter-Reformation
Catholic Church response to the Protestant Reformation beginning with the Council of Trent (1545–1563) and running through the mid-seventeenth century.

Union of Utrecht Treaty signed in 1579 unifying the twelve northern and Protestant provinces of the Netherlands; independence not recognized by Spain until 1609.

commercial capitalism
Preindustrial form of capitalism centered on trade rather than production.

trading enterprises. Wealthy individuals formed **joint-stock companies** and sold shares, or stocks, and in so doing raised huge amounts of capital. The English and the Dutch of the Low Countries—both rising maritime commercial empires— most vigorously promoted commercial capitalism, and the English Channel and the North Sea began to surpass the ports of the Mediterranean as the primary economic routes of Europe. Through the late 1500s, Antwerp was the hub of European commerce and at times had some 2,500 ships from distant lands in its harbor. By the 1620s, Amsterdam was the center of Europe's transatlantic capitalist commerce, and increasingly, as wealth and goods flowed into the city from overseas, it was the center of Europe's most prosperous, diverse, and tolerant society.

joint-stock companies Private business entity in which individuals purchase various shares of ownership, providing the company the equity to invest in its operations.

2-2
Opening up the Ocean World

Sometimes known as the Hakluyt Martyr map because it accompanied Richard Hakluyt's translation of *Peter Martyr's De Orbe Novo (the Eight Decades)*, this map refers to Sir Francis Drake's circumnavigation of the globe and encompasses most of what Europeans knew about the world nearly a century after the voyages of Columbus. It is the first map to include the colonies of New Mexico and Virginia.

How does this map compare to the T-O map presented earlier? ▶

Go to MindTap® to practice history with the Chapter 2 **Primary Source Writing Activity: The World Encompassed**. Read and view primary sources and respond to a writing prompt.

Private Collection/Peter Newark American Pictures/Bridgeman Images

Between 1450 and 1550 as Europe and the Mediterranean world underwent many internal transformations, Europeans also began to set off across the Atlantic Ocean on voyages of exploration, conquest, and trade. With new technologies that allowed them to harness the ocean's winds and currents, the Spanish, Portuguese, Dutch, and English reached the west coast of Africa as well as what came to be known by Europeans as the *New World*. Colonists started trading with the locals, including for slaves. They also experimented with crops, such as sugar, in new forms of production that quickly proved incredibly profitable but enormously destructive to native laborers. Finally, the colonists sent back reports of opportunities for wealth and land, spurring on even greater voyages. By the early decades of the sixteenth century, European navigators had circumnavigated the globe.

☞ As you read, look for the different contributions that rival nations made to the Age of European Expansion. What motivated Europeans to move beyond the Mediterranean, and how did their understandings of the Atlantic and the world change as a result?

2-2a The Age of European Expansion

Legend holds that in the fifth century CE, an Irish monk, St. Brendan, sailed out into the Atlantic and discovered enchanted islands. Five hundred years later, in the year 1001, Scandinavian seafarers sailed west from Iceland and under Eric the Red established settlements on Greenland. Soon thereafter, Leif Ericson founded a settlement in northern Newfoundland that he called *Vinland*. But Vinland was very far from Europe, and its colonization did not lead to a lasting bond between the colonists and the homeland.

{ Economic goods and new technologies drive Europeans to explore far beyond the Greater Mediterranean.

Centuries later, the Chinese became the first great oceanic naval power under the leadership of Muslim Admiral Zheng He (1371–1433) who initiated voyages to the Middle East, East Africa, Southeast Asia, and India. Although the Chinese were the most advanced mariners of their day, they saw little value in trade with foreign nations.

They also lacked the economic strength or the religious zeal to follow their voyages with colonies and conversion campaigns.

Western Europeans developed their own maritime technologies, but used them to different effect. In what is known today as the Age of European Expansion (1450–1650), Italian, Portuguese, French, and Spanish mariners explored the Atlantic, hoping to reach Asia and thereby bypass overland trade routes controlled by the Ottoman Turks. These expeditions were also spurred by new technologies. They were also propelled by Europeans' desires for greater access to gold and slaves from West Africa and a militant Catholicism that wanted not only to push Islam back but also to win new converts for Rome. Other reasons included the increasingly confident and competitive European states and merchants who vied for economic supremacy in the Greater Mediterranean and the economic markets of Europe. Early explorations failed to yield a direct route to what Europeans called the *Indies,* yet they unwittingly achieved something far more influential: They encountered the people of the Americas, bringing them, mostly against their will, into the European economic system.

The ships that proved most useful for European voyages of exploration were built after centuries of innovation in ship design and construction. In the Middle Ages, Europeans constructed two basic types of ships, one propelled by oars and the other by sails. Both were suited for the Mediterranean and the waters of Europe's Atlantic coastline. The oared vessel, or galley, was long and thin. When outfitted for war, it might hold several hundred men. These ships were ill suited for long voyages because they had limited space in which to carry provisions and were not trustworthy on the open seas. The sailing ships, or round ships, depended primarily on the wind and were therefore much cheaper to operate than a galley. Early sailing ships were almost as wide as they were long and usually propelled by a single square sail. They could not sail into the wind. Thus, they too were ill suited for long voyages on the open sea.

In the fifteenth century, a revolution in ship design resulted in a new kind of ocean-going boat. The sternpost rudder replaced steering oars as standard equipment. Ships added more sails, and many gained a third mast. By using a variety of sails, mariners could take advantage of a variety of wind conditions. Although the new ships were relatively small, they could sail into the wind.

The most important navigational tool during the Age of European Expansion was the magnetic compass, an instrument developed by the Chinese, brought west by the Muslims, and adopted by Europeans in the twelfth century. For travel in the Mediterranean, pilots carried charts indicating coastlines, ports, crucial geographical features, and compass directions for sailing from port to port. Mariners who sailed in uncharted ocean waters, however, had to rely on the compass, the **mariner's astrolabe**, and their powers of observation and calculation.

mariner's astrolabe
Astrological instrument used to determine a ship's north-south location while at sea.

Portuguese bronze nautical astrolabe, 1608, by Francisco de Goes, diameter 19.7 cm. /Istituto e Museo di Storia della Scienza, Florence, Italy/De Agostini Picture Library/Bridgeman Images

Mariner's Astrolabe, Thirteenth Century. Seafarers used a mariner's astrolabe—a large brass ring with a needle—that allowed the measurer to determine the height of the midday sun and therefore the ship's latitude, or north-south position. More difficult, and problematic, was the calculation of the ship's speed and east-west position, which could only be approximated. Despite these limitations, by the mid-fifteenth century, mariners had the ships and basic tools necessary to venture into the Atlantic, far beyond the sight of land. ▲

2-2b Iberian Pioneers at Sea

The Portuguese, who lived along the western coast of the Iberian Peninsula, first explored the Atlantic by following the west coast of Africa south. Portuguese traders were frustrated with limited access to the overland routes to the Far East and angered that the city-state of Venice had monopolized the commerce of the eastern Mediterranean. Portuguese leader Prince Henry (1394–1460), who declared "if you are strong in ships, the commerce of the Indies is yours," became a leading proponent of maritime exploration. Once the Portuguese modified their ships for the high seas of the ocean, their narrow-hulled ships known as *caravels* became ideal for the exploration of the Atlantic Ocean and the shallow coastal rivers and waters of West Africa.

In 1420, the Portuguese began to explore the West African coast in search of direct access to gold and another

> Portuguese mariners venture down the coast of Africa and eventually discover a maritime route to the Far East.

precious commodity, salt. In the 1440s, Portuguese ships passed the southern boundary of the Sahara desert, allowing them to trade directly with Africans. In the region where the coast of Africa turns east, the Portuguese established a series of forts, and soon African gold, salt, and slaves began arriving in Portugal by sea.

Portuguese ships may have been agile, but explorations advanced slowly. Some were simply blown off course into the Atlantic. Portuguese exploration continued eastward. With the Far East as the ultimate goal, in 1487 Bartolomeu Dias sailed around the southern tip of Africa into the Indian Ocean. The Portuguese soon established trading posts on the East African coast, violently pushing aside the Muslim traders who had formerly controlled the region. A decade later, Vasco da Gama sailed from Portugal to India. Europeans had finally found a sea route from Europe to the east. Portuguese traders established posts in Kolkata (formerly known as "Calcutta") and Goa, and da Gama returned to Portugal with a fortune in cinnamon, cloves, ginger, pepper, gems, and textiles. Before long, Portugal, a small country of only 1 million people, had established a maritime empire with trading posts that stretched as far east as China and Japan.

2-2c Colonization of the Atlantic Islands

In addition to opening up new seafaring routes down the coast of Africa and to the Far East, the Portuguese colonized islands off the coast of Africa—the Canary and the Madeira Islands. There they initiated a process of conquest and exploitation that would be repeated again and again in different ways as Europeans encountered new lands. On these islands, the Portuguese established brutal plantation systems that produced valuable staple crops for sale and export by using the labor of African slaves.

{ The Portuguese create slave plantations on islands off the coast of Africa. }

On Madeira Island, the Portuguese set fires for seven years to clear forests so that they could introduce new crops. Then, in 1425, after raising cattle, pigs, wheat, and grapes did not prove profitable enough for Portuguese merchants, they introduced sugar cane imported from Sicily. By the end of the fifteenth century, Madeira was well on the way to leading the world in sugar production. The Portuguese planters relied on slaves. Among the earliest were a small number of Jews and Muslims still remaining in Portugal as well as African slaves whom the Portuguese had purchased on their excursions down the African coast. The majority were Guanches, natives taken from the Canary Islands during the height of the Portuguese conquest.

The Guanche had settled the Canary Islands from Africa at least a thousand years before and had had no contact with Europeans until the late 1200s or early 1300s.

In 1402, Spaniards first attempted to conquer the Canary Islands, and they finally succeeded in 1478. They were able to subdue the Guanches, who probably numbered about 20,000 but who were not united, had no ships, spoke different languages, and had no weapons that could match European iron. Above all, the Guanches lacked immunity to the diseases that Europeans carried to the Islands. In the mid-1490s, two virgin soil epidemics, one of them typhus, killed nearly two-thirds of the Guanches on the two largest of the Canary Islands.

As the Guanches died by the thousands, the Portuguese seized or purchased West Africans to replace them as laborers in the sugar plantations they were establishing on the Canary Islands and on those that already existed on the Madeiras. The European trafficking in slaves would prove far more disastrous to the African continent than indigenous slave systems had been. On Madeira and the Canary Islands, the Portuguese learned how to introduce valuable crops to new and promising lands, how to conquer and subdue native peoples, and how to either enslave those natives or replace them with enslaved Africans. The deadly and exploitative plantation system that the Portuguese pioneered in the islands off Africa would change the course of world history.

2-2c Spain and Portugal in the Caribbean and Brazil

The Portuguese voyages of exploration and colonization provided opportunities for a generation of men to find glory and riches. Among these men was Christopher Columbus, who was born in the important Italian commercial town of Genoa and lived for many years in Lisbon, the capital of Portugal, where he became steeped in maritime culture. Columbus married the daughter of a Portuguese governor of the Madeira Islands, and he visited the Canary Islands and the Azores. Most likely he sailed on Portuguese ships down the coast of West Africa.

{ Sailing for Spain, Columbus reaches the Caribbean, mistaking it for Asia. }

Columbus was a devout Catholic fascinated by the writings of Marco Polo. He dreamed of sailing to China to open up a direct trade route with Asia and to introduce Christianity to the Chinese. The Portuguese believed that Columbus would fail, so Columbus sold his vision to Ferdinand and Isabella of Spain, whose recently united kingdoms had no experience with maritime exploration. Spain provided Columbus with three ships manned by eighty-seven men for what the most advanced maps of the day suggested would be a short journey to China.

In the summer of 1492, Columbus sailed west and in October made landfall at a number of Caribbean islands where he encountered the Taino, an Arawak-speaking people. He then sailed to the island of Hispaniola (today,

March 1500 and six weeks later made landfall in a harbor of present-day Brazil, a land that at that time had between 2 and 4 million indigenous inhabitants known as the Tupi. Cabral ordered a massive cross to be raised, claimed the land for his king, and sent news to Portugal to tell the king of this new discovery.

2-2e The World Encompassed

Without realizing what they had done, explorers like Columbus and Cabral had initiated a revolution: They had transformed the world's oceans from barriers to seaways and in the process shifted the center of their commercial world from the Mediterranean Sea to the Atlantic Ocean. This revolution set off a scramble among European nations to sponsor their own voyages of discovery and conquest. John Cabot, an Italian, claimed the eastern coast of North America for England in 1497. Two years later, the Italian Amerigo Vespucci sailed on a Portuguese expedition to South America, where he determined that Brazil was not part of Asia but rather the edge of a continent previously unknown to Europeans. Another Italian, Giovanni Verrazano, claimed Canada for France in 1524. Both of these explorers had set out in the hope of reaching Asia directly; although they were unsuccessful, the expeditions fueled the hopes of Europeans that a sea passage could be found through the North American continent.

{ Thirty years after Columbus's first voyage, mariners circumnavigate the globe.

Spain continued to sponsor voyages of exploration, some of which probed the interior of the Americas (see Map 2.3). In 1513, Vasco Núñez de Balboa crossed the isthmus of Panama and came upon the Pacific Ocean—which he claimed for Spain. In 1519, Ferdinand Magellan, a Portuguese mariner in the employ of Spain, set out to fulfill the dream of Columbus and others by finding a western sea route to Asia from Europe. Magellan's fleet of five ships and 270 men set sail in September 1520. They wintered on the coast of present-day southeast Argentina, rounded the southern tip of the continent that November, and then sailed northwest into the Pacific. In March 1521, the expedition reached the Philippines, where Magellan was killed by locals whom he had hoped to convert to Christianity. Sixteen months later, in September 1522, the expedition's sole remaining ship dropped anchor in Spain. The surviving crew had sought a more direct route to the East, but they had accomplished something more pivotal. They were the first men to circumnavigate the earth, and their voyage greatly advanced Europeans' understanding of the world and its seas, thereby accelerating the integration of distant regions into a nascent Atlantic economy and expanding European empires.

Portrait of Christopher Columbus, 1519. Before his departure, Columbus signed contracts with the Spanish monarchs authorizing him to "discover and acquire islands and mainlands in the Ocean Sea" for Spain. Once in the Far East, Columbus planned to set up a small trading settlement for the crown. ▲

Tomas Abad/Alamy Stock Photo

the island that Haiti and the Dominican Republic share) and back to Europe by way of Cuba. Columbus believed he had been to the outskirts of China. He brought back to Spain two very important discoveries: tobacco, which his men had acquired in Cuba, and an understanding of the winds of the Atlantic, which allowed Europeans to sail to the Western Hemisphere with the confidence that they would be able to return to Europe.

Isabella was disappointed that Columbus had not actually made contact with China and sponsored three more expeditions that he led. He returned to the Caribbean in 1493 with a fleet of seventeen ships and 1,200 men, including a priest, farmers, artisans, and laborers, in the hope of founding a colony. Not until his fourth expedition in 1504 did Columbus begin to realize that he had discovered an entirely unknown land. Eventually, he and others began to refer to the Caribbean Islands as the *West Indies* and to the native inhabitants of the Americas as *Indians*.

Less than a decade after Columbus had stumbled onto the West Indies, Portugal did the same in Brazil. Pedro Alvares Cabral, like Columbus, believed he could find a more direct route to Asia by sailing as far west as possible off the coast of Africa rather than the more southerly route taken by da Gama. His fleet left Lisbon in early

Map 2.3 European Explorations, 1492–1610 Beginning in the late fifteenth century, Spain and Portugal, followed by France and England, explored and then set out to colonize the Americas. Of the European powers, Spain claimed and controlled the greatest expanse of territory in the Americas. ▲

2-3

Spain's Empire in the Americas

This image, which shows Indians led by an Eagle Warrior attacking besieged Spaniards, illustrated a history of New Spain published in 1581 by the Spanish friar, Diego Durán (Codex Durán, folio 30a.) Durán was fluent in Nahuatl, the Aztec language, and worked with Aztec informants to write his book, which was in many ways sympathetic to Native peoples.

As you look at the contrasting weapons, postures, and clothing of these two groups, what can you deduce about their military strategies and the place of war in their societies? ▶

Codex Duran: Pedro de Alvarado (c.1485–1541) companion-at-arms of Hernando Cortes (1485–1547) besieged by Aztec warriors (vellum), Duran, Diego (16th century)/Biblioteca Nacional, Madrid, Spain/The Bridgeman Art Library

Following Columbus's expeditions, Spain explored and conquered many lands and peoples of the Americas. Spain brought the systems honed on Madeira and the Canary Islands to the West Indies, provoking a native population decline and moral outrage among some Spanish clerics. But Spain justified its colonization on religious, legal, economic, and moral grounds. Spain conquered the empires of Mexico and Peru, seizing much gold and silver and prompting Spanish conquistadores to search the Western Hemisphere for other wealthy civilizations to conquer. Once this initial period of excitement passed, Spain set out to rule its new lands and peoples by creating administrative structures designed to exploit and control native peoples. East and north of Mexico, Spain explored both Florida and what would become the American Southwest, but by the mid-sixteenth century, it had all but abandoned the dream of easy wealth in these lands.

☞ As you read, think about the motivations that lay behind the Spanish conquest. What reasons did the Spanish use to justify their control of unfamiliar lands and peoples?

2-3a Spanish Beginnings in the Caribbean and West Indies

Most Spaniards had little difficulty justifying their New World conquests. Like other Christians, they believed that their god had given them "dominion" over all creatures on the earth. In 1493, Pope Alexander VI—in what is known as the *Papal Donation*—decreed that he had the right to "give, grant, and assign" newly discovered lands to the Spanish and Portuguese monarchs so that they might bring the indigenous peoples to Christianity. The next year the Pope formally granted to Spain sovereignty over "all islands and mainlands, found or to be found" beyond a demarcation line negotiated by Spain and Portugal running 370 miles west of the Azores. Under the Treaty of Tordesillas (1494), Spain was granted rights to all lands to the west of the southeastern edge of South America, and Portugal to those to the east of the line. Thus, within a few years of Columbus's first voyage, the Spanish and Portuguese

{ Spain finds legal justification for its Caribbean colonies even as they prove deadly and exploitative.

and the Roman Catholic Church had obtained what they understood to be exclusive control over the New World and its peoples.

In exerting authority over Indians, Spaniards relied on policies that Spanish and Muslim armies had used during their long battle for control over Iberia. The Spanish **Requerimiento** ordered Indians to "acknowledge the [Catholic] Church as the ruler and superior of the whole world, and the high priest called

Pope, and in his name the king and queen [of Spain]." Indians who accepted the authority of the crown and the supremacy of Catholicism would be treated reasonably well. Those who refused to submit were informed that they would be enslaved or killed.

On the island of Hispaniola, Columbus and his countrymen faced challenges that would characterize virtually all European efforts to colonize the Americas. Europeans brought disease to the Americas, just as they had done to Madeira and the Canary Islands. Hispaniola had a native population of at least 500,000 Tainos before the arrival of Columbus. By 1496, perhaps as many as 350,000 had died, most likely from typhus, the same disease that had felled the majority of Guanche. By 1518, smallpox had further decimated a Taino population also reeling from virgin soil epidemics of measles and pneumonia. Smallpox soon spread to Puerto Rico, Jamaica, and Cuba, and by the 1550s, had reduced the population of the Caribbean by 90 percent.

Although Spain conquered Hispaniola and Santo Domingo (1508), Puerto Rico (1508), Jamaica (1509), and Cuba (1511) with relative ease thanks to superior weaponry and epidemics, it was not immediately clear whether and how the islands would generate income for Spain. In theory, Spaniards in Hispaniola would get rich by trading with the Tainos for gold. The Tainos, however, had little of the yellow metal, and what they did have had come from elsewhere. When his dreams of gold went unfulfilled, Columbus shipped Tainos to Spain to be sold as slaves. Isabella, however, ended the slave trade because she consistently affirmed that Indians, once they accepted Spanish sovereignty, were vassals of the crown and therefore free. Two loopholes, however, allowed Spanish slave-raiding expeditions to continue scouring the Caribbean in search of potential slaves: Indians who rebelled against Spanish authority were considered legitimate targets for enslavement, and Indians enslaved by other Indians could be obtained through purchase or barter.

The fact that the Spanish could not easily or legally enslave Indians presented colonizers with two problems: Who would work in the plantations and mines they planned to establish? And if those operations could not be made profitable through enslaved Indians, why should Spaniards risk life and limb to settle distant lands? The governor of Hispaniola, Nicolás de Ovando, found the answer in 1503 when he initiated in the Caribbean a system that had evolved in Spain during the long war against Islam. During the *Reconquista*, Spain had relied on a system known as the **encomienda** in which conquered Muslim villagers were assigned as laborers to conquering Spanish military leaders. In Hispaniola, the *encomenderos*—the men who held the grants of Tainos labor—were to look after the welfare of their Indian charges and ensure that they were instructed in the Catholic faith. Ovando also mandated that Indians be brought from the countryside into central towns where they would be easier to control and convert. Moving the surviving Tainos into towns, however, only made them more susceptible to European diseases. Forced labor, resettlement into towns, and the

Requerimiento Spanish legal document read to Indians during early phase of Spanish conquest demanding peaceful submission to Spain and Catholicism to avoid war, enslavement, or death.

encomienda System in which Spain granted an *encomendero* the right to Indian labor and tribute in a conquered community and required the *encomendero* to educate Indians in Catholicism.

Dea Picture Library/Getty Images

Global Americans In the wake of Columbus's voyages and the Spanish conquest of the Caribbean, thousands of Spaniards crossed the Atlantic in search of their fortunes. Among those who enriched themselves was the father of **Bartolomé de las Casas** (1484–1566) who sailed with Columbus on his second voyage and settled in Hispaniola. In 1498, the father returned to Spain with a present for his son: a Taino slave. Four years later, at age twenty-eight, Bartolomé sailed for the West Indies in the footsteps of his father. There he was a conquistador: He worked to suppress Indian rebellions and was rewarded with *encomiendas* on Hispaniola and Cuba. Eventually, however, he began to see the Spaniard's treatment of Indians in the West Indies as "unjust and tyrannical" and moved from exploiting to protecting Indians. He renounced his own *encomiendas*, became a Dominican friar in 1523, and became history's most vocal and effective critic of Spanish colonialism. He always believed in converting Indians to Catholicism, and in 1540, he met with King Charles and denounced the "murder and destruction" of the Indians by *encomenderos*. Las Casas's pleas led to the New Laws of 1542, sealing his reputation as a great reformer. But his views and writings also laid the foundation for the "Black Legend," the incorrect belief that Spaniards were the cruelest of colonists. The English would embrace and popularize this idea to justify their anti-Catholicism and explain away their own treatment of Indians in North America, which at times was worse.

diseases that accompanied the Spanish invasion all but destroyed the Taino within several decades of the arrival of Columbus.

The catastrophic depopulation and ruthless exploitation of the indigenous people of Hispaniola and other Caribbean islands conquered by Spain in the early 1500s prompted moral outrage among some Spaniards. One priest and *encomendero*, Bartolomé de las Casas, surrendered his encomienda grant in 1514 and spent the next half century trying to secure the humane treatment of Indians under Spanish rule. Eventually, his efforts bore fruit. In 1542, the Spanish crown promulgated "New Laws" that reformed the *encomienda* system and abolished the enslavement of Indians in Spain's American possessions.

On Hispaniola, however, long before the New Laws curtailed the *encomienda*, Spaniards had introduced sugar cultivation and had begun to rely less on Indian laborers. In the early 1500s, they constructed a mill whose Spanish managers came from the Canary Islands, which Spain had taken from Portugal in the 1470s and where it had already cultivated sugar. By 1518, the Spanish crown had worked with the Portuguese to bring enslaved Africans to Hispaniola to work in sugar cultivation. Two decades later, more than thirty mills were on the island; they were the earliest example of plantation slavery in the Caribbean. Despite these advances, the Spanish sugar industry on Hispaniola peaked in 1570 and then declined, undone by competition from Brazil. Spanish trade to and from the West Indies also remained vulnerable to predation because ships had to travel narrow and undefended shipping lanes and negotiate the Trade Winds, which blew west most of the year and complicated sailing east across the Atlantic.

2-3b Conquests of Mexico, Peru, and Brazil

With confidence in the justness of their conquests, Spanish **conquistadores** radiated out from the Caribbean to discover and conquer new territories. In 1518, Diego Velázquez, governor of Cuba, placed Hernán Cortés in charge of an expedition to explore and take control of the interior of Mexico but at the last minute revoked his commission. In an act of mutiny, Cortés stuck to his plan and in 1519 sailed from Cuba with eleven ships and more than 600 men. He soon formed an alliance with the Tlaxcala, who resented the rule of the Aztecs. Cortés then marched on the Aztec capital of Tenochtitlán and boldly seized the Aztec ruler Moctezuma, throwing the empire into chaos. Cortés had by his side an Indian woman of noble birth—baptized as Doña Marina—who was his translator and legitimator. In June 1520, Aztec warriors forced the Spanish invaders from the capital city. Velázquez sent Pánfilo de Narváez to arrest Cortés, but Cortés defeated Narváez. Soon smallpox arrived and spread quickly through the thickly settled countryside of Mexico. Within a year, the Aztecs had fallen to disease and Spanish military might as had the Guanches and Tainos. After a seventy-five-day siege in the summer of 1521, Cortés took the ruined city of Tenochtitlán, thereby giving Spain nominal control over an empire of 25 million people.

> Spain conquers America's largest and wealthiest Indian empires.

conquistadores Spanish or Portuguese soldiers or leaders who conquered much of the Americas between the sixteenth and eighteenth centuries.

Benson Collection, University of Texas, Austin

Global Americans The conquest of the Americas was anything but an exclusively male affair. Few women, however, played a more direct and controversial role in early American history than **Malintzin,** or Doña Marina. She was born in 1500 in a remote region of Mexico that stood on the periphery of the Aztec world. When she was a child, her mother sold her to Aztec traders who in turn sold her to the Maya, among whom she lived for many years. In 1519, when Cortés overwhelmed the town of Tabasco where she was enslaved, she was among twenty slave women offered to him as a gesture of submission. Baptized and renamed Marina, she was then given by Cortés to another Spaniard. Soon though, she became invaluable to Cortés, who took her back. He had with him a Spaniard who spoke Maya but not Nahuatl, so he was unable to communicate with the emissaries sent by Moctezuma, the Aztec leader. When Malintzin realized Cortés's predicament, she stepped forward and made it known that she spoke Maya and Nahuatl, her native tongue. With her assistance, Cortés built an Indian alliance that allowed him to conquer central Mexico, and for that some have judged her harshly. But she had no loyalty to the Aztecs, who had sold her into slavery, and she sensed that the powerful Cortés could best ensure her own survival. She and Cortés had a son together, the first *mestizo*, or person of Spanish and Indian ancestry. She later married a lesser conquistador and died of illness in 1529 at a young age, as did so many in colonial Mexico.

In search of gold to enrich themselves, Spaniards quickly moved to the south, west, and north of Tenochtitlán, reaching what are now Guatemala, El Salvador, Honduras, Florida, and California. As early as 1523, however, word had reached Spanish Mexico of a rich and powerful state—the Inca—somewhere to the south. The conquistadores Francisco Pizarro and Diego de Almagro set out to find it.

By 1532, when Pizarro arrived on the coast of Peru, the Inca empire was reeling from three successive virgin soil epidemics and a civil war. Pizarro, following the approach taken by Cortés, seized the Inca ruler, Atahualpa. He then demanded an enormous ransom in gold for his return. Once the Spaniards received some eleven tons of gold and thirteen tons of silver, they baptized and then murdered Atahualpa. In the wake of Atahualpa's death, civil war among the Inca continued, and the Spaniards began to fight among themselves for the riches of the Inca empire. Indian resistance continued until the Spaniards murdered Túpac Amaru, the last Inca ruler, in 1572. What remained of the Americas' greatest empire was then ruled by Spaniards.

In the same years that Spain was conquering Mexico and Peru, Portugal was beginning to settle Brazil, which it had first reached a generation earlier. The Portuguese—like the Spaniards on Hispaniola—relied on the system they had first employed on the Atlantic Islands. In 1530, the Portuguese divided Brazil into vast "captaincies," each composed of some 75 miles of coastline that stretched deep into the interior. Those Portuguese who received captaincies were expected to settle them at their own expense, and, in return, they received generous economic privileges.

The Portuguese in Brazil had trouble identifying a valuable export commodity until they settled upon dyewood, which could be used to produce a red dye of great value to European textile manufacturers. But the industry languished because the local Tupi had little need for the cheap trade goods that the Portuguese offered them in return for the wood. Some Portuguese enslaved the Tupi, many of whom fled into the interior. Countless others died of smallpox and other epidemics.

In the 1520s, a series of circumstances dictated that sugar would become the mainstay of the Brazilian export economy. Because of their experiences with plantations in Portugal and on the Atlantic islands, the Portuguese knew how to produce sugar. Coastal Brazil was suitable for the crop, and in the absence of the discovery of any precious metals in the colony, the Portuguese crown granted tax exemptions for new sugar plantations. In 1559, it authorized the opening of a slave trade between Africa and Brazil, and in 1570, the Portuguese crown abolished Indian slavery in the colony. Sugar production increased rapidly. The first mill opened in 1526. In 1576's the colony's 57 mills produced 2,500 tons for export, and a half century later 346 mills produced more than 20,000 tons.

2-3c Spanish Imperial Structures of Governance and Commerce

Within a decade of Columbus's first voyage, Spain had in place colonial systems of exploitation and governance. To govern and make profitable their American conquests, Spaniards often worked through Indian leaders to organize labor drafts and extract tribute. They allowed Indian communities to govern themselves as

{ Spain moves quickly to organize and exploit its colonies.

Map 2.4 The Viceroyalties of Colonial Latin America The Spanish and Portuguese monarchs delegated their authority in the Americas to viceroys, men who ruled over large administrative units. Within each viceroyalty were smaller administrative units, such as territories, which in turn were ruled by royal governors in concert with other royally appointed officials. ▲

Territories claimed by Spain

- Viceroyalty of New Spain
- Viceroyalty of New Granada
- Viceroyalty of Peru and Audiencia of Chile
- Viceroyalty of Rio de la Plata

Territories claimed by Portugal

- Viceroyalty of Brazil

✕ Silver mine

long as they submitted to Spanish authority and met their labor and tribute obligations (see Map 2.4). In addition to the *encomienda*, the Spaniards instituted the **repartimiento**, a forced rotational labor draft requiring Indians to work for Spaniards for a specific amount of time and for wages. After the discovery of silver in northern Mexico in 1550, silver became the most plentiful, valuable, and dependable export. Where there were no Indians to work the mines, Spaniards imported African slaves by the tens of thousands.

repartimiento Spanish labor organization system that compelled a certain number of Indians from each community to hire themselves out weekly to Spanish employers. Superseded the *encomienda*.

The Spanish crown delegated its authority in the Americas to **viceroys**, who ruled in the king's name over the expansive regions of New Spain, New Granada, Peru, and Río de la Plata. Viceroyalties were divided into smaller governmental units known as *audiencias*, which in turn were divided into *corregimientos*. At the local level, individual towns created their own municipal councils. During the first decades of the conquest, Indian leaders and nobles often staffed these councils. In the Indies, the Spanish crown followed a precedent set during the *Reconquista* and retained the power to organize the church in conquered regions. This meant that royal officials could appoint church officials such as bishops, thereby giving the crown nearly absolute religious authority in Spain's overseas territories.

The crown also funded legions of missionaries who set out to convert Indians to Catholicism. Franciscans first arrived in Mexico in 1524. By the middle of the century, a thousand missionaries were in New Spain, and the church claimed to have baptized millions of Indians. Many of the conversions were partial at best, aided by superficial similarities between Catholicism and Indian beliefs. Many Indians fused their god, Quetzalcoatl, with Saint Thomas; others likened an Indian rain god to Saint Peter. The Spanish practice of building Catholic churches above or in close proximity to Indian sacred places furthered the blending of religions.

The crown desired the natural wealth of the Americas, in particular silver, and colonists believed that they needed European commodities that they could not produce for themselves. Thus, transatlantic commercial networks developed quickly, linking Spain and its American colonies and reflecting the ascendant economic philosophy of **mercantilism**. A central tenet of mercantilism was the belief that overseas trade should be regulated in ways that supported strong national monarchies. The main goal of this system was to allow the state to amass bullion, which was equated with domestic prosperity and power at home and abroad.

Charles V, who ruled Spain's Empire from 1519 until 1556, regulated the transatlantic trade. Because it was a reliable source of taxes and he was a mercantilist, he believed that the overseas market should strengthen the central state. Charles required that all transatlantic trade be carried on Spanish ships, that only Spanish goods be shipped to the colonies, and that merchants obtain special licenses to trade certain goods. All goods—mostly precious metals, hides, cochineal, and sugar—had to travel to Spain in the *Carrera de Indias*, the heavily guarded Spanish fleet.

In Spain, the *Casa de Contratación*, or House of Trade, founded in 1503 as a royal trading house, organized the fleets and collected the duties on exports and taxes on imports. Charles's successor, Phillip II (1556–1598), tightened royal control over the transatlantic trade. For instance, he restricted trade outbound from Spain to the ports of Seville and Cadiz and designated four legal ports of entry in Spanish America. He also granted trade monopolies to the leading commercial concerns in the viceregal capitals of Mexico City and Lima. In effect, these changes gave the Spanish crown the ability to carefully regulate and tax the transatlantic trade, thereby creating a Spanish mercantilist system that remained in place for more than a century.

The *Casa*, and therefore the Spanish crown, controlled immigration to the Indies. Would-be immigrants needed royal approval to emigrate, and foreigners, Jews, Muslims, and heretics were prohibited from emigrating altogether. The Spanish crown did not see a pressing need for mass immigration because the colonies could rely on Indians and African slaves for labor. Still, in the sixteenth century, about 80,000 Spaniards immigrated to New Spain. About two-thirds of the early immigrants were men, but over time, more families crossed the Atlantic. In 1570, the Spanish population in the Americas was about 150,000.

2-3d Spanish Exploration of Florida and the Southwest

Not until 1513 did Spanish explorers venture into lands that would one day be part of the United States. That year, Juan Ponce de León, the former governor of Puerto Rico and one of the richest men in the Caribbean, claimed the Atlantic Coast of North America from southern Florida to Newfoundland for Spain. Early exploration focused on Florida because it was adjacent to the Caribbean. Contrary to legend, there is no proof that Ponce de León hoped to find a fountain of youth in Florida. In reality, he was in search of gold and slaves. He died in 1521 after being wounded by an arrow shot by a Calusa Indian in Florida.

> Spanish dreams of Indian cities of gold persist in Florida and the American Southwest.

Pánfilo de Narváez ventured to Florida in 1528 at the head of the expedition that included Estebanico, who was discussed in the chapter opening. One of the other survivors of that disastrous expedition, Álvar Nuñez Cabeza de Vaca, published a narrative of his journey in 1542, writing of emeralds and the great towns in the Mexican north. Even before their publication, however, Cabeza de Vaca's tales inspired a generation of would-be conquistadors. In 1539, Viceroy Antonio Mendoza sent a small group led by a Franciscan, Fray Marcos de Niza, and Estebanico north. Before long, Niza was back in Mexico telling all who would listen of lands in the north that were even richer than Mexico. He spoke of having seen Cíbola, one of seven cities in the north rumored to hold great wealth.

To determine the veracity of Niza's claims, Mendoza commissioned an expedition led by Francisco Vázquez de Coronado. In 1540 Coronado set out with 300 Spanish soldiers, 6 Franciscans, 1,000 Indian allies, and 1,500 horses

viceroys Royal officials who manage a region or country in the name of a monarch.

mercantilism Economic theory and policy to regulate a rival nation's economy to increase the power of Spain, England, Portugal, and France.

and pack animals. Niza guided the expedition. After they reached Cíbola, a village of 100 families, Coronado wrote despairingly to the viceroy, "He [Fray Marcos] has not told the truth in a single thing that he said, but everything is the opposite of what he related, except the name of the cities and the large stone houses." Coronado and his men pushed their explorations further into the northern interior (see Map 2.5), soon encountering the Pueblo Indians, a local people. Food shortages became acute in the winter of 1540–1541, and warfare broke out when the Indians tired of the Spaniards' demands for food, wood, and women.

Determined to make an example of a village he deemed uncooperative, Coronado attacked the pueblo of Arenal and burned alive its people who resisted. In the spring of 1541, Coronado gave up the dream of Cíbola and turned his considerable energies to finding Quivira, another city fabled for its riches. Coronado's Indian guide,

known as the Turk because of his attire, led the Spaniards through what are now Texas, Oklahoma, and central Kansas. There, on the trackless Great Plains, Coronado's dreams died. Coronado strangled the Turk with an iron collar, having learned from him that the Pueblo Indians had asked him to "take us to a place where we and our horses would starve to death."

In Florida, another Spanish expedition grew similarly disillusioned. Hernándo de Soto arrived in Florida in the early summer of 1539 with perhaps a thousand soldiers, two hundred horses, and swine, which he planned to use to feed his men. De Soto had made a personal fortune in the conquest of Peru, but he believed that Florida held greater riches. He and his men looted Indian villages and enslaved their occupants. Casualties on both sides ran high. "At night," one Spaniard recalled, "we dressed our wounds with the fat of the dead Indians as there was no medicine left." In 1542, de Soto died of a fever, and several

Map 2.5 Spanish Exploration of New Mexico, Mid-Sixteenth Century Motivated by the erroneous belief that the region north of Mexico City contained a kingdom of unfathomable wealth, Spanish conquistadores ventured to the far north. They encountered numerous groups of sedentary Indians but not the gold and silver of their dreams. ▼

hundred of his soldiers—after three years of a fruitless search for wealth in Florida—retreated down the banks of the Mississippi and into the Gulf of Mexico.

By the 1540s, it was clear to Spaniards that northern North America was not home to rich empires comparable to those they had conquered in Mexico or Peru. When the Spanish settled the north, it was not of the monarchy's doing. Instead, the private initiative of rich men funded the settlements and to a large degree delegated the task of reorganizing Indian lives to Catholic missionaries who sought poverty and anonymity with the same zeal that men like Coronado and de Soto had craved wealth and fame. Still, the viceroy of New Spain did see a pressing need for a military presence in Florida to protect Spanish treasure fleets from pirates. A Spanish post along the southeast coast of Florida, the viceroy reasoned, would keep pirates at bay and provide sanctuary for Spanish ships that on occasion ran aground in the region. In 1557, Phillip II, on his subordinate's advice, ordered the construction of a fort on the Gulf of Mexico and another along the Atlantic Coast at the Point of Saint Elena, known today as Tybee Island, Georgia.

2-4

Europe in the Americas to 1585

The inscription of this watercolor drawing *Indian Village of Pomeiooc* by John White (created in 1585 to 1586) reads, "The towne of Pomeiock and true forme of their howses, couered | and enclosed some wth matts, and some wth barcks of trees. All compassed | abowt wth smale poles stock thick together in stedd of a wall."

Examine the architecture of these buildings and the layout of this village. What they do they reveal about Indian life in this place and time? ▶

World History Archive/Newscom

In the decades after the conquest of Mexico, other European powers launched their own expeditions of exploration and conquest, challenging Spain's dominance in the Americas. At first, such was the power of the Spanish navy that other nations largely avoided direct confrontation. France explored deep into the interior of the continent's far north, for instance. But the destruction of the Spanish Armada in 1588 opened the seas to other powers. The English joined the competition for overseas colonies, especially once Queen Elizabeth and British merchants had been swayed to the view that the English, as Protestants, would be more successful in securing the wealth of the Americas than Catholic Spain (see Table 2.1). The first attempts by England and France to colonize in North America were failures. Although many early settlements proved ephemeral, the biological consequences of European expansion and settlement were nothing short of cataclysmic for the Americas and its peoples.

☞ As you read, focus on the different national cultures of colonization and expansion that Europeans brought to America. What are the similarities and differences between early French, English, and Spanish colonies in the New World?

2-4a The French

In the wake of Magellan's circumnavigation, French Atlantic merchants sponsored Giovanni Verrazano's exploration between today's Georgia and Maine in an attempt to find the Northwest Passage. The French arrived in North America in 1534 when Jacques Cartier made the first of his voyages to the New World. He was in search of a passage to the Far East. To avoid lands claimed by Spain and Portugal, he sailed to the north of the continent, making landfall in Newfoundland, which he quickly dismissed as worthless. Cartier then made his way up the St. Lawrence River, where he met a group of Haudenosaunees from the village of Stadacona, which would become Quebec. Sailing further north, he concluded mistakenly that the St. Lawrence River was a path to the orient.

The following year, Cartier returned, set up a winter camp at Stadacona, and traveled up river to a much larger

{ Indians and Spaniards drive French explorers and Huguenots out of eastern North America.

village, Hochelaga, the future site of Montreal. Although the Hochelagans received Cartier well, he withdrew to Stadacona fearing an attack. There he learned of the kingdom of Saguenay to the west. Indians said it was rich in gold, silver, and other precious resources. Cartier abandoned finding a passage to the Far East, but he decided that a French colony on the St. Lawrence could be used as a staging area from which to explore the interior of the continent and to conquer Saguenay. To further his plans, Cartier kidnapped the Indian leader Donnacona and his sons and took them back to France so that they could tell their stories to French officials. When Cartier returned in 1541, the now openly hostile local Indians killed more than thirty-five of his men. By 1543, the French had abandoned Stadacona and would not return until the fur trade lured them back in the following century. Canada was no longer of interest to the French, especially after Donnacona's description of Saguenay was revealed to be an invention.

The French, however, had continued to probe elsewhere for weaknesses in Spanish and Portuguese claims because they had never fully accepted the Treaty of Tordesillas. They sponsored encroachments on Portuguese Brazil. And in 1562, French explorer Jean Ribault established Charlefort in what is now South Carolina. The settlement of thirty men struggled, and the Spaniards destroyed it in 1563.

In 1564, a group of French Huguenots established Fort Caroline near the St. John's River in what is now Jacksonville, Florida, in a region previously explored by Ribault, who had intended to establish a "New France." He returned the following year with five ships and hundreds more French Huguenots who believed that by settling in the New World, they were striking a blow against Catholic Spain and securing a refuge for Protestants. The settlers also dreamed of gold, silver, and subservient Indians, none of which they found. Tensions rose with the local Indians, and the French decided to abandon the colony. Before they could, Pedro Menéndez de Avilés, a veteran of Spain's New World colonial ventures, marched five hundred soldiers and Indian allies to Fort Caroline. He found a poorly defended colony manned by a few sickly Frenchmen. Menéndez spared the women and children but hanged the men, apparently under a sign that read "I do this not as to Frenchmen, but as to Lutherans." Menéndez then headed south and killed all Frenchmen he could find. With the French Protestant threat eliminated from Florida, Menéndez established a town at Santa Elena on the site of the destroyed Charlefort and created a permanent settlement at St. Augustine in 1565. By 1567, Menéndez had established five military bases along the Atlantic coast and two forts along the Gulf coast to keep other Europeans at bay.

2-4b The Spanish, the Chesapeake, and War over the Seas

{ Spain establishes a mission on the Chesapeake that comes to a violent end.

In 1561, two years before Spain went to war against the French in Florida, a Spanish ship sailing north of Florida was blown off course and made landfall in the Chesapeake Bay, or what the Spanish called the *Bahía de Santa María*. There they encountered a small group of Woodlands Indians in a land the Spanish knew as Ajacán. The ship's commander, Antonio Velázquez, took two of these Indians—a leader known as Paquinquineo and his servant—back to Spain. Paquinquineo, who became known to the Spanish as Don Luís de Velasco, was presented to King Phillip II, who looked favorably on him. After years of unexpected adventures, in 1570 Don Luis led a group of Jesuits to a village near the James River where he was given a joyful greeting by friends and family who had long assumed he was dead.

But by that point, the land of plenty that Don Luís had described to Spaniards no longer existed following six years of famine. And the Jesuits' hopes that they could establish a mission and convince the Indians to plant communally were

TABLE 2.1 Major European Explorers and Conquerors of the Americas, 1492–1564

Date	Explorer/Conqueror	Sponsoring Country	Region
1492	Christopher Columbus	Spain	Caribbean and Central America
1497	John Cabot	England	Newfoundland
1500	Pedro Cabral	Portugal	Brazil
1513	Juan Ponce de León	Spain	Florida
1513	Vasco Nuñez de Balboa	Spain	Isthmus of Panama
1519–1521	Hernán Cortés	Spain	Mexico
1519–1522	Ferdinand Magellan	Spain	The world (circumnavigation)
1524	Giovanni Verrazano	Spain	Canada
1530s	Francisco Pizarro	Spain	Peru
1534–1541	Jacques Cartier	France	Canada
1539–1541	Hernando de Soto	Spain	Florida and the Southeast
1540–1541	Francisco Vazquez de Coronado	Spain	Southwest
1562–1564	Jean Ribault	France	Florida

Archive Photos/Getty Images

Global Americans It is a commonplace that during the colonial period, Europeans and Africans moved west and crossed the Atlantic to the Americas. But a number of Native Americans also went from America to Europe. Most became slaves or curiosities until they sickened and died. A surprising number, however, through luck, determination, and even cunning, returned to their homelands where they resisted colonization. Among these was **Paquinquineo**, also known as Don Luis de Velasco, whom Spaniards took from the Chesapeake in 1561. In Madrid, he became a favorite of the king, but in 1562, when Don Luis grew homesick, King Phillip supported his return to his homeland. Although he sailed for Mexico in the summer of that year, it would be many years before he reached Mexico City. He fell seriously ill and was nursed by Dominicans, who also baptized him. In 1566, Phillip II sent Don Luis and two Dominicans to explore the Chesapeake, but their ship was blown off course and landed in Seville. Don Luis lived in Spain among Jesuits for four more years. By then he spoke Spanish and understood the Spaniards, offering to help establish a mission in his homeland and lead them to "great kingdoms." In 1570, finally, he returned home accompanied by eight Jesuits. Before long, he led a bloody rebellion against the missionaries, killing many himself, and disappearing without a trace into the countryside. Years later, however, he was probably among a group of Indians who, dressed in the black robes of Jesuits, tried to lure a Spanish ship to shore so that he could attack it. And a half century later, he was almost certainly involved in an attack that nearly wiped out the Jamestown colony. Having left his own culture and learned what European settlements would mean for his people, he devoted his life to keeping them at bay.

dashed. As the mission failed and the Jesuits banned trade with the Indians, Don Luis abandoned the Spaniards to live with his uncle, a chief, in a distant village. Eventually, he led an attack on the Spaniards, all of whom except a boy, Alonso, were killed. The boy related the tragedy years later to none other than Pedro Menéndez de Aviles who had come to investigate the fate of the Jesuits. When he learned that the missionaries had been killed, Menéndez took revenge by killing nearly thirty local Indians. The Indians would not forget this violent intrusion into their homelands.

Although the French had failed to establish a settlement in Spanish Florida, they (and later, the English) turned to **privateering** in order to prey on the riches that Spain had extracted from the Americas and to deny the legitimacy of Spain's overseas possessions. Privateers were not the same as pirates; pirates stole for themselves whereas privateers were state-sponsored sailors of fortune who plundered the ships of another country. Typically, the sponsoring monarchy took one-fifth of the plunder. During the first half of the sixteenth century when Spain and France were at war almost continuously, France granted licenses to men willing to attack the Spanish treasure fleet. In the final decades of the century, when England and Spain were at war, the English did the same.

Among the most successful English privateers was Francis Drake.

In 1572, he stole a fortune in Spanish gold and silver from a mule train that was traversing the Isthmus of Panama. Five years later, he set off on another voyage to attack the Spanish treasure fleet. Within three years, he had stolen 800,000 pounds in Spanish treasure and sailed around the globe. In 1579, toward the end of that voyage, Drake sailed up the Pacific Coast, claiming northern California for England.

Drake had not only challenged Spain's claim to the west coast of the continent and the Pacific Ocean but also destroyed Spanish settlements on the Atlantic Ocean. In 1586, before heading back to England laden with Spanish treasure, he sacked Spanish Florida, prompting Spain to abandon its settlement at Santa Elena and transfer its residents and the colony's capital to the sole remaining Spanish settlement in Florida, St. Augustine.

2-4c The English, Ralegh, and Roanoke

In 1585, to spread Protestantism and beat back Catholic Spain, England established its first outpost in North America. The settlement at Roanoke, however, was a dismal failure, undermined by the English crown's emphasis on privateering over colonization. In

{ England's first attempt to plant a colony in North America ends in failure.

privateering Person or ship authorized by a government to attack foreign ships during wartime; in essence, a legalized pirate.

Watercolor drawing of *An Indian Man and Woman Eating* by John White. White's early realistic images of Indians challenged reigning European notions of Indians as naked savages cannibals. Here, a man and a woman eat maize rather than human flesh, and they appear sociable, not barbaric near-humans who live through hunting alone. ▲

British Library Board/Robana/Art Resource, NY

1578, Queen Elizabeth had given Humphrey Gilbert a six-year grant to explore and settle unclaimed portions of North America, but he died at sea before he could carry out his expedition. In 1584, the grant passed to his half-brother, Walter Ralegh, a favorite of the queen and a militant Protestant. Ralegh imagined a vast estate for himself on Roanoke Island in a land he would name Virginia in honor of Elizabeth, known as the *Virgin Queen*. Colonists devoted to agriculture would enrich him through rents and a share of the crops they raised. The colony would also be a base for privateering expeditions, which would benefit the monarch. As preparation for this settlement, the English scouted Roanoke, situated off of today's North Carolina.

The following year, Ralegh's cousin, Richard Grenville, and some 100 settlers, including the artist John White, sailed for Roanoke. Bad weather, the captain's desire to spend weeks privateering, and the queen's decision to divert many of the ships to the war against Spain, weakened the settlement before it even began. When one of the ships ran aground off Roanoke, the 107 Englishmen of the expedition found themselves with only twenty days' provisions. Later that summer, Grenville returned to England, leaving in charge the veteran military commander Ralph Lane who expected a supply ship later that fall. Through the long winter of 1585–1586, Lane's men searched for food, gold, and a water route to Asia. They also spread disease among the native population and grew desperate for food because the Indians had no provisions for men who offered nothing in return.

To the colonists' surprise, Drake arrived in June 1586 with a fleet of twenty-three ships fresh from sacking St. Augustine. The privateer, however, had no provisions to spare. After a hurricane laid waste to Drake's fleet, Lane abandoned the colony, sailing to England with nearly all of the colonists. When Grenville arrived in July with supplies, he found a colony nearly abandoned. He too then returned to England with his ships and several hundred colonists, leaving behind fifteen Englishmen.

Despite these setbacks, Ralegh sponsored another plan for Virginia. The "Cittie of Ralegh," governed by John White and peopled by 110 recruits who had paid their way to the colony and would receive grants of hundreds of acres of land, was to be founded in the Chesapeake Bay, which Ralegh considered a better base for privateering than Roanoke Island. A second settlement was to be established in Roanoke, and it was to be run by an Indian named Manteo, whom the English had captured during their first attempt at colonization. Ralegh intended to dub him "Lord of Roanoke."

Under White's command, Ralegh's ships arrived in Roanoke in July 1587 carrying 117 colonists. They found no settlers. Just a single skeleton remained of the men whom Grenville had left. The local Croatoans refused to subject themselves to Lord Manteo's authority or provide the settlers with food. Hoping to rescue the colonists from starvation, White returned to England in late August for provisions. But in England, he encountered the hard reality of England's priorities. The war with Spain took precedence over the survival of a hundred souls on the margins of the English empire.

To punish England for its support of privateering, Phillip II of Spain in 1588 had sent his Armada to destroy the English fleet and attack the nation itself. Only after English forces under the command of Drake defeated the Armada did White make his way back across the Atlantic although as a passenger on a privateering ship that carried neither provisions nor more settlers.

Setting foot on Roanoke Island in August 1590, White discovered the settlement vacant and overgrown and the word *CROATOAN* carved in a post near an abandoned house. White could not linger in Roanoke to investigate the colony's disappearance. The privateers who carried him were eager to move on, and he soon sailed with them to the West Indies where they searched for Spanish ships to plunder.

2-4d Biological Consequences

Although European settlements in America from Mexico and Peru to New France and Roanoke all played out on vastly different scales and trajectories, there was one common denominator: The interactions between newcomers and Natives

> The opening up of the Ocean World transforms both Europe and the Americas.

History without Borders

Chocolate

Anne of Austria, the daughter of Spain's Philip III, brought a taste for drinking chocolate to Paris when she became Louis XIII's queen in 1615.

Stationed in Asunción Mita in 1756, a Spanish judge described war captives who were destined to be sacrificed as wearing necklaces of cacao beans.

Mayan drinking vessels found in Colhá, and dated from ca. 600 BCE, contained cacao residues.

Legend:
- Intensive pre-colonial cultivation of cacao, ca. 1500
- Additional areas of cultivation, 16th and 17th centuries
- Spanish shipping route
- Aztec Empire, ca. 1500

Territorial claims, ca. 1585
- Portuguese
- Spanish

The Production and Trade of Chocolate during the Early Modern Period Chocolate was produced in specific regions of Mesoamerica and widely consumed. The Spanish carried chocolate back to Europe, where it was accepted across the continent. ▲

Europeans came to the Americas convinced in their cultural superiority over Native Americans. They believed that they were the bearers of civilization and that Indians were savages, peoples whose customs and beliefs were not only primitive but infused with idolatrous and even diabolical practices. Europeans looked at Indians' clothing, dwellings, and temples and saw the antithesis of their culture. Thus, Europeans believed that in colonizing the Americas, they would become the Indians' teachers and that

Indians would adopt key elements of European culture or risk annihilation and damnation. Yet Spaniards and then most Europeans adopted intact a central Mesoamerican practice: the ritual consumption of chocolate. Europeans did not modify chocolate to suit their own tastes but learned to drink it like Mesoamericans. In a reverse of European expectations and assumptions regarding the consumption of chocolate, culture flowed from the colonized to the colonizer. Indians taught; Europeans emulated.

When Spaniards came to settle and colonize the Americas, cacao— the bean from which chocolate is produced—had long been a staple across Mesoamerica. Cacao grows best in tropical lowland regions and thus many groups obtained it through the sprawling trade networks of Mesoamerica. The Aztecs so prized cacao that they demanded it as tribute from their subject peoples. From Central America to Northwest Mexico, cacao beans functioned as a currency. Mesoamericans consumed cacao in the

De Agostini/DEA/Getty Images

**Woman Turning Chocolate, Codex Tudela,
1553.** As this image suggests, indigenous women
produced, prepared, and served chocolate. They
roasted cacao "beans" over a fire; pounded them into
paste; flavored the paste with flowers, chilies, black
pepper, and vanilla; diluted the mixture with water;
and, in an indispensible preparation of the drink,
poured the concoction between vessels until a froth
formed as shown here. Finally, they served the drink
in lacquered gourds or specially prepared cups. ▲

Fine Art Images/Heritage Images/Getty Images

Still Life with an Ebony Chest, 1652, Antonio Pereda y Salgado. By
the 1590s, chocolate had become an item of consistent trade across the
Atlantic. By the 1620s, thousands of pounds were sent to Spain each year.
Between 1650 and 1700, Venezuela exported more than 7 million pounds of
chocolate to Spain. Shown here are the accoutrements of chocolate preparation and service, which were becoming a part of cultured life. To the right are
cacao and sugar. On the cabinet and to the left are various vessels necessary
to properly prepare, froth, and consume the beverage. ▲

form of chocolate as a beverage, hot
or cold. The emphasis Mesoamericans
placed on the color, fragrance, taste,
temperature, and presentation of the
drink suggests that it was designed to
appeal to many senses.

Initially, Europeans found the drink
disgusting. One observer concluded
that it "seemed more a drink for pigs,
than a drink for humanity." Another
likened the froth to feces. These views
faded as Spaniards, who comprised
a distinct minority in Mexico in the
sixteenth century, found themselves
in a chocolate consumption culture.
Spanish men constituted the majority of immigrants to New Spain, and
many married Indian women
and employed others as domestic
servants who prepared and served
Mexican chocolate the Mesoamerican
way. Markets, villages, and town

plazas abounded with the drink. And
everywhere, in a continuation of pre-
Hispanic practices, Indian leaders,
Spanish nobles, and leading clerics
served chocolate beverages as a form
of sociability.

As Spaniards traveled back to
Iberia, they brought chocolate with
them, and they continued to consume it as a drink, accented with
pepper and topped by a frothy foam.
In the seventeenth century, long
after the drink had become common
in Spain, Europeans added sugar to
their chocolate to approximate the
Mesoamerican drink, which Indians
had commonly flavored with honey.
Similarly, when Europeans added
cinnamon, black pepper, anise, and
rose to their chocolate, they were
replacing hard-to-find Mesoamerican
fragrances and flavors. In the

eighteenth century, Europeans, aware
that they had assimilated Indian
tastes and eager to support a Spanish
ideology of conquest, claimed to have
"improved" the drink and separated
it from its pre-Hispanic origins when,
in fact, Europeans had adopted
Mesoamerican tastes and practices
that were of ancient origin.

Critical Thinking Questions

▶ What other New World beverages
and foods did Europeans add to their
diets?

▶ In what other ways might one argue
that Europeans assimilated Native
American practices?

Native American Aztec people of Mexico dying of Small Pox introduced by the Spaniards, copied from the Codex Florentine, c.1540 (colour litho).. Private Collection/ Peter Newark American Pictures/The Bridgeman Art Library

Aztec Doctor Examining Indian with Smallpox, circa 1540. This image, created by a Native American scribe or artist in sixteenth-century postconquest Mexico, indicates the rapid spread of smallpox throughout the body of a victim. ▲

Columbian Exchange Transfer of plants, animals, people, ideas, and technologies between Europe and the Americas over the centuries in the wake of Columbus's 1492 voyage.

diseases introduced by Europeans claimed tens of millions of Indians across the Americas in one of the most tragic chapters in human history. In Central Mexico alone, the population fell from 25 million in 1519 to less than 2 million in 1580.

The plants and animals that Europeans brought to the Americas contributed to this tragic episode as well. European crops displaced local species, altering ecological balances and upending Native American societies. At the same time, Europeans' horses, cattle, pigs, sheep, goats, and chickens thrived in the Americas, disrupting Indians' long established ways of life and putting their societies in peril.

Eventually, American plants, animals, and microbes flowed to Europe as well, although with not nearly the same dire consequences. Europeans imported avocados, cashews, coca, cocoa, maize, manioc, papayas, pecans, pineapples, potatoes, quinoa, rubber, squash, sunflowers, strawberries, sweet potatoes, tomatoes, and vanilla. They also contracted a virulent form of syphilis as well as yellow fever and yaws from the Americas. This two-way traffic across the Atlantic is known today as the **Columbian Exchange** (see Map 2.6). Its effects ensured that European expansion across the Atlantic transformed Europe, not just the Americas.

were shaped by the diseases that Europeans introduced to the Native world. Just about everywhere in the Americas, virgin soil epidemics of smallpox, measles, influenza, and typhus were the handmaidens of European imperial expansion. Deadly

Map 2.6 Major Items of the Columbian Exchange With the linking of the Eastern and Western Hemispheres through commerce, trade carried plants, animals, people, and microbes back and forth across the Atlantic, dramatically altering the societies, economies, and ecosystems of the Americas, Europe, and Africa. ▲

Summary

In one way, at least, the sixteenth century closed much as it had begun. Because every French and English settlement along the Atlantic Coast had failed or been destroyed, Spain remained unrivaled in the New World. But in every other way, both Europe and the Americas had been transformed. In the Americas, the Spanish conquests and colonial policies killed untold millions of Indians and greatly increased Spain's power. In Europe, the discovery and conquest of the Americas reoriented commerce and intensified competition among nations. Suddenly, Europeans who had felt hemmed in by the Ottoman Turks had other avenues for trade and expansion. The most dynamic trade then proceeded across the Atlantic rather than around the Mediterranean. European powers began competing for advantage in the Americas while Indians in the Americas sought to preserve their cultures and lives under European rule.

<Thinking Back, *Looking Forward*>

As you review this chapter, think about the role that organized religion played in European society and the effects on Europe and Africa of the Age of Expansion. What drove Europeans to venture so far beyond the Mediterranean? How did Europeans justify their overseas colonies? What unintended effects did the European discovery of the New World have? Why did Europe "discover" Africa and the Americas rather than vice versa? Are the processes of exploration and expansion universal human goals? In the next chapter, look for patterns in European settlement in the Americas and think about how different nations had their own goals and strategies for colonization.

To make your study concrete, review the timeline and reflect on the entries there. Think about their causes, consequences, and connections. How do they fit with global trends?

Additional Resources

Books

Alchon, Suzanne Austin. *A Pest in the Land; New World Epidemics in Global Perspective*. Albuquerque: University of New Mexico Press, 2003. ▶ Cogent discussion of epidemic disease in a global context.

Clendinnen, Inga. *Ambivalent Conquest: Maya and Spaniard in Yucatán, 1517–1570*. Cambridge, England: Cambridge University Press, 1987. ▶ Best account of early missionary activity in colonial Mexico.

Crosby, Alfred. *The Columbian Exchange: Biological and Cultural Consequences of 1492*. Westport CT: Greenwood Press, 1972. ▶ The pioneering discussion of the movement of plants, animals, and germs across the Atlantic after Columbus.

Elliott, J. H. *The Old World and New, 1492–1650*. Cambridge, England: Cambridge University Press, 1970. ▶ Illuminating essays on what Europeans made of the discovery of the Americas.

Kupperman, Karen O. *Roanoke: The Abandoned Colony*. Totowa, NJ: Rowman & Allanheld, 1984. ▶ Excellent account of England's failed first North American colony.

Lockhart, James. *The Nahuas after the Conquest*. Stanford, CA: Stanford University Press, 1992. ▶ Brilliant exploration using the study of language to examine Indian life under Spanish rule.

Mancall, Peter C. *Hakluyt's Promise: An Elizabethan's Obsession for an English America*. New Haven, CT: Yale University Press, 2007. ▶ A penetrating examination of Hakluyt, England's most vociferous promoter of overseas colonization.

Phillips, Carla Rahn, and William Phillips. *The Worlds of Christopher Columbus*. Cambridge, England: Cambridge University Press, 1992. ▶ Brilliant and readable account of the world's most famous maritime explorer.

Reséndez, Andrés. *A Land So Strange: The Epic Journey of Cabeza de Vaca*. New York: Basic Books, 2007. ▶ Exciting account of the transcontinental journey of Cabeza de Vaca.

Townsend, Camilla. *Malintzin's Choices: An Indian Woman in the Conquest of Mexico*. Albuquerque: University of New Mexico Press, 2006. ▶ Complex and sympathetic biography of the Indian woman who helped Cortés conquer Mexico.

> Go to the MindTap® for **Global Americans** to access the full version of select books from this Additional Resources section.

Websites

1492: An Ongoing Voyage. (http://www.loc.gov/exhibits/1492/) ▶ Website devoted to the Columbian voyages.

Early Canada Online. (http://eco.canadiana.ca/) ▶ Complete archive relating to most aspects of New France.

MindTap®

Continue exploring online through MindTap®, where you can:
- **Assess your knowledge with the Chapter Test**
- **Watch historical videos related to the chapter**
- **Further your understanding with interactive maps and timelines**

Joining the Hemispheres, Europe, Africa, and the Americas

3,000 BCE–1 CE	2–999 CE	1000–1249	1250–1349	1350–1499
3000 BCE Agriculture emerges in the eastern Mediterranean.	**117** Romans exert control over the Mediterranean.	**1001** Ericson establishes Vinland in Newfoundland.	**1260** Mongols initiate the largest land empire in history, extending from the Black Sea to the Pacific coast of China and Korea.	**1420s** Portuguese explore the coast of West Africa.
2,000 BCE Minoans become first maritime power in the Mediterranean.	**400** Christianity becomes official religion of Rome.	**1095** Catholic Church launches first Christian Crusade to the Holy Land (Palestine).	**1275** Marco Polo travels the Silk Road to China.	**1425** Portuguese introduce sugar cultivation to Madeira Island.
1,000 BCE Phoenicians dominate Mediterranean trade with Asia.	**570** Muhammad is born.	**1182** France expels Jews.		**1454** Gutenberg invents movable type.
323 BCE Alexander the Great creates empire stretching from Greece to Asia.		**1215** King John of England signs *Magna Carta*.	**1300** Capitalism emerges The Renaissance begins.	**1492** Columbus makes landfall in the Caribbean. Spain expels Jews and Muslims and completes *Reconquista*.
			1347 Black Death plague devastates Europe.	**1493** Papal donation grants Spain control over New World lands.
				1494 Spanish and Portuguese sign Treaty of Tordesillas.

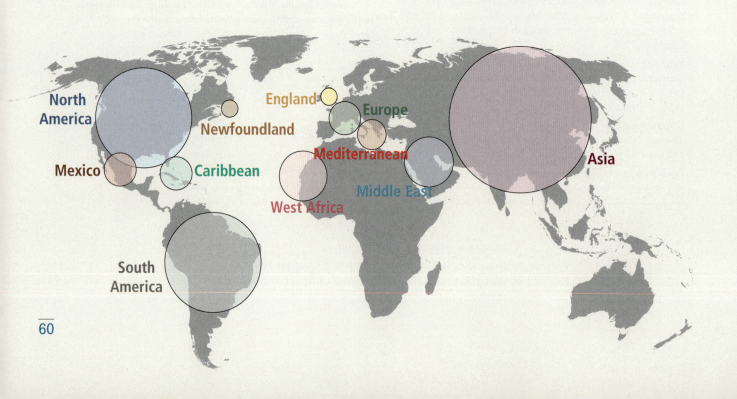

1500–1519	1520–1539	1540–1559	1560–1579	1580–1590
1500 Cabral sails to Brazil.	**1521** Cortés conquers Mexico.	**1540** Coronado explores the American Southwest.	**1565** Menéndez de Aviles destroys Fort Caroline and establishes St. Augustine.	**1581** Union of Utrecht creates United Provinces of the Netherlands.
Istanbul becomes Europe's largest city.	**1522** Magellan's crew completes circumnavigation of the globe.	**1542** Spain's New Laws abolish slavery in the New World.	**1572** Spaniards murder Túpac Amaru, the last Inca ruler.	**1585** English establish settlement on Roanoke Island.
1503 Spain establishes the *Casa de Contratación*.	**1528** Narváez expedition ventures to Florida.	**1543** Counter-Reformation begins with Council of Trent (1563).	**1579** Drake claims California for England.	**1588** English navy destroys Spanish Armada.
1517 Protestant Reformation begins.	**1532** Spain initiates conquest of Peru.			**1590** English find Roanoke settlement abandoned.
1519 Cortés sails from Cuba to mainland to begin conquest of Mexico.	**1534** Cartier voyages to New France.			
	1539 De Soto explores Florida.			

Go to MindTap® to engage with an interactive version of the timeline. Analyze events and themes with clickable content, view related videos, and respond to critical thinking questions.

3

Experimentation, Resistance, and Persistence

1585–1650

Tisquantum, who is known to most Americans as Squanto, was taken as a slave to Spain and made his way back to his village of Pawtuxet as an interpreter for a colonial English venture.

Every Thanksgiving, Americans commemorate the American creation story. The tale goes something like this: When a handful of English settlers first arrived in 1620 in what would become New England, they were cold, tired, and hungry. Had it not been for the generosity of an Indian named Squanto who taught them how to plant corn and how to fish, these settlers, the Pilgrims, would have perished. The next fall after a bountiful harvest, the Pilgrims welcomed Squanto and other Indians to a great feast of thanksgiving to celebrate their survival. This familiar story suggests that the Indians and English formed friendships and partnerships that

This carved elm burl porridge bowl is a work of Wampanoag craftsmanship and may date to the 17th century. It carries an inscription that in part reads: "A Trophy from the Wigwam of King Philip When he was Slain in 1676." ▲

Massachusetts Historical Society

were at the core of the early American experience. It also suggests that the English were the first Europeans to come to America and that their early relations with Indians were peaceful.

Although most Americans know this tale, few are familiar with the biography of Squanto and the degree to which he, like most people in colonial America, moved between worlds and crossed boundaries. Squanto's full name was Tisquantum, or "powerful other than human." In 1614, English explorers captured him and twenty-seven other Pawtuxet Indians to sell them into slavery. Transported to Spain, Tisquantum was taken in by Franciscan friars. Somehow he made his way to London by 1617. He subsequently returned to his homeland in March 1619 as an interpreter attached to an English colonial expedition.

He found that his tribe, the Pawtuxet, was gone. Between 1616 and 1618, a catastrophic epidemic, most likely transmitted by French fur traders, had devastated his people. The land that the English had once described as "the Paradise of all those parts" had become, said a later settler, "a new found Golgotha," the biblical "place of skulls." A refugee in his own homeland, Tisquantum was taken captive by the Pokonokets, a tribe within the larger group of affliated peoples known as the Wampanoag. Soon Tisquantum befriended their chief, Massasoit. Through Massasoit, Tisquantum contacted the Pilgrims, who had unknowingly founded their colony where his people had once lived. Realizing that his survival was tied to the English, Tisquantum taught the newcomers Pawtuxet methods of maize cultivation. Thus, by the time he encountered them, he was a global traveler well versed in English ways who acted as much out of self-interest as out of concern for the struggling Europeans. The colonial world he knew was not one of harmonious coexistence between Native Americans and Europeans but of conflict, enslavement, disease, and tense negotiation. Tisquantum succumbed to disease in 1622 and passed into myth as Squanto, the noble and generous Native American behind our Thanksgiving celebrations.

In Tisquantum's experiences, we can see the outlines of so many others who lived in early America. From the late sixteenth century through the middle of the seventeenth century, the Spanish, French, Dutch, and English had extensive contacts with other Native Americans as they sought to expand their existing colonies or begin new ones. With the colonization of various regions of North America (see Table 3.1), Europeans brought disease and dislocation to the local peoples. Indians

How do Tisquantum's experiences with the English and other Native American groups reflect the tensions, hardships, and opportunities of those who lived in early America?
    Go to MindTap® to watch a video on Tisquantum and learn how his story relates to the themes of this chapter.

responded in creative ways, as Tisquantum had, as they tried to adjust to what was for them in many ways a vastly different world. Europeans also suffered in their early attempts to create settlements out of lands they knew poorly and came ill prepared to colonize. Just as Tisquantum had crossed the Atlantic under what were unique circumstances, great numbers of Europeans—some free, others bound laborers—voyaged across the sea, hoping to find new opportunity. Some did, but later generations of settlers would be the ones to most enjoy the fruits of the labors of the first colonists. Hardship—not bountiful feasts—was the common denominator of the first decades of intensive European settlement in North America.

3-1

Spain and France in the Borderlands

This rock carving on the El Morro National Monument is among the earliest records of the Spanish exploration and settlement in New Mexico. It reads, "The adelantado Don Juan de Oñate passed by here from the discovery of the Sea of the South [as the Spanish knew the Pacific Ocean] on April 16, 1605."

Why would Juan de Oñate carve his name into this rock? How does Oñate describe himself? ▶

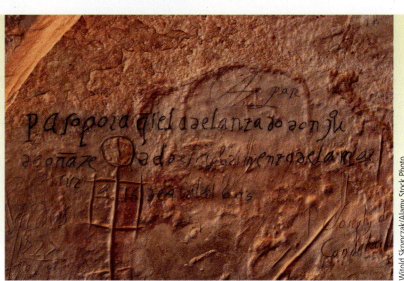

Witold Skrypczak/Alamy Stock Photo

In the late sixteenth century, Spain expanded existing settlements in the Caribbean and northern Mexico and founded colonies in Florida and New Mexico. In both regions, the Spanish monarchy relied on wealthy men to fund and organize the new settlements, but in both areas, the colonies struggled and were eventually taken over by the crown. Another similarity was that in both regions, the Spanish exploited native people for food and labor. In New France (present-day Eastern Canada), in contrast, the French treated Indians far better than the Spanish, relying on them for help in hunting animals for fur, which was extremely valuable in Europe. Only later did France establish full agricultural settlements in Quebec and Montreal. Life for the mostly young and male Europeans in these colonial settlements varied greatly because Spain and France administered their colonies in different ways.

☞ **As you read, consider how the different colonial strategies of Spain and France led to remarkably varied settlements in the regions they claimed as their own. What distinguished one colonial region from another?**

adelantamiento Royal grant of economic and political privilege to a man in return for his undertaking the conquest of a frontier territory.

adelantado Person to whom an *adelantamiento* is granted.

royal colony A crown-controlled colony ruled by a governor appointed by the monarch.

situado Annual payment or expense from the Spanish crown to maintain the province of Florida.

3-1a Florida and the Timucuas and Guales

With the death of Menéndez de Aviles in 1574 and the abandonment of St. Elena in 1576, Spain was left with a single military outpost in Florida, St. Augustine. Well into the seventeenth century, Spanish Florida remained a defensive enterprise intended to protect the Spanish treasure fleet as it sailed for Spain. King Phillip II of Spain had offered an *adelantamiento*, a royal concession of economic and political privilege to a wealthy man who planned to undertake, at his own expense, the conquest of a frontier territory. But defending Florida's long coastline against a French return and the potential arrival of the English required more money than any *adelantado* possessed. So Florida quickly became a **royal colony** for which the crown spent nearly sixty-five thousand pesos per year to defend. The bulk of the *situado*, as the cost of sustaining Florida was called, went to support Spanish soldiers stationed at St. Augustine.

> Spain establishes a foothold in Florida through fortifications, missions, and Indian labor, seeking to protect the sea-lanes that carried treasure from New Spain to Iberia.

Beyond St. Augustine, the second major Spanish institution in Florida was a sprawling chain of Catholic missions. Although the Jesuits had failed to create missions among the Florida Indians, the Franciscans who began to arrive in 1573 succeeded, founding dozens of missions in the region that today encompasses Florida, Georgia, South Carolina, and Alabama. By 1655, more than forty missions in Florida manned by seventy Franciscans ministered to at least twenty-six thousand Indians. Many of these Indians were Guale, Timucua, Apalachee, and Apalachicola refugees whose tribes had been decimated by diseases introduced by De Soto in the 1530s.

The Spanish governors of Florida cultivated allies among the native elite, known to them as *caciques*, by offering them clothing, knives, beads, cloths, scissors, and hatchets. With the support of these elites, Spanish soldiers and the Franciscans instituted the *repartimiento*, drawing laborers from Indian villages, who were compensated by their *caciques* with the gifts they received from the Spaniards.

A final pillar of Spanish colonization in Florida was the *sabana* system in which Indians affiliated with missions planted corn, wheat, beans, and other crops to support not only the Franciscans and themselves but also the soldiers at St. Augustine. The *repartimiento* turned Indian men into conscript laborers for only a week each year, but the *sabana* turned Indian women into peasants for months on end. Nevertheless, the Spanish system in Florida was built on well-established Indian practices. Spanish governors worked through Indian leaders who had long appropriated agricultural labor and tribute from their vassals. But the Indians did not always tolerate their Spanish overlords and rebellions became common.

3-1b New Mexico and the Pueblo Indians

New Mexico lacked the strategic importance of Florida, but the colony's settlement was similar: It began with a violent conquest and failed *adelantamiento*. The crown soon took over sending missionaries and soldiers. New Mexico emerged from the fantasies and treasure of Juan de Oñate, scion of one of New Spain's most successful silver mining families. Oñate won a contract from Phillip II to conquer New Mexico and promised to deliver to the king "a new world, greater than New Spain."

With such dreams dancing in his head, in 1598, Oñate crossed the Rio Grande River with 129 soldiers, a number of settlers, seven Franciscans, and several thousand sheep, horses, goats, oxen, and cattle. He asked the Pueblo Indians to "voluntarily" accept the supreme

> In New Mexico, Juan de Oñate establishes Spanish settlements that exploit Indians.

authority of the crown and the Pope. With the memory of how Coronado had burned alive villagers from Arenal, few challenged Oñate.

Oñate established his headquarters among the Tewa in the pueblo of Okhe, which he renamed San Juan. The Tewa were agricultural and lived in permanent multistory adobe and stone dwellings. Unprepared for winter in New Mexico, Oñate's soldiers and officers made increasing demands on the Tewa for food and clothing, and some even resorted to murder, torture, and rape. At the pueblo of Acoma, cultural misunderstandings and Spanish aggression led to crisis. When a Spanish soldier stole two turkeys, a bird sacred to the Acomas, and then raped an Indian woman, the Acomans attacked and killed Spaniards, including a nephew of Oñate.

In revenge, a Spanish army of 72 men destroyed Acoma, killing more than 800 men, women, and children and taking hundreds more captive. Oñate found the Indian captives guilty of murder. He sentenced those over the age of 12 to 20 years of servitude. In a bloody spectacle, Oñate's men severed one foot of all male captives over age 25.

A central institution of the colonization of New Mexico (see Map 3.1) was the *encomienda*, which the New Laws had phased out in central New Spain. But in 1601, Oñate revived the system to reward himself and his followers, requiring the dozens of pueblo communities under his jurisdiction to pay annual tribute in return for military protection, which the Indians did not need. Perhaps even more oppressive was the *repartimiento*, which was more harsh than in Florida.

Despite the wealth that he gained from the *encomienda*, Oñate was soon bankrupt, and in 1606, King Phillip replaced him with a royal governor. Oñate remained in the colony until he was finally banished for abusing Indians. But the colony survived. The 90 leading Spaniards in the region eked out a living growing corn, wheat, and vegetables, and raising cattle. They extracted what wealth and labor they could from Indians and depended on provisions from Mexico. In 1608, after Oñate's departure from the colony, the Spanish established Santa Fé, which became the capital of New Mexico in 1610.

If the Franciscans had not bestowed **baptism** on Indians in New Mexico, the crown would have abandoned the colony. But missionaries successfully argued that the crown could not forsake baptized Indians. By the late 1630s, nearly one thousand settlers controlled most of the land and water in New Mexico, and they still depended on thousands of Indians for labor and goods. This exploitative colonial system endured through the 1670s, in part because the Spanish in New Mexico, as in Florida, enriched Indian leaders with gifts.

caciques Title derived from the Taino language that the Spaniards across their possessions applied to Indians they identified as among the leadership elite.

sabana System in Florida in which Spaniards forced Indians at missions to raise agricultural products to feed the mission, missionaries, and soldiers.

baptism Christian sacramental process of formalizing admission into the Christian Church.

3-1c New France and the Wendats (Hurons)

Far to the north of Florida in what is now eastern Canada, the French developed a far less coercive colony, one based on a cooperative relationship between themselves and Indians. In the decades after Cartier abandoned his St. Lawrence River settlements, low-level trade between the French and Indians resumed in the dry fishery camps on the Atlantic Coast. There the French processed their catch from the Grand Banks. Before long, this trade became an industry of its own. The French would trade metal, glass, and cloth to Indians for food and animal skins. The French valued beaver fur above most other goods because beaver fur was scarce in Europe where the animals had been hunted to extinction. The production of fur did not require French laborers or the coercion or enslavement of Indians. Instead, Indians trapped the animals, processed the fur, and transported it to the coast for purchase by the French. When the broad-brimmed beaver felt hat became fashionable in western Europe in the early sixteenth century, the Canadian fur trade exploded.

> In New France, the French and the Wendat cooperate to create a commercial frontier centered on beaver skins.

In 1598, the French King Henry IV renewed a grant to the nobleman Troilus de Mesgouez, marquis de La Roche, giving him a **monopoly**, which granted complete control of specific goods, over trade between Canada and France. Yet neither La Roche nor his successor, Pierre Du Gua, sieur de Monts, was able to enforce the monopoly. There were simply too many places along the coast where Indians and the French could trade. In 1607, de Monts's men abandoned Canada, but the following year, one of his associates, Samuel de Champlain, ventured to a narrow point up the St. Lawrence River and established Quebec, which was his rendering of the Algonquin term for *narrow passage*.

Champlain wanted to secure furs in the interior before they could make their way to coastal trading posts frequented by rival traders. His plan was to forge trading partnerships with the local Algonquins, Algonquin-speaking Innus (Montagnais), and the Iroquois-speaking Wendats (Hurons), whose villages lay hundreds of miles farther west (see Map 3.2).

The trade at first proved beneficial to all involved. The French profited by exchanging a knife for a pelt that could later be sold for 200 times the knife's original value. The local people profited too. For millennia, the Wendats had traded with Indians beyond their own region, eager to acquire exotic goods like those the French now brought. To maintain the trade, the French had to learn the Wendats

monopoly The complete control of the entire supply of goods or a service in a certain area or market usually granted by the government.

Map 3.1 Colonial New Mexico and Its Native Peoples, Sixteenth and Seventeenth Centuries Pueblo Indian communities were concentrated along the Río Grand River more than a thousand miles north of Mexico City. ▼

Map 3.2 European Settlements in Eastern North America, 1565–1625 Between the 1560s and the 1620s, European powers established numerous competing settlements along the coast of eastern North America as they jockeyed with one another for control over lands and native peoples. ▲

Map labels:
NEWFOUNDLAND
Tadoussac 1600
Sable I. 1598
St. Croix 1604
Québec 1608
Port Royal 1604
Kennebec R.
St. Lawrence R.
Bay of Fundy
Sagadahoc 1607
Plymouth 1620
40°N
Mohawk R.
Hudson R.
Fort Nassau 1614
New Amsterdam 1625
ATLANTIC OCEAN
Jamestown 1607
Chesapeake Bay
James R.
Jacán 1570
Roanoke 1587
30°N
70°W
Santa Elena 1566
Charlesfort 1562
0 100 200 Km.
0 100 200 Mi.
San Mateo 1565
Fort Caroline 1564
St. Augustine 1565
Tocobaga 1567
Santa Lucia 1565
Calos 1567
Tequesta 1567
80°W

● Dutch settlement
● English settlement
● French settlement
● Spanish settlement

The French decision in 1627 to transfer de Monts's monopoly to a new group, the Company of 100 Associates, signaled a new era in New France. Composed of a large number of especially devout Catholics, the Company pressured Champlain to give Jesuit missionaries a leading role in French relations with Indian trading partners. Jesuit missionaries became most active in an area controlled by the Wendats, who accepted missionaries only after Champlain threatened them with the end of the trade. The years in which the Jesuits lived in Wendat lands coincided with devastating epidemics that reduced the Wendat's numbers, made them vulnerable to Haudenosaunee attacks, and undermined French control of the fur trade.

3-1d Missionaries and Indians

Catholic missionaries were integral to Indian–European relations in most frontier regions settled by France and Spain in the Americas. But

> Catholic missionaries across the Americas prompt change and rebellion among Indians.

nearly everywhere the missionaries appeared, disease, conflict, and tragedy undermined their ambitions and legacies and brought destruction and pain to Indians. The leaders of Spain and France saw it as their responsibility to bring Catholicism to Native Americans, and they concluded that Catholic missionaries, who took vows of poverty and were often funded by their own orders, were an inexpensive means of colonizing. But missionaries were not restricted to the Americas. As part of the Counter-Reformation, they also spread across Europe and Asia, attempting to bring their version of Christianity to millions of people.

In North America, the most active missionaries were **Franciscans**, whose blend of piety, poverty, and zeal made them a favorite of the Spanish crown. They came to the Americas by the thousands, establishing missions in Florida, Texas, New Mexico, Arizona, and California. Followers of the Society of Jesus, known as **Jesuits**, established missions in New France, Florida, Arizona, and Lower California.

Catholic missionaries had a common approach to Indians. Missionaries directed their efforts at children, who they believed were easier to convert than adults. They demanded that adult Indians live in sedentary communities, avoid premarital sex, practice lifelong monogamy, adopt European agricultural techniques, and attend catechism and Mass. Some Indians converted, but others rejected the missionaries and their beliefs. Most Indians were more interested in the food and trade goods the missionaries provided than the religious instruction they offered. Nearly all missionaries met with opposition and thus depended on soldiers for their survival.

Franciscans Members of a devout Roman Catholic order who adhere to teachings of Saint Francis of Assisi (1181/1182–1226), who preached poverty and the spread of the Gospel.

Jesuits Roman Catholic male religious order founded in 1540 by Francis Xavier and Ignatius of Loyola.

language and pledge to support the Wendats in their conflict against their traditional enemies to the south, the Haudenosaunees (Iroquois). Except for urging the Indians to collect larger numbers of furs, at first the French did not disrupt their lives. French traders often dressed like Indians, learned to paddle canoes and wear snowshoes, and joined in many ritual activities, such as hunting and steam baths. Some traders lived with Wendat women.

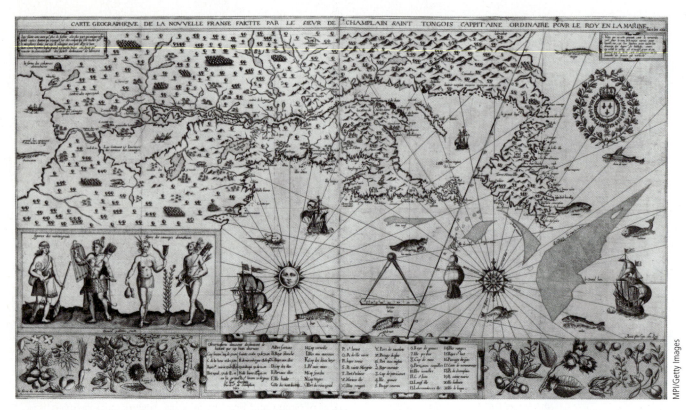

Detailed Portraits of Indians from Champlain's 1612 Map Archaeology suggests that the fur trade in the early sixteenth century ushered in a period of change in Wendat culture. Wendat peoples began to substitute tools of iron for those of stone. They put unfamiliar items to new uses, making arrowheads and ornaments out of copper kettles. With access to tools that simplified daily tasks, the Wendat had time for other pursuits and enjoyed a burst of creativity revealed in surviving artifacts including combs, pipes, masks, and pendants. ▲

MPI/Getty Images

Indians who failed to attend Mass or committed what the missionaries considered to be sexual transgressions, theft, or acts of idolatry were imprisoned or whipped. Missionaries believed that once Indians had consented to baptism, they were the missionaries' spiritual children who had agreed to live according to Catholic notions of morality, marriage, and sexuality.

Lethal epidemics that coincided with the arrival of missionaries created chaos in Native American communities. In humid Florida, where contagion spread quickly, epidemics in 1595, 1612, 1616, 1649, 1650, and 1655 wiped out entire villages. Those that survived were unable to meet Spanish demands for male laborers. In response, Indians launched coordinated attacks on the Florida missions. In 1577 and 1597, the Guales killed missionaries and burned missions. In both instances, the Spanish responded by killing hundreds of Indians and torching numerous villages. In New Mexico, Indian resentment exploded periodically, including in December 1639 when Indians at Taos and Jémez Pueblos killed their Franciscans and two soldier–settlers and then destroyed the mission church.

In New France in the 1630s, half of the thirty-five thousand Wendats died from smallpox after the arrival of the Jesuits. Some Wendats believed that the Jesuits—who remained healthy—deliberately spread disease. They saw the Jesuits' celibacy as indicative of supernatural power and came to associate baptism with death. The Wendats had relied on Jesuit assurances that they would protect them in the event of a Haudenosaunee attack. During the late 1640s, however, when the Wendats were reeling from epidemics and the Haudenosaunees attacked, the French accompanying the Jesuits did little. By 1650, the Haudenosaunees had dispersed the Wendats. Missionaries then abandoned the interior of New France and retreated to the St. Lawrence River Valley with their converts. The French fur trade also collapsed, undone by missionaries, diseases, and the Haudenosaunee onslaught.

3-1e Life in New France and New Mexico

As long as the fur trade had been profitable, the French had little reason to settle Canada. Thus, in the 1620s, there were only seventy French colonists in New France.

{ In both New France and New Mexico, colonial society is marked by economic inequality and political instability.

Over the following decades, however, French settlement gradually expanded up the St. Lawrence River with the

Mary Evans Picture Library/Alamy Stock Photo

Global Americans **María de Jesús de Ágreda** was a Franciscan nun who lived in Spain between 1601 and 1665. Born into an exceptionally devout Catholic family, she was said to have manifested extraordinary spiritual gifts from an early age. A well-known mystic, she wrote a series of influential books in which she recounted what she claimed were revelations from the Virgin Mary. She lived at a time when exceptionally spiritual Catholics claimed to experience levitation and many other paranormal phenomena. María de Jesús claimed to have been carried to what is now present-day New Mexico and Texas on the wings of saints and to have been protected there by angels. She asserted that she had preached the Gospel to Indians in their native languages in what is now the Southwest and awakened in Indians a desire for Catholic conversion. Although no Spaniard had ever seen her in New Spain and she was said never to have left her convent, her stunningly accurate descriptions of the Indians of New Mexico won over many who had been detractors and skeptics. Franciscan missionaries found her writings deeply inspirational and took from them and her claims to have traveled to the Americas proof that God favored them in the evangelization of the New World and was aiding the spread of the Gospel in miraculous ways.

establishment of Trois-Rivieres in 1634 and Montreal in 1642. At the same time, the lower St. Lawrence increasingly became the home of displaced native peoples. Montaignais groups, having hunted the beaver to extinction in their desire to trade with the French, settled near Quebec in 1638. Algonquins fleeing the Haudenosaunees migrated to Trois-Rivieres and Montreal in the 1640s, and Wendat refugees arrived in Quebec in the early 1650s. Nearly all lived in Jesuit missions, separate from the French settlers.

Socially, the French colony strongly resembled rural France. The Company of 100 Associates granted dozens of **seigneuries**, or tracts of land, to nobles, the Jesuits, merchants, and a few commoners. Those granted *seigneuries* were required to recruit settlers to live and work on them to make the concessions profitable or at least self-sustaining. The early *seigneuries* were long narrow lots on the St. Lawrence River encompassing hundreds of square miles. Lots such as these were common in France, particularly in Normandy, from which many early settlers recruited to live on the seigneuries came. Such lots could be easily surveyed and provided all who lived on them access to a river or a public road. In France, the families who lived on the lots were known as **habitants** and paid annual rents to their **seigneur**.

To populate and work the land of the Canadian *seignuries*, the Company did not recruit French families because few would have risked the long journey to a harsh land. Nor did it look to refugee Indians. Rather, it recruited nearly two thousand penniless, male **indentured servants**, known to the French as **engagés**. They committed themselves to three years of work in return for room and board and the promise of a small tract of land when their obligations had been fulfilled. If all went well, they became *habitants* on their own land.

In comparison, life across the continent in New Mexico was riven by conflict to a far greater degree than in New France. Pueblo Indians, Spanish Franciscans, and

soldier–settlers all competed for limited resources in an exploitative and divided colony. Most of the early settlers were single men who often married Pueblo Indian women or took them as concubines. There was no *presidio*, or military garrison, in New Mexico. Rather, the king expected settlers to bear arms and defend the colony.

After the collapse of Oñate's rule, the governors who followed him viewed the office as a path to wealth. Each knew that in a land without mineral wealth, his gains would depend on the exploitation of Indians. But each successive governor was undermined by powerful Franciscans who believed that soldiers' demands on Indians threatened the Christian society they hoped to establish among the Indians. In the five decades after Oñate stepped down, seventeen men assumed the governorship, and nearly all suffered ruin as a result of Franciscan resistance.

In New Mexico, land and Indian laborers were the key to wealth, and more than sixty soldiers received *encomienda* grants. The yields of the *encomienda* grants, however, declined along with the Pueblo Indians, who suffered terribly from introduced diseases. A smallpox epidemic killed about twenty thousand Pueblo Indians in 1636, reducing their number by one-third. With the population in decline across the Rio Grande Valley, the Spanish forced the Pueblo people to congregate into some forty-three towns, and in 1643, the Spanish shifted the onus of the *encomienda* tribute from the declining communities to the surviving individuals. Each Indian was then required to provide one cotton blanket and 2.6 bushels of corn each quarter.

seigneuries Large tracts of land granted in New France.

habitants Free settlers in New France who generally farmed land they leased from a *seigneur*.

seigneur Holder of a *seigneurie*.

indentured servants Person bound by contract to work for another for a specified time, usually in return for payment of travel expenses and maintenance.

engagés French term for indentured servants.

3-2
New Netherland

View of New Amsterdam, painted by Johannes Vingboons in approximately 1664, shows the city as seen from the Hudson River. The windmill in the background and the architecture of the buildings are typically Dutch.

What does this image tell us about the nature of Dutch settlement in New Amsterdam? ▶

Niday Picture Library/Alamy Stock Photo

Long before the Haudenosaunees overran the Wendats in the 1640s, the Dutch had begun to challenge the French for dominance in the fur trade with Northeastern Woodlands peoples. In fact, the Dutch colony of New Netherland at first resembled New France in that it relied on the capital of private investors, trade with Indians, and the presence of large property holders. But the similarities largely end there. New Netherland developed along its own trajectory, which was shaped by the priorities of the Netherlands, a rising and tolerant Protestant maritime nation that devoted scant resources to the colony, offered few incentives to those who might immigrate, and was more concerned with its intense rivalry with Spain than growing this remote colony.

☞ As you read, consider how settlement and life in New Netherland compared to that in New France, New Mexico, and Florida. What was most distinctive about each colony?

3-2a Rise of the Dutch

During their struggle for independence from Catholic Spain in the late sixteenth century, the Dutch emerged as a great maritime power. As part of his plan to punish the Dutch for their revolt, in 1585 Phillip II imposed an embargo on all Dutch ships, forbidding them to trade directly with Spain or Portugal. Rather than breaking the Dutch merchant marine or the movement toward independence, Phillip's initiatives spurred the Dutch to new heights. Opting for the Atlantic over the continent, Dutch traders began to trade directly with merchants and producers in Africa, the Americas,

> The Dutch reject mercantilism and concentrate on trade, not the creation of overseas colonies.

and the East Indies. By the time the Spanish had lifted their ill-fated embargo, the Dutch merchant marine was the largest in Europe and had ties to traders in every corner of the known Atlantic. In 1602, the Dutch created the **Dutch East India Company (VOC)**, referred to as the *Company*, which allowed the Dutch to take the dominant position in trade with Asia from the Portuguese.

In 1609, the Company hired the Englishman Henry Hudson to search for a **Northwest Passage** to Asia with the aim of discovering the long-elusive direct route to the East Indies. The Company's goal was to establish a secure trading monopoly in Asia on behalf of the Netherlands. When Hudson found the northern route in the Arctic blocked by frozen seas, he sailed south along the Eastern coast of the North American continent and then inland, 160 miles up the river that was to bear his name. At present-day Albany, New York, he reached shallow water. Local Indians approached with furs they hoped to exchange for beads and other goods. In subsequent years, Dutch trading vessels returned to trade for beaver pelts with Mahicans and their neighbors to the West, the Haudenosaunee Mohawks. By 1614, the future site of Albany had become one of numerous places of annual exchange between Native American and Dutch traders, all under the direction of the New Netherlands Company. The optimistic Dutch began to refer to the whole region as New Netherland.

3-2b Dutch West India Company

Dutch exploration in New Netherland had begun during a short period of peace between the Netherlands and Spain. In 1621, however, Spain and the Netherlands slid back into war, and the Spanish attempted to destroy the Dutch trade in Europe and the Atlantic. In response, the Netherlands

> To challenge the Spanish and establish overseas colonies, the Dutch create the West India Company.

Dutch East India Company (VOC) Dutch trading company founded in 1602 and granted a twenty-one-year monopoly over trade with Asia.

Northwest Passage Passage by sea linking the Atlantic and Pacific Oceans searched for by Europeans but not discovered until the mid-twentieth century given the severity of the Arctic climate.

National Maritime Museum, Greenwich, London, Caird Fund

A [Dutch] Ship in a Rough Sea When Spain and the Dutch signed a truce in 1609, the Dutch used the respite from hostilities to extend their power throughout the Atlantic. For the most part, the Dutch staked their prosperity on organizing and carrying the trade of other nations. ▲

immediately created the **Dutch West India Company (WIC)** to challenge the Spanish, and bolster or create Dutch settlements in Africa and North and South America. By the 1640s, the WIC had control over nearly 1,000 merchant or war ships and had captured or destroyed more than 600 Spanish vessels.

In 1624, the Dutch renamed their trading post on the Hudson Fort Orange, and, to bolster their claim to the territory and to protect the mouth of the Hudson from foreign incursions, they officially established the colony of New Netherland. The colony was bounded by the Delaware and the Connecticut Rivers and populated by several dozen French-speaking refugees from what is now Belgium. In its first decades, New Netherland subsisted through its monopoly over the beaver trade, and the WIC exported 16,300 beaver pelts in 1635. Eventually, the WIC sought to encourage people to migrate and trade at their own expense by suspending the monopoly on the trade of fur. By the mid-1650s, Dutch traders were exporting 80,000 pelts per year from New Netherland, but the WIC still struggled to make a profit from the colony.

Despite its investment in New Netherland, the WIC's main interest was in the South Atlantic and the coast of Africa. During peacetime, Dutch ships had carried large amounts of sugar directly to Amsterdam's twenty-nine sugar refineries. But in the early 1620s, when Spain and the Netherlands were again at war, Amsterdam had no supply of sugar. In 1624, Holland shocked Spain by seizing Bahia, the capital of Brazil, but a Spanish fleet carrying 12,500 soldiers forced the Dutch out within a year. Over the following two decades, the Dutch were able to conquer half of the fourteen captaincies of Brazil, naming them New Holland, and established sugar plantations. Needing a steady supply of laborers for these plantations, the Dutch through the WIC became very involved in the transatlantic slave trade. In these years, the Dutch also established a colony in Guiana along eight hundred miles of the South American coastline as well as one at the Southern Cape of Africa, known as Cape Colony or Cape Town. New Netherland, however, languished in obscurity, attracting few settlers and little interest from the Netherlands.

Dutch West India Company (WIC) Dutch trading company founded in 1621 to develop and promote Dutch trading interests in competition with Spain, Portugal, and England.

Manhattan Situated on the North River, 1639 In 1628, the WIC fortified the town that became known as New Amsterdam. By 1630, about 270 settlers, including many whole families, lived along the island's southern tip. ▶

Vinckeboons, Joan/Library of Congress Geography and Map Division Washington, D.C. 20540–4650 USA dcu

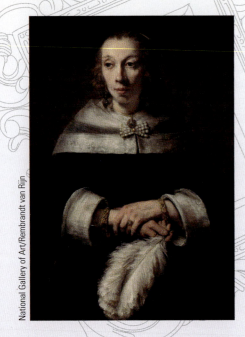

National Gallery of Art/Rembrandt van Rijn

Global Americans Born in Amsterdam in 1627, **Sara Kierstede** was the child of Scandinavian immigrants who came to the Netherlands earlier and most likely moved to New Netherland in 1630 in search of work. Her family was among the first to settle in the patroonship of Rensselaerswijk where they spent several years as tenant farmers. When her father became a member of the patroonship's governing council, the family moved to Manhattan where they became the first tenant farmers for the WIC and later farmed on their own land. Sara was likely multilingual from an early age. As a child in Rensselaerswijk, she probably learned Mahican from Indian children in the area and may have learned Scandinavian and German from her parents. Daily contact with Indians provided women like Sara with many of the foods and household items they needed. As an adult, she acquired fluency in Munsee. She became a key translator for the Dutch colony and took part in important negotiations between the Munsee and the Dutch in the lower Hudson in the late 1650s and early 1660s. Remarkably, during these years, Sara, like many Dutch housewives, gave birth to ten children. While she may have seemed an unlikely person to play a key role in the colony's intercultural relations, her mastery of the Munsee language emerged from her transatlantic background and her daily contact with Native Americans who frequented Manhattan markets and provided women like Sara with many of the foods and household items they needed.

3-2c Life in New Netherland

Unlike French and Spanish Catholics, the Protestant Dutch were more concerned with their own salvation than with converting Indians. They had no great plans to convert Indians and did not send missionaries to the colony. Nor did they demand that Indians be incorporated into their society and laws. Yet Dutch plans for agricultural settlements still led to tension, especially over the issue of land. On the lower Hudson, Dutch pigs, cattle, and farms encroached on Indian lands. In 1640, the colony began requiring local Munsee villagers to pay tribute in corn, furs, or beads, which provoked a bloody war that raged until 1645.

> New Netherland emerges as a small and diverse colony with great disparities of income and privileges.

For coastal Algonquins, the arrival of the Dutch ushered in an era of transformation and hardship, but not one rooted in Spanish-style labor exploitation or the pressures of Catholic missionaries. The Algonquin-speaking peoples of Long Island Sound had traditionally crafted valuable items out of clamshells. When they acquired iron tools in trading with the Dutch, they began fashioning strings of shell beads called **wampum** that had great value to Dutch traders. In the 1620s, a representative of the WIC secured a virtual monopoly on Pequot wampum, which the Dutch in turn traded in the interior for furs. The Dutch monopoly over Pequot-produced wampum fanned rivalries among the Pequot and their Narragansett neighbors, who were soon at war.

As in New Spain and New France, the Europeans also brought disease with them, adding to the Indians' woes. In 1634, Dutch traders reported with horror that more than 950 of 1,000 Indians in one village along the Connecticut River Valley had died from smallpox.

The directors of the WIC hoped that the New Netherland and Cape Town colonies would produce valuable commodities for export. But neither did. And because the Netherlands boasted a strong economy and tolerant religious environment, the WIC had trouble recruiting settlers. Thus, in 1629, company leaders created New Netherland's original governing laws, the **Freedoms and Exemptions**, intending to build up the colony through **patroonships**—huge tracts of manorial lands similar to the French *seigneuries*—granted to influential shareholders in return for a pledge to transport laborers to the colony. **Patroons** had the right to trade in pelts and could administer their fiefdoms largely as they wished. Unlike Spanish *encomenderos*, they had no claim to Indian labor or tribute. The Freedoms and Exemptions also offered independent settlers as much land as they could cultivate but specified that if they did not occupy the land, it reverted back to the WIC. This provision denied settlers the ability to sell their property or bequeath it to their children. Over time, however, as the colony liberalized its landholding laws, its population increased to about two thousand by 1643. Over the next two decades, settlers established seventeen towns in New Netherland, and agriculture,

wampum Shell beads manufactured by Northeast Woodland peoples that served as currency and memory devices.

Freedoms and Exemptions Dutch West India Company governing document (1629) to promote settlement of the New Netherland colony; created patroonships for those who could bring over at least fifty settlers.

patroonships Large tract, as deep as sixteen miles, deeded by Dutch West India Company to investors bringing at least fifty settlers to the New Netherland colony.

Patroons Holder of a patroonship.

especially growing tobacco, became more central. By 1664, the value of tobacco exported from the colony had surpassed that of peltries.

The local authorities tightly controlled the economic and religious life of New Amsterdam. They fixed the prices for all goods and made the Calvinist Dutch Reformed Church the official church of the colony. Membership was restricted to those who showed outward signs, such as church attendance and prosperity, that they were chosen by God for salvation.

In 1654, a small group of Jews arrived in the colony from Recife, Brazil, fleeing the Portuguese conquest of the Dutch colony there. New Netherland's director, Peter Stuyvesant, wanted to bar them from settling, but he was overruled by officials in the Netherlands who knew that the Jews had supported the WIC in Brazil and had lost everything. These Jewish settlers were not allowed to open businesses and were expected to live together in an ethnic enclave on the edge of New Amsterdam. But at the same time, the Dutch authorities were tolerant of Jews and other non-Calvinist groups as long as they practiced their religion in the privacy of their homes.

In 1655, New Netherland extended its influence in the Delaware River Valley by bloodlessly conquering New Sweden, a colony sponsored by the Swedish West India Company in 1638. Hundreds of Swedish, Finnish, German, and Dutch settlers lived in the region, and they put up little resistance to the Dutch invasion. Under Dutch rule, they enjoyed local autonomy, controlling their own courts and lands. New Netherland endured as a diverse colonial region until the mid-1660s when the growing Anglo-Dutch rivalry led to warfare between the two nations.

3-3
Establishment of Virginia

Powhatan Indians made this decorated leather tent by sewing together four white-tailed deer hides with sinew thread. The shell beadwork decoration consists of a central standing human figure flanked by two upright quadrupeds and surrounded by dozens of disks. Each of the disks most likely represents one of the communities tied together in the Powhatan chiefdom. This item is often identified as *Powhatan's mantle*. ▶ Ashmolean Museum/Mary Evans/The Image Works

What does the careful beadwork suggest about native culture and craftsmanship in early Virginia?

Go to MindTap® to practice history with the Chapter 3 **Primary Source Writing Activity: Expectations and Realities.** Read and view primary sources and respond to a writing prompt.

Although England eventually established more colonies in North America than any other European nation, it was slow to extend its influence overseas. Late sixteenth century English attempts to settle North America had met logistical challenges, poor leadership, and false expectations. Under the rule of King James I (1603–1625), England renewed its push for settlements on the mainland. Ultimately, growing tobacco brought a measure of viability to English settlements in the Chesapeake region. But as they expanded tobacco cultivation, the English encroached on Indians' land. By the middle of the seventeenth century in the wake of two major Indian rebellions, the Virginia colony had made killing Indians, or pushing them off their lands, a major goal.

☞ As you read, consider the divergent goals of Indians and the English and the evolution of their views toward the other. In what ways were English views of Indians typical of all European colonists?

3-3a Jamestown Settlement in the Shadow of Spain

In the early 1600s, even after the debacle of Roanoke, the English established overseas colonies amid rising pressures to join the Spanish, French, and Dutch in the race for American colonies. Merchants wanted to exploit the fish, furs, and timber of northeast North America and grow tobacco, hops, and hemp in the Chesapeake (see Map 3.3).

{ In the early years of the Virginia colony, the settlement nearly collapses and has tense relations with surrounding Indians.

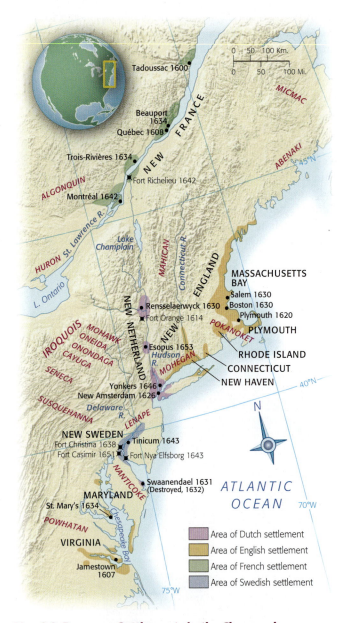

Map 3.3 European Settlements in the Chesapeake, Mid-Atlantic, and New England, 1607–1650 European settlements in eastern North America in the first half of the seventeenth century clung to the Atlantic Coast and interior rivers as commerce and connections to Europe proved vital to their survival. ▲

Many in England believed that England was overpopulated and needed colonies to alleviate this situation. England's defeat of the Spanish Armada in 1588 had opened the seas to England's ships that could provision overseas colonies. The English, in the wake of Las Casas, believed that they as Protestants could act more humanely to the New World's peoples than Spanish Catholics. And the landed gentry who invested in overseas colonization wanted to destroy the Spanish and engage in privateering. For all of these reasons, the crown in 1606 granted charters and monopoly rights to two privately funded joint-stock companies overseen by the newly created Council of Virginia. The Western Merchants' Virginia Company, based in

Plymouth, funded a doomed colony at Sagadahoc (Maine) in 1606. The following year, in April 1607, the London Virginia Company established a settlement at Jamestown in a region that the local Paspahegh people called Tsenacomoco, or *densely inhabited land*.

In the early seventeenth century, Tsenacomoco was governed by a paramount chief named Powhatan. A generation earlier, Spaniards had come to the region to establish a mission, ostensibly with the support of the Algonquin known to Spaniards as Luís de Velasco, who was almost certainly a contemporary and relative of Powhatan. The Spanish attacks—and Luís's knowledge of Spain and its other colonies—prompted Indians of the region to create new alliances with one another, leading to the expansion of the Powhatan paramount chiefdom over most of the Chesapeake. By the early sixteenth century, Chief Powhatan had at his disposal a fighting force of nearly one thousand warriors and ruled over about twenty thousand villagers.

Fearful of a Spanish attack from the sea, Captain Christopher Newport founded the Jamestown colony on a small island some fifty miles up the James River. From the start, it struggled. Many of the colonists were "gentlemen" who dreamed of easy riches in the colony. They had money to invest in the colony but few skills to ensure its survival. Only

Powhatan and His Countrymen with John Smith, 1624
Powhatan, in a bid to demonstrate his power, invited Smith and his men to leave Jamestown, live under his rule, and trade "Hatchets and Copper" for food. Smith declined, but, as he later wrote, he was dragged before Powhatan, his head was placed on stones, and the Indians prepared to "beat out his braines." Yet one of Powhatan's many daughters, the 11-year old Pocahontas, "got his head in her armes, and laid her owne upon his to save him from death." With Pocahontas acting as an intermediary, the English and the Powhatan entered a period of tense coexistence. ▲

National Portrait Gallery/Smithsonian Institution/Art Resource, New York.

Matoaks als Rebecka daughter to the mighty Prince Powhatan Emperour of Attanoughkomouck als Virginia converted and baptized in the Christian faith, and Wife to the wor:tt Mr Tho: Rolff.

Global Americans The westward crossing of the Atlantic Ocean by millions of Europeans and Africans is a central and well-known aspect of American colonial history. Less familiar are the far smaller, yet still significant, contingents of Native Americans who traveled from their homes across the Atlantic to Europe. Like Paquinquineo, **Pocahontas** was one of these travelers. She was among 175 Indians who visited England between 1500 and 1776. In 1616, two years into her marriage, Pocahontas, John Rolfe, their baby son Thomas, and perhaps ten other Indians traveled from Tsenocommah to England. Their voyage was an attempt by the Virginia Company to show off Pocahontas, who was then known to the English as Lady Rebecca, as proof of the English conquest. Powhatan, who saw the trip as a fact-finding delegation that might learn more about the English, supported it. In January 1617, King James I ceremoniously welcomed Pocahontas and the other Native Americans with her to his court where they attended a performance of a theatrical work by the noted playwright Ben Jonson. In the eyes of the English elite, the Indians were something of a sensation and became instant celebrities. Unlike Tisquantum, who had survived his trip to and from Europe, Pocahontas did not. Roughly one in four of the Indians who traveled across the Atlantic died on foreign soil. Pocahontas became sick and weak as she waited to sail home and died in England at age twenty. With her death, the dream of a long-term English-Indian alliance in Tsenacomoco died.

a dozen were skilled craftsmen. There were no missionaries among them. Their royal charter spoke of bringing Christianity to the Indians, but the colony was a profit-seeking venture.

Suffering marked the first years of the settlement. Meager rations, Indian attacks, a humid summer, and the approach of winter caused tensions to rise. The first governor of the colony, Edward Wingfield, was accused of hoarding food and plotting with the Spanish to destroy the colony. Stripped of his authority, he returned to England. Some men deserted to Indian villages in search of food. More than 100 succumbed to hunger. By January 1608, only 38 still inhabited the settlement, and they had become dependent on the Paspahegh for sustenance.

More Englishmen would have died had not John Smith, one of the colony's six "councilors," taken control. He forced the settlers to build cabins and begin the hard work of preparing the ground for crops. He used deadly force to coerce the Indians into trading corn.

In 1608, some additional one hundred settlers arrived in Jamestown. Most of them also expected easy wealth and had no interest in rebuilding the colony's fort. They sent ore back to England, but it was found to be worthless, and despair overtook the colonists. Food stores dwindled again in 1609. Powhatan told Smith that if the English provided him with a grindstone, fifty swords, some firearms, copper, and beads, he would give the colony corn, avoiding war. But the English did not have the goods Powhatan desired. As Powhatan plotted to kill the English settlers, his daughter, Pocahontas, alerted Smith to the plan, and he survived it. But he was injured in a firearm mishap, was then ousted in a coup, and was sent back to England in the fall of 1609. In Smith's absence, the starving colonists and the aggrieved Indians went to war.

3-3b Conflict in Tsenacomoco, 1609–1614

For five years, the English and the Powhatan Indians fought a nearly continuous battle. When the English tried to pillage Indian stores, Powhat-

> The colonists grow desperate and use all means to survive.

ans laid siege to Jamestown. Holed up in their fort with scant food, the settlers became desperate. Some resorted to cannibalism. Before other settlers executed him, one man confessed to having murdered his pregnant wife and "chopped" her into "pieces and salted her for his foode." When word of these horrors reached London in 1609, the Virginia Company reduced the price of its shares, promised land in Virginia to all investors, and launched a public campaign to promote interest in the colony.

By the winter of 1609–1610, more than 900 settlers had been sent to Virginia, but just 60 remained alive. Six hundred more Englishmen ended up traveling to Virginia, yet their arrival in the spring of 1610 only hastened the colony's disintegration. In June, the survivors abandoned Jamestown and set sail for England, but before they reached the open sea, they were met by three ships carrying new leaders, 400 settlers, and provisions to last a year. The arrival of Sir Thomas Dale with 300 settlers in 1611 further strengthened Jamestown, as did Dale's imposition of martial law. He put every settler to work, and those who resisted faced severe punishment.

In the spring of 1613 amid the ongoing war, the settlers kidnapped Pocahontas. The English at first hoped to ransom her but soon decided that she would be more valuable as the first Christian convert in Virginia. The English held her captive for a year in the remote outpost of Henrico. During her incarceration, a settler named John Rolfe taught her English. Rolfe believed it was God's plan for the two to marry so that he could redeem the English pledge to bring civilization to the Indians. Pocahontas's feelings for Rolfe are unclear. In 1614, when Chief Powhatan agreed to the marriage, the eighteen-year-old Pocahontas was baptized and given the name Rebecca. With the marriage, the English secured peace with the Powhatan.

3-3c Reorganization and Tobacco

After years of failure, the directors of the Virginia Company shifted their strategy again and began sending over higher numbers of men who could build a colony, not just men who dreamed of riches and a quick return to England. During the early seventeenth century, nearly 200,000 people from England, Wales, and Scotland who wanted to leave their homeland had simply gone to Ireland. Getting those who wanted more land or more freedom of religious expression to cross the Atlantic, however, was another matter. The most common inducement to get people to migrate to Virginia was indentured servitude that promised laborers free ocean passage and free land at the end of seven years of labor. As a further inducement, in 1619, the company offered one hundred acres of land to anyone willing to travel to Virginia. The company also instituted what became known as the **headright system** under which anyone who paid his or her own passage to Virginia would receive fifty acres for each additional person they brought with them. This system was intended to encourage entire families to immigrate but rarely did so. In 1619, the company also ordered Jamestown's governor to allow the election of a representative legislative assembly, the first in North America. It became known as the **House of Burgesses**. In response to these changes, 4,500 colonists, including a large number of women, arrived in Virginia between 1619 and 1624.

> Tobacco cultivation rescues the floundering colony.

John Rolfe's dream of converting the Powhatan to Christianity proved impossible. But the West Indian tobacco he planted in 1612 changed Jamestown's fortunes in another way. By the early seventeenth century, England had been swept by a craze for smoking. Despite efforts, including those by the king, to dissuade people from smoking, by 1638, Virginia was exporting 3 million pounds of tobacco annually grown in fields worked largely by English indentured servants.

headright system System to promote settlement in English colonies that gave land to those who brought in new settlers, usually by paying for the transportation of settlers.

House of Burgesses Virginia's legislative body, the first in British North America; established in 1619.

proprietary colony Colony granted by a monarch to an individual with full governing rights.

3-3d Opechancanough's Rebellions

The expansion of tobacco cultivation upended relations between the colony and the Powhatan. Thousands of recently arrived Englishmen ventured up the rivers that flowed into the Chesapeake, carving vast tobacco plantations out of the forest. The Powhatan realized that the English threatened to overwhelm them. With the death of Chief Powhatan in 1618, leadership passed to Opechancanough and the charismatic war leader Nemattanew. In early March 1622, two English servants claimed that Nemattanew had killed their master, and when he resisted arrest, they shot him. The murder greatly affected the Powhatan. On March 22, 1622, Opechancanough led a large-scale, well-coordinated attack on the English. The Powhatan caught the settlers by surprise, killing 347, about one-quarter of the English inhabitants. Among the dead was John Rolfe.

> Fearing that the English will push them off all of their land, the Powhatan attack, provoking a vicious English counterattack.

The slaughter provoked the collapse of the Virginia Company, and the crown took over the colony in 1624. Opechancanough's attack also fundamentally altered English–Indian relations. Those English who survived pursued a ruthless policy of extermination, seeing Indians as a savage people whose culture and values they deemed the antithesis of their own. In one 1624 battle, the Virginians massacred 800 Indians. In 1632, after a decade of war, Opechancanough sued for peace. Some English wanted to continue the war, but the Indians offered land, and a peace was made. In 1644, in their final offensive, the Powhatan killed 500 Englishmen, but this did little to slow the colony's growth. In 1646, the English captured the elderly Opechancanough. The governor hoped to ship him to London, but an English soldier shot and killed the Indian leader. Soon thereafter, a punitive peace was imposed on the Powhatan. With the threat of Indian attack no more, Jamestown prospered through the mid-1670s, a remarkable turnaround from the colony's disastrous early years.

The English established Maryland, a second colony on the Chesapeake, in 1634. Maryland was a **proprietary colony**, meaning that it was the sole property of its proprietor, George Calvert, first Lord Baltimore, who had received the grant as a gift from King Charles I. Calvert, who had previously tried to found a colony in Newfoundland and had been thrown out of Jamestown because of his Catholicism, planned the colony as a refuge for England's persecuted Catholics. He died in 1632 just as his grant was being approved. His son, Cecilius Calvert, second Lord Baltimore, governed the colony from England until his death in 1675. The family's views on religious toleration were embodied in Maryland's 1649 Act of Religious Toleration, which granted freedom of religious expression to all Christians.

The Chesapeake colonies, Maryland and Virginia, were marked by social instability. In the Chesapeake,

75 percent of the seventy-five thousand indentured servants who had arrived before 1680 were men. As a result, men outnumbered women in the region three to one. Although single women quickly found husbands, they, like the men, faced a life made difficult by heavy fieldwork and dangerous disease. Men in the colony typically lived to their mid-forties and women to their late thirties. And half of all English children born in the Chesapeake died before age twenty. Late marriage, early adult death, and high mortality of infants and children meant that English society in the Chesapeake could not reproduce itself.

3-4

Formation of New England

In this first Seal of the Massachusetts Bay Colony, an Indian man beseeches the English to "Come over and help us." The man's words were inspired by a similar passage in the Bible (Acts 16: 9) in which the apostle Paul encounters in a dream a pagan man from Macedonia, who begs him to "Come over to Macedonia and help us." ▶ Seal of the Massachusetts Bay Company, the first settlement, founded in 1630 (litho), American School/Private Collection/Peter Newark American Pictures/Bridgeman Images

Look at the man in the seal. How is he portrayed, and what does his image suggest about the Massachusetts Bay Colony's view of Indians?

If the Chesapeake colonies were motivated by profit and marked by death and disease, the settlements of New England (see Map 3.4) were prompted by a desire for freedom of religious expression and characterized by a healthy and stable population. Fearing oppression in England, two very different groups of Protestants had sailed to New England. One group settled in Plymouth, and the other landed in Massachusetts Bay. Each group, seeking freedom to worship as it pleased, was intolerant of others, routinely expelled dissenters, and did not attempt to evangelize among the Indians. The English in New England built a society based on family ties and religious devotion. Ultimately, they fought a war against the Indian people that was tragically similar in intent to that waged in Virginia.

☞ As you read, consider the nature of the Puritan settlements in Plymouth and Massachusetts Bay. How did colonial life in New England and the Chesapeake vary?

3-4a Separatists of Plymouth Plantation

Like the Virginia settlements, Plymouth Plantation was shaped by earlier Indian–European interactions. For a century, Europeans fishing the Grand Banks of the Atlantic had come to the mainland to trade with the local population. In the early 1600s, the French had explored the Northeast in search of furs, and

{ A small number of English colonists establish Plymouth Plantation, breaking with the Anglican Church and separating from England.

in 1608 the English had founded the short-lived colony at Sagadahoc. In 1614, John Smith returned to North America and thoroughly mapped the region, naming it New England, and promoting its colonization. That same year, Thomas Hunt, an associate of Smith's, took twenty-seven Indians prisoner, intending to sell them into slavery in Spain. Among them was Tisquantum, the Pawtuxet man better known today as Squanto.

Among the English who first settled in New England were radical Calvinists known as **Separatists**. These **Puritans** had broken from the Church of England because they believed it had not moved far enough from Catholicism. In 1607, these settlers had moved to the Netherlands, where they worshipped openly. But fearing that their children would grow up more Dutch than English, they sought a new home. The Virginia Company granted them the right to its northern lands in the North American continent. In 1620, thirty-five Separatists and more than sixty-five others sailed across the Atlantic on the *Mayflower*. During the voyage, non-Separatists challenged the authority of the colony's leaders after realizing that they were headed to land well north of the Company's jurisdiction. In response, men on board drafted the **Mayflower Compact**, a temporary governing charter that established a "Civil Body Politic" binding all the men of the ship together. The document provided for the election of a

Separatists Puritans who severed ties to the Anglican Church in the belief that it was hopelessly corrupt.

Puritans English Protestants who regarded the reformation of the Church of England as incomplete and sought to simplify and regulate forms of worship.

Mayflower Compact First governing document of Plymouth Plantation subjecting settlers to a government of their own making; signed on ship on November 11, 1620.

Table 3.1 North American European Settlements, 1585–1650

Year Founded	Colony/ Settlement	Founding Nation
1585	Roanoke	English
1607	Virginia	English
1608	Quebec	French
1608	Santa Fé	Spanish
1620	Plymouth	English
1624	New Netherland	Dutch
1630	Massachusettes Bay	English
1634	Maryland	English
1634	Rhode Island	English
1636	Connecticut	English
1638	New Sweden	Swedish

governor by the male colonists, regular meetings over matters of self-governance, and various laws for all to abide.

In November 1620, the colonists landed on what is now known as Cape Cod and soon relocated across the bay to the place that John Smith named Plymouth. They were not soldiers, indentured servants, or men who dreamed of gold, but families of husbands, wives, children, and servants committed to the construction of a Protestant utopia in the wilderness. They did not expect the Indians to work for them and planned instead to farm and fish—but they lacked the skills to do either. Soon, like the English at Jamestown, they starved. The Indians avoided them, appalled that the colonists had settled on the grounds of an Indian village destroyed by an earlier epidemic.

Only in the spring of 1621, after half of the colonists had died of starvation, did the Indians reach out to establish relations. Massasoit, a local chief, wanted to forge a trade and military alliance with the English that might give him leverage against his neighbors, the Narragansetts. With Tisquantum acting as an intermediary, Massasoit and the settlers agreed to a treaty of mutual defense that paved the way for trade, including Indian corn for English goods. Massasoit used the agreement to enhance his status across the region, bringing together disparate Indian groups into a new people known as the Wampanoag. They continued to rise in power under the leadership of Massasoit's sons, Wamsutta and Metacom, or as the English were to know them, Alexander and Philip.

By the late 1620s, the several hundred settlers at Plymouth enjoyed a stable existence based on subsistence agriculture and trade with the Indians. As among the English at Jamestown, the rights to own land and participate

in a representative government attracted settlers. At first, the Separatists held all their land, tools, livestock, and horses in common, but few were happy with this arrangement. In 1623–1624, each family received a permanent assignment of land on which to plant corn, and in 1627, each settler was granted twenty acres. The colonists elected their own governors and in 1636 formed a legislative body composed of representatives elected by landowning males. The colony's well-governed, industrious population grew exponentially. By 1643, nearly two thousand people were living in Plymouth, and by 1675, the number neared five thousand.

3-4b Establishment of the Massachusetts Bay Colony

During the 1620s, Puritans, faced increasing concern for their religious expression. With the coronation of Charles I (reign from 1625 to 1629), who took a French, Catholic wife, some Puritans

{ A large group of Englishmen establish the Massachusetts Bay Colony in the belief that their utopian society will lead to the spiritual reformation of England.

Map 3.4 Seventeenth-Century New England Settlements As the seventeenth century progressed, the initial English colonies of Massachusetts Bay and Plymouth spawned other English settlements throughout New England. ▲

from crown oversight. The crown revoked the charter in 1637 but lacked the resources to seize the colony. By then, its leaders had turned the company's leadership council into the **Massachusetts General Court**, which soon became a colonial legislature. Men who owned property and were members of the church were considered freemen and were allowed to vote in the colony's elections.

With a clear religious vision and the prospect of autonomy awaiting them, an unprecedented number of English people sailed for Massachusetts. In 1630, one thousand made the journey. By 1635, ten thousand had come, and by 1642, twenty-one thousand. Only the outbreak of the English Civil War (see Chapter 4) ended what is known now as the *Great Migration*. Although families made up the majority of these first immigrants, one-third of those before 1650 had been single adult males, and single men outnumbered single women four to one. Eventually, nearly all the women married, and had children. They and their husbands could expect to far outlive those who settled in the Chesapeake.

In its early years, the Massachusetts Bay Colony offered Englishmen unprecedented economic opportunity. In 1629, the colony's directors enacted a policy akin to Virginia's headright system. Settlers who paid their way to the colony would receive fifty acres of land and fifty more for every servant they brought with them. There were to be no *patroons, seigneuries,* or peasantry in Massachusetts Bay. The colonists, convinced that in the eyes of God the Indians had no title to land that they did not enclose or use to graze domesticated animals, worried little about the morality, ethics, or legality of appropriating Indian territory.

The Puritans in the colony practiced a different form of Calvinism than did those in England. Across the colony, like-minded believers signed covenants, chose and ordained their own ministers, and determined church membership. The goal of the **New England Way** policy was to restrict membership to those who appeared predestined for salvation. After 1636, the Massachusetts Bay Company gave highly selective town proprietors the power to grant acreage to those they deemed spiritually worthy. Most of the acreage was reserved for the children and grandchildren of the colony's founders. Newcomers not related to the prominent families could hope only for small lots, meaning that many families had little to pass on to their children and grandchildren.

John Winthrop, c.1640 (oil on canvas), Dyck, Sir Anthony van (1599–1641)/Private Collection/Peter Newark American Pictures/The Bridgeman Art Library

Portrait of John Winthrop This portrait by an anonymous painter captures John Winthrop, a wealthy English Puritan lawyer who was the leader of the Massachusetts Bay Colony. He was the colony's governor for most years between 1630 and 1649, and his son served as governor of Connecticut from 1635 to 1639. ▲

concluded that the only way to reform English society was to do so from afar, beyond the reach of a society they viewed as corrupt. They dreamed of creating a model Christian Utopia dedicated to industriousness, community, and the worship of God. After Charles appointed William Laud, an autocratic Puritan foe, to be Bishop of London in 1628 and then tried the following year to rule without Parliament, these Puritans created the Massachusetts Bay Company, securing a royal grant to settle land north and east of Plymouth. "We must consider that we shall be as a city on a hill, the eyes of all people are upon us," wrote their leader, John Winthrop. These settlers were **non-separating congregationalists** in that they did not officially break with the Anglican Church as had the Plymouth Separatists.

The first Massachusetts Bay colonists enjoyed spiritual satisfaction and political autonomy not available to them in England. The colony admitted to church and town membership only those who met high standards of spirituality and behavior; those who did meet these standards saw themselves as a select group. The colony's charter, issued in 1629, did not articulate where the company had to hold its meetings. When the principal investors decided to hold their meetings in the colony, they effectively broke free

non-separating congregationalist
Puritan who did not officially separate from the Anglican Church and hoped to lead it to reformation by modeling the life of a Christian fundamentalist.

Massachusetts General Court Governing council of the Massachusetts Bay Colony established in 1630.

New England Way Policy reflecting emphasis that the first Massachusetts Bay settlers placed on the conversion experience; restricted church membership to those deemed likely to be destined for salvation.

History without Borders
Climate Change

Major disruptive natural events and insurrections, 1600–1700

- Drought, with date
- Flood, with date
- Severe cold, with date
- Volcanic eruption, with date
- Major outbreak of violence, 1636–1666

EUROPE

SCOTLAND · DENMARK · ENGLAND · IRE. · DUTCH REP. · FRANCE · SWITZ. · AUSTRIA · PORT. · SPAIN · NAPLES

Poland had frost in summers of 1664, 1666, 1667.

Thames River froze in 1641, 1683, 1685.

RUSSIAN EMPIRE

1627

EUROPE
1620, 1628
1617

OTTOMAN EMPIRE

Qing overthrew Ming Dynasty, 1643–1645.

ASIA

JAPAN
1649–1650
CHINA
1618

NORTH AMERICA

1616–1621
Pequot War, 1637

Nile River fell to lowest recorded level, 1641.

MUGHAL EMPIRE
1630   1632

PHILIPPINES

ATLANTIC OCEAN

1616–1621
1641–1642

AFRICA
1614–1619

INDIAN OCEAN

PACIFIC OCEAN

PERU   **SOUTH AMERICA**   **BRAZIL**
1600

1641

Java experienced its longest drought in 400 years, 1643–1671.

KONGO
1614–1619

AUSTRALIA

1640

Territorial claims, ca. 1650

- British
- French
- Netherlands
- Portuguese
- Spanish

The Little Ice Age Unbeknownst to European explorers and settlers, the mid-seventeenth century was a period of unusually cold winters across much of the Northern Hemisphere. This period, known as the Little Ice Age, brought suffering and desperation to Indians and Europeans across the Americas. ▲

European settlement in the New World and Indian-European interactions often were shaped by climate and mistaken notions of geography and weather. Europeans believed that the earth's hemispheres were symmetrical, that is, that the continents of both hemispheres were mirror images. They also believed that lands situated midway between the equator and the poles would have a moderate climate similar to that of Europe. Thus, most of the settlers who came to the North American Atlantic coast in the seventeenth century arrived there expecting to find mild winters and manageable summers. Ill-prepared for extremes of weather, the settlers were baffled and then alarmed by the North American cold winters and hot summers. The Europeans did not understand that much of North America's climate was shaped by its own great landmass, which was quick to dissipate heat in the summer and slow to release it in the winter. Europeans also mistakenly believed that through their own actions—planting crops and grazing animals—they could modify the land, which would in turn modify the climate in ways that would render it more habitable for them.

The ill effects of these mistaken notions were exacerbated by dramatic climate change in the seventeenth century. Scientists have shown that

The Gallery Collection/Corbis

The Hunters in the Snow, **Pieter Brueghel the Elder, 1565** This image shows the encroachment of winter into urban life and people frolicking on frozen ponds. ◄

Heritage Images/Hulton Fine Art Collection/Getty Images

The Frozen Thames, **Abraham Hondius, 1677** London was particularly hard hit by blasts of cold winter air. One man in London recorded "fantastic" occurrences, and noted with surprise that "one honest woman (they say) … had a great longing to have her husband to get her with child upon the [frozen] Thames [River]." ◄

the period in which much of North America was explored and then settled by Europeans was one of enormous, perhaps even unprecedented, environmental stress. Indeed, the Northern Hemisphere experienced such severe cold and extreme drought in the mid-seventeenth century that scientists now refer to this period as the *Little Ice Age.* Data from a variety of sources— tree-ring studies, diaries, letters, sermons, glacial activity, ice cores, and sunspot activity—demonstrate that the seventeenth century was the coldest century in the past millennium. This most likely resulted from a decline in solar activity and volcanic eruptions that created dust clouds that lowered the earth's temperature.

The Little Ice Age was global. It affected Europe as well as North America. Indian oral traditions describe the winters of the early 1600s as unusually harsh, and archaeological evidence suggests that it was a period of crisis and change for many peoples. Similarly, in major cities of Europe and Asia, temperatures plunged, harvests failed, rivers froze, and peasant rebellions erupted. Europeans could not help but comment on the unusual weather and peoples' responses to it. One man in London, for example, recorded "fantastic" occurrences, and noted with surprise that "one honest woman (they say) . . . had a great longing to have her husband to get her with child upon the [frozen] Thames [River]." In 1641, John Winthrop, governor of the Massachusetts Bay Colony, noted in his journal "that all the Bay was frozen over, so much and so long, as the like, by the Indians relations, had not been so these forty years."

In this period of unusual climate change, Europeans and Native Americans struggled not only against one another but also against a challenging and changing climate that brought upheaval to much of the world.

Critical Thinking Questions

▶ How might Europeans and Native Americans have sought to understand climate change?

▶ What aspects of climate change would have been apparent to people of the seventeenth century? What aspects would not have been visible to them?

Go to MindTap® to engage with an interactive version of **History without Borders: Climate Change.** Learn from an interactive map, view related video, and respond to critical thinking questions.

3-4c Dissenters in New England

Puritans in Massachusetts Bay strove for homogeneity in all aspects of their society and warned those with divergent religious or political views to conform or face expulsion. The Massachusetts General Court punished civil offenders, regulated prices, and mandated church attendance. Neighbors monitored one another's behavior. But there were differences among Puritans over how best to express their religious beliefs, and these disagreements drove many to secede from the colony. In 1636, two Puritan leaders, Thomas Hooker and John

> Heavy immigration and rapid population growth brings challenges to the Puritan elite, who banish deserters from the colony.

Davenport, sought independence from the colony's leadership and established towns and churches at Hartford and New Haven without crown sanction. Eventually, these settlements combined with an earlier one at Saybrook founded by John Winthrop Jr. made up the colony of Connecticut.

Not every act of secession was as peaceful. The theologian and Salem pastor Roger Williams claimed that the colonists should break with the Church of England and that nonmembers of the Congregationalist Church should not be forced to attend as the Massachusett's Bay Colony's leaders insisted. He based his claim on the ground that only God, not the colony's leaders, could articulate proper forms of worship. Williams also challenged the colony's claim to own all Indian land that fell within its grant as well as the belief that Indians had no title to their ancestral homelands. In 1635, with Williams refusing to be silenced, the General Court banished him. He eventually moved south and settled on land given to him by the Narragansetts. The town he established, Providence, became the core of the colony of Rhode Island, which received its own charter from Parliament in 1644.

Equally troubling to colony leaders was Anne Hutchinson who threatened not only the religious leadership of New England but also prevailing gender norms. Hutchinson held meetings in her home to discuss her minister's sermons, arousing concern, for women were to have no public role in religious or civil affairs. She and several others also challenged the Calvinist notion of predestination. Hutchinson was put on trial in 1637 and banished and excommunicated as a result. In 1638, she and many of her followers headed to Rhode Island, joining Roger Williams's new settlement.

In addition to independent-minded and outspoken Puritans, the colony's leadership had to contend with thousands of arriving settlers who did not share their religious convictions. Gradually, the General Court became a secular colonial legislature, and, as the colony expanded, it was no longer possible for neighbors to watch one another closely or for everyone to easily attend church. Rooted from the beginning in religious rather than economic pursuits, the colony began to leave behind its original mission as merchants gained power in the colony.

The South part of New-England, as it is Planted this yeare, 1634.

Beinecke Library, Yale University

William Wood's South Part of New England This early map of New England as it appeared to English eyes in 1634 shows a large number of English settlements indicated by a circle and a cross. Native American villages and their leaders are shown as triangles, some of which are surrounded by palisades. ▲

3-4d Puritans and Pequots

In the midst of these emerging divisions in New England society, settlers found common cause in war against the Indians, whom they saw as savages, the opposite of civilized man (see Table 3.2). The first major conflict was the Pequot War of 1636–1638, which erupted in the Connecticut River Valley. The war's causes included the English greed for land, the Pequot's willingness to trade with the Dutch, the desire on both sides to avenge previous attacks by the other, and the English ambition to demonstrate their supremacy over Indians in New England.

> Puritans defeat the Pequot in battle and find in their victory an affirmation from God.

Table 3.2 Major Anti-Colonial Indian Rebellions and Wars, 1585–1650

Year of Rebellion	Colony Indians Attacked
1597	Florida
1622	Virginia
1637	New England
1639	New Mexico
1644	Virginia

In 1633, the Pequot attacked a trading vessel they believed was Dutch but was in fact English. Among the nine dead was the prominent Englishman John Stone. In 1636, when another Englishman, John Oldham, was found dead in Pequot country, the Massachusetts Bay Colony's leaders decided to demonstrate their supremacy by doing "justice upon the Indians" rather than waiting for the Pequot to surrender the killers of Stone and Oldham.

Volunteers from the colony headed to Block Island, intent on killing the local men and enslaving their women and children. But the raiders found few Indians and had to settle for torching their villages. In retaliation, the Pequot attacked the English in Hartford, New Haven, and Saybrook. In May 1637, John Underhill and John Mason led a combined force of 90 Englishmen, 70 Mohegans, and 500 Narragansetts against a Pequot village of about 700 on the Mystic River. The English and their Indian allies encircled the village and set fires that burned to death nearly all of the Pequot villagers. Horrified, the Narragansetts abandoned their English allies. As the battles continued, the English killed more Pequots and sold captives into slavery in the West Indies and Bermuda. The war ended in 1638 by which time the Pequots had almost ceased to exist. Like those Powhatans who remained in Virginia, the survivors largely were excluded from English society.

To the Puritans, their victory was proof that they were still God's chosen people. They now controlled most of southeastern New England along with access to the region's valuable trade in furs and wampum. In 1643, the colonies of Massachusetts Bay, Connecticut, New Haven, and Plymouth allied themselves for a common defense against the French, Dutch, and Indians, creating the **New England Confederation**. This was the first significant effort by English colonists to form an intercolonial alliance for mutual benefit.

3-4e Life in the Chesapeake and New England

Colonial life in the Chesapeake and New England diverged, largely because the regions attracted a dramatically different type of colonist. Immigrants to the Chesapeake were, for the most part, poor, unattached men who gambled that they would be able to find a better livelihood in Virginia. Immigrants to New England, by contrast, were by and large economically comfortable families who had left England out of religious conviction.

> Daily life in the Chesapeake and in New England varies greatly.

In the Chesapeake, the Virginia Company was motivated by profits, sending single male laborers to cultivate tobacco. Of the 120,000 settlers who moved to the Chesapeake in the seventeenth century, 85 percent were indentured servants, nearly all were male and single, and half were between the ages of twenty and twenty-nine. These servants worked every day but Sunday, from sunup to sundown, in an environment where malaria, typhoid, and dysentery were endemic and often lethal. With high mortality and an imbalanced ratio between the sexes, immigration was the source of the colony's population growth in the seventeenth century. In contrast, nearly 90 percent of all immigrants to New England arrived with relatives. Almost half were women or girls. Because the ratio between the sexes was roughly equal in New England, the vast majority of men and women married and had large families. The colonial population in New England not only was self-sustaining from the beginning but also its settlers found an environment conducive to agriculture and general good health. They could reasonably expect to outlive their peers in England.

In the Chesapeake, where there was no overriding imperative for literacy, schooling often completely depended on parents, who were often uneducated. In New England, childrearing was a major focus of life, particularly for women. Puritans believed that infants, as inheritors of original sin, were depraved and that baptism might grant them some measure of God's grace. However, children needed proper cultivation through strong parenting and formal education so that they could study the Bible and thereby fulfill their spiritual promise. Boys were often better educated than girls were in writing, mathematics, and Latin, the main areas of study.

The contrast between lives in the two regions was no more apparent than in the settlers' dwellings. Most dwellings in the Chesapeake were temporary because, as once the soil of a particular plot of land was exhausted, planters moved with their servants to a new area. Small planters and their servants most often lived in wood dwellings with dirt floors while poorer households in the Chesapeake lacked basic necessities, such as chairs, beds, and mattresses, and might have had only one iron pot for cooking cornmeal mush. These households were devoid of books and all other nonessential items. New Englanders, who lived on stable family plots, built wooden-frame homes that were meant to endure and furnished them with simple but sturdy furniture. In the Chesapeake, only the wealthiest planters lived like modestly prosperous New England Puritans.

In Virginia, where tobacco was cultivated across a vast landscape, settlers lived on isolated plantations. There were few communities other than Jamestown, and, therefore, the settlers had none of the bustling fairs and market days or crowded taverns and inns that were so common to the towns of colonial Massachusetts.

New England Confederation
Confederation of Puritan colonies in British North America designed to protect them against Indian or Dutch attack. In existence from 1643 to 1684.

African Slavery in the Americas

This engraving shows activities associated with sugar making in the Caribbean. Central to the scene is the sugar works. Also shown are the huts of the enslaved and the planter's home in the background.

As you look at this illustration depicting the many steps in the processing of sugar cane, what social relations do you see at work? How does the illustration reveal the sharp social divisions between slaves and planters? ▶

Sugar Refinery, Colored engraving from Jean Baptiste du Tertre, *Histoire Génerale des Antilles Habitées par les Francois* (Paris, 1667), vol. 2, p. 122. Bibliotheque Nationale, Paris, France/Bridgeman Images

As important as Jamestown, Plymouth, and the Massachusetts Bay Colony were to English colonization in North America, the West Indies, because of the dramatic rise of sugar cane cultivation on those islands, became not only the crown jewel of England's overseas empire but also the most profitable of any European colonies in the Americas. In creating the modern plantation dependent on enslaved African labor, Caribbean sugar planters sparked a revolution in sugar production that had global importance. As demand for sugar increased, so did West Indies planters' demand for slaves. A highly profitable and destructive slave trade was the result. A slave-driven society, the English West Indies witnessed unparalleled tragedy in this era and instituted policies of labor exploitation that eventually spread to the English colonies on the mainland. So rich did the planters become that the mainland colonies began to emulate them. By 1650, all the English mainland colonies had slaves, and each colony began to articulate the proper place of slaves and the institution of slavery within their emerging societies. Moreover, because West Indian planters focused almost exclusively on sugar, they had to import food to sustain their slaves, much of which came from British North America. Thus, with the explosion of sugar cultivation in the Caribbean came a greater integration of the disparate parts of England's emerging transatlantic empire.

☞ As you read, think about the similarities and differences between the development of slavery in the West Indies and on the mainland of North America. What were the distinguishing features of West Indian sugar plantations?

3-5a Sugar Revolution in the West Indies

First developed in the Mediterranean, Europeans carried the production of sugar to Iberia, the Atlantic islands

> The English cultivation of sugar takes off in the West Indies where the English revolutionize the production of sugar.

of Madeira, the Canaries, and Sao Tome in the fifteenth century and then to the Caribbean and Brazil. By the sixteenth century, sugar was sold in all major towns and cities of western Europe. The rich used sugar to create spectacular culinary displays whereas shopkeepers, artisans, and peasants used it to preserve fruits and make jams. In the seventeenth century, as sugar became available at lower prices, its appeal broadened. Europeans used it to sweeten tea, coffee, and chocolate, and the market for sugary breads, pastries, cakes, and candies expanded.

The price of sugar dropped as its supply increased with European colonization of the West Indies (see Map 3.5). Sugar was a natural fit for the islands of the Caribbean because sugar cane grows best in the tropics where rain is frequent and heavy. The distance from Europe was not problematic because sugar can be stored a long time without spoiling. And because land on the islands was scarce and expensive to clear for agriculture, sugar was one of the few profitable crops that offered a high enough yield per acre to justify the investment.

The production of sugar was an intensive process in which Europeans came to rely almost exclusively on forced slave labor. Sugar had to be extracted from the cane, the stalk of the sugar plant, within two days of harvest or it would dry up. Thus, slaves processed the cane in mills near where it was cultivated. Slaves extracted the sugar from the cane by feeding it quickly into a mill's cylindrical rollers, which crushed it. Slaves then boiled the resulting juice in a series of large copper pots until it crystallized. Then they ladled the sugar into barrels. The **molasses** that might seep out of the barrels was processed again to produce additional crystallized sugar or rum. The harvesting, milling, boiling, curing, and distilling kept a large work force of slaves busy from January until May. The rest of the year slaves tended the cane fields or worked on other aspects of the plantation.

The English who settled the island of Barbados in 1627 had planted sugar cane, relying on a mixed labor

Map 3.5 Caribbean Colonies, 1660 The islands of the Caribbean, once Europeans stripped them of their native vegetation and populated with enslaved Africans, proved to be enormously profitable centers of sugar production that enriched Dutch, English, Spanish, and French planters. ◄

force of English indentured servants and African slaves. By the mid-seventeenth century, however, the planters realized that African slaves were a better investment than Englishmen who would work for only five or six years. At the same time, English merchants invested heavily in the planters, allowing them to expand their processing of cane by purchasing the necessary slaves. With Dutch ships transporting provisions to Barbados and sugar to Europe, the Barbados sugar boom began. By the 1650s, Barbados was a world leader in the production of "white gold." The planters continuously expanded their crops by destroying rainforests and planting new cane. By 1665, the island was denuded of nearly all of its native vegetation.

The English planters had achieved their success by revolutionizing the production of sugar. Previously, on the Atlantic Islands, in Brazil, and in the Spanish Caribbean, sugar cane had been grown in small quantities and brought to a mill owner whose slaves processed the sugar. On Barbados, planters owned not only the fields where the cane was grown but also their own mills and laborers. Barbadian planters also introduced **gang labor**, which involved rigid discipline and whipping to force slaves to work as hard as possible. Sugar cultivation on Barbados was a harbinger of modes of production in the mainland colonies.

The "sugar revolution" drove social, economic, and environmental change throughout the Atlantic world. The sugar industry spread across the Caribbean to French Guadeloupe in the 1650s, Martinique a decade later, and then St. Kitts, Nevis, Antigua, and Montserrat in the 1670s. With the arrival of sugar, these islands shifted from diverse agriculture to monoculture, from small-scale to large-scale cultivation, from sparse to dense settlements, and from indentured labor to slavery. English sugar production became extraordinarily profitable, rivaling silver mining in Mexico and dwarfing English exports from the mainland. In 1686, London merchants imported £674,518 worth of goods from the West Indies compared to £141,600 worth from all of the mainland colonies combined. Sugar also tied all of the English colonies together. West Indian planters devoted all their land to sugar cane, forcing them to import food and other necessities. As early as the 1640s, farmers in coastal New England exported grain and salt pork to the West Indies, which provided the colonists the ability to buy goods from England.

3-5b Plantation Laborers: Servants to Slaves

Sugar did not bring slavery to Barbados, but it accelerated a shift already underway from a reliance on predominantly male English indentured

molasses Thick dark to light brown syrup that is separated from raw sugar in the production of sugar.

gang labor Brutal form of labor on a plantation that forced slaves to work unrelenting hours from sunup to sundown.

{ Barbados planters shift from a reliance on servants to slaves.

"Cutting the Sugar Cane" This image shows slaves harvesting sugar cane. Note the woman and child in the foreground sorting the cane, the elderly slave in the left supervising the crew, and the English planter, the only man on horseback, which suggests his social and political power. ▶

servants to a labor force of African slaves. In the colony's earliest years, indentured servants had produced most of the sugar. Some had arrived in Barbados voluntarily, but many had been kidnapped and transported to the island against their will. Others were thieves and vagabonds sent to the island as punishment. Seeking higher and higher profits, the planters began to treat their servants like slaves. To prevent them from rebelling, the planters passed laws that restricted their movement and imposed harsh punishments for any acts of resistance. In the mid-1640s, Barbadian planters began to construct fortified homes to protect themselves from their debased English laborers. In one incident, the planters executed eighteen conspirators who they feared were plotting an islandwide rebellion.

After potential immigrants in England grew wary of the labor regime in the West Indies, their supply dried up. The planters turned to African slaves, paying £25 for a slave's entire lifetime of labor, although many slaves died long before they reached old age. In comparison, an English indentured servant cost £12 for five years of work. The English also came to believe that Africans were better laborers than English indentured servants because they were more accustomed to hot climates.

In 1640, a few hundred black slaves were on Barbados. In 1685, there were 46,000 black slaves and only 20,000 whites. In the eighteenth century, well over 1 million African slaves were sent to the English sugar islands. Most died during the first months of the **seasoning** process to their new environment as the result their exposure to new foods, new diseases, and a brutal labor regime. Slaves who did not perish in the first year endured, on average, between seven and seventeen more years of brutal labor.

The planters, meanwhile, became wealthy beyond their wildest dreams. A well-run plantation on Barbados generated up to a 200 percent annual return on investment. The planters built great houses stocked with imported furnishings, china, and silver and, despite the tropical environment, insisted on wearing fine multilayered English clothing and consuming a meat-heavy diet. Still, most planters longed to return to Europe with their wealth and health intact. Even though they held nearly absolute political and economic power, they loathed the climate and what they saw as their primitive surroundings.

3-5c Slave Life in the West Indies

African slaves in the West Indies led lives of nearly unending suffering. They were forbidden from marrying, tied to one plantation for life, and denied any chance of freedom. Medical care was minimal, and nutrition was grossly inadequate. Slaves lived in flimsy huts and had few possessions, nothing more than mats for sleeping, gourds for drinking, and pots for cooking. Everywhere in the West Indies, slave deaths consistently outnumbered births, and only through the continued importation of new slaves did planters maintain their labor forces of between 100 and 500 slaves per plantation.

{ *Slaves live under an oppressive regime against which they occasionally rebel.* }

In the cane fields, slaves worked in gangs of about twenty people supervised by a driver, usually an older slave who carried a whip to enforce discipline. Other slaves toiled by themselves as carters or wagoners and transported cane to the mills or barrels of sugar to the wharves. A small number worked as watchmen, coopers, masons, carpenters, or domestic servants, attending to the needs of planters. All worked six days a week for 10 or 11 hours per day. Children went to work at age four or five and worked until they died. Cane cutting was usually confined

seasoning Process through which immigrants to the Americas adjusted to changes in climate, food, and working conditions. Often resulted in death.

to daylight hours, but mills and boilers ran day and night, and some slaves worked through both.

Because slavery had all but vanished from England in the thirteenth century, English law had no precedents for the governance of slaves. Planters in Barbados developed their own slave code in 1661, which characterized Africans as savage heathens and allowed a planter to punish his slaves as he saw fit without fear of punishment. A slave guilty of a minor offense was whipped and had his nose slit. Murder, rape, arson, theft, and assault were all capital crimes for slaves. They could not leave their plantations without explicit permission from their masters.

The masters believed that if the slaves could move freely, they would plot rebellions. Masters lived in constant fear of a slave uprising and reacted with great violence to suspected plots. In 1675, after they discovered plans for a slave revolt, Barbados officials arrested the suspects, burning six alive and beheading another eleven. The following year, in response to the failed rebellion, planters further restricted slaves' activity and mobility.

Despite the punitive slave code, slaves on Barbados planned major rebellions in 1683, 1685, 1692, and 1701, only to be found out on the eve of the uprisings. In Jamaica, another English sugar colony, six major slave revolts occurred between 1673 and 1694. Throughout the West Indies, runaway slaves became common and often persisted for generations in independent settlements known as **maroon communities** in remote locations of each island.

Compared with the laws and customs of Spanish America, the English slave codes that emerged in the West Indies and later in the English mainland colonies were far more restrictive, offering no path to manumission. In New Spain, especially in urban areas, a free African labor force began to outnumber that of slaves by 1700. But in the Caribbean, slaves vastly outnumbered free blacks, and those very few who had gained manumission saw their own freedom diminish over the seventeenth century.

3-5d African Slavery on the Mainland: The Early Years

The shift in Barbados from a society with a handful of slaves to a society entirely reliant on them foreshadowed the experience of some but not all of the colonies of mainland North America. African slaves had been brought to Virginia in 1619, New Netherlands in 1628, and New England in 1638. But through 1650, English indentured servants vastly outnumbered slaves.

> The enslavement of Africans is widespread across the European colonies in North America.

Far more than any other colony in eastern North America, tiny New Netherland depended on slaves in its early years. By 1640, some 100 African slaves were living in New Amsterdam, composing about 30 percent of the city's population. In contrast to those on Barbados, the New Amsterdam slaves soon were allowed to live and work on their own in return for a certain amount of labor and an annual payment to the Company. They joined the Dutch Reformed Church, served in the militia, and eventually accumulated their own property. In 1644, eleven enslaved men and their wives petitioned for and gained "half-freedom" from the WIC. They had to pay the Company an annual tribute of twenty-two bushels of grain and "one fat hog" or return to slavery.

The more densely populated New England, where large families did most of the labor, was slower to adopt slavery. Puritanism itself was not irreconcilable with slavery. In 1630, the same year of the establishment of the Massachusetts Bay Colony, Puritans founded a colony on Providence Island, off the coast of Nicaragua. Planning to grow tobacco, these colonists purchased slaves from the Dutch and later sold some of their slaves to traders who took them to New England where they became among the first slaves sold in the region. This is only one example of the trade connections between the mainland colonies and the Caribbean slave societies. Although slaves never became indispensable to the survival of Massachusetts colonies, Africans and English indentured servants were the main source of menial labor for the most affluent families. The few slaves in New England worked in households or as field hands. Notably, the Puritans also approved laws allowing the enslavement of Indians captured in a "just war," such as the Pequot War of 1637.

With its tobacco fields in need of cultivation, Virginia purchased more slaves than other mainland colonies. African slaves had been in Virginia at least since 1619. Some of these early slaves had Spanish or Portuguese names, were nominally Christian, and had grown up or lived near the commercial centers that Europeans had established in West Africa. In their dress, behavior, and familiarity with European languages, these slaves understood European ways. A few found that, through luck and industry, they could win their freedom. Yet it soon became impossible for others to follow this path. In the 1640s, the colony passed the first of many laws excluding people of African descent from entry into white society. In 1643, Virginia enacted legislation that all adult men who worked the land were tithable and thus occupied the lowest social status in society. Crucially, the law also classified "Negro" women as such, thereby placing black and white women servants in separate social categories before the law. White European servant women were considered more appropriate for domestic work, whereas, in the words of one Virginia planter, "Yet som wenches that are nasty and beastly and not fit to be employed are put [to work] in the ground."

Maryland adopted legislation similar to that of Virginia in 1654. Most important, at this time Virginia planters enshrined in law lifelong servitude for slaves. In 1646, Francis Pott sold a Negro woman and a boy to another man, "to the use of him … forever."

maroon communities
Independent communities formed by African refugees who had escaped slavery.

Six years later, William Whittington sold to Pott "one Negro girle named Jowan; aged Ten yeares and with her Issue and Produce duringe her (or either of them) for their Life tyme. And their successors forever."

African slavery was on the ascendance in the English colonies in 1650, but in New Spain, it had long since peaked. Slaves were common only in wealthy urban areas such as Mexico City where the affluent could afford them. Relative to slaves working on sugar plantations in the West Indies, these slaves lived well, although they were still always at the mercy of their masters. They had a better chance of marrying and having children. They could become artisans or skilled laborers and thereby win their freedom. Across New Spain, slaves formed lively confraternities within the Catholic Church, creating for themselves a rich religious and associational life. In New France, meanwhile, colonists held Indian slaves, but not until the establishment of the colony of Louisiana in the early eighteenth century did the French on the mainland hold African bondsmen.

Summary

Between the 1580s and the 1650s, Europeans shifted from exploring to settling North America. Their motivations were diverse, including wealth, religious expression, political freedom, and national rivalries. Most failed to find what they sought, but a few enjoyed spectacular success. Almost all Europeans who came to the Americas had incorrect notions about the geography, climate, and Indians. The immigrants optimistically imagined rivers that did not exist, a mild climate, and Indians who could easily be brought into European religions and systems of labor. Faced with repeated invasions, Indians confronted Europeans as best they could, trying variously to understand, profit from, and fend off Europeans. But to just about every corner of native North America, Europeans brought disease, depopulation, war, dispossession, and even enslavement or genocide. Although these forces raged across much of North America between 1580 and 1650, they did not completely destroy native North American peoples. Still, by the middle of the seventeenth century, a continent that had been shaped by hundreds of diverse Indian cultures was giving way to one increasingly dominated by a handful of European nations that held extremely dismissive views of Indians. In the same years that England was experimenting with diverse forms of settlements in Virginia and New England, it was causing a revolution in the organization and management of the production of sugar in the West Indies, which would have global import. By mid-century, Barbados had emerged as a world leader in the production of sugar, enriching England as Mexican silver had enriched the Spanish and knitting together Africa, the Caribbean, and North America in a web of commerce and brutality of transatlantic proportions. In these years, African slavery also began on the mainland colonies, in New England, and the Chesapeake, and New Netherland.

‹Thinking Back, *Looking Forward*›

As you review this chapter, compare European colonization in the Americas. How many different forms of colonization can you discern during the first century and a half of European expansion in the Americas? How did different patterns of empire and immigration shape European societies in the Americas? Similarly, how many different ways did Native American peoples respond to European settlements and colonization? What made possible the intersection of European, Caribbean, and African worlds in the West Indies?

In the next chapter look for the various ways that Europeans sought to develop coordinated transatlantic empires and try to understand the origins of the rebellions that convulsed many American colonies in the late seventeenth century.

To make your study concrete, review the timeline and reflect on the entries there. Think about their causes, consequences, and connections. How do they fit with global trends?

Additional Resources

Books

Bushnell, Amy Turner. *Situado and Sabana: Spain's Support System for the Presidio and Mission Provinces of Florida.* **New York: American Museum of Natural History, 1994.** ▶ Careful study that captures the intersection of Spanish and Native American worlds in early Florida.

Dunn, Richard S. *Sugar and Slaves: The Rise of the Planter Class in the English West Indies, 1624–1713.* **Chapel Hill: University of North Carolina Press, 1972.** ▶ Classic study of the sugar revolution in the English Caribbean.

Greer, Alan. *Mohawk Saint: Catherine Tekakwitha and the Jesuits.* **Oxford, England: Oxford University Press, 2005.** ▶Fascinating biography of Tekakwitha and the Jesuits who saw her saintly Catholic devotion.

Gutierrez, Ramón A. *When Jesus Came, the Corn Mothers Went Away: Marriage, Sexuality, and Power in New Mexico, 1500–1846.* **Stanford, CA: Stanford University Press, 1991.** ▶ Stunning and controversial study of sex and power in colonial New Mexico.

Horn, James. *Land as God Made It: Jamestown and the Birth of America.* **New York: Basic Books, 2005.** ▶ Lively account that places Jamestown in an Atlantic context.

Morgan, Edmund S. *The Puritan Dilemma: The Story of John Winthrop.* **Boston: Little, Brown. 1958.** ▶ Probing biography of the tensions at the heart of the leader of New England Puritans.

Romney, Susanah Shaw. *New Netherland Connections: Intimate Networks and Atlantic Ties in Seventeenth-Century America.* **Chapel Hill: University of North Carolina Press, 2014.** ▶ Reconstruction of the indispensable role of women in the Dutch colony in the seventeenth century.

Rushforth, Brett. *Bonds of Alliance: Indigenous and Atlantic Slaveries in New France.* **Chapel Hill: University of North Carolina Press, 2013.** ▶ Path-breaking examination of Indian slavery in New France.

Townsend, Camilla. *Pocahontas and the Powhatan Dilemma.* **New York: Hill and Wang, 2004.** ▶ Stirring and sympathetic biography of the Indian woman whose history is intertwined with that of the Jamestown settlement.

Weber, David J. *The Spanish Frontier in North America.* **New Haven, CT: Yale University Press, 1992.** ▶ Magisterial overview of Spanish exploration and settlement in North America.

> Go to the MindTap® for **Global Americans** to access the full version of select books from this Additional Resources section.

Websites

Virtual Jamestown. http://www.virtualjamestown.org/ ▶ Website covering most aspects of the Jamestown colony.

Plymouth Colony Archive. http://www.histarch.illinois .edu/plymouth/ ▶ Extensive online materials relating to early settlement of Plymouth.

Continue exploring online through MindTap®**, where you can:**
- **Assess your knowledge with the Chapter Test**
- **Watch historical videos related to the chapter**
- **Further your understanding with interactive maps and timelines**

Experimentation, Resistance, and Persistence

1585–1600

1573

Franciscan missionaries replace Jesuits in Florida.

1588

England destroys Spanish Armada.

1597

Guales rebel in Florida.

1598

Oñate claims New Mexico for Spain.

Spanish soldiers attack Acoma Pueblo.

1601–1609

1602

Dutch East India Company (VOC) is established.

1603

Queen Elizabeth I dies; James I (monarch1603–1625) is crowned.

1606

Oñate is ousted and replaced by a royal governor.

1607

English establish Jamestown.

1608

Champlain establishes Quebec City.

Spain establishes Santa Fé in New Mexico.

1609

John Smith is sent back to England.

1610–1615

1610–1611

Hudson searches for Northwest Passage.

1612

Rolfe introduces tobacco to Virginia.

1613

The English kidnap Pocahontas.

1614

Pocahontas marries John Rolfe.

Tisquantum (Squanto) is kidnapped.

1616

Epidemic begins in New England, killing nearly all the Pawtuxet by 1620.

1619–1621

1619

First African slaves arrive in Virginia.

Headright system is established in Virginia.

Elected assembly is established in Virginia.

1620

Pilgrims establish Plymouth Plantation.

Pocahontas dies in England.

1621

Dutch West Indian Company (WIC) is established.

1622–1625

1622

Rebellion of Opechancanough kills 347 Englishmen in Virginia.

Tisquantum (Squanto) dies.

1624

Dutch establish New Netherland.

1625

James I dies; Charles I is crowned.

1626–1630	1631–1635	1636–1640	1641–1644	1645–1655
1628 First African slaves arrive in New Netherland.	**1630s** Jesuit missionaries begin working with Wendats.	**1636** Pequot War breaks out.	**1642** French establish Montreal.	**1647** Charles I is arrested.
1629 Freedoms and Exemptions becomes governing document in New Netherland.	Smallpox overwhelms Wendats.	**1637** Massachusetts banishes Anne Hutchinson.	English Civil War begins.	**1649** Charles I is executed for treason.
Massachusetts Bay Colony gets charter.	Opechancanough sues for peace.	**1638** New Sweden is established.	**1644** Indian rebellion in Virginia kills 500 Englishmen.	**1650** Haudenosaunees defeat Wendats.
	1632 *Great Migration* to New England.	First African slaves arrive in New England.		**1654** Jewish settlers arrive in New Amsterdam from Brazil.
	1635 Massachusetts banishes Roger Williams.	**1639** Indians at Taos and Jemez rebel.		**1655** Dutch conquer New Sweden.
Charles I dismisses Parliament.		**1640** Dutch in New Netherland demand tribute from Munsees.		
1630 John Winthrop sails for New England with approximately 700 Puritans.		Charles I summons Parliament.		

North America

North American Southwest

New England

New Netherland

Virginia

Florida

England

Netherlands

Spain

4 Empires across the Atlantic World

1650–1700

William Penn dubbed his colony, gifted by King Charles II, the "Holy Experiment" and led a group of Quakers there.

The Peaceable Kingdom, 1832–34 (see also 84503)/Hicks, Edward (1780–1849)/Phaidon Press/Private Collection/ Bridgeman Images

Trained as a commercial painter, Edward Hicks painted more than a hundred versions of *The Peaceable Kingdom* between 1820 and 1849. This detail shows Hicks's rendering of William Penn meeting with Native American leaders who he attempted to treat fairly and with respect. ▲

Few men have experienced the vicissitudes of fortune—or embodied the conflicts and contradictions of their age—as William Penn Jr., who went from privilege to imprisonment, from being among the world's largest landholders to being debt ridden, all in a matter of decades. Penn was born in 1644, the son of a famous naval officer during a period of English history that saw civil war, the beheading of a king, a Puritan Commonwealth, the restoration of the monarchy, and the creation of new colonies in British North America. He was raised in affluence, afforded a fine education, and groomed to take over his father's properties. As a young man, Penn was sent to Ireland to check on some of the family's estates, and there he became most interested in Quakerism, a religious sect that Anglicans, Puritans, and Penn's father considered dangerous and heretical. Members of The Society of Friends were known derisively as Quakers because of their desire to "tremble at the word of the Lord." Central to Quaker belief is the conviction that people's souls can communicate directly with God, a God that makes itself known through an "inner light." To Quakers, trained ministers and religious ceremonies are unnecessary and an impediment to spiritual enlightenment. Penn's father was so displeased with his son's beliefs that he banished him from the family home. Homeless and cut off from his family, Penn's Quaker beliefs deepened. He soon became one of the great defenders of the Quakers, and he suffered imprisonment numerous times in the 1670s for his beliefs.

With his father's death in 1670, Penn gained a modest inheritance, and in 1677, he was among a group of Quakers who purchased land in the newly established province of West Jersey. In 1681, seemingly to repay a long-standing debt to the Penn family and rid England of its Quakers, King Charles II granted Penn some 45,000 square miles of territory west of New Jersey and north of Maryland, making him overnight the owner of an estate that dwarfed even the largest in England. In the following year, Penn led a large migration of Quakers to his colony, one that he dubbed the "Holy Experiment." He envisioned Pennsylvania as a place where colonists could worship in accordance with their beliefs and where Native Americans would be treated fairly by colonists. In 1684, he traveled back to England, and although he did not die until 1718, he would spend only two more years in Pennsylvania. Nevertheless, his vision of a colony that allowed free religious expression drew tens of thousands from across western Europe.

Although an ocean separated England from North America, Penn's life shows that political, religious, and economic events on European soil and elsewhere shaped the colonies. In England, a new king sought to reward loyal supporters like Penn with colonies in North America.

How does William Penn's founding of Pennsylvania reflect the religious and economic developments of the age in England and North America?

Go to MindTap® to watch a video on Penn and learn how his story relates to the themes of this chapter.

Later, however, a revolution in England meant that Penn's royalist contacts had become his greatest liability. He was branded a traitor, forced into hiding, and eventually imprisoned for debt. Penn's life and career were also shaped by the economic currents of his age. As proprietor of Pennsylvania, he was charged with the enforcement of the trade legislation that came to embody the imperial rivalries of Spain, England, and the Netherlands. Furthermore, his city, Philadelphia, emerged as a commercial center and became a central port for the disembarkation of slaves in the mid-Atlantic colonies. Remarkable for its scope, brutality, and widespread acceptance, the transatlantic slave trade expanded dramatically in the second half of the seventeenth century as plantation agriculture took hold, European empires solidified, and commerce quickened. Penn clearly espoused liberty for individuals, but he held a dozen slaves on Pennsbury, the estate from which he sought to administer his "Holy Experiment," and Pennsylvania itself profited by exporting food to West Indian slave plantations. Penn's life fully reflected the contradictions of the era in which he lived.

4-1

English Civil War and Restoration Colonies

This painting, titled *The Execution of Charles I*, 1649, shows the execution of Charles I by forces backed by Parliament and the Puritan general Oliver Cromwell. Charles I was found guilty of treason for fighting a war against Parliament and executed on January 30, 1649.

Consider the various scenes and people in this painting. What story or stories are being told here and from what point or points of view? ▶

Fine Art Premium/Corbis

For much of the seventeenth century, England was in political turmoil. The execution of Charles I, the Civil War, the Puritan Commonwealth, and finally, the restoration of the Stuart kings were English events that shaped politics in the colonies. The rise to power of the Puritans in England ended the Puritan migration to New England and convulsed politics in the Chesapeake. Later, a new king sought tight control over existing colonies and rewarded his most loyal followers in England by granting them five colonies in British North America: Carolina, New York, New Jersey, Pennsylvania, and Delaware. Across these colonies, political institutions developed according to local circumstances and the visions of the men who organized them.

absolute monarchy Form of monarchical rule in which the monarch, unencumbered by laws or a legislature, enjoys unrestrained power.

☞ As you read, consider how the restoration colonies were established. How did they differ from colonies that England had founded decades earlier?

4-1a English Civil War and Restoration Colonies

With the death of Queen Elizabeth in 1603, the English crown passed to James I (who ruled from 1603 to 1625) and then to his son Charles I (who reigned from 1625 to 1649) (see Table 4.1). James also passed to Charles his belief in the unrestricted power of **absolute monarchy**. Charles I made enemies by granting commercial monopolies to his political favorites and promoting Anglicanism as the only recognized faith, thereby antagonizing Puritans and Presbyterians alike. Starting in 1629, he tried to rule the country without parliamentary consultation, but in the late winter of 1640, a major fiscal crisis forced him to recall the governing body. Nevertheless, the monarch's relationship with the realm's legislators disintegrated soon after. In 1642,

{ Violent political upheavals in England create turbulence in the colonies of British North America.

Table 4.1 Seventeenth-Century English Rulers

Ruler	Reign
Elizabeth I	1558–1603
James I	1603–1625
Charles I	1625–1649
Oliver Cromwell	1653–1658
Richard Cromwell	1658–1659
Charles II	1660–1685
James II	1685–1688
Mary II	1689–1694
William III	1689–1702

Source: Voyages: The Trans-Atlantic Slave Trade Database.
www.slavevoyages.org

Charles tried to raise an army without parliamentary support to suppress a rebellion in Ireland. An outraged Parliament raised an army against the king and began passing laws that favored Calvinism over Anglicanism. In 1645, Parliament banned the Anglican **Book of Common Prayer** and then ordered the execution of Archbishop Laud. In the ensuing **English Civil War**, 200,000 English died in battle and from disease. In 1649, the victorious Parliamentarians beheaded Charles I, and for the next decade, England was a kingless "commonwealth." In 1653, the Puritan general Oliver Cromwell staged a military coup, pledging to impose order on a war-torn society. With his army, he seized Ireland and Scotland, which by then had become largely Presbyterian, and then banned Catholicism.

The English Civil War brought trade with British North America almost to a halt, prompting an economic crisis in the colonies that led New Englanders to increased self-sufficiency and to create their own merchant fleet. The colonists began exploiting the Atlantic fisheries off Newfoundland for food and the hardwood forests near their settlements for shipbuilding. New England merchants participated in a trade of commodities that connected colonial ports in the Azores and Madeira, West Africa, and the Caribbean. This trade resembled a triangle in its overall shape, but the same ship did not complete each leg of the trade. Merchants carried timber and grains to the Azores and Madeira Island. Ships from there sailed to the coast of Africa where they bought slaves, which experienced slavers then transported to Barbados. Finally, to complete the triangular circuit, merchants returned to New England with Barbadian molasses and a handful of remaining slaves.

The English Civil War also curtailed the Great Migration because Puritans chose to stay and fight Charles and then supported the rule of Cromwell, who held the title of Lord Protector. In fact, 15 percent of Puritans and 30 percent of Puritan ministers who had left for New England in the Great Migration returned to England during the Civil War. The other English colonies were affected by the war as well. The Virginia legislature denounced the execution of the king but in return for supporting Parliament was granted the right to choose its own council and governor. In Maryland, tensions between Catholics and Protestants erupted after the assembly passed the Maryland Toleration Act of 1649, which guaranteed Puritans the right to worship in a colony that had been dominated by Catholics.

By 1654, Cromwell had triumphed over Ireland and Scotland and negotiated peace with the Dutch, one of England's bitterest rivals. The devout Puritan next plotted to conquer Catholic Spain's holdings in the West Indies through a series of military adventures known as the **Western Design**. Admiral William Penn and General Robert Venables, who had gained glory in his suppression of the Irish, assembled an armada of more than fifty ships and 9,000 men. In the spring of 1655, the fleet arrived at Hispaniola. But within three weeks, 1,700 of Venables's men were dead from disease, starvation, and Spanish ambushes. When the English attacked neighboring Jamaica, they suffered similar losses but ultimately succeeded. At the cost of 5,000 troops, Venables seized the colony's capital and renamed it Spanish Town. The English hoped to use the island as a base from which to plunder Spanish treasure fleets but did not achieve that goal because of poor military organization. Eventually, Jamaica proved profitable for the English crown through sugar cultivation. Cromwell died in 1658, and with his death ended the Western Design and Puritan rule in England.

4-1b Establishment of Carolina

> England established the colony of Carolina as a buffer between Florida and the Chesapeake.

Upon Cromwell's death, Charles II, son of the beheaded Charles I and king from 1660 to 1685, reclaimed the throne in what became known as the **Stuart Restoration**. He pledged to support the Church of England, work with Parliament, expand England's territorial holdings, and continue to challenge England's main commercial rivals, the Netherlands and Spain. Over the next dozen years, the English seized New Netherland and in the formerly Dutch territory established the colonies of New York, New Jersey, Pennsylvania, and Delaware. Farther south, the English founded Carolina as a bulwark against Spanish expansion north from Florida (see Map 4.1). In what are now known as the *Restoration colonies*, proprietors of the colonies promoted religious toleration, worked toward increased governmental control, and tried to ground the social order with a landed elite in power (see Table 4.2).

Book of Common Prayer Anglican book of standardized prayers revised and republished in 1662.

English Civil War Political and military conflict pitting Parliamentarians against Monarchists over the nature of government in England between 1642 and 1651.

Western Design English attack on Spanish holdings in the West Indies to secure a Caribbean base from which the English could threaten Spanish treasure routes.

Stuart Restoration Period in England during which the monarchy was restored following civil war and Puritan rule.

Map 4.1 The Restoration Colonies, ca. 1681 Once the Stuart's were restored to power in England, they established five new colonies in British North America: Carolina, New York, New Jersey, Pennsylvania, and Delaware. ▲

Fundamental Constitutions Outlines for the government of Carolina, written by one of the colony's proprietors and John Locke; it granted freedom of religion, upheld slavery, and proposed a feudal social order.

The first of the Restoration colonies, Carolina, was created in 1663 when Charles granted eight courtiers the vast expanse of land between Virginia and Florida. The proprietors hoped to earn money by renting land to immigrants, but few were willing to live in their new

Table 4.2 Restoration Colonies and Proprietors

Year	Colony	Proprietor
1664	New York	James, Duke of York
1664	New Jersey	Sir George Carteret, John Land Berkeley
1665	North Carolina	Carolina Proprietors
1670	South Carolina	Carolina Proprietors
1681	Pennsylvania and Delaware	William Penn

Source: Voyages: The Trans-Atlantic Slave Trade Database. www.slavevoyages.org

society. In 1667, one of the proprietors, Anthony Ashley-Cooper, persuaded the others to invest their own money in the colony. They sent 300 settlers, only 100 of whom were still alive when the small fleet landed at Port Royal on the Carolina coast. Nearly half were from Barbados, which had become overcrowded as a result of the sugar boom and offered little opportunity for the children of planters to advance themselves. These Barbadian migrants were rich, and many arrived with slaves. At first they attempted to grow tobacco, cotton, and silk and then turned to producing beef and naval stores, but they met with little success.

In 1669, Carolina's proprietors issued the **Fundamental Constitutions**, a political treatise coauthored by proprietor Ashley-Cooper and his secretary, a brilliant young man named John Locke. Because the Fundamental Constitutions were based on landed nobility extracting labor from tithing serfs, they proved highly unpopular with settlers, who knew that Massachusetts, Virginia, and the other existing colonies had a social order based on settlers owning land. As a result, the colony's legislature did not ratify the Fundamental Constitutions.

By the early eighteenth century, the northern region of Carolina was oriented around tobacco cultivation. The southern region centered on a trade in deerskins, enslaved Indians, and cultivated rice, the colony's principal commercial crop. The technical knowledge to produce rice and the labor required to plant and harvest were often the province of slaves, many of whom had been brought to the colony from rice-producing regions of West Africa. In 1729, the two regions of Carolina became separate colonies both ruled by the crown.

4-1c New England, New York, and New Jersey

Not all of the colonies fully accepted the Stuart Restoration, and Charles II was alarmed by reports that Massachusetts magistrates had come to see their colony as a free state and refused to swear fealty to the

> In the 1660s, Charles II establishes three new colonies in northern North America, cementing England's control over a large contiguous territory.

king. Moreover, Puritans not only balked at the idea of religious tolerance but had in fact banned the Anglican Book of Common Prayer. Charles believed that part of New England's

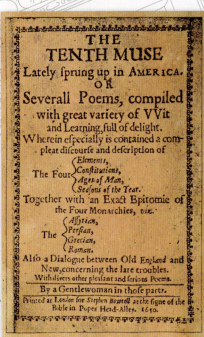

The Granger Collection, New York

Global Americans

Often overlooked because of their near invisibility in a world of letters dominated by men, women were nevertheless important readers and writers in seventeenth-century New England. Puritanism put a high priority on reading literacy because it was the way into the Bible and god's words. Some Puritan women in New England could write, but none seems to have done so with the skill and acclaim of **Anne Bradstreet**. Her collection of poetry, *The Tenth Muse*, was the first volume published by a woman in New England. Bradstreet was born in 1612 in England and came to Massachusetts in 1630 with other Puritans. Like most Puritan women, she had a large family, giving birth to eight children between 1633 and 1652. But her writing set her apart even as it focused on her role as mother and a deeply religious woman. Near the end of her life, she composed a spiritual autobiography for the benefit of her children. In typical Puritan fashion, it was filled with doubts about her own spiritual state. She advised her children to find faith in adversity: "If at any time you are chastened of God, take it as thankfully and joyfully as in greatest mercyes, for if yee bee his yee shall reap the greatest benefitt by it." She concluded with modesty and self-deprecation, traits that were typical of women of her time and place: "This was written in much sicknesses and weakness, and is very weakly and imperfectly done; but, if you can pick any Benefitt out of it, it is the marke which I aimed at." Bradstreet died in 1672.

intransigence was a result of the presence of New Netherland, which stood between Virginia and Massachusetts. The king believed that conquering New Netherland, which England had long insisted was an illegitimate encroachment on its territory, would not only strike a blow against his Dutch rivals but also help him control New England.

In England's confrontation with the Dutch in North America, the king's brother, James, the Duke of York, played a central role. Charles gave him control over virtually all unsettled land England claimed between Virginia and Nova Scotia, a region that included New Netherland. In 1664, James sent some three hundred troops commanded by Colonel Richard Nicolls, who were joined by a militia from Connecticut, to take New Amsterdam, which surrendered without a fight. Under the terms of the surrender, known as the **Articles of Capitulation**, the Dutch West India Company and the city's inhabitants, regardless of nationality, retained their property, New Amsterdam became New York City, and the trading post Fort Orange became Albany. Dutch settlers in New York City and on Long Island lived under English rule, but settlers elsewhere continued to live under Dutch law. The transfer of Albany to the English forced the Mohawks, who had lost their Dutch trading partners, into an alliance with the French to secure the trade goods and arms that they desired.

In 1665, James gave the land between the Hudson and Delaware Rivers, as well as lands farther north, to two proprietors, Sir George Carteret and Lord John Berkeley, both of whom had helped plan Nicolls's expedition. In 1676, the large grant was divided into East and West New Jersey. Presbyterians from England and Scotland came to East New Jersey and Quakers from England and Scotland immigrated to West New Jersey. But economically, both colonies struggled, and in 1702, the crown took control and united the two as a single colony, New Jersey.

The charter that the king gave James to govern New York was the briefest of any of the seventeenth-century colonial charters. It gave James nearly absolute power to control all governmental appointments in New York, set customs duties and taxes, regulate trade, direct the local militias, make the colony's laws, and adjudicate legal matters as though he were a judge. James had few opportunities to act on this power himself, however, because he never set foot in the colony, which was instead administered by a series of governors, the first of whom was Nicolls.

In writing and promulgating the **Duke's Laws**, the code that governed much of the colony, Nicolls imposed the Stuarts' vision of absolute rule on a colony that had previously enjoyed a great deal of autonomy, if not self-rule, under the Dutch. The Duke's Laws made no provision for an elected assembly or town meetings, granted religious liberty to Christians, and protected slavery, decreeing that no law prevented masters from taking "Servants for the Term of years or Life." Finally, the code decreed that no settler could purchase land from Indians without permission from the governor and that only licensed traders could engage in commerce with the Indians.

Yet Anglo-Dutch relations in New York inevitably became strained, reflecting the long rivalry between the two nations, and the larger currents of that rivalry were soon felt in the colony. New York, poorly defended by the English, was retaken by the Dutch in 1673 during the third Anglo-Dutch War. The Dutch sent Nicolls back to England and asserted their political and economic control over the region. But the Dutch once again relinquished the colony as part of the 1674 settlement that ended the war.

Articles of Capitulation Document through which the Dutch formally surrendered the colony of New Netherland to the English.

Duke's Laws Fundamental laws governing New York under the English that outlined an absolutist government but granted religious toleration to individuals.

The new English governor of New York, Edmund Andros, tried to thoroughly anglicize the colony, requiring all official records to be kept in English. He also made all residents of the colony take an oath of fidelity to the English king. But the people of New York—Dutch, English, and otherwise—became restless with their lack of say in these matters. In 1683, in response to popular clamoring, James allowed the election of a colonial assembly for the first time, and the assembly promptly drafted a **Charter of Liberties and Privileges**. The Charter mandated that elections be held every three years among male property owners and the freemen of New York City and granted the right of trial by jury and religious toleration for all Protestants. Suddenly, New Yorkers enjoyed greater power and autonomy than colonists elsewhere in British North America.

4-1d Pennsylvania and Delaware

In 1681, Charles II granted William Penn an extensive tract of land south and west of New York, a territory known as Pennsylvania in honor of Penn's father. In 1702, the lower half of the territory became the colony of Delaware. Given the power to create

> William Penn establishes Pennsylvania, bringing Quakers and greater religious diversity to British North America.

his own government, Penn set forth his ideas in a document known as the **First Frame of Government** (1682). He guaranteed settlers liberty of conscience, freedom from persecution, an elected assembly with the sole power to set taxes, and due process of law, all of which made the colony very attractive to people across western Europe, many of whom lived in countries with greater restrictions on religious expression and far fewer rights and liberties.

Penn promoted his colony throughout England, Ireland, and Germany, and in 1685 alone, about 8,000 immigrants arrived. Between 1675 and 1690, more than 10,000 **Quakers**, nearly half of the total number in England at that time, immigrated to the colony. Philadelphia, situated on the Delaware River, quickly emerged as a busy port city, and by 1690, had 3,900 residents and rivaled Boston and New York for commercial supremacy in British North America. By 1700, the colony had almost 18,000 residents and was sending large quantities of wheat and meat to the West Indies, where planters relied on the imported food to feed their slaves. In 1701, Penn further modified the colony's government, signing the **Charter of Privileges**, which created a one-house legislature and made it fully independent of his influence. Pennsylvania's relations with neighboring Indians were among the most progressive in colonial America because of Quaker pacifism and Penn's insistence on purchasing land fairly from Indians before advancing settlement. Penn's growing reputation among Native Americans for treating them justly led the colony to become a refuge for Indians who clashed with colonists in Maryland, Virginia, and Carolina.

4-2
Expansion of Imperial Rivalries for Trade and Territory

This painting, *A Dutch Merchantman Attacked by an English Privateer, off La Rochelle*, by Cornelis van Wieringen, shows two ships approaching one another. The Dutch ship is in the middle, while the English privateer is on the right. Both ships have opened fire. In the background, a French ship approaches.

As you look at the image, and the positioning of the ships, try to imagine this sort of warfare. What motivated this type of piracy and privateering, and what was its effect on colonial America? ▶

National Maritime Museum, Greenwich, London, Caird Collection

In the second half of the seventeenth century, as Spain's transatlantic trade declined, England and France created new rules of commerce designed to prevent them and others, in particular the Dutch, from profiting from their overseas colonies. English colonies resisted new commercial regulations, but this legislation eventually brought wealth to British North America and integrated its colonies into an expanding empire. The French took control of New France and embarked on further explorations and settlements in Canada's interior and in the lower Mississippi Valley. Spain, which had long pursued similar policies, expanded into the Southwest but was unable to integrate these frontiers into its empire other than as defensive peripheries. In these same years, in response to the rivalry of the French and English, the Haudenosaunees, who also had imperial and economic ambitions of their own, reached an agreement with the colony of New York, allowing them to expand their own influence in the Northeast.

☞ As you read, consider the origins and structures of European empires. What were the strengths and weaknesses of eighteenth-century transatlantic empires?

4-2a Anglo-Dutch Rivalry for Transatlantic Trade

Compared to Spain, England was slow to regulate trade between the home country and its colonies. Spain had created its House of Trade a decade after Columbus returned from his first voyage, but it was nearly half a century after the establishment of Jamestown before England regulated its overseas trade.

> European imperial rivalries play out not only in the contest for territory but increasingly in the arena of trade and commerce.

In the early seventeenth century, no gold was found in Virginia, and England lacked the resources of a strong navy or a powerful monarch to tighten trade rules. But by the mid-seventeenth century, Barbados sugar and Virginia tobacco appeared profitable enough to form the basis of a very lucrative transatlantic commerce, and by then, England had the largest navy in the world. During Cromwell's rule and the Stuart Restoration, therefore, England committed not only to regulating its transatlantic trade but also to capturing an increased share of all of the commerce between Europe and the Americas (see Map 4.2).

During the English Civil War, the Dutch had so increased their dominance of trade between Europe and the New World that the Dutch shipped more than the combined total of the rest of Europe. This Dutch supremacy was seen as a mortal threat to the English government. To combat the Dutch, Parliament passed the **Navigation Acts**, mercantilist laws that greatly enhanced state control over England's portion of the transatlantic trade. In 1650, Parliament banned foreign ships from trading with English colonies. The following year, it mandated that trade between England and its colonies travel in ships owned by Englishmen and that all European goods imported to England had to be carried either by English ships or ships belonging to the country where the products originated. In effect, this law was

Navigation Acts A series of English laws that mandated that trade between England and the colonies traveled in English ships and promoted specific industries through bounties and reduced tariffs.

Map 4.2 Seventeenth-Century Transatlantic Trade Routes During the seventeenth century, the Atlantic became a veritable highway with goods and people moving quickly and regularly between Europe, Africa, South America, the Caribbean, and North America. ▼

designed to cut Dutch merchants out of English commerce because the Dutch produced few if any exports. The Dutch offered the lowest shipping rates for sugar and tobacco, so planters in Barbados and the Chesapeake objected, but they capitulated when the greatly strengthened English navy approached their shores to enforce the law.

In 1651, Parliament passed the **Enumeration Act**, which required that key commodities and goods produced in English colonies—tobacco, sugar, cotton, indigo, dyewoods, and ginger—be exported only to England or an English port, where import duties would be collected. In 1663, the newly passed Staple Act mandated that European commodities destined for the English colonies be shipped through England. The Dutch saw all of these laws as part of a commercial attack on their trading empire, and to reverse these policies, they fought losing wars against England in 1652–1654, 1665–1667, and 1672–1674.

In North America, the lengthy coastline and the relative lack of English civil servants made it easy for smugglers and importers to evade the new trade regulations. Thus, in 1673, Parliament passed the Plantation Duty Act, requiring English ship captains to either post bond that they would deliver commodities to an English port or immediately pay the appropriate duties. To enforce the law, the crown initiated a colonial **customs service** that extended to British North America the corps of inspectors that had long been a presence in English ports. These inspectors boarded ships and searched for enumerated commodities and foreign manufactures. A generation later, the Navigation Act of 1696 further strengthened enforcement. Colonial governors had to swear to enforce trade laws. The crown directly paid the customs inspectors who received new tax-collecting powers. The crown also brought **vice admiralty courts** to the colonies. To the colonists' ire, judges in these courts instead of juries rendered verdicts, a process that impinged on the rights of due process long enjoyed by the English. The Navigation Act of 1696 also incentivized prosecutions by granting whistle-blowers, the governor, and the crown a share of any fines collected. Just as important, that act created the **Board of Trade** in England, which recommended legislation to Parliament and instructed royal governors in the colonies how to protect and expand legitimate trade. England's ability to enforce its new trade regulations as well as its supremacy in the Anglo-Dutch wars ultimately ended Dutch dominance of transatlantic commerce. By the early eighteenth century, England was the most important Atlantic naval power with only France as its main commercial rival.

The legislation regulating trade during this period—although controversial—brought the disparate colonies of British North America into an increasingly coherent and powerful empire. Across much of colonial America, but in particular British North America, the increased access to markets of consumer goods transformed dietary and consumption patterns of all colonists. Although the expansion and globalization of Atlantic commerce was a complicated development after 1650, the tropical items—tobacco; sugar; sugar products such as molasses and rum; and caffeinated drinks, such as chocolate, tea, and coffee—that brought energy and seemed to satisfy the appetite became paramount. By 1700, these seemingly frivolous products had altered the dietary habits of millions of people within reach of the Atlantic. Nearly 75 percent of the goods coming into Amsterdam and 85 percent coming into London from the Americas were tobacco and sugar products.

4-2b New France and Empire Building

Like the English, the French king Louis XIV (reigned from 1643 to 1715) and his chief minister, Jean-Baptiste Colbert, who served from 1665 to 1683, pursued a mercantilist strategy to combat Dutch dominance of the transatlantic trade. The French crown took control of its overseas colonies, passed laws that allowed it to directly profit from them, and tried to increase its share of transatlantic trade. In 1664, Colbert also oversaw the creation of the French East India Company, which controlled commerce between France, Africa, and the East Indies with Canada, and ensured that all trade goods were carried on French ships. Furthermore, to promote domestic industry, Colbert placed high tariffs on imported foreign goods and regulated nearly all domestic industries.

{ New France grows in population and settlements.

In Canada, France set out to rebuild a colony that had been nearly destroyed in the 1640s and 1650s when the Haudenosaunees overran the Wendats (Hurons) and the Jesuit missions. In 1663, the crown took over the management of the colony and increased the number of *seigneuries* granted in the St. Lawrence Valley where 75 percent of the colonial population lived. Hoping to create a feudal order in Canada, France sent thousands of *habitants* to populate the *seigneuries*. Agriculture, however, remained at the subsistence level, and fur was the principal export.

Like most militarized frontier regions, New France had far fewer women than men. And of the men who immigrated, only one in twenty was married. Royal officials scoured orphanages in France, offering women the prospect of a husband, land, and a dowry in New France. In the decade after 1663, eight hundred of these *filles du roi* made the journey at royal expense, and most married quickly. After 1673, female immigration to the colony virtually ceased, but

Enumeration Act 1651 law in which England designated that high-value commodities could be exported only from colonies to England or an English port.

customs service English officials in charge of collecting import and export taxes and duties on goods shipped between the English colonies and England.

vice admiralty courts English military-style courts that oversaw the prosecution of those accused of smuggling.

Board of Trade English governmental committee established in 1696 to oversee the economic development of its colonies.

filles du roi French term, literally *daughters of the king*, referring to some eight hundred women who were transported at royal expense to provide marriage partners for the male settlers of New France.

with the emergence of stable families, the population grew steadily, climbing from three thousand in 1663 to fourteen thousand in 1700. Although there was no elected legislature, crown officials running the colony built schools, hospitals, and churches.

None of this expansion and development would have been possible had the crown not sent one thousand additional soldiers to Canada in 1665. Their commander, Viceroy Alexandre de Prouville, sieur de Tracy, who was fresh from a victory over the Dutch in Guiana, had orders to "exterminate" the Mohawks in revenge for their earlier attacks on French settlements. The ensuing French campaign led to few Mohawks deaths but caused widespread destruction in their communities. Weary of battle, weakened by disease, and deprived of Dutch arms after the English conquest of New Netherland, the Mohawks sued for peace in 1667.

With New France self-sufficient and secure, the French looked beyond Quebec and Montreal, hoping to spread their empire into the interior. French fur traders, known as **coureurs de bois**, ventured into the western Great Lakes region known to the French as the *pays d'en haut*. As in the days of Champlain, these men often took Native American wives, spoke local languages, and generally lived as Indians. French explorers also headed south. In 1673, Louis Joliet and Jacques Marquette traveled down the Mississippi River to its juncture with the Arkansas River. In 1682, René Robert Cavalier, sieur de La Salle, followed the Mississippi River to the Gulf of Mexico, naming the region *Louisiane* in honor of Louis XIV and claiming coastal land with an ideal port that he called *Nouvelle Orléans*. La Salle tried to return to Canada in 1684, but having overshot the Mississippi River, he wandered for three years in Texas looking for the river until he his own men murdered him.

To counter the growing presence of the French in Canada and the interior of the continent, England's Charles II chartered the Hudson's Bay Company in 1670. The company received a monopoly over an immense territory, known as *Rupert's Land*, which encompassed one-third of today's Canada. The company established six coastal forts on Hudson Bay and began diverting valuable trade from the French. In response in 1682, the French established the Compagnie du Nord. Four years later, the governor of the company sent out various expeditions to capture the English forts, and through the 1690s, the English and French battled for control of Hudson Bay and its peltries. Among those who led the French attack on the English forts was Pierre le Moyne d'Iberville, a native of Montreal.

In 1698, Iberville began the French settlement of the lower Mississippi Valley, intending to complete what La Salle had left unfinished. In April 1699, he established Fort Maurepas on the eastern side of what is now Biloxi Bay. It was the first capital of the colony of Louisiana and served as a base for further exploration of the region. But the eighty French men posted there survived only by trading with the neighboring Biloxi Indians for provisions;

disease, boredom, heat, bad water, and the failure of the settlement's crops doomed the settlement. In 1701, with England and France officially at war, the fort was moved some sixty miles east to present-day Mobile, a site that was closer to the settlements of the Spain, a French ally.

4-2c Spain's Decline

In the sixteenth century, Spain had integrated its overseas commerce into an imperial system and ensured that much of the wealth from American mines and plantations flowed back to Spain and, in turn, supported colonial expansion. But in the seventeenth century, just as the Netherlands, England, and France pursued their own mercantilist agendas, Spain's system began to collapse. By 1700, it was in tatters.

> Spanish transatlantic trade declines and its frontier settlements stagnate.

The decline in Spain's revenue from transatlantic trade was a consequence of the growth of smuggling, a drop in silver production, the challenges posed by imperial rivals, and New Spain's production of items previously imported from abroad. From 1606 to 1650, the value of official trade between Spain and New Spain fell 60 percent, and from 1650 to 1699, the value of New Spain's exports dropped 75 percent. Furthermore, Spain spent more money each year on the defense of its overseas colonies, which constantly needed new fortresses, arms, garrisons, ships, and *situados* to defend against the growing Dutch and English ambitions. At the same time, foreign merchants began to use Spaniards as front men to win official Spanish trading contracts to the extent that by the turn of the eighteenth century, only 10 percent of the goods shipped to the Spanish Indies actually originated in Spain. Notably, while Spain's transatlantic system frayed, the Spanish colonies themselves moved toward self-sufficiency and an integrated economic system in which each region specialized in particular commodities.

Spain's desire to protect remote areas of New Spain from foreign encroachment had led it into new territories that had little economic value. To a large degree, these lands, north, west, and east of the silver mines of northern New Spain, remained isolated, undeveloped, poorly provisioned, and expensive to maintain. For example, on behalf of Spain, Jesuits and Franciscans explored Sonora, Baja California, and Texas, establishing isolated missions that attracted only small numbers of Indians. Florida, also a defensive periphery, probably never had more than seven hundred and fifty soldiers and settlers and rarely grabbed royal attention. That changed in 1668, when the English corsair *Robert Searles* sacked St. Augustine, ransomed its women, and sailed off with many captives. Spanish alarm increased with the English establishment of Charles Town in Carolina, which prompted

coureurs de bois French term, literally, *runners of the woods*, referring to male French fur traders in New France who traveled to the interior, often in the company of Indians.

History without Borders

The Spread of the Horse

Wild horse herds developed in Utah, Arizona, Oregon, Montana, and Wyoming.

Sioux and other Plains Indians used horses in their buffalo hunts by the 1770s.

1730

1770

1730

1770

1775

1700

SIOUX

NORTH AMERICA

Pueblo Revolt 1680

1719

1608

1690

1650

APACHE

1567

1565

Gulf of Mexico

from France *1665*

from Netherlands

from England *1629*

1660

1620

from England

ATLANTIC OCEAN

from Spain

Apaches raided Santa Fé and other Spanish outposts for horses, beginning in the early 1600s.

1519

1511

1493

from Netherlands

1526

Caribbean Sea

1514 *1509*

Europeans reintroduced horses to the Americas with Columbus's second voyage, 1493.

1538

The spread of the horse

→ 1400s
→ 1500s
→ 1600s
→ 1700s

Territorial claims, ca. 1700

British
French
Portuguese
Spanish

SOUTH AMERICA

1655

1630

1629

1532

PACIFIC OCEAN

from Spain and Portugal

1536

1531

1542

1626

1541

1584

The Spread of the Horse, North America, after 1500 Among the most important European imports to the Americas was the horse, which spread gradually throughout the Americas transforming Native peoples and their environments and cultures. ▲

Ancient Horse Skeleton from the La Brea Tar Pits The first horses—small animals the size of a dog—inhabited the forests of North America 55 million years ago. Some of these horses evolved into large animals. Ten thousand years ago, at the end of the Ice Age, just as humans were beginning to settle the Americas, ancient horses died out as their habitat dwindled. But they continued to live in the grasslands of eastern Europe and central Asia where humans domesticated them. ▲

Petroglyph Showing Indians Hunting from Horseback, Utah These images from Newspaper Rock show Indians of the Southwest mounted on horseback hunting. The figure in the foreground is depicted shooting an elk. They date from the historic period after Europeans reintroduced horses to North America. ▲

When Europeans came to the Americas, they brought not only calamities but also opportunities. Trade goods temporarily improved the lives of some Indians, and some European items—such as metal tools and woolen blankets—had advantages over bone tools and animal hides. But of all the things that Europeans brought with them to the Americas, probably none was more beneficial to Indians than the horse. To the people of eastern Europe and central Asia, horses offered advantages in trade, hunting, and especially warfare. From the chariots of Ancient Rome to the armored knights of the Middle Ages, horses had figured prominently in European warfare. Among the most successful adopters of horse culture were the Spanish who knit together the cultures of chivalry and warfare, both of which found their basis in the horse. After the expulsion of the Moors from Iberia, Spaniards brought horses with them as they sought to conquer the Americas.

American Indians hoped to take advantage of all that this animal had to offer, but it would be centuries before they could. Spaniards knew that in the horse they had a decisive military weapon, and they did their best to keep horses out of the hands of Indians.

In North America, Indians gained access to large herds of horses only after the Pueblo Revolt of 1680. Once they did, horses proved transformative, allowing Indians to hunt with greater speed and efficiency and move from place to place more rapidly than previously imagined.

By 1700, the tribes of the Great Basin had horses, and thirty years later, those of the northern Rocky Mountains and the southern Great Plains had them. And in every place, horses led to a modification of Native American culture. Only a century after the Pueblo Revolt, horse culture had spread across the western half of the continent from the Columbia River basin to the Great Plains. In these regions, through the horse, Indian peoples were finally able to harness all the energy stored in the grasslands, for by riding horses that fed on grass, they took advantage of the horses' ability to turn grass into energy, something that humans cannot do.

Critical Thinking Questions

▶ How did the domestication of the horse lead to changes in human culture?

▶ If horses changed humans, how have humans changed horses?

Go to MindTap® to engage with an interactive version of **History without Borders: The Spread of the Horse**. Learn from an interactive map, view related video, and respond to critical thinking questions.

Stan Honda/AFP/Getty Images

Global Americans Among the most important and influential ideas that some Europeans brought with them to the Americas were various forms of Christianity. In the dislocations of war and the wake of epidemics, missionaries often found some Native American people who seemed to hear their messages and answer their pleas to convert. Emblematic of these converts is **Kateri Tekakwitha**, a woman who was born in 1656 to an Algonquin woman who had been taken captive and then married to a Mohawk man. Smallpox epidemics of the early 1660s left her an orphan with a scarred face and damaged eyes. Her disability and her refusal to marry rendered her an outcast in her own community. In 1676, she accepted baptism and the following year she fled her community for Kahnawake, a mission village that had been recently established by Jesuits near Montreal. There she preached a cult of virginity and practiced self-flagellation until she died in 1680. In the centuries since her death, she has reportedly worked miracles. She was canonized in 2012, making her the first Native American saint.

Spain to build a stone fortification in St. Augustine, the Castillo of San Marcos, at great expense. The fort kept pirates at bay, and the colony itself proved an irritant to the English over the next century as it attracted servants and slaves from Carolina with offers of freedom.

Of the Spanish colonies in North America, isolated New Mexico developed the most elaborate local economy. Although often threatened by raiding, disease, and the governors' greed, the Spanish of New Mexico profitably traded iron goods and firearms to Indians of the Plains, who had long exchanged buffalo robes for cotton goods and corn produced by the Pueblos. The most lucrative trade on the Great Plains involved captives in wars between tribes, whom Indians often sold as slaves to the Spanish of New Mexico, who put them to work as farm hands or domestic servants. The economy of New Mexico, while at times vibrant, nevertheless remained disconnected from larger systems of intercolonial or international trade.

4-2d Imperial Realignment and Indians in the Northeast

The English and French imperial reorganizations of the mid-seventeenth century changed the colonies as well as the lives of Native Americans in and around them. The Haudenosaunees endured the most drastic change, losing power and prestige in the 1660s. Since the 1650s, the Susquehannocks and the English in Maryland had tried to prevent the Haudenosaunees from monopolizing trade in the upper Chesapeake. Meanwhile, Algonquian-speaking New England Indians pushed the Mohawks out of the territory between the Hudson River and Boston. Diseases, most likely spread through contact with Europeans, added to the Haudenosaunees' woes, killing about one thousand. In 1664, when the English conquered New Netherland, the Haudenosaunees suddenly found themselves depending on an unfamiliar European nation for trade and in their struggles against the French. The one thousand French soldiers sent to Canada in 1665 largely spelled the end of the Haudenosaunees' way of life.

> French and English colonial expansion and imperial reorganization create turmoil for Indians.

When the Mohawks sued for peace in 1667, they accepted Jesuit missionaries into their villages, much as the Wendats had. The Haudenosaunees became divided between Catholics and traditionalists. Nearly four thousand Haudenosaunees left traditional Mohawk villages for French Native American Catholic settlements such as Kahnawake near Montreal. In 1676, the Jesuits baptized a woman

Castillo de San Marcos, St. Augustine, Florida To protect St. Augustine, Indians and master workmen toiled on the fort from 1671 to 1695, costing the crown 138,375 pesos in wages and rations, an enormous investment in a colony that never produced a valuable export. ▼

Ron Chapple Stock/PhotoLibrary

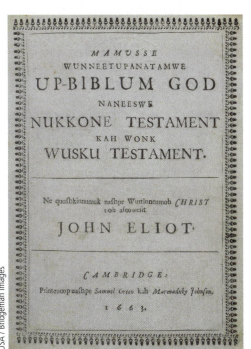

'Mamusse Wunneetupanatamwe up-Biblum God' ('The-Whole Holy his-Bible God'), title page from 'The Bible', also known as the 'Eliot Indian Bible', translated into the Massachusett language by the Reverend John Eliot (1604–90), published by Samuel Green and Marmaduke Johnson, 1663 (engraving), American School, (17th century)/Massachusetts Historical Society, Boston, MA, USA / Bridgeman Images

Eliot Bible, 1663 In 1646, the Massachusetts colony banned Native American religious practices and authorized John Eliot, a Puritan minister, to "civilize" and Christianize the Massachusetts. Funded and encouraged by people in England, Eliot began working with Indians to translate the Bible into the Massachusetts' language. In 1663, he began to print and circulate the "Eliot Bible" with an initial run of one thousand copies. ▲

from one of these settlements. Kateri (Catherina) Tekakwitha's devotion to Catholicism won her the admiration of Jesuit missionaries.

In 1678, the weakened Haudenosaunees entered into the first of several agreements with the English that established what became known as the **Covenant Chain**.

In Massachusetts, Indians surrounded by English settlers and facing increasing encroachment on their lands also found temporary haven in Christian enclaves. By 1674, some 2,300 Indians resided in at least fourteen **Praying Towns**, under the Protestant missionary John Eliot. In these separate Indian Christian communities in New England, Indians lived like the English yet apart from them, electing their own magistrates, speaking English, and praying regularly. The English continued to regard these communities with suspicion and disdain and never fully accepted their presence in New England.

In the Southeast, an infusion of English trade goods brought turmoil to Indians. In return for rum and firearms, Indians traded deerskins that were valued by the English to produce belts, gloves, and hats. More important was the swift expansion of an Indian slave trade promoted by the English. Rival Indian groups, in particular those in the **Creek Confederacy**, seized captives for sale to the English. This trade became the most profitable in Carolina in the final decades of the seventeenth century. The English put some Indian slaves to work on plantations but, because Native Americans often fled to their homelands, sent most to New York, Boston, or the West Indies. As many as fifty thousand Indian slaves—more than the number of Africans brought to the mainland colonies in the same period—were sold in Charles Town between 1670 and 1715. At the same time as this trade flourished, the growth of English settlements in Carolina put pressure on Indian landholdings, setting the stage for conflict in the following decades.

Covenant Chain Seventeenth-century treaties between the Haudenosaunee and the English that promoted peace and the Haudenosaunee claims to supremacy over other Indian groups.

Praying Towns A series of English mission towns established under the Protestant missionary John Eliot in Massachusetts in the mid-seventeenth century.

Creek Confederacy Confederacy of Southeastern Woodlands Indians.

4-3

Transatlantic Slave Trade and Slavery

This engraving, created from sketches made in the late seventeenth century, depicts canoes ferrying enslaved Africans from shore to larger vessels. This was just one small part in the slaves' long journey from freedom to enslavement in the Americas.

How does this image depict a crucial moment in the transatlantic slave trade? ▶

Go to MindTap® to practice history with the Chapter 4 **Primary Source Writing Activity: The Slave Trade.** Read and view primary sources and respond to a writing prompt.

Rare Books Division, NYPL.

Royal African Company (RAC)
English royal trading company that held a monopoly in the English slave trade from 1660 through 1689.

In the second half of the seventeenth century, the slave trade expanded and moved to the center of the transatlantic economy driven by growth in the production of sugar in the Americas. For slave traders, profits ranged from 3 percent to 30 percent per ship, and by the 1680s, half of all imports and exports to and from Africa were related to the trade. For the enslaved, the horrors began when they were taken captive in Africa, continued through a harrowing transoceanic voyage, and continued with their sale in the Caribbean or North America. The slave trade produced human suffering of unparalleled proportions as millions of Africans were taken from their homelands and scattered across the Americas. The majority of slaves were consigned to Caribbean or Brazilian sugar plantations where they endured miserable conditions until they died of disease and overwork.

☞ As you read, look for key moments in the process through which Africans were enslaved. In what different ways were slaves put to work in the Americas?

4-3a Slave Origins, Ages, and Sex

The transatlantic slave trade spanned half the globe and was well documented. European countries taxed the traders, merchants insured their ships and human cargo, and ports and customs officials recorded the comings and goings of ships brimming with slaves. The trade increased over time because slave traders became more efficient, slave ships became larger, and the sugar colonies' demand for slaves was unceasing. The trade began in earnest as early as 1500 and was not abolished until 1867. During that period, at least 12.5 million men, women, and children were taken from Africa on at least forty thousand

{ The flow of slaves from Africa is enormous and shaped by European and African priorities.

ship voyages. About 10.7 million survived the ocean crossing to the New World. More than any other factor, the sugar boom shaped the transatlantic slave trade in the seventeenth century. All told, 90 percent of all slaves carried to the Americas were destined to labor in the production of sugar. The trade grew steadily over the centuries and increased dramatically between 1600 and 1700, more than doubling over the second half of the seventeenth century, rising from 155,687 slaves shipped in the 1650s to 339,557 in the 1690s (see Figures 4.1 and 4.2). Despite the enormity of these numbers, not until 1700 did the value of slaves from Africa surpass the value of the metals, spices, and other goods Europeans took from the African continent.

At mid-century, the Portuguese dominated the slave trade. They carried slaves to the sugar-producing colonies of the Spanish Caribbean and Portuguese Brazil. In 1660, however, King Charles II of England chartered the Company of Royal Adventurers in Africa as part of his broader strategy of challenging Dutch trade. In 1663, the company was reorganized as the **Royal African Company (RAC)**, with Charles's son James as its governor. The company held a monopoly over the English slave trade from the purchase of slaves in Africa to their sale in the New World. With the creation of the RAC, the English participation in the slave trade grew dramatically. In 1664, England for the first time shipped more slaves to the Americas than Portugal did. By the 1690s, the English were responsible for 34 percent, or 116,495 slaves, taken from Africa, up from their share of 6 percent before the RAC.

All told, the British carried about 2.5 million West Africans to the English colonies in North America and the Caribbean before 1800. They delivered 2.2 million to the Caribbean, including 925,000 to Jamaica and another 450,000 to Barbados. By comparison, about 310,000 slaves had disembarked on mainland North America before 1800 (see Map 4.3). Half of the slaves (primarily men) shipped to the British Caribbean died within three years of arrival, and the majority of survivors never had children, meaning that English sugar colonies never developed

Figure 4.1 Number of Slaves Disembarking in the Americas by Region, 1651 to 1750 In the century between 1651 and 1750, some 3,131,146 slaves arrived in the Americas, with the brutal and lethal sugar colonies continuing to be the final destination of most. The overwhelming majority disembarked in Brazil (1,362,560), the British Caribbean (921,278), and the French Caribbean (332,612). Of the 3,131,146, some 161,021 slaves disembarked in mainland North America, and nearly all arrived between 1700 and 1750, a period when plantation owners had greater access to African slaves. ▶

Source: Voyages: The Trans-Atlantic Slave Trade Database. www.slavevoyages.org.

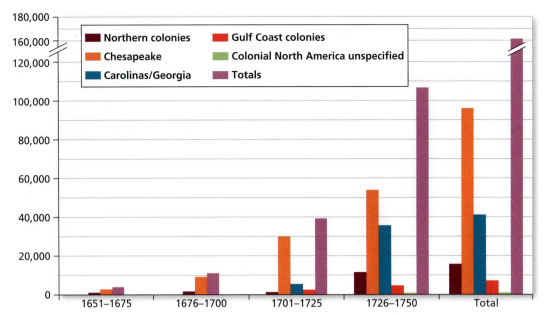

Figure 4.2 Number of Slaves Disembarking on Mainland by Region, 1651 to 1750 Some 161,021 African slaves disembarked in the North American mainland colonies between 1651 and 1750. Of these, nearly all (145,324) arrived after 1700, with 95,978 going to the Chesapeake and 41,143 to Georgia. ◀ Source: Voyages: The Trans-Atlantic Slave Trade Database. www.slavevoyages.org.

Map 4.3 African Origins and American Destinations of Enslaved Africans Europeans Brought to the Americas, Sixteenth to Eighteenth Centuries European slave ships carried millions of enslaved Africans across the Atlantic during the Early Modern period. The overwhelming majority were taken to the sugar plantations of the Caribbean and Brazil, where most died within a few years of their arrival. ▲

sustainable slave populations and thus constantly imported more slaves. In contrast, in the mainland colonies, the number of slaves increased rapidly as many took mates and produced children born into slavery. In 1800 in what had become the United States, there were 900,000 slaves while at the same time—despite the arrival of nearly nine times as many slaves—there were only 800,000 in the British Caribbean.

Overall, the majority of slaves were taken from west central Africa, a region that today includes part of Gabon, Congo, Zaire, and Angola. But between 1676 and 1725, the majority came from the **Slave Coast**, a coastline today in eastern Ghana, Togo, Benin, and western Nigeria. This shift had more to do with the rise and fall of African peoples and empires than the preferences of European slave traders. African cultures, systems, and conceptions of gender and work determined the age and sex of the exported slaves in each region. For instance, in some parts of Africa, women could be sold for more in domestic African slave markets, whereas men commanded higher prices in slave sales across the Atlantic.

The slave trade proved disastrous for Africa as a whole. Millions of Africans died even before they could be sent to the Americas, and millions more were displaced. As slavery in Africa became a major industry after the arrival of European traders, African leaders involved in the trade became increasingly violent, oppressive, and militarized. The slave trade reduced the population of Africa and in some areas vastly reduced the number of men, leading to an increase in polygamy and other cultural transformations. Before the onset of the slave trade, Africa's share of the overall Atlantic trade was small, yet it further declined once the slave trade began. The slave trade robbed the continent of laborers and provoked enduring and devastating conflict and poverty.

Slave Coffle, from a Slave Merchant's Journal, 1793–1794 Like other African commodities that Europeans prized, slaves were sold from one group of African traders to another as the slaves were driven from the interior in small groups bound to each other. Often they were kept in pens and fed minimally, and as a result, one in four slaves died on the journey from the interior to the coast. Some resisted but with little chance of gaining freedom. ▲

National Maritime Museum, Greenwich, London

4-3b African Captivity

Most slaves brought to the Americas were first captured by African slave hunters and bandits or sold into slavery by their countrymen or their families. Few slaves left a record of their captivity. One recounted how "a people came from a far and unknown country . . . and burnt all their towns." Another, Peter Kondo, stated that he was "kidnapped in the Basare country, where he had gone to buy corn." A man named Fije explained that he "was sold by his uncle because he had not presented him with a female slave and cows on his father's death." And another named Asa recounted that he had killed a man, "on which account he was sold [into slavery] by the king."

> For millions, the horrors of slavery begin in Africa with kidnapping and forced marches.

Slaves who survived the forced march to the coast faced a dire situation, for they were then confined in one of the numerous large-scale prisons built by European traders, often in swampy, disease-ridden areas. For weeks or months, slaves languished in dark, stale dungeons. Untold numbers died. Corpses were unceremoniously dumped in the swamplands in such numbers that human landfills formed. Only those few slaves who had connections to the local rulers could potentially be set free. When European slave traders arrived, African and European merchants transferred the slaves by canoes or small boats to the traders' ships.

This short trip from shore to ship afforded slaves one last chance to escape, but most failed. Their final moments in Africa were terrifying. An elderly enslaved woman, doomed to a life of servitude in the Caribbean and known today only as 'Sibell, described her terror after she had been taken to the coast and sold into slavery, "me nebber see de great ships pon de water before, me nebber hear de Waves before which me frighten so much-ee dat me thought me would die."

4-3c The Middle Passage

The transatlantic crossing that 'Sibell and 12.5 million of others were forced to embark on is known today as the **Middle Passage**. The term is Eurocentric in that it describes the middle leg of the European slave trader's journey that began with a passage from Europe to Africa with trade goods, continued with a "middle" passage from Africa to America with slaves, and

> The Middle Passage kills many and destroys aspects of the culture of survivors.

Slave Coast Coastline of West Africa from which millions of Africans were enslaved and transported across the Atlantic.

Middle Passage Transatlantic voyage between Africa and America.

National Museum of American History/Kenneth E. Behring Center/Smithsonian Institution

Restraining Irons, Eighteenth Century Slaves at every point in their descent into bondage in the Americas were bound and restrained, often with impregnable irons. ▲

concluded with a final passage from America to Europe with goods purchased in the colonies. In the seventeenth century, roughly 20 percent of slaves died on the Middle Passage, though the figure fell steadily to 10 percent by the late eighteenth century as traders paid more attention to the health and cleanliness of their human cargo. Slaves already weak from famine and disease were the most likely to die on ship, and they often did so soon after embarkation. During the voyage, dysentery, fever, measles, smallpox, and scurvy often spread, causing further deaths. Slaves were often deprived of food and water, only worsening their condition. Women suffered slightly lower mortality than average, and children had the highest mortality.

Hygiene onboard was primitive but understood as important for the survival of the cargo. Some shipmasters would smoke the ship with tobacco or wash the decks with vinegar to prevent the spread of illness. Fresh air was probably the most important factor in health, and in good weather, slaves were allowed on deck. They were usually fed twice a day. Like animals, they were placed in front of a trough of rice and beans ten at a time and given spoons to feed themselves.

In the hold, men were bound together in pairs, left leg to right leg, left wrist to right wrist. Some masters removed the chains once the ship was at sea, others removed them during the day, and some did not remove them at all until the destination had been reached. Women were rarely shackled and often held above deck, only to suffer sexual abuse at the hands of their captors. Captives were naked, without possessions, and at the mercy of men who held guns, knives, whips, and branding irons. So grim were the conditions that some slaves concluded that they had in fact died and entered an underworld.

On ships crowded with traumatized strangers, many elements of African society began to dissolve. Family, kin, lineage, social status, even names now held little or no meaning in a new society composed of people unmoored from the village and family communities that had reared them. Sometimes, however, slaves did find familiar faces or fellow countrymen or form new bonds on the ship as 'Sibell recounted, when "me go in de ship me find my country woman Mimbo, my country man Dublin, my Country woman Sally."

Enough social bonds survived the journey into slavery or were formed on ships that slaves, working together, rebelled against their captivity and the conditions of their confinement. Rebellions took place on 10 percent of all slave ships, and on average about 10 percent of rebelling slaves would be killed in each instance. In total, about 100,000 rebel slaves died on the Middle Passage. Although most rebellions never gained the slaves' freedom, they did have a significant effect on the slave trade as shipmasters, fearing insurrection, spent an additional 20 percent of their budgets on security, a sum that if used to purchase and transport more slaves would have led to the enslavement of an additional one million Africans.

Once on land, survivors of the Middle Passage were again inspected, prodded, and then sold, often in small numbers so as to erase any sort of community that might have survived the voyage or been forged in the ships' holds. Perhaps as many as 300,000 slaves who had survived the Middle Passage were shipped to other parts of the Americas. In a grim reminder of their captivity in Africa, newly arrived slaves in North America were frequently marched in chains for days or weeks from coastal ports to

The Art Archive/Alamy Stock Photo

***Slaves Below Deck*, Francis Meynell, 1846** Millions endured the horrors of the transatlantic passage but few recorded it for posterity. This rare image shows the misery and monotony of slaves held below deck. ▲

plantations, where they were again subjected to physical violence intended to render their servitude both hopeless and permanent. The lash, the stocks, dismemberment, and even death awaited those who resisted. For many, this was the final step in a tragic African diaspora as well as the beginning of another horrific ordeal, one whose legacies continue in both Africa and the Americas to this day.

4-3d Slavery in the Northern and Chesapeake Colonies

In 1700, some 5,700 people of African descent lived in the Northern and Middle Colonies. In the agricultural areas of Pennsylvania and

{ Slaves work in a variety of capacities, but most toil in agricultural pursuits.

New Jersey, the Hudson Valley, Long Island, southern Massachusetts, Connecticut, and Rhode Island, most male slaves worked as jacks-of-all-trades on farms that raised livestock and crops destined for the West Indies. A smaller number worked in tanneries, mines, forges, and foundries. At the same time, wealthy whites in the North began buying female slaves to work in their kitchens instead of continuing to rely on white servants who were more expensive. Slaves in the North lived in whatever extra space existed in their masters' homes or estates, such as closets, backrooms, cellars, or shacks. Some raised gardens to supplement their diets and used their free time to work for other whites who would pay them for their labor. Significant numbers of slaves worked in towns and ports as either common laborers or skilled craftsmen.

The Chesapeake had by far the largest number of people of African descent with some 19,600 in 1700 and had the most laws regulating slavery. It was in the Chesapeake that elite planters became the first colonial Britons on the mainland to enshrine slavery in law. In 1655, Elizabeth Key, a mulatto woman born to a slave mother and a free white man, successfully claimed her freedom on the basis of her father's status. The county court had made the decision based on English common law, which held that "the Child of a Woman slave begott by a freeman ought to be free." But the decision was superseded in 1662 when the Virginia legislature, which was controlled by the wealthiest slave-holding planters, mandated that all children born in Virginia "shall be held bond or free only according to the condition of the mother," thereby creating a system in which slavery became self-reproducing. Under this law and a similar one adopted by Maryland the following year (see Table 4.3), the children of slaves across the Chesapeake were considered property of their parents' owner, and the paternity of the child born to a slave woman was irrelevant. This law not only relieved planters of any responsibility for children born to slave women they raped but also was a reversal of English law in which children followed the status of their father.

A 1667 Virginia law declared that the baptism of a slave did not confer freedom, thereby closing another avenue slaves had often turned to that supported the claim that their children should be free. Previously, European Christians had typically refrained from enslaving other Christians, but in Virginia, Christians then could and did enslave black Christians. In 1669, planters in the colony granted themselves nearly complete control over the management of their slaves, declaring that it was not a felony if a slave died while being "corrected" by an owner. Finally, in 1672, the colony committed itself to policing slaves and compensating owners from the public treasury if a fugitive slave was killed while being recaptured. Slaves in Virginia were whipped for minor offenses and had little freedom of movement. Furthermore, to guard against slave conspiracies, not more than four slaves were allowed to meet, and any meeting of four or fewer was allowed for only a short period of time.

Because most slaves in the Chesapeake lived on small plantations and travel among plantations was restricted, it was difficult if not impossible for them to create a settled community or social life. Because planters imported more males than females, men had little opportunity to find wives, fathered

Overseer and Slaves, 1798 Everywhere male and female slaves who resisted slavery were beaten. This watercolor by Benjamin J. Latrobe depicts an overseer armed with a whip watching over enslaved women as they work. ▲

The Granger Collection, New York

Global Americans When captured in his native Angola, Antonio had no idea that he would become a prosperous slaveholder. After being sold to Arab slave traders, "Antonio a Negro" was sold to a Virginia Company representative in 1621 as a "servant" but actually was a slave. For a dozen years, Antonio worked alongside white indentured servants on Richard Bennett's tobacco plantation. There, he married "Mary a Negro woman." She and Antonio eventually farmed independently, and they had their children baptized, all actions of a couple assimilating into English society. Eventually, Antonio and Mary gained their freedom by purchasing it with funds they had saved while working for Bennett. Antonio changed his name to **Anthony Johnson** and ultimately purchased 250 acres and used black and white indentured servants on his own plantation. Anthony and Mary were part of a very small group of blacks in the Chesapeake in the mid-seventeenth century who had arrived in a period when race and slavery had not yet rigidified in the North American colonies. Africans could amass assets within a generation or two of their immigration and even purchase their own freedom. Between 1650 and 1700, however, such opportunities were numbered as planters pursued profitable and inhumane methods of extracting wealth from their imported laborers, as laws began to draw firm distinctions between African slaves and European servants in society, and as vast new systems of trade, commerce, and exploitation became central to not only the emerging colonies but also the Atlantic world that they shaped.

Like many others in the early modern period, Anthony Johnson could not sign his own name; thus in a 1666 legal proceeding, he left his own distinctive mark.

Table 4.3 Major Virginia Laws Related to Slavery

Year	Law
1662	Slavery inherited from mother regardless of status of father
1667	Christian baptism no longer alters status as a slave
1669	Planters who kill a slave while punishing him or her no longer guilty of a felony
1672	Colony commits to compensating owners from slaves killed while being recaptured

few children, and could not carry on their family's lineages, which were of paramount importance in Africa. Furthermore, because pregnant slave women were allowed no additional rest, they often suffered miscarriages. Planters could sustain this brutal order only with force. Maiming and beatings, sanctioned by law, became routine in the second half of the seventeenth century, as the Chesapeake transitioned from a society with slaves to a slave society.

Paradoxically, masters believed their slaves were part of their households and families. The planters were proponents and defenders of a **patriarchal** family structure in which wives, children, servants, and slaves all lived under the authority of the father. A good father provided protection and sustenance for his dependents while maintaining strict control of his household. For example, one Virginia planter told his slave that "If you will be good I shall be yr Loving Master," and at the same time threatened to have him "Slasht Severly, and pickled" if he was disobedient. In the late eighteenth century, masters began to imagine themselves as enlightened paternalists and created the fiction of the happy slave.

Because slaves were cheaper in the long run than indentured servants, planters moved away from servants and bought slaves in greater and greater numbers throughout the second half of the seventeenth century. This shift had a number of effects on slaves. First, it eroded the already minimal standards of decency and respect that they had been accorded when working alongside white servants. In the absence of white laborers, slaves were forced to work even longer hours, under tighter supervision, and with greater regimentation. They received less food, worse shelter, and poorer medical attention than white servants. Many slaves were forced to work on Sunday, and holidays were limited to Christmas, Easter, and Pentecost. As they assumed near total control over their slaves, Chesapeake planters also denied slaves the right to any sort of independent economy.

Slaves resisted this new regime. Some plotted, albeit with little success, against planters, and others feigned ignorance and incompetence. Some ran away, usually only to be recaptured. At the same time, opportunities for the dwindling number of free blacks in the Chesapeake dried up. They were denied the rights to employ white servants, to hold office, to bear arms, to participate in the militia, and to vote. And as blackness became synonymous with slavery, many free blacks were kidnapped and sold into slavery.

4-3e Slavery in the Lowcountry

In 1700, the coastal region of Carolina known as the Lowcountry or Lower South counted only about 3,400 African slaves. Slaves in the Lowcountry grew rice and indigo under the **task system**. After slaves completed a set amount of work each day or week, time was their own. Lowcountry planters offered their slaves little food, clothing, or medical attention. Although many African slaves had a sickle-cell trait that gave them some immunity against malaria, the living and working conditions in Carolina still proved fatal to many. Thus, the region's slave population increased only as planters imported them.

The task system and the persistence of African culture characterize slavery in the Lowcountry.

patriarchal Manifestation or institutionalization of male dominance over women and children in the family and in society in general.

task system Form of labor organization in which slaves were given an assignment to complete in a specific amount of time.

Slaves in this region lived together in unhealthy quarters. Yet these lodgings became the centers of their nonworking lives as well as outposts of African life and culture. Slaves built their quarters themselves, often using African construction techniques. Sitting in the shadow of the planter's mansion, these villages allowed slaves a modicum of permanence and stability. Within their villages, slaves asserted their rights to rest on Sunday and to own small plots of land where they cultivated vegetables, fowl, and rice. They spoke African languages, practiced African customs, celebrated African holidays, and kept their African names. Fewer slaves in the Lower South converted to Christianity than in the Chesapeake and the North.

As in the Chesapeake, planters used new laws and violence to support their rule. By 1690, planters in South Carolina were legally blameless if a slave died while being "corrected," even if the death was caused by a planter's "willfulness, wantonness, or bloody mindedness." As in regions to the north, slaves in the Lower South began to resist, in ways small and large, the brutal regime they found themselves living under.

4-4
Colonies in Crisis

There are no images of King Philip, Wampanoag leader, that date to the period in which he lived. In this image published in 1722, *Depiction of Metacomet, also known as King Philip of Wampanoag* by Paul Revere, note how Philip is dressed and the artifacts that are associated with him.

How is King Philip portrayed? What do his clothing and accoutrements of leadership say about him? ▶

PHILIP. KING of Mount Hope.

Yale University Art Gallery

By the late seventeenth century, after decades of settlement and the integration of colonies into expanding imperial frameworks, it was evident that the European colonies in North America would endure. But, at the same time, most faced grave challenges. New Mexico weathered one of the most destructive and successful Indian counteroffensives in the history of the North American colonies. New England did as well, and was also unsettled again by political upheaval whose origins lay across the Atlantic. Virginia, meanwhile, confronted a servant rebellion that escalated into civil war. None of these crises proved fatal, but all permanently changed the colonies in which they occurred.

☞ As you read, focus on the nature of conflict and crises in specific regions. Is there a common source of the various rebellions that shook colonial America in the late seventeenth century?

4-4a The Pueblo Revolts

After a steady accumulation of grievances, Pueblo Indians in 1680 rose against a colonial order that threatened their existence. In the previous decades, the number of Indians had declined as the result of disease, and the Spanish had raised tribute levels, compounding Indian hardship. Spanish demands disrupted the Pueblos' relations with their neighbors because the agricultural surplus that the Pueblos had long traded

{ Indians across New Mexico rebel, expel the Spaniards, and force a lessening in the terms of Spanish rule.

with the Apache on the Great Plains began instead to go to the Spanish. Viewing their own survival as imperiled, the Apache launched violent raids on Pueblo communities to take by force what they could no longer acquire through trade. The onset of drought and famine in the 1660s only led to additional violence. In 1673, Apache raiders torched the community of Hawikuh, killing 200 people and taking a thousand captive. Amid the crisis, many Pueblos who had practiced Catholicism at Spanish insistence returned to their Native religion. In 1675, New Mexico's governor responded by trying to stamp out what remained of Pueblo spirituality, taking particular aim at traditional dances. The governor had three Pueblo religious leaders hanged for sorcery and sedition and another forty-three beaten for practicing their religion.

The confrontation exploded in August 1680 with the **Pueblo Revolt**, a carefully planned rebellion by more than two dozen Indian communities. The rebellion was led by Po'pay, a religious leader from San Juan Pueblo who was one of the forty-three Indians beaten by the Spaniards. Within days, the rebels had killed a fifth of the province's 2,500 settlers, most of whom were caught off guard. Spanish survivors first took refuge in the capital of Santa Fé where they fought off an Indian siege. Eventually, the Spanish governor Antonio de Otermín led 1,500 refugees, many of whom were Indian servants, three hundred miles south to El Paso del Norte where they lived for the next twelve years.

Po'pay had his followers target all evidence of Catholicism. The rebels killed twenty-one of thirty-three missionaries in the province and destroyed most of the mission churches. A Pueblo man captured by the Spanish reported that Po'pay ordered his men to "break up and burn the images of the holy Christ, the Virgin Mary and the other saints, the crosses, and everything pertaining to Christianity." The rebels also called for male Indians to disavow the marriages that Franciscans had performed among them and to "separate from the wives" they had been forced to wed. To cleanse them of Christianity, Po'pay made all baptized Indians plunge themselves into the closest river in an attempt to have them wash away the baptism.

Po'pay's revolt succeeded because he had been able to unify many disparate groups that all shared common grievances against Spanish rule. But once the Spaniards had been driven out, the Pueblo coalition fractured. In 1692, a new Spanish governor, Diego de Vargas, led eight hundred Spaniards back into New Mexico and began exploiting divisions among the Pueblo. He quickly re-established Spanish rule, which included the economic exploitation of Indians and the prominence of Catholicism. Another Pueblo rebellion in 1696 left five Franciscans dead. In response, the Franciscans began to tolerate some aspects of Native religion and the colony's tribute system was abolished. But by that time, decades of drought and famine had reduced the Pueblo Indians' numbers to about fourteen thousand. These survivors no longer posed a serious threat to the Spaniards, and as a result, New Mexico entered a period of peace and unchallenged Spanish rule.

4-4b King Philip's War

The Puritan society that had emerged from the Great Migration of the 1630s was exclusionary, ruled largely by zealous church founders and laymen who did not fully admit settlers deemed spiritually lacking into their society. The children of the first generation of Puritan immigrants inherited property, church membership, and

> The Puritans' religious inflexibility and continued encroachment on Indian lands prompts crises in church membership and a new Indian war.

political power from their parents. But their children, like the mid-century immigrants to the colony, did not gain church membership and the political and economic opportunities that went with it unless they could demonstrate through a conversion experience that they indeed had saving faith. To arrest the decline in church membership, church leaders instituted the **Half-Way Covenant** (1662) under which the children and grandchildren of church members received partial church membership even if they had not had a conversion experience. Though they were granted membership, they were denied communion and a vote in church affairs. Still, church membership continued to decline. Frustrated and concerned ministers across New England subjected their congregants to angry sermons, known as **jeremiads**, in which they condemned their congregants for straying from the fundamentalism of the first generation of colonists.

If Puritan New England suffered internal turmoil because settlers found to be spiritually lacking were denied full participatory rights, it suffered nearly total ruin because most New England settlers refused to grant Indians any place at all in their world. Whereas colonists in New Mexico had attempted to exploit and convert the Pueblos, who vastly outnumbered them, New Englanders in the late 1670s sought to do away with the Native Americans in their midst whom they increasingly outnumbered. In the nearly forty years after the Pequot War, settlers and Indians had confronted one another numerous times. But the conflict that the English called **King Philip's War** (1675–1678) represented a new level of violence and hatred.

The spark for the war was the death of John Sassamon and the prosecution of three Indians for his murder. Sassamon was a longtime aide of the Wampanoag leader Metacom, or Philip, son of Massasoit, and had worked with the Puritan minister John Elliot to translate the Bible. Before his death, Sassamon had informed the Plymouth governor, Josiah Winslow, that Philip and other Indians were plotting to destroy the English and that he feared that Philip would kill him if he knew of their conversation. Soon thereafter, Sassamon was found dead in a frozen pond. Philip denied his involvement, but the Plymouth authorities arrested three of his counselors who were found guilty and executed.

A few days later, a group of Wampanoags, seemingly acting on their own, attacked the Plymouth town of Swansea, killing nine settlers. English militias supported by the governments of Plymouth, Massachusetts Bay, and Connecticut prepared a counterattack. Many were eager to push the Indians off of the

Pueblo Revolt Anticolonial rebellion of Pueblo Indians across New Mexico that temporarily forced the Spanish out of the province.

Half-Way Covenant Partial church membership in New England begun in 1662 that granted limited membership to the children and grandchildren of church members.

jeremiads Sermon full of lament and bitterness intended to provoke congregants to action; name derived from the biblical prophet Jeremiah.

King Philip's War Armed conflict (1675–1678) in New England between the Wampanoag and Narragansett Indians on one side and the English and their Indian allies on the other.

lands that remained in their control, and they feared that those Indians who had moved to Eliot's Praying Towns had become an enemy within. By the fall of 1675, the English militias had confined all of the Native Americans at the Praying Towns on an island in Boston Harbor.

As the region spiraled into war, Philip organized a large-scale attack on the English. Of the ninety towns in New England, Wampanoags and Narragansetts attacked fifty and destroyed thirteen. But the English proved more deadly. In an echo of the massacre of the Pequots decades earlier, New England militiamen surrounded a Native American village in Rhode Island, set it afire, and killed some one thousand Narragansetts. Philip and many of his followers fled south, perhaps mistakenly believing that New York's governor would aid them as New Netherland's governor once had. But Governor Edmund Andros, along with Mohawk allies he had armed, forced Philip and his people back into Massachusetts where English forces surrounded and killed Philip in the spring of 1676. By the end of the war, five thousand Indians, or half the Native American population in New England, had been murdered, killed in battle, or had died from the privations the war had brought. The English sold one thousand survivors into slavery and exiled another two thousand.

The English did not escape the war unscathed. Nearly one thousand English died in the conflict, and the cost of the war led to tax increases that sparked popular resentments. Moreover, the war so destabilized the colonies that they were unable to fend off the crown's plan to bind them more tightly into an imperial structure.

4-4c Bacon's Rebellion

Virginia, too, was riven by rebellion although of a different kind. In 1676, planters allied with Governor William Berkeley confronted men who followed Nathaniel Bacon, a recently arrived planter. **Bacon's Rebellion** came without warning, but the seeds of the conflict had been planted in an earlier era. As the result of a boom in tobacco production, Virginia had grown rapidly since mid-century, and by 1670, the colony's population stood at around thirty-five thousand. But most of the profits in the tobacco economy went to the richest and most powerful planters. Small planters also suffered more than their richer counterparts under the 1660 Navigation Act, which declared that goods and commodities produced in the colonies could be sold only in English ports. The result was diminished demand for tobacco, prompting the price of the crop to drop by half.

Bacon's wealth made him an unlikely rebel, but he and others were troubled by the declining opportunity

{ Declining social mobility for an increasing number of disgruntled servants prompts a rebellion.

for less wealthy men to rise, especially now that more and more indentured servants were outliving their terms of indenture. Bacon and others were especially upset with Berkeley's Indian policy, which had led to the removal of the Powhatans from the vicinity of the most settled areas of Virginia but assured them land above the York River. This area, however, was considered crucial to the economic ambitions of a frustrated generation of servants and former servants who had no land. Servants in Virginia, many of whom had gained their freedom after years of toil and could now not afford land, had little choice but to become tenants, virtually ensuring them a life of poverty. Bacon spoke to these struggling planters' fears and gave them hope that they could grow more tobacco by seizing Indian lands.

On the other side of the conflict stood Berkeley, who owned a 1,000-acre plantation and one of the colony's largest contingents of slaves at a time when there were only two thousand Africans in the colony. Berkeley and his planter friends, known as the *Green Spring faction*, used their connections and power to amass large landed estates. They imported servants and slaves and got 50 acres per head, allowing them to control virtually all of the good land suitable for tobacco cultivation, except that which was held by Indians. Berkeley, like other colonial governors of the time, favored the creation of a landed aristocracy. One of the largest slave owners in the colony, Berkeley supported the expansion of slavery. He had signed the legislation in the 1660s and 1670s that had enshrined slavery in the colony's laws. Furthermore, Berkeley was an absolutist. He called elections in 1661, just after he was appointed royal governor, but not again until 1676. Four years later, he signed legislation that denied the vote to men who did not own property.

Because there were few Indians living above York River, Bacon and his followers believed, incorrectly, that they could easily expel them (see Map 4.4). In January 1676, Chesapeake planters and militiamen marched out to the frontier, surrounded a group of Doegs and Susquehannocks, enticed their leaders to negotiate, and then murdered them. Further violence soon followed, leading to widespread fear among people in northern Virginia of a pan-Indian attack. Soon, 60 out of 71 plantations in the region were abandoned, and by March, three hundred Virginians had been killed.

To settle the dispute, Berkeley proposed a line of forts to keep Indians and settlers separate, but those who already had plantations believed that this would cost them too much in additional taxes. At this point, Bacon asked Berkeley for permission to go to war against any Indians he could find. When Berkeley refused, Bacon forced him at gunpoint to grant the requested military commission. Declaring Bacon a rebel, Berkeley went after him with three hundred planters and English soldiers. In May 1677, at the end of the conflict among Berkeley, Bacon and the local Indians, the surviving Powhatans had been

Bacon's Rebellion Armed rebellion led in 1676 by Nathaniel Bacon against William Berkeley, governor of Virginia, primarily over the colony's Indian policy and access to land.

Map 4.4 Bacon's Rebellion and English Expansion in the Chesapeake to 1700 By 1700 English cultivation of tobacco in Virginia had pushed far into the interior. In the wake of Bacon's Rebellion, Indians' loss of land in the Chesapeake accelerated. ▲

4-4d The Glorious Revolution in British North America

> A political revolution in England sparks popular rebellion across British North America.

In the late seventeenth century, many of the challenges the colonies faced originated in events in England. King Charles II attempted to establish greater control over the colonies. Most influentially, he encouraged Massachusetts leaders to make their government more secular. In response to their refusal, he revoked the colony's charter in 1684 and disbanded the General Court. He also jeopardized the colonists' landholdings, causing significant popular anger.

When Charles died in February 1685, his Catholic brother, James II, succeeded him. In England, James pushed Protestants out of government office in favor of Catholic appointees. James II imposed his authority on the colonies in 1686 by combining Plymouth, Massachusetts, Rhode Island, Connecticut, New Jersey, and New York into one colony, known as the **Dominion of New England**. He also promoted the Anglican Sir Edmund Andros to the dominion's governorship (see Map 4.5). Puritan fears about Andros were realized when he converted a Puritan church in Boston into an Anglican one. He alienated other groups in Massachusetts when he officially terminated the colony's representative assembly, imposed new taxes, and limited the power of town meetings.

Dominion of New England Administrative unit encompassing northern colonies in British North America from 1686 to 1689 that colonists bitterly opposed.

defeated by Bacon's men, who had also burned the capital of Jamestown to the ground. Bacon died of a fever during the conflict, and almost two dozen of his followers were captured and executed by the Virginia authorities after the conflict ended.

Bacon's Rebellion revealed that colonial government was largely powerless to prevent murderous attacks by settlers who wanted to establish their own plantations. Although the rebellion by Bacon and his followers had been put down, the expansion of English settlement onto Indian land above the York River continued given the destruction of the Powhatans as a fighting force. The Native Americans of the region recognized that the price of their survival was submission to English society. Over the coming decades, as the Powhatans declined, new English tobacco planters profited immensely on lands that were formerly Indian.

Map 4.5 The Dominion of New England, 1686 When James II became king of England, he sought to consolidate his power in the colonies by creating one large colony composed of Plymouth, Massachusetts, Rhode Island, Connecticut, New York, and New Jersey. ▲

Andros was unpopular in Massachusetts, but James was hated in England. In view of his appointment of Catholics to high office and cultivation of the Pope, many English Protestants feared that he would make England a Catholic nation again. In June 1688, James's queen, Mary of Modena, gave birth to a boy, which seemed to open the possibility of a dynasty of absolutist Catholic kings in England. The opponents of James—namely aristocrats and Anglican bishops—invited William, the Dutch Prince of the Netherlands, who was married to the king's Protestant daughter, Mary, to intervene and force James to accept a Protestant successor and recognize the authority of Parliament. In the fall of 1688, William assembled an enormous fleet of five hundred ships and forty thousand men and invaded England. He did so to pursue his own agenda: Fearing a renewed war with France, the Dutch military leader wanted to ensure that the English did not ally with France against the Netherlands. When James showed little interest in fighting for the throne, his regime collapsed, allowing William to conquer the island with little resistance. In 1689, Parliament transferred the throne to William and Mary as joint sovereigns.

Glorious Revolution Largely peaceful overthrow of James II and ascent to the throne of William and Mary who agreed to a limited monarchy.

Declaration of Rights Document crafted by English Parliament in 1689 during the Glorious Revolution that listed the wrongs committed by James II and the rights that all English citizens hold.

Bill of Rights Act of English Parliament in 1689 that essentially endorsed the Declaration of Rights and established basic civil rights for English citizens.

constitutional monarchy Governmental system in which the monarchy is constrained by a written constitution.

British Constitution Body of laws and principles that define the scope of the English government and guarantee English citizens basic rights and privileges.

Leisler's Rebellion Anti-authoritarian rebellion (1689–1691) in New York prompted by the Glorious Revolution in England.

As part of the **Glorious Revolution**, an event that shaped politics in the distant colonies, William and Mary decreed that Catholics could never hold the throne of England. They also extended religious toleration to various groups of dissenting Protestants through the Toleration Act of 1689, a law that, despite its name, denied freedom of religion to Jews and Catholics. Significantly, the new rulers assented to Parliament's **Declaration of Rights**, which amounted to a **Bill of Rights**. William and Mary disavowed absolutist rule by accepting a **constitutional monarchy** and agreeing to limits on the crown's power imposed by Parliament. The monarchs could no longer simply suspend or ignore acts of Parliament. They could not levy taxes or maintain a standing army without Parliamentary approval. Debate in Parliament was to be free. Elections were to occur regularly. Moreover, all Englishmen could now petition the crown without fear of retribution, had the right to trial by jury, were free from excessive bail or fines, and no longer subject to cruel and unusual punishment. With the overthrow of James II, Englishmen came more firmly to believe that

these "ancient rights and liberties" were the birthright of all Englishmen and that the crown was forever subject to the rule of law enshrined in a series of documents and precedents known as the **British Constitution**.

The British in the colonies followed suit; Protestant denominations, mainly the established churches of Anglicans and Presbyterians, dominated the political and religious life of most colonies. Similarly, in many English colonies, settlers rose against the representatives of royal authority. In New England, the Dominion was overthrown, and the original colonial charters again became the basis of law and governance. In Maryland, Protestants rose up against Lord Baltimore, the Catholic proprietor, and defeated his government without resorting to violence. Backed by the king, the rebels established a largely Protestant government. Catholics could still practice their religion but could not vote or hold office.

When news reached New York that William and Mary had taken the throne and then that Andros had been imprisoned by his rivals in Massachusetts, New York militiamen removed Lt. Governor Francis Nicholson, and seized New York City's fort to "save" the city from a much-feared Catholic and Indian invasion from Canada. A week later—in what is known as **Leisler's Rebellion**—Jacob Leisler, the son of a German Calvinist pastor, emerged as captain of the fort and then as commander of the colony.

Leisler's proficient rule came to an end in the spring of 1691 when the new crown-appointed governor, Henry Sloughter, arrived from England. He was determined to put down's Leisler's revolt. When Leisler finally surrendered, he was arrested, charged with treason, and sentenced to death. From the scaffold, on May 16, 1691, Leisler made an eloquent plea for his life, professing that he had not been motivated by personal gain but by the cause of Protestantism. Nevertheless, Sloughter had Leisler and his assistant hanged and cut down and beheaded while still alive.

4-4e King William's War and the 1692 Witchcraft Panic

Although many English colonists cheered the bloodless assent of William to the crown, his coronation meant more bloodshed in the colonies. William quickly started a war known in Europe as the *Nine Years' War* and in the colonies as *King William's War* (1689–1697). His enemy was France, England's longtime religious, cultural, territorial, and economic rival. William built up the English navy, and his early naval victories enhanced England's position in world trade and finance. In the colonies, however, the conflict provoked

> Indian warfare and religious fundamentalism lead to a witch panic in New England.

devastating frontier warfare and instability. England's Indian allies attacked the French, and France's Indian allies attacked English frontier outposts across New England, causing havoc and paranoia. Unbeknownst to the colonists at the time, King William's War was the first of a series of four bloody and extraordinarily expensive intercolonial wars, whose origins lay in Europe. These wars, largely fought between the English and the French pulled in Indians along the frontier between New England and New France, and would not be concluded until the defeat of the French and their Indian allies in the Seven Years War (1754–1763).

With the outbreak of King William's War, colonists in Massachusetts and Maine feared that neither their colonial governments nor a distant England could protect them from Indian attack. To fight the war against France, England had to build a much larger navy and army, create a state bureaucracy to run them, and then increase taxes to pay for it all. England, therefore, quickly moved from the lightest-taxed nation in Europe to among the heaviest taxed. Even so, the national debt increased each year. The beefed-up army and navy did little to help the colonists. England focused on protecting itself from invasion, and any remaining resources were sent to protect the lucrative West Indies. As fear pervaded the northern colonies, English defenses on the Massachusetts frontier collapsed because of the desertion of the men whom the then-deposed Andros had pressed into military service. When Indians who were aided by the French attacked in the winter of 1689–1690, the English suffered terrible losses and hundreds, if not thousands, abandoned their frontier settlements.

Not coincidentally, at that very moment, scores of colonists across Essex County, Massachusetts, gripped by fears of an Indian attack, began to level accusations of witchcraft against their neighbors and community members. The panic started in Salem Village, a small farming community about fifteen miles north of Boston, when a group of adolescent girls began to have bizarre fits. Samuel Parris, father of one of the girls and uncle of another, called a local physician. The physician suspected the girls were "under an evil hand." In February 1692, warrants went out for the arrest of three women whom the girls claimed were their tormentors. Two of the women denied the charges, but a third, a West Indian slave named Tituba, confessed. In the early spring, numerous women were tried and sentenced to death for witchcraft. One man, Giles Cory of Salem village, was accused of being a wizard, and for this crime, he was pressed to death by heavy weights progressively piled on top of his body. As the panic spread, 150 people were formally charged. As in previous episodes in the witch hysteria that gripped Europe from 1450 to 1750, three-fourths of the accused witches in New England were women who seemed to disrupt social expectations or norms. Women who had no husband or children or who had inherited property were vulnerable to charges of witchcraft.

In late September 1692, after twenty executions and with more than one hundred suspected witches in jail, the panic came to a close when ministers from eastern Massachusetts prevented the use of "spectors," or apparitions, as evidence. From that moment, it became almost impossible to prosecute anyone for witchcraft, and the remaining suspects, including Tituba, were eventually freed. The Peace of Ryswick (1697) ended the Nine Years' War in Europe, but it was not until the Grand Settlement of 1701 that war ended in America with the Haudenosaunees pledging neutrality in future wars between England and France. By the war's end, the Haudenosaunees had lost 2,000 of their total population of 8,600 and had narrowly saved themselves from destruction.

Illustration of a Witch from Cotton Mather Account, 1689 Witchcraft was a crime because a witch was believed to have made a pact with the devil. A large number of those seemingly tormented by the devil were refugees from various Indian attacks on the frontier and were haunted by fears and memories of violence, captivity, and murder. ▼

British Library/Granger, NYC—All rights reserved.

Summary

In the second half of the seventeenth century, revolutions and rebellions shook the emerging colonies. In the Caribbean, a revolution in the production of sugar sparked not only new dietary habits in England but also more plantations in the West Indies that depended on hundreds of thousands of enslaved Africans. To supply these laborers, Europeans kidnapped or purchased and sent into captivity millions of Africans who suffered horrible violence and indignities. A smaller number of Africans were transported to the mainland colonies where they were consigned to a slaves' existence without hope of liberation as new laws remade the lives of Africans in America. In the realm of international affairs, nations battled one another not only for territory but also for commerce as mercantilist thought revolutionized the way that the English and French colonies traded with one another and their own mother countries. Overall, England was on the ascendance, having defeated the Dutch in various conflicts, and Spain's focus remained on the consolidation of its long-established colonies. Although many English colonists resisted the new regulations, they in time strengthened local economies and the ties between colonies and the homeland. The greatest threat to the colonies in the late seventeenth century resulted from internal challenges as frustrated servants, oppressed Indians, ambitious leaders, and panicked believers challenged their leaders and neighbors in their attempts to find peace and security in a world beset by change and transformation.

‹Thinking Back, *Looking Forward*›

As you review this chapter, think about how events on the continent of Europe continued to shape the American colonies and locate the origins of the transatlantic slave trade in other earlier slave systems. To what extent was commerce a key factor in the integration of American colonies into larger imperial frameworks? How important were coercion and absolutism to the new societies taking root in colonial America? To make your study concrete, review the timeline and reflect on the entries there. Think about their causes, consequences, and connections. How do they fit with global trends?

Additional Resources

Books

Berlin, Ira. *Many Thousands Gone: The First Two Centuries of Slavery in North America.* **Cambridge, MA: Harvard University Press, 1998.** ▶ Best single-volume study of slavery across all the regions of colonial America.

Brown, Kathleen M. *Good Wives, Nasty Wenches, and Anxious Patriarchs: Gender, Race, and Power in Colonial Virginia.* **Chapel Hill: University of North Carolina Press, 1996.** ▶ Rereading of early Virginia history through the intersecting axes of gender and race.

Elliot, J. H. *Empires of the Atlantic World: Britain and Spain in America, 1492–1830.* **New Haven, CT: Yale University Press, 2006.** ▶ Thorough and engaging exploration of the economic, political, and intellectual foundations of England and Spain's transatlantic empires.

Eltis, David. *The Rise of African Slavery in the Americas.* **Cambridge, England: Cambridge University Press, 2000.** ▶ Stunning quantitative study of the transatlantic slave trade based on an examination of the shipping records of the trade itself.

Morgan, Philip D. *Slave Counterpoint: Black Culture in the Eighteenth-Century Chesapeake and Lowcountry.* **Chapel Hill: University of North Carolina Press, 1998.** ▶ Comprehensive and comparative study of slavery across the southern colonies.

Nash, Gary B. *Quakers and Politics: Pennsylvania, 1681–1726.* **Princeton, NJ: Princeton University Press.** ▶ Classic study of the Penn family's colony in America.

Norton, Mary Beth. *In the Devil's Snare: The Salem Witchcraft Crisis of 1692.* **New York: Alfred A. Knopf, 2002.** ▶ Painstaking and evocative reconstruction of the witchcraft crisis and the larger context within which it unfolded.

O'Malley, Gregory E. *Final Passages: The Intercolonial Slave Trade of British America, 1619–1807*. Chapel Hill: University of North Carolina Press, 2014. ▶ A rediscovery of the movements of thousands of slaves between the English colonies.

Ritchie, Robert C. *Captain Kidd and the War Against the Pirates*. Cambridge, MA: Harvard University Press, 1986. ▶ Swashbuckling account of England's most famous pirate.

Smallwood, Stephanie E. *Saltwater Slavery: A Middle Passage from Africa to American Diaspora*. Cambridge, MA: Harvard University Press, 2008. ▶ Gripping study of the Middle Passage and the meaning of slavery.

Websites

Voyages: The Transatlantic Slave Trade Database. http://slavevoyages.org/tast/index.faces ▶ Easy-to-search database with stunning set of records detailing more than forty thousand slave ships and their human cargo..

Salem Witch Trials Documentary Archive and Transcription Project. http://salem.lib.virginia.edu/home.html ▶ Archive of court records and other documents related to the trials in 1692.

> Go to the MindTap® for **Global Americans** to access the full version of select books from this Additional Resources section.

Continue exploring online through MindTap®**, where you can:**
- **Assess your knowledge with the Chapter Test**
- **Watch historical videos related to the chapter**
- **Further your understanding with interactive maps and timelines**

Empires across the Atlantic World

1647–1655	1656–1660	1661–1664	1665–1670	1671–1675
1647 George Fox establishes Quaker religion. **1649** Charles I is executed. **1651** Enumeration Act passes. **1653** Oliver Cromwell assumes control of England. **1654–1655** Cromwell launches the Western Design.	**1658** Cromwell dies. **1660** Charles II assumes control of England beginning the Stuart Restoration.	**1662** Virginia legislature rules that slavery is a status inherited from the mother. Church leaders institute Half-Way Covenant. **1663** Royal African Company is founded. Eliot Bible is first published. English Parliament passes the Staple Act. English establish Carolina. **1664** England conquers New Netherland and founds New York. Dutch formally surrender New York under the Articles of Capitulation.	**1665** English establish the Colony of New Jersey. **1667** Mohawks sue for peace with French. **1668** English sack Jamaica. **1669** Carolina adopts the Fundamental Constitutions.	**1673** English Parliament passes the Plantation Duty Act. Joliet and Marquette explore upper Mississippi River. **1675** King Philip's War breaks out.

North America

New Mexico

New York

Spain

England

Europe

British North America

Carribean

1676–1680	1681–1685	1686–1690	1691–1695	1696–1702
1676 New Jersey is divided into East and West Jersey. Kateri Tekakwitha is baptized. Bacon's Rebellion breaks out. **1678** Haudenosaunees and New York form Covenant Chain. **1680** Pueblo Revolt erupts.	**1681** Penn establishes Pennsylvania. **1682** Penn outlines his First Frame of Government. La Salle explores the Mississippi River to the Gulf of Mexico. **1683** Penn issues the Charter of Liberties. New York issues Charter of Liberties and Privileges. King Philip's War ends. **1684** Charles II revokes Massachusetts Bay Colony charter.	**1689** William and Mary ascend to the throne in the Glorious Revolution. Parliament suspends the Royal African Company's monopoly. Leisler takes over New York City's fort in Leisler's Rebellion. King William's War breaks out between the English and French. Witchcraft panic begins in Salem and spreads throughout New England.	**1692** Vargas leads reconquest of New Mexico.	**1696** Second Pueblo Revolt breaks out. Board of Trade is established in England. **1697** Peace of Ryswick ends the Nine Years' War. **1698** French settle lower Mississippi Valley. **1701** Haudenosaunees declare neutrality. **1702** Crown unites East and West Jersey in single colony.

5

Colonial Society and the Bonds of Empire

1700–1750

Born in Africa, taken captive in his youth, and carried to British North America, Broteer Furro, also known as Venture Smith, experienced the horrors and humiliations of the transatlantic slave trade. Through luck and perseverance, he survived and purchased his own freedom after decades of hardship.

In an age defined by the exchange of commodities across the Atlantic and the movement, forced or voluntary, of hundreds of thousands of people to the Americas, the story of Broteer Furro is both distinct and emblematic. Born in 1729 in Dukandarra, Guinea, Furro lived a peaceful life until he was eight, when slave hunters raided his town. "The very first salute I had from them," Furro recalled, "was a violent blow on the head with the fore part of a gun, and at the same time a grasp around the neck." Furro then saw his father "tortured to death," a "shocking scene" that was always "fresh" in his mind.

Broteer was imprisoned in a coastal slave station and eventually sold to Robertson Mumford, a Rhode Island slave trader, who purchased him "for four gallons of rum, and a piece of calico," a common form of cotton cloth. Mumford renamed the young boy Venture. After a transatlantic crossing, in which 60 of the 260 slaves on board Mumford's ship perished, Venture disembarked in Rhode Island.

Without much help, Venture fought his own battle against slavery for the remainder of his life. For refusing Mumford's son's orders, he was bound and threatened with death. Years later, Mumford beat him

A View Taken Near Bain, on the Coast of Guinea in Africa.
Engraved by Catherine Prestell, published by J. Phillips, London, 1789, after sketches on location by Carl B. Wadstrom.

"with a club two feet long and as large around as a chair-post." This brutality defined slavery in America throughout the early eighteenth century, an era when slaves worked in a variety of capacities, not just on plantations. To be black, whether free or enslaved, was to be despised and treated, in Venture's words, like "the black dog." Venture was purchased by one Captain Oliver Smith, and from then on he went by the name Venture Smith. Against all odds, Smith survived decades of the humiliation and brutality of slavery and ultimately purchased his freedom and that of his family and friends.

Venture Smith's story is distinctive because it ends in his hard-won freedom. But it is also emblematic in that it reflects the terrible experiences of slaves in early America. Smith is a reminder that across the eighteenth century, slavery was expanding in colonial America. His life also suggests the challenges overcome not just by slaves but also by the great numbers of people who came to the Americas from Europe and Africa as laborers. Moreover, Smith's life demonstrates the degree to which the global trade of people and commodities had knit together African, American, and European communities. Smith, purchased as a child for four gallons of rum and a piece of calico, was not only witness to the transnational commerce that shaped colonial America but also was its tragic embodiment.

How does Venture Smith's journey from slavery to freedom reflect the realities of transnational commercial development of the colonial age?

Go to MindTap® to watch a video on Smith and learn how his story relates to the themes of this chapter.

5-1
Peoples in Motion

This plan for *The Brookes*, an actual slave ship, from Carl B. Wadstrom's *An Essay on Colonization, particularly applied to the Western coast of Africa... in Two Parts* (1794, 1795), shows how Africans were stowed in the holds. In an added touch of realism, the inset depicts a revolt aboard a slave ship with the crew shooting the rebels. This ship was designed to carry 609 slaves (351 men, 127 women, 90 boys, and 41 girls).

Look closely at the detailed plan of this ship. How is its hold portrayed? How are slaves depicted? ▶

The Art Archive

After the crises of the late seventeenth century, the British colonies entered a period of stability, and the transatlantic economy continued to expand. As a result, vast numbers of people came to British North America in the early eighteenth century. Some came as slaves from Africa or as convicted felons from England. Others, most notably Germans, sold themselves or their children into years of labor to gain passage across the Atlantic. Still others left increasingly impoverished homelands in Ireland or Scotland. At the same time, the birthrate in the colonies rose to new heights, and the population of much of colonial America exploded. All of these factors contributed to a population increase in eastern North America from 251,000 non-Indians in 1700 to 1,186,000 by 1750 (see Table 5.1). These swelling numbers forced Indians into migrations of their own. Many went to Detroit and the Ohio River Valley as refugees.

☞ As you read, consider the range of circumstances under which people came to colonial America. Did they in any way share a common experience?

5-1a Unwilling Voyagers: African Slaves

In comparison to New Spain or Peru, where Spaniards built colonies on the backs of large populations of indigenous laborers, England's North American colonies were sparsely populated by local peoples. When the English colonists needed laborers and indentured servants were in short supply, as they were in the first half of the eighteenth century, colonists turned to African slaves. As a consequence, in the first half of the eighteenth century, slavery dramatically expanded on the mainland.

{ The population of slaves continues to grow through the transatlantic trade.

In 1700, only about 28,000 blacks lived in British North America. By 1750, there were 252,000. As in earlier periods, the vast majority of slaves were taken to the Caribbean or Brazil, but now 6.5 percent of those sold in the Americas were sold on the North American mainland, up from 1.5 percent in the previous half century. Of the slaves imported to British North America in this half century, nearly 84,000 disembarked in the Chesapeake, 41,000 in the Carolinas and Georgia, 7,000 in the Gulf colonies, and 13,000 in the northern colonies. These Africans came from many different ethnic groups and regions of Africa, and buyers often selected them based on their origins. For instance, South Carolinians and Georgians expressed a preference for slaves from Senegambia, where Africans knew how to cultivate rice, the most important crop in these areas.

Although African slaves constituted about half of all new arrivals to the colonies through 1750, they represented about 80 percent of all women who sailed to North America before 1800, largely because few European women had incentives to do so of their own volition. The forced migration of enslaved African women—who performed much of the domestic work in the colonies that women in Europe did—compensated for the deficit of European women in British North America through the early decades of the eighteenth century.

The importation of African women to the colonies led to the **natural increase** of the slave population in North

Table 5.1 Population of British North America by Broad Colonial Region, 1700–1750

Across the first half of the eighteenth century the population of British North America exploded because of massive immigration and a steady natural increase.

Year	Total	New England	Middle Colonies	Chesapeake	Lowcountry
1700	251,444	92,763	53,537	88,164	16,980
1710	327,360	115,094	69,592	117,254	25,420
1720	467,465	170,893	103,084	153,890	39,598
1730	636,045	217,351	146,981	211,713	60,000
1740	912,742	289,704	220,545	296,533	105,960
1750	1,1864,08	360,011	296,459	377,754	152,184

Source: *Historical Statistics of the United States*, millennial ed. Cambridge, England: Cambridge University Press, 2006.

St. George's Castle at Elmina and St. Jago, Gold Coast, Late Seventeenth Century Slaves brought to the Americas were first imprisoned in coastal forts notorious for the miserable conditions. This engraving shows some of the European forts built for this purpose along the coast of Africa. ◄

HANDOUT/KRT/Newscom

natural increase Population growth resulting from more births than deaths.

Act of Union Act of 1707 unifying the kingdoms of Scotland and England.

Scots-Irish Person of Scottish ancestry who immigrated from Ireland to British North America.

America. The climate and work regimes on the mainland, although brutal, were never as lethal as those in the Caribbean, meaning that women on the mainland were more likely to survive and bear children. Slaveholders knew that their future wealth was tied to the reproductive capacities of slave women. Later in his life, Thomas Jefferson expressed a widely held belief when he wrote that he considered an enslaved woman "who brings a child every two years more profitable than the best man of the farm. What she produces is an addition to the capital, while his labors disappear in mere consumption."

5-1b The Irish and Scots-Irish

In England, the conditions that had prompted immigration in the seventeenth century—a weak economy and religious persecution—changed after the Glorious Revolution, and the number of immigrant English people to North American plunged. But that of the Scots and the Irish increased as a result of high rents, famine, and religious oppression in those lands. These immigrants arrived in America in large numbers, especially after the **Act of Union**, which formally allowed Scots to move to the English colonies. More than 150,000 people from Ireland or Scotland went to North America, usually in whole families. Among those who left were Ulster Scots from Northern Ireland, who as Protestants were persecuted by the dominant Catholic population. Some 70,000 Ulster Scots immigrated, often in groups organized by their Presbyterian ministers. To distinguish themselves from Irish Catholics, they called themselves the **Scots-Irish**. Overall, the majority of immigrants from Ireland and Scotland settled in western Pennsylvania because they had trouble acquiring land closer to the coast (see Map 5.1). Many took land claimed by Indians, speculators, or the colonial government; over time this became a source of conflict on the frontier.

{ Very large numbers of immigrants come from Scotland and Ireland.

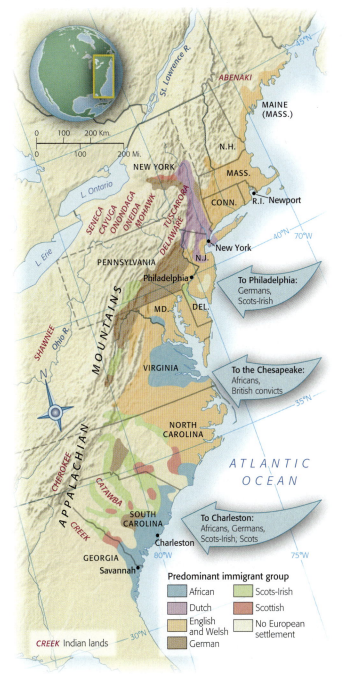

Map 5.1 European Immigration and Slave Transports to British North America, Mid-Eighteenth Century Through the eighteenth century, immigrants from western Europe and slaves from Africa swelled the population of British North America. ▲

OpenLibrary/Princeton Theological Seminary Library

SOME ACCOUNT

OF THE EARLY PART OF THE

LIFE

OF

Elizabeth Ashbridge,

WHO DIED, IN THE TRUTH'S SERVICE, AT THE HOUSE
OF ROBERT LECKY, IN THE COUNTY OF CARLOW,
IRELAND, THE 16TH OF 5TH MONTH,
1755.

WRITTEN BY HERSELF.

" Her sins, which are many, are forgiven; for she
loved much." *Luke*, vii, 47.

" A little leaven leaveneth the whole lump." *Gal.* v, 9.

PHILADELPHIA:

PRINTED FOR BENJAMIN AND THOMAS KITE,
NO. 21, SOUTH FOURTH STREET.

1807.

Global Americans In an age marked by spiritual and economic uncertainly, **Elizabeth Ashbridge** led an especially tumultuous life marked by personal, economic, and spiritual travails. She was born in England in 1713. Her father, a ship's surgeon, was at sea during most of her childhood. She rebelled against her parents and eloped at age fourteen only to find herself a widow five months later. To escape her father's scorn, she moved to Ireland. Soon she became disillusioned with Catholicism. Desiring change, Ashbridge ventured to Pennsylvania in 1732, only to be forced to sign a four-year contract as an indentured servant to pay for her voyage. Like so many servants of her time, she found her master cruel, but after three years, she bought out the remainder of her contract with money she had earned doing various odd jobs. She had less luck extricating herself from a bad marriage to a schoolteacher with whom she moved frequently as he pursued one job after another. But she eventually found happiness in the Quaker faith and in her third marriage. In 1753, Ashbridge became a Quaker minister—something that would have been unimaginable to her in youth—and traveled to England and Ireland to speak about her own spiritual journey. After nearly two years, she fell ill, attributing her growing infirmities to "bodily hardship in traveling" and "spiritual exercise in mind." She died in Ireland in 1755, having completed her spiritual journey not far from where she spent much of her difficult youth chasing not only financial independence but also religious ideals.

5-1c Convicts, Redemptioners, and Huguenots

In the early eighteenth century, English policymakers actively discouraged English-men and women from leaving the home country in the belief that a large population of workers in the mother country was one foundation of a mercantilist empire. These policy makers did want supposedly troublesome people—vagabonds, criminals, and supporters of the now-deposed Stuart monarchs—to leave. In the first half of the eighteenth century, England deported some 50,000 convicts, many of whom were sold into seven- or fourteen-year terms of labor. Male convicts cost one-third of the price of an African slave, and female convicts sold for two-thirds the price of their male counterparts.

In the hopes of creating a more robust labor force in the colonies, English policy makers also encouraged German and French Protestants to relocate to British North America, which was particularly attractive to Germans. Some 500,000 left the Rhineland in the eighteenth century with around 70,000 of them moving

> Indentured servants from many life experiences continue to arrive from western Europe.

Moravians Protestant denomination originating in central Europe often dedicated to missionary work.

Pietism Seventeenth-century Protestant religious movement originating in Germany stressing Bible study and personal religious experience over engagement with the world.

redemptioners European immigrants who gained passage to American colonies by selling themselves or their children into indentured servitude to pay for the cost of the transatlantic voyage.

Edict of Nantes Law promulgated in France in 1598 granting Protestants (known in France as *Huguenots*) a measure of religious and civil liberties in some parts of the country but revoked by Louis XIV in 1685.

Table 5.2 Major Sources of Immigration to British North America, 1700–1750

Africans	145,000
Ireland	80,000
Scotland	79,000
Germany	70,000
English Convicts	50,000

to Philadelphia (see Table 5.2). About 37,000 Germans arrived between 1749 and 1754 in one of the largest and most concentrated immigrations to North America since the Puritan migration of the 1630s. The majority of German and French immigrants were Protestants, but they came from many different denominations: Lutherans, **Moravians**, Baptists, and **Pietists**. Most were seeking affordable land, religious toleration, and low taxes—all of which could be found in Pennsylvania. Most went as families, although some entire neighborhoods and communities moved, too. The majority paid their own way across the Atlantic, yet roughly a third—known as **redemptioners**—sold their own labor, or that of their children, to pay for the transatlantic voyage. Meanwhile, in 1685, the French king Louis XIV revoked the **Edict of Nantes**, effectively outlawing the Huguenot (Protestant) faith and spurring 150,000 Huguenots to flee. French laws prohibited Protestants from moving to New France, so most resettled in Switzerland, Germany, Holland, and England. About 10,000 eventually made it to British North America.

5-1d Indian Refugees

The expansion of the British colonies' population forced many Indians out of their homelands. Thousands abandoned the Northeast for the new French post of Detroit. Similarly, Indians fleeing New England in the wake of King Philip's War and the outbreak of King William's War in 1689 streamed into the region between New England and New France.

> Massive population growth and increased settlement in the colonies drives Indians out of their homelands.

Colonial expansion also created conflict and refugees in the Carolinas. In South Carolina, the Shawnee Savannahs, after being attacked by the Catawbas, who had been armed by the English, fled west to live with the Creeks or north to Pennsylvania, a colony that welcomed Indians on its frontier. In North Carolina, colonists and their livestock crowded out the Iroquoian-speaking Tuscaroras. In 1711, the Tuscaroras sought to expel the colonists, killing more than a hundred settlers. But in the war that ensued, nearly fifteen hundred Tuscaroras were killed and another one thousand sold into slavery. In 1717, most survivors fled north, and in 1722, they became the sixth nation in the Haudenosaunee confederacy.

In a chaotic colonial world, rivalries and animosities between Indians persisted, and some groups worked with Europeans to dispossess other Indians. Even though the English had supported the Yamasees of South Carolina against the Tuscaroras, the Yamasees too felt the sting of encroaching settlers. In 1715, they rose in a conflict known as **The Yamasee War**, supported by Creeks, Catawbas, Cherokees, and French allies, killing hundreds of English settlers in South Carolina. In 1716, however, when the Cherokees entered the war in hope of defeating the Creeks, the Yamasees were forced to find refuge in Spanish Florida. Similarly, when Pennsylvania officials produced a blatantly forged treaty asserting that the Delawares had agreed to sell a swath of land whose size would be determined by how far a man could walk in a day and a half, the Iroquois Confederacy supported the colony in the swindle. In 1737, in what is known as the **Walking Purchase**, the colony hired two professional walkers who, after a good deal of practice, walked 64 miles in the allotted time. When the Delawares refused to vacate nearly 1,200 square miles of their land, the Haudenosaunees forced them out. Many Delawares took refuge in the Ohio Valley, where numerous other tribes had gone as well. These groups created new interethnic communities that sought political independence from France and England yet desired to trade freely with both, stoking an increasingly heated imperial rivalry for control over the Ohio Valley.

The Yamasee War Conflict in 1715–1717 between Indians and English settlers in South Carolina.

Walking Purchase Fraudulent agreement between the Penn family and Indians in Pennsylvania that dispossessed the Delawares of much of their land; supported by the Haudenosaunees.

5-2

Regional Cultures and Social Change

This engraving from Peter Cooper's *The Southeast Prospect of the City of Philadelphia* (1720) shows a view from the harbor of Philadelphia, where ships wait to pick up or drop off cargo. This was a typical scene in one of the busiest commercial entrepôts in British North America.

How does the painting portray the city? What might the range of ships in the harbor suggest about commerce at the port? ▶

Fotosearch/Getty Images

With the natural increase of colonial populations and the arrival of very large numbers of European immigrants and African slaves, new regional cultures emerged and old ones changed. New England's population exploded, largely through natural increase. This growth led to the establishment of new towns and far-flung settlements, further fraying bonds of community and family. The Middle Colonies received the bulk of free immigrants from Europe, and the region soon became characterized by ethnic and religious diversity and craft production. The Chesapeake's population expanded as the result of natural increase and the arrival of Europeans and tens of thousands of slaves, and towns and cities grew in a region known mostly for its isolated plantations. The populations of New France and New Spain, meanwhile, grew more slowly, and the lives of settlers in the colonies changed little over the decades. Across nearly all of colonial America, even in regions without plantations, coerced labor of Indians or Africans remained a common feature of daily life.

☞ As you read, consider the range of regional cultures that developed across colonial America. What accounts for the differences from region to region?

Table 5.3 White Population of British North America by Broad Colonial Region, 1700–1750

Year	Total Number	New England	Middle Colonies	Chesapeake	Lowcountry
1700	223,071	91,083	47,541	68,547	13,565
1710	284,662	112,509	60,229	89,959	18,820
1720	398,798	166,937	87,574	114,832	24,770
1730	538,424	211,233	126,606	157,893	34,000
1740	755,539	281,163	185,258	212,502	57,781
1750	934,340	349,029	248,515	227,204	82,384

Source: *Historical Statistics of the United States*, millennial ed. Cambridge, England: Cambridge University Press, 2006.

5-2a New England and the Middle Colonies

In New England (Massachusetts, Connecticut, Rhode Island, and New Hampshire), population growth from 93,000 in 1700 to 360,000 by 1750 meant that many people had to leave existing towns and settled areas if they hoped to establish viable farms of their own. Many in the rising generation of adults set out for the frontier, which helped accelerate the decline of local church and religious observance as the center of life in the region. As a result, the religious institutions that had differentiated New England from the rest of colonial America in the seventeenth century withered. Ports such as Boston and Salem were transformed by merchants and new patterns of consumption, and in the process became more like their cosmopolitan English counterparts than the self-contained and austere villages created by the Puritans. For many New Englanders, the pursuit of wealth became as important, if not more so, than concerns about personal salvation, and material gain trumped community and consensus.

{ Population growth and the consumer revolution drive the growth of towns and port cities.

The Middle Colonies (Delaware, Pennsylvania, New Jersey, and New York) also experienced social change driven by population growth and economic development. Largely the result of immigration, the non-Indian and non-slave population increased sixfold from 53,000 in 1700 to 296,000 in 1750 (see Table 5.1). Most immigrants were English, but 40 percent were ethnic Germans, Quakers, Jews, or Catholics, who continued to practice their beliefs in America. As a result, the Middle Colonies emerged as the most diverse region in colonial America. As in New England, settlers were increasingly devoted to economic advancement (see Map 5.2).

Slavery remained an important but not defining institution in New England and the Middle Colonies. The number of slaves imported depended on the Atlantic labor market. When the European economy was in decline and sea-lanes to colonial America were open, indentured servants immigrated. But when the European economy was

Map 5.2 Major Economic Industries, British North America, Mid-Eighteenth Century By the middle of the eighteenth century, regions continued to specialize in certain industries but overall the economy of British North America was increasingly diversified. ▲

expanding or war prevented transatlantic travel, the supply of available laborers fell and slave imports to Boston, New York, and Philadelphia rose. However, because the European population increased so quickly because of immigration, slaves constituted a large percentage of the population only in a few urban centers. By 1750, a quarter of all slaves in the colony of New York lived in New York City, and one-third of all Massachusetts slaves lived in Boston. Many urban slaves labored on wharves, in shipyards, or on ships. Nearly all worked alongside white laborers. Tradesmen and artisans owned some slaves. A few lived on their own and worked for wages that they then turned over to their masters. Most did not marry or have children because their masters did not want to be responsible for wives or offspring.

Table 5.4 Black Population of British North America by Broad Colonial Region, 1700–1750

Year	Total Number	New England	Middle Colonies	Chesapeake	Lowcountry
1700	28,373	1,680	3,661	19,617	3,415
1710	42,698	2,585	6,218	27,295	6,600
1720	68,667	3,956	10,825	39,058	14,828
1730	97,621	6,118	11,683	53,820	26,000
1740	159,224	8,541	16,452	84,031	50,200
1750	252,068	10,982	20,736	150,550	69,800

Source: *Historical Statistics of the United States*, millennial ed. Cambridge, England: Cambridge University Press, 2006.

5-2b The Chesapeake

The Chesapeake colonies of Virginia and Maryland also experienced social change as a result of population growth. The white population of the Chesapeake grew from 69,000 in 1700 to 227,000 in 1750, largely the result of the founding of permanent settlements, which improved life expectancy and, by extension, increased the birthrate. Soon the many new settlements were connected by an expanding and extensive system of roads, bridges, and ferries. Across the Chesapeake, life remained largely secular, even if by mid-century the Church of England had made inroads in the colony.

> As the white population increases, so does the demand for slaves, which creates a divided society based on ideas of free and slave as well as white and black.

The racial makeup of the Chesapeake was starkly different from that of New England and the Middle Colonies. In a society dominated by plantations, slaves were the foundation of economic life. In 1700, slaves composed 22 percent of the population in Maryland and Virginia, a figure that reached 40 percent in 1750 (see Map 5.3). In 1700, 19,617 blacks were enslaved in the Chesapeake, and by 1750, there were 150,550 (see Table 5.4). By the 1760s, more than half of the households in the most prosperous areas had slaves.

The slaves came from Africa, for the most part, which represented a change from the previous century. In the mid-1600s, slaves constituted only 3 percent of the Chesapeake's population and most arrived by way of the Caribbean on the ships of the Royal Africa Company. But the company's monopoly on the shipment of slaves to the English colonies collapsed in 1689, and in 1698 Parliament suspended it. The direct shipment of slaves to the Chesapeake from Africa rose more than tenfold from fewer than 3,000 in the 1680s to nearly 35,000 in the 1730s. Between 1700 and 1750, nearly 120,000 African slaves were sold in the region, six times as many in the previous 50 years.

Map 5.3 African American Population Distribution, Mid-Eighteenth Century In the middle of the eighteenth century, enslaved African Americans lived throughout British North America with the greatest numbers in the Carolinas and the Chesapeake. ▲

The British viewed these newly arrived slaves direct from Africa as strange, libidinous, heathenish, and frightful, although they valued the slaves as laborers. Chesapeake masters ordered them not to converse with fellow slaves in their native languages. They were put to work weeding between rows of tobacco plants, using only their bare hands or simple tools. Planter William Tatham wrote that slaves worked "from daylight until the dusk of the evening and some part of the night, by moon or candlelight, during the winter." Under these harsh conditions, new arrivals sickened, and many died soon after coming to the Chesapeake. Children born into slavery in the Chesapeake, in contrast, were healthier than their African parents and conversant in English.

As the enslaved population in the Chesapeake increased in size, slaveholders' fears of rebellion grew. Many whites believed that their slaves were united against them when, in fact, the slaves in the Chesapeake were characterized by many variations in homeland, language, and personal experiences.

5-2c The Lowcountry

Farther south, in the Low-country (North Carolina, South Carolina, and Georgia), immigration had increased the non-Indian population from 17,000 in 1700 to 147,000 by 1750, despite the ravages of various diseases, including malaria. In South Carolina, the English wars with neighboring Indians—the Tuscaroras and the Yamasees—resulted in an Indian slave labor force of about 2,000 people. But this did not satisfy planters' desires for slaves, and they started importing them from Africa at a high rate. By the 1720s, Africans outnumbered whites two to one in lowland South Carolina and three to one along the coast. By 1750, the colony had 49,000 slaves, or 66 percent of its population, the highest proportion in any colony in North America.

> Rice and indigo production in the South drives the need for more slaves and land in Georgia, which also acts as a buffer against the Spanish.

Georgia was established in 1732 as a utopian experiment and a buffer against Spanish Florida. It was intended for settlement by the "worthy poor" who had been released from prison in England. Because of its rules limiting private landholdings to five hundred acres, prohibiting rum, and banning the importation of slaves, the colony attracted only five thousand settlers by 1750. When Georgia's charter expired in 1753, the colony reverted to the crown. Soon thereafter, royal officials relaxed the colony's ban on slavery and loosened restrictions on landholding, creating a foundation for the colony's growth in the 1760s.

The Lowcountry had two distinct slave populations by 1750. Slaves on plantations lived in unhealthy quarters, which became outposts of African life and culture. These were often small villages where life achieved a modicum of permanence and stability. Slaves asserted their rights to Sundays free from work and to their own small plots of land, where they cultivated vegetables, fowl, and rice. Common languages and experiences rooted in memories of Africa and the Middle Passage bound many Lowcountry plantation slaves together. As in previous decades, Lowcountry rural slaves practiced African customs, celebrated African holidays, and one in five carried an African name. This cultural continuity and the lack of command of the English language meant that Christianity made little impact among these slaves.

A different slave world developed in Lowcountry urban areas where wealthy Carolina planters often maintained a second residence staffed by slaves. By 1720, Charles Town had one thousand four hundred whites and almost as many slaves. Most of these slaves lived in back rooms, basements, or attics in their master's residence. They spoke English and came into contact with large numbers of other slaves in port towns, where they worked as porters, drayers, stevedores, skilled craftsmen, seamstresses, and weavers. Highly skilled urban slaves arranged for their own employment and lodging and paid their master a portion of their wages. Some urban slaves dressed in extravagant clothing and powdered wigs, and, like their masters, scorned plantation slaves whom they viewed as wretched.

5-2d New France and New Spain

The population growth, expanding diversity, and social upheavals that characterized the English colonies were not fully mirrored in the French or Spanish possessions. At the turn of the eighteenth century, the bulk of French settlement in Canada was situated along the St. Lawrence River where fifteen thousand French settlers lived. Over the next half century, the population of New France grew to nearly eighty-five thousand, mostly owing to natural increase because French policies prohibited Protestants from immigrating and Catholics had little incentive to leave France. There were small minorities of Catholic Scots, Irish, Germans, Basques, and New Englanders who were taken captive or who had deserted, and *métis*.

> In the continent's interior, French settlers cultivate relations with their Indian neighbors and enslave those they receive in exchange for goods while Spanish settlement in northern New Spain proceeds slowly.

As in the English colonies, slavery was an important institution in the French colonies, although it was not nearly as important on the mainland as it was in the French Caribbean. Few if any of the slaves in New France came from Africa. Rather, they were captive Indians who in the early 1700s constituted about 5 percent of the population. They worked as farmhands, stevedores, domestic servants, and assistants in craft and artisanal industries. In Montreal, half of all home-owning colonists came to hold at least one slave. In Louisiana, by contrast, most Indians successfully resisted enslavement, leading French plantations to import African slaves. By the 1720s, the colony had about fourteen

métis Offspring of a Native American woman and a European man in the colonial era, most common in seventeenth-century New France.

hundred enslaved Africans compared to about one hundred sixty Indian slaves, many of whom were women.

To govern their growing number of African slaves in Louisiana, in 1724, slaveholders adopted the **Code Noir**. This Black Code set minimum standards of conduct for masters so that slaves would have less desire to rebel. It ostensibly prevented masters from torturing their slaves, but it allowed planters to beat them with rods and whips. It prohibited intermarriage, denied slaves the right to appear in court, and mandated their instruction in Catholicism. The Black Code forbade masters from breaking up slave families by selling individuals. It also gave slaves the right to charge their masters with poor treatment. But there is no record of a slave bringing such a case. Few slaves, it seems, even knew of the Black Code's existence.

By 1731, the enslaved African population of the lower Mississippi Valley reached four thousand, meaning that there were more slaves than French colonists. Above New Orleans, slaves grew tobacco; below the city, they raised the **indigo plant** used in the production of dye. In New Orleans, slaves built levees, canals, and docks. Some became skilled artisans and dominated certain trades. Like the slaves of English Charles Town, New Orleans' slaves with free time hired themselves out as laborers. Some even bought their freedom.

In the frontier regions of New Spain, meanwhile, population growth was slow. Officials continued to rely on Catholic missions and military fortifications to secure New Spain's claims to its northern regions, where diseases eroded mission populations, and government officials increasingly saw missionaries as holdovers from the past. Remote pockets of Spanish settlement in New Mexico and parts of the Gulf Coast and Texas had no easy access to trade with the Atlantic world or even with each other and thus attracted few immigrants. News of the larger world arrived rarely and almost always in the form of government newsletters, bulletins, and edicts. The military and its forts were poorly staffed, badly organized, and inconsistently provisioned. By 1765, after eighty years of settlement, the population of New Mexico approached ten thousand, nearly a third of whom lived in and around El Paso, where they had remained after the Pueblo Revolt of 1680. Under Spanish law, slavery was illegal in New Mexico, and the colony had no African slaves. But Spanish residents throughout New Mexico often held Indian domestic servants and farmhands, whom they effectively treated as slaves.

Code Noir French code of 1724 intended to regulate slaves and masters in Louisiana; based on code issued by Louis XIV in 1685.

indigo plant Source of blue dye.

5-3

The Colonial Economy in the Atlantic Age

Joseph Van Aken, an Antwerp-born English painter, depicts here an elite family having tea in what was usually an elaborately staged social event. In this detail of the 1720 painting, *An English Family at Tea*, a servant woman pours as a manservant brings more tea and another guest to the party. In the first half of the eighteenth century, wealthy English colonists enjoyed regular tea parties, but so too did increasing numbers of the less affluent.

How does the artist portray this scene? What gender roles are demonstrated in this image? ▶

Tate, London/Art Resource, NY

A dynamic transatlantic economy widened the social gap between people at the top and at the bottom of the income scale. Planters and merchants enriched themselves, most often at the expense of common laborers and slaves. Income inequality increased as the economy grew, especially in urban areas. With their newfound wealth or because sugar- and caffeine-based commodities were so cheap, both the elite and the middling classes engaged in new forms of ritual and consumption. The wealthy enjoyed tea and liquors, clothing, and other finery. Others, in particular laborers, depended on sugar products for energy and on caffeine products in the form of tea and coffee for stimulation as they tried to keep up in an economy that demanded more work and offered less leisure time.

5-3a Economic Diversification and Growth

Across much of colonial America from 1700 to 1750, particularly in the English colonies, population growth accompanied the expansion of trade, and economic production became more diverse as settlers moved from subsistence farming to the production of staples and commodities for the commercial market. In New England, farmers began to produce food for large, distant markets, bringing higher profits and increasing uncertainty to their economic lives because they came to depend on overseas demand. The fish and lumber export industries employed thousands, and a large shipbuilding industry grew to supply the vessels needed to transport commodities to Europe or the Caribbean.

{ Diverse economies develop across colonial America.

Wheat and other grains remained central to the society and economy of the Middle Colonies. Increased production of grain and surplus production of fish, livestock, lumber, barrel staves, and other basic goods lifted the export economy. With this economic expansion, New York and Philadelphia surpassed Boston as the largest and most important centers of economic activity in British North America.

In the Chesapeake, the economy diversified beyond tobacco, which remained profitable for the largest planters but less so for others because the price of tobacco declined from overproduction. Increasingly, small-scale planters' families turned to the production of grains and other goods that were necessary to feed the region's expanding population. In South Carolina, even though rice cultivation dominated the export trade, the economy diversified as indigo grew in importance in the 1740s. North Carolina, like the Chesapeake, exported tobacco to England; it also produced naval stores, lumber, shingles, and barrel staves.

In New France, in the far northeast of the colony, inhabitants focused on fishing, whereas along the St. Lawrence, settlers farmed their extensive riverine plots and shipped their small surpluses to Montreal and Quebec. Isolated settlements of the interior, such as St. Louis and Des Moines, sustained themselves through fur trade with Indians.

In much of northern New Spain, settlers focused on their own survival more than the search for a staple export commodity. In New Mexico, merchants traded iron goods, firearms, horses, and mules to Plains Indians, who had long exchanged buffalo robes for cotton goods and corn produced by Pueblo Indians. The most lucrative trade item on the Great Plains remained Indian captives, especially young women, who were often taken on the Plains and then sold to the settlers of New Mexico.

5-3b Colonial Regulations and International Trade

England continued to pursue mercantilist policies with its colonies in North America. By 1720, the bureaucracy in the colonies dedicated to policing transatlantic commerce had expanded to twelve thousand men, who reported to the Board of Trade. But smugglers continued to evade capture and prosecution. Meanwhile, import merchants continued to oppose the Navigation Acts, believing that the policies increased their expenses and reduced their profits. The acts, however, did benefit the economy overall. They helped sustain the English navy, which reduced the risk of piracy, thereby allowing ships to travel with more goods and fewer arms. Furthermore, in the south, the acts promoted the production of indigo. Elsewhere they supported a booming shipping industry. The acts had little effect in the Middle Colonies, which largely produced goods not protected by the acts, such as fish, flour, and meat. In the South, those who produced staples such as tobacco, which could not be sent directly to foreign markets, attacked the acts as oppressive and damaging.

{ Mercantilist trade regulations shape the economy at the same time that consumer preferences remake patterns of consumption in the English colonies.

Of particular frustration to colonists were English laws that prevented or curtailed the production of certain goods. The Wool Act of 1699, the Hat Act of 1732, and the Iron Act of 1750 were all designed to protect England's economy by preventing the colonists from producing those goods. The Molasses Act of 1733 imposed a heavy tax on the importation of molasses from the French West Indies, which the colonists distilled to make rum. The goal was to protect British West Indies sugarcane growers against French competition. American colonists, however, insisted that the British West Indies alone could not produce enough molasses to meet their needs. Colonists bypassed the Molasses Act through smuggling, but it remained a source of conflict.

5-3c The Consumer Revolution in British North America

If the latter decades of the seventeenth century were marked by the increased production and consumption of tropical goods—tobacco, tea, chocolate, and sugar—the first half of the eighteenth century was characterized by a spike in the consumption of consumer goods manufactured in England. Small manufacturers produced more and more cloth, ceramics, cutlery, glassware, paper, and textiles in response to rising demand. People increasingly purchased goods that were prominently displayed in shop windows and widely advertised

{ The middling classes begin the consumption of imported goods.

in journals, magazines, and newspapers. In British North America, colonists took part in this consumer culture. Stores proliferated, and peddlers fanned out across the countryside as the simple and austere world of homespun cloth and wooden plates gave way to store-bought linens and tableware.

The goods that colonists consumed were not in themselves revolutionary, for they did not constitute technological breakthroughs in the way that the wheel, the compass, or the musket had. Rather, what was revolutionary about these goods was what they communicated about the people who purchased them.

In British North America, the traditional signs of prosperity, such as houses, land, and livestock, no longer effectively communicated social rank, especially in a society that was growing more urban and more commercial by the year. Moreover, in a society undergoing massive immigration and in which titles and ranks meant little, there was great desire for inexpensive and fashionable items that would be recognized immediately as indicators of social status. Ordinary men and women—not just the wealthy—began to buy consumer goods, including embroidered waistcoats, clay pipes, fancy snuff boxes, card tables, sets of carved chairs, china plates, and silver forks. Colonial women also bought more practical items, such as soap, cloth, candles, and clothing, which saved them the time and labor they otherwise would have devoted to producing themselves. Poorer folks, and even some slaves, tried to keep up as best they could.

To pay for what they wanted to consume, colonists produced and exported more tobacco, rice, indigo, and foodstuffs. They also took advantage of new forms of credit. For instance, the passage of the Tobacco Inspection Act of 1730 proved influential in the Chesapeake. It mandated that all tobacco exported from Virginia be inspected and stored at one of forty warehouses in the region. Planters sold their tobacco to the warehouses and in return received credits, which functioned as currency and could be used with local merchants. In the six years after the passage of the act, the quantity of British goods imported to Virginia and Maryland doubled. Similar forms of credit also emerged in the northern colonies at this time.

As this consumer revolution took hold, the value of colonial imports increased from 450,000 pounds to 1.5 million pounds per year, increasing the colonies' importance to England. In 1700, colonists consumed 10 percent of British exports, and by the 1770s, the figure was 37 percent.

5-3d The Refinement of the Colonial Elite

The expansion of trade increased the wealth and size of the colonial elite, and although many of these people were born in America, they started

{ The colonial elite increasingly style themselves after the upper classes in England.

to emulate European codes of genteel behavior. For the elite, gentility was a means of asserting cultural superiority and their growing interest in establishing the legitimacy of their institutions and political power.

The richest colonists adopted ostentatious lifestyles best symbolized by their homes. At the end of the seventeenth century, a small group of merchants in Boston and Philadelphia built grand houses in the fashionable **Georgian style**. Soon, similar houses were under construction across British North America. These houses were not only very large but boasted a ballroom or parlor, whose sole purpose was entertainment. They also typically had manicured gardens, where the genteel walked and conversed.

Within their houses, the genteel tried to build a world of order and beauty. They donned ruffled shirts, dined with fine silver, and moved about with studied grace. They hired teachers and tutors for their children, hoping to send them to college, something that had formerly been the province only of those destined for careers as clergymen. Most importantly, they steeped themselves in manuals of genteel comportment. As a boy of age ten or twelve, George Washington's tutor required him to copy some "110 Rules of Civility and Decent Behavior in Company and Conversation." Washington learned, "Bedew no man's face with Spittle by approaching him when you speak" and "In the Company of those of Higher Quality than yourself Speak not ti[ll] you are ask'd a Question then Stand upright put of[f] your hat and Answer in few words." Washington's firm mouth in portraits of him later in life reflected this early study of composure.

Side table and pair of spindle back chairs, Lancashire (oak)/English School (18th century)/Private Collection/Bridgeman Images

Carved Chairs These carved chairs were emblematic of the fine finished goods enjoyed by the affluent in British North America. ▲

Georgian style Architectural style popular in England and the colonies between 1720 and 1830 characterized by symmetrical two-story houses with a central entryway.

History without Borders

Piracy

Spanish shipping routes
- → Inbound
- → Outbound
- ■ Pirate stronghold
- ✶ Selected pirate raid

Territorial claims, ca. 1750
- British
- French
- Netherlands
- Portuguese
- Spanish

Notes:

1. Dutch privateer Pieter Pieterszoon Heyn, commanding a fleet of 31 ships, captured a Spanish silver treasure fleet of 16 ships in September 1628. Heyn's raid yielded more than 11 million guilders of silver, gold, and other booty, a sum that funded the Dutch army for eight months and yielded a 50% dividend to investors in the Dutch West Indian Compnay.

2. A small and rocky island, Tortuga became a base for pirates who fled Hispaniola after the arrival of Spanish settlers in the 1630s.

3. In the 1660s and early 1670s, Sir Henry Morgan used Port Royal as a base of operations for raids on the Spanish settlements of Portobello, Cartagena and Panamá City.

4. Due to its ideal location in the Spanish shipping lanes, New Providence became a major pirate stronghold, reportedly home to more than 1,000 English pirates by early 1700. Blackbeard was known to frequent its taverns.

The Golden Age of Piracy Pirate havens and pirate attacks were concentrated around the major shipping routes to and from Spain, especially where sea lanes narrowed and ships laden with treasure and merchandise proved vulnerable. ▲

Few economic activities are more lawless than piracy, which flourishes in the interstices between nations and on the open seas. The first half of the eighteenth century is often referred to as a "Golden Age of Piracy," for between 1700 and 1730, it experienced a booming industry that extended to most of the world's oceans. In this period, the famous pirate, Edward Teach, better known as Blackbeard, was most active. With the conclusion of the Queen Anne's War in 1713 and in 1714, the wider conflict of which it was part—the War of the Spanish Succession—thousands of sailors and ship captains found themselves unemployed. Many became pirates, and piracy expanded in the coasts of the Caribbean, the Atlantic of North America, West Africa, and the Indian Ocean.

Pirates of the era preyed on the growing transatlantic trade that kept

Granger, NYC — All rights reserved

Blackbeard the Pirate The details of Blackbeard's early life are murky. Most likely he was born into a respectable family in Bristol, England's second most important port. By the late 1690s, he was in the Caribbean and during Queen Anne's War (1701–1713) seems to have operated from Jamaica, where he served on board a ship that was engaged in "privateering," piracy sponsored by the English and against Spanish ships. ▲

Granger, NYC — All rights reserved

Black Bart Capt. Bartholomew Roberts, also known as "Black Bart," raises his sword to his two ships after capturing a fleet of eleven English, French, and Portuguese slave ships off the coast of Africa. ▲

the sea-lanes busy between Africa, the Caribbean, North America, and western Europe. In 1718, Blackbeard and his fleet blockaded Charles Town and ransacked nine ships that were awaiting entrance to the harbor. Such activities alarmed Virginia's governor, Alexander Spotswood, who dispatched two ships to track down Blackbeard. They found him anchored in an inlet in North Carolina, overpowered his men, and killed him. They severed his head from his body and hung it from the rigging.

As piracy took its toll, more nations, especially after the signing of the Treaty of Utrecht in 1714, began to increase the size of their navies in order to protect their merchant fleets. By the 1730s, the Golden Age of Piracy in the Atlantic was over. Nevertheless, piracy continued to offer opportunities to sailors and to create problems for government officials wherever there was a valuable and unprotected maritime trade. This was especially true in the Mediterranean, where pirates from the coast of North Africa (often referred to as *Barbary Pirates*) attacked Italy, Spain, and islands in the Mediterranean. Scholars estimate that between the sixteenth

and the nineteenth centuries, perhaps as many as 1 million European sailors were captured by Barbary Pirates and sold into slavery in North Africa. But after the 1720s, at least, piracy no longer hindered the expansion of global trade.

Critical Thinking Questions

▶ What events led to the rise and fall of piracy across the Atlantic?

▶ What was the life of a pirate like?

5-3e Inequality

The benefits of the expanding economy were not shared equally. Poverty was common in cities, where urban laborers often went unemployed or moved from job to job. Indentured servants struggled, and most lived in desperation. Elizabeth Sprigs, an indentured servant in a Maryland household, wrote her father in England that she worked day and night, was fed a meager ration of salty corn, and was "tied up and whipp'd." She slept wrapped "up in a Blanket . . . on the Ground," and begged her father to send her clothing as she was "almost naked" and had "no shoes nor stockings to wear."

Elizabeth Sprigs may have suffered more than most indentured servants, but few English women held wealth of their own, and few slaves and Native Americans had an opportunity to amass wealth in the first place. But white, property-holding men had chances for a reasonable income and more opportunity to advance than in England or continental Europe. Few free settlers seem to have been poor, and at least two-thirds of rural householders owned their own land by 1750.

On the mainland, white Southerners were the richest, largely because they held nearly twice as much land as the average landowner in other colonies and because they owned laborers who reproduced themselves. The landed elite—those controlling more than a thousand acres of land and holding at least ten slaves—controlled half of the wealth in the Chesapeake. Whites who could not afford slaves or land often had no choice but to settle in the interior, where the lack of roads made tobacco cultivation far less profitable. The distribution of land in New England, by contrast, was fairly egalitarian because of the custom of dividing land among heirs.

In the Middle Colonies, wealth became less evenly distributed as a small group of merchants amassed large fortunes. Roughly 20 percent of the population—mostly widows, children, and persons with infirmities—remained mired in poverty. In response, some merchants established almshouses and workhouses to care for the growing numbers of urban poor. Pennsylvania offered easy land for those who could afford their own passage to America, but it also had the largest number of indentured servants.

In British North America outside of regions dominated by plantations, roughly 70 percent of land was worked by those who owned it. In contrast, land ownership in New France, and therefore wealth, was far less equitably distributed. Land was first granted to a *seigneur*, a lord, who then "sold" small portions of the property to settlers. Settlers, however, never truly owned the land. Rather, they had to provide roughly 8 to 10 percent of their annual income, in the form of produce, to the *seigneur*. Under this system, wealth became concentrated among a small number of *seigneurs* who spent their riches on fineries imported from France, not goods produced in the colony.

> Inequality is a defining feature of colonial America.

5-4
Imperial Rivalries, Territorial Expansion, and Border Warfare

This painting, attributed to José de Páez, ca. 1765, shows a Franciscan view of the 1758 destruction of Mission San Sabá, in Texas. Franciscans venerated missionaries who were killed in Indian rebellions, believing that their deaths and the miracles that might follow would attract Indian converts.

How does the artist portray the Indians' attack on the mission? What are the central images in this dramatic rendering? ▶

DeAgostini/Getty Images

Across the first half of the eighteenth century, wars over European succession and trade roiled the margins of American colonies. The War of the Spanish Succession prompted Queen Anne's War in the colonies, pitting England against Spain and France and leading to frontier warfare across northern New England. Farther south, the war sparked conflicts between English Carolinians and Spanish Floridians. Soon thereafter, the War of the Quadruple Alliance—pitting Spain against France, England, Holland, and Austria—prompted the French and Spanish to spar over Texas and the Gulf Coast. Later disputes led England to charter the colony of Georgia to protect the Carolinas from incursions from Spanish Florida. Amid all of this territorial jockeying, the French formally established

New Orleans as an anchor to their growing ambitions in the lower Mississippi River Valley. The War of the Austrian Succession brought renewed violence to some of the colonies. And later, on the other side of the continent, Russian fur hunters ventured down the Pacific Coast, one factor that led Spain to establish outposts in Alta California. More often than not, Indian peoples, who had already been pushed to the edges of European settlement, saw their own fortunes decline as they became pawns in European disputes or impoverished when trading partnerships collapsed in war.

☞ As you read, consider the relationship between European conflicts and those that erupted in the colonies. How did these wars reshape colonial America?

5-4a War on the Northern Frontier

The peace that England and France had agreed to in 1697, ending King William's War, was brief. The eighteenth century opened with a war that quickly engulfed the colonies (see Table 5.5). The **War of the Spanish Succession** (1701–1714) began when the king of Spain, Carlos II, died heirless. Louis XIV of France put forward his own grandson, Philip, as heir to the Spanish throne. Leopold, the Holy Roman Emperor, countered with his own son, Charles. England's Queen Anne, fearing the unified might of Spain and France if Philip became king of Spain, backed Charles. The conflict that resulted was known in the colonies as **Queen Anne's War**. Unlike King William's War, which ended in a stalemate, England won, at least in Europe, seizing territory from both Spain and France and blocking the feared unification of the two monarchies.

In North America, however, the English did not fare so well. Because the British crown's priorities were in Europe, not the colonies, an English fleet intended to attack the French by

{ Conflicts that begin in Europe bring violence to the northern frontier.

Etow Oh Koam, King of the River Nations

Sa Ga Yeath Qua Pieth Ton, King of the Maguas

No Nee Yeath Tan no Ton, King of the Generath

Tac Yec Neen Ho Gar Ton, Emperor of the Six Nations

The Four Indian Kings In 1710, leading English colonists, hoping to lure the Iroquois out of neutrality and gain added English support for the war, organized a delegation of four "Iroquois Kings," who traveled to England for an audience with Queen Anne. They were in fact not kings or even noted leaders, and one was a Mohican. But they were a sensation in London and boosted Parliamentary support for an all-out offensive against the French. ▲ Etow Oh Koam, King of the River Nations, 1710 (oil on canvas), Verelst, Johannes or Jan (b.1648–fl.1719)/Private Collection/The Bridgeman Art Library; (top left) Sa Ga Yeath Qua Pieth Ton, King of the Maguas, 1710 (oil on canvas), Verelst, Johannes or Jan (b.1648–fl.1719)/Private Collection/The Bridgeman Art Library; (top right) No Nee Yeath Tan no Ton, King of the Generath, 1710 (oil on canvas), Verelst, Johannes or Jan (b.1648–fl.1719)/Private Collection/The Bridgeman Art Library; (bottom left) Tac Yec Neen Ho Gar Ton, Emperor of the Six Nations, 1710 (oil on canvas), Verelst, Johannes or Jan (b.1648–fl.1719)/Private Collection / Bridgeman Images (bottom right)

Table 5.5 The Intercolonial Wars, 1690–1748

Across much of the late colonial period, wars on the continent sparked wars in the Americas. These related conflicts often carried different names.

	War's Name in North American Colonies	Corresponding War in Europe	Nations Involved
1689–1697	King William's War	Nine Years' War	E, H vs. F, S
1702–1713	Queen Anne's War	War of the Spanish Succession	E, H, A vs. F, S
1718–1720	War of the Quadruple Alliance		S vs. F, E, H, A
1739–1748	King George's War	War of the Austrian Succession	E, H, A, vs. F, S, P

E = England; H = Holland; F = France; S = Spain; A = Austria; P = Prussia

War of the Spanish Succession European conflict of 1701–1713 triggered by the death in 1700 of the infirm and childless King Charles II of Spain. See also Queen Anne's War.

Queen Anne's War Conflict in North America that emerged from Europe's War of the Spanish Succession.

sailing up the St. Lawrence was twice diverted to other war fronts. Not until 1710 did the English send warships to Boston. Meanwhile, French troops and their Abenaki allies besieged New England frontier towns. The war led to hundreds of English captives being taken to New France, where they were adopted, sold into slavery, or used as bargaining chips in negotiations.

In the spring of 1711, England launched its largest invasion yet in the New World. It consisted of fourteen battle ships and some eight thousand men. Hundreds of Iroquois took part. Yet, as the ships made their way up the St. Lawrence River, fog obscured their passage and several ran aground, killing some nine hundred Englishmen. To the shock of the Iroquois, who had agreed to give up their neutrality to fight with them, the English abandoned the battle and sailed home.

The war ended in 1713, when the **Treaty of Utrecht** resulted in the Bourbon Philip V being crowned as king of Spain. But it also required him to renounce any claim to the French throne, thereby preserving the balance of power in Europe. In the settlement, France gave Acadia, Newfoundland, and the Hudson Bay to England, and Spain agreed to give up its monopoly over the transport and sale of slaves to Spanish colonies.

In 1740, during the **War of the Austrian Succession**, known in British North America as **King George's War**, Britain allied with Austria against much of Europe, and the English again tried to conquer New France. In 1745, with the assistance of some four thousand volunteers from New England and a British naval squadron, Massachusetts governor William Shirley took the French fort at Louisburg in the Gulf of St. Lawrence. After nearly half a century of attempting to dislodge the French from Canada, the English colonists were thrilled with their victory. They were then shocked when the English returned the fort to France in the 1748 peace of Aix la Chapelle, which ended the conflict. By relinquishing the fort, the English regained lands that the French had taken from them in India and Flanders. Once again, the English colonists realized that imperial priorities lay elsewhere.

5-4b Conflict on the Southern Borderlands

{ France and Spain jockey for territory in the South in wars originating in Europe.

Farther south, wars and new alliances repeatedly remade international boundaries along an arc of land stretching from Texas to the Carolinas

(see Map 5.4). France had established forts on Biloxi Bay and the Mississippi River in 1699 and had laid claim to Louisiana, all in Spanish territory. But because of the alliance between Spain and France during Queen Anne's war, Spain did not destroy the French settlements. France did little to develop Louisiana other than establishing trade relations with the local Choctaws, Chickasaws, Alabamans, and Caddos.

After the Treaty of Utrecht, Spain remained wary of French intentions along the Gulf Coast. The arrival in 1714 of the French trader Saint-Denis at the Spanish Mission San Juan Bautista, just south of the Río Grande, prompted Spain to reoccupy Texas. Meanwhile, the French established a trading post at Natchitoches, creating a western boundary between French Louisiana and Spanish Texas. To ensure that the French would move no farther west, the Spaniards established two more missions among the Caddo tribe. In 1718, the new governor of Texas, Martín de Alarcón, established a presidio, San Antonio de Béjar (whose chapel would later be known as the *Alamo*), and the *villa* of San Antonio along the San Antonio River.

In 1718–1720, in the **War of the Quadruple Alliance**, Spain hoped to destroy Charles Town but instead lost Pensacola in a surprise attack by the French. Spain, fearing a French thrust from Louisiana into Texas, relocated soldiers and missionaries to San Antonio. And in 1721, Spanish soldiers evicted the French from east Texas and established a fort near Natchitoches. By 1727, however, the Spanish abandoned its missions in east Texas, which were difficult to provision.

Meanwhile, Spanish troubles on the southern Great Plains increased when Pawnees, Wichitas, and Comanches, who already had large supplies of Spanish horses, received guns from the French. Horses had first reached the Plains in the Spanish *entradas* of the sixteenth century, but no significant herds had remained behind after the Spaniards departed. Spanish mustangs eventually spread across northern New Spain and reached the southern Great Plains by the early eighteenth century. In the 1730s, as their horse herds grew, the Comanches made the conversion to full-blown equestrianism with remarkable speed.

In 1740, during King George's War, South Carolinians invaded Florida, taking the smaller posts of northern Spanish Florida, yet failed to conquer St. Augustine. Spain then retaliated by attacking coastal Georgia, which the English were able to defend. After the war's conclusion, Spanish missionaries abandoned Florida, unable to win converts among Indians who preferred English trade goods.

In the 1740s and 1750s, the Comanches pushed the Apaches from the Northern Great Plains. To the Spanish, the southern Great Plains became known as the *Comanchería*. In 1757, to protect the San Antonio missions, bring the Apaches into the Spanish fold, and keep the Comanches at bay, the Spanish established another fort and mission at San Sabá in central Texas. In March 1758, Comanche raiders destroyed the mission, blocking a Spanish–Apache alliance and securing their control of the southern Great Plains.

Treaty of Utrecht Agreement concluding War of the Spanish Succession in 1713 that confirmed Philip as king of Spain with his renunciation of the French throne.

War of the Austrian Succession European conflict of 1740–1748 over the succession to the throne of the Holy Roman Empire.

King George's War Name in North America given to Europe's War of the Austrian Succession.

War of the Quadruple Alliance European conflict over terms of Treaty of Utrecht and territories in Italy.

Comanchería Region of today's New Mexico, west Texas, and adjacent areas occupied by the Comanches once they had mastered equestrianship.

Map 5.4 European Expansion across Colonial America to 1750 By the middle of the eighteenth century, Spain, France, and England all had extensive claims to much of North America. Spain sought to control the region stretching from Florida to Baja California with missions and forts; France maintained a sprawling fur trading empire across the American interior; and England had established populous settlements from Georgia to Maine. ▲

5-4c European Expansion and the Pacific Coast

> Russian and Spanish settle on the Pacific Coast.

With the major European nations warring over territory and trade in North America, the Russian crown hoped to establish its own power in Europe through the exploration of the Northern Pacific. In 1741, Danish mariner Vitus Bering and Russian officer Alexei Chirikov led an expedition that sailed east from Siberia. After a harrowing winter that killed Bering and many of his men, the survivors returned to Russia carrying some nine hundred sea otter pelts, which commanded huge prices in China. In subsequent years, Russia launched more expeditions to hunt otter, seals, and sea lions. These voyages lasted years and often proved fatal to many of those who staffed them. Moreover, the voyages devastated the indigenous people they encountered.

In 1781, Russian merchants organized the **Russian-American Company** to establish fur-trading colonies on the North Pacific Coast. Three years later, the company founded Russia's first permanent settlement east of Siberia on Kodiak Island. A decade later, more than three hundred thirty colonists were on the island, all of them men. The Russian colonial venture remained the most limited European enterprise in North America, yet it did prompt Spain to defend Alta California against Russian encroachment.

In 1765, largely as a result of the new Russian presence to the north, José de Gálvez, a high-ranking official who King Carlos III had sent to New Spain to inspect the Spanish colonies, ordered the settlement of Alta California. In 1769, Gálvez sent five expeditions to Alta California, three by sea and two by land. They headed for the port of Monterey to take possession of the province for Spain. However, these expeditions were plagued by illness, shortages of food, and the inability to find Monterey, which they did not locate until 1770.

Alta California developed along the same trajectory as other Spanish territories, with the establishment of missions serving as the foundation for later settlements. Leading

Russian-American Company
Russian joint-stock company that received royal monopoly in 1799 to settle and hunt fur-bearing animals from the Aleutian Islands to today's Alta California.

Global Americans

Granger, NYC — All rights reserved

Missionaries embodied the international nature of the colonial encounter between Indians and Europeans, and few more than Father **Junípero Serra**. Serra was born on the Spanish Mediterranean island of Mallorca in 1713. Raised in a small agricultural village, he then studied for the priesthood in Palma, the island's capital and a center of Catholicism in the western Mediterranean. At age thirty-five, Serra gave up a professorship to become a missionary in New Spain. He worked for eight years organizing missions north of Mexico, where he also was an investigator for the Mexican Inquisition. He then spent another decade traveling around the countryside leading popular religious revivals. After a short stint as an administrator of missions in Baja California, Serra went north to Alta California in 1769 when he was 56 years old. There he spearheaded the establishment of Franciscan missions, starting at San Diego. A tireless advocate of the missions, he walked thousands of miles over frontier trails and roads seeking to spread the gospel. Serra was a staunch defender of the use of corporal punishment and believed that Indians needed to take up European modes of agriculture. His commitment to his faith was extraordinary, although the effects of his and other missionaries' actions were often disastrous for Indians. In 2015, Pope Francis canonized Junípero Serra, calling him a "founding father" and "the evangelizer of the Pacific Coast."

the missionaries into Alta California was Father Junípero Serra, a zealous Franciscan. The military, which depended on the missions for basic foodstuffs, established forts at San Diego (1769), Monterey (1770), San Francisco (1776), and Santa Barbara (1782) and the agricultural settlements of San José (1777) and Los Angeles (1781).

The missions proved as deadly to Alta California Indians as they had to the Wendats and other Indians across colonial America. In 1820, the Franciscan overseeing the Alta California missions wrote that the missionaries found themselves "with a people miserable and sick, [and] with rapid depopulation of *rancherías* [villages] which with profound horror fills the cemeteries." By the mid-1830s, the Franciscans had baptized more than eighty thousand Indians, but almost sixty thousand had died.

5-5

Politics, Religion, and Daily Life

This 1747 painting captures an elite New England family, that of the artist, John Greenwood. Note the basket of needlework and the flame stitch canvas work on the table that suggest the accomplishments of the women. The book on the middle of the table in the painting's center hints at their literacy.

As you examine this painting, what sense do you get of these women's lives, circumstances, and responsibilities? ▶

> Go to MindTap® to practice history with the Chapter 5 **Primary Source Writing Activity: Daily Life in the Colonial Regions.** Read and view primary sources and respond to a writing prompt.

The Greenwood-Lee Family, c.1747 (oil on canvas), Greenwood, John (1727–92)/ Museum of Fine Arts, Boston, Massachusetts, USA/Bequest of Henry Lee Shattuck in memory of the late Morris Gray/Bridgeman Images

Colonial society in North America by 1750 was firmly rooted in beliefs and practices that were European in form but everywhere shaped by local attitudes, immigrant peoples, colonial circumstances, and new intellectual currents and religious practices. In their politics, colonists in British North America subscribed to English notions of liberty and power and deferred to their betters but enjoyed far more access to freedom and a free press than their counterparts in England. In their religious beliefs, colonists in New England looked back to an idealized Puritan past yet were at the same time changed by the circulation of contemporary religious views and practices. Women, the illiterate, and African Americans played an increasing role in affairs of religion. Yet on the whole, the patriarchal organization of society persisted, and gender roles were slow to change despite the efforts of those who challenged them. African Americans suffered enslavement and, even if free, terrible indignities. Daily life in the colonial regions of New France and New Spain continued apace but—with the exception of New Orleans—these regions were not fully integrated into the Atlantic economy. In these areas, patriarchy and Catholicism structured daily life, population increased slowly, and economies remained local.

☞ As you read, consider how gender and wealth shaped peoples' lives. How did different colonial communities reflect them?

Library of Congress. William Harvey

Image of Veins from Harvey's *Exercitatio Anatomica de Motu Cordis et Sanguinis in Animalibus* By using the scientific method, William Harvey established the circulation of the blood throughout the human body. His findings were first published in an illustrated volume in 1628. ▲

5-5a The Enlightenment in Europe and America

In the late seventeenth century, many vestiges of the medieval worldview gave way in the face of the Scientific Revolution. On a foundation of breakthroughs made by earlier Western, Muslim, and Asian thinkers, European scientists overturned the belief that the earth was at the center of the cosmos, discovered the fundamental laws of the universe, and developed more accurate understandings of the human body. Galileo Galilei (1564–1642) proved that the sun was the center of the solar system, which in turn was just a small part of an enormous galaxy. In his *Mathematical Principles of Natural Philosophy* (1687), Sir Isaac Newton used the scientific method and his own discovery of gravity to explain for the first time the movements of the seas, the moon, planets, and stars. William Harvey (1578–1657) discovered that blood circulates through the body and determined how the heart functions. These and other discoveries allowed Europeans in the century after 1650 to create more accurate clocks, invent the modern blast furnace, develop basic steam engines, build new and more efficient spinning machines, and take the first steps to the science of medicine.

> New intellectual currents, based on previous ideas, reshape the thoughts of many colonists.

Moreover, these developments in the natural and human sciences helped to launch a philosophical movement known as the Enlightenment, which rejected many traditional beliefs, including religious ideas, and venerated human reason as the only means to understand the world and improve society. Although they worked in many different fields, Enlightenment thinkers shared a common desire to substitute the search for objective truth for a trust in religious faith. Because of their beliefs and writings, the idea of human free will began to replace the notion that human destiny was determined by God.

In the Americas, Enlightenment ideas first gained acceptance in the British colonies. Anglicans and some other religious groups welcomed the writings of Newton and the political philosopher John Locke and attacked Puritan churches and their emphasis on Calvinist notions of predestination. Benjamin Franklin (1706–1790) was the quintessential Enlightenment figure in America. He combined an interest in science with a belief that human reason could improve the lot of mankind. Franklin was a printer, a politician, a scientific investigator, a humorist, and an autobiographer. He was also a **Deist**, believing that God had created the universe but no longer intervened in human affairs. With little more than a kite, he conducted a famous experiment proving that lightning and electricity were one in the same.

Deism Belief that a supreme being had created the world that was run by natural laws rather than supernatural interventions.

Great Awakening Mid-eighteenth century religious revival in Great Britain and British North America.

In New Spain, the Catholic Church, the Inquisition, and the universities rejected the new ways of thinking. As a result, the Enlightenment did not gain traction in the colony until the end of the century.

5-5b The Great Awakening in British North America

During the mid-eighteenth century, a series of religious upheavals known as the **Great Awakening** swept through England and British North America. It was a reaction to the waning of orthodox Calvinist belief in the colonies and the rise of Enlightenment rationalism and Deism. The revival spread through existing transportation and commercial networks and was

> Religious revivals spread across British North America.

The Reverend Mr Samson Occom, engraved by Jonathan Spilsbury, 1768 (mezzotint), Chamberlin, Mason (1727–87) (after)/Private Collection/© Michael Graham-Stewart/Bridgeman Images

Global Americans During the colonial period, some Indians were brought to Europe as captives. Others, like Pocahontas, went out of curiosity and to represent their people. **Samson Occom**, a Mohegan preacher from New England, crossed the Atlantic to raise money for an Indian school in his homeland. Born in the early 1720s, Occom was exposed to Christianity during the Great Awakening, and he began to study for the ministry under the leading Protestant missionary, Eleazer Wheelock. Exceptionally gifted, Occom learned to read and write English and mastered Greek, Latin, and Hebrew. He was ordained in 1759, and in 1765, he traveled throughout the southern colonies with George Whitefield, one of the leaders of the Great Awakening who was then on his sixth preaching tour of British North America. Later that year, Occom traveled to England on his own preaching tour. Over the next two years, he delivered more than three hundred sermons in the British Isles and helped raise more than £12,000 for his cause. Occom achieved such fame on this trip that the University of Edinburgh offered him an honorary degree, which modesty led him to decline. When Occom returned home, he was shocked to learn that Wheelock had not fulfilled his promise to care for his wife and children but had abandoned them. Occom spent the remainder of his life as a teacher and preacher, and he is widely considered to be the first Native American to publish his own writings. He died in 1792, having not only straddled Indian and European worlds but also ventured across the Atlantic and throughout the colonies.

facilitated by newspapers, other printed materials, and new forms of marketing. No similar revival occurred in New France and New Spain, where Catholic missionaries and parish priests enforced the observance of Catholic rituals, and where, as a result, the Enlightenment had less impact.

The Great Awakening is most closely associated with three Protestant preachers: Jonathan Edwards (1703–1758), George Whitefield (1714–1770), and Gilbert Tennant (1703–1764). In the colonies, the revival began in the mid-1730s in Jonathan Edwards's congregation in Northampton, Massachusetts. He found it alarming that his congregants believed that humans were not innately sinful and could gain salvation by divining the will of God. In response, he preached highly emotional sermons rooted in orthodox Calvinist principles of the arbitrariness of predestination and the horrors of hell. He also urged that only by surrendering to God's will and reforming their behavior could individuals achieve salvation and heavenly joy. Edwards believed that "scarcely a single person in the whole town" was left untouched by the revival and that his emotional preaching style was the reason.

Meanwhile, George Whitefield, a traveling minister from England, became the movement's leading figure, connecting various revivals across the colonies and inspiring a truly broad religious movement. Along with John Wesley (1703–1791), Whitefield was one of the founders of Methodism, an evangelical form of Protestantism that believed in itinerant preaching by unordained ministers and was particularly devoted to salvation of the poor and common folk. Perhaps the most powerful public speaker of his day, Whitefield spoke before an estimated thirty thousand gatherings in his career, often in front of tens of thousands of people. He made fifteen tours of Scotland, three of Ireland, and seven of the North American colonies between 1739 and 1741. As the cost of printing materials dropped, Whitefield was able to publish his

Library of Congress Prints and Photographs Division[LC-US262–108255]

Cartoon Lampooning George Whitefield, 1763 Preacher George Whitefield was among the most recognizable figures in eighteenth-century British North America. His charismatic and dramatic preaching drew crowds, admiration, and derision, as shown in this cartoon. ▲

sermons in all the colonies and use newspapers to advertise his upcoming visits. Although he denounced the growing consumerism of his age, he advertised widely in print and offered quantity discounts, prepayment incentives, and home delivery of his materials—all inventions of the consumer revolution. Whitefield was so prolific that American printers, the most prominent of whom was Ben Franklin, produced some eighty thousand copies of Whitefield's works.

Whitefield preached discipline, morality, and social harmony, but New England preachers such as Gilbert Tennent radicalized the conservative religious movement by attacking the established clergy as passionless. Itinerant preachers such as Tennent offered alternatives to the bland palate of religion often provided by local ministers. As a result of their work, once-peaceful congregations became engulfed in disputes between "Old Lights"—orthodox clerics—and "New Lights"—evangelicals— over the religious fitness of their ministers.

The overall impact of the Great Awakening went far beyond debates over ministerial authority. Lay preachers—often women and even Native Americans— shattered elite white men's hold on religious speech. With a new set of preachers coming to the fore, many people felt liberated from the belief that their destinies were tied to the beliefs of their social superiors. The upheavals of the Great Awakening weakened and recast the bonds between individuals, families, communities, and society.

5-5c English Liberty and Liberalism in the Eighteenth Century

The Enlightenment influenced political theorists in England, who came to believe they had perfected the art of politics and governance. They conceived of three forms of government: monarchy (the rule of one), aristocracy (the rule of a few), and democracy (the rule of many or all). These thinkers believed that these forms could degenerate respectively into tyranny, oligarchy, or mob rule, and they argued that a stable government included elements of each form, balancing them within a single constitution. Many believed that England had achieved its great power through the establishment of a **mixed and balanced government** after the Glorious Revolution. In England, the monarchy was represented in the figure of the king, aristocracy in the House of Lords, and democracy in the House of Commons. The crown executed the law but was checked by courts and controlled by aristocratic and popular elements in Parliament that also restrained one another.

The concept of **liberty** occupied the center of English political identity during the eighteenth century even if the presence of slavery within the empire revealed that it did

> The English develop very precise ideas about politics and rights in the eighteenth century.

not extend to all. For the English, liberty meant not only the rights they enjoyed under the English Constitution but also, more generally, the right to resist arbitrary government. The English by 1700 had come to believe passionately that liberty and power were always in conflict. Thus, it was necessary, the English believed, for the rule of law to mediate between the contending forces of power and liberty and for the laws themselves to have been approved by representatives elected by the people themselves. Not all English people believed that the system worked. Many **radical Whigs**, notably John Trenchard and Thomas Gordon, asserted that the crown, through patronage, bribes, and collusion, had gained control over the English government and threatened to deny Englishmen their proper liberty. This view was widely accepted in the colonies by an elite who was suspicious of English imperial objectives and concerned about England's rising debt and costly military.

In addition to liberty, the English believed that **liberalism** was crucial to individual freedom. In this respect, no thinker was more important than John Locke, author of *Two Treatises of Government*, which was published in 1689 but did not achieve a wide readership until the first half of the eighteenth century. Locke dismissed the idea that governments were divinely sanctioned and that they, like families, had to be governed by authoritarian fathers. He argued that government existed as a social contract between the people and their rulers. Men surrendered some liberty to their rulers in return for the protections of the rule of law. But the people always retained their natural rights, and, according to Locke, a government that broke the social contract could be overthrown, by violence if necessary.

5-5d Politics and Power in the Colonies

In British North America in particular, politics was the province of white men. Only those who had property could vote, but because of the widespread availability of land, between 50 and 80 percent of adult white males were eligible. This was far more than the 5 percent who held the privilege in Britain at that time. Colonial politics, however, were anything but democratic. In many of the colonies, Jews, Catholics, Baptists, and Quakers could not vote. Some free blacks who held land could vote but

> The well-established governors and upper houses of the colonial assemblies lose power to the rising lower assemblies.

mixed and balanced government Form of government that integrates elements of democracy, aristocracy, and monarchy.

liberty Right recognized under the British Constitution to resist arbitrary government as understood by eighteenth-century Britons; the antithesis of power.

radical Whigs English political commentators who feared moral decay in English society and the royal encroachment on the powers of Parliament.

liberalism English belief that government was a social contract entered into freely between the people and their chosen representatives and rulers.

most lost the right as the eighteenth century progressed. A small number of women, usually propertied widows, voted in New England. Indians were denied the right to vote everywhere. And even the white men who voted often did so in ways that were not fully independent. **Deference** was common in all colonies, particularly in the South. In the Chesapeake, political power became concentrated in the elite planters, who built towns and colleges and were only marginally responsive to the people. Leading families also tended to intermarry so that an ever-smaller number of families controlled society. Over time, disadvantaged whites were cut off from power.

Throughout the first half of the eighteenth century, England was preoccupied with wars in Europe and managing its commercial empire and thus devoted little energy to governing the colonies. In this period of "salutary neglect," the colonies developed their own systems of governance. By 1700, nearly all the colonies had a governor, a lower house, and an upper house. Colonial governors, who were largely selected by officials in England, were quite powerful. They advised on judicial appointments, vetoed legislation in the upper houses, and dissolved assemblies or simply denied them the right to meet. But soon enough, colonial governors lost power to the lower assemblies as colonists fought back, inspired by England's own theories about the proper functioning of politics. New assemblies of colonists acted as if they were their own House of Commons. They asserted control over tax legislation, the militia, and, at times, the governor's salary. When the governors, their councils, and the Upper Houses objected, their opponents saw threats to liberty and the onset of tyranny, as predicted by the radical Whigs.

In New France, politics and governance reflected the institutions of the home country: an absolutist monarchy backed by an army but without a parliament. Only the king's sense of obligation to his people tempered his ultimate authority. To govern New France, the king appointed three officials. The most powerful was the governor-general, but just below him was the intendant who controlled finances and much of the daily administration of the colony. Both had to respect the bishop, who was in charge of parish priests and wielded enormous moral authority. They shared power with a crown-appointed council composed of five to seven *seigneurs*, the largest landholders.

New Spain boasted a large bureaucracy, but on the frontier, from Alta California to Florida, there was strict oversight by colonial governors but no elected legislatures. Spanish governors presented themselves as impartial judges, but most were absolutists who looked to profit from their offices. In the remote corners of northern New Spain, state authority was checked only by Catholic missionaries and their powerful leaders. The locus of local political power in New Spain's communities was the town council, which was not a democratic forum but rather an avenue for local elites to carry out their will.

5-5e The Press and Political Culture

In the rural areas of British North America, formal politics intruded on daily life only during elections, but in cities such as Boston, New York, and Philadelphia, men interested in discussing and debating politics formed clubs and associations that met regularly. In 1727, Benjamin Franklin created a weekly club, the Junto. Wealthy men usually founded these societies, but the less affluent created their own, too, meeting in coffee houses and taverns. All of these clubs helped create an increasingly informed citizenry, a process also advanced through the creation of the first circulating libraries in colonial America and the expansion of newspaper culture. Franklin established the first of these, the Library Company of Philadelphia, in 1731. By 1740, thirteen colonial newspapers were published in the colonies, and they were increasingly affordable to an expanding literate populace.

> Literacy, politics, and freedom of the press emerge in the English colonies.

Although the right to freely express one's ideas in most cases extended to legislators so that they could represent their constituents and express their views without fear of reprisal, this right was not afforded to ordinary citizens or publishers under the British Constitution. Similarly, freedom of the press was not guaranteed by law and was discouraged by local assemblies, who feared that the public would be swayed by printed materials, which could be inaccurate. Although the government could not censor printed materials, authors and publishers could be prosecuted for defaming government officials.

In 1734, for example, the New York government jailed newspaper editor John Peter Zenger and charged him with seditious libel for writing in his paper, *The New York Daily*, that Governor William Cosby was a corrupt tyrant. Andrew Hamilton, a lawyer from Philadelphia, rose to Zenger's defense, claiming that Zenger's allegations about Cosby were true and therefore could not constitute seditious libel. The jury sided with Zenger, declaring him not guilty and freeing him from jail. The **Zenger case** established the right of the colonial press to criticize the government, decreed that the truth cannot be considered defamatory, and suggested that future prosecutions of this sort would be hard to win.

In comparison, in neither New France nor the distant corners of Spanish America did movements for freedom of expression emerge. Spanish and French officials censored printed materials, but these mostly consisted, in the first place, of religious texts and legal manuals. The size and distance of Spain's colonial empire also worked against the spread of ideas and the creation of a shared political

---

deference Respect or esteem granted to an elder or a social superior.

Zenger case Landmark New York libel case of 1735 that resulted in protections for free expression in printed materials.

culture. New Spain spanned some 5 million square miles, and few of its distant colonies were connected by trade. In comparison, the thirteen English mainland colonies encompassed only about 322,000 square miles and inter-colonial trade was robust.

5-5f Patriarchy and Gender Roles

Martin Luther, the founder of Protestantism, reflected early modern beliefs about the abilities of women when he stated that "woman is a different animal to man, not only having different members, but also being far weaker in intellect . . . she . . . does not equal the dignity and glory of the male." From these misogynistic ideas, rooted in scripture and embedded in law, flowed a set of patriarchal beliefs that shaped society and granted men formal powers over women and children. Compared to women, men were seen as more able to control themselves. Women were viewed as weak and vulnerable and thus likely to succumb to sexual or demonic temptation.

{ Traditional roles and institutions dominate life in colonial America.

In British North America, women could not hold public office, serve in the military, or train in a profession. Unmarried white women above the age of eighteen and widowed women had a few limited rights: They could sue and be sued, transfer property, and write wills. But once married, a woman—and nearly all women in the colonies eventually married—could not transfer property, enter into a contract, initiate a lawsuit, or make a will without the consent of her husband. According to William Blackstone, the most important interpreter of English law, marriage meant that the husband and wife were considered one person. A married woman's state was called *coverture*, in that it was under the "cover" or protection of "her husband, her baron or lord," that "she performs everything."

Women's work responsibilities varied across class, region, and season, but throughout colonial America, women bore the greatest responsibility for tending the home fire, preparing meals, rearing children, baking bread, making cheese, carrying water and waste, spinning wool, sewing, cleaning and ironing clothes, slaughtering pigs and chickens, brewing beer, and working in the household garden. In urban areas, women spent more time in marketplace exchanges than in domestic production, but no matter where they lived, they were responsible for their family's medical care and basic education.

Most men, meanwhile, performed heavy domestic labor, maintaining structures and buildings, tending to animals, producing crops, and managing lands. In urban areas, some worked as artisans, craftsmen, or common laborers or as lawyers, merchants, or ministers. Men were expected to bring their sons into their line of work, teaching them their trade just as women were to teach their daughters how to serve their husbands and care for their families. In Protestant New England, girls and boys were taught to read and write so they could study the Bible. In the Chesapeake and the Carolinas, rates of literacy were lower except among the male children of planters. In Catholic New France and New Spain, where literacy and religious practice did not go hand in hand, few boys and fewer girls attained literacy.

5-5g Sexuality, Marriage, and Reproduction

Because there were few forms of reliable contraception and because families needed children for labor, a white woman in colonial America typically had a child every two to two-and-a-half years. Women gave birth at home under the care of female relatives and a midwife. By and large, white families were healthy and grew quickly in size with most women bearing six or seven children during their lives.

{ Conservative notions about marriage and sexuality structure life across colonial America.

Throughout colonial America, as in Europe, infant mortality (death in the first year of life) occurred in between 15 and 25 percent of births although that figure could reach 40 percent during epidemics. Thus, parents chose not to immediately attach themselves to their children and often treated boys and girls similarly at first, waiting until they were six or seven to dress and raise them in gender-specific ways.

Across colonial America, sex between unmarried persons was forbidden by law but common in practice. In Virginia and Maryland, where laws of indentured servitude prevented women from marrying, as many as one in five servant women became pregnant out of wedlock. And in New England, one in three brides was pregnant at the time of marriage. According to the laws across the British colonies, if the offending couple did not become engaged, they could be jailed for three days, whipped, and fined. If the couple were engaged, however, the fine would be halved.

In the British colonies, adultery was seen as sinful and a threat to society and thus was grounds for divorce and punishment by death. The death sentence, however, was hardly ever imposed. Adulterers were fined, jailed, placed in the stocks, whipped, branded, or forced to wear signs indicating their crime. In Catholic New Spain, many Hispanic men believed that they could enhance their honor by protecting the sexual purity of their female relatives, especially their wives and daughters. Thus, Hispanic wives and daughters in New Spain often lived in seclusion at the insistence of their husbands, fathers, and brothers.

The response to all forms of nonheterosexual relations was general revulsion. Male homosexuality was deemed a capital offense, but female homosexuality was never even acknowledged in the criminal codes of British North America. Advice books suggested it could be fatal.

Reproductive knowledge and health were largely the concern of women because they stood to be most affected by sex. Ignorance about the biology of human sexuality was widespread, especially among men. Many people believed that sperm originated in the spinal cord, that copulation during menstruation would beget a monstrosity, and that conception was deemed impossible without simultaneous orgasm.

Couples usually delayed marriage until they had sufficient resources to live independently. Free men tended to marry in their mid-twenties and free women a few years younger. In some British colonies, women could divorce on the grounds of their husbands' desertion, adultery, bigamy, or impotence, but divorce was not common, and divorce with the right to remarry was exceptionally rare. Divorced women had no legal status and no legal right to their children or what had formerly been their property, including inheritances and their dowry. More common than divorce, especially among the lower classes, was the informal dissolution of marriage. It was also common for a spouse to die and for the widow or widower to remarry. As a result, there were many blended, sprawling families, and some mothers and fathers came to refer to children who were not their own but under their care as "sons- or daughters-in-law."

Given their comparative rarity, elderly relatives were often appreciated and cared for by their family. Religion provided rituals and meaning to those in their final hours and to those who sought to comfort them. Hell, for Protestants and Catholics, was as real as heaven, and death's approach inspired terror or provided comfort to the faithful of all Christian denominations.

5-5h Slave Resistance and Rebellions

In comparison to white families, the families of slaves were far more fragile in every respect. The hardships slaves faced in starting and maintaining families was just one aspect of their lives, however, that prompted them to resist their masters. Nearly every aspect of slave life—clothing, drumming, dancing, dressing, singing, eating, speaking, worshipping, and mourning—could become a form of resistance. Slaves sometimes turned to violence or to poisoning and arson. When flames destroyed Charles Town in 1740, slaveholders assumed that slaves had set fire to the city.

{ As varied as the slaves and the conditions of slavery were across colonial America, so too was slave resistance.

Slaves damaged tools, sabotaged machines, and ruined crops of tobacco, rice, or corn by harvesting it too soon or too late. Others worked slowly or lackadaisically. Still others "stole" from their masters or "stole" themselves by running away to maroon communities. Spanish Florida essentially invited runaways after 1693 when the Spanish king, Carlos II, issued a proclamation "giving liberty" to all fugitive slaves.

Slave rebellions were common in the Caribbean, where slaves often vastly outnumbered planters, but they were rare in British North America, where the chances of survival, much less success, were very low. In 1712, twenty-four Africans burned a New York building and killed nine men who sought to douse the flames. In response, civil authorities killed twenty-one suspected rebels and six others committed suicide. In 1741, when mysterious fires plagued New York City, some two hundred people including at least twenty poor whites were arrested out of fear that they and slaves were conspiring to overthrow the city government. Even with little evidence to support their fears, officials executed thirty-five slaves and four alleged white accomplices.

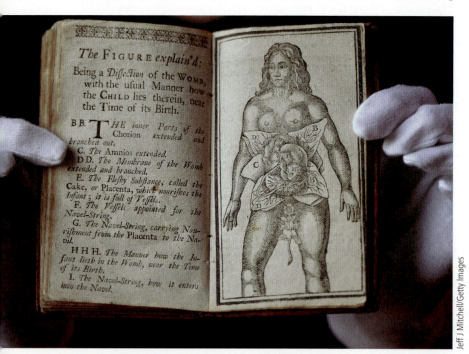

Detail from Aristotle's Masterpiece *The most widely circulated and printed sex and midwifery manual in the eighteenth century was published by an author who falsely claimed to have been Aristotle. The book gained popularity for the advice it dispensed as well as its illustrations of the male and female bodies. It was published in three editions and one hundred printings.* ▲

Jeff J Mitchell/Getty Images

The largest slave uprising in British North America was small relative to those in the Caribbean. In South Carolina in 1739, one hundred armed slaves killed several whites and fled toward Florida. A white militia, aided by Indian auxiliaries, defeated the slaves in a pitched battle. This uprising, known as the **Stono Rebellion** after the river where the slaves' attack began, was put down ruthlessly and the rebels' severed heads were mounted on fence posts.

Many whites recognized that slaves toiled in subhuman conditions, yet few voiced opposition to slavery. In New England, Puritan ministers such as Cotton Mather owned slaves and argued that their conversion to Christianity and education were more important than their manumission.

Only among Quakers did arguments for the liberation of slaves advance, albeit slowly. In 1754, John Woolman, a Quaker tailor and bookkeeper from New Jersey, published *Some Considerations on the Keeping of Negroes*, the first antislavery tract in British North America. Four years later, Philadelphia Quakers, led by Anthony Benezet, outlawed slavery among local members. But it would be another generation until manumission became a matter of open discussion, even in the North.

The few slaves in colonial America who attained freedom lived in isolation and impoverishment. Lawmakers denied free blacks the rights associated with freedom. They were forbidden from testifying against a white person, punished more severely than whites for crimes, taxed more heavily, prevented from owning firearms, and discriminated against when they tried to purchase property, borrow money, or move from place to place. Of the several hundred free blacks living in Boston in 1742, 110 lived in a church-sponsored poor house and another 36 lived in a public workhouse.

Stono Rebellion South Carolina slave rebellion, the largest in British North America.

Summary

The first half of the eighteenth century was a period of dramatic transformation for much of colonial America. Spain, France, and England competed for territory and trade. Wars over European succession and trade roiled the edges of many colonies, leading to the destruction and seizure of some frontier settlements. Native Americans, who had already been pushed to the margins of the colonies, in many cases became pawns in European disputes. Moreover, their proportion among the overall population continued to decline because of illness and war as well as the explosion of the colonial population.

In this period, the colonies in British North America proved the most dynamic and expansive. They attracted hundreds of thousands of immigrants, nearly half of whom were, in one way or another, unwilling migrants, coming either from Africa as slaves or from western Europe as transported convicts or refugees from their homelands. With their arrival, distinctive cultures emerged in New England, the Middle Colonies, the Chesapeake, and the South. Population growth and the increasingly dynamic transatlantic economy also led to a widening of the gap between rich and poor. Yet the elite, the middling, and the poor all engaged new patterns of consumption and, at times, religious practice.

By 1750, life in the colonies of British North America had been transformed. English colonists debated notions of liberty and power in their political clubs and enjoyed far more access to the franchise and a free press than did Englishmen. The Great Awakening had remade Protestant religious views and practices and had allowed women, the unlettered, and a few free African Americans to take on roles of religious authority.

Slaves, however, experienced none of the excitement and opportunity that characterized this half century, even though their labor was in many respects the foundation of both. A small number gained a modicum of autonomy in port cities along the Atlantic Coast, both in the North and South of British North America. Although most remained enslaved, their lives were far more manageable than Africans transported to the Caribbean sugar colonies. Many married and had families, but the satisfaction they took in these accomplishments must have been tempered by the realization that the children they created were born into slavery. Finally, daily life in the frontier regions of New France and New Spain changed less in these years. as the dynamic centers of French and Spanish colonial life developed elsewhere. Nevertheless, local populations continued to shape regions and create cultures of their own.

<Thinking Back, *Looking Forward*>

As you review this chapter, think about the large-scale immigration to the Americas from the earliest days of settlement through 1750 and evaluate the roles labor, religion, and politics played in the movement of peoples across the Atlantic. To what extent did people cross the Atlantic of their own volition? Why did they do so? By and large, why did European women not immigrate in large numbers to the colonies?

In the next chapters, look for the ways in which European conflicts continued to shape life in colonial America.

To make your study concrete, review the timeline and reflect on the entries there. Think about their causes, consequences, and connections. How do they fit with global trends?

Additional Resources

Books

Bailyn, Bernard. *The Origins of American Politics*. New York: Alfred A. Knopf, 1968. ▶ Best concise discussion of politics in British North America.

Barr, Juliana. *Peace Came in the Form of a Woman: Indians and Spaniards in the Texas Borderlands*. Chapel Hill: University of North Carolina Press, 2007. ▶ Pioneering study of the role of women in Indian-Spanish relations in the Southwest.

Berkin, Carol. *First Generations: Women in Colonial America*. New York: Hill and Wang, 1996. ▶ Concise overview of women's experiences in British North America.

Bushman, Richard. *The Refinement of America: Persons, Houses, Cities*. New York: Alfred A. Knopf, 1992. ▶ Study of the evolution of an elite material culture in the eighteenth century in English colonies.

Greene, Jack P. *Pursuits of Happiness: The Social Development of Early Modern British Colonies and the Formation of American Culture*. Chapel Hill: University of North Carolina Press, 1988. ▶ Sweeping synthesis describing the evolution of a common English culture across the English colonies by 1750.

Hackel, Steven W. *Junípero Serra: California's Founding Father*. New York: Farrar, Straus, and Giroux, 2013. ▶ Penetrating biography of the Mallorcan imperial priest who founded California's missions and was canonized in 2015.

Hofstadter, Richard. *America at 1750: A Social Portrait*. New York: Alfred A. Knopf, 1971. ▶ Brief and riveting account of the English colonies' social development through 1750.

Norton, Marcy. *Sacred Gifts, Profane Pleasures: A History of Tobacco and Chocolate in the Atlantic World*. Ithaca, NY: Cornell University Press, 2008. ▶ Intellectual and economic history of Europeans' gradual reception of tobacco and chocolate in the seventeenth century.

Shammas, Carole. *The Pre-industrial Consumer in England and America*. New York: Oxford University Press, 1990. ▶ Path-breaking economic study of changing patterns of consumption in British North America.

Usner, Daniel H. Jr. *Indians, Settlers, and Slaves in a Frontier Exchange Economy: The Lower Mississippi Valley before 1783*. Chapel Hill: University of North Carolina Press, 1992. ▶ Examination of how economic exchange created points of cultural contact and understanding among blacks, Indians, and the French in Louisiana.

Go to the MindTap® for **Global Americans** to access the full version of select books from this Additional Resources section.

Websites

Early California Population Project, Huntington Library. (http://www.huntington.org/Information/ECPPmain .htm) ▶ Online and searchable database of baptisms, marriages, and burials of Indians, soldiers, and settlers in colonial California, 1769 through 1850.

Canada: The Research Program in Historical Demography. (http://www.genealogie.umontreal.ca/en/LePrdh) ▶ Online and searchable database for Quebec and French Canada, 1621 through 1849, including all baptisms, marriages, and burials.

Continue exploring online through MindTap®, **where you can:**

- **Assess your knowledge with the Chapter Test**
- **Watch historical videos related to the chapter**
- **Further your understanding with interactive maps and timelines**

Colonial Society and Bonds of Empire

1693–1711	1712–1716	1717–1720	1721–1725	1726–1730
1693 Spanish Florida offers freedom to fugitive slaves from British North America.	**1712** Slaves rebel in New York City.	**1717** The Tuscaroras move north from North Carolina.	**1722** The Tuscaroras join the Haudenosaunees.	**1729** Russian explorers Bering and Chirikov undertake their first expedition.
1698 Parliament suspends the Royal African Company's monopoly on the transport of slaves from Africa to British North America.	**1713** Treaty of Utrecht is signed, ending the War of Spanish Succession and confirming Philip as king of Spain.	**1718** Mission San Antonio de Béjar is established in Texas.	**1724** *Code Noir* is decreed in Louisiana.	
1701 Queen Anne's War/War of the Spanish Succession begins.	**1715–1716** Yamasee War breaks out in Southeast between Indians and English settlers.	**1718–1720** The War of Quadruple Alliance pits Spain against France, England, Holland, and Austria.		
1702–1704 Carolinians wage attacks on Spanish Florida.				
1704 French-Mohawk raid Deerfield, Connecticut.				

1731–1735	**1736–1739**	**1740–1748**	**1746–1769**	**1770–1799**
1731 Spanish missions in Texas relocate to San Antonio.	**1737** The Delaware Indians fraudulently dispossessed of their land through the Walking Purchase.	**1740** King George's War/ War of the Austrian Succession breaks out.	**1753** Georgia's original charter expires.	**1770** Spain takes possession of Alta California at Monterey.
1732 Georgia is established.	**1739** Slaves rise up in the Stono Rebellion.	**1741** Bering and Chirikov undertake their second expedition.	**1754** Woolman publishes his first antislavery tract.	**1777** Pueblo of San José is established in Alta California.
1733 Molasses Act taxes molasses from the French West Indies. Jonathan Edwards's sermons spark a religious revival in Northampton, Massachusetts, beginning the Great Awakening in the colonies.			**1758** Mission San Sabá is destroyed.	**1781** Pueblo of Los Angeles is established in Alta California.
1735 Zenger is found not guilty of libel.			**1769** Junípero Serra establishes Mission San Diego in Alta California.	**1799** Russian-American Company is chartered.

Go to MindTap® to engage with an interactive version of the timeline. Analyze events and themes with clickable content, view related videos, and respond to critical thinking questions.

6

Imperial Conflicts and Revolution

1750–1783

Thomas Paine claimed that the American people were strong because they were unified, but people living in North America were divided by economy, culture, and imperial connections.

Thomas Paine grew up making foundation undergarments in a small English town but soon ran away to sea to become a privateer. Paine and the other 250 crewmen aboard the *King of Prussia* in 1757 were sanctioned by British King George II to attack enemy merchant ships and sell the spoils for personal profit. A new, global war among European powers made this kind of work lucrative and plentiful, but also dangerous. After eight months at sea, Paine returned to corset making, followed by a new career as a government tax collector. In London, Paine published a pamphlet on behalf of his fellow tax collectors, contrasting their poverty and misery with "the rich, in ease and affluence." He became acquainted with a group of men who called themselves "The Club of Honest Whigs" that gathered every two weeks in a coffee shop to talk politics and philosophy. One of its members, Benjamin Franklin—a Philadelphia printer, inventor, and politician—gave Paine the letter of introduction that set him on course to be an international revolutionary.

German artist Balthasar Friedrich Leizelt created this idealized image of Philadelphia, making it look similar to European ports engaged in Atlantic trade. ▲ Library of Congress Prints and Photographs Division

With Franklin's letter in hand, Paine crossed the Atlantic to the bustling port of Philadelphia in 1774, where new political associations were organizing North American colonists to protest what they saw as Britain's unfair treatment. Paine began publishing essays criticizing British corruption and praising American colonists' virtue. He created a sensation in January 1776, when his pamphlet *Common Sense* became the bestseller that urged colonists to reject reconciliation with Britain and support independence. He championed the revolution that erupted, boosted spirits during the war, and celebrated victory afterward.

In 1787, Paine moved to Europe, where he joined a new revolutionary movement, this one in France. In 1791 and 1792, he published his most famous work, *The Rights of Man*, praising the French Revolution and proclaiming that God had created all people equal and equally deserving of political rights. He was a champion of the poor who believed that governments in which the people ruled made better societies than monarchies did. "I see in America," he wrote, "the generality of people living in a style of plenty unknown in the monarchical countries."

Paine traveled in a world of competing imperial structures—armies, courts, trade monopolies—that had broad reach but uneven strength. The British Empire deployed him as a tax collector and privateer to keep profits away from rivals, but he also found ways to cross boundaries and seek his fortune, a strategy many adopted. Native Americans used strategic alliances with European empires to gain access to trade goods and military strength against those who would claim their land. At the

In what ways do Thomas Paine's actions within and against empires reflect the struggles of the various peoples who lived within the Atlantic World?

Go to MindTap® to watch a video on Paine and learn how his story relates to the themes of this chapter.

same time, colonial American farmers disregarded boundary lines drawn by distant empires, hoping to make their own deals locally. American colonists eagerly imported European goods along trade routes protected by powerful navies. But many colonists chafed at rules demanding that they trade only within their own empire and smuggled their way to new markets. Enslaved people were ruthlessly exploited as profitable commodities by empires that then needed them as soldiers in the ongoing warfare of the eighteenth century.

With each war over trade and territory, Europe's empires redrew borders and swapped colonial holdings. Both the Seven Years' War and the American Revolution were part of the ongoing eighteenth-century contest of Britain and its allies against France and its allies. Yet the cycle launched a new trajectory in 1763, setting in motion what would become second and third dimensions of colonial revolution: between Native Americans and colonists and between British colonists and the government in London. In all three, the desires of average people for land, personal freedom, and self-governance were prominent and often in conflict with one another.

In calling for the creation of a new country, Thomas Paine claimed that the American people's greatest strength was "in unity," but the sense of common cause needed to wage a war of independence came from different political and economic motivations. People across North America wanted personal freedom, access to land, and economic opportunity. These desires led some to join the cause for colonial independence and reject monarchies in favor of a republic. For thousands of others, especially enslaved Africans and displaced Indians, those same desires confirmed their sense in 1783 that although they lived in North American territory, they were not part of the new United States.

6-1

Seven Years' War, Years of Global Warfare

This image depicting 1764 negotiations for the return of 206 colonial captives taken from the Virginia and Pennsylvania backcountry during wartime was created by American artist Benjamin West. Around a council fire, British Colonel Henry Bouquet and his aides use paper and ink while a group of Senecas, Shawnees, and Delawares use a wampum belt to record diplomatic agreements. Both wear fabrics made in Europe.

How does this image use space, framing, posture, and props to illustrate the bargaining positions of Indians and Europeans at council fires? Why are the colonial captives not pictured? ▶

Library of Congress Prints and Photographs Division Washington, D.C.[LC-US262–104]

European empires competed for wealth and power by warring over territory and trade. Between 1689 and 1748, a series of wars had focused on the European continent but included armed conflict in North America. In 1754, a new cycle in these imperial contests began, and this time North America was the primary focus rather than an afterthought. Fighting among European empires and their Indian allies in this conflict, called the *French and Indian War* in North America but the *Seven Years' War* in Europe, in fact lasted for more than nine years. British victory ended French claims to North America but did not stop ongoing warfare between Native Americans and American colonists. In the Great Lakes and Ohio Valley

Charleston Museum

Eliza Lucas Pinckney's Silk Shoes, Ordered from London

Global Americans **Eliza Lucas Pinckney**, born Eliza Lucas on the island of Antigua in 1722, finished her education in England like many daughters of wealthy British families posted around the empire. Her family moved to become plantation owners in South Carolina when she was a teenager. With her father sent back to the Caribbean as an army officer, Lucas took over management of the family plantations, overseeing the labor of enslaved Africans and experimenting with new crops. Joining business and scientific interests, she developed a strain of indigo, a blue dye plant, and a method of producing dye cakes, which became the second most prominent and profitable export of South Carolina after rice. South Carolina indigo competed with French dyes to color the quickly expanding international commerce in new printed fabrics.

In 1744, Eliza Lucas married Charles Pinckney, a much older lawyer and politician. Raising her children "according to Mr. Lock's method" to "play [themselves] into learning," she lived to see two of her sons become revolutionary leaders. The occupation of Charles Town resulted in the loss of many of her trappings of wealth and taste. Widowed, she wrote to one creditor that her slaves had been seized for military work, her house filled with foreign soldiers, and her elegant trees cut down for army use. Like most wealthy South Carolina slave owners at the time, her identity was oriented toward the Caribbean and transatlantic commercial and intellectual networks; only during the Revolution did she remake herself as an American. At her funeral in 1793, George Washington was a pallbearer.

regions, allied Indians, inspired by religious visions and a charismatic leader named Pontiac, continued to violently oppose British and colonial American presence in the North American interior.

☞ As you read, think about how local struggles between neighbors in North America influenced imperial actions between 1754 and 1763. What types of alliances were possible? How did war change them?

6-1a **Trade and Empire**

In 1757, one French diplomat observed that the "balance of commerce of the nations in America" and the "balance of power in Europe" were ultimately the same. Integrated global trade shaped settlement patterns, alliances, and the shifting fortunes of empires in the eighteenth century. Around the Atlantic, British, French, and Dutch governments sponsored companies that shipped guns and cloth to West Africa in exchange for captive humans who were transported to work on plantations in the Americas. From the Americas, slave-grown sugar, tobacco, indigo, and rice traveled back to Europe, transforming daily diets and enriching investors. The wealth generated by this trade established Dutch banks and English factories that in turn spurred global investment and local economic development. Another global circuit, connecting French and British traders with Indian fur trappers in North America, built substantial fortunes in Europe and dressed men and women on three continents.

Across the Pacific, the Spanish empire dominated global trade, shipping the silver mined by coerced laborers

> Trade goods shape power politics locally and globally.

in Mexico and Peru to China in exchange for silks, spices, and porcelain. But the Russians were rising competitors, in the form of traders crossing from Siberia to the Aleutian Islands in search of valuable seal, fox, and sea otter pelts. Imperial taxes on the trade plumped state coffers. By the 1770s, the fur trade yielded 8 percent of Russian revenues. Spain, France, and Britain likewise depended on import taxes from their colonies to fund wars they waged to expand their territories.

Oceanic circuits for goods needed Native American labor, expertise, and trading connections. To keep relations friendly and access to animal skins open, France sent cloth, tools, cooking pots, guns, and ammunition to Indian allies as gifts. England learned to do the same with the Haudenosaunee confederacy, now known as the Six Nations. But trade-based alliances also spread disease and spurred overhunting that profoundly disrupted Indian lives. White settlers followed early traders and set up cabins as **squatters** on Indian land.

In the late 1740s, North American alliances began to break down. European wars had drained the reserves of European kings and left them with less money for diplomatic gifts. Native Americans wanted to negotiate new diplomatic and trade terms. A group of displaced Delaware and Shawnee Indians living in the Ohio River valley firmly proclaimed their neutrality and insisted on the right to deal with any trader, regardless of political ties. As they watched Scots-Irish and German migrants freely settle on their lands, claimed by both Pennsylvania and Virginia, Delawares and Shawnees rejected Haudenosaunee efforts to negotiate on their behalf and broke the old Covenant Chain that had bound allied tribes together and to the British.

squatter Person who lives on land without legal or customary claim to it, often insisting that working on land confers ownership. Squatters often claimed Indian lands.

The region between the Ohio River and the Great Lakes had long been one of the great crossroads of cultures because it linked two essential waterways of trade and travel: the route from the Atlantic along the St. Lawrence River into the Great Lakes and the Mississippi watershed that connected the interior of the continent down to the Gulf of Mexico. In 1753, French officials responded to escalating tension in the region by constructing a new line of forts between Montreal and New Orleans to secure their trading posts from British competition and American colonists in search of farmland. The crossroads of cultures became a proving ground of power.

6-1b Seven Years' War

In 1754, threatened by new French forts and Indian alliances, British authorities convened the **Albany Congress**. Delegates from seven British colonies met with representatives of the Six Nations to try to repair the Covenant Chain and secure support against the French. Extensive gifts and the naming of influential trader William Johnson to a new office, the Superintendent of Indian Affairs, convinced the Haudenosaunees to pledge limited military assistance in the form of individual warriors and scouts. Delegates also passed Pennsylvanian Benjamin Franklin's proposed Albany Plan of Union, which would have created a central government made up of representatives from British North American colonies and a crown-appointed "president general" to oversee Indian land treaties, trade, and military affairs. Preferring to retain local control, colonial assemblies rejected the idea.

As the delegates debated, fighting was breaking out. Seeking to assert authority on Virginia's borderlands, Governor Robert Dinwiddie sent a small force commanded by twenty-two-year-old George Washington to seize Fort Duquesne, a new French fort at the forks of the Ohio River, where it controlled access to the Mississippi River. Washington and Dinwiddie were shareholders in the **Ohio Company of Virginia**, a land speculation company with claims to the same valuable Ohio territory claimed by France, Britain, the Haudenosaunees, the Shawnees, and the Delawares. This gave both men personal and political reasons for expelling the French. Tanaghrisson, a Seneca chief who accompanied Washington, hoped that war between the French and British would drive both out of Indian territory, and he encouraged Washington to launch an attack. The ill-planned ambush resulted in multiple French casualties and the

> Imperial conflicts reignite, involving people around the world.

Join or Die Borrowing imagery from European emblems, Benjamin Franklin published this illustration of an eight-segmented snake in the May 9, 1754, edition of the *Pennsylvania Gazette*. The image represented his belief that only centralized colonial government with power to govern North American affairs would ensure the health of the empire as a whole. The colonies, represented in this image by their initials, disagreed. Georgia and Delaware were not included in the Albany Plan or the snake image. ▲

capture of twenty-one prisoners but left Washington's small force exposed and vulnerable at a quickly constructed Fort Necessity. More French troops soon forced Washington's ignominious retreat. Although there was no formal declaration until 1756, the **Seven Years' War** between France and its allies and Britain and its allies had begun. In the words of one British politician, "A volley fired by a young Virginian in the backwoods of America set the world on fire." People around the world were caught in the conflagration.

From the perspective of European power centers, the war was another clash of empires. As Britain, France, and then Spain sought to defend and expand colonial holdings in North America, they pursued similar designs in Central America, India, and the Philippines. In Europe, Britain, France, and Spain formed new strategic alliances and fought over territory in response to the rising military power of Prussia under Frederick the Great. From West Africa to the Caribbean, European empires battled to control valuable international trade routes fueling the enormous profits in enslaved people, sugar, and coffee. The British and French East India companies took advantage of political turmoil in the Mughal empire, a Muslim dynasty ruling much of India, to pursue control over textile-producing hubs. As before, European empires depended on a combination of their own troops, auxiliaries hired from other countries, and local fighting forces, many of whom had their own agendas in taking up arms (see Map 6.1).

In North America, Britain had great difficulty convincing colonists that the war was their fight. Colonial defense forces relied on **militia** units consisting of adult

Albany Congress Meeting in 1754 of representatives from British colonies and Six Nations to reestablish alliances at which Franklin proposed centralized multicolony government.

Ohio Company of Virginia Land development company with powerful investors who hoped to sell land in contested Ohio River Valley.

Seven Years' War Conflict involving European empires, their colonies, and indigenous people around the globe.

militia Local defense force in every colony headed by a governor and led by local elite officers in Indian warfare and patrolling runaway slaves.

Library of Congress Prints & Photographs Division, [LC-USZC4-5315]

Events of the Seven Years' War

1. Virginia-Pennsylvania-Ohio, 1753–1764
2. Nova Scotia, 1754
3. Hudson River-Lake Champlain, 1755–1760
4. Minorca, 1756
5. Central Europe, 1756–1762
6. Bengal, 1757
7. Louisbourg, 1758
8. West Africa, 1758
9. Madras, 1758–1759
10. Québec and Upper St. Lawrence, 1759–1760
11. Eastern Caribbean, 1759–1762
12. Iberian Coast, 1759
13. French Coast, 1759–1761
14. Upper Great Lakes, 1759–1764
15. Pondicherry, 1760–1762
16. Spain, 1762
17. Newfoundland, 1762
18. Havana, 1762
19. Manila, 1762
20. Pontiac's Rebellion, 1763–1764

Territorial claims, ca. 1750
- British
- French
- Netherlands
- Portuguese
- Russian
- Spanish
- Ottoman Empire

Map 6.1 Seven Years' War as a Global Conflict, 1754–1763 As with all clashes between empires in the eighteenth century, this war involved colonial settlers, indigenous people, and imperial soldiers in violent conflict around the world. In the Seven Years' War, territorial claims in North America and Native American alliances were a primary cause, but events in one theater shaped outcomes for people thousands of miles away. ▲

property-owning men. Mirroring community social structure, militias were led by local elite officers who presided over occasional public mustering exercises and organized runaway slave patrols. Militias were local in their outlook. When the war began, therefore, members of the Virginia militia refused to leave their farms unworked

and their enslaved population unguarded to fight at the forks of the Ohio River. Virginia's House of Burgesses was forced to draft men to fill Britain's military quotas. Because the militia was composed of men who were also voters, elected authorities tried to conscript poor men and outsiders.

Following shocking early losses, in 1757, British cabinet secretary William Pitt took over control of the war effort and made North America his first priority. Relying on Britain's ally, Prussia, to fight the alliance of France, Austria, and Russia that had entered combat on the European continent, Pitt poured money and supplies into North America, ultimately amassing forty-five thousand troops to overwhelm France's ten thousand. Pitt also promised British Americans compensation for their participation in the war effort. Telling colonists that this was a global war of Protestants against Catholics, he drew on religious antagonisms to fuel loyalty to the British Empire.

The new investment in North American colonies paid off in battlefield victories that won support from Haudenosaunees in the North. The siege and capture of Quebec in 1759 was the dramatic turning point of the war. After three months of skirmishes, General James Wolfe led four thousand British troops over steep cliffs behind the city and engaged French forces on the Plains of Abraham outside city walls. Following a short engagement, in which both Wolfe and the French general Louis-Joseph de Montcalm were mortally wounded, the British took the field and the city. Within a year, after British forces had captured Montreal, the French surrendered all of Canada. The victory, which cost the British more than ten times what the French had spent, was a testament to Britain's economic power and organization, especially its large and well-funded navy. That same navy helped defeat France in other theaters of the war.

Britain's victory over France had profound consequences for native people around the globe who had used the strategy of playing one empire against the other. In India, the **British East India Company** wielded a combination of military and commercial might to exploit Indian riches in cotton textiles, silk, and tea on behalf of the British Empire. Native Bengal leaders had relied on an insistent French presence to counterbalance the company's power. When the French were defeated and driven out in 1761, Bengal Indians lost their main leverage against consolidating British control. The same happened in the Great Lakes region of North America. With the defeat and departure of the French, the Wendats (Hurons) and the Potawatomis lost negotiating leverage.

Death of General Wolfe The capture of Quebec was a military victory that turned Wolfe into a martyr and national hero celebrated in songs and sermons across the British Empire. Pennsylvania-born artist Benjamin West mixed classical poses with contemporary settings and costuming to create a painting that was a sensation when exhibited in London in 1771. It was quickly copied onto affordable textiles, ceramics, and engravings—materials of eighteenth-century consumer culture. ▲

On February 10, 1763, the **Treaty of Paris** marked the formal end of the Seven Years' War that had claimed a million lives. Confident in their power to redraw political maps moving people and land from one empire to another, diplomats in Paris upended the balance of power, granting enormous territorial claims to Great Britain. France lost all its territory in North America with the exception of two fishing islands off the coast of Newfoundland and a handful of islands in the Caribbean, including sugar-producing Saint-Domingue. Spain, a latecomer in declaring war on Britain in 1762, lost Florida but gained Louisiana in a separate agreement. Britain claimed all lands from the Atlantic coast to the Mississippi River. Native Americans, no matter on which side they had fought, were excluded from peace negotiations.

6-1c Postwar Landscape

New boundaries dictated displacements. Britain split its new colony of Florida in two, creating West Florida and East Florida. Thousands of Spanish-speaking colonists, officials, soldiers, and enslaved Africans living in the region evacuated permanently to Spanish Cuba as did a group of Catholic Yamasee Indians. Creeks who objected to the terms of the treaty had to sail to Havana to seek Spanish military support against encroaching English settlers. They were "surprised," the Creeks said, "how People can give away Land that does not belong to them."

British soldiers took a more violent approach to removing the **Acadians** from Nova Scotia. These French Americans, who often intermarried with local Micmacs, had lived under British rule since the end of the War of

{ Displacements fragment communities and force new identities.

British East India Company Joint-stock company originally chartered in 1600 that by mid-eighteenth century had a trade monopoly in the East Indies and substantial military and administrative powers.

Treaty of Paris Agreement signed in 1763 ending the Seven Years' War among European powers in which France lost claims to North America and Native Americans were not represented.

Acadians Culturally mixed French and Native people who lived in British Nova Scotia; those who refused to pledge loyalty to Britain in 1755 were driven from homes, many to Louisiana.

Spanish Succession in 1713. In 1755, those who refused to take a loyalty oath to Britain were forced from their homes. Some fled north, some escaped to France, but many were exiled to other British colonies. British troops continued to seize territory and burn homes and fields, removing Acadians and sending them into servitude in New England or imprisoning them in ships and workhouses. Thousands died during the eviction. Eventually, several thousand Acadians moved to Louisiana, where their descendants became known as *Cajuns*.

Thousands of British American colonists died in the war, either in battle or from diseases contracted at forts and garrisons, and their deaths prompted more relocations. As families left behind struggled to support themselves, cities such as Boston filled with widows and orphans seeking financial support. Unable to raise enough money to aid them, communities in New England increased the practice of "warning out," whereby local authorities sent residents back to the town of their birth (or, in the case of free married women, their husband's town) to receive charitable assistance there. Economic losses compounded demographic ones. Lucrative military contracts for ships, weapons, clothing, and provisions dried up, and the removal of forty thousand British troops meant no more customers for food, lodging, and other services. At the very moment that they were celebrating victory in what some called the Great War for Empire, many in the colonies faced economic misery.

Less miserable, but equally uncertain, were new members of the British and Spanish empires. By claiming vast lands inhabited by mixed villages of French, Spanish, and Native American people, Britain gained an empire that was more heterogeneous than it had been in 1754. Some new subjects spoke French or Spanish; many were Catholic. But British authority was spread thin in lands once claimed by France. Kinship ties forged between French fur traders and Indian women were more influential in many places than British administrators and merchants sent to enforce the new map. Likewise, Spanish officials in Havana struggled to administer and defend the large and distant Louisiana territory. They relied on experienced French traders and a regular supply of gifts to encourage Indian allegiance. Consequently, for many living in Louisiana, the new Paris-born lieutenant governor's declaration that "we are all Spaniards" meant little. Osage traders near St. Louis took advantage of the limited colonial oversight to expand their commercial power over the Mississippi River by partnering with French, British, or Spanish traders as opportunities arose.

6-1d Pontiac's Rebellion

French troops withdrew from North American forts after the fall of Montreal, but warfare in the Great Lakes region continued between Indians and the British. Although it was in some ways a continuation of the Seven Years' War,

{ Allied Indians continue to fight for territory and sovereignty.

the conflict was also a war for independence fought by a diverse group of Native Americans newly united by a shared desire to drive the British out of the Ohio Valley and stop further colonial settlement. This common cause drew strength from a sense of spiritual purpose. Since the 1730s, Native American prophets from various communities had called for a renewal of old rituals. By the 1750s, Delaware prophets had a new message: The Master of Life wanted them to "destroy the poison among them." Neolin, the most influential of these prophets, proclaimed that the path to heaven was blocked by European vice. He urged his followers to cease trading with the French and English and stop using their goods. His words inspired Pontiac, an Ottawa war chief, who emphasized the most militant part of Neolin's message: Indians must join together not only to resist European contact but also to force European colonists from the land. Spiritual and tactical arguments created a new sense of unity, a belief that Native Americans were a distinct people with a common identity, regardless of tribe or clan.

In the spring of 1763, a coalition of Native American people seized all but three of Britain's dozen forts and besieged Fort Niagara and Fort Pitt. During **Pontiac's Rebellion**, Indian warriors attacked settlements on the Pennsylvania and Virginia frontiers, forcing colonists to flee to refugee centers near the coast. Some turned against their Native American neighbors. In late December 1763, the Scots-Irish "Paxton Boys" murdered unarmed Christian Indian families near Lancaster and then marched to the capital city of Philadelphia, determined to kill the Indians who had fled there. Colonial officials, led by Franklin, turned them away after hearing their demands, which included military protection and increased political representation.

British Commander-in-Chief Jeffrey Amherst, who had declared a desire to "remove that Vermin" of Native Americans, was short on troops, and Pontiac's forces lacked ammunition and had to contend with devastating illness. The result was a stalemate rather than clear victory for either side. News in October 1763 of the signing of the Treaty of Paris extinguished Pontiac's hope for aid from the French, and some tribes, such as the Senecas, made their own separate peace. Pontiac and Charlot Kaské, a Shawnee war chief, continued to recruit warriors and mobilize resistance, but in 1766 they accepted a peace negotiated by William Johnson at Oswego, New York. Twelve years of warfare that had begun in 1754 ended.

Although it was incomplete and did not last, joint Indian resistance did compel the British to abandon their plan to dictate terms to them. Amherst was removed as commander, and former French forts were re-established with British soldiers and officers who restored the trading and gift exchanges that had made diplomacy possible

Pontiac's Rebellion
Coordinated warfare in 1763 by Indians in Great Lakes against continuing British presence that ended in stalemate.

Royal Proclamation of 1763
Decree setting a line of settlement along the Appalachian Mountains marking the limit of legal colonial settlement.

before the war. Troops enforced the **Royal Proclamation of 1763**, a decree planned before the outbreak of Pontiac's Rebellion that forbade colonial governors from granting land patents west of the Appalachian Mountains. Those lands were to be the possession of "several Nations or Tribes of *Indians*" under the protection of the British Empire (see Map 6.2). Although a type of declaration of property rights for Native Americans, the prohibition meant little to settlers and squatters who already lived in the territory. By formally walling off Indian land, however, the Proclamation Line was a blow to those colonial elites who had formed the Ohio Company of Virginia, launched the war, and hoped to profit from land speculation once the French were gone. Indians kept copies of the Proclamation and the wampum belts that had circulated with it to hold Britain to its promises.

Map 6.2 North America in 1763 The Treaty of Paris ended French claims to vast territories on the continent. Drawing new boundaries, the British and Spanish empires forced the migrations of thousands of people living in newly claimed land. In the same year, the British established a Proclamation Line along the Appalachian Mountains, officially dividing Indians' and British colonists' lands within the empire. ▶

6-2
Imperial Reorganization and Colonial Resistance

This creamware teapot, protesting British tax policy for the American colonies, was made in Britain for export to those colonies. Potters in Cornwall, England, used local clay to develop this new form of ceramic in the 1750s in order to compete internationally with Chinese porcelain. Benjamin Franklin, testifying in Parliament in 1766, said that the goods Americans imported from Britain were "either necessaries, mere conveniences, or superfluities," all of which could be replaced.

What does this teapot suggest about the cultural and economic relationship between Britain and the British colonies? Why were goods exported from Britain the focus of British colonial policy? ▶

National Museum of American History, Smithsonian Institution, Behring Center

War brought Britain and Spain vast new territories at great cost. To reduce their war debt—and to tighten imperial control—Spain boosted trade within its empire while Britain decided to shift more costs of empire onto the colonists by taxing imports. These policy shifts signaled the recognition of colonies as markets for goods, not merely sources of raw materials. In return, American colonists soon recognized that, as consumers, they could assert power and

influence policy by refusing British goods. Just as Pontiac had united diverse groups of northern Indians behind a rejection of European goods, so, too, did colonial boycotts unite disparate colonies though a sense of shared sacrifice. But new protest measures also tapped into a rumbling sense that the inequalities of colonial society—whether at the hands of local elites or British agents—were fundamentally unjust.

☞ As you read, identify the various forms of resistance that developed in North America after the Seven Years' War. What was the relationship between imperial actions and colonial reactions?

6-2a Tightening Imperial Ties

The Seven Years' War left Europe's empires deeply in debt and maneuvering to re-establish themselves in the global balance of power. Spain and Britain, empires that seemed to have gained the most during the war, attempted to capitalize on their gains by raising more revenue from their American colonies, imposing closer political control, and establishing a military presence along borderlands.

> Spain and Britain re-assert political and economic power over their colonies.

In a series of actions later known as the **Bourbon Reforms**, Spain pressured its silver mines in New Spain and Peru to increase their output and send more money back to Spain. The empire opened Spanish ports to direct trade with Spanish colonies. And the crown counteracted local colonial elites by appointing loyal Spanish to the *audiencias*. In 1767, the viceroy of New Spain reminded colonial subjects of their subordinate status, declaring that they "should know once and for all that they were born to keep silent and obey, and not to discuss or express opinions on high matters of government." Residents of Spanish New Orleans, accustomed to free-flowing trade with the English under a distracted French government, refused to keep silent, and in 1768 revolted against their crown-appointed governor, Antonio de Ulloa. Spain sent a replacement, but French language and culture remained dominant.

Trade around the Pacific was also essential to refilling Spanish coffers, and Spanish King Carlos III sought to extend control over Alta California in the aftermath of war. In 1776, the year Spanish settlers and soldiers founded San Francisco, Carlos III separated the large region covering California, New Mexico, and Texas into its own province, the "Provincias Internas" (Interior Provinces) under direct control of the crown.

Britain likewise concentrated on raising revenue and tightening control. The Seven Years' War had nearly doubled Britain's national debt, and interest on it consumed half the government's annual revenues. Faced with a home population that paid ten times what a colonial American one paid in taxes, the British government concluded that Americans should pay more.

According to the outraged reports of officials, American colonists were openly ignoring trade regulations, thus evading payments rightfully due to Britain. During the Seven Years' War, New England merchants continued to import molasses from French sugar colonies to make their rum, bribing customs officers to avoid having to pay the duties intended to force them to buy British. To stop smuggling, customs officers in Boston asked the Superior Court to issue general search warrants, called **writs of assistance**, to aid them in their searches for illegal goods. In a 1761 court case, James Otis of Boston challenged the writs as an unconstitutional violation of rights. He further charged that England was crippling the American economy with measures that "destroyed all our security of property, liberty, and life." Few debated Great Britain's right to make laws regulating colonial commerce, but Otis's choice of words, equating unimpeded trade with security, liberty, and life, shortly became core principles of resistance to British authority.

In 1764, the British government took the first step in raising revenues to support its global empire with the American Revenue Act, better known as the **Sugar Act**. This law, backed by a vigorous lobby of British Caribbean sugar planters who stood to gain, actually lowered the tax on British molasses from six pence per gallon to three pence per gallon. But it sought to eliminate the illegal trade in French molasses by funding new customs officers, requiring merchants to post bonds pledging their observance of the law, and strengthening the vice admiralty courts where accused smugglers and tax evaders would be judged by crown-appointed judges, not a jury comprised of sympathetic neighbors. The Currency Act of 1764 outlawed another common practice—that of colonies printing their own paper money and using it, rather than silver or gold, to pay their debts. These acts generated local opposition but no coordinated response.

6-2b Stamp Act

Pushing for a more direct way to raise revenue from the colonies, British prime minister George Grenville proposed that a stamp tax, long in force in England, be applied to the colonies. The **Stamp Act**, passed in February 1765, required that paper to be used for newspapers, playing cards, or legal documents carry a stamp indicating that the tax had been paid. Those who wanted the paper had to buy it from licensed distributors and pay the tax. The new tax revenue would support soldiers stationed in the North American interior, recently vacated by the Spanish and French. To British officials, the tax seemed reasonable, but to colonists, it was an outrageous new way to extract money from them.

> A new British tax sparks widespread opposition in its colonies.

Slated to take effect in November 1765, the Stamp Act drew unprecedented public opposition from all ranks of society because of its broad reach. Editors, lawyers,

Bourbon Reforms Policies of Spanish King Carlos III influenced by European Enlightenment ideals placing state power over church power to strengthen imperial control over New Spain.

writs of assistance General search warrants that permitted customs officials to search merchant warehouses for smuggled goods.

Sugar Act British 1764 law that lowered the tax on British molasses but increased enforcement of mercantilist principles to strengthen the empire.

Stamp Act Law proposed in 1765 to raise revenue on daily colonial legal and commercial transactions that sparked protest across British colonies.

merchants, and tavern keepers objected to paying a tax on something they used every day. They formed associations called the **Sons of Liberty**, who organized protests and wrote letters that were circulated between colonial centers and printed in local newspapers. Prosperous tradesmen and common laborers employed the **politics of the streets**. They staged mocking "stamping" rituals to ridicule the regulations. On the evening of August 14, a Boston crowd hanged an effigy of stamp distributor Andrew Oliver and destroyed his home. Similar protests, including the violent tarring and feathering of stamp distributors, occurred in colonial port cities from Rhode Island to St. Kitts and Nevis in the Caribbean. Loosely coordinated crowd protests, denigrated as "mobs" by their targets, were common in the 1760s. In England, Spitalfields weavers marched in London and hanged effigies to protest unemployment and the importation of French silk.

In some protests, outrage at the provisions of the Stamp Act merged with deeply running tensions over economic inequality. Two weeks after attacking the stamp distributor's home, thousands of average Bostonians turned on the mansion of Boston-born Lieutenant Governor Thomas Hutchinson, seizing and destroying the French wines, Spanish silver, and English furniture and fabrics that marked him as a man of wealth and style.

Urged on by the Sons of Liberty, American merchants also devised a new protest measure, the **nonimportation** pledge. Merchants who signed these agreements promised to stop all trade with Britain. By refusing to import cloth, ceramics, tools, and other goods, they believed that they would hurt British manufacturers, prove their own self-sufficiency, and force a repeal of the law. A 1765 pamphlet by Pennsylvanian John Dickinson urged Americans to follow the Swiss, whose "coarse clothes and simple furniture" helped them "defend their liberty." Although the idea was innovative, commitment was uneven, and British imports continued to flow into North American colonies.

Assemblies in nine colonies elected delegates who met in October in New York at a Stamp Act Congress to draft a unified response to Parliament, objecting to the stamp tax as a dangerous break with past methods of ruling the empire. As participants in Britain's empire of trade, colonial North Americans grudgingly accepted the government's right to regulate imports and exports to strengthen the empire. The stamp tax was different because it was a direct tax on daily life intended to raise revenue that had no connection to trade policy. Without conceding its right to tax the colonists for this purpose, Parliament responded to the unprecedented opposition by repealing the Stamp Act in March 1766.

6-2c Rights and Liberties

Globally, the British Empire had no single method of colonial government after the Seven Years' War. In India, the British East India Company established courts, collected revenues, raised troops, and commissioned officers to lead them, all on behalf of Britain. In Quebec, a crown-appointed governor and his council made and administered local laws. Long-standing British colonies in North America and the Caribbean had representative assemblies in which elite local men made law. In theory, all were **virtually represented** by members of Parliament, who supposedly represented the needs and interests of subjects all over the empire, not just the small group of propertied men in Great Britain who voted for them.

> Protesters draw on multiple ideologies of rights.

By the 1760s, many adult white men in British North America objected to the idea of virtual representation. Their experience of their own assemblies, in which voters had **actual representation** by individuals directly answerable to them, gave them an expectation of self-governance. The majority of people living in the colonies still had to accept virtual representation because age, sex, color, or lack of land disqualified them from the vote. Yet because the Stamp Act was imposed by Parliament rather than locally elected assemblies, the men of the Stamp Act Congress believed that Parliament had violated their rights. Their resolutions proclaimed it "inseparably essential to the freedom of a people, and the undoubted rights of Englishmen" to be taxed only by their own representatives.

Americans familiar with British political thought sensed another threat to liberty. Since the 1720s, the Radical Whigs had been convinced that the British government was being destroyed from within by corruption in Parliament and a tyrannical king. They promoted their conspiratorial outlook in essays that literate Americans such as Patrick Henry reread in light of the Stamp Act. Henry, fiery new member of Virginia's House of Burgesses, declared that any attempt to give taxation power to a nonrepresentative assembly "has a manifest Tendency to destroy British as well as American Freedom."

Individual liberty was at the core of British identity by the 1760s, bolstered by national pride in the English mixed and balanced constitution. Yet protests following the Stamp Act cracked open the broad implications of a commitment to individual rights when enslaved men and women took to street protest and transformed its politics. In fall 1765, the avenues of Charles Town, South Carolina, were filled with

Sons of Liberty Intercolonial associations of men protesting British imperial crackdown in the 1760s and 1770s.

politics of the streets Public protest rituals that included parades, tarring and feathering, and effigies; called *mob rule* by opponents and victims.

nonimportation Protest measure consisting of written promises to stop importing British goods with the intention of using economic pressure to force a change in tax laws.

virtual representation Political theory dominant in Britain that members of Parliament represented the interests of residents in the entire empire.

actual representation Political theory emerging from colonial experience with representative assemblies maintaining that elected legislators should respond to the specific needs of constituents.

white protestors shouting "Liberty and no Stamp Act." In January 1766, enslaved Charlestonians followed suit, shouting "Liberty!" as they marched. Whites in power immediately understood the radical implications for the tens of thousands of recently arrived Africans. The South Carolina assembly stopped all slave importations for three years, and the city enforced a strict curfew for two weeks. Riders traversed the colony warning slave owners to restrict the freedoms of their human property as more than one hundred slaves escaped to the woods and swamps.

Fear of a slave rebellion overpowered British colonists' desire for self-government in the Caribbean, even though the Stamp Act specifically targeted them for higher taxes. The tax on wills and estate documents in the islands was double that of the mainland colonies and taxes on land grants triple. Yet with the exception of St. Kitts and Nevis, Caribbean colonies largely complied with the Stamp Act. Fearful of their enslaved population, which vastly outnumbered them, white West Indians had accepted the imperial clampdown. They even offered to pay the costs of additional troops to protect them from slave uprisings. New England traders were disgusted. Calling the West Indians "poor, mean spirited, Cowardly, Dastardly Creoles," New Englanders stopped shipping provisions to the islands, cutting off food for enslaved workers.

6-2d Nonconsumption and Nonimportation Movements

Parliament tried again to raise revenues in 1767 with a new set of taxes. The **Townshend Duties** taxed paper, lead, glass, paint, and tea imported into the colonies and created a new Board of Customs Commissioners to enforce them. New taxes sparked another round of protests, once again centered on a nonimportation movement that gained support in the southern colonies for the first time. This new round of boycotts not only specified forbidden imports but also drew average consumers into a growing **nonconsumption** movement. Although nonimportation depended on merchants to accept or refuse shipments of goods, nonconsumption could be practiced by anyone who bought muskets or wore calico.

> Boycotts tie politics to daily life.

Army and Church in the British Caribbean British slave owners in West Indian colonies encouraged imperial shows of force to subdue the colonies' majority enslaved population and fend off attacks from French ships. Thomas Hearne's watercolor of Antigua places the large army barracks and the spire of St. John's Anglican church at its center. No slaves are depicted working in the sugarcane fields; instead, they relax together with a mixed-race free soldier in the shadow of the hospital. ▲

Yale Center for British Art, Paul Mellon Collection

Free women, often calling themselves the **Daughters of Liberty**, were at the forefront of the nonconsumption movement, signing public pledges not to buy imported fabric, thread, hats, ceramics, silverware, furniture, pins and nails, cheese, and dozens of other goods. They denounced merchants who violated nonimportation agreements and advocated the use of American-made goods. Championing **homespun**, a textile made by local families, women made their protest public by staging spinning contests on town greens. As one poem celebrating spinning bees proclaimed, "Britain, behold thy Trade stole from thy Hand." For some women, these movements connected their daily life's work to larger political importance and imparted a new sense of public power. Enslaved women seldom reaped power, but they did occasionally receive training in new kinds of work such as spinning and weaving when slave owners wanted to avoid purchasing imported cloth.

The renewed nonimportation and nonconsumption movements achieved the goal of disrupting British commerce. In 1769, the value of British North American exports

Townshend Duties Taxes imposed in 1767 on imported lead, glass, paper, paint, and tea, paid at colonial ports.

nonconsumption Boycott agreement engaging regular consumers—most prominent of whom were women—who agreed to stop purchasing and using British imports.

Daughters of Liberty Self-identification of women who protested British policies by boycotting imports and creating substitutes.

homespun Rough fabric spun and woven by families in colonial America and worn primarily by slaves until it became a political rallying point.

exceeded the value of imports for the first time. Parliament responded the way that many merchants had hoped by repealing nearly all of the Townshend taxes in 1770. Merchants resumed importing and consumers returned to stores.

6-2e Violent Conflict in the Interior and on the Coast

In the **backcountry**, a region of mixed colonial and Native American settlement bordering New York, Pennsylvania, and the Carolinas, colonists

> British troops become embroiled in local conflicts.

developed their own politics of protest, although often the flashpoint was land rather than import taxes. Residents and British officials clashed frequently over who had the right to live on, use, and profit from land on the border of settlements. Native Americans sold land through agreements arranged by chiefs, warriors, and matrons in public councils. They marked territory with slashes on trees and piles of stones. British colonists relied on mortgages signed with speculators, most of whom had received land grants from colonial governors in defiance of the Proclamation Line of 1763. These colonists were frequently in debt and faced eviction when lenders demanded payment. Under British law, debtors could be imprisoned until they or their families sold property or found some other way to pay what they owed. Because backcountry colonists were underrepresented in colonial assemblies, they seldom found institutional solutions to their problems. Petitions to colonial assemblies and letters to newspapers demanding tax relief and judicial reform got little response.

As boycotts roiled the coast, white farmers in the backcountry who felt exploited by Indians, speculators, and government officials staged a series of popular uprisings known as the **regulator movement**. North Carolina farmers turned increasingly to violent measures, forcibly closing courthouses to prevent foreclosure hearings, whipping lawyers, and breaking debtors out of jail. In 1770, they broke into the house of Assembly member Colonel Edmund Fanning and destroyed it the same way crowds in Boston had

destroyed Andrew Oliver's home. Herman Husband, a leader of the North Carolina Regulators, denounced "the unequal chances the poor and weak have in contention with the rich and powerful."

While western colonists demanded the attention of colonial elites, Indians sought aid from the British army as diplomatic allies against those colonists. In 1768, in return for an enormous gift of trade goods, Haudenosaunees signed away rights to land occupied by Shawnees and Delawares on the border with Pennsylvania and Virginia. The **Treaty of Fort Stanwix** (1768) essentially moved the Proclamation Line of 1763 west to the Ohio River. From the Haudenosaunee perspective, it was a strategic move to secure British friendship and enforce a new boundary between colonists and Indians. For the Shawnees and Delawares, who had already relocated, it was one more Haudenosaunee betrayal. Militant Shawnees and Delawares organized a series of diplomatic conferences on the Scioto River to convince southern Cherokees and Creeks to join them in an anticolonist alliance independent of the Six Nations. British officials, fearing a large coordinated Indian attack, attempted to hold back Virginia speculators and settlers.

Unable to defend the Proclamation Line and facing street protests over the Stamp Act and Townshend Duties, Britain shifted troops from the interior to the coast. In 1768, the first of four regiments of British troops arrived in Boston Harbor, ultimately bringing two thousand fighting men and more than one thousand women and children as supporters and dependents with them. The **standing army** not only patrolled the streets but also lived in Bostonians' houses and yards. Soldiers shared meals, joined families through marriage and godparentage, and competed with Bostonians for scarce jobs by taking on part-time work to supplement insufficient wages.

In March 1770, tensions between British soldiers and Boston teenagers turned a taunting snowball fight into a deadly shooting; five Bostonians died, including Crispus Attucks, a forty-seven-year-old runaway slave of African and Indian ancestry who worked as a sailor. Lawyer John Adams defended the soldiers and officers in a prominent trial and won their acquittal, but his cousin, political organizer Samuel Adams, turned the event into anti-British propaganda. He arranged a funeral procession of ten thousand mourners and, by calling the incident the **Boston Massacre**, linked it to the recent St. George's Field Massacre (1768) in which British soldiers in London had killed seven people by firing into a crowd. The London crowd, too, was protesting British displays of arbitrary power. That group demanded the release from prison of radical British politician John Wilkes, a champion of freedom of speech, a critic of governmental corruption, and an opponent of the Townshend Duties who had corresponded with Boston's Sons of Liberty. In the hands of Sam Adams, Boston's conflict, rooted in labor competition, became part of transatlantic opposition to imperial might.

backcountry Region bordering Indian lands and colonial settlements in Western New York, Pennsylvania, and the Carolinas unified by intermarriage and undermined by competing land claims.

regulator movement Coordinated activities of backcountry colonists to protest their lack of political representation and vulnerability to Indian warfare and debt collectors.

Treaty of Fort Stanwix Agreement between Britain and the Six Nations signed in 1768 marking the Ohio River as the western border of British land claims. It voided the 1763 Royal Proclamation.

standing army Permanent military force in peacetime or wartime. British standing army was controlled by Parliament.

Boston Massacre Inflammatory label given to a violent clash between British soldiers and Bostonians in which five Americans died.

From Resistance to Revolution

Thomas Paine's *Common Sense* was a widely read seventy-seven-page pamphlet urging "the Inhabitants of America" to separate from Great Britain. Published after fighting had begun but before independence was declared, it combined political theory and history with polemic, as this portrait and cover page text suggest. By using common language and familiar stories, Paine declared "it is my design to make those that can scarcely read understand."

How did the timing and style of *Common Sense* influence those who read it? How would its influence on the people living in the American colonies differ from the influence of protests or boycotts? ▶

Go to MindTap® to practice history with the Chapter 6 **Primary Source Writing Activity: From Resistance to Revolution.** Read and view primary sources and respond to a writing prompt.

COMMON SENSE; ADDRESSED TO THE INHABITANTS OF AMERICA, On the following interesting SUBJECTS.

THOMAS PAINE.

The Charles J. Tanenbaum Collection of the Eighteenth Century/British Museum

Turmoil on the East Coast and in the North American interior intensified in the early 1770s as conflicts between British colonists and London on the one hand and between Native Americans and colonists on the other, hardened into opposing camps. People across colonial North America connected their personal grievances to larger political goals. Initially, Britain attempted to treat colonial rebellion as a police matter, focused on subduing rowdy Bostonians. For some colonists, however, 1774 marked a transformation from separate colonial protests into a coordinated opposition movement. In a matter of months, debate and protest turned to armed conflict and a new political body linked thirteen of Britain's North American colonies. By 1776, one segment of the population was committed to political independence from Britain. Another—enslaved African Americans—sought liberty with Britain.

☞ As you read, think about how the events between 1754 and 1776 changed the context and meaning of colonial protests and shaped the Declaration of Independence.

6-3a Imperial Laws and Escalating Colonial Reactions

When it repealed the Townshend Duties in 1770, Parliament retained the tax on tea to affirm its right to tax colonies directly. As an Asian-grown, British-imported daily habit, tea held powerful symbolic significance for the nonconsumption movement. "The produce of the West-Indies

{ The increasing presence of tax collectors and imperial troops begins to create a sense of shared colonial struggle.

debauches the country," declared one critic, bemoaning the fact that many continued to buy and drink that "Chinese drug," often from smuggled Dutch sources. Their inability to give up tea seemed to demonstrate colonial Americans' inability to sacrifice for the common good.

Sacrifice was a key theme of the nonconsumption movement as it turned from its original goal—to hurt Britain financially—into a broader critique of colonial society. Boycotters drew on a blend of Protestant belief and classical **republicanism** in promoting the ideal of self-sacrifice. As a philosophy of governance, republicanism rested on a moral, utopian model in which leaders sacrificed individual interests for the sake of the greater good. This selflessness, called public **virtue**, was what entitled leaders to their power. A society of people willing to sacrifice for the common good could govern itself whereas a society of weak and selfish people would fall under the rule of a tyrant. Sons and Daughters of Liberty used the ideas of republicanism to rally supporters.

The 1773 Tea Act tested American virtue by making taxed British tea cheaper than the smuggled Dutch alternative. Under its provisions, the British East India Company gained permission to ship tea directly to America rather than stopping in England first to pay a tax, as was required of all other tea merchants. The law rescued the East India Company, which faced debts it could not pay, and tempted North American customers to buy British. Rather than celebrate cheaper tea, though, Americans in New York,

republicanism Originating in antiquity, political theory arguing that a class of independent citizens, sacrificing self-interest for the common good, can best govern society.

virtue Bravery and selflessness expressed by free men acting to protect their societies from corruption within or tyranny from without.

Library of Congress Prints and Photographs Division [Robert Sayer and John Bennett/LC-DIG-ppmsca-19468]

British View of Patriotic Ladies British satirists mocked American revolutionaries as bullies or fools, using revolutionary politics for personal gain. This English cartoon ridicules the women of Edenton, North Carolina, who signed a pledge to boycott British tea. The artist depicts the women flirting and neglecting their duties as mothers. A dog chews on the child's ear while urinating on a tea canister. ▲

Philadelphia, Charles Town, and Boston organized to refuse the shipments of the British monopoly. On December 16, 1773, a group of colonists—merchants, builders, artisans, farmers—dressed in Indian styles boarded three ships carrying East India tea and dumped £10,000 worth into Boston Harbor. Shoemaker George Hewes remembered that to prevent scavenging, sailors and Bostonians rowed out to sink any floating remains by beating them with their paddles "to render its entire destruction inevitable."

Parliament responded to what became known as the *Boston Tea Party* with a series of laws designed to punish and isolate the city. Conceived as Coercive Acts (to coerce obedience), the laws closed the port of Boston to international commerce, forbade most coastal trade (see Table 6.1), and replaced Massachusetts's representative government and public meetings with appointed officials. These appointments removed the beleaguered Thomas Hutchinson, putting commander Thomas Gage in his place. They also gave British officers the right to commandeer privately owned uninhabited buildings and house troops in them, a practice called **quartering**.

Finding themselves economically isolated and under military occupation, Bostonians called the laws **Intolerable Acts**. Stories of food scarcity and the brutal behavior of imperial officials, which spread through newspapers, pamphlets, and letters circulating among the Sons of Liberty, helped to engender sympathy for Bostonians. From other regions, colonists sent sheep, rice, firewood, and other provisions to Boston's poor in the crisis. One group in Durham, New Hampshire, noted, "the methods by which the ministry sought to divide, have happily united us."

That same spring of 1774, Parliament's **Quebec Act** addressed turmoil in the backcountry with another sweeping assertion of power. The act merged the Ohio Valley region

Table 6.1 The Escalating Crisis

Between 1764 and 1774, the British government sought tighter economic and political control over its American colonies from Quebec south to the West Indies. People in the coastal mainland colonies responded with increasingly coordinated resistance. Twice, Britain had to back down, repealing the Stamp Act and most of the Townshend Duties.

Act	Provisions	Reactions
Sugar Act 1764	Reduced tax on molasses and added tax on sugar, coffee, calico, etc.; established vice-admiralty court	Individual colonies petition for repeal
Currency Act 1764	Outlawed colonial paper money	Scattered protests; circulation of pamphlets
Stamp Act 1765	Placed tax on printed materials to be purchased with specie	Street protests; nonimportation movement; formation of Sons of Liberty; Stamp Act Congress; repealed in 1766
Declaratory Act 1766	Asserted Parliament's authority to tax American colonies	Scattered protests
Townshend Acts 1767	Placed tax on imported paper, lead, glass, paint, tea; revenues to pay British administrators	Nonconsumption movement; formation of Daughters of Liberty; repealed in 1770 except for tax on tea
Tea Act 1773	Permitted East India Company to sell tea in colonies with lower tax	Protests dumping and confiscating tea
Coercive (Intolerable) Acts 1774	Closed Boston port, cut powers of Massachusetts elected officials, permitted troop quartering in private buildings	First Continental Congress, 1774
Quebec Act 1774	Acknowledged large British colony with protected Catholicism and French civil law	First Continental Congress, 1774

with former French Canada into a single colony with a centralized administration. In keeping with former French colonial practice, there was no representative government, and Catholics could continue practicing their religion freely. To the Protestant community on the North Atlantic coast, the act seemed to endorse arbitrary and tyrannical authority on the continent, a threat to all. Even more pressingly, colonists who wanted Ohio Valley land for themselves—as speculators, traders, or farmers—believed themselves to be shut out, victims of British tyranny.

6-3b Continental Congress

In May and June 1774, political leaders in Boston, Providence, Philadelphia, New York, and Williamsburg called for an intercolonial congress to address Britain's

> A new political body coordinates protest movements in individual colonies but neglects borderland conflicts.

escalating measures. When royal governors attempted to stop the election of delegates by dismissing colonial assemblies, organizers created independent conventions to choose representatives. In September 1774, fifty-five men from twelve North American colonies attended the **First Continental Congress** in Philadelphia. Delegates came together intending to use protest measures developed over the previous ten years in a newly coordinated style. They drafted a petition to King George III for relief from the Coercive Acts and the tea tax. They agreed to nonimportation and nonconsumption of British goods. They resolved to cut off Britain and the British West Indies from North American products. And they committed themselves to commercial independence by starting cloth manufactories.

To enforce these agreements, Congress authorized local **Committees of Observation and Inspection** to operate outside British law but within the spirit of boycott. Committee members, totaling seven thousand to eight thousand throughout the mainland colonies, were elected by the same men eligible to vote for colonial assemblies. Over time, these committees became temporary governments, aligning practical administration with the emerging rebellion. The **patriot** cause, opposed to the existing British rule, built on this shared structure of self-rule and sacrifice. Americans who still felt loyal to Britain accused the committees of mob mentality. Anglican clergyman Samuel Seabury warned New Yorkers about this quasigovernment "chosen by half a dozen fools in your neighborhood" who claimed the right to "examine your tea canisters, and molasses-jugs, and your wives' and daughters' petty-coats . . . if I must be enslaved, let it be by a king at least, and not by a parcel of upstart lawless committee-men."

The Continental Congress's *Declaration of Resolves* included a bill of rights for "the inhabitants of the English colonies in North America" that they believed to be fundamental: the right to life, liberty, and property; the right to local representative government; and the right to be free from a standing army imposed without consent. Overall, the Congress hoped to return to the situation of 1763 before the new taxes and increased presence of British imperial agents as well as the imposition of what they called "a ruinous system of colony administration . . . evidently calculated for enslaving these colonies, and with them, the British Empire."

Native Americans were not represented in the Continental Congress and most did not share its desire to roll back the presence of the British Empire. The Creeks in the Georgia backcountry valued British support against the tide of farmers and land speculators simultaneously attending the Continental Congress. Shawnees, Mingos, and Delawares in the Ohio River valley were combating a similar pattern of American land speculation and settlement and hoped British officials would intervene in the local violence. They were disappointed. In April 1774, Virginians who had crossed the Appalachians attacked and killed a group of Shawnee women and children. Retaliatory raids escalated into **Dunmore's War**, named for Lord Dunmore, royal governor of Virginia, who led the militia against the Shawnees and their allies. Typical of frontier fighting, Dunmore's War had members of the same family on both sides. John Ward, who as a child had been kidnapped and raised a Shawnee, fought for his adopted family; his father James, fighting for the Virginians, died in battle against him. When the Indians were defeated and forced to yield significant land in Kentucky territory, their ally the British government offered little real assistance. From Boston, Gage ordered the Virginians to retreat; he was ignored.

6-3c Early Fighting

Although the Continental Congress had put its grievances in the form of a loyal petition to King George, he received the request as defiance and declared the colonies in rebellion: "blows must decide whether they are to be subject to this country or independent." His ministers agreed, and in April 1775, the king ordered Gage to seize military supplies in Concord, outside of Boston. British soldiers and the Massachusetts

> Local militias take up arms while British leaders hope to put down opposition.

quartering Practice of housing occupying soldiers in civilian buildings rather than in separate barracks.

Intolerable Acts Protestors' name for Coercive Acts of 1774, British police actions that closed the port of Boston and removed Massachusetts's elected government to quash rebellion.

Quebec Act Parliamentary law passed in 1774 that created a large British colony retaining Catholicism and a nonrepresentative government that had existed under French control.

First Continental Congress Philadelphia meeting of representatives from twelve British North American colonies in 1774 to coordinate protests against escalating punitive British measures.

Committees of Observation and Inspection Elected groups in each colony who enforced the agreements of the Continental Congress.

patriot Term identifying someone who openly supported the cause of independence in the American Revolution. Also called Whig or rebel.

Dunmore's War Conflict in 1774 in which the Virginia militia and a Shawnee alliance fought over violations of the 1763 Royal Proclamation.

Global Americans **Daniel Boone** was born into a large Pennsylvania family in 1734 and grew up with Indians as neighbors. After serving with British forces in the Seven Years' War, Boone, his wife, and their children settled in backcountry Virginia. Supporting his family as a hunter and trapper brought him deep into Native American hunting grounds west of the 1763 Proclamation Line. In 1773, he and a group of Virginians attempted to establish a settlement there; they were turned back by Delawares, Shawnees, and Cherokees in a clash that killed Boone's son and fueled Dunmore's War. Two years later, the families established Boonesborough on the Kentucky River. Defending his town during the fighting of the Revolutionary War required shifting alliances because neutrality was not possible. In 1778, Boone was captured and adopted into a Shawnee community and then was charged with treason by Virginians for his negotiations with Shawnee and British allies. By the end of the war, Boone had become a Virginia militia officer and elected assemblyman.

Boone's 1784 biography made him into an American folk hero who fought Indians to clear the path for the "sweets of liberty." In Europe, he was celebrated as a "natural man" uncorrupted by civilization. After the war, a disputed land title sent him in search of a new identity once more, and he moved with his family across the Mississippi to live on Spanish-claimed land as a local official of Spain. As with many in the late eighteenth century, Boone was committed to land and personal independence and was willing to seek them within empires or as part of new polities.

militia had been in a stalemate for months and when Britain forced the issue by sending 700 troops to capture ammunition, fighting broke out. Militiamen defeated British soldiers at Lexington and nearby Concord, forcing them to retreat, with 272 casualties against 93 American casualties. The following month, Ethan Allen, Benedict Arnold, and a small force seized Fort Ticonderoga in northern New York, capturing British artillery that they then transported to Boston.

Such conflicts were typical of the first year of undeclared war: Standing British troops fought local colonial militias with little oversight from the rebel side. The Continental Congress initially relied on militias for practical and political reasons. Politically, members of Congress believed that adult male citizens were the best defenders of the community. Practically, there was

neither money nor time to raise an army, and so in May 1775, the Continental Congress turned the Massachusetts militia into the Continental Army, supplemented with expert riflemen from Pennsylvania, Maryland, and Virginia and under the command of George Washington, a Virginian.

Initially, the Continental Congress insisted that the conflict with Britain was a limited one. In July 1775, it prepared a speech for the Six Nations to accompany wampum belts that referred to Native Americans as "brothers." Attempting to re-establish the Covenant Chain as an American, rather than a British, alliance, agents representing Congress urged neutrality: "This is a family quarrel between us and Old England. You Indians are not concerned in it. We don't wish you to take up the hatchet against the king's troops. We desire you to remain at home, and not join on either side, but keep the hatchet buried deep." Six Nations chiefs largely agreed, at least temporarily, waiting to see how best to use the British–American conflict to their own advantage.

Although they called themselves the Continental Congress, the rebellious alliance did not include the northern territories won from France in the Seven Years' War. Early on, Congress authorized an attack on Quebec, hoping to win it from Britain as a fourteenth rebelling colony. In December 1775, two forces led by General Richard Montgomery coming from New York and Colonel Benedict Arnold traveling across Maine arrived at the walls of Quebec city. The soldiers were exhausted and weakened by smallpox. Yet knowing that

Newspapers Forge Connections Eighteenth-century newspapers circulated beyond their hometowns via packet ships and family correspondence. Papers in one city frequently reprinted material from another. This masthead of the *Massachusetts Spy*, published in the wake of fighting at Lexington and Concord, used a familiar image of Liberty and a quotation—"Liberty or Death!"—from a British play about the last Roman republican in order to appeal to "Americans" as a group. ▼

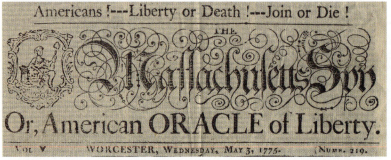

Americans !---Liberty or Death !---Join or Die !

The Massachusetts Spy

Or, American ORACLE of Liberty.

VOL V   WORCESTER, WEDNESDAY, MAY 3, 1775.   (NUMB. 219.

short-term militia enlistments would expire on January first, on December 31, in the midst of a blizzard, the American generals attacked. Montgomery was killed, Arnold wounded, and hundreds of Americans wounded or captured. Arnold's siege that followed was a disaster and by the summer of 1776, American forces had been permanently driven from Canada.

Faced with disloyal militias, Britain turned to potentially loyal enslaved men. As early as September 1774, a group of New England slaves had written to Gage, offering to fight for him in return for their freedom. Parliament discussed a measure to emancipate enslaved people in order to humble "the high aristocratic spirit of Virginia and the southern colonies." In November 1775, Virginia's royal governor Dunmore declared martial law in his province and offered freedom to any servants or slaves belonging to rebels who joined the king's forces. Dunmore's intent was tactical: to mobilize slaves and unnerve white rebels, not spark a general uprising. But enslaved people interpreted **Lord Dunmore's Proclamation** much more broadly. Among the first to join his "Ethiopian regiment" were eight of the twenty-seven slaves on the plantation of Peyton Randolph, a delegate to the Continental Congress. Within months, nearly one thousand slaves had joined and hundreds were captured trying. Outfitted in uniforms with "Liberty to Slaves" stitched across their chests, the men of the Ethiopian Regiment fought the patriot Virginia militia in December 1775 near Norfolk but were defeated. They retreated with the governor onto ships in the Chesapeake Bay. Only a fraction made it farther; most contracted smallpox in the close quarters of military accommodations and perished or were abandoned to die on Gwynn's Island.

In the same month that Dunmore issued his proclamation, the Continental Congress formally declared all blacks, slave or free, ineligible for military service. They gave many of the same reasons that opponents to the idea in Britain had: that merchants owed their livelihood to the slave trade, that arming enslaved people violated the honor of soldiers, and that it would provoke retaliation. Many whites also feared that enslaved people in colonies such as Jamaica would take the opportunity to launch an Atlanticwide slave insurrection. Washington, himself a slave owner, initially agreed but soon, in need of troops, changed his mind.

6-3d Declaration of Independence

Even as Congress formed an army and engaged in combat, many were reluctant to support a full independence movement that, should it fail, would mark them as traitors. Conservative members of the Continental Congress feared wartime instability would

{ Thirteen American colonies resolve to separate from Britain.

ignite rebellions from below, and those who profited from trade with or protection from the British Empire opposed the idea of separation. Thomas Paine's *Common Sense*, published in January 1776 and broadly distributed, reminded American colonists of the blood already shed and told them it was too late for reconciliation. Instead, they could "begin the world over again." Theirs was a struggle not "of a city, a country, a province, or a kingdom, but of a continent—of at least one eighth part of the habitable globe."

Paine linked independence with republicanism, highlighting the dangers of hereditary privilege and the corruption of European politics and optimistically envisioning a society united by a common good. John Adams, long a vigorous advocate of independence, complained that *Common Sense* was "a tolerable summary of the arguments which I had been repeating again and again in Congress for nine months." Those arguments, familiar on both sides of the Atlantic, came together in a new, compelling way in Paine's writing. Paine instructed readers to see European history as leading inevitably to the independence of North American colonies. It was only common sense for them to separate. And when they did, they would be leading a world-changing movement away from monarchy and toward republican freedom.

On June 7, 1776, Richard Henry Lee of Virginia proposed to Congress: "That these united colonies are, and of right ought to be, free and independent states, that they are absolved from all allegiance to the British crown, and that all political connection between them and the state of Great Britain is, and ought to be, totally dissolved." Voting on the proposal was postponed until July; in the meantime, a five-man committee, consisting of Adams, Franklin, Thomas Jefferson of Virginia, Roger Sherman of Connecticut, and Robert Livingston of New York, set to work writing a declaration. Because it would mark the point of no return in the conflict between Britain and the colonies, the declaration had to explain the reasons for separation and establish the new nation. It also would proclaim the ideals of the "one people" it spoke for. Jefferson wrote a draft that was edited and revised by the committee and Congress as a whole. To secure the support of slaveholding South Carolina, Congress removed a paragraph in which Jefferson blamed the English king for the slave trade, which he called a "cruel war against human nature itself, violating it's most sacred rights of life & liberty."

The **Declaration of Independence** drew on the experience and rhetoric of the anti-Stamp Act protests, the nonimportation and nonconsumption movements, and the Regulators. The document pulled together the political theories that had influenced Paine. Its opening section declared that "all men are created equal" and

Lord Dunmore's Proclamation
Policy announced in 1775 that slaves belonging to patriots could win freedom by joining the Virginia governor's forces.

Declaration of Independence
Document establishing the United States as an independent nation, enumerating the causes for separation, and declaring the classically liberal ideas of its signers.

History without Borders
Declarations of Independence

Republic of Texas declared independence from Mexico, 1836.

United States declared independence from Britain, 1776.

South Carolina declared independence from the U.S., 1860.

Mexico declared independence from Spain, 1821; Central American Provinces followed, 1823.

Brazil separated from Portugal as an independent empire, 1822.

Crimea first declared independence, 1991.

Korean self-determination movement declared independence from Japanese Empire, 1919.

Palestine National Council declared independence from Israel, 1988.

Minority white government declared Southern Rhodesia independent from Britain, 1965; Britain and United Nations deemed it illegal.

NORTH AMERICA

SOUTH AMERICA

EUROPE

ASIA

AFRICA

AUSTRALIA

PACIFIC OCEAN

ATLANTIC OCEAN

INDIAN OCEAN

PACIFIC OCEAN

Year independence declared

	Independence gained	Unsuccessful or not recognized
Age of revolutions, 1776–1847		
World War I dissolutions, 1917–1919		
Anti-colonial movements, 1945–1988		
Fall of Soviet Union, 1990–1992		
Other declarations, 1849–1993		

—— International boundaries, 1993

Declarations of Independence, 1776–1993 More than 100 nations have issued declarations of independence, in four main waves. In the first "Age of Revolutions," the people of Haiti and of Spanish and Portuguese America broke away from their European rulers. After World War I, nations demanded the right to separate from the large land empires of Europe. A third round of anticolonial independence movements accompanied the end of World War II. Most recently, many states sought independence with the fall of the Soviet Union. ▲

From the beginning, the Declaration of Independence was both a distinctively American artifact and a global one. The fifty-five original signers dipped their pens into an inkstand crafted by an Irishman from silver mined in Spanish America by enslaved Africans and native South Americans. Nine signers had been born in England or Ireland; a quarter of them had been educated in Europe. Thomas Jefferson and the other men who wrote the Declaration of Independence blended global ideals, such as that of natural rights, with a specific claim to have become "one people," a new state in the international community.

The first printed copies of the Declaration began their global journey as Dutch undershirts. Papermakers in the Netherlands collected linen rags from old shirts, shredded them into a pulpy soup, dipped frames set with a fine mesh into the mixture, and smoothed and dried each sheet to

Library of Congress, Manuscript Division

John Adams Library copy transferred from the supervisors of the Temple and School Fund. Quincy, Mass., 1894

Draft of the Declaration This detail of Thomas Jefferson's handwritten draft of the Declaration of Independence shows the edits added by Adams and Franklin. The final document was a product of negotiation and discussion. ▲

French Translation of the Declaration of Independence, 1778 Philadelphia printers arranged for translations of the Declaration of Independence that they then sold abroad with translated copies of state constitutions and other Revolution-era political documents. In this way, a document intended for one audience was repackaged and circulated in another context. ▲

create fine-grained paper. The paper traveled to England, where it was taxed and placed on a British ship, as imperial law demanded, and next exported to Philadelphia. John Dunlap, the man who bought the paper in 1776, had emigrated from his home country of Ireland in the middle of the Seven Years' War. He used a British printing press to stamp words on Dutch-made paper to announce a new entity to the world, the United States of America.

Assembled in Philadelphia in the summer of 1776, copies of the Declaration of Independence soon traveled the oceans again. Within a month, the document was reprinted in London newspapers. The following month, people in Copenhagen and Warsaw were reading translations of the Declaration in their publications. A vast communication network of newspapers, businessmen, soldiers and spies carried copies around the world. Some foreign readers pointed out the hypocrisy of slaveholding authors claiming "life, liberty, and the pursuit of happiness" as universal rights. Others were inspired by

the idea of colonized people breaking away from the imperial power that ruled them and establishing a government that had to respond to its citizens.

More than one hundred times since 1776, foreign states have broken off from their earlier affiliations, declared independence, and presented themselves as sovereign to face the international community with written proclamations. The 1918 Czechoslovak Declaration of Independence explicitly cited the "American Declaration of Independence." Ho Chi Minh proclaimed an independent Vietnam in 1945 with 150-year-old words. Internationally, declarations of independence marked the change from a world of empires in the eighteenth century to a world of independent states in the twenty-first century.

Passages from the Declaration opposing tyranny and promoting equality became the tools of international revolutionaries and reformers. French radicals published the *Declaration of the Rights of Man and Citizen* in 1789. In 1848, Elizabeth Cady Stanton launched the American women's suffrage movement

with a "Declaration of Sentiments" that included the line "all men and women are created equal." Independent states formed after World War II, joined together at the United Nations, likewise embraced revolutionary claims of human equality. The UN's 1948 Universal Declaration of Human Rights recognized the equality not only of nations, but also of "all members of the human family."

Critical Thinking Questions

▶ Why has this eighteenth-century document, a product of a specific context, proved so versatile a tool for radically different groups?

▶ Which parts of the Declaration have had the widest resonance in the years since its publication?

Go to MindTap® to engage with an interactive version of **History without Borders: Declarations of Independence.** Learn from an interactive map, view related video, and respond to critical thinking questions.

asserted humanity's rights to "life, liberty, and the pursuit of happiness." It went on to accuse the king of planning to establish "an absolute tyranny over these states," and to object to Parliament's acts regarding taxation and the presence of British troops, objections that had filled the petitions of previous years.

The Declaration asserted that "these United Colonies are, and of Right, ought to be free and independent states." It did not define territorial borders but referred to a western "frontier" as a place where the king encouraged "the merciless Indian savages, whose known rule of warfare is an undistinguished destruction of all ages, sexes and conditions." Frontier warfare was vicious, but by tying the backcountry conflict to alleged indiscriminate Indian warfare, the Declaration tried to dismiss specific grievances over treaty violations that drew Native Americans into the larger conflict.

By proclaiming a distinct nation, the Declaration of Independence invited European involvement in what had been a contest within the British Empire. France and Spain both covertly gave substantial sums to the rebelling colonists through a company created to launder the money on its way across the Atlantic. This fund purchased 80 percent of the gunpowder American forces used that year. The Declaration's assertions about natural rights held by "all men" would prove to have a significant international legacy in the long run, even though their short-term relevance seemed precarious.

6-4

War for Independence

Jean Baptiste Antoine de Verger, a French officer in Rochambeau's army, painted this watercolor in the diary he kept as eyewitness to war. It depicts four soldiers of the Continental forces at Yorktown in 1781: a black soldier from the First Rhode Island Regiment, a New England militiaman, a backcountry rifleman, and a French officer.

What does this painting indicate about the makeup of pro-independence forces? What can you surmise about their different motivations? How did that makeup matter politically? ▶

Soldiers in Uniform, 1781–1784 (w/c on paper), Verger, Jean Baptiste Antoine de (1762–1851)/Brown University Library, Providence, Rhode Island, USA/The Bridgeman Art Library

As a war fought in towns and villages as well as on battlefields, the American Revolution profoundly altered the daily lives and political fortunes of all involved. Everyone contended with shortages and death as the fighting dragged on for more than six years in North America and two more around the globe. For Continental soldiers, early enlistees' confidence that the virtuous cause of independence would ennoble warfare gave way to the grinding reality of military discipline and insufficient resources. For noncombatants caught between warring forces, the fighting was a bloody civil war manifested in racial and gender violence. For European empires, the war was a chance to settle old imperial scores in the global balance of power. The resolution of the war redrew the map of the world for a second time in two decades by creating a new, large, and independent United States.

mercenary Professional soldier who fights for a country other than his own, many of whom were employed by the British army during the Revolutionary War.

☞ As you read, seek to understand the Revolution from various perspectives. In what ways was it an imperial conflict? In what ways was it a civil war?

6-4a Military Strategy in the Early Stages of War

In 1776, the government of Prime Minister Lord North planned to defeat the Continental Army the way that Britain had defeated the French army a decade earlier—by outmaneuvering it in battlefield engagements, winning, and then dominating peace negotiations. British forces concentrated on taking colonial centers such as New York City, which they occupied by fall of 1776, forcing Washington to retreat through New Jersey, which the British soon controlled as well. Britain relied on its powerful navy, standing army, and thousands of soldiers from northern Germany, whom the colonists called *Hessians*. The Hessians were **mercenaries**, men who fought on behalf of the foreign country that hired them. The British also expanded Lord Dunmore's policy of recruiting runaway slaves. Although his Proclamation had called for able-bodied warriors, one-third of those

> British and U.S. leaders devise and revise their strategies.

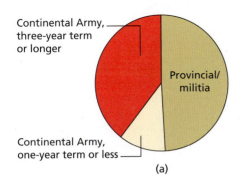

Massachusetts Recruits, 1777

Continental Army, three-year term or longer

Provincial/militia

Continental Army, one-year term or less

(a)

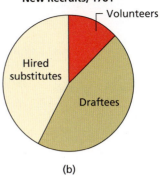

Loudoun County, Virginia New Recruits, 1781

Volunteers

Hired substitutes

Draftees

(b)

Figure 6.1(a) Massachusetts Recruits, 1777 The year 1777 marked a turning point when soldiers signed enlistments of three years or more in the Continental Army. Nonetheless, many men in Massachusetts preferred the shorter commitments of the militias, which were sent on brief expeditions of a month or two. ▲ Source: Walter Sargent, "The Massachusetts Rank and File of 1777," in *War and Society in the American Revolution*, ed. John Resch and Walter Sargent (Northern Illinois University Press, 2006).

Figure 6.1(b) Loudoun County, Virginia, New Recruits, 1781 In 1781, the Virginia Assembly set quotas for counties to supply recruits for the Continental Army. In Loudoun County, those who enlisted voluntarily were all landless laborers who were promised a bounty of cash, land, and a slave if they served for the duration of the war. Draftees and substitutes hired by draftees served eighteen months. ▲ Source: Michael A. McDonnell, "'Fit for Common Service?': Class, Race, and Recruitment in Revolutionary Virginia," in *War and Society in the American Revolution*, ed. John Resch and Walter Sargent (Northern Illinois University Press, 2006).

who reached British lines were women and children. Soon, anywhere there were British ships, there were slaves trying to get to them. Most ended up in noncombat support roles, segregated and underfed. The lucky ones traveled with the troops; the unlucky suffered disproportionately from malnutrition and smallpox.

Underfunded and underequipped, the Continental Congress ran the war in the North as one of attrition, depending on hit-and-run strikes and hoping for enough local successes to convince the British public that fighting Americans was not worth the cost. Often in retreat, the Continental Army had a few victories. Crucially, on Christmas Day in 1776, Washington, with soldiers eager for their enlistments to end in the new year, crossed the frigid Delaware River to surprise Hessians camped at Trenton, New Jersey. Capturing most of the garrison, the soldiers stayed with Washington to attack again, at Princeton, on January 3, 1777, forcing a British retreat.

As the initial enthusiasm and prospect of quick victory faded, Congress abandoned the idea of a militia-style force in favor of a standing army. In April 1777, it approved a draft and encouraged enlistment standards that changed the profile of the Continental Army (see Figures 6.1a and 6.1b). Many states permitted draftees to send substitutes, either free or enslaved, to serve in their stead. In New Jersey, as many as 40 percent of soldiers were substitutes. Pennsylvania and New Jersey also enlisted large numbers of recent German and Irish immigrants who had been working as bound servants.

To attract a fighting force for the duration, Congress offered varieties of freedom to enlistees. To recent immigrants and indentured servants, it promised land, which for most colonists was the bedrock of individual liberty. To enemy deserters, prisoners of war, and people who had failed to pay their taxes, Congress granted freedom from

imprisonment or execution. For slaves, Congress changed the existing policy and offered freedom from enslavement. To free blacks, it offered the dignity of service, which had long been associated with civil rights. Although a majority of African Americans sided with the British, about five thousand served in the Continental Army and still more in racially integrated state militias. The result was that more soldiers served longer terms and were subject to stricter discipline, but the idea of a patriot–citizens' army died. Congress also sent Silas Deane to Europe to attract officers with expertise that the Americans lacked. Among his recruits was the young and idealistic Marquis de Lafayette, a French army officer who became a close friend of Washington.

These American regulars marched against British forces in New York and Philadelphia in the summer and fall of 1777 (see Map 6.3). Britain planned a pincer movement to deal a decisive defeat to American armies and cut off New England, the center of colonial resistance. Because the pincer's timing failed, separate engagements yielded opposite results. Outside Philadelphia, General William Howe defeated Washington at Brandywine Creek and Germantown with troops outnumbering the Americans three to one. The British occupied the colonial capital of Philadelphia while Continental Army units retreated to nearby Valley Forge for the winter, hungry, injured, and undersupplied. To the North, British General John Burgoyne made slow progress from Quebec. After skirmishes with American troops, he was forced to surrender his entire force to American General Horatio Gates at Saratoga in October 1777. Britain sent Sir William Howe to replace Burgoyne.

The experience at Valley Forge, where two thousand of eleven thousand soldiers spent the winter shoeless, forced

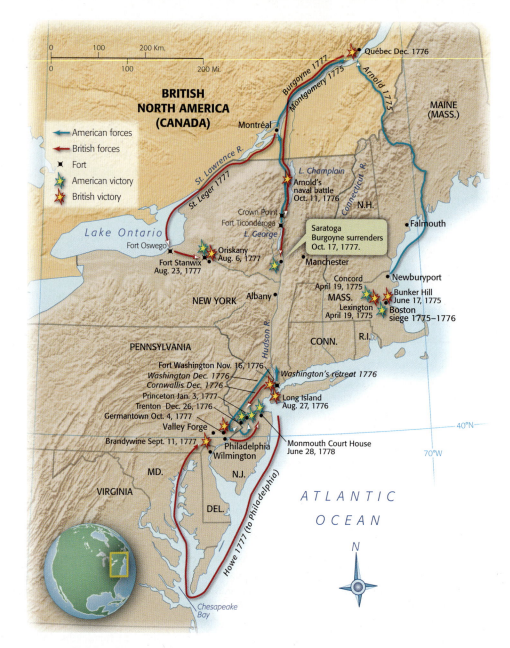

Map 6.3 Fighting in the North Revolutionary warfare began in Massachusetts. The British hoped to isolate rebellious New Englanders by occupying New York City and then Philadelphia. Troops of British general Burgoyne were successful at Quebec and in engagements along the St. Lawrence River and its connected waterways, but the American rebels defeated him at Saratoga. ▲

Americans to reconsider their scorn for British military organization, starting with support staff. While the British army maintained a standard of one woman for every ten men to do the work of cooking, cleaning, mending, and nursing, the Continental Army had only one woman for forty-four men. Washington, like other American generals, assumed that women among the troops encouraged prostitution and immorality. Consequently, two thousand five hundred soldiers died that winter and spring from disease, malnutrition, and hypothermia. Frederich Wilhelm, Baron von Steuben, a Prussian officer, arrived at Valley Forge and promptly hired more women. He also imposed a regime of drill and discipline for American soldiers that began to convert them into a more effective force. In June 1778, Washington's army fought a more evenly pitched, though inconclusive, battle against Henry Clinton's army at Monmouth, New Jersey, and the theater of war shifted to the South.

6-4b American Revolution as Imperial Conflict

American victory at Saratoga brought France openly into the war as an ally, decisively turning the American Revolution into one more imperial conflict. Hoping to see their longtime enemy Britain thwarted, the French court and French public had been inclined to the pro-independence side from the beginning. "There is a hundred times more enthusiasm for this Revolution in any Paris café than in all the colonies together," claimed Louis Duportail, a Frenchman who worked as chief engineer of the Continental Army. Benjamin Franklin, envoy of the Continental Congress living in Paris during the war, stoked that enthusiasm by entertaining French high society, but the French government wanted evidence that the United States could win, and Saratoga provided it. In February 1778, Franklin and French foreign minister Charles Gravier, Comte de Vergennes signed the **Treaty of Alliance** between the two countries, promising military and financial support in return for French dominion over any Caribbean islands it captured in the course of fighting. France and the United States also signed the Treaty of Amity and Commerce promoting open trade between the two. Spain declared a separate war against Britain in June 1779. Seeing an opportunity to seize valuable plantations, France and

> People around the world experience the Revolution as an imperial conflict with local consequences.

Spain spent heavily on troops in the Caribbean, India, and elsewhere. France also sent six thousand French regulars under the command of Comte de Rochambeau to Rhode Island in 1780 (see Map 6.4).

The Caribbean was the main focus of France's attempts to avenge the losses of 1763 because of its tremendous wealth and the shaky loyalties of merchants and traders there. Although West Indian colonial assemblies proclaimed loyalty to Britain—largely because they needed military protection from slave revolts and American privateers—traders from British, French, Dutch, and Spanish islands all smuggled military supplies to the American forces in small, nighttime boat deliveries. The people in ostensibly neutral Dutch St. Eustatius (with a population that included 40 percent British merchants) supplied a weekly convoy of French merchant ships to aid the war effort.

The entry of France, Spain, and finally the Netherlands into the American Revolution in 1780 turned a colonial uprising into a far-flung conflict in which multiple empires had a stake. Following the early examples of Lafayette and Von Steuben, aristocratic officers from Poland, France, and Germany journeyed to America to offer their expertise to the Continental Army. Except for some troop support from Prussia, Britain had no European allies. Its navy attacked

Treaty of Alliance Agreement signed in 1778 by the United States and France confirming French military and financial support in exchange for French territorial expansion in the Caribbean.

Map 6.4 The Revolution Worldwide, 1775–1783 Like the Seven Years' War, the American Revolution was in part an imperial conflict over trade and territory between Britain and its adversaries around the world. Many of the earlier sites of warfare reignited as Europe's empires sought to undo Britain's earlier gains. ▼

merchant ships from any nation suspected of transporting military supplies to the United States. In 1780, Russia, the Holy Roman Empire, the Ottoman Empire, the Scandinavian countries, and others signed a League of Armed Neutrality, insisting that any ship under the flag of a neutral country should be able to travel and trade freely.

6-4c American Revolution as Civil War

> Native Americans and Loyalists discover that neutrality is impossible.

In the streets, villages, farms, and forests of North America, people experienced the American Revolution as a civil war. A significant minority—perhaps 20 percent—in the thirteen colonies openly opposed the patriot cause; others resisted passively. Called **Loyalists**, for their loyalty to Britain, or Tories, by their enemies, to link them with political enemies in Parliament, these people did not share a single ideology or motivation for remaining committed to Britain. Some living in the backcountry, as well as religious and ethnic minorities, considered the empire to be their protector against locally powerful colonial Americans. Many Native Americans, too, saw the British Empire as the only remaining counterweight to colonists' encroachments on their land. For wealthy elites with close ties to British leadership, the empire was the source of their livelihood and identity.

Neutrality proved impossible. Thomas Brown, an English-born plantation owner in Georgia believed that events in New England had "no connection or concern" to his life, but when he refused to sign a patriot association list in 1775, six of his neighbors attacked him. They broke his skull, tied him to a tree, poured tree sap on him, burned him, and scalped him. He recovered sufficiently to rally backcountry residents into a Loyalist militia renowned for its brutality.

Wherever rebel militias, loyal militias, Indian forces, and regular British and Continental troops converged, civilians suffered. Soldiers commandeered livestock and burned crops. Both European and American colonial armies used rape to terrify and conquer. The Continental Congress commissioned a report on wartime rape to document British atrocities but was unable to get fearful women to report the attacks. Indian warriors viewed terror tactics and captive-taking differently. They, too, sought revenge on enemy communities but did not rape. Starving and fearing for their safety, thousands of Native Americans,

National Portrait Gallery, London

Diplomat Benjamin Franklin Scientist, printer, and politician, Franklin served as a minister to the French court during the Revolution. French people loved his "American" identity, typified by the backwoods fur hat he wears in this French portrait. His credibility, however, came from his highly respected position as a learned scientist and erudite "citizen of the world." Across the Atlantic, his son, William Franklin, was the loyalist governor of New Jersey who was arrested, imprisoned, and then exiled from the United States. ▲

The War at Sea French involvement in the American Revolution expanded the naval war. John Paul Jones of the Continental Navy commanded the *Bonhomme Richard*, a ship he received from France and renamed after Franklin's *Almanac*. In September 1779, Jones attacked the British vessel *Seraphis* off the West Coast of England, where it was protecting a merchant convoy. Jones's victory, against long odds, made him a celebrated hero; depictions of the battle were copied and republished across Europe as in this French engraving. ▼

Library of Congress Prints and Photographs Division

George Romney/Getty Images

Global Americans

Joseph Brant (or **Thayendanega**) was born to a Mohawk Wolf clan family along the Ohio River in 1743. As a young teenager, he followed his sister Molly Brant's husband Sir William Johnson into battle during the Seven Years' War. He attended Moor's Charity School (later Dartmouth College) in Lebanon, Connecticut, where he converted to the Anglican religion and became skilled in English language and European history. He also met his first wife, Margaret, an Oneida with whom he had two children before she died. When the American Revolution broke out, Brant organized Haudenosaunee warriors to attack American settlements. His success and leadership against the American rebels earned him a captain's commission in the British army, although he continued to fight as a Haudenosaunee war chief and labored to forge a pan-Indian alliance to hold back U.S. settlement.

After the Treaty of Paris, Britain rewarded him for his loyalty to the empire with a grant of land for his family (he had married a Mohawk woman, Catharine) and his followers along the Grand River in British-held Canada. His decision to side with Britain had made him and his people exiles. Brant committed to international missionary work, traveling to England to raise money and translating selections of the Bible into the Mohawk language, before dying in 1807. His comfort both in front of the English court and at the Haudenosaunee council fires exemplified his skill in manipulating imperial structures for the benefit of Indian peoples.

colonists, and enslaved people fled, often to live as refugees in cities occupied by the British.

The Haudenosaunee alliance broke apart over whether to continue support for the British. Joseph Brant and Molly Brant, Mohawk siblings with deep ties to British institutions and officials, organized raids on American settlements and mobilized warriors to add troop strength to British campaigns in New York and Pennsylvania. In return, British outposts such as Fort Niagara sheltered and provisioned thousands of Indians from nearly twenty-two different tribes and family groups. Yet Oneidas and Tuscaroras, members of the Six Nations Confederacy, fought on the side of the rebelling Americans at the Battle of Oriskany in August 1777. In 1779, when American troops burned their towns and fields, the Onondagas, another member of the Six Nations, joined the British. Mary Jemison, kidnapped as a child to live as a Seneca in New York, recalled that the American forces destroyed her town, "burnt our houses, killed what few cattle and horses they could find, destroyed our fruit trees, and left nothing but bare soil and timber."

For Cherokees, the decision to join the fighting in the South grew from a generational power struggle that split the community into its own civil war. Like the allied Shawnees to the North, Cherokee families faced frequent border attacks from colonists eager for land. Led by matrons and older clan leaders such as Attakullakulla, who urged a limited response to frontier murder, many Cherokees attempted to maintain neutral relationships. As their economy had grown more focused on the deerskin and slave trades, they had become more dependent on the gunpowder, bullets, and trading partnerships offered by British connections. But younger warriors strongly opposed the program of neutrality and appeasement, especially as it involved selling off Cherokee land to mixed-race traders. Well aware of the ambivalent

loyalties within the Cherokees, both South Carolina patriots and British Indian agents sought in 1775 and 1776 to win them over with trade goods and diplomatic missions. Delegates from Shawnee and Delaware communities who had been urging unified action since the Treaty of Fort Stanwix joined new emissaries from northern Six Nation tribes to press for a British alliance. Young Cherokee warriors were less interested in alliance than in attacking the immediate threat to their well-being. Declaring that it was "Better to die like men than to diminish away by inches," Attakullakulla's son, Dragging Canoe, launched an attack in 1776 against South Carolinians living on the Cherokee side of the 1763 Proclamation Line. The fighting lasted into the 1780s.

Britain's strategy in the South exploited the civil war dimension of the conflict. Enlisting the assistance of Loyalists, enslaved people, and pro-British Indians, the British seized territory in Georgia and South Carolina between 1778 and 1780, occupying Savannah and Charles Town (later Charleston). Soldiers commanded by Lord Charles Cornwallis crushed American forces dominated by militiamen at the Battle of Camden in August 1780. As retribution and revenge intensified the violence in the South, prisoners on both sides suffered the consequences. In North Carolina in 1781, patriot militiamen "hewed [Loyalist prisoners] to pieces with broadswords."

The British hoped to hand control of the South over to Loyalists and then sweep northward. Instead, the British army under Lord Cornwallis became dispersed and overextended as it pursued Continental forces, trying to force an engagement (see Map 6.5). In 1781, Nathanael Greene, the new commander of the American Southern Department, devised a strategy of divide and

Loyalists People who opposed the cause of independence, some of whom were motivated by personal gain, others by a desire for protection offered by the British Empire.

Map 6.5 Fighting in the South British strategy depended on loyal militias, enslaved runaways, and supportive Indians in the South. British troops, however, became overextended as rebellious Americans divided and evaded them. The final continental confrontation at Yorktown depended on timing and the arrival of the French. ▲

conquer that eventually outmaneuvered the British forces. Separate contingents of the American army joined with local patriot militias to engage the British army at different times and different places: Cowpens in January 1781; Guilford Court House in March; and Hobkirk's Hill in April. Cowpens was a surprising victory for Americans; the other two were losses but inflicted heavy casualties. Between battles, the American army used strategic withdrawals to force British troops to chase them beyond established supply lines. By the summer, Cornwallis

moved his diminished forces north to Virginia and encamped at Yorktown on orders from General Clinton to fortify an anchoring point for the British Navy.

6-4d Surrender and Settlement

In August 1781, when Washington learned that a French fleet was heading north from the Caribbean, he and French commander Rochambeau abandoned plans to retake New York and rapidly marched south to meet Cornwallis's

{ The United States wins independence.

Treaty of Paris Agreement between Britain and the United States ending the war and redrawing the map of North America without reference to the claims of Native Americans.

The New York Public Library/Art Resource, NY

Reconciliation at War's End The Revolutionary War ended with another treaty in Paris that from the European perspective left the future open. This 1782 British cartoon, "The Reconciliation between Britania and Her Daughter" depicts the United States as a Native American embracing her "mother." On the left, a Frenchman tugs at America, worrying "Begar they will be friends again if you don't pull a little harder here." A Dutchman, leaning on a barrel, vows to wait before choosing sides again. ▲

own benefit. The British, who wanted American trade for themselves, offered territory belonging to Native Americans to sweeten the deal. The **Treaty of Paris**, signed in September 1783, set the boundaries of the newly independent United States to the north at the border with Canada, to the west at the Mississippi River, and to the south just above East and West Florida, which once again passed to Spain. Britain also signed peace treaties with France, Spain, and the Netherlands (see Map 6.6).

Wyandot chiefs, calling themselves "your children," had pressed to be "remembered in the Treaty," but the territorial claims of Native Americans—not present at the treaty negotiations—were ignored. They felt betrayed by their allies and asserted that Britain did not have the right to give up land it did not possess. Furthermore, they recognized that they were now left to deal with enemy Americans on their own.

troops. By September, the fleet of Comte de Grasse had defeated a British fleet and blockaded the mouth of the Chesapeake. Washington and Rochambeau arrived at Yorktown and with 7,800 Frenchmen, 5,700 Continental soldiers, and 3,200 militiamen, surrounded Cornwallis on land. The allied army dug besieging trenches and bombarded the British with artillery fire. In little over a week, Cornwallis surrendered. At the surrender ceremony, October 19, 1781, Cornwallis's representative attempted to deliver his sword to Rochambeau, who deferred to Washington, crediting the new United States with a victory that had depended upon French assistance.

Fighting in the Caribbean, however, did not stop. Although U.S. independence had been won, the imperial balance of power around the globe was still in play. France captured St. Kitts but failed to conquer St. Lucia and Jamaica. On the other side of the world, France fought in West Africa and India while Spain tried and failed to capture Gibraltar. These actions shaped each empire's standing as they went into final peace negotiations although in the end, most of what had been won was returned.

Meeting in Paris, Spanish and French representatives attempted to manipulate negotiations to support their own imperial ambitions against Britain. They hoped the new United States would become a politically and geographically limited nation dependent on its commercial connections to them. But the American commissioners, Franklin, Adams, and John Jay, moved first to establish a separate peace with Britain, hoping to use European rivalries to their

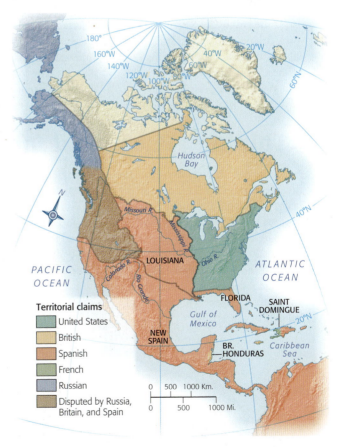

Map 6.6 North America in 1783 The 1783 Treaty of Paris redrew territorial boundaries, creating the new nation of the United States. As with the 1763 treaty meetings, Indians were not represented. The 1783 treaty disregarded Indian claims altogether. ▲

Territorial claims
- United States
- British
- Spanish
- French
- Russian
- Disputed by Russia, Britain, and Spain

Summary

People seeking land and trade shaped North America at mid-eighteenth century. Native American and European fur trappers pursued dwindling animal populations deep into the interior. European settlers migrated north along the West Coast and west from the East Coast in search of farmland. Thousands of African people were forced ashore to live as slaves. Migrations fueled competition among European empires that saw North America as a proving ground of power. Native coalitions and colonial settlers had their own stake in global struggles over land and trade, which had yielded decades of conflict. Early in the 1750s, these conflicts erupted again in the Ohio River Valley among refugee Indian groups, land speculators, French soldiers, and European settlers. Local conflict escalated into global war.

At the end of the Seven Years' War, Britain won a lopsided victory that changed the terms of these ongoing struggles. The ejection of France left Indian diplomatic alliances and trade patterns in disarray. The assertion of unified British authority over a multicultural population seemed at odds with local ideas about identity and self-government. A wave of protests, incorporating new formats such as the boycott and forging new alliances among Great Lakes Native Americans, challenged new policies. In coalescing resistance movements, colonists, Indians, and Africans debated power and human rights. But they did not agree on an answer. Because trade and land remained core issues, people frequently turned against neighbors rather than joining with them. Over a decade of resistance, two main dimensions of conflict emerged: between Indians and colonists and between British colonists and the central government.

The Declaration of Independence asserted the existence of a "United States," but the process of deciding who was part of this new nation took decades. The long Revolutionary War was fought as a civil war that itself cemented alliances. Indians from the Mohawks in New England to the Cherokees in South Carolina formed a resistance movement in opposition to the new United States. Enslaved people who saw that rebel calls for "liberty" would not end slavery took their chances with the British army. Backcountry farmers who hoped to remain neutral were drawn into patriot or loyalist ranks in reaction to brutal home front fighting that targeted crops, homes, and families as well as soldiers.

The third dimension of the American Revolution—the global struggle of France, Spain, and the Netherlands against Britain—emerged after the Declaration as these empires all supported the rebel Americans in order to halt British imperial power. The 1783 Treaty of Paris acknowledged that the United States had won independence and emerged as a new separate nation in the world, but the people living within its boundaries did not all agree on what kind of nation it would be.

‹Thinking Back, *Looking Forward*›

As you review this chapter, evaluate the role of rebellion in American history. How did the anticolonial protests of the 1760s and 1770s compare with the Pueblo Revolt or Bacon's Rebellion? How did rebel leaders bind followers together? How did local struggles over money and status intersect with the global balance of power?

In the next chapters, trace the aftermath of rebellion. How did the American Revolution disperse people across the continent and around the world? What ideas about liberty or rights did they take with them?

To make your study concrete, review the timeline and reflect on the entries there. Think about their causes, consequences, and connections. How do they connect events in North America to global trends?

Additional Resources

Books

Anderson, Fred. *The Crucible of War: The Seven Years' War and the Fate of Empire in British North America, 1754–1766.* **New York: Vintage, 2001.** ▶ Narrates the Seven Years' War as a global struggle over empire.

Armitage, David. *The Declaration of Independence: A Global History.* **Cambridge, MA: Harvard University Press, 2007.** ▶ Comparative examination of the influence of the U.S. Declaration of Independence on subsequent movements.

Calloway, Colin. *The Scratch of a Pen: 1763 and the Transformation of North America.* **New York: Oxford University Press, 2004.** ▶ Explores the consequences of the Seven Years' War for Native Americans, both locally and in global context.

Frey, Sylvia. *Water from the Rock: Black Resistance in a Revolutionary Age.* **Princeton, NJ: Princeton University Press, 1992.** ▶ Explores the Revolutionary War in the South as a three-way struggle between Britain, American rebels, and African Americans.

Gould, Eliga. *Among the Powers of the Earth: The American Revolution and the Making of a New World Empire.* **Cambridge, MA: Harvard University Press, 2012.** ▶ Political and economic history of the emergence of the United States as a "treaty-worthy" nation.

Gray, Edward G., and Jane Kamensky, eds. *The Oxford Handbook of the American Revolution.* **New York: Oxford University Press, 2012.** ▶ Wide-ranging collection of essays covering multiple dimensions of the revolutionary conflict and its aftermath.

Hartigan-O'Connor, Ellen. *The Ties That Buy: Women and Commerce in Revolutionary America.* **Philadelphia: University of Pennsylvania Press, 2009.** ▶ Places revolutionary boycotts in broader context of Atlantic urban economies with women at the center.

Nash, Gary B. *The Unknown American Revolution: The Unruly Birth of Democracy and the Struggle to Create America.* **New York: Penguin Books, 2006.** ▶ Lively account of the perspectives of native, working, and enslaved people toward the war for independence.

O'Shaughnessy, Andrew Jackson. *An Empire Divided: The American Revolution and the British Caribbean.* **Philadelphia: University of Pennsylvania Press, 2000.** ▶ A study of the American Revolution in the nonrebelling British Caribbean colonies.

Saunt, Claudio. *West of the Revolution: An Uncommon History of 1776.* **New York: W.W. Norton, 2014.** ▶ Examines native and imperial relationships in 1776 North America away from the East Coast.

> Go to the MindTap® for **Global Americans** to access the full version of select books from this Additional Resources section.

Websites

American Revolutionary War Era Maps (1750–1800). **http://maps.bpl.org/highlights/ar/american-revolutionary-war-era** ▶ Norman B. Leventhal Map Center links to multiple libraries' digitized maps of the Revolution.

Common-Place. http://www.common-place.org/ ▶ Journal covering Revolution-era topics cosponsored by the American Antiquarian Society and the University of Connecticut.

A Guide to the American Revolution, 1763–1783. https://www.loc.gov/rr/program/bib/revolution/memory.html ▶ Organizes links to the thousands of digital sources on the Revolutionary era at the Library of Congress.

Continue exploring online through MindTap®, where you can:
- **Assess your knowledge with the Chapter Test**
- **Watch historical videos related to the chapter**
- **Further your understanding with interactive maps and timelines**

Imperial Conflicts and Revolution

1754–1762

May 1754
Seven Years' War breaks out in Ohio Valley.

June–July 1754
Albany Congress brings representatives of Six Nations and seven British colonies to discuss anti-French alliance.

1762
Spain declares war on Britain and is defeated at Havana.

1763

February
Treaty of Paris formally ends war, stipulating that France give up territorial claims to North America.

May
Coalition of Native people seizes British forts around the Great Lakes in Pontiac's Rebellion.

October
King George III issues Royal Proclamation marking line of settlement between colonial and Indian lands.

1764–1767

April 1764
Sugar Act lowers tax on British molasses while increasing enforcement of customs laws.

Currency Act outlaws colonial paper money.

March 1765
Stamp Act places tax on newspapers, playing cards, and legal documents; repealed in 1766.

Stamp Act Congress meets in New York with delegates from nine British colonies.

Nonimportation movement in response to Stamp Act urges merchants to boycott British imports.

January 1766
Slaves march in Charles Town streets, shouting "liberty!"

June 1767
Parliament passes new taxes on everyday goods, called Townshend Duties; most repealed in 1770.

Nonconsumption movement urges regular consumers to boycott British goods.

1768

October 1768
Treaty of Fort Stanwix cedes Shawnee and Delaware land to Pennsylvania.

Creole-dominated Superior Council in New Orleans banishes Antonio de Ulloa, first governor of Spanish Louisiana.

1769–1773

March 1770
Tensions between occupying British troops and Bostonians leads to Boston Massacre.

June 1770
Junipero Serra establishes Franciscan mission in Monterey.

May 1773
Tea Act makes British tea cheaper than smuggled Dutch tea.

December 1773
Boston protestors dump 90,000 pounds of East India Company tea into harbor.

1774	1775	1776	1777–1779	1780–1783
March–June	**April**	**January**	**1777**	**Summer 1780**
Parliament passes series of Coercive Acts that close Boston Harbor, remove colonial representative government, and allow military quartering in private buildings.	Boston stalemate between British forces and colonial militia breaks with fighting at Lexington and Concord.	Thomas Paine publishes *Common Sense*.	Congress approves a draft, changing the profile of the Continental Army.	League of Armed Neutrality pledges European countries to free trade for ships under neutral flags.
June	**November**		**February 1778**	**December 1780**
Quebec Act consolidates larger Canadian colony, confirming no representative government and toleration of Catholicism.	Dunmore's Proclamation promises freedom to rebels' slaves who join the British cause.	**June**	France and the United States sign Treaty of Alliance and Treaty of Amity and Commerce, pledging military support and open trade.	Britain declares war on the Netherlands.
May–October		José Joaquin Moraga, with soldiers, American-born colonists, and nearly three hundred cows, establishes military garrison and Franciscan mission in San Francisco Bay.	**1779**	**October 1781**
Governor of Virginia leads militia against Shawnees and allied Indians, defeating them in Dunmore's War.			Spain declares war on Britain.	British troops under Cornwallis surrender the Continental Army of Washington.
September–October		**July**		
First Continental Congress meets in Philadelphia with fifty-five delegates from twelve colonies.		Continental Congress passes Declaration of Independence.		**September 1783**
		September		Britain and United States sign Treaty of Paris, officially ending war and redrawing boundaries of United States.
		British troops occupy New York City.		

7

American Experiments

1776–1789

John White Swift, purser aboard the *Empress of China*, sailed from New York to Canton and back, 1784–1785

In August 1784, when ship's purser John White Swift sailed into Canton harbor, he was optimistic about U.S. trade with China. The officers on the *Empress of China* were experienced Revolutionary War veterans. The ship had sailed out of New York harbor on George Washington's fifty-first birthday. The newly independent United States was eager to establish its own commercial relationships, especially because Britain had cut off trade between its former colonies and remaining colonies. Those aboard the *Empress* hoped that expanding commerce could help pull the new nation's economy out of its postwar slump.

Fan Depicting the *Empress of China* ▲
© Philadelphia History Museum at the Atwater Kent/Courtesy of Historical Society of Pennsylvania Collection/Bridgeman Images

The *Empress of China* had set out to the east, crossing the Atlantic Ocean and sailing around the tip of Africa and then through the Indian Ocean to China—an eighteen-thousand-mile journey that took six months. In Canton, the Chinese who watched the ship arrive were cautious. It flew an unfamiliar red-and-white striped flag that looked curiously like the flag of the East India Company, but the ship was too small to be a vessel of that powerful British firm. Nor was the Chinese empire looking for more trading partners. It confined foreign sea traders to a single port and dictated all the terms of exchange, viewing it as a privilege for foreigners to associate with the Qing Dynasty.

The initial meeting with Chinese merchants was awkward, as Swift later wrote to his father: "the Chinese had never heard of us, but we introduced ourselves as a new nation." To back up that claim, the ship's captain John Green pulled out a letter of introduction stamped with the new United States seal, copies of diplomatic treaties with European powers, and the Declaration of Independence itself. Samuel Shaw, another officer, tried to impress the Chinese with a map conveying "the extent of our country, with its present and increasing population." Americans would make good customers, he asserted. But the Chinese customs officials were not impressed. Four months later they still listed U.S. ships as British.

Chinese wariness was justified. These newcomers spoke English and wanted the same goods as the English but claimed to be different. They had arrived with a French escort but insisted they were from an independent nation. Their map was continental but the United States was not. Most important, the only goods that the Americans had to offer were ginseng, a medicinal root, and furs, both trade goods provided by Native Americans. The Chinese would not have known that relationships between Native Americans and U.S. merchants were in tatters after years of brutal warfare and forced treaties.

In what ways does the fate of the *Empress of China's* trade mission to Canton reflect the problems facing the new United States?

Go to MindTap® to watch a video on the Empress of China and learn how the sailors' journey relates to the themes of this chapter.

The problems facing the *Empress of China*'s backers were the problems of the United States as a whole in the years between the Declaration of Independence (1776) and the ratification of the United States Constitution (1789). Thirteen states were independent of Britain but, although joined in a confederation, were still largely independent of each other. The conflicts that had sparked the Revolution—over land, political power, and international trade—were still urgent and unresolved. So were the imperial rivalries that could destabilize the new nation. And decades of warfare had forced tens of thousands from homes and homelands, undermining the very notion of unity.

Some liked it that way. Between 1776 and 1789, Americans engaged in a prolonged debate over whether unified or dispersed power best served an independent people. States reorganized their governments to make them more responsive to the people and then revised them when the people seemed to have gained too much control. The same process happened at the national level as new institutions dispersed and then centralized economic and political power. The United States rejected the old hierarchies of birth, but many doubted that average people deserved power and trust.

The *Empress of China* returned to New York in 1785, bearing tea, silks, nankeen trousers, and porcelain, earning backers 25 percent on their investment. The sailors re-entered a world of uncertainty and experimentation. People across the political and social spectrum, from Creeks to enslaved Africans to western farmers, knew that the end of British control meant fewer restrictions but also fewer protections. Average men and women tested the limits of revolutionary devotion to liberty and equality. Enslaved people sought freedom through courts, governments, and individual owners. Free women pressed for equal education and egalitarian marriages. Native Americans insisted that their property rights were valid. Some experiments were resolved after long debate by the principles and structures set forth in the new Constitution of the United States. But for many, like the common sailors on the *Empress of China*, the resolutions worked out in the thirteen years following 1776 felt like a revolutionary promise unfulfilled.

7-1

Institutional Experiments with Liberty

This miniature in watercolor on ivory depicts Elizabeth Freeman, painted by Susan Ridley Sedgwick in 1811. It is one of the few portraits of an African American from this period. Born into slavery, "Mumbet," as she was known, won her freedom and took her new name in a lawsuit advanced by Sedgwick's father-in-law; she became a paid servant in his home. As an old woman, Freeman was a midwife, churchgoer, property owner, and taxpayer in Massachusetts.

How does the painter use the details of costume, pose, and expression to depict her subject as a free, rather than enslaved, woman? ▶

Go to MindTap® to practice history with the Chapter 7 **Primary Source Writing Activity: Experiments with Liberty and Equality**. Read and view primary sources and respond to a writing prompt.

© Massachusetts Historical Society, Boston, MA, USA/Bridgeman Images

In 1776, rebelling Americans rejected the institutions of monarchy and aristocracy in favor of independence, self-governance, and fundamental rights. Provided that they were successful in winning the war, the implications for government seemed clear. The United States would become independent, and elected lawmakers would replace royal governors sent from Britain. Putting these principles into practice was not easy, however, because there were practical problems of who should vote and who could lead. Furthermore, the language of "liberty" and "rights" promised a broad social transformation in which traditions of deference upholding the wealth and power of the "better sort" would be replaced with fair competition among equals. How far should that transformation go? Would the institutions of slavery, family, and church also be transformed by new ideas about human liberty? Would controls over trade be abandoned? Putting liberty into practice required rethinking basic assumptions about who had the right to power over others.

☞ As you read, look for the appearance of ideas about freedom and self-governance. How did they transform institutions such as legislatures, slavery, families, and churches?

7-1a State Constitutions

The Declaration of Independence asserted that governments derive "their just powers from the consent of the governed." The people, rather than God or a hereditary monarch, gave the government its power and legitimacy. One of the first proving grounds for this idea, known as **popular sovereignty**, was in the state constitutions created during and after the American Revolution. Connecticut and Rhode Island revised their old colonial charters, keeping most structures in place, but other states wrote new **constitutions** that spread power to a wider group of people. They strengthened elected legislatures, long considered the voice of free men, and weakened governors, who had previously represented imperial power. Elected legislatures, not governors, appointed judges and the governor's council, and governors lost veto power. State constitutions allocated more representation in the legislature to regular farmers living in the backcountry; in five states, representation was linked directly to population numbers. Writing new constitutions, legislators reexamined qualifications for voting.

Deciding who was eligible to vote became an exercise in defining "the people" empowered by popular sovereignty. Most states required voters to own some form of property, most commonly land, as they had throughout the eighteenth century. By holding onto this requirement, these states were following influential political theories maintaining that only free adult men who owned land and therefore had an independent stake in decisions about property could put aside selfish desires and act for the common good. Renters, wives, servants, and slaves owed their livelihoods to others, and so they were not considered able to exercise independent judgment. Many state constitutions reduced property requirements to allow more ordinary taxpaying men a voice in political decisions, but they were cautious about turning government over to what they feared was a "mob" of popular opinion. Massachusetts legislators

> State constitutions institutionalize popular control.

even considered but then rejected a plan to confiscate private landholdings of more than one thousand acres and redistribtribute them to landless men in order to turn them into stakeholding farmers who could then be trusted to vote responsibly.

The most radical experiment in government was the Pennsylvania Constitution of 1776. Under its provisions, there was only a single legislative body, elected annually, whose debates were open to the public. Rather than a governor, Pennsylvania had a committee selected from among the legislators to handle executive functions. Voting was open to all free men over twenty-one years of age who had lived in the state for a year and paid any public taxes, such as the head tax levied on adult men without property, which meant that recent German immigrants and propertyless laborers could vote. Like six other early state constitutions, Pennsylvania's had a bill of rights guaranteeing citizens religious freedom, trial by jury, and freedom of speech. Pennsylvania also mandated public elementary education and forbade imprisonment for debt. The goal was both to restructure government to make it more responsive and to educate and cultivate a society of people who could become "persons most noted for wisdom and virtue," and therefore trusted with such political power.

Most states did not go as far as Pennsylvania. They retained governors and upper houses of the legislature. They required candidates for political office to own more property than average voters. But more generous voter laws and the experience of wartime self-governance led to political change. State legislatures' lower houses increasingly consisted more of artisans, backcountry farmers, and men of moderate wealth (see Figure 7.1). Governments, in the form of state capitals, moved away from the East Coast and closer to the average farmers geographically. Albany replaced New York, Harrisburg replaced Philadelphia, Richmond replaced Williamsburg, and Columbia replaced Charleston.

7-1b Challenges to Slavery

Enslaved people, especially those in New England who could **petition** courts and legislatures, seized on the Revolutionary rhetoric of freedom to make the case for their release. In 1774, a group of Massachusetts slaves petitioned legislators to grant their freedom on the grounds that they had "in common with all other men a naturel right to our freedoms without Being depriv'd of them by our fellow men." The request was denied, but everywhere slaves asserted that ideas about liberty should apply to them, and they used notions

> Slaves seek freedom through courts and new state governments.

popular sovereignty Political theory that legitimate power resides with people who then authorize governments to act on their behalf.

constitutions Documents defining the use and limits of governmental power. State constitutions, like colonial charters, were written contracts. The British Constitution was an unwritten group of customary practice.

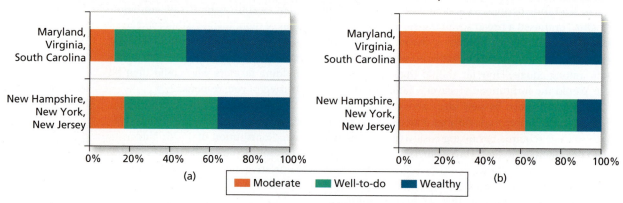

Colonial Representatives before the Revolution

State Representatives after the Revolution

Legend: ■ Moderate ■ Well-to-do ■ Wealthy

(a)　　　　　　　　　　　　　　　　(b)

Figure 7.1a Colonial Representatives before the Revolution In the decade prior to the Revolution, men elected to serve in the colonial assemblies were prosperous, and even wealthy, as determined by the value of the property they owned: moderate (£500–£2,000), well-to-do (£2,000–£5,000), and wealthy (more than £5,000). Note that only 30 percent of the free adult male population owned property valued at more than £500; the majority owned less and were below the "moderate" level. ▲

Figure 7.1b State Representatives after the Revolution In the decade after the Revolution, legislatures were larger and more men were elected to represent western farmers to balance out the domination of men from the coast. Assemblies in the South tended to have a higher proportion of wealthy representatives, even after the war. ▲ Source: Adapted from Jackson Turner Main, "Government by the People: The American Revolution and the Democratization of the Legislatures," *William and Mary Quarterly*, 3rd ser., 23, no. 3 (July 1966)

free state State in which slavery is not permitted under law.

gradual emancipation laws State laws passed during and after the Revolutionary War that ended slavery for the future children of slaves.

about fundamental equality embedded in the language of the Declaration of Independence to try to dismantle the institution of slavery.

In Massachusetts, slaves used the first article of the new state constitution, which declared that "All men are born free and equal" and "every subject is entitled to liberty" to challenge the legality of their enslavement in court. Quok Walker, who had been promised and then denied freedom, was awarded his own freedom by the Massachusetts Supreme Court in 1781. The justices went further and declared that the words of the state constitution "effectively abolished" slavery. Elizabeth Freeman likewise won her freedom the same year. The Massachusetts legislature discussed but then failed to pass a general emancipation law that would have applied to all people held as slaves. The burden was on individual slaves to find lawyers and bring suit.

Enslaved people in other northern states had specific new laws to support their bids for freedom (see Table 7.1). In 1777, when Vermont declared independence from New York and New Hampshire, its new state constitution abolished slavery outright, and it entered the United States in 1791 as a **free state**. Connecticut, Rhode Island, and Pennsylvania followed by enacting **gradual emancipation laws**. Under these laws, people who were enslaved

remained slaves for life, but their children born after the passage of the laws were freed following prolonged indentures during which they continued to work for former masters. Most gradual emancipation laws worked to protect the property rights of owners and to ensure continued access to the labor of former slaves. Once they outlawed slavery, however, free states became destinations for enslaved people seeking liberty.

In Virginia and Maryland, the doctrines of the expanding Methodist and Baptist churches that discouraged

Table 7.1 A Slow Legal End to Slavery in the North

Of the original thirteen colonies, only Vermont banned slavery outright in the Age of Revolution; other northern states relied on gradual legal processes. Because gradual emancipation laws did not apply to people born before a law was passed and because they included long periods of "apprenticeship" before freedom, thousands of people were still held in bondage in the North in the 1830s. Gradual emancipation laws were debated in Virginia and Delaware but never passed.

Year	State	Legislation
1777	Vermont	Constitution bans slavery
1780	Pennsylvania	Law frees the children of enslaved mothers at age 28
1780	Massachusetts	Constitution declares "all men are born free and equal"; courts interpret statement to refuse to uphold slavery
1783	New Hampshire	State constitution declares "all men are born equal and independent"; legal interpretation remains ambiguous
1784	Rhode Island	Law frees children of enslaved mothers at age 18 (girls) and 21 (boys)
1784	Connecticut	Law frees children of enslaved mothers at age 25
1799	New York	Law frees children of enslaved mothers at age 25 (girls) and 28 (boys)
1803	Ohio	Constitution bans slavery
1804	New Jersey	Law frees children of enslaved mothers at age 21 (girls) and 25 (boys)

Source: Joanne Pope Melish, *Disowning Slavery: Gradual Emancipation and "Race" in New England, 1780–1860* (Ithaca: Cornell University Press, 2000).

slavery, along with some pressure to remedy the hypocrisy of slave owning in a free republic, merged with a strong sense of property rights to convince legislatures to pass laws that made it easier for masters to free individual slaves. In a process called **manumission**, owners could take the initiative to free their human property; no longer did they have to seek special permission from the state assemblies to do so. In some cases, slave owners manumitted people by selling slaves to themselves, transferring title to and ownership of the human body to the person who inhabited it. In other cases, slave owners manumitted their slaves gradually. Prominent Virginian Robert Carter II manumitted five hundred slaves during his lifetime and at his death, but he was the exception. Only a minority of owners took part in manumission before laws tightened again; in fact, the number of slaves in Virginia and Maryland increased in the 1780s and 1790s.

Between the 1770s and 1790s, the number of free black people grew from a few thousand to tens of thousands, but emancipation and manumission increased racial divides and intensified hostility to blacks. Gradual emancipation laws and antislavery court decisions in New England coincided with new laws forbidding a white person to marry "any Negro, Indian, or mulatto." Even those whites who embraced the idea of natural rights rarely thought of black people as equals. The New York legislature deadlocked over a gradual emancipation bill when key supporters insisted on simultaneously denying blacks the right to vote.

7-1c Women and Familial Power

Revolutionary leaders wanted to dismantle a world that put aristocrats in charge of ordinary people, but most of them preferred to keep intact a patriarchal family supported by laws that limited the rights of free women. Some women had other ideas. Writing to her husband John Adams in 1776 while he attended the Second Continental Congress, Abigail Adams asked him to "remember the ladies" in creating the new government. "Do not," she warned, put "unlimited power into the hands of the Husbands. Remember all Men would be tyrants if they could" and women "will not hold ourselves bound by any Laws in which we have no voice, or Representation." Abigail Adams ran the family farm and managed the family finances for years at a time while he was away, but John Adams belittled her request. Noting that revolutionary struggle "has loosed the bands of Government every where," that "Children and Apprentices were disobedient—that schools and Colleges were grown turbulent—that

> Families recalculate shared power of women and men.

Ellen Kellearan Gardner Fund

Republican Family Revolutionary ideals praised the free family as a place of virtuous restraint rather than abundant reproduction. In this 1788 portrait, *Samels Family* by Johann Eckstein, the mother is at the center, at the same level as her husband. An adolescent daughter is painted with a book in her hand, signifying the importance of reading and education for girls. ▲

Indians slighted their Guardians and Negroes grew insolent to their Masters," he cautioned, "We know better than to repeal our Masculine systems."

The "masculine system" was not repealed. After the Revolution, as before, common law denied married women the right to make wills, control their own earnings, or move away from their husbands. But in the new nation, Annis Boudinot Stockton wrote to her daughter, "the Empire of reason is not monopolized by man," and free women prided themselves on their virtue and self-restraint. Many argued that raising generations of virtuous citizens required educated, self-disciplined mothers, and their commitment to a special kind of female republicanism made long-standing female duties newly political. Free mothers made a virtue of their legal and political limitations by proclaiming their freedom from the corruptions of money and power that came with masculine political maneuvering.

Free black and white women also began cooperating with their husbands to reduce the number of children they bore, starting their families later, spacing their children's births, and ending childbearing by their mid-30s. They used methods already available, including prolonged breastfeeding and abstinence, as well as herbal medicines to avoid or end unwanted pregnancies. Their new focus on a smaller, intensively managed family began a long decline in fertility rates that would not appear in western Europe for another century.

Enslaved black women, in contrast, bore increasing numbers of children as their owners recognized that reproduction increased their wealth. Watchful owners encouraged the birth of more children into slavery and invested more in the health of the people they owned to boost the slave population.

manumission Process by which an individual owner frees an individual slave.

disestablishment Act of ending state support for particular churches.

Act for Establishing Religious Freedom Virginia law passed in 1786 creating separation between church and state.

civil rights Personal rights, often including freedom of speech and freedom from discrimination, to which all individuals are entitled.

Motherhood lost, rather than gained, political power for women in many eastern Indian tribes. The matrilineal Cherokees, for example, had long recognized the influence of mothers as negotiators and diplomats. "We are your Mothers; you are our sons," announced Nancy Ward (Nanye'hi) to the U.S. Treaty commissioners in Tennessee in 1781. "Our cry [is] all for Peace . . . Let your Women hear our Words." But the prolonged frontier fighting and accelerated wartime diplomacy of the late eighteenth century had elevated sacrifice in battle. European commanders seeking armed support increasingly rewarded young warrior chiefs with supplies rather than entering into diplomatic relations with warrior chiefs, clan chiefs, and matrons. As young warriors distributed those goods among their allied families and clans, they increased their power relative to older male and female leaders. Trade goods and warfare upset the familiar balance of authority between men and women as well as between generations in Indian communities.

7-1d Emerging Religious Freedoms

Prior to the Revolution, religious toleration was uneven, and in most colonies, a single denomination's clergy were supported by taxes and assessed fees. People who wanted the freedom to pursue their own religious beliefs without such payments used revolutionary political upheaval to challenge the idea of state-supported or established churches. New Protestant denominations such as the Baptists had flourished since the Great Awakening of the mid-eighteenth century, and their adherents chafed at being taxed to pay establishment clergy. Gradually,

> States separate religious and political authority.

state after state allowed residents to direct their taxes to a wider range of religious institutions. In some cases, state governments maintained a list of acceptable churches. Other states allowed taxpayers to choose which Protestant church (or, if they were Catholic or Jewish, which school or charity) was to receive their money. Eventually, states adopted **disestablishment**, and their governments stopped collecting taxes to pay ministers or maintain congregations. Instead, religious institutions competed openly for members and financial support.

In spite of the trend toward disestablishment, most states maintained legal preferences for Protestants and required testaments of religious belief from elected officials because lawmakers believed that piety and morality were essential to virtuous leadership. Even the radical Pennsylvania Constitution of 1776 required members of the General Assembly to swear belief in the Old and New Testaments as the word of God. Evidence of Christian belief, they maintained, was evidence of moral fitness for office.

Leading Virginians, however, where the established Episcopal Church had broken its organizational ties to the Church of England, began insisting on a stronger separation of church and state. James Madison and George Mason argued that each individual should be free to follow the religion of his or her choice. As they wrote in the 1776 Virginia *Declaration of Rights*: "all men are equally entitled to the free exercise of religion, according to the dictates of conscience; and that it is the mutual duty of all to practice Christian forbearance, love, and charity, towards each other." Thomas Jefferson introduced this sentiment to the Virginia assembly in 1779 and, as the **Act for Establishing Religious Freedom**, it passed into law in 1786. The act ended compulsory taxes to support churches, mandatory church attendance, and religious oaths for those serving in political offices. Under this law, religious authority and civil authority were strictly separate. In Virginia, those who were not Protestant Christians of any denomination could profess their beliefs with no effect on their **civil rights**.

7-2
Political Experiments in the Politics of Alliance

This 1763 painting by Miguel Cabrera, *From Spanish [man] and Mestiza [woman], Castiza,* was from a popular genre known as *casta* paintings that depicted the mixed-cultural relationships common in Spanish colonialism. These paintings both categorized people by race and asserted a multiplying variety of individuals born in colonial societies.

How does this painting use clothing, pose, and background to suggest the identity of the *castiza* child born in New Spain? Is it optimistic or pessimistic about this alliance? ▶

Iberfoto/Superstock

Most people who lived in the territory claimed by the United States experienced independence and political representation as a local phenomenon. Their alliances were to family, community, or state. But after 1783, American states, European empires, and Indian tribes all experimented with ways to construct larger alliances to replace those torn apart by the war for independence. To organize on this larger level, institutions had to be calibrated to bind people together, and individuals had to accept new identities. A Virginian had to decide she was an American; a Wind Clan Creek had to decide he was an Indian. New laws were only modestly successful in pushing personal transformations, in part because all of these entities were relatively weak and could not compel adherence.

☞ As you read, think about the broad consequences of political experimentation during and immediately after the American Revolution. How important was shared identity in holding governments or military alliances together?

7-2a Articles of Confederation

The **Articles of Confederation**, written in the wake of the British occupation of Philadelphia and formally adopted by the Continental Congress in 1777, codi-

{ A written agreement loosely unites states to conduct the war.

fied the U.S. government as a loose confederacy joined to fight a war for independence. They institutionalized Congress as a legislative body representing the states and responsible for their common defense, whose members were selected annually by local voters, special conventions, or state legislators. Congress had the power to print money and seek loans, regulate relations with Native American tribes, and conduct foreign policy, including declarations of war and peace. Congress was to establish a post office and fix standard weights and measures to facilitate trade among the states. Calling the United States of America "a firm league of friendship," the Articles also affirmed the states' sovereignty equality: Each had one vote in Congress. The men who drafted the Articles wanted to prevent the concentration of power that they felt had led to abuse under the British colonial system. Congress had no upper legislative body reserved for aristocrats but only a single elected house. There was no prime minister and no king. The President of the Congress presided but had no separate powers.

The Articles reserved so much power for the states that Congress had trouble raising money to fight the Revolution and handling diplomacy after the war was won. Congress could not tax; it could only request revenues from the states. Because amending the Articles required the unanimous support of all thirteen states, multiple measures proposed to cope with the financial crises, such as attempts to set a national **tariff** to raise money on imports, were squashed by a single state's no vote. Most states remained committed only to their individual interests. Interstate trade, for example, was impeded by competing currencies, import taxes, and regulations that each state maintained on its own behalf.

Although the Articles established a league of equals, geography and colonial history gave some states advantages that could translate into greater power. Small states and those without long-standing colonial charter claims to lands beyond the Appalachians refused to ratify the Articles for years, fearing domination by their more populous neighbors. In fact, the Articles were not ratified by all of the states until March 1781, just six months before the Siege of Yorktown ended the war. Only when Virginia, which claimed vast expanses of northwestern land under its charter, promised to give its **western lands** to the United States as a whole under Congress did its neighbor Maryland sign the confederation agreement (see Map 7.1).

With limited powers over jealous, independent, and autonomous states, Congress under the Articles of Confederation was more successful fighting the war than managing the aftermath. Under its oversight, the United States achieved victory in the American Revolution. Its agents won concessions to the United States in the 1783 Treaty of Paris that ended the war with Great Britain. But peacetime diplomacy was a series of failures in the context of shifting Indian alliances and hostile Britain and Spain that still contested North American territory. Because it lacked the ability under the Articles to enforce its own treaty agreements, Congress could do little to counteract actions of Europeans or Native Americans. Power remained firmly in the hands of the states themselves, and their interests were local.

7-2b Native American Alliances

The 1783 Treaty of Paris negotiations did not acknowledge the tens of thousands of Indians who participated in the Revolutionary conflict and for

{ Eastern Indians re-establish alliances as fighting continues on the borderlands.

most of them, documents signed in Europe did not end the war. Fighting continued with Chickamauga Cherokees and Shawnees embroiled in border warfare with South Carolinians and Georgians. Their war became the center

Articles of Confederation Agreement of thirteen states passed in November 1777 to establish a confederacy for the purpose of winning independence from Britain.

tariff Tax placed on imported goods, usually to protect domestic manufacturers by making them cheaper.

western lands Areas west of the Appalachian Mountains occupied by numerous Indian groups and claimed by multiple early states under their colonial charters.

History without Borders

Vermillion

Significant Producers and Consumers of Vermillion, 8000 BCE–1800 People living near large deposits of cinnabar processed the pigment for cosmetic, decorative, and ceremonial uses. They also produced quantities for export overland and overseas, often relying on coerced labor because of the dangers of mercury poisoning. Synthetically produced vermillion also became a valuable trade good. ▲

In the eighteenth century, people around the world tapped into global trade networks because the goods they purchased improved their lives: Cooking was quicker in a bronze kettle, socializing centered on tea sweetened with sugar, and warfare was more deadly with muskets and gunpowder. Imported goods also played a role in emerging racial identities, as in the case of vermillion. Artists across the globe had long favored this orange-red pigment. Titian used it to color the gown Mary wore as she ascended to heaven in his Renaissance fresco. Qing Dynasty artists covered their carved boxes and ewers with vermillion lacquer.

A pigment of mercuric sulfide, vermillion came from two sources: powdered cinnabar, the naturally occurring ore, and an artificial process that synthesized mercury and sulfur. Mining the ore was dangerous work because of high levels of mercury, and Roman dealers sent slaves to dig it out of the rock in Almaden, Spain. Chinese chemists perfected the synthetic process in the eighth century, creating a valuable product that emperors treasured and traders sought out. Eighteenth-century records of the Hudson's Bay Company reveal that the pigment became an important part of the fur trade that connected Asia, Europe, and North

America because Haudenosaunees and other Indians bought it to use for body paint, replacing the clay they had formerly used with an import that yielded more vivid hues.

Red body paint reinforced new ideas about Indian identity in the late eighteenth century. In the earliest encounters between Europeans and Native Americans, skin color garnered little attention; Indians and Europeans focused instead on differences in religion and daily life. By the end of the Revolution, however, Euro–Americans and Indians alike were dividing the world into groups of people identified as having "white," "red," or "black"

Eighteenth-Century Chinese Carved Cinnabar Lacquerware To make lacquerware, Chinese artists covered wooden bowls, trays, and vases with lacquer, a tree resin colored with powdered mercury sulfide. They carved designs into the lacquer, creating objects that became desirable trade goods in Europe and North America, traveling alongside porcelain and silks. ◀

Dennis Cox/Alamy Stock Photo

Joseph Brant In this 1797 portrait by Charles Willson Peale, Brant presents a different appearance than in the one in Chapter 6, painted by George Romney. Here his role as diplomat is prominent; he is unarmed and wearing the half-moon gorget he received earlier from the British government. Aware that the painting was intended for a collection of statesmen's portraits in Peale's Philadelphia Museum, Brant applied vermillion paint high on his cheekbones. ◀

Charles Willson Peale/Independence National Historical Park

skin. Those markers, in turn, were used to justify exclusion and separation. In the early nineteenth century, a Mikasuki chief told the governor of Florida that the Creator had initially made three men: one white, one black, and one red. He gave each a present. The white man, whom the Creator pitied, chose pens, paper, and instruments of learning. The red man, the Creator's favorite, chose weapons of war and hunting. The black man received axes, hoes, and buckets. He concluded that "the negro must work for both the red and white man, and it has been so ever since." Such explanations made racial identity seem a clear distinction of skin color, ability, and aptitude. In fact, however, as an earlier world of fluid racial identities was replaced with newer color lines, those identities were created and reinforced by global trade. North American merchants purchased redness from the Chinese to sell to the Indians.

Critical Thinking Questions

▶ How did globally traded goods assume different meanings for people in different locations?

▶ Why did people in the eighteenth century use purchased goods to communicate their sense of who they were? Did they do this differently than we do today?

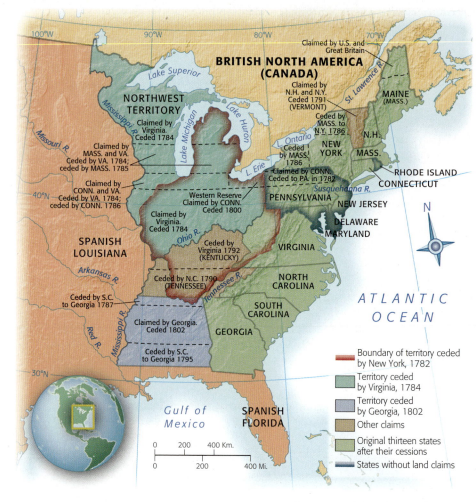

BRITISH NORTH AMERICA
(CANADA)

NORTHWEST TERRITORY

SPANISH LOUISIANA

Map 7.1 Western Lands Old colonial charters and competing Indian treaties created an overlapping patchwork of land claims in the western portion of the new United States. Turning that land into a reserve of potential future states owned by the United States as a whole was a significant diplomatic and economic goal of those who wanted to strengthen the confederation of united states. ▲

Legend:
- Boundary of territory ceded by New York, 1782
- Territory ceded by Virginia, 1784
- Territory ceded by Georgia, 1802
- Other claims
- Original thirteen states after their cessions
- States without land claims

evacuate its forts on the Great Lakes. Joseph Brant, the Mohawk diplomat who had coordinated attacks with Britain during the Revolution, traveled again to London in 1785 to win British support against Euro-Americans' land claims, hoping that the British and allied Indians could make common cause against the United States. He returned with a pension, compensation for wartime losses, and a silver snuffbox but only vague promises for more. While actively seeking military support, the allied Native Americans also worked to make the United States think that they were more numerous and more strongly backed by Britain than they actually were. They spread stories of treaty meetings with the British and sent false messages by British officials still stationed in the West.

Indians in the South hoped that the Spanish, who now claimed Florida and the Louisiana territory, would provide similar leverage against the United States. Alexander McGillivray, a leader with a Creek mother and a Scottish father who had been educated in Charleston, South Carolina, dealt with the Spanish in Florida to request ammunition and support. Declaring that sovereignty over their land was one of Indians' "natural rights," McGillivray secured treaties that preserved Creek lands as a buffer between the United States and Spanish Florida. Working with the Creek National Council, which consisted of chiefs from multiple autonomous villages, he bolstered the power of Creek headmen over the traditional power of clans. McGillivray hoped that centralized power over warfare, captivity, and treaty making would strengthen Creeks as a nation and build the larger Indian alliance.

Although the British Empire had treated Haudenosaunees as spokesmen for a wide range of Indians, the United States wanted to divide and conquer individual tribes and villages by having their Indian agents meet with them separately. Piteasewa, a Shawnee speaker, countered in 1785 that "we are unanimous." The alliance was successful in forming war parties to push back white settlement in Georgia and Tennessee, but unity was always

of a strengthened pan-Indian alliance ranging from the Creeks in the South to the Delawares in the Ohio River Valley to the Wyandots and Haudenosaunees in the North. In 1783, Indians from thirty-five native nations met at the Wyandot town of Sandusky to form an alliance. Their first goal was to roll the line of white settlement from the 1783 Treaty of Paris line back to the Ohio River border negotiated between the British and the Six Nations under the treaty of Fort Stanwix in 1768. Their larger aim was to forge a unified counterweight to American power. Among themselves, they agreed that none could sell land without the agreement of all. Looking outward, they knew that their alliance's ability to hold back the United States depended upon material support from European empires in North America.

In the North, this meant a continuing alliance with Great Britain, which still held Canada and refused to precarious. Individual Indian clans sometimes decided that a separate peace could buy them some relief from frontier warfare.

Indian alliances depended on strategic calculations, but they also increasingly drew on a sense of shared identity. Identity as Indians, unifiers argued, could combat others' efforts to seize more of their land. One group of Choctaws told the Creeks, "Brothers! . . . The same father made us all red people and desired us to live in peace . . . [I]f we continue united they can never take [our lands] from us." It was an ideology reinforced by the blood vengeance of frontier warfare during which American settlers indiscriminately raided both allied and enemy Indians.

7-2c Spanish North America after the War

By the end of the American Revolution and the ensuing treaty settlements, Spain claimed vast territory in the Americas, including North America west

{ Spain struggles to organize its American colonies for profit.

of the Mississippi River, East and West Florida, much of Central and South America, and islands in the Caribbean including Cuba and Santo Domingo. Most valuable, and most closely governed, was the region in Mexico and to the south where large populations worked silver mines and ranches and paid taxes. In 1780, tens of thousands of Indians from multiple clans joined by *mestizos* rose up against Spanish rule and new imperial taxes in Peru and New Granada. The leader of the Peruvian revolt, Tupac Amaru, called on a shared Inca heritage to unify the insurgents and promised the return of Inca rule. The revolt turned into a house-by-house racial conflict that lasted until 1783 before pro-Spanish troops defeated it.

North of central Mexico, Spanish Texas and New Mexico consisted of presidios, towns, and missions surrounded and often dominated by Indian groups. Spanish political power was wielded by governors and Franciscan friars who competed for authority over the settlers and who often acted on their own, only later seeking approval from officials in Mexico City.

Comanches, Apaches, Caddos, and Wichitas had drawn both French traders from the north and Spanish officials into the Indian slave trade that was a key part of diplomacy and warfare in the region. These southwestern groups raided enemy communities to capture women and children, whom they then ransomed, traded as slaves, employed as slave labor, or incorporated into new families. Although enslaving and selling Indians was illegal in New Spain, trade in female captives became a key component of Spanish diplomacy. Spanish traders profited by selling Indian slaves in North America or transporting them to Havana. Retaliatory raids by Indians carried away Spanish and Indian women living in Spanish settlements. The children they bore with their captors became part of a growing *mestizo* population.

In asserting new domain over Louisiana, Spanish officials took an approach toward trade, settlement, and relationships with Native Americans that relied on negotiation as well as the exchange of goods and captives. British, French, and Indian traders along with American farmers used the interconnected Ohio, Missouri, and Mississippi Rivers to transport goods to New Orleans and from there to the Gulf of Mexico and the ocean. After the Seven Years' War, Spain had followed French practices of signing treaties with Native Americans as independent entities rather than declaring them subjects of the king. The diverse community of traders and agents made it difficult for Spain to unite its commercial and political goals for its North American colonies. The mixed loyalties of people who lived in Spanish Louisiana often thwarted Spanish efforts to retaliate against its European foes. When, at the end of the Revolution, Spain sought to deny British ships access to the central port of New Orleans, merchants in that city—many of whom were themselves British or French—violently opposed the measure.

The 1783 Treaty of Paris named the Mississippi River as the western boundary of the United States and granted the new nation right of access to trade on this major artery, worrying Spanish officials, who called people of the United States "active, industrious, and aggressive." As Spain moved to secure its borders from encroachment, it came to see the United States as more dangerous to its colonial holdings than England or France. In 1783, Britain signed East and West Florida over to Spain, rendering it a transcontinental power in North America. Yet the United States disputed the boundary of West Florida, and Georgia's government began selling land occupied by Creeks, Chocktaws, and Chickasaws to speculators (see Map 7.2).

In 1784, Spain closed the lower Mississippi River and the port of New Orleans to the United States, depriving backcountry settlers access to global markets. Instead, Spain offered land grants to lure white American settlers to migrate and become Spanish subjects. Spanish officials hoped that as these American farmers brought their African American slaves with them, the frontier trading community would develop into a profitable agricultural export economy. Spanish governors opened New Orleans to the international slave trade in order to support plantations of cotton and sugar, both of which depended on intensive slave labor, and, with tobacco and deerskins, became the most profitable crops in the lower Mississippi. These policies altered the population balance in the region as the numbers of white settlers and their slaves came to equal the number of Native Americans.

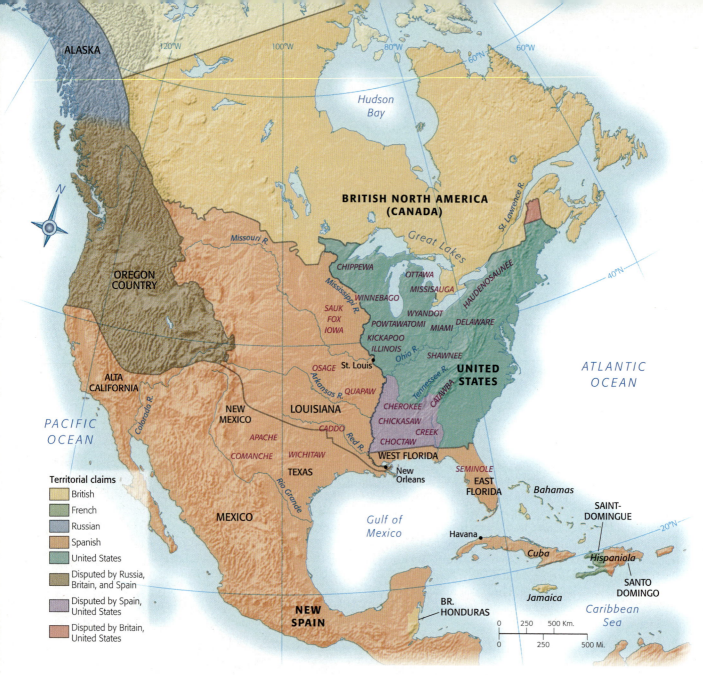

Map 7.2 Spanish America and Contested Borderlands, 1783 At the end of the American Revolution, the Spanish empire's territorial claims in the Americas were vast. Political borders drawn by overlapping treaties, as well as geographical boundaries such as the Mississippi River, created contested borderlands where Native American power and Indian alliances determined daily life, trade, and governance. ▲

New migrants were also potential allies against U.S. expansion from the east and ongoing raids by the powerful Osages and Apaches to the west. Spanish officials therefore welcomed the waves of Indian families from the Ohio River Valley and the Southeast, including Shawnees, Miamis, and Chickamauga Cherokees, who moved west of the Mississippi to live in Spanish-claimed territory. Eastern Indians likewise hoped the Spanish could provide a counterweight to U.S. expansion. In 1784, a delegation of allied Indians complained to the Spanish governor at St. Louis that the Americans were pushing into Indian lands "like a plague of locusts." The Spanish agreed.

Global Americans **James Wilkinson** was born to an Irish family in Maryland in 1757. As a young man, he trained as a physician in Philadelphia before entering the Continental Army, where he was quickly promoted. In 1783, he moved to Kentucky as a merchant trader and property broker. Wilkinson dreamed of establishing an independent republic west of the Appalachians and in 1787 traveled to New Orleans to propose an independent Kentucky allied with Spain. Other western republics, he suggested, would break away from the United States and form a separate confederacy linked economically and politically with Spanish America along the Mississippi River. That scheme collapsed, but Wilkinson, commander of the U.S. Army, pursued other plans for an independent West. Appointed governor of the new Louisiana Territory in 1805, Wilkinson corresponded with Aaron Burr over a speculative plan to break Louisiana from the United States.

Court-martialed by President James Madison in 1811, Wilkinson was found not guilty and went on to be named U.S. envoy to Mexico where he promoted another war of independence, that of Mexico from Spain. He died in Mexico City in 1825, still hoping for a large personal land grant in Texas. His shifting identity and alliances, what his detractors called treachery and treason, were products of the mobile world of imperial rivalries and new republics in flux.

Everett Collection Historical/Alamy Stock Photo

7-3

Postwar Migrations

Cato Rammsay carried this Loyalist Certificate when the British evacuated New York at the end of the American Revolution. Guy Carleton, commander-in-chief of British forces in North America in 1782, ordered the issuance of these "Birch Certificates" to secure the passage of black Americans freed by the wartime promises of the British army. Samuel Birch, who signed most of them, was the last commandant of New York City under British occupation.

What freedoms does this certificate grant Cato Rammsay and on what basis? ▶

Black Loyalist Heritage Society

NEW-YORK, 21ˢᵗ April 1783.

THIS is to certify to whomsoever it may concern, that the Bearer hereof *Cato Rammsay* a Negro, resorted to the British Lines, in consequence of the Proclamations of Sir William Howe, and Sir Henry Clinton, late Commanders in Chief in America; and that the said Negro has hereby his Excellency Sir Guy Carleton's Permission to go to Nova-Scotia, or wherever else *He* may think proper. —

By Order of Brigadier General Birch,

Certificate of Freedom, 1783

The American Revolution unleashed unprecedented migration in North America. Fighting in the countryside sent tens of thousands of refugees into the cities. Indians allied with the British fled to Niagara, Detroit, and St. Louis. White Loyalists and their slaves lived under protection of British garrisons in New York City, Charleston, and Savannah, but when the British were defeated, these people became refugees who were ultimately dispersed throughout the then smaller British Empire. The end of the war also ended British restrictions on settlement and trade, releasing new waves of voluntary migration west. Merchants and sailors, like those on the *Empress of China*, sought new trading partners to replace British monopolies. Blacks freed from slavery by gradual emancipation laws or individual owners migrated to U.S. cities in search of paid work and mutual support.

☞ As you read, compare the various postwar migrations of groups and individuals. How did these migrations, both forced and voluntary, reshape American societies? How did the departure of some change the communities left behind?

7-3a Loyalist Diaspora

Men and women who had supported the losing side in the Revolution faced tough options at the war's end. Some, uprooted and with their property seized by patriots, lived on temporary pensions funded by the British treasury while hoping to go back to their old lives. Others remained on their land and claimed that they

Loyalists in exile reshape the British Empire.

had been neutral. Slave-owning Loyalists moved to the Caribbean to secure their property rights in exile. Slavery had been challenged as illegal in Britain since a 1772 court decision, but it remained widespread in British colonies. Between 1783 and 1785, the population of the Bahamas increased by almost seven thousand people, largely slaves taken from the rice swamps of South Carolina and Georgia to work in the sugar cane fields.

Black Loyalists, most of whom were former slaves freed during wartime, struggled to establish themselves as loyal citizens deserving refugee rights. Former owners insisted they were illegally seized property; British soldiers sometimes sold them or bestowed them as spoils of war. Many black Loyalists were ill equipped to defend their freedom in court or to recover wartime losses. When William Cooper claimed he had lost a house and land worth £500, the commission in charge of hearing claims dismissed him: "all these blacks say that they were free born and that they had property, two things that are not very probable; we did not believe one syllable of his case." But British institutions were black Loyalists' best chance to claim their freedom. The Earl of Dunmore, former Virginia governor who had issued the first promise of freedom to slaves who joined the king's forces, became governor of the Bahamas and created a "Negro Court" to rule on cases of contested freedom there.

In the final evacuation, about sixty thousand Loyalists left with the British, taking fifteen thousand enslaved people with them (see Map 7.3). Together, 2.5 percent of the British North American population dispersed around the world. One-third went to the Canadian communities of Nova Scotia, New Brunswick, and Quebec, as well as new settlements that Britain had established for them. South of Halifax, Nova Scotia, one group of white Loyalists received land grants to construct a brand-new town, Shelburne, which soon had a population of eight thousand people. Black Loyalists were directed to build their own town, Birchtown, elsewhere on Port Roseway harbor. Many did not receive the land grants promised to war veterans. Looking for a more secure footing in freedom, a third of the free black community emigrated within a decade to **Sierra Leone**, a British colony on the west coast of Africa sponsored by British antislavery activists. Located a few miles from Bunce Island, a major British slave-trading fort, the colony of Sierra Leone promised migrants land, opportunities for trade, and the chance to live in a "Province of Freedom" although still under white leaders. It was a kind of qualified freedom that would be familiar to men and women freed from slavery in North America.

Great Britain saw West Africa as a potential resettlement colony for criminals as well as for loyal free blacks. The loss of its North American colonies meant that Britain could no longer exile thousands of its convicts, most of whom had been convicted of petty property crimes, to North American ports. For a short time, the country experimented with an ill-fated venture that sent these men and women to West Africa, to operate the forts that collected and traded captured slaves. When this failed, Britain developed a prison colony in New South Wales, Australia, in 1788. First claimed for Britain by Captain James Cook in 1770, the new colony further redirected the flow of people and goods from the Atlantic empires into the Pacific.

7-3b Free Black Communities

Most black Americans did not leave with the British, remaining instead enslaved in the newly independent United States. But gradual emancipation and manumissions swelled the numbers of free black people, who congregated in cities. Before the Revolution, free blacks in the British North American colonies were only one-tenth of 1 percent of the U.S. population, but by 1820, they represented 2.5 percent (see Table 7.2). Many did similar kinds of work in freedom that they had done in slavery, especially hard manual labor and domestic service. In southern cities, some ran shops or negotiated their own work as carters or laundresses, and many supplemented meager wages with odd jobs and small street sales of food. Husbands and wives rented rooms in houses belonging to

> Free blacks form urban communities.

Table 7.2 Free People of Color in 1790

The greatest concentrations of free people of color in the new United States were in the middle coastal states of Delaware, Maryland, New Jersey, Pennsylvania, and Virginia. Rhode Island had a high percentage of free blacks although the overall number of people was not large. Both the size of the community and their relationship to the white population shaped daily life for free people of color.

State	Free People of Color	Percentage of Total Population (%)
Connecticut	2,808	1.2
Delaware	3,899	6.6
Georgia	398	0.5
Kentucky	114	0.2
Maryland	8,043	2.5
Massachusetts	5,463	1.4
New Hampshire	630	0.4
New Jersey	2,762	1.5
New York	4,654	1.4
North Carolina	4,975	1.3
Pennsylvania	6,537	1.5
Rhode Island	3,407	5.0
South Carolina	1,801	0.7
Vermont	255	0.3
Virginia	12,866	1.7

Source: 1790 U.S. Census.

Sierra Leone West African British colony created as a refuge for freed slaves.

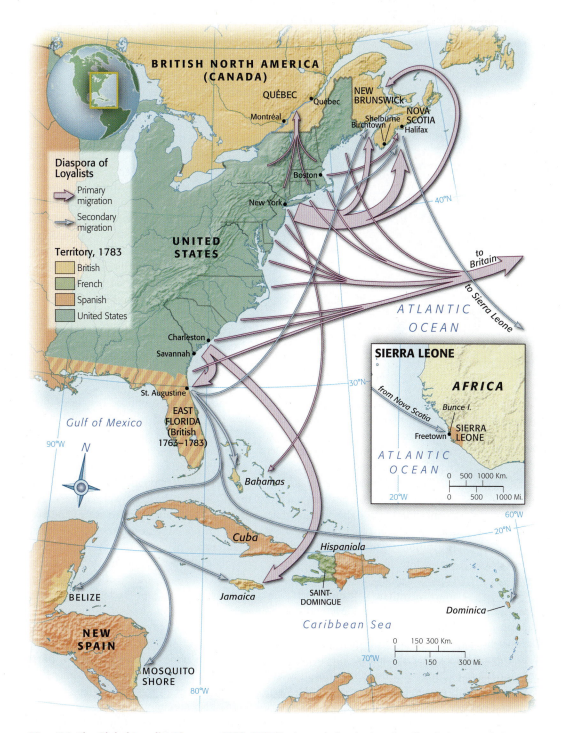

Map 7.3 The Global Loyalist Diaspora, 1783–1793 During and after the American Revolution, a total of 60,000 free Loyalists—black and white—left the United States, taking 15,000 slaves with them. Many migrated more than once. Refugees who settled in East Florida migrated a second time to the Caribbean and elsewhere when Britain returned Florida to Spanish control with the Treaty of Paris. Likewise, free blacks in Nova Scotia sought a better life in Sierra Leone. ▲

whites, scraping together income from multiple jobs. Free blacks with family members still in slavery sought to earn enough to purchase them, a process that required years of savings and, in some cases, careful petitions to state authorities.

In leaving behind slavery, free men and women created new identities, starting with new names. They shed the degrading nicknames of slavery—"Fortune," "Cesar," "Mistake"—for full, often English-sounding names such as Thomas or Sarah. They selected last names for the first

Global Americans The girl who grew up to be **Phillis Wheatley** was born in West Africa, "Gambia" as she remembered it, and captured into slavery around the age of seven. Massachusetts slave trader Timothy Fitch paid to transport her to North America on a voyage in which 25 percent of her fellow captives died. Purchased by the Wheatley family of Boston and named Phillis, the name of the ship she disembarked, she became a house slave. The Wheatleys oversaw her conversion to Christianity, and their daughter Mary taught her to read English and Latin and to write. In 1767, Phillis published her first poem. In 1773, when she was about 20 years old, she traveled to London to publish and promote a volume of her work; while there, she met Benjamin Franklin and secured her own manumission. Back in the United States, Wheatley became a celebrated patriot poet. Her poem "To His Excellency George Washington" depicted the Revolution as a worldwide cause against Britain's "thirst of boundless power."

In 1778 she married John Peters, a free black shopkeeper, and had several children, all of whom died young. Caught in the postwar economic depression with her husband frequently jailed for debt, she supported her remaining child by working as a servant and living in a boardinghouse. Frustrated in her attempts to publish a second volume of poetry, she died in 1784, around the age of 31 and was buried alongside her last child in an unmarked grave, her death a testament to the difficulty of free black lives after slavery.

Library of Congress Prints and Photographs Division[LC-DIG-ppmsca-02947]

Free African Society
Organization established in multiple U.S. cities by former slaves after the Revolution to pool resources and start schools.

Treaty of Fort Stanwix of 1784 First forced treaty between Indians and the United States after the Revolution that gave up Six Nation claims to the Ohio Valley but was rejected by Indians living there.

time, and although some, such as Elizabeth Freeman, proclaimed their transformation with a descriptive last name, most selected common English names such as Smith or Brown.

Former slaves were no longer owned as property, but they lacked political and civil rights within white society. Instead, they founded new institutions to provide the support that white institutions would not. Absalom Jones, a former slave who together with his wife purchased their own freedom, and Richard Allen, a black Methodist minister, founded Philadelphia's **Free African Society** in 1787. Similar societies appeared in other northern cities, adopting "African" as a new shared identity. They sponsored schools for black children and established mutual aid funds to assist members with loans and charity in the face of illness and poverty.

7-3c The Trans-Appalachian West

Even before the ink was dry on the 1783 Treaty of Paris, white Americans flooded across the Appalachians, especially to the Ohio country and the Tennessee River Valley, deep in the southern borderlands. As they moved, they hunted extensively, driving the bison out of Kentucky by the end of the century. They also transformed the landscape with farms and fenced pastures. Their desire for land in the West had motivated many in

> U.S. and Indian migrants struggle over who should "settle" the West.

the backcountry to oppose Britain in the first place, and now they expected to reap the benefits of victory. Veterans who had been promised land in exchange for enlistment pressured states to open territory to development and sales. Land ownership, they insisted, would give them security as well as political and financial independence. In the 1780s, two-thirds of whites living in Kentucky did not own land but rather rented from landlords, an ominous trend for revolutionaries who believed that the lord-and-tenant relationships of Europe encouraged tyranny. Many people did not wait for the state and the surveyors but claimed land as squatters, often fighting to stay put.

Already living on the land west of the Appalachians were tens if not hundreds of thousands of Indians, including many displaced refugees from the Revolution who had moved west to escape being killed and the destruction of their fields and towns. A significant portion of Haudenosaunees followed Joseph and Molly Brant to refuge in Canada, but many moved onto land no longer under nominal British dominion and protection. As they moved and regrouped, they formed multiethnic communities along backcountry rivers.

The U.S. government insisted that Indian allies of the British were a defeated enemy with no right to live, farm, or hunt on land won by the United States. Like the white Loyalists (who were acknowledged in treaty negotiations), these Indians had forfeited their rights to property by choosing the losing side in the Revolution. To assert its claim to the spoils of war, the United States negotiated a series of Indian treaties at gunpoint. The second **Treaty of Fort Stanwix of 1784** was typical. When Haudenosaunee representatives tried to insist that the Ohio River, not the Mississippi, was the western boundary of the United States, they were told "You are a subdued people" who "stand out *alone* against our *whole* force." The fact that neither the Haudenosaunees nor the United States had the undisputed authority to negotiate over these lands, which were claimed by New York and Pennsylvania and were home to Senecas, caused more problems for the Indians who signed away lands than for the Americans who gained them. Haudenosaunee negotiators returned home to face angry Senecas who insisted that the Haudenosaunee delegates could not speak for them.

Federal commissioners exploited such divisions within Indian groups. Similar treaties took land from Delawares, Wyandots, and others at Fort McIntosh in 1785 and from Senecas at Fort Finney in 1786. Even Indians who had fought on the patriot side, such as the Pequots in Rhode Island and the Oneidas in New York, were forced to sign treaties by state and federal commissioners and burdened with neighbors who disregarded their property rights.

Treaty of Fort Stanwix, 1784 Both Haudenosaunee chiefs and U.S. agents signed and placed vermillion wax seals at the bottom of this treaty page. The treaty, which ceded the Ohio country to the United States, recognized each of the Six Nations as sovereign states and established the first Indian reservation in the United States. The United States ratified the treaty in 1785; the Six Nations never did. ▼

National Archives

7-3d **Pacific Connections**

{ Traders spread commerce and disease.

Ships and crews that had fought in the American Revolution turned to ocean trade after the war, freed from British trade restrictions but also no longer protected by British monopolies or the British navy. Investors hoped that by developing independent trade relations with China, the United States could integrate itself into the Pacific Rim trading world. The Pacific Ocean had been a conduit of trading voyages for many years. In the Spanish-occupied Philippines, traders exchanged silver from Spanish mines in South America for Chinese luxury goods. In the icy waters of the North Pacific, Russian and Native American traders exchanged sea otter pelts. In 1778, British explorer Captain Cook sailed from the Pacific islands of southeast Asia toward the west coast of North America, searching for the Northwest Passage that would connect Asia, America, and Europe by an all-water route. Reports of his encounters in the Hawai'ian Islands, the territory of Alaska, and the Pacific Northwest spread interest in trade in the rest of the world.

The traders who followed Cook helped establish an expanded region of Pacific commerce linking North America, Asia, and Europe. The Spanish controlled ports in Alta California and dominated supply ships from Mexico through the early 1800s, but U.S. merchants soon came to predominate in the volume of Pacific trade, which involved traders from two dozen countries. Alta California was by the early nineteenth century a transit point where trade ships stopped to obtain sea otter pelts, timber, fish, and other commodities collected by Native Americans before heading along the Northwest coast to Alaska or to Hawai'i. Even more than in the Atlantic, entrepreneurs frequently evaded imperial boundaries and laws to create an international trading world.

Traders also brought diseases, such as tuberculosis, syphilis, and smallpox, with devastating results for Indian populations. Indigenous Pacific peoples quickly grasped the connection between disease and trading vessels. Cook islanders who fell ill developed the phrase *kua pai au*, or "I am shippy," to describe their suffering and pinpoint the obvious agent of their illnesses: the

Global Americans Born in Connecticut in 1751, **John Ledyard** studied to be a missionary to Native Americans but instead joined a trading voyage to see the world. After stints in the British navy and army, he served as a marine officer on British Captain Cook's third exploratory voyage around the Pacific. His 1783 account of Cook's 1779 death in Hawai'i at the hands of Pacific natives was the first book to receive a copyright in the United States.

Having seen the commercial potential of Pacific trade first hand, Ledyard dreamed of leading a sea voyage across a Northwest Passage to trade in Asia. Philadelphia merchant Robert Morris eventually funded a voyage using Ledyard's scheme of trading furs for Chinese porcelain and silk and sent his ship, the *Empress of China*, to Canton. In 1785, conversations in Paris with Benjamin Franklin, Thomas Jefferson, and the Marquis de Lafayette inspired Ledyard to undertake an overland trip through Siberia that was intended to cross Alaska and end in Virginia but was cut short in Yakutsk by suspicious Russian authorities. As he met native Asian people in Siberia, he concluded that they were related to North American Indians, and historians who had "written the History of Man have begun at the wrong end."

Funded by a British antislavery activist, Ledyard took a final journey to follow the Niger River in Africa, where he died in Cairo in 1789. His global travels linked exploration, imperial influence, and commercial opportunity. Ledyard himself insisted he was "commissioned by myself to serve the World at large."

Ledyard described the walrus hunt that was part of Cook's voyage.

trading ships. Rates of infertility and death rose dramatically along indigenous trading routes as virgin soil epidemics spread into the interior of Indian country.

Terrible losses of life from disease forced new migrations and relationships. From the late 1770s to the 1780s, a smallpox epidemic transmitted by soldiers in the East, fur traders in Canada, and horse raiders across the plains spread across North America. When it hit previously unexposed settlements of Indians in the interior, death rates were far higher than was typical in Europe, wiping out entire villages. The epidemic of the 1780s killed as much as 80 percent of the population of the agrarian Mandans, Hidatsas, and Chipeweyans living in the Northern Plains. Sioux records referred to the 1779–1780 season as "Smallpox Used Them Up Winter." Those who survived moved west into lands emptied by dead and fleeing neighbors. The Sioux came to dominate their new territory on the northern and central plains, hunting and trading buffalo in mobile bands on horseback.

7-4
Power in Crisis

Congress printed this Continental one-third of a dollar designed by Benjamin Franklin to finance the American Revolution. It was the first American paper money to be in dollar denominations rather than pounds, shillings, and pence. After the war, the value of these dollars fell so dramatically people began to use the phrase "not worth a Continental" when talking about useless things.

What does the image of linked rings surrounding a sun suggest about the political and financial bonds of the states? ▶

Wartime dislocations contributed to an economic depression in the 1780s. During war, farms produced less for national and international markets, and plantation production sharply declined as thousands of enslaved people fled to the British. The costs of war heightened these difficulties. It was a bitter truth that to pay for a war opposing British taxation, American states had to raise their own taxes to new highs. In a republic where the people taxed themselves, the implications of popular sovereignty were felt keenly in the pocketbook, and the result was social turmoil in North America and vulnerability abroad. In another ironic twist, freedom from the British trading empire also meant isolation from the benefits of trade within the empire, and Americans struggled to establish trade connections in a world still influenced by mercantilism. Some thought the answer lay in enlarging the United States itself.

☞ As you read, consider the ways that debt, access to land, and political power were connected in the 1780s. How did people seek political solutions to their economic crises? Who succeeded and who was ignored?

7-4a Trade within and around Imperial Systems

Once the war was over, British merchants flooded American markets with finished goods. The patriotic efforts of the nonimportation and non- { Americans struggle to establish new international trading circuits in a world plagued by war debt.

consumption movements fell away and were replaced with eager purchasing after years of deprivation. British ceramics manufacturers revitalized their own industry by creating patriotic dishware decorated with eagles and images of George Washington that they sold to American consumers. Personal debt grew with the new purchases, sparking a familiar call from political leaders for women to purify the nation through self-sacrifice. "Feathers and fripperies suit the Cherokees," one wrote, but they were inappropriate for "the fair daughters of independent America." Groups of free women once again took up the cause of virtuous restraint in consumption, signing agreements to dress simply as an example to all.

Planters in South Carolina and Georgia resumed the importation of Africans as slaves in 1783 after a wartime suspension of the trade. Tens of thousands of slaves had died, escaped, or been evacuated over the course of the war. In some regions, half of the slaves—representing labor and capital—were lost to owners. One Savannah merchant observed that to replace them, "the Planter will as far in his power sacrifice every thing to attain Negroes." To meet the high demand, slave traders from Great Britain, France, Denmark, the Netherlands, and the United States shipped 11,000 enslaved people into South Carolina and Georgia from Africa and the Caribbean between

Patriotic Dishware Produced in Britain, circa 1800 As they had before the Revolutionary War, British craftsmen made objects specifically for American markets, such as this jug featuring George Washington's portrait, surrounded by the figures of liberty and justice. Purchasing British imports such as these sunk postwar Americans deeper into debt. ▲

Brayton, George/The New York Public Library Digital Collections

1783 and 1785. In 1787, now with an oversupply, South Carolina closed the trade again.

Consumers in the United States were eager to buy British manufactured goods and cargoes of African people, but imperial trade laws made it difficult to earn the money to do so. Britain closed the British West Indies, which had remained loyal, to American ships, ending the lucrative trade of fish, grain, and livestock in exchange for sugar and molasses that had enriched colonial merchants. The French were not able to fill the gap by providing the same kind of long-term credit with which all trade was conducted. Yet there was little Congress could do to address the intertwined trade and diplomatic problems. Under the Articles of Confederation, Congress lacked power over commerce, so it could not close U.S. ports to British traders in retaliation for the British ban. Because Americans bought more than they sold internationally, they had to send scarce **specie** (gold and silver) out of the country to pay for their goods. The result was a staggering trade deficit in the millions (see Figure 7.2). An indebted nation was a weak nation. In 1783, British Lord Sheffield published a pamphlet on American commerce stating that the United States "should not be, for a long time, either to be feared or regarded as a nation."

specie Gold and silver coins preferred for payments that were believed to have a more stable, intrinsic value than other forms of money.

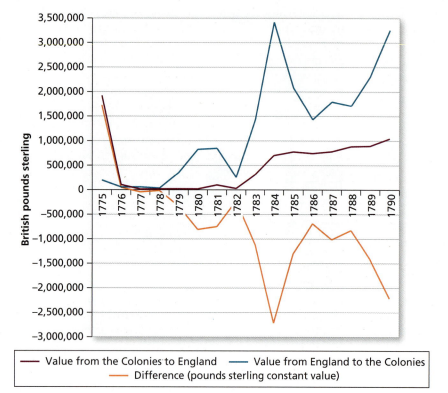

Figure 7.2 Trade Deficit with England Just as the Revolutionary War broke out, the value of goods that Britain's thirteen North American colonies exported to England was higher than the value of the goods imported from England. As the war ended, the United States resumed importing English goods, sending the new country deep into debt to its former empire. ▲ Source: *Historical Statistics of the United States*, millennial ed. Cambridge University Press, 2006.

7-4b American Debt Crisis

Congress paid for the American Revolution by borrowing money from European allies, printing paper money, and issuing promissory notes.

> { Government debts threaten political stability at the national level.

France loaned the United States $7 million and gave several million more outright. Dutch investors loaned $2.8 million at the end of the war. Following a practice of British colonies during earlier eighteenth-century wars, Congress paid salaries and military costs with paper money, known as **bills of credit**. It declared these bills to be legal tender, meaning that people could use them, rather than specie, to pay their debts. And it planned to redeem bills of credit with specie collected from the states, which had been charged with taxing their residents to pay for the war. States, struggling to recruit and equip soldiers themselves, sent very little to Congress. Congress printed more bills, called Continentals, but they were backed by nothing more than the hope of future tax payments from the states, which were not forthcoming. Military losses undermined faith in Congress, and counterfeiting

bills of credit Issued by the Continental Congress and states to fund the American Revolution, paper money backed by the promise of future tax payments.

war bonds Interest-bearing notes used in exchange for money, supplies, and labor given to the revolutionary cause on which governments paid interest but could not redeem after the war.

undermined faith in Continentals, whose purchasing power plummeted. By the end of the war, Congress was ordering states to accept the bills at 2.5 percent of their printed face value. Creditors rejected paper money, and the very state governments that had printed their own bills of credit refused to accept them.

To supplement the nearly worthless Continentals, Congress (and the states) used a variety of promissory notes to pay soldiers, farmers, and other wartime suppliers. By the end of the war, Congress had converted these notes to interest-bearing **war bonds** that it was unable to redeem. Rachel Wells of New Jersey petitioned Congress in 1786 to repay her war bond loan because "I have done as much to carry on the war as many that now sit at the helm of government." Desperate to pay their bills and rebuild their farms and businesses, bondholders sold them at a discount to speculators in exchange for usable money. Abigail Adams was a dedicated bond speculator who bought up such bonds at reduced prices. Profits were guaranteed for those who, like Adams, were wealthy enough to invest. Governments paid her interest on the face value of the bonds, not on the discounted price she had paid for them. Meanwhile, the farmers, widows, and soldiers who had originally received the war bonds lost their investment in the revolutionary effort.

At the war's end, paying interest on war bonds alone took up two-thirds of the money most states collected in taxes. Because that money was the only revenue available to run the U.S. government, state debts raised serious questions about the continued existence of the country. With no independent power to tax, Congress was unable to meet international obligations. If the United States could not pay back France, Spain, and the Netherlands for money borrowed during the Revolution, would those countries send troops to collect? Britain refused to remove its soldiers from western American forts until the United States repaid money owed to British merchants and Loyalists whose property had been seized. Furthermore, how could the United States attract foreign investors if it could not collect its own taxes?

Thomas Jefferson, serving as U.S. envoy in Paris, tried to interest French aristocrats in loaning money to Americans for land speculation, canal building, or other developments, but money was tight everywhere. Commerce had slowed for everyone during the war as British naval blockades had disrupted the business of Spanish, French, and Dutch merchants. These countries had all borrowed money from banks and private financiers to fight the war, and as much as half of their governments' income was spent on repaying that debt. European governments, like the United States, raised taxes. In France, a new finance minister proposed a stamp tax and new land taxes that would obligate nobles to pay for the debts rising out of a century of imperial wars. Nobles refused to give up their privileges, ultimately sparking another round of Atlantic revolutions that began in Paris in 1789.

7-4c Popular Uprisings

States responded to the debt crisis by raising taxes to three or four times higher than they had been before the war and insisting that they be paid in

{ Western farmers violently protest debt, taxes, and unrepresentative government.

scarce specie. Debtors pushed back. Conflicts reminiscent of the mid-eighteenth-century Regulator movement broke out between western farmers and the merchant-dominated legislators along the coast. In 1786, the Massachusetts legislature passed one of the harshest new taxes on people and on property to pay off war bond debt. Those who could not pay had their property seized; if that was not sufficient to pay the debt, they were sent to jail, even for small sums.

Western Massachusetts farmers, mobilized in public meetings, protested the tax and its enforcement by closing the courthouses from which arrest warrants and property foreclosures were issued. The dissidents freed debtors and protestors from jail, carrying liberty poles and other emblems from the Revolutionary era. Many of the protestors were Revolutionary War veterans, still waiting for their back pay and desperate to find new markets for farm products because trade with the British Caribbean was closed. In January 1787, one veteran, Daniel Shays, led a group of more than one thousand protestors against the federal armory in Springfield to capture weapons and ammunition for their cause. A force of militiamen funded by Boston merchants engaged them, killing four and chasing the rest across New England for weeks.

Although Boston elites called the event **Shays's Rebellion**, the depth of unrest went beyond a single leader. A similar uprising in Greenbrier County, Virginia, broke out in the spring of 1787 when western farmers blocked the courthouse doors to prevent judges from issuing warrants to collect overdue taxes. The immediate goal of both uprisings was debt relief and in both cases, it was met. In Massachusetts, voters replaced the existing legislators with new men who pardoned the remaining rebels and enacted debtor relief laws. These laws reduced financial pressure on average people by letting them pay taxes in paper money, reduced the legal payments owed to bond speculators, and extended the amount of time debtors had to repay their debts. In Virginia, the legislature responded to the rebellion by repealing the tax that had sparked it.

The larger issues motivating these revolts were the responsiveness of state governments to the needs of average people and the right to determine what those needs

were. Massachusetts's state constitution, like many written or rewritten in the 1780s, was conservative in apportioning power to its citizens. Although earlier constitutions, such as the Pennsylvania Constitution of 1776, had attempted to make government as responsive as possible to the people, representatives soon discovered that grassroots pressure made tax collection and tight money control difficult. By 1790, even Pennsylvania had revised its constitution to give the state government more centralized and executive power. Protestors, sensing that the government was no longer accessible through its elected representatives, took popular sovereignty into the streets.

Jefferson, U.S. minister to Paris at the time, considered these uprisings as a normal part of democratic governments. He wrote to James Madison that for the health of elected governments, "a little rebellion now and then is a good thing." But to elites in the United States, rebellion against elected government was deeply troubling. The problems of the 1780s, reported Alexander Hamilton of New York and Elbridge Gerry of Massachusetts to their fellow representatives in Congress, were due to an "excess of democracy."

7-4d Northwest Territory

To the men in Congress, selling Indian land in exchange for war bonds seemed to be a way out of the debt crisis that would simultaneously provide

{ Political experiment in the Northwest provides a blueprint for U.S. expansion.

economic opportunities to disgruntled farmers and reward Revolutionary War veterans. The Confederation government pinned its hopes on 160 million acres of land north of the Ohio River, which had been violently contested for decades. But to achieve their goals, they had to work with the divided confederacies of the United States itself and of allied American Indians.

First, the United States had to assert national power over treaty making in the region. Massachusetts, Connecticut, and Virginia claimed parts of the territory under their old colonial charters and were reluctant to relinquish these rights and the potential profits from land sales to a shaky confederation of states. Between 1784 and 1802, states formally ceded their claims to the United States as a whole. Next, Congress had to establish a plan for surveying and selling land at auction. In the optimistic **Land Ordinance of 1785**, Congress divided the territory into a grid of six-square-mile townships, divided into 640-acre sections that could be sold individually (see Map 7.4). The hope was that by selling some smaller parcels directly, American farmers, as well as land speculators, could take ownership.

The orderly plan immediately clashed with reality on the ground.

Shays's Rebellion Insurrection by Western Massachusetts farmers (1786–1787) protesting harsh taxes, lack of adequate representation, and money policies that favored East Coast elites.

Land Ordinance of 1785 Congressional plan for land north of the Ohio River that divided the region into townships and lots to be sold to settlers and speculators.

Map 7.4 The Land Ordinance of 1785 This ordinance established a plan for surveying and selling land as well as creating townships in the Northwest Territory. The experience of people in the region was at odds with the orderly plan for drawing lots along a grid. Most importantly, Indians living on the land had not ceded or sold vast portions of the Northwest Territory to the United States, and they insisted on their legal right to their homelands. ▲

With no U.S. military to protect Americans who purchased land in the Ohio River Valley, sales were slow and not profitable enough to rescue the fortunes of the new United States. Ohio River Valley Indians, rejecting the idea that the territory belonged to the United States, disrupted surveys and walked away from treaty meetings. In 1786, delegates from the Haudenosaunees, Wyandots, Delawares, Shawnees, and others sent a message to Congress repudiating earlier land treaties signed by individual tribes. For land west of the Ohio River, they reaffirmed, the United States must deal with "the united voice of the confederacy." At the same time, speculator companies formed to pressure Congress to carve land grants out of the territory.

The **Northwest Ordinance of 1787** attempted to solve the U.S. side of the stalemate. First, it promised that Indian lands could not be seized and sold unless in "just and lawful wars authorized by Congress." Second, it established a procedure for converting the land in the Northwest into states by inventing a new type of temporary colonial status. The provisions of the Ordinance divided the region into districts. As the land was surveyed and sold, districts became **territories**, each with its own appointed governor and elected assembly. When the population reached 60,000, a territory could ratify a state constitution and become a sovereign state of the United States. This model for expansion was a departure from that of existing empires. Rather than creating colonies to channel wealth into a metropolitan center as European empires did, the Ordinance proposed territorial status as a step toward equal statehood.

The men who devised plans for the Northwest Territory envisioned a particular social order for new states in the United States. The Northwest Ordinance outlawed slavery but provided for the capture and return of **fugitive slaves** who escaped to the territory in pursuit of freedom. Building on the Land Ordinance's provision of one lot in each township for a public school, the Northwest Ordinance stated "Religion, morality, and knowledge being necessary to good government, and the happiness of mankind, schools and the means of education shall forever be encouraged." Free white farmers—independent because of the availability of land and virtuous because of the education they had received from their mothers and their teachers—would, the designers hoped, supply the ideal citizens for an expanding republic.

Northwest Ordinance of 1787 Charter signed by the Second Continental Congress establishing a government, a bill of rights, and a path toward statehood for the Northwest Territory.

territories Region under the authority of the U.S. government with an appointed governor but its own elected legislature. Nineteenth-century territories gradually gained statehood.

fugitive slaves Enslaved people who escaped to states in which slavery was illegal but were subject to territorial and national laws that supported owners' rights to reclaim their human property.

U.S. Constitution

This cartoon, published in the *Massachusetts Centinel* in 1788, depicts a hand from the clouds propping up the Massachusetts pillar to the "Federal Superstructure." It was printed as the divided convention of Massachusetts debated whether to ratify the new Constitution that would replace the Articles of Confederation.

What does the cartoon suggest about the nature of the new U.S. government? How does it differ from Benjamin Franklin's 1754 image of the "join or die" snake in Chapter 6? ▶

The Massachusetts Centinel/Library of Congress Serial and Government Publications Division Washington, D.C. 20540 USA

The C E N T I N E L.

States—like the gen'rous vine fupported live,
The ftrength they gain is from th'embrace they giv
THE FEDERAL PILLARS.

DEL. PEN. N.JER. GEOR. CON. MASS.

UNITED THEY STAND—DIVIDED FALL.

The struggles of the period between 1776 and 1787 over unity, identity, debt, and power culminated in a Constitutional Convention. Originally convened to revise the agreement among the states, the Convention produced a new governing document for a stronger, more centralized federal government. In designing and debating this Constitution, people in the new United States faced the problems of representation and taxation that had sparked the American Revolution. They also sought political solutions to the social, military, and financial upheavals of the 1770s and 1780s. The Constitution's preamble stated that "We, the People" composed the United States, replacing the Articles of Confederation's compact of states with a collective body of citizens. But as the debates over the ratification of the new Constitution revealed, national unity and shared identity were still weak at the local level.

☞ As you read, focus on the ways in which the relationship between local and federal power was central to the framing of the Constitution and the debates over its ratification. Which side won the debate? Initially? Ultimately?

7-5a The Constitutional Convention

The movement to reform the Articles of Confederation started small, when delegates from five states met in Annapolis, Maryland, in the fall of 1786 to seek a remedy for barriers to interstate trade, which was stifled by state taxes on imports across state lines. The group, calling themselves the Commissioners to Remedy Defects of the Federal Government, issued a vaguely worded report calling for a

{ The Constitutional Convention rethinks the new nation's political structure.

1787 convention to discuss the Articles. In fact, their plan was more ambitious. Led by men who wanted a stronger national government, they hoped that a separate convention might be able to accomplish what the Confederation Congress could not: shift enough power away from the states to unify national and international goals. Shays's Rebellion added urgency to their desires for stronger central control. With the approval of Congress, states appointed delegations for a late spring convention in Philadelphia.

The fifty-five delegates who arrived over the course of May 1787 included Revolutionary War veterans (George Washington, Charles Cotesworth Pinckney, Alexander

Rare Books Department of Special Collections at the J. Willard Marriott Library, The University of Utah

THE SPIRIT OF LAWS.

Translated from the FRENCH of
M. DE SECONDAT,
BARON DE MONTESQUIEU.

With Corrections and Additions communicated by the Author.

VOL. I.

LONDON:
Printed for J. NOURSE, and P. VAILLANT, in the *Strand*.
MDCCL.

Montesquieu's *Spirit of Laws* Among the works that James Madison consulted prior to the Constitutional Convention was Baron de Montesquieu's *Spirit of Laws*, published in France in 1748. Montesquieu theorized that history and climate shaped nations' political structures. Working from an idealized model of the English constitutional monarchy, he thought governments that granted executive, legislative, and judicial powers to separate bodies best preserved liberty. He emphasized that each of these bodies should be bound by the rule of law. ◀

Constitutional Convention
Private meeting of delegates in 1787 to draft a constitution for the United States that would establish a strong centralized government.

Virginia Plan Madison's proposed structure for a new federal government that favored greater power to more populous states and limits to voters' power.

checks and balances
Enlightenment political theory favoring government structures designed to curb political corruption by allowing one branch of government to overturn another's actions.

New Jersey Plan Alternative to the Virginia Plan that proposed maintaining equal representation of each state in the U.S. government.

Hamilton) and representatives to the Confederation Congress (forty-two of the fifty-five had served at some point). Most were lawyers; all were comfortably wealthy white men. Worried about public interference, they agreed to conduct business with the windows closed and with no communications to the press. Madison's detailed notes on delegates' speeches and deliberations, which give modern readers an eyewitness account, were locked away and not made public until 1840. The convention's use of secrecy, which Jefferson, from his diplomatic post in Paris, called an "abominable precedent," was not in keeping with revolutionary politics and revolutionary state constitutions, which had insisted on open debate and the publication of government proceedings. The secrecy did allow delegates to hammer out a delicate compromise.

Madison, part of the Virginia delegation, prepared for what would become known as the **Constitutional Convention** by immersing himself in European Enlightenment treatises on political philosophy, studies of what would later be called political science. These texts gave histories of specific kingdoms, republics, and empires since antiquity. They also proposed general theories about how governments should use and manage power. Influenced by these works, Madison believed that a proper structure of government could fix many of the problems that arose from human nature. He therefore set the terms of the delegates' discussion from the start by proposing a comprehensive plan for a new U.S. government. Called the **Virginia Plan**, it scrapped the structure of the Articles of Confederation in favor of an expanded central government. The new federal government would divide its powers among three branches with distinct roles: a congress for legislation, a president for executive authority, and a supreme court for judicial powers. The three branches would operate through a series of what came to be called **checks and balances** (see Figure 7.3). Because each branch could overturn some decisions made by another branch, none would become too powerful.

Vague on many details, Madison's plan focused on addressing what he saw as one of the main problems of the confederation: that local interests could thwart the larger common good. Under the Articles, self-interested states had equal representation in the Continental Congress; important votes required a supermajority of nine of thirteen states' support, and amending the Articles required all thirteen to agree. Under such circumstances, little legislation passed. Fixing this problem required a new approach to representation. In the proposed new structure, each state would be represented in Congress

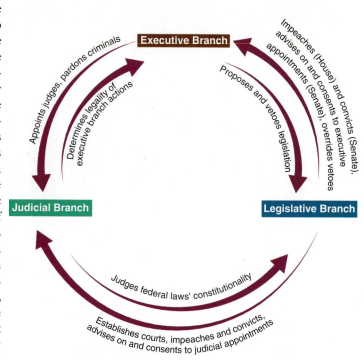

Figure 7.3 Checks and Balances in the Constitution The 1787 U.S. Constitution was designed to balance power among the branches of the federal government as well as the power between the federal government and the states. Unlike the English "mixed" government, the new U.S. government granted each branch distinct powers and gave each branch ways to check the actions of the others. ▲ Source: John G. Geer et al., *Gateways to Democracy*, 3rd edition. Boston: Cengage Learning, 2015.

in proportion to its population. At the same time, the dangers of majority rule would be counterbalanced by making representation more indirect. Madison proposed that voters would elect only members of the House of Representatives.

Delegates from smaller states objected that the new apportionment of representation would allow states with larger populations to overrule their interests and needs. The **New Jersey Plan**, prepared as a rebuttal to Virginia's scheme, recommended a structure much more like the Articles of Confederation with a single legislature in which each state had an equal vote. This plan was appealing to small states that hoped to retain their power.

7-5b United States Constitution of 1787

The final version of the **Constitution of the United States**, signed in 1787 after months of negotiation, resolved the two approaches to representation by establishing two houses of Congress: the Senate in which each state had an equal vote and the House of Representatives in which

{ The new Constitution creates a stronger central government.

Birch, William Russell, 1755–1834, artist Charles Desilver (Firm)

Pennsylvania State House Yard The Constitutional Convention that met behind closed doors in the Pennsylvania State House in 1787 chose a location with deep significance for the Revolution. The Second Continental Congress had met in the same building in 1775, and revolutionaries rang its tower bell in 1776 to announce the passage of the Declaration of Independence. British soldiers turned the building into a barracks during their occupation of the city. ▲

states were represented in proportion to population. As stated in Article I, each state would have two senators in the Senate and, for every thirty thousand inhabitants, one representative in the House of Representatives. All funding bills would originate in this lower house, meaning that the majority population would control taxation. This concession to popular sovereignty was important because the Constitution granted the U.S. government extensive new powers over the economy. Congress, not the states, could coin money and regulate foreign and interstate commerce. It would have the right to tax American citizens directly rather than relying on states to raise all of the revenue.

Although slavery was not directly named in the new document, multiple clauses supported the slave system, starting with how Americans were counted. For the purposes of apportioning representatives and for the direct taxes that the federal government could demand, the government counted all free people who lived in that state as well as three-fifths of the slaves. This did not mean that a slave was three-fifths of a person or a person with three-fifths of the rights of a free citizen. Instead, the **three-fifths compromise** was a way to grant power in Congress to slave owners in exchange for acknowledging, and taxing, the slaves who produced the wealth in

their states. Article I also prohibited Congress from ending the importation of slaves until 1808.

Other articles of the Constitution contained additional compromises that reflected the tension between popular sovereignty and central control. Article II outlined the executive powers of the president—an entirely new position—and put the election of the president in the hands of an **electoral college** rather than directly with voters. State legislatures chose citizen-electors in numbers equivalent to the total number of senators and representatives the state had in Congress. Those electors, in turn, chose two candidates, at least one of whom had to be from another state, and sent the names to Congress to be tallied. The person with the majority of votes became president and the one in second place became vice president. In this and other measures, the authors hoped to protect the new government from mob rule, although the final version

Constitution of the United States Document signed in 1787 establishing a new structure of U.S. government and the allocation of power within it as well as limits to that power.

three-fifths compromise Method for determining population numbers for the purposes of federal taxation and representation that counted only three-fifths of a state's enslaved people.

electoral college Institution created by the Constitution to select the U.S. president indirectly, channeling the popular vote through electors more likely to think nationally than locally.

Doolittle, Amos, 1754–1832, engraver

"Federals" and "Antifederals" in Connecticut The ratification debate connected state issues to the proposed U.S. Constitution. At the top of this cartoon, Connecticut is a wagon, sinking into the mud because of its heavy load of debts and paper money. On the left, Federals urge viewers to "Comply with Congress"; on the right, Antifederals cry "the People are oprest." At the bottom, merchant vessels sailing from Connecticut to New York complain about taxes on interstate trade. State politicians feud in the middle. ▲

Federalists Supporters of the 1787 U.S. Constitution who praised its structures of shared power between states and the national government.

federalism System of government in which a central body and regional governments share power.

Federalist Papers Eighty-five newspaper essays written by James Madison, Alexander Hamilton, and John Jay and published anonymously in New York to support constitutional ratification.

Antifederalists People who opposed the 1787 U.S. Constitution, usually on the grounds that it consolidated power at the expense of state and individual freedoms.

still allocated more power to the people than either the Virginia or New Jersey plan had. Most votes in Congress required only a simple majority to pass.

Supporters of the new Constitution called themselves **Federalists**, a term that referred to **federalism**, the sharing of power between the central government and states. Overall, however, the document was a strong statement of centralized power. Article VI stated that the Constitution and U.S. law were "the supreme law of the land," binding people in every state. Article IV declared that citizens in each state had the right to "all privileges and immunities of citizens in the several States." Finally, the Constitution itself, under Article VII, would be ratified if nine state conventions voted in favor of it. Unanimity was no longer the mark of legitimacy.

7-5c Ratification Debates

When the delegates emerged from their closed negotiations with the final draft of the new federal Constitution in September 1787, public debate began. As was typical in British political culture, printed debate engaged

> The debates over ratifying the Constitution center on federal powers and the nature of a republic.

public opinion that then continued in taverns, homes, workshops, and alleyways. The proposed Constitution was quickly published in every U.S. newspaper. Drafters Hamilton, Madison, and John Jay also published a series of essays, later known as the **Federalist Papers**, making their case for the new form of government. In their essays, originally printed anonymously between October 1787 and May 1788 in New York newspapers, they elaborated on the philosophy behind the governmental structure, arguing that the new Constitution resolved problems of representation, preserved popular sovereignty, and created a state strong enough to provide defense and regulate trade in the world.

Opponents of the new Constitution likewise published numerous essays in addition to speaking to friends, family, and colleagues. **Antifederalists**, as they were labeled, were not unanimous in their reasoning but united in believing that the 1787 Constitution had betrayed the principles of the Revolution with its compromises and inventions. They were especially alarmed at the perceived restrictions on state and individual rights. Antifederalist sentiment was strong in the backcountry and in northern New England. It involved elites (including dissenting delegates to the Constitutional Convention such as George Mason) as well as middling businesspeople and struggling farmers.

Antifederalists argued that the new government was too powerful at the federal level. Instead of a union of sovereign states, the country would become a centralized state with a government that acted directly on the people. Patrick Henry, a leading patriot during the Revolution and former governor of Virginia, dismissed the celebrated checks and balances promised by the three branches of government as distracting "rope-dancing" and "chain rattling" rather than a real separation of power. Sooner or later, powers such as those to sign treaties would consolidate in the hands of a few men, he feared.

More pressing, the central government gained new powers to command a permanent army, raise taxes, and take on debts. All of these were features of European empires and all, argued the Antifederalists, threatened the liberty of U.S. citizens. While taking the power to raise troops for an army away from the states, the Constitution also granted the central government the right to control and use state militias to "suppress Insurrections and repel Invasions," a power that had been wielded against debt-burdened farmers, rebelling slaves, and Indians. In the eyes of its opponents, the Constitution was an attempt to turn the United States into a European-style empire, when, as many Antifederalists pointed out, a revolution had just been fought to separate from a European empire, its standing armies, and its corruptions.

Critics also believed that the new republic was too large to be responsive to the greater good of the community. It replaced local control by leading elected men with the distant power of those who might not know their constituents, given the large size of each congressional district. Madison, writing in *Federalist 10*, countered that the large size safeguarded the republic from special interests called **factions**, which were a great danger, Madison argued, because they favored a particular interest or passion that was at odds with the rights or needs of the community as a whole. Whereas factions representing a minority of the population would be voted out in a democracy or republic, a faction composed of the majority could easily tyrannize the country. To combat a **tyranny of the majority**, the new constitution created a large republic. In a large republic, the pool of qualified representatives was larger, and better men could be elected who could filter out the effects of faction. A larger district would also likely contain several factions that would balance each other. Madison's innovation turned around the common wisdom of republicanism by stating that its goals—a virtuous society of shared interests— were best met by increasing the size of the country rather than keeping it small.

7-5d The Bill of Rights

One of the most concrete objections to the new Constitution was that it had no bill of rights to protect individual liberties from a powerful, consolidated government. Seven state constitutions had bills of rights securing freedom of the press, trial by jury, and other individual liberties. The absence of a similar statement of rights in the proposed Constitution held up ratification for months.

> The continuing importance of protecting individual rights against a powerful central government reflects the Revolution's legacy.

Table 7.3 State Ratification of the Constitution

The campaign to ratify the Constitution in state conventions began with quick success but then slowed as conventions grappled with the document's lack of a bill of rights. Votes were especially close in Massachusetts, New Hampshire, Virginia, and New York, where Antifederalist sentiment was strong. The last two states to ratify, North Carolina and Rhode Island, did so only after the First Congress sent the first twelve amendments to the states for ratification.

State	Date of Vote	State Convention Votes
Delaware	December 7, 1787	30–0
Pennsylvania	December 12, 1787	46–23
New Jersey	December 18, 1787	38–0
Georgia	January 2, 1788	26–0
Connecticut	January 9, 1788	128–40
Massachusetts	February 6, 1788	187–168
Maryland	April 28, 1788	63–11
South Carolina	May 23, 1788	149–73
New Hampshire	June 21, 1788	57–47
Virginia	June 25, 1788	89–79
New York	July 26, 1788	30–27
North Carolina	November 21, 1789	194–77
Rhode Island	May 29, 1790	34–32

Source: State-by-State Ratification Table, http://teachingamericanhistory. org/ratification/overview/, a project of the Ashbrook Center at Ashland University.

Even states that ratified the Constitution sent in a total of 124 proposed amendments focused on protecting civil liberties. Some called for a second Constitutional Convention to address these additions. The U.S. Constitution became law when New Hampshire ratified it in June 1788, but the vitally important states of Virginia and New York, which were home to significant Antifederalist feeling, followed only when their ratification was linked to an insistence that a bill of rights be added as amendments. Rhode Island held out until 1790 (see Table 7.3).

The lack of a bill of rights in the 1787 Constitution was not an oversight. Elbridge Gerry, a delegate from Massachusetts, had proposed one at the end of the Constitutional Convention and refused to sign the final draft when it failed to include a statement of rights. The majority of those assembled argued that a bill of rights was unnecessary. Because the Constitution gave the federal government only specific powers, Americans retained their liberties. Enumerating specific protected liberties would only imply that rights not listed were subject to federal intervention.

Most voters rejected this logic. As one of its first acts, therefore, the new Congress created what became the **Bill of Rights**, ten amendments

factions Group of people whose interests oppose the interests and freedoms of others. Considered by many to play a divisive and corrupting role in politics.

tyranny of the majority Concept that minority civil rights are violated in a system of majority rule addressed by *Federalist Papers* author Madison.

Bill of Rights First ten amendments to the U.S. Constitution, preserving individuals' civil rights. In several states, including it was a condition of ratification.

to the Constitution that the individual states ratified (see Table 7.4). The First Amendment protected Americans' right to speak, assemble, publish in the press, and petition the government and prohibited Congress from passing any law "respecting an establishment of religion, or prohibiting the free exercise thereof." The Second and Third Amendments countered the dangers of a standing army by protecting individuals' rights to "keep and bear arms" and form a militia as well as banning the quartering of soldiers in individuals' homes without their consent. Amendments 4 through 8 established legal rights in trials. The last two amendments covered anything left out. Amendment 9 explicitly affirmed that the rights protected in the first eight amendments were not the people's only rights. In an effort to reassert the principles of federalism, Amendment 10 confirmed that any powers not specifically given to the federal government remained powers of the individual states or of the people. The Bill of Rights therefore turned the goals of the early Revolutionaries—personal liberty, local control, freedom from tyranny—into law. Whether the Constitution could maintain these rights was an open question.

Table 7.4 The Bill of Rights

The Bill of Rights consists of the first ten amendments to the U.S. Constitution. Other amendments were sent to the states in 1789, but not ratified, including one that would have forbidden Congress to vote itself a pay raise. That amendment was eventually ratified in 1992.

Number	Subject
Amendment 1	Freedom of religion, speech, the press, assembly, petitioning
Amendment 2	Right to bear arms and form a militia
Amendment 3	No quartering of soldiers without consent
Amendment 4	No unreasonable searches and seizures
Amendment 5	Right to due process, not to testify against oneself, to compensation for property taken
Amendment 6	Right to public trial, to know charges, to confront witnesses, to legal counsel
Amendment 7	Right to a jury trial
Amendment 8	No excessive bail or fines, no cruel and unusual punishments
Amendment 9	Rights not enumerated are still maintained
Amendment 10	Powers not delegated to the federal government remain with the states

Summary

The period of experimentation between 1776 and 1789 tested the limits of the American Revolution as a true revolution as opposed to a war for independence. States, confederacies, and empires responded to wartime pressures to redistribute power among a broader group of people. Many individuals, from refugee children to freed slaves to urban mothers, wondered how the changing patterns of power might offer them new liberties. The answer they got was mixed. Wartime idealism initially motivated people to revise some old hierarchies. Slaves in northern states used petitions and new gradual emancipation laws to secure freedom; some southern masters, citing the natural law of human freedom, manumitted their slaves. Free mothers pressed for better education for girls. Many argued that freedom of religion was as important as political liberty. New state constitutions within the United States granted average men a stronger voice in their governments.

As the war dragged to its end, economic depression and bitter race warfare hardened lines between "us" and "them" that ran counter to the inspiring principles of liberty and equality that Jefferson had asserted as being self-evident. The end of the Revolution sent tens of thousands into exile around the globe, and fighting continued in borderlands, destroying long-standing sources of group identity including the Six Nations and the British Empire. Debt and its vulnerabilities ensnared everyone from western farmers to urban merchants to the governments of France, Spain, and the new United States. Disease sapped native communities across the interior of North America and down the West Coast with significant implications for U.S. efforts to secure borders and expand trade.

The United States Constitution was born in a mood of caution among political leaders who worried that the Revolution had gone too far. It also reflected a pragmatic concern for the way government could work rather than the idealistic views of the early years. As one of the *Federalist Papers* essays remarked, "If men were angels, no government would be necessary." By turning independent cooperating states into a single nation, the Constitution attempted to affirm a unity not yet cemented and to assert stronger centralized control over American citizens not yet ready to relinquish their individual rights. A hastily amended Bill of Rights addressed some of these persistent concerns. But the more radical potential of revolutionary ideals would be reignited in the decades to come, sparking first with revolution in the United States' ally, France.

‹Thinking Back, *Looking Forward*›

As you review this chapter, think about the lasting consequences of the American Revolution. What expectations for liberty and self-government did the Revolution raise, and how were they met and unmet? In the next chapters, look for new hierarchies of race and gender that solidified in the absence of nobility and royalty. Which new rights proved permanent? Which would be denied, and to whom? Observe, too, the continuing conflict between centralized government and dispersed power.

To make your study concrete, review the timeline and reflect on the entries there. Think about their causes, consequences, and connections. How do they connect events in North America to global trends?

Additional Resources

Books

Cornell, Saul. *The Other Founders: Anti-Federalism and the Dissenting Tradition in America, 1788–1828.* **Chapel Hill: University of North Carolina Press, 1999.** ▶ Study of the diverse thought and influence of Antifederalism.

Duval, Kathleen. *Independence Lost: Lives on the Edge of the American Revolution.* **New York: Random House, 2015.** ▶ Global story of individuals on revolutionary borders and their postwar lives.

Holton, Woody. *Unruly Americans and the Origins of the Constitution.* **New York: Hill and Wang, 2007.** ▶ Explanation of the role of popular protest in shaping the U.S. Constitution through ratification.

Igler, David. *The Great Ocean: Pacific Worlds from Captain Cook to the Gold Rush.* **New York: Oxford University Press, 2013.** ▶ Intercultural history of the maritime Pacific.

Irvin, Benjamin. *Clothed in Robes of Sovereignty: The Constitutional Convention and the People Out of Doors.* **New York: Oxford University Press, 2014.** ▶ Social and cultural history of the Continental Congress and its public reception.

Jasanoff, Maya. *Liberty's Exiles: American Loyalists in the Revolutionary World.* **New York: Alfred A. Knopf, 2001.** ▶ The lives and migrations of Loyalists after the end of the Revolution.

Klepp, Susan. *Revolutionary Conceptions: Women, Fertility, and Family Limitation in America, 1760–1820.* **Chapel Hill: University of North Carolina Press, 2009.** ▶ Innovative examination of the Revolution's impact on families.

Nash, Gary. *Forging Freedom: Philadelphia's Black Community, 1720–1840.* **Cambridge: Harvard University Press, 1991.** ▶ Detailed look at the lives of African Americans before and after the Revolution in Philadelphia.

Rakove, Jack N. *Original Meanings: Politics and Ideas in the Making of the Constitution.* **New York: Vintage, 1997.** ▶ Political and intellectual history of the Constitutional Convention.

Wood, Gordon. *The Creation of the American Republic, 1776–1787.* **Chapel Hill: University of North Carolina Press, 1998.** ▶ Classic study of politics and state constitutions in the Revolutionary era.

Go to the MindTap® for **Global Americans** to access the full version of select books from this Additional Resources section.

Websites

The American Revolution, 1763–1783. http://www.gilderlehrman.org/history-by-era/american-revolution-1763–1783 ▶ Gilder Lehrman Institute of American History site with timelines, sources, and essays.

Charters of Freedom http://www.archives.gov/exhibits/charters/constitution.html ▶ National Archives site on the context and meaning of the U.S. Constitution.

Documenting the American South. http://docsouth.unc.edu/support/about/ ▶ University of North Carolina at Chapel Hill site with primary documents regarding the Revolutionary South.

Free Black Communities at the Library Company. http://www.librarycompany.org/blackfounders/#.Vden6879MiQ ▶ Exhibition including documents of free black communities after the Revolution.

Nova Scotia Museums. http://museum.novascotia.ca/our-museums ▶ Research and resources on the Loyalist diaspora, as well as other Canadian topics.

Continue exploring online through MindTap®, **where you can:**
- **Assess your knowledge with the Chapter Test**
- **Watch historical videos related to the chapter**
- **Further your understanding with interactive maps and timelines**

American Experiments

1772

June

English Justice Mansfield decides case in favor of James Somerset, a Virginia slave, challenging the legality of slavery in England.

1776

July

Continental Congress adopts Declaration of Independence, marking formal break with Britain.

September

Pennsylvania State Constitution establishes government with single legislature, broad voting rights, no governor.

1777

July

Independent Vermont's constitution outlaws slavery.

November

Continental Congress adopts Articles of Confederation as governing structure for the United States in rebellion against Britain.

1778

January

James Cook reaches Hawai'an island of Kauai on voyage seeking Northwest Passage.

1780–1781

March 1780

Massachusetts State Constitution's first article asserts all men born free and equal.

November 1780

Anticolonial Indian revolt led by Tupac Amaru in Peru opposes Spanish taxes and imperial policy.

August 1781

Elizabeth Freeman secures freedom in Massachusetts court.

1782–1783

Twelve thousand Loyalists arrive in Spanish East Florida.

September 1783

Britain and United States sign Treaty of Paris ending Revolutionary War and redrawing national boundaries.

Fall 1783

South Carolina reopens the import of enslaved Africans and then closes it again in 1787.

Western Alliance of Native Americans meet in Sandusky to coordinate opposition to Treaty of Paris border.

November 1783

Twenty-nine thousand Loyalists evacuate New York for Nova Scotia.

1784

March

Spain bars U.S. trade on the Mississippi River, blocking access to New Orleans.

August

Empress of China, the first U.S. trading ship in Asia, reaches Canton.

October

Six Nations sign Treaty of Fort Stanwix with United States, relinquishing claim to Ohio territory.

1785–1786

May 1785

Land Ordinance divides Northwest Territory into townships.

November 1785

Joseph Brant travels to London to request British aid for Western Indian alliance.

January 1786

Virginia Legislature passes Act for Establishing Religious Freedom.

1787–1788

January 1787

Daniel Shays and supporters attack Springfield armory to seize weapons for the cause of western farmers but are defeated.

May 1787

British abolitionists establish West African settlement of Sierra Leone.

Delegates at Continental Congress begin debate on new national government.

July 1787

Northwest Ordinance establishes political blueprint for land north of Ohio River.

September 1787 –May 1790

States debate and gradually ratify the U.S. Constitution.

October 1787 –May 1788

New York newspapers publish the *Federalist Papers* arguing in favor of ratification.

1789–1791

January 1789

Ratified U.S. Constitution takes effect.

December 1791

Bill of Rights ratified.

Go to MindTap® to engage with an interactive version of the timeline. Analyze events and themes with clickable content, view related videos, and respond to critical thinking questions.

8

Inventing Republics in the Age of Revolutions

1789–1819

From Philadelphia to Saint-Domingue, Leonora Sansay saw the spread of the revolutionary ideals of freedom and natural rights, and the violence that accompanied change.

The Library Company of Philadelphia

Incendie du Cap [Burning of Cap Francais] depicts whites fleeing the 1793 slave rebellion in Saint-Domingue. ▲

Leonora Hassell, stepdaughter of a Philadelphia tavern keeper, spent her adolescence observing American politicians. Her family's tavern, the Sign of the Half-Moon, was located across the street from the Philadelphia statehouse, where the Continental and Confederation Congresses met. In the statehouse, at the taverns, and on the pages of newspapers, men like Leonora's friend New York senator Aaron Burr struggled—often violently—over how to interpret and implement the results of the American Revolution. In 1800, after months of intrigue and character assassination, Burr became the nation's third vice president in an election that inaugurated a new political party. That same year, Leonora married Louis Sansay, a French refugee from the revolution on the Caribbean island of Saint-Domingue. Soon after their marriage, when France moved to take the island back from black revolutionaries, Louis and Leonora Sansay sailed there too, optimistic, she said in a letter, that "order would be established" and they could reclaim the lucrative plantation.

Instead, Leonora Sansay witnessed the violent birth of another new nation. Revolutionaries defeated French troops, burned the capital city of Cap Français, and in 1804, issued their own Declaration of Independence. They called the new nation Haiti, the name the island's native Taino inhabitants had given it before Europeans arrived. Sansay fled to Spanish Cuba but within a year ran again, this time from her abusive husband. She returned to Philadelphia and reconnected with Burr, who embroiled her in a plot that he and James Wilkinson had devised to colonize the Louisiana territory, which had been recently sold to the United States.

Leonora Sansay's life read like a novel and she knew it. To support herself as a woman alone in Philadelphia, she published fictionalized versions of the racial warfare and domestic violence she had witnessed in Haiti. Although novels about young women in trouble were very popular, her books, *Laura* and the *Secret History*, did not sell well. So she started over again and with the help of personal and bank loans, opened her own business making artificial flowers. A woman raised on revolution became an urban entrepreneur.

Leonora Sansay grew into adulthood in the Age of Revolution. She witnessed the spread of revolutionary ideals about freedom and natural rights that sparked uprisings in North America, France, the Caribbean, and South America as people claimed the right to govern themselves. Sansay also witnessed the violence that accompanied revolutionary change. Public protests turned to public executions on Paris streets, and the new French republic launched two decades of warfare in Europe to topple monarchies and expand French power. Millions died as French armies and the opposing forces of Britain, Austria, Prussia, and Russia sacked towns and crushed uprisings across the continent. Bound to European empires through trade

How do the events of Leonora Sansay's life reflect the uncertainties and violence of emerging nations in the Age of Revolution?
Go to MindTap® to watch a video on Sansay and learn how her story relates to the themes of this chapter.

and political alliances, the United States and Native American confederacies were drawn into global conflict; soon their towns burned and their people perished, as well. In Saint-Domingue, slaves destroyed plantations and killed the owners who had forced them to labor in the sugar fields, sending the island into thirteen years of warfare. In 1810, war spread across Latin America as colonists fought to end Spanish rule and slavery. Haiti and several Latin American republics achieved independence. Elsewhere, empires reasserted their sovereignty over colonies and territories.

The birth of revolutionary republics raised philosophical and practical questions for the United States. Should it support fellow revolutionaries or try to remain neutral in a world of constant commercial rivalry and imperial warfare? Should it follow the most radical examples, committing to citizens' rights and the end of slavery, or temper idealism with stability? Factionalism rent the political fabric of the republic as people struggled over the best direction for a country professing "Life, Liberty, and the pursuit of Happiness."

With such uncertainty, many feared, and some hoped, that the United States would collapse back into the British Empire. Instead, the United States asserted itself as a sovereign nation and extended itself as an empire. As early as 1780, Thomas Jefferson had proposed that the United States become an "empire of liberty." This new kind of empire, supported through agricultural exports, would be one that linked self-governing republics together to resist the corrupt powers of Europe. Yet implementing the vision required political and cultural choices that limited universal liberty. Commercial agriculture required land and laborers to work it, which meant driving Native Americans off their territory and expanding the institution of slavery from the coast into the interior of the continent.

8-1
The Fragile Republic

These two portraits of George Washington were both painted during his presidency. The one on the left is *General George Washington at Trenton* (1792) by John Trumbull. The one on the right is *George Washington* (1796) by Gilbert Stuart. The Charleston City Council commissioned the Trumbull painting but rejected it, preferring "a more matter-of-fact likeness." The Stuart portrait was commissioned as a gift to the Marquis of Landsdowne, British supporter of U.S. independence.

What props does each artist use to evoke the authority of Washington? How do the two portraits tell different stories about why Washington is the first president? What does each suggest about the people he leads? ▶

Trumbull, John (1756–1843)/Bridgeman Art

Painting/Alamy Stock Photo

The U.S. Constitution of 1789 created a structure for a republic with a strengthened centralized government. The future of that republic, however, seemed shaky in the next decades. The American population was culturally divided and regionally dispersed. The empires of Britain and France had deep and influential ties to the U.S. economy and government that persisted after independence. France, Spain, and Britain all formed alliances with Native Americans, who controlled the majority of North America and were pushing back against the U.S. government and individual American squatters and speculators. George Washington, the first president, was a war hero and a nationally revered figure, which helped him establish a legitimate tone of authority, and he set precedents for asserting presidential power. But powerful executives could, many feared, erode the power of the people.

☞ As you read, think about the forces pulling at the republic created by the U.S. Constitution. What held people together—culture? laws? force?

8-1a First Presidency

George Washington took office in New York City, temporary capital of the United States, in April 1789, having been elected unanimously by the first Electoral College. As the first president, he walked a fine line between demonstrating sufficient authority and appearing too kingly. For his inaugural suit, he sent General Henry Knox, future secretary of war, to acquire American-made cloth in the color "Congress Brown" and silver buttons stamped with eagles. He used the title "Mr. President" rather than some of the more impressive ones proposed, including the florid "His Highness, the President of the United States, and Protector of Their Liberties," favored by John Adams.

{ A new executive projects national power.

With Washington secured as president, Congress bolstered the executive by creating departments of War, State, and the Treasury, as well as Attorney General and Postmaster General. The heads of those departments appointed by the president became a **cabinet** system of advisors. Washington's two most influential advisors were Secretary of State Thomas Jefferson and Secretary of the Treasury Alexander Hamilton, men with often dramatically different ideas about the expression of federal power. Hamilton, citing the clause in the Constitution that gave Congress power "to make all laws which shall be necessary and proper" to carry out its duties, argued that the national government should be proactive. His position, later described as **loose construction** of the Constitution, was that Congress had the power to develop new offices, programs, and laws that would strengthen the economy. In his 1790 *Report on Public Credit*, Hamilton promoted the creation of a national bank, a joint venture between private investors and the federal government, that could make loans, manage government funds, and issue reliable money. Jefferson opposed the bank, insisting that only a **strict construction** of the Constitution—one that gave the government only the powers specifically mentioned in the document—could protect the people's rights to govern themselves. In the end, the Congress supported Hamilton's vision, chartering the **Bank of the United States** in 1791.

Hamilton also pushed for the United States to transform itself from a nation of farmers into a manufacturing power. As he expressed in his *Report on the Subject of Manufactures* (1791), he believed that the United States needed to nurture the "spirit of enterprise" in its citizens. First, the U.S. government had to tackle the problem of its war debts, both the money still owed to foreigners and the money that the national government and the states owed to citizens who had bought war bonds, loaned animals and tools, fed and clothed the army, and fought in the Revolutionary War. Hamilton recommended that the U.S. government pay all of these debts with money from taxes and land sales. He proposed, and Congress passed, a tariff on what he called "foreign luxuries" and an **excise tax** on distilled spirits made within the country, which damaged "the health and the morals" of the American people. The tariff, which for the next half century would provide the most reliable federal income, was relatively easy to collect at port customs houses and encouraged American manufactures by making foreign goods more expensive.

The excise tax, collected by federal revenue officers in the U.S. hinterlands, sparked a national political and military crisis that dramatized the consequences of a powerful executive. Farmers in western Pennsylvania, Kentucky, Maryland, and the Carolinas, unable to sell their grain via the Spanish-controlled Mississippi River, frequently distilled their corn and wheat into whiskey, which was cheaper and easier to transport to urban customers. Because the excise threatened their livelihoods, they resisted with violence, tarring and feathering excise officers who attempted to collect and arming themselves in preparation for a larger revolt. These protests, called the **Whiskey Rebellion**, were most violent in Pennsylvania. In September 1794, Hamilton and Washington personally led thirteen thousand federalized militia troops to put down the rebellion, which collapsed quickly. Seated on his horse, Washington was both an official elected by the voice of the people and a commander-in-chief ready to aggressively enforce federal law.

cabinet Group of presidential advisors made up of the heads of executive departments plus the vice president.

loose construction Method of interpreting the U.S. Constitution that grants the federal government powers not specifically forbidden including passing laws to accomplish its aims.

strict construction Method of interpreting the U.S. Constitution that permits the federal government only those powers specifically mentioned and reserves other powers for the states.

Bank of the United States National bank supported by private investors and federal government that held U.S. Treasury funds and controlled the money supply. It was allowed to expire in 1811.

excise tax Tax on the manufacture or sale of specific goods, such as alcohol, produced domestically that was added to the cost of the product.

Whiskey Rebellion Armed protests by backcountry farmers and distillers who opposed the excise tax on whiskey and were defeated by nationalized militia forces.

8-1b Conflicts on the Continent

Neither the Treaty of Paris's boundary lines or the Northwest Ordinance's blueprint for future states resolved the question of who owned and controlled the Ohio and Tennessee River valleys, and the borderlands remained a tinderbox of conflict. Initially, the U.S. Congress thought to control relations between whites and Indians with the 1790 Indian Trade and Intercourse Act, which stated that only licensed traders could work in Indian country and all land treaties and sales had to be approved by Congress. But states, squatters, and speculators regularly ignored this law. At the same time, British soldiers, stationed stubbornly at seven forts in U.S. territory, encouraged Indian warfare, hoping that an Indian state in the Northwest would act as a barrier between the United States and British Canada.

{ Indian confederacies and European empires contest U.S. sovereignty on unstable borders.

Treaty of Greenville
Agreement signed between
the United States and allied
Indians after the Battle of Fallen
Timbers, granting much of the
Ohio Territory to the United
States.

annuities Goods or money
provided annually to Indian
leaders by the government as
dictated by treaties conferring
Indian land to the United States.

Southwest Ordinance U.S.
law outlining process for
territory south of the Ohio River
to become states of the United
States. Unlike the Northwest
Ordinance, it permitted slavery.

Most of the land included in the Northwest Ordinance was under the control of a confederacy of northwestern Indian tribes led by Miamis and Shawnees. Miami chief Little Turtle and Shawnee Blue Jacket successfully led the confederacy in battle against U.S. troops in 1790 and 1791, delivering crushing defeats with the loss of hundreds of soldiers and the near destruction of the U.S. army. The confederacy maintained a strong alliance for two years, but constant warfare requiring the coordination of numerous Indian groups proved difficult. In 1794, General Anthony Wayne led four thousand army and militia troops to defeat the unraveling confederacy at the Battle of Fallen Timbers. Retreating Indians hoped for assistance from nearby Fort Miami, still occupied by British soldiers, but the gates closed against them while Wayne's troops burned their cornfields and scalped defeated warriors. In 1795, Wayne negotiated the **Treaty of Greenville**, which both sides hoped would end the violence. The treaty handed much of Ohio and the lower Northwest Territory—lands of the Shawnees, Delawares, and Wyandots—to the United States and established **annuities** by which the federal government made annual payments to favored Indian chiefs to distribute among followers.

Abandoning their Indian allies, the British tried to undermine the United States by luring citizens back as British subjects. In the Canada Constitutional Act of 1791, Britain divided its North American colony in two: Lower Canada, a French-speaking region in the East around Quebec, and Upper Canada, along the St. Lawrence River and Great Lakes, which was already populated by English-speaking Loyalists who had left the United States. A new lieutenant governor, John Graves Simcoe, offered families two hundred acres of farmland in exchange for a loyalty oath to the king of England and a small fee. Canada's Constitution further promised that subjects could not be taxed to raise revenue for the empire. Although Simcoe insisted that political loyalty to the British Empire motivated thousands of migrants and called them the "Late Loyalists," most of the migrants themselves were less political and more practical. As one said: "We fought seven years to get rid of taxation, and now we are taxed more than ever!"

Learning from its mistakes with the thirteen rebellious colonies, Great Britain designed the Canadian Constitution to limit the people's power and quash any rumblings of independence. To meet American migrants' expectations for self-government, the Constitution established an elected assembly. But the number of representatives, who shared power with a group of elites appointed for life, was kept low. A powerful lieutenant governor, appointed from London, decided when to summon or suspend the assembly. The same people regularly served in legislative, executive, or judicial positions simultaneously, so power was concentrated in a few hands.

Fights over land and trade also continued in the Southeast as one faction of Creeks and Cherokees battled U.S. settlers pressing into Kentucky, Tennessee, and Georgia. Congress passed the **Southwest Ordinance** in 1790, attempting to organize the Southwestern Territory as it had done with the land north of the Ohio River. Anticipating the spread of plantation agriculture, the Southwest Ordinance permitted slavery. As in the northern territory, however, laws could not contain struggles over power. One Cherokee headman told South Carolinians that his people were forced to move because "the Creeks and the white people . . . both love fighting." Creek Indian raids took white and black captives as prisoners who could then be ransomed back to families, sold to slave traders, or exchanged with Spanish officials for cash or livestock.

Spain, claiming jurisdiction over the continent west of the Mississippi River, hoped to lure disaffected U.S. farmers into its empire. In 1788, the Richards family of Kentucky floated down the Mississippi River to Natchez with

U.S. Diplomacy with Native Americans, 1795 The United States gave this peace medal to Wyandot chief Tarhee at the signing of the Treaty of Greenville. The United States followed European imperial protocols in distributing medals to Indian chiefs as part of treaty negotiations. At the council, General Wayne told Indians that the medals were from "your father, the Fifteen Great Fires of America," referring to the fifteen states. The treaty recognized Indian rights to all land that had not been formally ceded, a significant change from the postrevolutionary policy of conquest and forced treaties. ▲ Treaty of Greeneville Peace Medal, 1795, American School, (18th century)/© Philadelphia History Museum at the Atwater Kent,/Courtesy of Historical Society of Pennsylvania Collection,/The Bridgeman Art Library their only possession—an ax. The Spanish colonial governor granted them—and thousands more—land for family farms in exchange for their pledged loyalty to the Spanish king and commitment to send their Protestant children to imported Irish Catholic priests for religious conversion. As individual families Americanized the border, Spain tried to use taxes on river trade and riverside forts to restrict the expansion of the U.S. nation by impeding its access to the Mississippi River. Spain also expanded its military presence in Louisiana and Florida by establishing forts on disputed territory and, in 1793, signing the Treaty of Nogales, which promised mutual assistance between the Spanish and the confederation of Cherokees, Chickasaws, Choctaws, and Creeks against U.S. expansion in the region.

Worried about the shifting loyalties on its western borders, the U.S. Congress swiftly admitted Kentucky and Tennessee as new states in 1792 and 1796. Turning disputed Indian land into national territories and national territories into states became a key strategy for the United States as it expanded its power west, adding Ohio in 1803.

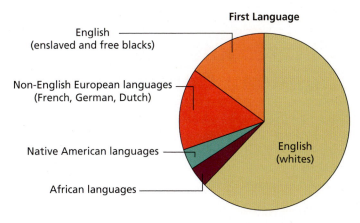

First Language

English (enslaved and free blacks)

Non-English European languages (French, German, Dutch)

Native American languages

African languages

English (whites)

Figure 8.1 Language Diversity in the United States in 1790 The first U.S. census revealed that nearly one of four people living within the boundaries of the United States did not speak English as a first language but spoke German, French, and West African and Native American languages. English speakers had different degrees of proficiency and often used regional pronunciations and local terms. ▲ Source: Adapted from Jill Lepore, *A is for American.*

8-1c American Populations

A year after Washington took office, the United States undertook its first census to count the residents of the United States and its organized territories. Census takers walked through communities, recording the name of the head of household, the number of free white males over and under the age of sixteen, the number of free white females, "all other free persons" (meaning people of color and Indians living in U.S. settlements), and slaves. By their count, the U.S. population was 3.9 million and growing. With birthrates higher than Native American or European settlements, the expanding U.S. population put pressure on its borders. But internal pressures divided that populace by culture, race, and language.

{ Art and language highlight tensions within a growing population.

Jokes, essays, and plays underscored the fact that Americans regarded those living on the other side of the country as foreigners. The first play written and professionally performed in the United States, Royall Tyler's *The Contrast* (1787), featured an honest country bumpkin character, Jonathan, who lived up to all of the stereotypes of New England "Yankees" as unsophisticated and stubborn.

Noah Webster, Massachusetts teacher and lawyer, concluded that "A National language is a national tie, and what country wants it more than America?" Webster, like his mentor Benjamin Franklin, thought that a distinctive, official "American" language would unify the new country (see Figure 8.1). He started with spelling and pronunciation. In *The American Spelling Book* (1788), the most popular textbook for decades, Webster explained rules for reading and writing everyday words and simplified several common usages: *honour* became *honor*, and *musick* became *music*. Some of his later proposals to further simplify the language sparked racist satire. One newspaper

mocked Webster's efforts to unify the public through language by printing fake fan mail from Irish, German, and black readers. A supposed black correspondent urged Webster as a "fello Cytzen" to add words like "hommany" and "banjoe" to the lexicon, but the satire made it clear that Native American cuisine and West African musical instruments were as unwelcome to the national culture as their words were to the national language.

Another immigrant, starring in the first U.S. bestseller, amplified the vulnerabilities of people set adrift in a mobile, polyglot country. Charlotte Temple, an English schoolgirl impregnated by a British soldier who brought her to America and abandoned her, was the heroine of *Charlotte: A Tale of Truth* (1791), written by English-born, Massachusetts-raised Susanna Haswell Rowson. Novels, a new form of literature in the eighteenth century, focused on stories of regular people rather than historical heroes or Biblical characters. People could rent copies of these books in the circulating libraries that sprung up in cities and towns.

Readers loved **seduction novels** like *Charlotte Temple* and Leonora Sansay's *Secret History* for their exciting plots and complicated moral messages. Young women, who were both the main characters and a large proportion of the audience, were free to choose their own husbands and newly independent in attaining education away from home and familiar neighborhoods. Yet with freedom came danger. In these novels, female heroines were vulnerable to tricks and betrayals from the very people who should have been reliable authorities: teachers, parents, and fiancés. The narrative of virtue under attack resonated personally and politically with Americans cast in unfamiliar surroundings. With corruption at home and betrayal abroad, many felt that the security of the young republic was at risk.

seduction novels Popular fictional stories centered around the seduction of innocent young women by male scoundrels.

Atlantic Revolutions and American Consequences

William Blake, the English poet and engraver, created this erotic image, *Europe Supported by Africa and America* (1796), to illustrate a book by J. G. Stedman, a Dutch officer sent to put down a slave rebellion in South American Suriname. The armbands on the women representing Africa and America recall the shackles of slavery. The rope, held by the white woman, binds all together.

What does the illustration suggest about the relationship among the continents in an age of emancipation? Is it to be egalitarian or hierarchical? Why are the continents represented by nude female figures? ▶

Stedman, John Gabriel/The Bridgeman Art Library

The American Revolution was part of an age of revolutions that overturned rulers and upset traditional hierarchies, military alliances, and borders. Sailors, slaves, writers, and merchants traversed the oceans, bringing with them ideas about freedom and equality, but their experiences demonstrated the social upheaval unleashed. Revolutions in France and Haiti shared dedication to liberty and natural rights and shunned the idea of privileges based on birthright. They also involved widespread participation of poor, formerly ignored people who fought for their own reasons that did not always coincide with those of the elites. Almost immediately, these revolutions became part of renewed warfare among European powers, leaving the United States clinging to neutrality abroad and politically divided at home. As war raged around the new country, political parties came to shape government decision making.

☞ As you read, think about how the American experience of revolution influenced responses to revolutions around the Atlantic. How did people understand the United States's position in global events? Did subsequent revolutions change how they thought about the American Revolution?

8-2a Revolution in France

France, like Britain and Spain, was economically devastated by the continuous warfare of the eighteenth century. Turning to a combination of new taxes and borrowing to pay its debts, the kingdom soon found itself in political and economic crisis. When the French government proposed a stamp act in 1787, protesters revived arguments from anti-Stamp Act pamphlets published 20 years earlier in North

> French revolutionaries express the radical potential of rights.

French Revolution Political and social revolution in France overturning the monarchy and establishing a republic.

Declaration of the Rights of Man and Citizen Document written by the French National Assembly asserting natural rights, freedom of religion and the press, and the idea of government as contract.

America. That same year and the next, failed harvests and harsh winters pushed peasants to riot over bread prices. To deal with the crisis in 1789, King Louis XVI convened the Estates General, a representative body that had not met for 175 years. By tradition, this assembly was divided into orders, or "estates," the first being the nobility and the second the clergy, both exempt from most taxes. The third estate—everyone else—not only paid almost all the taxes but also expected to be outvoted by the nobility and clergy because each estate had one vote. Members of the third estate wanted voting in this assembly to be by numbers of delegates. On July 14, the people of Paris seized the Bastille, an old royal prison, in a protest. Claiming a new order of "Liberty, Equality, Fraternity," they established a Constituent Assembly, overturned the traditional tax system, and voted for a constitutional monarchy. The following year, the Marquis de Lafayette, who initially supported the emerging revolution, handed the key to the Bastille to Thomas Paine, the radical writer who had rallied American patriots to the cause of independence with his *Common Sense*. Lafayette told him to deliver it to George Washington because "the principles of America opened the Bastille."

The **French Revolution** seemed at first to affirm the American Revolution. The Constituent Assembly's **Declaration of the Rights of Man and Citizen** of August 1789 drew on Enlightenment thought and rhetoric from the American Revolution (see Table 8.1) Expressing his admiration of the revolutionaries' goals, Paine in 1791 published the *Rights of Man*, in which he argued that human rights are inborn and governments merely human creations that can be revised and changed if they do not serve the people. French revolutionaries created a new constitution and a new elected assembly through

Table 8.1 Comparison of Revolutionary Declarations

The French *Declaration of the Rights of Man* shared ideas about human equality and inalienable rights with the 1776 U.S. Declaration of Independence. The French declaration of 1789 also proclaimed specific rights soon to be enshrined in the U.S. Bill of Rights (1791), demonstrating the transatlantic intellectual currents of the Age of Revolution.

Issue	United States (1776)	France (1789)
Motivation	"A Prince, whose Character is thus marked by every act which may define a Tyrant, is unfit to be the Ruler of a free People."	"The ignorance, neglect, or contempt of the rights of man are the sole cause of public calamities and of the corruption of governments."
Source of rights	"All men are created equal"	"Men are born and remain free and equal in rights. Social distinctions may be founded only upon the general good."
Unalienable rights	"Life, Liberty, and the Pursuit of Happiness"	"Liberty, property, security, and resistance to oppression"
Relationship of government to people	"Governments are instituted among Men, deriving their just Powers from the Consent of the Governed."	"Law is the expression of the general will. Every citizen has a right to participate personally, or through his representative."
Citizens' responsibilities	Not specified	• Submission to legal arrest • Determination and payment of taxes • No infringement on others' natural rights
Rights affirmed in law	Not specified	• Fair legal process of accusation, arrest, and imprisonment • All innocent until proven guilty • Freedom of thought, expression, religion • Property ownership

which the common people could exert power. In the new constitutional monarchy, the king—like any citizen—was subject to the rule of law. Seeing their ideals confirmed by the French revolutionaries, many in the United States celebrated with French fashions and toasts to the friendship of the United States and France. The town of Hopewell, Kentucky, renamed itself Paris. In 1793, one young Virginian vowed to cross the Atlantic to join the army of the republic and "*serve* the noblest cause in the world."

Some French revolutionaries pushed at the radical edge of universal rights. In 1791, French intellectual and playwright Olympe de Gouges published the **Declaration of the Rights of Woman and the Female Citizen**, rewriting all seventeen articles of the 1789 Declaration to explicitly include women as well as men. She insisted: "Woman, wake up . . . the tocsin of reason is being heard throughout the whole universe. . . . What advantage have you received from the Revolution?"

That was a question American women asked themselves as well. In 1790, Massachusetts author Judith Sargent Murray published an essay entitled "On the Equality of the Sexes" challenging prevailing ideas that women were unequal in society because of their fundamental inferiority. Murray, like de Gouges and English author Mary Wollstonecraft, argued that men and women were born equal, but a limited education debased women. "Is it reasonable," Murray asked, that women "be allowed no other ideas, than those which are suggested by the mechanism of a pudding, or the sewing of the seams of a garment?" Murray and Wollstonecraft believed the solution to the problem lay in educating girls in writing, mathematics, sciences, and languages, not merely cooking and sewing. Only then could women realize their true potential. Their

transatlantic influence encouraged the growth of private academies for girls who could afford them and educational books for those who could not. De Gouges's more radical proposals, including a new kind of secular egalitarian marriage and easy divorce, were not widely championed. In 1793, she was executed as the French Revolution devolved into mass executions of political rivals.

8-2b Revolution in the West Indies

People in the French Caribbean colony of Saint-Domingue largely welcomed news of the revolution in Paris, although for divergent reasons. A French colony of about six hundred thousand people located on the western third of the island of Hispaniola, Saint-Domingue generated enormous wealth for the French, producing 40 percent of the sugar and 50 percent of the coffee grown worldwide. Early on, elite white planters in the colonial assembly hoped that the Revolution would yield economic gains by transforming Saint-Domingue from a colony into a province. They wanted to be released from mercantilist restrictions and bound only by laws passed by locally elected leaders and subsequently sanctioned by the king. For the large numbers of free people of color, in contrast, the Revolution promised rights and protections that would make them equal to their free white neighbors.

{ Haitian Revolution overturns slavery.

Declaration of the Rights of Woman and the Female Citizen Document penned by de Gouges asserting the rights of women as being equal to those of men and claiming the Revolution for women.

Haitian Revolution Slave revolt on the French colony of Saint-Domingue that grew into a political independence movement, abolishing slavery and establishing a new nation.

Ultimately, it was the enslaved majority, who outnumbered the free population by ten to one and who seized on the notion of equality, that pushed revolution to its radical extreme. In August 1791, thousands of enslaved people marched across the island in a coordinated insurrection, killing a thousand whites, burning hundreds of sugar and coffee plantations, and plunging the island into civil war (see Table 8.2). Clearly inspired by the revolution in France, the enslaved rebels also drew on West African symbols and ideas. One rebel, when captured and killed, was carrying revolutionary pamphlets printed in Paris as well as an African amulet made of hair, herbs, and bone.

In demanding an end to slavery, the **Haitian Revolution** from 1791 to 1804 appealed to a growing international movement that proclaimed universalist messages of liberty and equality. The movement initially targeted the inhumanity of the slave trade, graphically depicted in Thomas Clarkson's 1788 engraving of the cruel crowding below decks on a slave ship. In 1789, English antislavery activists published *The Interesting Narrative of the Life of Olaudah Equiano*, which served as a template for explaining the injustice of slavery in a world speaking of liberty and equality. In 1794, France abolished slavery in the entire French Empire and declared that all were citizens with rights.

White and mixed-race slaveholders fled Saint-Domingue, taking their slaves with them to cities around the Atlantic. Between 1791 and 1805, tens of thousands of refugees arrived in

Table 8.2 The Course of the French and Haitian Revolutions

The French and Haitian Revolutions spanned more than a decade of intertwining legal, political, and military developments. Both ended with self-proclaimed emperors taking command of the nations that had emerged from the global conflict.

1789	French Estates General convenes in Versailles
	National Assembly organizes
	Paris crowd storms the Bastille
	National Assembly issues *Declaration of the Rights of Man*
1791	Assembly creates French constitutional monarchy
1791	Free people of color in French colonies are granted citizenship
	Slave insurrection begins in Saint-Domingue
	Thousands of slave owners flee to the United States
1792	French National Convention abolishes monarchy and declares France a republic
1793	French King Louis XVI is executed
	Toussaint L'Overture, leader of former slave army, allies with Spain to prevent France from reinstituting slavery in Saint-Domingue
1794	France abolishes slavery in entire empire
	L'Ouverture sides with French forces
	Napoleon stages coup, establishes Consulate
1796	L'Ouverture is declared governor of Saint-Domingue
1801	L'Ouverture proclaims new constitution, is declared governor for life
1802	Napoleon sends troops to re-establish French power in Saint-Domingue and re-instate slavery.
1803	Napoleon's troops in Saint-Domingue are defeated
	United States buys Louisiana territory from France
	L'Ouverture is imprisoned in France
1804	Declaration of independence is issued in Haiti
	Napoleon crowns himself emperor of France
	Jean-Jacques Dessalines proclaims himself emperor of Haiti
1806	United States passes Haitian Embargo Act

Inhumanity of the Slave Trade First published in 1788 by the Plymouth Chapter of the Society for Effecting the Abolition of the Slave Trade, Thomas Clarkson's engraving *The Brookes Ship* became a widespread image of the dehumanizing Middle Passage. Reproduced on pamphlets, tokens, and other emblems of the international antislavery movement, it quickly circulated among activists. ▶

The Art Archive

Global Americans According to his autobiography, **Olaudah Equiano** was born an Ibo in the kingdom of Benin in the middle of the eighteenth century. Kidnapped as a child and sold into the international slave trade, Equiano was shipped first to Barbados, then to Virginia, and then around the Atlantic Ocean working on merchant ships, sold and resold several times. In 1766, his Philadelphia owner allowed him to purchase his freedom, and he made his home in England. He continued to travel on trading voyages and in 1773 accompanied a polar expedition that was looking for a water passage from Europe to Asia.

In 1789, Equiano published his autobiography with the backing of British abolitionists; it had multiple editions in his lifetime and was translated into Dutch, German, and Russian. Alone and with a group called the Sons of Africa that he founded, Equiano traveled around Britain and Ireland speaking against slavery and the slave trade. He married Englishwoman Susan Cullen in 1792, and they had two daughters. He died in 1797, ten years before Britain abolished the Atlantic slave trade. Some recent scholarship suggests that Equiano was in fact born in South Carolina before beginning his journeys around the Atlantic. His autobiography, which so vividly captured the dislocation and misery of the Middle Passage, may actually be a combination of personal testimony and the collective experience of American slavery as an Atlantic phenomenon. ▲ Everett Collection Historical/Alamy Stock Photo

North American cities of New York, Philadelphia, Charleston, Savannah, and New Orleans. Initially, states such as Virginia created relief funds to provide for them, but the refugee presence was profoundly destabilizing. Many enslaved people living in the United States were inspired and encouraged. In 1793, enslaved Baptist Preacher Gowan Pamphlet was reportedly found carrying a letter stating that people of "our color" would "be in full possession of the hole country in a few weeks" aided by West Indian slaves. One Virginian claimed to have overheard his slaves discussing "how the blacks *has* kill'd the whites in the French Island." Soon white Virginians and slave owners across the United States were blaming "the example in the West Indies" for discontent in the slave population.

8-2c U.S. Diplomacy in the Age of Revolutions

Americans who had celebrated the early French revolutionaries' declarations of liberty and natural rights had different reactions as the Revolution

> The United States seeks to maintain trade relations and avoid being drawn in to Europe's wars.

entered a far more violent phase. In 1792, revolutionary France declared war on Austria, initiating more than two decades of warfare. By 1793, Britain and France were at war again, with Spain allied with Britain. That same year, revolutionaries executed the French king, queen, and thousands of priests and aristocrats who had been part of the old aristocratic world. Those killings were followed by months of "The Terror" as rival political factions arrested and executed each other in the tens of thousands as "enemies of the revolution."

Confronted with such violence, Americans were divided over whether to support France and Haiti as embodiments of republicanism or back their old imperial parent Britain, which still supplied nearly 90 percent of imports to the United States. Taxes charged on British imports were the main source of income for the new federal government. In addition, the more radical sentiments of revolutionaries pledging racial and gender equality worried political leaders, who had spent a decade experimenting with controls on the revolutionary impulse.

In April 1793, the recently reelected Washington proclaimed neutrality in European wars, which neither France nor Britain accepted. Edmond Genêt, representing the new French republic, arrived on American soil and promptly began using U.S. resources for French purposes, commissioning American privateers to attack and seize the cargo of British merchant ships in the Caribbean and organizing local troops to march against Spanish-controlled New Orleans. In spite of his repeated violations of U.S. sovereignty, Washington did not extradite him when a new French regime recalled him to be executed and instead, Genêt became a U.S. citizen. Britain likewise refused to accept U.S. declarations of neutrality, directing its navy to seize any American merchant ships trading with the French in the Caribbean. Washington sent Supreme Court Chief Justice John Jay to negotiate. The resulting **Jay's Treaty** (1794–1795) avoided war and gained some concessions for the United States, including a promise to remove British forces from western forts and permission to trade in the British East Indies. Opponents in Congress, outraged that the 1778 alliance with France had been violated, demanded to see the details of treaty negotiations. Washington refused, invoking **executive privilege**.

Jay's Treaty Agreement between Britain and the United States designed to ensure peace and maintain commercial ties but unpopular with some Americans.

executive privilege Concept that the president can withhold sensitive information from Congress or the courts if it concerns national security or communications within the executive branch.

Hoping to win the United States as an ally against the British on the North American continent, Spain made new trade concessions. In 1795, Spain signed the **Treaty of San Lorenzo** with the United States, opening the Mississippi River to untaxed U.S. trade and permitting American merchants to store and ship goods from the valuable port of New Orleans. The treaty betrayed Spain's promise of mutual assistance with allied southeastern Indians by establishing a U.S. border at the thirty-first parallel north of Florida, land occupied by Creeks, Choctaws, and Chickasaws. It also removed one more barrier to U.S. expansion to the west. Observing the one thousand-mile Mississippi River that now joined, as much as separated, Spanish and U.S. claims, one Spanish official concluded "You can't put doors on open country."

8-2d First Political Parties

The divide between supporters and opponents of the French Revolution helped give rise to the first U.S. political parties. Factions had long been feared as promoting selfish personal interests at the expense of the public good. But in the early 1790s, those who opposed the anti-French philosophy of Jay's Treaty or Hamilton's economic plan began to express their disagreement in "democratic-republican societies." Modeled on the revolutionary Sons of Liberty, these clubs consisted of middling-rank urban artisans. Asserting that centralized power had reached too far, they supported local and state legislative caucuses. They were branded as "democrats," a term that suggested support for mob rule, by their opponents, who dug in their heels as **Federalists**. By the late 1790s, national political leaders began to draw on these coalitions, and the **first party system** took shape (see Table 8.3).

> Coalitions with competing policies and ideologies harden into two parties.

The issues that divided Federalists and **Democratic-Republicans** were not identical to those that had separated the Federalists and Anti-Federalists of the Constitutional debates. The new Federalists, many of whom were New Englanders and urban commercial people, favored a strong national government run by the rich and well born, closely tied to business and commercial elites and backed by a substantial army. They preferred a passive citizenry that deferred to its leaders. Democratic-Republicans advocated a weaker national government that preserved the revolutionary elements of the Constitution. They optimistically welcomed trade with the world and did not fear rule by the common people, either because they themselves were farmers and lower-rank men or because, as white Southerners, they lived where the common folk could not vote or were already deferential. Many believed that a radical transformation of power and social relationships around the world was still ongoing, with the United States at the forefront.

In 1796, Washington linked domestic partisanship and "foreign entanglements" as two kinds of dangerous alliances that threatened the young republic. In a letter later called his **Farewell Address** announcing that he would not seek or serve a third term as president, Washington reiterated republicanism's stress on sacrifice and unity of interest. "The common and continual mischiefs of the spirit of party" were jealousy and desire for revenge that would enflame people's passions, leading to riot or tyranny. Just like blind adherence to a party, a "passionate attachment of one nation for another" could destroy a republic by dragging it into distant wars or rendering it a "satellite" of powerful nations. Better to take advantage of the geographical distance between the United States and Europe, Washington urged, and practice a policy of **free trade** without mercantilist restrictions, as well as neutral politics toward all other nations. As republican revolutions around the Atlantic expanded into imperial wars, this idea proved difficult to realize, although it remained an enduring ideal of U.S. foreign relations.

Treaty of San Lorenzo Agreement between Spain and the United States granting Americans trading access to the Mississippi. It negated promises of military support to southeastern Indians.

Federalists Political party in power after the American Revolution that favored commercial development and ties with Britain.

first party system Emergence after 1796 of two main political parties identifying themselves as Federalists and Democratic-Republicans.

Democratic-Republicans Political party opposing the Federalists and favoring agriculture supported by recent immigrants and poor whites.

Farewell Address Letter written by Washington to "Friends and Fellow Citizens" at the end of his second term as president, cautioning against partisanship and foreign entanglements.

free trade System of international commerce with few taxes or other restrictions. It was a political ideal contrasted with mercantilism and took various forms.

Table 8.3 Comparison of the First U.S. Political Parties

Anglo-American political culture had long deplored political parties as dangerous "factions." Although a true republic could have only a single common good, competing ideas about how to deploy power abroad and at home led to the first party system in the United States.

Federalists	Democratic-Republicans
Supported protective alliance with Britain	Supported political alliance with France
Distrusted mass politics	Encouraged mass politics
Favored strong central government	Opposed strong central government
Had strongest support from merchants, property owners, city dwellers	Had strongest support from farmers and southern planters
Had Alexander Hamilton, John Adams as national figures	Had Thomas Jefferson, James Madison as national figures

8-3

Membership and Participation in the Republic

In this 1796 cartoon, newspaper editor William Cobbett, who wrote under the name "Peter Porcupine," says "I hate this country and will sow the seeds of discord in it." Columbia, with the liberty cap and the American eagle, weeps over a memorial to the Declaration of Independence to the left. On the right, the Devil and the British Lion offer money to destroy liberty, trampling on the Magna Carta, U.S. flag, and 1778 Treaty of Commerce with France.

How are elements of revolutionary imagery used in this satire of politics in the 1790s? What does the presence of these elements suggest about the emerging identity of the United States? ▶

The Granger Collection, New York

Go to MindTap® to practice history with the Chapter 8 **Primary Source Writing Activity: Political Inclusion.** Read and view primary sources and respond to a writing prompt.

In his Farewell Address, Washington asserted that "with light shades of difference," Americans had "the same religion, manners, habits, and political principles" to unify them. He attempted to minimize the very real divisions that stoked the political crisis over belonging in the new United States. As people in the United States hammered out the details of who should lead and who should follow, who could participate in governance, and whose power should be checked, they crafted new forms of citizenship. In the process of defining individual rights and to whom they would apply, a set of hierarchies rooted in race and gender hardened.

☞ As you read, reflect on the development of U.S. political culture in the decades following the ratification of the Constitution. How did people decide who deserved full participation in the republic?

8-3a Political Culture and Presidential Power

Accustomed to political participation by revolutionary boycotts, spinning bees, and other politics of the streets, non-elites remained deeply involved in public demonstrations. Print culture and debating societies further encouraged voters and nonvoters to participate in political debate. This democracy of information allowed for wide participation, and disgruntled elites sarcastically complained that "Every body is wise enough to be secretary of state."

> Popular political culture yields to partisanship.

Political debate grew more sharply barbed once Washington left office. John Adams, Washington's vice president, was a leading political and intellectual figure of the Revolution and Confederation periods but personally much pricklier than the first president. When elected in 1796, Adams could not command the same loyalty as his predecessor and objections to executive power grew stronger. Jefferson, who received the second highest vote in the Electoral College, became vice president, placing partisan rivals together in the executive branch.

National leaders took a deeply personal view of political action. Like many high-ranking gentlemen, they relied on their own reputations to establish power in their communities, and their ideas about honor shaped the way they conducted business. Elected officials used the aristocratic practice of dueling, called **affairs of honor**, to appeal to the public when they felt a partisan rival had demeaned them. In an affair of honor, one man challenged another to shoot pistols at each other from an agreed-upon distance. Typically, the matter ended in negotiation before shots were fired, but the willingness to risk death to preserve one's reputation was regarded as a sign of leadership fitness. In 1804, Vice President Aaron Burr shot and killed Hamilton in a duel over reputation. For the less refined, fists could serve as well as pistols, and personal grievance coexisted with policy debates at all levels of government. In 1798, Roger Griswold, representative of Connecticut, brawled with Vermont congressman Matthew Lyon on the floor of the House of Representatives over a dispute rooted in name-calling and tobacco spit.

affairs of honor Polite name for dueling that emphasized the importance of reputation defended by face-to-face violence and was most common among southern elites and national politicians.

Global Americans

William Duane was born in colonial New York in 1760. Widowed by colonial-Indian warfare, his mother moved the family back to Ireland, where he grew up to be a printer. He moved to Calcutta, and began *The Indian World*, a paper critical of the powerful East India Company. Deported back to England, he soon ran afoul of the government there for criticizing its crackdown on a free press and freedom of assembly. In 1795, Duane moved to the United States, where he supported himself as an assistant to Benjamin Franklin Bache's Democratic-Republican newspaper in Philadelphia. When Bache died from yellow fever, Duane took over the paper along with Bache's wife, Margaret, whom he married.

A harsh critic of Federalist policies and political repression, Duane was arrested under the Sedition Act and targeted as an alien. Together with a group of exiles from the Society of United Irishmen movement in Ireland, he helped his friend Thomas Jefferson win the presidency in 1800 and in 1802 became a naturalized U.S. citizen. He fought in the U.S. army during the War of 1812 and in 1822 traveled to Latin America to observe revolutionary developments there, publishing his experiences in *A Visit to Colombia*. Duane's influence on American politics showed the significance of international radicals who championed participatory democracy, religious freedom, and economic independence from European empires. ▲ Saint-Mémin, Charles Balthazar Julien Fevret de, 1770–1852, artist

Brawls were unusual, but nasty words were not. Revolutionary leaders who had promoted public education in the 1780s hoped that increased literacy would produce sober, moral citizens to help keep order in the new country. Instead, newly independent Americans eagerly expanded print culture to communicate ideas about society and culture that challenged the status quo. By 1790, there were more than one hundred newspapers and other periodicals in the United States, five times as many as had been available in 1760, and they accelerated partisanship in the 1790s. Colonial newspapers had mainly reprinted news from Europe, but editors in the 1790s took aggressively political stances, printing personal attacks against political opponents. The motto of *The Federalist Gazette of the United States* was "He that is not for us, is against us." Subscribing to a partisan paper signaled membership in a group of like-minded citizens.

During Adams's administration, Democratic-Republican newspapers, often edited by Irish immigrants, became the voice of political dissent over foreign policy.

Following Washington's precedent, Adams attempted to remain neutral in the war between England and France, but both countries attacked U.S. merchant ships engaging in trade with the other. Finally, in 1798, Adams cut off trade with France, sparking an undeclared conflict later called a **Quasi-War** (1798–1800). He strengthened the U.S. army, supported Congress's buildup of a navy, and sent ships to the Caribbean to engage French privateers who were seizing U.S. ships. He sent ammunition, food, and other supplies to Toussaint L'Ouverture, the former slave who had become the military leader of the Haitian Revolution, thereby serving two purposes at once: opposing France and repaying a debt to the seven hundred fifty free black soldiers in L'Ouverture's army who had fought with American patriot forces during the siege of Savannah in 1779. Newspapers such as the *Aurora* lambasted Adams for betraying the American Revolution by warring against the country that had aided Americans in their fight for independence. Personal in its attacks, the *Aurora* called him "old, bald, blind, querulous, toothless."

In retaliation, Federalists in Congress passed the **Alien and Sedition Acts (1798)**, a series of laws designed to silence pro-French newspaper editors. These laws made it a crime to speak, write, or print anything against the U.S. president that would bring him "into contempt or dispute" or to oppose "any measure or measures of the United States." These extremely broad laws gave the president power to deport any foreign resident whose activities he considered dangerous. More than twenty Democratic-Republican newspaper editors and politicians were arrested and several sent to prison under these laws. Similar laws in England, also passed in the 1790s, treated dissent as an unlawful attack on government. In 1794, Thomas Paine was tried and found guilty of seditious libel in English courts (although he had escaped to France) for publishing *The Rights of Man*.

Opponents of the Alien and Sedition Acts insisted that they violated the First Amendment of the Constitution, which protected freedom of speech and the press. Vice President Jefferson and Congressman Madison

Quasi-War Naval conflict between the United States and France conducted mainly in the Caribbean over trading rights and alliances during which the U.S. navy experienced a buildup.

Alien and Sedition Acts (1798) Targeting recent immigrants and critics of the president, four U.S. laws that many interpreted as a Federalist attack against Democratic-Republicans.

secretly drafted resolutions later passed by the state legislatures of Kentucky and Virginia, denouncing the acts. In these **Virginia and Kentucky Resolutions**, Democratic-Republicans articulated the idea of **nullification**, which argued that a state could refuse to enforce or obey federal laws that it deemed unconstitutional.

8-3b Citizenship and Political Rights

Before the Revolution, colonists were British subjects by birth. In the new United States, people proclaimed themselves citizens, a word that implied active political participation. Because it was active, citizenship could be chosen by those born on other continents, and the first Congress had to establish the rules with naturalization laws. Under the **Naturalization Law of 1790**, any "alien" who had lived in the United States for more than two years could become a citizen as long as she or he was "a free white person" who could present proof of good character. After taking a loyalty oath, they and their children under twenty-one years of age became citizens.

Imperial powers insisted that loyalty could not be shed so easily. Desperate for sailors to fill its ranks in its ongoing struggles with French forces, the British navy practiced **impressment**, seizing sailors on U.S. merchant ships and forcing them into service, claiming that any person born a British subject remained so until death. The seizure of thousands of U.S. citizens born before the Revolution or naturalized was a direct rejection of U.S. sovereignty, and in 1796, Congress passed a law allowing any American sailor who paid 25 cents to receive a "certificate of citizenship" that he could present to British officials trying to impress sailors into the Royal Navy. Seeking something more permanent, sailors also used tattoos of eagles, liberty poles, or the date 1776 to proclaim their allegiance to the United States. Of course, actual British deserters could do the same.

Those particular inked emblems of citizenship evoked support for Democratic-Republicans and republican revolutions worldwide, demonstrating that struggles over citizenship were closely tied to partisan politics. Democratic-Republicans supported the easy inclusion of immigrants into the political body of the United States; Federalists opposed this. William Cobbett, popular Federalist editor who was himself a British migrant, sneered that "As well might we attempt to tame a Hyena, as to Americanize an Irishman." In Cobbett's Pennsylvania, tens of thousands of Irish migrants fleeing poverty and political unrest arrived in the first decades after independence. Naturalized as citizens and

> States expand and contract political rights.

granted the right to vote under a 1790 state constitution that enfranchised free taxpaying men, they began voting with the newly forming Democratic-Republican party. As political control of the U.S. Congress shifted between parties, so, too, did naturalization laws. In 1798, Congress under Federalist control passed a new Naturalization Act that extended the period a person had to live in the United States before becoming a citizen to fourteen years. When Democratic-Republicans rose in power in Congress, they passed the 1802 Naturalization Act, which reduced the residency requirement to five years.

The Bill of Rights protected citizens' rights to political participation through freedom of speech, the press, and assembly. The states, however, determined who could vote. The reshuffling of voting from a privilege associated with property holding to a right associated with white adult male citizenship had begun in the Revolution-era state constitutions. In New Jersey, the state constitution granted the right to vote to "all inhabitants . . . of full age who are worth £50." Taking the gender-neutral language at its word, property-holding single women began to vote in local elections, a practice that was soon acknowledged in election laws of the 1790s, referring to voters as "he or she." In fact, when lawmakers proposed a state amendment in 1800 that would explicitly allow women to vote in congressional elections, others declared it unnecessary. One legislator said "Our Constitution gives this right to maids or widows black or white." In New Jersey, property holding, not gender or race, was what qualified a voter. It was a logic that prevailed in Canada, where unmarried women with property voted until 1834.

In New Jersey, however, Democratic-Republican claims of voter fraud during an 1807 election led to a revision of voting rights law. The new law not only banned women from voting but also took the right away from black men. Other states followed suit in the first four decades of the nineteenth century, striking down laws requiring that a voter own property and simultaneously disenfranchising white women and all blacks. Faced with a democratic population filled with rowdy and unreliable citizens, legislators decided to draw lines by color and gender rather than wealth. The Revolution had been a victory for popular sovereignty in which the people rule; the two decades that followed defined who would be included in "the people" for political purposes.

Virginia and Kentucky Resolutions Measures passed by the legislatures of Virginia and Kentucky asserting states' rights to interpret the constitutionality of laws and opposing the Alien and Sedition Acts.

nullification Legal theory that the states, as sovereign parts of the United States, retain the right to void laws passed by the federal government.

Naturalization Law of 1790 Act establishing process by which a free white person born outside the United States could become a legal citizen after two years.

impressment Practice of seizing people and forcing them into military service conducted by navies against the crews of enemy or neutral ships.

8-3c Political Exclusion and the Limits of Choice

Citizenship could be chosen, but political choices, like economic choices, were often constrained. Free women, like free men, could become

> Race and gender constrain political inclusion.

naturalized citizens, but only single women were obligated to pay taxes to support state and local government. Married women under the old English principle of coverture were folded within their husband's economic identity. Nor were married women held to the same standard of loyalty to the state. In the case of *Martin v. Commonwealth of Massachusetts* (1805), the Massachusetts Supreme Court ruled that a married woman Loyalist who had fled during the Revolution could not have her property confiscated. Federalist Judge Theodore Sedgwick explained, "A wife who left the country in the company of her husband did not withdraw herself—but was, if I may so express it, withdrawn by him." As Sedgwick's words suggested, free women made a single politically significant choice—the choice of a spouse—and that determined their citizenship status. In fact, American-born women who married foreigners frequently found their status as U.S. citizens challenged.

Free black Americans found their ability to function as citizens sharply curtailed by laws that attempted to link them with the enslaved population. The **Fugitive Slave Law of 1793** put the power of the federal government on the side of slave owners trying to recapture runaways. It established a $500 fine for interfering with the recapture of a supposed runaway and permitted slave owners to establish ownership by making a case to an individual judge. Black people kidnapped by slave catchers—whether fugitives or free people—were denied the right to jury trial and even to present evidence supporting their own case for freedom. All were presumed to be slaves unless proven otherwise, revealing the fragile protections of living in so-called free states. Even in places where slavery was prohibited, **Black Laws** reduced free black men and women to a permanent underclass. First enacted in Ohio in 1804, Black Laws in states created from the

Fugitive Slave Law of 1793 U.S. law that authorized the capture and return of people who escaped from slavery and established a fine for anyone who helped a runaway.

Black Laws Acts passed in Northwestern states where slavery was illegal to exclude African Americans or limit their access to education, voting, and the legal system.

Gabriel's Rebellion of 1800 Virginia slave rebellion led by a skilled artisan slave who claimed the legacy of the American Revolution and planned to march on Richmond.

American Colonization Society Organization founded in 1816 by clergymen and politicians to raise money to send former slaves and free blacks to settle in Africa.

Liberia Colony founded by the American Colonization Society on land purchased in West Africa that was designed for the settlement of free blacks from the United States.

Northwest Territory forbade any "black or mulatto person" from testifying in court against a white person, joining the militia, or attending public schools. The laws required free black immigrants to carry identity certificates and to sign guardianship bonds with property holders who would be responsible for them.

Enslaved people faced violent opposition to claiming citizenship. In 1800, a skilled artisan slave named Gabriel organized a rebellion in Richmond, Virginia. He was inspired by revolutionary ideals as they recirculated during the ongoing Haitian Revolution. He also hoped to take advantage of partisan divisions within the white community. Organized among skilled urban slaves and free blacks, the rebels of **Gabriel's Rebellion of 1800** planned to march on Richmond, seize the ammunition and guns stored in the Capitol Square Building, take Governor James Monroe hostage, and demand freedom and economic justice for Virginia's poorest. Gabriel predicted that as word spread, more slaves as well as poor whites, who shared free blacks' economic and political hardships, would join the rebel army, forcing a bargain with city leaders.

When the rebellion was exposed by nervous plantation slaves and the conspirators captured and tried, several participants explicitly called upon revolutionary words. One claimed: "I have nothing more to offer than what General Washington would have had to offer, had he been taken by the British and put to trial. . . . I have adventured my life in endeavouring to obtain the liberty of my countrymen, and am willing to sacrifice in their cause." Gabriel was sentenced to death. Many of the other alleged conspirators were distributed to slave traders to sell to the Spanish in Louisiana.

The presence of free American-born blacks in Gabriel's conspiracy confirmed many white Virginians' belief that the republic could not accept them as citizens. In 1806, the state passed a new manumission law, requiring any newly freed person to leave the state within the year. Some thought moving to a new state was not enough. In 1816, a group of wealthy white ministers, lawyers, and politicians formed the **American Colonization Society** whose purpose was to raise money to deport free African Americans. Some members feared that free blacks could never find equal treatment in the United States and were better off forming their own community elsewhere. Others thought the existence of free blacks undermined the institution of slavery and to protect it, the United States needed to expel former slaves. Using private funds and money from the U.S. Congress, the Society ultimately sent thousands of African Americans to **Liberia**, a new colony they founded on the West Coast of Africa, next to Sierra Leone, the colony for freed slaves that Britain had established in 1787.

8-4
Agrarian Republic or Empire of Liberty?

This circa 1805 painting by an unknown artist is known as "Plan of Civilization." It depicts a man like Benjamin Hawkins, superintendent of Indian Affairs for the Southeast United States from 1796–1816, who was sent to introduce European-style farming techniques to Creek Indians. In this painting, slave cabins with distinctive West African peaked roofs are visible in the background.

Compare this picture with the first seal of Massachusetts Bay Colony presented in Chapter 3. What does each image suggest about the artist's attitude toward Indians? What has changed from the colonial era to that of the early United States? ▶

Courtesy of Greenville County Museum of Art, Greenville, S.C.

Thomas Jefferson was elected president in 1800 after a bitter partisan campaign. In his first inaugural address, he attempted to draw the country back together, proclaiming "Let us, then, fellow citizens, unite with one heart and mind. . . . We are all Republicans, we are all Federalists." He spoke optimistically about the "experiment" of the United States, "Kindly separated by nature and a wide ocean from the exterminating havoc of one quarter of the globe; too high-minded to endure the degradations of the others." He praised the small farmers whose independence, he believed, would preserve the virtue of the republic. Reality did not match his rhetoric, however, because the United States could not avoid the rest of the world. As a trading nation, it depended on merchants and exchange with other countries. As a country that shared a continent with multiple groups, families, coalitions, and empires, it had to negotiate its boundaries. Although politicians articulated a fantasy of virtuous expansion, the desires and ambitions of people living on the land drew the United States into positions similar to the empires that patriots had criticized. Meanwhile, people debated whether a republic could, or should, become a new kind of empire.

☞ As you read, compare the emerging U.S. empire to other early nineteenth-century empires. How was it similar? How was it different?

8-4a Democratic-Republicans in Power

The election of 1800 was, in the minds of Democratic-Republicans, a chance to redeem the promise of the American Revolution and to turn away from the drift toward national consolidation that had taken place under the Federalists. Campaigning against the Alien and Sedition laws, new taxes, and the undeclared

{ New national political leadership envisions the United States as a new type of republic.

war with France, Jefferson called on the voting public not to endorse the extremes of the French Revolution but to reinvigorate American republicanism. Celebrating their victory and the nonviolent transfer of power, Democratic-Republicans began to dismantle some of the Federalist program—repealing the excise on whiskey, shrinking the army, eliminating district courts, and withholding appointments for Federalist justices of the peace.

One of the justices deprived of his appointment, William Marbury, brought his case, **Marbury v. Madison** (1803) to the U.S. Supreme Court. Marbury did not get his job back, but in his decision, Chief Justice John Marshall established the practice of judicial review by which the Supreme Court had the power to judge whether executive actions and laws passed by Congress or the states were constitutional. Laws in conflict with the Constitution were void. It was a precedent that formally expanded the checks on congressional power by asserting the independence of the judiciary.

As his Kentucky Resolution had illustrated, Jefferson saw the United States as a compact between states as much as a centralized nation. He and the other Democratic-Republicans championed a small national government that loosely held together a country of independent farmers who sold their surplus to distant markets. Jefferson argued that the country could consist of an expanding set of politically equal states spreading freedom across the hemisphere, a concept he referred to as an "empire of liberty." Jefferson's expansionist vision initially confronted demographic and economic challenges. In 1800, 75 percent of North America was in Native American hands, including half of the supposed territory of the United States and most land claimed by Spain. The population of the United States was about 5.3 million, in contrast to the 13 to 17 million people living in neighboring Spanish America.

Marbury v. Madison U.S. Supreme court case that established the court as an equal branch of the federal government, with the power to overturn laws that violated the Constitution.

Peale, Rembrandt (1778–1860)/Collection of the New-York Historical Society, USA/
The Bridgeman Art Library

Jefferson as Natural Man Like George Washington, Jefferson was a Virginia slave owner, but he cultivated a public image different from that of the first president. Rembrandt Peale painted this portrait in 1805 at the beginning of Jefferson's second term. In it, the president wears his own hair rather than a wig, a plain, unruffled neck cloth, and a fur collar. Fur and clean linen were luxuries, but they were not aristocratic, befitting an executive who also discontinued formal presidential receptions. ▲

Jefferson's ideal of free trade on the world's oceans was undermined by the perils of merchants in the Mediterranean, where the North African states of Algiers, Morocco, Tunis, and Tripoli licensed privateers to capture ships and take hostages. In gaining independence, U.S. merchants lost the protection of the British navy, and its sailors were captured and enslaved by the **Barbary States**, which demanded millions of dollars in tribute to release them. Lurid novels and sensationalistic press accounts alarmed the American public with tales of innocent white hostages sold into slavery by dark-skinned Muslim pirates, and the government had limited tools to fight back. Treaties failed, tribute payments drained federal accounts, and U.S. shipbuilding lagged. When Tripoli declared war on the United States in 1801, Jefferson stopped the payments, sent ships to blockade Tripoli's port, and supported the building of a navy to defend U.S. sovereign rights. Conflicts, including a second war with Algiers, continued until a series of treaties was made in 1815.

Democratic-Republicans' ideals also were tested by ongoing global crises. After a decade of warfare around the Atlantic and across Europe, some revolutionaries sought stability in strong

Barbary States Group of North African states, some with allegiance to the Ottoman Empire, that captured merchant ships on the Mediterranean and demanded tribute payments for their return.

civilizing mission Rationalization for U.S. territorial expansion into Indian lands that involved converting natives to Protestant Christianity and spreading new family and farming patterns.

military leaders. In France, General Napoleon Bonaparte claimed the highest political office of First Consul in 1799. In 1801, the revolutionaries of Saint-Domingue chose military commander Toussaint L'Ouverture to be governor-general of a semi-independent country. Determined to retake the island, Napoleon dispatched sixteen thousand soldiers to defeat the rebels and terrorize the population. The French captured L'Ouverture, who warned them that the "tree of liberty" would "spring up again by the roots." On January 1, 1804, new leader Jean-Jacques Dessalines announced the nation-state of Haiti with a Declaration of Independence that demanded former slaves be incorporated into society on equal terms. Haitians purged the island of white influence, first with mass killings of remaining French people and then with law. Haiti's 1805 Constitution forbade white men from owning land and declared that all Haitians would be called "black." The U.S. Congress responded by placing an embargo on trade with Haiti, and Jefferson refused to recognize the self-styled "black republic." Fearing the spread of slave rebellion, Jefferson opted for economic isolation, and other empires followed suit. The U.S. embargo and refusal of acknowledgement lasted until 1863, when President Abraham Lincoln opened diplomatic ties.

8-4b Indian Accommodation and Resistance

The people most pressingly facing U.S. expansion were Native American neighbors. After the Treaty of Greenville in 1795, the United States temporarily abandoned its policy of military conquest in favor of a **civilizing mission**. The federal government signed dozens of land treaties with tribal groups who ceded land to the United States. In exchange, the United States pledged to bring what leaders called "civilization" to Indians, permitting them to coexist with Americans and eventually melt into American society through intermarriage and the casting off of Indian ways. For men like Benjamin Hawkins, the U.S. Indian agent to the Creeks from 1796–1816, "civilizing" Indians meant converting them to Protestant Christianity, reorienting their economic and family lives, and pushing them toward centralized political authority. Hawkins directed Creek men to take over farming from Creek women and to employ more intensive forms of cultivation that required less land. He urged women to expand their household tasks, including spinning and weaving. He convinced the Creek National Council to take over the responsibility of punishing Creek lawbreakers rather than leave it to individual clans. The United States also supported religious schools in Indian territories that focused on training young Indians. Nancy Reece, a Cherokee girl who attended the Brainerd Mission School in Tennessee, wrote that "When school hours are over, the girls attend to domestick concerns and learn to

> Eastern Native Americans confront U.S. plans for their future.

make their own clothes and the clothes of the boys so they can do such work when they go home, to assist their parents. . . . and perhaps can learn their parents something that they do not understand."

Cherokee parents who sent their children to such schools were adopting the strategy of **accommodation**, going along with the U.S. plan in the hope of preserving their land and families. For many Southeastern Indians, including Cherokees and Creeks, the practices that white Americans called "civilized" were not distant from their own. Most were already farmers. Cherokee and Creek clans had also long been involved in the slave trade. Using slave labor to grow cotton that women could process into fabric appeared to be a good economic strategy among elite Native Americans. By accommodating to the U.S. civilization project, they hoped to confirm their sovereignty as an independent nation located next to the United States.

Their accommodation, moreover, was often selective; many adopted economic practices but not gender roles. Hawkins claimed that Creek men made "slaves" of their wives by having them work in the fields, but Creek women preferred to add spinning to their farming work rather than replace one with the other. One Creek grandmother insisted to Hawkins that "she could not consent that the woman and children should be under the direction of the father" as in Euro-American families.

Other Indians looked at the losses of land they had already suffered (see Map 8.1) and concluded that accommodation would not stop the flow of white migrants. The Senecas, who had once claimed 4 million acres in New York and Pennsylvania, were by the turn of the century confined to fewer than 200,000 acres. The formerly powerful

accommodation Indian strategy of accepting some U.S. social, cultural, and economic interventions to maintain land and political sovereignty.

Map 8.1 Indian Land Cessions and Resistance The backcountry in the Age of Revolution was the site of prolonged warfare and forced treaties by which Indian groups lost their land to British American colonists and then the United States. Indians made and remade alliances between the Seven Years' War and the War of 1812 in an effort to resist the devastating loss of their lands. ▼

Iroquois Confederacy could no longer provide protection and diplomacy. Alcoholism, poverty, and violence plagued Indian communities torn apart by decades of war and U.S. land seizures. In 1799, Handsome Lake, a Seneca, had a religious vision that turned him away from alcohol to lead a religious revival among the Iroquois. Handsome Lake began to preach "the Good Message," a group of teachings that combined Christian and Iroquois beliefs and focused on self-renewal. He urged Indians to stop using alcohol and cease intertribal violence. Other prophets followed Handsome Lake, and the period from 1795 to 1815 became an "Age of Prophesy" for Northwestern Indians, inspiring resistance rather than accommodation.

The Shawnee Tenskwatawa (known as The Prophet) was the most influential of this group. He warned Shawnees that Americans were "children of the Evil Spirit," and Indian adoption of U.S. culture was to blame for their suffering. Denouncing Christianity, metal tools, domesticated animals, and private property, Tenskwatawa drew hundreds of Shawnees, Delawares, Ottawas, and others to the new village of **Prophetstown** on the Tippecanoe River in Indiana. Indian unity depended on turning away from white culture; prophets even argued that mixed-race children should grow up with their white relatives. Those who doubted the prophets were accused of witchcraft and some were tortured or burned at the stake.

8-4c The Louisiana Territory

Faced with the options of resistance and accommodation, substantial numbers of Native Americans instead moved across the Mississippi River.

> { Global revolutions and rivalries give the United States an opportunity to expand.

The territory of Louisiana, stretching west from the Mississippi and including the valuable port of New Orleans, was inhabited by a diverse group of Native Americans; French, Spanish, and British traders; and U.S. farmers. In the minds of European leaders, Louisiana was also a key piece in the global balance of power. The first wave of the Haitian Revolution in 1791 had brought thousands of planters and slaves to New Orleans as refugees. Drawing on their sugar-growing and processing expertise, these refugees turned the local economy from one based on Indian fur trading and the cultivation of tobacco and indigo into one focused on slave-labor-based sugar production. New Orleans quickly became one of the main slave markets for North America.

The region's potential as a plantation-based economy attracted Napoleon, who hoped to turn Louisiana into a supply colony for the French Empire in the Caribbean. In 1800, faced with rising debt, Spain agreed to give up its Louisiana claims to France, provided that the French not sell it away again. However, recapturing the

Prophetstown Indian town on the Tippecanoe River where Tecumseh and Tenskwatawa forged a pan-Indian alliance. It became the target of an attack by U.S. troops.

Louisiana Purchase Acquisition of the Louisiana Territory from France that was financed abroad and doubled the size of the United States.

island of Saint-Domingue and re-enslaving the population proved more difficult than Napoleon had anticipated. The strength of Haitian generals L'Ouverture and Dessalines, as well as the deadly toll that tropical diseases took on French forces, caused Napoleon to abandon his vision of an integrated French Caribbean power. Without Saint-Domingue's profitable sugar plantations, Louisiana's value to France diminished. Needing money to fund imperial conquest in Europe and eager to encourage U.S. neutrality, Napoleon sold Louisiana in 1803 to the United States for $15 million, doubling the size of its territory (see Map 8.2).

The **Louisiana Purchase** of 1803 was celebrated by hunters and farmers who wanted Louisiana land and permanent trading rights on the Mississippi. What the United States lacked was the money to make the purchase. British and Dutch banks signed the loans, at 6 percent interest, which suited British political calculations because it stripped its old adversary France of a large piece of its global empire.

For Jefferson's Louisiana vision to become reality, American farmers needed water routes to the Pacific Ocean connecting the river systems of the new territory to the Missouri and Mississippi Rivers. The president commissioned the Corps of Discovery Expedition, led by Meriwether Lewis and William Clark, to cross the new

Free Black Culture in New Orleans At the time of the Louisiana Purchase, the population of New Orleans was 38 percent enslaved and 20 percent free people of color. In 1786, the Spanish colonial governor had required all women of color to wrap their heads in kerchiefs, a style that women in West Africa had pioneered by using imported Indian textiles. By the nineteenth century, the practice had evolved into a fashion statement for free and enslaved women of color as depicted in François Fleischbein's *A Portrait of Betsy* (circa 1837). ▼

The Historic New Orleans Collection

Global Americans Born around 1788, Sacagawea was a Shoshone Indian who as a girl was kidnapped by a raiding group of Hidatsas and taken as a slave to the northern Plains. As a teenager, she was traded to French Canadian fur trader Toussaint Charbonneau to be his wife. In the winter of 1804–1805, carrying her newborn son, Sacagawea accompanied William Clark and Meriwether Lewis in their journey across the North American continent to investigate the territory purchased from France. She provided practical skills of gathering edible plants and acting as interpreter and guide. According to Clark, her presence also "confirmed . . . our friendly intentions, as no woman ever accompanies a war party." She was unexpectedly reunited with the family of her birth, who agreed to help equip and guide the expedition over the treacherous Rocky Mountains and on to the Pacific Ocean.

After her return, Sacagawea moved with her husband and son to St. Louis, where the boy was enrolled in a boarding school that trained children in the civilization program. Sacagawea died of illness in 1812. Her short life demonstrated how much U.S. diplomacy and discovery, like that of all empires, depended on the participation of Indian women. Her experiences dramatize how people in the middle of a vast continent served as pivots of global economic flows. Yet no depictions of Sacagawea were made in her lifetime. When she was chosen in 1998 to appear on a new U.S. dollar coin, artist Glenna Goodacre used modern Shoshone college student Randy'L He-dow Teton as a model. ▲ United States Mint

Map 8.2 Louisiana Territory and Haitian Revolution, 1803 The Louisiana Purchase connected slave rebellion with the expansion of the United States onto Indian land. Some in the United States believed that foreign ownership of Louisiana threatened U.S. security and encouraged Indian resistance to U.S. expansion. North Carolina congressman Samuel Purviance warned Congress in 1803 that if France kept Louisiana, "the tomahawk of the savage and the knife of the negro would confederate in the league, and there would be no interval of peace." ▲

territory in search of a Northwest Passage that would link his empire of liberty to Asia. In addition to staking a claim to the northwest border of the territory, the expedition was charged with gathering information on plant and animal life as well as establishing direct contacts with Native American groups. Lewis and Clark's two-year trip did not find an easy route to the Pacific; they reached its shores in an arduous journey over land. The artifacts and samples they collected were exhibited in the first American museum as unique elements of a new empire.

8-4d Cotton Frontier

Although Democratic-Republican politics and ideas about the economy praised free and independent producers, U.S. engagement with a global

{ The booming market for cotton expands American slavery.

marketplace ultimately boosted a dramatic expansion of slavery in the early nineteenth century. Since the 1780s, industrialists in England had been building factories to produce colorful printed cotton fabrics previously imported from India. The factories needed cotton, and the United States soon became their main source. The first cotton grown in the American colonies was sea island cotton from Barbados, which flourished in very wet areas of Georgia and South Carolina but not farther inland. Another kind of cotton, called *short-staple cotton*, could grow widely, but the seeds were hard to remove from short, fuzzy fibers. In 1794, Eli Whitney devised a machine he called the *cotton gin* that could separate the seeds from the fibers more quickly than could be done by hand. Farmers spread cotton cultivation rapidly across the lower South. The money it brought enabled the United States to buy manufactured goods from Europe, pay off foreign debt, and invest in industry.

Enslaved men, women, and children produced this wealth. Although at the time of the Revolution some politicians had predicted a gradual decline in U.S. slavery, the expansion of the cotton frontier instead encouraged a dramatic increase. In the first two decades after the ratification of the Constitution, more than one hundred thousand enslaved African people arrived on North American shores and were quickly transported inland. When Congress debated whether to allow slavery to continue in newly purchased Louisiana, James Jackson of Georgia and Jonathan Dayton of New Jersey both insisted that slavery was the only way to make the land a productive part of the U.S. republic.

In 1807, Britain banned the Atlantic slave trade, and the U.S. Congress followed suit, officially ending the importation of African captives effective January 1, 1808. To enforce these laws, both countries' navies

Cotton Gin Enslaved people used Eli Whitney's cotton gin to remove seeds from cotton fibers with combs turned by a hand crank. Mills in England were ready to process cleaned and baled fibers into cotton fabric, and less than a decade after Whitney secured his patent, the United States was producing 45 percent of the raw cotton for British mills. By 1803, cotton had become the leading U.S. export; by 1820, the United States had become the world's leading producer of cotton (surpassing India); and by 1850, it produced 68 percent of total world production. ▲

policed the Caribbean, where the illegal slave trade continued for decades. Yet the number of U.S. slaves, increasingly laboring in cotton fields, continued to grow (see Figure 8.2).

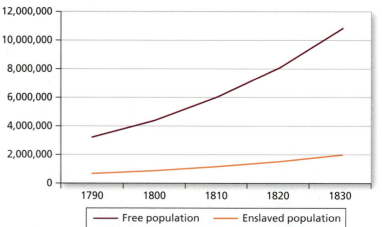

Figure 8.2 Growing U.S. Population, Free and Enslaved Although the United States banned the transatlantic slave trade in 1808, its enslaved population increased in the early nineteenth century. Under U.S. law, the children of enslaved women were deemed slaves for life. These children, in turn, gave birth to another generation of people held in slavery to increase the wealth of their owners. The free population grew through "natural increase," too, and also through immigration. ▲ Source: Historical Statistics of the United States Online Millennial edition.

National Museum of American History/Kenneth E. Behring Center/Smithsonian Institution

Historical Statistics of the United States, online millennial ed.

Life on the cotton frontier was grueling. Enslaved people cleared the land and created the fields. Each year, men, women, and children planted, thinned, picked, ginned, baled, and shipped cotton. They also grew food crops, raised livestock, and repaired fences and buildings.

Their status as valuable property made them frequent targets of Southeastern Indian raids seeking to plunder their enemies. Some captives were sold into the continental slave trade; others were enslaved by Creek and Cherokee plantation owners.

8-5

Erosion and Expansion of Empires

In John Archibald Woodside's patriotic painting *We Owe Allegiance to No Crown* (1814), revolutionary symbols such as the liberty cap are joined with new symbols, including the stars and stripes flag. The sailor representing the United States crushes a crown beneath his foot. Broken chains, evoking slavery and "enslavement" to Britain, lie on the ground. Woodside specialized in painting signs for taverns and hotels; he also decorated fire engines and painted banners for private military companies.

How would Americans have known about the symbols depicted in this painting? How would that influence the way people interpreted the painting's meaning? ▶

Erik Arnesen (c) Nicholas S. West/National Portrait Gallery, Smithsonian Institution/Art Resource.

The European wars of 1803 to 1815 marked the end of a century of conflict among European empires over land, trade, and power. Those conflicts had embroiled people around the globe, at sea and on land, and in 1812, the United States, which had vowed to stay out of foreign wars, declared war on Britain. As with the earlier conflicts, North American Indians' claims to their own territory and trade became an essential part of the global conflict, and its resolution further weakened their ability to use European antagonisms to hold back the taking of their land. For the United States, what some saw as the second war for independence cleared the way for land acquisition, cross continental expansion, and international trade.

☞ As you read about U.S. participation in the global wars of the early nineteenth century, consider the significance of the War of 1812. Was it really a second "war for independence"? Was it an entirely new conflict?

8-5a War of 1812

Jefferson's vision of an empire of liberty was possible only if international trade allowed farmers in the West to sell their goods. In 1803, after a two-year pause, Europe plunged into another round of warfare, making U.S. trade and territory once again targets. For the next twelve years, Europe was embroiled in the Napoleonic Wars as French forces numbering in

{ Americans contest independence in a second war against Britain.

the hundreds of thousands under Napoleon invaded and conquered much of the land and people from Spain to Russia. Napoleon crowned himself emperor of France in 1804, pledging to bring stability to the French and to secure equality under the law. He pledged the same for the nations he conquered, but they allied to fight back, and battles raged across Europe, at sea, and at colonial outposts around the world.

The wars were commercial as well as military. Both Britain and France passed resolutions forbidding neutrals such as the United States from trading with the other empire or its colonies in the Caribbean. Some Americans saw these as attempts to reinstate the mercantilist trade policies, forcing the United States back into colonial status. In retaliation, Congress passed the **Embargo Act of 1807**, which cut off exports to foreign ports. Jefferson hoped that the consequences would convince France and Britain to respect the trading rights of neutrals, but the result was a crushing economic downturn for the United States. American farmers could not export their crops; American merchants could not sell their goods; and American sailors, dockworkers, and boardinghouse keepers could no longer make a living from networks of global trade. James Madison,

Embargo Act of 1807 U.S. law advocated for by Jefferson that cut off foreign trade in an attempt to assert U.S. rights against European empires.

who was elected president in 1808 at the end of Jefferson's two terms, initially sustained the embargo, but strong opposition resulted in its replacement with the Nonintercourse Act of 1809, which resumed trade with all countries except France and Britain.

Attempts to remain neutral and trade freely failed, as did U.S. efforts to coerce powerful European empires to follow its wishes. In frustration, Democratic-Republican congressmen from the South and West elected in 1810 demanded an aggressive assertion of U.S. power. Called **war hawks**, they pushed for a declaration of war, citing Britain's violations of national sovereignty: its impressment of American sailors, its alliances with enemy Indians in the West, and its encouragement of backcountry violence. In June 1812, the war hawks got it.

Canada was the first target of the U.S. offensive in the **War of 1812**. Looking at its small population of British subjects, Jefferson had declared that conquering Canada was "a mere matter of marching" up to get it and achieving, within a year, "the final expulsion of England from the American continent." Some even thought the Canadians would welcome membership in the republic of the United States. Between 1812 and 1814, U.S. forces attempted several invasions in the area around the Great Lakes, all of which failed.

U.S. soldiers ran into difficulties immediately because of their lack of experience. British soldiers, many of them recruits from Ireland, were veterans of the Napoleonic Wars, but most American soldiers were inexperienced recruits from militia units. Because soldiers were armed with smoothbore muskets that were accurate only to about one hundred yards, companies depended on disciplined, coordinated firing to disperse the enemy—just the kind of maneuver that required drill and obedience in the confusion of battle. To become an effective fighting force, as Major Thomas Melville, Jr., insisted, these men had "to forget *the Citizen* and become *the Soldier*." U.S. soldiers were also poorly paid and equipped. In 1812, Congress initially offered $5 a month to men capable of earning at least $10 per month as civilians. Even though Congress increased pay and created incentives including land in the West, the United States could not meet its targets for a fully staffed army. Nevertheless, Congress refused to accept free blacks into the army, reversing the precedent of the Continental Army of the Revolution.

The powerful British navy blockaded ports along the Atlantic and Gulf coasts, raiding eastern towns and bringing American foreign trade to a standstill. British warships, outnumbering the fledgling U.S. fleet four to one, engaged in naval battles along the coast, but the Great Lakes became the main focus of naval warfare. The United States quickly built ships to defend against British offenses and in September 1813, Commodore Oliver Hazard Perry destroyed British forces at Put-in-Bay on Lake Erie. Control of Lake Erie meant control of supply lines in the West, but neither side could gain ground, and troops at the border with Canada were in a stalemate.

8-5b Tecumseh's Confederacy

As it had during the Revolution, the British army depended on its alliances with Indians to combat the United States, and when formal hostilities broke out, the United States was already engaged in extensive Indian warfare. In 1808, Tecumseh, brother of prophet Tenskwatawa, revived the confederacy of Blue Jacket and Little Turtle by transforming the Prophet's religious following into a pan-Indian military alliance. As a teenager, Tecumseh had fought with allied Indian forces under Joseph Brant. Perhaps, he reasoned, this new alliance of diverse Indians groups could form its own united "state" neighboring the United States. In its early stages, the alliance was vulnerable. In the fall of 1811, William Henry Harrison, governor of Indiana Territory, led troops toward Prophetstown, outnumbering and defeating the Indians there at the **Battle of Tippecanoe** and burning the community to the ground. As Prophetstown was rebuilt, Tecumseh turned to the British. Together, British and Indian soldiers captured strategic forts on the Great Lakes, took Detroit (see Map 8.3), and fought U.S. armies in Kentucky. But long supply lines through Canada and the fact that many Indian warriors returned to their families after battle weakened Tecumseh's ability to hold together his forces. Coordination with supporters in the South was difficult. In October 1813, Tecumseh was killed in a final confrontation between his warriors and the army headed by Harrison at Moraviantown, a Canadian town established by a Pennsylvania missionary for English-speaking Christian Indians. The war continued, but the Indian alliance was fatally wounded.

Fighting in the South pitted a militant confederacy of Creeks, called the **Red Sticks** because of their war clubs, allied with British troops against the U.S. forces led by General Andrew Jackson of Tennessee. Inspired by their own group of prophets preaching spiritual renewal and rejection of white ways, the Red Sticks had military backing from the Spanish. In 1813, divisions between accommodationist Creeks and the Red Sticks dissolved into a civil war that overlapped the conflict between Britain and the United States. Creeks fought on both sides over U.S. expansion into their territory. In 1814, Jackson, with Cherokee, Choctaw, and Creek allies, defeated Red Stick Creeks at the Battle of Horseshoe Bend, killing eight

Wide-scale Indian alliance mounts its last stand.

war hawks Name for a group of Democratic-Republicans led by Henry Clay who favored war against Britain to resolve trade, territorial, and impressment disputes.

War of 1812 War between the United States and Britain concerning trading rights, territory, and alliances with Native Americans.

Battle of Tippecanoe Attack by U.S. troops led by William Henry Harrison against pan-Indian alliance led by Tecumseh.

Red Sticks Members of radical faction of Creek Indians who allied with the British against the United States and were defeated by Andrew Jackson and allied Indians in 1814.

Map 8.3 Fighting the War of 1812 U.S., British, and Native American forces fought the War of 1812 in disparate locations across the eastern portion of North America. As in previous imperial conflicts, privateers and naval ships also attacked one another in the seas around Britain and the Caribbean. ▲

hundred warriors. In the **Treaty of Fort Jackson** that followed, the United States took two-thirds of Creek territory, land that belonged to both the defeated Red Sticks and the Creeks who had fought alongside Jackson. Red Stick leaders largely refused to sign the treaty; instead, they moved south to join the mixed communities of Seminole Indians and runaway slaves who lived in Spanish East Florida.

Defeats in the War of 1812 ended the pan-Indian alliance that had existed in various forms since the Seven Years' War. The many groups in the eastern woodlands—weakened by disease, outnumbered by the increasing migration of white Americans onto Indian lands, impoverished by the erosion of the animal skin trade, and divided over how much to adopt so-called civilization projects and respond to federal interference—were no longer able to sustain alliances and contain U.S. territorial

claims. Pockets of militant resistance remained, particularly among the Seminoles, but the majority of Indians adjusted to new economic conditions and attempted to coexist with their neighbors.

8-5c Restoration

In Europe, the tide turned against the French in 1812 with uprisings in France and Germany and France's failed invasion of Russia, which cost its army staggering losses. By April 1814, Paris was under foreign occupation and Napoleon was in exile. Britain then launched its most striking attack against

Treaty of Fort Jackson Agreement following Jackson's 1814 defeat of Red Stick Creeks at the Battle of Horseshoe Bend that ceded the majority of Creek land to the United States.

{ The end of fighting reshuffles the balance of power in Europe and returns the status quo to the United States and Britain.

History without Borders

The Great Comet of 1811 and Political Prophesy

Sightings of the Great Comet, 1811–1812 People across the globe saw the Great Comet and looked for meaning in its blaze of light. In some locations, viewers wrote down their observations about the comet and its connection to earthly political events. Their accounts circulated internationally, fostering shared culture and to some degree, a shared experience. ▲

From the spring of 1811 until the summer of 1812, people around the world watched a blaze of light in the sky and wondered what it signified. Visible during the day and night, the Great Comet was first spotted with a telescope by Frenchman Honoré Flaugergues in March 1811, and could be seen by the naked eye longer than any other in history. The comet at its peak visibility in October 1811 was as bright as the third largest star in the sky and had a split tail. By the time of its last spotting by telescope in Russia in August 1812, people around the world had

come to interpret this global phenomenon in the context of local circumstances, seeing in it the prophesy of dramatic changes in the balance of power among people. Others thought profit, not prophesy, would be its greatest legacy.

In America, it was called "Tecumseh's Comet" after the Creek leader whose name, chosen at birth, meant "shooting star." Drawing on a coincidence that seemed prophetic, Tecumseh and his brother The Prophet used the appearance of the comet to enhance their spiritual and political power to unify Eastern Indians against U.S. squatters. The

comet coincided with a series of severe earthquakes in southeastern Missouri, northern Arkansas, and Tennessee and Kentucky between December 1811 and February 1812. These quakes, called the New Madrid Earthquakes, could be felt as far as Charleston, South Carolina, and Boston, Massachusetts. In Missouri, the land cracked and sank, and sailors on the Mississippi River reported that entire islands disappeared. The celestial object seemed a portent of earth-shattering reversals in the balance of power between native alliances and the United States.

Caricature on the 1811 Comet, c.1811 (coloured engraving), French School, (19th century)/Musee de la Ville de Paris, Musée Carnavalet, Paris, France/ Bridgeman Images

French cartoon *La Comete* (1814) This French cartoon lampoons the fashionable and foolish people who go comet viewing. Looking through telescopes, magnifying glasses, and a funnel, they are distracted from urban disorder and shady characters. The humorous image presents a stark contrast to the deadly consequences of military leaders' use of the comet. ◄

Tankard, London, 1811–12 (silver)/Emes, Rebecca & Barnard, Edward I (fl.1808–29)/CLARK ART INSTITUTE/Sterling and Francine Clark Art Institute, Williamstown, Massachusetts, USA/Bridgeman Images

Tankard, Rebecca Emes and Edward Barnard I (London 1811/12) This tankard is engraved with the image of the Comet of 1811, three planets, and multiple stars. The comet decoration made it a souvenir of the event that would be shared as the tankard owner drank with others long after the light in the sky had faded. ◄

The comet also coincided with an earthquake in Cape Town, South Africa. William Burchell, a visiting British scientist and collector, wrote in his journal that people in town "drew from this two-fold portentous sign, the certain prognostics of the annihilation of the Cape." In fact, British and Dutch colonizers soon plunged into the Fourth War of Dispossession that pitted the Europeans against resisting Africans. In China, leaders of the Eight Trigram Sect viewed the comet as divine encouragement to plan and launch an attack on the Forbidden City to overthrow the Manchu Qing Dynasty in 1813. More than seventy thousand died as the rebellion was defeated.

In Europe, the light in the sky was called "Napoleon's Comet" and linked with another set of military prophesies and another power shake-up.

Napoleon and some of his advisors saw the comet as a favorable sign to begin his assault on Russia in 1812. He was mistaken, lost most of his army in the failed invasion, and within a year was in retreat. He later wrote of this pivotal turn in the empire's fortunes that "my star was fading."

With Napoleon's army defeated and the Napoleonic Wars at last at an end, numerous enterprising Europeans turned the globally shared experience of comet watching into commercial opportunity. They sold prints of the comet, painted fans with its likeness, and etched it into beer tankards. Drawing on the belief that comets had a strong effect on the earth's atmosphere that enhanced plant and animal growth, French winemakers credited the comet with a particularly good Bordeaux crop, and "comet wine" was advertised and pursued at high

prices until the 1880s. Others used a more remote connection to the comet to invoke a shared, exciting experience and encourage people to spend their money. Henry Bell, a Scottish inventor and businessman, named his new paddlewheel steamship on the River Clyde, the first commercially successful service in Europe, *The Comet*.

Critical Thinking Questions

▶ How did different leaders use the Great Comet of 1811 to justify military action and why?

▶ What role did commemoration of the Great Comet play in turning it into a type of shared culture across national boundaries? Who was included and who excluded?

the United States. British forces landed in Maryland and marched into Washington, D.C., the new capital of the United States. They burned the president's house and the capitol building as Congress and President Madison, who had been reelected in 1812, fled.

Taking advantage of southern Indian hostility and potential rebelling slaves, the British opened a southern front in Florida and Louisiana. They brought in West Indian regiments, consisting of men born in Africa and enslaved in the Caribbean, under white officers. These regiments, assigned some of the most dangerous and unhealthy work, were intended to inspire slaves to run away to the British lines as they had during the Revolution. Once again, the tactic worked. Five of Indian Agent Benjamin Hawkins's slaves escaped to join the British. But Britons were growing weary of the sprawling war.

After enforcing the punitive treaty at the end of the Creek War, Jackson took the lead in the southern fight against the British. He supported the creation of a free black battalion of soldiers drawn from the New Orleans region to defend the port from the British but also relied heavily on enslaved laborers to build fortifications and reinforce the levees. Jackson placed the city under martial law to await the final battle, which came on January 8, 1815. The **Battle of New Orleans** was a lopsided victory for the Americans, who lost only thirteen soldiers to Britain's nearly three hundred dead. Jackson was celebrated as a defender of freedom from British enslavement. Yet when the British ships retreated, several hundred enslaved Africans went with them, preferring the losing side to a life of slavery in the United States.

The **Treaty of Ghent**, which officially ended the war in December 1814, restored the territorial borders that had existed prior to the fighting. At the peace talks, the British initially proposed the creation of an Indian state in the Northwest between the United States and Canada, which the United States rejected. With no Indian representatives to speak for any of the groups in Tecumseh's alliance, the British abandoned their allies. The final treaty contained only a promise that Indian lands held before the war would be restored. They were not.

Jackson's victory took place after the treaty had been signed but before news of it had arrived in the United States. It made him the most celebrated hero of the war and a political leader on the rise. At the same moment, New England Federalists were meeting in Connecticut to pursue a new attack on Democratic-Republican power. Many opposed the war, most supported the idea of state nullification of federal laws, and some even contemplated leaving the United States to make a separate agreement with New England's strongest trading partner, Britain.

At the **Hartford Convention**, these Federalists proposed amendments to the Constitution that they hoped would protect them from the tyranny of the majority that Madison, now president, had warned about during the ratification of the U.S. Constitution. Their proposals called for limiting the representation of slaveholders, new immigrants, and backcountry farmers, all of whom tended to support Democratic-Republicans. In a piece of bad timing, they published their proposals just as the country was celebrating the end of the war. What the Federalists called dissent was attacked as treason, severely wounding the party. U.S. political culture was soon reduced to a single party, the Democratic-Republicans. In 1816, the third Virginia Democratic-Republican president in a row, James Monroe, was elected president.

In Europe, diplomats attempted to settle one hundred years of international warfare and remake the balance of power at the 1814–1815 **Congress of Vienna**. Once again, they drew lines on world maps and restored the rule of royalty. In France, the younger brother of the executed king was crowned monarch; he, like restored monarchs in Spain and Portugal, now ruled a constitutional monarchy. The defeat of Napoleon's France was interpreted as a defeat of French revolutionary ideas more broadly on the continent. One anti-French insurgent song stated, "Here's an end to equality. Here's an end to liberty. Long live God and his Majesty."

8-5d Independence in Spanish America

The heavy toll of European war ultimately brought Spain's colonies into a third wave of revolutions (see Map 8.4). In 1808, the royal government in Madrid collapsed, and Napoleon placed his own brother on the throne. With the metropolitan center in turmoil, conspiracies and coups proliferated in Spanish America as American-born elites tried to take back powers eroded by the Bourbon Reforms. In 1809, the Spanish government accommodated them and declared that its American dominions were not just "colonies," but "an essential and integral part" of the kingdom, deserving of representation in the Spanish legislative body. Spain, unlike Britain in the 1770s, was willing to allow elected representation for its American entities, but it was not willing to grant equal representation. Spanish America, with a population between 15 and 16 million, was allotted nine representatives; metropolitan Spain, with 10 million people, had thirty-six. Disputes over representation and the difficulties of balancing central authority with local autonomy and popular sovereignty plagued Spanish America as it had the new United States in the 1780s.

Spanish America enters an age of revolution while the United States strengthens national bonds.

Battle of New Orleans Final military engagement of the War of 1812 that was a significant U.S. victory after the signing of the peace treaty.

Treaty of Ghent Peace treaty ending the War of 1812 that returned territorial claims to prewar status for the United States and Britain and promised the same for Indians.

Hartford Convention Meetings in the winter of 1814–1815 by New England Federalists who opposed the War of 1812 and proposed new amendments to the Constitution.

Congress of Vienna Peace convention ending the Napoleonic Wars and restoring monarchies, some with constitutions. It re-established a balance of power.

Map 8.4 American Hemisphere in the Age of Revolution A wave of independence movements ended most of Spain's imperial claims to the Americas. Negotiations with the United States redrew boundaries that took on new meaning in the wake of Mexican independence. In spite of these changes, Spanish language, culture, and religion remained widespread. ▲

Transcontinental Treaty (Adams-Onis Treaty)
Agreement between the United States and Spain acknowledging Spanish control of Texas and granting Florida and Oregon to the United States.

nationalism Identification with and feeling of loyalty to a nation, often as opposed to another group interest, such as religion.

An attempt at compromise, a new Spanish constitution of 1812 proclaimed a unified "nation" spanning the Eastern and Western Hemispheres. It granted the vote to most free adult males while taking it away from women who headed households. At the same time, the constitution formally excluded anyone with African ancestry from full rights as Spaniards and sustained legal slavery. A new, freer press spread word of the more liberal constitution. But word spread quickly, as well, when King Ferdinand VII was restored to the throne in 1814, abolished the constitution, and attempted to turn back the clock.

Revolutionaries who had spent time in the United States and Europe were already drawing on universal ideals and local cultures to lead independence movements in Spanish America. A movement in Mexico, begun in 1810, continued for a decade before ending in a new nation whose borders stretched from the Yucatan up to the Canadian border and from the Pacific to the edge of the Louisiana Territory. Simón Bolívar, leader of an independence movement in Venezuela, praised the United States as a model nation "maintained by liberty alone" in 1819. Revolutions in Latin America and South America followed, and by 1830, Cuba and Puerto Rico were all that was left of Spain's once vast Western Hemisphere empire. Many of the newly independent nations declared themselves republics but spent years in conflict over the details of how to allocate power within their multiracial communities.

The United States was slow to recognize these fellow republics and did not give official assistance to revolutionaries. It did take advantage of Spain's imperial turmoil to consolidate its own territorial claims. In 1819, the two countries signed the **Transcontinental Treaty (Adams-Onis Treaty)**, which established borders between territory claimed by Spain and territory claimed by the United States, most of it inhabited and controlled by Indians. The U.S. claimed Florida; Spain claimed land from Texas to the Pacific and down through Mexico.

In 1819, John Quincy Adams, who negotiated both the Treaty of Ghent and the Transcontinental Treaty, wrote in his diary that the "United States and North America are identical." Although far from true, his

Simón Bolívar in Caracas The South American "Liberator" initially appealed to American politicians, who toasted him as "the George Washington of the South." The relationship later soured over political and economic power. Bolívar said of Latin American people, "We are a microcosm of the Human Race, a world apart, neither Indian nor European, but a part of each." ▲

statement reflected the kind of optimistic, expansionist **nationalism** that spread in the United States after the War of 1812. This new type of patriotic loyalty and identification rested on images that had been developing since before the Revolution. The Stars and Stripes, approved by the Continental Congress in 1777 as the flag of the United States, became a prominent symbol of the nation. One flag, which had flown over Fort McHenry during its attack by British forces in 1814 inspired Francis Scott Key's poem and song "The Star-Spangled Banner." The Flag Act of 1818 formally linked the familiar symbol with the nation's expansion. Under its provisions, each time a new state joined the United States, the official flag was to gain another star. There were stars for Louisiana (a state since 1812), Indiana (1816), Mississippi (1817), Illinois (1818), and soon Alabama in 1819 as borderlands became cotton frontier states where free white men held political power through their citizenship and votes.

Summary

The War of 1812 was in one sense a second war for independence of the United States. It was part of the final confrontation of a century of warfare between Britain and its allies on one side and France and its allies on the other. Although the war itself did not change British policies toward the United States or the border with Canada, its conclusion established that the fate of the U.S. republic diverged from those of other revolutionary republics, including France, Haiti, and the new nations in Latin America. After twenty years of turmoil, the United States had not collapsed from external pressure or turned to self-proclaimed emperors to restore political order. Its political system had endured the wrenching divisions of partisan politics and dissent without dissolving into anarchy or giving way to a dictator.

Many of the American revolutionary experiments in governance and economy survived the test of the Age of Revolution, and a new form of participatory citizenship was taking hold.

There were ironies in the emerging continental empire that had come into focus by 1819. The War of 1812 solidified U.S. conquest of Indian land to the Mississippi River and beyond. With the vast territory of the Louisiana Purchase, Jefferson's vision of a continental empire seemed closer to reality. The United States had used familiar tools of empire: war, diplomatic negotiation, purchase, and national economic policy. Although the United States had joined Britain in abolishing the international slave trade in 1808, it relied heavily on a thriving interstate trade that expanded slavery to economically and politically support the nation that Jefferson had branded the empire of liberty. Finally, the egalitarian concept of citizen had replaced the old hierarchies of political subjects to a monarch, but the evolving meaning of citizenship on the ground remained contested.

<Thinking Back, *Looking Forward*>

As you review this chapter, critically evaluate Jefferson's idea that an "empire of liberty" could exist. Think about the laws, trading relationships, and military agents of empires in the colonial period. When did they restrict liberty, and when did they promote it? How did the United States in the early nineteenth century differ from the empires that had come before it?

Consider the new United States in its global context: Which political and economic relationships survived the Age of Revolution and the subsequent restoration of European monarchies, and which were transformed?

In the coming chapters, evaluate the consequences of the Age of Revolution for different groups.

How did the rights and obligations of citizenship change over the nineteenth century?

To make your study concrete, review the timeline and reflect on the entries there. Think about their causes, consequences, and connections. How do they fit with global trends?

Additional Resources

Books

Dowd, Gregory. *A Spirited Resistance: The North American Indian Struggle for Unity, 1745–1815.* Baltimore, MD: Johns Hopkins University Press, 1993.
▶ Decades-spanning exploration of eastern Indian alliances.

Egerton, Douglas R. *Gabriel's Rebellion: The Virginia Slave Conspiracies of 1800 & 1802.* Chapel Hill: University of North Carolina Press, 1993. ▶ Exploration of the political and social context of slave revolt.

Freeman, Joanne. *Affairs of Honor: National Politics in the New Republic.* New Haven, CT: Yale University Press, 2002. ▶ Lively depiction of the uses and abuses of honor in national politics.

Klooster, Wim. *Revolutions in the Atlantic World: A Comparative History.* New York: New York University Press, 2009. ▶ Engaging comparisons of the motivations and trajectories of Atlantic revolutions.

Taylor, Alan. *The Civil War of 1812: American Citizens, British Subjects, Irish Rebels and Indian Allies.* New York: Vintage, 2011. ▶ Portrayal of the northern front of the War of 1812.

Zagarri, Rosemarie. *Revolutionary Backlash: Women and Politics in the Early American Republic.* Philadelphia: University of Pennsylvania Press, 2007.
▶ Study of the mixed political legacy of the Revolution for American women.

Go to the MindTap® for **Global Americans** to access the full version of select books from this Additional Resources section.

Websites

European Explorations and the Louisiana Purchase. (http://www.loc.gov/collections/louisiana-european-explorations-and-the-louisiana-purchase/) ▶ Library of Congress collection of maps and other sources about Louisiana.

War of 1812. (http://www.nps.gov/subjects/warof1812/index.htm) ▶ National Park Service site providing maps, primary sources, and personal stories.

MindTap®

Continue exploring online through MindTap®, where you can:
• **Assess your knowledge with the Chapter Test**
• **Watch historical videos related to the chapter**
• **Further your understanding with interactive maps and timelines**

Inventing Republics in the Age of Revolutions

1789–1790

February 1789
George Washington is elected the first U.S. president.

July 1789
Parisians storm the Bastille, beginning the French Revolution.

March 1790
First U.S. Naturalization Law offers a pathway to free white immigrants to become citizens.

May 1790
Southwest Ordinance establishes plan for territory south of the Ohio River to become states.

August 1790
First U.S. census counts a population of 3.9 million people, free and enslaved.

1791–1793

August 1791
A slave revolt on Saint-Domingue launches the Haitian Revolution.

1791
Tens of thousands of refugees begin to flee Saint-Domingue for the United States, Cuba, and French Louisiana.

February 1793
Washington is reelected president.

Fugitive Slave Law commits federal government to help slave owners recover runaways.

1794

March 1794
Eli Whitney patents a cotton gin, making the hand processing of cotton fiber faster and easier than without it.

August 1794
Battle of Fallen Timbers ends in Indian defeat but begins more moderate relations with the United States.

September–November 1794
Hamilton, Washington, and federalized militia troops put down the Whiskey Rebellion tax revolts in Pennsylvania.

1795–1799

October 1795
Treaty of San Lorenzo between the United States and Spain opens the Mississippi to trade.

February 1797
Congress certifies that Adams, Washington's vice president, is elected president.

June–July 1798
Congress passes the Alien and Sedition Acts, targeting a press critical of the Adams administration.

1798–1800
France and the United States engage in an undeclared war over neutral trading rights.

1800–1802

February 1800
Jefferson is elected president in the House of Representatives, transferring executive power from one political party to another.

September 1800
Skilled slave Gabriel plans a large-scale revolt in Virginia that is uncovered and brutally put down.

1801
Barbary States begin to wage war on the United States over demands to pay tribute for captured merchant ships on the Mediterranean.

Western Alliance
United States
Creeks
Spanish America
Britain
France
Spain
Barbary States
Europe
Haiti
China
Peru

1803

February 1803

Supreme Court case *Marbury v. Madison* establishes the principle of judicial review and the independent judiciary.

October 1803

Louisiana Purchase from France adds 530 million acres of territory to the United States.

1804–1806

November 1804

Jefferson is reelected president.

January 1804

New republic of Haiti declared, ending the revolution on Saint-Domingue.

December 1804

Napoleon crowns himself emperor of France in the midst of war with European powers.

1804–1806

Lewis and Clark expedition crosses the Louisiana Territory to the Pacific Ocean and returns.

1805

Shawnee Tenskwatawa begins preaching a message of unity for Eastern Indians to shun American culture.

1807–1809

February 1807

New Jersey disfranchises unmarried women and free black men who had previously voted legally.

1807–1809

Embargo Act cuts off foreign exports, plunging the United States into an economic downturn.

1808

Leonora Sansay publishes *Secret History; or the Horrors of St. Domingo.*

January 1808

U.S. law banning the import of enslaved Africans from overseas goes into effect.

February 1809

Congress certifies that Madison, major author of the U.S. Constitution, is elected president.

1810–1815

1810

Independence movement breaks out in Mexico against imperial Spain.

November 1811

Harrison defeats Tecumseh's forces at the Battle of Tippecanoe, weakening the Indian alliance.

1812–1814

War of 1812 pits the United States against Britain and its Indian allies.

February 1813

Congress reports that Madison is reelected president.

August 1814

Treaty of Fort Jackson claims two-thirds of Creek territory for the United States.

1814–1815

Congress of Vienna ends Napoleonic Wars and restores monarchies in Europe.

December 1814–January 1815

Jackson turns Battle of New Orleans into a major victory for the United States over Britain.

1816–1819

November 1818

Monroe is elected president.

February 1819

Transcontinental Treaty establishes a new border between the United States and Spanish America, granting Florida to the United States.

Go to MindTap® to engage with an interactive version of the timeline. Analyze events and themes with clickable content, view related videos, and respond to critical thinking questions.

9

Markets and Democracy

1790–1840

C&O agents recruited men in Ireland to work on the Chesapeake and Ohio Canal, where they earned 50 cents per day, plus whiskey, for each day they worked.

In their shanty on the bank of the Potomac River in 1834, Irish immigrants Patrick and Mary Ryan bet their futures on a construction project. Patrick was a contractor hired to build a section of the Chesapeake and Ohio Canal. Funded by private investments and generous state loans, the canal joined two great waterways of North American trade—the Atlantic Ocean and the Mississippi River—to transport crops to market cheaper and faster. Patrick had to advance the capital to complete his section of the canal, so while they waited for his speculative venture to yield profits, Mary, Patrick's wife, ran a boardinghouse for the laborers, cooking, washing, and bringing in vital additional income.

The Granger Collection, New York

Barges at the Entrance to the Erie Canal, 1825 ▲

Canal work was physical and grueling. Men spent twelve to fifteen hours each day blasting through rock with gunpowder, clearing the rubble using horses and handcarts, digging deep into the dirt, and draining the passes through which barges and later steamships could travel. In return, they made fifty cents per day plus whiskey, but only for the days they worked. It was a bargain that could appeal only to men with few options, such as the men recruited in Ireland by C&O agents and transported to the Ryans' camp.

On the evening of November 8, 1834, long-simmering tensions in the camp exploded into violence. As the men gathered with their boss, drinking and gambling, John Brady, too ill at the time for canal work, got up from the table and stumbled into Mary's kitchen, where he had been helping with the cooking to pay his room and board. An argument broke out, and Brady hit his landlady, who brandished a candlestick in retaliation, shouting that she would "hammer the life out of him." Patrick ran into the kitchen. Brady, battered and bloody, staggered out into the cold alleys of the workers' camp. After Brady died the next morning, Mary and Patrick Ryan were charged with murder.

Testimony at the trial suggested that the community held Brady's life cheaply. One witness commented that "such disturbances are common in the shantees." The Ryans themselves, dismissing Brady as a despised "County Clare man," attributed the conflict to ethnic tensions brought from Ireland. The jury, considering Patrick "an excellent contractor," acquitted the Ryans. But the struggles of poor immigrant laborers were increasingly hard to ignore. Canal workers on the C & O led at least ten strikes protesting working conditions and pay. Federal troops intervened repeatedly to put down labor unrest.

Relationships between workers and employers underwent dramatic changes in the first half of the nineteenth century. American sons and daughters left their farms, and immigrants fled their homelands for work in U.S. factories where new machines set the pace of a workday measured by the clock, not the task. Canals such as the C&O, as well as turnpikes, steamboats, and railroads, moved people, products, and information faster, making goods widely available through an internal

How did the treatment of the workers who were recruited from Ireland to build the Chesapeake and Ohio Canal reflect the United States's early-nineteenth-century political and labor landscape?

Go to MindTap® to watch a video on the workers and learn how their experiences relate to the themes of this chapter.

trade. Americans' daily lives were shaped by economic forces they could not control and struggled to comprehend. New ways of organizing the production of goods devalued craft skills, altered household production, and challenged ideas about who should lead and who should follow.

Transformations in the United States were linked to global markets and industrialization. Industrial innovation, advances in transportation, and complex financial instruments created an integrated global marketplace that turned raw materials grown in one region into finished goods produced in another. Around the world, powerful empires, including the British in China, the Spanish in South America, and the Russians on the Pacific Northwest coast, competed economically with the United States, revealing the new nation's political and financial vulnerability. Global events—demand for cotton, displacement by landlords, regional famines, and political revolutions—set in motion two streams of migrating laborers: enslaved African Americans across the South and free European immigrants to the United States. The government forcibly relocated a third migrant group—Eastern Native Americans—to use their land to supply the global cotton boom.

The new market landscape raised cultural and political questions about competition. Some Americans placed their faith in its creative power, insisting that lively competition—of businesses, goods, ideas, and individuals—produced the best society. Others thought that fair competition must include protections to shelter minority viewpoints, promote valuable regional interests, and incubate emerging industries. A new national political system arose in response to this debate but excluded most individuals from formal participation because of their sex, race, or immigrant status. They expressed political will though labor organization, petitions, and protest.

9-1

Industry and Labor

This two-dollar bank note from the Sanford Bank in Maine (1861) depicts three women making textiles: the one on the left is spinning thread; those in the center are operating power looms. Artwork on bank notes was designed to foil counterfeiters but also became a cultural vehicle. Engravers produced dies with pastoral scenes or historical vignettes, and printers could select a combination of images to make an appealing or inspiring note.

The Granger Collection, New York

Why does this bank note contain multiple images of women at work? What does it suggest about the place of women in the nineteenth-century economy? ▶

Go to MindTap® to practice history with the Chapter 9 **Primary Source Writing Activity: Labor and the Global Marketplace.** Read and view primary sources and respond to a writing prompt.

In the first half of the nineteenth century, new technologies used water, steam, and human muscle power to increase the speed and profitability of U.S. manufacturing. A global flow of free workers poured into cities, where they toiled for wages in sugar refineries, distilleries, breweries, and in new factories that produced cotton cloth. New production processes reinforced dependent relationships between workers and their supervisors as the economic system increasingly treated workers as interchangeable commodities to be hired at the lowest wages possible and fired in hard times. Industrial development commandeered the labor of Indians on the Pacific coast and slaves in the South who produced the raw materials that became manufactured goods.

☞ As you read, think about how technology transformed labor patterns and the meaning of work in the United States. How did businessmen respond? How did workers respond?

9-1a Growth of Manufacturing Systems

The **Industrial Revolution**, which transformed the production and distribution of goods worldwide, was built on the trade networks, political power, and wealth that European empires had developed through centuries of colonialism. In Britain, money from colonial trade allowed entrepreneurs to experiment with water-powered spinning machines and mechanized looms that could produce cotton textiles to compete in global markets with cloth made in India. Cotton textile production led the way to more innovations, including steam- and coal-powered machinery and centralized factories where workers used complex machines to mass-produce finished goods of uniform quality.

> European technology and new labor arrangements change the scale of production.

What began in Britain spread across Europe and North America. In 1789, English farm boy-turned-factory-worker Samuel Slater arrived in the United States armed with a good memory and a plan for adapting British technology to American social conditions. Flouting the British law that forbade workers in its renowned factories from sharing industrial secrets, Slater built his own mill in Pawtucket, Rhode Island. That mill, powered by a wheel turned by falling water, carded and spun cotton into thread. He employed entire households, advertising for "men with growing families" and constructing apartment buildings to house them and company stores to take their credit. Fathers managed the work of their dependents, just as they did on farms.

Once the thread was spun, Slater's mill "put out" the product to local farm families to finish. This **putting-out system** enabled manufacturers to tap into local labor markets and pay only for work completed; there was no responsibility to house or feed workers. Children and unmarried women wove thread into cloth and in some cases, sewed fabric into clothing. Returning the finished goods earned the family store credit to purchase tools and imported goods, including finer printed cloth. Manufacturers could not, however, control quality or flow of product and profit.

The Embargo of 1808 and the trade disruptions of the War of 1812 shut consumers off from English imports and opened the door for local entrepreneurs like Slater. Francis Cabot Lowell, who spent two years touring the mills of Manchester, England, returned to the United States to cofound the Boston Manufacturing Company in 1813. After building early mills in Waltham, near Boston, the company expanded in 1821 with a fully integrated cotton manufactory at Lowell, Massachusetts. The **Waltham-Lowell System** brought all of the processes of fabric production (carding, spinning, weaving, and fulling) under one management. Company salesmen promoted its cloth to urban merchants and dealers, who in turn distributed it to markets across the United States and around the world (see Map 9.1). Some cloth was shipped as far as China, where it rivaled cloth made in India by the British East India Company.

Unlike the earlier Slater-style mills, Lowell mills employed single women. The mills recruited from the same group of young farm women who had performed putting-out work for decades; in some ways, the new system reassured people anxious that industrialization destroyed families by dismantling household economic unity. In other ways, the Waltham-Lowell system marked a sharp break with the past. The "mill girls," as they called themselves, worked long hours set by the clock and enforced by a system of bells. Workers were supervised during the day by men who were not family members and at night by landladies who ran the company-approved boarding houses where they were required to live. The women could choose how to spend their wages of $12 to $14 each month—on imported fabrics, novels, or lessons. They sent some money home to help relatives. In the evenings, they organized prayer groups and published a literary

Canned Food to Feed an Army During the Napoleonic wars, Frenchman Nicolas Appert discovered a method for preserving food by cooking it in a sealed jar. British inventors improved on the technology with mass-produced tins filled with food for long military campaigns like this tin of roast veal prepared by the British firm of Donkin, Hall, and Gamble in 1823. The Industrial Revolution linked technology, mass production, and military power. ▲ Science & Society Picture Library/Getty Images

Industrial Revolution Eighteenth- and nineteenth-century transformation of economies and societies as the result of new machinery, energy sources, and labor organization.

putting-out system Early manufacturing method of distributing raw or partially processed materials to people who completed them at home using their own tools.

Waltham-Lowell System Fully integrated textile manufactory system originating in Massachusetts that centralized production and distribution and housed workers in company-managed boardinghouses.

Map 9.1 Global Webs of Cotton For thousands of years, people picked, spun, and wove cotton and wore cotton clothing in warm regions of the Americas, Africa, and Asia. From local roots, this labor-intensive product became an important trade good. In China and India, manufacturers drew on nearby sources, but European and U.S. manufacturers used imperial conquest and transatlantic financing to acquire raw materials from one region and turn them to profit in another, aided by new technologies of water and steam power. ▲

surplus labor Working members of a family whose labor was not needed on the farm for household subsistence. Some found wage work that contributed to family security or comfort.

magazine, called the *Lowell Offering*. As the Waltham-Lowell System spread to other New England towns, so did paid female employment. By the 1830s, women made up 30 percent of workers in manufacturing and 80 percent of textile workers.

9-1b Spread of Wage Labor

The women employed in the Lowell Mills were part of a larger movement of migrants pushed out of farms along the East Coast and the villages of Europe and pulled into the developing cities and industries of the United States. As American farms became more productive, families faced a new phenomenon of **surplus labor**—young men and women who were not needed to work year-round on farms. Alternatives

> Migrants and immigrants create a dynamic supply of waged workers, changing manufacturing systems.

in manufacturing, land speculation, and urban service work drew men and women from country to city and from east to west. In the 1810s, the U.S. population in the Great Lakes region and the southern Mississippi Valley region tripled.

These same opportunities appealed to men and women thousands of miles away. Hundreds of thousands of British, Irish, and German migrants arrived in the United States in the first four decades of the nineteenth century. English textile workers brought expertise in weaving to New England's mills. Coal miners from Scotland and Wales moved to Pennsylvania where their knowledge earned them far higher wages than they had at home. Poor German immigrants labored in cities and along the canals of the expanding transportation systems of the United States while wealthier German families established trades or became Midwestern farmers. Some later became land speculators in central Texas.

The greatest proportion of immigrants came from Catholic Ireland. Largely single women and men, they were seeking relief from poverty and English repression. A few

Henry H. and Zoe Oliver Sherman Fund

Global Americans When he commissioned his portrait in 1825, wealthy Philadelphian **Patrick Lyon** insisted that he be depicted as the working blacksmith he had been at the beginning of his career. Lyon was born in 1779 in London and trained in Scotland to become a master blacksmith. Migrating to Philadelphia in 1793 to establish his own business, Lyon suffered the tragedies of early urban living when his wife and child died in a yellow fever epidemic. In 1798, he was hired to forge the locks for the vault of the Bank of Philadelphia. When the vault was breached and more than $160,000 stolen, Lyon was jailed for three months in spite of his strong alibi. After the real criminal confessed, Lyon was finally released and sued the bank directors for false imprisonment and loss of reputation. He was awarded a large settlement, equal to several years' wages, but until his death in 1829, he was resentful of the moneymen who had imprisoned an honest artisan. His portrait, depicting the nobility of work, was a response to the internationally connected bankers who had orchestrated his imprisonment and the industrialization that was undermining his craft specialization. Having immigrated for economic opportunity, he became a symbol of American egalitarianism. The judge at his trial proclaimed that "in our country . . . neither wealth nor office create an unequal standing."

with money speculated on western land, but most men worked in mills, on wharves, or they supplied the labor to build canals and roads. Irish women labored as laundresses and maids and hoped for employment in the mills. Their presence in urban enclaves and along transportation routes peaked between 1846 and 1851 when a potato blight and famine Ireland called the "Great Hunger" drove more than a million Irish to cross the ocean in desperation.

Artisan trades were transformed by the spread of cheap, flexible waged labor. In a traditional artisan's workshop, a master who was both a skilled worker and a business owner signed long-term contracts with two groups: young apprentices, who worked in return for training and board, and fully trained journeymen, who were saving money until they could open their own workshops. Living and working together in the same business, these men and women developed a sense of occupational identity that was nourished by the fact that workers could not be fired for sickness or business downturns. In contrast, immigrants, runaway servants, and teenagers on the move could be hired for a wage and fired with no lasting obligations to train and support them, making them an appealing alternative to nineteenth-century business owners.

If they were not going to invest in training workers in all aspects of a craft, business owners had to simplify the work. Artisan masters increasingly subdivided projects into smaller tasks that could be successfully completed by an untrained labor force, implementing a **division of labor** in the manufacturing process that was efficient but monotonous for workers. Merchants who wanted to compete with established workshops bypassed the old system completely, hiring a mixture of skilled and unskilled laborers to produce goods.

Standardization helped unlock the profitable potential of divided labor. In 1790, French gunsmith Honoré Blanc

called politicians, intellectuals, and military officers to Paris to demonstrate how his workshop produced muskets made of **interchangeable parts**. Taking pieces of gunlock from a line of bins, he constructed a working whole. His system, developed in the workshops of Swedish watchmakers and from sketches of French military engineers, depended on precision tools and gauges as well as uniform measurements. In the United States, Eli Whitney sought to copy Blanc's success directly but struggled with musket production. Yet the idea of standardization soon permeated the manufacture of products such as clothing. While an eighteenth-century gentleman paid a master tailor for a custom-crafted suit, a businessman in the nineteenth century bought a ready-made suit. A skilled cutter used a standardized pattern to create the fabric pieces, which he then sent to a woman to sew together in her home. Because each garment earned her only a few cents, she took on as much piecework as possible to scrape out a living.

9-1c Workers and Labor Organization

The expansion of a market economy, in which prices of goods and labor fluctuated rather than adhered to custom or law, had profound social and political implications. For native-born women in the textile mills, earning money of one's own meant freedom from the

> Industrialization challenges the meaning of work and independence.

division of labor Production process in which different workers specialize in different parts of a larger task.

interchangeable parts Nearly identical components made from standardized instructions, allowing them to be exchanged for one another when assembled.

family-based credit that dominated the countryside. But for native-born white men, working for a wage seemed a threat, not a boon, to autonomy. Journeymen found their upward mobility severely limited by masters' efforts to pay the least and profit the most from their work. By 1815, half of the journeymen in New York were over thirty years old, typically married with several children and yet unable to afford a shop or home of their own. Since the eighteenth century, land ownership had served as the basis for independent male adulthood and civic participation. Artisans argued that their ownership of tools and craft knowledge offered them similar independence. But waged workers depended on others for basic subsistence, a status that meant they did not fit the model of republican citizenship.

Organizing to resist the changes that stripped them of their independence, journeymen wanted to maintain set fees for completing finished products and used a combination of joint demands and limited strikes, called **turn outs**, to press their case with employers. Initially, U.S. judges, relying on common law, deemed such labor actions to be illegal conspiracies, but later they began to accept limited worker's rights, opening the door to increased labor organization. In 1833, New York house carpenters, leather-dressers, cabinetmakers, and type foundry workers, among others, formed the **General Trades Union** to organize strikes and push for higher wages.

The crowded conditions in mills and factory boardinghouses also fostered collective action. In 1834, female workers at the Lowell Mills turned out for several days and paraded in the streets of Lowell to protest a wage cut—unsuccessfully. When the company in 1836 proposed to raise rents in the boardinghouses, resulting effectively in another pay cut, between fifteen hundred and two thousand women walked off the job for several months. Faced with the loss of one quarter of the work force, the company conceded and kept rents low.

Working men and women justified labor action by talking about their families. Sarah Bagley, an organizer in Lowell, explained to a skeptical public, "The whip which brings us to Lowell is NECESSITY. We must have money; a father's debts are to be paid, an aged mother is to be supported, a brother's ambition to be aided, and so the factories are supplied." Men in trade unions typically paired demands for fair wages with an insistence on their rights as householders. Like their counterparts in Europe, many agitated for a **family wage** that would supposedly allow a man to earn enough that his wife and children would not have to look for paid employment. Acutely aware of the oppressive conditions of factory workers in England, organizing workers in Philadelphia insisted that while in Europe, "slavery, labor [and] degredation" had descended since medieval times, the American "community of freemen" should award dignity to labor. Although they cast themselves as breadwinners to employers, such men depended on their wives and children to scrimp, save, salvage, and barter to make ends meet.

Expanding commercial businesses demanded a robust service industry to keep the books, sell the goods, and house and feed the workers who had left their homes. Clerks and boardinghouse keepers, two rapidly expanding ranks of service workers, embodied the challenges to ideas about independent work and household unity. Nineteenth-century clerks ran errands, moved goods, served customers, and spent days making deliveries. By the middle of the nineteenth century, New York City had fourteen thousand clerks, just over 40 percent of whom had immigrated from western Europe. Clerking appeared to be an opportunity to European immigrants and farm boys, but in their daily lives, clerks got no respect. Some critics complained that service work was too soft for a man; others scorned the physical tasks that clerks did as meaningless unskilled labor. Women expanded the service economy by taking in borders; by one estimate, 30 percent of all nineteenth-century households housed and fed nonrelatives for money. Companies such as the Lowell mills hired women to run boardinghouses that enforced church attendance, curfews, and limited mixed-sex socialization. Mary Ryan on the C & O Canal worked as part of a husband-wife team that had looser standards. All boardinghouses were suspect for selling the services that Americans expected female relatives to provide for free. Even if the food was tasty, it was tainted because the landlady had to be paid to make it. One critic claimed, "In the cold heartless atmosphere" of the boardinghouse "interest takes the management instead of affection."

9-1d The Pacific Coast in the Global Marketplace

Eastern industries needed more than a boardinghouse full of workers to keep profits flowing; they needed the labor of workers thousands of miles away. Slaves on the Gulf Coast picked cotton that was spun in New England mills. Mid-Atlantic miners dug coal to fuel steam engines.

> Eastern manufacturing demands transform Pacific workplaces.

A vast network of European, Indian, and multiracial laborers turned the plants and animals of the Pacific into usable raw materials to keep the new machines running. In California, the emerging independence movement disrupted annual Spanish supply ships that had brought finished goods to California's missions, pueblos, and presidios. Into the breach came European, South American, and Euro-American traders who plied the coast. Missionaries reoriented production in the missions in response to what these foreign traders wanted, directing Indians to raise and slaughter tens of thousands of cattle annually for

turn out Collective labor action, also called *strike*, in which workers leave the workplace for days or weeks to protest working conditions by revealing company dependence on them.

General Trades Union Umbrella organization of multiple separate trade unions created in 1834 New York City to coordinate labor protests across the economy and with other cities.

family wage Earnings that were theoretically sufficient to allow a man to support a wife and children who did not work for wages but were never a reality.

their hides and fat. Stripped of their hides, cattle carcasses littered California's countryside, leading to an explosion in the population of grizzly bears and other predators. Once Mexican independence officially opened California ports to global commerce (see Chapter 11), New England merchant houses sought to dominate the hide-and-tallow trade. Packaged on ships that sailed around the Cape of South America to the eastern United States, California hides became leather for shoes and machine belts. Tallow, crafted into soap and candles, brightened homes and workplaces not only along the East Coast of the United States but also in Peru, where silver miners deep underground depended on the light from tallow candles.

Factories that needed leather belts to run their machinery also required oil to keep gears turning, and the favored source of that oil was the fat of whales swimming in the waters of the Pacific Ocean. The eighteenth-century U.S. whaling industry had concentrated on short-term voyages from Massachusetts's Nantucket Island. After the War of 1812, American whalers turned in earnest to the vast number of whales in the Pacific for bones, blubber, and spermaceti, the oily liquid filling the head cavity of sperm whales that made superior, clean-burning candles. Deep-sea voyages took sailors from their homes for years as they worked on international crews.

Work on a deep-sea whaling ship followed a grueling schedule that some thought resembled factory work. Because they were away from port for such long periods of time, whaling vessels had to process and store the products of their hunt while at sea. Risking injury from sharp knives, heavy kettles, and boiling oil, sailors earned wages similar to those of factory workers, but the idea of a family wage meant little. While officers' wives back home received some company wages, the families of common sailors had to find other paying work during their long absences.

9-1e Expansion of Slavery

The Waltham-Lowell system produced a coarse grade of cotton fabric used to clothe the enslaved people who had picked the fibers to begin with. In the early nineteenth century, a thriving **interstate slave trade** transported people from the farms of the Chesapeake, where depleted soil made slave labor less valuable, to the cotton plantations of the Deep South and the West (see Map 9.2). As British and then New England mills demanded increasing inputs of raw cotton, the profitability of the global cotton trade drove up the prices people were willing to pay for human beings to grow, pick, and process the cotton.

The interstate slave trade began as individual speculative ventures. A trader traveled from plantation to plantation in the upper South, purchasing groups of about ten people whom he chained together in **coffles** and marched south, selling them as they walked. A slave purchased for $300 in Maryland could sell for $600 in Georgia. Soon, slave-trading firms centered in cities such as Baltimore and Alexandria took over the business from individual entrepreneurs. Crowding people into "pens" in urban centers, including the capital, Washington, D.C., slave traders shipped human beings by steamship, canal, and improved roads to auctions in New Orleans and Natchez. Between 1800 and 1840, the state of Virginia exported more than 300,000 enslaved people; Mississippi alone gained more than 130,000. One-third of slaves in this migration moved with owners as part of a familiar group; two-thirds were separated from family and sold in distant marketplaces.

Slaves caught up in forced separation experienced firsthand what it meant to be both a person and a commodity. Owners told them, "[I'll] put you in my pocket," vowing to sell a boy for a pocketful of bills to be used to purchase new goods, slaves, or land. Jacques, one slave boy in Louisiana, was mortgaged three times and sold twice between his eighth and twelfth birthdays. Slaves did anything they

interstate slave trade Forced migration of hundreds of thousands of slaves from the coastal Atlantic states to the cotton-growing Gulf states in the first half of the nineteenth century.

coffles From the Arabic word *cafila*, a chained caravan designed to prevent humans or animals from escaping.

{ Legal and illegal slave trade accelerates the movement of labor.

The Business of Whaling The log of the Nantucket-based *Washington* records capturing, killing, and processing whales. Each day, Captain Coffin noted the ship's location and drew blood-spouting whales to tally the daily kill. After chasing and killing their quarry, sailors sliced blubber from the animal's side and hoisted strips up to the deck for boiling. One observer commented that the work "somewhat resembled the unwinding of a lot of tape from a long bobbin." ▼

Courtesy of the Nantucket Historical Association

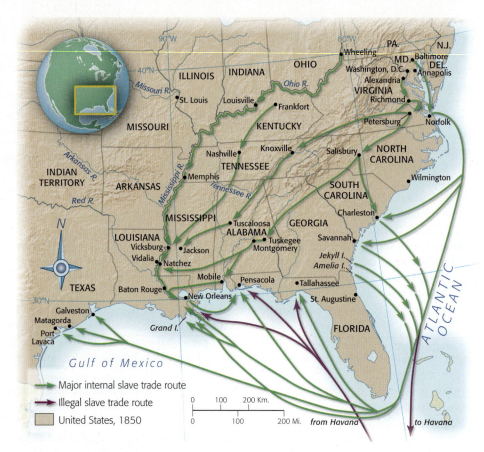

Map 9.2 The Interstate Slave Trade More than 875,000 enslaved people were dragged to the Lower South between 1820 and 1860. In addition to being a forced migration, the trade generated millions in profits for the sellers and transporters as well as income for the lawyers, doctors, blacksmiths, clothing providers, provisioners, and insurers who made the trade possible. An illegal slave trade centered on Spanish Cuba intersected with the legal slave trade across the Gulf of Mexico. ▲

Sale of Human Beings This 1812 advertising flyer categorized people as if they were exchangeable parts rather than individuals, highlighting their sex and relative age or their work experience. The advertisement did not note the names, individual preferences, or unique relationships of the people who were treated as a mobile source of cash for owners. ▶

could to hold on to some part of their lives. Mothers bargained with owners to stay with their children; husbands threatened to run away if they were not sold to a plantation where a beloved wife lived.

Although the United States had outlawed the importation of Africans in 1808, demand for slave labor boosted a thriving illegal Atlantic trade into the mid-nineteenth century, bringing Africans into Texas, Louisiana, and Florida from Spanish Cuba. U.S. shipbuilders constructed new vessels to transport captive African men and women across the Gulf of Mexico. Traders in the illegal business depended on smugglers or bribable U.S. customs agents in New Orleans and elsewhere to classify their cargo as products of the legal interstate trade, not the illegal international trade. In the slave pens of New Orleans, legally and illegally enslaved people suffered together in the interest of global profits.

Library of Virginia

9-2
Time, Space, and Money

Process of Excavation, Lockport, George Catlin (1826). This image depicts the work of Irish laborers digging a channel for the Erie Canal at Lockport, New York, where a system of locks on the canal raised the level of the water.

What does the scale of this image—the canal, the workers, and the wooden cranes—suggest about the relationship of workers to their work in an expanding industrial and commercial economy? ▶

New York Public Library

U.S. commerce depended on a political system that encouraged businessmen and investors. Federal and state governments organized and sold public land, subsidized transportation, and passed protective laws making American-produced goods cheaper than imports. Nationally minded congressmen advocated a future United States that combined commercial agriculture with manufacturing in order to make the country more independent. However, connections among markets for labor, credit, and goods meant that individuals were already dependent on global economic forces that they could not control or fully comprehend.

☞ As you read, consider the various ways that Americans promoted and paid for national economic development. Who benefited from this intersection of politics and the economy?

9-2a Transportation Revolution

A spreading web of turnpikes, canals, steamship lines, stage-coach routes, and railroads covered the United States in the first half of the nineteenth century (see Map 9.3). Backers called these projects **internal improvements** to stress that improved transportation strengthened the national economy. These large-scale, risky undertakings depended on unprecedented levels of government sponsorship. Early turnpikes were funded by private companies that raised capital by selling shares to individual investors and earned profits from the tolls collected periodically along their course. Canals needed state support. The **Erie Canal**, running 364 miles from the Hudson River near Albany to Lake Erie at Buffalo, completed a long-desired all-water route between the Atlantic Ocean and the Great Lakes. When it was finished in 1825, New Yorkers celebrated with bonfires, songs, cannon salutes, and speeches praising national unity

> New modes of transportation and communication shorten the experience of distance.

through better transportation. Such patriotic displays slighted the international effort involved. The state of New York raised funds for its construction through a lottery and a tax on the auction sales of goods; English investors loaned the balance of the money. Irish immigrant laborers and pardoned convicts dug the channel, modifying the specifications of Dutch and English engineers for North American landscapes.

Like canals and turnpikes, steamboats on the Mississippi River brought the global economy to the U.S. interior by making communication faster and freight fees cheaper. Robert Fulton, who developed the American steamboat in 1807, envisioned it bringing "a little Paris, a section of Broadway, or a slice of Philadelphia" to "the very doors of our cabins." By harnessing the potent power of steam, boats could travel upriver as well as down. In 1817, seventeen steamboats opened for business on the Mississippi; within thirty years, there were more than seven hundred, each larger and carrying more cargo and passengers. In 1814, it took six days and six hours for the *Orleans* to make the 268-mile trip from New Orleans to Natchez. By 1844, the *Sultana* made it in just under twenty hours. Whereas an old-style boat with a keel transported goods from New Orleans to Louisville at the rate of 5 cents per pound, the flat-bottomed steamboat took them for a half-cent a pound. Furs from animals trapped near the Great Lakes and grain and livestock from the western plains all traveled south. Cotton and sugar went north.

Railroads, first constructed on a major scale in the 1830s, were even faster and more direct. Steamships transported goods north and south on the Mississippi River, but the early railroad companies such as the Baltimore and Ohio and the Reading Railroad connected east and west, altering the axis of major

internal improvements
Infrastructure and transportation projects with the goal of improving commerce that were funded in part with public money.

Erie Canal New York water route between Albany and Buffalo completed in 1825 to speed transportation of goods and people from East Coast to Great Lakes networks.

Map 9.3 Transcontinental Travel and Commerce by 1840 Canals and roads funded by states and private investors, followed by railroads and telegraph lines, formed a network with navigable rivers to connect port cities to communities in the continent's interior. New communication and transportation lines also linked up with overland trade routes in the West. The migration of people and goods became easier and cheaper, boosting commercial agriculture because farmers could transport goods to distant markets. The result was increased U.S. settlement onto lands previously or simultaneously occupied by Indian groups. ▲

ATLANTIC OCEAN

BRITISH NORTH AMERICA (CANADA)

MAINE
N.H.
VT.
MASS.
R.I.
CONN.
NEW YORK
Portland
Lowell
Boston
Providence
New Haven
New York
Trenton
Albany
Springfield
Utica
Rochester
Buffalo
Catskill Tpk.
Erie Canal
Lake Ontario
Lake Erie
PENNSYLVANIA
N.J.
Philadelphia
Trenton
DEL.
MD.
Baltimore
Washington, D.C.
Harrisburg
Pittsburgh
Pennsylvania Rd.
Hagerstown
Valley Tpk.
Cleveland
Toledo
Columbus
Dayton
OHIO
Ft. Wayne
South Bend
INDIANA
Indianapolis
Vandalia
National Rd.
Cincinnati
Louisville
Lexington
KENTUCKY
Portsmouth
Richmond
Norfolk
VIRGINIA
Lynchburg
Great Valley Rd.
NORTH CAROLINA
Raleigh
Fayetteville
Wilmington
Charleston
SOUTH CAROLINA
Augusta
Savannah
St. Augustine
FLORIDA TERRITORY 1822
GEORGIA
Macon
Atlanta
Montgomery
ALABAMA
Mobile
New Orleans
Nashville Rd.
Chattanooga
Knoxville
TENNESSEE
General Jackson's Military Rd.
Natchez Trace
Memphis
Jackson
Vicksburg
Natchez
MISSISSIPPI
LOUISIANA
Gulf of Mexico
Galveston
MICHIGAN 1837
Lake Huron
Lake Superior
Lake Michigan
WISCONSIN TERRITORY 1836
Chicago
Evanston
ILLINOIS
Nauvoo
St. Louis
Pike
Ohio R.
IOWA TERRITORY 1838
Mississippi R.
Independence
Ft. Leavenworth
MISSOURI 1837
ARKANSAS 1836
Little Rock
Ft. Smith
INDIAN TERRITORY
REPUBLIC OF TEXAS
San Antonio
Chihuahua
El Paso del Norte
DISPUTED AREA
Santa Fe
Taos
El Camino Real
Rio Grande
Red R.
Arkansas R.
Santa Fe Trail
Cimarron Crossing Trail
Ft. Smith–Santa Fe Trail
Butterfield Overland Trail
Emigrant Trail
MEXICO
GREAT PLAINS
UNORGANIZED TERRITORY
Ft. Laramie
Ft. Kearny
N. Platte R.
Platte R.
Missouri R.
Milk R.
Yellowstone R.
ROCKY MOUNTAINS
Ft. Smith
Mormon Trail
Oregon Trail
Santa Fe Trail
OREGON COUNTRY
Astoria
Ft. Vancouver
Portland
Columbia R.
Snake R.
Ft. Hall
Ft. Lane
Lassen's Trail
California Trail
GREAT BASIN
Great Salt Lake
Salt Lake City
Green R.
Colorado R.
Gila R.
CALIFORNIA
Sacramento (Sutter's Fort)
San Francisco
Santa Barbara
Los Angeles
San Diego
Sacramento R.
Old Spanish Trail
Salt Lake to Los Angeles Trail
Butterfield Overland Trail
Emigrant Trail
PACIFIC OCEAN

300 Mi.
300 Km.
150
150
0
0

N

Settled areas
1820
1840
U.S. territory largely unsettled

— Road
— Railroad
— Canal
— Navigable river
···· Telegraph line
— Trail to the west
— Boundaries as of 1840
● Principal manufacturing city

commercial traffic. When construction began on the Baltimore and Ohio Railroad in 1828, Charles Carroll, the last living signer of the Declaration of Independence, told the gathered crowd that launching the new railroad was "among the most important acts of my life, second only to my signing the Declaration of Independence, if even it be second to that."

9-2b Corporations

New businesses from cotton mills to steamboat lines were organized as corporations, entities legally able to buy and sell poperty. Shareholders

{ State governments join public and private ventures.

pooled their money and obtained **corporate charters** issued by state legislatures. In 1808, John Jacob Astor, a German immigrant who had spent decades building a beaver fur-trading business with Indians in New York and the Great Lakes, received a charter from the state of New York to found the American Fur Company. He hoped that a state charter would help him drive his British rival, Hudson's Bay Company, from U.S. borders and trade routes. Inspired by reports from the Lewis and Clark expedition, Astor chartered a subsidiary, the Pacific Fur Company, in 1810 to establish a base called Astoria at the mouth of the Columbia River on the Pacific coast and issued one hundred shares of stock in the company.

Although the pooling of investors had existed since the joint-stock companies that funded much of European colonialism, state governments in the nineteenth century created new incentives for private investment in transportation projects. Corporate charters typically granted the protection of limited liability, which reduced investor risk by preventing creditors from seizing shareholders' personal assets to satisfy business debts. Most transportation charters also included the power of **eminent domain**, a corporation's legal right to force landowners to sell property along the route of a turnpike, canal, or railroad, whether they wanted to or not. Eminent domain had previously been a power only governments could invoke to serve a common good. Because states in the nineteenth century were trying to tap into private resources to undertake major projects, state governments transferred some of their powers to corporations serving a quasi-public function.

Courts supported the sanctity of corporate charters, bolstering the power of businesses. In the 1819 Supreme Court decision *Trustees of Dartmouth College v. Woodward*, Chief Justice Marshall declared that a private corporation had the same protected rights as a U.S. citizen. In this case, the state of New Hampshire was prevented from turning Dartmouth College into a public college. Such an alteration in the school's charter, Marshall contended, would amount to an illegal seizure of private property, and protecting private property was a cornerstone of U.S. law and politics.

9-2c National Institutional Supports

Nationally minded politicians believed that the federal government should directly support economic development by backing internal improve-

{ Nationalists mobilize the federal government.

ments. With the end of the War of 1812, they insisted that the United States should cultivate markets within its own borders, free from Europe's problems and dependencies. "The crops of our plains would no longer sustain European armies," declared Daniel Webster. Instead, interstate commerce could promote the integration and independence of the United States. Tench Coxe, who before the Revolution had been a merchant with strong ties to English businesses, envisioned a new system by which farmers would feed manufacturers, who would in turn provide farmers' tools. Merchants would supplement this domestic interdependency with additional products from "foreign climates." Coxe's vision drew on decades of experience with manufacturing societies that invested in new factories and lobbied for laws to shield their products from foreign competition while permitting trade.

The federal government called the first **Patent Act** (1790) an Act to Promote the Progress of Useful Arts. It gave inventors a fourteen-year monopoly on machinery and processes that they had created, described, and licensed. As Coxe had envisioned, patents encouraged innovation in manufacturing, agriculture, and trade. Charles Newbold, David Peacock, and Jethro Wood patented cast iron plows between 1797 and 1819 that immediately outpaced damage-prone wooden plows clad in iron plates. Cyrus McCormick patented a horse-drawn reaper in 1834 that could harvest as much as fourteen individuals could with scythes. Inventions patented outside the United States were excluded from protection; the federal government sanctioned and even encouraged industrial espionage at the heart of New England's new power looms.

Recognizing that entrepreneurs needed to take big risks, lawmakers also experimented with laws to cushion their losses. Under the short-lived national Bankruptcy Act of 1800, merchants, bankers, brokers, and insurance underwriters who could not repay their creditors could be compelled to declare **bankruptcy**, have a commission divide their assets, and start fresh.

corporate charters Written license granted by a government detailing the structure and plans of a business that often included limits on the duration and privileges of the business.

eminent domain Legal power of a government or its agent to take private property to serve a public good with compensation.

Trustees of Dartmouth College v. Woodward U.S. Supreme Court decision protecting the sanctity of private corporate charters, deeming corporations to have constitutionally protected rights.

Patent Act First federal patent law passed in (1790) that protected registered inventions from competition for fourteen years, following English practice.

bankruptcy Legal process that distributes assets among creditors and cancels the remaining debt status of a person deemed unable to pay his or her debts.

Joseph Kriehuber/The Granger Collection, New York

Global Americans Born in Germany in 1789 and largely self-educated, economist **Frederich List** fled Austria for the United States in 1825 on the advice of Revolutionary War hero General Lafayette. List worked as a newspaper editor, coal prospector, and railroad builder, all the while advocating strongly for the American System. Opposing the free-trade policies of Adam Smith, List argued in favor of the protective tariff, claiming that such a measure was well in the spirit of the U.S. Founding Fathers. At the same time, he used examples from Europe to argue that other governments were far ahead of the United States in cultivating knowledge about commerce and economy. Pointing to the polytechnic schools of France, Austria, Switzerland, and Germany, he argued that such institutions yielded not only productivity gains but also "moral riches." A fully engaged participant in the American System, List articulated the moral and ideological dimensions of taxes, banks, and internal improvements. He became a U.S. citizen and traveled back to Germany as a diplomat and railroad promoter, but financial failures contributed to the despair that drove him to suicide in 1846.

Once through bankruptcy, a commercial debtor had no enduring legal or moral obligations to make all of his or her old promises good; instead, the individual was released to make new ones. Fears of collusion between debtors and creditors forced the act's repeal in 1803.

Robust commerce also depended on good communication, and the United States Post Office, formally organized in 1792, soon employed more people than the rest of the civilian bureaucracy put together. Thousands of post offices opened in the third decade of the nineteenth century as settlers in distant parts of the country petitioned for service. Postal policies and direct investment were a boon to local economies and transportation between communities. The office subsidized stagecoaches because the mail traveled along with passengers. The mandate that post offices be open every day meant that local postmasters, commonly tavern keepers and shopkeepers, could keep their businesses open and even sell liquor on Sundays because they were exempt from laws forbidding the practice. Because printed material, such as newspapers and political pamphlets, traveled at a much cheaper rate than personal letters, the Post Office fostered a closely networked business and political world.

Building on these targeted laws and private initiatives, Kentucky congressman Henry Clay suggested a comprehensive, centralized plan for national development. His proposed **American System** consisted of a protective tariff on imports, a national bank, increased federal land sales, and federal money for internal improvements. By uniting the interests of agriculture, commerce, and industry, Clay hoped to promote success for individual Americans and make U.S. exports stronger. The American System had unifying potential across regions. John C. Calhoun, congressman from South Carolina, supported using federal funds to "bind the republic together with a perfect system of roads and canals. Let us conquer space."

McCormick's Patent Virginia Reaper Advert, 1850 (litho), American School (19th century)/Private Collection/Peter Newark American Pictures/Bridgeman Images

Advertisement for Mechanical Reaper Cyrus McCormick invented and manufactured the Virginia Reaper, but a patent did not guarantee profits. In its first decade, his company made little money. Moving to the emerging grain belt of the Midwest, developing an extensive advertising campaign, and introducing regular improvements were essential steps to success. ▲

But should the federal government take such an active role in commercial development? U.S. officials had debated this since Hamilton and Jefferson took opposing sides on the question of strict versus loose construction of the Constitution. One faction of Democratic-Republicans, in the tradition of Hamilton, favored expanding the powers of the federal government to serve what its proponents saw as the interests of the United States as a nation. Other

American System Program of political assistance proposed for the economic development of the United States in the 1810s and 1820s. Some elements were adopted; others were contested and rejected.

lawmakers were more cautious about pushing beyond measures such as post and patent offices, which were clearly authorized by the Constitution. In 1817, President James Madison, although a supporter of economic development, vetoed a bill that would have earmarked U.S. Bank dividends to pay for transportation projects.

9-2d State Banking and Western Lands

Clerks, landladies, canal diggers, and spinning machine operatives who were no longer directly involved in farming created new markets for

> The spread of farming in the Midwest sends produce east and speculators west.

foodstuffs across state lines. To capture this market, farmers wanted more land and were willing to speculate on future profits to get it. Governments and entrepreneurs eased their way, connecting the East and Midwest through land sales.

Acquired through treaty, sale, or warfare with the Indian people who lived on it, the land these farmers desired was transformed into federal territories. Following practices established by the 1785 Land Ordinance, the U.S. government hired surveyors to assess difficult terrain, marking an orderly grid over swamps, fields, forests, mountains, and rivers. As they had in the Northwest and Southwest Territories, Americans moved onto land in the Mississippi Valley long before the surveyors arrived. Congress frequently permitted squatters who had "improved" their land by building barns, houses, and fields the chance to purchase it at a minimum price of $1.25 an acre. But many white migrants who arrived after the squatters had to buy their farms from speculators, who had bought them at Land Office auctions and then resold them on credit with interest rates as high as 40 percent. The fastest way to pay back such loans was with earnings from cash crops exported east and on to Europe.

Speculators and farmers depended on **state banks** created by investors who deposited assets—usually bonds—with a state government and then began issuing money. Banks supported land booms and dramatically expanded the supply of circulating money. Under the U.S. Constitution, only the federal government could coin money; paper money, in contrast, could be issued by a wide range of institutions. State banks hired engravers to design and print **bank notes**, slips of paper promising to pay an equivalent amount of gold or silver coin when the note was presented for redemption at the bank. Other businesses, including insurance companies, railroads, and private banks printed their own paper notes. By the 1850s, more than ten thousand different kinds of paper were in circulation. These paper dollars, easily portable across distances, were a much-needed circulating medium that enabled people to undertake varied transactions.

A bank note's value rested on what the people who used it agreed it to be. As long as all users had faith that two different $5 bills could be exchanged for equivalent amounts of gold and silver, the system worked. But banks and other corporations issued far more paper money than they could redeem in gold and silver, hoping to raise more money in interest payments from the people to whom they extended loans. While the notes circulated through the hands of farmers and land agents, the system worked. But if all the holders of a bank's notes came at once for their gold and silver, the speculative bubble would burst.

9-2e Panic of 1819

The bubble did burst, first in 1819, followed by a series of panics throughout the nineteenth century. The trouble began in Europe. During the

> A financial crisis reveals the vulnerabilities of the new political and economic systems.

Napoleonic wars, many western Europeans were desperate for food, and the price of U.S. corn and wheat surged, prompting midwestern farmers to expand their fields to grow crops to export. British factories' demands for cotton ensured that prices for U.S. cotton increased as well. By 1818, however, European farmers had recovered from wars and crop failures and were growing their own foodstuffs. Britain turned back to India to supply its mills, and the price paid for a pound of cotton fell 50 percent. Land purchased on the promise of high prices was not worth the money that had been borrowed to buy it.

The **Second Bank of the United States** compounded American credit woes. Chartered in 1816 for a twenty-year period, it was the most powerful of all of the new banks. In addition to having branches in multiple states, 20 percent of its stock was held by the federal government. The bank loaned money to the federal government, state banks, and individuals. It also acted as the federal government's banker, making transactions and holding its revenues. Because its paper notes alone could be used to pay federal taxes, customers daily visited its branches to exchange their various notes for Bank of the United States paper. By taking those state bank notes back to their origins for immediate redemption into specie, the Bank could exert some control over the money supply in the United States.

In late 1818, faced with worrisome evidence of a speculative bubble, its directors called in loans and contracted credit. To make their redemptions, state banks had to call in their loans and send their gold and silver to the Second Bank. Indebted farmers could not pay, nor could land speculators, who in turn owed far more to

state banks Corporation licensed by a state to print money, accept deposits, and make loans. Predominated in the nineteenth century.

bank notes Paper certificate issued by banks that circulated as currency with the promise to repay the holder the face value on demand.

Second Bank of the United States National bank chartered by Congress in 1816 to conduct business for the federal government and issue notes that could be used to pay federal taxes.

History without Borders

Paper Money

Sweden 1745 3

Denmark 1713 3

Sweden 1661 2

Britain 1830s 5

Russia 1860s 5

Québec 1685 3

Britain 1694 4

Russia 1769 3

EUROPE

France 1701 3

NORTH AMERICA

ASIA

United States 1780s 5

3 **Massachusetts 1690**

Austria 1762 3

France 1840s 5

Germany 1850s 5

China 960 1

6 **United States 1861**

ATLANTIC OCEAN

AFRICA

PACIFIC OCEAN

SOUTH AMERICA

INDIAN OCEAN

AUSTRALIA

1 Traders in China began using "flying money" in place of cumbersome coins, **960.**

2 The Stockholm bank received permission to issue paper money, redeemable for copper coin, **1661.**

3 Warfare between France and England led colonial Québec and Massachusetts to create paper money, to pay for soldiers and supplies, **1685–1690.** European kingdoms drawn into the conflict followed, **1701–1769.**

4 The need to fund the war against France led to the founding of the Bank of England, a joint-stock company that then handled government money, **1694.**

5 Private banks took over printing and circulation of paper money in the United States, **1780s.** Private banks in Europe also issued circulating money, **1830s–1860s.**

6 U.S. Congress ordered the Treasury Department to print paper "greenbacks" for the United States during the Civil War, **1861.**

Paper Money, 960–1861 As paper money systems developed around the world, their legal status and who had the right to issue bills created tensions among traders, investors, and governments. This map shows some key turning points, as paper money came to be tightly linked to the power and credibility of nations. ▲

Barter—the immediate, face-to-face exchange of one good for another—is one of the simplest methods of exchange, but every trading society has had to cope with how to transmit exchanges across distances and over time. Global trading regions developed unique markers to denote value and smooth transactions. In Africa, India, China, and other regions connected by the Indian Ocean, cowrie shells served as small-denomination money of exchange. Merchants and traders in the East Indies used small, low-value bronze coins with a hole in the center, which Europeans called *cash*.

Fur traders in North America used wampum, beads that Native Americans on Long Island Sound made out of whelk and clamshells. Spanish invaders minted large deposits of gold and silver in South America into coins as part of colonial conquest. These "pieces of eight" circulated around the world as familiar global currency by the seventeenth century. Each of these forms of money had benefits, but all were bulky to transport and vulnerable to theft.

The appeal of paper money—lightweight, foldable, and easily printed with financial and political information—was clear, but its spread depended on

political and financial developments. Chinese merchants in the Song Dynasty (960–1279 CE) were the first to use paper IOUs called *flying money* to transmit exchanges over long distances. By the Middle Ages, traders around the Mediterranean also used paper IOUs called *bills of exchange* that functioned as checks do today except that the bills could then circulate as money in transactions that had nothing to do with the original agreement. Florentine bankers, traders, and growers of commodities all welcomed the bill of exchange as a method of importing in one place, exporting from another, and settling up accounts in a third.

Great Ming Circulating Treasury Note, 1375 This is the earliest surviving example of government-issued paper money. Paper money began in China as a convenient private tool used by traders, but Chinese emperors took over and used paper money to control international trade and centralize holdings of gold and silver. By the 1450s, however, overprinting money had made the notes lose value, and China abandoned a paper money system for silver coins. ◄

Banknote of China, Ming Dynasty, 1368–1644 (paper), Chinese School/ Ashmolean Museum, University of Oxford, UK/Bridgeman Images

Bank of Henderson Five Dollar Bill, 1818 This bill is signed in ink by bank directors, linking these five dollars with earlier bills of exchange, signed by merchants. The Bank of Henderson was one of the unregulated banks of the nineteenth-century United States. Located in Kentucky, its notes were not backed by the reserves suggested by its issuing practices. ◄ Library of Congress/ University of Chicago. Library. American Currency Collection

Governments also began to use paper IOUs to fund their largest projects: wars. In British North America, Massachusetts authorities first issued paper money in 1690 to pay for troops and supplies in battles against the French in New France. These Massachusetts shillings promised holders gold or silver equivalents at the end of the conflict, but instead, paper money typically circulated and was used to purchase goods and pay taxes. For paper money to succeed, users had to believe that it could be exchanged for something of value, such as gold or silver. Too much paper money in circulation led to inflation, causing bills to be worth far less than the values printed on them. The disastrous experience of paper bills in the American Revolution led the framers of the Constitution to forbid states from printing money.

Between the Revolution and the Civil War, most paper money in the United States was printed and circulated by private commercial sources with state charters: banks, insurance companies, railroad and canal companies, and companies without charters. These notes, frequently counterfeited or backed with little or no security, circulated alongside thousands of different gold, silver, and copper coins minted by governments from around the world. A profusion of forms of money, intersecting with global financial flows, fed the economic growth and boom-bust cycles of the nineteenth century.

Critical Thinking Questions

▶ How does the form that money takes influence who can use it? How does it influence who can issue it?

▶ Why is the history of paper money directly linked to both trade and warfare?

Go to MindTap® to engage with an interactive version of **History without Borders: Paper Money.** Learn from an interactive map, view related video, and respond to critical thinking questions.

state banks than the land was then worth. Banks failed, the western land bubble popped, and people around the country suffered. For the next four years, Americans lost their homes and jobs as foreclosures rose and businesses collapsed. Unemployment reached 75 percent in Philadelphia. Tens of thousands were jailed for debt, and the *National Gazette* reported that debtors in New York prisons had no bedding and no food other than a quart of soup every twenty-four hours.

Who was to blame? Individuals referred to the Panic of 1819 as "hard times." Few had the idea that something as abstract as "the economy" or as difficult to grasp as the speculative value of paper money could cause such real anguish. Many assumed that moral failures were the root of the trouble. One newspaper quipped, "To dress, to visit, and to play, / To get in debt, and run away, /Are common vices of the day." Victims countered that fraud was to blame and talked of shady dealers who "laughed in their sleeves" at others' misfortune. A growing number pointed to the Second Bank, charging that insiders ran banks as monopolies. Although times improved after 1822, debt and poverty remained and suspicions about the banking system simmered. The **boom-bust cycle** of the U.S. economy persisted.

9-3

Global Markets and Regional Alliances

Hauling the Whole Week's Picking (1842), William Henry Brown. This collage, depicting a surprisingly well-dressed family of slaves, is part of a series created to decorate the rooms of the masters' children on the Nitta Yuma plantation in Vicksburg, Mississippi. Brown specialized in the art of silhouette, which involved using scissors to cut portraits of people from black paper.

What does the placement and relative size of humans, wheels, and baskets of picked cotton suggest about the way cotton cultivation shaped human lives? How are the slaves' work lives depicted in comparison with the men digging the Erie Canal? ▼

Hauling The Whole Week's Picking, c.1842 (w/c on paper), Brown, William Henry (1808–83)/The Historic New Orleans Collection/Bridgeman Images

HAULING THE WHOLE WEEKS PICKING

Americans viewed their place in the global economy in starkly different ways. Farmers favored policies that sent products across borders easily to generate profit. Manufacturers opposed the idea of open competition with European products, arguing that the United States needed to favor its own industries over those of foreigners. Merchants looked for new regions to exploit, forging uneasy partnerships across racial and ethnic lines. Cotton growers, dependent on global markets, invested deeply in expanding racialized slavery. Looking inward, these competing regional economic interests threatened national political unity. The credit system concentrated profits in developed parts of the country, leaving the South and the West dependent on the East and on Britain—a relationship more fitting for a colony than a republic. Looking outward, the United States tried to project strength as part of a larger hemispheric region of linked former colonies.

☞ As you read, consider the ways that economic interests reconfigured regional politics and identities in the first half of the nineteenth century. Which new interests emerged on the national scene?

9-3a **Export Economy**

In spite of the development of manufacturing in the United States, the vast majority of Americans lived on farms practicing **composite farming**, which included some production for the family's own use and some for sale in local and more distant markets. Husbands and wives worked all day to raise crops and livestock, maintain vegetable gardens, and process dairy products. Children performed essential labor and ran errands. To purchase goods they could not produce, families ran long credit accounts with local storekeepers that they paid off in extra eggs or homespun thread. Large families meant that new generations often had to move away to establish farms of their own, but they took the familiar forms of work and exchange with them.

{ Agriculture unites and divides Americans.

boom-bust cycle Economic course typified by expansion and then contraction of business activity that came to exemplify the U.S. economy in the nineteenth century.

composite farming Farming system that grows crops for household use and also for market exchange.

Like their urban counterparts, farm families also responded to the opportunities of market development, labor migration, and improved transportation. Women in Delaware increased their dairy businesses to earn surplus profits that could be reinvested in land, opening more fields to wheat cultivation. Midwestern farmers used improved plows and mechanical reapers to specialize in corn and wheat as cash crops. Farmers, like merchants, replaced long-term worker contracts with seasonal waged work, which meant that the people who helped with the harvest did not have to be supported over the winter. Transportation opened new markets across regional lines and internationally (see Figure 9.1).

International markets meant international competition, and Americans disagreed about which industries needed protection. In 1816, Congress established a federal tariff on imports into the United States, hoping to protect the emerging textile, ironwork, and tannery industries by making their imported competitors more expensive. American businesses could be protected as they experimented with the technology, labor, and distribution systems necessary to compete with imports on their own. With subsequent revisions, by 1830, most imported goods that competed with U.S.-made goods were taxed one-third to one-half of their value.

Opponents of the tariff asked why U.S. manufacturing should be protected but not commercial agriculture. Southern planters of rice, cotton, and tobacco exported most of their crops, where they competed in markets not under U.S. tariff protection. Because their customers were abroad, southern planters earned their money in the form of credit abroad. The protective tariff that made

English imports expensive meant that the credit Southerners received from English buyers was worth less than the credit U.S. manufacturers earned within the United States. Many feared that the British, who already protected their own farmers with Corn Laws, would retaliate with additional tariffs and price American export-based farmers out of their livelihood.

9-3b Global Fur Trade

While farmers kept their eyes focused on the trade routes of rivers emptying into the Atlantic Ocean and Gulf of Mexico, fur trappers and traders fixed their attention on the Pacific. Following the first voyage of the *Empress of China* in 1784, U.S.–China trade had grown dramatically. By 1840, it was a $6.6 million business, making China the third largest exporter to the United States behind England and France. U.S. traders scoured the natural resources of the globe to find goods they could exchange for Chinese silks, tea, and porcelain. They soon added Hawaiian sandalwood, Rocky Mountain furs, Pacific otter skins, and Turkish opium to their shipments to Canton.

{ Indian workers supply global markets with western plants and animals.

Tapping into the natural resources of North America for the China trade meant collaborating with Native Americans. In the Rocky Mountains, fur traders from the United States relied on the connections and expertise of Indians and French-speaking traders to obtain beaver fur and bison hides. Men employed by the Rocky Mountain Fur Company traveled up the Missouri River and along

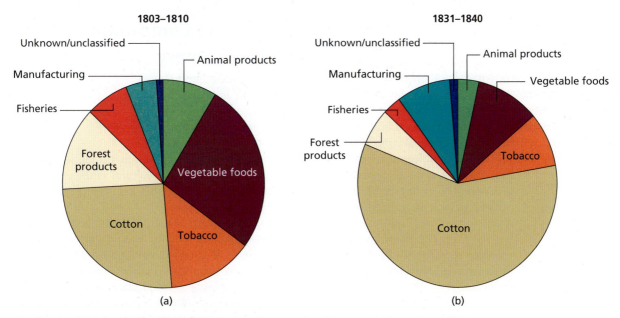

Figure 9.1 Changing Profile of U.S. Exports In the first decades of the nineteenth century, cotton increasingly dominated U.S. exports, pushing aside earlier important commodities such as tobacco. Grains and other vegetable foods also declined as exports because more U.S. grain was traded between states across new transportation lines. ▲ Source: *The Cambridge Economic History of the United States, Volume 2.*

Montana Historical Society

Global Americans Born in 1825 to an influential Blackfeet family, **Medicine Snake Woman** (Natawista) married Alexander Culbertson, a trader with the American Fur Company twice her age, when she was 15. Their marriage bolstered the fur company's ambitions to replace the mobile rendezvous system with a chain of settled trading forts on the Upper Missouri River. Medicine Snake Woman's married life looked in two directions: toward the United States, where she sent five of her children to be educated in Catholic schools in St. Louis, and toward the contested West, where she worked with Culbertson to negotiate land treaties between the United States government and Blackfeet and Gros Venture Indian groups. From her home at Fort Union on the Upper Missouri River, she hosted Assiniboine, Crow, Sioux, and Blackfeet hunters; U.S. railroad surveyors; and European artists who all came to trade beaver and buffalo furs for English rifles and Chinese glass beads. Retiring in wealth to Peoria, Illinois, in 1858, Medicine Snake Woman left Culbertson ten years later to live with her Native American relatives. She died in 1893 on a Canadian Indian reservation. Through her economic, diplomatic, and family life, she negotiated the intersection of global business and Native American kinship practices, which defined life in western North America.

Native American roads to live year-round with Indian families. Indian women agreed to partner with trappers, teaching them how to treat, process, and pack furs. Traders, trappers, and Indians from multiple tribes met together at annual **rendezvous** points that were marked by peeling the bark off a set of trees near a river junction or constructing a five-foot tall mound of earth marked red with vermillion. When the parties met at these trade fairs, they exchanged goods for furs, which then traveled through St. Louis and down the Mississippi River to New Orleans, a hub of the global economy.

Native American labor, Chinese consumers, and Russian, U.S., and English ships all came together in the "great hunt" of the Eastern Pacific sea otters. Traders on the border between Russia and China had treasured and exploited the velvety fur of these small animals since the mid-eighteenth century. By kidnapping the indigenous hunters of the Aleutian and Kodiak Islands and putting them to work, the traders emptied the northern Pacific of otters, pushing the hunt down the coast toward Baja California, where British, U.S., French, and Spanish traders competed for the profitable business. In the years between 1803 and 1812, Americans and Russians joined forces in otter-hunting ventures that used U.S. ships to transport Indian men and women specializing in canoe-based hunting and pelt preparation, together with Russian overseers, to the shores and bays of California, paying bribes to the Spanish to look away. In the 1830s, sharpshooters targeted the remaining otters from the shore and within a decade, all of the "soft gold" of sea otter pelts had been hunted to near extinction.

American fortunes in the Pacific, however, continued to grow. In 1839, the Chinese government decided to halt the illegal flow of Indian and Turkish opium brought by competing U.S. and British ships. Confiscation of the contraband drug sparked the Opium War between the British and Chinese, which ended in an 1842 treaty that expanded British trading power. Not to be excluded, in 1844, the United States and China signed the **Treaty of Wanghia**, which granted the United States similar most-favored nation trading status, meaning that U.S. businessmen paid the same tariffs and received the same benefits as those from Britain, France, or any other nation. American merchants gained access to the five Chinese ports established at the end of the Opium War. In those ports, Americans could buy land, establish churches and hospitals, learn the Chinese language, and be subject to U.S. rather than Chinese law, an arrangement that put China in a subordinate position.

9-3c Political Compromise over Slavery

{ Internal developments reshape political regions.

By 1820, the most important regional split in the United States was no longer the East Coast versus the borderland West but rather states with slavery versus those without. This hardening sectionalism was economic, political, and cultural as the congressional crisis provoked by Missouri's admission to the United States highlighted.

Since the passage of the Northwest and Southwest Ordinances, national politics had sought compromise on the question of slavery in the republic, although free-state lawmakers grumbled that the Three-Fifths Compromise permanently granted states with slavery the edge in representation. In 1818, Missouri, where slavery existed, applied to be admitted as the second new state of the Louisiana Purchase, forcing Congress to confront the expansion of legal slavery in the United States. At the time, the country had eleven free states and eleven slave states.

rendezvous Annual gathering in which white and Indian trappers exchanged furs for manufactured goods as part of the Rocky Mountain fur trade industry.

Treaty of Wanghia Agreement that granted the United States the same access to Chinese ports and to trading as Britain had and that guaranteed that trading Americans remained under U.S. law.

Map 9.4 Missouri Compromise, 1820 The law passed by the U.S. Congress maintained a balance of free and slave states. Nationalists were gratified that the Union could be strengthened through internal compromise and independence from European political maneuvering. But seventy-seven-year-old Jefferson lamented that the compromise was "a reprieve only, not a final sentence" on the question of extending slavery. ▲

Admitting Missouri would upset the balance between the two sides in the Senate. In addition, Missouri was geographically northern—its profile reached up over the Ohio River, which had been the dividing line between interior states that permitted slavery and those that outlawed it. Free-state congressmen moved to place conditions on Missouri's admission, including a gradual emancipation amendment, and slave-state congressmen protested that the federal government lacked the power to compel what was properly state law.

After long debate, Congress passed the **Missouri Compromise** in 1820, which allowed Missouri to enter the United States as a slave state balanced by Maine (formerly part of Massachusetts) as a free state (see Map 9.4). Seeking to pre-empt future debates, the bill also prohibited the extension of slavery in the territory of the Louisiana Purchase north of the 36–degree parallel but permitted it south of that line. Like other dividing lines in the history of imperial expansion in North America, the Missouri Compromise line helped to turn complicated political and familial identities on the ground into a starker sense of "us" versus "them." Missouri's new constitution, which prohibited free blacks from settling in the state, indicated that individual citizenship rights would continue to resist compromise.

9-3d A Hemispheric Vision

Statesmen hoping to promote U.S. economic development faced other contradictions that had always accompanied Jefferson's "empire of liberty." Lacking a strong navy and still relying on British banks for loans and seed money, the United States was vulnerable on both coasts. On the Atlantic, a Holy Alliance of European monarchies declared its commitment to put down revolutionary movements and help Spain retake its former American colonies. On the Pacific, Russian Czar Alexander I declared in 1821 that no foreign ships could come within one hundred miles of the coast of Alaska, claiming his empire's intention to maintain and extend its fur-trading operations in the Pacific Northwest. To protect itself from these perceived imperial threats, the United States needed a standing army, navy, higher taxes, and more centralized power. Yet these measures all undermined the ideals of a republic and long-standing opposition to a permanent military.

> External dangers reshape political regions.

Missouri Compromise Law that admitted Missouri as a state permitting slavery and Maine as a state outlawing slavery, an attempt to maintain sectional political balance.

South America presented a political and economic solution. There, new republics and gold and silver mines offered the indebted United States a way to repay European investors and curb paper money speculation. Congressman Clay urged the United States to recognize South American independence movements and establish lucrative hemispherical trading ties that would create a region of "National Independence and Liberty" in contrast to the Old World monarchies. Others were skeptical of tying U.S. diplomatic fortunes to fledgling republics and urged a political alliance with Britain, which wanted to keep U.S. markets open and the Spanish and Russians out as colonial powers.

Monroe and his secretary of state John Quincy Adams crafted a message to Congress in 1823 that came to be called the **Monroe Doctrine**. Its central ideas were that North and South America were joined in republicanism, anticolonialism, and economic independence. Asserting that the Americas were "not to be considered as subjects for future colonization by any European power," the message warned that the United States would look on any "interposition" in the Western Hemisphere by European empires as a threat to American safety. The president's message further promised "not to interfere in the internal concerns" of Europe.

Such bold words presented a vision of regional influence that served the political interests of the United States. They did not specify what the United States would do in the event of European intervention. In fact, U.S. statesmen counted on the British Royal Navy to deter other European empires. And the Doctrine's words failed to acknowledge that in terms of trade, Britain, not the United States, was the major source of loans, trading relationships, and banking expertise to the new republics of Latin America. British traders, European diplomats, and Latin American revolutionaries all understood it as a statement of ambition rather than strength.

9-4

Democracy in Practice

The County Election (1852), by George Caleb Bingham, depicts election day in Missouri at mid-century as a social event. On the right side of the image, voters debate their options. On the left side of the image, the lone African American serves alcohol. Voting in this period was done either by voice vote or with tickets printed and handed out by political parties, decorated to make the voter's choice clear to the crowd.

How does this painting use the details of a local election day to portray the atmosphere of mid-nineteenth-century democratic participation? Who would feel welcome casting votes? ▶

The County Election, 1852 (oil on canvas), Bingham, George Caleb (1811–1879)/Saint Louis Art Museum, Missouri, USA/Gift of Bank of America/Bridgeman Images

Americans buffeted by the forces of migration and industrialization pressed for a political system that could represent new regional and class divisions. States replaced an older conception that voting was a privilege of stable landowners who had a clear stake in society with an emerging one that the vote was connected with citizenship for adult white men. To reach this new constituency, politicians innovated an open, competitive, masculine culture focused around elections. Embracing private interests, a new party system revived partisanship. As global political movements in favor of democracy offered inclusion to some but excluded others, disenfranchised Americans experimented with alternative forms of political action.

☞ As you read, think about the social and political consequences of new laws granting most adult white men the right to vote. Did political developments extend or reverse the achievements of the American Revolution?

9-4a Revival of Partisan Politics

In the first decades of the nineteenth century, states removed religious tests and property requirements for voters, replacing them with the requirement that voters be male and white. In 1821, New York widened the right to vote to all white men with no property requirements and declared that only free black men who owned

{ A new electorate requires new electioneering.

Monroe Doctrine Foreign policy statement by Monroe asserting U.S. opposition to European efforts to colonize in North or South America.

$250 worth of property could vote. Of the 30,000 African Americans in New York, only 298 were eligible to vote. Similar patterns emerged in the new states created by territorial expansion. All of the states admitted to the Union after the War of 1812 permitted white men to vote without any requirement for property holding. At the same time, all of the states admitted after 1819, except Maine, prohibited black men from voting.

The consequences of enfranchising almost all white men transformed political life. In 1820, James Monroe was elected president without significant challenge. But opponents of the American System that he supported awakened from the lull in political partisanship and began to coalesce around Andrew Jackson. In 1824, Jackson was a war hero famous for his victory at the Battle of New Orleans and a wealthy lawyer and slaveholder. His origins, however, allowed him to portray himself as a striking alternative to the East Coast elites who had dominated the U.S. presidency. Son of Irish immigrants, Jackson grew up in the borderlands of the Carolinas and Tennessee, was orphaned at age fourteen, and had only sporadic education. In the 1824 presidential election, Jackson received more popular and electoral votes than any of the other four candidates for the presidency but no overall majority. Under the provisions of the Constitution, the outcome was therefore decided in the House of Representatives. Clay, who came in fourth in the Electoral College, threw his support to John Quincy Adams, a fellow **National Republican**, as their faction of the party was known. Jackson was defeated, and Clay became secretary of state. Jackson's supporters charged that a "corrupt bargain" had vanquished the will of the people. A new **Democratic Party** unified around opposition to Adams and what its members called *elitist minorities.*

The Democratic Party mobilized and secured the loyalty of new voters, embracing the idea that voters should choose party leaders who would promote their interests rather than espousing old ideas that elections should select independent men to act for the common good. The 1828 campaign used mass-produced newspapers and printed handbills with slogans such as "Who do you want—John Quincy Adams, who quotes the law, or Andy Jackson, who makes the law?" Parades, rallies, and barbecues emphasized white men's camaraderie as enfranchised citizens. Beating Adams, who ran again, Jackson won the presidency in 1828 with the overwhelming support of new voters. In the next years, political parties, following the tactics developed in evangelical reform movements (see Chapter 10), began to hold national conventions to craft platforms and select nominees. Rather than choose candidates in Congress, parties relied on popular participation to shape the careers of national politicians. The new tactics worked. In 1824, fewer than 30 percent of eligible voters cast ballots, but in 1840, 80 percent voted.

9-4b Andrew Jackson as National Executive

> Jackson champions the majority by strengthening the power of the presidency.

Proclaiming that "parasitic minorities" should not rule over the majority, Jackson mobilized a diverse group who felt victimized by the economic changes of the nineteenth century. Artisans feared the loss of independence foisted by a small owner-manager class. Southern and western white farmers thought Indians should be expelled from valuable farmland. Indebted farmers worried that a cabal of moneymen were exploiting the legal and banking system for selfish gain.

The Second Bank of the United States became a prime target for Jackson's attacks that the privileges of the few should not prevail over the rights of the many. Since the Panic of 1819, opponents had argued that the Second Bank was so big and powerful that it threatened to put state banks out of business, and if it became the only source of money in the United States, the bank could do whatever it wanted. Jackson agreed. He wanted to destroy the bank and replace its paper money with a national currency of gold and silver coins. When bank president Nicholas Biddle requested a recharter for the Second Bank in 1832, Jackson vetoed the bill and then withdrew all federal deposits and put them in selected state banks. In doing so, he acted against the wishes of Congress and his secretary of the treasury, who pointed out that by law the deposits were supposed to go to the Bank of the United States.

Jackson's 1832 veto statement attacking the "Monster bank" demonstrated that his hatred for the bank was political as much as economic. He told people to blame the bank and outside corruption for the uncertainties of the market economy and played up a class warfare argument. He argued that the bank was an example of "the rich and powerful" bending "the acts of government to their selfish purposes." He pointed out that many of its stockholders were wealthy foreigners. And he argued that he, as elected president of the people, had a duty to participate directly in lawmaking because he represented the majority of Americans while congressmen, elected from state districts, represented only minorities within the whole.

The largest group to become the target of Democratic attacks on "minority" privileges was made up of southeastern Indians. Although many Creeks, Cherokees, and Choctaws had responded to the civilizing mission of the early nineteenth century, the federal government targeted them for removal to western lands. Echoing earlier ideas about the spread of U.S. civilization but with a new hardened racial edge, Jackson mischaracterized Indian-controlled lands as "covered with forests and ranged by a few thousand savages." In contrast, he declared, "our extensive republic" was "studded with

National Republican Faction within the Democratic-Republican party that supported the American System.

Democratic Party Political party formed around Andrew Jackson that opposed entrenched elitism, favored white male franchise, and pioneered boisterous mass politics.

Indian Removal Act U.S. law authorizing the president to offer Native Americans lands west of the Mississippi in exchange for their eastern homelands.

Cherokee Indian Cases U.S. Supreme Court legal decisions in 1831 and 1832 that affirmed Native American Indian tribes as sovereign entities but that Jackson refused to enforce.

cities, towns, and prosperous farms, embellished with all the improvements that art can devise or industry execute, occupied by more than 12 million happy people." The needs of the "12 million" in his eyes, trumped those of the "few thousand." In 1830, Congress passed the **Indian Removal Act**, which called for almost 100,000 Indians to relocate voluntarily from areas up and down the western borderlands of the United States across the Mississippi River to Indian Territory.

The American millions pushing Congress and the states to buy Indian land gained a new motive in 1829 when a north Georgia farmer and prospector discovered gold on a tributary of the Chattahoochee River, setting off a rush of migrants in search of quick wealth. The Cherokee Nation, a republic-style government established in 1820, owned most of the gold-producing land. The state of Georgia quickly passed laws designed to strip Cherokees of this land and their rights. As Native Americans had long done, Cherokees brought their grievance against Georgia to U.S. courts. In his *Cherokee Nation v. Georgia* (1831) decision, Chief Justice John Marshall ruled that the U.S.

Supreme Court had no jurisdiction under the Constitution to hear Indian cases, but he did define the Cherokee Nation as a "domestic dependent nation," a ward rather than an independent country, that nevertheless had rights to its lands until it decided to cede control. In 1832, the Cherokee Nation brought a new test case with a U.S. citizen: Samuel Worcester, a Vermont missionary who had refused to obey Georgia's new law that non-Indians in Cherokee country pledge allegiance to the state of Georgia. In this decision, *Worcester v. Georgia* (1832), Marshall declared that the Cherokee Nation was "a distinct community" and Georgia laws had no force within its borders. Taken together, the **Cherokee Indian Cases** defined the legal status of Native American tribes as entities under the protection of the U.S. government that maintained sovereignty within their own borders.

Jackson, acting as executive, refused to enforce the decisions and supported the forcible removal of Indians in the Southeast. Seminoles in East Florida held out the longest, fighting a guerrilla war against U.S. Army and militia troops from 1835 to 1842. Some stayed in the Everglades, but ultimately most were expelled to follow the Choctaws, Creeks, Chickasaws, and Cherokees.

9-4c Global Democratic Experiments

The Cherokee Nation was one of many entities expanding men's access to their governments. In 1827, it ratified a written constitution that established a bicameral elected

{ People around the world experiment with democratic reforms through law and independence movements.

legislature as well as executive and legislative branches. The document extended the right to vote and to serve in office to all free adult Cherokee men. It excluded Cherokee women and all people of "negro or mulatto parentage."

In Britain, after a decades-long campaign, Parliament passed a Catholic Emancipation Act in 1829 that permitted Catholics to serve in Parliament. Three years later, the English Reform Act of 1832 further reconfigured representation. Rural districts long emptied of residents lost their members of Parliament, and urban and industrial centers such as London and Manchester gained more proportional representation. The old idea that each representative spoke for the entire empire was replaced with a more democratic model of representatives closely linked to their constituents' needs. Poor working men had protested for the right to vote, but the Reform Act took only gradual steps, granting adult men whose homes were worth £10 in annual rents the vote. The expansion increased the number of voters from about 14 percent of men to nearly 20 percent, a far more modest change than in the United States.

Inadequate representation spurred other European states to overthrow autocratic kings in favor of constitutional monarchies who would sanction freedom of the

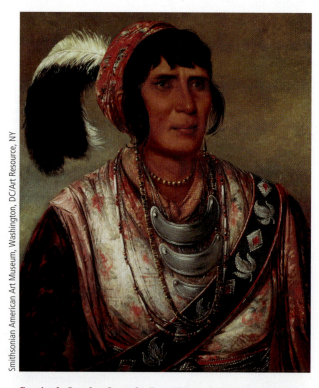

Smithsonian American Art Museum, Washington, DC/Art Resource, NY

Seminole Leader Osceola Born William Smith, Osceola rose to become a leader in the Seminoles' armed resistance to removal in the late 1830s. George Catlin painted this portrait in 1837, during the final months of Osceola's life in a South Carolina prison, after he was captured under a flag of truce. Catlin's gallery of hundreds of portraits of American Indians, called "Nature's dignitaries," toured the United States and Europe. ▲

press and assembly as well as economic policies associated with free trade. In 1830, wealthy urban Frenchmen forced autocratic King Charles X to abdicate and replaced him with Louis-Philippe. A member of the royal family who had spent time in the United States in the 1790s, he was hailed as the "citizen king." Belgians, who had been united with the Netherlands at the end of the Napoleonic Wars, objected to a union in which they outnumbered the Dutch but did not enjoy greater representation in government. When petitions to William I failed, Belgians declared independence in 1830. Other peoples demanded recognition as independent nations with less success. Poles were defeated in their revolt against the Russian czar in 1831.

The wave of independence movements in Latin America produced constitutions establishing representative governments. Uruguay's first constitution of 1830 drew on U.S. and French models in creating separate branches of government to oversee lawmaking, enforcement, and judicial decision making. Chile's 1833 constitution created a republic whose government was declared to be "popular and representative," granting the right to vote to those free men over twenty-one who could read and write.

9-4d Participatory Politics

Americans who could not vote did have the right to petition, and beginning in the late 1820s, this traditional form of gaining access to political leaders became a tool of the masses. By collecting signatures and making political demands, Americans with vulnerable political rights tried to amplify their voice as citizens. The right to petition was so closely tied to U.S. citizenship that in 1837, the U.S. House of Representatives passed a resolution forbidding slaves from submitting petitions on the grounds that they were not citizens.

{ Petitions seek democracy for nonvoters.

Shut out from voting, white women petitioners tried to make their exclusion from partisan politics a point in their favor. Catharine Beecher, part of an influential family of educators, preachers, and writers, organized the first national women's petition drive to flood Congress with petitions opposing Cherokee removal. Claiming that "women are protected from the blinding influence of party spirit," these petitions made a nonpartisan moral case against the forcible removal of Indian men, women, and children. They highlighted feelings of distress for the Christianized Cherokees, forced out of their homes and the mission schools that many of the petitions' signers had supported for decades.

Working people hoped that petitions would form a bridge between labor actions and political change. In the 1840s, the **Lowell Female Reform Association**, together with blacksmiths and carpenters in Philadelphia, joined forces with an international **Ten-Hour Movement** to petition lawmakers to limit the workday to no more than ten hours. Factory workers in the United States and Britain regularly toiled over 12 hours a day, six days a week. Pressure in Britain to regulate work, especially child labor, was gaining strength, and activists hoped to achieve results in the United States as well. In 1845, three-fourths of those who signed ten-hour petitions addressed to the Massachusetts legislature were women. The movement was a moderate success, and in 1840, the federal government mandated a ten-hour workday on federal projects. By the end of the decade, New Hampshire and Pennsylvania had adopted ten-hour days. But in many states, including Massachusetts, the Ten-Hour Movement was decried as "un-American."

Lowell Female Reform Association Organization of female factory operatives in Massachusetts in 1845 that grew out of the earlier Lowell Factory Girls' Association.

Ten-Hour Movement International labor movement that pushed governments to legislate maximum ten-hour workdays.

9-5

Limits of Majority Rule

"Specie Claws" (1837), by H.R. Robinson, links the hard times of 1837 to national policies. In this image, rent collectors appear at the door while an out-of-work carpenter, with his tools strewn on the bare floor, tells his hungry wife and children "I have not the means, and cannot get any work." Faint portraits of Democratic presidents Jackson and Van Buren are hanging on the walls.

According to this cartoon, who is to blame for the financial crises of 1837? Who suffers? ▶

Library of Congress Prints and Photographs Division Washington, D.C[LC-USZ62–36585]

The boom-bust economy of the 1830s and 1840s brought the flaws in majority rule into sharp focus as some regions rose and others suffered. In response, some states tried to renegotiate the terms of their participation in the Union. New coalitions formed political parties more responsive to the needs and interests of those states. When global markets entangled the United States in another crushing economic depression, elected representatives redesigned laws and institutions to cope with seemingly anonymous global forces. In doing so, they debated the proper balance between open competition and necessary shelter.

☞ As you read, reflect on the ways Americans used democratic politics to rethink the meaning of individual rights. How did lawmaking reflect changing ideas about rights?

9-5a States' Rights

Alexis de Tocqueville, a French aristocrat and political thinker who toured the United States in the 1830s, wrote critically about the

{ A revived focus on state political power emerges as a counterweight to majority rule.

social dimensions of American democracy. The much-celebrated majority rule, he claimed, restricted true liberty: "I know of no country in which there is so little independence of mind and real freedom of discussion as in America." Madison had warned against the political consequences of this "tyranny of the majority" during the constitutional debates of the 1780s, cautioning that because the essence of democracy is the rule of the majority, government must be carefully designed to protect the rights of the minority. Tocqueville focused on social costs, arguing that democratic despotism oppressed people who did not even realize it. While the aristocratic rulers of Europe controlled people's bodies with decrees about forbidden behaviors, democracy in the United States coerced conformity by insisting that the majority was correct and opponents should be ostracized.

The political realities of majority rule combined with a rising sense of **sectionalism** dividing the country reinvigorated debate over the proper balance between the rights of states and the interests of the country as a whole. When Congress passed the **Tariff of 1828**, white South Carolinians believed that it blatantly favored northern industry at the expense of southern commercial agriculture. But how could they stop the measure, given that a majority vote had passed it? In an anonymous essay, Vice President Calhoun proposed a method for states to nullify federal laws they deemed unconstitutional. His *doctrine of nullification* stated that the federal Constitution was a compact between individual states that retained their own sovereignty. When

sectionalism Political loyalty to one's own region of the country in opposition to other regions that in the nineteenth century was increasingly between North and South.

Tariff of 1828 Federal tax on imported manufactured goods that prompted a political crisis dividing the cotton-producing South from the North and Midwest.

Whigs Political party created to oppose the Democrats and to champion a strong federal government and, in some cases, moral reform.

there was a disagreement about that compact, states kept the right to interpret it as they saw fit. In other words, the states, not the federal courts, had the final say on whether a federal law was constitutional. Calhoun suggested that South Carolina hold a state convention and vote the tariff null and void and then take its cause to the other states in a specially called convention. If three-quarters of the other states disagreed, the nullifying state had two choices: either live with the law or withdraw from the United States.

The doctrine of nullification was a way to protect minority rights. In this case, southern planters were the minority. Supporters claimed to be following in the patriotic tradition of the Kentucky and Virginia Resolutions, which had suggested that sovereign states were the best check on tyrannical power. Opponents disagreed, declaring the U.S. Constitution an agreement among "we the people" of the United States, not merely a compact between independent states. That same Constitution, they argued, gave the power to regulate commerce to the federal government.

Andrew Jackson was known as a strong states' rights supporter. He was a cotton planter and a slave owner, but he opposed nullification, insisting "Our Federal Union. It must be preserved." He thought that the tariff would temporarily help the United States raise money to pay its debts and increase its military defense. He therefore signed a tariff act in 1832 that reduced the rates but insisted on the principle of protectionism. South Carolina held a convention and declared federal tariffs null and void in the state. Jackson asked Congress to pass what was called a *Force Bill*, giving him the power to use the military to collect tariff revenues. Even those representatives who opposed nullification thought that this was going too far. Pushed to the brink, Senator Clay devised a compromise to gradually lower the tariff and eventually end protectionist measures. South Carolina promptly nullified the Force Bill, an action that the federal government ignored. The crisis died down, but the issue of states' rights, particularly a state's right to protect legal slavery, would not go away.

9-5b New Political Parties

Native-born businessmen, defenders of displaced Indians, and antitariff Southerners saw Jackson as a tyrant. "King Andrew," they claimed,

{ Opposition parties challenge Democrats and push for a more active government.

manipulated gullible supporters by using the "tyranny of the majority" to crush opposition to his power. Gathering together in a new political party that first ran candidates in the 1836 election, they named themselves the **Whigs** to honor revolutionary patriots and eighteenth-century British opponents of kingly tyranny (see Table 9.1). Whigs saw the expansion of the right to vote and the boisterous political culture of rallies, party platforms, and parades as the collapse of the Founding Fathers' vision, not its logical next step, as Democrats did. "*The Republic has degenerated*

Table 9.1 Comparison of U.S. Political Parties

Both the Democratic and Whig parties of the second party system were coalitions, made up of voters with diverse views on religion, slavery, and regional economic power. In terms of style, both parties adopted imagery that presented politics as a battle of rugged masculinity.

Democrats	Whigs
Favored weaker federal government	Favored stronger federal government
Supported state control of internal improvements	Supported federal investment in internal improvements
Encouraged immigration	Distrusted immigration
Were motivated by local rights and the "common man" against monopolies	Were motivated by social reform issues
Had strongest support from laborers, Catholic immigrants, Southerners	Had strongest support from businessmen, native-born Protestants, New Englanders, free blacks
Had Andrew Jackson, Martin Van Buren as national figures	Had Henry Clay, William Henry Harrison as national figures

into a Democracy" one Virginia newspaper lamented, using the term *democracy* in its negative eighteenth-century sense of mob rule. Whigs preferred a system in which the passions of the majority were filtered through the judgment of elites. Influenced by evangelical Christianity, they praised self-control and domesticity for men.

Whigs advocated an active central government. They championed many of the elements of the American System, including a national tariff, a new national bank, and renewed support for internal improvements. Mostly native-born Protestants, Whigs tended to concentrate in the Upper South, the North, and parts of the West focused on commercial development.

Working people's struggles to improve their conditions highlighted the importance of the ballot box. Laws forbidding unionization, imprisoning debtors, and seizing the property of bankrupts could change only by the action of elected officials, and the major parties seemed unconcerned with the suffering of workers and debtors. Inspired by similar organizations in England, Philadelphia workers formed the first Working Men's Party in 1828 to represent "the interests and enlightenment of the working classes." In 1837, workers and farmers in Utica, New York, established the Equal Rights Party to demand a legal system that would protect average people, not just propertied investors. Working Men's political parties championed several causes, including free public schools, an end to imprisonment for debt, the payment of all wages in hard currency, and a ten-hour workday. Dissatisfied with the candidates of the Democrats and then the Whigs, these **third parties** defined and spoke for a specific constituency. Most were short lived. Their success, typically, came when one of the two major parties took up their issue as its own.

9-5c Credit Crash and Its Consequences

The year 1836 began on a bubble of enthusiasm for speculation in the U.S. economy. The transatlantic cotton business was booming again as British firms purchased U.S. cotton at ever-higher prices and sent desirable manufactured goods to American ports. Gold and silver flowed in as well. Imported from Mexico where it was mined, silver had long been funneled to China in exchange for imports. In the 1830s, Chinese merchants preferred paper bills on British banks, which were more easily integrated into the opium trade with India. Flush with borrowed British paper that they passed on to the Chinese, U.S. state banks began to accumulate Mexican silver. To many of these banks, more silver in the vault justified the printing of more paper money. Individuals eagerly borrowed that new money, in turn, to purchase western land sold by the federal government. Borrowers speculated that the value of land would rise quickly enough to enable them to pay off their debts. But just as in 1818, such practices were vulnerable to sudden credit contractions.

> Americans face the consequences of speculation.

Contraction came first from England, where a bad grain harvest forced the Bank of England to restrict its credit, leading to a domino effect of firms calling in their transatlantic debts. The panic spread and deepened as the consequences of new U.S. financial policies took over. Jackson, at the end of his presidency, had tried to curb speculation in 1836 by adopting the **Specie Circular**, which prohibited the federal government from accepting anything but gold and silver coin as payment for government land. Martin Van Buren, Jackson's vice-president who was elected president in 1836, left the policy in place even as the panic took hold. The effect was to reduce the value of the notes that farmers held. People rushed to the banks to obtain specie with which to repay their debts, but the banks lacked sufficient reserves to pay depositors. More than half of the nation's banks failed. As banks desperately called in their business loans to obtain specie, businesses failed in turn. Unemployment soared, and wages fell by as much as 50 percent. Following the philosophy of the Democratic Party, which called for limits on federal power, Van Buren refused to involve the federal government in stopping the panic or depression that followed.

The **Panic of 1837** had international causes, but many read the hard times that followed as an indictment of U.S. democracy. With more than 30 percent of workers in New York City unemployed, many wondered whether the U.S. government could still respond to the needs of the people or if it had become completely captive to the interests of bankers and bosses.

third parties Political parties other than the main two that have often coalesced around a specific cause.

Specie Circular Jackson's executive order requiring payments for public land in specie rather than credit or bank notes that was repealed in 1838.

Panic of 1837 Financial crisis of international origins that led to bankruptcies, bank failures, and unemployment.

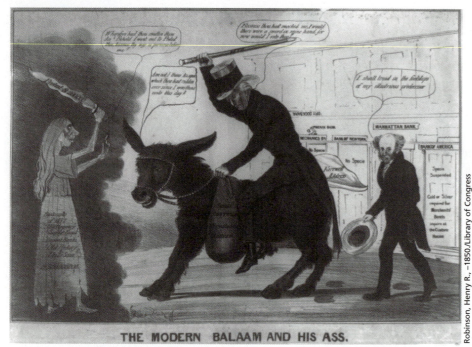

THE MODERN BALAAM AND HIS ASS.

Andrew Jackson Rides the Democratic Donkey This 1837 political cartoon references a Biblical story to criticize Jackson for being a false prophet indifferent to the suffering he has caused as president. With a "Farewell Address" trailing out of his pocket, Jackson beats his donkey with a cane marked "veto." Newly elected Van Buren follows in the footsteps of his predecessor, oblivious to the specter brandishing a flaming sword to protest their actions. ▲

Robinson, Henry R., –1850./Library of Congress

Increasing suspicion about the legality and utility of state charters combined with a rash of states defaulting on their loans led to the sharp curtailment of such charters in the years after the panic. Whereas 70 percent of canal construction had been financed by state and local sources, 70 percent of railroad construction came from private investment. The U.S. Supreme Court, in *Charles River Bridge vs. Warren Bridge* (1837), ruled against the types of state monopolies that had been at the heart of early nineteenth-century commercial development, preferring to bolster the rights of individual entrepreneurs to compete. The case revolved around a state-chartered toll bridge linking Charlestown and Boston that had been extremely profitable for its owners. When Warren Bridge, a rival, constructed in 1828 less than a hundred yards from the first cut into those profits, the Charles River owners sued for protection of their corporate rights. The court's decision supported the new bridge and private competition.

To cope with the fallout of so many Americans "going smash," Congress tried again to fashion a bankruptcy law that would satisfy creditors without destroying debtors. The Bankruptcy Act of 1841 offered a fresh start to anyone who obeyed court orders and gave over assets to a bankruptcy assignee. For the next two years, forty-one thousand Americans were designated bankrupts. They were not imprisoned or branded for life as cheats; most went on to waged work that offered steadier, although less potentially lucrative returns, than entrepreneurship. For some creditors, the idea of such a safety net was galling—should gamblers be allowed to cheat the people who had trusted them with no consequences? Under political pressure, Congress revoked the Bankruptcy Act in 1843.

Most free Americans continued to believe that financial failure was the fault of the individual in spite of the fact that the expanding economy had exposed average people to international and transcontinental forces they could not control. Disappointed European investors, who held the bonds that U.S. states refused to repay in the crisis, blamed governments unwilling to tax voters.

Summary

In the early decades of the nineteenth century, political revolutions and industrialization eroded imperial trade monopolies as nations competed for position in global markets. Market transformations changed labor and family patterns. Although many farm families continued to operate under an integrated household economy, urban and immigrant families increasingly consisted of a collection of waged workers who pooled their disparate resources to survive. Global labor flows further broke up and reassembled families as free sons and daughters migrated within the United States and immigration brought in new workers and communities. Enslaved families long established in the tobacco-producing coastal regions were torn apart by an interstate slave trade serving the demands of continent-spanning cotton and textile businesses.

Projects such as the C & O canal helped promote a unified United States, bridging old regional divides between the coast and the western borderlands by constructing vital links between them. But new divisions threatened to destabilize the American union. The relationship between the developing economic system and the U.S. political system underwent profound flux in the opening decades of the century as the East–West political divide of the Revolutionary era was replaced by a North–South divide over slavery. Working against these sectional trends, a new party system tried to knit together coalitions that reached across regional divides. Slave-owning Southerners and poor Irish immigrants in northern cities became Jacksonian democrats.

Faced with an economy they could not control, Americans struggled to use their political system to speak for their interests. Old debates over the contest between majority rule and minority rights in a republic took new sectional shape in the democratic system that had emerged by 1840.

‹Thinking Back, *Looking Forward*›

As you review this chapter, compare the global forces behind early colonial migrations, both free and forced, with the global forces that were behind migrations, again both free and forced, in the first decades of the nineteenth century. How did the changing nature of labor itself affect families? How did work lives and family ties change from the mid-eighteenth century to the mid-nineteenth century?

In coming chapters, be alert to how families, religious practices, new institutions, and cultural forms responded to the disruptions caused by nineteenth-century economic transformations.

To make your study concrete, review the timeline and reflect on the entries there. Think about their causes, consequences, and connections. How do they connect events in North America to global trends?

Additional Resources

Books

Beckert, Sven. *Empire of Cotton: A Global History*. New York: Knopf, 2014. ▶ Sweeping study of capitalism and the global cotton trade.

Igler, David. *The Great Ocean: Pacific Worlds from Captain Cook to the Gold Rush*. New York: Oxford University Press, 2013. ▶ Portrayal of the international Pacific World of the nineteenth century.

Johnson, Paul. *Sam Patch, the Famous Jumper*. New York: Hill and Wang, 2004. ▶ Story of a competitive waterfall jumper and the Industrial Revolution.

Johnson, Walter. *Soul by Soul: Life inside the Antebellum Slave Market*. Cambridge, MA: Harvard University Press, 1999. ▶ Illumination of the dynamics of human commodification in the domestic slave trade.

Larson, John. *Internal Improvement: National Public Works and the Promise of Popular Government in the Early United States*. Chapel Hill: University of North Carolina Press, 2001. ▶ History of the connections between transportation projects and the shift from republic to democracy.

Mihm, Steven. *A Nation of Counterfeiters: Capitalists, Con Men, and the Making of the United States*. Cambridge, MA: Harvard University Press, 2009. ▶ Exploration of the making and distribution of counterfeit bills.

Rockman, Seth. *Scraping By: Wage Labor, Slavery, and Survival in Early Baltimore*. Baltimore, MD: Johns Hopkins University Press, 2009. ▶ Detailed study of enslaved and free workers in nineteenth-century Baltimore.

Watson, Harry L. *Liberty and Power: The Politics of Jacksonian America*. New York: Hill and Wang, 2006. ▶ Classic, engaging survey of culture and politics in the early nineteenth century.

Wilentz, Sean. *The Rise of U.S. Democracy: Jefferson to Lincoln*. New York: W.W. Norton, 2005. ▶ Interpretive synthesis of the political and cultural ramifications of nineteenth-century democracy.

Zaeske, Susan. *Signatures of Citizenship: Petitioning, Antislavery, and Women's Political Identity*. Chapel Hill: University of North Carolina Press, 2003. ▶ Study of the form and use of petitions as political tools by women.

Go to the MindTap® for **Global Americans** to access the full version of select books from this Additional Resources section.

Websites

Capitalism by Gaslight at the Library Company. (http://www.librarycompany.org/shadoweconomy/index.htm) ▶ Exhibition with documents featuring the illicit economies of the nineteenth century.

Cotton Town. (http://www.cottontown.org/Pages/default.aspx). ▶ Extensive collection of documents and analysis of the English cotton industry.

Railroad Maps at the Library of Congress. (http://www.loc.gov/collection/railroad-maps-1828-to-1900/about-this-collection/). ▶ Collection of 623 railroad maps and associated documents.

Transatlantic Slave Trade Database. (http://www.slavevoyages.org). ▶ Detailed numbers and maps of the slave trade into the nineteenth century.

Women Working, 1800–1930. (http://ocp.hul.harvard.edu/ww/index.html). ▶ Valuable collection of primary sources and essays on women at work.

Continue exploring online through MindTap®, **where you can:**

MindTap®
- **Assess your knowledge with the Chapter Test**
- **Watch historical videos related to the chapter**
- **Further your understanding with interactive maps and timelines**

Markets and Democracy

1790–1792

April 1790

Congress passes the first patent act, granting fourteen-year monopoly on registered inventions.

November 1790

Blanc demonstrates the principle of interchangeable parts on gunlocks in Paris.

February 1792

Congress formally organizes the United States Post Office.

1807–1810

March 1807

Congress abolishes the international slave trade, effective 1808.

November 1808

Madison wins election as president.

June 1810

Astor charters the Pacific Fur Company to establish a fur trading post on the Pacific Coast.

1812–1816

November 1812

Madison wins reelection as president.

1812–1814

War of 1812 pits the United States against Britain and its allies.

April 1816

Second Bank of the United States created.

Congress passes a protective tariff on imported cotton and wool textiles.

November 1816

Monroe wins election as president.

1819–1820

1819

Panic of 1819, sparked by European postwar recovery, sends U.S. economy into downturn.

March 1820

Missouri Compromise admits Missouri to the United States as a slave state and Maine as a free state.

November 1820

Monroe wins reelection as president.

1821–1825

1821

Boston Manufacturing Company creates cotton textile manufactory in Lowell, Massachusetts.

September 1821

Russian Czar Alexander I declares the Alaskan coast forbidden to non-Russian ships.

December 1823

Monroe Doctrine states that the American Hemisphere must remain free from European interference.

February 1825

John Quincy Adams wins election as president in a decision made in the House of Representatives.

October 1825

Erie Canal connecting Albany to Buffalo is completed.

Britain
Belgium
France
Netherlands
Europe
Russia

United States
Southeastern Indians
Seminoles

China

Uruguay

276

1828–1829

May 1828
Congress passes Tariff of 1828 over South Carolina's objections.

July 1828
Construction begins on the Baltimore and Ohio Railroad, connecting the Potomac and Ohio Rivers.

November 1828
Jackson wins election as the first president from the new Democratic Party.

April 1829
British Parliament passes Catholic Emancipation Act, permitting Catholics to serve in government.

1830

May
Jackson signs the Indian Removal Act, authorizing land grants for Indians west of the Mississippi.

July
Independent Uruguay models first constitution on U.S. and French examples.

August
French King Charles X abdicates in favor of Louis Philippe, the "citizen king."

November
Belgians declare independence from the Netherlands.

1832

July
Jackson vetoes the recharter of the Second Bank of the United States.

November
Jackson wins reelection as president.

1833–1836

August 1833
Workers from diverse trades form the General Trades Union in New York.

1835
Seminoles fight guerilla war against the United States to oppose removal (to 1842).

1836
Female mill workers in Lowell organize a turn-out that lasts months.

November 1836
Van Buren wins election as president, defeating candidates from the new Whig Party.

1837–1844

1837
Bank failures and unemployment soar in the Panic of 1837.

February 1837
House of Representatives resolves that slaves lack the right to petition because they are not citizens.

August 1841
Congress passes Bankruptcy Act that applies to average Americans, not just elite businessmen.

July 1844
Treaty of Wanghia with China grants the United States trading privileges equal to those of Britain and France.

10 Personal Transformations and Public Reforms

1800–1848

Lucretia Mott and Elizabeth Cady Stanton met when both traveled to London for the World's Anti-Slavery Convention, where the younger Stanton in particular was awakened to a larger world.

When they met in 1840, Elizabeth Cady Stanton was a 25-year-old bride on her honeymoon and Lucretia Mott was a 47-year-old international activist. Both had traveled to London for the World's Anti-Slavery Convention, Stanton as a supportive observer and Mott as a delegate from the Philadelphia Female Anti-Slavery Society. The British and Foreign Anti-Slavery Society, organizer of the convention, had invited "the friends of the slave of every nation and every clime" to come to coordinate international efforts. Britain had legally emancipated slaves in its colonies in 1833, and British abolitionists wanted to end slavery everywhere. Responding to the call, nearly five hundred activists from across England and Ireland, the Caribbean (Jamaica, Antigua, Barbados, Haiti, and Mauritius), Africa (Sierra Leone), France, Spain, Canada, and the United States met in London.

The Library of Congress

Elizabeth Cady Stanton with Her Daughter, Harriot, 1856

The U.S. delegation included seven women, many of them Quakers like Mott, who were leaders in American antislavery societies. But when the women tried to present their credentials and take their places, the conference organizers refused, stating that it was against "English custom and usage" to permit women equal participation in men's antislavery work.

The first day of the conference was devoted to debating this issue with opponents stating that they would be "embarrassed" to talk about the horrors of slavery in front of ladies. One black male delegate from Jamaica thought that including women would "lower the dignity" of the proceedings and make it a subject of ridicule. London attorney William Ashurst called these delegates out for their hypocrisy. How could it be, he asked, that a convention in favor of universal humanity was opening by "disfranchising one-half of creation"? The delegates were unconvinced and voted overwhelmingly to make the women sit silently behind a divider. Some American men, including leading abolitionist William Lloyd Garrison, joined them in solidarity.

To Mott and the other longtime activists, the debate highlighted a familiar dilemma. Efforts to reform social ills—from drunkenness to prostitution to poverty to slavery—depended on women as speakers, writers, fund-raisers, and organizers. Yet women could not vote, and powerful cultural ideals demanded they remain in the background. Undaunted, Mott continued with her European tour, lecturing and meeting allies interested in ending these limitations to women's rights. Stanton was electrified by her new transatlantic acquaintances: "It was intensely gratifying to hear all that . . . I had dimly thought, so freely discussed by other women."

Many in the nineteenth century experienced a newfound sense of living in a larger world. Some, like Stanton, were energized and inspired. Garrison's antislavery newspaper bore the motto "Our country is the world—our countrymen are mankind." Cheaper travel, faster printing presses, and more widespread literacy made it possible to spread culture and ideas quickly through neighborhoods and across international political boundaries. New ideas about human nature and human capacities made forging these connections imperative.

At the same time, industrialization, displacement, and urbanization created social problems that divided people in new ways. Manufacturing

What do Lucretia Mott and Elizabeth Cady Stanton's experiences at the World's Anti-Slavery Convention reveal about the relationship between democracy and reform in the nineteenth century?

Go to MindTap® to watch a video on Mott and Stanton and learn how their stories relate to the themes of this chapter.

boomtowns and cities were crowded with poor and transient people competing for low-wage work. The territorial expansion of the United States forced Native, French, and Spanish communities to adapt their own legal systems and family patterns. Regimented labor brutalized slaves on cotton fields and demoralized workers in factories. The boom-bust economy left farmers and clerks scrambling to plan for the future. An economy and political culture built on competition was ruthless to losers.

Remedies took one of two main approaches: strengthening communities or asserting individual rights. In city neighborhoods, free black people created mutual aid societies. In rural areas, men and women experimented with new forms of communal living. Everywhere, churches hoped to change behavior and reform society by reinforcing the bonds between believers. At the same time, and often in the same regions, men and women stressed autonomy as much as community. Thinkers sought wisdom in self-reliance. Slaves escaped to free themselves. Women, white and black, continued to expand the claims of equality.

10-1
American Communities

George Catlin's *Five Points* (1827) depicts black and white New Yorkers working, fighting, and socializing in the streets. The painting details nineteenth-century urban life, including people pumping and carrying water, a prostitute soliciting customers from an upper-story window, and the proliferation of grocery shops, most of which sold alcohol. Catlin's picture also highlights contrasts: A pig is foraging in the garbage at the feet of a man in a top hat.

How does the artist portray relationships among these neighbors? Is he depicting one community? ▶

The Five Points, Junction of Baxter, Worth and Park Streets, New York (hand-coloured engraving), Catlin, George (1796–1872) (after)/© Museum of the City of New York, USA/Bridgeman Images

Migration, industrialization, and global trade restructured nineteenth-century U.S. communities, gradually in some regions and dramatically in others. From the countryside and from Europe, people flocked to cities to work in factories, offices, and service industries. In search of productive land, farmers pushed west onto former Indian territory. Across the South, export-minded cotton growers dragged enslaved African Americans away from families and work lives. Up streams and over mountains, Native Americans and fur traders joined distant markets. All confronted new lives among strangers who differed in wealth, religion, and culture. In most cases, families bore the brunt of economic change.

☞ As you read, think about how the economic forces of the early nineteenth century, including migration, industrialization, and global trade, reshaped communities in the United States. Were people aware of larger patterns, or was their context mainly local?

10-1a U.S. Cities

The majority of Americans lived rural lives in the nineteenth century, but between 1820 and 1850, a significant proportion of the population was caught up in a quick urbanization (see Table 10.1). Old ports grew as industries in them expanded, and transportation networks created new boomtowns along canals and railroads. In 1820, only 7 percent of Americans lived in cities of more than twenty-five hundred people, but thirty years later, 18 percent did. Three groups—migrants from rural surroundings, free black people, and immigrants from abroad—accounted for the bulk of this increase.

> Urban communities fracture along lines of class, race, and religion.

They found, especially in the larger cities, the same problems of poverty, crowding, and illness that American

Table 10.1 Urban Population and Growth around the World (in thousands)

In the first half of the nineteenth century, city populations in the United States increased dramatically. By mid-century, some equaled the size of European urban centers, although most were dwarfed by the major cities of Asia and Europe. Slave labor and transatlantic trade led to large population increases in Brazil's Rio de Janeiro, where slave-grown coffee became a significant export, and in England's Manchester, home to industrial cotton manufacturing.

City	Population in 1800	Population 1850–1851	Percent Increase (%)
New Orleans	8	116	1,350
Boston	25	137	448
Baltimore	26	169	550
New York City	60	696	1,060
Philadelphia	69	340	393
Rio de Janeiro	43	166	286
Mexico City	137	170	24
Manchester	90	303	237
Berlin	172	419	144
Amsterdam	217	224	3
Vienna	247	444	80
St. Petersburg	336	485	44
Paris	581	1,053	81
London	1,117	2,685	140
Edo (Tokyo)		1,150	
Osaka		330	
Beijing		850	
Suzhou		700	

Sources: International Historical Statistics; Saito Seji, "Edo jidai no toshi jinko [Urban Population of the Edo Period]," Chiiki kaihatsu [Local Development], September 1984, pp. 48-63, Sekiyama Naotaro, Kinsei nihon no jinko kozo [The Population Structure of Early Modern Japan], Tokyo: Yoshikawa Kobunkan, 1958: Chinese statistics are for the 1840s, from G. William Skinner, The City in Late Imperial China.

statesmen and wealthy travelers had always condemned in European cities. In poor neighborhoods, men worked for low wages as manual laborers, women took in sewing and did cleaning work, and children scavenged in the streets for trash that could be resold. They lived in crowded wooden buildings with nowhere to dump garbage but out the window. The infamous **Five Points** neighborhood of Lower Manhattan sat at an intersection of streets and had once been a skating pond. Decades of garbage and run-off from urban tanneries and landfill turned it into a place where disease passed quickly through the water supply.

Filthy conditions and international trade exposed Americans to global epidemics. Cholera, a disease originating in South Asia, had begun traveling with sailors by 1817 (see Map 10.1). An 1831 outbreak in London spread to Canada and then to New York in 1832, hitting the poor of the Five Points especially hard. Children who seemed well in the morning died by evening, their bodies shaking with cramps. Of the city's 250,000 residents, 3,515 died before the epidemic subsided. As they fled, traveling on mail coaches and canal boats, people carried the disease as far north as Maine, deep into the Midwest, and down the Mississippi to New Orleans, where it claimed thousands more lives. No one at the time knew that water contaminated by human and animal waste was to blame. Instead, cholera was called the "poor man's plague," both because the poor were disproportionately victims and, some wealthy New Yorkers believed, they were the perpetrators. "They have brought the cholera this year," wrote former mayor Philip Hone, "and they will always bring wretchedness and want." Charles Dickens, the popular British author, likened the Five Points to London slums on his visit in 1842: "All that is loathsome, drooping, and decayed is here."

Competition for work among free blacks, native-born poor whites, and recent European immigrants was intense. Male laborers could earn $1 a day for construction or dock work, but work was not available every day. A woman in Baltimore might earn six cents for every pair of pants she sewed, but in the next building would be another woman, sewing faster and enlisting her children to help. Discriminatory laws barred African Americans from many jobs and membership in institutions.

Sometimes hostility among neighbors erupted into violence. On the evening of July 7, 1834, a group of musicians from the New York Sacred Music Society arrived at the Chatham Street Chapel and discovered an African American choir had

Five Points Neighborhood in New York City named for the "points" created where three streets intersected that was internationally known for poverty, crowding, and violence.

Map 10.1 The Global Cholera Epidemic of 1829–1836 The cholera epidemic spread along the same routes as imperial armies, religious pilgrims, and traders. Death tolls were highest in urban areas, leading many observers to conclude that it was a disease of the urban poor. But improved transportation, including canals, turnpikes, trails, and steamships also spread the disease to rural parts of Europe and Asia, and deep into the North American interior. ▲

received permission to use the large hall to celebrate the seventh anniversary of New York's final, full emancipation of slaves. A brawl between musicians escalated into days of violent rioting as thousands of white New Yorkers pulled down the houses of African Americans, desecrated black churches, and assaulted blacks in the city.

In response to this environment of violence and discrimination, African Americans formed tight-knit subcommunities around racial solidarity that often transcended class or family background. They organized mutual aid societies and established their own churches. They protected runaways from slave catchers and protested attempts to enslave free people. Even blacks who had been born to free parents participated in annual public commemorations of the end of the Atlantic slave trade in 1808.

nativism Ideology opposing immigrants in favor of preserving the privileges of existing citizens.

Using the Catholic church as a foundation, Irish immigrants built their own subcommunities supported by a network of aid associations, schools, militia companies, and political organizations. In Philadelphia, the Hibernian Society for the Relief of Immigrants met incoming ships at the docks with clothing, cash, and offers of assistance to help immigrants find work and housing. Skilled Irish workers joined together in businesses and craft associations to form contracts that competed with U.S.-born workers, often by working for less money.

Cultural and religious clashes between immigrant Irish Catholics and native-born Protestants layered on top of labor competition. Nineteenth-century American Protestants inherited anti-Catholic biases that had taken root during centuries of Europe's wars of religion. Sensational Protestant publications, such as the 1836 *Awful Disclosures of Maria Monk*, accused Catholic priests and nuns of secret immorality and asserted that Catholic institutions in the United States were populated by conspiracists hoping to undermine American institutions. Popular publications fed the political **nativism** that opposed immigrant rights.

10-1b The Middle Class

On the outskirts of crowded cities lived a group of U.S.-born white Americans who worked with their brains rather than their muscles and

New ideologies of the home structure middle-class life.

lived not on the streets but in homes as part of the **middle class**. This class, created by the developing system of capitalism, was in one sense an economic standing between poverty and aristocratic wealth. It was also a culture practiced initially in the urban Northeast but expanding into the South and West. Middle-class Americans were self-conscious about their economic standing and anxious that the boom-bust economy could take it away. They placed their faith in a culture of sober respectability involving Protestant churchgoing, thriftiness, and moderation to keep them secure.

The most significant social hallmark of the middle class was the separation of home and work. Factories, banks, loan offices, canal companies, and other expanding industries created new occupations for men as lawyers, engineers, bankers, and managers. Rather than toil side-by-side with their wives and children in shops or on farms, these men went out to work. Farm life had always involved a gendered division of labor in which men plowed and harvested, repaired tools, and built fences while women made and preserved food, washed and repaired clothing, and cared for children. But as adult men moved into paid work away from home, the gendered division of labor became a profound separation in the daily lives of middle-class men and women. Middle-class wives still engaged in housework and child care, alone and with the help of servants, but out of the sight of men and for no compensation.

As unpaid domestic work lost its status as an overtly economic contribution, many came to see it as a labor of love. Across industrializing Europe, women's skills in cooking, cleaning, and nurturing were loudly praised as evidence of their natural destiny, and the U.S. middle class took up the message. For centuries, philosophers and ministers had insisted that men needed to be in charge of children and household because they were more rational and God had granted them more power. But new times demanded new explanations for family life. Magazines like *Godey's Lady's Book* founded in 1830 promoted a new culture of the home, led by women, called **domesticity**. Through pictures and text, the magazine insisted that men and women lived in different "spheres" of life, each one appropriate to inborn differences in the sexes. Men dominated business and politics because they were fundamentally rational, aggressive, and competitive. Women presided over homes because these spaces required people who were emotional, nurturing, and self-effacing. In the evenings, men and women reunited.

Domesticity contained many contradictions at the heart of middle-class life. Superior mothering depended on having fewer children. Over the course of the nineteenth century, the white birthrate fell from seven to five children per woman as husbands and wives cooperated to use periods of abstinence, herbs such as savin and pennyroyal, and, after mid-century advances in rubber technology, condoms and other devices. On farms, additional children meant additional laborers, but in a middle-class urban setting, more children required more resources to educate, place in careers, and establish in marriages. Domesticity also praised the home but required regular trips out to obtain the appropriate clothing, toys, and home decoration from an expanding consumer culture. Finally, although domesticity celebrated women as natural caregivers, a growing industry offered expert instruction. In her 1841 *Treatise on Domestic Economy*, educator Catharine Beecher outlined a chore for middle-class women to do every hour of the day.

Domesticity also highlighted the distance between middle-class lives and those of poorer neighbors. Black, white, immigrant, and U.S.-born poor people lived in crowded, chaotic spaces that doubled as workplaces; they had no hope of practicing the ideals of domesticity.

10-1c Families in the West and Midwest

From St. Louis to Santa Fe and north along the Pacific Coast, men from the United States claimed a place in the fur trade. Just as the French

Mixed-race communities bind western settlements.

and Spanish had, they forged trading networks centered on families formed through marriage, adoption, and guardianship. In 1800, in the fur-trading hub of St. Louis, 80 percent of people born were *métis*, meaning that they had Indian as well as European ancestors. New cross-cultural families formed when Euro-American men sought Indian wives who possessed the skills and connections to help them succeed in the trade. A. P. Chouteau, West Point graduate and oldest son of a powerful fur-trading family, left his wife, Sophie, and children in St. Louis in 1822 when he obtained a U.S. license to trade with Osages and Kickapoos along the Arkansas River. The new venture depended on strong Indian allies, and for Chouteau, that meant Osage wives. Just as powerful Osage men did, Chouteau married several women over the course of his time on the Arkansas and Missouri Rivers, creating a broad network of allies whom he depended on for the business and eventually for diplomatic missions between the United States and Indian tribes on the Plains. His Osage household raised the next

middle class Part of society that had to engage in work to survive but had enough income to enjoy leisure and self-improvement with the aid of consumer goods.

domesticity Ideology praising home life as a peaceful oasis sheltered from the public in which middle-class women oversaw the emotional comfort of the family.

History without Borders

The Middle Class

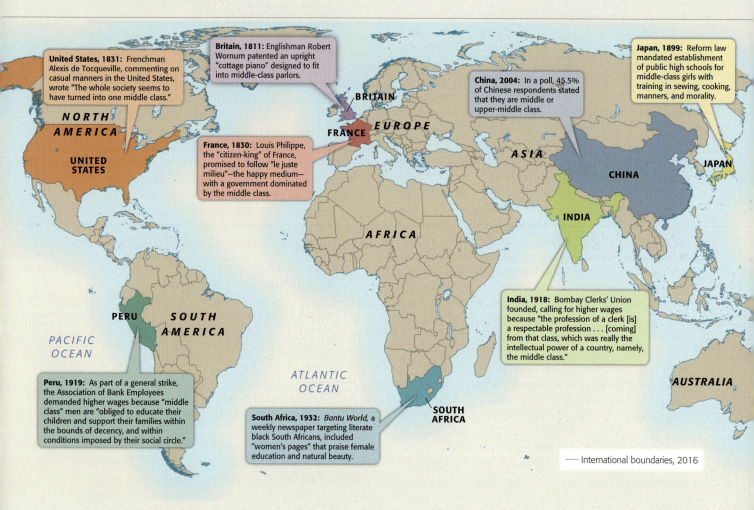

United States, 1831: Frenchman Alexis de Tocqueville, commenting on casual manners in the United States, wrote "The whole society seems to have turned into one middle class."

Britain, 1811: Englishman Robert Wornum patented an upright "cottage piano" designed to fit into middle-class parlors.

France, 1830: Louis Philippe, the "citizen-king" of France, promised to follow "le juste milieu"—the happy medium—with a government dominated by the middle class.

China, 2004: In a poll, 45.5% of Chinese respondents stated that they are middle or upper-middle class.

Japan, 1899: Reform law mandated establishment of public high schools for middle-class girls with training in sewing, cooking, manners, and morality.

India, 1918: Bombay Clerks' Union founded, calling for higher wages because "the profession of a clerk [is] a respectable profession . . . [coming] from that class, which was really the intellectual power of a country, namely, the middle class."

Peru, 1919: As part of a general strike, the Association of Bank Employees demanded higher wages because "middle class" men are "obliged to educate their children and support their families within the bounds of decency, and within conditions imposed by their social circle."

South Africa, 1932: *Bantu World,* a weekly newspaper targeting literate black South Africans, included "women's pages" that praise female education and natural beauty.

—— International boundaries, 2016

The Middle Class Around the World Arising along with industrialization at different periods, middle classes around the world often announced their existence in order to claim political rights. The term "middle" was not usually a measure of wealth; instead, it was meant to imply the group's separation from corrupt aristocracy on the one hand and ignorant poor on the other. ▲

Emerging in different locations at different points in the late eighteenth, nineteenth, and twentieth centuries, middle-class status was made in manufacturing enterprises, private homes, and elected governments. Industrialization created more opportunities for men to work as professionals, bureaucrats, and business owners who earned incomes in the form of profits and wages. The consequences were financial: economic comfort and access to consumer goods unknown to most people. The results were also political because income and financial independence, not family background,

increasingly qualified men to participate in political leadership. As the middle class expanded, nations adopted new laws abolishing privileges associated with birth. The British Reform Bill of 1832 extended the vote to industrialists and shopkeepers. The Meiji Reforms in late nineteenth-century Japan abolished feudal ranks and created railroad and mining industries that they sold to newly made businessmen. Those businessmen held political offices formerly reserved for elite samurai families.

Middle-class women's work in their own homes was the stabilizing counterpart to marketplace activity. Just as

Godey's Lady's Book trained middle-class American women to preside over families in the 1840s, a half century later *Jogaku zasshi* (*Women's Educational Journal*) used articles about child rearing, temperance meetings, and inspiring literature to turn young urban women in Japan into "good wives and wise mothers." Domesticity ensured morality, whether joined to formal religious observance or not.

Middle-class people proudly identified themselves as moderate in their behavior and material lives: neither too showy nor too coarse, neither too passionate nor too lazy, and neither

Godey's Lady's Book, March 1850

THE SPHERE OF WOMAN.

TRANSLATED FROM THE GERMAN OF GOETHE.

Mother-Centered Domesticity After 1836, Sarah Josepha Hale, a young widow supporting five children, edited the women's magazine *Godey's Lady's Book*. Because it cost only $3 per year, mill workers as well as middle-class wives could afford it, and circulation reached one hundred fifty thousand by mid-century. The magazine introduced readers to new images of family, centered around a fashionable mother dedicated to the emotional comfort of her children. The domesticity industry also offered literate women new opportunities to support themselves. ▲

Jogaku zasshi

Jogaku Zasshi, **December 1890.** This page from the popular Japanese ladies' magazine features a parlor pump organ, an instrument for entertaining in the home. Middle-class domesticity required consumer purchases and leisure time to cultivate artistic skills and emotional expression. Music lessons for children or adults were part of cultivating social development. As with the pump organ, middle-class purchases were also for performance, allowing the user to demonstrate status to guests. ▲

aristocrat nor peasant. The concept that most middle-class people used, whether they lived in London in 1780, in Baltimore in 1830, or Johannesburg in the 1930s, was "respectability," which described self-controlled, law-abiding, educated, moral, thrifty families. Respectability, they claimed, was what kept them secure in a modern market susceptible to dramatic swings in fortune. Middle-class status knit together a comfortable level of wealth and a culture demonstrating that the possessor of that wealth deserved it.

These ideals became a central plank of colonialism and conquest in the nineteenth and early twentieth centuries. Whereas early fortune seekers and traders in the American Northwest lived in racially mixed outposts, conquest by the United States in the second half of the nineteenth century brought the shuttering of multiracial dance halls and the

creation of reform societies, a pattern that repeated in other regions. Colonial guides for Frenchwomen traveling to Indochina in the early twentieth century told them they were "auxiliary forces" for the French empire by making sure their homes were "happy and gay and that all take pleasure in clustering there." Native people who did not live by middle-class codes were barred from political privileges.

In some times and places, middle-class respectability became a tool that racially marginalized people used to secure better treatment. Black women in 1896 formed the National Association of Colored Women, whose motto, "Lifting as We Climb," stressed the significance of middle-class charity work among poor blacks for improving the image and status of all African Americans. Black men and women in Sophiatown, South Africa, in the 1940s united around an

identity as respectable property owners to establish better schools and demand that the police respond to urban crime in their neighborhoods.

Critical Thinking Questions

▶ Why did groups of people identify themselves as being part of a shared "middle class"? From whom were they separating themselves?

▶ What did "middle-class values" offer people engaged in power struggles over land, resources, and political access?

Go to MindTap® to engage with an interactive version of **History without Borders: The Middle Class.** Learn from an interactive map, view related video, and respond to critical thinking questions.

Bent's Fort Trading outpost built in 1833 by William and Charles Bent for their business in furs and buffalo hides, connecting Indian hunters to global markets.

generation of bicultural children to own land and conduct trade in the Midwest by educating them in mission schools (see Table 10.2) and sending them to St. Louis to spend time with French-American relatives.

Mixed-culture families also anchored the trading posts and forts in the contested West. **Bent's Fort**, located at the foot of the Rocky Mountains in 1833, was a center for trade in buffalo robes, tools, and horses. William Bent gained diplomatic and economic power from his Cheyenne wife, Owl Woman, daughter of a chief who acted as an intermediary between U.S. traders and warring Indian groups. Their children went to schools in St. Louis but spent much of their time with their Cheyenne communities; one observer talked of them

The Granger Collection, New York

A Fur-Trapping Family American men in the fur trade married into Indian families, such as those depicted in *The Trapper and His Family* (1840–1841), by Charles Deas. Deas had a studio in St. Louis, which was a trading hub populated by generations of families with Indian and Euro-American members. In the painting, the trader and his wife have a canoe filled with children, a dog, and a covered pile of animal skins. ▲

"chattering now Indian, and now Spanish or English." Life in and around the adobe fort involved frequent moves among cultures, and Bent's employees typically had families that included European and Indian members. Seasonal trading patterns brought camps of Arapaho, Sioux, Kiowa, and Comanche hunters and their families.

As they moved in and out of the orbit of trading posts, mixed-culture families helped negotiate the strain of migration and overhunting west of the Mississippi River in the 1830s and 1840s, when the political power of the United States and Mexico was distant and often weak. Mixed families on the Southwestern Plains brokered deals between Comanches and Cheyennes who warred over who would control the lucrative hide trade. As refugee Indians moved or were forced west from their origins east of the Mississippi River, they sometimes intermarried with existing Indian and mixed-culture families as an alternative to warring over land.

Intercultural marriages between wealthy California women and ambitious traders settling in Alta California formed the core of an elite group of landholders who rose to power after the province became part of independent Mexico in 1821. Beginning in 1833, successive Mexican governors won approval from their country's central government to break apart the mission system in a process known as *secularization*. They exiled Franciscans, converted missions into parish churches, emancipated Indians from the missions, and granted enormous tracts of land to their friends, subordinates, and relatives. Some native people formed refugee communities with Indian groups nearly depleted by disease. Others became servants or laborers on the reconfigured farms, ranches, and manufactories. Intercultural marriages, representing 15 percent of marriages recorded in California, helped cement "respectable society" that controlled the area's wealth.

Table 10.2 Harmony School Population, 1824–1825

Missionary records from the Harmony School in Missouri document the multicultural backgrounds of children of the fur trade in the early years of Missouri statehood. They also hint at the personal toll of the civilizing mission. Mary E. Sibley was the daughter of Osage chief Sans Oreille and one of his three wives. She was briefly adopted by the Sibleys and renamed before her own mother came to Harmony to bring her home.

Name	Parentage
Catherine Strange	U.S. and Osage
Susan Larivive	Sioux, French, Osage
Rebecca Williams	Pawnee, French, Osage
Mary Ludlow	Pawnee, French, Osage
Louisa Anna Bean	Pawnee, French, Osage
Maria Seward	Osage
Mary Williams	Osage and U.S.
John B. Mitchell	Osage and French
James Chouteau	Osage and French
Julia Michael	Osage and French
Lewis Michael	Osage and French
Gabriel Marlow	French and Pawnee
Augustus Chouteau	French and Osage
William C. Brownlee	Delaware
William Rogers	Pawnee
John B. Packett	Sauk
John McDowell	Osage
Mary E. Sibley	Osage
Jane Renick	Osage and French

Sources: Louis F. Burns, *A History of the Osage People* Anne Hyde, *Empires, Nations, Families.*

10-1d Plantations and Slavery

The global cotton economy enmeshed southern communities along with the rest of the country in industrialization and territorial expansion, and the South's distinctive plantation slavery systems adapted. Slave owning itself was concentrated in a minority of the population: In 1830, only 36 percent of southern whites owned slaves (see Figure 10.1). The average slave owner was a farmer who bet that an investment in owning another human being would allow him to build something bigger. Such slave owners worked in the fields with their slaves—male or female—and hoped to earn enough to purchase additional human property, which would lift them into the upper levels of southern society.

> An expanding institution shapes all southern lives.

If the average white Southerner lived with one or no slaves, the average enslaved Southerner lived with both whites and blacks. Half of the slaves in the South lived on plantations with between ten and fifty other slaves. The overwhelming majority were U.S. born, which set the South apart from other major slave populations of the nineteenth century. Brazil and Cuba, where slaves numbered more than 40 percent of the population in the 1840s, relied on a constant supply of captured Africans to work—and die—on sugar plantations and in towns and industries. The enslaved majorities in South Carolina and Mississippi who emerged by mid-century, in contrast, shared language, culture, and history with the free population.

Close contact between slaves and owners meant close supervision, which intensified on the expanding cotton plantations of the lower South. On Lowcountry rice and indigo plantations, slaves worked a set task and then turned to different crops—corn, squash, potatoes—that they grew in their own gardens to supplement inadequate food supplies. But most enslaved people sold to the cotton growers were from Chesapeake tobacco farms or Caribbean sugar plantations, where they labored from dawn to dusk as part of a gang. On cotton plantations, they found gang labor intensified by a "pushing system" driven by a white overseer hired to whip more work out of them. Cotton planters kept detailed records of each slave's daily work and devised quotas to demand increased productivity. When in the 1830s Israel Campbell picked only ninety pounds in one day rather than one hundred, his owner declared he would suffer "as many lashes as there were pounds short."

Slaves who labored in workshops, stables, or homes avoided some of the physical strain of the fields but suffered even closer attention from slave owners. A plantation was both home and workplace; there could be no isolated domesticity. Cooking, cleaning, sewing, and caring for large families required the work of mistresses and slaves. Slave masters prided themselves on offering hospitality to travelers and visiting family members because the gifts of food, lodging, and conversation expressed a man's honor as well as his wealth. More visitors meant more laundry, however, and failure to perform daily household drudgery sparked violence against slaves just as unmet cotton quotas did.

Slave families tried to mitigate the personal costs of violence and exhaustion by creating networks of love and support. Even though marriages between slaves were not legally recognized, many owners encouraged them, either with people on the same plantation or on neighboring ones, in what were called **abroad marriages**. Slave owners hoped that giving people a stake in family life would keep them docile and prevent runaways. They used the threat of separation to bind mothers, who were more likely to live together with their children, to their owners. Harriet Jacobs, a slave in North Carolina, remembered that her owner threatened to send her children away to a distant plantation unless she did as he commanded. When she resisted, he said, "Your boy shall be put to work, and he shall soon be sold; and your girl shall be raised for the purpose of selling well." In fact, one-third of slave marriages in the nineteenth century ended in forced separation, and parents could expect owners to sell their children away.

The majority of white Southerners supported slaveholding even though they did not themselves own slaves. All free white men were required to donate time to serve on slave patrols, which rode through the countryside on horseback, looking for and capturing runaways. White men elected elite planters with multiple plantations to serve the highest

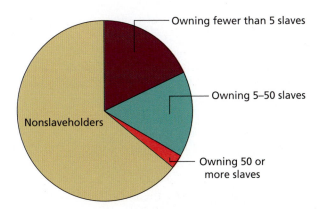

Figure 10.1 Slaveholding in the South, 1830 (in percentages)
Slave owners in the South wielded economic, political, and cultural power, but this wealthy group was greatly outnumbered by those who owned no slaves. Over the course of the middle of the century, the number of slaves increased, but the proportion of slaveholders decreased. By 1860, just 25 percent of white Southerners owned slaves. Yet most white Southerners supported slavery, practically and ideologically. ▲ Source: U.S. Bureau of the Census.

abroad marriages Marriages between enslaved people who lived on separate farms or plantations in which the husband's visit to his wife and children required permission or secrecy.

brawling Style of bare-knuckle
fighting used by white men
in the backcountry South to
defend their honor.

political offices rather than insisting
on representatives closer to their own
rank. In part, white men and women
supported the power of slave owners
because they hoped one day to own
slaves themselves. Even without the direct use of slave
labor, small white farmers operated within an economy
organized around plantation agriculture and planter
dominance. Big plantation stores bought these farmers'
surplus produce to feed their slaves, and skilled artisan
slaves provided services for the community.

10-1e Farming Communities

Whites who lived in the borderland South, far from cotton
fields or growing markets,
developed a more insular
culture. They farmed for their

{ Farm families develop
distinct rural cultures.

own use and hunted and pastured animals in woodlands
shared with neighbors. They lived in a local, kin-based
society of rural villages. Impassable roads isolated people
from the types of internal improvements and international
commerce that fed the cotton trade. In contrast to the
cities of the North or the plantations of the deep South,
work was not specialized or rationalized. Family life, too,
was strikingly different from the middle-class ideals of the
industrializing areas because men and women toiled all
day to meet basic needs.

Masculinity for these families was grounded in
toughness and ferocity, not reliable breadwinning or gentlemanly hospitality. Told they were political equals, poor
white men held little economic or social power as compared to that of the slave owners who dominated southern public life. Instead, these men often fought over small
insults to assert their own honor in a **brawling** style of
fighting that involved kicking, pulling hair, biting ears,
and especially gouging out an opponent's eyes. Mike
Fink, a celebrated gouger and hunter, boasted: "I can out-
run, out-jump, out-shoot, out-brag, out-drink, an' out-
fight, rough-an'-tumble, no holts barred, ary man on both
sides of the river from Pittsburgh to New Orleans an'
back ag'in to St. Louiee."

Some upland farmers left the South and joined the
migrating New Englanders and New Yorkers who settled
in the Northwest. Treaties signed at the end of the War of
1812 pushed the Kickapoos, Potawatomis, and Chippewas
from their land in the Ohio River Valley. U.S. agents and
private speculators sold that land, in turn, to farmers from
New England, New York, Pennsylvania, and Kentucky.
Some were in search of profits from land booms, but many
desired the independence and stability that land brought.
Initially, these families practiced mixed farming. They
bartered small surpluses of corn, hogs, and homespun
cloth for salt, coffee, and tools sold by traveling peddlers.
They raised larger families than Americans in the East
or their remaining Indian neighbors. Women married in
their late teens or early twenties and gave birth to children

German Immigrants' Dream versus Reality German migrants, like those from the East coast, hoped for
the good life on farms in the Midwest. Some were disappointed, as this 1845 German cartoon, "The German
Emigrant," depicts. This man dreams of the life of a southern planter but finds "I perish here a poor wretch
behind the plow/Whilst lion and vulture devour my wife and child." ▲

every two years until their forties. Visiting from New York, Washington Irving joked that he was "in [a] house with nineteen children and thirty-seven dogs."

Over time, developments of the transportation and industrial revolutions transformed these communities. Settled families accumulated land and better tools, including mechanical harvesters that allowed them to increase the size of their surpluses. Ohio canals, stagecoaches, and railway lines meant cheaper access to markets in New York and New Orleans. Soon, Midwestern grain fed New York seamstresses and Mississippi slaves. Transportation lines also carried new immigrants to the Midwest. In the 1840s, German-speaking migrants joined native-born Americans and descendants of French and Indian traders in the Midwest. Many of the newcomers were unable to purchase independent farms and instead became tenants of landowners, locked into rental agreements that earmarked a portion of their proceeds to landlords.

10-2

Religious Awakenings and Social Experiments

Certificate of the Missionary Society of the Methodist Episcopal Church (engraved circa 1838), registers a $20 contribution by Philip Harper. The certificate is both a receipt and a decorative object to be displayed at home. Nathaniel Currier, later part of Currier and Ives, was the most successful commercial lithographer of the nineteenth century, using new printmaking techniques to offer inexpensive popular art to wide swathes of the U.S. and, eventually, European public.

Look at the circle of seated Indians wrapped in blankets and the dark-skinned family on their knees, surrounded by palm trees. What do these images suggest about the relationships among missionaries and the people they served? Why would Philip Harper have wanted to join this society? ▶

Bettmann/Corbis

By accelerating impersonal labor, low wages, and disruptive migrations, industrialization led many individuals to rethink their religious lives. Uprooted from settled places of worship and religious leaders who had guided communities for decades, they searched to understand the individual's relationship to God. Originating in the borderlands, religious revivals swept the Midwest, the South, New York, and New England. Expanding Protestant denominations espoused a mixed message of both individual freedom and community responsibility. Enslaved people adopted Christianity's emphasis on liberation whereas slave owners and other elites chose messages that stressed social control. Missionaries sought converts and established schools and churches that linked salvation and U.S. power from the Middle East to the far West.

☞ As you read, consider the ways that evangelical Christianity spread new ideas about an individual's connection to God. What were the implications for how the people of the world should live together?

10-2a Evangelical Christianity

In 1801, twenty-five thousand people gathered in Cane Ridge, Kentucky, to pray, sing, and listen to sermons as part of a life-changing religious revival. As they tied up their wagons, pitched their tents in the woods, and gathered in front of the stages that organizers had built for the visiting ministers, the crowd became part of an outpouring of religious feeling and enthusiasm known as the **Second Great Awakening**. This Protestant movement of the early nineteenth century greatly increased church attendance and made evangelical Christianity a powerful cultural force in the United States.

{ Expanding Protestant denominations reinvigorate religious practices.

Second Great Awakening
Name of a series of religious revivals and expanded church attendance that made evangelical Christianity the main religious force in the United States.

Camp Meeting Part of the appeal of outdoor revivals was that dancing, singing, and extreme emotions were welcomed as part of the religious experience. Benjamin Latrobe, who sketched the layout of an 1809 camp meeting in Fairfax, Virginia, noted that right in front of the stage there was "a boarded enclosure filled with straw, into which the converted were thrown that they might kick about without injuring themselves." In this picture, observers are fascinated, but skeptical. ▲

Library of Congress Prints and Photographs Division [LC-DIG-ds-030915]

In the early years of the republic, few Americans attended church regularly; some estimate that perhaps only one in twenty were frequent churchgoers. By 1830, that number had swelled to one in seven. New members joined congregations of Methodist, Baptist, and African Methodist Episcopal churches that were experimenting with ways to reach potential believers. Following disestablishment, states no longer compelled citizens to support a particular church; instead, Americans attended and paid to support those churches that appealed to them in message and method.

Evangelical Christians believed that all humans had the potential for salvation but it was up to the individual to accept God's grace in an act of free will. Once she did, she could conquer sin in herself, a doctrine of self-transformation known as **perfectionism**. Offering believers a vision of individual self-respect and collective self-confidence, the evangelical movement asserted that people had the obligation and the right to read the Bible, pray, and decide for themselves on spiritual matters rather than relying on an educated elite to instruct and test them. Lay speakers as well as ordained ministers strove to reach individual souls. One of the most famous Awakening preachers, Charles Grandison Finney, asserted that "we must have exciting, powerful preaching, or the devil will have the people." At **camp meetings** such as the one at Cane Ridge, the result was a full-body

experience. In 1832, British observer Fanny Trollope described "Hysterical sobbings, convulsive groans, shrieks and screams" as participants "threw about their limbs." Although Trollope claimed to feel "sick with horror" at the spectacle, the outdoor meetings increased evangelical denominations' influence.

Evangelical culture spread through travel and publications. Ministers themselves traveled to audiences, either at revivals or as part of a regular circuit, visiting communities with no established churches. Evangelical publishers supported ministers' work by selling pamphlets to help organizers plan their own revivals. In a constant transatlantic exchange, U.S. and British Methodist magazines reprinted affecting stories of sinners converted by the power of God. The American Bible Society, founded in 1816, raised money to print and distribute Bibles in English and by 1823 had arranged for a Spanish translation to spread Protestant Christianity throughout the hemisphere.

Perfectionism was an individual undertaking whose results could be multiplied across societies. Business owners tapped into the personal responsibility vein of evangelical theology and linked a strong work ethic to salvation. In the winter of 1830–1831, Finney accepted an invitation to bring revival to the Erie Canal boomtown of Rochester, New York. Drawn by exciting preaching and often led by the women in their families, hundreds converted and established Bible study groups in their homes. Inspired by their own conversions, Rochester residents founded churches for workers and set up savings banks

perfectionism Protestant tenet holding that humans can work to free themselves from sin during their lives.

camp meetings Outdoor religious revivals held in the United States and Britain at which people stayed for several days to pray, sing, and listen to a variety of ministers and lay preachers.

Oberlin College Archives

Global Americans Connecticut-born, New-York raised **Charles Grandison Finney** (1792–1875) studied to be a lawyer, but a conversion experience in 1821 led him to abandon the law and become a Presbyterian minister. In the 1820s and 1830s, his preaching tours, with their message of universal salvation delivered to women and men in exciting, relatable language, sparked revivals across the northeastern United States and Britain. In 1835, he became a professor at Oberlin College, where he later (1851) was president. Oberlin, the first U.S. college to regularly admit white women and African Americans, was part of abolitionists' efforts to help runaway slaves escape to freedom in Canada.

Finney's tours and publications ensured that the Second Great Awakening was a transatlantic religious movement. In 1835, he published *Lectures on Revivals of Religion*, in which he explained that enthusiastic preaching worked only on a soul that was prepared. He urged readers, "You must begin by looking at your hearts" and write down an inventory of specific sins committed (pride, envy, lying) as well as sins of omission (ingratitude, neglect of the Bible, failure to pray with family). The book was soon translated into French and Welsh. He and his second wife, Elizabeth, traveled to Britain in the 1850s where he preached and she held religious meetings for women, spreading the "new measures" of revival.

to encourage thrift in others. Women started the Female Charitable Society to collect and distribute relief funds for families and the unemployed. Poverty, drunkenness, and laziness, they concluded, were not regrettable consequences of hard lives but sins to be redeemed.

10-2b American Missions

Catholic missionaries had worked in the Americas for centuries, and their efforts continued in the nineteenth century. Religious orders ran convent schools in cities such as St. Louis, where they educated Indian and métis children. Privately funded organizations expanded in Catholic countries in the early nineteenth century, backing missions to Africa and Asia as well as to the Pacific islands of Hawai'i. Increasingly, those priests and nuns competed with Protestant missionaries from New England for converts.

> Missionaries forge international networks.

Protestant evangelical missionaries believed that salvation in an individual life was part of a larger, thousand-year cycle of sin and redemption set by God's time. A belief called **millennialism** held that mass conversion would bring about the final thousand-year reign of Jesus Christ on earth. The belief inspired particular attention to the Middle East because some evangelicals were convinced that the conversion of Jews in the old city of Jerusalem was essential to securing Jesus's return. In 1810, a group of ministers, businessmen, doctors, and lawyers in New England founded the

American Board of Commissioners of Foreign Missions (ABCFM) as the first U.S. missionary organization. Through its fund-raising and organization, it sent missionaries—often a husband and wife—to China, Ceylon, and the Ottoman-controlled territory of the Middle East. Missionary couples inspired by religion and nationalism established schools and churches teaching spiritual salvation through the adoption of English language and middle-class culture. Missionary Elizabeth Dwight wrote in a letter from Constantinople to *Mother's Magazine*, an American publication, "The heathen want not only ministers of the word, but *pious, well-educated families* . . . to be the living, bright examples of the doctrines of Christianity."

Evangelical missionaries also targeted American Indian settlements, where they became embroiled in the power politics of U.S. expansion. In 1819, African American lay minister John Stewart began a mission to the Wyandot Indians in Ohio. Working with a former slave who had been captured by the Wyandots and knew their language, Stewart converted several high-ranking members. His efforts soon inspired the Methodist Episcopal Church to open its own missionary society in the region. Converted Wyandot Indians, in turn, convinced missionaries to intervene in border disputes with the United States and used evangelical fund-raising channels to purchase clothing and food.

millennialism Belief held by some Christian denominations that there will be a one thousand-year period of Christ's reign on earth before the final judgment.

American Board of Commissioners of Foreign Missions (ABCFM) Organization established in 1810 as the first U.S. society dedicated to sending Protestant missionaries to convert people in Asia, Africa, and the Middle East.

Native Americans in more distant settlements found missionaries' messages less compelling. In 1835, ABCFM sponsored newlywed Marcus and Narcissa Whitman's journey from New York to Oregon Country. There, they built a mission for the Cayuse Indians in the Walla Walla Valley, urging the seasonally migratory people to take up permanent farming and Protestant Christianity together. Unsuccessful in its conversion efforts, their mission became a way station and first-aid center for settlers traveling into the Oregon territory in the 1840s. Those migrants soon brought a devastating measles epidemic to the Cayuses, who saw in their misery the fulfillment of their own prophesy, that strangers would bring destruction followed by community rebirth into a new world. When Marcus Whitman, a doctor, was unable to cure the suffering people, a group of Cayuses killed both Whitmans and twelve others at the mission in 1847. Subsequent retaliatory violence escalated into a decade of warfare.

10-2c Christianity's Multiple Messages

Evangelical Protestantism became a major religious and cultural force in the nineteenth-century United States in part because it carried messages of both liberation and conservative control. In the slaveholding South, Baptists and Methodists gained converts among whites by abandoning their earlier insistence on the equality of souls and preaching instead the duty of fathers to lead the members of their households to Christian conversion. Sermons and print culture stressed the responsibility of masters and the necessary obedience of inferiors, including children and slaves. Baptist congregations in the South encouraged women's prayers but revoked their power to speak on church business.

> Christianity fills divergent purposes in a pluralistic society.

At the same time, the Bible offered profoundly moving stories for enslaved people. Some found inspiration in the story of Exodus, in which Moses led Israelites out of slavery, and in the nobility of Jesus Christ's suffering. One song sung by slaves in the nineteenth century drew direct parallels between Bible stories and their own lives: "He delivered Daniel from the lion's den, / Jonah from the belly of the whale, / And the Hebrew children from the fiery furnace, / And why not every man?" Regular, enthusiastic group worship gave enslaved people chances to meet and form relationships. All of these practices, essential to Christianity's message about a deep, personal religious experience, at the same time

African Methodist Episcopal
First independent black denomination in the United States, recognized in 1816.

utopian communities
Settlement that experimented with communal living arrangements organized around religious or philosophical principles designed to perfect society.

Shakers Utopian community founded by Briton Ann Lee that believed in celibacy; men and women lived and worked apart.

nurtured independence, knowledge, and the networks that enabled resistance to slavery.

Mixed messages of inclusion and exclusion sparked the creation of new Protestant denominations. Evangelical churches initially encouraged black participation and nurtured free black preachers, encouraging them to speak to mixed-race groups. Blacks and whites both attended the Cane Ridge camp meeting and because revivals welcomed new authorities, the number of black ministers and lay speakers increased. But many congregations retained discriminatory practices. Some did not allow black members to be buried in the same church cemeteries, and others required African American participants to sit upstairs in special galleries around the sanctuary rather than joining white congregants. The **African Methodist Episcopal** (AME) church, which had begun as an all-black affiliate of a Philadelphia congregation created by the Free African Society, sought and won legal recognition as an independent church in 1816. It was the first fully independent black denomination in the United States with its own bishops and national structure. Like other evangelical churches, it encouraged black women to speak as lay ministers although it did not make them full ministers.

Slavery itself divided denominations as they debated whether slavery was a sin or was part of the God-ordained order of the world. The American Presbyterian (1837), Methodist Episcopal (1844), and Baptist (1845) churches each divided into separate conferences that either accepted slavery or rejected it.

10-2d Experimental Communities

Significant numbers of Americans despaired at the divisions between rich and poor created by industrialization as well as the social isolation of both middle-class parlors and urban construction sites. They decided to withdraw into communities that would pursue cooperation rather than competition. Some of these **utopian communities** were based on a religious vision. Others were living expressions of carefully designed blueprints informed by scientific principles. All shared a conviction that a good society required reformed relationships between men and women.

> Social experiments counter the culture of individualism.

One of the oldest utopian communities, the **Shakers**, decided that separation of the sexes was the only way to preserve the dignity of both. Founded in late eighteenth-century Britain by Ann Lee, the community was officially called the United Society of Believers in Christ's Second Appearing. Lee preached that God was both male and female and that each individual communicated personally with the divine in the form of artistic expression and work. The Shakers, whose name came from the religious ecstasy of their dancing, believed in total celibacy. Men

Buttre, John Chester, 1821–1893, engraver, Gorbitz, J., artist

Global Americans Born in Scotland in 1795, orphaned as a toddler, and raised in London, **Frances ("Fanny") Wright** became an international traveler and writer in her early twenties, befriending the marquis de Lafayette and touring with him across the United States in 1824. The following year, she became a U.S. citizen, purchased land in western Tennessee, and published *A Plan for the Gradual Abolition of Slavery in the Western United States without Danger of Loss to the Citizens of the South*, outlining a plan to establish a colony for freed slaves. Her own colony, Nashoba, was a failure, and in 1828 she joined Robert Dale Owen's New Harmony utopian society in Indiana.

Wright became a popular public speaker not as a moral reformer but as a freethinker dedicated to equality. Labeled a "female Tome Paine" by one of her critics in 1829, Wright was sharply critical of evangelical preachers who, she charged, preyed upon "the minds of weak and deluded women" who were easy, poorly educated victims. She championed women's education as well as sexual and economic rights within marriage. She traveled frequently between France and the United States and stumped for the Democratic Party in 1836 and 1838. She died in 1852 in the midst of a legal battle with her ex-husband over her own earnings, a symbol of both international radicalism and its limits for women.

and women lived and worked apart, each group contributing to the success of the whole. They relied on converts, including orphans, widows, and poor families who asked to join. Because they did not recognize blood ties as more significant than other connections, a mother and daughter who joined together became "sisters."

Other British transplants created societies that were not religiously inspired but equally radical in re-envisioning the ties binding humans into a society. Robert Owen, a Scottish factory owner, traveled to the United States in 1824 to invest his industrial fortune in an experimental community, New Harmony, in Indiana. Having witnessed the misery of British mill towns, Owen declared that human beings needed to be liberated from "the trinity of evils responsible for all the world's misery and vice: traditional religion, conventional marriage . . . and private property." In spite of his business experience, Owen was unable to secure a solid financial footing for the community, and he returned to Europe to promote what he had come to call *utopian socialism*.

Frances Wright, another Scot, purchased former Chickasaw land in Tennessee to found the society of Nashoba, where she believed that she could help end slavery and thus bolster American liberty. She planned to fill the model farm at Nashoba with enslaved African Americans who, working under a cooperative labor system, would earn enough to buy their own freedom within five years and pay for their own relocation to Haiti or Liberia. She predicted that as the idea spread, slavery would become unprofitable and ultimately extinct. Unable to acquire enough investment or slave labor, Wright

re-tooled Nashoba as a utopian community of whites, but ultimately that vision collapsed in scandal.

The miseries of industrialization in France inspired the most successful imported utopian movement. Frenchman Charles Fourier believed that the progress of civilization depended on a very specific form of community living: 1,620 people living in a large building complex set on six thousand acres of well-tended land. Leisure, not work, would fill their days. A dazzled American visitor, Albert Brisbane, brought the Fourierist movement to the United States in the 1840s, eventually involving fifteen thousand Americans in communal living experiments, clubs, mutual insurance associations, and cooperative stores.

American Joseph Smith's vision of new religious and social bonds proved far more enduring and influential in the United States than any of the transatlantic experiments. Smith grew up poor in a farming family in western New York who had lost everything in a speculative ginseng shipment to China. As a boy, he witnessed multiple revivals sweeping through the region and concluded that none of these competing factions represented the true church. In his 20s, Smith experienced visions in which God called him to be a prophet, redeeming society from its excess of individualism. In 1830, he published his revelations in the *Book of Mormon* and established the Church of Jesus Christ of Latter-day Saints, or **Mormons** in New York. They resolved the conflicts between the claims of the individual and the need for social order by establishing a highly controlled, patriarchal society.

Mormons Church founded by Joseph Smith in 1830. Organized in New York, the group moved west after being the focus of attacks.

American Cultures

A.W. Graham, Laurel Hill (1844). This engraving, depicting a new "rural cemetery" outside of Philadelphia, appeared in *Godey's Lady's Book* and was later reprinted in a cemetery guidebook. Carefully landscaped rural cemeteries offered urban Americans a respite where they could picnic in nature. Nearby, merchants sold industrially produced monuments, iron fences, and outdoor furniture to decorate these "cities of the dead."

How does the artist use costume and scale to suggest human beings' relationship to nature? What does the image imply about the relationship between the living and the dead? ▶

The Library Company of Philadelphia

The boom-bust economy of the first half of the nineteenth century generated new wealth but also great insecurity. Surrounded by strangers and stalked by financial failure, Americans developed cultural responses to the difficulty of judging truth from fiction in an expanding world. Some sought authenticity, in manners that conveyed genuine emotions or in time spent in nature. Others turned harmless frauds into public amusements. The technologies of the early nineteenth century, including expanding transportation systems, cheaper printing processes, and robust communication networks, allowed performers and publications to transmit culture around the world as never before.

☞ As you read, identify the ways that culture helped people interpret new social and economic conditions. How did books, newspapers, lectures, and songs shape behavior?

10-3a Feelings and Behavior

Middle-class Americans believed that they had earned their wealth, but because it was held in paper mortgages, bank notes, and insurance certificates, they knew it could quickly be lost. So they struggled to act as if their status was secure. They bought etiquette books that explained in minute detail how a middle-class person should dress and behave with rules that stressed restrained and predictable movements: "The general positions for the arms are about the level of the waist, never hanging down or being quite stiff, but being gently bent, the elbow a little raised, the fingers not

{ Middle-class culture cultivates sincere feeling as a sign of respectability.

sentimentalism Theory that humans can understand each other through sympathy for others' feelings and that those feelings allow people to bond in societies.

parlor music Popular songs with subjects such as family, love, patriotism, and history sold as sheet music for families to sing in their parlors.

stretched out stiffly, but also a little bent, and partially separated." Proper behavior would demonstrate true worth. "The manners of a gentleman are the index of his soul," one book pronounced. Yet people in a city of strangers feared that fakers surrounded them. How could one know whether a well-mannered new clerk was an honest associate or an ambitious fraud? What kind of society would there be if each member were only pretending to belong? Middle-class Americans looked for sincerity in others and worked to foster it in themselves.

Sincere feeling, they hoped, was the true glue of society. **Sentimentalism**, the idea that human beings could connect emotionally by understanding each other's feelings, pervaded nineteenth-century middle-class life. Men and women believed that sensitivity to the feelings of others was the most refined character trait a person could possess. It was a mark of superiority and the only true motivator of benevolent behavior. To cultivate those feelings, middle-class Americans developed new forms of leisure focused on the home. In the evenings, families gathered in their parlors, special rooms that were devoted to reading out loud, sincere conversation, and music. **Parlor music** sung to the accompaniment of a wife or daughter playing the piano offered short, melodic songs that evoked powerful emotions of love and loss, such as the wildly popular "Home! Sweet Home!" Originally written in 1823 by American actor John Howard Payne for an English opera, it proclaimed "Be it ever so humble / There's no place like home."

Mourning culture was another way to experience and demonstrate sentimentalism. Middle-class women wove connections between the living and the dead by making jewelry out of the hair of deceased loved ones. They embroidered "mourning pictures" with weeping willows and the names of the deceased. Men and women visited vast new cemeteries. Mourners believed that their experience of deep grief helped awaken them to Christian sympathy and realize the emptiness of worldly happiness.

10-3b Nature and Self-Improvement

"Nature," wrote Ralph Waldo Emerson in 1836, is "essences unchanged by man; space, the air, the river,

{ Urbanizing, competitive Americans seek truth in nature.

the leaf." In these essences, he believed, was a truth obscured by nineteenth-century society. With like-minded thinkers, he founded **transcendentalism**, an intellectual movement in New England during the 1830s and 1840s that came to have a major influence on U.S. culture. Transcendentalists were inspired by European romanticism, a movement in art and thought that challenged Enlightenment rationalism. They also read translations of Chinese Confucian and Indian Hindu texts brought home by missionaries. Transcendentalists argued that human reason was not the best tool for understanding; instead, humans should seek to transcend their senses and come to understand truth.

The term *transcendentalism* originated with the German philosopher Immanuel Kant, who argued that there was a kind of "transcendental" knowledge in intuition. Emerson, a former Unitarian minister who ultimately deemed the denomination a "corpse cold" form of Christianity, championed "Self-Reliance," the title of an essay he published in 1841. Calling on readers to defy conventions and "trust thyself," Emerson's celebration of individualism suited U.S. democratic politics and the middle-class ideal of the self-made man. His friend Henry David Thoreau experimented with solitary existence, moving to a cabin on Massachusetts's Walden Pond in 1845, but it was intellectual rather than physical independence that the transcendentalists sought. In his cabin, Thoreau entertained like-minded reformers and had regular visits from his mother and sisters.

Transcendentalists benefited from the **lyceum movement**, which also emerged in the 1830s in New England. Local associations, called *lyceums* after the school in Athens where Aristotle taught, promoted adult education in the form of public lectures and debates that by the middle of the century reached four hundred thousand people weekly. Each local lyceum collected subscriptions to pay for speakers, who traveled along regular circuits. Arriving in town by stagecoach or rail car, lyceum speakers gave talks on reform, women's rights, science, art, medicine, and politics. In 1838, a young Abraham Lincoln spoke about "The Perpetuation of our Political Institutions" to the Young Men's Lyceum in Springfield, Illinois. Middle-class self-improvers believed that adult education could reform society by training citizens in the arts of public speaking and persuasion.

Tomas Abad/Alamy Stock Photo

Romanticism and the Natural Landscape European romanticism inspired American painters to portray the beauty and power of nature in harmony with or in contrast to settled farmland as in this painting, Thomas Cole's 1836 *The Oxbow*, which measures six feet wide. Cole, who emigrated from England to Ohio with his family as a child, founded the Hudson River School, a group of landscape painters greatly admired by transcendentalists. ▲

10-3c Print and Public Performance

The industrial revolution made printing faster and cheaper, allowing publishers to reach a new public. In 1825, the cyl-

{ Truth and fraud compete in new cultural media.

inder printing press, combining German technology and English steam machinery, reached the United States. It was self-inking and had a continuous process, which meant that fewer operators could produce thousands of copies an hour rather than hundreds. In 1833, Benjamin Day brought the benefits of mass printing to crowds of urban workers with his *New York Sun*, four pages of opinionated essays, crime reporting, and sensational stories of life on the moon and in the Five Points neighborhood. Costing only a penny a paper, the *Sun* and others of the **penny press** pioneered a new kind of news. Before the *Sun*, newspapers were called "blanket sheets"—large papers that were four feet by three feet when opened. Businessmen subscribed to them, paying six cents an issue for political and international economic information. The penny press, in contrast, was supported by advertising and sold on street corners.

The new audience demanded a new kind of reporting. Penny press reporters did not wait for information to be submitted but instead interviewed crime victims and gathered evidence to wrap in sensationalist language for an eager public. Coverage of the 1836 trial of New York clerk Richard Robinson, accused of murdering the prostitute Helen Jewett, typified the new relationship between the people and

transcendentalism Literary and philosophical movement organized around the belief that people have an intuitive knowledge of themselves and the world that does not depend on rational belief.

lyceum movement Network of organizations that sponsored adult education through public lectures on political and literary subjects.

penny press Daily and weekly urban newspapers, sold on street corners for a penny, that covered local crime and sensational stories and pioneered investigative journalism.

minstrel show Popular musical theatrical performance by white Americans dressed to look like stereotypical African Americans presented on national and international tours.

the press. Highly emotional reporting from the scene of the crime combined with investigations into the family backgrounds of Robinson and Jewett turned the trial and Robinson's hasty acquittal into lucrative entertainment. Most readers believed in Robinson's guilt and thought the whole event a cautionary tale about young people in the anonymous city and the dangers of prostitution.

Printed sensations took advantage of improved roads and faster steamships to advertise public amusements to an extended crowd. One of the most popular show promoters of the nineteenth century, P. T. Barnum, won national attention and a personal fortune by inviting audiences to test the truth of his outrageous claims. He exhibited a "feejee mermaid," a sewn-together taxidermy creature combining animal parts that he insisted was an actual mermaid. Thousands lined up to pay to be tricked in this new form of mass entertainment. In 1843, Barnum enlisted his five-year-old distant cousin, Charles Stratton, who had a form of dwarfism, to tour Europe and then Cuba under the name of "General Tom Thumb," singing, dancing, and impersonating Napoleon.

Another type of dress-up and trickery was the basis for a new American form of popular culture, the **minstrel show**. These productions featured white performers who blackened their faces with burnt cork and sang and acted out stereotyped African American characters. Stock types, such as "Zip Coon," a free black man who boasted of his independence yet misused complicated words, populated minstrel shows, which also included songs about southern slave plantations (such as "Dixie" and "Old Folks at Home"). The most eager audiences for minstrel shows were urban white working men, who felt themselves threatened on one side from free black laborers and on the other by religiously minded reformers who scolded them and spoke of their need to adopt sobriety and self-discipline. Minstrel shows also toured Europe, and Stephen Foster's "Oh! Susanna!"

Image courtesy of Images Musicales

Music for Stephen Foster's "Oh! Susannah!" The cover of this sheet music notes that the song was popularized by the Ethiopian Serenaders, a blackface minstrel group that performed in various places in the United States, including at the White House, and in Europe. This copy of the music was printed in London, meaning that the emerging middle class there could sing songs about the U.S. South in their parlors. ▲

was performed by buskers on the streets of London and sung by Juan Bega, an African American boatman working on the Isthmus of Panama, within months of its publication.

10-4
Ideologies of Race and Slavery

These lithographs of "Black and White Slaves" by Edward Williams Clay (New York, 1841) contrast the supposed paternalism of the U.S. South with the cruelty of English factory owners. The slave owner on the left says "These poor creatures are a sacred legacy from my ancestors"; the industrialist on the right tells the starving family to "pack off to the work house." Clay was a Philadelphia artist and cartoonist whose stereotyped images helped develop a visual culture of race and racism.

How does the artist, a Northerner, depict the lives of "slaves" in the United States and England? What does he suggest about their relationship to those who own them? ▶

Smithsonian Institution National Museum of American History, Behring Center

Slavery expanded in the nineteenth century to fill the labor demands of global trade and industrial production. Scientists, ministers, politicians, and slaveholders devised racial and religious ideas that argued with new strength and conviction for the cruel system of racial hierarchy that supported slavery. At the same time, the Age of Revolution and the agreement of European nations and the United States to abolish the international slave trade increased debate about the morality of holding humans in permanent bondage. People trapped in slavery drew on their intimate knowledge of law, faith, and the personal lives of their enslavers to carve out moments of independence in an exploitative world that occasionally widened into rebellion.

☞ As you read, note the ways that slavery adapted to changing global politics and economies in the nineteenth century. How had discussions linking race, slavery, and politics changed?

10-4a Legal Contexts for Slavery

The laws governing American slavery developed over centuries of experimentation within European empires, and they continued to adapt

> Slave laws respond to evolving national and international contexts.

in the nineteenth century. The abolition of the Atlantic slave trade in 1808 was followed by treaties designed to enforce it, which altered the landscape of slavery along the U.S. coast. The **Anglo-Spanish Treaty of 1817** pledged Spain to end the slave trade north of the equator immediately and to the south by 1820. It also gave the British navy the right to board suspected slave ships, seize human cargo, and fine the captain. Yet slavery thrived on the plantations of Brazil and on Spanish Cuba, where ships from West African kingdoms such as the expanding Dahomey still delivered hundreds of thousands of captive humans.

In 1839, this international framework was put to the test in U.S. courts when U.S. forces seized forty-three Africans aboard the ship *Amistad* in Long Island Sound. Captives on the Cuban-bound voyage had waged a shipboard revolt, killing the captain and cook and demanding that the remaining crew divert the ship to Africa. When they ended up in the United States instead, the question for the courts was: Were they murderous pirates or freedom fighters? The verdict hinged on uncovering the captives' origins. If they were slaves in Cuba, they should be returned as property; if they were newly enslaved victims of the outlawed international slave trade, they deserved freedom. They were ultimately declared free, acquitted of murder, and allowed to return to West Africa.

Within the United States, legislators in Alabama, Georgia, and Louisiana responded to charges that slavery destroyed families by passing laws in the 1820s and 1830s that prevented owners from selling children under ten away from their mothers. To get around such

laws, however, owners often rented out their slaves, including very young children they sent to farms needing "little negroes" who could be trained to babysit white children or help in the fields. Slave owners viewed small black children, just like adults, as flexible laborers who could produce income for them during plantation slack times.

Industries in the South took advantage of the practice of slave rentals to fill out their labor force. The **Tredegar Iron Works** in Richmond, Virginia, which provided material for the expanding railroad system in the United States, had a 50 percent enslaved workforce. The company, chartered in 1837, bought some of its slaves but rented the rest through contracts signed with Virginia slave owners. Through such contracts, slave owners held on to their human property but handed the management and maintenance of these workers to company supervisors.

10-4b Proslavery Arguments

Whites who justified slavery in the eighteenth century typically cited the economic benefits of an enslaved labor force. By 1820, a new **proslavery doctrine** had

> Defenders reimagine slavery from a necessary evil to a positive good.

emerged in the United States. Building on the concepts of paternalism forged on eighteenth-century tobacco plantations, this notion held that slaves by their natures were unable to take care of themselves, and whites had been appointed by God to watch over their bodies and souls. Southern slave owners said that they were providing what blacks required, oversight and protection: "The Southerner is the negro's friend, his only friend."

Proslavery speakers embraced the paternalistic view of U.S. slavery in part because it was economically self-serving. With the international slave trade abolished, slave owners had to rely on "home-grown" slaves. Breeding human beings, like breeding animals, was a concept they embraced eagerly. One planter wrote from Texas in 1849 to his nephew: "Get as many young negro women as you can. Get as many cows as you can. . . . It is the greatest country for an increase that I have ever saw in my life." Slavery increased dramatically. By 1860, the United States had 4 million slaves in a population of 31 million people. Evangelical religion also bolstered proslavery paternalism. White Southerners converted in large numbers during the Second

Anglo-Spanish Treaty of 1817 Agreement signed between England and Spain in which Spain pledged to end the slave trade and to permit the British navy to inspect Spanish ships suspected of carrying slaves.

Amistad Spanish schooner carrying rebellious illegal slaves that landed in the United States, leading to a series of trials to determine the status of the people aboard.

Tredegar Iron Works Virginia plant manufacturing iron hardware and locomotives established in 1836 by Francis B. Deane that employed slave laborers alongside free blacks, immigrants, and United States-born workers.

proslavery doctrine Ideology drawing on law, religion, history, and racist science in defense of slavery as a positive institution for whites and blacks.

William H. Townsend. Sketches of the Amistad Captives. General Collection, Beinecke Rare Book and Manuscript Library, Yale University

Global Americans The woman who became **Sarah Mar'gru Kinson** was born Mar'gru to a large family around 1832 in Bendembu, West Africa. After her father pawned her for a debt, she marched with a group of captives to the coast of Galinhas and was sold into the Spanish-Cuban slave trade. Mar'gru was confined in slave pens on Lomboko Island and then transported to Cuba, where she was sold at auction as a slave. On route to her new plantation aboard the ship *Amistad*, Mar'gru was caught up in a mutiny led by Cinque, one of the adult slaves on the ship. After three grueling months at sea, the ship ended up near Long Island Sound, where it was seized by U.S. maritime forces. Its occupants became the focus of a famous trial. Abolitionists demanded their freedom; Cuba insisted that they were legal slaves.

Along with the other *Amistad* survivors, Mar'gru traveled to Sierra Leone in 1841, sponsored by the Amistad Committee and Union Missionary Society. Then going by the name Sarah Kinson, she was unable to integrate into Mende culture. Instead, she returned to the United States in 1846 and studied at Oberlin, the first college in the United States to accept black and white students together. She returned to West Africa to teach at a mission school and married Edward Green in 1852. Soon after, she disappeared from written records. Sarah Mar'gru's life was extraordinary, but its Atlantic dimensions demonstrate that the expansion of slavery and the emergence of abolition in the nineteenth century were fundamentally international developments.

Great Awakening and began to use Biblical rather than economic language to talk to and about their slaves. They quoted Paul's letter to the Ephesians in the Bible: "Servants, be obedient to them that are your masters according to the flesh with fear and trembling, in singleness of your heart, as unto Christ."

Forged in paternalism, proslavery language became a sectional strategy for the South. Southerners claimed that they were maintaining the true bonds of caring dependence that had been disrupted by industrial growth elsewhere. They accused northern industrialists of merely exploiting those who labored, giving them no guidance, training, compassion, or security in return. Slave owners, they countered, had a duty to support their slaves even when they were sick or old. Northerners were vulnerable to these claims, because they heard the same arguments from a growing labor movement. Proslavery barbs targeted Britain as well. In 1833, South Carolina planter James Henry Hammond condemned the British as hypocrites who forced the Irish into "absolute & unmitigated slavery."

Proslavery ideology ignored the basic truths of American slavery. Slaveholders declared themselves committed to supporting enslaved people throughout their lives, but the thriving interstate slave trade demonstrated that they were quick to sell human property to pay debts. The myth of the large benevolent family was especially cruel. Slave masters were legally free to rape their slaves, father children with enslaved women, and continue to hold those children as property rather than family members. White women reacted to this open secret with rage, beating and punishing the enslaved women, or with bitter resignation.

scientific racism Body of knowledge created by so-called scientific studies of human traits that declared permanent hierarchical differences among distinct racial groups.

10-4c Scientific Racism

New ideas about human origins bolstered proslavery arguments and spread racism in free states and territories.

> The "science" of difference links race, slavery, and conquest.

Earlier race prejudice had various explanations for physical differences between groups of human beings, but most Euro-Americans had believed in the Biblical story that all humans came from a single origin. In the nineteenth century, this idea, called *monogenesis*, was challenged by *polygenesis*, the idea that human beings had fundamentally different origins. Polygenecists believed that from these different origins had grown separate races that were fundamentally and permanently different. In fact, proponents argued that a hierarchical chain of races separated the people of so-called superior appearance, intelligence, culture, and temperament from those with "inferior" qualities.

Scientific racism linked physical appearance to character, a connection that had broad support in the nineteenth century. Phrenologists, who believed that bumps on one's skull corresponded with over- or underdeveloped parts of the brain, applied their analysis to individuals. A person with a bump near the part of the brain that controlled envy had an envious temperament. Scientific racism insisted that entire groups of human beings, or races, shared physical traits linked to intellectual and moral capacity. Philadelphia physician Samuel George Morton measured the size and capacity of thousands of skulls and, in his 1839 *Crania Americana*, published his conclusions about the link between skull capacity, intellect, and moral character. He divided humanity into four groups: Caucasians, Mongolians, [Native] Americans, and Negroes. According to his reported measurements, Caucasians had the largest brains and were the most intellectual and cultured whereas Negroes had the smallest brain capacity although they were talented in music. The idea that human beings fell into unchangeable categories that could be easily perceived gained popular appeal among scientists and the public. Even the *Amistad* captives were subjected to a phrenologist's scrutiny while they awaited their legal fate.

Scientific racism blurred categories of culture and appearance, forging a tool for expansionist political rhetoric. In 1844, Mississippi senator Robert J. Walker argued that Mexico did not deserve independent status because Mexicans were an "ignorant and fanatical race" due to their Catholicism and the prevalence of multicultural families. In fact, race was neither obvious nor fixed, and nineteenth-century migrations allowed people to shift from one race to another, passing with a new identity. Joshua Peavy was born a free black farmer in North Carolina in the early nineteenth century. Converting to Methodism in the Second Great Awakening, he moved to Alabama to become an ordained minister. Neighbors described him as a "Frenchman" with a "very dark complexion."

10-4d Resistance to Slavery

White Southerners deepened their commitment to slavery; enslaved people continued to resist it daily. To disrupt the punishing workday, some broke tools or pretended to be sick. They ran away for short periods of time to visit family members on nearby plantations. Some retaliated against vicious treatment by poisoning masters and mistresses. The multiple forms of resistance to slavery depended on an individual's calculation of the personal risks of each action, and many relied on slave owners' misunderstanding of the people they claimed to know. Frederick Douglass, a former slave who became one of the most prominent U.S. antislavery crusaders, wrote in his autobiography that whites often thought slaves' singing was evidence of their contentment, but they were profoundly mistaken: "The songs of the slave represent the sorrows of his heart; and he is relieved by them, only as an aching heart is relieved by tears."

Although large-scale rebellions coordinated by multiple slaves were rare in the United States, one of the largest occurred in 1831 when enslaved Virginian Nat Turner, inspired by a religious vision, led dozens of slaves in an uprising known as **Turner's Rebellion**. Armed with axes, knives, and guns, the group killed sixty people, starting with Turner's owners. Terrified whites called in militias and vigilantes from Virginia and North Carolina. Thousands went on a rampage of retaliation, killing two hundred slaves at random in Virginia and neighboring states. Turner was caught. While he was in prison, awaiting conviction and then execution, he was interviewed by a slave-owning lawyer named Thomas Gray, who published *The Confessions of Nat Turner*. In this

{ Enslaved people use a range of methods to resist slavery in their daily lives.

Public Domain

Frederick Douglass Born into slavery in Maryland, Douglass learned to read and write in Baltimore in spite of bans on slave literacy. He escaped to freedom in New York in 1838 and became active in the American Anti-Slavery Society. His 1845 autobiography, *Narrative of the Life of Frederick Douglass*, countering proslavery claims, was a best seller in the United States. Within a decade, it had been translated into Dutch, French, and German. ▲

account, Turner did not claim that he was mistreated by specific owners. Rather, he saw in the Bible and in heavenly visions the truth that slavery was a sin committed by whites against blacks. When the lawyer asked if he had any regrets, Turner reportedly said, "Was not Christ crucified?"

White Southerners took two lessons from Turner's Rebellion. First, the killings graphically reminded those clinging to paternalism that slavery was in fact violent and dangerous. The following year, the Virginia legislature debated a measure that would have gradually ended slavery and sent all free blacks out of the state. Those in favor of the measure argued that the safety of whites depended on eliminating black people from their communities; those opposed insisted that they could not afford to end slavery in the state. Virginia legislators ultimately defeated the measure seventy-three to fifty-eight. The second effect of Turner's Rebellion was to convince white Americans in the South that Christianity and literacy could be dangerous because they encouraged enslaved people to think about and act on their desire for freedom. In the early 1830s, both before and after the Turner rebellion, southern states passed or tightened laws against teaching enslaved people to

Turner's Rebellion Slave uprising led by Nat Turner in Southampton County, Virginia, that had the most casualties of any U.S. revolt.

read, hoping to close off access to the Bible and antislavery works. After the rebellion, Virginia and Alabama forbade teaching enslaved or free black people to read or write.

A violent uprising in Jamaica also in 1831 had a starkly different effect on the British Atlantic. Led by Samuel Sharpe, an enslaved Baptist deacon and speaker, the protest began as a labor strike after Christmas. Peaceful protest soon turned to armed conflict between fifty thousand slaves and British colonial authorities. Fourteen whites and one hundred eighty-six slaves died in the **Christmas Rising**; more than five hundred more slaves were captured, tried, and

hundreds executed in the aftermath. British public opinion, shocked by the uprising and its brutal suppression and at the same time comfortably separated from the realities of living among freed and enslaved people, finally supported the British abolitionists' cause. They pushed Parliament to vote for emancipation, which passed in 1833. The **Slavery Abolition Act**, which took effect on August 1, 1834, declared most enslaved people in the British Empire free from slavery and instead put to work as apprentices for several more years. The British government compensated former slave owners for the loss of their property with money.

10-5
Individual Rights and Social Good

The image on the left was originally created for the Society for the Abolition of Slavery in England in the 1780s and became widely used on both sides of the Atlantic. In the United States, Maria M. Stewart, a free black abolitionist, used the image on the right in the 1830s to accompany her publications.

Compare the bodies, clothing, and poses of the people in the two images. What are the key differences between the earlier image and the later one, and how do they influence the universalism of the message? Do they present different rationales for emancipation? ▶ Everett Collection, The Granger Collection, New York.

Go to MindTap® to practice history with the Chapter 10 **Primary Source Writing Activity: Social Ills and Social Good.** Read and view primary sources and respond to a writing prompt.

The problems of nineteenth-century American societies, including poverty, prostitution, alcoholism, crime, slavery, and inequality struck many Americans as incompatible with democracy and the evangelical mission. Some reasoned that a self-governing society needed healthy, informed, equal citizens. Others believed that achieving God's kingdom on earth required the eradication of sins. But how could they best achieve reforms when many reformers and their targets lacked the vote? The answer came from private organizations that drew on networks of churches and intellectuals to spread ideas. They used technologies of print, publicity, and transportation to gain supporters. Public opinion, they hoped, could be a political tool.

Christmas Rising Slave rebellion on the British colony of Jamaica led by Samuel Sharpe, an enslaved Baptist lay preacher that helped push Britain toward abolition.

Slavery Abolition Act Legislation (1833) that abolished slavery in most British colonies although former slaves had to serve a period of apprenticeship. Slave owners received financial compensation for their lost property.

American Temperance Society Organization founded in 1826 to promote reducing the use of alcohol that sparked a national cause and eventually had numerous local branches.

☞ As you read, think about how connections of people, ideas, and publications shaped the development of reform movements in the first five decades of the nineteenth century. How did Americans use international movements to address local issues?

10-5a Temperance Movement

For centuries, Americans drank ale, cider, and beer with meals, at public celebrations, and as medicine. In the early nineteenth century, people began to drink more, replacing ale with increasingly high alcohol beverages. Employers such as Patrick Ryan served whiskey rations to the men performing difficult and dangerous work on canals. Binge drinking and drinking alone were also on the rise as people moved far from their families and familiar communities. By 1830, per capita alcohol consumption by U.S. adults peaked; across Europe, only the Swedish and French drank more (see Figure 10.2).

{ Efforts to get Americans to curb alcohol consumption gain diverse supporters.

American religious leaders viewed these developments with alarm. Minister Lyman Beecher condemned excessive drinking for "the moral ruin which it works in the soul," with consequences for Americans and "the hopes of the world, which hang upon our experiment of civil liberty." In 1826, he and other Boston ministers founded the **American Temperance Society**, which soon inspired the opening of thousands of local chapters. Their goal was to encourage people to moderate their

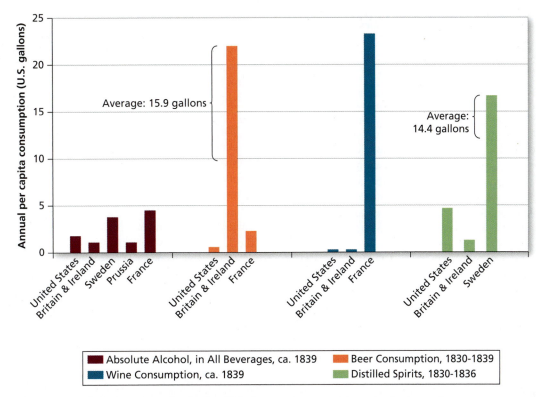

Figure 10.2 Alcohol Consumption in the 1830s Improved transportation, urbanization, and international trade increased the amount of alcohol that people drank in the early nineteenth century and influenced what they drank. Western U.S. farmers distilled surplus grain into whiskey, which was less bulky and expensive to transport. For American drinkers, this meant that whiskey was more widely available than in previous generations. In France, rural farmers moved to cities and became wine drinkers, in part to avoid the contaminated water common to urban centers around the world. ▲ Source: W. J. Rorabaugh, *The Alcoholic Republic.*

drinking by limiting consumption and switching to beer and wine rather than the "ardent spirits" of whiskey or rum.

The expanding movement had wide appeal, as well as support from churches and business leaders. The Georgia State Temperance Society, founded in 1828, initially held its annual meetings with the state Baptist convention. Baptists charged that drinking violated the Sabbath because workers who had only a single day off in the workweek spent it in the bar rather than in church. Others focused on the social costs of excessive drinking. Men and women argued that alcoholic fathers failed in their duties as head of household by drinking up the family's earnings and physically abusing their wives and children. By the mid-1830s, the American Temperance Society claimed that 1 million people had signed pledges to give up drinking, and temperance stories, songs, and poems rolled off printing presses.

Increasingly, temperance movements pushed for total abstinence from alcohol. Thomas P. Hunt, a Presbyterian minister, founded the Cold Water Army to recruit children to the cause, getting them to sign pledges that they would drink cold water, not alcohol. In 1840, working-class people formed the **Washingtonian movement** whose members drew on their pasts as hard drinkers and shared stories of lives destroyed by drink. By focusing on the links between drinking, poverty, and family violence, Washingtonians encouraged a type of grass-roots reform. As they lectured, they offered one another practical assistance in the form of food and clothing to restore families torn apart by alcohol abuse.

Temperance leadership was male but depended on female members to work for the cause. Maria Stewart, a widowed free black woman speaking in Boston in 1832, linked temperance with better living conditions for free blacks, proclaiming that were "the American free people of color to turn their attention more assiduously to moral worth and intellectual improvement, this would be the result: prejudice would gradually diminish, and the whites would be compelled to say, unloose those fetters!" But by saying these words in a public hall rather than in her home, Stewart and other female speakers were challenging expectations about proper female behavior. Stewart's audiences pelted her with tomatoes and jeered at her presumption.

Washingtonian movement Group of working-class societies in the 1840s that advocated total abstinence from alcohol by using the stories of former alcoholics as cautionary tales.

10-5b Institutions of Rescue and Reform

Temperance was the first and most widely supported reform movement, but it encouraged and trained generations of reformers who tackled other social problems. As the case of Helen Jewett demonstrated, rootless men and women moving into cities contributed to a significant expansion in the commercial sex trade. The number of established brothels in New York City tripled between 1820 and 1860, where as many as 10 percent of women engaged in prostitution at some point to make ends meet. In 1834, middle-class women established the **American Female Reform Society** in New York, targeting both the men and women caught up in the sex trade. Decrying the sexual double standard that permitted middle-class men to visit prostitutes discreetly, female reformers published the names of men seen exiting brothels in newspapers and organized raids to drive them onto public streets. Challenging the idea that poor prostitutes deserved ostracism, they tried to rescue them with training to be domestic servants in Magdalen charities, modeled on English institutions that took prostitutes away from their former neighborhoods.

> Expanding institutions combat social ills.

American Female Reform Society Organization founded in New York in 1834 by women dedicated to ending prostitution and helping former prostitutes.

asylum movement International campaign led in the United States by Dorothea Dix to establish institutions in which the mentally ill could receive care and treatment.

Philadelphia Quakers were at the forefront of another transatlantic development in reforming institutions: the penitentiary. Most existing jails held a mix of offenders, including debtors, people awaiting trial, and convicted criminals held for whipping or branding. Rather than punish the body, reformers insisted that time in a penitentiary, properly supervised, could reform a criminal's character. Philadelphia's penitentiaries used a combination of clean conditions, strict routine, religious self-reflection, solitary confinement, and training in a marketable skill to transform prisoners. In 1816, New York State modified these methods in its new state penitentiary where inmates toiled in gang labor during the day but were confined to solitary cells at night. Alexis de Tocqueville journeyed to the United States specifically so that he could pay twenty-five cents to observe prisoners.

When Dorothea Dix, daughter of an alcoholic Methodist itinerant father and mentally ill mother, entered a Boston-area jail in 1841 to teach religious classes, she discovered that numerous inmates were not criminals but mentally ill. Chained to walls, inadequately clothed, and generally ignored, these women and men were confined with convicted criminals because their families were unable to care for them. Drawing from the ideas of French and British doctors, Dix plunged into research and writing, presenting her findings to the state legislatures of Massachusetts, New York, New Jersey, and Pennsylvania. She became a leader of the **asylum movement**, which pushed states to establish public institutions for the treatment of the mentally ill.

Prisoners at the State Prison at Auburn.

Penitentiary Prisoners New York's Auburn System combined a form of slave labor with progressive belief in human self-improvement. Prisoners wore uniforms, marched in formation, and kept silent. The state of New York sold the shoes and furniture made by prisoners behind bars for a profit. Initially, neighboring industries objected to having to compete with prison laborers; soon, prison officials began to contract out inmates' labor. ▲ The Granger Collection, New York

Concentrating the "insane" within institutional walls created a laboratory for reformers and physicians. Doctors and directors of asylums in the United States, Europe, and Asia published studies and shared correspondence concerning the proper definition and treatment of people with this baffling illness.

Other reformers targeted schools. Physician Samuel Gridley Howe was a veteran of the Greek War of Independence (1821–1832) when he retuned to head the New-England Institution for the Education of the Blind in 1832. He joined with educator Horace Mann to promote a new kind of teacher training emphasizing patient guidance, rather than threats of physical punishment, to instruct students. Mann, like Howe and Dix, urged state legislators to fund institutions that would develop Americans' capacities. Mann argued in 1832 that a system of **common schools** offering basic education to all children was essential in a democracy: "For what value is it, that we have the most wisely-framed government on earth," he asked, "if this people has not the intelligence to understand" or uphold it?

10-5c Expansion of Antislavery

By the 1830s, the United States stood as a contradiction to its neighbors. It permitted the broadest range of citizens to vote, yet those citizens supported an expanding population of people held in permanent slavery. Independent Mexico abolished slavery in 1829. Britain had ended slavery in its North American colonies in 1833. Charles Follen, a German immigrant, asked in 1833, "Shall the United States, the Free United States, which could not bear the bonds of a King, cradle the bondage which a King is abolishing?"

Local contexts shape the international movement to end slavery.

Follen was part of a transatlantic network of antislavery activists whose message had grown increasingly radical. Antislavery organizations first emerged in England, where Quakers, who had previously prospered in the slave trade, rejected the institution as a violation of their faith in the equality of human souls. In their commitment to egalitarianism, Quakers opposed hierarchical titles, refused to practice rituals of deference to elites, and welcomed both men and women as public speakers of the faith. From those origins in the 1750s, a network of antislavery activists grew, championing the abolition of the international slave trade, gradual emancipation, and the resettlement of former slaves in African colonies such as Sierra Leone and Liberia.

Originating in the free black community, **abolitionism** demanded the immediate and universal end to slavery. Abolitionists identified slavery as an entrenched social system of violence and immorality that had to be actively defeated. In 1829, David Walker, a free black man born to a white mother and an enslaved father, published his ***Appeal to the Coloured Citizens of the World***, tracing the global history of slavery and its spread throughout the United States. He called out the hypocrisy of the Founding Fathers and all Americans celebrating the Fourth of July for espousing equality while upholding both slavery and racism. "America is more our country, than it is the whites—we have enriched it with our blood and tears," he wrote, appealing to free blacks and those in slavery. He directed Americans to look to Spain and Portugal, where repression and revolution had men "cutting each other's throats" and see the judgment of God on countries that had been "oppressing the Lord's people" in their former American colonies. Walker argued that the violence of slavery could be met with violent antislavery: "kill or be killed."

Whites and blacks formed the **American Anti-Slavery Society** in 1833, committed to the immediate and full abolition of slavery. Eschewing the violence of Walker, their early tactics drew on the experience of reformers in the temperance and evangelical movements at home and in Europe. Hoping to create an intense antislavery moral climate by evoking sympathy for slaves, they published a flood of antislavery literature, totaling more than 1 million pamphlets in 1835. They produced children's picture books and parlor music. Their message stressed the sins of slavery, including the sexual abuse of slave women, the separation of families, and the murderous violence that was part of slave discipline. Southern states passed laws forbidding the post offices from carrying or delivering such literature, cutting abolitionists off from moderate whites in the South.

Abolitionists turned to spreading their message among Northerners, many of whom cared little about what they saw as someone else's problem. Angelina and Sarah Grimké, two sisters who had grown up in a slave-owning family but became Quakers and leading abolitionists published *American Slavery As It Is: Testimony of a Thousand Witnesses* with activist Theodore Dwight Weld in 1839. The book brought the voices of former and escaped slaves to northern readers. Former slaves Sojourner Truth and Frederick Douglass spoke to audiences of the horrors of slavery, describing their experiences in vivid detail. Revival-style abolitionist meetings won converts but also stoked violent opposition from mobs.

Simultaneously, the Anti-Slavery Society bombarded Congress and other legislative bodies with more than seven hundred thousand petitions designed to chip away at the more vulnerable parts of the laws supporting slavery. These petitions called for the abolition of slavery in Washington, D.C.; the abolition of the interstate slave trade; the removal of the Three-Fifths Compromise from

common schools Tax-supported public elementary and secondary schools designed to educate all children equally.

abolitionism Political movement demanding the immediate end to slavery and the emancipation of all slaves without compensation for slave owners.

Appeal to the Coloured Citizens of the World Radical abolitionist essay written by David Walker calling for the violent overthrow of slavery.

American Anti-Slavery Society Abolitionist organization founded in 1833 led by William Lloyd Garrison dedicated to nonviolent moral opposition slavery by women and men.

the Constitution; and the denial of admission of new slave states to the United States. In response, Congress in 1836 passed a **gag rule** that forbid the national legislative body from even discussing antislavery petitions.

10-5d Women's Rights

The accumulated experiences of nineteenth-century reform produced another transformative movement for social justice: women's rights. From the start, critiques of women's degraded status depended on international comparisons and connections. American women who traveled as missionaries used their experiences in Asia to highlight the inferior condition of women outside the United States. Anne Hasseltine Judson, a missionary who worked in India, Thailand, and Burma in the 1810s and 1820s, returned to the United States in 1822 and told U.S. women that supporting missionary work would elevate the position of women around the world. Shocking her audience, she claimed that Hindu women were kept ignorant and debased, that "mothers consider female existence a curse." Christian education and conversion, she declared, would elevate these women to the privileged status of their white sisters in the United States because Protestant Christianity proclaimed the spiritual equality of men and women.

Missionaries were not the only ones debating women's status worldwide. In France, female socialists demanding wage equity for working people concluded that the fruit of women's labors should belong to them, not to the men of their families. They moved beyond most male activists in promoting financial autonomy for women. In England, a Chartist movement of working people had formed following the limited gains of the 1832 Reform Act. But when movement leaders demanded "universal suffrage," and yet intendeded to extend the vote only to men of the working class, female activists began to advocate on behalf of women. In German states, women in "free congregations" that rejected Christian establishments and emphasized free thought objected when these churches limited female opportunities for leadership.

The contradictions that women faced in reform movements forced them to confront the larger question of equality and human capability. When Angelina Grimké was called "unnatural" and unfeminine for speaking publically against slavery, she asked: "What then can *woman* do for the slave when she is herself under the feet of men and shamed into *silence*?" At the same time, connections forged through one type of reform strengthened work for women's rights. English activist Anne Knight wrote to American abolitionist Maria Weston Chapman, recommending that she read Scottish author Marion Reid's *A Plea for Woman* because "These things ought to be sent darting off like lightning to all the world if possible." Women's rights activists built international networks through personal correspondence and printed pamphlets that connected efforts across the oceans.

Women and men deepened these networks by holding conventions, which enabled them to meet and develop policy programs. In 1848, Lucretia Mott and Elizabeth Cady Stanton organized a Women's Rights Convention at Seneca Falls, New York, where Stanton lived. Mott knew the town from her missionary work there with a community of Seneca Indians. At this convention, three hundred people, including prominent abolitionist Frederick Douglass, met to listen to speeches about the social, political, and economic condition of women. They also presented the **Seneca Falls *Declaration of Sentiments***, written largely by Stanton. Signed by sixty-eight women and thirty-two men, the document was modeled on the Declaration of Independence and presented the demands of a wide-ranging "woman movement" that claimed both rights and a central place in public life for women. The declaration objected to laws that gave husbands the right to their wives' earnings and awarded child custody in divorce cases to fathers, never mothers. It protested practices that denied women access to higher education and higher wages for their work. And it insisted that women should have the right to vote. This last, most radical demand became the main goal of the women's suffrage movement that spanned the next seventy-two years. Of the one hundred people who signed the Declaration, only two were still alive when the U.S. Constitution was amended to allow women to vote.

State legislatures, responding to political pressure, began to pass laws modifying the status of married women who lived under coverture. Under these acts, which began in Arkansas territory (1835) and Mississippi (1839), married women were permitted new rights to own and eventually control property in their own names. In 1848, New York passed a comprehensive **Married Women's Property Act** that became a model for other states in the 1850s (see Table 10.3). This act determined that the property a woman owned at the time of her marriage, whether it was the clothes on her back or the land her parents had given her, belonged to her, not her husband. His creditors could not seize her property. She controlled the profits that her property yielded. These early laws focused on wealthier women; only later in the century did married women who worked for wages gain legal rights to those wages.

> Wide-ranging women's rights movements emerge from religious and reform activism.

gag rule (1836) Resolution passed in the U.S. House of Representatives forbidding the consideration of antislavery petitions. It was rescinded in 1844.

Seneca Falls *Declaration of Sentiments* (1848) Document by Elizabeth Cady Stanton signed at the Seneca Falls Convention that was modeled on the Declaration of Independence and demanded rights for women.

Married Women's Property Act Name for diverse state laws in the nineteenth and twentieth centuries that granted married women relief from coverture and gave married women rights to their own inheritances and wages.

Table 10.3 Married Women's Property Acts, 1808–1860

Laws expanding the property rights of free women fell into broad categories concerning wills, property holding, and earnings. Individual states attached specific limitations. For example, a state that permitted married women to write their own wills might require the husband's permission. Years later, that provision could be eliminated in another law. The result was a complex patchwork of legal rights that changed in response to husbands' and fathers' demands as well as those of women themselves.

	Married Women Permitted to Write Their Own Wills	Married Women Permitted to Own Poperty Free from Husband's Debts	Married Women Permitted to Control Their Own Earnings
1800–1820	1808 Ohio		
	1809 Connecticut		
	1810 Ohio		
	1818 Massachusetts		
1820–1840	1823 Florida		
	1825 Florida		
	1833 Pennsylvania		
		1835 Arkansas Territory	
		1839 Mississippi	
1840–1845	1840 Ohio		
	1841 New Hampshire		
	1842 Massachusetts		
	1843 Maryland	1843 Maryland	
		1844 Maine, Michigan	
		1845 Florida, Connecticut, Vermont, Texas, Massachussetts	
1845–1850	1846 Alabama	1846 Alabama, Arkansas, Iowa, Kentucky, New Hampshire, Ohio	
	1847 Indiana		
	1848 Pennsylvania	1848 Alabama, Arkansas, New York, Pennsylvania, Rhode Island	
	1849 New York	1849 Connecticut, Missouri	
	1850 Michigan	1850 Oregon, Tennessee, Wisconsin	
1850–1855	1852 Tennessee, Ohio	1852 New Jersey	
	1853 Oregon		
	1854 New Hampshire		
	1855 Massachusetts	1855 Florida, Michigan	1855 Massachusetts, Pennsylvania
1855–1860	1856 Rhode Island		
			1858 Kansas
			1860 Maine, Maryland, New York

Source: Joan Hoff, *Law, Gender, and Injustice: A Legal History of U.S. Women* (New York: New York University Press).

Summary

Economic and political developments in the first half of the nineteenth century transformed religious practice, personal life, and culture. Migration for jobs created new multiethnic urban communities that divided along racial and religious alliances. Boom-bust cycles of economic instability drove some to drink and others, as part of a new middle class, into a sober celebration of private home life. Global markets in cotton and animal skins rewarded families that could take on new members and abandon others, leaving Indian wives, enslaved husbands, and mixed-race children behind. In every region of the United States, individuals and communities adapted their personal beliefs and private lives to cope with the opportunities and uncertainties of national and global forces.

Evangelical Christianity, with its emphasis on both personal perfectionism and community obligation, became a powerful force in the United States and was soon exported by missionaries around the globe. Reformers insisted that sin was the poison causing most social problems and personal effort was the antidote. At times, reformers' message seemed to punish those suffering. In other cases, they demanded that the powerful invest time and money to help weaker members of the community. Both enslaved people and enslavers found support in Biblical messages, but as Native Americans had discovered, religious goals intersected with political ones in ways that could be difficult to control.

Improved transportation and printing technologies encouraged cultural forms created locally to be exported globally. Songs written in the North about slavery in the South entered popular culture across the Atlantic. American artists, inspired by European celebrations of untamed nature, painted wild North American landscapes. Escaped slaves shared their testimony with Midwesterners through public speaking and with Europeans in the pages of their autobiographies.

New cultures and new ideas, in turn, shaped the politics and economy of nineteenth-century America. Notions about middle-class domesticity bolstered the practice of paying women workers less. Scientific racism, nurtured in transatlantic intellectual circuits, offered an explanation for why slavery was expanding in a democracy and ensured cotton planters' reliance on an enslaved labor force. The conviction that humans had an obligation to choose their own church and actively seek salvation fueled a profitable international marketplace in religious publications and speakers. The national political system, oriented around individualism and competition among free men, could not remain aloof to the interests of non-voters.

‹Thinking Back, *Looking Forward*›

As you review this chapter, think about the history of culture and how seemingly essential concepts, such as sex, religion, and human nature, were transformed by local circumstances and global trends. How did circulating scientific knowledge or new ideas about natural rights alter the ways people worshipped God? Why were ideas about women's "nature" in the nineteenth century different from those in the seventeenth century? In the chapters to come, look for the consequences of cultural change. How did new ideas about race determine foreign policy and the growth of new empires? Did nineteenth- and twentieth-century conquests in the West and the Pacific draw on different cultural ideas than sixteenth- and seventeenth-century European conquests?

To make your study concrete, review the timeline and reflect on the entries there. Think about their causes, consequences, and connections. How do they connect events in North America to global trends?

Additional Resources

Books

Anderson, Bonnie. *Joyous Greetings: The First International Women's Movement, 1830–1860*. New York: Oxford University Press, 2001. ▶ Intellectual history of transatlantic women's rights movements.

Boydston, Jeanne. *Home and Work: Housework, Wages, and the Ideology of Labor in the Early Republic*. New York: Oxford University Press, 1994. ▶ Pioneering study of women's household labor in the nineteenth century.

Camp, Stephanie. *Closer to Freedom: Enslaved Women and Everyday Resistance in the Plantation South*. Chapel Hill: University of North Carolina Press, 2004. ▶ Provocative interpretation of how gender shaped slave resistance.

Cook, James. *The Arts of Deception: Playing with Fraud in the Age of Barnum*. Cambridge, MA: Harvard University Press, 2001. ▶ Study of nineteenth-century popular entertainments.

Davis, David Brion. *Inhuman Bondage: The Rise and Fall of Slavery in the New World*. New York: Oxford University Press, 2008. ▶ Sweeping portrayal of American slavery in global context.

Dunn, Richard S. *A Tale of Two Plantations: Slave Life and Labor in Jamaica and Virginia*. Cambridge, MA: Harvard University Press, 2014. ▶ Comparative study of slave experiences in Jamaica and Virginia in the nineteenth century.

Hatch, Nathan. *The Democratization of American Christianity*. New Haven, CT: Yale University Press, 1999. ▶ Historical study that links the Second Great Awakening with democratic impulses.

Howe, Daniel Walker. *What Hath God Wrought: The Transformation of America, 1815–1848*. New York: Oxford University Press, 2007. ▶ Synthetic history of nineteenth-century politics, economy, and culture.

McDaniel, Caleb. *The Problem of Democracy in the Age of Slavery: Garrisonian Abolitionists and Transatlantic Reform*. Baton Rouge: Louisiana State University Press, 2015. ▶ An interpretation of American abolitionism that highlights its transatlantic contexts.

> Go to the MindTap® for **Global Americans** to access the full version of select books from this Additional Resources section.

Websites

Ardent Spirits at the Library Company. (http://www.librarycompany.org/ArdentSpirits/index.htm) ▶ Exhibition exploring the many dimensions of the temperance movement.

Home, Sweet Home: Life in Nineteenth-Century Ohio. (http://lcweb2.loc.gov/diglib/ihas/html/ohio/ohio-home.html) ▶ Library of Congress collection of parlor music with explanatory essays.

Immigration to the United States, 1789–1930. (http://ocp.hul.harvard.edu/immigration/) ▶ Harvard University Library collection of sources on nineteenth-century immigration.

Inland Waterways. (http://americanhistory.si.edu/onthewater/exhibition/4_1.html) ▶ Smithsonian National Museum of American History exhibit on life along inland waterways.

Continue exploring online through MindTap®**, where you can:**

- **Assess your knowledge with the Chapter Test**
- **Watch historical videos related to the chapter**
- **Further your understanding with interactive maps and timelines**

Personal Transformations and Public Reforms

1801–1810

August 1801
Camp meeting in Cane Ridge, Kentucky, draws tens of thousands.

1808
Charles Fourier publishes his first major work, influencing utopian communities.

June 1810
New England ministers and businessmen found the American Board of Commissioners of Foreign Missions (ABCFM).

1816–1817

1816
New York builds a state penitentiary following the Auburn System of prisoner control.

April 1816
African Methodist Episcopal Church becomes an independent denomination.

May 1816
American Bible Society dedicated to printing and distributing Bibles is founded.

September 1817
Anglo-Spanish Treaty commits Spain to ending the international slave trade to be enforced by Britain.

1821–1826

September 1821
Mexico achieves independence from Spain.

May 1823
American John Howard Payne premiers "Home! Sweet Home!" in London.

1825
Robert Owen founds New Harmony, an experimental community, in Indiana.

February 1826
Boston ministers found the American Society for the Promotion of Temperance to encourage moderation in alcohol consumption.

1828–1830

November 1828
Andrew Jackson elected president of the United States.

1829
David Walker publishes *Appeal to the Coloured Citizens of the World*, decrying slavery and racism.

September 1829
Independent Mexico abolishes slavery.

1830
Joseph Smith publicizes the *Book of Mormon*, the founding text of the Church of Jesus Christ of Latter-day Saints, also known as the Mormon Church.

June 1830
Godey's Lady's Book begins publication.

1831–1832

1830–1831
Finney leads religious revival in Rochester, New York, during high point of Second Great Awakening.

August 1831
Turner leads largest U.S. slave rebellion of the nineteenth century.

December 1831
Sharpe leads Christmas Rising slave revolt in Jamaica, resulting in two hundred deaths.

1832
Cholera outbreak in New York City kills thousands of mainly poor residents.

Cayuses
United States
Britain
France
Spain
Europe
Mexico
Spanish Cuba
Jamaica

1833

August 1833
British Parliament passes the Slavery Abolition Act, ending slavery in most of the British colonies.

September 1833
Day publishes the *New York Sun*, first of the penny press papers.

December 1833
Garrison and others found the American Anti-Slavery Society.

1834–1836

May 1834
New York women found the American Female Reform Society to combat prostitution.

July 1834
Antiblack riots in New York City are sparked by anniversary celebrations for state emancipation.

1834–1836
Mexican officials break up the Franciscan missions in Alta California.

1835
ABCFM sends missionaries Marcus and Narcissa Whitman to Cayuse Indians.

May 1836
Congress passes a gag rule, forbidding the further consideration of antislavery petitions.

1837–1839

February 1837
Richmond, Virginia, businessmen receive charter for the Tredegar Iron Works.

June 1839
Chartists' Petition demanding universal male suffrage presented to Parliament.

August 1839
U.S. navy seizes the *Amistad*, launching a series of trials concerning the passengers' free status.

1839
Physician Samuel George Morton publishes *Crania Americana*, fueling scientific racist thought.

1840–1844

June 1840
World's Anti-Slavery Convention meets in London with nearly five hundred delegates.

1841
Ralph Waldo Emerson publishes "Self Reliance."

1843
U.S. promoter P. T. Barnum tours Europe and Cuba with his distant cousin posing as "Tom Thumb."

1845–1848

May 1845
Baptist Church splits over whether to accept slavery, forming two conferences.

July 1848
One hundred women and men sign the Seneca Falls Declaration of Sentiments for women's rights.

Go to MindTap® to engage with an interactive version of the timeline. Analyze events and themes with clickable content, view related videos, and respond to critical thinking questions.

11

A Continental Nation

1815–1853

Texas in the 1830s and 1840s was a difficult place for *Tejanos*. By the time he died in 1890, Juan Seguín had exiled himself to Mexico. People on both sides of the border questioned his loyalty because he had fought for both Mexico and the United States during his lifetime.

On the night of February 25, 1836, Juan Seguín slipped out the back of Mission San Antonio de Valero in Texas. Mexican forces had surrounded him and his comrades in the Spanish mission, better known today as the Alamo. The situation appeared hopeless for the Texas rebels who were fighting for their independence from Mexico. Their commander sent Seguín to ride north and bring back reinforcements to help save the men from certain attack, capture, and perhaps death. Although Seguín carried his message to Sam Houston, president of the newly formed Texas Republic, he was too late. The Mexican army attacked before he returned, killing virtually every man who stayed to defend the Alamo. Seguín later helped defeat Mexican forces at the Battle of San Jacinto. He was among the victors who accepted General Antonio Lopez de Santa Anna's surrender when he laid down his arms and recognized Texas independence.

Juan N. Seguín, Jefferson Wright (1838)/The State Preservation Board, Austin, Texas

Seguín, a wealthy and prominent man, was elected as a state senator, the only *Tejano* (Texan) in that body, and later mayor of his hometown, San Antonio. As he returned to domestic life, he envisioned a world where former Mexican citizens would live side-by-side with their Anglo neighbors who had emigrated from the United States over the past two decades. Together they would all be *Tejanos*, a people united by the shaping of a new democratic nation.

But Texas in the mid nineteenth century was a difficult place for Mexican Americans, even those as wealthy as Seguín, to maintain their status in the Lone Star Republic's evolving society. By the time Seguín died in 1890, he had held many offices, been exiled to Mexico because people questioned his loyalty to Texas, lived on both sides of the U.S./Mexican border, and fought for both the Lone Star Republic against Mexico and for the Mexican government against the United States. He eventually lost all of his property and died a destitute man who wondered in his memoir how he had become a "foreigner in my native land." The world was changing around Seguín. He and others born in Mexico's northern provinces were remade as Americans as the United States expanded its border to the Pacific.

The story of Juan Seguín reveals the complexities of living in the territories between the Mississippi River and the Pacific Ocean, which in 1815 were either colonies of Spain and Britain or the unorganized Louisiana Territory, which had been a colony of both Spain and France. By 1850, the American West would be organized into U.S. territories. The process of incorporation was marked by experimentation, violence, political turmoil, and accommodation. Across these vast spaces, imperial nations and Indian empires competed for trade monopolies and power even as individuals—Native Americans, Mexicans, and Euro-Americans— competed for land and wealth.

On the northern Great Plains, the Sioux sought to dominate their neighbors. In Indian Territory, tribes from the southeast United States re-established themselves. In Texas, white U.S. settlers and their slaves crossed international boundaries to establish cotton plantations. In Oregon, fur

> How does Juan Seguín's experience as a *Tejano* in Texas illustrate the complexities of living in the territories between the Mississippi River and the Pacific Ocean?
> Go to MindTap® to watch a video on Seguín and learn how his story relates to the themes of this chapter.

trappers from around the world created monopolies for their enterprises even as families from the eastern United States worked to build farming communities. In California, the discovery of gold drew men and women from all over the world. As these peoples and cultures clashed, the U.S. government asserted its control by sponsoring expeditions, relocating Native Americans, improving transportation and communication to promote commerce, negotiating treaty settlements, and making war that forced territorial transfers. Between 1815 and 1850, the nation expanded by more than 50 percent.

The repercussions were not limited to the United States. As Spain's empire contracted in the face of independence movements throughout the Americas, France and Britain threatened to seize new territories. The British took a renewed interest in Pacific Coast enterprises. France intervened in Mexico. The Texas province of Coahuila y Tejas broke away to form an independent nation (the turmoil in which Seguín was caught). Aggressive overtures by Britain in what would become the Pacific Northwest accelerated annexation by the United States.

11-1
Pulled and Pushed West

Winter Counts, or as Lakotas call them *waniyetu wowapi*, are calendars that tell history. They were drawn on bison hides, and each year people added information. They were called Winter Counts because they were created during the cold months when people were inside and not engaged in hunting, planting, or harvesting. ▶ Fine Art Premium/Corbis

As you study the image, describe the narrative being told. How could it help historians tell a more comprehensive account of migrations on the Great Plains?

Continuing the migrations of the early nineteenth century, Americans pushed beyond the former frontier lands of Ohio, Kentucky, and Tennessee, across the Mississippi River. Establishing plantations that used slave labor as in the South and small farms with commercial connections as in the North, these pioneers came into direct contact and conflict with Indians up and down the western frontier. The settlers' presence dispossessed Sac, Fox, and Sioux in the North and Cherokees, Seminoles and others in the South. The importance of Mississippi River towns, including New Orleans and St. Louis, increased as hubs for trade in cotton, wheat, and slaves. Pushing farther west, fur trappers and traders from the United States, France, Britain, and Mexico competed for the region's rich resources of beaver pelts and bison hides. In an attempt to bring order and control over this mix of people, the U.S. government sent mapping and scientific expeditions to bolster knowledge about the region and to help formulate plans for increased influence.

Indians were not the only people pushed unwillingly west. Black slaves were chained and marched from the failing tobacco fields of the Chesapeake to the southwestern frontiers. Mormons, adherents to a new American religion, fled to Utah beyond the reach of their persecutors and

the U.S. government. Like the traders and planters, many migrants in the trans-Mississippi West paid little regard to national boundaries or Indian lands, eager to get what they wanted and willing to move farther west. In the vast places not yet mapped or even marched over by Euro-Americans, control by the United States, Mexico, or Britain was not much in evidence but that of the Indians was clear.

☞ As you read, consider why people were pushing —or being pushed—across the Mississippi River. How did they interact with those they encountered?

11-1a Sioux Destiny on the Great Plains

Sioux, who referred to themselves as *Oceti Sakowin*— Seven Council Fires—did not always live on the Great Plains or hunt bison. By studying

{ Sioux dominate the trade of the region's natural resources.

Winter Counts, historians know that although the Sioux originally lived in the Great Lakes region, white and other Indian migrations earlier in the nineteenth century had pushed them out of the Upper Missouri Valley and westward. The move disrupted not only their day-to-day lives but also their sense of themselves as a people. To combat that disruption, the Sioux told a story of their origin to explain their migration onto the Great Plains.

In their explanation, **White Buffalo Calf Woman** came to the Sioux and prophesized their success if they moved onto the Great Plains. The Sioux then reimagined themselves as a nation destined to live on the Great Plains and control the magnificent bison herds that roamed that portion of North America. This narrative provided them a religiously ordained justification for the conquest of their neighbors and their dominance of the bison hide trade, which were in high demand globally. The first population pressure on other Indians living on the Great Plains came not from Euro-Americans looking for "free" land but from the Sioux, who were pushing westward to fulfill their own prophesized destiny.

The Sioux created alliances in order to move freely along the plains and control the regions' resources. The Sioux could not do all the hunting and preparing bison hides themselves, so they acted as intermediaries between other Indians and European and U.S. traders. The Sioux were spared the most dramatic impact of a smallpox epidemic when it swept through the Missouri River Valley in 1837 because their mobility allowed them to disperse themselves, fleeing the settled villages where disease spread easily. In contrast, almost half of the Indian population, forced to stay in their circumscribed territory because they feared Sioux depredations, perished in the epidemic (see Figure 11.1). The Sioux took advantage of rivals' population loss and pushed farther west and south, displacing Mandans, Hidatsas, Pawnees, Crows, and others from their hunting lands and agricultural plots. Moreover, Sioux population increased from five thousand in 1804 to more than twenty-five thousand in 1850.

Sioux expansion and ties to global markets began to decimate the vast bison herds. They moved away from hunting for subsistence and the demands of a regional economy toward fulfilling the greater demands of a market economy in bison hides, which were increasingly used for making industrial grade leather as well as fur coats. In partnership with the increasing number of Euro-American traders, the Sioux began to overhunt to meet the market demands from competing fur trade companies. To dominate this trade, the Sioux relentlessly attacked their neighbors. Although U.S. citizens, who by the early 1840s were moving across the Plains on their way to Oregon, were rarely the target of Indian attacks, they were often caught in the cross fire and competition over territory.

To settle Great Plains warfare among Indians and to open a path across the continent for those heading west,

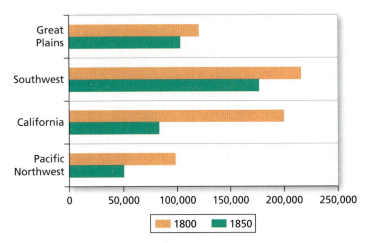

Figure 11.1 Decline in Native Populations in the U.S. West by Region, 1800–1850 Inaccuracies of census data make determining the population of Native Americans during this period difficult. For instance, the Great Plains census shows a slight decline, but historians know that the population of the Mandan decreased more than 75 percent whereas that of the Lakotas increased. These relative numbers, however, reflect the population decline that would continue through the mid-twentieth century, when they finally began to increase. ▲ Source: D. H Ubelaker. "North American Population Size, A.D. 1500 to 1985." *American Journal of Physical Anthropology* 77 (1988): 292.

the U.S. government negotiated the **Fort Laramie Treaty** in a 1851 conference to secure safe passage so that the migrants could move west unimpeded. In addition to securing safe travel for Americans, the treaty established set boundaries (the beginnings of reservations) for many of the weaker Plains groups and defined all political relationships on the Great Plains until the 1890s. The Sioux, in alliance with Cheyennes and Arapahoes, kept other groups away from the proceedings and dominated the conference. They made a treaty that solidified their alliance with the Americans. Although the signed treaty proclaimed U.S. military presence on the Plains, it was also the U.S. government's recognition of the power of the Sioux.

11-1b Indian Removal

During the same period, Choctaws, Chickasaws, Cherokees, Creeks, and Seminoles continued their ongoing warfare with the state and federal governments in the Southeast (particularly in Georgia) and the U.S. government. In the North, tribes constantly resisted their forced movement imposed on them by the Indian Removal Act of 1830.

> The U.S. government pushes Indians west.

In 1828, the "British Band" of the Sauk led by Black Hawk resisted U.S. expansion and dismissed the treaty of 1804, which they had signed, as corrupt and unjust. Black Hawk said, "Whites were in the habit of saying

White Buffalo Calf Woman
Protagonist in the Sioux origin narrative that justified tribal migrations onto the Great Plains and domination over their neighbors.

Fort Laramie Treaty
Agreement between the U.S. government and Plains peoples to establish boundaries and to allow white immigrants to pass safely through Indian country.

one thing to the Indians and putting another thing down on paper." The **Black Hawk War** in 1832, however, was not just a military engagement between the United States and the Sauks; it also involved a complicated set of previous alliances and enmities between France, Great Britain, the United States, Sauks, Meskwakis, and Potawatamies.

Black Hawk and his allies won an initial round of skirmishes that left the Illinois militia stunned. In response, President Andrew Jackson ordered General Winfield Scott to take over the operations and promise no treaty negotiations. Jackson wanted Black Hawk to be made an example so that other Indians would not resist the U.S. government and their removal. Black Hawk surrendered and was taken to prison in Virginia. Before being released a few months later, he toured Baltimore, Philadelphia, and New York City. He was to report back to his people about the power and size of the United States and to counsel against any future resistance to U.S. removal policy. The conclusion of the Black Hawk War opened Iowa to white settlement.

Black Hawk War Battle between the United States and the "British Band" of Indians led by Black Hawk, who crossed into U.S. territory trying to avoid conflict in their homelands.

Indian removal had long been U.S. government policy, which had been engaged in convincing Indians to move west across the Mississippi River (see Map 11.1). Along the western frontier from Michigan to Georgia, the U.S. government pushed Indians west to the Great Plains, which were already under pressure from the Sioux. The Plains were also being populated by Indians such as Kiowas and Apaches, who were fleeing the expansion of the Comanche in the southern Plains.

John Ross, the principal chief of the Cherokee nation, condemned the Indian Removal Act. In two Supreme Court case decisions, the Cherokees prevailed (see Chapter 9). The court victories, however, proved to be merely symbolic. Rather than enforce the Court's rulings granting Cherokee sovereignty, Jackson worked with officials in Georgia and the U.S. Congress to forcibly remove the Indians. He also called on a Cherokee ally, Major Ridge, who led the opposition to Ross. Ridge and Jackson had fought together during the War of 1812. Ironically, Ridge had risen to a position of power partly because in 1807 he had killed Doublehead, a Cherokee leader in the pay of the United States who had been bribed to violate a blood oath against

Map 11.1 U.S. Removal of Indians, 1830–1845 After the passage of the 1830 Indian Removal Act, the federal government legally pushed Indians from their homelands in the regions noted in the map to the far West. Tens of thousands lost their property and family networks and had to start over in Indian Territory, part of which was later organized as the state of Oklahoma. By 1837, the Jackson administration had relocated more than fifty thousand people and opened 25 million acres of land for white settlement. ▼

signing treaties that ceded Cherokee lands. But twenty-eight years later, Ridge led the Cherokees, who believed that it was pointless to oppose removal and instead sought the land in the West as compensation.

In 1836, the U.S. government negotiated the **Treaty of New Echota** with the Treaty Party, a small group of Cherokees led by Major Ridge and his son John Ridge; they did not represent the majority and were not the elected government. The Treaty promised to pay $5 million to Cherokees to be paid in per capita payments, promised to cover the traveling costs of those who moved, and gave Cherokees an amount of land, equivalent in acreage to that lost in Georgia, in **Indian Territory** (present day Oklahoma). Many Americans who opposed the treaty saw the inherent unfairness to the Cherokees. Others questioned the wisdom of siding with President Jackson against the Supreme Court. Some who opposed the treaty would eventually become antislavery advocates in Congress—most famously, the former president, John Quincy Adams. Despite heated opposition, the U.S. Senate ratified the treaty by a margin of one vote. It gave the Cherokees two years to remove themselves to Indian Territory.

Those who followed Ridge left almost immediately. Many in the Ross party, however, continued to hope that they could negotiate to stay in their homes. But the state of Georgia ignored their petitions and held a lottery in which whites received Cherokee lands, houses, and improved fields. As the 1838 deadline approached, General Scott arrived to round up Cherokees from their homes, put them into holding pens, and then lead them overland in the winter to Oklahoma in what has become known as the **Trail of Tears**. The conditions on the trail were brutal as families struggled to stay together and survive in the face of inadequate provisions, drought, harsh weather conditions, and disease. In the winter of 1838–1839 as they moved to their lands across the Mississippi, leaving behind their property and most of their possessions, more than 25 percent of those who had set out on the trail died. Estimates range from 4,000 to 8,000 lives lost during the entire removal process. Quatie, the white wife of John Ross, died of exposure after giving her only blanket to a small child who had none. No Cherokee family was left unscathed by the process of removal.

In Oklahoma, Cherokees came into conflict with U.S. settlers who were pushing into Mexican-controlled Texas to the south and other Indians who were fleeing from Sioux and Comanche dominance. Despite a harsher and drier climate than the one they had left in Georgia, Cherokees built homes and businesses and created a new government while the Ross and Ridge factions vied for political power. The bitter division between the factions escalated as the majority of Cherokees blamed the Ridge family for their hardships in Oklahoma. On June 22, 1839, Major Ridge, his nephew, and his son were murdered for what many Cherokees considered their treason in selling land in Georgia. Revenge killings continued until 1845 when U.S. federal troops were called in to prevent a civil war among the Cherokees.

Cherokee Alphabet, developed in 1821 (print), American School (19th century)/Private Collection/Peter Newark American Pictures/Bridgeman Images

Sequoyah and the Syllabary In the late 1810s, Sequoyah developed a syllabary (a series or set of written characters) so that Cherokees could communicate with one another in writing. Sequoyah did not know how to read or write in any other language. Each of the eighty-five characters in his syllabary represents a syllable. Within a decade, Cherokees had achieved almost 90 percent literacy (much higher than anywhere else in North America). The Cherokee community had a printing press that published a newspaper, books, fliers, and hymnals. ▲

11-1c Maps, Trails, and Trade

After the success of the Lewis and Clark Expedition and the acquisition of territory from the Transcontinental (Adams-Onis) Treaty, the U.S. government wanted to explore and map these new acquisitions (see Map 11.2). Its curiosity extended far beyond the North American continent. In 1836, President Jackson authorized the U.S. Exploration Expedition to survey and collect data from the South Pacific and Antarctic regions. The military venture included civilian scientists who collected plant samples, drew images, and wrote scientific entries about all they encountered. Between 1838 and 1842, the expedition of six ships commanded by Navy Lieutenant Charles Wilkes encountered many indigenous peoples, often using violence. Wilkes

> Global and local economies become increasingly intertwined.

Treaty of New Echota Agreement signed by the U.S. government and the Treaty Party of the Cherokees, who agreed to remove themselves to present-day Oklahoma.

Indian Territory Area of federal lands in the western United States that was set aside for Indians who were removed from their ancestral homelands.

Trail of Tears Name of a series of forced migrations of Native Americans from their homelands in the southeast United States to federal territories in the U.S. West.

Map 11.2 Trails to the West, 1804–1850 Far from being an empty space when white settlers began their migration, what would become known as the U.S. West was already filled with thousands of Native Americans who had complex economies and thriving communities. These routes into the interior of the West show how white settlers followed rivers and Indian trading trails to make their incursions. These were well-known paths that had served indigenous communities for generations but became the highways that brought settlers into Indian country. ▲

found it difficult to balance the military and scientific missions. Upon the expedition's return, its collections became the basis for both the National Botanical Garden and the newly created **Smithsonian Institution**.

Exacerbating the contest over lands and trading routes in the middle part of the North American continent, thousands of Americans and Europeans came in search of economic opportunities. Throughout the first part of the nineteenth century, the Mississippi and Missouri Rivers had been the highways on which trade was conducted through the continent's interior. The U.S. government sent out expeditions and created bureaucracies to control and map these lands in preparation for settlement. In addition to these government-sponsored explorers and some early settlers trekking along the trails, U.S. and European fur trade companies led by John Jacob Astor, Manuel Lisa, and the Choteau family dominated the region economically.

The Lewis and Clark expedition was only the first of many government-sponsored forays into the West to map and explore the region from the Mississippi to the Pacific Ocean and, when possible, from the northern reaches of Mexico's territories north to British territory. In 1806, Zebulon Pike headed west to map the Louisiana Purchase and to find the headwaters of the Arkansas and Red Rivers. He entered Spanish territory in present-day southern Colorado and built a fort for the winter. The Spanish government arrested Pike for trespassing and took him to Mexico City where he was able to observe and then report back on the landscape, resources, and peoples of the region.

Smithsonian Institution
U.S. national museum with headquarters in Washington, D.C., funded by a bequest from the British scientist, James Smithsonian.

Global Americans William and Charles Bent

made their lives on the edge of three cultures: the United States, Mexico, and Indian country. The brothers came from a large prosperous family in St. Louis, Missouri. They headed west to find their fortunes in the emerging fur markets. In 1833, along with their friend Ceran St. Vrain, they established Bent's Fort, which sat on the Santa Fe Trail and in Mexican territory.

Bent's Fort was the only outpost between St. Louis and Santa Fe and functioned as a free trade zone. It was not under the control of the United States, Mexico, or any particular Indian tribe, although the Bents worked closely with the local Indians to establish the post. This freedom extended beyond the economic and into the social realm. It was a place where people from many nations intermingled with Americans and Indians from a wide range of plains groups. The Bents also brought three slaves, the Green family, to the Fort.

The Bents made strategic marital alliances. William married Owl Woman, the daughter of White Thunder, a Cheyenne elder of considerable stature. They had four children. Charles wed Maria Ignacia Jaramillo, who was from a prominent *Hispano* family. He used this connection to promote the trading posts and to acquire thousands of acres of land. The Bents' network across this borderland between nations represented a world where exchanges flowed freely with little constraint from government or society.

▲ (Left) The Granger Collection, New York. (Right) Center for Southwest Research, University Libraries, University of New Mexico

The **U.S. Army Corps of Engineers** had been established in 1779 to coordinate military efforts, propose infrastructure improvements, and to map the West. In 1824, Congress passed the **General Survey Act**, which provided the authorization for the Corps to survey road and canal routes into the interior of North America. One of the most effective surveyors during this period was Stephen H. Long. He completed five surveys, covered 26,000 miles, and was the first to label the Great Plains as the Great American Desert.

Official government expeditions acquired much knowledge and shared it through informal trade networks. For example, William Clark kept a map in his St. Louis office where fur traders, explorers, and travelers to the West would come and add to the map what they had seen or just study it to understand what type of terrain they were heading into. The **Clark Map**, as it came to be known, was the physical embodiment of knowledge about the American West as it changed over time.

Enterprise and trade often preceded the government into the West. The development of the **Santa Fe Trail** from St. Louis to Santa Fe, where it met the Chihuahua Trail, began in earnest after Mexico had gained independence from Spain in 1821. The trails, which were based on known Indian trade routes, created a highway of multinational people who traded everything from furniture and cloth to foodstuffs and raw goods in a trading system that linked the West to New York, Mexico City, London, and China. By the 1830s, fur trapping had also become an important part of this developing economy along the Santa Fe Trail. In 1833, William and Charles Bent and their partner Ceran St. Vrain established Bent's Fort. Long

Clark's Map, 1810 Upon his return from the Lewis and Clark expedition, William Clark drew a map of the trans-Mississippi West. During his time as territorial governor of Missouri, he kept the map in his office where returning travelers would stop by to talk about their travels and make additions and edits to the map. ▼

American Memory, Geography and Map Division, Library of Congress

U.S. Army Corps of Engineers
Military division created to provide domestic and military engineering services including the building of canals, roads, and dams.

General Survey Act
Legislation passed after *Gibbons v. Ogden* decision that gave the federal government authority over interstate commerce to fund the building of roads and canals.

Clark Map Master map created by Clark in 1810 when he returned to St. Louis after his expedition with Lewis, providing essential cartographic information for the next twenty-five years.

THE MORMON HAND-CART COMPANY CROSSING THE PLAINS.

Mormon Migration

Mormon migrations differed significantly from other white migrations into the U.S. West. Whereas most families who migrated brought as many possessions and provisions as they could carry, Mormon families traveled light because they wanted to get to Utah as quickly as possible. As a result, families used these pushcarts, taking only what would fit and what one man could pull over more than 900 miles from Winter Quarters to Salt Lake City. ◀

North Wind Picture Archives/Alamy Stock Photo

before the U.S. government could dominate the region, these traders and their Indian allies had created a thriving economy and multinational community.

The West was crisscrossed with various trade routes that would eventually become overland trails for settlers moving from the East into California and Oregon. By the early 1840s, settlers moved across the Oregon Trail, the Santa Fe Trail, the Platte Road, and what became known as the **Mormon Trail**. Migration to the West depended on the U.S. government's ability to control Indian violence by creating a system of forts that could aid settlers.

Unlike the market-driven movement of fur traders and trappers, the Mormon migration by members of the Church of Jesus Christ of Latter-day Saints (see Chapter 10) was one of the most organized and hierarchical migrations into the U.S. West. Because they were persecuted for their religious beliefs, their forced westward trek from 1831 to 1838 took them through western New York, Ohio, Illinois, and Missouri. They created thriving communities that grew rapidly but were always harassed by suspicious locals. In 1843, their prophet Joseph Smith claimed to have received a revelation regarding **polygamy**.

The revelation was immediately controversial. Smith constantly defended himself against outsiders, and many Mormons doubted the revelation and the place of polygamy in their religious practice. After a series of confrontations between Smith and the Illinois government, Smith turned himself in to the local sheriff at Carthage. While he was in jail, a mob attacked, killing him and his brother Hiram. To avoid more attacks, the Mormons, under the leadership of their new prophet, Brigham Young, pushed westward to find a new home.

Fearing interference from the U.S. government, Young wanted to move the immigrants westward into Mexican territory in February 1846. He then struck a bargain with President James K. Polk, who had just declared that a state of war existed with Mexico. The Mormons were allowed to make their encampment on U.S. government land in Nebraska and agreed to send 543 men, the Mormon Battalion, to fight Mexico. The government wages provided much needed cash to aid Mormon families who were slowly moving westward. They, like the Sioux in the Treaty of Fort Laramie, exchanged their military cooperation for access to land.

In the spring of 1847, after making his way across the Great Plains, Young stood atop the Wasatch Range and looked into the Utah Valley and proclaimed, "This is the place." But "this" turned out to be territory held by Utes, who were not interested in sharing the fertile valley with the Mormon immigrants. Sensing that they could not challenge the powerful Utes, Young moved south and settled in the arid and desolate Salt Lake Valley. The advance group began planting crops, building shelter and fences, and preparing for an onslaught of immigrants while Young returned to Nebraska to lead his flock to the Salt Lake Valley. Sixteen thousand men, women, and children with their household goods and animals walked to Utah. The poorer immigrants took only what they could carry in handheld pushcarts or on their backs. In 1849, to ensure their success, Young, under the guidelines of the Northwest Ordinance, established a territorial government and the state of Deseret (meaning honeybee) of which he was the governor.

Santa Fe Trail Overland trade route from Franklin, Missouri, to Santa Fe, New Mexico where it connected with the *Camino Real*, linking the region directly to Mexico City.

Mormon Trail Overland route used by Mormons fleeing persecution, linking Nauvoo, Illinois, with Salt Lake City, Utah.

polygamy The practice of one man marrying multiple women that Joseph Smith declared in 1831 to be a tenet of the Mormon Church.

11-2

National Destiny

The Fall of the Alamo by Robert Jenkins Onderdonk (1903) depicts the way that many Americans, Texans in particular, choose to remember the battle at the Alamo. It depicts Davy Crockett, out of ammunition, beating off Mexican soldiers before he dies a valiant martyr's death. Although contemporary witnesses and historians later disputed the events as shown here, some suggesting that Crockett had been captured and executed, most chose to believe the myth that had been created about the defenders of the Alamo.

How does Onderdonk portray Davy Crockett in the painting? How does he depict the Mexican army's attack on the Alamo? ▶

MPI/Archive Photos/Getty Images

In the 1830s and 1840s as Indian treaties and removals opened land across the Mississippi to settlement, many Americans began thinking of themselves as part of a continental nation. What would it take to realize a nation that would stretch from the Atlantic to the Pacific? Already, American settlers were ignoring national boundaries to take up residence in the Mexican province of Coahuila y Tejas, as well as in Oregon where a joint occupation with Britain had followed treaties negotiating the withdrawal of both Russian and Spanish claims. By the 1830s, the presence of Americans in Texas and Oregon accelerated interest in making these regions part of the United States. But with that land came the people who had inhabited it for centuries, and Americans reacted in different ways to the prospect of incorporating them into the United States.

☞ As you read, consider how U.S. settlers regarded national boundaries. Why did Americans continue to look beyond their established borders to expand U.S. influence?

11-2a Conflict in the Texas Borderland

After the Louisiana Purchase in 1803, the boundary with Mexico was uncertain. The United States sponsored explorers such as Pike and John C. Fremont to mark the boundaries of the nation and spy on their Mexican neighbors. Illegal explorations, **filibusters**, also crossed these unmarked borders. For example, Augustus Magee, a former lieutenant in the U.S. army, raised a force of three hundred men to cross into Texas to help free the province from the Spanish in 1812. While the expedition was unsuccessful, it revealed a pattern of U.S. citizens crossing borders to further U.S. interests, even if unsanctioned by the government. Although the Treaty of 1819 specified the U.S.-Mexico border and renounced all U.S. claims to Texas, the border still remained a porous and

> A new republic breaks away from Mexico.

largely symbolic line that few recognized. Southerners in particular resented that Texas, along with Florida, had not been ceded by the Spanish as they wanted to push slavery farther west into Texas's cotton-growing areas.

Tejas y Coahuila was sparsely populated by Spanish, and later Mexican citizens. Because of its distance from Mexico City, the province was poorly served by the government. The outposts continually confronted Comanches who raided their communities for horses, cattle, and captives. Nevertheless, the province's struggling missions, along with the settled population of farmers, maintained cattle ranches and strong communities that drew the attention of slaveholders in the U.S. South.

Once Mexico gained independence from Spain in 1821, the Mexican government worked to secure its northern border against the United States. The government worried that foreigners—Americans, Russians, and the British—would overrun New Mexico, Alta and Baja California, and Tejas y Coahuila. Because Texas seemed the most susceptible of these to foreign and Indian incursions, the Mexican government encouraged foreigners, particularly Americans, to emigrate under the Mexican government's terms. These immigrants would gain property rights to millions of acres if they agreed to become Mexican citizens and convert to Catholicism. Thousands of U.S. citizens, particularly those moving from Tennessee and Kentucky, accepted the offer and started new lives as Mexican citizens. Many of them married into elite, property-owning *Tejano* families, like the Seguíns (see Table 11.1).

In 1821, Moses Austin, a New Englander who had sought his fortune in lead mining in upper Louisiana, was drawn by Mexico's offer and negotiated an *empresario* contract whereby he would settle 300 families on 100,000 acres of Texas land. Austin died before he could fulfill his contract, and in 1821 the colonial government was overthrown and the Republic of

filibusters A person who enters a foreign territory with the intention of starting a rebellion or uprising, which was associated with U.S. presence in Latin America.

empresario A person to whom the Spanish and later Mexican governments granted large areas, sometimes millions of acres, of land.

Table 11.1 Racial Terminology Used in North America circa 1820–1850

The historical terms listed here describe ethnic groups mentioned in this chapter who populated the North American continent. In addition to these terms, groups would have also had derogatory terms to describe one another.

Term	Definition
Tejana/o	People of Mexican descent residing in Texas and who became U.S. citizens after 1845
Hispana/o	People of Mexican descent residing in New Mexico and who became U.S. citizens after 1912
California/o	People of Mexican descent residing in California and who became U.S. citizens after 1848
Mestiza/o	People of mixed racial or ethnic backgrounds
Mexicana/o	U.S. citizens of Mexican descent
Mexican	Citizen of Mexico
Mexican–American	U.S. inhabitants of Mexican descent
Anglo	People of European descent
Gentile	Term used by Mormons to describe non-Mormons; could apply equally to Catholics, Protestants, and Jews
Indian	General term used to describe indigenous peoples of North America
Métis	People of mixed heritage from European and Indian parents; used mostly by the French
Pueblos	Native Americans who lived along the Rio Grande Valley in New Mexico

Mexico soon established. Moses Austin's son, Stephen, renegotiated the arrangement with the newly independent Mexico, fulfilling the requirement that he convert to Catholicism, and eventually settled more than nine hundred people in Texas. Ninety percent of them were southerners who intended to grow cotton using slave labor. Although Mexico abolished slavery in 1829, Tejanos ignored the law and blacks remained enslaved.

Texas, like New Mexico and California, was far from the seat of political power in Mexico City. Like the Regulators in backcountry North and South Carolina, these *Tejanos* on the nation's northern frontier often felt neglected in receiving adequate government financial aid and military protection against Indians. Most of the immigrants to Texas had strong ties to the United States, looked eastward for cotton markets, and hoped for eventual union with the United States. In 1826, Haden and Benjamin Edwards rebelled against the Mexican government and formed an alliance with Indians and *métis*. The group seized Nagadoches, Texas, in an effort to wrest independence from Mexico. Stephen Austin, who supported the emerging Mexican republic, and his men subdued the rebellion. Perceiving the revolt to be a result of southern U.S. influence, the Mexican government banned the further importation of slaves and prohibited any further immigration from the United States. Austin and other Texas leaders accepted these limitations reluctantly.

Eight years later, however, General Antonio Lopez de Santa Anna renounced the republican, federal form of government and declared himself dictator, preferring a more centralized form of government. Santa Anna dissolved the Constitution of 1824, angering the Texans who expected to live under a democracy. Austin and other leaders, including Juan Seguín, pushed for Texas independence. In rhetoric recalling the American Revolution, leaders stated that they were preserving the Mexican Republic and were rebelling only against Santa Anna's tyranny.

While many immediately hoped for Texas to be granted U.S. statehood, their public rhetoric merely called for a return to Mexico's own republican ideals. On March 2, 1836, Texas leaders declared independence from Mexico and wrote a constitution that borrowed heavily from the U.S. Constitution but prohibited the Texas legislature from interfering with slavery and free blacks from residing in the territory. A number of prominent *Tejanos* signed their names to the document, including Lorenzo de Zavala who became vice president of the new republic.

General Santa Anna amassed a force of seven thousand troops to squash the rebellion outside the **Alamo** in San Antonio. William Travis, the commander at the fort, sent Juan Seguín to tell the newly elected president, Sam Houston, of the Alamo's siege and to bring back reinforcements. After a two-week siege, he attacked the garrison, killing almost all of the 187 men, 10 percent of whom were *Tejanos*. Santa Anna sustained a serious loss of 1,500 men, but he continued his march north wiping out the Texas forces at Goliad, including summary executions of 300 *Tejanos*.

Following a month of preparation and recruiting volunteers from the United States, President Sam Houston, the commander of the Texas forces, led a surprise charge on Santa Anna's forces at San Jacinto. In just over fifteen minutes, Houston's troops defeated the Mexican forces and captured Santa Anna. After such a humiliating defeat, Santa Anna could do little but accept Texas independence under the terms of the **Treaty of Velasco**. The Mexican Congress, however, repudiated the treaty, refused to recognize Texas independence, and stripped Santa Anna of his power, banishing him to Cuba. The United States recognized Texas as a sovereign nation but did not consider it for statehood because doing so would shift the balance of free and slave states. From 1836 to 1845, Texas was known as the *Lone Star Republic*.

Alamo A Texas mission in which the Mexican government laid siege to Texas rebels for 13 days in the spring of 1836 before defeating them.

The Treaty of Velasco The 1836 treaty that ended hostilities between the Mexican government and the Texas rebels after the defeat of Santa Anna at San Jacinto.

AP Images/Harry Cabluck

The Surrender of Santa Anna, **1896** This painting by William H. Huddle depicts Santa Anna surrendering to Houston, who is shown injured, lying under an oak tree with a bandaged leg. The defeated Santa Anna is depicted wearing the white pants of a private. ◄

11-2b The West as the Future

In 1839, John L. O'Sullivan, a prominent political commentator and editor of *The Democratic Review*, published "The Great Nation of Futurity." He argued that Americans were uniquely free from the brutality of European history. He wrote, "The expansive future is our arena, and for our history. . . . We are the nation of human progress." O'Sullivan often spoke for the expansionist wing of the Democratic Party, extolling the need to push west for the sake of expanding the nation's democratic principles to those in the Mexican and British provinces, which he claimed would not otherwise enjoy those freedoms.

> Politicians discuss the West and the expansion of slavery.

National politics between 1835 and 1845 increasingly focused on the West. The slavery issue came into play with each new territory that petitioned for statehood (see Table 11.2). Politicians strove to maintain the precarious balance between free and slave states in the Senate that had been achieved with the Missouri Compromise in 1820.

Presidential elections began to reflect the increasing political importance of the West. In 1828, Andrew Jackson became the first president elected from a state west of the Appalachian Mountains. In 1840, the Whigs ran William Henry Harrison of Indiana, another famed Indian fighter and the military hero of the Battle of Tippecanoe. Although born wealthy on a Virginia plantation, he was recast as a hard-drinking westerner, a man of the people born in a log cabin. John Tyler, a former Democrat, was his running mate. The Whigs rallied their supporters with parades featuring barrels of hard cider, miniature log cabins, and the slogan "Tippecanoe and Tyler Too!"

The Democratic nominee, President Martin Van Buren of New York, had faced the Panic of 1837 and the ensuing depression. Whigs blamed the economic downturn on the inactivity of the federal government and

Table 11.2 Free and Slave States Admitted between 1800–1850

During the first half of the nineteenth century, the balance of power between free and slave states was precarious. The eight states admitted as slave states allowed settlers to import their human property without fear of confiscation. National confrontations over the place of slavery played out in the western territories to which immigrants moved. To make way in these regions for the settlers and their new labor systems, whether free or slave, Indians were removed from their homelands.

Year	State	Status
1803	Ohio	Free
1812	Louisiana	Slave
1816	Indiana	Free
1817	Mississippi	Slave
1818	Illinois	Free
1819	Alabama	Slave
1820	Maine	Free
1821	Missouri	Slave
1836	Arkansas	Slave
1837	Michigan	Free
1845	Florida	Slave
1845	Texas	Slave
1846	Iowa	Free
1848	Wisconsin	Free
1850	California	Free

lampooned the president as "Martin Van Ruin." In contrast to Harrison's tough warrior image, they derided the president's masculinity, declaring "Van, Van is a used-up man." James G. Birney, a former slaveholder, ran on the **Liberty Party** ticket, a single-issue, electorally weak party that aimed to bring opposition to slavery to the forefront of national

Liberty Party Third-party that broke away from the U.S. Anti-Slavery Society to advocate the use of the Constitution to abolish slavery.

politics. For the next twenty years, every national politician would need to address the issue directly.

Harrison won the election of 1840 by a landslide, taking 234 electoral votes to Van Buren's 60. Refusing to wear a hat or overcoat on a cold, wet day, Harrison gave a nearly two-hour inaugural address, the longest in U.S. history. He developed pneumonia and died only a month after taking office, leaving the presidency to John Tyler. A lifelong Democrat, Tyler had joined the Whig Party only because he opposed Jackson's promise to use force against South Carolina during the nullification crisis. As president, Tyler opposed all efforts by the Whigs to pass their program of federally financed improvements, vetoing their efforts to raise the tariff and create a bank. Furious over his vetoes, which Whigs compared to Jackson's veto of the Bank Bill, they expelled Tyler from the party. For the next four years, the federal government was gridlocked.

The only policy the parties could agree on was westward expansion and allocation of public lands (see Map 11.3). Congress enacted the **Preemption Act** in 1841, which allowed squatters on public land to purchase 160 acres at the minimum price of $1.25 an acre. Much of this land was in newly acquired territories in the old northwest and southeast, sites of intense efforts to remove Indians and promote white settlement. Western expansion was one of the few areas of bipartisan consensus at a time when the parties were deadlocked over the proper role of the federal government. Ever since Jefferson had bought the Louisiana Purchase, Democrats had understood that western expansion was an exception to their philosophy of limited federal government. Southern Democrats rallied to the idea of more slave states and called for the annexation of Texas, and nationalists denounced the British and called for the annexation of Oregon Territory. Even President Tyler, a "states' rights" politician who was otherwise suspicious of vigorous federal power, could see the political benefits of western expansion.

The issues of westward expansion, particularly the issue of Texas **annexation**, and slavery dominated the election of 1844. The Democratic Party was divided on the issue of slavery. Antislavery Democrats, such as Van Buren, opposed

Preemption Act Legislation that permitted settlers, also known as squatters, to purchase the land they occupied on federal claimed lands for $1.25 an acre.

Map 11.3 U.S. Geographic Expansion, 1800–1860 During the first half of the nineteenth century, the United States more than doubled its territory and became a continental nation. In the process of expansion it overtook Native American communities as well as pushed out foreign nations such as Great Britain, France, Spain, Russia, and Mexico. The U.S. military and settlers used well-established trails to make their incursions, and by 1850 most of the continent was occupied and controlled by the United States. ▼

annexation, but proexpansion Democrats engineered the presidential nomination of James Polk, a Tennessee congressman who pushed for the annexation of both Oregon and Texas. On the other side, most Whigs were hostile to the idea of adding a slave state to the Union. Their nominee, Henry Clay, took an ambiguous position on the annexation of Texas. In a close race, Polk won on a platform of expansion.

Tyler, a lame-duck president, denied Polk the chance to annex Texas by pressing Congress to pass a joint resolution inviting Texas to join the Union. Unlike a treaty, the resolution did not require a two-thirds vote in the Senate and, therefore, could not be blocked by antislavery Democrats and Whigs. Proslavery Americans had been migrating in large numbers to Texas for a decade, and they outnumbered *Tejanos* by a margin of eight to one. Even influential *Tejanos* such as Juan Seguín were marginalized. Not surprisingly, the Texas legislature ratified the annexation resolution treaty, and Texas joined the Union as a slave state on December 29, 1845. Once Texas was open to U.S. settlement, southerners pushed westward into the area around its eastern rivers where cotton plantations worked by slaves had sprung up and was ripe for the expansion of slavery. The annexation also created a diplomatic crisis with Mexico.

Two earlier events contributed to the crisis. In March 1845, Florida, a former colony of both Spain and Britain, had joined the Union as a slave state. Then, in the summer of 1845, in the midst of the debate over Texas, O'Sullivan suggested in the *Democratic Review* that it was the "manifest destiny" of the United States "to overspread the continent allotted by Providence for the free development of our yearly multiplying millions." He articulated the ideology underlying the U.S. expansion, which had been in place since President Jefferson had sent Lewis and Clark west to explore the northwest. The term **manifest destiny** resonated in public and political discourse. O'Sullivan warned that "other nations" had "intruded" themselves in Texas, a violation of the Monroe Doctrine. He also asserted the superiority of U.S. political institutions over those of Mexico and predicted that California would naturally "next fall away" from Mexico's tenuous ("imbecile and distracted") hold. "The Anglo-Saxon foot is already on its borders." O'Sullivan's words spoke to Americans who wanted to secure territory for the expansion of the U.S. economy in general and slavery specifically. Just as the Sioux used the White Buffalo Calf Woman narrative to justify their claims, so the U.S. found in the ideology of Manifest Destiny a religious justification for expansion.

The U.S. annexation of Texas portended war against a neighboring republic. Since 1824, Mexico had been an independent republic with a constitution that had established a federal republic of nineteen states and four territories. Unlike the U.S. Constitution, the Mexican Constitution included Indians as citizens, outlawed slavery, and had fewer racial or property restrictions regarding suffrage or holding public office. But the Mexican Constitution proved incapable of constraining the power of the central government. As the rhetoric of Manifest Destiny became heated, most Americans willingly set aside Mexico's sovereignty to take advantage of its weaknesses.

11-2c U.S.–Canada Border and the Oregon Question

{ The U.S. government finally resolves its border issues with Great Britain.

With the nation's political focus on the West and the escalation of hostilities with Mexico over Texas, pressure built to settle the question of the Oregon border peacefully. Since the Revolutionary era, Britain and the United States had been in constant dispute about their shared border at various locations from Maine to Oregon. In an effort to avoid hostilities, the two nations had jointly occupied Oregon since 1818. In 1842, after clashes over the boundary between New Brunswick and Maine, the two countries signed the **Webster-Ashburton Treaty** to clarify the northeastern border between the two nations.

In the far west, Great Britain had discouraged settlement in order to protect its fur trade, but the U.S. government promoted the settlement of family farms. What began in the late 1830s as a trickle of missionaries, such as the Whitmans (Chapter 10), and fur traders trekking westward picked up momentum, and by 1843, almost one thousand immigrants were making their home in the jointly occupied territory. By 1845, two thousand five hundred people had crossed the Great Plains through Indian lands to get to Oregon. As John C. Calhoun noted, it was "wise and masterly inactivity" that had allowed what was called the **Great Migration** and would also allow the Oregon Question to be decided by the settlers in the territory.

Tensions with Mexico made the settlement even more imperative. The settlers and their expansionist allies pressured the newly elected President Polk to resolve the dispute as he had promised in his 1844 campaign slogan of "Fifty-four forty or fight!" that is, setting the northern border of Oregon at the latitude line of fifty-four degrees, forty minutes. In the Oregon Treaty of 1846, however, Polk compromised and retained only half of the U.S. claim, making the **forty-ninth parallel** the border with Canada. Great Britain kept the Vancouver Islands. As tensions with Mexico rose, Polk wanted to avoid a simultaneous war with a much stronger British foe. Because Oregon Territory was not conducive to slavery, Polk's settlement also provided a way to balance the recent annexation of Texas, a slave territory. It was a precarious balancing act for Polk.

annexation The addition of territory, sometimes by force, to another nation, state, or city.

manifest destiny Popular belief in the United States in the early nineteenth century that the nation was destined to rule over North America.

Webster-Ashburton Treaty Agreement between the United States and Great Britain that established the border between the two countries in the eastern half of North America.

Great Migration (1843) Movement of almost one thousand U.S. settlers to Oregon Territory, overwhelming their British counterparts.

forty-ninth parallel Latitude used by the Oregon Treaty of 1846 to mark the international boundary between Canada and the United States.

History without Borders
Violence on Settler Frontiers

Migrations and Frontier Conflicts, 1825–1890 During the nineteenth century, other nations, as well as the United States, were expanding their global reach through warfare, trade, and colonialism. These countries tended to migrate towards the temperate zones where they found comfortable climates and abundant natural resources. These colonizing enterprises also found resistant native peoples who did not want to share their resources with the interlopers. The nineteenth century, as depicted on this map, is marked by violence as settler societies imposed themselves on native communities. ▲

Once we discard the myth that the American interior was unoccupied land, it becomes another example of borderland conflict that spread globally as Europe's descendants pushed inland onto continents they claimed. Territorial expansion, settler migration, and dispossession of native peoples in the young United States paralleled events taking place simultaneously on other nineteenth-century frontiers. In the temperate-zone, new nations of the Americas, and the British

colonies of Australia and South Africa, white-dominated "settler societies," embarked from coastal settlements to pursue wealth and opportunity in the continents' interior.

Such frontiers were often violent places. Because pioneer settlers preceded lawful government, vigilante justice prevailed. Miners fought over conflicting claims during gold rushes. Ranchers and farmers who had rival agendas for land use competed for government support. In the United States, the expansion

of slavery caused a frontier war with Mexico and western settlers. The most common source of violence, however, was settlers' determination to push aside native inhabitants of the land.

In Argentina, General Juan Manuel Rosas, a frontier rancher and military strongman whom historians have compared to Andrew Jackson, initially negotiated peace agreements with the Indians of the Pampas but then turned to conquest and removal. During the Campaign of the Desert (1833–1836), Rosas led a

MPI/Getty Images

Geronimo with Apache Warriors, 1886 Geronimo (far right), Apache leader, fought against the encroachment of Mexican settlers. In 1885, Geronimo and his band fled the San Carlos Reservation in Arizona, fighting against and eluding U.S. troops before finally surrendering in September 1886. Geronimo later claimed that the surrender had been conditional, a fact disputed by the U.S. government. ◄

CAPE WAGGON.

The Granger Collection, New York

Voortrekkers Make the Great Trek in South Africa, 1835–1843 Beginning in 1835, wagon trains like this one made the Great Trek from the Cape Colony to Natal as the Boers sought frontier in the eastern interior outside of British rule. ◄

military drive to force Indians south of the Rio Negro, which divided the nation into north and south. He allowed tribes that agreed to stay south of the line to be provided rations and horses and attacked those who refused. A similar situation occurred in Australia where white settlers, many of whom were convicts transported from Britain, collided with aboriginal people on several frontiers and perpetrated notorious massacres despite the efforts of missionaries and humanitarians.

In the British Cape Colony of South Africa, the Boers, descendants of the original Dutch colonizers, stretched the frontier as they sought land for cattle ranching and resisted British edicts that had ended the enslavement of African natives. In 1835, twelve thousand Boers embarked on a Great Trek into the eastern interior, where they set up three republics in defiance of British rule. The Great Trek and the U.S. "Trail of Tears"

happened simultaneously and made a striking contrast. In South Africa white ranchers pushed past native peoples toward the far frontier, protesting Britain's refusal to seize native lands.

In the United States, the full force of state and federal governments bore down on Native Americans in order to remove them farther westward and open lands for white settlers. Even so, in the 1870s, when gold was discovered in the Boer regions of South Africa, the British quickly seized the land and exploited the natives brutally as mine workers. In the United States, Argentina, Australia, and South Africa during the 1870s, campaigns against native peoples resumed with greater force on the next frontiers, transported by railroads and with powerful new weapons to confine natives to out-of-the-way colonies, "homelands," or reservations.

Violence was only part of the settler frontier story, which also included

transnational immigration, family homesteading, and boom-and-bust economies. Expansion was tied to economic development as frontier farm products were shipped internationally. The United States promoted the growth of banks and factories in eastern cities. Almost everywhere, however, indigenous peoples were targeted for removal and faced painful choices about whether to adopt white ways, accept forced relocation, or organize resistance.

Critical Thinking Questions

► How did European and U.S. expansion into the interior of North America compare with similar migrations in other parts of the world?

► How did Native peoples, both in North America and elsewhere, respond to these violent encroachments?

UniversalImagesGroup/Getty Images

11-3
Transcontinental Nation

This lithograph depicts the U.S. army's victory over Mexican forces in the heart of Mexico City. The battle, in which the United States captured the San Patricio Brigade, was brutal and included hand-to-hand combat. It marked the first time that the United States had occupied the capital of a foreign nation.

This painting appeared just one year after the end of the war. How do you think Americans reacted to images such as this one, which depicts U.S. armed forces taking the capital of Mexico? ▶

Between President Polk's election in 1844 and the Treaty of the Guadalupe-Hidalgo in 1848, which ended the hostilities between the United States and Mexico, the two countries fought a fierce military and ideological battle over who would control what later became known as the U.S. Southwest. The United States pushed across national boundaries and directly attacked Mexico's capital. When the war ended and U.S. troops occupied Mexico City, both U.S. citizens and politicians wondered what to do with this conquered nation. Now that the territory had been won, what were the consequences of bringing thousands of Mexicans and Indians into the Union? The debate that ensued publicly exposed U.S. nativist prejudices against Mexicans and Indians. For some Americans, the potential acquisition of so much territory also fueled the national debate about the spread of slavery to the territories. But with the ratification of the treaty, some U.S. politicians realized the promise of Manifest Destiny—a country that spread from the Atlantic to the Pacific coasts.

☞ As you read, consider the results of U.S. expansion. As the country became a nation that stretched from coast to coast, how did it deal with the issues raised by the incorporation of nonwhite citizens from Mexico and the potential spread of slavery?

11-3a Start of and Opposition to the U.S.–Mexican War

Tension between Mexico and the United States had been rising since the founding of the Republic of Texas in 1836. Mexico never recognized Texas as an independent republic and warned the United States that its annexation of Texas would be considered an act of war. Complicating the diplomatic situation between the two nations was the political instability in Mexico and the covetous gaze of the United States on Mexico's north.

{ Americans debate the merits of the war.

Nueces Strip The territory between the Nueces River and the Rio Grande, which was the source of territorial dispute between the United States and Mexico prior to their war.

Between 1821 and 1876, the presidency of Mexico changed fifty-five times, most often through coup and violent overthrow. Santa Anna served eleven times as president during crucial moments of U.S.–Mexican diplomacy and hostilities. The constant change in governments made diplomatic negotiation difficult.

President Polk sent John Slidell, Louisiana congressman and diplomat, as his envoy to negotiate with the Mexican government about acquiring territory and settling U.S. citizens' claims against the Mexican government. Slidell offered Mexico $30 million to purchase California and New Mexico territories. The Mexican government never officially recognized his diplomatic mission, and the public was angered by the audacity of the "yankees" who thought they could purchase their way out of the dispute. Slidell left Mexico disgusted by the government's unwillingness to negotiate and suggested to Polk that he station troops at the border to pressure Mexico to negotiate.

The most sensitive issue was their shared border. Mexico believed that the border between Mexico and the renegade Texas was the Nueces River. Texas, however, and consequently the United States, insisted it was farther south, along the Rio Grande. Even before Slidell had left Mexico, President Polk ordered General Zachary Taylor to move his troops across the Nueces River and into the disputed territory, the **Nueces Strip**. On April 12, 1846, Mexican forces ordered Taylor to retreat across the river. He refused and directed the U.S. navy to blockade the mouth of the Rio Grande, thus cutting off supplies to the Mexican troops. On April 25, the Mexican army attacked the U.S. military in the strip, killing eleven, wounding five, and taking forty-seven prisoners. This was the provocation that Polk needed. When he received the news on May 9, 1846, he announced to Congress that "by the act of Mexico" a state of war existed. Mexico, he said, "has invaded our territory and shed American blood upon the American soil." Despite opposition from both Whigs and Democrats, many of whom recognized the duplicity of Polk's claims, the war resolution passed Congress on May 13, 1846.

The war garnered significant initial public support, including a massive rally in New York City in May. The rally included speeches that vilified Mexicans as Catholic, half-breed mongrels and called for the United States to invade their land. Newspapers such as the *New York Herald* supported the war. Walt Whitman, the editor of the *Brooklyn Daily Eagle*, wrote that "Mexico must be thoroughly chastised" for its aggression.

Others viewed the war as a southern Democratic ploy to acquire territory for the extension of slavery. In August 1846, David Wilmot, an antislavery congressman from Pennsylvania, tried to add a proviso to an appropriation bill to outlaw slavery in any territory that might be gained from war with Mexico. Denouncing both the war and slavery, Henry David Thoreau penned "On Civil Disobedience." He refused to pay taxes to support the war, spent a night in jail, and argued that if government "is of such a nature that it requires you to be the agent of injustice to another, then, I say, break the law." His call for **civil disobedience** has reverberated to the present. Some northern women, who were antislavery as well, opposed the war on moral grounds. Women's rights advocate Lucretia Mott read a public antiwar statement to a large crowd in Philadelphia in June in response to a petition from the women of Exeter, England. The women of these two cities did not want war. More than three thousand women signed Mott's antiwar speech, and the British Consul forwarded their antiwar response to their counterparts in Exeter.

> **civil disobedience** Refusal, often in the form of nonviolent resistance, to obey laws considered to be immoral or unjust.

11-3b Waging of the War

Once Congress acknowledged the state of war with Mexico in 1846, the military struggle was fought on three fronts across the present-day U.S. Southwest, northern Mexico, and Mexico City (see Map 11.4). President Polk ordered General Taylor to move his troops farther south into Mexico's territory in

> The United States invades Mexico and meets resistance on multiple fronts.

Map 11.4 Major Campaigns of the U.S.–Mexican War The war that the United States waged against Mexico covered much territory and was fought on at least three fronts at any given point in the war. While U.S. troops fought on foreign territory, Mexicans fought on their home territory. Involving civilians made the war more difficult to wage, making the progress of U.S. troops slow but steady through Mexico's interior. ▼

Global Americans

Riley was taken prisoner at the Battle of Churubusco, about a year after the capture of Monterrey, shown here.

John Patrick Riley, born in County Galway Ireland around 1818, was a British soldier before migrating to Canada during the Great Famine. He quickly crossed into Michigan and joined the U.S. army. Immigrants often joined the military because of the wages it paid, the stability it provided, and the path to citizenship it offered. These immigrants, however, often faced anti-immigrant and anti-Catholic prejudice from enlistees and officers, at which Riley bristled. With the outbreak of the U.S.–Mexican War, he was sent south to fight against Mexico.

After six months, Riley and Patrick Dalton deserted the U.S. army and formed the Saint Patrick's Battalion to fight for the Mexican army. The battalion, made up of hundreds of deserters of mostly Irish and German descent, also included former slaves who had crossed into Mexico for their freedom. The men who joined the battalion did so for a number of reasons: prejudice they faced in the United States made them eager to leave, sympathy for Catholic Mexico for what they perceived as U.S. aggression, and the promise of free land for their service to the Mexican cause.

Captured by U.S. troops at the Battle of Churubusco, battalion members were tried for treason and desertion. Although Riley escaped execution, he was convicted of desertion and branded with a "D" on his cheek. He never returned to the United States but remained in Mexico where he and his battalion members were revered as heroes in Ireland, Mexico, and among Irish immigrants in the United States.

---

the summer of 1846. On September 25, Taylor's troops captured Monterrey, Mexico. Taylor's men captured Saltillo in November and by the end of the year controlled all of northeastern Mexico. In early 1847, Taylor's troops continued to take territory, culminating in the battle of Buena Vista in February, the bloodiest confrontation of the war. It cost the lives of 665 Americans and more than 3,500 Mexicans.

While Taylor fought on the southern side of the Rio Grande, Brigadier General Stephen Watts Kearny pushed west along the Santa Fe Trail from Kansas toward New Mexico and California. Although his main mission was to secure Mexico's northern territories, he was also under orders to intimidate the Plains Indians, particularly the Comanches. Kearny told them that "the road opened by the dragoons [horse-mounted infantry] must not be closed . . . and that the white people traveling upon it must not be disturbed, either in their persons or property." His expedition highlighted U.S. military presence on the Great Plains. It signaled that the U.S. government was willing to protect its citizens during violent encounters with Indians. Polk also asked Kearny to incorporate the 543 men of the Mormon Battalion that Brigham Young had sent to re-enforce Kearny's march west.

Kearny and his troops met relatively little resistance as they entered New Mexico in the summer of 1846. New Mexico Governor Manuel Armijo mustered a defensive force that met Kearny's troops east of Santa Fe. But Armijo abandoned his troops and fled more deeply into Mexico, leaving a small, overmatched force. When Kearny and his troops entered Santa Fe, they met no resistance. Many

New Mexico residents welcomed the Americans, whom they regarded as potentially wealthy trading partners who would boost the economy and develop the region. Kearny and his men set up a U.S. territorial government with Charles Bent as governor. The occupation happened so quickly that Kearny left Santa Fe after little more than a month and took most of his men west toward California to aid the uprising there.

A year earlier, the U.S. government had sent John C. Frémont and a small group of men to find the headwaters of the Arkansas. Without explanation, Frémont headed to the far west. While in California, Frémont met with Thomas O. Larkin, the American consul to Mexico, and they discussed California's revolting from Mexico in the same way that Texas had done nine years earlier. The Mexican government, suspicious of Frémont's exhortations to American citizens, encouraged him to leave. But, after crossing into Oregon, Frémont retraced his steps and headed back into the heart of California. Frémont spent June and July inciting military unrest. On July 4, 1846, the Bear Flag Republic declared its independence from Mexico. Once the new republic received word that the U.S. had declared war on Mexico, it allied itself formally to the United States.

Conquering California was an involved and bloody conflict for the United States. Frémont, placed under the command of naval Commodore Robert F. Stockton, led the California Battalion south toward San Diego and the onslaught of Mexican troops. Taking San Diego and Los Angeles proved difficult because the *Californios* and the Mexican army protected the two cities from U.S. capture. By January 1847, Kearny, Stockton, and Frémont had taken control of California, but at a significant cost to U.S. troops. Kearny was wounded and lost one-third of his men. In that month, however, General Andres Pico signed the **Treaty of Cahuenga**, which turned California over to the United States but guaranteed *Californios* the same rights as U.S. citizens.

New Mexico also did not submit easily to U.S. rule. Despite the appearance of calm when Kearney had left, tensions ran high. A rebellion against U.S. rule erupted in December 1846 in the northern town of Taos. A coalition of *Hispanos* and Pueblo Indians intended to assassinate Governor Charles Bent and attack the U.S. troops. Bent had the plotters arrested and went to Taos in January 1847, believing his trading and family connections would calm any lingering hostile feelings. During his visit, rebels attacked his entourage and murdered Bent and a number of the group. Over the next few weeks, more than three thousand rebels mounted a counterinsurgency, and U.S. troops had to be sent north from Santa Fe. They crushed the rebellion after three months of skirmishes. Eventually, twenty-eight *Hispano* and Pueblo men were convicted and executed for treason and murder.

With the U.S. troops' steady success in taking the northern provinces of Mexico, President Polk decided to send troops under the leadership of Major General Scott into central Mexico. His troops landed in Veracruz on the eastern coast of Mexico and marched toward Mexico City. Between November 1846 and September 1847, U.S. troops made steady progress across the interior of Mexico. Their invasion provoked resistance and bloody battles at Cerro Gordo, Puebla, Contreras, Churubusco, and the climactic battle in Mexico City at Chapultepec Castle, which housed a military academy. On the morning of September 13, 1847, U.S. forces began attacking the castle. Shelling continued throughout the day. The next morning, infantrymen attacked and pushed into the castle and through the city, where they met troops and citizens led by their president and military commander, General Santa Anna. By September 16, the U.S. flag flew over the capital city of Mexico—the first time that the U.S. flag had flown over a foreign country. The war that President Polk had proclaimed a defensive measure against Mexican encroachments across the Rio Grande had become a war of conquest and domination. For Mexicans, the war brought political turmoil and humiliation with the presence of an invading force in their capital.

11-3c Politics of Victory

> The United States comes to terms with massive land acquisition and new citizens.

The U.S. military success created a host of problems in dealing with a conquered Mexico and its people. The United States could now lay claim to more than half of Mexico's territory from the capital of Mexico City north to California's boundary with Oregon. Those who pushed for keeping all of this land were part of the **All Mexico** movement. These supporters tended to be Democrats who either wanted to expand slavery or who saw it as the U.S. mission to bring "progress" to Mexico and its peoples. In the All Mexico movement, supporters of Manifest Destiny had to confront its logic. If it was the Manifest Destiny of the United States to acquire all the lands between the Atlantic and Pacific Oceans was it also its destiny to incorporate all of the land's inhabitants, including Mexicans and Indians? What was the meaning of citizenship for those who had been conquered by U.S. aggression? The U.S. public and politicians had to contemplate what the results of this war meant within the context of a democratic and republican society.

Most Americans opposed the naked aggression reflected in the All Mexico movement. Conscience Whigs had opposed the U.S.–Mexican War on ideological grounds. Abraham Lincoln, a young congressman from Illinois, voiced the position that true democracies should not be in the business of conquering foreign nations, their people, and their land. These actions stood in opposition to the principles on which the United States was founded. In addition, those who opposed slavery also were against the acquisition of Mexican territory because they feared the spread of slavery farther west. Because of their history, isolation, and arid geography, neither California nor New Mexico seemed likely candidates for the extension of slavery, but Texas encouraged slaveholders to bring their human property to the state and extend cotton culture. Finally, racist and anti-Catholic arguments surfaced as Americans confronted the prospect of thousands of Catholic Mexicans becoming U.S. citizens. John Calhoun, one of the most outspoken critics of the All Mexico movement said, "Ours, sir, is the Government of a white race. The greatest misfortunes of Spanish America are to be traced to the fatal error of placing these colored races on an equality with the white race."

In 1848, the **Treaty of Guadalupe Hidalgo**, which required Mexico to give up all claims to Texas and recognize the Rio Grande as the international boundary, was negotiated in this political context and after a difficult series of diplomatic exchanges. When negotiations broke down over the extent of U.S. territorial ambitions, President Polk recalled his envoy, Nicholas P. Trist, believing there was no room for negotiation. The war and occupation would simply continue. The Mexican government, sensing that Trist was their best option in obtaining a somewhat favorable treaty, hurriedly finished negotiations, which clearly favored the U.S. position. Although some Mexicans wanted to continue the fight, the defeat at Chapultepec combined with political upheaval in the Mexican capital made it difficult to launch a united front.

The treaty established the U.S.-Mexican border along the Rio Grande and then due west along a surveyed and marked border through the desert. The United States agreed to

Treaty of Cahuenga Agreement that ended the California front of the U.S.–Mexican War and gave *Californios* the same rights as U.S. citizens.

All Mexico Political movement at the close of the U.S.–Mexican War that pushed to acquire and take over all of Mexico as opposed to annexing only the northern provinces.

Treaty of Guadalupe Hidalgo Agreement ending the U.S.–Mexican War that required the United States to pay $30 million and Mexico to give up the present-day U.S. Southwest.

pay Mexico $15 million for the territory it would acquire. It also assumed claims that U.S. citizens had against the Mexican government for any losses they suffered during the war or from hostile encounters with Indians along the border. The two governments also committed themselves to arbitrating their future differences. Two points, however, were not amicably negotiated: citizenship and property rights of former Mexican citizens (see Table 11.3).

Table 11.3 Treaty of Guadalupe Hidalgo

Two important clauses of this treaty affected former Mexican citizens who came under U.S. jurisdiction. Article IX provided that they would become full U.S. citizens "as soon as possible." However, the Senate changed this to "be admitted at the proper time (to be judged of by the Congress of the United States)," causing many to wait more than sixty years for citizenship. Article X promised to recognize property rights existing under Mexican law. However, the Senate forced these Mexicans to go through an arduous legal process to document their land titles.

As Written during Negotiations	As Ratified by U.S. Senate
Article IX	**Article IX**
The Mexicans who, in the territories aforesaid, shall not preserve the character of citizens of the Mexican Republic, conformably with what is stipulated in the preceding Article, shall be incorporated into the Union of the United States, and admitted as soon as possible, according to the principles of the Federal Constitution, to the enjoyment of all the rights of citizens of the United States. In the mean time, they shall be maintained and protected in the enjoyment of their liberty, their property, and the civil rights now vested in them according to the Mexican laws. With respect to political rights, their condition shall be on an equality with that of the inhabitants of the other territories of the United States; and at least equally good as that of the inhabitants of Louisiana and the Floridas, when these provinces, by transfer from the French Republic and the Crown of Spain, became territories of the United States.	The Mexicans who, in the territories aforesaid, shall not preserve the character of citizens of the Mexican Republic, conformably with what is stipulated in the preceding article, shall be incorporated into the Union of the United States and be admitted at the proper time (to be judged of by the Congress of the United States) to the enjoyment of all the rights of citizens of the United States, according to the principles of the Constitution; and in the mean time, shall be maintained and protected in the free enjoyment of their liberty and property, and secured in the free exercise of their religion without; restriction.
The same most ample guaranty shall be enjoyed by all ecclesiastics and religious corporations or communities, as well in the discharge of the offices of their ministry, as in the enjoyment of their property of every kind, whether individual or corporate. This guaranty shall embrace all temples, houses and edifices dedicated to the Roman Catholic worship; as well as all property destined to its support, or to that of schools, hospitals and other foundations for charitable or beneficent purposes. No property of this nature shall be considered as having become the property of the American Government, or as subject to be, by it, disposed of or diverted to other uses.	
Finally, the relations and communication between the Catholics living in the territories aforesaid, and their respective ecclesiastical authorities, shall be open, free and exempt from all hindrance whatever, even although such authorities should reside within the limits of the Mexican Republic, as defined by this treaty; and this freedom shall continue, so long as a new demarcation of ecclesiastical districts shall not have been made, conformably with the laws of the Roman Catholic Church.	
Article X	**Article X**
All grants of land made by the Mexican Government or by the component authorities, in territories previously appertaining to Mexico, and remaining for the future within the limits of the United States, shall be respected as valid, to the same extent that the same grants would be valid, if the said territories had remained within the limits of Mexico. But the grantees of lands in Texas, put in possession thereof, who, by reason of the circumstances of the country since the beginning of the troubles between Texas and the Mexican Government, may have been prevented from fulfilling all the conditions of their grants, shall be under the obligation to fulfill said conditions within the periods limited in the same respectively; such periods to be now counted from the date of exchange of ratifications of this treaty: in default of which the said grants shall not be obligatory upon the State of Texas, in virtue of the stipulations contained in this Article.	*Stricken*
The foregoing stipulation in regard to grantees of land in Texas, is extended to all grantees of land in the territories aforesaid, elsewhere than Texas, put in possession under such grants; and, in default of the fulfillment of the conditions of any such grant, within the new period, which, as is above stipulated, begins with the day of the exchange of ratifications of this treaty, the same shall be null and void.	

Source: http://www.ourdocuments.gov/doc.php?flash=true&doc=26.

The U.S. Senate ratified the Treaty of Guadalupe Hidalgo on March 10, 1848. Finally, in 1853, the last piece of what is known today as the continental United States was acquired when President Franklin Pierce directed James Gadsden, the minister to Mexico, to purchase a parcel of land in present-day southern Arizona. Manifest Destiny, as envisioned by many U.S. citizens, had finally been realized. Americans were then free to push westward in search of new lives and lands.

11-4
The World Rushed In

As "gold fever" caught in 1849, people from the East Coast, the Midwest, and outside the U.S.—Britain, France, Central America, Chile, Hawai'i, and China—flocked to try their hand at panning for gold and getting rich quick. Many advertisements induced forty-niners to take the stemship route rather than the overland route to the goldfields of California. This Nathaniel Currier cartoon titled "The Way They Go to California" offers a fantastical satire on the desperation of miners looking to make a fast journey by any means—even rocket.

How did new modes of transportation and communication promote passage to California? ▶

Go to MindTap® to practice history with the Chapter 11 **Primary Source Writing Activity: Promise of the West.** Read and view primary sources and respond to a writing prompt.

The Granger Collection, New York

THE WAY THEY GO TO CALIFORNIA.

People in San Francisco learned about the end of the U.S.–Mexican War just as news of the discovery of gold at Sutter's Mill, outside of Sacramento, spread through the city. The irony of discovering gold just as Mexico had turned California over to the United States was not lost on *Californios*. Now that this *El Dorado* had been discovered, it belonged, from the perspective of *Californios*, to Americans who poured across the Great Plains on their way to California.

Farther north in Oregon, immigrants were drawn by the promise of fertile and plentiful land rather than gold. Eastern families sold their land, homes, and belongings and packed up wagons for the move west. This decision was often an agonizing one that meant leaving behind all community ties and comforts. Life on the trail was difficult and often treacherous. Families had to redefine how work was divided and accomplished to survive. Thousands of migrants took a toll on the environment along the trail, which could barely sustain such a vast movement. This massive migration also forced new relationships between Euro-Americans, indigenous peoples, and Mexican-Americans. Both violence and accommodation marked these new relationships.

☞ As you read, consider the consequences of this migration. How did it affect the Indians, *Californios*, and the landscape? How did the end of the war and the Gold Rush shape Americans' perceptions of themselves?

11-4a The Move to the West

California's Indian and *mestizo* population had been under Spanish control until 1820 followed by Mexican rule until 1848. The Spanish

{ Families remake themselves in the new territory.

military, Catholic missionaries, and Spanish settlers had colonized California Indians. The Spanish encouraged the Indians to move to missions and worked them as unfree labor to bring intensive agriculture to the region. The *Californio* population thrived during the Mexican period by engaging in extended trade with merchants from all over the world who came into the ports of San Francisco, Monterey, and Los Angeles to buy cowhides and tallow. The California Indian population continued to decline, however, particularly after smallpox spread through the region in 1836 and 1844. Forced labor, disease, and land loss through privatization of property for eight hundred *ranchos* were responsible for the Indians' rapid population decline. In California, Americans remade the economy and society based on gold, commerce, and immigration.

On January 24, 1848, two weeks before the Treaty of Guadalupe Hidalgo was signed, James W. Marshall, a foreman working for Sacramento businessman John Sutter, found pieces of shiny metal near a lumber mill along the American River in what is now Coloma, California.

The two men privately tested the findings and confirmed that indeed it was gold. Sutter wanted to keep the news quiet because he feared the onslaught of settlers into his valley in a frenzied search for gold. However, rumors soon started to spread and were confirmed in March 1848 by a San Francisco newspaper publisher who strode through the streets of San Francisco, holding aloft a vial of gold, shouting "Gold! Gold! Gold from the American River!"

News of the gold discovery met with skepticism. On August 19, 1848, the *New York Herald* was the first major newspaper on the East Coast to report the news. But not until December 5, when President Polk confirmed in an address to Congress the discovery of gold did the vast majority of Americans take the news seriously. That winter, families discussed whether to allow their husbands, fathers, and sons to head off to the goldfields. The migration of 1849 primarily included young white men from the East Coast and Midwest who used any means necessary to get to California. Some boarded ships in Boston and sailed around Cape Horn or through the Straits of Magellan in South America. Some traveled on ships down the East Coast to Panama where they disembarked, walked across the Isthmus of Panama, and then boarded another ship on the Pacific side and sailed north into the port of San Francisco. Most packed their wagons with supplies of food staples, tools, and animals and headed west across the open prairie to make it to California before all the gold was gone. As word spread about a gold rush, people caught what the Sioux leader, Black Elk, described as "gold fever." They impulsively abandoned their homes and families and went west in search of easy riches.

The Gold Rush and ensuing migration of hundreds of thousands of people, mostly men, as well as the wealth that the gold rush created transformed the way Americans thought about money and the definition of success. In the first year after news of the gold rush hit the eastern United States, eighty thousand people headed west, four times as many as had gone in the past. By the end of the Gold Rush in 1854, more than three hundred thousand people, mostly men, from around the world had gone to California to try to make a quick fortune. About one-third of these migrants came from abroad. Mexican and Chilean miners came to try their expertise in the goldfields. Chinese immigrants came in search of *Gum Sham* (Gold Mountain). And Europeans, mostly German and French, fled the revolution of 1848 to find prosperity and a new home. These adventurers (later called **forty-niners**) and settlers were not entering empty territory but a region that had a long and rich history of Indian and Mexican expansion, conquest, and settlement.

Between 1849 and 1855, $300 million worth of gold was pulled out of the Sierra Nevada Mountains and its foothills and rivers. The California Gold Rush combined with the discovery of gold in Australia in 1852 influenced families' behaviors around the globe. Friedrich Engels noted to Karl Marx in 1852, "California and Australia are two cases not provided for in the [*Communist*] *Manifesto*: the creation of large new markets out of nothing. We shall have to allow for this." The Gold Rush caused Americans to question how democracy would work in a frontier society and what it meant to have potential access to so much money in such a short time. For example, Eddin Lewis, a farmer in Sangamon County, Illinois, who exported livestock and corn, recorded that he had earned $350 in 1847. Meanwhile, C.C. Mobley, one of the first to reach the California goldfields recorded that he and his companions had made $205 each that week and the week before had made $150 each. Mobley and his friends, with just a pick and shovel, had made as much in two weeks as Lewis, one of the most prosperous farmers in Sangamon County, had made in a year from a farm he had built over a lifetime.

11-4b Life in the Goldfields

Those who left their homes in 1848 to search for the precious substance did not arrive in California until 1849. Travelers arriving in San Francisco described the city as a ghost town because all able-bodied people had left the city to head into the Sierras to try their luck at getting rich quick. That first season of panning for gold in 1848 was a family venture with *Californio* and Indian families working the rivers for their own benefit or for the benefit of California *rancheros*. Panning for gold required little investment or infrastructure. People just put a pan in the water, dropped in the gravel, and swished it around looking for pieces of gold. Prospectors competed for places along the river to use **placer mining**, which used the technology of panning but could require more intensive labor.

{ Gender imbalance and racial diversity characterize the Gold Rush.

In many ways, class divisions softened. One American noted of the changes brought by the discovery of gold, "The millionaire is obliged to groom his own horse, and roll his own wheelbarrow; and the *hidalgo*—in whose veins flows the blood of Cortes—to clean his own boots." Economic competition, however, seemed to fuel racial tensions. After the spring of 1849, thousands of foreigners poured into California and upended what had emerged as a precarious balance among Californians. This mix of Americans, Europeans, Chinese, Chileans, and Mexicans led to violence and legal restrictions.

In particular, the Chileans faced the most overt hostility because of their long history of mining and their immediate success. They attracted the animosity of the less capable Americans, who asserted that because California was a U.S. territory, the mines should be reserved for U.S. citizens. Physical violence and racial harassment plagued the miners from Chile, Peru, Mexico, and China. This prejudice peaked with the passage of the

forty-niners Adventurers from around the world who came to the California goldfields in 1849.

placer mining Process of removing mineral deposits from river beds by placing dirt in a pan, swishing it with water, and letting the heavy metals sink to the bottom of the pan.

Chinese during the Gold Rush, 1852 Chinese, like other sojourners, were looking to get rich quickly, send money back to their families, and then return home. Unlike white migrants, however, Chinese men faced nativist hostilities from men who resented their mining skills and were suspicious of their different appearance and religion. The Chinese were quickly barred from the goldfields and found a niche providing domestic services such as laundry and cooking to other miners. They were also segregated into separate camps and Chinatown neighborhoods in cities such as Sacramento and San Francisco. ◄

Art Resource

Foreign Miner's Tax of 1850, which charged non-U.S. citizens a $20 fee to mine, essentially barred all foreigners from working the goldfields. Some groups, particularly the French, complained, but the law remained in place, although the tax was eventually lowered to $3 a month—still a hefty sum given that the mines were not as lucrative as more people mined.

The majority of Chinese did not arrive until 1852, after the height of the rush was over. More than twenty-five thousand disembarked in San Francisco, and like the other immigrants, they were drawn by stories of quick wealth. Most of them came from the Pearl Delta Region, an area with a long history of trade with the Pacific Coast of North America. Because many American Christian missionaries had come to that region, the Chinese were familiar with the United States and English and had connections that brought them news of the Gold Rush. Most of the Chinese who went to California were men with some means who were capitalizing on their knowledge of gold mining, trade routes, and sense of adventure. Like all other immigrants to the goldfields, the Chinese, too, had dreams of getting rich quickly and returning to their families in China.

These dreams were quickly shattered. Upon their arrival, the middle-class Chinese immigrants became the primary target of amplified American nativism because the boom days of the gold rush had passed. The miners who were still working their claims worked long and difficult hours with little profit. The Chinese were not only worthy competitors but also had a culture and appearance that seemed frightening to many Americans. Some people found Chinese clothes, food, and worship of Buddha curious and intriguing, but most found the Chinese

threatening and wanted them to go away. Americans quickly pushed them out of the goldfields through violence and intimidation. But the Chinese adapted and found a niche open to them because there were few women in the goldfields. They did work that American men did not want to do for themselves and for which they were willing to pay: cooking and laundry.

Panning for gold was anything but easy and very few people made themselves rich by it. The money made was quickly spent on the few consumer items and services available, which came with a steep price tag. The people who did make fortunes were those like Levi Strauss (the inventor of jeans) and Henry Wells and William G. Fargo (creators of California's early bank) whose businesses supplied the hungry and desperate miners. Those who did work the placer mines struggled to find lucrative spots and to maintain their claims. Many of the Americans banded together in groups that adopted constitutions and rules for how they would work communally once they reached California. Others chose to work as individuals or in pairs, preferring more informal arrangements for balancing work on the actual claim with the "support" work of cooking, purchasing supplies, cleaning, and accounting.

Because this was primarily a migration of men, the lack of women to provide "support" work created an opportunity for arrangements that defied conventional gender norms. Plentiful gold dust circulating through the economy created a situation in which men were willing to pay for domestic work. Chinese immigrants filled part of the void. Some enterprising white women who came out with their

Foreign Miners Tax of 1850
A $20-per month tax placed on foreigners who wanted to prospect in California during the Gold Rush.

Few people who came to the Gold Rush got rich. Those who did made their money from servicing the forty-niners rather than mining. Such was the case with the Ghirardellis. **Carmen Alvarado Domingo Ghirardelli** was born in Lima, Peru, in 1829. She married a French physician, and had one daughter, Carmen. Her husband's ship, however, was lost at sea and Carmen was widowed in 1845. In 1847, she met and married Domingo Ghirardelli, who was also recently widowed. He had been born near Genoa, Italy, and apprenticed with a confectioner. He left Italy in the 1830s during the violent reunification process. He first went to Uruguay, and then to Lima where he set up a sweet shop. He caught gold fever and headed to California, leaving Carmen behind with three young children. Like thousands of women worldwide, she stayed behind, kept the house and children, and ran the business in Lima, while Domingo pursued his dream in California.

In California, Domingo started prospecting but soon found that he made more money selling provisions to the miners than by mining himself. He and his friend had brought six hundred pounds of chocolate with them. He opened stores in both Stockton and San Francisco before founding the Ghirardelli Chocolate Factory in San Francisco in 1852. In 1853, Carmen sold the business in Lima and moved to San Francisco to join her husband. Their growing family lived above the factory and by the 1860s, they were importing thousands of pounds of chocolate and gaining a reputation for their exquisite confections. ▲ National Portrait Gallery

menfolk or by themselves ran successful bakeries, restaurants, and boarding homes that appealed to men who missed domestic comforts. The balance between the sexes was so skewed (in 1850 there were twelve men for every woman) that women had their choice of husbands. Many men complained about the lack of marriage prospects, and a few feared that their wives would find someone more to their liking.

Others viewed the imbalance as an opportunity to make money by exploiting the sexual desires of men. William Stewart told the story of a man who created quite a scene when he brought his young wife into a camp and allowed the men to look at her as she peeked out from the wagon's curtains. "She repeated this performance several times, and I kept slowly moving back so the boys could have a good view of her." Other women sold their time and company to men who were eager for their attention. In many situations, sex was exchanged without fear of reprisal because there were no laws to prevent prostitution. Some encounters did not involve sex. An attractive woman could earn up to $20 for the evening just to sit at a poker table and entertain the men.

11-4c Families in the West

The Gold Rush disrupted the lives of most families who were pulled into the vortex of its power. The influx of prospectors from around the world upended the delicate balance that the families already living in the region had created for themselves. Western families were a diverse group, who, prior to the

> Diverse peoples form new communities.

gold rush, had come together to create stable economic and social groups that provided nurturing homes. These families tended to congregate around the emerging institution such as the town, mission, military garrison, or trading post. At Fort Vancouver on the banks of the Columbia, mixed families made up of British, American, and Indian peoples came together to trade and develop one of the strongholds of the Pacific Northwest. Bent's Fort on the banks of the Arkansas was such an enterprise that provided a safe haven for families from the depredations of the Comanches.

By the early 1840s, however, fur-trading families began to realize that the world was shifting, and their place as successful intermediaries between Indians in the Far West and the trading houses in the East was being eroded. These traders worked hard to find a place for their mixed families in this rapidly changing world that would come to see mixed-race children as a problem. Kawsmouth (Kansas City), on the banks of the Missouri River, had been founded by the Chouteau family in 1821 as a trading post. By the 1840s, it was almost a mixed race community where fur-trading families could purchase property and raise their children in relatively stable conditions with access to schools provided by both Protestant and Catholic churches. Prominent fur traders, such as the Bents, Bridgers, and McKenzies, ensconced their families there. The families worked as guides, farmers, and traders for the growing number of people who passed through. Places such as Saint Louis helped these families make the transition from frontier fur-trade economies to the more settled world of commerce and trade that was taking over the Great Plains and Mountain West with the increased traffic of immigrants from Europe and the eastern United States.

Fort Vancouver, WA, 1824 Encampments such as the one shown here became gathering points for the emerging mixed families in early nineteenth century North America. Places such as this one, Bent's Fort, and at Kansas City were fortified against outside incursion and provided a space for families to grow crops or hold livestock (notice the fences). These places also fostered the trade of goods, ideas, and cultures. ◄

The Granger Collection, New York

The Gold Rush unraveled the alliances that fur traders and their families had been nurturing. As word filtered back east from early migrants, many Americans began to look to the far west as a new place to take their families and make a living. From 1843 through the end of the 1850s, thousands of families made their way every year across the Great Plains or took ships to Oregon and California. This migration was a movement of whole families who came to a collective decision about their permanent move to a new place. Families began preparing in the early spring and sold all but the most essential items that they could load into their wagons. They took the cash they had raised from selling their homes, farms, businesses, and household goods and set out on the trail, not knowing whether they would have enough money or supplies to make it to California or Oregon by the time snow fell in late autumn.

Despite the hardships of such an arduous trip, thousands of families made the trek to their new homes. When they arrived, they encountered Mexican, Indian, and mixed-race families who had been living for generations in the region where they had established communities, churches, schools, and governments. At first, the settlers engaged peacefully with the local populations, but as the population pressure increased, these encounters became more violent.

11-4d Legacy of Colonialism

Between 1815 and 1850, the United States became a continental nation. Much of the land between the Mississippi River and the Pacific Ocean had been taken from Indians and came under U.S. control. It was mapped and organized into states and territories. Oregon, Colorado, New Mexico, Arizona, Nevada,

> The process of incorporating territories was uneven and arduous.

and Utah became territories in 1848 with the transfer of Mexican territory, which had been owned at various times by Britain, France, Spain, and Mexico. The transfer of this territory to U.S. control had a lasting impact on those arriving in the West. They felt as if they were bringing their nation with them to this new territory. But the transition placed a deep mark on those who were already settled there, mostly Mexicans and Indians. They suffered land loss and death at the hands of encroaching settlers and then had to remake themselves to fit their property, customs, and families into the legal, social, and economic regime that the United States imposed.

Through the process established by the Northwest Ordinance in 1787, these newly acquired western territories were to be incorporated into the United States as equal states with citizens. This was the promise also made in the Webster-Ashburton Treaty and the Treaty of Guadalupe Hidalgo. The reality of the process, however, differed from the ideal and the earlier incorporation of lands acquired by earlier treaties and the Louisiana Purchase. Some areas—Utah, because of the presence of Mormons, and New Mexico, Arizona, and Oklahoma, because of their mixed race populations—had exceptionally long territorial periods before they were granted statehood. Mixed-race fur-trading families as well as Mexican and Indian families experienced first-hand the hardening racial structures in the United States. As tensions over the place of slavery in the western territories mounted and conversations concerning race, citizenship, and rights became more fraught, violence often erupted.

By 1850, the United States had managed to become a continental nation and strove to be the "empire of liberty" that Thomas Jefferson had envisioned. That expansion came, however, with difficult growing pains as some of the multiracial population was not convinced that it wanted to be incorporated into the new nation.

Summary

Following Lewis and Clark's trek across the West, Americans thought about how to incorporate the western territory into the nation. Some used diplomacy and war, and others, such as the fur traders, used their economic power to subdue Indians and conquer territories. Some Americans had conflicting ideas about their place within the encroaching United States. In the case of the Sioux, accommodation in the form of the Fort Laramie Treaty of 1851 secured safe travel across the Great Plains for immigrants going to California. In the case of Cherokees and Sauks, the conflict with whites ended in forced removal to Indian Territory. The Mormons were also pushed west, not out of a desire to take land but because their neighbors persecuted them for their religion. The tensions over ideologies, power, land, and resources marked this period as contested and violent.

Many Americans embraced Manifest Destiny, which justified taking territory and displacing its inhabitants, primarily Mexicans and Indians, from their homes. Many believed that their actions were justified because they were improving the land they conquered and the peoples they encountered. Throughout this period, the national political parties vied with one another to determine how to incorporate the West into the new nation. This conflict defined political parties and set the stage for the sectional conflicts of the 1850s.

The first test of Manifest Destiny was the U.S.–Mexican War. The U.S. military attacked Mexico, which ended with the acquisition of Texas, New Mexico, Arizona, and portions of Colorado and Utah. In the last days of the war, the United States occupied Mexico City. The Treaty of Guadalupe Hidalgo established a new boundary between the two nations and then specified how former Mexican citizens and their property would be incorporated into the U.S. system.

As continental dreams became a reality, Americans migrated west. The lure of the Gold Rush drew people, mostly men, from around the world. They hoped to strike it rich and then return home to their families. Although the majority never earned vast riches, many decided to stay and make their homes in California. The rush to the West also fueled a later wave of immigrants who moved with their families to start new lives. With all of these people moving through the Great Plains and creating new communities in the West, conflict and accommodation emerged as these new immigrants came into constant contact with Indians and Mexican Americans who had been making their homes there for generations.

‹Thinking Back, *Looking Forward*›

As you review this chapter, think about the role that westward expansion played in the development of the United States as a diverse nation. How were these various groups incorporated into the expanding nation? In what ways was their participation limited? What was the role of violence in westward expansion and incorporation? In the next chapters, think about how violence continues to play a role in U.S. conquest. Also consider how the lessons learned from the U.S.–Mexican War and U.S. westward expansion play a role in U.S. conquest after the Civil War.

To make your study concrete, review the timeline and reflect on the entries there. Think about causes, consequences, and connections. How do they fit with global trends?

Additional Resources

Books

Chavez, Ernesto. *The U.S. War with Mexico: A Brief History with Documents.* **New York: Bedford/St. Martins Press, 2007.** ▶ Comprehensive history and analysis of the war from the perspective of people on both sides of the border.

Faragher, John Mack. *Frontiers: A Short History of the American West.* **New Haven, CT: Yale University Press, 2007.** ▶ Comprehensive work on this period and the U.S. West.

Greenberg, Amy S. *A Wicked War: Polk, Clay, Lincoln and the 1846 Invasion of Mexico.* **New York: Knopf, 2012.** ▶ Description of the political landscape and antiwar sentiment prior to the U.S.–Mexican War.

Hämäläinen, Pekka. *The Comanche Empire.* **New Haven, CT: Yale University Press, 2008.** ▶ The rise of the Comanches as they came to dominate the southern Great Plains against other Indian and Euro-American groups.

Holliday, J.S. *The World Rushed In: The Gold Rush Experience.* **Norman: University of Oklahoma Press, 2002.** ▶ Widely considered the most comprehensive study of the Gold Rush.

Hyde, Ann. *Empires, Nations, and Families: A History of the North American West, 1800–1860.* **Lincoln: University of Nebraska Press, 2011.** ▶ Award-winning narrative that looks at the relationships between families and how empires developed in the U.S. West.

Johnson, Susan. *Roaring Camp: The Social World of the California Gold Rush.* **New York: Norton, 2000.** ▶ Award-winning account of the multifaceted nature of the Gold Rush and the ways the event upended social mores.

Montejano, David. *Anglos and Mexicans in the Making of Texas, 1836–1986.* **Austin: University of Texas Press, 1987.** ▶ Analysis and explanation of the complex racial relations during the economic development of Texas.

Purdue, Theda, and Michael Green. *Cherokee Nation and the Trail of Tears.* **New York: Penguin, 2008.** ▶ Comprehensive examination of the federal policies that led to the Cherokee tragedy and the response to it.

Weber, David. *The Mexican Frontier: The American Southwest Under Mexico.* **Albuquerque: University of New Mexico Press, 1982.** ▶ Study of the region's history prior to its conquest and occupation by the U.S. government.

> Go to the MindTap® for **Global Americans** to access the full version of select books from this Additional Resources section.

Websites

100 Milestone Documents. www.ourdocuments.gov ▶ Primary source site from the U.S. government with full text of important U.S. government documents.

Smithsonian Winter Count Project. www.wintercounts .si.edu ▶ Comprehensive digital collection of numerous Winter Counts with explanations.

Continue exploring online through MindTap®, **where you can:**
- **Assess your knowledge with the Chapter Test**
- **Watch historical videos related to the chapter**
- **Further your understanding with interactive maps and timelines**

A Continental Nation

1815–1821

October 1818
The U.S. Senate ratifies the Treaty of 1818, establishing the joint occupation of Oregon Territory with Great Britain.

February 1819
The U.S. Senate ratifies the Transcontinental Treaty, establishing the boundary with Spain in North America.

November 1820
James Monroe is elected president.

August 1821
Mexico and Spain sign the Treaty of Cordoba, which grants independence to Mexico.

1822–1829

April 1824
General Survey Act passes and allows the president to commission surveys for roads and canals.

August 1824
Republic of Mexico is established.

October 1824
Mexican Constitution abolishes slavery and frees all current slaves.

November 1824
John Quincy Adams is elected president.

November 1828
Andrew Jackson is elected president.

1830–1833

May 1830
Indian Removal Act authorizes the president to negotiate with tribes for their removal to western federal territories.

July 1831
Joseph Smith, leader of the Church of Latter Day Saints, reveals the practice of polygamy to his followers.

November 1831
Chocktaws begin their forced migration to Indian Territory in a process known as the *Trail of Tears*.

April 1832
Black Hawk War between the United States and Sauks begins.

November 1832
Andrew Jackson is reelected president.

May 1833
Bent's Fort is established as a major trading post for fur trappers.

1834–1836

December 1835
United States and Cherokees sign the Treaty of New Echota.

March 1836
Texas convention declares independence from Mexico, forms a government, and adopts a constitution.

April 1836
Sam Houston defeats General Santa Anna at the Battle of San Jacinto.

November 1836
Martin Van Buren is elected president.

1837–1841

Spring 1837
Smallpox epidemic in the Missouri River Valley kills thousands of Indians on the Great Plains.

August 1838
U.S. Exploration Expedition, led by Charles Wilkes, leaves Virginia.

December 1838
Cherokees begin their one-thousand-mile forced migration along the Trail of Tears.

November 1840
William Henry Harrison is elected president.

April 1841
John Tyler becomes president after the death of President Harrison.

September 1841
Preemption Act passes, allowing squatters living on federal lands to purchase up to 160 acres for $1.25 an acre.

Great Britain

Sauks   United States

Texas   Cherokees

Spain

Mexico   Choctaws

1842–1845

August 1842

U.S. Senate ratifies the Webster-Ashburton Treaty, resolving the territorial disputes between the United States and Great Britain.

October 1843

Almost a thousand immigrants, in what became known as the *Great Migration* to Oregon, arrive in the Willamette Valley.

November 1844

James K. Polk is elected president.

March 1845

Tyler annexes Texas to the United States. Florida joins the Union as a slave state.

December 1845

John Slidell arrives in Mexico and offers $30 million for California and much of the U.S. Southwest.

1846

February

Brigham Young leads his followers onto the Mormon Trail westward.

May

U.S. Congress approves a declaration of war against Mexico.

June

California declares its independence from Mexico and name it the Bear Flag Republic.

July

Mexico declares war on the United States.

1847

January

Taos Revolt against the United States occurs, killing Governor Charles Bent.

Treaty of Cahuenga is signed, and Mexico releases all claims to California.

June

Mormons under the leadership of Brigham Young arrive in present-day Utah.

August

At the Battles of Contreras and Churubusco, most of St. Patrick's Battalion are killed or captured.

September

After the Battle of Chapultepec, General Winfield Scott occupies Mexico City.

Polk recalls Trist from Mexico, but he remains.

1848–1850

January 1848

Gold is discovered at Sutter's Fort in California Territory.

February 1848

United States and Mexico agree to the terms of the Treaty of Guadalupe Hidalgo.

July 1848

Last U.S. troops depart from Mexican territory.

August 1848

New York Herald reports that gold has been discovered in California Territory.

December 1848

Polk confirms report of gold in California Territory.

Spring 1849

Thousands from around the world migrate to the California goldfields.

September 1850

U.S. Congress grants California statehood as part of the Compromise of 1850.

1851–1853

September 1851

The Fort Laramie Treaty between the United States and representatives from the Cheyennes, Arapahoes, Crows, Assiniboines, Mandans, Hidatsas, and Arikaras is signed.

December 1853

Gadsden Purchase adds territory from Mexico for a transcontinental railroad

Go to MindTap® to engage with an interactive version of the timeline. Analyze events and themes with clickable content, view related videos, and respond to critical thinking questions.

12 | Expansion, Slavery, and the Coming of the Civil War

1848–1861

John Brown left rural New York for the Kansas territory, where he and his sons engaged in guerrilla warfare between his antislavery bands and proslavery militias. Brown would later launch the unsuccessful raid on Harpers Ferry and be executed for his efforts.

William Walker sailed from San Francisco to Nicaragua, eventually declaring himself president, legalizing slavery, and offering land grants to American plantation owners. Walker was eventually killed by a Honduran firing squad.

In the spring of 1855, William Walker and John Brown, two Americans of opposing sectional backgrounds and views, set out to resolve the status of slavery in new lands open to settlers. Walker sailed to Central America, whose tropical climate and fragile governments tempted U.S. adventurers, especially Southerners eager to extend U.S. rule and slave-labor plantations. Brown headed to the Kansas territory, where

Boston Athenaeum

John Brown

Library of Congress Prints and Photographs Division[LC-USZC4-10802]

William Walker

Congress had recently set off a small-scale civil war by declaring that the settlers themselves should decide whether to allow or ban slavery. Consumed by visions of fame and righteousness, both men believed themselves agents of destiny.

A mildly successful lawyer from Tennessee, Walker had caught the fever for U.S. expansionism in Latin America. In May 1855, he sailed from San Francisco to Nicaragua with a small volunteer army that gained local allies in Central America, defeated the Nicaraguan army, and installed a puppet regime there. Following a sham election, Walker declared himself president of Nicaragua and legalized slavery. Describing Nicaragua as better suited to plantation agriculture than Kansas, he offered land grants to Southerners who would bring their slaves to grow cotton, sugar, and coffee.

John Brown was a restless tanner, sheep farmer, and land speculator who moved among several northern states seeking to support his large family. Although he was white, Brown settled for a few years in a rural New York black community on land donated by the wealthy abolitionist Gerrit Smith. Before long, Brown became convinced that he was divinely appointed to destroy slavery. In 1855, he followed his sons to Kansas territory to spearhead the fight against slaveholding settlers. There Brown led a raid on a proslavery settlement that killed five residents. For months afterward, guerrilla warfare raged in Kansas between Brown's antislavery bands and armed proslavery militias, some sent from neighboring Missouri.

Walker and Brown failed in their missions. A Central American army led by Costa Rica forced Walker out of Nicaragua, while Brown, his men badly outnumbered by proslavery guerrillas, fled Kansas to safety in New England. Yet these self-styled freedom fighters remained undeterred. Walker launched several more expeditions to Nicaragua, the last an attempt in 1860 to penetrate the country through neighboring Honduras. Meanwhile, in October 1859, Brown electrified Americans by leading an unsuccessful raid on the federal arsenal at Harpers Ferry, Virginia, in hope of stirring a rebellion among local slaves. Captured by U.S. marines, he was convicted of treason and executed by hanging. Less than a year later, Walker was taken into custody and killed by a Honduran firing squad.

How do the fanatical actions of John Brown and William Walker in the name of their causes reflect America's intensifying divisions in the mid-nineteenth century?

Go to MindTap® to watch a video on Brown and Walker and learn how their stories relate to the themes of this chapter.

Not all proslavery and antislavery enthusiasts were as fanatical or as prepared as Walker and Brown to die for their cause. During the 1850s, however, Americans became increasingly divided into opposing camps. As the nation's borders expanded in the Southwest and settlers filled in the Great Plains, the contest between proslavery and antislavery advocates intensified. Each expansionist move—the purchase of California and New Mexico as prizes of the U.S.–Mexican War, the opening of Kansas and other western prairie lands, and the prospect of annexing Cuba and other Caribbean territories—led to a showdown between impassioned citizens of the northern and southern states over the issue of extending the South's slave society into the nation's territories. Despite a temporary congressional compromise in 1850, sectional tensions mounted in the following years during a series of crises based in one way or another on differences over slavery. The confrontation culminated when the majority of slave states seceded from the Union and war broke out between the United States and the rebellious Confederacy.

Viewed in global context, the American sectional struggle over slavery in the territories was part of a transatlantic upsurge in nationalist feeling in the 1840s and 1850s. Nationalist and republican revolutions swept through Europe in 1848 while wars of national unification or expansion raged in Mexico and South America. Almost everywhere, competing visions of national futures led to conflicts over territorial boundaries, forms of representative government, central versus local control, and degrees of personal freedom. Many Americans sympathized with overseas struggles against kings and tyrants, but when their own nation's expansion became intertwined with fierce sectional divisions over slavery versus freedom, its political leaders inched step-by-step toward a homegrown nationalist war.

12-1

Continental Expansion, Conflict, and Compromise

This 1852 engraving by Henry S. Sadd after a painting by Tomkins Harrison Matteson, entitled *Union*, commemorates the Compromise of 1850, an agreement forged in Congress to resolve the dispute over the status of slavery in territories acquired after the U.S.–Mexican War. Most of the key individuals who debated the compromise are posed formally, including General Winfield Scott, Lewis Cass, Henry Clay, John C. Calhoun, and Daniel Webster.

Analyze the symbolism of the print. Why are Webster, who approved the compromise, and Calhoun, who opposed it, both depicted next to a bust of George Washington? Why do they rest their hands on the U.S. Constitution? Why is Clay seated at the center? Why does an eagle help to part the curtain in the background, revealing a gleaming classical temple? What is meant by the engraving's title? ▶

Library of Congress Prints and Photographs Division[LC-DIG-pga-02601]

Many Americans took pride in their nation's expansion across the continent, but some wondered whether the growing "empire of liberty" should extend the institution of slavery. Victory in the U.S.–Mexican War aroused northern fears that southern politicians would turn the new territories thus gained into slave states. Some claimed to detect a conspiracy to expand the South's "peculiar institution" and use slave-state votes to control national politics. At stake in the struggle over the West were the competing political fortunes of the North and South and the future of the nation. Out of this volatile mix of ambitions and fears emerged a proposal to outlaw slavery in the new territories that opened a fierce debate in Congress and sparked talk of southern states' quitting the Union. Tensions were neutralized only when Congress approved a shaky sectional compromise.

☞ As you read, consider the opposing positions Americans took on the issue of slavery in the territories. How did the Compromise of 1850 attempt to reconcile them?

12-1a Debate over Slavery in the Territories

A few months into the U.S.–Mexican War, David Wilmot, a Pennsylvania Democrat, offered an amendment to a funding bill pledging that

Partisans of free soil, states' rights, and popular sovereignty vie for control over western lands.

"neither slavery nor involuntary servitude" would be permitted in any lands acquired from Mexico. The **Wilmot Proviso** echoed the wording of the Northwest Ordinance to emphasize that Congress was empowered by the framers of the Constitution to prohibit slavery in federal territories. Although it never passed both houses, for the next few years, the proviso focused and escalated the national controversy over the expansion of slavery.

In the debates of 1846–1848, three main positions emerged, two aggressively sectional and one aimed at compromise. Wilmot's idea that the federal government could and should prohibit slavery in the territories was labeled **"free soil."** A diverse coalition of Northerners rallied under its banner. Political abolitionists supported the free-soil position as a key step toward ending slavery. Yet one could oppose slavery's extension without being an abolitionist. Wilmot, for example, declared that "the negro race already occupy enough of this fair continent." He and many white Northerners believed that slave plantations in the West would shut out the North's aspiring white farmers. Promotion of white economic opportunity in the West was often tinged with prejudice against blacks, free as well as slave. In 1848, Illinois voters approved a law forbidding free blacks from entering the state, and Indiana soon followed suit.

Alarmed by Northerners' support for free soil, prominent Southerners sought a secure future for their slave society. John C. Calhoun argued that the Constitution and the Fugitive Slave Law of 1793 defined slaves as property and that protection of owners' rights meant that they could take their slaves into territories. This position extended Calhoun's states' rights doctrine beyond state borders. It reflected not only slave owners' ambitions to expand their realm but also the hopes of nonslave-owning Southerners who looked to western territories for the chance to raise their social and economic standing.

A potentially attractive compromise beckoned in the idea of **"popular sovereignty,"** which was formulated by Lewis Cass of Michigan and later championed by his fellow Democrat, Stephen Douglas of Illinois. Why not let the territorial settlers decide for themselves the status of slavery? This formula took the controversy out of Congress and invoked U.S. traditions of self-government and local control. It fudged crucial questions with ambiguous language by not specifying how and at what stage slavery could be banned. Both proslavery and free-soil settlers warmed to "popular sovereignty" because each saw how it might bring victory.

12-1b Election of 1848

The question of slavery in the territories remained unresolved during the election of 1848. Polk declined a second term, so the Democrats turned to Cass, a party veteran who ran on the

Party divisions over slavery give the presidency to the Whigs' Zachary Taylor.

platform of popular sovereignty. The Whigs again sought victory by running a war hero; this time it was General Zachary Taylor of U.S.–Mexican War fame. Because Taylor was a southern slaveholder and the Whigs refused to endorse the free-soil position, many southern Democrats crossed party lines to vote for the general. Meanwhile, Northerners opposed to extending slavery, who were snubbed by the two parties, formed a new organization. The **Free-Soil Party** appealed to Democrats who favored the Wilmot Proviso, antislavery Whigs, and former Liberty Party men. It nominated former president Martin Van Buren.

Van Buren attracted one in seven northern voters, not enough to win any northern state but sufficient to play "spoiler" by dividing these states along East-West lines between Taylor and Cass. As a result, the soldier-planter Taylor, who was stronger than Cass in the South, won a narrow victory. The Free-Soil Party won ten seats in Congress, another sign that the major parties were beginning to crack under the strain of the slavery question. It was left to the aged General Taylor, who had no political experience and had never even voted, to resolve the conflicted legacy of the war he had helped the United States to win.

12-1c The Compromise of 1850

By the time Taylor took office in March 1849, the slavery issue had become pressing because the Gold Rush had populated California so

After much maneuvering, Congress adopts measures to settle the sectional dispute over slavery.

quickly with new settlers that it skipped territorial status and qualified for statehood. A strong proponent of Manifest Destiny, Taylor believed that the slavery controversy should not block the path to continental empire. Encouraged by the new president, California voters drew up a state constitution that prohibited slavery. Southerners closed ranks to oppose the state's admission. Because the ratio of free to slave states was fifteen to fifteen, admitting California would give the North a critical edge in the Senate and add to its majority in the House.

With Congress deadlocked, Henry Clay, the venerable Whig leader who had helped forge compromises over Missouri in 1820 and

Wilmot Proviso Proposal in 1846 for Congress to ban slavery from all territory gained from the U.S.–Mexican War that touched off heated sectional debate.

free soil Political platform declaring that Congress should exercise its constitutional power to prohibit slavery in the western territories.

popular sovereignty Position taken by many Democrats in the debate over slavery in the territories that asserted local, not congressional, control over the issue.

Free-Soil Party Third political party organized in 1848 by Democratic and Whig dissidents who opposed the expansion of slavery into western territories.

the tariff in 1833, constructed a compromise "omnibus bill" that addressed several contentious issues, including California statehood and the status of slavery in other lands acquired from Mexico. Clay's bill touched off a six-month debate in which the Senate's aging giants, John C. Calhoun and Daniel Webster, mustered their best arguments and oratory. Calhoun warned that the Union was doomed unless Northerners ceased attacking slavery and Southerners were given a permanent veto over laws related to it. Webster rose, speaking "not as a Massachusetts man, nor as a Northern man, but as an American," to support sectional compromise.

In July, hopes for compromise were shattered when Congress defeated Clay's proposal. Calhoun was dead, the exhausted Clay left Washington, and Webster, bitterly attacked in Massachusetts for his concessions, resigned to become secretary of state. Just when all appeared lost, two events allowed a deal to be struck. First, President Taylor, who had opposed Clay's bill, died suddenly of an intestinal ailment. His successor, Millard Fillmore of New York, was a milder man and a political veteran who persuaded other Whigs to join the compromise. Second, Clay's younger ally, Stephen Douglas of Illinois, took charge of the bill, and the "Little Giant," a five-feet, four-inch dynamo, brought new energy to the fight. Douglas shrewdly broke up Clay's package and introduced the measures separately, building a different coalition to pass bills that admitted California as a free state, placed the New Mexico and Utah Territories under popular sovereignty, adjusted the Texas state boundary, strengthened federal sanctions against fugitive slaves, and banned slave trading in the nation's capital. Few senators voted for all these measures, but taken together, they became known as the **Compromise of 1850** (see Table 12.1).

President Fillmore hailed the deal as the "final and irrevocable" settlement of the sectional dispute over slavery. For all its shortcomings, the Compromise of 1850 had two big advantages. First, massive victory rallies in Washington and other cities seemed to indicate that the majority of voters was relieved to end the crisis.

Compromise of 1850 Cluster of five bills passed by Congress to resolve the dispute over the status of slavery in lands acquired after the U.S.–Mexican War.

"THE HOME OF THE OPPRESSED."

CAPITOL OF THE UNITED STATES. "HAIL COLUMBIA."

Library of Congress Rare Book and Special Collections Division[LC-USZ62–40900]

A Capital under Slavery's Shadow This abolitionist engraving dramatizes a national embarrassment: a line of shackled African Americans being marched past the U.S. Capitol on their way to slave markets. This blatant juxtaposition of white liberty and black slavery stunned many foreign visitors and appalled Illinois congressman Abraham Lincoln, who introduced a bill in 1849 to abolish slavery in the District of Columbia. The Compromise of 1850 outlawed slave trading, but not slaveholding, in the nation's capital. ▲

Second, the status of slavery in all U.S. territories was now confirmed. Although there was still the potential for overseas expansion, within the nation's boundaries there were no new lands to fight over.

In the presidential campaign of 1852, both major parties endorsed the sectional compromise, but the Democrats were the more united party. Torn between "Conscience" Whigs who opposed Fillmore and "Cotton" Whigs who appeased the South, the Whigs nominated another U.S.–Mexican War hero, the Virginian Winfield Scott. Some antislavery northern Whigs bolted to support John P. Hale of the Free-Soil Party. The Democrats chose Franklin Pierce, a New Hampshire politician whose enthusiasm for expansion and silence on slavery satisfied the party's southern wing. Pierce won easily with 254 electoral votes to Scott's 42.

Pierce interpreted the results as popular approval of the 1850 congressional deal. His inaugural address contrasted Europe convulsed by revolutions and the United States, which was blessed with prosperity and calmed by sectional compromise. Proclaiming the United States exempt from "their wars, their tumults, and anxieties," Pierce called "unfounded" the fear that "extended territory [and] multiplied States" posed dangers to the republic. Events at home and abroad soon challenged such confidence.

Table 12.1 The Compromise of 1850

Because only a handful of senators voted for all of its measures, the Compromise of 1850 did not represent an agreement forged by concessions on both sides. In hindsight, it may be more accurate to label it an uneasy truce than a genuine compromise.

Pro-North Provisions	Pro-South Provisions
California admitted as a free state	Slavery permitted in New Mexico and Utah territories under "popular sovereignty"
Texas boundary dispute settled by granting lands east of Rio Grande to New Mexico Territory	Texas given $10 million by U.S. government to pay state debts and drop its claim to New Mexico lands
Slave trade prohibited in Washington, D.C.	Tough new Fugitive Slave Law adopted

12-2
The United States Overseas

On July 8, 1853, U.S. naval commodore Matthew Perry led a flotilla of steamships under a cloud of black smoke into Tokyo Bay to force the long-secluded country to open its doors. Oceangoing steamships were unfamiliar to Japanese artists, and this colorful woodblock print dramatically portrays Perry's vessel.

What kind of human features did the Japanese artist give Perry's ship, and why? Does the image convey fear of Western technology, fascination with it, or both? ▶

Glenn Asakawa/The Denver Post/Getty Images

Once the United States spanned the continent, the nation's leaders looked beyond its borders to project American power. President Pierce held visions of U.S. global influence that reflected agreement among business and political elites from both parties that American ideals, trade, and territory should spread wherever possible. Many hoped that European nations would adopt the U.S. republican model, especially after nationalist and democratic revolutions broke out in 1848. Some sought new U.S. territories in Mexico and Central America. Others, eager to follow up on overland expansion to California, pushed American commerce to the Pacific and predicted fabulous profits from the China trade. As an added benefit, Pierce hoped that initiatives abroad would divert Americans' energies from festering domestic divisions. Yet Europe's revolutions and U.S. initiatives in Latin America quickly became entangled in controversies at home over the slavery question.

☞ As you read, consider the various locales, goals, and methods of U.S. expansionism after 1848. Where did U.S. expansionists look to project the nation's power, and how? How successful were they? How did the slavery issue intrude?

12-2a Americans and the Revolutions of 1848

President Pierce was part of **Young America**, a cohort of emerging journalists and politicians who rose to prominence as Clay, Webster, and Calhoun faded with age. The group's label replaced *United States* with *America*, a term that absorbed the entire hemisphere and referred to national ideals as well as a particular place. The label also reflected transatlantic crosscurrents. "Young Italy" and "Young Germany" were nationalist movements of the 1840s whose members, inspired by the U.S. example,

> Support for European revolutions reflects Americans' international ambitions and their internal divisions.

sought to unify their nations under republican governments. The Young Americans were energized by this European ferment and by pride in their nation's prosperity and territorial gains. They became a vocal faction in the Democratic Party, promoting an aggressive, male-dominated literary and political nationalism. Their leading magazine, the *Democratic Review*, championed a unique national identity for American literature, publishing works by Ralph Waldo Emerson, Henry David Thoreau, Nathaniel Hawthorne, and Walt Whitman. In politics, Young Americans updated the Democrats' agrarian stance by accommodating banks and promoting railroads. They advocated aggressive expansion into western territories and support for republican movements abroad.

Young America's hopes for the spread of democratic institutions seemed to be confirmed by the **Revolutions of 1848** that swept through Europe. Popular demands for reform first erupted into revolution in Paris, where a crowd invaded the royal palace and proclaimed the Second French Republic. This was followed by nationalist uprisings in the German states, Italy, and the Austrian empire. In Germany and Italy, revolutionary leaders aimed to unify a patchwork of small states under a national republic. In the Austrian empire, the Hungarians and other ethnic groups sought independence. Whether they promoted breakaway or consolidating nationalism, most European revolutionaries fought to create republican governments.

Americans welcomed news of the uprisings against kings with massive rallies in several American cities. The United States was the first nation to recognize the new French republic. Beyond this, what form American assistance to European revolutionaries should take proved controversial. To aid an insurrection against Britain planned by the "Young Ireland" movement, a band of Irish Americans sailed across the Atlantic, but they were arrested and detained until U.S. diplomats apologized to the British

Young America Circle of writers and Democratic politicians promoting expansion of U.S. influence and institutions through North America and overseas.

Revolutions of 1848 Wave of nationalist and republican uprisings that swept Europe in 1848, most of which failed or were suppressed.

Library of Congress

Global Americans The Young America movement not only inspired writers and politicians; it also spawned ambitious entrepreneurs who promoted U.S. business ventures abroad and coupled them with republican values. William Wheelwright built railroads in Chile; Freeman Cobb set up stagecoach lines in Australia; and Perry Collins proposed constructing a telegraph line across Russia. None of these men was more colorful than **George Francis Train**, a publicity-seeking Massachusetts merchant who became a shipping magnate, railroad organizer, travel writer, and confidant of European revolutionaries. In 1853, Train sailed to Melbourne, Australia, to set up a shipping business connected to England and California. He described his return journey in *Young America Abroad* and *An American Merchant in Europe, Asia and Australia*, books published in 1857. A zealous believer in the United States as a model for the world, Train urged the Australians and Irish to declare independence from Britain, rejoiced to find Crimean War soldiers swigging New England rum, and promoted democratic ideas wherever he went. "He would have every place Americanized, including Jerusalem and Athens," an English critic complained. In the 1850s, Train built London's first horse-drawn street railway and then returned to promote a U.S. transcontinental railroad. Two decades later, he circled the globe in record time, a feat that inspired Frenchman Jules Verne's adventure novel, *Around the World in Eighty Days* (1873). Increasingly eccentric, Train died a forgotten man in 1904. Fifty years earlier, however, his colorful promotion of American technology and ideals abroad made him a famous "Young American" on three foreign continents.

government. Despite public pressures, Polk and later U.S. presidents adhered to the policy of noninterference in European affairs, and Congress sent no military aid to Europe's freedom fighters.

After 1848, the forces of European reaction regrouped to suppress the nationalist revolts. French conservatives rallied around Louis Napoleon, nephew of the former emperor, who declared himself Emperor Napoleon III in 1852. In Austria, the Hapsburg monarchy accepted the revolutionaries' decree ending serfdom but ruthlessly put down uprisings in Vienna, Prague, and Budapest, the last with aid from Russia.

Americans' reactions to the failures of 1848 reflected their stance toward growing sectional divisions at home. Some Northerners blamed Europe's aristocratic classes for squelching reforms and vowed to fight against undemocratic "despots" at home and abroad. To anxious onlookers in the South, the revolutions showed that popular agitation could easily slide toward radicalism. In 1848, France's revolutionary government abolished slavery in overseas colonies, and legislators influenced by socialist ideas set up National Workshops that guaranteed workers employment. That same

year, a pair of exiled German revolutionaries, Karl Marx and Friedrich Engels, published the *Communist Manifesto*, which predicted that class struggles would soon topple capitalism and inaugurate rule by the working class ("proletariat") for the equal benefit of all.

In practical terms, the suppression of European revolutions strengthened the free-soil movement by sending a vocal group of German "Forty-Eighters" into exile. Deeply influenced by democratic ideas, these immigrants settled chiefly in free midwestern states and often voted against proslavery interests. In the 1850s,

Kossuth in America In 1851, exiled Hungarian patriot Louis Kossuth arrived for a U.S. fund-raising tour. A Kossuth mania overtook Americans as they renamed towns for him and beards like his became fashionable, replacing the clean-shaven look of the Founders. But Kossuth alienated many Americans with his noncommittal stance on slavery. This Hungarian Fund certificate shows Kossuth in the center and promises the donor repayment one year after Hungary wins independence. Kossuth departed with meager donations and no pledge of U.S. government aid. ▼

Facsimile of a fifty dollar note of the Hungarian Fund, signed by Kossuth (engraving), English School, (19th century)/Private Collection/© Look and Learn/Illustrated Papers Collection/Bridgeman Images

leading Forty-Eighters such as Carl Schurz of Missouri and Friedrich Hecker of Illinois rallied support among German Americans for the newly formed Republican Party and its free-soil platform.

Despite their failure, the European revolutions heightened popular zeal to have the U.S. republican experiment succeed and its institutions imitated elsewhere. Whether such institutions should include slavery and whether American influence should be spread by example or intervention remained divisive questions.

12-2b American Commerce and Markets in Asia

In the 1850s, Asia was another focal point for Americans' overseas ambitions, with trade the primary objective. Since Jefferson, U.S. presidents and diplomats had pursued a strategy of finding markets abroad for the nation's goods and of keeping sea-lanes open for commerce. As the nation reached the Pacific, this strategy stretched to Asia. Senator William H. Seward, later secretary of state, urged U.S. businessmen to "multiply your ships, and send them forth to the East," declaring that the nation that dominated Pacific trade would become "the great power on earth." Like Seward, many Americans viewed the plunge into the Pacific as the culminating phase of frontier expansion. Protestant missionaries eyed the West Coast as a staging ground for evangelizing in Asia. Congressional orators predicted that the United States would carry Western science and republican institutions to China and Japan while American farms became Asia's granary.

> U.S. commercial influence extends with pressure on China, Japan, and Hawai'i.

The reality fell short of the rhetoric. Americans' desire to trade with Asia ran up against the desire of China and Japan to fend off Western pressures. U.S. shippers traded ginseng, furs, and (in some cases) opium to obtain tea, textiles, and porcelains from Chinese merchants, but Western rivals outpaced them. The British, French, and Russian empires vied for colonies as well as **spheres of influence**, concessions that included control over certain territories, ports open to foreign ships, access for missionaries, and even "extraterritoriality," the right to enforce European rather than indigenous laws. In the 1850s, U.S. policy makers' most realistic goals in Asia were treaties that granted the same trade privileges given to other Western nations.

In China's second opium war, called the *Arrow War* (1856–1860), the United States offered modest naval support when the British and French invaded Beijing. At the war's end, the United States obtained access to treaty ports that Europeans forced China to open. This conflict occurred in the middle of the **Taiping Rebellion** (1850–1864), the century's bloodiest civil war, in which

more than 20 million Chinese people perished, mainly from starvation and disease. Britain, France, and Russia took advantage of the crisis to grab territory on China's coast and borders, and some Americans proposed seizing Formosa (now Taiwan). But U.S. leaders' vision of empire did not yet include annexing land in Asia. The China trade failed to meet Westerners' inflated expectations, and the United States lagged behind Britain in gaining a share.

American relations with Japan were a different story because the United States took the lead in prying open the Japanese market. The Shogun, Japan's military ruler, had prohibited all but a few contacts with Westerners after European missionaries and traders were expelled in the 1630s. That isolation ended suddenly. Ordered by President Fillmore to survey the Asian coast and to negotiate a trade treaty with Japan, U.S. naval commodore Matthew C. Perry cruised up Tokyo Bay in July 1853 with a squadron of steam-powered warships. The Americans believed that a show of strength would win concessions that the British and Russians had failed to get. After much hesitation, Japanese officials, aware of China's recent military defeats against Western powers, relented. By agreeing to the **Treaty of Kanagawa** (1854), modeled on the **unequal treaties** that China had signed, Japan opened two ports to American ships, offered protection for shipwrecked crews, and allowed American vessels to buy provisions. A second treaty in 1858 opened full diplomatic relations between the United States and Japan and placed a low tariff on imported American goods. Such treaties set the unequal, and to the Japanese, humiliating, terms of Japan's commercial relations with Western powers for the rest of the century.

Increasing trade with Japan amplified Hawai'i's importance as a stopover where steamships could refuel. Already significant as a whaling port and the site of sugar plantations owned by Americans, Hawai'i allowed U.S. businessmen and missionaries to exercise growing influence on its government. In the 1840s, rival U.S., French, and British officials pledged to respect Hawai'i's independence under King Kamehameha III, but their truce was uneasy. Americans who held key ministerial posts in the Hawaiian government pushed for closer ties. In 1854, an envoy of President Pierce negotiated a treaty of annexation, but it was never signed because of foreign protests and disputes over whether slavery would be permitted. U.S. policy makers remained determined to dominate the Hawaiian economy and to prevent other nations from taking over the islands.

spheres of influence Areas outside a nation's territory but still under its sway; in the case of empires, lands that conceded trading and other rights to imperial powers.

Taiping Rebellion Long and bloody Chinese civil war that allowed Western powers to increase their local influence.

Treaty of Kanagawa Agreement between the United States and Japan that opened Japanese trade to American merchants.

unequal treaties Nineteenth-century treaties signed by China and Japan under duress ceding trading privileges, missionary access, or territorial concessions to Western powers.

12-2c U.S. Expansionism in Latin America

When Hawaiian annexation failed, southern politicians' hopes for slave plantations in the Pacific turned to the Caribbean, whose nearby location, tropical climate, and colonial history appeared hospitable to slavery. Sugar plantations worked by half a million slaves still thrived in Spanish Cuba and Puerto Rico, and unstable governments in Spain's former Central American lands seemed to invite intervention. Potential U.S. possessions in the Caribbean and Latin America might become slave states that could, one proslavery politician claimed, give the South "more power & influence than . . . a dozen wild deserts" of the Southwest. Such lands (see Map 12.1) might be purchased or seized by filibusters. Southern expansionists had found important allies in Presidents Polk, Pierce, and Buchanan, who were strong supporters of slavery, Manifest Destiny, and expanded overseas trade.

> American moves to purchase or seize Caribbean lands heighten the domestic dispute over slavery.

The defensive part of Southerners' strategy involved quarantining Haiti. For decades after Haiti's blacks had abolished slavery and won independence from France, the United States withheld diplomatic recognition of the country. Trade in sugar and grains flourished between the two nations, and many U.S. merchants and abolitionists supported formal relations, but southern politicians stood in the way. A free black republic was too dangerous to befriend for American slaveholders, who feared the influence of Haiti's example and its refugees among their slaves.

In contrast, Cuba, just ninety miles off the Florida coast, struck white Southerners as a candidate for annexation. Before the 1840s, U.S. officials backed Spanish rule in Cuba to preserve regional stability and to avoid a "second Haiti." When wealthy Cuban exiles began agitating for Americans to assist Cuban independence, southern politicians saw a chance for the Democrats to acquire it "for the planting and spreading of slavery," as a Mississippi senator admitted. In 1848, President Polk authorized $100 million to purchase Cuba, but Spain's foreign minister ruled out selling the island, which he considered a jewel in the Spanish empire's crown.

One response to Spain's refusal came from Narciso López, a Venezuela-born Cuban who recruited a private invading force in the U.S. South. In 1850 and 1851, he sailed from New Orleans to Cuba with a small army. The first time, López failed to win local support in Cuba and retreated in defeat to Florida. The second time, Spanish soldiers killed two hundred of his men and executed fifty, including López himself. Another

response to Spain's defense of Cuba was to escalate U.S. pressure to purchase the island. The U.S. minister to Spain, Pierre Soulé of Louisiana, tried to use an incident involving the illegal seizure of an American ship to threaten Spain with war. In October 1854, Soulé and the U.S. ministers to England and France met in Belgium and drafted a memorandum to Pierce declaring that the United States should seize Cuba if Spain refused to sell it. But this **Ostend Manifesto** was leaked to the public, and an outcry among Northerners forced the Pierce administration to disavow it. The dream of a Cuban slave state died hard, however, and purchasing Cuba remained on the Democratic Party's platform until the Civil War.

Another target for expansion southward was Mexico. The All-Mexico movement had faltered after the U.S.–Mexican War (see Chapter 11), but the cession of California and New Mexico whetted some expansionists' appetite for additional chunks of Mexican land. Southern-born filibusters launched unsuccessful private invasions of Mexican border provinces from California in the 1850s. In 1853, President Pierce sent an envoy to offer Mexican ruler Santa Anna up to $50 million for several areas, including Baja California. In the Gadsden Purchase, Pierce settled for a much smaller addition to southern New Mexico to ease construction of a transcontinental railroad (see page 352).

As it turned out, Americans built the first transcontinental railroad outside, not within, their nation's borders. U.S. interest in Central America intensified after the Gold Rush showed the importance of a shorter passage between the Atlantic and Pacific Oceans than sailing around Cape Horn. In 1855, after New Granada (present-day Colombia) ceded the right of transit across Panama, a U.S. company completed the forty-eight-mile Panama Railway connecting Colón on the Atlantic coast to Panama City on the Pacific. Westward expansion across the continent came to depend heavily on the steamship route to and from the isthmus and the railroad route across it, which transported more gold seekers than the Overland Trail. In the next decade, the Panama route carried the bulk of U.S. mail as well as gold and silver shipments from California to eastern banks.

In Nicaragua, where a large interior lake aided the crossing between oceans, the United States confronted Great Britain's prior claim to coastal lands. The two nations agreed in the **Clayton-Bulwer Treaty** of 1850 not to exclude others from any waterway they built. Although high costs and engineering difficulties prevented construction of a canal, U.S. business tycoon Cornelius Vanderbilt established a road and steamship route through Nicaragua that carried two thousand Americans between the oceans each month.

Into this strategic and contested terrain came William Walker, seeking fame, fortune, and territory for slavery. In May 1855, he sailed from San Francisco to Nicaragua with a band of fifty-six men that was later reinforced by local opponents of the Nicaraguan government. Aided by repeating rifles, Walker's men defeated the Nicaraguan army and

Ostend Manifesto Letter from U.S. ministers in Europe to President Pierce in 1854 recommending purchase or seizure of Cuba from Spain.

Clayton-Bulwer Treaty Accord in which the United States and Britain disavowed plans to colonize Central America and agreed to permit mutual access to any canals constructed there.

installed a puppet government. In 1856, Walker declared himself president of Nicaragua, legalized slavery, and announced plans to reopen the African slave trade.

Despite bitter opposition from antislavery politicians, the Pierce administration immediately recognized Walker's government. Nicaragua's tropical farms could "never be developed without slave labor," the U.S. minister to Nicaragua explained. But Walker's triumph was short lived. Troops from Costa Rica, inspired by nationalist hero Juan Santamaria and subsidized by Walker's rival Vanderbilt as well as Great Britain, invaded and helped the Nicaraguans defeat Walker's army. Southerners' dream of a proslavery empire in the Caribbean did not become reality, but it scarred U.S. politics throughout the 1850s. Pierce and other Young America supporters had hoped that overseas expansion might quell the domestic debate over slavery, but filibustering and overtures to buy territory only sharpened the sectional conflict.

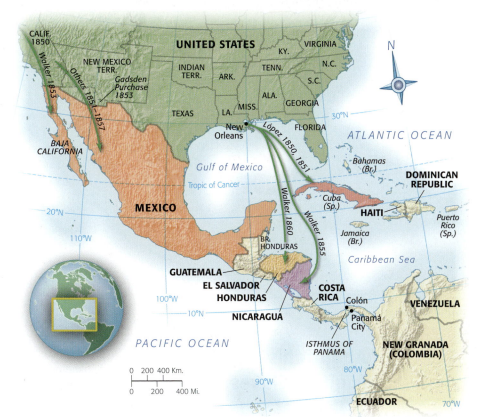

Map 12.1 Filibustering Expeditions in Latin America, 1850–1860 Throughout the 1850s, U.S. adventurers mounted illegal private expeditions to grab land from northern Mexico, independent Central American republics, and the Spanish colony of Cuba. Filibusters sought fame and fortune as well as expanding U.S. territory, including areas where slavery could take root. ▲

12-3

Reemergence of the Slavery Controversy

In the climax to Harriet Beecher Stowe's bestselling novel, *Uncle Tom's Cabin* (1852), the runaway slave Eliza crosses the half-frozen Ohio River to freedom with her child. This poster for a British-American theatrical coproduction shows Eliza making the treacherous nighttime crossing while fending off hounds sent by slave catchers visible on the far shore.

How would this scene, taken from Stowe's novel, evoke the northern public's sympathies for slaves and suggest slavery's relevance to their lives? ▶

Library of Congress Prints and Photographs Division[LC-USZC4-1298]

Plans for expansion beyond existing U.S. borders escalated sectional divisions over slavery. Closer to home, the controversy over fugitive slaves showed how the Compromise of 1850 had heightened Northerners' awareness of their entanglement with slavery and its impact on their daily lives. African American and white abolitionists' challenges to the strengthened Fugitive Slave Law combined with a best-selling novel dramatizing the plight of the South's slaves captured the public's attention. Tensions reached the boiling point, but only after the question of slavery in the territories reemerged unexpectedly in 1854. That year, a law that opened the Kansas territory to slave owners shattered the sectional truce.

☞ As you read, consider the events that reignited controversy over slavery in the United States in the early 1850s. How did black and white abolitionists revive the debate over slavery after the Compromise of 1850? How did the question of slavery in the territories resurface?

Library of Congress Prints and Photographs Division

Global Americans The most famous of the Underground Railroad's "conductors," **Harriet Tubman** exemplifies the transnational dimension of U.S. slaves' journey to freedom. Born into slavery on a Maryland plantation, Araminta "Minty" Ross became a muscular laborer and a habitual rebel who married freeman John Tubman in 1844. Emboldened by stories of successful runaways he told and by fears that her family would soon be sold, she fled to Philadelphia in 1849, where she adopted her mother's name, Harriet. Determined to lead others to freedom, Tubman returned to Maryland and, after the Fugitive Slave Act of 1850 raised the risk of capture, began to guide escaped slaves on a long and dangerous route through Pennsylvania and western New York to Canada, where Britain had outlawed slavery in 1833. Carrying a revolver and using the North Star as a guide, Tubman traveled with her "passengers" at night and relied on local free blacks and white abolitionists for assistance. Slaveholders posted rewards for her capture, but she was never apprehended. After Tubman established her home in St. Catharines, Canada West (present-day Ontario), she made it a haven for fugitive slaves, including many friends and family members. In the 1850s, she returned to the South more than a dozen times to conduct runaways to Canada. Abolitionist William Lloyd Garrison called her "Moses" for leading hundreds of escapees to the "Promised Land"—which before the Civil War meant Canada for those seeking legal protection from recapture.

12-3a Abolitionists and Fugitive Slaves

Abolitionists played a major role in keeping the moral issue of slavery in public view after the Compromise of 1850. Fearing recapture after his escape from slavery, Frederick Douglass left the United States in 1845 to lecture in England and Ireland, where abolitionist sympathizers purchased his freedom. When he returned, Douglass resolved to take an independent stand against all forms of white racism. Breaking with his antipolitical mentor, William Lloyd Garrison, Douglass supported the Free Soil Party's campaign against slavery in the territories. His newspaper, the *North Star*, supplemented news of the antislavery movement with exposés of segregationist practices in northern schools, streetcars, and railroads. In an 1852 Independence Day speech, Douglass asked pointedly "What to the slave is the Fourth of July?" His answer: "A day that reveals to him, more than all other days in the year, the gross injustice and cruelty to which he is the constant victim."

> Abolitionist agitation and the new fugitive slave law bring slavery home to Northerners.

Douglass hoped to change attitudes and practices—North and South—with appeals to conscience, but not all black leaders were as optimistic as he was. In the wake of the Compromise of 1850, Martin Delany promoted plans to leave the United States. Delany, who had been dismissed from Harvard Medical School after white students objected to a black man's presence, suggested in *The Condition, Elevation, Emigration, and Destiny of the Colored People of the United States* (1852) that free blacks and slave runaways build a black homeland in Central America or West Africa. In 1859, he negotiated a treaty with Yoruba leaders to settle free African Americans on land that is now part of Nigeria. However, the vast majority of northern blacks remained in the free states, determined to fight for civil rights and an end to slavery. Even male and female delegates to the 1854 National

Emigration Convention in Cleveland approved a resolution demanding "every political right, privilege and position to which the whites are eligible in the United States."

Some northern blacks organized campaigns to end discrimination in employment and education. After five-year-old Sarah Roberts was refused admission to a nearby white school and assigned to a distant and poorly funded all-black school in Boston, her father took the case to court. Robert Morris, the first black lawyer to argue a jury case in the United States, cocounseled with Charles Sumner to challenge Boston's segregated school system. They lost their case in an 1850 state court decision that was later cited to justify segregation laws. But through protests, boycotts, and alliances with white abolitionists, Boston's free blacks eventually won over the state's lawmakers. In 1855, Massachusetts became the first state to legally desegregate its public schools.

African American abolitionists and white allies also formed associations to protect runaway slaves against capture and re-enslavement. More than a thousand southern slaves managed to escape north to freedom each year, often with assistance. The loose network of abolitionist agents and safe houses that became known as the **Underground Railroad** helped many escaped slaves reach the relative safety of the North's cities or a more certain refuge in Canada (see Map 12.2).

The new **Fugitive Slave Law**, part of the Compromise of 1850, was intended to stem this northern flow, but its effects were broader. It tightened enforcement of the federal law of 1793 by adding restrictions on runaways and their sympathizers. Captured suspects were denied a trial by jury or the right to present evidence to federal commissioners who heard their case, and local governments were prevented from intervening. The law

Underground Railroad
Secret network of abolitionist safe houses and conductors that helped southern slaves escape to northern free states or Canada.

Fugitive Slave Law
Legislation passed as part of Compromise of 1850 that strengthened federal government control over the capture and prosecution of runaway slaves.

Map 12.2 Escape from Slavery A few thousand slaves successfully escaped each year from slavery in the South. Although some fled south to Mexico and the Caribbean, most headed north by roads, trains, or boats and were often assisted by Vigilance Committees on the Underground Railroad. Many runaways followed routes to Great Lakes ports or other border crossings to seek a safe haven from slave catchers in British Canada. ▲

threatened free blacks with potential enslavement, decreed that citizens could be compelled to join the hunt for fugitives, and made it a felony for anyone to harbor them.

A string of dramatic rescues and court cases intensified opposition to the new law. In 1851, a group of black resistance fighters in Christiana, Pennsylvania, led by escaped slave William Parker killed a Maryland slave owner who was attempting to recapture fugitives. Parker fled to Canada, assisted by Frederick Douglass. Three years later, an interracial crowd of abolitionists stormed a Boston courthouse to free the captured runaway Anthony Burns, and a prison guard was killed in the failed attempt. President Pierce sent federal troops to Boston to escort Burns south. Each episode attracted new sympathizers. Enraged by the Burns case, Massachusetts

businessman Amos Lawrence declared that he and his friends "went to bed one night old fashioned, conservative, Compromise Union Whigs & waked up stark mad Abolitionists."

12-3b *Uncle Tom's Cabin*

The plight of fugitives and the horrific fate of relatives they left behind were the subject of a best-selling novel published in 1852, Harriet Beecher Stowe's ***Uncle Tom's Cabin***. A white abolitionist, Stowe had never seen a slave plantation, but her family had harbored runaways at their home in Cincinnati. Her book

> An influential antislavery novel dramatizes the evils of slavery.

Uncle Tom's Cabin Stowe's best-selling novel that dramatized the evils of slavery and plight of fugitive slaves.

settler societies New World nations or British colonies where European settlers dispossessed native peoples and African slaves, pushed inland, and transplanted their way of life.

Gadsden Purchase Agreement with Mexico by which the United States paid $10 million for southwestern lands to ease construction of a transcontinental railroad.

Kansas-Nebraska Act Law pushed by Democrat Douglas that repealed the Missouri Compromise and opened Kansas Territory to slavery under popular sovereignty.

absorbed their stories into a fictional saga that brought the cruel realities of the slave quarters and the whipping post into tranquil northern parlors.

Unabashedly sentimental, Stowe's novel traced the fate of several slaves, including Eliza, who flees northward carrying her child across ice floes on the Ohio River; Lucy, who commits suicide when her infant is sold away; and the saintly Uncle Tom, who forgives a cruel master even as he is beaten to death. All suffer the evil effects of the slave system. Stowe drew on ideas of womanhood that transcended racial and class differences by highlighting the agony of enslaved mothers. Convinced that slavery also corrupted the master class, she avoided blaming southern slaveholders, portraying most as good Christians trapped in their roles and making the cruelest master a New England-born overseer. Her intent was to stir readers' consciences and awaken them to their complicity with slavery.

Uncle Tom's Cabin tugged at the heartstrings of the quarter of a million Americans who read it in its first year as well as those who attended theatrical adaptations. Many Northerners accepted Stowe's portrait of slavery as accurate whereas white Southerners condemned it as misleading propaganda. Translated into many languages, *Uncle Tom's Cabin* became the world's best-selling novel in the nineteenth century. It was a huge hit in Europe, where Romantic literature prevailed, the South provided an exotic setting, and the recent abolition of slavery in British and French colonies allowed readers to pity Americans. At the end of the novel, Stowe linked the antislavery movement to the European revolutions of 1848. Both gave voice to the hunger for freedom among the oppressed, she declared, and every nation that failed to heed this call would face God's wrath on the Day of Judgment.

12-3c The Kansas-Nebraska Act

Despite controversies over *Uncle Tom's Cabin*, fugitive slaves, and Central American filibusters, the most explosive issue in the struggle over slavery in the 1850s remained the question that the U.S.–Mexican War had raised: the status of slavery in the western territories. The man who shattered the sectional truce of 1850 was the same one who had steered it through Congress. When Stephen Douglas proposed in 1854 to organize the remaining Louisiana Purchase lands west of the Missouri River into territories where slavery might take hold, he created a furor that convulsed American politics.

> Stephen Douglas reopens the political fight over slavery in western territories.

The dispute grew out of two manias that nineteenth-century Americans shared with **settler societies** such as Canada and Argentina: land hunger and railroads. Midwestern farmers had long coveted fertile lands in the vast prairies between the Mississippi River and the Rockies. Attempts to open them for sale and settlement were held back because the federal government had set aside some tracts in 1830 as a permanent Indian reserve. Meanwhile, plans for a transcontinental railroad anchored the dreams of many U.S. expansionists. Enormous profits could be made by linking existing lines east of the Mississippi with the Pacific. For the eastern terminus, Northerners' hopes focused on Chicago, the booming Great Lakes port and commercial hub. Southerners pushed for New Orleans, Memphis, or St. Louis, all located in slave states. As sectional rivalry for the transcontinental railroad heated up, it inevitably became entangled with slavery.

Prodded by expansionists, federal officials opened new western lands to settlers and railroads. In 1853, the Pierce administration purchased from Mexico thirty thousand square miles of desert land south of the Gila River in present-day Arizona and New Mexico. Costing $10 million, the **Gadsden Purchase** skirted the southern end of the Rocky Mountains to create a level railroad route from the South to the West Coast. The path was less smooth than expected. This borderland had long been contested between the Apache people and Mexican frontiersmen, and the U.S. government joined the violent struggle as a third party. Farther north, the Pierce administration pressured tribal leaders in Nebraska to give up their lands for railroads and white settlement. In treaties signed early in 1854, the Delawares, Shawnees, Iowas, and Kickapoos ceded all but a few small reservations. Most Indians were eventually forced to move to Oklahoma territory, where they were squeezed onto small grants bordering the Native Americans who had been sent there earlier by the Indian Removal Act in the 1830s.

Early in 1854, Douglas, eager to promote a transcontinental railroad that would benefit his state of Illinois, introduced a bill to organize the remaining Louisiana Purchase lands into two territories, Kansas and Nebraska. To attract Southerners' support, Douglas's bill raised the possibility that slavery could be established in these territories by leaving the issue to local voters, his trademark formula of popular sovereignty.

This time the Little Giant had miscalculated. Douglas was indifferent to slavery and believed it had little chance to take root on the Great Plains. By 1854, however, many Northerners and Southerners were ready to argue vehemently over that possibility. Free-soil advocates saw popular sovereignty as a proslavery formula, especially after the Utah Territory had used it to legalize slavery in 1852. Besides that, the Kansas and Nebraska Territories lay above the line where slavery had been forbidden in the Louisiana Purchase lands by Congress in 1820. After a heated debate, the **Kansas-Nebraska Act** was passed by Congress in May 1854 (see Map 12.3).

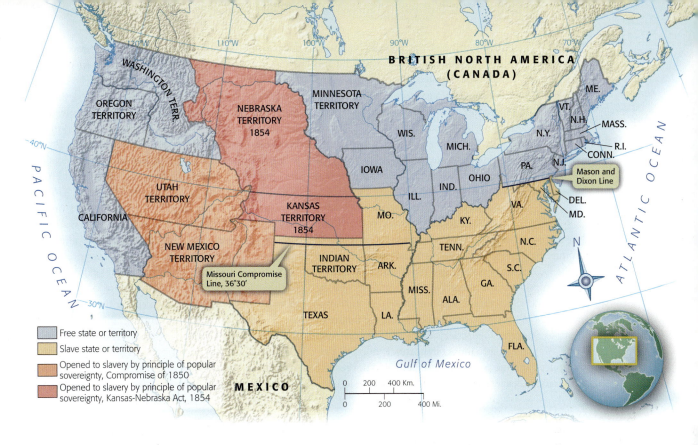

Map 12.3 The Kansas-Nebraska Act and Slavery in the Territories, 1854 Stephen Douglas's Kansas-Nebraska Act reopened the slavery controversy by applying the formula of popular sovereignty from the Compromise of 1850 to new territories in remaining lands from the Louisiana Purchase. The Missouri Compromise of 1820 had banned slavery from those lands, but the new law repealed it, causing a political firestorm. ▲

Douglas's victory reopened sectional divides and strained existing political parties to the breaking point. Southern Democrats strongly backed the Kansas-Nebraska Act while Democrats in the North, wary of a popular backlash, split their votes. Their fears proved well founded in the 1854 elections, when northern Democrats lost most of their seats in Congress and were left in control of only two free-state legislatures. As the Democratic Party became more southern dominated, dissatisfied northern members began to seek alternatives. Meanwhile, the Whig coalition shattered entirely. Northern Whigs voted unanimously against the Kansas-Nebraska Act, southern Whigs decisively for it. The national Whig Party, already weakened by divisions over the Compromise of 1850, simply dissolved. The stage was set for a dramatic realignment of the American political system.

12-4

The Politics of Sectionalism

After the Kansas-Nebraska Act became law, settlers rushed into the new territories and formed free-soil and proslavery factions who vied for control, sometimes violently. This northern cartoon blames Democratic Party leaders such as Franklin Pierce and Stephen Douglas for forcing a "freesoiler" to swallow slavery.

Why did the struggle over popular sovereignty devolve into armed conflict? How does the cartoon link slavery's spread to western territories with U.S. expansionism in Latin America? ▶

Library of Congress Prints and Photographs Division,[LC-US262–92043]

political machines Urban political organizations, often headed by a boss, that rely on party discipline and distribution of rewards to gain power and retain voters' loyalty.

Know-Nothings Secret society founded in the 1850s to prevent Catholics from voting and holding office that elected members to Congress through the American Party.

In the wake of the Kansas-Nebraska Act, old political parties splintered and new ones emerged, one of them a short-lived anti-immigrant coalition, the other a rapidly growing northern party dedicated to preventing slavery's spread. The shake-up signaled a move toward political parties that starkly reflected sectional ideas and interests. As each of the major parties, the older Democrats and the new Republicans, consolidated their control over voters in the South and North, respectively, the venerable tradition of sectional compromises engineered by cross-sectional parties, long the glue of the U.S. political system, was rapidly melting away.

One symptom of the intensifying sectional rift was the outbreak of guerrilla warfare between proslavery and antislavery settlers in the territories. Another was the failure of an ambitious Supreme Court decision to settle the question of slavery's expansion into those territories. If political parties, the courts, and the people themselves could not resolve their differences peacefully, what alternatives were left?

☞ As you read, consider the impact of the Kansas-Nebraska Act, the formation of new political parties, and the Dred Scott decision. How did these developments escalate sectional tensions over slavery?

12-4a Anti-immigrant Sentiment and the Know-Nothings

When northern voters sought new political moorings after the Whig Party dissolved, substantial numbers rallied around nativism. Almost 3.5 million

{ A short-lived nativist coalition bids to disrupt the political party system.

immigrants landed in the United States between 1848 and 1860, the largest influx in U.S. history in proportion to the resident population (see Figure 12.1). Native-born American Protestants generally welcomed the German Forty-Eighters and middle-class German Protestants, who scattered on farms in the Midwest, established prosperous businesses in river ports, and shared northern Protestants' free-soil beliefs. But Catholic immigrants, especially 1 million poor Irish Catholics escaping the "Great Hunger," a potato blight and famine that lasted from 1846 to 1851, aroused opposition. Nativist fears focused on poverty, crime, and cultural differences between Catholics and Protestants over temperance laws and separate schools. After a republican revolt in Rome was suppressed and the Papal States restored, Protestant propagandists portrayed Catholic immigrants as the advance troops of a papal plot to take over the United States and destroy free institutions.

Political opposition to immigrants crystallized when the newcomers began voting. Irish immigrants and German Catholics preferred the Democratic Party, which organized their votes into urban **political machines**, which distributed jobs and favors in return for party loyalty and promised protection from religious persecution. In response, secret anti-Catholic organizations such as New York's Order of the Star-Spangled Banner (1850) were formed in northern states. Going public, these secret societies nominated local candidates who attacked crime and corruption and stirred voters' Protestant loyalties and patriotic sentiments. By 1851, nativist parties succeeded in electing prominent city officials in Boston, Philadelphia, New Orleans, and San Francisco.

In 1854, the anti-immigrant crusade went national, in part to fill the void left by the Whigs' demise. Nativist organizations coalesced into the American Party, also called the **Know-Nothings**, after a secret organization whose members were supposed to reply "I know nothing" to inquirers.

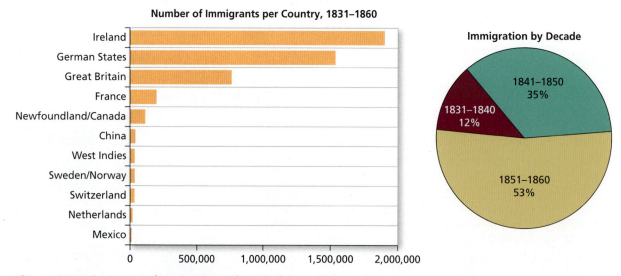

Figure 12.1 Major Sources of Immigration to the United States, 1831–1860 The majority of immigrants into the United States came from Ireland and the German states with Great Britain a distant third. More than half arrived during the sectional struggle over slavery in the 1850s. By 1860, 15 percent of the white population was of foreign birth, and 90 percent of immigrants lived in northern states.

▲ Source: Data from Stephan Thernstrom, ed., *Harvard Encyclopedia of American Ethnic Groups* (Cambridge, Mass., and London: Harvard University Press, 1980), 1047.

Know-Nothings pledged to extend the time to citizenship for immigrants (naturalization) from five to twenty-one years, to restrict voting rights to native-born Americans, and to bar Catholics from holding office. The new party achieved a stunning success in the 1854 elections by running its own candidates or forming alliances with local parties, usually Whigs. Know-Nothings captured most state offices in Massachusetts, Delaware, and Pennsylvania, gained ground in Upper South cities such as Baltimore and Louisville, and elected seventy-five congressmen pledged to their program.

Fearing that the question of slavery could destroy the Union, the Know-Nothings tried to ignore it by appealing to constitutional agreements and patriotic sentiments. But the issue was impossible to avoid, and playing on religious and ethnic prejudice proved an unsuccessful diversion. In short order, the Know-Nothings, like the Whigs before them, split along North-South lines over slavery. When Know-Nothing leaders introduced a platform in 1856 that endorsed the Kansas-Nebraska Act, most Northerners walked away from the new party.

12-4b Republicans and the Sectional Debate

Another new coalition, the **Republican Party**, got off to a later start than the Know-Nothings but proved more durable. The party sprang up in 1854 in midwestern states out of spontaneous protests over the Kansas-Nebraska Act and then spread eastward. Its coalition of antislavery Whigs, dissenting northern Democrats, and Free Soilers began with divergent views on such issues as immigration and tariffs, but they agreed on one powerful cause: opposition to slavery's extension westward. Its clout was demonstrated in the 1854 elections when the fledgling party won a surprising victory, capturing a majority of northern states' seats in the House of Representatives.

> A new northern party polarizes the political dispute over slavery.

The Republicans' motto, "Free Soil, Free Labor, Free Men," summarized their appeal. Free-soil antagonism to slavery in the territories reflected varied concerns, ranging from prejudice against blacks in the North to the search for economic opportunity in the West unhindered by competition with slave labor. Only a small minority of prominent Republicans held abolitionist views; others, like northern bankers and manufacturers of clothing, profited directly from the trade in slave goods. Most were willing to leave southern slavery alone and did little to improve the condition of the North's free blacks.

The ideology of **free labor** highlighted Northerners' confidence in their prosperous system of competitive capitalism. Northern farms and factories had created a high standard of living compared to that of the "backward" South. A free-labor society, Republicans believed, dignified work and rewarded initiative. Prominent Illinois lawyer Abraham Lincoln and other Republicans tied free labor to U.S. nationalism, asserting that the North's thriving economy and open frontier exempted the United States from class antagonisms that divided Europeans. Preserving western lands as a **safety valve** that offered an escape for discontented eastern wage workers would guarantee America's fortunate difference into the future.

For the great majority of Republicans, free men meant free white men unpressured by the "Slave Power," a conspiracy of influential planters that threatened majority rule and compromised the nation's global posture. The South's promotion of slavery, Lincoln and other Republicans believed, tarnished the image of the United States abroad and prevented foreign liberals from adopting its republican institutions. Despite the emphasis on free men, Republicans celebrated middle-class women's moral influence and encouraged their participation in political events in contrast to the Democratic Party's emphasis on male mastery of households and plantations.

The Republican Party was the first major sectional party in U.S. politics. In their heyday, the Whigs and Democrats, with substantial membership in the North and South, often put aside sectional views to promote compromise. Without southern members to appease, Republicans appended a northern-flavored economic program to their platform. They updated the old Whig American system of federal support for internal improvements with calls for federal subsidies for a Pacific railroad and free homesteads of one hundred sixty acres for western settlers. This economic package and, after party leaders denounced nativist views, a friendlier attitude toward immigrants attracted additional northern voters.

The Democratic Party remained a cross-sectional coalition but became increasingly dominated by southern leaders. Franklin Pierce and other "northern men of southern principles," called "doughfaces" for their pliable views, rose in the party at the expense of neutral nationalists such as Stephen Douglas. The core strategy of the Democrats' vocal Deep South **"fire eaters"** was an aggressive defense of slaveholders' rights. Their growing influence among Democrats pushed aside the Upper South tradition of sectional compromise. Without a viable opposition party to replace the Whigs, Southern politics became a one-party system dedicated to sectional loyalty and defense.

Southern Democrats' growing militancy derived from other sources besides party reshuffling. The cotton boom required expansion, and access to western lands promised social mobility for poor whites who aspired

Republican Party Political coalition created to oppose extension of slavery to western territories that adopted the economic program formerly advocated by Whigs.

free labor Ideology that celebrated the virtues of property ownership, waged work, self-discipline, and upward mobility under competitive capitalism.

safety valve Idea that access to western lands offered relief for poor or discontented eastern workers and farmers, and a chance for upward mobility.

fire eaters Outspoken defenders of white Southerners' rights to own and dispose of slaves under government protection; the first advocates of the South's secession.

Architect of the Capitol

Global Americans Born in Germany, **Emanuel Leutze** was brought to the United States as a child by his immigrant parents. He took painting lessons in Philadelphia and returned to Germany for advanced training. At first practicing his craft abroad, Leutze specialized in historical subjects painted dramatically and in painstaking detail, many of them illustrating the virtues of America. A strong supporter of the Revolutions of 1848, Leutze painted his iconic *Washington Crossing the Delaware* (1850) to inspire European liberals with the example of the American Revolution. In 1859, he returned permanently to the United States. As the sectional struggle over slavery in the territories heated up, Congress commissioned Leutze to produce a stairway mural for the U.S. Capitol Building. *Westward the Course of Empire Takes Its Way* portrayed Manifest Destiny on an epic scale. It features a procession of pioneer men and women, including recent Irish and German immigrants, who pilgrimaged from the Valley of Darkness toward the golden light of San Francisco Bay. Like many German immigrants, Leutze warmed to the Republicans' free-labor ideology. For the mural's final version, Leutze linked westward expansion with antislavery sentiment by inserting a freed black boy guiding a mule near its center.

to own slaves—a southern white version of the free-labor safety valve. In the eyes of southern Democrats, Republicans looked no different from abolitionists, for both threatened to strangle the slave system. Also at stake was the shifting balance of sectional power in Congress. Additional free states remained to be carved out of the Oregon, Louisiana Purchase, and Northwest Ordinance territories whereas slaveholders could count only on dry and distant New Mexico. Unless slavery could be extended, the Democrats' control of Congress and the presidency appeared doomed. Finally, Deep South politicians worried about the loyalty of Upper South farmers, who were less tied to the cotton boom and might compromise slaveholders' interests. The fire eaters believed that confrontations over slavery would ensure a united southern front.

During the intensified sectional debate of the 1850s, proslavery advocates extended the religious, racial, historical, and economic arguments they had developed earlier to defend their views and attack opponents (see Chapter 10). Josiah Nott, an Alabama physician, claimed in *Types of Mankind* (1854) that black Africans and their descendants constituted a separate, unchanging racial type unable to rise from "barbarism." International perspectives also informed the controversy. South Carolina senator James Henry Hammond, in his famous "mud-sill" speech, used Roman history to argue that a servile laboring class was necessary to support "civilized" free men. To discredit the North's free-labor system, proslavery spokesmen borrowed heavily from British and French critics of industrialism. Northern workers toiling in factories and living in squalid new industrial slums were "wage slaves" whose plight was far worse than that of southern blacks, the Virginia proslavery apologist George Fitzhugh charged in *Sociology for the South; or The Failure of Free Society* (1854). At the same time, proslavery politicians' aggressive stance fed on their discomfort that slavery and other forms of bound labor were in obvious decline throughout the western world. The revolutionary upheavals of 1848 outlawed slavery in French colonies and ended serfdom in the Austrian empire and German states. To antislavery Northerners, these developments showed that the tide of history was rising with them. Both sides were determined to make a stand in Kansas.

12-4c Violence in Kansas, Congress, and California

Far from resolving growing tensions over slavery, the Kansas-Nebraska Act simply shifted animosities from Congress to Kansas. Goaded by the popular sovereignty provision, a race began between proslavery and antislavery forces to recruit settlers and build a majority among Kansas voters, and their animosity degenerated into a mini-civil war. Southerners initially gained the upper hand because Kansas lay west of slave-state Missouri. In 1855, thousands of Missouri "border ruffians" crossed over and voted fraudulently to give proslavery candidates a large majority in the territorial legislature, which established Lecompton as its capital. Northern

> Conflict over territorial slavery produces bloodshed in western lands and the U.S. Senate.

abolitionists and religious societies responded by sponsoring free-soil settlers, in some cases providing them with guns. Abolitionists such as Angelina Grimké and Lydia Maria Child who had previously embraced pacifism now declared that violence was necessary to defend Kansas free soilers. Republican politicians declared that Americans in Kansas faced a homegrown Revolution of 1848 between the forces of freedom and despotism. When the Lecompton legislature legalized slavery, the free soilers convened in Topeka and established their own territorial government and constitution.

By early 1856, guerrilla warfare had erupted between partisans of the two Kansas governments, and President Pierce pledged armed federal support for the proslavery regime. In May, a posse organized by a federal marshal sacked the free-state town of Lawrence. In retaliation, abolitionist agitator John Brown led four of his sons and a few followers in a raid on a proslavery settlement on Pottawatomie Creek. Wielding broadswords, they hacked five men to death. After that, armed bands of guerrillas roamed through eastern Kansas, clashing over slavery and rival claims to turf. What the eastern press called **"Bleeding Kansas"** became a living symbol of sectional polarities.

Meanwhile, violence reached the floor of Congress when Massachusetts Republican Senator Charles Sumner gave a stinging speech condemning "The Crime Against Kansas." An abolitionist and florid orator, Sumner portrayed proslavery voter fraud as "the rape of a virgin territory" and singled out Senator Andrew Butler of South Carolina as one who had taken "the harlot, slavery" as his mistress. Sumner's abusive personal references provoked an attack by South Carolina representative Preston Brooks, a relative of Butler, who beat Sumner unconscious with his cane. The injured Sumner became a hero to Republicans, his vacant senate chair a symbol of slaveholder violence. Brooks was censured by Congress but reelected by South Carolina voters and received dozens of congratulatory canes as replacements for the one he broke in the attack.

The presidential contest of 1856 provided a snapshot of the political divisions and realignments that followed the Kansas-Nebraska Act. Passing over Pierce and Stephen Douglas as too controversial, the Democrats turned to Pennsylvania's James Buchanan, a reliable doughface who had been an overseas diplomat during the sectional debate. For their first national election, the Republicans chose John C. Frémont, a military hero and western adventurer who relied on his youthful good looks—and his politically savvy wife, Jessie Benton, the daughter of a powerful Missouri senator—to unify the new party's ranks. The Know-Nothings, now split by slavery into northern and southern wings, fretted as the first organization endorsed Frémont while the second nominated former president Millard Fillmore.

With the support of southern voters, who preferred Buchanan to Fillmore in every slave state but Maryland, the Democratic candidate won the three-way election. Frémont, however, ran remarkably well, carrying eleven of the sixteen free states. If the Republicans had taken Pennsylvania and one other heavily populated free state, Frémont would have entered the White House; by this time, a northern sectional party could win the presidency without even campaigning in the South.

That lesson was not lost on James Buchanan. Perhaps seeking to appease Republicans, who had campaigned against the "twin relics of barbarism," polygamy and slavery in the West, the new president sent U.S. forces to the Utah territory to replace Mormon leader Brigham Young as governor. The expedition led to a prolonged standoff known as the *Utah War* (1857–1858) whose worst casualties were not armed men from either side but a band of one hundred twenty California-bound emigrants ambushed in a remote area by local Mormon militiamen. Eventually, the two sides negotiated an agreement whereby Young stepped down, federal troops remained as peacekeepers, and those who took part in the "Mormon Rebellion" were pardoned.

Buchanan also took steps to resolve the Kansas question but only made things worse. The new president announced that he supported Kansas's admission to the Union as a slave state. A proslavery constitution was drafted at Lecompton in 1857 and eventually submitted to Kansas voters, who rejected it. Nevertheless, Buchanan insisted that the **Lecompton constitution** was legitimate and pressured northern Democrats in Congress to join southern colleagues and admit Kansas to statehood under it.

Stephen Douglas broke with the administration. Angered by Buchanan's violation of popular sovereignty, Douglas believed that midwestern Democrats like him could not cave in to proslavery politicians without endangering their own reelection. Douglas's independent stand infuriated southern Democrats and ended his dream of winning the South's support for his presidential ambitions. The Lecompton controversy revealed a growing sectional fissure in the Democratic ranks.

In California, where the Democrats were divided between migrants from the free and slave states, the Lecompton rift sparked intraparty violence. Newly elected U.S. Senator David Broderick was a second-generation Irish American and a Democratic political boss who sided with Douglas. His bitter rival, Kentucky-born David Terry, had been chief justice of the California Supreme Court and led the state's proslavery Democratic faction. The two men exchanged insults and then fought a duel south of San Francisco, where Terry shot Broderick in the chest. "I die because I was opposed to a corrupt administration and the extension of slavery," the senator reportedly proclaimed on his deathbed. In 1854, the Whig Party had shattered over slavery; a few years later, the nation's Democrats headed toward their own breakup.

"Bleeding Kansas" Label given by northern newspapers to guerrilla war in Kansas Territory after 1854 as armed conflict raged between antislavery and proslavery supporters.

Lecompton constitution Proslavery constitution that was drafted for Kansas Territory but not approved by Congress when Democrats split into sectional factions.

Library of Congress Prints and Photographs Division (LC-USZ62–107588)

Missouri History Museum, St. Louis

Roger Taney and Dred Scott These photographs suggest the gravity of the *Dred Scott* case and the dignity of both principals. Roger Taney was a Maryland attorney and Jackson appointee who had freed his own slaves but who championed white man's democracy and condemned antislavery agitation as "northern aggression." Dred Scott's master had allowed him to marry and promised that he could earn his freedom, but when the master died, his widow reneged, prompting Scott's suit against her and her brother, John Sandford. Shortly after the Supreme Court's decision, the sons of Scott's first owner purchased him and his family and freed them. ▲

12-4d *The Dred Scott* Case and Lincoln-Douglas Debates

In his inaugural address, President Buchanan referred to a pending Supreme Court decision that he hoped would settle the slavery controversy once and for all. Dred Scott, a Missouri slave, had been taken by his owner, an army surgeon, to various posts in Illinois and Wisconsin, the latter a territory where slavery had been banned by the Missouri Compromise. In Wisconsin, Scott met and married another slave, Harriet Robinson. When their owner took them back to St. Louis, Harriet Scott, who attended an abolitionist church, convinced her husband to sue for freedom. Arguing that residence in a free territory had made him and his family free, Scott's lawyers pursued his appeal to the Supreme Court.

{ A Supreme Court decision opens the territories to slavery and deepens sectional divisions.

At stake were two key issues. First, did Scott have the right of U.S. citizens to sue in federal court? Second, did Congress, or a federally sanctioned territorial legislature, have the power to prohibit slavery in a territory? In March 1857, Chief Justice Roger Taney delivered the majority opinion of a court that tilted toward the South. Scott, Taney declared, could not be a citizen. Ignoring African Americans' citizenship in several

Dred Scott decision Supreme Court case (*Dred Scott v. Sandford*) that declared blacks ineligible for U.S. citizenship and overturned federal laws prohibiting slavery in territories.

northern states since the 1780s, Taney asserted that the founding generation had agreed that blacks were "beings of an inferior order" with "no rights which the white man was bound to respect." Moving on to the question of slavery in the territories, Taney declared that the Missouri Compromise was unconstitutional. The Constitution did not give Congress authority over territory acquired after 1787. More important, said Taney, the Fifth Amendment to the U.S. Constitution forbade taking a person's property, including slaves, without their consent or "due process of law."

Instead of settling the controversy over slavery, the **Dred Scott decision** of 1857 deepened it. Southern whites, whose constitutional arguments had won crucial support, rejoiced whereas Republicans, whose free-soil views the Court dismissed, were outraged. African American conventions held in northern cities denounced the decision. For northern Democrats such as Stephen Douglas, the Court's decision posed a fatal obstacle. Because territorial legislatures were then prohibited from interfering with slave owners' property rights, Douglas's formula of popular sovereignty became meaningless: Kansas could not prohibit slavery even if its citizens wished. Polarized reactions to the decision indicated that by 1857, the Supreme Court could not keep together a union of states that slavery was pulling apart.

The biblical adage that "A house divided against itself cannot stand" struck Abraham Lincoln as an apt metaphor for the situation in the United States. Either the opponents of slavery would blockade it into extinction, as Republicans proposed, or its advocates would press until the nation legalized slavery everywhere inside its borders. During the Illinois senatorial campaign of 1858, Lincoln, the Republican challenger, engaged the incumbent Douglas in a series of debates. Lincoln charged that the *Dred Scott* decision prefigured the spread of slavery to free states. Declaring slavery a "vast moral evil," Lincoln asked Douglas whether popular sovereignty remained a viable way to curb it.

In reply, Douglas asserted that despite the *Dred Scott* decision, citizens in territories could exclude slavery by denying it legal protection—a response that appeased Illinois voters but further damaged the Little Giant's standing in the South. When Douglas labeled Lincoln a "Black Republican" who favored racial equality, Lincoln responded that he was not in favor of "bringing about the social and political equality of the white and black race." Lincoln's racial views stood at the moderate Republican center, positioned between the abolitionists and antiblack free soilers, and his debate performance enhanced his reputation among Republicans nationally. Douglas hung onto his seat, but other northern Democrats felt the backlash from the *Dred Scott* decision in the 1858 elections. Propped up by the solid South, the party kept control of the Senate but it lost its majority in the House, which only tightened the political deadlock in Washington.

12-5

Road to Disunion

This political cartoon produced by New York printmakers Currier & Ives depicts the movement among southern states to leave the Union in the winter of 1860–1861. It shows Florida, Alabama, Mississippi, and Louisiana as men riding donkeys, following South Carolina's man riding a pig toward a dangerous cliff. South Carolina's rider shouts that "Old Hickory [Andrew Jackson] is dead, and now we'll have it," while Alabama declares that "Cotton is King!" The Georgia rider detours down a hill, expressing "doubts about 'the end' of that road."

What does this northern cartoon suggest about the motives of the seceding southern states? How does the cartoonist view their prospects? ▶

Go to MindTap® to practice history with the Chapter 12 **Primary Source Writing Activity: Domestic Divisions.** Read and view primary sources and respond to a writing prompt.

Library of Congress Prints and Photographs Division (LC-USZ62-32995)

THE "SECESSION MOVEMENT".

With the status of Kansas unresolved, an unpopular Supreme Court decision under debate, and Congress locked in stalemate, the issue of slavery in the territories seemed to paralyze the U.S. political system. Some white Southerners, surveying the gains that opponents of slavery had made at home and abroad, preached disunion as the only solution. By withdrawing from the Union, southern whites could transform themselves instantly from a minority to a majority and build a new nation founded on slavery and states' rights. Disunion remained a distinctly minority view among white Southerners, however, until an attempted slave insurrection in 1859 and the Republicans' presidential victory the following year seemed to confirm the fire eaters' dire prophecies. When South Carolina renounced the federal union after Lincoln was elected president, it set off a chain reaction that led to civil war. As it turned out, Americans disagreed just as fiercely over the meaning and permanence of the Union as they had over the extension of slavery within it.

☞ **As you read, examine key events along the road to the Civil War. What did the response to John Brown's raid**

reveal? Why did several slave states secede from the Union following Lincoln's election? Why did Republicans reject political compromise and Northerners refuse to let the secessionists depart? How did the Civil War break out?

12-5a John Brown's Raid

As political positions on slavery polarized, John Brown again pushed the conflict over the line into violence, as he had in Kansas. On October 16, 1859, Brown led an interracial band of eighteen followers in a raid on the federal arsenal at Harpers Ferry, Virginia. His intent was to steal firearms and establish a fortress in a mountain hideaway in Virginia, inspiring slaves to rebel and take refuge there. Brown knew about successful Latin American maroons—colonies of runaway slaves—and he absorbed tactics of guerrilla warfare from writings of the Italian revolutionary of 1848, Giuseppe Mazzini. But his raid failed badly, and his men were besieged in the arsenal's engine

> An abolitionist attempt to provoke a slave insurrection electrifies the nation.

John Brown Confers with Frederick Douglass Brown sought the support of abolitionist Douglass shortly before leading the raid at Harpers Ferry. Douglass disapproved, warning that attacking federal property was suicidal and would provoke a violent backlash. After the raid, Douglass fled for a time to Canada, fearing arrest as a coconspirator. To the South's whites, the web of guilt by association spread beyond abolitionists like Douglass to include mainstream Republicans. In this 1941 painting by black artist Jacob Lawrence, Brown makes his appeal and Douglass resists. A cross on the wall suggests their shared religious inspiration. ▶

U.S. National Archives and Records Administration

John Brown's Raid Failed 1859 attack by militant abolitionists on the federal arsenal at Harpers Ferry, Virginia, intended to spark a slave insurrection.

house by the local militia and then U.S. troops commanded by Colonel Robert E. Lee. After surrendering, Brown and six of his followers were convicted of treason against Virginia and executed.

John Brown's Raid electrified the nation, and his death stirred strong emotions at home and abroad. Impressed by Brown's courage, transcendentalist Henry David Thoreau praised him as a martyr who "would make the gallows as glorious as the cross." In an impassioned plea to stay Brown's execution, the French romantic novelist Victor Hugo published a letter calling Brown a "liberator" and "the champion of Christ." Southern planters' reactions formed a stark contrast, for the raid revived their worst nightmare: a violent insurrection by their own supposedly loyal slaves. Once it became known that Brown had received financial support from a circle of New England abolitionists, Southerners saw proof that northern abolitionists aimed to incite a slave rebellion. Proslavery leaders had threatened to desert the Union for a decade, but Brown's raid convinced many rank-and-file white Southerners that they were no longer secure in confederation with free states.

12-5b Election of 1860

When Congress reconvened after John Brown's raid, tensions ran so high that according to one senator, many members carried concealed revolvers and knives on the floor of Congress. In February 1860, Democratic Senator Jefferson Davis of Mississippi demanded congressional action against states harboring fugitive slaves and federal guarantees that slavery would be protected in the western territories. For the South's fire eaters, the Davis resolutions were the minimum price the North had to pay to keep southern states in the Union.

> A four-party contest gives the presidency to Republican candidate Lincoln, elected by a sharply sectional vote.

That price was too high even for northern Democrats. Fearing rejection by voters in their own states, Stephen Douglas and other free-state champions of popular sovereignty refused to switch to Davis's position. In April 1860, the Democrats met to nominate a presidential candidate, and when Douglas secured the majority, the Deep South delegates walked out. The same drama was repeated at a later convention. Hopelessly divided, the Democrats offered two candidates to the public: Douglas for the northern wing of the Party, and Vice President John C. Breckinridge of Kentucky for the southern.

Republicans, sensing victory, sought a moderate candidate and a broad platform. Lincoln appealed as a Midwesterner who could win interior states. He was untainted by Know-Nothing views and less militant on slavery than the early favorite, Senator William Seward of New York. The Republican platform condemned John Brown's raid and pledged noninterference with southern slavery but held the line against its extension. Republicans also widened their appeal by advocating immigration, homestead laws, and a transcontinental railroad.

None of these candidates pleased political veterans in the Upper South. Desperate to preserve the Union, they hastily formed the Constitutional Union Party. Their nominee, John Bell of Tennessee, conjured the spirit of Henry Clay but had no specific compromise to offer.

The election of 1860 became a four-way race that was sharply sectional in character. Lincoln took every northern state except New Jersey, which he split with Douglas. Breckinridge carried nine states in the Deep South. The Upper South was divided among Bell, Breckinridge, and Douglas, who won only Missouri. Lincoln won just under 40 percent of the popular vote, but his margin in the Electoral College was decisive. The Republicans had learned the lesson of 1856: A presidential candidate no longer needed Southerners' votes to win. South Carolina's proslavery leaders understood this, too.

12-5c The Secession Crisis

In December 1860, not long after the election results were official, South Carolina passed an ordinance of **secession**, withdrawing the state from the Union. Proslavery politicians in that state were emboldened by lame-duck president Buchanan, who denied the right of secession but said the federal government could do nothing to stop it. South Carolina leaders argued that the incoming "Black Republican" Lincoln would do all he could to abolish slavery. The Republicans' victory signaled that the Democrats' control over the presidency and Congress was ending, and their dominance of the Supreme Court would soon follow. Because the Union was no more than a compact among sovereign states, proslavery leaders contended, state conventions or legislatures could vote to withdraw from it. Secessionists portrayed their cause as the true heir to the American Revolution's revolt against tyranny and the proper response to Republicans' abandonment of the Framers' constitutional guarantees to slave owners. The only course left was to form a new nation dedicated to slavery and states' rights.

> Deep South states bolt from the Union, and the Republican Party rejects compromise.

South Carolina's secessionists hoped to force other southern states to declare their slave-state loyalties and forswear sectional reconciliation. The response was mixed. State conventions in the Deep South passed secession ordinances, and by February 1861, six states—Georgia, Florida, Alabama, Mississippi, Louisiana, and Texas—had joined South Carolina to form the Confederate States of America (see Map 12.4). Convened in Montgomery, Alabama, the delegates drafted a constitution little different from that of the United States with a few telling exceptions: It declared the Confederacy a union of sovereign states (not of "the people"), prohibited tariffs, and protected slavery in Confederate states and territories. The delegates chose Jefferson Davis as their president, organized the Confederate legislative and executive branches to function as an independent government, and began seizing federal forts and installations in the South.

This show of southern unity was deceptive. Four states of the Upper South—Virginia, North Carolina, Tennessee, and Arkansas—rejected secession, at least for the time being. Slaves constituted less than one-third of these states' population. Many Upper South voters were "conditional Unionists" who advocated waiting to assess the new Republican administration's policies on slavery and secession. Others were nonslaveholders who had always been wary of planter domination. As the South's poor whites weighed their class interests against their sectional loyalties,

secession Formal withdrawal from the United States declared by the southern states that formed the Confederacy in 1861 but was not recognized by Unionists.

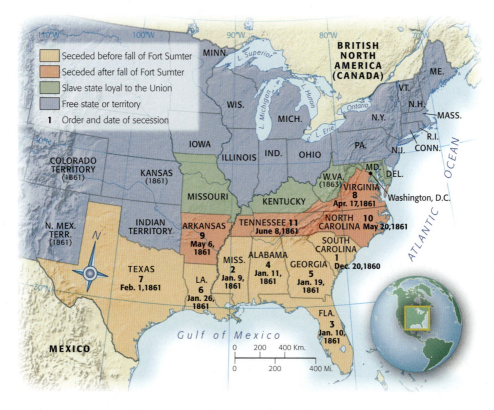

Map 12.4 The Course of Secession, 1860–1863 Secession from the Union occurred in two waves that reflected white Southerners' response to events and the regional importance of slavery to states' economies. After Lincoln's election, South Carolina passed an ordinance of secession and was soon joined by six Deep South states. Four Upper South slave states waited and seceded only after fighting began in April 1861. Four border slave states remained loyal to the Union. ▲

History without Borders

Secession

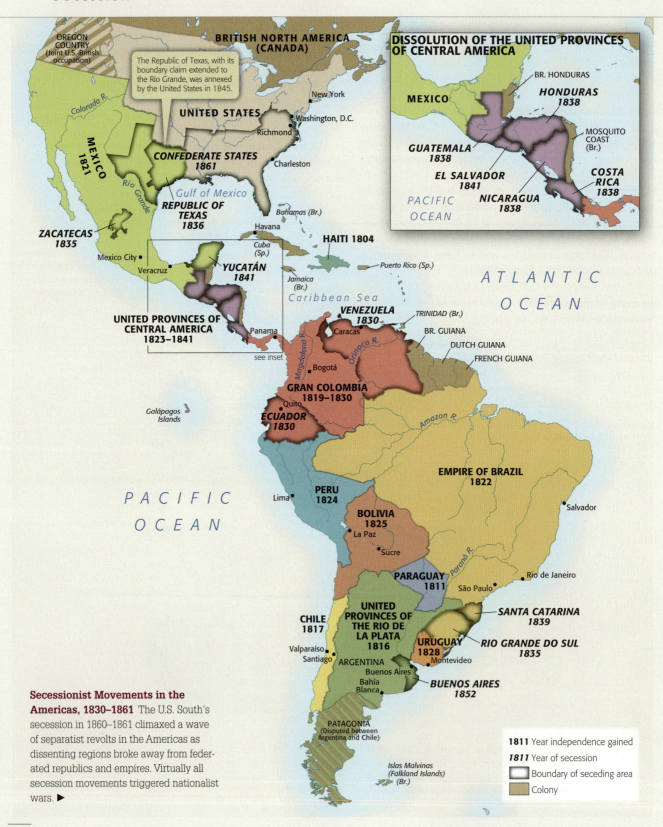

DISSOLUTION OF THE UNITED PROVINCES OF CENTRAL AMERICA

MEXICO

BR. HONDURAS

HONDURAS
1838

GUATEMALA
1838

MOSQUITO
COAST
(Br.)

EL SALVADOR
1841

COSTA
RICA
1838

NICARAGUA
1838

PACIFIC
OCEAN

OREGON
COUNTRY
(Joint U.S.-British
occupation)

BRITISH NORTH AMERICA
(CANADA)

The Republic of Texas, with its
boundary claim extended to
the Rio Grande, was annexed
by the United States in 1845.

New York

UNITED STATES

Washington, D.C.

Richmond

MEXICO
1821

Colorado R.

CONFEDERATE STATES
1861

Charleston

Rio Grande

Gulf of Mexico

REPUBLIC OF
TEXAS
1836

Bahamas (Br.)

ZACATECAS
1835

Havana

Cuba
(Sp.)

HAITI 1804

Mexico City

Veracruz

YUCATÁN
1841

Puerto Rico (Sp.)

ATLANTIC
OCEAN

Jamaica
(Br.)

Caribbean Sea

UNITED PROVINCES OF
CENTRAL AMERICA
1823–1841

Panama

see inset

VENEZUELA
1830

TRINIDAD (Br.)

Caracas

BR. GUIANA

DUTCH GUIANA

FRENCH GUIANA

Magdalena R.

Bogotá

Orinoco R.

GRAN COLOMBIA
1819–1830

Galápagos
Islands

Quito

ECUADOR
1830

Amazon R.

EMPIRE OF BRAZIL
1822

PACIFIC

OCEAN

PERU
1824

Lima

Salvador

BOLIVIA
1825

La Paz

Sucre

Paraná R.

PARAGUAY
1811

Rio de Janeiro

São Paulo

SANTA CATARINA
1839

CHILE
1817

UNITED
PROVINCES OF
THE RIO DE
LA PLATA
1816

URUGUAY
1828

RIO GRANDE DO SUL
1835

Valparaíso

Santiago

ARGENTINA

Buenos Aires

Montevideo

BUENOS AIRES
1852

Bahía
Blanca

**Secessionist Movements in the
Americas, 1830–1861** The U.S. South's
secession in 1860–1861 climaxed a wave
of separatist revolts in the Americas as
dissenting regions broke away from feder-
ated republics and empires. Virtually all
secession movements triggered nationalist
wars. ▶

PATAGONIA
(Disputed between
Argentina and Chile)

Islas Malvinas
(Falkland Islands)
(Br.)

1811 Year independence gained

1811 Year of secession

☐ Boundary of seceding area

▨ Colony

Alfredo Dagli Orti/The Art Archive at Art Resource, NY

Garibaldi in Two Worlds Italian nationalist hero Giuseppe Garibaldi fought for republican self-government on both sides of the Atlantic. Committed to national self-determination, Garibaldi veered between supporting secession movements in Brazil (1835) and the Papal States (1848) and fighting wars of national consolidation in Uruguay (1842) and, most famously, Italy. By conquering Sicily in 1860, Garibaldi and his Redshirt army helped create a consolidated Kingdom of Italy free from foreign control. When the U.S. Civil War broke out, President Lincoln unsuccessfully offered Garibaldi a generalship in the Union army. ▲

WOJTEK RADWANSKI/AFP/Getty Images

The Confederate Flag Abroad Despite its removal from South Carolina's capitol building in 2015, the Confederate battle flag remains embroiled in controversy at home and abroad. It flies around the world, sometimes expressing white supremacist ideology (as with neo-Nazi groups in Germany) and other times symbolizing defiance by ethnic or regional minorities. In this photo, a Polish far-right activist holds a Confederate flag and a "White Pride" banner during a July 2015 demonstration against accepting over two thousand Middle Eastern immigrants to Poland. In recent years, Confederate flags have also been displayed by pro-Russian separatists in Ukraine. ▲

The slaveholding South's strategy of secession was not unique. The mid-nineteenth century was a global age of nationalism in which popular fervor was mobilized not only to incite democratic revolutions or unify small states into national governments but also to carve new nations out of centralized republics or monarchies through acts of secession. In the latter category, the European revolutions of 1848 featured revolts intended to establish Hungary and Poland as independent nations throwing off Austrian and Russian imperial rule. But the closest parallels to the U.S. secession crisis were the separatist movements that threatened new nations in Latin America.

After winning their independence from Spain and Portugal by the 1820s, many Latin American nations adopted federal-style governments, often modeled on the United States, to forge national unity out of local differences. Like the young United States of America, these countries were "unions" that had not yet become tightly knit nations. Some, like the United

Mexican States and the United States of Colombia, copied the name of their northern neighbor, and they experienced many of the same sectional tensions. Disputes over tariffs, political representation at the capital, church-state relations, and powers of national versus local government provoked regional secession movements and wars to suppress such revolts in Brazil, Argentina, Colombia, and other new Latin American republics.

Next door to the United States, the republic of Mexico faced a series of regional revolts in the antebellum decades. The struggle for Texan independence was, from the viewpoint of the Mexican government, one of several linked secession movements. In the mid-1830s, after President Santa Anna suspended the federal constitution, enlarged his powers, and decreed new local taxes, the Mexican states of Yucatan, Zacatecas, and the section of the state of Coahuila known as Tejas declared themselves in revolt. The Texans' secession movement, which was led by transplanted white Southerners, set a precedent that South Carolinians followed twenty-five years later.

The Yucatan Republic maintained its fragile independence for more than a decade before internal divisions and lack of foreign support caused its demise. To suppress a revolt by native Mayan peoples, Yucatan's leaders sought an alliance with the United States during

the U.S.–Mexican War, but Congress declined to take on another war. In desperation, Yucatan secessionists agreed in 1848 to rejoin Mexico in exchange for military assistance against the Mayans.

Mexico's violent divisions persisted to the late 1850s, when a revolt by conservatives who were outraged by a new republican constitution of 1857 that separated church and state ousted Mexico's reform administration and forced its leader, Benito Juárez, into internal exile. The resulting civil war (the Reform War of 1857–1861) overlapped the U.S. secession struggle. North of the border, president-elect Lincoln supported Juárez and likened seceding Southern slaveholders to the Mexican usurpers. Both groups, he declared, were attempting to destroy legitimate republican constitutions through illegal means, substituting bullets for ballots.

Critical Thinking Questions

▶ How was the secession of the U.S. South in 1860–1861 similar or different from other secessionist movements in the age of nationalism?

▶ Why did nineteenth-century secession movements nearly always result in civil wars?

Go to MindTap® to engage with an interactive version of **History without Borders: Secession.** Learn from an interactive map, view related video, and respond to critical thinking questions.

Crittenden Compromise
Eleventh-hour proposal to stop secession and prevent sectional war that Republicans rejected because it allowed slavery in future territories.

Fort Sumter Federal fort in harbor of Charleston, South Carolina, whose bombardment by Confederates began the Civil War in April 1861.

border states Four slave states in the Upper South—Maryland, Delaware, Kentucky, and Missouri—that remained in the Union after secession.

many hesitated or even opposed secession. Whites in Kentucky and Missouri had additional reasons to waver, for if a sectional war followed secession, it would divide their families and almost surely be fought on their soil. Before Lincoln took office in March 1861, secession was a half-successful revolution but a determined one.

At first, Lincoln considered secession a bluff staged by the South's proslavery minority to gain concessions from the national government. As the breakaway movement gathered momentum, Lincoln marshaled arguments against it. The Union, he asserted, was not a revocable agreement among the states but a perpetual trust inherited from the Founders' generation. Secession violated the nation's fundamental right to ensure its survival, a task that was especially critical, Lincoln believed, because the failure of the U.S. experiment in self-government would set back the global spread of democracy for a century.

In the midst of the secession crisis, Senator John J. Crittenden of Kentucky proposed a compromise intended to prevent further defections and perhaps lure back the seceded states. Its main provision extended the old Missouri Compromise line to the Pacific and declared all present or future territories above the line free and those below it open to slavery. Lincoln, not yet sworn in as president, urged Republicans to oppose the **Crittenden Compromise** of 1861. To accept it would be to renounce the antiextension platform on which he had just been elected. Lincoln was willing to concede defeat in New Mexico, whose territorial legislature had approved black and Indian bondage, but he stood adamantly against proslavery expansionism in the Caribbean. Recalling William Walker, he warned that Crittenden's proposal would encourage "filibustering for all South of us," including Nicaragua and Cuba, and "making slave states of it." The prospect of slavery expanding outside U.S. borders, not its extension within, became the final obstacle to negotiating a halt to secession. Lacking the Republicans' support, Crittenden's proposal died in Congress. Whether proslavery extremists would have accepted it is debatable, but its failure guaranteed that the nation would be divided into contending governments when Lincoln assumed office.

12-5d "And the War Came"

After the lower-South states seceded, two questions remained: Would the remaining slave states leave the Union? Would secession lead to war? The second was answered first.

> Confederates fire the first shot when the Union tries to provision Fort Sumter.

In his inaugural address of March 1861, Lincoln appealed to Southerners' unionist sentiments and pledged not to touch slavery in states where it existed. While committed to maintaining federal authority over the South, Lincoln sought to avoid war by adopting a cautious strategy. No federal troops were sent to punish secessionists or to collect tariffs. Instead, Lincoln resolved to hold onto key forts off the coast of the rebellious states.

At **Fort Sumter** in Charleston harbor, the decisive collision occurred. When federal soldiers stationed there ran low on supplies, Lincoln notified South Carolina authorities that he would dispatch a relief ship to off-load food but no guns or ammunition. Faced with the choice of accepting this show of federal authority or attacking the fort, the Confederates chose war. On April 12, the Confederate government ordered local commanders to compel the surrender of Fort Sumter. Lincoln had maneuvered Confederates into firing the first shot, which signaled to Unionists that the South's action was a rebellion against legitimate national authority. "Both parties deprecated war," he later wrote, "but one of them would *make* war rather than let the nation survive, and the other would *accept* war rather than let it perish, and the war came." After two days of relentless bombardment, the federal garrison surrendered Fort Sumter. Miraculously, no soldiers were killed in the battle that began the bloodiest war in American history.

In response to the attack on Fort Sumter, Lincoln called for seventy-five thousand Union militiamen and began mobilizing the North for war. Political leaders in the Upper South, who had been waiting to see whether Lincoln would force secessionists to return, now cast their lots. During the next two months, four more slave states seceded to join the Confederacy: Virginia, Arkansas, Tennessee, and North Carolina. In recognition of Virginia's importance, the Confederate capital was moved to Richmond. Four **border states**—Maryland, Delaware, Kentucky, and Missouri—remained in the Union, held there by intense political pressure and, in the case of Missouri and Maryland, the firm presence of federal troops. By the summer of 1861, the two sides were formed to settle the issues of slavery and secession on the battlefield.

12-5e Slavery, Nationalism, and Civil War in Global Perspective

Focusing on the raging domestic conflict over slavery in the territories helps explain the nation's descent into civil war, but seen from a global perspective, this outcome was highly unusual. Popular opposition to slavery mounted throughout the nineteenth-century Western world, but it led to civil war almost uniquely in the United States. Besides Haiti, where the abolition of slavery had merged into a war for colonial independence, all other slave

> The South's commitment to slavery prevents peaceful emancipation, and the cotton boom feeds Southern nationalism.

societies in the Americas abolished slavery peaceably through national laws or imperial decrees in the 1800s.

In an age of intense nationalist feeling, slavery's entanglement with rival definitions of nationhood dramatically raised the stakes of the U.S. conflict. Lincoln's insistence that the Union could not endure half-slave and half-free represented an ambitious program to enact the Founders' ideals and make freedom national. Meanwhile, Southern states opted to form an independent nation in 1860–1861 to protest Republicans' "betrayal" of a tradition of compromise going back to the 1787 Constitution. Both the North's consolidating version of nationalism and the South's breakaway version followed transatlantic precedents. The Republicans' push for uniformity under the central government echoed contemporary national unification movements in Italy and Germany. In contrast, Southern proslavery spokesmen resorted to a familiar contemporary strategy by seceding from the federal union. On both sides of the Atlantic, secession movements led to wars between competing national claimants.

Only in the United States, however, was slavery at the root of the nation's splintering. In the face of growing antislavery sentiment, Southern leaders were fiercely determined to preserve their slave system. Unlike European colonists in the West Indies and slave owners in South American nations, the South's planters rejected plans for gradual or **compensated emancipation** and looked toward the nation's expanding frontier to extend the plantation system. Because slavery was highly concentrated in one U.S. region (unlike in Brazil, for example), Southern politicians formed a powerful sectional bloc against Republicans' efforts to contain the slave system. Also, because of the booming global demand for cotton, Southern elites wielded enough economic clout on the world market to envision the Confederacy as a successful independent nation. When Northerners disputed the South's right to quit the Union, the sectional conflict rooted in slavery exploded into civil war.

compensated emancipation
Process to end slavery by reimbursing owners after slaves were freed by manumission or legal decree.

Summary

In the 1850s, the expansion of slavery westward and its potential extension south of U.S. borders triggered a national crisis. Inflamed by national pride, most Americans favored spreading their nation's territory across the continent and its influence around the globe. Yet national expansion added fuel to the sectional rivalry over slavery. The nation's rapid westward push set off a prolonged debate over extension of the South's slave system into newly acquired territories. Involvements abroad provided no respite. American reactions to the European revolutions of 1848 reflected domestic divisions over slavery, and the nation's threatened movement south into Cuba and Central America injected the slavery question directly into foreign affairs.

The U.S. acquisition of California and New Mexico following the war with Mexico brought the slavery issue to center stage. Most white Northerners were not abolitionists; they refused to attack slavery in the South or support African Americans' push for racial equality in the North. But northern free soilers clashed with militant slaveholders over western lands, which both sides saw as the key to economic opportunity and the nation's future. Political divisions heightened sectional tensions as new northern-dominated coalitions such as the Republicans and the Know-Nothings appeared in the wake of the Whig Party's collapse. The Compromise of 1850, the Kansas-Nebraska Act (1854), and the Supreme Court's Dred Scott Decision (1857) failed to resolve the territorial dispute. In Kansas, guerrilla fighting between free-soil and proslavery partisans presaged a national civil war. John Brown's raid at Harpers Ferry raised the specter of abolitionist-inspired slave insurrections in the South itself.

In 1860, slaveholders' demand for federal guarantees of slavery in the territories split the Democratic Party, giving the presidency to the Republicans' Abraham Lincoln. Seeing that the control over the national government they had exerted since Presidents Jefferson and Jackson was now over, proslavery leaders resorted to a common practice in federative nations of the Americas: They seceded. As happened elsewhere, secession led to armed conflict, but only in the United States did the struggle over slavery provide the spark for secession and civil war. Whose vision of nationalism prevailed—the Union's or the Confederacy's—and the fate of the root cause of division, slavery itself, would be decided on the battlefield.

‹Thinking Back, *Looking Forward*›

As you review, consider how the contest over slavery in the territories culminated two nineteenth-century topics discussed earlier: continental expansion and the growing debate over slavery and race. How did westward expansion heighten tensions between free and slave labor in America's "empire of liberty"?

How was U.S. abolitionism connected to freedom struggles in other nations? Why was antislavery such an explosive cause in the United States? Did the outbreak of Civil War mean that the U.S. republican experiment had failed? In the next chapters, look for the consequences of a nationalist war rooted in slavery.

How did the Civil War play out as a war of competing nationalisms? As a struggle over freedom and equality?

To make your study concrete, review the timeline and reflect on the entries there. Think about their causes, consequences, and connections. How do they fit with global trends?

Additional Resources

Books

Anbinder, Tyler. *Nativism and Slavery: The Northern Know-Nothings and the Politics of the 1850s*. New York and Oxford: Oxford University Press, 1992. ▶ Explanation of the rapid rise and fall of the influential anti-immigrant political party.

Fleche, Andre M. *The Revolution of 1861: The American Civil War in the Age of Nationalist Conflict*. Chapel Hill: University of North Carolina Press, 2012. ▶ Placement of the divergence of northern and southern nationalism in a transatlantic context, including the revolutions of 1848 in Europe.

Foner, Eric. *Gateway to Freedom: The Hidden History of the Underground Railroad*. New York: W. W. Norton, 2015. ▶ Presentation of fresh evidence to reconstruct the network of black and white abolitionists who assisted fugitive slaves.

Freehling, William W. *The Road to Disunion: Secessionists Triumphant, 1854–1861*. New York and Oxford: Oxford University Press, 2007. ▶ A powerful analysis of how secessionist fire eaters overcame Upper South-Lower South divisions.

Gienapp, William. *The Origins of the Republican Party, 1852–1856*. New York and Oxford: Oxford University Press, 1987. ▶ A comprehensive history of the party's rapid rise.

Horwitz, Tony. *Midnight Rising: John Brown and the Raid That Sparked the Civil War*. New York: Henry Holt, 2011. ▶ A riveting account of the raid and its background, including a complex portrait of Brown.

May, Robert E. *Manifest Destiny's Underworld: Filibustering in Antebellum America*. Chapel Hill and London: University of North Carolina Press, 2002. ▶ An eye-opening history of nearly forgotten expansionist adventures.

Potter, David M. *The Impending Crisis, 1848–1861*. New York: Harper & Row, 1976. ▶ The best single-volume overview of the coming of the Civil War.

Stampp, Kenneth M., ed. *The Causes of the Civil War*. New York: Simon and Schuster, 1991. ▶ Indispensable collection of documents, essays, and interpretations.

Wiley, Peter Booth. *Yankees in the Land of the Gods: Commodore Perry and the Opening of Japan*. New York: Viking, 1990. ▶ A colorful account of the historic encounter of East and West.

Go to the MindTap® for **Global Americans** to access the full version of select books from this Additional Resources section.

Websites

Brady-Handy Collection of Photographs, Library of Congress. (http://www.loc.gov/pictures/collection/brhc/) ▶ Archive of ten thousand photographs of political and social leaders of the 1850s and the Civil War era.

Civil War Primary Sources. (http://www.civilwar.org/education/history/primarysources/#photos) ▶ Source of political speeches, acts of Congress, and party platforms of the 1850s as well as secession ordinances of the thirteen Confederate states.

Harpers Ferry National Historic Site. (http://www.nps.gov/hafe/index.htm) ▶ Gateway website for the well-preserved West Virginia town with exhibits on John Brown, munitions technology, and antebellum African American life.

Library of Congress Primary Documents in American History: *Dred Scott v. Sandford*. **(http://www.loc.gov/rr/program/bib/ourdocs/DredScott.html)** ▶ The text of the 1857 Supreme Court decision and dozens of related primary sources.

Lincoln-Douglas Debates of 1858. (http://lincoln.lib.niu.edu/lincolndouglas) ▶ Complete text of the seven debates of the Illinois senatorial campaign plus newspaper commentary.

Continue exploring online through MindTap®**, where you can:**
- **Assess your knowledge with the Chapter Test**
- **Watch historical videos related to the chapter**
- **Further your understanding with interactive maps and timelines**

Expansion, Slavery, and the Coming of the Civil War

1846

August

Wilmot Proviso opens congressional debate over slavery in territories acquired through U.S.–Mexican War.

1848

February

Republican revolution erupts in France and spreads antimonarchy uprisings across Europe.

April

Revolutionary government in France abolishes slavery in French colonies.

August

Free-Soil Party is formed to ban slavery from U.S. territories.

September

First wave of German "Forty-Eighters" arrives in United States as German revolutions are suppressed.

November

Whig candidate Zachary Taylor is elected president.

1849

December

California applies for admission to statehood.

1850

September

Congressional compromise admits California as free state and enacts new Fugitive Slave Law.

1851

September

Filibusterer Narciso López is captured in Cuba and executed.

December

Defeated Hungarian nationalist Louis Kossuth lands in the U.S. to seek official support.

1852

March

Uncle Tom's Cabin is published and becomes a best-selling antislavery novel in the United States and Europe.

November

Democrat Franklin Pierce is elected president.

December

Louis Napoleon declares himself Emperor Napoleon III of France, signaling end of 1848 Revolutions in Europe.

1853

July

U.S. Commodore Matthew Perry sails into Tokyo Bay to force open trade with Japan.

December

Gadsden Purchase adds territory from Mexico for a transcontinental railroad.

1854

March

In Treaty of Kanagawa, Japan agrees to open specified ports to the United States and other Western nations.

May

Kansas-Nebraska Act rekindles political controversy over slavery in the territories.

FORCING SLAVERY DOWN THE THROAT OF A FREESOILER

July

Republican Party forms political coalition in opposition to Kansas-Nebraska Act.

August

U.S. negotiates annexation treaty with King Kamehameha III of Hawai'i, but it goes unsigned.

October

U.S. foreign ministers draw up Ostend Manifesto urging purchase or forced cession of Cuba from Spain.

November

Know-Nothing movement organizes nationally as the American Party after winning local elections.

1855

January

New York company completes Panama Railroad crossing the isthmus between the Atlantic and Pacific Oceans.

October

William Walker's filibustering expedition overthrows Nicaragua's government.

1856

May

Massachusetts Senator Charles Sumner attacked in Congress after speech against extending slavery to Kansas.

Guerrilla war rages in Kansas territory between free-state and proslavery partisans.

October

Arrow War (Second Opium War) opens as England and France attack China, resulting in U.S. access to additional Chinese ports.

November

Democrat James Buchanan is elected president.

1857

March

Supreme Court issues *Dred Scott* decision permitting slavery in territories and denying blacks U.S. citizenship.

December

Mexican civil war (Reform War) begins over new republican constitution and laws separating church and state.

1858

August–October

Abraham Lincoln and Stephen Douglas debate free soil versus popular sovereignty in the Illinois race for U.S. Senate.

1859

October

John Brown attacks arsenal at Harpers Ferry, Virginia, in an attempt to spark a slave insurrection.

1860

April

Deep South's demand to guarantee slavery in the territories splits the Democratic Party.

September

Filibuster William Walker is executed in Honduras.

November

Republican candidate Lincoln is elected president in sectional four-party election.

December

South Carolina convention approves ordinance of secession from the Union.

1861

January

Last-minute Crittenden Compromise fails to pass Congress.

February

Six Deep South slave states join South Carolina in seceding from the Union, forming the Confederate States of America.

April

Civil War erupts when Confederates bombard Fort Sumter off South Carolina coast.

April–June

Four additional slave states join the Confederacy.

13 The American Civil War

1861–1865

In 1863, William Andrew Jackson toured England, Scotland, and Wales, giving vivid testimony about slave life in the Confederacy to help rally British public opinion behind the Union.

L ike many Americans, William Andrew Jackson, a twenty-nine-year-old slave from Virginia, was transformed by the Civil War. Born in the countryside, he was taken to Richmond and hired out by his master, eventually as coachman for Confederate President Jefferson Davis. Davis's slaves constantly talked about fleeing bondage, Jackson recalled, making sure that "when the time came they would be found ready." Jackson seized his chance in April 1862. When Davis left Richmond to confer with his generals, Jackson escaped to nearby Union camps, where he provided details of Richmond's fortifications and Confederate troop movements.

As Jackson made his way north, he became a celebrity. "Jefferson Davis's Coachman" was profiled in *Harper's Weekly* and the New York press. Literate and an eloquent speaker, he was, said the *New York Tribune,* as "black as a Congo negro" yet "much more intelligent than a good many white folks." Pressed for details about the Davis family, Jackson revealed that Varina Davis, the Confederate first lady, lacked faith in the Confederacy, which she privately declared was "about played out."

New York: Harper & Brothers, June 7, 1862.

Varina Davis "used to talk a great deal about England and France helping them [the Confederates]," Jackson recalled, and in the fall of 1862 he sailed to England to prevent such an outcome. With letters of introduction from abolitionist William Lloyd Garrison, Jackson spoke at public meetings in Britain, giving vivid testimony about slave life and stressing that the Confederates were fighting to preserve slavery, not simply to win independence. In 1863, he toured England, Scotland, and Wales as an agent of the Union and Emancipation Society, which had organized to support President Lincoln's Emancipation Proclamation. Jackson's campaigning and that of other former slaves on tour helped rally British public opinion behind the Union.

Jackson's transatlantic journey from the stables of the Confederate White House to speakers' platforms in British lecture halls was unique. Yet his experience illustrates two of the Civil War's most far-reaching developments: the way that the South's slaves and their northern allies seized wartime opportunities to achieve emancipation and the way that the war threatened to escalate from a domestic dispute into an international conflict. Union leaders announced that their objective was to restore the Union, but a year and a half into the war, President Lincoln declared his intention to free secessionists' slaves. Emancipation had enormous implications for the war's outcome overseas as well as at home because the political leaders of Britain and France, although eager to support the South's independence, were reluctant to defend slavery, having abolished it in their own colonies decades earlier.

The end of slavery in the United States and the struggle over foreign intervention were only two of the wartime developments that wrought huge changes in American life. In the North, the demands of war

How do William Andrew Jackson's experiences as coachman to Jefferson Davis and later rallying Union support in the United Kingdom illustrate the role of emancipation in the war's outcome both domestically and overseas?

Go to MindTap® to watch a video on Jackson and learn how his story relates to the themes of this chapter.

production boosted industrial capitalism, and in both sections of the divided nation, the reach of central governments expanded. The war itself, begun as a gentlemanly affair between West Point generals, devolved into fierce campaigns in which powerful new cannons crumbled masonry forts and marching armies destroyed farms and homes. When the Union finally prevailed in 1865, all Americans faced adjusting to personal traumas and the social and economic transformations brought by war.

The American Civil War was not the only mid-nineteenth century nationalist conflict between centralizers and secessionists, republicans and aristocrats. The North's aim to unify the states under the national government and the southern states' resistance aligned with similar struggles in Latin America and Europe. In Germany and Italy, centralized nation-states replaced weak federations and alliances between dukes or kings. In Mexico and South America, national governments triumphed by tightening constitutional controls. The creation of new national governments often coincided with movements to end forced labor and extend political participation to common people. Almost everywhere, entrenched elites opposed democratic changes, and clashes over the meaning of freedom and nationhood were settled on the battlefield.

13-1
Beginning of the War, 1861

This Union propaganda map, published in 1861, shows General Winfield Scott's Anaconda Plan to surround the Confederacy by land and sea and squeeze it into submission. Notice how Georgia's cotton factories close down and Mississippi slaves rise up, "burning massa out." Northern farms prosper while North Carolinians are reduced to eating rosin (cakes of pine resin).

How does the map envision the Anaconda Plan's operations and its success? How are states in the Upper South portrayed? ▶

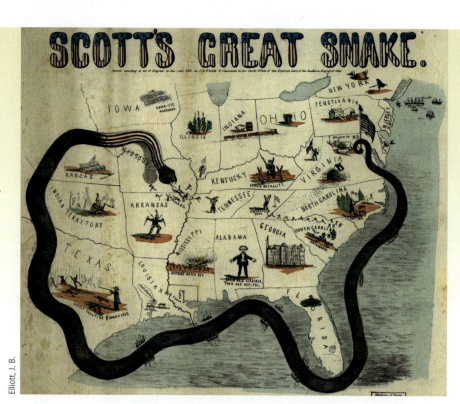

Elliott, J. B.

Each side in the Civil War predicted a quick and easy victory, the Union by penetrating and blockading the South, the Confederacy by repulsing the invaders. The Union's superior industrial and labor force resources promised an important material edge. Confederates, however, counted on their fighting spirit and the advantages of defending their homeland. Linked to Europe by ties of trade and national self-interest, the South also hoped to secure an alliance with Britain and France that would tip the war scales in its favor. Neither side was prepared for combat. The Confederacy lacked an army and navy, and the regular Union army totaled only seventeen thousand men, most of whom were deployed on the western frontier. It took time and effort to mobilize for the war. In the meantime, the first major battle at Bull Run and the struggle over the allegiance of border states such as Missouri demonstrated that the war would be neither brief nor painless.

☞ As you read, consider the resources, war aims, and strategies of the Union and the Confederacy. What were each side's strengths and weaknesses?

13-1a Mobilization and Strategy

President Lincoln's call for seventy-five thousand volunteers after the attack on Fort Sumter spurred both sides to action. Northern politicians

Planning a war to restore the Union, the North invades while the South defends.

closed ranks behind the Union. Stephen Douglas, Lincoln's northern opponent in the 1860 presidential election, pledged his support, as did many prowar Democrats. A quarter of a million New Yorkers attended a patriotic rally in Union Square, the largest public gathering in North America up to that time. In the South, conditional Unionists in Virginia, North Carolina, Tennessee, and Arkansas responded to Lincoln's call for troops by siding with the Confederacy. They joined earlier secessionists at enlistment rallies and elaborate balls held to celebrate departing troops.

Both sides invoked the nation's history and principles to justify their cause. Northerners declared that Union victory would preserve the Founders' legacy and promote democracy around the world. "If we should fail," one Ohio soldier wrote, "the onward march of Liberty in the Old World will be retarded at least a century, and Monarchs, Kings and Aristocrats will be more powerful against their subjects than ever." In contrast, Confederates likened their cause to the patriots of 1776 who had declared their independence against a tyrannical king. A young Virginia officer wrote his mother that the North's "war of subjugation against the South" was just like "England's war upon the colonies."

At the war's outset, Lincoln and Congress emphasized that their goal was to restore the Union. They viewed the Confederacy not as a sovereign nation but as a conspiracy of states in rebellion against the national government. Taking a global view, Lincoln felt a kinship with advocates of national unification in Mexico, where President Benito Juárez had just defeated a conservative revolt, and in Italy, where a patchwork of kingdoms and states was coalescing through diplomacy and war into a unified constitutional monarchy. Impressed by the Italian nationalist hero Giuseppe Garibaldi, Lincoln offered him a generalship, but Garibaldi refused because the Union was not committed to abolishing slavery.

For Lincoln, preserving the Union required leaving slavery untouched. On the day before Lincoln's inauguration, Czar Alexander II, intent on modernizing Russia after its humiliating defeat by the French, British, and Ottoman Turks in the Crimean War (1853–1856, see also figure 13.2 on page 396), freed Russia's 23 million serfs by edict. Lincoln applauded the Czar's action but rejected similar steps against U.S. slavery. Most Northerners were not abolitionists, and many were Democrats who might withhold their support if the war targeted slavery. Pressing the issue might also drive slave owners in the border states to the Confederacy. In his July 4, 1861, message to Congress, Lincoln reaffirmed that he had "no purpose, directly or indirectly, to interfere with slavery in the states where it exists." Congress agreed.

Lincoln's assurances meant little to Confederates, who sought independence without interference. To fend off invasion and blockade, Confederate leaders planned a defensive war. This strategy had several advantages. Confederate forces could rely on local knowledge and assistance to outmaneuver invaders. Defense required fewer soldiers than occupation, and Southerners had only to hold on while their troops won enough military victories or Northerners grew weary enough to call the war off. Prolonging the war, however, risked stretching Confederate resources to the breaking point (see Figure 13.1).

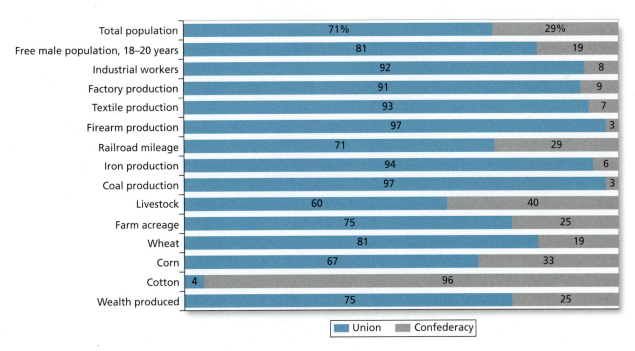

Figure 13.1 Comparison of Union and Confederate Resources, 1861 At the start of the war, the Union enjoyed huge quantitative advantages in population, industry, railroad mileage, and wealth. Confederates had the advantage of fighting a defensive war and relying on slave labor to sustain domestic production while white men fought. The South's strategists believed that a short war might give the Union insufficient time to mobilize its resources and that a prolonged one would allow Confederates to rely on the global demand for cotton to attract funds and foreign support. ▲

Battle of Bull Run First major battle of the Civil War, fought in northern Virginia in July 1861, in which Union troops' panicked retreat gave Confederates a decisive victory.

King Cotton Diplomacy Confederate strategy of withholding cotton from Britain and France as pressure to recognize the South's independence and provide armed support.

Trent Affair Anglo-American diplomatic crisis in 1861 that was resolved peacefully after Union officials apologized for seizing Confederate envoys on a British ship in the Caribbean.

To counteract the Union's material advantages, the Confederacy hoped for European allies.

Both sides' ideas about a quick and decisive victory were tested in July 1861 when Union general Irvin McDowell marched thirty-five thousand raw recruits into Virginia. Awaiting them across a stream called Bull Run at Manassas, a railroad junction thirty miles southwest of Washington, were twenty thousand Confederates. With little expectation of bloodshed, some Washington dignitaries picnicked on a nearby hill to watch the action. The Union soldiers initially pushed back the enemy, but the Confederates, rallied by General Thomas ("Stonewall") Jackson, held firm. When Rebel reinforcements arrived by train in the middle of the battle—a first in the history of warfare—the Confederates counterattacked, and Union soldiers fled in disorganized panic, some all the way to Washington. The **Battle of Bull Run** boosted Confederates' confidence and revealed to Northerners that the war would be no afternoon picnic.

13-1b Potential European Involvement

Most nineteenth-century civil wars became international wars, and the U.S. war threatened to join the list. The nation's growing economic

{ Britain and France tilt toward the Confederacy, and the Union escapes a diplomatic crisis.

stature made it a rival that European powers would have been pleased to see splintered. Especially because the South's cotton exports were important to their economies, Britain and France leaned toward intervening on the Confederacy's behalf. France also sought to regain a New World empire in Mexico. In December 1861, Britain, France, and Spain sent troops to collect debts owed by Mexico's beleaguered liberal government under President Juárez. Britain and Spain soon withdrew their forces, but Napoleon III, who aimed to install a Catholic monarch beholden to France, sent additional soldiers.

Europeans held conflicting attitudes toward the Civil War. Although British mill owners depended on cotton, factory workers and abolitionists sympathized with the Union and the idea of free labor. Writing in exile from London, Karl Marx predicted that the defeat of slave owners would help liberate workers everywhere. Meanwhile, Britain's landed elites, like Europe's ruling classes generally, identified with wealthy southern planters and opposed democratic reforms. National self-interest influenced European policies more than public opinion. But before

allying with the Confederacy, European rulers wanted assurance that it was a viable nation. They also eyed each other with suspicion, worrying that intervention might drag them into a distant war to the benefit of rivals. Napoleon III resolved not to recognize the secessionists unless Britain did.

Thus, the Confederates' diplomatic objective became securing Britain's recognition, which Union leaders aimed to prevent. If Britain allied with the South, it could destroy the Union navy, supply the Confederacy with war materiel, and open a second fighting front on the Canadian border. Cotton was the Confederacy's primary lure. In the war's first year, Southerners imposed a voluntary embargo, gambling that withholding cotton would increase pressure in Britain on their behalf—a strategy that became known as "**King Cotton Diplomacy**."

Union leaders sought to stop Confederate overseas trade entirely. A few days after Fort Sumter fell, Lincoln proclaimed a naval blockade of Confederate ports, opening a prolonged diplomatic controversy with Britain. Under international law, the blockade implied that the Confederacy was a sovereign state free to trade with neutral nations like Britain and France—exactly what the Union was trying to prevent. Union leaders were fortunate that Britain did not challenge the blockade directly but relied on Confederate ships to carry goods. Initially, most Confederate merchant ships passed through unscathed, but by 1863, the blockade tightened enough to deter Rebel runners.

Long before that, the South's cotton strategy faltered. British merchants warehoused a surplus of cotton when the war began, and a year later, when the cotton famine loomed, they developed alternative supply sources. The South reversed its embargo policy in 1863, but it was too late. Meanwhile, European trade with the North increased, and poor grain harvests in England meant that Britain needed the North's wheat even more than the South's cotton.

Despite the blockade and the cotton embargo's failure, a brisk trade flourished in arms and ships between the British and the Confederates. British shipyards supplied powerful commerce raiders such as the *Alabama* to the Rebel navy, which used them to sink Yankee merchant ships on the high seas. In November 1861, a confrontation in international waters came close to sparking an Anglo-U.S. war. A federal warship stopped the British mail packet *Trent* as it left Havana carrying Confederate envoys James Mason and John Slidell, who were bound for London and Paris. The two diplomats were removed and imprisoned in Boston, outraging British officials, who began preparing for war. Cooler heads prevailed when U.S. secretary of state Seward acknowledged that the Union captain had acted without authorization, and President Lincoln ordered the diplomats' release. The **Trent Affair,** the first of several war scares with Britain, blew over, and the Rebels resumed their mission to secure British and French support.

Minard, Charles Joseph, 1781–1870.

King Cotton Diplomacy Fails

These maps created by French cartographer Charles Joseph Minard in 1866 show the dramatic shift in cotton imports to Europe before (1858) and during (1864) the Civil War. The South's voluntary embargo and the North's coastal blockade brought the huge flow of cotton from the United States (blue band) to a virtual halt. To compensate, England and France developed new sources of supply in India and China (orange band), Egypt and Syria (brown band), and Brazil and the West Indies (lavender band). ◀

13-1c Struggle for the Border States

After Fort Sumter and the secession of four upper-South slave states, the fate of four remaining slave states— Maryland, Delaware, Kentucky, and Missouri—remained undecided. Gaining these states would shift badly needed resources to the Confederacy and give it strategic advantages. Lincoln viewed holding the border states, especially Kentucky, as key to Union victory. "I think to lose Kentucky is nearly to lose the whole game," he fretted.

> The Union retains four border slave states by various strategies.

The centerpiece of Lincoln's border-state strategy was his emphasis on restoring the Union, not attacking slavery. Otherwise, the president varied his tactics according to local conditions. Tiny Delaware, with few slaveholders, was safe for the Union, but in neighboring Maryland, slaveholders and pro-Confederate sympathizers were a serious threat. In mid-April 1861, a Baltimore mob attacked a Massachusetts regiment en route to Washington, killing four soldiers. Acting swiftly, Lincoln placed the state legislature under military watch, suspended the writ of **habeas corpus** (which prevented arbitrary arrest and detention), and put pro-Confederate officials behind bars. One case was appealed to the Supreme Court's chief justice, Roger Taney, who in *ex parte Merryman* (1861) declared that only Congress could suspend habeas corpus. Lincoln ignored the ruling, outraging but neutralizing dissenters in the North.

Whereas Maryland was saved for the Union by force, Kentucky was won by restraint. In the native state of both Lincoln and Jefferson Davis, the conflict became a "brothers' war" that divided family members. Kentucky's officials attempted to remain neutral, threatening to turn against whichever side sent an army across its borders. The federal army shrewdly outwaited its foe. In September 1861, a Confederate army seized the heights commanding the Mississippi River at Columbus, Kentucky. The state legislature denounced the "invaders" and invited Union troops to drive them out. Kentucky officially became a Union state, although the Confederates also claimed it and recruited soldiers there.

A more complex and drawn-out series of events took place in Missouri, where the pro-Confederate state militia and German-American Unionists from St. Louis squared off and regular Union and Confederate armies massed for a showdown. In August 1861, the Confederates under General Sterling Price pushed northward, claiming half the state. John C. Frémont, the Union's local commander, drove Price back but could not control the feuding population. For much of the war, bands of **guerrillas** roamed Missouri, "bushwhacking" (ambushing) enemy patrols, terrorizing neighborhoods, and carrying on local feuds. In the pro-Confederate gang of William Quantrill, from whom postwar outlaws Frank and Jesse James learned their trade, guerrilla tactics descended into robbery and wanton killing.

habeas corpus The right of an arrested person to be brought before a judge or into court.

guerrillas Armed bands of civilians or irregular combatants rampant in Civil War border states and Appalachia who attacked soldiers and civilians.

West Virginia New Union state created when pro-Union counties of western Virginia separated from Confederate Virginia under protection of occupying federal troops.

Some states that were firmly committed to the Union or Confederacy divided geographically. In the backcountry of eastern Tennessee and western Virginia, nonslaveholding whites sabotaged Confederate operations and fought Rebel guerrillas. In the summer of 1861, the Union army cleared Confederate forces from western Virginia. Protected by a strong federal presence, local officials seceded from Virginia and entered the Union as the state of **West Virginia** in 1863. In contrast, the southern counties of Ohio, Indiana, and Illinois, where many migrants from Tennessee and Kentucky resided, became hotbeds of resistance to Union war measures. In distant California, many transplanted Southerners sided with the Confederacy. Around San Francisco Bay, Union officials foiled plots to divert shipments of California gold to Confederate coffers.

13-2
The Seesaw War, 1862

The Civil War was the first to be extensively captured by camera. Photographers accompanied the armies, and in October 1862, Mathew Brady displayed photographs of *The Dead of Antietam* at his New York City studio, including this view of slain Confederate artillerymen at Dunker Church. One reporter wrote, "Mr. Brady has done something to bring home to us the terrible reality and earnestness of war. If he has not brought bodies and laid them in our door-yards and along the streets, he has done something very like it."

What emotions did photographs of the battlefield dead evoke in viewers? How did such pictures contrast with participants' expectations of the war's fighting and outcome? ▶

Library of Congress Prints and Photographs Division Washington, D.C.[LC-DIG-cwpbh-03384]

The war's second year demonstrated that it would not be over soon. Momentum on the battlefront tilted in opposite ways in different regions. In the West, Union forces secured key areas and penetrated southward along the Mississippi River. In the East, where fighting concentrated in Virginia, Confederate generals turned back offensives by larger Union forces aiming to capture Richmond. Both sides struggled to care for the unprecedented number of sick and wounded soldiers. Only after a Confederate move northward into Maryland was thwarted did Lincoln's administration seize the initiative by shifting its strategy on slavery.

☞ As you read, look for reasons the Civil War proved to be so long and deadly. What geographic, military, and medical factors contributed to the toll?

13-2a Union Gains in the West, Confederate Victories in the East

After Bull Run, Lincoln turned to General George B. McClellan, fresh from success in western Virginia, to command of the Army of the Potomac. He had been an official U.S. military observer at the Crimean War, where he watched British and French forces practice maneuver and siege against Russia. As a northern Democrat, McClellan wanted to avoid an all-out war that might loosen the South's control over slavery. Hailed as the "Young Napoleon" by the press, McClellan

{ Lincoln and Davis split victories, but both find fighting generals.

Map 13.1 The Civil War, 1861–1862 Victories in Kentucky, Tennessee, and Missouri swung momentum in the West to the Union in 1862. Two Tennessee forts surrendered to forces led by Grant, who continued south. In the East, Confederates dominated on battlefields between Washington and Richmond. "Stonewall" Jackson outmaneuvered the federals in western Virginia and then joined Lee in the Seven Days' Battle to turn back Union forces near Richmond during McClellan's Peninsular Campaign. ▲

had all of his namesake's vanity but none of his daring. An excellent organizer, he trained the Union's new recruits into a disciplined army but hesitated to deploy it. He stalled for several months despite public clamor to march his huge army toward Richmond.

Across the Appalachians, the Union army fared better (see Map 13.1). The Mississippi River and its tributaries allowed federal troops and gunboats to penetrate the Confederacy. Lincoln also found an aggressive commander in Ulysses S. Grant. A quiet, unpretentious man, Grant was a Mexican War veteran who entered civilian life in the 1850s and struggled to earn a living. Rejoining the army when the war broke out, Grant displayed determination, calmness in battle, and grasp of military strategy. In February 1862, he coordinated a land and river campaign against Fort Henry on the Tennessee River and nearby Fort Donelson on the Cumberland River that forced the surrender of thirteen thousand Rebel soldiers. These first major Union victories boosted morale in the North and pushed the Confederates out of Kentucky and half of Tennessee.

As Grant advanced south toward Corinth, Mississippi, the Confederates launched a surprise attack in the two-day **Battle of Shiloh**, April 6 and 7, 1862. Initially driven back, the federals were reinforced by troops arriving by steamboat and recovered their ground. Shiloh introduced Americans to the bloodbath of the Civil War: More than 23,000 of the 77,000 soldiers engaged were killed or wounded. Grant's career suffered a temporary setback, but Union forces soon occupied Corinth. These victories on the Mississippi River were complemented by an attack farther south in which Union Admiral David Farragut forced the surrender of New Orleans. By the summer of 1862, only two hundred miles of the Mississippi remained in Confederate hands.

West of the Mississippi, Union forces also made gains. They chased Confederate Missourians into Arkansas, where at Pea Ridge in March 1862, they repelled a Rebel attack. Eight hundred miles farther west,

Battle of Shiloh Bloody Union victory fought in southwestern Tennessee between forces under Union general Grant and Confederate generals Johnston and Beauregard.

Confederates from Texas drove up the Rio Grande to occupy Albuquerque and Santa Fe. A band of Colorado miners who enrolled in Union regiments marched over the Rockies to confront the Texans at **Glorieta Pass** on March 26–28 and sent them homeward in retreat. This battle, combined with the advance of California volunteers eastward along the Gila River, secured Arizona and New Mexico for the Union and thwarted Confederates' hopes for an overland connection to gold and sympathizers in California.

In the compact Washington-Richmond corridor, Confederates could concentrate their forces more effectively than in the sprawling West. Against the Atlantic blockade, they unveiled a new weapon, the ironclad ram *Virginia*, rebuilt from the captured Union frigate *Merrimack*. The *Virginia* destroyed several U.S. Navy ships off Hampton Roads, Virginia, before it encountered a Union counterpart, the *Monitor* on March 8, 1862, in history's first battle between **ironclads**. The ships fought to a draw, but the *Virginia*, unable to escape to open water, was soon scuttled by the Confederates. The superior *Monitor* became the model for dozens of shallow-draft ironclads the Union used to tighten the blockade.

In April 1862, General McClellan finally advanced toward Richmond (see Map 13.1). His **Peninsular Campaign** was an elaborate offensive in which one hundred thousand federal troops were transported by ship to the peninsula between the James and York Rivers from which to fight their way to Richmond, seventy miles northwest. It took six weeks for them to reach the outskirts of Richmond, where Confederate general Joseph Johnston's men attacked, and the two armies fought to a draw in the Battle of Seven Pines (May 31–June 1). When Johnston was wounded, President Davis replaced him with General Robert E. Lee.

Born into a prominent Virginia family, Lee had served in the U.S-Mexican War and later commanded the federal troops that forced John Brown's surrender at Harpers Ferry. Although personally reserved, Lee preferred an aggressive strategy of mounting swift counterattacks wherever Union forces appeared vulnerable. Sensing McClellan's hesitation, Lee attacked the separated Union lines. For the next week, the armies fought almost daily as the unnerved McClellan retreated down the James River. The Seven Days' Battles left thirty thousand men dead or wounded. Although the Union army fought well, McClellan gave up the Peninsular Campaign and returned to Washington. Emboldened by his success, Lee moved north to attack McClellan's replacement, General John Pope. In the Second Battle of

Bull Run (August 29 and 30), Lee's nimble army isolated elements of Pope's forces and routed them. An exasperated President Lincoln removed Pope from command and, lacking alternatives, reappointed McClellan to restore the discipline and morale of the Army of the Potomac.

13-2b Death, Medical Care, and the Soldiers' Life

{ The war compels advances in medicine and nursing.

As Shiloh and the Seven Days' Battles showed, most Civil War engagements were deadly contests whose victor was determined only by which side retreated afterward. One reason for high death tolls was new weaponry to which generals were slow to adjust. Taught at West Point to concentrate foot soldiers for frontal attacks, they continued the practice even though modern rifles had greater range and accuracy than older smooth-bore muskets. Armed defenders behind earthworks or in trenches decimated lines of advancing soldiers, and their fire was often supplemented with artillery that spewed canister or grapeshot (clusters of small metal balls).

Civil War doctors refined amputation and other surgical techniques, but they could not stop infections. Disease killed twice as many soldiers as bullets. Overcrowded and unsanitary conditions in soldiers' quarters bred smallpox, dysentery, typhoid ("camp fever"), pneumonia, and malaria. The Peninsular Campaign revealed that neither side could effectively care for the wounded. Building on a report by Crimean War observers, the Union army organized an ambulance corps that became a model for all armies into the twentieth century. Away from the front, federal authorities constructed more than three hundred fifty hospitals, many in an airy pavilion style that retarded the spread of disease.

Many women seized the chance to aid the war effort by assisting sick and wounded soldiers. Northern women, already schooled in activism through temperance, abolitionist, and other reform movements, were especially well organized. They formed the rank and file of the **United States Sanitary Commission**, founded in the spring of 1861. Patterned on the British Sanitary Commission, which had improved hospital care during the Crimean War, the Commission donated blankets and medical supplies procured with funds raised by volunteers. Northern women also learned from British nurse Florence Nightingale's success in mobilizing care for the Crimean War's wounded. Over the objection of most army doctors, a corps of female nurses was added to the service. Dorothea Dix, a veteran of mental health reform, became superintendent of nurses in Washington. More than three thousand Union women worked as paid army nurses and many more, including Susie King Taylor, an escaped slave from Georgia attached

Glorieta Pass (1862) Westernmost major battle of the Civil War, in which Union soldiers drove an invading Confederate army from New Mexico Territory.

ironclads Iron-protected gunships, a key Civil War technological innovation, developed by both sides in 1862 to contest the Union's river and coastal blockade.

Peninsular Campaign (1862) Massive offensive planned by McClellan to attack Richmond via the Yorktown Peninsula but defeated by indecision and Lee.

United States Sanitary Commission Private agency chartered by the federal government to assist sick and wounded Union soldiers, a key outlet for women's volunteer work.

JT Vintage/Glasshouse Images/Alamy Stock Photo

Global Americans Before her career as a pioneer nurse and humanitarian, Massachusetts-born **Clara Barton** worked as a teacher and then as a clerk in the Washington, D.C., Patent Office, to which she returned at the start of the Civil War. Seeking a more active wartime role, Barton joined other women volunteers to gather food, clothing, and bandages for Union soldiers. In 1862, after the battles of Second Bull Run, Antietam, and Fredericksburg, she gained permission to work at field hospitals tending wounded men. Later in the war, she distributed supplies and oversaw hospitals for Union armies in South Carolina and Virginia. The Civil War served as a springboard for Barton's career as a global humanitarian. At first, she ran the government's Office of Missing Soldiers, established to find and identify individuals imprisoned, killed, or missing in action. On vacation in Geneva, Switzerland, she learned about the International Committee of the Red Cross, a neutral relief society founded by Swiss activist Henry Dunant in 1863. During the Franco-Prussian War (1870–1871), Barton helped to run German hospitals and distributed supplies to civilians in Paris. After returning to America, she campaigned for the U.S. government to recognize the Red Cross and the Geneva Convention that enabled its operations. In 1881, she organized the American branch of the Red Cross and for two decades directed relief efforts during wars and emergencies in the United States and overseas, including Cuba and Ottoman Turkey. Honored for her humanitarian work in Europe as well as at home, Clara Barton believed that charity recognized no national borders.

to a black Union regiment, served as volunteers. This collective effort turned nursing into a female occupation and helped professionalize it after the war. Although the Confederacy lagged behind the Union in providing adequate hospitals and medical care, Confederate women organized locally to furnish clothing and bandages to Rebel soldiers, and many served selflessly as nurses. Sally Louisa Tompkins, who ran a model hospital for wounded Confederates in Richmond, was commissioned a captain by Jefferson Davis so that she could remain in charge after the military took it over.

Some women accompanied troops in camp as cooks or laundresses, and others sold sexual services. Still, for soldiers who escaped death, wounds, or disease, camp life was monotonous. "The first thing in the morning is drill," one Pennsylvania soldier explained, "then drill, then drill again. . . . Between drills, we drill and sometimes stop to eat a little and have roll call." Soldiers relieved boredom with gambling, sports, drinking, and letter writing. As the war dragged on, many soldiers became hardened and fatalistic, but patriotism, duty, and comradeship kept them at their posts.

13-2c Debate over Emancipation

Wherever the North's army penetrated, African American slaves escaped to seek freedom behind Union lines. These fugitives forced the issue that Lincoln's administration had tried to avoid. In response, Union generals improvised. Some returned the runaways under the Fugitive Slave Law, but others crowded them into makeshift camps. When two Union generals

{ "Contrabands" and Congress open the path to emancipation.

proclaimed them free, Lincoln countermanded their orders. Union general Benjamin Butler found a halfway solution: declaring the fugitives "**contraband**," or captured enemy property, he refused to return them and put them to work.

Butler's policy was aligned with the first Confiscation Act passed by Congress in August 1861, which permitted the seizure of property employed by the Rebel army, including slaves, but did not give them freedom. Lincoln remained committed to a hands-off policy, but mounting pressures and the logic of the war pushed him toward bolder measures. Emancipation, Lincoln admitted in August 1862, would "help us abroad." Britain and France had previously abolished colonial slavery and both would hesitate to oppose a U.S. antislavery war. Republican abolitionists argued that slavery was the root cause of rebellion and should be eradicated. Frederick Douglass tied emancipation to the advantage that black soldiers, initially rejected by recruiters, could give the Union. Others pointed out that encouraging slaves to escape would cripple the Confederate economy. In July 1862, a second Confiscation Act allowed the seizure of land from rebellious Southerners, freed runaway slaves, and authorized the president to use blacks as soldiers.

Lincoln still preferred gradual, compensated emancipation and offered such a proposal to the loyal border states coupled with a plan to resettle willing former slaves in the West Indies or Central America. He pleaded with Delaware and Kentucky to take the deal. When they refused and northern blacks angrily rejected resettlement, Lincoln changed course.

In mid-1862, Lincoln decided to proclaim slaves in Rebel states free, striking a moral and a practical blow against the Confederacy. He prepared

contraband Term that fixed the legal status of slaves who fled to Union lines prior to the Emancipation Proclamation as captured, unreturnable enemy property.

Map 13.2 The Civil War, Late 1862 In 1862, Union armies made steady progress penetrating Tennessee and clearing Confederate regulars from Missouri. In the East, Lee, after success at the Second Battle of Bull Run, invaded Union territory. McClellan's defenders repulsed Lee's advance at Antietam Creek in Maryland. Although a limited victory, Antietam allowed Lincoln to announce his pending Emancipation Proclamation. Union fortunes in Virginia were again set back at Fredericksburg, where Lee's men inflicted a lopsided defeat. ▲

northern public opinion by linking emancipation to Union victory. "My paramount object in this struggle is to save the Union," he wrote antislavery editor Horace Greeley. "If I could save the Union without freeing *any* slave, I would do it; and if I could save it by freeing *all* the slaves, I would do it; and if I could do it by freeing some and leaving others alone, I would also do that." Lincoln had already decided on the third option. After informing his cabinet, he agreed to wait for a decisive Union military victory so his announcement would not look like an act of desperation.

Battle of Antietam Standoff in which McClellan stopped Lee's advance into Maryland, the Union victory that allowed Lincoln to announce plans for emancipation.

That victory came in September 1862 at the **Battle of Antietam** (see Map 13.2). Lee had invaded Maryland, hoping to secure that state for the Confederacy, impress European powers, and scare Northerners into

voting for peace. He collided with McClellan's army near Sharpsburg, on Antietam Creek, on September 17. With twenty-three thousand men killed or wounded, it was the bloodiest one-day battle of the war. Technically, Antietam was a Union victory because Lee's offensive was stopped, but McClellan failed to break Lee's lines or to cut off his retreat to Virginia. Frustrated by the missed opportunity, Lincoln again removed McClellan from command, this time for good.

Although Antietam was not the crushing blow Lincoln sought, it served his purpose. Five days later, he issued a Preliminary Emancipation Proclamation announcing that all slaves in rebellious states would be freed on January 1, 1863, unless those states declared loyalty to the Union before the deadline. No Rebel states accepted the offer.

Turning Points, 1863

After the Emancipation Proclamation, Frederick Douglass, William Forten, and other African American abolitionists issued a national call for black recruits. This poster from 1863 appealed to free and newly freed blacks to "join the Battles of Liberty and the Union." Invoking the revolutionary heroes of 1848 in Europe and black Union soldiers who had already fallen, the signees declared, "Let us rather die freemen than live to be slaves."

How did these abolitionists give global significance to black enlistment? What did they mean by "fail now & our race is doomed"? Why did they ask, "Are freemen less brave than slaves"? ▶

Go to MindTap® to practice history with the Chapter 13 **Primary Source Writing Activity: A War for the Union, A War against Slavery**. Read and view primary sources and respond to a writing prompt.

MEN OF COLOR
To Arms! To Arms!
NOW OR NEVER
THREE YEARS' SERVICE!
BATTLES OF LIBERTY AND THE UNION
FAIL NOW, & OUR RACE IS DOOMED
SILENCE THE TONGUE OF CALUMNY
VALOR AND HEROISM
PORT HUDSON AND MILLIKEN'S BEND.
ARE FREEMEN LESS BRAVE THAN SLAVES
OUR LAST OPPORTUNITY HAS COME
MEN OF COLOR, BROTHERS AND FATHERS!
WE APPEAL TO YOU!
STRIKE NOW!

Archive Photos/Getty Images

By officially aligning the United States with the global movement to end slavery, Lincoln's decision for emancipation deterred foreign support for Confederates. Closer to home, it helped tip the war's balance by weakening the South's economy and enlisting thousands of black Union soldiers. Later in 1863, Union military forces won strategic victories in Pennsylvania and Tennessee and on the Mississippi River. Much bloodletting remained, including continued conflict in Indian country. But after the summer of 1863, the Confederate army was permanently on the defensive, and the path to Union victory became visible.

☞ As you read, look for several key turning points in the Civil War during 1863. How did each help to turn the tide in the Union's favor, and how did each reinforce the others?

13-3a The Emancipation Proclamation and African American Soldiers

Issued on New Year's Day 1863, Lincoln's **Emancipation Proclamation** fell short of complete abolition. It freed slaves in states still in rebellion, but specifically excluded slaves in the loyal border states and in areas under federal occupation, just as the president had hinted to Greeley. Lincoln's approach was both conservative and radical. Declaring emancipation a "military necessity," he pacified the North's conservatives by stressing its damage to the Confederacy. By casting it

{ Emancipation transforms the Union's war aims and armies.

as an "act of justice," he pleased abolitionists and turned Union soldiers into liberators. Most important, the proclamation grafted a war against slavery onto the war for the Union.

Reactions to the Proclamation underscored this change. Confederate spokesmen deplored it as a revolutionary measure intended to provoke a race war in the South. Some northern Democrats stoked fears about white intermarriage with free blacks. Most Northerners, however, supported Lincoln's decree, seizing on either its military or moral justifications as they saw fit. African Americans in the North celebrated the news at impromptu rallies, and as word spread to southern plantations, slaves voted for freedom with their feet. More than one-fifth of the South's blacks ran away. This massive exodus reduced the South's plantation output and boosted the Union's potential resources.

The Proclamation cleared the way for the Union to enlist African American soldiers. Frederick Douglass, Martin Delany, and Sojourner Truth joined recruiting tours through the North, and freedmen were signed up in refugee camps near the front. By the war's end, 186,000 African Americans served in the Union army and another 20,000 in the navy. More than half were former slaves and free blacks from Confederate states. Douglass claimed that military service would cement black claims to legal equality: "Once let the black man get . . . a musket on his shoulder and bullets in his pocket, and there is no power on earth which can deny that he has earned the right to citizenship." His optimism was premature. Black soldiers served in

Emancipation Proclamation
Lincoln's edict of January 1, 1863, freeing slaves in rebellious states and encouraging their recruitment as Union soldiers.

History without Borders

Slave Emancipation in the Americas

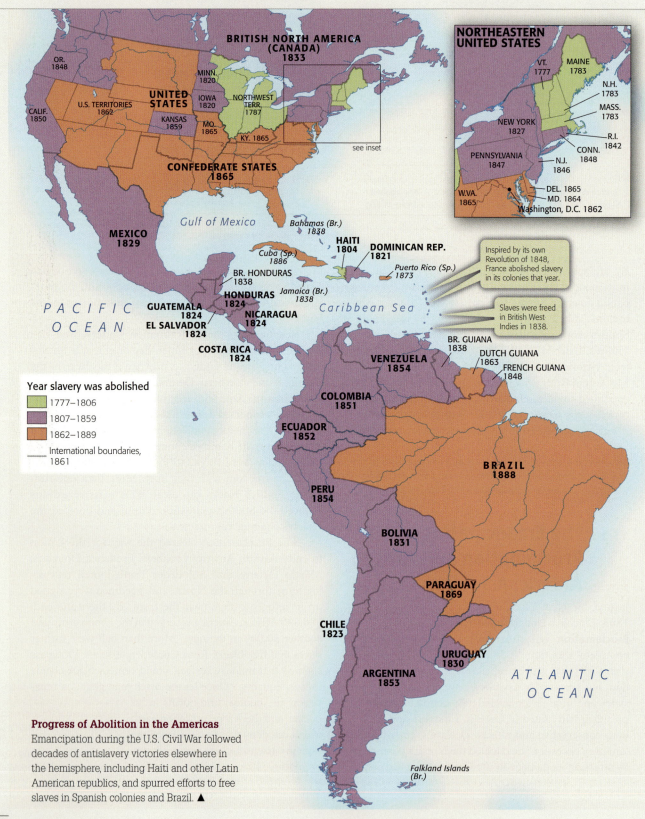

NORTHEASTERN UNITED STATES

VT. 1777
MAINE 1783
N.H. 1783
MASS. 1783
NEW YORK 1827
R.I. 1842
CONN. 1848
PENNSYLVANIA 1847
N.J. 1846
W.VA. 1865
DEL. 1865
MD. 1864
Washington, D.C. 1862

BRITISH NORTH AMERICA (CANADA) 1833

OR. 1848
MINN. 1820
UNITED STATES
IOWA 1820
NORTHWEST TERR. 1787
CALIF. 1850
U.S. TERRITORIES 1862
KANSAS 1859
MO. 1865
KY. 1865
see inset

CONFEDERATE STATES 1865

Gulf of Mexico

Bahamas (Br.) 1838

MEXICO 1829

Cuba (Sp.) 1886

HAITI 1804
DOMINICAN REP. 1821

BR. HONDURAS 1838
Puerto Rico (Sp.) 1873

HONDURAS 1824
Jamaica (Br.) 1838

GUATEMALA 1824

Caribbean Sea

PACIFIC OCEAN

EL SALVADOR 1824
NICARAGUA 1824

COSTA RICA 1824

VENEZUELA 1854

BR. GUIANA 1838
DUTCH GUIANA 1863
FRENCH GUIANA 1848

> Inspired by its own Revolution of 1848, France abolished slavery in its colonies that year.

> Slaves were freed in British West Indies in 1838.

COLOMBIA 1851

ECUADOR 1852

BRAZIL 1888

PERU 1854

BOLIVIA 1831

PARAGUAY 1869

CHILE 1823

URUGUAY 1830

ARGENTINA 1853

ATLANTIC OCEAN

Falkland Islands (Br.)

Year slavery was abolished
- 1777–1806
- 1807–1859
- 1862–1889
- International boundaries, 1861

Progress of Abolition in the Americas

Emancipation during the U.S. Civil War followed decades of antislavery victories elsewhere in the hemisphere, including Haiti and other Latin American republics, and spurred efforts to free slaves in Spanish colonies and Brazil. ▲

Liberation of Slaves by Simon Bolívar (1783–1830) (w/c on paper), Cancino, Fernandez Luis (19th century)/Casa-Museo 20 de Julio de 1810, Bogotá, Colombia/Bridgeman Images

Liberation of Slaves by Simón Bolívar This watercolor by F.L. Cancino presents a top-down view of Bolívar's declaration ending slavery during the independence war in Gran Colombia (present-day Venezuela). Although he personally opposed slavery, Bolívar also acted to ensure the support of Haiti's president and Gran Colombia's blacks in the war against Spain. ▲

mauritius images GmbH/Alamy Stock Photo

Samuel Sharpe Monument in Jamaica These statues in Montego Bay memorialize the Jamaican slave uprising of 1831–1832. Sharpe, a Baptist convert, preached nonviolence and led a general strike against slavery that evolved into the Christmas Rebellion of 1831, during which Sharpe and hundreds of slaves were captured and murdered. The statues show Sharpe preaching to a group of Jamaican slaves, dramatizing their active struggle for freedom. ▲

By the time the Civil War began in the United States, slavery in the Americas had been under attack for nearly a century. Despite resistance from planters and their political allies in imperial centers and national governments, the abolition of slavery progressed in three overlapping waves. The first coincided with wars for colonial independence and the second followed efforts to outlaw the African slave trade after 1807. In the third, which was spurred by the American Civil War, emancipation spread to the United States, Brazil, and the Spanish Caribbean, plantation societies where global trade in cotton, sugar, and tobacco had kept the institution profitable.

The Age of Revolution (1776–1830) spread ideals of freedom and equality through the Atlantic world. All the northern U.S. states took measures to extinguish slavery after independence, and the Haitian Revolution (1791–1804), which evolved from a slave rebellion, provided inspiration for slaves elsewhere. Several new republics in Latin America adopted gradual emancipation measures between 1814 and 1830 during their struggle for independence from Spain.

Great Britain, whose Parliament banned the slave trade in 1807, exerted strong pressure on remaining slaveholding nations. The moral agitation of evangelical reformers blended with economic incentives as England transitioned to contract labor in colonial lands and sought to deny cheap slave labor to its rivals. In 1808, the United States outlawed the slave trade, and the Netherlands and France soon followed. By the 1850s, Britain's powerful navy had effectively ended the transit of slaves to the Americas except for Spanish Cuba and Puerto Rico. With their enslaved populations dwindling, Colombia, Argentina, Venezuela, and Peru abolished the institution.

Britain also took the lead in ending colonial slavery. Frightened by a massive slave rebellion in Jamaica in 1831–1832, Parliament emancipated seven hundred fifty thousand slaves in the West Indies, effective in 1838. The French Revolution of 1848 freed three hundred thousand slaves in France's overseas colonies. These actions bolstered antislavery efforts by U.S. reformers and transatlantic ties between Anglo-American abolitionists.

Despite antislavery activism, slavery was still thriving in 1860 in Dutch Surinam, the Spanish Caribbean, and the two largest slave societies of the Americas, the United States and Brazil. Union victory in the Civil War dealt the death blow to slavery in the U.S. South and sealed its fate in the hemisphere. The remaining slave strongholds in the Americas were pressured by Britain and the United States, which joined Britain in 1862 in suppressing the African trade. The Dutch Empire ended colonial slavery in 1863. Spain abolished slavery in Puerto Rico in 1873 and Cuba in 1886. Brazil began gradual abolition in 1871, which culminated in 1888.

Throughout the Americas—with the exceptions of Haiti and the United States—emancipation occurred by legislation or decree without causing a war of its own. Many governments adopted compensation schemes that appeased masters and gradually freed their slaves. In the British West Indies, slaves had to endure a six-year "apprenticeship" to their owners prior to freedom. Because emancipation in the U.S. South began as a wartime measure, it was more abrupt and radical. As announced by Lincoln's Proclamation, emancipation was immediate and uncompensated. By aiding the Union cause, African American men and women, many of them former slaves, laid the basis for claims to full citizenship and voting rights.

Just as moral and military motives mingled in Lincoln's Emancipation Proclamation, historians have argued over the main drivers of abolition in the wider Atlantic world. Growing moral and religious revulsion over slavery, preference for wage-labor capitalism, crises prompted by wars for independence and slave revolts, national self-interest, and the courageous struggles of slaves and abolitionists all played roles in ending this long-standing injustice.

Critical Thinking Questions

▶ What shared or unique factors spurred the emancipation of slaves in the Americas? What considerations slowed the abolition movement?

▶ What role did Great Britain play in ending transatlantic slavery? How and why did the United States follow its lead?

Go to MindTap® to engage with an interactive version of **History without Borders: Slave Emancipation in the Americas**. Learn from an interactive map, view related video, and respond to critical thinking questions.

segregated units and faced opposition from white officers, some of whom resigned their commissions. Others only grudgingly accepted "anything that will kill a rebel."

Initially, black soldiers were paid less than white soldiers. They were given lackluster training and inferior equipment and assigned to labor detachments or garrison duty. African American soldiers protested these inequities, and one black South Carolina sergeant was executed for leading his men in a camp walkout. Attitudes began to change when black soldiers fought heroically at Milliken's Bend in Louisiana and in a futile assault on Fort Wagner, near Charleston, by the 54th Massachusetts regiment. Finally, in June 1864, Congress equalized the pay of black and white soldiers. That same month, black soldiers in the Army of the Potomac won the personal thanks of President Lincoln when he visited the Virginia front.

Confederate policy classified captured black soldiers as insurrectionists who could be enslaved and even executed. The Lincoln administration responded by suspending prisoner exchanges until the Confederates treated black prisoners equally with whites. The standoff meant that after 1863, Confederate and Union prisons became overcrowded, deadly pens. More than fifty thousand soldiers of both sides died in captivity, a quarter of them Union soldiers at the infamous Confederate prison at Andersonville, Georgia.

In April 1864, two Confederate armies committed mass murder against black soldiers. Led by General Nathan Bedford Forrest, a founder of the Ku Klux Klan after the war, Confederate soldiers massacred more than two hundred black soldiers who had surrendered at **Fort Pillow**. Farther west, a Confederate regiment of Choctaw Indians scalped and mutilated a similar number of captured black soldiers at Poison Spring, Arkansas.

Despite such atrocities and prejudice in their own army, African Americans who joined Union forces took pride in their service. Putting on the federal blue uniform, one remembered, was "the biggest thing that ever happened in my life." Like slave runaways of both sexes, African American soldiers and those who toiled in Union camps seized their freedom, rather than being given it.

13-3b The Contest over European Intervention

By announcing the end of slavery in the South, Lincoln reduced the probability that Britain would support the Confederates. A few weeks

> Britain and France back away from supporting the Confederacy.

after the Proclamation, Henry Adams, son of Charles Francis Adams, the U.S. minister to London, wrote his brother in the Union army that Lincoln's action meant more than "all our former victories and all our diplomacy. . . . If only you at home don't have disasters," Adams continued, "we will give . . . a checkmate to the foreign hopes of the rebels."

Yet more Union disasters awaited. In May 1863, General Joseph Hooker's army was outmaneuvered by General Lee's bold splitting of his smaller force into separate wings at the **Battle of Chancellorsville**. Although Lee lost Stonewall Jackson, who was mistakenly shot by his own men, Chancellorsville sealed Lee's reputation for daring generalship and lent his army an air of invincibility.

Lee's victories impressed British and French authorities. French bankers awarded the Confederacy a $15 million loan and their government resumed backroom scheming for Anglo-French mediation of the conflict. British shipyards secretly contracted with Confederates to build ocean-going ironclad rams that could destroy the Union blockade's wooden ships. Only when U.S. Minister Adams threatened war did the British government seize two warships known as "Laird Rams" that were under construction. At the same time, the Union victories at Gettysburg and Vicksburg (see page 386) demonstrated that the tide of battle had turned decisively in the Union's favor. These events put an end to the Confederates' hopes for British support.

Yet British-built commerce raiders continued to stoke Anglo-American tensions. The *Alabama* destroyed more than sixty merchant vessels before the *U.S.S. Kearsage* sank it off Cherbourg, France, in June 1864. Later that year, Confederate agents crossed the border from British Canada to rob banks in St. Albans, Vermont, and set fires in New York City. Union leaders protested to British officials, but none of these incidents led to war.

Once Britain backed off, Confederate hopes for foreign intervention rested on Napoleon III and his intrigue in Mexico. After the Mexicans defeated French forces in the Battle of Puebla on May 5, 1862 (commemorated as *Cinco de Mayo*), Napoleon sent reinforcements, seized Mexico City, and overthrew President Juárez in June 1863. Allying with Mexican royalists, Napoleon installed Archduke Maximilian of Austria as emperor of Mexico. Confederates hoped the Lincoln administration would condemn this takeover and declare war on France or that Napoleon III would recognize the Confederacy if Confederates recognized Maximilian's **Second Mexican Empire**. Neither happened. Napoleon shied away from provoking the Union, and although secretary of state Seward condemned France's invasion as a violation of the Monroe Doctrine, President Lincoln understood that Union forces already had their hands full. "One war at a time," he advised his cabinet.

New York: Harper & Brothers

Russian Fleet Visits New York City, 1863 In October 1863, Russia's Czar Alexander II dispatched squadrons of warships to New York and San Francisco harbors. The move was intended to protect Russia's navy from winter freezing and British threats in Europe, but the North's public interpreted it as a promise of Russian assistance should Britain and France intervene in the Civil War. Union officials gave the Russians a hero's welcome. ◄

13-3c The War in Indian Country

The peculiar legal status of Native American peoples in the United States as "domestic dependent nations" shaped their Civil War experience. As "nations," they negotiated treaties of alliance with the Union or Confederacy; as "dependents," they remained subject to white domination no matter which side they chose. Approximately 20,000 Native Americans served in Civil War armies, the majority with the Confederacy. Either way, most tribes emerged worse off than before the war.

> The war divides Indian peoples and inflames frontier disputes.

In Indian Territory—present-day Oklahoma—the southeastern tribes forced there by Indian Removal were bitterly divided during the Civil War. Full-blooded Cherokees who had opposed removal generally favored neutrality, while mixed bloods who had married southern whites and sometimes owned slaves favored the Confederacy. Initially, Confederate sympathizers held the upper hand. Leaders of the Cherokees, Creeks, Chickasaws, Choctaws, and Seminoles signed treaties of alliance with the Confederacy, held seats (but could not vote) in the Confederate Congress, and organized Confederate units. Meanwhile, pro-Union Cherokees rallied around John Ross, principal chief of the Cherokee Nation, who enrolled three of his sons in the Union army. Cherokee factions staged raids against each other, vandalizing homes and burning crops.

In the summer of 1863, the momentum shifted toward the Union. Federal troops invaded Indian Territory, forcing pro-Confederate Cherokees to flee southward. Confederate authorities failed to aid their Indian allies, and more than 10,000 huddled in refugee camps, their tribal governments and economies devastated. After Cherokee chief Stand Watie became the last Confederate general to surrender in June 1865, the U.S. government treated the Cherokees as if all had supported the Confederacy, compelling new cessions of land as punishment for alleged wartime disloyalty.

Some Indians on the northern Plains seized on the absence of federal soldiers to oppose oppressive treaties and corrupt white agents. In August 1862, the eastern (Santee) Sioux of Minnesota, led by Little Crow, killed more than 400 whites. President Lincoln dispatched a Union force commanded by General Pope, who suppressed the revolt. Thirty-eight Sioux leaders were executed, and the tribe fled west to the Dakotas.

Farther west, Union volunteers who had organized to fight Confederates turned on local Indians. In New Mexico, Army colonel Christopher ("Kit") Carson, who had helped stop Confederate advances in the Southwest, led his troops into Navaho country in retaliation for Indian raids on Anglo settlers. After Carson destroyed cornfields and villages, 8,000 Navajos were marched four hundred miles south to a reservation at Bosque Redondo. Several hundred died along the way, and the rest were held captive until released by a treaty in 1868.

A similar hatred of Indians festered among the Colorado volunteers returned from the Battle of Glorieta Pass. Under the command of Col. J. M. Chivington, they indiscriminately attacked Native American groups who resented tribal cessions of vast lands during the Pike's Peak gold rush. In November 1864, Chivington's army attacked a village of friendly Cheyennes and Arapahos encamped near Fort Lyon, killing and mutilating more than one hundred fifty Indians, mostly women and children. A congressional committee condemned the **Sand Creek Massacre**, but no charges were brought. The massacre enraged young Indian warriors who opposed treaty concessions, and the cycle of retaliatory raids continued after the war.

Sand Creek Massacre Brutal attack on a peaceful village of Cheyenne and Arapaho Indians by a Colorado militia under Union officer Chivington in November 1864.

Map 13.3 The Civil War in 1863 Three Union victories turned the military tide in 1863. Vicksburg's surrender to Grant gave the federals control of the Mississippi River and isolated western Confederates. Meade's forces stopped Lee's second invasion of the North after his success at Chancellorsville during a massive three-day struggle at Gettysburg, and Lee retreated to Virginia. At Chattanooga, Grant avenged an earlier Union defeat at Chickamauga, solidified Union control of Tennessee, and opened the route to Atlanta. ▲

13-3d Gettysburg, Vicksburg, and Chattanooga

In the summer of 1863, Union forces turned the tide of the war in three key battles (see Map 13.3). Lee again invaded the North, believing

> The Union wins three crucial battles.

that a victory there would demoralize the Northerners and win European recognition of the Confederacy. In mid-June, his army of 75,000 men crossed the Potomac, where they foraged for food and demanded payments from frightened townspeople. When Hooker followed Lee too cautiously, Lincoln replaced him with the steadier George G. Meade. In the **Battle of Gettysburg**, an epic three-day struggle, Meade's Union troops

Battle of Gettysburg Crucial three-day Civil War battle of July 1863 in which Meade's Union forces defeated Lee's Confederates in Pennsylvania, forcing a retreat to Virginia.

Vicksburg Fortress town in Mississippi surrendered by Confederate defenders to Grant on July 4, 1863, after a prolonged siege, ensuring Union control over the Mississippi River.

repulsed repeated attacks by Lee's army. Total casualties of nearly 50,000 men made it the largest battle ever on North American soil. Lee lost one-third of his soldiers and retreated south. Although Meade failed to cut off Lee's escape, the Union victory at Gettysburg was decisive. President Lincoln, dedicating the battleground cemetery the following November, honored the Union dead for sacrificing their lives so that "government of the people, by the people, for the people, shall not perish from the earth."

The day after the Gettysburg victory, General Grant occupied **Vicksburg**, climaxing a prolonged struggle for that Confederate stronghold on the Mississippi River. After a six-week siege in which Vicksburg's soldiers and civilians were reduced to eating rats, Confederate John C. Pemberton surrendered 30,000 men to Grant on July 4. When the Confederate garrison at Port Hudson, Louisiana, surrendered a few days later, Union forces controlled the entire Mississippi River, cutting the Confederacy in half.

Bettmann/Corbis

Global Americans Carl Schurz, a military officer in the failed Frankfort revolution against the German monarchy, sought exile in France and England and then migrated to the United States. Like most of the four thousand German "Forty-Eighters," Schurz had strong antislavery convictions. Settling in Wisconsin, he helped to organize the state's Republican Party, attacked the Fugitive Slave Law, and gave rousing speeches—often in German—at pro-Lincoln rallies. Once elected, Lincoln sent him to Spain as an ambassador to help dissuade it from supporting the Confederacy. In 1862, Schurz was commissioned a Union general; he later fought at Second Bull Run, Chancellorsville, Gettysburg, and Chattanooga, and became the best known of the German-American Union officers, a group that included Franz Sigel, Friedrich Hecker, and Alexander von Schimmelfennig. News of their military exploits and antislavery efforts heightened the interest of European liberals and revolutionaries, including their fellow German exile, Karl Marx, in the Union cause.

At the war's end, Schurz turned to politics. A prominent advocate of clean government and aid to former slaves, he was elected to the U.S. Senate from Missouri in 1868, becoming its first German-American member. He later served as secretary of the interior under President Rutherford Hayes. Schurz fervently hoped that U.S. institutions would spread worldwide, but his belief in self-government made him an outspoken critic of U.S. imperialism. Throughout his career, Schurz was an authoritative and influential transatlantic voice for freedom.

Lincoln next sent Grant to Chattanooga, Tennessee, where Union General William Rosecrans was in danger of surrendering to a siege by Confederate Braxton Bragg. In the **Battle of Chattanooga**, November 23–25, Grant's troops stormed the heights east of the city and drove Bragg's disorganized Confederates back into Georgia. Although less celebrated than the Union victories at Gettysburg and Vicksburg, the capture of Chattanooga was equally important. It secured all of Tennessee for the Union and cleared the path to Atlanta, the gateway to the southern Confederacy.

Battle of Chattanooga
Victory by Grant over Confederates under Bragg that secured Tennessee for the Union and opened the route to Atlanta.

13-4
War on Two Home Fronts

These two engravings by American artist Winslow Homer featuring women's wartime activities appeared in *Harper's Weekly*, the North's most popular illustrated magazine. The first is titled *Filling Cartridges at the U.S. Arsenal, Watertown, Massachusetts.* The second, *The Influence of Woman: The Sister of Charity, Sewing Shirts, Washing, Home Tidings,* appeared in a series "Our Women and the War."

Compare and contrast the two illustrations. How do the activities they portray suggest both continuities and changes in gender roles during the war? ▶

Library of Congress Prints and Photographs Division[LC-USZ62-96445]

Homer, Winslow (1836–1910) (after)

"An army marches on its stomach," Napoleon once declared, and his campaigns demonstrated the success of massive wartime mobilization overseen by a powerful government. Union and Confederate political leaders took this lesson to heart. Both sides raised revenue, drafted soldiers, and stimulated factory and farm production to sustain their armies. In the process, they enlarged the powers of the national government in ways that alarmed dissenters. The war's outcome hinged on how well each side handled home front political and economic problems, not simply on how their armies fought.

☞ As you read, consider the political, social, and economic transformations that took place on the Union and Confederate home fronts. How did they help or hinder each side's war effort?

13-4a Centralization and Resistance

Among the war's changes, none was more startling to Southerners than the growing power of their new national government. Waging the best possible fight required subordinating states' rights and local prerogatives to war needs. Understanding this, Confederate President Jefferson Davis asserted government

> Drafts, taxes, and martial law arouse dissent in the Union and Confederacy.

control over arms, supplies, and troops. The Confederate Congress established a draft in April 1862, passed a 10 percent tax to be paid in farm products, and gave the executive control over railroads. The army impressed slaves to build fortifications and confiscated crops and animals to feed troops. Overnight, a bureaucracy sprang up in Richmond that rivaled the Union's in proportion to the overall population.

As the Rebel government's claim on men and resources escalated, opposition to its centralized power grew. Vocal states' rights zealots, led by Vice President Alexander Stephens and the governors of Georgia and North Carolina, denounced the Davis administration as despotic. More damaging dissent arose among ordinary Southerners. Nonslaveholders in the backcountry refused to cooperate with tax collectors and impressment officers. The Confederate draft law, which allowed men to hire substitutes and exempted one white man on a plantation with twenty or more slaves, spurred charges that the conflict was "a rich man's war but a poor man's fight." Many poor whites who resented planters refused to "go fight for their infurnal negroes." Conscription bolstered the desperate Confederate army—more than 25 percent of Confederate soldiers were draftees and substitutes, compared to 8 percent for the Union (see Table 13.1). But the Confederacy paid a price in home front morale and unity.

The Confederate Congress prevented Davis, who had invoked martial law in embattled Confederate districts early in the war, from detaining draft and tax evaders.

Table 13.1 Social Profile of Civil War Soldiers

Despite complaints over "a rich man's war and a poor man's fight," both sides in the Civil War organized an army of soldiers that roughly reflected their population's social origins. The major exception was the Union's recruitment of African American men after 1862 and the Confederacy's refusal to do so. Union recruiters also benefited from a sizeable pool of white men, including many immigrants, whereas the Confederacy faced shortages and relied heavily on the draft to supply soldiers.

	Union	Confederate
Total number who served in the military	2.1 million	0.9 million (est.)
Percentage of total who were drafted	2	20
Percentage of total who paid for substitutes	6	8
Percentage of living West Point graduates who joined	66	23
Social Origins (approximate percentage of total)		
Native-born whites	67	89
Foreign born	24	9
African American	9[a]	0[b]
Native American	<1	2
Farmers and farm laborers	48	62
Unskilled laborers	16	9
Skilled laborers	25	14
White collar and professional	8	12

[a] Approximately half of this number were runaways or recently freed slaves from Confederate states.

[b] Southern slaves were often impressed into assisting the Confederate army in camps, hospitals, and defensive lines, but the government did not officially enroll any as soldiers until the war was virtually over.

Sources: Steven Woodworth and Kenneth J. Winkle, *Atlas of the Civil War* (New York: Oxford University Press, 2004), 364; James McPherson, *Ordeal By Fire*, 4th ed. (New York: McGraw-Hill, 2009), 387–388; E.B. Long, *The Civil War Day by Day* (Garden City, NY: Doubleday, 1971), 705–708.

Stephens declared that losing the war would be preferable to curbing Southerners' liberties. Such sentiments underscored the dilemma of white Southerners' fixation on individual and states' rights during wartime, signaling the failure of Confederate nationalism.

On the Union home front, the Lincoln administration pursued similar policies of centralization and also met with opposition. Yet discontent in the North was muted by several factors, including a strong political and military response, the increasingly positive momentum of the war, and general wartime prosperity.

In 1861, Congress created the nation's first income tax. In the following year, the **Internal Revenue Service** began collecting it and a new series of excise taxes on tobacco, liquor, and other items, which had been eliminated by President Jackson. These measures met little opposition, partly because the income tax was progressive, with rates rising according to income. Congress raised the tariff to produce additional revenue. In the end, the Union covered 21 percent of its war costs through taxation, compared with the Confederacy's less than 10 percent.

The Union's draft lottery, enacted in 1863, aroused heated opposition. Like the Confederate measure, it allowed draftees to hire substitutes or pay a fee to avoid serving. Workers and immigrants in the North's cities condemned the system as discriminatory, although statistics showed that they were not selected disproportionately (see Table 13.1). Among working-class Northerners, the war was increasingly unpopular for its enrichment of bosses and the threat of competition for jobs posed by newly emancipated slaves. Anger erupted into violence in New York City in July 1863 when the first draft lists were posted. A predominantly Irish mob destroyed local draft headquarters, looted homes of the rich, and turned on African Americans, burning the city's Colored Orphan Asylum and murdering black bystanders. Class resentments and racism fueled three days of street warfare that claimed more than one hundred lives. Army units rushed from Gettysburg and gunboats borrowed from the Union blockade finally suppressed the **New York City Draft Riot**.

The Lincoln administration asserted military control over civilian dissenters more forcefully than its Confederate counterpart. After September 1862, when Congress gave the administration permission to suspend habeas corpus at will, Lincoln authorized the arrest of those suspected of evading the draft, trading with the enemy, or "any disloyal practice." All told, military authorities detained more than thirteen thousand civilians during the war, and federal courts refrained from interfering. After the war, in *ex parte Milligan* (1866), the Supreme Court ruled that federal authorities had overstepped their bounds and that citizens could not be tried by military tribunals in areas where loyal civilian courts were functioning. The decision came too late to assist wartime detainees, however. The Union's practice of aggressively using courts and prisons to deter disloyalty created abuses but was undeniably effective.

13-4b Comparative Politics and Leadership

{ The Union's political institutions and leadership help ensure its success.

Contrasts between political systems and leadership added to the Union's comparative advantage over the Confederacy. In a display of unity, members of the Confederate Congress renounced party affiliations, yet this strategy backfired. Lacking a disciplined party organization, President Davis could not assemble votes to pass legislation or build loyalty through patronage. As a result, Confederate politics splintered into multiple warring factions divided along personal or ideological lines. Congressmen engaged in fistfights and brandished weapons. The Confederate Cabinet was similarly unstable. Most of the South's ablest leaders chose to join the army, and Davis relied on a dwindling cadre of efficient advisers. Resignations and cabinet reshuffling produced five Confederate secretaries of war in four years.

Davis was too icy and inflexible to guide the Confederacy through its embattled infancy. An honorable but proud aristocrat, he combined the self-assurance of a wealthy planter with an engineer's penchant for micromanaging the war. He quarreled with key generals, took political criticism personally, and lacked the common touch to inspire affection among ordinary Southerners.

Internal Revenue Service Federal agency established in 1861 to collect income and excise taxes during the Civil War.

New York City Draft Riot Violent protest against Union conscription, targeting wealthy residents, antislavery journalists, and especially African Americans.

ex parte Milligan Supreme Court ruling against military tribunals in the case of pro-Confederate civilians in Indiana who plotted to take over the state's government.

Library of Congress

Brady National Photographic Portrait Galleries, photographer

Two Civil War Presidents Photographs of Jefferson Davis (left) and Abraham Lincoln (right), both taken by Mathew Brady, show similarities in appearance and bearing between the two. Beneath surface appearances, however, Davis and Lincoln had important differences in temperament and political skill that gave an edge to the Union war effort. ▲

In the 1863 elections, openly antiadministration candidates came close to winning majorities in the Confederate Congress. Meanwhile, as the Union army occupied more and more Confederate territory, Davis's government lost control over local conditions. Dissenters took possession of several mountain districts. A group of non-slaveholding whites in isolated Jones County, Mississippi, declared the Free State of Jones and defied Confederate authorities.

The North's political institutions and leadership proved more resilient than the South's. Like Davis, Lincoln faced opposition to his policies, but he used his personal skills, the North's reservoir of talent, and the tools of party politics to neutralize foes and further the war effort.

Although reduced to a minority, the Democratic Party remained a powerful force in Union politics and a conduit for wartime dissent. The Democrats contained war and peace factions, both of which promised a return to "the Union as it was," the former by force and the latter by negotiation. Democrats closed ranks by blaming the Lincoln administration for the war's high death toll, its economic upheavals, and especially the emancipation of slaves. Many Democratic leaders also condemned the draft and martial law. These positions, along with warnings that freed slaves would inundate the North, appealed to many Midwesterners with southern roots and to workers and immigrants in northern cities.

Lincoln both accommodated and countered the Democrats. He lured War Democrats by offering appointments to federal offices and commissions as Union generals. He played tough politics, too, secretly subsidizing Indiana's budget so the state's Republican governor could dismiss its Democratic-controlled legislature. Outspoken **Peace Democrats** were accused of disloyalty. When Ohio congressman Clement L. Vallandigham denounced emancipation and the draft and labeled Lincoln a "dictator," military authorities imprisoned him for treason. Lincoln commuted Vallandigham's sentence, avoiding a judicial confrontation, and shrewdly exiled him to the Confederacy. A small cadre of Peace Democrats formed shadowy secret societies and hatched plots to sabotage Union communications or free Rebel prisoners in the North. Such activities gave Republicans the chance to label all Peace Democrats "**Copperheads**" (after the poisonous snake) and associate them with treason.

Within his own party, Lincoln faced near-constant challenges from radicals who decried his caution on emancipation or his management of the war. But the president maneuvered deftly to balance Republican factions and preserve party unity.

He appointed factional leaders to his Cabinet, a talented group that included Seward and Treasury secretary Salmon Chase, and he managed this "team of rivals" with skill. As a result, his administration was efficient with little of the turnover that plagued Davis's cabinet.

"This is essentially a people's contest," Lincoln had told Congress on Independence Day, 1861. He identified the Union with the goal of "afford[ing] all an unfettered start and a fair chance in the race of life." In such speeches, Lincoln voiced the egalitarian aspirations of American nationalism. In contrast to Davis's aristocratic demeanor, "Old Abe" offered plain speech and folksy humor that captured the Union public's imagination and held their allegiance through the war. Lincoln's leadership, together with his able cabinet and the Republicans' domination of politics, sustained the Union in wartime.

13-4c Economic and Social Transformations

The war's economic impact dramatically highlighted contrasts between the Union and Confederate home fronts. By 1861, the North had a large network of factories and railroads, and its farms were increasingly mechanized. Wartime government spending pumped enormous sums into the economy, including nearly $2 billion on weapons, supplies, food, horses, and wagons. To oversee such expenditures, the War Department built a bureaucracy of one hundred thousand employees and established procedures for issuing contracts and inspecting goods. Nevertheless, fraud occurred. Corrupt contractors sold the government blankets and uniforms made from "shoddy," compressed wool that quickly disintegrated. Some government agents accepted bribes or handed contracts to relatives and cronies. In the short term, the War Department's close relations with business filled the massive needs of military mobilization; in the long term, the relationship prefigured the fraud and scandals of the postwar "Gilded Age."

Republican legislation also fostered the partnership between capitalism and government. With their congressional majority bolstered by the exit of southern members, Republicans passed probusiness measures from their prewar agenda. They raised the tariff to protect the North's industries. They approved the **Pacific Railroad Act** (1862), which gave railroads land grants and loans to build a line to California. In 1863, Congress created a national banking system that issued a paper currency of **greenbacks**, which were not backed by gold or silver but nevertheless held their value during the war. These and similar measures expanded the reach of the federal government into Northerners' daily lives.

Such laws benefited affluent groups at the expense of average Northerners. Central banking created a more

> The Union booms while the Confederacy busts.

Peace Democrats Faction of the North's Democratic Party that opposed wartime legislation and emancipation, calling for negotiations to restore "the Union as it was" peacefully.

Copperheads Republican label for Northerners who sympathized with the Confederacy, smearing them as traitors by likening them to poisonous snakes.

Pacific Railroad Act Federal law that subsidized construction of a transcontinental railroad from Omaha, Nebraska, to Sacramento, California.

greenbacks Paper money, printed in green ink on one side, issued by the U.S. government during the Civil War and not backed by gold or silver.

stable currency but also tighter credit that squeezed western farmers. Republicans, however, specifically added two laws to promote Lincoln's goal of opportunity for all. The **Homestead Act** granted one hundred sixty acres of public land to settlers who remained for five years. The **Morrill Act** used sales of other public land to establish state universities specializing in agriculture and engineering. Before the war ended, twenty thousand homesteaders had taken up new western farms, and eleven campuses in the Northeast and Midwest had been designated state land-grant colleges.

Despite the wartime boom, many ordinary Northerners experienced hardship. Taxes and inflation raised the price of consumer goods while wages lagged. Faced with replacement by labor-saving machines or competition from young rural migrants, workers organized protests. Some, including tailors, cigar makers, and railway engineers, formed national unions and threatened strikes. Employers denounced worker activism as unpatriotic and recruited women, blacks, and immigrants as strikebreakers. One spark that lit the New York City Draft Riots, for example, was the hiring of African Americans to break a longshoremen's strike. In other cases, federal troops were called in to suppress labor protests at arsenals and munitions factories. Overall, the North benefited from an economy balanced between farms and industry, but its wartime prosperity was far from evenly shared.

The South's economy, ill prepared for the agricultural and industrial demands of war, simply collapsed under the combined weight of declining production and escalating destruction. Understanding their comparative disadvantages, Confederate officials asserted control over the economy, hastily building new railroad lines, factories, and foundries. Through trade and domestic production, Confederate soldiers received enough rifles and ammunition to persevere. But the South's food production could not meet basic civilian and military needs. As young men enlisted, farms declined, and slaves who escaped to Union lines left plantations shorthanded. The shrinking grid of working railroad lines could not distribute corn and hogs. And as Union troops occupied the South, they consumed or destroyed most livestock and crops.

By 1863, shortages of food and clothing were severe. Food riots broke out in Richmond and Atlanta to protest high prices and the scarcity of bread and salt. Marching under banners that read "Bread and Peace," the women of Mobile, Alabama, looted stores for sustenance. Some families on the home front lined their threadbare clothes with newspapers to keep warm; others stripped furniture for fabric.

Unable to finance the war, the Confederates printed paper money. For the Union, "greenbacks" solved a shortage of cash, not goods; for Confederates, the shortage was goods, and inflation surged. By mid-1864, Confederate dollars were practically worthless. It was said that Southerners had earlier gone to market with money in their pockets and returned with potatoes in carts, but this time, they brought carts of money to return with a single potato in their pocket. Despite hardships, people managed by bartering, improvising, and sacrificing. The South's unbalanced agricultural economy, overly dependent on cotton and tobacco exports, never adjusted to the demands of war.

13-4d Women and the War

Wartime requirements opened new opportunities for women. In the North, prosperity widened women's sphere, and many drew on prewar experiences in reform movements or factory work to take advantage. More than one hundred thousand women toiled in northern factories, stitching boots, manufacturing ammunition, and canning foods for soldiers at the front. Less than a decade after Americans Elias Howe and Isaac Singer had introduced the first commercially viable sewing machines, women in the North used them to mass-produce Union uniforms, tents, and flags. The federal government hired thousands of women as clerks and copyists. In private businesses, unlike government, women were often paid less than men for the same work, yet in both cases, war work for wages gave women a measure of independence and a way to contribute publicly to the Union cause.

> Wartime needs bring welcome opportunities and unwelcome hardships for women.

How far the war permanently changed women's roles in the North is unclear. Clerical work, nursing, and teaching (where women replaced men who had gone to fight) continued to be "women's work" after the war, but opportunities in factories declined when soldiers came back. After the war, several state universities permitted women to enroll and more private colleges went coeducational. Women's rights advocates used women's war work to call for social and political rights, especially the vote. Nevertheless, conservative ideas about women's domestic role remained popular, and many middle-class women—and their soldier husbands—longed to return to home and hearth. The war chipped away at rigid restrictions on women's lives but brought no large-scale changes.

On both the Union and Confederate sides, a few hundred women disguised themselves as men to fight in the armies. Some had identified as men before the war; others joined from a sense of patriotism, adventure, or loyalty to the brothers and husbands they accompanied. Both sides benefited from well-placed female spies. Rose Greenhow picked up gossip in Washington for the Confederacy, and actress Pauline Cushman toured Confederate camps for the Union. Locally, civilians often provided valuable intelligence to Union and Confederate army officers.

In comparison with northern women, white women's lives in the South were more rigidly shaped by traditional gender

Homestead Act Federal law that granted one hundred sixty acres for a small fee to settlers on public lands in the West.

Morrill Act Federal law allotting land grants whose sales funded state colleges for agriculture and the mechanical arts.

roles. In the war's early days, newspapers and magazines urged women to remain exemplars of purity and self-sacrifice. Staying within the domestic context, Confederate women joined together to sew flags, roll bandages, and collect jewelry and silverware to donate. As war needs escalated, many took on traditionally male tasks. Like their Union counterparts, they managed farms in their husbands' absence and made tents and munitions at nearby factories. Young women migrated to capitals to take government jobs as clerks and secretaries or to serve as nurses. Schooled by traditional ideals, many regarded these tasks as temporary and often distasteful necessities, recording in their diaries their longing to return to the ordered and peaceful prewar world.

Unlike Northerners, southern women faced the ordeal of invasion, dislocation, and economic collapse. As the war turned against the South, battlefield deaths and everyday hardships chipped at their loyalties and undermined any enthusiasm for expanded roles. By 1864, many women focused on nothing but survival. For northern reform women, the Civil War was building the ground for progress and equality; for southern white women, the war was destroying the ground under their feet.

13-5
Union Success, 1864–1865

This photograph by George Barnard depicts the ruins of Charleston's railroad station after its destruction by Union general William T. Sherman's troops in early 1865.

What effects did the wholesale destruction of railroads, factories, and public buildings have on the South's resources and morale? Why did Union armies target civilian property? ▶

Library of Congress

By the spring of 1864, the stage was set for coordinated offensives that, Union leaders hoped, would bring victory. Lincoln appointed the tenacious Grant commander of all the Union armies, leaving tough-minded General William T. Sherman in charge of the western army at Chattanooga. Grant advanced toward Richmond to force Lee's army into a decisive battle while Sherman pushed southeast to take Atlanta. Both offensives took longer than expected, complicating Lincoln's bid for reelection in the fall. Not until April 1865 did the two major Confederate armies surrender. Northerners at last won the Civil War, but their celebration was cut short when an assassin's bullet felled the president who had led them to victory.

☞ As you read, think about what forced the Confederate armies to surrender. Why did the North win and the South lose?

13-5a Grant and Sherman on the Move

In May 1864, Lee's 75,000 soldiers repulsed Grant's massive 115,000-man army in the thick underbrush of the Wilderness, near Fredericksburg, Virginia. Undeterred, Grant resumed his southward march, hoping to outflank Lee and draw him into open battle. Lee, on the defensive, fought behind earthworks. Fighting broke out with brutal regularity during the **Overland Campaign**, and the blood flowed apace (see Map 13.4). In four weeks, the two armies fought five pitched battles. At Cold Harbor, Grant lost seven thousand men before calling off the morning assault. Some Union

The Union begins its final offensives in Virginia and Georgia.

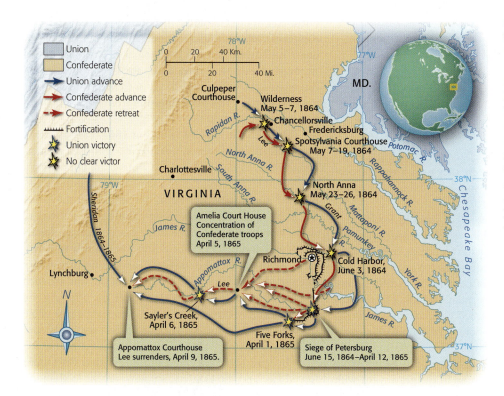

Map 13.4 Grant and Lee in Virginia, 1864–1865 Grant's relentless attacks during the Overland Campaign eventually wore down Lee's smaller army and stretched its lines to the breaking point. From the Wilderness to Petersburg in spring 1864, the Confederates withstood almost daily Union assaults and inflicted horrendous casualties. The next year, Grant's forces slowly encircled Petersburg, and Lee's dwindling army fled westward before he surrendered to Grant at Appomattox Court House. ◀

soldiers, sure they would die, pinned their names to their uniforms so their bodies could be identified.

Checked in front of Richmond, Grant bypassed the capital to seize the railroad center at Petersburg twenty miles south. There his army settled into a prolonged siege. The Overland Campaign had cost Grant 65,000 casualties to Lee's 35,000, but the Union army could replace lost soldiers while the Confederate force could not.

In Georgia, Sherman's flanking moves pushed Joseph Johnston's Confederates back ninety miles into Atlanta's stout defenses. But in mid-July, when Davis replaced Johnston with the combative John B. Hood, the Confederates counterattacked, slowing Sherman's progress. After a month of frustration, the Union army circled south to cut off Atlanta's supply lines, forcing Hood to evacuate the city. "Atlanta is ours, and fairly won," Sherman telegraphed Lincoln triumphantly on September 2.

13-5b Election of 1864

Sherman's victory at Atlanta came just in time for the president, who was fighting a battle of his own to be reelected. The Republicans renominated Lincoln in July but with little support from the party's radicals, who decried his lenient plans for readmitting conquered southern states. At the Republican convention, Lincoln's managers engineered a bipartisan National

{ Lincoln wins reelection thanks to timely Union victories.

Union ticket by nominating Andrew Johnson of Tennessee, a strongly prowar Democrat, as vice president. His place on the ticket was meant to expand Lincoln's base of support and exploit division among Democrats.

The Democrats nominated Lincoln's former commander, George B. McClellan, who favored continuing the war until the Union was restored. When vocal Peace Democrats passed a platform calling for an immediate armistice and negotiations, Republicans charged treason, and McClellan was forced to repudiate the platform. Despite the Democrats' divisions, there was concern that Lincoln could lose an election that was widely seen as a referendum on the war. In August, Grant's army was bogged down at Petersburg and Sherman's was stalled before Atlanta, and the North's public was stunned by the war's death toll.

Quite suddenly, the military situation improved. The Union navy closed the port of Mobile, Alabama, on August 23. Ten days later, Sherman occupied Atlanta, and by October, General Philip Sheridan had secured Virginia's Shenandoah Valley. This string of victories lifted Unionist morale and ensured Lincoln's reelection. In November, he won 55 percent of the popular vote and 212 of 233 electoral votes. Despite their grief and fatigue, the northern public voted to see the war through. Lincoln's reelection—the first of a sitting American president during wartime—was the war's most important political turning point.

Overland Campaign A six-week series of bloody battles between Grant's Union army and Lee's troops defending Richmond.

13-5c Surrender and Assassination

While Grant pinned down Lee's army in Virginia, Sherman cut loose in Georgia. Exemplifying the Union's new hard war strategy, Sherman aimed to "make war so terrible" to Southerners "that generations would pass away before they would again appeal to it." From Atlanta, he led sixty-two thousand soldiers on a **March to the Sea** toward Savannah (see Map 13.5). Abandoning their supply lines, the federals foraged for food and destroyed everything else that could support the South's war effort: railroads, foundries, barns, crops, courthouses, and livestock. Advancing ten miles a day, they left a sixty-mile wide wake of devastation. Nearly twenty thousand slaves followed Sherman's troops. Their defection and Sherman's pillaging led Confederate women to plead with soldiers to return home. "If you put off a-coming," one wife wrote to her husband at the front, "'twont be no use to come, for we'll all hands of us be out there in the garden in the grave yard with your ma and mine." In response to such desperate appeals, Confederate desertions soared.

Sherman entered Savannah by Christmas and in February turned north into South Carolina, where his men gutted the state capital of Columbia, and then marched into North Carolina. Confederate General Johnston, with a ragtag army of twenty-two thousand men, faced the Union juggernaut. Sherman's objective immediately switched from destroying property to preventing Johnston from linking up with Lee in Virginia.

Through the fall and winter of 1864–1865, Grant's army had been locked in a stalemate with Lee's dwindling forces, stretching the thin Confederate lines along a seventy-mile front and slowly encircling Petersburg. Confederate authorities became so desperate that they took the previously unthinkable step of offering freedom to slaves who would enlist. The irony was not lost on southern whites and blacks. "The South went to war to defeat the designs of the abolitionists," a Virginia newspaper thundered, "and behold! in the midst of the war, we turn abolitionists ourselves!" Few slaves took the offer. As one prominent slave owner recognized, why fight for possible freedom in a slave society when all blacks "are pretty sure of having it anyway" after a Union victory.

On April 1, 1865, a Union breakthrough at Petersburg forced Lee and the Confederate government to abandon Richmond (see Map 13.4). Grant's army pursued Lee's haggard remnants and cornered them at Appomattox Court House. On April 9, Lee accepted Grant's respectful terms and surrendered. Two weeks later, Johnston surrendered to Sherman in North Carolina. In May, the

> The war ends with triumph and tragedy for the Union.

March to the Sea Sherman's destructive path from Atlanta to Savannah, intended to crush the Confederacy's resources and morale.

Map 13.5 Sherman's Campaign in the South, 1864–1865 While Grant tied Lee down in Virginia, Sherman pushed south to Atlanta. He maneuvered Confederates under Hood into abandoning the city and then led a rapid March to the Sea, destroying Confederate resources and morale. Hood invaded Tennessee trying to divert Sherman but was badly defeated at Franklin and Nashville. From Savannah, Sherman turned north to ravage South Carolina and prevent Johnston from joining Lee's retreating forces. News of Johnston's surrender reached Washington during mourning over Lincoln's assassination. ▼

Confederates' trans-Mississippi army under General Kirby Smith gave up its arms. The Civil War had finally ended.

Northerners had barely begun celebrating when unprecedented tragedy struck. Five days after Lee's surrender, John Wilkes Booth, a rabid Confederate sympathizer and the brother of a well-known stage actor, assassinated Lincoln. Booth had stalked the Union president for months, initially with a kidnapping plan in mind, but he turned to murder after Lincoln began supporting voting rights for blacks. On the night of April 14, he shot the president at Ford's Theatre in Washington. Fleeing across the Potomac, Booth was tracked down by Union soldiers and killed. Eight of his accomplices, one of whom stabbed Secretary of State Seward (who recovered) and another who was assigned to kill Vice President Johnson but balked, were arrested. Four were convicted in the murder conspiracy and hanged. On April 15, the day Lincoln died, Andrew Johnson was sworn in as president.

A month earlier, in his Second Inaugural Address, Lincoln had noted the "fundamental and astounding" changes the war had brought. "Neither party expected for the war the magnitude or the duration which it has already attained," he said. "Neither anticipated that the cause of the conflict [slavery] might cease with or even before the conflict itself should cease." Lincoln had skillfully guided the Union through these transformations. As he considered the coming peace, the president reaffirmed his commitment both to end slavery forever and to "bind up the nation's wounds." Now this daunting dual agenda was left to his successors.

13-6
National and Global Impacts of the War

After Appomattox, Union veterans were sent to the Southwest to pressure France's puppet regime in Mexico. This sheet music conveyed their message in song. The lyrics explain that Napoleon III had sneaked in a Hapsburg prince "while Old Uncle Sam was busy . . . with his dear rebellious children." But "now our cruel war is over, we're united all once more. . . . Poor Max, there's no use talking, so pack up your kit and go, for the Universal Nation says 'Get Out of Mexico!'"

How does the illustrator portray the victorious Union's strong international posture? Why do the lyrics refer to the Civil War and call the United States "the Universal Nation"? ▶

Lyon and Healy, Chicago, 1866

The Civil War was the most traumatic event to date in the nation's history. As many as 700,000 soldiers died in the conflict, fourteen times the number killed in the Revolutionary War. Confronted with death on a monumental scale, Americans struggled to ennoble it. Northerners took pride in the Union's preservation and prosperity while white Southerners bewailed their lost pride and privilege. Emancipation, the war's most radical change, aligned the nation's laws with its ideals but also opened a hotly contested social revolution in the South. Outside the nation's borders, the conflict industrialized warfare and escalated its destructiveness. Its outcome solidified republican government in Mexico and inspired European reformers to press for democratic changes. Cleared of slavery's taint, many Americans hoped that their reunited states might be a beacon of freedom to the world's peoples.

☞ As you read, consider the many ways the Civil War changed Americans and others. How did the political, social, economic, and technological effects of the war reverberate inside the nation and beyond it?

13-6a Legacies of the War for the Nation

The war had devastated the South, where most battles were fought, destroying railroads, industries, and farms and defacing the landscape. Defeat

{ The war strengthens the national government, hardens sectional loyalties, and ends slavery.

Lost Cause Nostalgic postwar defense of the Confederacy by southern whites.

also scarred white Southerners' consciousness, ending a way of life based on slavery and instilling harsh memories of invasion and occupation. The experience fed their regional pride and defiance, cementing their devotion to the **Lost Cause**. Talk of secession ended, but states' rights remained a potent dissenting ideology. In this sense, the Civil War did not close the book on sectionalism but added a new chapter to its history.

Economically, the war had brought prosperity to the North and set the foundation for future growth. Whereas the South's share of the nation's wealth fell by more than 60 percent, the aggregate wealth of the North increased significantly. This bonanza was not distributed equally, however. Industrialists and entrepreneurs benefited but business and government did little to moderate class and gender inequalities.

Battlefield victories enforced Lincoln's claim that the Union was perpetual and achieved its preservation. In fact, the national government emerged from the war more powerful than before, having exercised authority over banking, taxation, railroads, and the disposition of western lands. For African Americans and their abolitionist allies, emancipation was the war's most far-reaching achievement. At the war's outset, most Northerners were not abolitionists, and few observers foresaw that Lincoln would align the goal of "assur[ing] freedom to the free" with "giving freedom to the slave." Yet white racial attitudes shifted only gradually. Many Northerners still balked at extending voting rights to blacks and considered them racially inferior. White Southerners stiffened their defense of white supremacy.

The Civil War ended slavery and secession but left other questions unresolved. Disputes over the balance of federal and state authority persisted, and issues that cut across sectional lines, such as the tariff, currency, and immigration, remained controversial. Most immediately, the war's outcome left two pressing and fundamental questions: On what terms would northern and southern states be reunited, and what place would the freed slaves take in American society? Answering them became the central challenge of the postwar years.

13-6b The Transnational Technology of War

Because it was the first great conflict fought with the weapons of the Industrial Revolution, the Civil War changed the nature of warfare. Some

{ The Civil War revolutionizes weaponry, making future wars deadlier. }

new weapons, such as British sharpshooter rifles and French conical bullets (minié balls), had not been previously used on a massive scale. Others, such as repeating rifles, submarines, and land mines, were U.S. innovations. These new weapons helped to make the Civil War the deadliest of the era's nationalist conflicts outside of Asia (see Figure 13.2). The war conclusively demonstrated the importance of railroads and telegraph lines in conducting large-scale combat and the superiority of ironclad warships over wooden fleets. Taken together, the Civil War's technological changes marked it as the first "modern war." Its new weaponry made subsequent wars even deadlier.

European military observers criticized America's volunteer soldiers as "armed mobs from which nothing could be learned," as one Prussian general concluded. Few realized how the Civil War's repeating guns, trench warfare, and indecisive battles foreshadowed the devastation of World War I. Yet the U.S. experience did influence European practice. Successful bombardments demonstrated that new rifled cannons made masonry forts obsolete. After observing Union monitors and Confederate rams, European navies rushed to build fleets of ironclad warships. The world's first ocean battle between ironclads occurred between Austria and Italy just one year after the Civil War ended.

Figure 13.2 Death Toll of Mid-Nineteenth-Century Nationalist and Civil Wars Although it was dwarfed by China's Taiping Rebellion (1850–1864), in which 20 million people lost their lives, the U.S. Civil War was the deadliest Western conflict in an age of many nationalist and civil wars. Disease continued to cause most war deaths, but conscription and massive armies, more powerful and accurate weapons, and civilian targets increased casualties in the mid-1800 conflicts and later wars. ▶ Source: Estimates derived from annotated lists in *Statistics of Wars, Oppressions and Atrocities of the Nineteenth Century* (http://necrometrics.com/wars19c.htm)

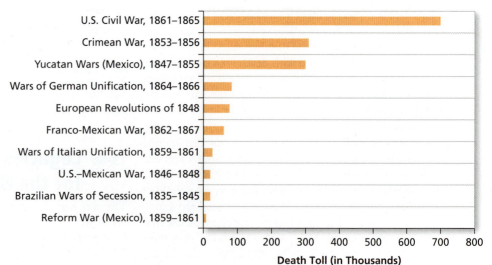

NOTE: Figures are approximate and include soldier and civilian deaths.

Harper's Weekly

Global Americans Born in Massachusetts in 1831, **Frederick Townsend Ward** was an international adventurer who sought military glory and was willing to shift allegiances to achieve it. He sailed on clipper ships to China, joined a U.S. filibuster expedition to Mexico, and fought for the French in the Crimean War. On a trading voyage, Ward arrived in Shanghai in 1860 at the height of the Taiping Rebellion (1850–1864), a massive religious and political uprising against the Qing emperor. At first, he planned to join the rebels but switched sides when Shanghai bankers and merchants offered him financing. To defend the emperor, Ward organized the Ever Victorious Army, an elite body of five thousand Chinese troops led by Western officers and trained in modern weaponry and tactics. When news of the American Civil War reached China, Ward wavered but eventually sided with the Union. His army protected Shanghai's small American expatriate community from attacks by the British navy, and he pledged much of its booty to the Union cause. In 1862, Ward led the Ever Victorious Army to several victories over rebel Taiping forces that greatly outnumbered his men. His spectacular success ended when he was mortally wounded in the Battle of Cixi in September 1862. In the United States, the events of the Civil War overshadowed Ward's exploits during his lifetime and afterward, but he is better known in China. Some historians credit him with saving Shanghai for the Qing dynasty, but most believe that exporting Western arms and military training to China was his major legacy.

One U.S. military innovation aimed at humane effects. In 1863 at Lincoln's request, the German-American legal philosopher Francis Lieber drew up a code of conduct for Union soldiers. Known as General Orders No. 100, or simply the **Lieber Code**, it was prompted by Confederate brutality toward captured black soldiers. The code prescribed treatment of prisoners of war, civilians, and spies. It became the basis for later international agreements, including the Hague Regulations of 1907, which absorbed it into international treaty law. As modified by subsequent Geneva Conventions, it remains in effect today.

13-6c Political and Economic Reverberations Abroad

The North's victory not only reunited the Union but also helped to consolidate neighboring nations. Following the Confederates' surrender, fifty thousand federal soldiers under General Sheridan marched to the Texas-Mexican border. U.S. officials pressured France to withdraw from Mexico and established a naval blockade to prevent Austrian reinforcements. After Napoleon III withdrew French forces in 1866, Maximilian's monarchy collapsed, President Juárez was restored to office, and the Mexican republic was saved. The Civil War also spurred, more indirectly, the creation of modern Canada through the British North America Act of 1867 (see Chapter 14).

> The war encourages nation building in North America and liberal nationalism in Europe.

Trade disruptions spread the Civil War's effects around the globe. Cotton growers in India, Egypt, West Africa, Turkey, and Brazil expanded farms to replace exports from the South. After emancipation, production shifted from slave economies to sharecroppers, tenant farmers, and peasants. The South's cotton exports recovered but no longer monopolized the global market. Meanwhile, wartime Confederate raiding and the Union demand for ships devastated the American whaling industry in the Pacific. Merchants in Hawai'i lost their lucrative restocking business and turned to growing sugar, making it the island kingdom's chief industry by the war's end.

In rallying the public behind the war, Lincoln had described the United States as the world's "last best hope" for democracy. The European Revolutions of 1848 had failed to replace monarchies with lasting republics and constitutions. In some cases, such as Germany under Chancellor Otto von Bismarck, nationalist movements had embraced authoritarian politics. Lincoln, in contrast, had aligned U.S. national unification with political equality. The Union's victory reinvigorated the idea of democratic self-government and encouraged European liberals to promote reforms. Britain extended voting rights to workers and small landholders. French jurist Edouard Laboulaye, a strong supporter of the Union and emancipation, proposed constructing the Statue of Liberty as a congratulatory gift to the United States. In India, Australia, and elsewhere, emerging colonial nationalists took heart from the U.S. example. Confident American victors anticipated that the "new birth of freedom" forecast by Lincoln in his Gettysburg Address would spread worldwide. The most perceptive observers realized, however, that its promise first had to be kept at home.

Lieber Code Rules of warfare codified at President Lincoln's request by legal scholar Francis Lieber, which influenced later international agreements covering combat and prisoners.

Summary

The American Civil War took place among parallel struggles over national unity and the extension of freedom that had begun with the European Revolutions of 1848, continued with Latin American civil wars, and concluded with Italian and German unification in 1871. Although both the Union and the Confederacy anticipated a quick victory, the war became a long and deadly struggle as the Union's mobile troops and gunboats won victories in the Mississippi Valley that were countered by Confederate triumphs on the battlefields of Virginia. Mass mobilization of soldiers and civilians provided men and supplies, railroads and steamboats took them to battle zones, and the new technology of rifled muskets and cannons littered battlefields with the dead and wounded.

As the war dragged on, it took on larger dimensions, some of them unanticipated. Native Americans became involved as participants or as rebels against treaties imposed by white governments. Britain and France threatened to intervene, potentially tipping the scales in the Confederates' favor or embroiling Europe's powers in a global war. The Confederate and Union central governments expanded their powers, the latter in permanent ways. Above all, the war's erosion of social institutions, accelerated by occupying armies and runaway slaves, led to Lincoln's momentous decision to emancipate the South's slaves.

By 1864, the Union's superior leadership and resources began to take effect. After the Union's campaign of destruction in the lower South and gradual encirclement in Virginia, the Confederates were forced to surrender. The South's landscape lay devastated and its racial order overturned. Victorious Northerners cheered the Union's preservation and its example of republican self-government to the world. Looking ahead, Americans of all regions and races faced the formidable task of healing sectional wounds, deciding the proper role of government, and enacting the pledge of freedom given to former slaves.

<Thinking Back, *Looking Forward*>

As you review this chapter, think about how the Civil War continued a centralizing trend for the nation and the federal government. What other nations experienced similar nationalizing struggles, even civil wars, at this time? In the next chapters, look for the consequences of a strong central government and for continuing conflict over its powers. Compare slave emancipation in the United States with emancipation of unfree people elsewhere. Did governments translate freedom into equality?

To make your review concrete, review the timeline and reflect on the entries there. Think about their causes, consequences, and connections. How do they fit with global trends?

Additional Resources

Books

Berlin, Ira, et al. *Free at Last: A Documentary History of Slavery, Freedom, and the Civil War.* **New York: New Press, 2007.** ▶ A revealing collection of documents from enslaved and free African Americans.

Blight, David. *Race and Reunion: The Civil War in American Memory.* **Cambridge, MA: Harvard University Press, 2002.** ▶ Pioneering exploration of how the war was remembered and commemorated.

Clinton, Catherine, and Nina Silber, eds. *Divided Houses: Gender and the Civil War.* **New York: Oxford University Press, 1992.** ▶ Essays on the varied wartime roles of men and women.

Doyle, Don H. *The Cause of All Nations: An International History of the Civil War.* **New York: Basic Books, 2015.** ▶ An engaging history of wartime diplomacy and public opinion abroad.

Gallagher, Gary. *The Confederate War.* **Cambridge, MA: Harvard University Press, 1999.** ▶ An expert contribution to the debate over why the Confederacy lost.

Goodwin, Doris Kearns. *Team of Rivals: The Political Genius of Abraham Lincoln.* **New York: Simon and Schuster, 2006.** ▶ Colorful narrative of how Lincoln led his administration and the Union to emancipation and victory.

Guelzo, Alan. *Gettysburg: The Last Invasion.* **New York: Knopf, 2013.** ▶ Detailed, dramatic study of an epic battle and key military turning point.

Hauptman, Laurence M. *Between Two Fires: American Indians in the Civil War.* **New York: Free Press, 1995.** ▶ An informative survey of wartime activities and divisions among Native Americans.

McPherson, James. *Battle Cry of Freedom: The Civil War Era.* **New York: Oxford University Press, 1988.** ▶ The best single-volume overview of the period.

Sutherland, Daniel E. *A Savage Conflict: The Decisive Role of Guerrillas in the American Civil War.* **Chapel Hill: University of North Carolina Press, 2013.** ▶ Excellent overview of an often-neglected and sometimes romanticized aspect of the war.

Go to the MindTap® for **Global Americans** to access the full version of select books from this Additional Resources section.

Websites

Abraham Lincoln Papers at the Library of Congress. (http://memory.loc.gov/ammem/alhtml/malhome.html). ▶ A collection of twenty thousand documents by or relating to President Lincoln.

The Civil War Home Page. (http://www.civil-war.net). ▶ Excellent gateway to Civil War documents on the Internet from printed and archival sources.

The Civil War in *Harper's Weekly.* **(http://sonofthesouth .net/).** ▶ A complete file of the popular northern illustrated magazine during the war.

Civil War Photographs from the Library of Congress Collections. (http://www.loc.gov/pictures/collection/ civwar/). ▶ More than seven thousand photographs on varied aspects of the war.

Making of America: The War of the Rebellion. (http:// ebooks.library.cornell.edu/m/moawar/waro.html). ▶ Searchable copy of the one hundred twenty-eight-volume Official Records of the Union and Confederate Armies, originally published in 1880–1901.

National Park Service. (http://www.nps.gov). ▶ Gateway site to Civil War National Military Parks and Soldiers and Sailors database.

The Valley of the Shadow. (http://jefferson.village .virginia.edu/vshadow2/). ▶ A rich collection of sources on how the Civil War affected two counties, one in Pennsylvania, the other in Virginia.

 MindTap®

Continue exploring online through MindTap®**, where you can:**
- **Assess your knowledge with the Chapter Test**
- **Watch historical videos related to the chapter**
- **Further your understanding with interactive maps and timelines**

The American Civil War

1861

March

Czar Alexander II issues edict freeing Russia's serfs.

Benito Juárez is elected president of the Mexican Republic after Reform War ends.

Lincoln is inaugurated as U.S. president.

April

South Carolina bombards Fort Sumter, opening the Civil War.

June

Northern women form U.S. Sanitary Commission, modeled on British organization from Crimean War.

1861

July

Confederate army is victorious at First Battle of Bull Run in Virginia.

November

Trent Affair sparks Anglo-American diplomatic crisis and war scare.

1862

February

Grant's victories at Forts Henry and Donelson spearhead Union advances down the Mississippi Valley.

March

Standoff between *Monitor* and *Virginia* opens global era of ironclad warships. Union victory at Glorieta Pass, New Mexico, thwarts Confederate designs on California.

May

Federal Homestead Act offers free farms to loyal Northerners and immigrants.

1862

July

Peninsular Campaign ends in Union retreat from outskirts of Richmond.

U.S. Congress passes Pacific Railroad Acts, strengthening economic ties to West.

September

Battle of Antietam halts Lee's invasion of Maryland.

Lincoln announces Preliminary Emancipation Proclamation.

1863

January

Emancipation Proclamation frees slaves in rebel areas, welcomes black Union recruits, gains support for the U.S. abroad.

April

Lieber Code, written to counter Confederate mistreatment of black Union soldiers, prescribes globally influential rules of military conduct.

May

Battle of Chancellorsville caps Lee's successes, Union failures in Virginia.

June

West Virginia separates from Virginia and joins the Union, highlighting border-state divisions.

Napoleon III's French army seizes Mexico and installs Maximilian, Archduke of Austria, as emperor.

1863

July

Union victories at Gettysburg and Vicksburg turn military tide in the Union's favor.

New York City Draft Riot dramatizes dissent on Union and Confederate home fronts.

September

Russian fleet makes friendly visits to New York and San Francisco.

British government seizes ironclad *Laird Rams* intended for Confederacy.

1864

April

Confederates massacre surrendering black Union soldiers at Fort Pillow, Tennessee.

May–June

Overland Campaign in Virginia produces bloody stalemate between Grant's and Lee's armies.

1864

September

Sherman captures Atlanta, boosting Republican fortunes in election year.

October–November

Confederate agents enter U.S. from Canada to raid Vermont and New York City.

November

Lincoln is reelected over Democrat George McClellan, the war's pivotal political event.

Union soldiers annihilate Cheyenne and Arapaho Indians in the Sand Creek Massacre in Colorado.

November–December

Sherman's March to the Sea destroys Confederates' resources and resolve.

1865

April

After breakthrough at Petersburg, Virginia, major Confederate armies surrender, ending the Civil War.

Lincoln is assassinated, succeeded by Vice President Andrew Johnson.

June

Stand Watie, Cherokee chief, is last Confederate general to surrender.

1866

January

Under U.S. pressure, Napoleon III announces withdrawal of French troops from Mexico, hastening fall of Emperor Maximilian.

April

Supreme Court rules in *ex parte Milligan* against trying civilians in military tribunals when civil courts are functioning.

14

Reunion and Retreat: Reconstruction

1865–1877

The son of immigrants from Haiti and Cuba, Rodolphe Desdunes worked throughout his life for equal rights for people of color in Louisiana. This included organizing support for Homère Plessy, the plaintiff in the landmark *Plessy v. Ferguson* case, which ultimately upheld segregation and proved a deep disappointment to Desdunes.

For Louisiana people of color like Rodolphe Desdunes, emancipation was a transnational movement and a multigenerational commitment. Carried by slaves and other migrants, the ideal of racial equality coursed across the Atlantic and stretched in time from the French and Haitian Revolutions of the 1790s to the American antisegregation campaigns a century later. Desdunes's parents were from Haiti and Cuba; he grew up in the New Orleans community of Creoles or "free coloreds" whose French language associations protested racial restrictions and advocated abolition. When federal troops occupied New Orleans during the Civil War, many Creole men joined the Union army, cementing their claim to full citizenship. After the war, Louisiana's new Constitution of 1868 guaranteed "equal civil, political and public rights" to all citizens. Six years of Republican rule built freed people's schools, enlisted blacks in the state militia, and elected dozens of American-born and Caribbean-origin blacks to office.

Louisiana Division/City Archives

Desdunes was too young to vote for the 1868 Constitution, but he defended it when black civil rights came under attack by violent white-supremacist groups. Serving on the New Orleans Metropolitan Police, Desdunes was wounded in 1874 when more than three thousand armed White Leaguers, mostly Confederate veterans, stormed city hall and the statehouse. They withdrew only after President Grant rushed federal troops to the city.

As the rights of people of color were assailed, Desdunes began studying law to take their grievances to the federal courts, where postwar constitutional amendments could be used to challenge state laws. When Louisiana mandated racial segregation on railroads, Desdunes enlisted his son to test the statute and won a verdict that integrated interstate trains. Because railroad travel *within* Louisiana remained segregated, Desdunes organized support for Homer (born Homère) Plessy, another Creole of Haitian descent, to mount a legal challenge that climbed to the U.S. Supreme Court. *Plessy v. Ferguson* (1896), which upheld Louisiana's segregationist practices, broke the promise of Louisiana's 1868 constitution and signaled the final unwinding of Reconstruction. Heartbroken, Desdunes withdrew from public life to write a history of black Creole activism in New Orleans meant to inspire future generations to renew the struggle.

Desdunes's post-Civil War experience had unique features that stemmed from Louisiana's Afro-French community and its cosmopolitan outlook. Still, Louisiana blacks played an important role outside the state as prominent advocates for civil equality. Moreover, the struggle in Louisiana broadly resembled the course of postwar debates elsewhere in the nation. What political and social rights would be guaranteed to emancipated African Americans? How far would the northern victors and newly empowered freed people restructure southern society and politics to embody those rights? How would the former Confederate states be restored to the Union, and who would control that process? How much authority should the federal government exert over the states?

How do the experiences of Rodolphe Desdunes reflect the struggle of Louisiana blacks and the role that they played as prominent advocates for civil equality?

Go to MindTap® to watch a video on Desdunes and learn how his story relates to the themes of this chapter.

The answers to such questions were hotly debated among different political, economic, and racial groups. Control over events veered between the president and Congress, the states and the federal government. All knew that the outcome was as important as the Civil War's battles, for it was possible to win the war and lose the peace. The questions themselves implied a dilemma: Rapid and lenient restoration of Rebel states to the Union would mean letting go of transforming the South and enforcing racial equality, whereas determination to revolutionize the South's economic and racial order would mean a long, costly, and potentially bloody struggle.

Of the two main postwar tasks Americans faced—restoring political relations with former rebels and reshaping southern life after slavery—the first was the residue of civil war, and the second was the aftermath of emancipation. Viewed in a global context, the postwar political settlement resembled national unification in countries such as Italy and Germany, where the northern victors dominated the national government but North-South differences remained and regional resentments festered. The struggle over emancipation was also a familiar global theme. Around the world, other slaveholding nations, including Spain (in Cuba), Britain (in Jamaica), and Brazil, faced similar conflicts over emancipating slaves and defining justice once they were liberated. Emancipation during the Civil War gradually undermined the existence of slavery elsewhere, including Cuba and Brazil. Yet the abandonment of the North's Reconstruction program indicated that for the time being, the United States would follow a conservative path similar to that of other postemancipation societies in the Americas, which retreated from equality, limited the rights won by freed people, and appeased their former masters.

14-1
Wartime Origins of Reconstruction

As the Civil War ended, the Freedmen's Bureau, northern charities, and former slaves collaborated to construct local schools in the South. This photograph shows the Freedmen's School and its students on James Plantation in North Carolina.

Examine the photograph and the placement of its subjects. Who is the woman on the left? What can we learn from the varied heights and two sexes of the pupils? What can this photograph tell you about freedmen's schools and black Southerners' attitudes toward education? ▶

The Granger Collection, New York

Reconstruction began long before the Civil War ended. When the federal army occupied areas in Louisiana, Tennessee, and Virginia, local Unionists made preparations to rejoin the federal government. Before and after President Lincoln's Emancipation Proclamation, hundreds of thousands of runaway slaves migrated behind Union lines, seeking freedom and enlisting as federal soldiers or hospital workers. Wartime debates in Congress over readmitting rebellious states, addressing freed people's aspirations for land and labor, and adopting Union policies to meet the needs of the refugee influx provided a rehearsal for the postwar struggle over Reconstruction.

☞ As you read, consider how the Union's actions during wartime helped to set up conflicting expectations for postwar reconstruction. Were Union policies meant to raise former slaves' economic status or to keep them as farm laborers?

14-1a Lincoln versus Congress

{ The president and congressional Republicans quarrel over Reconstruction.

In his Proclamation of Amnesty and Reconstruction of December 1863, President Lincoln set lenient terms to entice Confederates back to the Union. While holding firm on emancipation, the president offered pardons and restoration of property to Confederates (except to high military and civil officials) who would swear an oath of allegiance to the United States. According to Lincoln's **Ten-Percent Plan**, as soon as 10 percent of those who had voted in 1860 took the oath, new state governments could be formed. He imposed no requirements for freed people's civil and political rights.

Most congressional Republicans criticized Lincoln's plan of "restoration" and favored a more thorough "reconstruction" of the South. Republican radicals, about one-third of the party's congressmen, wanted to "revolutionize Southern institutions, habits, and manners," according to spokesman Thaddeus Stevens. Moderates favored less drastic changes but agreed that Congress, not the president, should control reconstruction. The gap between Lincoln and **Radical Republicans** was exposed in the struggle over reconstruction in Louisiana, where the new state constitution of 1864, ratified by only 10 percent of Louisiana's adult white males, rejected black suffrage. In response, Congress denied admission to Louisiana's representatives.

In July, Republicans in Congress countered Lincoln's plan with the **Wade-Davis Bill**. It required 50 percent of voters to take an oath of allegiance to the Union and mandated that new state constitutions be drawn up by delegates elected by those who had never supported the rebellion. Lincoln, fearing that this bill would halt the process underway in Louisiana and Arkansas, killed the legislation by using a pocket veto, refusing to sign it before Congress's session ended.

Lincoln's reelection in 1864 paved the way for passage of a measure that the president and Republican radicals agreed on: the **Thirteenth Amendment**, abolishing slavery nationwide. Republicans feared that Lincoln's Emancipation Proclamation would be overturned by the courts in peacetime or reversed by new state governments in the South. The solution was to amend the federal constitution. Fall elections in 1864 gave the Republicans a strong congressional majority, and in January 1865, the House of Representatives passed the Thirteenth Amendment after several wavering Democrats were wooed by Republican lobbyists to their side. When the amendment was ratified by three-quarters of the states, emancipation became the law of the land in December 1865.

14-1b Emancipation on the Ground

{ Northern volunteers and the Union government assist the freed people.

In regions far from the invading Union armies, most black Southerners did not learn about emancipation until the spring of 1865. *Juneteenth*, the official announcement of emancipation in the holdout state of Texas on June 19, 1865, became a special day of celebration for African Americans. Long before that, slaves in coastal regions and the upper South had taken steps to free themselves. More than a million fled the South's plantations during the war, and half ended up in Union-occupied areas.

Union army officers' response to the influx of freed people was shaped by the desire to maintain order and agricultural production more than humanitarian motives. Herded into makeshift camps, some freed people were supplied rations and hired by the army and navy for meager wages as laborers, cooks, or hospital workers. Others were contracted to work on plantations seized by Union armies and leased to loyal southern whites or Yankee entrepreneurs.

For freedmen intent on staying in the agricultural South, leasing or buying confiscated lands was the preferred alternative. By the end of the war, nearly one-fifth of the farmland in areas under Union occupation was being worked by independent black families. When General Sherman passed through coastal Georgia and South Carolina in January 1865, local black leaders persuaded him to draft **Field Order No. 15** to give each freed family provisional title to forty acres of land confiscated from slaveholders. Union officials settled more than forty thousand freed people there. Elsewhere in the South, small pockets of freed people had been able to purchase land during the war.

Freed people's thirst for education was quenched more readily than their hunger for land. Freedmen's aid societies formed in the North sent more than one thousand teachers to the South during the war, and the influx increased after Appomattox. Three-quarters were women and perhaps one-fifth were black. Charlotte Forten, a young African American woman who journeyed from Philadelphia to teach in South Carolina's Lowcountry, told her

Ten-Percent Plan Lincoln's lenient wartime program to restore pacified Confederate states to the Union.

Radical Republicans Party faction intent on ensuring civil rights for former slaves and transforming the South's society and economy during Reconstruction.

Wade-Davis Bill Congressional measure that required stiff loyalty tests for readmitting former Confederate states but that Lincoln pocket vetoed.

Thirteenth Amendment Constitutional addition outlawing slavery in the United States that was ratified eight months after the Civil War ended.

Field Order No. 15 Sherman's 1865 decree setting aside land confiscated from slaveholders in coastal South Carolina, Georgia, and Florida for settlement by freed people.

Freedmen's Bureau Federal agency created under the War Department to oversee education, labor contracts, and welfare of former slaves.

students about "the noble Toussaint [L'Ouverture]," the black liberator of Haiti, so that they "should know what one of their own color could do for his race." Teachers like Forten promoted basic literacy and numeracy but also strove to help freed people "unlearn the teachings of slavery" by promoting pride, self-discipline, and the dignity of work.

Higher education for freed people was offered in seminaries, colleges, and "normal schools" (teacher training institutions) that were founded by northern charitable organizations and biracial missionary societies. Howard University in Washington, D.C., Fisk University in Tennessee, and Hampton Institute in Virginia trace their origins to Reconstruction; all were named after or led by prominent Civil War generals.

Congress assisted these philanthropic ventures and independent schools through the **Freedmen's Bureau**,

established in March 1865. Run by the War Department, the bureau allocated one-third of its budget to schools from primary education to colleges such as Howard and Fisk. It took over the Union army's wartime mandate to provide relief to refugees and to enforce labor contracts between planters and former slaves.

Prevailing stereotypes and ideologies compromised most types of help available to the freed people, whether it was provided by the federal government or private volunteers. Many army supervisors and Unionist whites envisioned southern blacks as permanent farm workers, not owners. Free-market practices meant that whites often outbid former slaves who had scraped together money to buy land. And the free-labor ideology decreed that blacks should be left to fend for themselves after a short period of aid and tutelage. These assumptions persisted and undermined Northerners' plans to reconstruct the South.

14-2
Postwar Conditions and Conflicting Agendas

Thomas Nast's widely distributed cartoons in *Harper's Weekly* magazine both shaped and reflected northern views of Reconstruction. This cartoon of August 5, 1865, features contrasting episodes. On the left panel titled *Pardon,* Columbia, a symbol of the United States, wonders "Shall I trust these men?" referring to the prostrate figures of Robert E. Lee, Jefferson Davis, and other former Confederate leaders. On the right panel called *Franchise,* Columbia clasps the shoulder of a disabled black Union veteran and asks, "And not these men?" The globe-shaped object on the pedestal is a ballot box.

How does the cartoonist contrast President Johnson's plan to pardon former Confederate leaders with mainstream Republicans' program to give voting rights to male African Americans? Which position does the cartoonist favor, and how does his portrayal indicate it? ▶

Library of Congress Prints and Photographs Division

Go to MindTap® to practice history with the Chapter 14 **Primary Source Writing Activity: Responses to Reconstruction.** Read and view primary sources and respond to a writing prompt.

At the end of the Civil War, white Southerners were demoralized and resentful while the region's blacks looked forward to free and independent lives. All realized that postwar life would require changes, and each group developed its own agenda. Dramatic divisions formed among white and black Southerners, political parties, the president, and Congress over restoring the Union and defining the role of former slaves. The debate over Reconstruction paralleled struggles that followed the emancipation

of slaves and other unfree laborers in overseas lands, but control by congressional Republicans seemed to promise a more equitable outcome than elsewhere.

☞ As you read, consider the agendas of different political groups in the North and South for postwar Reconstruction. How did the varied positions of former slaves, southern whites, President Johnson, and the Republican-dominated Congress lead to conflict, and over which issues?

14-2a Freedom in Action

At the war's end, slavery was gone and the Confederacy dissolved, but no new social or political system emerged to take their place. Despite the initial confusion, the lines were quickly drawn between southern blacks and whites over the fundamental issues of land, labor, and political power.

> African American families reunite and organize to secure equal rights.

Former slaves had firm ideas about what they expected from freedom. For many, the first task was to reunite families who had been separated by slavery or the war. Freed people used their communal grapevine to locate relatives and took to the roads to find them. They enlisted help from the Freedmen's Bureau or paid for newspaper advertisements. Some relatives were never found, but most families broken by slavery were mended in the postwar years, and by 1870, the two-parent household became the norm.

Reconstituted African American families had to decide where to live. Some returned to the familiar surroundings of their old plantation, but many others fled the places where they had labored. As one slave told her former owner, "If I stay here I'll never know I'm free." Thousands moved to cities, believing that life would be freer there and Union troops would provide protection. The black population of major southern cities doubled in the five years after the war. Urban black enclaves were segregated "across the tracks" from whites, and occupational choices were restricted by prejudice. The majority of males became unskilled manual laborers and women were hired as maids, washerwomen, or seamstresses. Still, their neighborhoods provided precious space where African Americans established schools, clubs, benevolent societies, and other community institutions.

Whether in towns or the countryside, African Americans organized and built separate Protestant churches. Predominantly Baptist and Methodist, they became focal points for religious life and other community activities from educational classes and festivals to political meetings. Black women played prominent roles in these events, and male ministers emerged as respected community leaders who dispensed political as well as spiritual guidance.

In an agricultural society, economic independence entailed access to land. Stimulated by the Freedman's Bureau, "forty acres and a mule" became the rallying cry for freed people who demanded a portion of the lands they had worked for generations. They were deeply disappointed when "Sherman's lands" were restored to white owners and various proposals to confiscate and redistribute Rebel plantations failed to win passage in Congress.

The majority of newly emancipated blacks had little choice but to work on plantations for wages. Determined to get their full worth, blacks bargained hard over wages and hours and turned to the Freedmen's Bureau for help in enforcing annual contracts with white employers. Many African American women refused to return to full-time fieldwork, eager to raise their children and tend their own households. Labor shortages gave freedmen bargaining power, but they hated working in gangs, which reminded them of slavery, and distrusted their former masters as employers.

Freedmen realized that political organizing was necessary to demand equal rights. Even before the war ended, freedmen had joined Union Leagues, Republican clubs that had been organized in occupied districts, and used them to call for the rights of "all loyal men, without distinction of color." In the summer and fall of 1865, freedmen's conventions assembled in most former Confederate states,

Image copyright © The Metropolitan Museum of Art. Image source: Art Resource, NY

Dressing for the Carnival In the 1870s, northern artist Winslow Homer captured this image of a freed Virginia family preparing for the Afro-Caribbean festival of Jonkonnu, a celebration that former slaves merged with the Fourth of July. In the painting, two women sew colorful shards on a man dressing like a harlequin, while children look on, one holding a lowered American flag. Homer celebrated the freed people's creative mix of cultures while subtly contrasting hopes for Reconstruction with its harsh realities. ◄

several in black churches. Delegates addressed petitions to white-dominated constitutional conventions, demanding equal participation and the right to vote. The new white governments ignored these demands, indicating how far apart former masters and former slaves stood at the dawn of the new era.

14-2b White Resistance

The war's physical and eco-nomic devastation demoral-ized white Southerners, who had controlled the region's resources. Much of Atlanta, Charleston, and Richmond lay in ruins. Slave emancipa-tion and farms destroyed by marching armies diminished planters' wealth, and the wartime deaths of one in five white southern men deprived households of traditional heads. With no new legal system in place, crime rates rose sharply.

> In defeat, white Southerners are devastated but defiant.

Many former Confederates feared being subject to occupying troops who had recently killed the South's sol-diers. White Southerners especially dreaded reprisals from their former slaves, who might claim former masters' pos-sessions or even murder them. In late 1865, rumors of a pending Christmas insurrection of violent freedmen, stirred by recollections of a similar revolt in Jamaica, sent chills through the South's white communities. A South Carolina planter's wife foresaw "the foulest demonic pas-sions of the negro, hitherto so peaceful & happy, roused into being & fierce activity by the devilish Yankees."

Paranoia about potential black violence prompted immediate attacks by whites. The Civil War left a legacy of guerrilla warfare, racial hatred, and gun carrying in the South that continued to fuel violence after Appomattox. On Christ-mas Eve 1865, a group of Confederate veterans gathered in Pulaski, Tennessee, to organize the **Ku Klux Klan**. This secret vigilante group pledged to suppress all freedmen's assertions of equality and restore white supremacy by intimidation and violence. Its membership grew rapidly in the following year as it allied with opposition to black voting. Even white South-erners who renounced the Klan's tactics could not imagine peaceful coexistence of the two races under legal equality.

Southern whites especially worried about losing the cheap and disciplined labor of African American slaves on their farms. In the summer of 1865, white-dominated state legisla-tures passed restrictive **Black Codes** designed to return freed people to conditions as close to slavery as possi-ble. They forbade blacks from owning guns, consuming alcohol, and marry-ing whites. Vagrancy laws forced black men and women to carry permits and mandated fines or imprisonment for the unemployed. The Black Code in South Carolina required freedmen

Ku Klux Klan White supremacist secret society organized by former Confederates that terrorized southern blacks and their supporters during Reconstruction.

Black Codes Restrictive laws passed by Democratic-controlled southern states that denied civil rights and economic advancement to former slaves.

to pay hefty fees to set up businesses, and Mississippi's made it illegal for blacks to own or lease farmland. These codes announced that southern whites' immediate postwar agenda was to reestablish social and economic dominance over African Americans.

14-2c Johnson's Reconstruction Plan

Ex-Confederates' aspirations were bolstered by the new president, Andrew Johnson, who developed a surprisingly lenient Reconstruction plan.

> President Johnson seizes the initiative and conciliates former Confederates.

In some ways, Johnson was a worthy successor to the slain president. Like Lincoln, he was born in humble cir-cumstances in the upper South's backcountry, had little formal education, and rose through hard work. Johnson was also an ardent Unionist. A Democrat and the only sen-ator from the South to remain in Congress after secession, he had been appointed military governor of occupied Ten-nessee and inserted as Lincoln's running mate in 1864 on a bipartisan Union ticket. Johnson once owned slaves but during the war supported emancipation, mainly as way to punish the South's aristocrats, whom he resented. At the war's end, he declared repeatedly that "treason is a crime and must be made odious." Some Radical Republi-cans who had criticized Lincoln's generous reconstruction terms saw Johnson as a potential ally.

Yet as a former southern Democrat with states' rights leanings and unreconstructed racial views, Johnson had as much in common with the war's vanquished as its victors. His plan, introduced in May 1865, called for swift restora-tion of the Rebel states, which he claimed had never legally left the Union. Nearly all Southerners who swore an oath of allegiance to the Union would regain their political and property rights. Confederate civilian and military officers and those owning more than $20,000 in property had to obtain a presidential pardon. Except for having southern states ratify the Thirteenth Amendment, the plan was silent on civil or voting rights for the freed people.

Over the summer of 1865, Johnson dropped his call to punish Confederate leaders and granted more than thir-teen thousand pardons to wealthy former Confederates. Meanwhile, southern states largely accepted Johnson's mild conditions and created new governments little dif-ferent from prewar regimes. Some refused to ratify the Thirteenth Amendment or repudiate their Confederate debts. No reorganized southern state allowed black votes, and the former Confederates who led those states adopted harsh Black Codes. To underscore their defiance, white Southerners sent Alexander Stephens, the former Confed-erate vice president, to the U.S. Congress along with ten Confederate generals and fifty-eight former Confederate congressmen. Eight months after the war's end, Republi-can leaders wondered aloud who had actually won it.

14-2d Congressional Response

When Congress reconvened in December 1865, angry Republicans refused to seat representatives from the former Confederate states. Moderates agreed that the former slaves' civil rights should be protected, and most Republicans believed that southern states should not be readmitted until they renounced secession and repudiated Confederate debts. Many worried that unrepentant southern Democrats might undo Republican wartime legislation. Emancipation had nullified the constitution's clause that African Americans represented three-fifths of a person or citizen. Because freedmen were then counted as one whole person, southern states stood to gain as many as two dozen representatives in Congress. These concerns moved congressional Republicans toward extending voting rights to the former slaves on political as well as moral grounds.

> Congress opposes Johnson and forges an alternative Reconstruction program.

Taking aim at the Black Codes, Congress in early 1866 reauthorized the Freedman's Bureau, directing it to prosecute state officials who violated blacks' civil rights. President Johnson vetoed the bill. Clinging to old racial fears, he was convinced that efforts to empower freedmen would come at poor whites' expense. Congress next sought to broaden its protection of freed people by passing the **Civil Rights Act of 1866**, a landmark bill that specified that blacks enjoyed the same rights guaranteed to other U.S. citizens. It directly aimed to overturn the Supreme Court's *Dred Scott* decision of 1857. Again, Johnson vetoed the measure, denouncing its expansion of federal power as well as its assertion of equal rights. In both cases, the president's refusal to compromise helped to unite his Republican opponents, who mustered the two-thirds majority necessary to override his veto.

To counter white Southerners' opposition, Republican leaders sought constitutional protection for equal rights. In June 1866, Congress passed the **Fourteenth Amendment**, which absorbed the new Civil Rights Act into the federal charter. It declared that all persons born or naturalized in the United States (except Native Americans) were citizens entitled to due process and equal protection of the law. When ratified by the states in 1868, this sweeping provision established a policy of **birthright citizenship**, automatic granting of citizenship to those born within the nation's borders. This policy was later adopted by nearly all Western Hemisphere republics—most immediately, Argentina in 1869—but was resisted by European nations that relied on ties of language or blood lineage to bind their nationality.

Other sections of the Fourteenth Amendment repudiated the Confederate debt and disqualified Confederate officeholders from state and national positions. Rather than give black people the vote outright, the amendment specified that states denying suffrage to black men would have their representation in Congress reduced proportionally. Many Republicans represented northern states that denied blacks the vote and balked at mandating universal male suffrage. Some hoped that Johnson would accept the amendment as a compromise and a minimum condition for Reconstruction.

Johnson flatly opposed the Fourteenth Amendment and encouraged white Southerners and northern conservatives to remain defiant. In the summer of 1866, he launched an unprecedented speaking tour across the

Civil Rights Act of 1866 Law that recognized citizenship rights of former slaves and gave the federal government power to enforce them.

Fourteenth Amendment Constitutional addition ratified by the states in 1868 that gave citizenship to nearly all persons born or naturalized in the United States, including former slaves, and penalized states that restricted male suffrage.

birthright citizenship Automatic provision of citizenship to children born within a nation's borders or territories, which became common practice in the Americas after U.S. adoption.

Memphis Riots, May 1866 Three days of violence erupted after a white policeman tried to arrest a black Union veteran. Memphis's whites, who resented policing by black Union soldiers and competition with former slaves for jobs, attacked a black shantytown, shooting at will and setting buildings ablaze. Forty-six blacks and two whites died and one hundred buildings were burned, but no arrests were made. Accounts of the riot influenced passage of the Congressional Reconstruction Act. ▶

Tennessee State Library and Archives

SCENES IN MEMPHIS, TENNESSEE, DURING THE RIOT—SHOOTING DOWN NEGROES ON THE MORNING OF MAY 2, 1866.—[SKETCHED BY A. R. W.]

Print Collector/Hulton Archive/Getty Images

Global Americans The son of a Cuban schoolmaster, **Ambrosio Gonzales** was educated in New York and returned to Havana to earn a law degree and teach languages. There he joined a secret organization that advocated U.S. annexation of Cuba without ending slavery. In 1849 and 1850, Gonzales helped organize two failed filibusters to invade Cuba from the United States. Through these activities he became associated with prominent southern planters, and in 1856, he married into a wealthy South Carolina slaveholding family. During the Civil War, Gonzales served as a Confederate artillery chief under General P.G.T. Beauregard, his former schoolmate in New York. Reconstruction turned Gonzales's privileged plantation life upside down. The family estate languished when black workers departed and cotton prices fell, and Gonzales's Caribbean import business in Charleston was destroyed in a race riot. An experiment in hiring Chinese and European contract laborers for his sawmill ended in bankruptcy. In 1869, the family sailed to Havana, counting on wealthy relatives and the legality of Cuban slavery to escape the reversals of Reconstruction. Less than a year later, Gonzales's wife died of yellow fever. Returning to the United States in the 1870s, he scraped together a living by teaching in various cities and repeatedly urged Grant and others to annex Cuba. Although his Cuban background was unusual for the South's planter elite, Gonzales's career embodied their Caribbean connections, expansionist dreams, and resistance to emancipation and Reconstruction.

northern states to rally public support for his resistance to equal rights legislation. Scheming to bypass Republicans and forge a new centrist coalition, Johnson labeled his congressional opponents traitors who should be hung.

These crude attacks alienated the North's public. Meanwhile, two bloody race riots that broke out in southern cities suggested the violence Johnson's stand appeared to encourage. In May 1866, a mob of whites stormed a freed people's neighborhood in Memphis, killing nearly fifty and burning schools and churches. Three months later, armed whites in New Orleans attacked a black parade for voting rights; nearly eighty citizens were killed or wounded, most of them African Americans. These outrages prompted a backlash against Johnson and his policies. The 1866 congressional elections returned a veto-proof Republican majority to Congress. Republicans were poised to replace the president's discredited program of "restoration" with a more sweeping "reconstruction" agenda.

14-2e Reconstruction in a Global Perspective

During the Reconstruction years, Americans battled over the aftermath of civil war and the meaning of emancipation. Viewed in global perspective, neither struggle was unique. In the mid-nineteenth century, many countries faced continued turmoil after civil wars and emancipations. Their histories served as important points of influence and comparison for U.S. developments.

Former Confederates complained that Reconstruction was unduly harsh on the South, but most groups

> The United States stands out among postemancipation societies in granting freed slaves the right to political equality.

defeated in nineteenth-century civil wars were treated more brutally. The victorious Chinese imperial forces who suppressed the Taiping Rebellion (1850–1864) executed more than 1 million captives. Defeated spokesmen for the 1848 revolutions in Europe, when not imprisoned, were forced into exile. After the failed Hungarian revolt, Louis Kossuth never returned to his native land, and thousands of his fellow secessionists languished in Austrian prisons.

Some Confederate partisans who refused to accept defeat went into voluntary exile. Confederate cabinet member Judah Benjamin fled to England, where he began a successful second career as a barrister. Colonies of Confederate expatriates were formed in Mexico, Cuba, and British Honduras (now Belize). About twenty thousand whites from the Deep South migrated to Brazil, whose emperor offered subsidized transport and cheap land and where slavery was still legal. These *Confederados* established cotton plantations and introduced Baptist Christianity to the region north of Sao Paolo.

In comparison to conquerors in civil wars elsewhere, victorious Unionists were remarkably lenient. A few Radical Republicans declared that "the leaders of this rebellion must be executed or banished," yet neither Jefferson Davis nor Robert E. Lee was tried for treason and the victors imposed no exile or mass imprisonments. Federal laws disfranchised a small number of high-ranking Confederates, but pardons and amnesty acts restored their property and political rights.

In contrast to this relatively mild political punishment, many Republicans favored wholesale social changes in the conquered South. Compared to emancipation elsewhere in the Western world, postwar Reconstruction made possible a more abrupt break with the past. In Russia, where Czar Alexander II emancipated the serfs, and in the British Caribbean and Brazil, where plantation slavery was abolished gradually, masters were compensated for losing their human property and strongly influenced the terms of emancipation. When Confederates rejected President Lincoln's offer of compensated emancipation, they triggered his Emancipation Proclamation—the largest confiscation of property in the nation's history. The Union's military victory meant that in the postwar period Congress excluded former masters from setting the terms of the new order.

In most plantation societies in the Americas, landed white elites retained the upper hand after emancipation and used it to keep political power and force former slaves back to work. In Jamaica, for example, freed people had to accept a four- to six-year apprenticeship working for their former masters without wages. Although full civil rights were supposed to follow, freed slaves were prevented from voting by prohibitive property requirements and eventually outright exclusion. Reconstruction in the United States got off to a more promising start. When the Republican-dominated Congress passed laws guaranteeing civil and political rights regardless of race, the United States became unique among postemancipation societies in granting freed slaves the right to political equality.

As Americans debated Reconstruction, they looked for lessons as emancipation unfolded in the Caribbean. In October 1865, freed black farm workers in Jamaica rose up to protest lack of access to land. The **Morant Bay Rebellion** was brutally suppressed, and Jamaican whites returned control of the colony to Britain. When news of the rebellion reached North America, the South's newspapers warned that demands for land and similar "incendiary teachings" would produce violent uprisings among former slaves. Meanwhile, northern abolitionists such as Lydia Maria Child compared the Jamaican freed peoples' restrictions to the South's Black Codes, declaring that such schemes for "legislating the blacks back into slavery" must be stopped.

Morant Bay Rebellion
Uprising in Jamaica by freedmen asserting their right to land to which whites retaliated by killing more than four hundred blacks and revoking colonial self-rule.

14-3
Congressional Reconstruction

This political cartoon was published during the impeachment trial of President Andrew Johnson in 1868 when Republicans in Congress charged him with obstructing enforcement of the Constitution and recent Reconstruction laws. "This little boy would persist in handling books above his capacity," the caption reads. "And this was the disastrous result." The cartoon reflects Republicans' confidence that Johnson would be convicted.

Why would political opponents portray Johnson as a "little boy" involved in matters "over his head"? Why is it significant that Johnson is shown crushed by "Vol. 14" of the Constitution? ▶

The Granger Collection, New York

THIS LITTLE BOY WOULD PERSIST IN HANDLING BOOKS ABOVE HIS CAPACITY.

AND THIS WAS THE DISASTROUS RESULT.

Under "radical" Reconstruction, congressional Republicans used their strong majority to impose plans to restore the Union and reconstruct the South politically. Their program did not distribute land to freed people; it did not enfranchise women or prevent indirect disfranchisement of African Americans. But it amended the constitution to make voting rights colorblind and federally protected. And it installed loyal Republican governments in the former Confederate states. This expansion of federal power paralleled the growth of national influence abroad following the Union's victory in the Civil War.

☞ As you read, think about how the Union victory in the Civil War and growing federal powers reconfigured sectional relations in the United States as well as foreign relations in North America. How did Congressional Reconstruction attempt to make over the South politically and socially? How did expanding U.S. power redraw the map of North America?

14-3a Military Occupation and Impeachment

After debating several proposals, Congress drew up a comprehensive blueprint for overhauling the South's political framework. The

{ Congress takes charge of Reconstruction during a constitutional crisis.

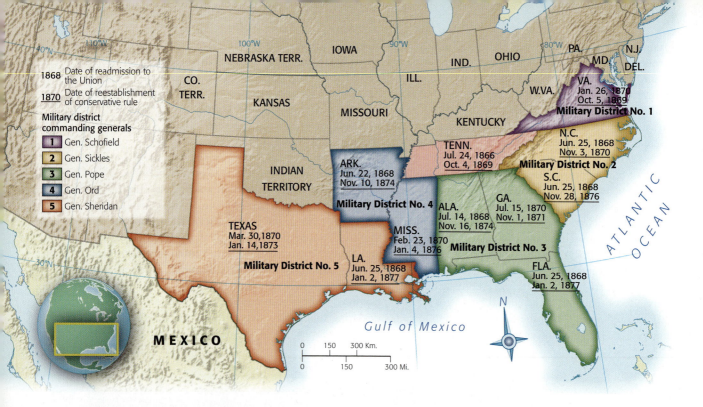

Map 14.1 Course of Reconstruction This map shows the five military districts established when Congress passed the Reconstruction Act of 1867. As the dates within each state indicate, by 1870 all southern states had been readmitted to the Union. Almost immediately, however, conservative Democratic forces began regaining control of state governments, and so-called radical Reconstruction was in retreat. ▲

Reconstruction Act of 1867 rolled back the restoration process begun under Johnson. It divided ten former Confederate states—excluding Tennessee, which ratified the Fourteenth Amendment—into five military districts overseen temporarily by the Union army (see Map 14.1). These states were required to call constitutional conventions with delegates elected by blacks and whites. For states to win readmission to the Union, their new constitutions had to guarantee black men's voting rights, Congress had to approve the new charters, and the states had to ratify the Fourteenth Amendment. Congressional Reconstruction met Republicans' call for freedmen's rights, loyal southern governments, and federal control of the process.

Expecting Johnson to oppose their plans, Republicans passed laws to limit his power. The **Tenure of Office Act**, which prohibited the president from removing cabinet members and other high officials without the Senate's consent, became the focus of conflict. It was designed to protect Secretary of War Edwin Stanton, a Radical Republican who supervised military occupation in the South. Johnson, believing the law unconstitutional, fired Stanton in February 1868. Congress responded immediately by initiating the first **impeachment** of a U.S. president. By a vote of 126 to 47, the House approved eleven articles of impeachment. Nine centered on the Tenure of Office Act; the others accused Johnson of insulting Congress and—the crux of the matter—holding up enforcement of its Reconstruction laws.

In the Senate trial in May 1868, Johnson escaped removal from office by a single vote short of the two-thirds required. A handful of Republicans who held the balance of power hesitated. Some believed that Johnson's political tussling with Congress fell short of the "high crimes and misdemeanors" required by the Constitution. Others distrusted Radical Republican senator Benjamin Wade, who was next in line for the presidency and a crude, combative figure much like Johnson himself.

Johnson remained publicly defiant after his narrow acquittal, granting amnesty to more Confederates and pardons to Jefferson Davis and Robert E. Lee. During the trial, however, Republicans obtained his private promise to accept the Reconstruction Act. The disgrace of impeachment ensured that Johnson would be a one-term president.

Reconstruction Act of 1867 Legislation that returned former Confederate states to military rule and set conditions for readmission, including new constitutions and ratification of the Fourteenth Amendment.

Tenure of Office Act Law passed in 1867 to prevent Johnson from firing cabinet members without Senate approval.

impeachment Constitutional process of bringing federal officials to trial in the Senate for "high crimes and misdemeanors" that requires a two-thirds vote to remove them from office.

14-3b Completion of Congress's Plan

Only six months intervened between Johnson's impeachment trial and the election of 1868. The Republicans turned to Civil War hero Ulysses S.

> Americans elect Grant and Congress finalizes Reconstruction legislation.

Grant as their nominee. Although he lacked political experience, Grant had won Republicans' respect by eagerly enlisting black soldiers and backing Congress in its dispute with Johnson. The Republican platform, however, placated conservatives by leaving the question of black suffrage in the loyal North to the states. Between 1865 and 1868, white voters in the North had rejected equal suffrage amendments in eight states, passing them only in Iowa and Minnesota.

The Democrats nominated former New York governor Horatio Seymour, who had opposed emancipation and wartime expansion of federal power. The party's platform denounced Congressional Reconstruction as a "military despotism" designed to secure "negro supremacy." The party used openly racist appeals in the North and furtive violence in the South, where the Ku Klux Klan and other white supremacist groups tried to prevent black and white Republicans from voting. Violence succeeded in a few states, including Louisiana, where armed whites negated black voting rights granted by the constitution of 1868 (see this chapter's introduction). But African American votes helped Grant win five southern states, ensuring his strong victory (214 to 80) in the Electoral College.

In February 1869, the Republicans used their large majority in both houses of Congress to impose a new Reconstruction requirement. The **Fifteenth Amendment**, adopted in direct response to voter suppression in the recent election, outlawed denial of the vote "on account of race, color, or previous condition of servitude." The amendment's language left open a loophole for literacy, property, or other restrictions. To boost the amendment's chances, Congress required three as yet unreconstructed states—Mississippi, Texas, and Virginia—to ratify it before readmission.

In February 1870, the Fifteenth Amendment became law. Although its language was not airtight, it was a landmark addition to the Constitution. African American men were guaranteed the vote in states where they had recently been slaves. Ironically, they were also given the vote for the first time in fourteen northern states where racial prejudices remained strong. The amendment's adoption sealed the readmission of all former Confederate states to the Union, almost all with Republican-dominated legislatures. Congressional Republicans had restored the southern states and, they believed, reconstructed southern politics.

In the process, these Republicans expanded the scope and power of the federal government over states in ways that they believed necessary but that many Americans found troubling. Reconstruction continued the nationalizing process begun during the Civil War. In 1870, Democratic politicians and the conservative majority on the Supreme Court began responding by reasserting state prerogatives. Before that, the Court handed congressional Republicans an important victory in *Texas v. White* (1869). The case hinged on the legality of Confederate state war bonds, which the justices invalidated, declaring that the South's unilateral secession had been unconstitutional. It was too late to save seven hundred thousand soldiers' lives, but the ruling codified the Union's victory in law.

14-3c Women's Suffrage and Electoral Reform

The post-Civil War battle in the United States over black voting rights took place at the same time that the British Parliament debated extending

> Feminists enter voting rights debates in the United States and Great Britain.

suffrage to most male workers. The example of radical Reconstruction influenced Britain's Reform Act of 1867, which lowered property requirements for voting. In both nations, women's rights advocates demanded to be included in electoral reform.

American feminists were angered by the Reconstruction amendments. The Fourteenth Amendment guaranteed voting rights only to male citizens, and the Fifteenth Amendment permitted denial of the vote on grounds of sex. Women's rights advocates, who had actively supported emancipation and the Union, felt betrayed. Elizabeth Cady Stanton vowed to oppose the Fourteenth Amendment unless the word "male" was deleted, but Republican leaders gave priority to racial justice over "the lesser question of sex." Even Frederick Douglass, a longtime women's rights supporter, argued that Reconstruction was "the Negro's hour." Mainstream Republican leaders believed that endorsing female suffrage would jeopardize the immediate task of enfranchising African American men.

Stanton and Susan B. Anthony next opposed the Fifteenth Amendment, whose passage, they claimed, would establish an "aristocracy of sex." By 1869, the dispute over Reconstruction amendments split women's rights advocates into rival organizations. Moderates in the **American Woman Suffrage Association** such as Lucy Stone and Julia Ward Howe cooperated with the Republican Party, supported the Fifteenth Amendment, and focused on winning the vote through state-level campaigns. The more radical **National Woman Suffrage Association**, led by Stanton and Anthony, attacked

Fifteenth Amendment Constitutional addition that became law in 1870, prohibiting states and the federal government from denying the vote on grounds of skin color or prior condition of servitude.

American Woman Suffrage Association Organization formed after women's rights advocates split over the Fifteenth Amendment and that supported black voting rights despite women's exclusion.

National Woman Suffrage Association Organization formed by a splinter group of women's activists who opposed Fourteenth and Fifteenth Amendments and other discriminatory laws.

Library of Congress, Prints & Photographs Division, [LC-US262–2023]

Women Press Congress for the Vote, 1871 Joined by Susan B. Anthony (second from the right in the foreground), Victoria Woodhull presented a petition to the House Judiciary Committee in January 1871 claiming that the Fourteenth Amendment gave women as citizens the right to vote—an argument that the committee rejected. Woodhull ran for president the following year as the candidate of the Equal Rights Party, becoming the first woman to do so. ◄

discrimination more broadly and pushed for a federal women's suffrage amendment.

Women's suffrage advocates in England watched U.S. developments closely, but they divided over class, not race. Moderates advised winning the vote incrementally beginning with educated and propertied women, whereas radicals pushed immediately for equal rights for all women. Parliament put off the former proposal and roundly rejected the latter in 1867 when the philosopher-politician John Stuart Mill introduced it.

Suffrage advocates won small victories in 1869 and 1870 when two western U.S. territories, Wyoming and Utah, enfranchised women, in part to attract female migrants. Elsewhere the state-by-state strategy met with strong opposition from traditionalists as women's suffrage proposals failed in New York and Kansas. The federal government also proved hostile to gender equality. When Susan B. Anthony voted in the 1872 presidential election, a federal marshal arrested her. Missouri suffragist Virginia Minor, who attempted to follow her example, sued the registrar who had blocked her, claiming that the Fourteenth Amendment's guarantee of citizenship enfranchised women. In **Minor v. Happersett** (1875), the Supreme Court ruled that national citizenship did not compel states to grant women the vote. American feminists' defeats during Reconstruction and British feminists' rejection in Parliament indicated that a long struggle would be necessary before the "women's hour" arrived in the Anglo-American world.

14-3d Reconstruction of the Nation's Borders

Increased federal power at home under Reconstruction was complemented by reaffirmed U.S. prowess in North

{ Union victory expands U.S. territory and influence in North America.

America. The Civil War had threatened to remake the continent's borders and reshuffle its deck of players, but U.S. leaders used the Union's victory to restore, and even enhance, the nation's continental preeminence.

Deploying troops freed by the war's end, U.S. officials helped Mexican liberals overthrow the French-imposed regime of Emperor Maximilian (see Chapter 13). Far north of the U.S. border, Americans seized an opportunity to extend the nation's reach into the Pacific by purchasing the vast territory of Alaska from Russia.

The imperial Russian-American Company had attempted to monopolize the fur trade, but it lacked the resources to colonize Alaska or to thwart the westward push of Britain's Hudson's Bay Company across Canada. To keep Alaska out of Britain's hands, Russia offered to sell it to the United States, and Secretary of State William Seward readily agreed. He had long championed a U.S. continental empire, and purchasing Alaska would end one more European power's presence in North America. Confederate attacks on Yankee whaling ships had convinced him that the nation needed advanced outposts in the northern Pacific. In the spring of 1867, the U.S. Senate ratified Seward's treaty, purchasing Alaska for $7.2 million.

Skeptics mocked the **Alaska Purchase** as "Seward's Folly." Although Americans did not organize a territorial government there until 1884, Seward was vindicated when a major gold deposit was discovered in the Yukon in 1896. Meanwhile, Alaska's Aleutian Islands, which stretched twelve hundred miles westward toward Japan, provided a safe harbor for American whaling boats, naval vessels, and merchant ships bound for Asia. For similar reasons, Seward authorized the navy to occupy the uninhabited Midway Islands eleven hundred miles west of Hawai'i in 1867, the nation's first seizure of overseas lands.

Some Americans saw purchasing Alaska as the prelude to annexing British Columbia, which Seward's deal sandwiched between two U.S. landmasses. Officials in

United States Coast Guard

Global Americans One of ten children of Michael Morris Healy, an Irish immigrant planter in Georgia, and his wife, Mary Eliza Smith, a mixed-race African American woman who had been his slave, blue-eyed **Michael Healy** "passed" for white. Because racial intermarriage was illegal in Georgia and the Healy children were technically born into slavery, they were sent to northern states and Canada to be educated in Catholic schools. Most pursued careers in the church, but free-spirited Healy signed aboard a U.S. clipper ship bound for Calcutta. During the Civil War, he entered the U.S. Revenue Marine Service (later the Coast Guard) and in 1868, cruised to the newly purchased Alaska Territory. Soon commanding his own cutter, Healy represented the U.S. government in Alaska for two decades, informally called "king" but acting as policeman, judge, rescuer, and medical officer to whaling crews, merchant seamen, and Alaskan natives. In the 1880s, Healy took the renowned naturalist John Muir on several scientific voyages. When commercial fishermen overhunted seals and whales, Healy steamed to Russia's Siberian coast and returned with herds of reindeer, which became an essential source of food and clothing for Alaska natives. "Hell Roaring Mike" was a hard drinker and larger-than-life figure, beloved and feared by subordinates and recognized as the dominant U.S. authority on the North Pacific rim. Not until Healy died in 1904 did his African American ancestry become public knowledge.

Canada eyed the United States suspiciously, aware of Americans' annexationist dreams and fearing reprisals for Canadian aid to Confederates. British Canadians were alarmed when the **Fenians**, a secret brotherhood pledged to promote Irish nationhood, launched raids in 1866 across the U.S. border intended to dismember Britain's empire. Joined by hundreds of Irish-American Union veterans, the Fenians aspired to conquer Canada and exchange it with England for Ireland's independence.

When Britain captured two Irish-American Fenians and charged them with treason, Congress responded with the Expatriation Act (1868), which denied other countries' claims that naturalized U.S. citizens still owed them allegiance. This law and the **Bancroft treaties** that the United States signed with dozens of foreign countries after 1868 struck a decisive blow for voluntary citizenship against the feudal doctrine of "perpetual allegiance" to monarchs. The same conflict underlay the impressment controversy that had sparked the War of 1812, but increased naval power allowed U.S. naturalization policies to prevail after the Civil War.

In response to threats from Fenians and U.S. annexationists, Britain took steps to unite its Canadian colonies under a single government. The **British North America Act** of 1867 created a federal Dominion of Canada that stretched from the Maritime Provinces to western Ontario, and four years later to British Columbia. Confederation was designed to fortify Canada against U.S. pressure to invade or annex it and to take the Civil War's lesson that a stronger government might prevent internal secessions.

Tensions over Canada added to difficult Anglo-American negotiations over Civil War damages. Americans recalled the wartime attacks on Union ships by the *Alabama* and other Confederate raiders built in Britain, and some demanded Canadian territory as reparation. Claims and counterclaims hummed over the undersea transatlantic cable, which, ironically, had begun operating in 1866 with friendly telegrams between Queen Victoria and President Johnson. Eventually, diplomats moderated their demands, and in 1871, the two nations signed the **Treaty of Washington**. The *Alabama* claims and others were submitted to a five-nation arbitration commission, which awarded the United States $15.5 million and England about half that sum. The treaty also resolved a standoff over the San Juan Islands, which occupied the Puget Sound between Vancouver Island and the Pacific Coast. This final U.S.–Canada boundary settlement fixed the northern U.S. border and put to rest the question of annexation.

Minor v. Happersett
Supreme Court decision declaring that citizenship rights were separate from voting rights and used by states to justify outlawing women's suffrage.

Alaska Purchase U.S. acquisition of Alaska Territory from Russia, designed to promote continental expansion and overseas trade.

Fenians Members of an Irish republican organization founded in the United States whose raids into Canada in 1866 aimed to coerce Ireland's independence from Britain.

Bancroft treaties Agreements between the United States and other nations signed after 1868 that recognized naturalized citizens as long as they resided in their new countries.

British North America Act Parliamentary law creating the federal Dominion of Canada from three British colonies to strengthen transcontinental ties and fend off U.S. expansion.

Treaty of Washington Pact that fixed the U.S.–Canadian border and addressed claims for Civil War damages between Britain and the United States.

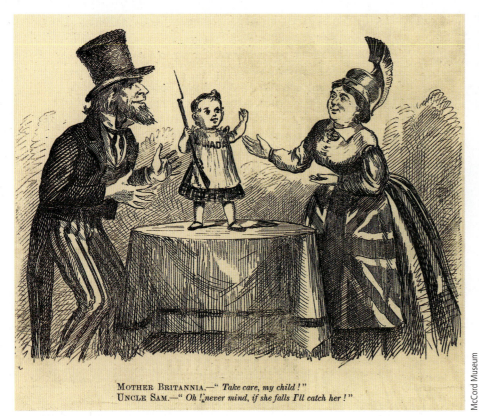

MOTHER BRITANNIA.—" *Take care, my child !* "
UNCLE SAM.—" *Oh ! never mind, if she falls I'll catch her !* "

McCord Museum

Canadian Confederation In this British cartoon of 1870, Mother Britannia exults that her child Canada can stand alone, while Uncle Sam urges "Oh! Never mind, if she falls I'll catch her!" The image reflects British anxiety about potential U.S. annexation of Canada after the Civil War, which might be disguised as economic assistance or protection against foreign "interference." ◄

14-4

Reconstruction and Resistance in the South

This lithograph, entitled *The First Vote,* was published in a northern magazine in 1867. It pictures the uniquely American—although temporary—postemancipation enforcement of equal political rights for former slaves under the terms of Congressional Reconstruction.

Whom does the artist portray as representative African American male voters in the South? Which party would they likely support? Why are they under an American flag? What problems might voting in public view create? ▶

North Wind Picture Archives/Alamy Stock Photo

Many Northerners were confident that with new laws and constitutional amendments, the South was being reconstructed as well as restored to the Union. Southerners, however, knew that a long struggle lay ahead. Ex-slaves and former masters argued over access to land and terms of labor, evolving the compromise system of sharecropping. Relying heavily on black voters, the South's Republican Party built a coalition that formed new state governments and enacted programs for education and economic development. But white Southerners refused to accept the Republican regimes and their challenge to the old order. Mobilizing through the Democratic Party and violent paramilitary groups, angry whites fought to reverse Reconstruction's gains for blacks and retake political control.

☞ As you read, consider the key issues under dispute in the postwar South. What important changes did Reconstruction bring to the South's politics and society? How were these changes contested and eventually reversed?

14-4a Transition to Sharecropping

The majority of the South's freed people aspired to become independent farmers, but this was a dream deferred. By 1867, federal authorities

> Postwar land and labor systems limit freed people's rise.

had restored almost all confiscated lands to planters, and several land redistribution bills had died in Congress. The **Southern Homestead Act** of 1866, modeled on the earlier national law, gave African Americans and loyal whites access to public lands in five states in plots of eighty or one hundred sixty acres. The law was not well publicized, however, and the acreage was often unsuitable for tilling. In the end, only a thousand free blacks were granted land certificates.

In some areas, the number of black farm workers dwindled to half its prewar total because freedmen migrated elsewhere and freedwomen withdrew from fieldwork. To relieve the shortage, southern states established agencies to encourage immigration. But as the result of local prejudices against Asian and Caribbean immigrants and opposition by the federal government, the effort to import cheap substitutes for the South's former slaves floundered.

Gradually, **sharecropping** and other forms of tenant farming evolved as the most widespread alternative to wage labor for freed people or contracts for imported workers. Landlords divided plantations into parcels of twenty-five to fifty acres, allowing families to settle on the land. In return, the owner received a share of the annual crop, usually half (see Map 14.2). In tenant farming, a variant that involved more poor whites than blacks, households received the crop's proceeds but used them to pay rent and to reimburse the landlord for the outlay of equipment and animals.

In theory, sharecropping and tenant farming represented a reasonable compromise between planters and former slaves. Planters gave up daily supervision of freedmen, who lived in separate cottages and set their own hours. Freed people rented land but hoped to accrue enough crop surpluses to buy their own farm. Both parties avoided outlays of cash, which was in short supply in the South. In practice, sharecroppers and tenants got the short end of the bargain. Unscrupulous landlords raised rents, cheated in weighing the crop, or evicted independent-minded tenants. Rural merchants (often planters themselves) advanced food, clothing, and other supplies to tenants on credit at interest rates as high as 50 percent. Under the **crop-lien system**, the landlord and merchant secured their

Southern Homestead Act Legislation that opened public lands in the South for settlement by free blacks and loyal whites initially, and later all Southerners, but was repealed in 1876.

sharecropping System of tenant farming by which renters worked a plot of land in return for paying half or more of the crop to landlords.

crop-lien system Legal restriction by which landlords and other creditors asserted priority rights to tenant farmers' crops.

1860

Wooded areas

1881

■ Tenant farmer's residence

Map 14.2 From Plantation to Sharecropping Maps of the Barrow plantation in Georgia in 1860 and 1881 illustrate the postwar transformation of southern agriculture. In 1860, about one hundred thirty-five slaves lived in quarters behind the master's house. After the Civil War and a brief interlude of growing cotton for wages, freed people moved to cottages on rented farms of twenty-five to thirty acres on plantation lands. The former master had become their landlord. Note the presence of some female-headed households as well as a church and school established by African Americans. ◄

History without Borders

After Slavery: Debt Bondage in Sugar and Cotton

Major migrations of indentured laborers
- Indians
- Chinese
- Pacific Islanders
- Africans
- Japanese
- Portuguese
- Filipinos

Major migrations of other contract laborers
- Chinese
- Japanese

Note: Numbers of migrants departing from their homelands do not equal number of migrants arriving at their destinations.

— International boundaries, 1913

CARIBBEAN AND GUIANAS

to U.S. South: 3,000*
to Cuba: 122,000
to other Caribbean: 4,000*
49,000
7,000
ATLANTIC OCEAN
17,000*
CUBA (Sp. to 1898; U.S. to 1902)
HAITI
Jamaica (Br.)
Caribbean Sea
Guadeloupe (Fr.) 260,000
Martinique (Fr.)
to all Guianas:
32,000*
18,000
16,000
283,000
Trinidad (Br.)
NICARAGUA
COSTA RICA
PANAMA
VENEZUELA
BRITISH GUIANA
DUTCH GUIANA
FRENCH GUIANA
to Hawai'i: 11,000
COLOMBIA

to Caribbean, Guianas, and Hawai'i: 48,000*
EUROPE
ASIA
CHINA 387,000
JAPAN 85,000
77,000*
65,000
50,000*
19,000*
330,000*
NORTH AMERICA
CA
UNITED STATES
1,000*
ATLANTIC OCEAN
see inset
Madeira (Port.)
WEST AFRICA
INDIA (Br.) 1,336,000
450,000*
Philippines (Sp. to 1898; U.S.) 32,000*
34,000
31,000*
2,000
Hawai'i (U.S.)
11,000
AFRICA
EAST AFRICA (Br.)
39,000
Réunion (Fr.)
Mauritius (Br.) 527,000
Pacific Islands (Br., Ger.) 96,000
PACIFIC OCEAN
26,000*
18,000
99,000
2,000
PERU
BRAZIL
SOUTH AMERICA
to Caribbean and Guianas:
58,000
17,000*
145,000
TRANSVAAL
CAPE COLONY (Br.)
37,000
34,000
64,000
152,000
INDIAN OCEAN
AUSTRALIA (Br.)
5,000
100,000*
63,000
56,000
26,000
Fiji (Br.)
543,000
*Estimate

Indentured laborers worked on Peru's guano islands as well as on mainland plantations.

Major Overseas Indentured Migrations, 1834–1919 Millions of workers from Asia, Africa, and the South Pacific were recruited overseas to replace emancipated slaves. Some were bound by strict indenture agreements while others worked under simple wage contracts. Whereas the majority of indentured laborers from Africa and Asia harvested sugar and similar plantation crops, other migrant workers were employed building railroads in the United States, mining gold in South Africa, or shoveling guano (valuable as fertilizer) in Peru. ▲

For millions of agricultural workers across several continents, the abolition of slavery led not to prosperity but to a subtler form of bondage based on indebtedness rather than ownership of persons. Looking for ways to boost production after emancipation, planters and merchants tied to the growing global market for cash crops created new forms of dependent labor.

To replace newly freed slaves, sugar planters worldwide recruited contract laborers from Asia, Africa, and the South Pacific. Great Britain opened the trade for *coolies* (a Tamil-origin term for hirelings) to its Indian Ocean sugar islands in 1834. As slave emancipation spread, Indian laborers were sent to Fiji and South Africa to harvest sugar, and Chinese and Japanese migrants worked in Caribbean sugar fields. The first Chinese contract workers arrived in Hawai'i in 1852, and within thirty years, they made up half of the sugar plantation

workforce. Altogether, more than 1 million contract laborers were recruited to harvest sugar between 1865 and 1885.

Customary indenture contracts compelled these workers to work for several years and repay the cost of their voyage. In practice, this arrangement was often brutal, and workers had little legal recourse. Some of them were kidnapped or coerced to sign contracts, and many never earned enough to pay off their debt. Such conditions and planters'

Historic New Orleans Collection

Chinese Contract Laborers in Louisiana
In 1867, hundreds of Chinese laborers were brought from Cuba to Louisiana to harvest sugar cane. Some cotton farmers were eager to follow suit to boost production and reassert white supremacy. "Give us five million Chinese laborers in the valley of the Mississippi," wrote a planter's wife, "and we can furnish the world with cotton and teach the negro his proper place." ◄

Universal History Archive/Getty Images

Cotton Cultivators in Egypt In this 1873 illustration, Egyptian farm workers deliver cotton in bags to a mercantile house, where it is weighed before packing and shipment overseas. By the 1870s, large landowners, small farmers, and tenants expanded Egypt's and India's cotton exports to more than triple their pre-Civil War total. But many peasant cultivators incurred debts to local moneylenders, suffered from declining cotton prices, and lacked access to food crops, resulting in regional food shortages and even famines. ◄

use of impoverished Asian workers to replace African slaves in tropical lands led critics to charge that a new form of racial slavery had emerged. When abuses were publicized and local protests erupted against "coolie labor," Britain and the United States restricted its trade in the 1880s. Latin American governments gradually followed, but the practice continued in modified forms elsewhere into the twentieth century.

Cotton growers chose a different option. During and after the Civil War, production of cotton went global, stimulated initially by the Confederacy's cutoff of shipments. Around the world, farm workers aspired to become growers and shunned picking cotton for wages. In contrast to sugar, cotton was increasingly produced by cultivators who worked their own small farms or rented land using family labor and outside capital.

In the U.S. South, planters and former slaves developed the sharecropping system, which dominated cotton production. In other lands, tenants and small farmers predominated and financial elites encouraged them to abandon subsistence crops to grow cotton for the world market. In India and Brazil, farmers used advances from European capitalists and local merchants to plant cotton. After 1860, cotton exports from India, Brazil, and Egypt increased dramatically. But whether they were landowners, sharecroppers, or tenants, small farmers depended on merchants and landlords, who were backed by harsh lien laws. Vulnerable to price fluctuations, subject to punitive laws, and politically marginalized, small cotton growers were technically free but often trapped in debt.

To indentured sugar workers and small cotton farmers, the postemancipation global economy appeared to offer opportunities for advancement. But the global market's demands for commodities and profits translated into

new forms of exploitation. Historians disagree when comparing migrant contract laborers to slaves, but most agree that indentures often led to agricultural "debt bondage." The United Nations Supplementary Convention on the Abolition of Slavery outlawed indentured labor in 1956. The practice continues, however, in South Asia, and the recent wave of globalization has resulted in the rise of other varieties of forced migrant labor.

Critical Thinking Questions

▶ How did the abolition of slavery transform global sugar and cotton production? What factors led to the establishment of indentured migrants and tenant farmers as dependent farm laborers?

▶ In what ways was agricultural debt bondage similar to slavery? How was it different?

Carpetbaggers Derisive term for Northerners who moved to the South after the Civil War and became active Republicans and whom southern Democrats saw as interlopers.

Scalawags Derogatory term for white Southerners who backed the Republican Party during Reconstruction and were marked as turncoats by southern Democrats.

advances by placing a legal claim on the farmer's next crop. The system guaranteed payouts for creditors but not their victims, and most tenants and sharecroppers fell into chronic debt.

By 1880, the division of plantations into tenant and sharecropping tracts encompassed the majority of farms in the cotton belt and nearly three-quarters of the South's black farmers. Because lienholders made borrowers grow cotton, which was easy to sell, the South's small farmers turned from diversified or subsistence farming to growing a single crop for the national and global market. Cotton production recovered to surpass prewar levels, but prices declined (see Table 14.1). Caught in a perfect storm of low cotton prices, spiraling debt, and reduced access to food crops, the South's freed people saw their dreams of economic independence fade. By the end of Reconstruction, few black sharecroppers had graduated to owning their own farms.

Table 14.1 U.S. Cotton Production and Exports, 1860–1880

After severe wartime declines and the adjustment to tenant farming and sharecropping, the South's production of cotton recovered in the mid-1870s to surpass prewar levels. U.S. cotton exports gradually approached their pre-Civil War share of the global market. At the same time, prices fell to half the immediate postwar level.

Year	Cotton Produced (Thousands of Bales)	Price (Cents per Pound)	U.S Share of British Cotton Imports (Percentage)
1860	3,841	12	80
1861	4,491	15	65
1862	1,597	30	4
1863	449	51	8
1864	299	53	9
1865	2,094	45	20
1866	2,097	25	38
1867	2,520	20	42
1868	2,366	16	43
1869	3,011	19	38
1870	4,352	18	54
1871	2,974	13	49
1872	3,933	15	35
1873	4,168	14	47
1874	3,836	13	49
1875	4,631	13	50
1876	4,474	12	57
1877	4,773	11	62
1878	5,074	12	73
1879	5,756	11	71
1880	6,606	12	71

14-4b Republican Governments in the South

{ Fragile Republican Party coalitions bring change to reconstructed southern states.

Freed people's political status improved under Congressional Reconstruction. Between 1867 and 1869, all states in the former Confederacy adopted new constitutions as required by Congress. These charters brought progressive changes to the South's electoral system, but the Republican coalitions that won the first statewide elections found it difficult to forge a common platform and even harder to win acceptance from southern whites.

The coalition was made up of three groups. **Carpetbaggers**, or transplanted Northerners, were caricatured by southern whites as transient opportunists, but most contradicted the stereotype. Their numbers included former Union soldiers who stayed in the South after the war along with businessmen, Freedmen's Bureau agents, and teachers. **Scalawags**, another derisive name invented by political opponents, were southern whites who joined the Republicans. Some were small farmers who had been wartime Unionists, others represented the South's business and financial elites, and a few others were planters who wagered that cooperating with Republicans was the best route to postwar recovery or personal gain.

African Americans were the third and by far the largest component of the South's Republican alliance. Their votes were essential for the party to control state governments. After the ordeal of slavery and years of political mobilization, they were eager to participate. "It is the hardest thing in the world to keep a negro away from the polls," a white Alabamian admitted as he watched former slaves respond to voter registration drives.

White Southerners opposed to Reconstruction stigmatized it as "Negro Rule." Taken literally, this charge was exaggerated. Fourteen blacks served during Reconstruction in the U.S. Congress and two in the Senate. South Carolina had a black majority in its House of Representatives, led by former slave and Union naval hero Robert Smalls. Yet African Americans held no major offices in Alabama, Georgia, North Carolina, or Texas. Despite providing four-fifths of the South's Republican votes, blacks received less than one-fifth of the offices, mostly local positions. Carpetbaggers and scalawags were determined to dominate Reconstruction politics.

If Reconstruction was not "negro rule," it was still a startling reversal of status for blacks and whites. Black mayors, sheriffs, town councilmen, and justices of the peace ran many small southern communities. Perhaps most galling to former Confederates, African Americans dominated the state militias called out to suppress local riots and protect black voting rights. The rise of the Ku Klux Klan and other white supremacist groups created an increasingly militarized environment, and there were not enough federal troops to patrol the entire South.

Beset by violent white opponents, the South's Republican Party also suffered internal tensions. Party supporters had divergent agendas. Moderates courted southern whites by promoting compromise whereas radicals relied on black voters. Yankee carpetbaggers pushed to modernize the South's economy while freedmen concentrated on voting rights, debt relief, and public schools. Poor whites sought economic relief but opposed racial integration. Each group had to make concessions, but all came to realize that most white Southerners would never join the Republicans. The party's continued rule depended on the national government.

While they lobbied for federal support, Republican leaders in the South enacted important changes in civil rights, public welfare, and economic development. New state laws empowered African American men to serve on juries and in police and fire departments. Reorganized southern states built public orphan and insane asylums and enacted laws against child abuse. Continuing the assault on illiteracy begun by freedmen's schools, Republican regimes set up public educational systems in every state in the South. Black leaders accepted segregated schools, often reluctantly, as the price for this improvement. Despite substandard facilities and shortages of funds, the literacy rate in 1875 among southern blacks had risen to more than 30 percent, three times the figure at the war's end. Educational gains were the most notable achievement of Republican rule in the South.

Republicans' economic programs were less successful. Seeking to diversify the South's economy and expand its markets, white Republican leaders chartered hundreds of new banks and encouraged construction of factories. Above all, state leaders promoted railroads, believing them an almost magical key to prosperity. According to one Tennessee Republican, "a free and living Republic [will] spring up in the track of the railroad . . . as surely as grass and flowers follow in the spring." Track mileage increased by 40 percent, a pace that outran farmers' needs and saddled state governments with huge debts.

Generous charters and subsidies for bonds led to a building spree. The construction boom overwhelmed southern state budgets. Republican lawmakers addressed deficits by raising taxes to levels unseen in the tax-hating prewar South. Soaring tax bills alienated landowners already reeling from the loss of $2.4 billion in slave "property" and spurred charges of waste and corruption. Some southern states had honest governments, but in others, such as South Carolina, Louisiana, and Florida, bribery, embezzlement, and profiteering were rampant. Political corruption was probably no more prevalent in the postwar South than in the North, but it lent a strong impetus to southern Democrats and others determined to end Republican rule.

14-4c Conservative White Resurgence

> Using politics and terror, southern Democrats restore white supremacy.

The high taxes and blatant corruption of some Republican regimes gave southern Democrats potent campaign issues. In reality, they had never considered Republicans legitimate participants in the South's politics. Many white Southerners saw Reconstruction as a foreign occupation, with the former slaves controlled by white Republicans who ruled with the backing of nearby federal troops.

Such attitudes sanctioned any form of resistance, from ballots to bullets. If policy differences failed to rouse the white public, racial hatred worked. Just as a shared belief in white supremacy had united prewar slaveholders and nonslaveholding whites, postwar Democrats used race baiting and violence to energize white voters. Violence against African Americans escalated as former slaves entered politics and served in local militias. White paramilitary groups spread spontaneously to punish "uppity" African Americans, sometimes after false accusations that they had raped or dishonored white women. The

Library of Congress Prints and Photographs Division

MISSISSIPPI KU-KLUX IN THE DISGUISES IN WHICH THEY WERE CAPTURED.
[FROM A PHOTOGRAPH.]

Ku Klux Klan in Mississippi, 1871 Mississippi Klan members pose for a photograph in the disguises they wore when they were arrested by federal authorities for attempted murder. None is wearing a pointed hood or white clothes, regalia that the Klan adopted in the early twentieth century. Enforcement of federal anti-Klan laws in the early 1870s netted hundreds of arrests, but violent resistance to black voting and office holding persisted among a variety of secret white supremacist organizations in the South. ▲

Redeemers Self-description of southern Democrats who rebelled against Reconstruction and restored Democratic rule and white dominance in the 1870s.

convict lease system Legal practice of hiring out convicts to employers for low wages that was combined with vagrancy laws to reduce many black Southerners to semislaves.

Ku Klux Klan, the most notorious of these groups, conducted night raids clad in costumed disguise, murdering dozens of blacks and several white Republican leaders before Congress sanctioned a campaign against it.

The Klan and its imitators served as the terrorist wing of the South's Democratic Party. Other Democrats adopted more subtle means of controlling black voters. In an era before the secret ballot, the party supervised polling places to identify Republican voters as potential targets of intimidation or retaliation. Employers required workers to sign contracts barring participation in political meetings, and landlords threatened politically active tenants with eviction.

One by one, southern states fell to conservative Democrats, who called themselves **Redeemers**. The counter-revolution succeeded first in 1869 in Virginia and Tennessee, upper South states whose black population was too small to sustain Republican electoral victories. In the Deep South, more violence was required to suppress Republican voters. In 1875, the White Line movement in Mississippi mobilized Democratic supporters to break up Republican meetings, patrol voter registration sites, and march in military formation through black neighborhoods.

Republican governors hesitated to call out black-dominated state militias to restore order, fearing it would enrage whites further or spark all-out race war. By 1876, the Democrats had toppled Republican regimes in all but three Deep South states.

Redeemer governments wasted no time in their effort to erase Reconstruction. Once in power, southern Democrats slashed taxes on land and state spending on schools and social services. Poll taxes, long-term residency requirements, and other restrictions not expressly forbidden by the Fifteenth Amendment were adopted to curtail black voting. Unable to reverse constitutional emancipation, the South's Democrats employed an arsenal of legal tactics to "re-enslave the colored race," as Texas Republicans charged in 1876. Toughened criminal codes restricted hunting and fishing and meted out prison terms for trespassing or petty theft. Redeemer legislators revived the Black Codes' vagrancy laws to imprison unemployed or loitering blacks. From overcrowded prisons, the **convict lease system** rented black inmates to private contractors for work on chain gangs harvesting crops, mining coal, or building railroads. Conditions were so bad that death tolls among prisoners averaged 15 percent annually and reached 41 percent in Alabama in 1870. Protesting this system, a Tennessee convention of freedmen in 1875 called it a "condition of servitude scarcely less degrading than that endured before the late civil war."

14-5

Abandonment of Reconstruction

A series of scandals damaged Grant's presidency. In the Crédit Mobilier affair, U.S. lawmakers accepted shares of stock for allowing payments to a phony railroad company. None were charged with crimes. In this cartoon, Uncle Sam, backed by public opinion, directs senators implicated in the scheme to commit hari-kari, or ritual suicide. In Japanese tradition, when a person is condemned to hari-kari, the victim's best friend stands by to complete the work.

Why would the cartoonist suggest suicide as the appropriate fictional punishment for the Crédit Mobilier conspirators? Why is Senator Roscoe Conkling, a spokesman for Grant, shown unsheathing a sword? How might Americans have learned about hari-kari in this era? ▶

Frank Leslie's Illustrated Newspaper. Image courtesy of Wikimedia.

White Southerners' violent return to power succeeded in part because Northerners abandoned their commitment to Reconstruction. After a decade of turmoil, many Northerners were impatient to leave the "Southern question" behind. Northern voters were preoccupied by the booms and busts of the national economy, distracted by overseas adventures, and frustrated by the difficulty of transforming southern ways. The Republicans were weakened by corruption and factionalism within their party and joined voters in turning against Reconstruction. The contested presidential election of 1876 completed the process by which the former Confederate states were restored without being truly reconstructed.

☞ As you read, consider the impact that political changes and economic fluctuations had on the federal government's enforcement of Reconstruction. What factors, attitudes, and events led Northerners to abandon Reconstruction?

14-5a "Grantism" and the Gilded Age

Grant moved into the White House pledging both to uphold Congressional Reconstruction and to restore sectional peace. This agenda was daunting and perhaps contradictory. Grant made a good-faith effort to assist embattled freed people in the South and even to reform federal Indian policy, but his prospects were hurt by the growing taint of fraud and corruption that surrounded his administration.

> Political scandals and unchecked corporate influence herald a new era.

To sustain black voting rights, Grant worked hard to pass the Fifteenth Amendment, whose adoption he believed "the most important political event since the nation came into life." To protect Native Americans from further dispossession and bring peace to federal-Indian relations, Grant overhauled reservation appointments and policies (see Chapter 15). Finally, to atone for his notorious wartime order expelling Jews (whom he stigmatized as cotton speculators) from his military district on the Mississippi River, he appointed several prominent Jews to government positions.

Yet Grant made serious mistakes with other appointments. Although scrupulously honest as a soldier, he had a lower standard concerning civilians. Some of his advisees and cabinet members were mediocre men, bumbling relatives, and wartime cronies to whom Grant remained loyal after their incompetence or deceptions were exposed.

Partly as a result, a string of scandals weakened his administration and fixed the label "Grantism" on political corruption. On "Black Friday" in September 1869, the price of gold plummeted after financier Jay Gould and his partner Jim Fisk tried to corner the market. They had involved Grant's brother-in-law in the scheme. In 1872, Grant's vice president, Schuyler Colfax, was reportedly among the thirty federal officeholders given shares in **Crédit Mobilier**, a phony construction company formed by the directors of the Union Pacific Railroad to multiply profits. Colfax was dropped from the Republican ticket that year, but the scandals continued. Grant's private secretary Orville Babcock was indicted in 1875 for allowing federal agents to accept bribes from whiskey distillers to avoid excise taxes. The next year, a House investigation revealed that Grant's secretary of war, William Belknap, sold rights to trading posts in Indian Territory. He was

impeached, but Grant allowed him to resign to avoid conviction. Grant's later cabinet appointees were able men who attacked corruption in the Interior, Treasury, and Justice Departments. But the damage to the president's relationship with Congress and the public had already been done.

The wave of scandals in railroads, finance, and government contracts showed that opportunities for illicit gain were legion during the postwar era's surge of economic growth. Industrial production nearly doubled during Reconstruction as did the number of workers in manufacturing and construction. Railroads, lavishly subsidized by federal and state governments, reached from coast to coast and incorporated new southern lines. The National Mineral Act of 1866 granted mining companies free access to millions of acres of public land.

To gain subsidies, win contracts, and avoid regulation, promoters of railroads and oil and mining corporations wooed politicians with shares of stock, appointments to boards, or outright bribes. Ethical standards were low and conflict of interest laws nonexistent. One wag wrote that John D. Rockefeller of the Standard Oil Company could do everything he wanted with the Pennsylvania legislature except refine it. Republican leaders increasingly catered to big business interests instead of tending to farmers' aspirations or freed peoples' rights.

Republicans were not alone in pocketing cash. The nation's mushrooming cities provided enticing opportunities for politicians who awarded contracts or distributed patronage. Many big-city bosses ran **political machines**. In New York City, Democratic boss William M. Tweed and his ring of operatives stole tens of millions of dollars from the city treasury through embezzlement, inflated contracts, and bribes. Tweed's headquarters, **Tammany Hall**, became a national byword for corrupt city government. One Tammany leader's epitaph, "I seen my opportunities and I took 'em," could serve as a motto for the frenzied speculation and flagrant corruption of an era that novelist Mark Twain and his coauthor Charles Dudley Warner labeled the **Gilded Age**.

14-5b Influence and Opportunities Overseas

As Reconstruction waned, American policy makers refocused on gaining markets and raw materials in Latin America and strengthening

> As postwar business booms, Americans seek influence in Latin America and Asia.

Crédit Mobilier Grant administration scandal in which railroad companies generated fraudulent profits and distributed shares of stock to government accomplices.

political machine Powerful political organization in which a party boss or elite rewards loyal supporters with jobs, money, or contracts, often acquired illegally.

Tammany Hall New York City's Democratic Party political machine, named after its headquarters and controlled by Boss William M. Tweed from 1869 to 1873.

Gilded Age Term coined in 1873 to critique an era of political corruption and economic inequality that stretched to 1900.

Virginia Baptist Historical Society.

Global Americans Born into a family of wealthy Virginia planters, **Charlotte "Lottie" Moon** and her sisters were given an unusually fine education. At first a nonbeliever, she underwent a religious awakening at age eighteen through revivals on her college campus. During the Civil War, Moon took teaching positions at various Virginia schools; after the war, she settled into a teaching career but felt called to overseas missionary work. Treaties with China opened the country to foreign missionaries, and in 1872, the Southern Baptists reversed their policy against sending single women abroad. The next year, Moon left for the treaty port of Tengchow, beginning a forty-year ministry in China. In 1885, she gave up teaching and evangelized full-time in China's interior. During her missionary career, Moon faced famine, plague, revolution, and war and responded with practical assistance to natives. (Here she is shown with students in Japan after fleeing China's Boxer Rebellion.) Moon's time in Asia coincided with renewed U.S. overseas expansionism after the Civil War and enlarged public roles for women. By 1900, 60 percent of American overseas missionaries were women. Missionaries spread Western religion and middle-class values, believing them superior to native peoples' ways. Moon advocated a similar paternalism of racial "uplift" for southern blacks. But Moon and other U.S. missionaries also fostered women's education abroad, introduced Americans to other cultures, and sometimes criticized colonial policies.

the nation's position in the Caribbean. Yet the issues of slavery and race continued to influence U.S. policies in complex ways. On the one hand, emancipation hastened the end of bondage in two New World societies where plantation slavery still thrived. In 1866, Emperor Dom Pedro II suggested that Brazil consider abolishing slavery, and five years later, a law declared that the children of slaves born thereafter would be freed. The Thirteenth Amendment also energized abolitionists in Cuba, many of whom sought U.S. assistance in winning the island's independence from Spain. On the other hand, Reconstruction disputes often spilled into foreign affairs, and motives of national interest competed with moral considerations in the struggle to define U.S. diplomacy.

Grant proved an inconsistent champion of both U.S. expansion and local freedom struggles in the Caribbean. Shortly after acquiring Alaska from Russia, Secretary of State Seward negotiated a treaty to purchase for $7.5 million two islands of the Danish West Indies (later called the *Virgin Islands*) to be used as naval stations. But President-elect Grant was hostile and the U.S. Senate, hounded by critics of the Alaska deal and preoccupied with the Johnson impeachment crisis, refused to act.

When Cuban colonists rose up against Spanish rule in 1868, Grant favored assisting them, but he feared war with Spain or a costly diversion from Reconstruction. Guided by cautious Secretary of State Hamilton Fish, Grant called the revolt "premature," accepted Spanish rule, and urged Madrid to adopt reforms. Even when Spain seized a hired American ship that transported supplies to the rebels and executed fifty-three persons aboard, the United States remained a bystander. The Ten Years' War, the Cuban struggle for independence and emancipation, ended in 1878. Spain freed slaves who had fought in the war (but not others) and enacted financial reforms but

maintained its colonial rule. Not until 1886 did Spain decree freedom for all of Cuba's slaves. Some Cuban rebels, including the young nationalist writer José Martí, refused to surrender and continued plotting from U.S. soil to free their homeland.

Although Grant hesitated over Cuba, he made strenuous efforts to acquire the small Caribbean republic of Santo Domingo (later the Dominican Republic), whose corrupt president, Buenaventura Báez, was willing to exchange annexation for debt relief. The U.S. navy, eager for Caribbean bases, coveted the island's protected Samaná Bay. Grant believed that the tropical land could become a refuge for the South's persecuted freed people, and he convinced Frederick Douglass that this would increase southern blacks' leverage at home. But opposition arose from many sides. U.S. newspapers derided the project as a financial risk, and some warned against "adding to our population nearly a million of creoles and West Indian negroes." Charles Sumner, Republican chair of the Senate Foreign Relations Committee, opposed annexation as the plot of unsavory speculators and a threat to neighboring Haiti. When the annexation treaty came before the Senate in June 1870, it fell short of the necessary two-thirds approval.

Across the Pacific, the reunified United States continued to seek trade concessions similar to those won by aggressive European powers. U.S. diplomacy veered between conciliation and force. The nation's minister to China, Radical Republican Anson Burlingame, saw parallels between Reconstruction's program of racial equality at home and respect for Asian peoples abroad. The **Burlingame Treaty**, ratified in 1868, recognized China's control of its territory and declared discriminatory anti-Chinese legislation in California illegal. But it did not remove the ban on naturalizing Chinese immigrants to the United States, and it reaffirmed the rights of American missionaries to China granted ten years earlier.

Burlingame Treaty U.S.–China pact promoting cooperation that recognized China's territorial sovereignty and rights of Chinese immigrants except for U.S. citizenship.

In Japan, the United States again sought a leading role, although the Civil War limited its ability to enforce the unequal treaties of the 1850s. Subdued by a flotilla of European ships that included a lone U.S. gunboat, Japan's Shogun agreed in 1864 to pay indemnities and allow Westerners access to local traders. Popular resentment of this national humiliation helped precipitate the Shogun's overthrow in the **Meiji Restoration** of 1868. Asserting power over samurai warriors and regional lords, the young emperor Meiji and his ministers embarked on a crash program to modernize Japan by abolishing feudal privileges, developing industry, and creating an efficient government bureaucracy.

Americans viewed this revolution as a potential bonanza for U.S. producers and traders, but the Japanese were determined to copy modern industrial methods without becoming subject to Western domination. During a seven-month "knowledge-seeking" mission to the United States in 1873, Japanese envoys paid special attention to new technologies and political reforms. Disappointed American political humorist Finley Peter Dunne complained through his Irish alter ego, "Mr. Dooley": "the throuble is whin the gallant Commodore [Perry] kicked open th' door, we didn't go in. They come out."

Still, more than three hundred U.S. experts were recruited in the 1870s to assist Japan's modernization. They taught scientific farming and brought new breeds of livestock to northern Japan. U.S. educators designed a college-level science curriculum and helped draw up Japan's blueprint for universal schooling. In 1873, Horace Wilson, a Union army veteran, introduced baseball at elite schools in Tokyo. Within two decades, the game had captivated the Japanese as it had the Americans.

Americans resorted to violence to pry open the Kingdom of Korea, which strongly resisted foreign trade. In 1866, a heavily armed U.S. merchant vessel, the *General Sherman*, landed at Pyongyang to impose a trade agreement. Angry Koreans set fire to the ship and killed its fleeing crew. In retaliation, the Grant administration sent a squadron of warships in 1871. Fired on as they approached Seoul, the Americans landed a squad of marines who killed some three hundred Koreans before departing. Eventually, the U.S. navy secured China's help to reach a pact with Korea in 1882 that granted concessions to American merchants and missionaries.

14-5c Republicans in Retreat

By the time Grant's first term ended, a Republican splinter movement had formed to voice several grievances against party policies. First, congressional expansion of federal power during Reconstruction worried such reformers, who subscribed to the **laissez-faire** doctrines that were gaining traction with transatlantic industrialists and intellectuals. Adopting as a model Britain's Liberal Party, whose leader William Gladstone became prime minister in 1868, the

> Despite Grant's reelection, Congress and the courts back away from Reconstruction.

Liberal Republicans advocated limited government, free trade, and unfettered enterprise. These policies, they argued, would create prosperity and reduce taxes and corruption. Liberals also called for a **civil service system** to replace appointed spoilsmen with professional managers. Finally, the Liberals opposed continued federal intervention to support black Southerners and prop up the region's Republican governments. Further progress, the Liberals declared, was up to freed people themselves. This retreat from Reconstruction allied them with southern white opponents of Reconstruction. The Liberals proposed a general amnesty for unreconstructed Southerners and a return to self-government by the "best men" among former Confederates.

The rise of the Liberal Republicans temporarily shook up existing party alignments. Unable to convert Republican "regulars," they formed an alliance with Democrats and nominated Horace Greeley, longtime editor of the *New York Tribune*, for president. Greeley, who had earlier supported Congressional Reconstruction, urged Americans to put the Civil War behind them and "clasp hands across the bloody chasm." Grant, running for a second term, defeated Greeley easily. Drawing on his reservoir of goodwill among the northern public and a high turnout among the South's black voters, Grant amassed 56 percent of the popular vote and carried all but six southern states.

The Liberal Republican revolt ended with the election but brought changes. Grant signed the nation's first civil service law in 1871 to select federal employees on merit, not political connections. Responding to Greeley's call for reconciliation, Congress passed the Amnesty Act, which allowed almost all former Confederates to hold office. More generally, the Liberal split forecast increased impatience among Republicans with their party's reconstruction program.

Toward the end of his first term and into his second, Grant remained committed to radical Reconstruction. When the South's Republicans clamored for protection from violent attacks, Congress responded with strong measures. To protect black voters, the **Ku Klux Klan Act** of 1871 and related enforcement acts authorized the government to prosecute members of groups that denied citizens' civil rights. Although these laws did not end racial violence, they resulted in hundreds of convictions of Klan members. Grant sent federal troops to South Carolina to break up the Klan and dispatched army units to North Carolina, Mississippi, and Louisiana to quell white supremacist insurrections. Congress

Meiji Restoration Rise to power of Japan's Emperor Meiji after widespread protests against unequal treaties, leading to modernization program for Japanese government, army, and industry.

laissez-faire Doctrine opposing government regulation or intervention in economic matters beyond a necessary minimum.

Liberal Republicans Party faction that favored limited government, free trade, and conciliation of southern whites and bolted to the Democratic ticket in 1872 under Greeley.

civil service system Arrangement for hiring and promoting government employees by professional merit rather than personal or political connections.

Ku Klux Klan Act Legislation also known as the Third Enforcement Act that allowed the president to impose martial law to combat attacks by the Klan and other white supremacist organizations.

followed with the Civil Rights Act of 1875, which banned racial discrimination in theaters, hotels, and other public places.

Before long, however, Congress realized that many Northerners had grown tired of southern tumult and the "negro question." Northern businessmen sought order and stability in the South to secure trade and investment. The number of Union soldiers in the South dwindled as they and Civil War generals such as O. O. Howard, the former head of the Freedmen's Bureau, were reassigned to the West to enforce the government's new reservation policy for Native Americans.

White Republicans who had supported African American rights primarily for partisan political advantage never shed their racial prejudice. In the 1870s, many northern Republicans swallowed tales of "black rule" and "barbarism" told by journalists touring the South. Increasingly, former supporters of black suffrage blamed southern violence and Republican losses on black voters, whom they condemned as ignorant and easily corrupted by Democrats.

Republicans who stood firm on African American rights suffered a major defeat when the Supreme Court, uneasy about Reconstruction's expansion of federal powers, restricted the government's authority to enforce civil rights. In its first ruling on the Fourteenth Amendment, the so-called **Slaughterhouse Cases** of 1873, the Court declared that freedom of speech, the right to a fair trial, and most other civil rights derived from state, not national, citizenship and were controlled by state law.

Another damaging decision concerned the **Colfax Massacre**, the bloodiest instance of racial violence during Reconstruction. In 1873, an armed mob of white Louisiana Democrats attacked a courthouse that was held by newly elected Republican officeholders (mostly black) and defended by the state militia. More than one hundred African Americans were killed, many while fleeing or surrendering. Prosecutors secured the conviction of only three men for murder and conspiracy. Reviewing their appeal, the Supreme Court ruled in ***U.S. v. Cruikshank*** (1876) that the Reconstruction amendments gave Congress the power to outlaw acts of discrimination only by state governments, not private individuals. This ruling was solidified in the Civil Rights Cases of 1883, when the Court declared the antidiscrimination strictures of the Civil Rights Act of 1875 unconstitutional. These decisions undermined federal protection of equal rights and gave a tacit go-ahead to white supremacist organizations in the South.

Radical Republicans began to lose in Congress as well as the courts. In the 1874 elections, the Democrats gained control of the House for the first time since the 1850s, proof that support for Reconstruction had dwindled. Grant cared about southern blacks' rights, but he understood which way the political winds were blowing. Responding to a call from South Carolina to suppress a massacre of black militiamen in 1876, Grant deplored the incident but weakly appealed to "the better judgment and co-operation of citizens of the State" to bring the offenders to justice "without aid from the Federal Government."

14-5d Panic and Compromise

> An economic crisis and a contested election end Reconstruction.

The North's shift away from Reconstruction accelerated when the postwar economic boom slid into a deep depression. Like earlier U.S. financial crises, the **Panic of 1873** originated in Europe. After its victory in the Franco-Prussian War (1870–1871), an increasingly powerful Germany demanded payments to it in gold rather than silver. This decree spurred bank failures in Vienna that spread through financial networks to northern Europe and North America. The U.S. economy was especially vulnerable because of speculation and overbuilding of railroads. The influential investment firm Jay Cooke and Company shut down, sparking a chain reaction among

RUN ON THE UNION TRUST COMPANY.

The Library of Congress

Bank Panic, 1873 The run on the Union Trust Company in New York City was among those on hundreds of banks that had to suspend operations in the Panic of 1873. Founded as savings banks, trust companies were virtually unregulated and prone to speculative schemes. Dramatic scenes of bank runs predominated in magazine depictions of the panic and depression. Such male-dominated images overlooked the depression's devastating effects on unemployed women and families. ▲

Slaughterhouse Cases Supreme Court ruling that weakened the Fourteenth Amendment by declaring that state, not federal, laws covered most civil rights.

Colfax Massacre Murderous attack by armed whites on black officeholders and state militia defending a county courthouse in Louisiana.

U.S. v. Cruikshank Supreme Court decision concerning the Colfax Massacre that exempted private individuals from federal prosecution for civil rights violations.

Panic of 1873 International financial crisis that led to U.S. economic depression, weakening Republican control and eroding support for Reconstruction.

banks and businesses. Over the next five years, one of four American railroads failed, hundreds of banks folded, and many businesses closed. Unemployment reached 15 percent, and those who hung onto their jobs faced seasonal layoffs and severe wage cuts.

For working-class victims of the depression, the crisis exposed the inadequacy of Republicans' free-labor ideology to the new industrial era. Unemployed workers in New York and other cities demanded that government officials create jobs or at least finance public relief. But Republican spokesmen and business leaders denounced such programs as interfering with the free market and discouraging hard work. According to laissez-faire tenets, workers in the North, like southern blacks, enjoyed mobility and civil rights and had to rise by their own efforts. As Reconstruction evolved, it hardened, rather than tempered, the creed of middle-class individualism that Republicans had fashioned in the 1850s.

The lingering economic depression and the Grant administration's continuing scandals gave the Democrats momentum going into the 1876 presidential campaign. They nominated Governor Samuel J. Tilden of New York, a reformer renowned for prosecuting the Tweed Ring in New York City. In addition to "corrupt centralism" in Washington, Tilden promised to end "carpetbag tyrannies" in the South. The Republicans nominated Rutherford B. Hayes, a former Civil War general with a clean record as governor of Ohio, who promised to crack down on graft and voiced conciliatory sentiments toward southern whites.

Tilden received 250,000 more popular votes than Hayes, but in the Electoral College, his total was 184, one shy of the number required for victory (see Map 14.3). Hayes received 166, but the votes of one Oregon elector and three southern states were disputed. South Carolina, Louisiana, and Florida were the only remaining Republican governments in the South. The contest there was marred by fraud, and both parties claimed victory.

Faced with this unprecedented situation, Congress created a fifteen-member commission composed of senators, representatives, and Supreme Court justices to examine the disputed returns. The commission voted eight to seven along strict party lines to give Hayes all the contested electoral votes and with them the presidency. Outraged Democrats threatened to block Hayes's victory in the House of Representatives. The impasse was broken when Democrats and Republicans appeared to negotiate a series of back-room deals just two days before the inauguration. The arrangement became known as the **Compromise of 1877**. In return for the Democrats' acceptance of Hayes as president, the Republicans agreed (among other concessions) to provide federal subsidies for a southern transcontinental railroad (the northern line had been completed in 1869). Most importantly, the Republicans pledged to withdraw federal troops that bolstered the remaining Republican regimes in the South.

The Compromise of 1877 broke down so rapidly that some historians question whether it was forged at all. The most important feature held, however: Shortly after Hayes

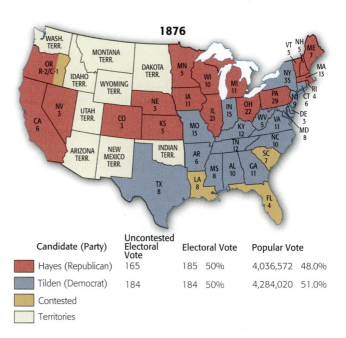

1876

Candidate (Party)	Uncontested Electoral Vote	Electoral Vote		Popular Vote	
Hayes (Republican)	165	185	50%	4,036,572	48.0%
Tilden (Democrat)	184	184	50%	4,284,020	51.0%
Contested					
Territories					

Map 14.3 Election of 1876 and Compromise of 1877 Democratic gains in the North and the collapse of Reconstruction governments in the South gave Samuel Tilden the majority of popular votes. However, Republican Rutherford Hayes captured the presidency after a special commission gave him all the disputed Electoral College votes and a private agreement assured Democrats that Reconstruction was over. ▲

was inaugurated, he removed federal troops stationed in the three contested states. Without the army to support them, the South's Republicans ceded control of Louisiana, South Carolina, and Florida to the Democrats. This closed the long sectional struggle over whether the postwar South would simply be restored to the Union or thoroughly reconstructed. Sectional peace returned, but at the price of relinquishing Reconstruction's transformational agenda. By abandoning the pledge of civil and political equality recently inscribed in the Fourteenth and Fifteenth Amendments, the North and South were reunited.

Compromise of 1877 Political deal that resolved the disputed election of 1876 by ceding electoral votes to Republican candidate Hayes in exchange for ending Reconstruction.

14-5e Reconstruction's Troubled Legacy at Home and Abroad

The end of Reconstruction had important consequences for relations between the South and the nation. Relinquishing rule to the South's large landowners enabled them to recapture their regional power and set the terms of southern race relations, but they no longer controlled national politics. Before the Civil War, white Southerners dominated the presidency, Supreme Court, and other federal leadership positions; afterward, the sectional balance of power was reversed. In the next fifty years,

{ Home rule in the South isolates it politically and entrenches racist practices.

Lost Cause Nostalgic praise of the plantation South and Confederate bravery voiced by white Southerners who were opposed to Reconstruction and racial equality.

only 7 of 31 Supreme Court appointees and 14 of 133 cabinet members were Southerners. Not until 1912 was a southern-born man, Woodrow Wilson, elected president. Nationally, political party allegiances were evenly divided, but the Republicans' economic agenda, including banking, land, tariff, and tax policies that favored the industrial North, prevailed.

Meanwhile, wartime destruction combined with unfavorable conditions in the international market to inflict lasting damage on the South's economy. While mechanized farming made rural communities in the North prosperous, the traditional hand-harvested staples of cotton, tobacco, rice, and sugar still dominated southern agriculture. All these crops suffered from global overproduction and declining prices. Industrialization and diversified farming might ensure future prosperity, but Southerners lacked the home-grown capital to make changes, and many resisted industry as an alien way of life. Southerners emerged from Reconstruction dependent on the North's banks, factories, and corporations to offset diminishing returns from staple crops. The South's subordination in the national government and its lagging economic development resembled the outcome of national consolidation in countries such as Italy and Germany, where north-south disparities continued to divide nations that were unified politically in midcentury.

Shaken by their declining status, southern whites idealized the prewar plantation economy, lamented the Confederacy's **Lost Cause**, and demonized their alleged oppressors during radical Reconstruction. Once the South's Republican regimes were toppled, white politicians launched systematic campaigns to disfranchise, intimidate, and segregate African Americans. To justify discrimination against blacks and nonwhite immigrants, white commentators and academics in both the North and South developed elaborate racial theories based on ideas of Anglo-Saxon superiority, immutable racial traits, or the evolutionary "backwardness" of nonwhite peoples.

By providing fodder for such racial theories, the abandonment of Reconstruction had damaging international repercussions. According to James Bryce, Britain's ambassador to the United States and a respected authority on American society, postwar turmoil in the South showed "the risk a democracy runs when the suffrage is granted to a large mass of half-civilized men." British imperialists in lands such as Australia and South Africa cited Bryce's view that Reconstruction was a mistake as proof that nonwhite peoples were incapable of self-rule. Such views produced segregation laws, racial exclusion from voting, literacy tests, and similar methods of disfranchisement in Britain's so-called white dominions that were based on models from the U.S. South.

Blacks in the American South, like their global counterparts, did not let such views go unchallenged. Beginning in the mid-1870s, emigration movements recruited heavily in the cotton belt. Perhaps 30,000 southern blacks left for Kansas in the so-called Exoduster movement (see Chapter 15) and another 4,000 sought new lives in Liberia. The vast majority remained in their adopted land, struggling to make a living and fighting for their rights. Despite legal restrictions and physical threats, the South's African Americans continued to vote in large numbers into the 1880s. When in the next decade southern states passed laws restricting voting and mandating segregation, people of color, including Louisiana's Rodolphe Desdunes and his friend Homère Plessy, reasserted equal rights against all odds.

Summary

Americans entered the post-Civil War era with conflicting agendas for restoring peace and distributing justice. Emancipated slaves sought political rights and economic independence. Former Confederates insisted on the freedom to retain regional power and racial dominance. Republicans in Congress held the balance of political power and debated plans for the postwar settlement. The contest between revolutionizing the South and restoring the prewar status quo galvanized the nation when the Republicans impeached their renegade president and framed a program to reconstruct southern life as a precondition to reunion. Congressional Reconstruction strengthened the federal government's domestic power at the same time that the purchase of Alaska confirmed the nation's continental dominance. In 1867, the United States became the only postemancipation society in the Americas committed to guaranteeing former slaves full civil and political rights.

Reconstruction shook southern society to its foundations as Republican state governments elected with African American votes enacted sweeping changes in politics, education, and public welfare. But in the South, as in postemancipation societies in Caribbean islands, white planters who had resisted emancipation led determined efforts to maintain their racial and economic supremacy after slavery's end. Using the Democratic Party and secret paramilitary groups, angry white Southerners arose to take control of their states. As political winds shifted, industrial upheavals and overseas expansion drew the public's attention, and the North's Republicans retreated from their commitment to enforce racial equality.

By the time Reconstruction officially ended in 1877, an informal settlement emerged by which Northerners dominated the newly powerful national government and traditional white elites regained control over the postwar South's politics, agriculture, and race relations. As in most nations undergoing unification struggles, sectional integration was incomplete and cultural and ideological rifts lingered. The North returned to peace, prosperity, and expansion, the South assumed a subordinate relationship in national politics, and the Union's promise of full freedom to the former slaves was sacrificed. Instead of serving as a model of political equality for other postemancipation societies, Americans provided examples of racial segregation and political disfranchisement amid glimpses of progress.

‹Thinking Back, *Looking Forward*›

As you review this chapter, think about how Reconstruction transformed American politics, the national economy, and social relations in the South. Which changes endured, and which were temporary? Did the North win the Civil War but lose the postwar peace? Why did Americans retreat from their unique pledge of postemancipation equality between races? How complete was U.S. national unification compared to that of other nations? In the next chapters, look for the lasting consequences of Reconstruction's battles. What did the South's segregationist regime mean for Reconstruction's legacy? What were the consequences of Reconstruction for Native Americans, immigration, and U.S. citizenship?

To make your study concrete, review the timeline and reflect on the entries there. Think about their causes, consequences, and connections. How do they fit with global trends?

Additional Resources

Books

Beckert, Sven. *Empire of Cotton: A Global History*. New York: Knopf, 2014. ▶ Documentation of the worldwide switch to tenancy and small-farm production after the U.S. Civil War.

Cook, Adrian. *The Alabama Claims: American Politics and Anglo-American Relations, 1865–1872*. Ithaca, NY: Cornell University Press, 1975. ▶ Scholarly history of U.S.–Great Britain relations during Reconstruction.

Dubois, Ellen Carol. *Feminism and Suffrage: The Emergence of an Independent Women's Movement in America, 1848–1869*. Ithaca. NY: Cornell University Press, 1978. ▶ Account of the break of women's rights' advocates from their abolitionist roots to focus on the vote.

Foner, Eric. *Reconstruction: America's Unfinished Revolution, 1863–1877*. New York: HarperCollins, 1988. ▶ The best single-volume history of the period.

Hahn, Steven. *A Nation under Our Feet: Black Political Struggles in the Rural South from Slavery to the Great Migration*. Cambridge, MA: Harvard University Press, 2005. ▶ Exploration of the hidden history of black political organizing during and after Reconstruction.

Hunter, Tera W. *To 'Joy My Freedom: Southern Black Women's Lives and Labors after the Civil War*. Cambridge, MA: Harvard University Press, 1997. ▶ Retelling of urban black women's lives and struggles as domestics.

Litwack, Leon. *Been in the Storm So Long: The Aftermath of Slavery*. New York: Vintage Books, 1980. ▶ Classic account, based on participants' testimony, of how blacks experienced freedom.

Scott, Rebecca J. *Degrees of Freedom: Louisiana and Cuba after Slavery*. Cambridge: Belknap Press, 2005. ▶ Comparison and contrast of emancipation and race relations in two sugar plantation societies.

Simpson, Brooks D. *The Reconstruction Presidents*. Lawrence: University Press of Kansas, 1998. ▶ A comparative assessment that rehabilitates Grant's reputation.

Stewart, David O. *Impeached: The Trial of President Andrew Johnson and the Fight for Lincoln's Legacy*. New York: Simon & Schuster, 2009. ▶ A dramatic narrative that criticizes Johnson for squandering Lincoln's hopes for emancipation.

Trelease, Allen. *White Terror: The Ku Klux Klan Conspiracy and Southern Reconstruction*. Baton Rouge: Louisiana State University Press, 1995. ▶ A comprehensive, state-by-state history of Klan activities during Reconstruction.

> Go to the MindTap® for **Global Americans** to access the full version of select books from this Additional Resources section.

Websites

Andrew Johnson Impeachment Trial. (http://www.law.umkc.edu/faculty/projects/ftrials/impeach/impeachmt.htm). ▶ A collection of documents, information, and links about the impeachment.

Freedmen and Southern Society Project. (http://www.history.umd.edu/Freedmen/). ▶ Essays and primary source documents related to emancipation, land, and labor.

Freedmen's Bureau Online. (http://www.freedmensbureau.com/) ▶ State-by-state reports and documents, many capturing African American voices.

Harper's Weekly. (http://blackhistory.harpweek.com/default.htm). ▶ Collection of reports on Black America 1857–1874 that includes editorials, news stories, and cartoons on Reconstruction from the popular northern magazine.

Ohio State University Libraries. (http://cartoons.osu.edu/digital_albums/thomasnast/index.htm). ▶ Extensive portfolio of Thomas Nast's political cartoons, which reflect changing Republican attitudes during Reconstruction.

Reconstruction: The Second Civil War. (http://www.pbs.org/wgbh/amex/reconstruction/index.html). ▶ Background information, documents, and access to two PBS documentary films about Reconstruction.

 MindTap®

Continue exploring online through MindTap®, where you can:

- **Assess your knowledge with the Chapter Test**
- **Watch historical videos related to the chapter**
- **Further your understanding with interactive maps and timelines**

1863

December

Lincoln's Proclamation of Amnesty and Reconstruction outlines lenient plan for restoring rebellious states to the Union.

1864

July

Lincoln pocket vetoes congressional Wade-Davis bill imposing strict terms for readmission to the Union.

1865

March

Congress establishes Freedmen's Bureau to assist former slaves.

April

Lincoln is assassinated and is succeeded by Vice President Andrew Johnson .

May

Johnson announces plan to disfranchise Confederate leaders and quickly restore former Confederate states.

Summer

White governments in restored southern states adopt Black Codes restricting freed people's rights.

October

Morant Bay Rebellion in Jamaica stiffens southern whites' resistance to freedmen's rights.

December

Thirteenth Amendment is ratified, outlawing slavery in United States.

Ku Klux Klan is organized in Tennessee to terrorize freed people.

1866

April

Civil Rights Act extends citizenship and accompanying rights to all persons born in the United States, including former slaves.

May–June

Fenian Brotherhood launches invasion of Canada aimed at securing Irish independence.

July

Armed U.S. merchant ship *General Sherman* is attacked and destroyed in Korea.

1867

March

United States purchases Alaska territory from Russia to promote continental expansion and Pacific trade.

Reconstruction Act returns former Confederate states to military rule and sets congressional requirements for readmission.

British North America Act creates Canadian Confederation in response to threat of U.S. expansion.

August

Reform Act in Britain expands voting rights to double the electorate but rejects women's suffrage.

1868

January

Japan's Meiji Restoration initiates modernization and increases U.S. influence in its industry and educational system.

February

Bancroft Treaties spread recognition of naturalized citizenship, beginning with pact between German states and the United States.

March

Johnson impeached but not convicted by Congress in dispute over Reconstruction policies.

July

Fourteenth Amendment gives citizenship to African Americans and establishes birthright citizenship as U.S. policy.

Burlingame Treaty between U.S. and China proclaims mutual respect and continues Chinese immigration to United States.

October

United States stays neutral as the Ten Years' War erupts in Cuba over abolition and colonial independence from Spain.

November

Republican candidate and Civil War hero Ulysses Grant is elected president.

1869 – 1870

April

In *Texas v. White*, the Supreme Court declares secession unconstitutional without consent of the United States.

May

Debate over Reconstruction amendments splits U.S. women's suffrage activists.

March

Fifteenth Amendment bans denial of vote on grounds of race.

June

U.S. Senate rejects annexation of Santo Domingo.

1871

January

Women's suffrage advocates appear before Congress to press their claims.

May

Treaty of Washington resolves U.S.–Britain disputes over Civil War claims and Canadian border.

June

U.S. expedition to Korea avenges *General Sherman* incident but fails to open trade relations.

September

Brazil, influenced by prior British and U.S emancipation, adopts a gradual emancipation law.

1872

September

Crédit Mobilier scandal rocks Grant administration, eroding support for Republican Party.

November

Grant is reelected president as Liberal Republican revolt fails.

1873

April

White Southerners murder black officeholders in Louisiana's Colfax Massacre.

U.S. Supreme Court weakens Fourteenth Amendment in Slaughterhouse Cases ruling.

September

Bank Panic in Europe triggers U.S. economic crisis and six-year global depression.

1874

November

Democrats win control of House of Representatives for the first time since the Civil War.

1875

March

U.S. Supreme Court rejects women's suffrage in *Minor v. Happersett*.

1876

March

U.S. v. Cruikshank drastically limits federal oversight of freed people's civil rights.

November

Republican Rutherford Hayes and Democrat Samuel Tilden deadlock in disputed presidential election.

1877

March

Electoral College and congressional compromise declare Hayes president and officially end Reconstruction.

Go to MindTap® to engage with an interactive version of the timeline. Analyze events and themes with clickable content, view related videos, and respond to critical thinking questions.

Russia

Britain   Germany

Canada

United States

Korea

The Caribbean

China

Brazil

15 Incorporation of the U.S. West

1862–1917

In the aftermath of the Sand Creek Massacre, the U.S. government removed Black Kettle and the remainder of his group to a reservation in Indian Territory along the Washita River in present-day Oklahoma. Black Kettle's story reveals the dangers Indians faced when they opted for peace with the U.S. government.

Black Kettle, a leader of the Cheyennes who advocated accommodation with the U.S. military and white society, left his home at Sand Creek, Colorado, and made his way to Fort Lyon. There, on September 26, 1861, he signed a peace treaty and surrendered. He asked Major Scott Anthony if he and his people could overwinter in the fort for safety and receive government food rations. Because the fort was already at capacity with other Cheyennes, Anthony told Black Kettle to return to his camp thirty miles away, where they could hunt for winter game and wait for further instructions. Anthony assured Black Kettle that his people would be safe despite U.S. military campaigns against other Indians nearby.

Bosse, Left Hand, White Wolf, Black Kettle, White Antelope, Bull Bear, Neva: (b/w photo), American Photographer, (19th century)/ Denver Public Library, Western History Collection/The Bridgeman Art Library

Chiefs of the Arapahoe, Sioux, Cheyenne, and Kiowa tribes, circa 1860–1868. Black Kettle is the figure seated on the far left side of the front row.

Not all Cheyennes accepted Black Kettle's surrender. The Dog Soldiers, a group of young men who had separated themselves to create a warrior culture, opposed accommodations to whites that almost always ended in Indian land loss and the suppression of Indian culture. During the Plains Wars of the mid-nineteenth century, increasing numbers of young men abandoned the Cheyenne leaders to join the Dog Soldiers. In Colorado, they were preparing to fight Colonel John M. Chivington as he and his regiment of seven hundred left Denver to attack the Cheyennes and Arapahoes.

It was a time of violence. Half a continent away, in the same month that Black Kettle moved to Sand Creek, Union general William T. Sherman conquered Atlanta. He marched through Georgia, destroying anything useful to the Confederacy. The Civil War's legitimization of force against civilians was perpetuated in the West where the U.S. military continued to use force to subjugate Indian peoples. Similar migrations and violent encounters were occurring in Australia, Argentina, and South Africa where European settlers pushed aside native peoples to take control of natural resources.

Early on the morning of November 29, 1864, Chivington, who was aware of the peace agreement, attacked Black Kettle's sleeping camp. Only a few men were present to mount a defense, so women and children scattered or burrowed into the ground to protect themselves from gunfire. By mid-afternoon, more than one hundred fifty Cheyennes lay dead. Miraculously, Black Kettle and his wife survived. The white fur trader, George Bent, living at Sand Creek, and other traders with mixed-race families tried to negotiate a peace, but Chivington's men burned the camp and then pushed on to destroy other Indian villages.

In the aftermath, the U.S. government removed Black Kettle and the remainder of his group to a reservation in what was known as *Indian Territory* (present-day Oklahoma). Four years later, in the winter of 1868, Colonel George Armstrong Custer attacked Black Kettle's encampment. This time neither Black Kettle nor his wife survived. Black Kettle's experiences reveal the dangers that Indians faced when they opted for peace with the U.S. government.

How do Black Kettle's experiences with warfare on the Great Plains reflect the dangers that Indians faced when they opted for peace with the U.S. government?

Go to MindTap® to watch a video on Black Kettle and learn how his story relates to the themes of this chapter.

Once southern members had vacated Congress during the Civil War, the overwhelmingly Republican majority was free to plan the future of the trans-Mississippi territories without the obstacle of southern slaveholders. In quick succession, Republicans passed three pieces of legislation that changed the West forever. The Pacific Railroad Acts funded the building of transcontinental railroads, the Homestead Act granted land to settlers who would improve it, and the Morrill Act encouraged land sales to establish state universities specializing in agricultural science and engineering. Together, these acts, which suggested the federal government's increasing power after the Civil War, opened the West to commercial development and a wave of white settlement.

In the decades following the Sand Creek Massacre, warfare on the Great Plains peaked and then subsided as the U.S. military destroyed Indian settlements and broke down resistance. By the 1890s, the U.S. government had placed the last of the Indian leaders—Sitting Bull, Chief Joseph, and Geronimo—on reservations and decimated the great herds of bison that had supported Indian life for centuries. The land was then enclosed into ranches and farms settled by white Americans and European immigrants. Railroads transported people and products to eastern factories and cities. Commerce and communications knit the continent and connected it across the Pacific to China and Japan, which opened new markets for U.S. goods and created opportunities for new immigrants. New markets, new agricultural methods, and new technologies united the nation and made the West less distinctive. In reality and in Americans' imagination, the West had been tamed and brought into the nation. As the violence that had begun with the arrival of the Spanish conquistadors faded into history, Americans romanticized the development of the West into a story of progress.

15-1
Ties of Commerce

John Gast completed *American Progress* in 1872. Notice the city on the right in the sunshine and the rugged mountains and darkness on the left. Find the horsemen, farmers, fleeing bison and Indians, and the train puffing black smoke. The crowned and classically garbed figure carries a book and trails a telegraph wire behind her as she floats, beneficently, over the landscape.

What do you think the floating female figure represents? How does Gast use light and imagery to tell a story about progress? ▶

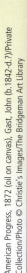

American Progress, 1872 (oil on canvas), Gast, John (b.1842-d.?)/Private Collection/Photo © Christie's Images/The Bridgeman Art Library

The economic development of the West intensified with the growth of the railroads, which were built across the trans-Mississippi frontier in advance of most commerce and white settlement. Americans' desire for commercial ties linking the nation with western ports for trade with Japan and China was the driving force behind railroad development. Transcontinental railroad projects were immense and expensive undertakings made possible only by the federal government, whose economic and political power surpassed that of the largest private corporations. The federal government also sponsored the establishment of state universities specializing in agriculture and engineering. These produced the managers and engineers who planned the railroad routes and directed these projects. But the work of carving rail lines into the landscape was accomplished by the labor of millions of men, often immigrants willing to take grueling and dangerous jobs.

☞ As you read, consider ways in which the transcontinental railroad knit the nation together. What problems did railroad development cause?

15-1a The Transcontinental Railroad

Building a transcontinental railroad was a dream of business and political leaders before the Civil War. After the war, underwritten by the

{ The transcontinental railroad draws the nation together through commerce.

federal government, it became a reality. The Pacific Railroad Acts (1862, 1864) financed the project through **land grants** from the public domain amounting to 174 million acres, larger than the size of Texas (see Map 15.1). The Union Pacific built west from Omaha, Nebraska, and the Central Pacific built east from Sacramento, California. Each received ten sections (sixty-four hundred acres) along the right of way for each mile of track laid. That incentive later increased to twenty, and then forty, sections per mile. The railroads sold these lands to settlers and speculators who built towns and created business that required rail traffic for the new lines.

Because of the magnitude of the transcontinental line, the federal government also financed the railroad by selling bonds that promised a return of 6 percent to the investors. Ultimately, the government advanced about $77 million

land grants Awards of public domain lands by Congress to railroad companies and to states to support the development of railroads and schools.

Map 15.1 Federal Land Grants Given to Railroads Building railroads after the Civil War would not have been possible without immense federal subsidies of land. Taken from Native Americans, who were increasingly confined to reservations, these lands were turned over to railway companies that sold them to raise revenue. While homesteaders could get "free" land, many who could afford it chose to pay a premium price to have easy access to the railroad, which opened a global market to them. ▲

in bonds to the railroad companies, which they were supposed to repay over the next thirty years, but in fact they repaid only a fraction of what was owed. The government also covered about $43 million in deferred interest payments to the railroads' bondholders. The magnitude of this infrastructure project succeeded only because of these massive government subsidies to private corporations.

The Central Pacific Railroad (CPRR) started the first transcontinental line in Sacramento, California, and began laying track east across and through the Sierra Nevada mountains and out onto the high plateaus of the interior West. A group of powerful tycoons financially underwrote the railroads. Known as the **Big Four**, Leland Stanford, Collis P. Huntington, Mark Hopkins, and Charles Crocker bought and sold the government-backed bonds to finance the railroad, amassing a huge profit. With the exception of timber, all of the materials—rails, equipment, and engines—had to be shipped from the East Coast to the West via the Isthmus of Panama or through Cape Horn on the southern tip of South America. The cost was enormous in terms of material, labor, and time.

From Omaha, Nebraska, the Union Pacific had the easier task, pushing westward across the plains. As the two lines neared each other, the nation waited in anticipation, as the workers engaged in a gripping competition. The Union Pacific laid the most track overall, but the CPRR held the record for most track laid in a single day—ten miles. On May 10, 1869, the two companies met at **Promontory Summit** in Utah, and when the hammer hit the last spike at 12:32 P.M., joining the two railroads, a telegraph sent to Washington, D.C., declared "Done." People across the nation celebrated as one newspaper columnist wrote that this was the marriage of "the gorgeous east and the imperial west of America, with the indissoluble seal of inter-oceanic commerce." The transcontinental railroad and the telegraph wire strung alongside it were the physical expression of the U.S. fascination with its Manifest Destiny (the belief that the U.S. was ordained to rule over North America), and its more benevolent version of *American Progress* as embodied in Gast's painting.

Although the nation's rail network had expanded rapidly, very little of it was standardized or compatible. Each line had been developed as a private enterprise without much government regulation, and each company used different railcars and coupling systems to link its railcars. Each rail line also used its own gauge (distance between the rails), and by the 1870s, more than two dozen gauges existed. Someone taking the train from New York to Chicago would have had to change trains and transportation companies at least three times. Freight had to be transferred by hand from one railway line's railcars to those of the next company as it moved through the system,

driving up shipping costs. The Pacific Railway Acts codified a standard gauge for the entire transcontinental railroad to avoid these problems. This type of standardization spread throughout the railroad industry after the Civil War to provide efficiency and convenience amid fierce competition and cutthroat practices among rival companies.

Until 1883, when the railroads adopted the policy of **standard time**, people in North America operated on "local time" or simply had an approximate sense of what time it was. With the advent of railroads and the need to coordinate transfers and rail use precisely, this practice had to change. Since the eighteenth century, mariners had used Greenwich Mean Time (GMT), based on the established longitude of zero degrees at Greenwich, England, to help navigate the seas. In 1847, British railroads had adopted GMT, which became known as *railway time*, to synchronize their schedules. Britain eventually adopted GMT as its legal time in 1880. Then in 1883, on the "day of two noons," railroad stations across the United States set their clocks to railway standard time, and time zones were established. Within a year, 85 percent of all U.S. cities were using railway time. In 1918, Congress passed the Standard Time Act that set official time zones in the United States. Globally, railroads literally set the clocks for the world as it became essential in terms of efficiency and safety to make sure that the trains ran on time and made their posted connections, particular at rail crossings.

15-1b Railroad Expansion at Home and Abroad

Railroad development in the 1860s went far beyond building the first transcontinental railroad. Once it was finished, other rail lines competed to access government funding and create their own cross-country roads. After the meeting of the Union and Central Pacific Railroads rails at Promontory Summit, the Big Four turned to developing the Southern Pacific Railroad Company to tap into the emerging markets in Mexico and to develop copper mines along the border. The Associates focused their attention on creating a line that would reach the growing California market from Sacramento to Los Angeles. They then built a line that eventually connected Los Angeles with El Paso, Texas, and all the way east to New Orleans, Louisiana. These railroads created a regional market that linked Mexico and the U.S. Southwest into an intricate web of cross-border commerce.

{ Railroads and transportation networks link the world together.

The southern line had the potential to draw much larger and international markets as they tapped into the Gulf of Mexico and Mississippi River trade that drew goods from the Caribbean and Central and South America. Under President Porfirio Diaz, Mexico had its own railroad boom. Because of his favoritism to

Big Four Businessmen, also known as the *Associates*, who used unscrupulous tactics to develop railroads across North America.

Promontory Summit The meeting point in northern Utah where the Central and Union Pacific Railroads joined to create the first transcontinental railroad.

standard time Synchronized time within designated zones conforming to one standard time rather than a local one.

Everett Collection Historical/Alamy Stock Photo

Global Americans **J.J. Hill** was born in Ontario, Canada, in 1838. At the age of eighteen, he saw an opportunity in the expanding transportation markets along the upper Mississippi River and moved to St. Paul, Minnesota, to work first on steamboats and then the railroad. In 1870, he started the Red River Transportation Company, which hauled coal, fuel, and passengers on steamboat lines from St. Paul to Winnipeg, developing cross-border commerce between Canada and the United States. A relentless worker, Hill had the motto "Work, hard work, intelligent work, and then more work." He was one of the very few who profited from the Panic of 1873 by buying a bankrupt railroad. During the Panic of 1893, when his competitors were failing, he stayed in business by lowering rates and extending credit to his customers. In 1879, he bought the St. Paul, Minneapolis, and Manitoba Railway with cash. Unlike all other railway owners, Hill never took government land grants, bonds, or loans to finance his businesses. He was the only railway owner never to go into bankruptcy. But in order to make his railways profitable, he created markets. He opened immigration offices in Germany and Scandinavia to encourage farmers to migrate to the upper Midwest. He also introduced hybridized wheat from Russia, which was hardier and could grow in the harsh Dakota winters. Hill was a globalized businessman who realized the advantages of open immigration and free markets. He was an early and strong proponent of free trade, always opposing any tariff bills that would inhibit his companies' profits.

U.S. businessmen, the Mexican government granted $32 million in subsidies to U.S. companies that would build railroads. Five railroad companies eventually constructed more than twenty-five hundred miles of track that ran south to north. In August 1884, Mexican Central Railway completed an international, transcontinental railroad that linked Mexico City with El Paso, Texas, and the Atchison, Topeka, and Santa Fe Railway. The road eventually went as far north as Santa Fe, New Mexico. Railroad **boosters** created an even more lucrative *Camino Real* than the one the Spanish had created in the colonial period. By 1910 and the Mexican Revolution, U.S. companies held almost 90 percent of all investments in Mexican railroads and owned fifteen thousand miles of track south of the border.

Railroad owners realized that trade did not end at the shores of the Pacific Ocean. They gambled that the transcontinental railroad combined with Pacific steamship service from San Francisco would make the United States a conduit for trade between Europe and Asia, serving as a constructed Northwest Passage, the imagined all-sea route that had enticed early European explorers. Their hopes were dashed when the **Suez Canal** opened in 1869 just after the railroads had been joined in Utah, providing a sea route between Europe and Asia that cut off the long trip around Africa. Nevertheless, railroad investors such as the Big Four saw potential growth in trade between the East Coast and Asia by means of the Pacific Mail and the Occidental and Oriental Steamship Companies, which provided bimonthly service between the West Coast and various ports in Asia. The United States exported cotton, wheat, silver, and opium whereas Asian countries shipped tea, silk, spices, porcelain, and laborers to California ports for distribution throughout the United States.

15-1c Railroad Workers

Railroad development happened because of the engineers who planned the routes and the physical labor of thousands of men who did

{ An international labor force builds the railroads.

the day-to-day work. As industrialization proceeded, the need for a new class of technical experts knowledgeable in the design and operation of machines emerged. The military had long trained engineers to build fortifications. But now, an entirely new array of engineers—mechanical, mining, and later chemical and electrical engineers— emerged. Many received training at the new land-grant institutions established under the Morrill Act. This act supported technical education by granting 30,000 acres of public domain land that could be used to fund agricultural, mechanical, and technical schools. Some states, such as Wisconsin, put the money into their existing educational systems; others, such as Michigan, created a new school, Michigan State University. These schools gave students the skills necessary to develop the nation's infrastructure and extract its natural resources. Such schools created a managerial class who oversaw the work of laborers and thus contributed to the class hierarchies evolving in industrializing America.

At the other end of the labor spectrum were the day laborers who did the arduous work of cutting the timber, preparing and shipping the rail ties, mining the coal that fueled the trains, laying the track, and then maintaining the entire system once it was in place. Like the urban areas of

boosters Local businessmen who wanted to draw settlers to their community by boasting of its advantages.

Suez Canal Sea-level canal that linked the Mediterranean and Red Seas, opening a trade route between Europe and the Middle and Far East.

the East Coast in the United States in this period, the U.S. West was an industrializing landscape that drew thousands of immigrants from around the world (see Figure 15.1). Chinese men worked on the northern and western lines, and Mexicans for the most part built the southwestern rail lines. African Americans made up the majority of the workers on the southern railroads. By the 1890s, women were also working for railway companies as clerks, machinists, and laborers in the roundhouse and on the tracks. The Northern Pacific employed more than two thousand women by the early twentieth century.

Not everyone who worked on the railroad was a new immigrant. When the Union Pacific started building west from Nebraska, it turned to the Irish, who made up more than half of its workforce. Irish immigrants had been coming to the United States since the early nineteenth century when they fled the famines in their home country. They found work as laborers in East Coast cities and later along the growing transportation routes as diggers for the Erie Canal and tracklayers for the emerging railroads across the interior of the nation.

In California, the CPRR turned to Chinese labor when white workers went on strike. It employed ten thousand Chinese laborers who constituted 90 percent of its workforce. The Northern Pacific employed fifteen thousand Chinese railroad construction workers, which was a majority of its workers. The Chinese, many of whom had come during the gold rush in the early 1850s, worked for $31 a month (or about $870 in 2014), which was much less than the white workers earned. Although they were given housing—usually in old boxcars—they had to pay for their meals from their wages. The work was difficult for these laborers who dug and dynamited the tunnels that went through the Sierra Nevada. Some men hung from baskets as they bored holes into the side of a mountain, stuffed nitroglycerin in the holes, and lit the fuse after which they were quickly whisked upward. Chinese laborers struck to protest low pay and dangerous conditions, but they were in the middle of nowhere and the company reduced their rations, and so the strike ended quickly.

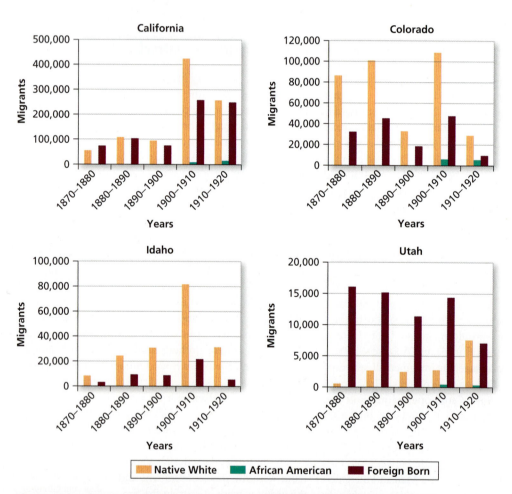

Figure 15.1 Migrations into Four Western States, 1870–1920 Although not as large or diverse as the immigration to the eastern United States during this period, the American West also became home to both migrants and immigrants. This table is a sample of four western states' migration patterns. Can you give historical reasons for why these patterns emerged as they did? ▲ Sources: Hirschman, Charles and Liz Mogford. "Immigrants and Industrialization in the United States, 1880 to 1920." (http://faculty.washington.edu/charles/pubs/Immigrants_Industrialization.pdf); Kuznets, Simon, and Dorothy Thomas. *Population Redistribution and Economic Growth: United States, 1870–1950.* Philadelphia: American Philosophical Society, 1957.

Chinese Workers on the Union Pacific Railroad, circa 1869 Regardless of race or ethnicity, life as a railway worker was difficult, low paying, and dangerous. Workers had to follow the track as they were laying it. They lived in makeshift shacks or abandoned railway cars and cooked meals over an open fire. Some brought their families, but most were single men who hoped to make enough money before returning home to settle down. ◄

Topham/The Image Works

Throughout the latter decades of the nineteenth century, railroads continued to employ both Chinese and Irish workers, while Mexicans began to make up a larger proportion of the railroad workforce. Because of the massive U.S. investment and development in Mexico, its economy began to shift from a subsistence to an export-driven market. The creation of the railroads that connected the two nations also made migration easier. Mexican men began leaving their homes in rural communities and moving to Mexico's urban centers, which were becoming overcrowded and could not provide enough work for all. Consequently, Mexican workers kept moving north along the railroad until they crossed the border, which had few barriers, and found work. Eventually families followed. Many settled in the emerging urban areas such as El Paso, Los Angeles, and Albuquerque. Some moved along with the railroad expansion, living in old boxcars that were pulled along behind the advancing track lines.

The railroad transformed the U.S. economy by drawing settlers and workers into the West. Many of these newcomers were Americans in search of economic opportunity. Many were foreign-born immigrants from all over the world, mostly from Asia, Mexico, and southern Europe, who hoped to start a new life. The railroad transformed U.S. trading relations with foreign countries such as Mexico, Canada, and Asia. The railroad was often the first step in drawing these markets and people into the U.S. orbit.

15-2
A Strong Federal Role

Daniel Freeman's Homestead certificate for one hundred and sixty acres of the U.S. public domain was issued January 20, 1868. Such certificates were the means by which the U.S. government distributed public domain land to heads of households.

What does this document suggest about the authority of the federal government to transfer land and organize society? Who benefited and who did not? ▶

National Archives and Records Administration

HOMESTEAD.

Land Office at *Brownville Neb*
January 20ᵗʰ 1868.

CERTIFICATE, } No. 1 }

{ APPLICATION, { No. 1

It is hereby certified, That pursuant to the provisions of the act of Congress, approved May 20, 1862, entitled "An act to secure homesteads to actual settlers on the public domain,"

Daniel Freeman has made payment in full for *E½ of NW¼ and E½ of NW¼ and SW¼ of NE¼* of Section *Twenty Six (26)* in Township *four (4) N* of Range *five (5) E* containing *160* acres.

Now, therefore, be it known, That on presentation of this Certificate to the COMMISSIONER OF THE GENERAL LAND OFFICE, *the said* Daniel Freeman *shall be entitled to a Patent for the Tract of Land above described.*

Henry M. Atkinson
Register.

U.S. Geological Survey (USGS) Federal agency created from the earlier General Survey to explore the West so that its lands could be developed for industrial and other uses.

Homestead Act Congressional act that provided citizens and immigrants 160 acres of free land.

Timber Culture Act Congressional act allowing homesteaders to acquire another one hundred sixty acres, in addition to land obtained from the Homestead Act, if they planted one-quarter of the new parcel with trees.

In addition to the Pacific Railway Acts and the Morrill Act, the Civil War Congresses also promoted the development of the West through a program of land distribution that attracted rapid settlement. Later legislation advanced the development of timber and mining resources. As federal troops left the South after the war, the military turned its attention to the West and reacting to the increasing conflicts between Indians and settlers. For the first time, the federal government was able to exert a consistent influence over the region. On the nonmilitary side, the federal government sent scientists through the **U.S. Geological Survey (USGS)**, founded in 1879, to map the West's natural resources. This information helped settlers, speculators, and developers to transform the West's economy, which provided the raw resources for the nation's continued economic development. Finally, the federal government politically incorporated the areas in and peoples of the West.

☞ As you read, consider how the federal government extended its power across the American West.

15-2a Land Distribution

Since the 1830s, the federal government had been distributing public domain land, all of it taken from Native Americans, to U.S. citizens and immigrants. The Free-Soil Party and later, in the 1850s, the new Republican Party promoted this distribution. In 1862, under the **Homestead Act**, anyone—a citizen or someone intending to become a citizen—who was twenty-one years old and head of a family could file for a quarter section (one hundred sixty acres) of land (see Table 15.1). Women who were heads of households or were single could file a claim. If the person lived on the land for five years and improved it by building a house, digging a well, plowing ten acres, and fencing at least part of it, the land was his or hers to keep for free. Those who wanted to own their land sooner could pay $1.25 an acre and forgo these requirements. This process of acquiring free or cheap land by settling on it and improving it was known as *homesteading*. Between 1870 and 1930, more than 270 million acres of land (10 percent of the United States) were given out to more than 1 million people who had completed their claims and received their land. In 1873, under the **Timber Culture Act**, people could also file for another one hundred sixty acres if they agreed to cultivate timber.

> The federal government passes a variety of laws to distribute western lands.

These acts did not deliberately discriminate. Some Indians and Mexican Americans who had lost land, freedmen, and some women had direct access to the Homestead Act and gained landholdings in the trans-Mississippi West. In 1866, Congress passed the Southern Homestead Act, which gave Southerners, even former members of the Confederate Army, the same rights to homestead land. In 1890, the Morrill Act was extended to include former Confederate states, where it funded state schools for African Americans that provided agricultural and technical education. The act also funded tribal colleges for Native Americans. Nevertheless, although the federal government distributed 250 million acres to the U.S. public, the system had faults. Only about one of every six acres distributed by the Homestead Act went directly into the hands of small farmers.

Table 15.1 Civil War and Reconstruction Legislation Related to the Development of the West

Historians tend to focus on this period as a time when the federal government was preoccupied with reintegrating the U.S. South into the nation. The government simultaneously passed a number of laws and signed two treaties that stimulated the economic development of the West. In addition to the two treaties, the legislation gave land that had formerly belonged to Indians to railroads, state governments, and individuals who created infastructure and businesses.

Date	Legislation	Summary
May 1862	Homestead Act	Allowed immigrants and citizens to claim and eventually own one hundred sixty acres of land
July 1862	First Pacific Railway Act	Authorized selling bonds and granting lands to finance railroad development
July 1862	First Morrill Act	Granted large parcels of land to state governments to raise funds for public higher education
June 1866	Southern Homestead Act	Opened 43 million acres to black and white farmers in former Confederate states
April 1868	Fort Laramie Treaty	Signed by the U.S. government and Lakotas, Dakotas, and Arapahoes to secure small reservations and prohibit further white settlement
May 1872	General Mining Act	Authorized and regulated mining on federally held lands
March 1873	Timber Culture Act	Allowed homesteaders to acquire another one hundred sixty acres if they planted one-quarter of it with trees
May 1875	Reciprocity Treaty with Hawai'i	Free trade agreement with Hawai'i that also ceded land to the United States for a military base

The rest was acquired by land speculators and by railroad companies through the Pacific Railway Acts.

Land development was just one aspect of the federal government's allocation of natural resources to individuals and private corporations. Through the Mining Act of 1872, individuals and corporations could purchase government lands for anywhere between $2.50 and $5.00 per acre to mine for gold, silver, platinum, copper, coal, oil, or uranium. Once the land was purchased, mineral rights could be freely developed without encumbrances. Purchasers did not have to pay royalties to the federal government or the state on any profit they made from the mine.

15-2b Land Surveys

The post-Reconstruction period in the West experienced a shift from an age of exploration to an age of surveying and mapping. On May 11, 1869, the day after the final spike was driven for the transcontinental railroad, John Wesley Powell joined the Colorado River Exploratory Expedition, which he was to command. Powell, a scientist and Civil War veteran who had lost most of his right arm at the Battle of Shiloh, was the first Euro-American to explore the Grand Canyon. Although less celebrated than the completion of the transcontinental railroad, the work done by Powell, his expedition, and, later, the USGS transformed the way Americans thought about the West and their use of the nation's natural resources. Under the central organization of the USGS, expeditions led by Powell and others created detailed maps that settlers could use to find the choice parcels of land for farming or ranching.

> The federal government sponsors surveys to explore and map the West.

Powell spent three months floating down the Colorado River, mapping its geology, and noting abandoned buildings and campsites everywhere. Simultaneously, three other surveyors—Clarence King, Ferdinand Hayden, and George Wheeler—also mapped and surveyed portions of the West. Each worked under contracts from private institutions and state governments with some federal funding appropriated by Congress or the Department of War. The days of government-sanctioned but loosely organized expeditions such as those by Lewis and Clark and Zebulon Pike gave way to a much more centralized mapping and cataloging of the West. No longer were such people sent to "discover" the West and its peoples; they were to write reports that detailed rainfall, mineral deposits, soil conditions, and waterways.

Some surveyors, such as Powell, also conducted ethnographic research on Indians, but for the most part government surveys assumed that Indians would disappear as immigrants moved westward. Surveys also were used by European and American speculators who wanted to exploit the West's mineral wealth such as coal, copper, silver, and gold, which had become much more accessible since the completion of the transcontinental

Clarence King King, first director of the U.S. Geological Survey, lived among the most elite in New York City but had a double life. In 1887, he met Ada Copeland, a former slave, and fell in love. He told her that his name was James Todd and that he was a Pullman porter. She believed he was African American. They raised five children and lived in a common-law marriage until his death. He never revealed his true identity to her. ◄

Bettmann/Corbis

railroad. This period also started the federal government's control over the West's natural resources that could be marketed.

Some USGS staff pandered to western congressional delegations and business boosters. For example, Ferdinand Hayden falsely touted the West as a well-watered and fertile place where Americans could settle and thrive. Powell thought differently. What Powell saw on his 1869 expedition convinced him that the West was so arid in comparison to the eastern United States that it could not be settled in the same way. He argued that the Homestead Act and U.S. land policy, based on an assumption that all of North America received as much rainfall as the land east of the Mississippi River, would not work because in most western regions "160 acres could barely support a field mouse." Powell was ignored because neither bureaucrats nor boosters wanted to hear this realistic assessment. Instead, they based both land and development policy on an overly optimistic vision of the West.

15-2c States and Citizens

Before the Civil War, the nation had expanded to the Pacific, but questions regarding statehood and citizenship had been tabled during the war. After the war and despite the process laid out in the Northwest Ordinance of 1787, most of the West's inhabitants endured exceptionally long periods in territorial status. Alaska's lasted ninety-two years. New Mexico and Arizona, with majority Mexican American

> Statehood evolves slowly in the West.

polygamy The practice of one man marrying multiple women that Joseph Smith declared in 1831 to be a tenet of the Mormon Church.

Reynolds v. United States U.S. Supreme Court decision that outlawed polygamy because religious belief did not exempt a person from criminal acts.

Edmunds-Tucker Act Legislation that unincorporated the Mormon Church and ended the Perpetual Emigration Fund.

The Manifesto Mormon Church's statement that polygamy was no longer a practice endorsed by the church.

Buffalo Soldiers African American cavalry regiments formed after the Civil War and stationed in the West to assert federal power and fight Indians.

populations, waited for sixty-two years before becoming states in 1912. Oklahoma, which had the largest Indian population, had become a state only five years earlier in 1907. Utah, with its majority Mormon population, waited forty-eight years. These states had populations not considered to be in the mainstream of U.S. society and so languished in the territorial period while Congress debated about how to incorporate them, an issue that would also arise with the Spanish-American War in 1898 (see Chapter 19). The exception was California, which had a similar mixed population but had been granted statehood in 1850.

Because residents of territories did not enjoy full citizenship rights, they were not represented in Congress and could not vote in presidential elections. Their governors were appointed, not elected, and like staffing decisions made in British and Dutch colonial settings, presidential appointments did not always reflect the interests of territorial residents. Governorships might be political plums, although some found them to be political death. General Lew Wallace, for example, was so disappointed at being sent to Santa Fe as governor of New Mexico that he locked himself in his office and focused more on writing the famous novel, *Ben Hur* (1880), than on governance. The consequences of territorial status were not only a lack of representation, about which residents complained bitterly to newspapers and Congress, but also lagging political and economic development.

Utah, largely settled by Mormons, reflected the nation's apprehension about incorporating outsiders. Most

Americans regarded the Mormon practice of **polygamy** as immoral and un-Christian, and by the Republican Party as, a "relic" of "barbarism." Brigham Young, the first territorial governor, had married at least twenty women, and other leaders in the Mormon community likewise practiced polygamy. But federal law prohibited bigamy. The U.S. Supreme Court ruled in ***Reynolds v. United States*** (1879) that the First Amendment protected religious belief but not practice. Congress then passed a series of laws restricting the practice of polygamy. The most extensive law, the **Edmunds-Tucker Act** (1887), not only prohibited polygamy but also unincorporated the Mormon Church and the Perpetual Emigration Fund, and dissolved the Mormon militia. As one of the most sweeping pieces of legislation since Reconstruction, the act sought to reorder Mormon society and bring it into the mainstream of U.S. culture.

Known polygamists went into hiding or were arrested and their wives were forced to testify against them. Their considerable assets were frozen, placing individuals, families, and communities in jeopardy. Finally, Wilford Woodruff, the president and a prophet of the Mormon Church, issued **The Manifesto** in 1890, telling his followers that God had revealed to him that U.S. law should be obeyed. With that official recognition of polygamy's illegality, the barriers to statehood for a population that was otherwise prosperous and politically powerful were removed. Utah became a state in 1896. Still, the following year, the federal government sent the **Buffalo Soldiers** to Salt Lake City to ensure that Mormons were obeying the order. As in the Reconstruction South, the U.S. government used its military power to enforce federal law.

Polygamy did not end immediately among Mormon families. It was difficult to unravel such complex social, economic, and emotional relationships. Many polygamous families stayed together because federal authorities were then much less likely to pursue cases following renunciation. Mexico and Canada provided havens for polygamous families who still believed in the covenant. The Mormon

Buffalo Soldiers These all-black federal forces were stationed in the U.S. West and most often dealt with problem populations such as strike breakers, Indians and Mormons. The soldiers were known for their horsemanship, dedication, and loyalty. They aided the federal government in opening territory so that settlement could continue, westward. ▶

Time Life Pictures/Time & Life Pictures/Getty Images

Church purchased more than one hundred thousand acres just across the border in Mexico to settle polygamous families in 1885. Charles Card escaped custody on his charge of practicing polygamy and fled across the Canadian border into Alberta, where he founded the town of Cardston. Until the early twentieth century, polygamy remained a national issue. One Mormon congressman was refused his seat on grounds that he was a polygamist, and Utah senator Reed Smoot came under intense scrutiny before he was seated in 1903.

The long period of territorialism in the West points to the fluid nature of how people thought about their relationship to the federal government and their citizenship. Although Americans who left the eastern United States retained citizenship once they headed into the territories, the extent of their political rights often remained unclear. The lack of a strong federal presence along the national borders complicated the issues of citizenship. As people crossed freely from both Canada and Mexico into the United States, they made communities among themselves, ignoring international boundaries along the **borderlands**. These areas were filled with families, often of mixed ethnicity and race. Mexican border towns such as El Paso, Texas, and San Diego, California, developed an economy and society allowing people to pass freely between the borders to go to school, work, and shop. As a result of this fluidity, people tended to think more about affiliations with their small towns or regions than with their identity as U.S. citizens. In these communities, persons who otherwise were marginalized in the national political scene worked at the local level, electing school boards, mayors, and council members to represent their interests.

White women found more opportunity in the West and made inroads into political office in the western states, where opposition to suffrage was much lower. In 1869, the Wyoming legislature granted equal and complete suffrage for its thousand female inhabitants, hoping to lure more to the territory. Susanna M. Salter was the first woman ever elected to political office in the United States when she won the election for mayor in Argonia, Kansas, in 1887. And in 1890, when Colorado women won the right to vote, journalist Caroline Nichols Churchill declared that the West "Shall be the Land for Women!" National citizenship and identity were complex issues that remained in flux for the many Americans living on the western edges of the United States.

borderlands Communities along international borders that have more in common with their neighbors across the border than they do with the majority population of their own nation.

15-3
Indian Resistance and Resettlement

This photograph was taken on Pine Ridge Reservation in 1890, just after the Wounded Knee Massacre. Note that most of the household items, including the tent, were government-issued to this family.

As you look at the photo, consider what the meaning of home is in the photo? Can you identity items that would have been traditionally used and items that were more modern, and issued by the U.S. government? Can you speculate as to why there is only one adult male in this photo? Who do you think took the photo and why? ▶

Go to MindTap® to practice history with the Chapter 15 **Primary Source Writing Activity: Indian Resistance.** Read and view primary sources and respond to a writing prompt.

The Sioux Reservation at Pine Ridge, South Dakota, c.1890 (b/w photo)/American Photographer, (19th century)/PETER NEWARK'S PICTURES/Private Collection/ Bridgeman Images

During the Civil War and into Reconstruction, conflict among Native American groups and violence between Indian and white settlers or U.S. troops disrupted life on the Great Plains. By the mid-1870s, violence had escalated as settlers pushed west and Indians competed for dwindling land and natural resources. In an effort to protect the western immigrants, the Department of War established a system of forts and increased military presence along the trails. These forts provided protection for travelers and created trading opportunities for those settlers eager to supply the troops. Even with this new effort to secure the trails, however, the U.S. military simply did not have enough personnel to cover all of the trouble spots in the West. By 1887, as a result of escalating violence, the federal government passed laws meant to move all Indians onto reservations and educate them in the ways of sedentary farming. Indians both resisted and accommodated the new regime, which lasted well into the twentieth century.

☞ As you read, reflect on the late nineteenth century as a turning point for Native Americans as they adjusted to westward expansion, industrialization, and technological developments. What forms did their adjustments take?

15-3a Settlement, Indians, and Bison

Violence escalated dramatically after the close of the Civil War all across the West as newcomers to the region put everyone in competition for land and resources. After the Sand Creek Massacre, violence on the Plains grew to such an extent that most U.S. troops felt they were penned inside the forts without enough soldiers to suppress the various Plains groups. When a young lieutenant, William Fetterman, ignored the orders from his superiors not to go beyond the boundaries of Fort Phil Kearny in Dakota Territory in 1866, he was ambushed by a group of Cheyennes, Arapahoes, and Sioux, who were waging Red Cloud's War against the U.S. troops. These Plains Indians had allied to keep settlers and the U.S. cavalry out of the Powder River Valley in Wyoming. Fetterman and his eighty-one men were entirely wiped out. The ambush made it clear to the U.S. public and the federal government that Indian warfare had to be dealt with forcefully by an increased military presence.

{ Migrants to the West confront and displace American Indians and bison.

In 1868, President Grant ran for reelection using the slogan, "Let Us Have Peace," which referred to both the South's Reconstruction and hostilities with Indians in the West. **Grant's Peace Policy** between 1868 and 1876 encouraged making treaties in an effort to bring Native Americans under U.S. control. By the late nineteenth century, the U.S. government realized that it could no longer just move Indians to places farther West but had to confine them on small parcels of land called *reservations*. The Grant Administration signed the **Treaty of Fort Laramie of 1868** with Lakotas, Dakotas, and Arapahoes, ending Red Cloud's War, promising to give Lakotas the entirety of the Black Hills, which was only a small part of their reservation, and closing it to white settlement. Under the Grant Peace Policy, reservations were run by religious organizations, particularly Quakers, who were supposed to help Indians incorporate into U.S. society. The federal government promised an ideal form of reservation life: private property, education, and the tools necessary to move from a hunting society to a settled (and supposedly) prosperous agricultural life that would conform to a Jeffersonian ideal of farming.

Grant's Peace Policy Set of policies initiated by a group of reformers who persuaded the federal government to take a more benevolent approach toward Indians.

Treaty of Fort Laramie of 1868 Treaty between the United States and the Lakotas (among others) who agreed to move onto a reservation in the Black Hills but that white settlers violated.

accommodation A political and cultural stance in which a group agrees to blend in with the dominant society rather than resist it.

But by the late 1870s, violence perpetuated by whites in tandem with inadequate supplies from the federal government and poor governance meant that the Peace Policy was a failure.

The U.S. military moved Indians onto reservations while simultaneously depleting their most important resource—bison. There has been much historical debate about how the near extinction of the bison happened in such a short period of time. To some extent, Indians themselves were partially responsible for the depletion as they became entwined in the developing market economy that placed a premium price on bison hides and tongues and consequently put pressure on the ecosystem and bison survival. Native groups competed with one another for the best hunting grounds and for access to the American and European traders who set up posts and forts in strategic locations.

White western migrants also helped decimate bison herds by overhunting them for the market and for sport. Buffalo hunters sought to exploit the abundant resource by indiscriminately killing vast herds, skinning them where they dropped, carrying off the hides and tongues, and leaving the open Plains littered with decaying waste. Finally, the western army realized that the main reason that Indians stayed on the Plains and away from the forts and reservations was that they could sustain themselves on their traditional economy that relied on bison. Therefore, the U.S. government sought to destroy the remaining bison to force Indians off the Plains and onto reservations where they could not hunt and would have to subsist on government rations. All these factors combined to create a desolate environment where few bison survived and Indians' options dwindled as the U.S. government's actions forced them to raid white settlements or move to the reservations.

15-3b Indian Wars

While the federal government advanced a policy of containment and removal, Native Americans imagined a different future for themselves. Even as new migrants pushed into their territories, many Native Americans thought it possible to live next to settlers as long as each side would leave the other alone and respect the other's rights. But as it became clear that settlers would never coexist with Indians, two factions arose within Indian communities, each side using different strategies to survive the onslaught. **Accommodationists** were leaders such Black Kettle who willingly cooperated with whites and lead their people into reservations or forts where they would be under the watchful eye of the U.S. government.

{ Indian removal takes on its most violent phase in the late nineteenth century.

On the other side were those, like the Dog Soldiers, who refused to be brought into the reservation system and fought all efforts by the U.S. military to subdue them (see Map 15.2). Until the late 1870s, Indians had significant success in resisting U.S. policies and pushing back the military. The greatest defeat of U.S. forces came against General George Armstrong Custer and the Seventh Cavalry. Custer was part of a larger military force that had been sent to the Black Hills of South Dakota to take the area for U.S. settlement in violation of the 1868 Treaty of Fort Laramie. Miners had been rushing into the area after gold was discovered. Boomtowns such as Deadwood required military protection if they were to survive.

Custer and his commanders set out to attack the encampment along the Greasy Grass River, which held the Sioux as well as their Cheyenne and Arapahoe allies. The U.S. military underestimated the size of the group encamped and attacked headlong into the middle of the camp, which held more than 3,000 people, including many survivors from Sand Creek. Custer ignored directions to wait until he had support from Major Marcus Reno and sent his men into the heart of the camp to engage them on the **Little Bighorn River**. The fight lasted "no longer than it takes a hungry man to eat his lunch." and when it was over, not one of Custer's 268 men survived. Ironically, news of the Seventh Cavalry's complete defeat reached the east coast around July 4, 1876, just as the nation was celebrating the 100th anniversary of the

signing of the Declaration of Independence. While Americans celebrated the birth of their republic, its future and security were not yet entirely certain.

After the defeat of Custer, the U.S. military launched an all-out effort to secure the West for settlement and mineral extraction by sending in thousands of troops. Two of the three leaders of the Lakotas (Sitting Bull and Gall) who had defeated Custer and his men retreated across the border to Canada to avoid pursuit by an enraged U.S. Cavalry. Crazy Horse, however, stayed in the area around the Little Big Horn and battled General Nelson Miles, who pursued Crazy Horse's forces throughout the winter. The constant military harassment as well as the dwindling bison population eventually forced Crazy Horse's group to surrender in May 1877. Gall stayed out until January 1881, when he brought his group into the Poplar River agency to surrender. Sitting Bull lived in Canada and rebuffed offers by the U.S. government to surrender until July 1881, when he finally agreed to come into the reservation at Standing Rock.

Little Bighorn River Location in present-day Montana where Custer and his men were defeated by a coalition of Plains Indians.

Map 15.2 Selected U.S.– Indian Battles, 1860–1890 Violent conflicts on the Great Plains were a constant background as Euro-American settlers pushed onto Indian lands and displaced families. After the Civil War, U.S. policy makers realized that Indians could no longer be pushed west and forcibly contained them on reservations. However, by 1887 with the passage of the Dawes Act, these reservations were further reduced by allotment. Violence, as depicted in this map, was then replaced with policy and law in an effort to further contain Indians. ▼

General Allotment Act, or Dawes Act Congressional act that allotted land, provided a path to U.S. citizenship, and set up schools for Native Americans.

The Sioux were not the only group who resisted placement on reservations. The borders between the United States with Canada and Mexico became important barriers and protections for those fleeing the U.S. military. Both Mexicans and Americans were pushing Apaches from their lands along the border between Sonora and Arizona. The Apaches constantly fought to maintain their land and to keep their families safe. After the Civil War, violence escalated as the U.S. military sought to quell border violence, and capturing or killing Geronimo became their main goal. Between 1858 and 1886, Geronimo and his group evaded the cavalry and became notorious nationwide for their attacks on both sides of the border. Slowly and steadily, both the Mexican and U.S. militaries, including the Buffalo Soldiers, pressured Geronimo's followers into increasingly smaller territory where they were barely able to survive. He surrendered at Skeleton Canyon, Arizona, in September 1886. Until his death in 1909, he was a prisoner of war held on various military installations.

In eastern Oregon, Chief Joseph (Hin-mah-too-yah-lat-kekt) led his group of Nez Perce along a 1,170-mile trek in an attempt to escape U.S. troops in 1877. For more than three months, seven hundred fifty Nez Perce moved across the Pacific Northwest and the upper West before the Cavalry captured them. The group was taken to Fort Leavenworth, Kansas, and then to a reservation in Indian Territory. They finally relocated to their own reservation in Washington Territory in 1885. Chief Joseph's widely published speech expressed the anguish Native Americans felt as they surrendered to a life of confinement and surveillance: "Hear me, my chiefs! I am tired. My heart is sick and sad. From where the sun now stands I will fight no more forever."

15-3c Dawes Act and Indian Resistance

Passed in 1887, the **General Allotment, or Dawes Act**, was the culmination of governmental policies that had been enacted after the failure of Grant's Peace Policy as a response to the brutality of the Indian Wars. As part of a moral reform movement that found its origins in abolitionism and in Reconstruction, a group of northeastern Republican reformers pushed for a government-sponsored project that would assimilate Indians into mainstream society, economy, and culture. These Republicans viewed reservations as obsolete and as barriers to Indians' progress and urged the federal government to break them up into individual plots of private property.

> An allotment program aims to assimilate Indians and make reservations obsolete.

One of the most forceful reformers, Captain Richard Pratt, called for Indian children to be taken from their families and placed in boarding schools where they would be educated in the U.S. tradition. In 1879, Pratt began opening schools such as the Carlisle Industrial Training School in Pennsylvania—which borrowed ideas from Reconstruction schools for newly freed blacks such as Hampton Institute and the training programs developed by Booker T. Washington at Tuskegee Institute. Pratt believed his educational institutions would prepare Indian children to leave their traditional culture and move into a modern world where they could farm or work in industry. Indian children and their families, however, saw the schools as places where their culture, language, and ties to kin and community networks were stripped from them. Pratt's idealism never matched the lived experience of those Indian

Breakfast Lesson in Home Economics Class, Carlisle Indian School, 1901 At Carlisle Indian School, Captain Richard Pratt put into practice his motto, "Kill the Indian, and save the man" or, as in the case of the photo, the woman. These schools were intent on "civilizing" Indian children, which first meant removing them from their families and homes and sending them to boarding schools such as this one. The curriculum forced isolated children to abandon their native language, foods, and customs and then adopt what Pratt believed to be the modern and progressive way of Euro-Americans. ▶

Johnston, Frances Benjamin, 1864–1952, photographer

The Granger Collection, New York

Global Americans

Wovoka was a member of the Northern Paiutes born around 1856 in Smith Valley, Nevada, in what was then Utah territory. While growing up, he worked for a white couple, David and Abigail Wilson. When dealing with whites, Wovoka often used the name Jack Wilson and later in life used it exclusively. The Wilsons were devout Christians who taught Wovoka various Bible passages and infused him with Christian theology. He was also exposed to Mormon theology as that group was migrating into and setting up communities near him. On January 1, 1889, during a solar eclipse, Wovoka had a vision from which he later prophesized three events: all whites would leave the U.S. West, allowing Indians to live in peace and prosperity; the bison, which were disappearing, would reappear as would the Indian dead; and Indians would be protected from bullets fired by whites. For this to happen, Wovoka said, believers had to perform the Ghost Dance and live righteous lives. He explicitly linked the prophecy with salvation for believers. Wovoka's prophecy mirrored other millenarian movements of the time such as Mormonism and Christian evangelicalism. His teachings spread throughout the North American West. In Saskatchewan, among Canadian Sioux who were refugees from the 1882 Dakota War, it became the New Tidings Congregation. Others, such as Lakotas, sent representatives via train to visit and learn from Wovoka. They then returned to their homelands, sometimes on reservations, where they spread Wovoka's message of salvation and spiritual renewal and taught the Ghost Dance. Until the massacre at Wounded Knee abruptly ended the movement, it was part of a broader religious awakening across North America.

children who were sent to his schools. A similarly tragic story played out in Canada, Australia, and New Zealand, where white governments established modified versions of U.S. Indian boarding schools to forcibly assimilate native peoples.

Passage of the Dawes Act came at the same moment that the last of the Reconstruction reforms in the South were receding in the face of virulent racism. The act had three broad provisions. First, it decreed that the remaining acres within the reservations would be allotted to Indian families in a system that duplicated that of the Homestead Act, forcing them to give up their communal reservation lands and become sedentary farmers. Once Native American families had chosen their land plots, the rest of the reservation land would be open to white settlement and sold at market rates. In theory, the monies generated from these land sales would be used for farming tools, seeds, and education to help Indians make the transition to farmers. The act's second policy provided more funding for expanding the educational system that Pratt had begun a decade earlier. Finally, it established a clear path to citizenship, promising it to those Indians who agreed to have land allotted to them and work toward becoming assimilated into U.S. culture. However, citizenship was not granted to Native Americans until 1924.

Although there was some opposition to the Dawes Act among Congress and Americans, most wanted to embrace a program that would assimilate and acculturate Indians into the U.S. mainstream. On the other hand, Native Americans were not entirely willing to embrace this new set of policies that stripped them of their land base, economy, culture, and, in many cases, their children. Most Indians accepted the act's terms and suffered terribly as a result. However, a few groups, notably Navajos and

Senecas, resisted the Dawes Act. In 1881, Indian reservation lands totaled some 155 million acres; by 1900, as a result of allotment, the figure had fallen to 78 million acres. Allotment remained U.S. policy until 1934 when Indians had lost 60 percent of their reservation lands.

The most dramatic reaction to the Dawes Act and the power of the federal government came in the form of a religious movement, the **Ghost Dance**. In 1889, Wovoka, a Paiute leader, revived a religious movement that had long been a part of Native American culture. He preached that if his followers performed the Ghost Dance, the depredations they had suffered would turn into triumphs. This message was a powerful and hopeful antidote to the reality of Native Americans' day-to-day experience of privation and hunger on the reservation. The Ghost Dance swept across the U.S. West as Indian leaders traveled to see Wovoka and then returned to their reservations to teach the dance and its meaning to followers. U.S. officials, who believed it to be a war ceremony, viewed the Ghost Dance with unease. They speculated that Indians would rise up against the army and Indian agents policing the reservations.

In December 1890, an inexperienced Indian agent at the Pine Ridge Reservation feared that the Ghost Dancers were turning violent as they repeatedly performed the ritual. Tensions came to a crisis point when the reservation's residents found out that Sitting Bull had been killed during his arrest at nearby Standing Rock Reservation. Indian agents there were convinced that Sitting Bull had been encouraging the Ghost Dance and other forms of resistance. When another leader, Big Foot, brought his band from the Cheyenne River Reservation toward Pine Ridge, the Seventh Cavalry (formerly Custer's

Ghost Dance Native American religious movement that preached salvation for believers who were morally upright and practiced the dance.

Wounded Knee Tragic event in which the Seventh Cavalry gunned down Indian families at the Pine Ridge Reservation.

Indian Question "Question" that concerned how best to deal with Indians and their place in U.S. society.

unit) stopped them near Wounded Knee Creek. On the morning of December 29, the unit's commander ordered Big Foot's band to surrender. When a shot rang out, the cavalry unleashed its full force and fired indiscriminately into the camp, gunning down 146 Sioux, including forty-five women and eighteen children. Other deaths were accounted for later, bringing the Sioux death toll to more than 250. The officers were later disciplined, and there was some public outcry about the massacre of subdued Indians and innocent women and children. **Wounded Knee** has come to symbolize the tragedy and brutality of U.S. Indian policy.

By the end of the nineteenth century, laws and military action contained Native Americans and brought them under the tutelage of reformers and the U.S. government, leaving them very little physical space or legal room to maneuver and create self-sustaining lives. Answers to the **Indian Question** changed as reformers worried—not if Indians could survive in the twentieth century but what their roles would be as integrated U.S. citizens. Indians in the twentieth century moved their resistance to U.S. courtrooms and, public arenas where Indians and their advocates would push for fair treatment and equal rights.

15-4
Development of the West as a Market

Postcard of the Chicago Union Stockyards, 1910 Here immigrant laborers processed unfathomable numbers of animals so that every last piece of an animal could be made into an edible product, from steaks, to hot dogs, to dog food. The leftovers were used to make gelatin, leather, and other by-products. One observer noted, "From the snout to the tail—everything but the squeal."

Notice the relationship between the city, the railcars, and the animals. Describe the journey that these animals took from the Great Plains to this stockyard. How did the railroad connect the city and countryside? ▶

Lake County Museum/Curt Teich Postcard Archives/Getty Images

Even before the Indian Question was settled, Americans saw the West as a place that they could safely invest in and develop. The completion of the transcontinental railroad as well as the development of the smaller intertwined rail systems created new markets. The new economic opportunities lured farmers, ranchers, and miners west. Through the end of the nineteenth century, people pushed into the Midwest and West by the thousands, but unlike pre–Civil War migrants, they came by train, not by horseback, pushcart, or covered wagon. Through their labor, these people continued the development of the West by selling their goods in global markets. Their crops, animal products, and minerals could be exported by rail to the east, for consumption or to export to Europe, across the border into Mexico, and to the Pacific Coast for trade with China, where demand for U.S. agricultural products had increased dramatically. Farmers populated the Great Plains and began planting cash crops. Cattlemen moved north and onto the recently opened ranges on the Plains. By the end of the century, Americans looked beyond the boundaries of the continental United States to exploit the trade opportunities in Hawai'i and Alaska.

☞ As you read, identify the commodities and markets that emerged in the West. How were they tied to the industrialization of the eastern United States?

15-4a Commercial Agriculture

Once the nation realized the limitations, if not the failures, of Reconstruction, many Americans looked west for the potential to rebuild their

{ Farmers use emerging technologies to expand large-scale agriculture.

lives with more promising opportunities. Union soldiers who took pay in land scrip were allowed to homestead under fewer restrictions than those that applied to other homesteaders. After 1866, southern farmers and former Confederate soldiers were allowed to take homesteads, and many left war-torn southern landscapes and the unstable labor conditions.

Former slaves with no land and few resources were also eager to leave the South, especially because Ku Klux

Klan violence threatened their lives and the return of white supremacy closed economic opportunity. Under the leadership of men such as Benjamin "Pap" Singleton, thousands of African Americans—by 1881 about fifty thousand—moved west, primarily to Kansas, to become farmers. Called **exodusters**, they packed what little they had and walked to the Mississippi River, where they caught steamboats going upriver toward Kansas. There they built new communities, mostly separated from white settlers. All-black towns such as Nicodemus, Kansas, had their own schools, markets, and churches. Although such communities never provided a huge haven for former slaves, the West and independent farming did offer an alternative to sharecropping. For people of varied backgrounds, the West held promise and hope.

Immigrants from around the world made their way to the Midwest to farm and create homes for their families. Railroads set up emigration offices in Scandinavian and German cities to entice successful farmers, who they believed would be potential clients. These immigrants, along with Bohemians, populated the upper Midwest as they fled economic downturns, landlessness, and political instability in their home countries. They built **sod homes** since there was no hard wood left on the Great Plains. Families tolerated these dark dwellings, which rarely had windows, but which kept them protected from both the harsh winters and summers.

With railroads, farmer's business methods became entwined in the global economy and relied on corporations to transport and market their goods. Corn and wheat could be stored, graded, and shipped from **grain elevators**. Grain was loaded and unloaded by steam power onto railroad cars and steamships. The grading system allowed for a futures market in agricultural products to develop into a commodities exchange centered in Chicago. Innovations in irrigation, windmill technology, and drought-resistant seeds transformed U.S. agriculture from primarily a local affair of trade and consumption and trade to a burgeoning national and international market.

Perhaps even more transformative than railroads and grain elevators was the mechanical **combine** that not only cut wheat but also raked it and bound it into bales. Benjamin Holt made improvements on Cyrus McCormick's earlier reaper, and both men launched the machines into mass production in the 1870s. With a combine, the time it took to harvest an acre of wheat dropped from sixty-one hours in the 1840s to just under three hours by 1890. When Holt and McCormick saturated the U.S. market, including New England and the South—which were the last places to adopt the combine—their companies began promoting combine sales to overseas markets such as China, Africa, and the Caribbean.

Despite geography, experience, and John Wesley Powell's dire warning about western aridity, farmers put as many fields into wheat and other grains as possible to meet expanding market demands. They ignored the twenty-year drought cycle on the Great Plains and instead followed the old adage that "rain follows the plow." Moreover, boosters aided by railroads, grain elevators, and the combine, encouraged farmers to invest in mechanized equipment even if it meant going into debt in order to survive in the competitive market economy.

15-4b Expanding the Cattle Range

The development of ranching in the trans-Mississippi West also depended on the railroad, expanding markets, and technological innovations. Patented in 1867, barbed wire allowed ranchers to fence large tracts of land. Prior to the late nineteenth century, cattlemen and families let their animals run freely across the open range. People branded their animals to signify which ones belonged to them. Each year, roundups sorted cattle by owner after which they were taken to market. Barbed wire also allowed farmers to enclose their own agricultural lands and protect them from animals that might destroy the crops. This relatively inexpensive fencing solved many problems and helped grow the market, but it also exacerbated conflicts between competing ranchers who quickly, and often illegally, tried to enclose land. These **range wars** led to violence, property destruction, and sometimes death, as in the case of the 1892 Johnson County War in Wyoming. The violence was so intense that President William Henry Harrison called in the Ninth Regiment of Buffalo Soldiers to keep the peace, and it remained as an occupying force for a year.

Prior to the railroad, cattle and pigs—key sources of protein—were driven "on the hoof" short distances to the local butcher. Chances were that the cow or pig that a town dweller saw alive by the side of the road was the "dressed" meat he or she would buy from the local butcher next week. People were intimately acquainted with the food they ate. With the advent of railroads, however, cattle that had been grazing on the open range were rounded up, branded, and then driven hundreds of miles to "cow towns" such as Dodge City, Kansas, or Fort Worth, Texas. These towns were known for their stockyards where animals were rested, fed, and watered before they were loaded and shipped by railroad to places such as Chicago. There, the live animals were slaughtered and butchered for mass consumption.

> Technologies and global capital expand ranching and exterminate the bison.

exodusters Groups of African Americans who migrated from the U.S. South to the Midwest looking to start farms.

sod homes Solid and warm, but damp, houses built by stacking squares cut from prairie grass, which had a deep root structure.

grain elevators Technological innovation that allowed grain to be deposited into a silo without bagging and where it was graded, mixed, and sold in large lots.

combine Machine that combined reaping and binding wheat into one machine, saving time in the harvesting process.

range wars Confrontation between ranchers over the use of private property and government lands to graze cattle.

History without Borders

Wheat

Map labels:

Transatlantic Cable: 1866

NORTH AMERICA

UNITED STATES

New York
Portland
Philadelphia

San Francisco

see inset

Transcontinental Railroad: 1869

ATLANTIC OCEAN

BRITAIN
Liverpool

EUROPE
Marseille
Livorno
Danzig
Odessa

RUSSIA
Rostov-on-Don

ASIA

PACIFIC OCEAN

Suez Canal: 1869

AFRICA

Karachi
INDIA (Br.)

PACIFIC OCEAN

SOUTH AMERICA

CHILE
Valparaiso
ARGENTINA
Buenos Aires

ATLANTIC OCEAN

from Australia

AUSTRALIA (Br.)
Adelaide

to Europe

Legend:
- Major wheat growing area
- Wheat shipping route
- International boundaries, 1880

THE MIDWEST
CANADA
Duluth
DAKOTA TERR.
UNITED STATES
MN
WI
IA
Chicago
Union Pacific R.R.
NE
IL
KS
MO
INDIAN TERR.
AR

Cultivation and Distribution of Wheat around the World Grains such as wheat developed into commodities that pulled the world closer together through trade and migration. The regions indicated on the map indicate the "bread baskets" that provided food to large portions of the globe's population. The availability of commercially grown and traded grains helped bolster the world's population. Immigrants brought seed varietals to their new homes, which helped develop new areas such as the Bonanza wheat farms in the upper Midwest of the United States.

Wheat, like all food commodities, weaves the globe together through trade, immigration, and technology transfer. Wheat production began around 8000 BCE in an area of the Middle East called the *Fertile Crescent*. It spread north to Europe and west to China and was introduced into North America during the Columbian Exchange. Cultivation of the grain began in the middle colonies of British North America. As settlers pushed west across the Appalachian Mountains, they took their cultivation techniques with them. Most of the grain they grew was for the local market, but after the development of road and canal systems during the early nineteenth century, for various other parts of the nation.

Technological innovations transformed the market for wheat. The invention of the reaper and later the combine, which "combined" cutting the wheat and removing its kernels, dramatically reduced the number of person hours needed to grow and harvest a bushel of the grain. Its market expanded with the invention of grain elevators, which allowed wheat to flow freely rather than be bagged and to be graded by quality. Finally, the expansion of rail and steamship networks allowed the grain to travel all over the nation and to be put on boats to Europe, Russia, and China, which became the largest customers for it. When the Chicago Board of Trade allowed contracts of "futures" to be bought and sold in 1864, a full-fledged commodity trading in wheat opened to national and global markets. By 1900, the United States produced 25 percent of the world's wheat and was being called the global "bread basket."

Hulton Archive/Getty Images

McCormick Machines Are the Best in the World, 1901 Advertisements like this one appeared in magazines all over the world and in dozens of languages. Note how it uses the image of an attractive woman to draw the reader's attention and then shows the practical uses in the smaller images. Other companies such as Kellogg's and Karo Syrup also used foreign language advertisements to increase their market share and to entice foreigners to purchase American foodstsuffs such as cereal and corn syrup. ▲

Detroit Publishing Co., publisher

Grain Elevator in Buffalo, New York, 1900 This grain elevator was located in a central location on the border between the United States and Canada, where steamships could easily load and unload grains for shipment to regional and global markets. Technological innovations, such as the grain elevator, combine, and railroad, in conjunction with marketing and the rise of business practice efficiencies, made the United States the largest exporter of grain at the turn of the century. ▲

bonanza farms Large acreage farm that used labor, mechanization, and hybrid seeds to produce huge yields for a global market.

Because wheat was farmed across the world, U.S. wheat exports had global effects. In Italy, cheap U.S. wheat undersold local farmers, prompting unemployed peasants to migrate to the Americas. Immigrant farmers from northern Europe brought different growing methods and seeds to the United States. Some were hybrids that had been cross-bred to thrive in colder climates, which was perfect for the upper Midwest. These immigrants created the **bonanza farms** (large acreage farms that used labor and mechanization to produce huge yields) in the Red River Valley. They fueled the production and export of wheat from the end of the nineteenth century through World War I. Flour producers, such as General Mills, distributed cookbooks in different languages, particularly Chinese, to stimulate demand for wheat, flour, and other wheat-based products in foreign countries.

New technologies associated with the Green Revolution in the late twentieth century ensured that global wheat production kept pace with that of rice and corn, although corn surpassed it around the beginning of the twenty-first century. Wheat has the highest protein content of any vegetable-based grain, still making it one of the most demanded food products around the world.

Critical Thinking Questions

▶ What made the North American landscape viable for wheat growing and exportation?

▶ What social, economic, and political forces helped develop the wheat market?

HISTORY WITHOUT BORDERS **451**

Goodnight-Loving Trail Path used by cattle drives from Texas to move the animals to markets in the upper Midwest where they could be placed in railroad cars.

vaqueros Herdsman or cowboy in North America and term from which *buckaroo* is derived.

At its peak production, the Union Stockyard could process twenty-one thousand cattle, seventy-five thousand pigs, twenty-two thousand sheep, and two hundred horses daily. With the advent of refrigerated cars (filled with ice cut from the Great Lakes), the animal flesh could be transported from Chicago to major cities as dressed meat, which urban consumers could purchase at the local butcher or corner store. By the end of the nineteenth century, most city dwellers had no idea where their meat originated. The railroads and the production of animal flesh had severed peoples' connection to food and nature.

Cowboys who worked the range and drove the cattle to the railroads came from a variety of ethnic backgrounds. Many had some sense that their work was tied to these larger markets. Most cowboys worked for large organizations run by men such as Charles Goodnight, who, with Oliver Loving, first opened the cattle market by driving thousands of cattle from Texas north to New Mexico and west to California, establishing the **Goodnight-Loving Trail** in the 1860s (see Map 15.3). Cowboys were a diverse group of workers who reflected the immigrant culture of the West. Many were **vaqueros** from Mexico where the cowboy culture originated, Indians who had left the reservations, and African Americans such as Nat Love.

Foreign businessmen from Scotland, England, and the Netherlands owned many of the large cattle ranching outfits. They found owning a cattle operation in the U.S. West to be a romantic adventure (see Figure 15.2). No doubt they wanted to make money, but few of these enterprises were very profitable. Ranching was a volatile business with high turnover in personnel (cowhands) and overwhelming obstacles (rain, drought, diseases) in getting animals from the range into the stockyards.

Map 15.3 Mining and Ranching Enterprises in the West, 1860–1890 In the late nineteenth century, the U.S. West developed economically at a phenomenal pace. All of these enterprises—whether ranching and mining as depicted here or farming, cutting timber, or other extractive endeavors—depended on the railroads. By the late nineteenth century, these enterprises also depended on money from the East Coast or foreign banks and investors. This infrastructure and investment capital connected the West intimately to the global economy. ▼

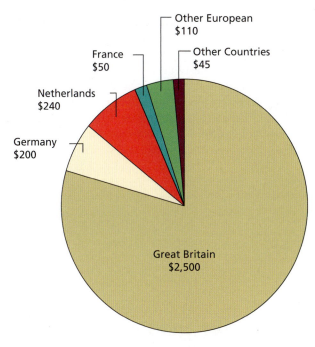

Other European $110

France $50

Other Countries $45

Netherlands $240

Germany $200

Great Britain $2,500

Figure 15.2 Sources of Foreign Investment in the United States in 1899 (Millions) This chart provides some sense of the extent to which the United States and the West, in particular, depended on investment from foreign capital markets. These investors were lured by the scope of development and put their money into building railroads, buying land, running cattle ranches, and extracting mineral wealth from the United States. ▲ *Source: Davis, Lance E., and Robert J. Cull. International Capital Markets and American Economic Growth, 1820–1914. Cambridge, UK: Cambridge University Press, 1994.*

15-4c Mineral Resources and Mines

Like farming and ranching, mining depended on the developing markets created by the railroad. All three activities changed the western landscape, and all were tied to the growth of the East Coast in the post-Civil War era. As factories produced more goods and more people moved to cities, the demand increased for the products of ranching, agriculture, and mineral resources.

{ Outside investment and immigrants lead to the intense extraction of mineral resources.

Whereas earlier mineral booms in the West had focused on precious metals such as gold and silver, by the late nineteenth century, the emphasis was on extracting minerals essential to industrialization. Coal played a vital role in the nation's development as it fueled homes and industry. Copper, primarily found in the southern half of Arizona and northern Mexico, was in high demand for wiring used in telegraphs and later telephones. Both copper and coal mining reshaped labor relations as well as people's relationship to the environment.

Industrial mining demanded immense amounts of capital, which was supplied by eastern bankers and industrialists, such as John D. Rockefeller, who was interested in diversifying his oil empire. He invested in the iron rich properties of the Mesabi Range in Minnesota and in the coalfields of Colorado. Both ventures involved teaming with other industrialists—including Andrew Carnegie to develop the iron fields and Jay Gould to develop the coal fields—to control not only the resources but also the railroad lines that took them to market. Massive capital investment from these eastern investors incorporated the West into the national and global economy.

Coal Miners Underground, circa 1910 Mining camps were some of the most multicultural and diverse communities in the nation. Miners from all over the world came to these camps to find work. Their work was dangerous and difficult, and a miner was in constant jeopardy of injury or death. As a result, union organization moved sporadically across these western enclaves as men and their families sought to create a better life and gain a fair wage and safe workplace from their employers. ▶

Detroit Publishing Co., publisher/Library of Congress

Utah State Historical Society

Global Americans **Leonidas Skliris**, a native of Sparta, Greece, emigrated and in 1897 set up a labor agency in the heart of "Greektown" in Salt Lake City, Utah, near the rail yards. He became successful and powerful, with offices in many towns where new immigrants flocked to find work. Known as the "Czar of the Greeks," he sent agents to Greece to recruit even more workers and ran a series of advertisements there and other places abroad. Skliris used his old-world skills as a *padrone* to recruit laborers. He charged each man for whom he found work $20 and a $1 to $2 monthly fee for as long as the laborer worked at that job. Skliris was accused of taking kickbacks from the companies to which he supplied laborers, especially strikebreakers, to the largest western companies, such as Carbon Coal Mines and the Denver and Western Rio Grande Railroads. He was adept at playing ethnicities against each other in labor disputes. By 1912, however, even his own countrymen tired of his manipulative ways, and in the midst of a nasty labor dispute between the United Mine Workers of America and the copper miners, the workers, including his countrymen, threw out Skliris as their leader. He left Utah quickly and eventually moved to Mexico where he purchased part ownership in a mine.

Immigrants and migrants formed the majority of the work force used in mining across the West. Until the 1890s, most of the miners were Irish, Italian, English, Welsh, and Mexican. They made their way into the West from other mining fields in North America, such as those in Kentucky, the upper peninsula of Michigan, and northern Mexico. By the turn of the century, workers from southern Europe, Japan, and China joined this initial group of immigrants. Mining camps across the West were multicultural work areas where laborers learned to work with one another on the job and in their personal associations. Management opposed the development of unions or camaraderie among workers because a divided labor pool kept wages as low as possible. Consequently, the U.S. West experienced some of the worst industry violence and the emergence of some of the most radical unions from the Knights of Labor to the Industrial Workers of the World (the IWW, or Wobblies.)

Even with the advent of rail transportation, much the West was remote from urban centers, and mining camps were isolated. Women who followed their husbands as they sought mining work often found substandard housing, few groceries, and a dangerous landscape on which to raise their children. Mining was not steady work, and for long periods, mines could lie idle and men were laid off. Most women adapted to the harsh economic and physical environment by growing vegetables, raising small animals, such as goats and chickens, and keeping a vigilant eye on their children who played on mining slag heaps or walked along the railroad tracks.

As a result of these harsh conditions, recruiting workers was difficult and retaining them more difficult. One solution that management employed to address this problem was to hire immigrant labor agents who recruited workers in their home country. Known as *patrons, padrones,* or *coyotes,* depending on the ethnic group, these agents shared the common purpose of persuading their countrymen to leave their homes, take a boat or train to the United States, and work for a mining company.

15-4d Alaska and Hawai'i: The West of the Future

As the nineteenth century progressed, U.S. business interests looked farther west to Alaska and across the Pacific for new opportunities. In 1867, as part of his vision of an expansive U.S. commercial empire across the Pacific, Secretary of State William Seward purchased Alaska from the Russian empire, which opened the region for U.S. exploration. In 1896, gold was discovered in the Klondike region of Canada's Yukon Territory and then, in 1899, in Nome, Alaska. These gold rushes brought more than one hundred thousand immigrants from around the world who established new comunities and put millions of dollars into the North American economy. The Nome rush alone produced more than one hundred twelve metric tons of gold ore, approximately one-third of the amount mined during the California Gold Rush.

> U.S. business looks even farther west to new markets.

After the Civil War, Hawai'i gained geostrategic importance as another crucial part of U.S. designs for commercial empire in the Pacific. In 1875, the United States and the Hawaiian Kingdom signed a trade agreement that allowed Hawaiian sugar to enter the U.S. market duty free and barred Hawai'i from extending territorial or economic concessions to any other nation. As a result, the sugar industry in the islands grew rapidly. Americans who owned the majority of the sugar plantations in Hawai'i built irrigation projects and imported Chinese and Japanese laborers. Production of Hawai'ian sugar increased tenfold while native islanders—their population severely depleted by epidemics—lost much of their political and economic autonomy. In addition to commanding Hawaii's economy, Americans also controlled its politics after 1887, when the Hawai'ian monarch was forced to agree to a new constitution that took away much of his authority. The naval station that the United States acquired at Pearl Harbor in 1875 provided coal to U.S. transpacific steamers and military vessels patrolling the Pacific to ensure the free flow of travel and trade.

15-5
West in the American Imagination

This painting, *Yosemite Valley*, was completed by Albert Bierstadt in 1866.

What mood is Bierstadt trying to invoke in his audience? Why did he paint in such a romantic style? What would someone who had never been to the West think about the place? ▶

Buyenlarge/Getty Images

In the 1890s, three events marked the incorporation of the American West into the nation. First, after the massacre at Wounded Knee, violent Indian resistance appeared to be coming to an end. Second, the Buffalo Bill Show, which set up just outside the gates at the Chicago World's Fair in 1893, presented both the West and Indians as entertainment for those who might never see the region in person. Finally, in Chicago that same year, a young historian named Frederick Jackson Turner pondered the significance of the closing of the western frontier, articulating ideas that would have a profound influence on U.S. thought for generations afterward. The confluence of these three factors allowed Americans to imagine the West—Indians on the land and white settlers moving westward—as part of the country's past and to begin to create idealized notions about what the West had been.

☞ As you read, consider why boosters, artists, and writers created mythical images about the U.S. West. What purposes did such images serve?

15-5a Literature and Art

The West had always held an important place in American literature and popular culture. Beginning with James Fenimore Cooper's leatherstocking tales in the early nineteenth century, which told of a "West" in upstate New York that existed just over the edge of eastern settlement, Americans became fascinated with stories of the U.S. frontier. In the late nineteenth century, writers such as Mark Twain (Samuel Clemens) chronicled the development of the West.

> American and European novelists and popular artists create images of the western past.

Twain, who grew up along the banks of the Mississippi River, understood the impulses that pushed people west. In the first paragraph of *Huckleberry Finn*, Twain described his young hero's inability to settle down and be "sivilized" by the Widow Douglas. Instead Huck "lit out" for the country where he could be "free and satisfied." Twain based some of his work on his travels west to California and then back to New York across the Isthmus of Panama, and he told easterners about the western world that was opening up to them. His novels portrayed a frontier society filled with characters capable of pushing the boundaries of language, etiquette, and racial norms set by eastern society.

Western literature and travel journal articles by popular authors such as Mary Halleck Foote and Bret Harte appeared in popular magazines including *National Geographic, Colliers, Harper's, and Scribner's*. These writers introduced their readers to the sights, landscapes, and peoples of the West. Some of these were truthful accounts, but most embellished on real life there.

Another popular way of portraying the U.S. West was through grand paintings that found large public audiences in the East and Europe. The most popular images were painted by the **Rocky Mountain School** painters, German-born Albert Bierstadt and Thomas Moran. They painted dramatic, almost unreal, mountain vistas and breathtaking landscapes. Bierstadt first went west with the Frederick West Lander Expedition, which was engineering an emigrant trail from Nebraska to Oregon in 1859. Bierstadt convinced Lander to provide an escort for him as he explored and painted. Bierstadt took the techniques and styles from his earlier work within the Hudson River School and began

Rocky Mountain School
Group of painters who were known for their majestic landscapes of U.S. western scenery.

applying them to the spectacular western landscapes of the Rocky Mountains. The paintings were huge, literally and figuratively. Bierstadt painted on canvasses that took up an entire wall of a large room. He always chose sweeping vistas with dramatic light as his subject.

Thomas Moran also gained his first exposure to the West and to what became Yellowstone National Park through a government-sponsored geological expedition led by Ferdinand V. Hayden. Moran first saw the Yellowstone region (northwestern Wyoming bordering Idaho and Montana) in 1870 and took this landscape as the subject of many of his dramatic paintings. He made field sketches and quick watercolors of the landscape while he was surveying the region and then returned to his studio to create the vast canvasses. Neither Bierstadt nor Moran made his home in the West but both were taken with its inspirational landscapes. Their work came to epitomize Americans' image of the West to such an extent that Congress appropriated tens of thousands of dollars to purchase some of their largest works.

15-5b Tourism to the West

Literature, travelogues, magazine articles, and paintings piqued the curiosity of Americans about the landscapes and peoples of the West. However, the greatest purveyors of the U.S. West as a tourist destination were the railroad companies, which were anxious to fill their trains with tourists and potential settlers to the region. Railroads advertised the dry and warm climates of the U.S. Southwest for those suffering from asthma, consumption, and gout in the damp eastern climate. The companies packaged and advertised the natural and spectacular beauty of places such as Yellowstone, the Grand Canyon, and Yosemite as destinations for wealthy Americans who could afford to vacation. Railroad advertisers made Native Americans into spectacles to be gazed on by tourists who sought to have an authentic experience by visiting reservations. Marketers relied on government surveyors such as Hayden and King to boost the image of the West as a place to be preserved, revered, and visited for the sheer emotional uplift of experiencing its landscape.

Yellowstone, which was made the first national park in 1872, fascinated Americans as they learned about the boiling cauldrons of sulfurous water and "Old Faithful" geyser, which blew a twenty-two-foot plume of water out every ninety-one minutes. Bierstadt's paintings of Yosemite in California made the park even more popular with his dramatic interpretations of the valley floor and the mountain peaks. The first tourists visited there in 1855, and by 1864, the region had so much commercial traffic that President Lincoln signed an act allowing for the Yosemite Valley and the nearby Mariposa Grove of giant sequoia trees to "be held for public use, resort, and recreation . . . inalienable for all time" (see Table 15.2). This act inspired other states to seek federal protection for their special lands. In 1890,

> Boosters lure tourists to the West to see the natural beauty.

Table 15.2 National Reserves and Parks Created, 1832–1916

The Organic Act, which set aside lands for national parks and created the United States Park Service was signed in August of 1916. But this was not the first time that the federal government had set aside land for preservation. Prior to that legislation, these thirteen sites were protected by Congress or the president to make sure that the areas were not developed for commercial use but instead could be enjoyed by visitors.

Date Protection Enacted	Site of Reserve or Park	State
April 1832	Hot Springs	Arkansas
March 1872	Yellowstone	Wyoming, Montana, Idaho
September 1890	Sequoia	California
October 1890	Yosemite	California
March 1899	Mount Rainier	Washington
May 1902	Crater Lake	Oregon
January 1903	Wind Cave	South Dakota
June 1906	Mesa Verde	Colorado
May 1910	Glacier	Montana
January 1915	Rocky Mountain	Colorado
August 1916	Haleakalā	Hawai'i Territory
August 1916	Lassen Volcanic	California
August 1916	Denali	Alaska Territory

Congress authorized the second national park, Yosemite, which epitomized to Americans the need to preserve wilderness areas to be enjoyed in their natural beauty.

15-5c Popular Images of the West

Although railroad literature, travelogues, paintings, and advertising reached a large audience, they were geared toward the middle class, encouraging them to visit the West. Other forms of entertainment were targeted more specifically at the mass of Americans who would never be able to afford to travel west. The drama of the West was brought to them by dime novels and popular traveling shows. Inspired by such tales and traveling theatrics, European authors such as Germany's Karl May wrote about a West they had never seen and told extremely popular tales of adventure.

> Western images appeal to the masses as well as the elite and middle class.

Dime novels became increasingly popular in the United States and in England, where they were called *penny dreadfuls*. The rise in literacy opened a new mass market of readers. Dime novels were sold at newsstands as part of the popular "rag" literature movement that targeted young working-class men and women who toiled in urban factories. Although the genre covered a wide array of subjects from detective fiction to tales of urban outlaws and working girls, some of the most popular series were westerns. Series about Nat Love (the black cowboy also known as Deadwood Dick), Jesse James (the infamous outlaw), and Buffalo Bill Cody (a scout for the U.S. military) were some of the most popular, aimed at young boys who lived in urban areas and could only dream of going west, being a cowboy, and fighting Indians.

Another popular venue portraying the West was **Buffalo Bill's Wild West Show**. Like popular shows presented by the showman and entrepreneur P.T. Barnum, Bill Cody drew millions into the world he created. In his two-hour show, which included hundreds of animals; sharpshooters, such as the ever-popular Annie Oakley; and Indians, such as Sitting Bull, Cody portrayed the winning of the West by white Americans over subdued Indians. Popular skits included the family homestead attacked and burned down by marauding Indians with Cody and the cavalry saving them from certain disaster, a staged buffalo hunt with real animals and Indians in pursuit, and, perhaps the most popular scene, a reenactment of the Battle of Little Big Horn.

Cody was able to portray the Indians as victorious because by the late nineteenth century, they appeared to be on an irreversible retreat in the face of U.S. expansion. Cody's show sought to re-create a fantastic West that had at least some basis in history and reality. Hundreds of Native Americans, called *show Indians*, toured with the Wild West Show. It played to huge audiences in the United States and across Europe. It was so popular that in 1887, Queen Victoria, who rarely was seen in public while mourning her husband, Prince Albert, came to a special showing that Cody arranged for her. Delighted by the dramatic display of western scenes, she encouraged her subjects to attend.

15-5d **End of the Frontier**

Frederick Jackson Turner began his presentation at the Chicago World's Fair in 1893 with the statement that,

> Myth making about the West depends on the fiction that the frontier had closed.

according to the 1890 census, "Up to and including 1880 the country had a frontier of settlement, but at present the unsettled area has been so broken by isolated bodies of settlement that there can hardly be said to be a frontier line." With that statement, Turner's provocative analysis of the American character declared the frontier closed. American identity had been so influenced by the movement west, he wondered how it would continue to develop when migrants would no longer be able to remake themselves and create new opportunities in the wide-open frontier. In so doing, he created a mythologized West that charted the progressive states of development that the U.S. frontier underwent. Starting with the era of "savagery" when Indians dominated the American continent, progressing through fur trading, ranching, farming, and eventually mercantile society, Turner connected frontier history to the stages of human history since prehistoric times. At the same time, he told a story of U.S. national development that was the direct product of Manifest Destiny and portrayed vividly in Gast's painting, *American Progress*.

The **frontier**, of course, never closed, and Indians did not disappear from the western landscape. During the remainder of the nineteenth century and well into the twentieth century, Americans and immigrants from around the world continued to press into the West and to create new homes in what was increasingly becoming one of the most multiethnic and diverse regions in the world. Indians continued to live and work in the country although within constricted political, economic, social, and educational boundaries established by the Dawes Act and the reservation system. Together, old settlers and new immigrants had created a new West based on the region's ties to eastern and global markets.

Buffalo Bill's Wild West Show Traveling variety show portraying the West of the United States that entertained thousands across the country and Europe.

frontier Region beyond Anglo-European settlements and control.

Summary

The end of the Civil War allowed Americans to look westward again. They and thousands of immigrants from around the world moved into the West to expand farming, ranching, and mining. Completion of the first transcontinental railroad, which was followed by other cross-continent lines, made possible the development of national and global markets. The railroad also drew a diverse group of laborers who found ample opportunity despite difficult working conditions.

Federal officials asserted power over western lands and the people who settled there. They incorporated them into the nation through land surveys, property distribution, and, ultimately, statehood, although residents in some regions were denied full rights as citizens for unusually long periods. Some who found their status as citizens questioned used the international borders of Canada and Mexico to create their own local communities or to flee the U.S. military. White women, however, found the West a more hospitable place than the rest of the nation for their political ambitions of equality and suffrage.

Incorporation also highlighted the legacy of the U. S. relationship with Native Americans who lived on these western lands. Violence was often the most common solution, and these groups were pushed onto reservations and forced to make accommodations to U.S. laws and customs. Despite strong resistance, by the end of the nineteenth century, Indians seemingly had been incorporated through the Dawes Act. In response to these changes, Americans began to indulge in a nostalgic fondness for the western past. They painted ethereal images, wrote novels, and created tourist destinations that recalled a distant romantic history. Most of these images were misleading or emphasized an idealized past, reassuring settlers about the West's development and progress, and providing escapism for East Coast or European city dwellers.

<Thinking Back, *Looking Forward*>

As you review this chapter, think about the ways that the U.S. West was transformed by violence, migration, and capital investment. How does this transformation compare to the changes in the West during the antebellum period? What role did immigrants and foreign capital play in the development of the West? As you read the next chapter, think about how changes in the West were driven by the industrialization of the eastern United States. To make your study concrete, review the timeline and reflect on the entries there. Think about their causes, consequences, and connections. How do they fit with global trends?

Additional Resources

Books

Cronon, William. *Nature's Metropolis: Chicago and the Great West, 1848–1893.* **New York: WW Norton, 1991.** ▶ Sweeping study of the U.S. West's economic ties to Chicago and points farther east.

Isenberg, Andrew C. *The Destruction of the Bison: An Environmental History, 1750–1920.* **New York: Cambridge Press, 2001.** ▶ Argues that white and Indian participants in the growing hide market caused the near extinction of the bison.

Lukas, J. Anthony. *Big Trouble.* **New York: Simon & Schuster, 1997.** ▶ Readable narrative of industrial violence at the turn of the century, focusing on the IWW.

Pasco, Peggy. *What Comes Naturally: Miscegenation Law and the Making of Race in America.* **New York: Oxford Press, 2009.** ▶ Comprehensive look at how laws regulating sexuality and race shaped the way Americans dealt with racism and segregation.

Sandweiss, Martha A. *Passing Strange: A Gilded Age Tale of Love and Deception Across the Color Line.* **New York: Penguin Press, 2009.** ▶ Gripping narrative about Clarence King, head of the USGS, and the secret life he led passing as a black man.

St. John, Rachel. *Line in the Sand: A History of the Western U.S. Mexico Border.* **Princeton, NJ: Princeton Press, 2012.** ▶ Comprehensive history of how the border was formed, maintained, and crossed between 1848 and 1940.

Scharff, Virginia. *Twenty Thousand Roads: Women, Movement and the West.* **Berkeley: University of California Press, 2002.** ▶ Biographies of six women illuminate the influence of women in the development of the West.

Warren, Louis. *The Rising of God's Red Son: The Making of an American Religion and the Road From Wounded Knee.* **2017.** ▶ Discussion that places the Ghost Dance movement within the context of America's religious traditions and shows its international implications.

West, Elliott. *Contested Plains: Indians, Goldseekers, and the Rush to Colorado.* Lawrence: University of Kansas Press, 1998. ▶ Gripping narrative about the multiethnic world of the Great Plains that involved competing groups struggling to control their futures.

White, Richard. *Railroaded: The Transcontinentals and the Making of Modern America.* New York: WW Norton, 2011. ▶ Comprehensive economic and political history of how railroads were financed and built during the Gilded Age.

Go to the MindTap® for **Global Americans** to access the full version of select books from this Additional Resources section.

Websites

Keeping History: Plains Indian Ledger Drawings. (http://americanhistory.si.edu/documentsgallery/exhibitions/ledger_drawing_2.html). ▶ Based on a Smithsonian exhibit, a good introduction to the system of recording Plains life.

National Park Service. (www.nps.org). ▶ Excellent resource from which to gather accurate and concise histories of particular places protected by the National Park Service.

Shadows at Dawn. (http://brown.edu/Research/Aravaipa/). ▶ Primary and secondary sources that help students understand the multiple perspectives of the Camp Grant Massacre in Arizona.

Women of the West Museum. (www.theautry.org). ▶ Primary and secondary sources regarding the experiences of women, particularly an important exhibit on suffrage.

Continue exploring online through MindTap®**, where you can:**

- **Assess your knowledge with the Chapter Test**
- **Watch historical videos related to the chapter**
- **Further your understanding with interactive maps and timelines**

Incorporation of the West

1862	1863–1864	1865–1867	1868–1870	1871–1873
May Lincoln signs the Homestead Act.	**June 1864** Lincoln signs law protecting Yosemite.	**April 1865** Barbed wire is patented.	**April 1868** Fort Laramie Treaty is signed.	**January 1872** Gast paints *American Progress.*
July Lincoln signs the Pacific Railroad Act.	**September 1864** Black Kettle signs Treaty of Fort Lyon.	**June 1866** Goodnight-Loving Trail is established.		
Lincoln signs the First Morrill Act.	**October 1864** General Sherman's march to the sea.	**June 1866** Congress passes the Southern Homestead Act.	**November 1868** Battle of Washita takes place in Oklahoma.	**May 1872** Congress passes the General Mining Act.
	November 1864 Indians are killed in the Sand Creek Massacre.		**May 1869** Transcontinental railroad is completed.	**June 1872** The combine is patented.
		December 1866 U.S. cavalrymen are killed in the Fetterman Massacre.	John Wesley Powell explores the Grand Canyon.	**March 1873** Congress passes the Timber Culture Act.
		March 1867 United States purchases Alaska from Russia.	**November 1869** Suez Canal is completed.	

1874–1879

May 1875

United States and Hawai'i sign the Reciprocity Trade Treaty.

July 1876

Custer and his men are killed at the Battle of Little Big Horn.

by the Sioux and their allies.

October 1877

Chief Joseph surrenders.

January 1879

U.S. Supreme Court issues ruling in *Reynolds v. United States*.

1880–1885

July 1881

Exoduster migration to Kansas reaches its peak.

November 1883

Railroads begin adopting standard time.

August 1884

Mexico completes its transcontinental railroad.

February 1885

Huckleberry Finn is published in the United States.

1886–1889

September 1886

Geronimo surrenders to the U.S. army.

February 1887

Congress passes the Edmunds-Tucker Act.

Congress passes the Dawes Act.

July 1887

Hawaiian king is forced to cede powers to the United States.

January 1889

Wovoka has vision and encourages the Ghost Dance.

1890

January 1890

Census Bureau data suggests the frontier closed.

August 1890

Congress Passes the Second Morrill Act.

September 1890

The Mormon Church issues The Manifesto.

December 1890

Massacre at Wounded Knee leaves more than two hundred and fifty dead.

1891–1910

April 1892

Johnson County war erupts in Wyoming.

December 1893

Turner presents "The Significance of the Frontier" at the Chicago World's Fair.

August 1896

Gold is discovered in the Klondike.

September 1898

Gold is discovered in Nome in Alaska.

November 1910

Mexican revolution begins.

Go to MindTap® to engage with an interactive version of the timeline. Analyze events and themes with clickable content, view related videos, and respond to critical thinking questions.

16 The Making of Industrial America

1877–1917

Mary Harris Jones immigrated to Toronto as a child to escape famines in her birthplace of County Cork, Ireland. Her life as a wife and mother took her to Tennessee. Later, she returned to Chicago and helped found the growing labor movement there.

Barely thirty years old, Mary Harris Jones sat alone in her darkened home wondering how her life had become so undone. Just a week earlier, she had been the wife of George Jones, an iron molder, and the mother of four small children. Now all five were dead from the yellow fever epidemic that swept through Memphis in 1867.

Jones had been a migrant all her life. She was born in County Cork, Ireland, in 1837 and immigrated as a child, first to Canada and then to Michigan and Chicago before settling with her husband in Memphis. She had worked as a teacher in Michigan and a seamstress in Chicago. And, although she took in sewing work while in Memphis, she focused on being a mother and wife in a working-class family.

National Photo Company Collection (Library of Congress)

Mother Jones Speaking to President Coolidge, 1924 ▲

With nothing left for her in Memphis, Jones returned to Chicago, where she settled in a small apartment and began work as a dressmaker for wealthy Lake Shore Drive clients. Her business thrived, but in 1871 she lost everything in the great fire that burned much of Chicago to the ground. With no money, no family, and very little hope, she embraced the growing labor movement in Chicago and joined the Knights of Labor, becoming an organizer. That choice provided the stepping stone that launched her career as one of the foremost labor leaders of the late nineteenth and early twentieth centuries.

The Knights' policy of organizing all workers regardless of gender, race, or occupation appealed to Jones. She quickly rose through the ranks and earned a reputation as a passionate speaker and compassionate advocate who was best when drawing women and children to labor's cause. Jones became increasingly radicalized with each strike. She rallied workers and their families at some of the most notorious strikes, including the Ludlow strike against the Colorado Fuel & Iron Company in 1914, which earned her a stay in federal prison. She became an outspoken advocate, who, as she aged, looked more like a dear grandmother than an anticapitalist hell-raiser. Yet her ability to incite workers earned her the moniker, "the most dangerous woman in America" from a U.S. attorney general who prosecuted her.

In 1905, Jones became one of the founding members of the Industrial Workers of the World (IWW) along with William D. ("Big Bill") Haywood and Eugene V. Debs. The IWW brought together a coalition of immigrants and workers who pushed for changes that affected all workers, not just skilled ones, and sought to reorder the relationship between the laboring and capitalist classes. The *Wobblies*, as they were called, built on their U.S. experiences and their interactions with union leaders, socialists, and Marxists from Europe and Russia.

"Mother" Jones had contradictory ideas about the place of women in society and in the world of work. She was known to use her grandmotherly persona to persuade men such as John D. Rockefeller Jr. and Theodore Roosevelt of the necessity to protect workers and families.

In what ways does the journey of Mary Harris Jones—from immigrant, wife, and mother to laborer and workers' advocate—illustrate the turbulence brought on by immigration, industrialization, and urbanization at the turn of the century?

Go to MindTap® to watch a video on Jones and learn how her story relates to the themes of this chapter.

She believed that men needed to earn a decent wage so that women could stay home and tend to their children. She reasoned that parental absenteeism was the single largest cause for juvenile delinquency, a problem that she thought dangerous to society and the fabric of the family. She also opposed women's suffrage, arguing that a woman did not need the franchise in order to "raise a little hell." Her campaign against child labor was meant to keep young girls out of the workplace and in the confines of their home with their families.

Jones was part of a massive immigration movement that uprooted families across the world. When she settled in the United States, she encountered immigrant workers from all over the globe and was influenced by the ideas of intellectual labor leaders from Europe. Given the tragedies she had experienced in early life, it is not surprising that Jones dedicated herself to advocating for the sanctity of the family, the right of men to earn a decent living, and the opportunity for children to have wholesome childhoods. Jones lived through turbulent times for families, women, and ethnic minorities, who felt the deep impact of the changes brought by immigration, industrialization, and urbanization at the turn of the century. In advocating for workers and their families, she faced global economic upheaval on the local level.

16-1
Age of Steel

The Bessemer process, as portrayed in this British painting, enabled molten pig iron to be turned into steel by blowing extremely hot air through it. The Bessemer Steel Converter made steel cheaper and stronger, leading to robust production that drove the global economic expansion of the late nineteenth century.

What does this image reveal about the labor conditions for factory workers? What were the dangers? ▶

SSPL/Getty Images

The end of the nineteenth century saw an unprecedented growth in technology and business innovation that transformed the way people worked and lived. Steel enabled the construction of high-rise buildings that became the hallmark of dense cities, which drew people into closer proximity with one another. Steamships became larger and faster as global trade expanded and immigrants poured into the United States, greatly increasing the pace of urbanization. Industrialists, such as Andrew Carnegie, John D. Rockefeller, and J.P. Morgan, capitalized on scientific breakthroughs to boost the consumption of their products and profits using new legal and business practices to consolidate their corporations and expand market share. This business expansion, however, was tempered by economic instability and a major economic downturn in 1893 that hurt not only the rich and powerful but also workers, immigrants, and farmers as the nation struggled to adjust to economic cycles of boom and bust.

☞ As you read, think about the specific ways in which technological innovation and business consolidation transformed the global economy. How did the economic cycles of boom and bust affect business owners, workers, and farmers?

16-1a International Advances in Technology and Manufacturing

{ Electricity and steel production drive new types of industrial development.

The marriage of theoretical science and its practical application in the late nineteenth century prompted what observers later described as the **Second Industrial Revolution**. Building on the major technological advances in British manufacturing made earlier in the nineteenth century, businesses capitalized on new technologies in industrial chemistry and the production of steel and electricity. These innovations combined with advances in railroad transportation after the Civil War created a synergy in which global markets in steel, grains, petroleum, and fertilizers flourished. This growth was most rapid in the United States, Great Britain, northwestern Europe, and Japan, but the effects were felt throughout the global economy (see Figure 16.1).

U.S. businessmen applied scientific research emerging in European universities to industrial markets. By the early twentieth century, more than one hundred fifty U.S. companies, such as U.S. Steel, DuPont, and Standard Oil operated research facilities that hired foreign scientists. These companies found practical uses for theoretical innovations in chemistry, engineering, and physics for consumer use. The companies also engaged in what is now called *patent trolling*, the practice of buying any new patents to lessen competition. The three most transformative technologies

during this period were electricity, Bessemer steel, and the automobile.

Of these innovations, electricity had the most dramatic initial impact in people's day-to-day lives by stimulating new types of inventions. In 1876, Thomas Alva Edison created the first U.S. commercial research lab in Menlo Park, New Jersey. Among the dozens of inventions that Edison produced over his lifetime, the first practical incandescent bulb transformed daily life. Although a number of inventors across Europe and the United States developed the bulb itself, Edison made it marketable by creating the first commercially successful electrical system in New York City in 1882. Streets, factories, and many homes were lit using electricity instead of gas. Edison declared, "We will make electricity so cheap that only the rich will burn candles."

By 1887, the United States had 121 generating plants that distributed electricity through Edison's direct current (DC). Meanwhile, George Westinghouse, another U.S. inventor, developed alternating current (AC), which was more practical because it allowed electricity to travel long distances at high voltage via transformers and then be transformed to low voltage for civic, commercial, and home use. After intense competition, AC current eventually became the voltage used in the United States. Able to run electrical machines around the clock, businesses then instituted both day and night shifts and extended the workday.

Communication also transformed rapidly at the end of the nineteenth century. In the 1840s, engineers in Russia, Germany, and the United States had developed the electric

Second Industrial Revolution Late nineteenth-century period of industrialization driven by technological innovations and advances in chemistry.

Figure 16.1 Highest Steel- and Wheat-Producing Countries, 1860–1900 (in metric tons)

Production of steel and wheat is a good indicator of a country's economic development and participation in the global market. Initially, steel production in the United States lagged behind that of both Great Britain and Germany but by 1900 almost matched the two combined. The United States was a leader in wheat production and exports throughout this period; by 1890, Japan and India, in addition to the countries shown here, had also begun producing wheat for their own consumption. ▼

Sources: Mitchell, B.R. *International Historical Statistics: Europe, 1750–2005*. New York: Palgrave Macmillan, 2007; *International Historical Statistics: The Americas, 1750–2005*. New York: Palgrave Macmillan, 2007; *International Historical Statistics: Africa, Asia, and Oceania, 1750–2005*. New York: Palgrave Macmillan, 2007.

Exposition Universelle or World's Fair, Paris, 1900 Panorama of the gardens of Trocadero and Champ-de-Mars. World's Fairs like this one and the Chicago World's Fair of 1893 were created to bring countries together to share ideas, inventions and to show off for others. The 1900 Fair was meant to celebrate the turn of the twentieth century and praised the trends in modernism and *Art Noveau*. ▲

telegraph that increased the speed of communication. In 1851, the United States and Europe had adopted Samuel Morse's patented telegraph and coded alphabet. By the middle part of the century, telegraph wires and poles had covered much of North America. The first transatlantic telegraph cable between Ireland and Newfoundland was laid in 1858, but broke after a month, and its investors lost confidence. A second cable weighing one ton per nautical mile laid in 1866 proved more durable. By the end of the nineteenth century, British, French, German, and U.S. telegraph companies had laid multiple cables that could carry more than one message at a time, thus making the connection between Europe and the United States closer. In 1876, the Scottish emigrant Alexander Graham Bell patented the telephone, which allowed sounds to be transmitted over wires.

The **Bessemer steel process**, first introduced into the United States from England, was a second technology during this period that transformed industry across the globe. Prior to the Bessemer process, steel was uneven in quality and too expensive to be used for anything other than small tools. Steel replaced pig iron, which was brittle and thus limited in its uses. After a conversation with Napoleon III, Emperor of France, about the poor quality of pig iron for manufacturing armaments, Sir Henry Bessemer improved his oxidation experiments that rid pig iron of its impurities. Convinced that the process had commercial potential, Bessemer patented it in 1856. The resulting steel was much stronger, 80 percent cheaper, took less time to manufacture, and was less labor intensive than manufacturing pig iron.

In 1873, Andrew Carnegie introduced the Bessemer process at his Homestead plant in Pittsburgh, Pennsylvania. The new steel transformed almost every industry. Buildings could be built taller and bridges made longer. Skyscrapers and suspension bridges began to dot the urban landscape, especially in New York, Chicago, London, and Paris. The transcontinental railroad system would not have been possible without Bessemer steel.

The automobile was the third technological innovation that had a profound impact on the global economy. Karl Benz of Germany, the inventor of the automobile, developed the commercially viable internal combustion engine. By 1896, his was the largest car manufacturing company in the world, selling a modest 596 units that year. But it was Henry Ford in the United States who mastered mass assembly, drawing on techniques such as

Bessemer steel process
Industrialized manufacturing of steel that used oxidation to produce a strong steel quickly and cheaply, revolutionizing machinery and construction.

Singer Sewing Machine Ad, _Revista Popular_, 1880
Advertisement for Singer sewing machines to be bought on credit system. The ad appeared in the 1880 edition of the Spanish publication _Revista Popular de Conocimientos Utiles_. Ads for U.S. companies such as Singer, Coca Cola, and International Harvester reveal the extent of U.S. commercial influence. ▲

Classic Image/Alamy Stock Photo

using interchangeable parts, developed during the First Industrial Revolution of the early nineteenth century in England and Massachusetts. Ford pioneered a new system of production by using machines and moving assembly lines to dramatically increase the speed of production. By 1914, Ford had cut the time to make an automobile from more than twelve hours to ninety-three minutes. The efficiency saved money as well as time, allowing Ford to slash the price of his popular Model T car from $950 in 1909 to $290 in 1924. Rapid technological and commercial innovation during the late nineteenth century reinforced a feeling of **modernity** among many Americans.

16-1b **New Business Practices**

In addition to applying technological innovations, businesses also transformed operations and marketing. **Industrial capitalism** fully replaced eighteenth-century economic views about merchant capitalism, as **surplus labor**, and goods entered the global market. One of the most useful concepts that industrialists applied to their enterprises was **vertical integration**, which allowed a company to control each part of the

> Organizational innovations make corporations more efficient and successful.

supply chain, from natural resources through production and delivery, to marketing and sales.

Andrew Carnegie was one of the first U.S. businessmen to perfect this system. He acquired iron and coal mines, as well as the coke ovens that produced the high-quality fuel needed to produce steel. He either owned or made close alliances with railroad lines that would ship and deliver his products. By controlling the entire supply chain, Carnegie maximized efficiencies and cost savings. Both reformers and workers, however, protested the immense power concentrated in vertically integrated corporations.

American businesses also used monopolies, which had been used by colonial governments and were the basis of the transatlantic economy. A true **monopoly** exists when one firm or a group of firms exerts total control over the supply of a good or service in order to control its price. Even though it did not reach that benchmark, John D. Rockefeller's Standard Oil owned 88 percent of all oil-refining facilities in the country, practically shutting out all other competition. Rockefeller then used vertical integration to control other parts of the oil supply chain. Until the Supreme Court ruled in 1911 that his company was an unfair monopoly, Standard Oil was the largest corporation in the nation.

Rockefeller's near-monopoly created a **holding company** that allowed Standard Oil to control many other corporations. This legal device allowed the board (or trustees) of one firm to govern dozens of others, ensuring that they did not compete with one another. During the **great merger movement** between 1895 and 1905, manufacturers of everything from paper bags to tin merged small businesses into gigantic holding companies. More than eighteen hundred firms disappeared and were replaced by consolidated firms prefaced with brand names connoting nationwide power, such as American, Standard, Union, or General. Many consolidated firms, such as Otis Elevator and International Harvester, controlled 70 percent or more of their respective industries. The reasons for the mergers remain controversial among historians. One reason could have been that the industries were trying to suppress competitive price wars by buying out competitors. Another reason could have been that the industries were simply trying to

modernity Term used to distinguish a historical era as "modern" based on the convergence of new technologies, lifestyles, and personal independence.

Industrial capitalism Economic system based on a free market in which all enterprises are privately owned.

surplus labor Farm workers whose labor was not needed year-round for household subsistence. Some found wage work that added security and comfort.

vertical integration Business practice that encourages ownership of all aspects of production from the natural resources to the delivery of the finished product.

supply chain System of organizations, people, activities, information, and resources needed to provide materials to manufacture a product for customers.

monopoly Also termed _horizontal integration_, exclusive control of ownership of every outlet for a good or service, thus allowing it to set the price.

holding company Entity that exists for the sole purpose of holding shares/stock of other companies, allowing a few people to control many companies.

great merger movement Period in U.S. economic history when companies consolidated into larger corporations.

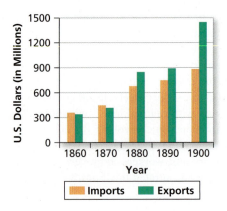

Figure 16.2 U.S. Exports and Imports, 1860–1900 During the latter half of the nineteenth century, the United States became increasingly enmeshed in the global economy by importing and exporting goods. The United States had a fairly even trade balance in 1870, but by 1880, its exports had surpassed imports. By the turn of the twentieth century, the value of exports was nearly double that of imports, indicating U.S. companies' ability to export wheat, steel, and finished manufactured goods, such as combines and sewing machines. ▲ Source: Mitchell, B.R. *International Historical Statistics: The Americas, 1750–2005.* New York: Palgrave Macmillan, 2007.

become more efficient through scale economies in transportation or capital investment.

These business practices and improved efficiency not only provided U.S. consumers a new array of choices but also expanded U.S. exports (see Figure 16.2). The Singer Sewing Machine Corporation, for example, had been selling its machines since the early nineteenth century. Innovations in marketing and production enabled Singer to begin exporting on a scale that would have been unimaginable earlier. By the early twentieth century, U.S. industrialized consumer products from typewriters and cameras to razor blades and packaged cereals had become popular items in Asia, Europe, and Latin America.

The global economy expanded dramatically in the late nineteenth century with every industrialized country seeing significant growth in productivity, exports, and imports. But even among this phenomenal growth, the United States stood out. The U.S. economy quintupled in size and accounted for 25 percent of global economic growth in the period between the end of the Civil War and the turn of the century. The U.S. economy was the largest in the world and was more than twice the size of the next largest economic powerhouses, Germany and the United Kingdom. These two economies had grown because of their access to new markets with the opening of the Suez Canal. U.S. growth depended on the extraction of the West's resources and the immigrant labor that was flooding into the country and providing the human power to develop those resources and markets.

boom-bust cycles Economic process typified by expanding and then contracting business activity that typified the U.S. economy in the late nineteenth century.

Panic of 1893 Economic depression brought on by the failure of railroads and banks, business bankruptcies, and high unemployment.

16-1c Risk and Economic Volatility

After 1865, the global economy grew as the United States built railroads and established new markets and European powers developed their colonial possessions. But two periods of economic depression were interspersed in this generally upward trend. These **boom-bust cycles** triggered dramatic upswings and downward spirals and contributed to income inequality. In 1873, both sides of the Atlantic experienced an economic depression brought on by the collapse of railroad expansion and the demonetization of silver (see Chapter 14). Banks in the United States, Germany, and Great Britain shuttered, and companies shut down production, laid off workers, and declared bankruptcy. The New York Stock Exchange closed for twenty days, and more than one hundred U.S. railroad lines failed or were in bankruptcy by 1874. In the United States, the depression lasted until 1877. Great Britain fared even worse and endured twenty years of economic downturn called the *long stagnation*.

In 1893, after almost a decade of economic growth in the United States, an economic depression again engulfed global markets. The downturn began in France in 1889, and Great Britain and Germany felt the recession by the following year. The collapse of speculative projects in European colonial outposts in South Africa, Australia, and Latin America caused both European and U.S. banks that had financed the speculation to falter. Like the 1873 depression, as the market became saturated, rampant railroad speculation and then railway failures also triggered the **Panic of 1893**. Many of these railroads had been financed by British banks, which were overly leveraged with bad debt. At the peak of the depression, fifteen thousand companies and five hundred banks in the United States had failed, and almost 20 percent of Americans were unemployed. Workers in the cities fared much worse. Unemployment reached nearly 35 percent in New York City. Europe did not fully recover from the recession until 1896. The worldwide depression showed just how interdependent the European and U.S. economies were. Both were also intertwined with the global speculative and growing markets. A downturn in one part of the world could trigger panic and decline in other markets.

Such economic volatility made life precarious for businessmen, workers, and their families. Small farms and businesses were particularly vulnerable to downturns. Those with more money and economic stability were able to better weather the crises. Mark Twain labeled this period the *Gilded Age* because a thin veneer of opulent wealth for the few gilded the problems, corruption, and inequalities associated with industrialization, urbanization, and immigration that accompanied such rapid growth.

{ Cycles of prosperity and depression destabilize the global economy.

16-2
Growth of Cities

This photograph, taken between 1900 and 1910, shows laundry hanging above the yard between tenement buildings in Manhattan. Many city dwellers left the crowded living conditions on the southern end of New York City. They spread north as a result of both the growing immigrant population and the desire of wealthy families to live uptown on Park Avenue and Central Park West, away from the masses.

What does the photograph suggest about the ways that families adapted to such crowded living situations? ▶

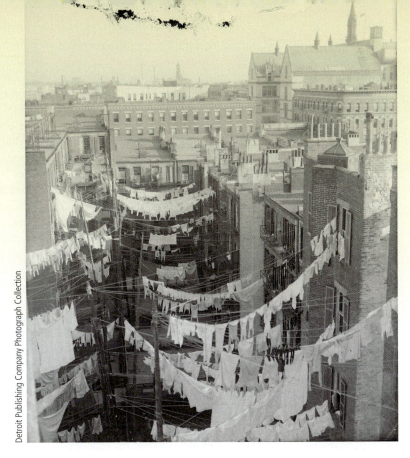

Detroit Publishing Company Photograph Collection

The technological innovations that drove the spectacular growth of the world economy also drove people to reconsider how and where they wanted to live. One of the most dramatic shifts at the end of the nineteenth century was the global migration of peoples to other countries and cities to take advantage of new economic and social opportunities. During this period, millions of people left their rural homes and made their way across international borders, oceans, and sometimes just across the state to find a new life in the emerging cities. The period between the end of the Civil War and the beginning of World War I saw the largest migration of peoples to date within the borders of the United States as well as from other nations.

☞ As you read, consider how the influx of these new migrants transformed cities. What types of infrastructure did cities have to create to accommodate them? How did living in urban areas reshape people's social lives?

16-2a Local and Global Migrations

The efficiencies created by technological advances—including the development of the combine, which required less demand for manual labor, and the railroads—allowed Americans to leave their farms in unprecedented numbers. Drawn to urban areas by jobs in manufacturing, sales, and distribution, people flocked to U.S. cities seeking jobs, homes, and the consumer goods associated with living there. Although families often moved, young rural single men and women made up the majority of the internal migrants. The urban population

{ Immigrants from around the world and migrants from the countryside transform U.S. cities.

of the United States increased by seven times in the last half of nineteenth century.

Western cities also grew rapidly, although they did not match the size or pace of eastern urban areas. Port cities such as San Francisco, Los Angeles, Portland, and Seattle became commercial centers that processed, marketed, and sold the natural resources of the U.S. West internally and to rest of the world. Interior hub cities such as Denver, Fort Worth, and Kansas City processed wheat and livestock and were connected by an expanding railroad system that tied rural America to the rest of the nation.

Although the South remained largely rural throughout this period with only 17 percent of its population living in cities, the region also felt the impact of internal migration (see Map 16.1). In addition to the freedmen who moved to both southern and northern cities, rural whites also took advantage of the new urban opportunities. Black and white women found new work as domestic servants as well as in factories. Migration to southern cities was part of an economic expansion pushed by southern elites in the wake of Reconstruction's end. Leaders such as Henry W. Grady, editor of the *Atlanta Constitution*, hailed the **New South** as the place where increased industrialization and an influx of capital would lift the region out of its economic devastation. This vision of economic uplift for the South, however, was not based on

New South Term used to describe the industrializing southern United States in the period between the end of Reconstruction and World War I.

racial equality because the Southern elite continued to believe in white supremacy and saw **Jim Crow** laws as a part of this new regime.

The movement of rural peoples into U.S. cities only partly explains the unprecedented pace of urbanization. The key factor that made cities grow rapidly and more diverse was the wave of immigrants who arrived between 1870 and 1920. Earlier immigrants were largely German, British, Irish, and Scandinavian sojourners who tended to arrive with skills and some capital to start a business. More than half of those from Germany traveled west to start farms using the Homestead Act, but the remainder stayed in the cities where they built tightly knit communities.

By the 1880s, the immigrant flow shifted to arrivals of the **new immigrants** from eastern and southern Europe, who were young—between the ages of fifteen and forty-five—and were mostly Catholic or Jewish. Seventy percent were young men looking for economic opportunity. Unlike earlier waves, these men were unskilled laborers who worked some of the dirtiest and most difficult jobs in the industrial economy. They left their countries of origin for a variety of reasons, including economic upheaval from the global depressions of the 1870s and 1890s and religious persecution from **pogroms**. The most prevalent factor, however, was the lure of employment in the expanding U.S. economy. Migrants who had been "pushed" from their homeland by famine or persecution came to start a new life. Those "pulled" by job possibilities often planned a temporary stay, but most settled permanently. The two major immigration stations, **Ellis Island** (1890–1964) in New York harbor and **Angel Island** (1910–1940) in San Francisco Bay together processed more than 13 million immigrants (see Map 16.2).

Although most immigrants to the United States in this era were Europeans, western cities took in thousands who came from Asia and Mexico. Immigrants from China and Japan and to a lesser extent Korea, India, and the Philippines came to West Coast ports on transpacific steamer ships that carried goods and people. Prior to 1924, Mexican immigrants easily crossed back and forth across the U.S.–Mexico border, which was unpatrolled in most places. These people lived and worked in the growing industries of mining, ranching, and agriculture in the West.

The confluence of migration and urbanization occurred worldwide. In Japan, the industrialization in Tokyo and secondary cities such as Osaka triggered tremendous growth driven by internal migration from the countryside. Berlin (Germany) and Sao Paulo (Brazil) grew at faster rates than Chicago during this period. Argentina, where 30 percent of the population was foreign

Map 16.1 Global Immigration Patterns, 1900 Immigrants from both Asia and Europe pressed into the Americas to make homes and find work in these booming economies. Notice that in this period, as opposed to the early nineteenth century, more immigrants came from southern, rather than northern, Europe. Consider what both pushed and pulled these immigrants to relocate. Notice that other places in the Americas also received large immigrant populations. Was the U.S. immigrant experience unique? ▼

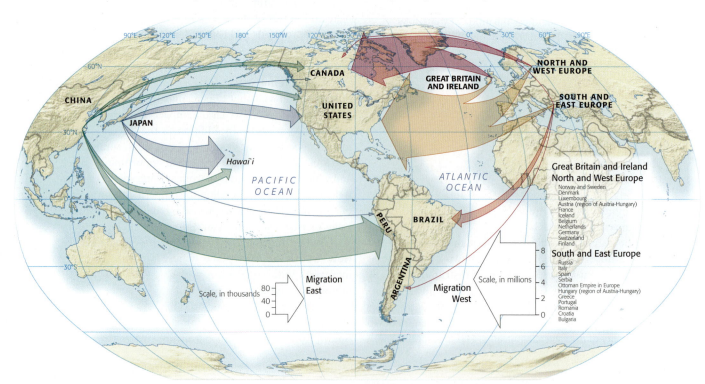

born, had an immigrant experience most similar to that of the United States. By 1914, the proportion of immigrants in Buenos Aires (70 percent) rivaled that of New York City, but they came from a more limited range of countries such as Spain and Italy. Labor markets, cultural preferences, ease of citizenship, and migration "chains" set up by relatives who preceded them influenced immigrants' destination choices. For many, migration within Europe or Asia preceded an overseas move.

The massive global migrations in the late nineteenth and early twentieth centuries affected the United States in two unique ways. First, it received more immigrants than any other country. From the 1830s to 1930, the United States took in 60 percent of all immigrants from Europe. Canada, in second place, received 12 percent. The ability to absorb so many foreigners reflected the availability of land and the rapid industrial growth in the United States. Second, the nation received a much broader diversity of newcomers than other countries. Canada's immigrants came mainly from Great Britain, and those to South America were overwhelmingly Iberian and Italian. Immigrants to the United States, however, came from all over the world. Arriving in U.S. cities, these diverse newcomers created ethnic neighborhoods (Little Italy, Little Tokyo, Greektown, Chinatown, etc.) that were often sealed off from each other and from mainstream society by heritage, language, culture, food, and social customs. Yet the new immigrants found themselves working side-by-side with people from other immigrant communities and together created civic organizations, unions, and religious communities that cut across ethnic lines. Such experiences and institutions advanced the process of assimilation through which immigrants developed common forms of communication and understanding while still maintaining distinct ethnic identities and practices. To the optimist, the merging of global, ethnic, and linguistic differences exemplified the United States as a **melting pot**, a timely metaphor drawn from a blast furnace, which forged different elements into solid metal.

melting pot Metaphor relating to a society's ability to assimilate newcomers who gradually make one community.

Map 16.2 U.S. Immigration and Urbanization, 1890–1900 Millions of immigrants spread across the United States to find economic opportunity in both rural and urban locations. The orange-shaded areas in the U.S. West show where immigrants flocked to work in the mining and agricultural industries. In the Northeast, immigrants were more concentrated in cities, with Chicago, New York, and Philadelphia totaling a million people, making them some of the largest and most vibrant cities globally. ▼

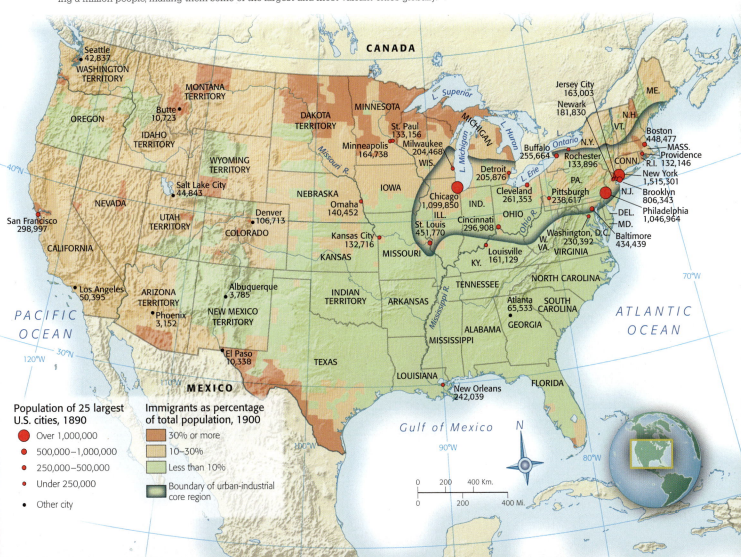

16-2b Urban Infrastructures

Thousands of people moving into such concentrated masses in the cities required local governments to build infrastructures that kept cities running efficiently and cleanly by addressing the most urgent problems: transportation and public health.

> Electricity and other technological innovations transform the urban landscape.

Prior to the Second Industrial Revolution, people in cities relied on their bodies (by walking) and horses (by riding in omnibuses or wagons) to move themselves and their goods. The crowding and the piles of animal waste on the streets convinced officials that horse-drawn transportation was not workable in this dense environment. After an outbreak of equine influenza that killed thousands of horses, it became clear that cities needed to find a new energy source for transportation.

In the early 1880s, a number of city governments such as those in Scranton, Pennsylvania, Richmond, Virginia, and Newark, New Jersey, experimented with public transportation powered by electricity. By the late 1880s, San Francisco, Chicago, and New York riders were using electric or cable trolley cars that moved along embedded rail lines laid in the middle of roads. There was also

Chicago frame Building term referring to the development of a structure's skeleton steel frame by Chicago architects that enabled construction of skyscrapers.

a surge in building elevated rail lines and, in 1897, Boston built the nation's first urban transportation system consisting of both subways and above-ground trains. By the beginning of the twentieth century, thousands of miles of subways, elevated trains, cable cars, and improved roads had been constructed in the nation's cities. These improvements enabled shorter travel times, allowing people to live farther from their workplaces.

The cheaper and stronger steel made possible by the Bessemer process produced a surge in civil engineering projects, building rail lines, bridges, and skyscrapers that transformed the nation's cities. The 1883 opening of the Brooklyn Bridge, which connected Manhattan and Brooklyn, then the fourth largest city in the United States, was celebrated as one of the great engineering feats of the century and expanded commerce between two thriving downtown areas. In the mid-1880s, architects and engineers developed the **Chicago frame**, which took advantage of steel rather than stone or brick to build lighter and taller structures. The earlier 1852 invention of the elevator had made skyscrapers practical. The new buildings, in turn, allowed for increased urban density as cities rose skyward, packing more people into fewer square feet of land. The price of this land shot up because a new building such as a high-rise apartment complex could house many more rent-paying tenants. Fortunes were made in urban real estate that rivaled those made in western land speculation.

Map of Chicago's Elevated Trains, 1897 This illustrated map shows the elevated train lines of the Chicago, Rock Island and Pacific Railroad in Chicago, Illinois. Also note the infrastructure of the city in term of the roads laid out in a grid, and the Chicago River, which had been reengineered to flow backwards so that the industrial waste of the city and the stockyards would flow away from the city center and into Lake Michigan. ◄

The Granger Collection, New York

City officials created intricate water and sewer systems to deal with public health issues in addition to building public transportation systems, bridges, and skyscrapers. Overcrowding made it dangerous for families to dump their **night soil** onto the streets or to dig outhouses in the back of apartment buildings. The United States had suffered a series of cholera, typhoid, and yellow fever epidemics because of poor sanitation systems. Mother Jones's family had been victims of such an epidemic in Memphis. The first sewer systems were built in London as the result of a devastating cholera outbreak in 1858. The first sewage treatment plant in the United States was built in Worcester, Massachusetts, in 1890. In one of the greatest hydraulic engineering feats of the time, the city of Chicago in 1887 changed the course of the Chicago River so that it could more effectively deal with its sewage problem from both humans and the Union Stockyards on Chicago's south side.

Public officials also lived in constant fear of a great catastrophe. The 1871 Great Chicago Fire killed three hundred people and burned almost the entire city's downtown. The fire that swept through Boston a year later burned sixty-five acres, caused $73.5 million in damages, and killed thirty people. These two fires prompted municipalities across the nation to make sure that there was ample public water available to fight fires and inspired the creation of city-funded professional firefighter services. But even this planning could not prevent the impact of natural disasters such as the 1906 San Francisco earthquake. In the quake and fires that ensued, more than three thousand people died and 80 percent of the city burned to the ground.

16-2c Cities and Their Countrysides

Urbanization transformed the cities as well as the surrounding countryside, drawing rural places into the economic orbit of cities. Agriculture and transportation systems developed rapidly to meet the demands of the cities, which did not have the physical ability to feed their growing populations. Moreover, as urban populations exploded, more affluent residents moved out of city centers. To escape the crowds in lower Manhattan, New York's wealthiest families moved farther north up Fifth Avenue, and after Central Park was finished in 1858 and transportation lines expanded, they moved to the Upper West Side. In the late nineteenth century, the rise of the popular streetcar and railroad allowed people to commute to the **suburbs**, such as the North Shore of Chicago, Brookline just outside of Boston, and Westchester north of New York.

> Transportation technologies bring rural and urban spaces together.

Although boosters of suburban communities espoused the idea that the countryside was separate from the teeming masses and dirty streets that epitomized the U.S. city, in reality, the two were intimately connected. These early suburbs were "bedroom" communities that housed middle-class workers who still depended on the city for their economic survival. Men traveled to work each day on the newly expanded commuter train lines. People depended on the city to provide their consumer demands. Department stores such as Bullocks in Los Angeles, Marshall Fields in Chicago, and Macy's in New York provided fancy clothes and household goods that could be purchased in the city centers and moved to new homes in the suburbs.

More subtly, and perhaps in ways that most city dwellers did not realize, the success of the cities depended on the countryside for their survival. They also depended on public funds, rather than private corporations, to build urban infrastructure projects. Cities utilized not only technological advances and public funding to create waterworks and sewers but also nearby natural resources to supply their fresh drinking water. New York built the forty-one-mile Croton Aqueduct to bring ample fresh water to holding lakes in Central Park and under today's New York Public Library. It was then distributed to a series of fresh-water fountains throughout the city for public use. (Piped indoor plumbing would not come to most city dwellers until the early twentieth century.) San Francisco completed one of the most ambitious public water works projects when it brought water 167 miles in a gravity-driven system from a newly built dam in Yosemite National Park. The controversy over damming the Hetch Hetchy River in California pitted President Theodore Roosevelt against John Muir, one of the earliest environmentalists and the founder of the Sierra Club in 1892, sparking the beginning of the modern environmental movement.

Burgeoning cities depended on the countryside for food as well as water. City dwellers provided almost no food for themselves because of the crowded conditions and lack of gardens. The rural areas closest to the cities provided eggs, milk, and fresh produce that could be trucked in daily. With the advent of better transportation and wide use of refrigerated train cars in the 1880s by companies such as Armour and Company, U.S. city dwellers could have clean, dressed beef shipped to their local stores. Grain grown in the countrysides was also delivered to cities. By the end of the nineteenth century, most city dwellers could expect to find most of the foods they needed at their local grocery or on the carts that lined city streets. That availability of these products depended on the intricate balance between technology, transportation, the market, and the countryside.

night soil Euphemism for human waste that people threw out of their windows or dumped into the street before indoor plumbing.

suburbs Community built outside the city limits primarily for families looking to escape the crowded urban areas.

Museum of the City of New York/The Art Archive at Art Resource, NY

16-3

Life in Industrialized America

This 1890 photo of an Italian immigrant family was taken by photographer and social reformer Jacob Riis. This family was living in a one-room apartment on New York's Lower East Side. Riis exposed the way poor and immigrant familes lived and worked during the late nineteenth century.

What does Riis's photograph reveal about this family and how its members could benefit from attempts at social reform? Why would this family pose for him? ▶

Go to MindTap® to practice history with the Chapter 16 **Primary Source Writing Activity: Life in Industrialized America**. Read and view primary sources and respond to a writing prompt.

Robber Barons Disparaging name given to wealthy industrialists who dominated corporate United States in the late nineteenth century.

Disparities in class and racial divisions in the United States became more apparent as the century came to a close. The concentration of wealth in the hands of a few people increased after the Civil War and by the end of the century, a small percentage of individuals controlled a majority of the nation's wealth, creating class divisions. Many Americans, however, interpreted this accumulation of wealth as something positive for the nation, a source for inspiration and aspiration. In this way, the working classes admired the rags-to-riches stories of commanding business leaders such as Andrew Carnegie because they held out hope that they too could become rich and powerful. At the same time, these stories, supported by interpretations of Charles Darwin's theory of evolution, taught Americans that their own limitations and failures—not the structure of the economy—prevented them from climbing out of poverty. Such theories, together with violent state repression, stymied reform efforts seeking to improve the conditions for millions of poor Americans and their families.

☞ As you read, think about the kinds of economic and racial tensions that emerged within a rapidly industrializing and urbanizing society filled with a range of new immigrants and internal migrants.

16-3a Inequality

Accelerating technological innovation created vast amounts of cash and capital as the global economy grew. Consumers

{ Economic inequalities lead to class divisions and explanations for those divisive disparities.

purchased new goods and services, which created more jobs and wealth. This increased wealth, however, was not evenly distributed. Capitalists, who were derisively called **Robber Barons** because of the opulent way they displayed their wealth and their apparent disregard for the working classes, accumulated wealth at a far higher rate than workers. James Bryce, an Englishman talking about the U.S. elite, noted in 1897 that "those who deem themselves ladies and gentlemen draw just the same line between themselves and the multitude as is drawn in [aristocratic] England, and draw it in much the same way." Americans, who liked to distinguish between their democratic republic and old world feudalism, found Bryce's comparisons offensive. Yet wealthy New Yorkers proved his point at the annual 1898 Christmas dinner they sponsored for the poor in Madison Square Garden. The elite came and sat in the galleries and watched twenty thousand of the city's poor line up to eat at the tables below them.

In fact, many of America's burgeoning elite often wanted to be like Europe's nobility. It became fashionable to take transatlantic ocean liners to visit famous sites and purchase art. Women returned from these trips dressed in the latest Parisian fashions. Some American elite also married their daughters off to European nobility in an attempt to gain an aristocratic pedigree. For example, Consuelo Vanderbilt, granddaughter to the railroad magnate Cornelius Vanderbilt, married Charles Spencer Churchill, the ninth Duke of Marlborough in England and the heir to Blenheim Palace. The $2.5 million from her wedding dowry kept the estate running. These *dollar princesses*, as they came to be known, were popular. By 1915, there were 42 American-born princesses, 17 duchesses,

Library of Congress Prints and Photographs Division Washington[LC-USZ62-102808]

Global Americans

Andrew Carnegie was born in Scotland where his father was a skilled weaver but struggled to provide for his family. In 1848, the Carnegies emigrated to Allegheny, Pennsylvania. At thirteen, he found work as a bobbin boy for $1.20 a week. Two years later, he found a job as a messenger boy for a telegraph company. Self-educated, Carnegie found another job as a secretary when he was eighteen at Pennsylvania Railway Company and began his upward climb into corporate America. During the Civil War, he worked to open rail and telegraph lines for the North, earning an excellent wage and making lucrative investments. By the end of the war, Carnegie recognized that real wealth and growth lay in the development of the steel industry to supply the expanding railways. He opened his own steel works, and eventually purchased the rival Homestead Steel Works in 1888. The introduction of Bessemer steel into the U.S. economy caused dramatic growth and development of the nation's infrastructure. By 1901, when Carnegie sold his interest to J.P. Morgan, U.S. Steel became the first $1 billion company. Carnegie faced criticism for his labor policies that included brutal strike breaking. In his later career, however, based on his teachings from "The Gospel of Wealth," he funded thousands of libraries both in the United States and abroad and endowed cultural institutions and recreational facilities for working families. During the Spanish-American War, which he opposed, he joined the Anti-Imperialist League and became an outspoken critic of U.S. imperial ambitions in both the Caribbean and the Pacific.

Andrew Carnegie (Far Right) with Booker T. Washington and Others at the Tuskegee Institute's 25th Anniversary

33 viscountesses, 33 marchionesses, 46 ladies, 64 baronesses, and 136 countesses.

American popular culture revered self-made men like Cornelius Vanderbilt. They were the heroes of popular novels by the prolific author Horatio Alger, who wrote almost one hundred books during his career. The formulaic narratives told the rags-to-riches stories of young, poor boys who worked hard and were thrifty and honest—virtues that led to their inevitable climb into the comfortable middle class. Wealth and success were tied to moral uprightness whereas poverty was ascribed to laziness and moral failings. Such views of rich and poor were backed by new but pseudoscientific theories, such as **Social Darwinism**, which argued that Darwin's theory of evolution as outlined in his famous *Origin of Species* (1859) could be applied to human societies. While Darwin limited his concept of **natural selection** to biological contexts, highly regarded English social thinkers, including Herbert Spencer and Darwin's half-cousin Francis Galton, ranked various groups in society based on evolutionary notions of the "survival of the fittest." In the United States, Social Darwinists such as William Sumner of Yale University applied the theory of evolution to the emerging U.S. industrialized society. In 1883, Sumner argued in his pamphlet "What the Social Classes Owe Each Other" against social reforms to help the poor because society worked best when it was left alone (laissez-faire) to let the strongest survive. He warned that the government must stay out of social and economic affairs and focus instead on individual rights and protections.

Unlike Social Darwinists, the powerful business leader Andrew Carnegie believed that the rich were duty bound to return capital to the working class. One of the wealthiest men in America, Carnegie embodied the Horatio Alger hero who was transformed from rags to riches. In decrying the new class of wealthy industrialists who lived opulently with no regard to the workers they employed, he developed a philosophy called the *gospel of wealth* that extolled his paternalistic vision of the obligations of the wealthy classes to the laboring poor. He favored Britain's high estate tax that penalized what he called "selfish and greedy" men who died wealthy and left their riches to their families. Carnegie believed that men of wealth needed to engage in paternalistic philanthropy, give away the majority of their money, and thus help guide the poor to live rewarding lives. He lived by his creed by donating $10 million to found the Carnegie Endowment for International Peace (which still exists today), the largest gift at the time to support harmonious global relations.

Carnegie had a very clear vision of those he believed to be worthy of his largesse. To advance educational opportunities, he built more than twenty-five hundred libraries across the world (sixteen hundred of them in the United States), endowed schools that eventually became the Carnegie Institute of Technology (later Carnegie-Mellon University), erected concert halls, and gave money to institutions that he believed would help working peoples improve their lives. He did not believe in charity or welfare but maintained that the poor were lazy and needed to be taught skills to improve their lives. The

Social Darwinism Popular theory at the end of the nineteenth century applying Darwin's theory of natural selection to human societies.

natural selection Biological process through which the strongest traits of a given species survive and thrive.

collective bargaining
Negotiation process between a company and its workers in which a group, not individual workers, present demands.

de jure Legitimate or legal, often used to describe segregation that is established and enforced by law.

de facto In fact or reality, whether legal or not, often used to describe segregation that is not necessarily legal but enforced by customs and practices.

philanthropist's largesse also did not extend to the thousands of workers at his own companies whose requests for **collective bargaining** he denied repeatedly. As a result, the workers educated themselves about the power of organized labor, which much to Carnegie's chagrin, led to many contentious strikes.

One great irony of the late nineteenth century is that while industrialists fought off the ever-looming threat of unionization, the gospel of wealth created a space for workers to develop their own class identity. Whether it was while sitting in a library endowed by Carnegie or working under the ever-present watchful eye of the foreman, employees came to see themselves as a distinctive economic class from their employers.

16-3b Ethnic Segregation and Racial Divisions

Racial segregation became the pattern in most U.S. cities during the late nineteenth and early twentieth centuries. For example, ethnic groups, such as the Bohemians, Poles, and Slavs, congregated into neighborhoods close to their industrial jobs at the Chicago stockyards where they worked on the killing floors of the Swift and Armour meatpacking plants. They joined earlier Irish and German immigrants, making up the multiethnic, neighborhood-centric cities that came to symbolize U.S. urbanism. Mexicans and African Americans remained segregated in less desirable locations farther from work. In many cases, their urban

> Although the Civil War ends slavery, conflicts over race and ethnicity continue.

neighborhoods became institutionalized as *barrios* and segregated neighborhoods for racial minorities. In addition to experiencing urban segregation in southern cities after the end of Reconstruction in 1877, African Americans faced restrictions on their voting rights. Ten of the eleven former confederate states passed new state constitutions that disenfranchised blacks. The laws inhibited blacks' ability to resist the imposition of discriminatory (albeit legal) Jim Crow laws and practices, which in many cases were reapplications of antebellum slave codes (see Table 16.1). Much of the anxiety that provoked Jim Crow was the fear of African American mobility and the loss of their labor. African American families began leaving their rural homes and moved to emerging southern cities such as Memphis, Atlanta, and Birmingham or north to the booming industrial centers of New York, Chicago, and Philadelphia. These migrations set the pattern for the largest black outflow from the South that started during World War I.

Even before Reconstruction officially ended, white Southerners returned to power and enacted laws prohibiting the equal treatment of blacks and whites, creating legal (**de jure**) racial classifications. All across the South "Whites Only" signs appeared as private businesses enforced new laws requiring racial segregation by refusing to serve African Americans. Public facilities and transportation, schools, theaters, restaurants, and bathrooms were separated into different spaces for blacks and whites. While this type of racial segregation occurred less frequently outside the South, local governments in the North and West practiced **de facto** racial segregation and discrimination rooted in common practices rather than overtly racist laws.

African Americans in the South contested the imposition of the new Jim Crow regime. After Louisiana passed the Separate Car Act in 1890, which stipulated that all public transportation would be segregated by race, a group of concerned citizens challenged the

Table 16.1 Select Jim Crow Laws

The term *Jim Crow* first was used in the early 1890s to describe laws that segregated blacks from whites in restaurants, schools, and public transportation. It regulated all aspects of African Americans' lives. This table gives a sense of how encompassing these restrictions were for black Americans.

State	Area Restricted	Restriction
Alabama	Health care	White nurses allowed to deny care to black patients
Arizona, Maryland, Wyoming	Marriage	Marriage between a Caucasian and a Negro, Mongolian, Malay, or Hindu declared null and void
Georgia	Burial	Whites and blacks separated by law in cemeteries
New Mexico	Education	Black and white children segregated in schools
North Carolina	Education	Black and white children not allowed to share the same textbooks
Oklahoma	Public utilities	Separate telephone booths for blacks and whites maintained by telephone companies
Texas	Public institutions	Public libraries segregated

The Granger Collection, New York

Global Americans In 1854, **Yung Wing** was the first Chinese man to earn a Bachelor of Arts degree at Yale University. He had come to the United States in 1847, accompanying the missionary Reverend S.R. Brown who was returning to the United States from his mission in southern China, where Yung and his family lived on a small farm. Yung became a naturalized U.S. citizen in 1852. After graduating, he returned to China where he found work in the government. After the signing of the Burlingame Treaty (see Chapter 14) that permitted Chinese immigration to the United States, Yung developed an educational program in China that enabled Chinese students to study in the United States for four years. He also founded the Chinese Education Mission, which eventually sent more than one hundred students to the United States who returned to China as engineers, teachers, and doctors. While running the program, he married Mary Kellogg and had two sons with her. In 1876, Yale granted him an honorary Doctor of Laws degree.

When Empress Dowager Cixi came to power 1898, she decided to end connections with the West. She was suspicious of Yung, who fled to Hong Kong. In 1902, he petitioned the United States to return to Connecticut, but the Department of State had revoked his citizenship as a result of the passage of the Chinese Exclusion Act of 1882 so that he could not legally reenter the United States. With the help of friends and his family, however, Yung returned illegally, just in time to see his youngest son graduate from Yale. He lived the rest of his life in Hartford, Connecticut. A portrait of him hangs at Yale, and PS 124 in Chinatown, New York City, is named after him.

MANDARIN YUNG WING.

law. This group included New Orleans editor and civil rights activist Rodolphe Desdunes (see Chapter 14) who enlisted Homer Plessy, an octoroon (seven-eighths white but categorized as "colored" under the law), to purchase a first-class ticket and board the Whites Only car on a New Orleans tram. Plessy had the blessing of the tram company, which opposed the law because of the high cost of separating blacks and whites. Local police immediately arrested him when he refused to leave the white section of the tram. The incident spurred a series of court rulings that led to an 1896 U.S. Supreme Court decision.

At issue in *Plessy v. Ferguson* was the plaintiff's claim that Louisiana's segregation of tram riders by race deprived him of the equal protection of the laws guaranteed by the Fourteenth Amendment and imposed involuntary servitude on him, a violation of the Thirteenth Amendment. In a seven-to-one decision, the Supreme Court held that Louisiana law could segregate citizens by race into separate physical spaces so long as those spaces were equal in quality and comfort because such segregation did not "stamp . . . the colored race with a badge of inferiority." In his lone dissent, Justice John Marshall Harlan, a Southerner familiar with Jim Crow practices, argued that Louisiana's law "put the brand of servitude and degradation upon a large class of our fellow citizens," because, regardless of the equal quality of the tramcars, "the real meaning of such legislation" was that "colored citizens are so inferior and degraded that

they cannot be allowed to sit in public coaches occupied by white citizens."

Although discriminatory laws were directed primarily against blacks, Asian immigrants became the first targets of exclusionary immigration laws. Congress enacted the Chinese Exclusion Act in 1882, which for a ten year-period barred laborers of Chinese ancestry from entering the United States. Despite attempts by Radical Republicans to naturalize the Chinese, they continued to be banned by a 1790 statute limiting U.S. citizenship to whites. Capitalists, such as the Central Pacific Railroad's Big Four, benefited from Chinese labor, which was hard to find in the sparsely populated West, and often paid them less than whites. Although a combination of industrialists and supporters of Pacific trade ensured that the door to Chinese migration remained opened, western laborers and workingmen's organizations had long pressed Congress to shut it.

The Chinese were discouraged from creating stable families as the immigration of women was all but prohibited by the Page Act (1875). The law barred only prostitutes from entering the United States, but its enforcement came to exclude most Chinese women. Only 2 percent of Chinese immigrants were female in 1855 and by 1890, that number had risen to just 4 percent. Asian exclusion policies were not unique to the United States in this era. Canada, Australia, and New Zealand, as well as other societies of British origin on the Pacific Rim, passed similar laws restricting the flow of first Chinese, and then Japanese, workers.

The exclusion of the Chinese initially focused on laborers (the vast majority of immigrants) but armed with further restrictions from Congress, immigration officials expanded the reach of exclusion to include the so-called exempt classes of Chinese (merchants, teachers, students, and travelers). By 1904, the ten-year period of exclusion (which had already been twice renewed) had been extended in perpetuity. The situation was dire for Chinese immigrants, but one bright spot was that their children were able to retain their U.S. citizenship. In *United States v. Wong Kim Ark* (1898), the U.S. Supreme Court protected immigrant rights under the Fourteenth Amendment's guarantee of citizenship. Customs officials had barred Wong Kim Ark from re-entering the United States after he had visited China because he was the son of Chinese nationals, even though Wong was born and had lived his entire life in California. The Court's decision allowed him to return to the United States and held that the Fourteenth Amendment's guarantee of citizenship to "all persons born . . . in the United States and subject to the jurisdiction thereof" applied to Wong, because, unlike a foreign ambassador's child, he was governed by U.S. laws when he was born on American soil. Since the *Wong Kim Ark* decision, all children born on U.S. soil who are subject to U.S. laws have been regarded as natural-born citizens, regardless of the nationality of their parents.

The *Plessy* and *Wong Kim Ark* decisions occurred against a backdrop of violence toward African Americans and Chinese. Between 1892 and 1901, whites **lynched** at least one hundred African Americans each year in racially motivated crimes. In 1892 alone, two hundred thirty blacks were murdered, mostly in the South. Sometimes racist whites acted as a mob and sometimes as individuals in what they believed to be vigilante justice. Each case had its own specific circumstances but tended to follow a pattern. White men would perceive some sort of behavior on the part of African American men as offensive. It might have been that a black man had become successful by opening a shop in town, had talked back to a white person, or perhaps had looked at or spoken with a white woman. These perceived transgressions of racial, economic, and sexual boundaries happened as people lived and worked among one another and often led to horrific race-based violence.

Ida B. Wells witnessed such brutality, and its impact transformed her life. She became an outspoken advocate for racial justice. Born a slave in Mississippi, Wells became responsible for the family after her parents died in a yellow fever epidemic in 1876 and she moved her five siblings to Memphis. Even at a young age, she was known for outspoken views on racial equality as the columnist for a local paper. In 1892, her world was turned upside down when a white mob attacked three of her friends who owned the Peoples Cooperative Grocery Store, which competed against a white-owned store. The mob set the store on fire and in the ensuing melee, three white men were shot but not killed. The police arrested Wells's three African American friends. While they were in jail, a second white mob attacked it, took them out, and lynched them.

In response, Wells called for African Americans to boycott white-owned establishments and even suggested that they leave Memphis where their property and bodies could not be protected. She then worked tirelessly to expose the evils of lynching, specifically that of her friends. She published the pamphlet "Southern Horrors: Lynch Laws in All Its Phases." This earned her the wrath of local whites who threatened her with violence and caused her to flee to Chicago, where she began working for the *Chicago Conservator*, a well-established African American-owned newspaper. From this platform, Wells broadened her campaign against lynching. She traveled across the North and even to England where huge crowds heard powerful evidence about the failures of Reconstruction and African American quest for racial equality.

While blacks faced racial persecution in the South, Chinese people suffered mob violence throughout the West. In 1871, more than five hundred whites invaded Los Angeles's Chinatown and killed eighteen people in retaliation for the murder of a white police officer who had intervened in violence among rival Chinese groups. The hostility was fueled by a deadly combination of white supremacist racial views and economic fears that Chinese immigrants were stealing jobs from white men. Pressured by the depressions of the late nineteenth century, white laborers took out their frustrations on Chinese immigrants.

Although violence was widespread throughout the West, one of the region's most horrific attacks occurred in 1885 at Rock Springs, Wyoming, where twenty-eight Chinese were murdered. The thousand or so Chinese people who lived in Wyoming had come to work on the Union Pacific railroad and stayed to work in the company's coal mines. They also found jobs as cooks, laundry owners, and various other service workers. The railroad paid Chinese laborers less than others and used them as strikebreakers against Cornish, Irish, and Welsh miners who belonged to the Knights of Labor. Encouraged by local Knights members, whites burned the Chinese camp and attacked fleeing residents. Federal troops had to be called in to quell the violence, and the next year at the urging of the U.S. secretary of state, Congress paid a large indemnity to China as compensation to the victims' families without accepting responsibility for the crime.

lynched Extralegal public execution meant to intimidate a particular minority group.

16-3c Recreation and Entertainment in the City

Amid spectacular growth, race riots, segregation, and an epidemic of urban squalor, philanthropists such as Andrew Carnegie and John D. Rockefeller sponsored recreation centers to uplift the poor and calm labor and racial tensions. Rockefeller sponsored the first U.S. branch of the Young Men's Christian Association (YMCA) in 1885. Founded in London in 1844, it provided wholesome activities and safe short-term housing for working-class youth of "healthy mind, body, and sprit." The organization began as an evangelical outlet for Protestantism but over time welcomed youth of all Christian faiths and peoples from every continent. YMCA leaders focused on issues of moral uplift, good citizenship, and the redeeming values of athletic competition and recreation.

> Cities create entertainment opportunities for all classes.

The Salvation Army was another organization seeking to uplift workers and immigrants from the drudgery of urban life. Methodists William and Katherine Booth founded the organization in England in 1865. They preached "soup, soap, and salvation" as the antidote for the ills suffered by alcoholics, drug users, prostitutes, and the poor. As an advancing "army of Christians," the organization came to the United States in 1880 and set up operations in urban immigrant communities.

Another form of moral and social uplift came from Catholic charities tied to neighborhood dioceses. At a time when government did not aid the poor and needy through social welfare programs, religious organizations, such as Catholic charities, joined with the YMCA and Salvation Army, forming the frontline of urban social services. These faith-based institutions provided a place where working people found companionship, recreation, and entertainment amid the alienating culture of the late nineteenth century city.

In addition, most immigrant communities provided mutual aid that benefited members of their own ethnic and national groups. Mexican Americans formed *mutualista* societies whose dues provided modest unemployment insurance, burial insurance, job references, and even personal counseling to families. Almost every small town or community group living in large urban centers had a group such as the *Sociedad Proteccion Mutua de Trabaiadores Unidos (SPMDTU)*. Chinese immigrants depended on their own benevolent societies (*huiguan*), and in 1882, the Chinese Consolidated Benevolent Association, also known as the Six Companies, was incorporated. It supported immigrants by emphasizing moral living and hard work, opposed anti-Chinese legislation and vigilante violence, and encouraged ties to their home provinces and villages.

Not all leisure and recreation in cities was organized or institutionalized. Increased transportation combined with new leisure time and cash in working people's pockets led to the emergence of an entertainment economy. In New York, working people could take the outbound train to **Coney Island** to enjoy what by the 1880s had become the largest amusement park area in the country. They also headed to the Bowery where they could dance, drink, and socialize among their peers. Chicagoans went to the lakeshore to swim or to visit sites such as the newly built **Field Museum of Natural History**. In southern California, people took the electric train to Coronado and Balboa Islands.

The impact on old-world immigrant families and young women transformed the way a generation of young working-class people interacted with the opposite sex, families, and workplaces. Women negotiated their newfound freedom and economic resources. Young people could more freely mingle in public with one another. Because the homes of many workers were crowded, many individuals spent their leisure time in the streets, in public parks, or at local diners and saloons where they could meet without being under the watchful eyes of their families. Single men and women were able to go to nickelodeon shows or dance halls together, which meant more intimacy between the sexes in public places.

The cities' elite also found new forms of entertainment. Often mimicking the European culture, benefactors created libraries, concert halls, opera houses, and museums. These cultural institutions became the pet projects of the rich and elevated their own social status and in some cases provided cultural venues for the working class. The Metropolitan Opera in New York was founded in 1880 and included the Vanderbilts, Roosevelts, and Morgans among its first subscribers.

By the end of the nineteenth century, much of the country was in upheaval, as the effects of migration, immigration, industrialization, and urbanization pressured people in their daily lives. This phenomenal interaction of people allowed for both the potential for understanding as well as the very real possibility of conflict, some of it violent. Although many fed that friction for numerous reasons including fear or prejudice, many others worked to solve the problems by joining reform movements and advocating for their causes. Nowhere were these frictions more apparent and more violent than in the upheaval that was caused by the industrialization of the U.S. workplace.

Coney Island Amusement park and boardwalk in Brooklyn, New York, on the Atlantic Ocean where working-class people spent leisure time and found entertainment.

Field Museum of Natural History Building from the World's Columbian Expedition held in Chicago in 1893 that presents scientific knowledge about the world and is named for its founder, department store magnate Marshall Field.

History without Borders

Baseball

Year professional or semi-professional baseball league established

- Before 1900
- 1900–1929
- 1930s
- 1940s
- 1950s
- 1960s–1992

— International boundaries, 1992

NORTH AMERICA

UNITED STATES

Hoboken

CUBA

Mexico: Liga Mexicana de Béisbol was founded, 1925.

Dominican Republic: Baseball was first played in 1870.

Panama: Earliest recorded games were played in the Canal Zone, 1903.

SOUTH AMERICA

PACIFIC OCEAN

ATLANTIC OCEAN

Sweden: Exhibition games took place at Stockholm Olympics, 1912.

UNITED KINGDOM

EUROPE

AFRICA

ASIA

JAPAN

Japan: Tokyo University students organized teams, 1872.

Zimbabwe: Hosted first Africa Cup Baseball Championship, 1992.

INDIAN OCEAN

AUSTRALIA

Baseball Organizations, 1870–1992 Baseball is considered the most American of all sports. Yet baseball found its origins in a game called rounders that emerged from England and may have been a derivative of cricket. Since its inception in the late nineteenth century, baseball has become a global phenomenon that has entertained both men and women. Increasingly, Major League Baseball, which is the largest professional league in the world, reflects the globalization of the sport as athletes from around the world come to compete in the United States.

Baseball has been called "America's Pastime," but it in fact originated in England and then spread around the globe. Nevertheless, it is still most closely associated with the United States, which is the most lucrative market for Major League Baseball (MLB).

Baseball is derived from a game called *rounders*, which was played in England during the late eighteenth century and may also have been a precursor to cricket. By the early nineteenth century, Americans in the Northeast—both men and women—were playing some form of

baseball as a leisure activity after work. In 1845, the New York Knickerbockers, a club of elite men, formalized the rules of what is now considered modern baseball. The first professional game was played in Hoboken, New Jersey, in 1846. However, almost ten years later in 1855, the New York sports pages were still devoting more space to coverage of cricket than that of baseball.

By the late nineteenth century, baseball had taken off as a major leisure time sport among both urban and rural youth. Groups like the YMCA created

youth leagues in order to provide activities for boys after school or work. John D. Rockefeller Jr. financed a baseball league in his Colorado mines. The league boasted state-of-the-art facilities, with scoreboards, spectator stands, and uniforms and stipends for the players. Mine superintendents would "trade" miners between various camps to ensure they had a championship team.

With the advent of the railway system, a professional national league developed where city teams could compete with one another despite long

The Granger Collection, New York

Engraving of a Baseball Game Between the Cincinnati Red Stockings and the Brooklyn Atlantics, 1870 This image captures the early years of baseball, in which professional teams would travel long distances in order to compete in front of ever increasing audiences. The rise in the popularity of baseball marked a moment when American workers began to have leisure time as well as extra money that they could spend to entertain themselves purely for pleasure. Baseball along with city parks, dances, and amusement parks like Coney Island provided public spaces for freedom and entertainment. ▲

National Photo Company Collection (Library of Congress)

Osaka Mairuchi Baseball Players Visit the White House, 1925 At the peak of the U.S.-Japanese trans-Pacific baseball exchange, the Osaka Mairuchi baseball players were invited to appear at the White House to visit with President Calvin Coolidge. ▲

Library of Congress Prints and Photographs Division, LC-USZC4-3227

Advertisement for Baseball Game, 1867 This poster advertised a match for the Cuban All Star Club team, which played in Havana. ▲

distances. In the 1870s, professional baseball was being played up and down the East Coast and across the Midwest. Blacks were allowed to play until 1888, when the league owners signed an agreement that imposed Jim Crow on baseball.

Black baseball leagues had been in existence since the Civil War and thrived alongside white teams, often playing them, even during the Jim Crow era. In 1887, the National Colored Baseball League, known as the Negro League, was formally founded. Meanwhile, baseball was also emerging as a national sport in Cuba. In 1889, the mixed-race team, the All Cubans, toured the United States playing both Negro-league and MLB teams. These leagues developed simultaneously and spread the sport throughout the Caribbean diaspora. Finally, in April of 1947, baseball was once again desegregated when the Brooklyn Dodgers signed and played Jackie Robinson.

During the same time period, Japan was also discovering the joys of playing baseball. In 1878, Hiroshi Hiraoka returned from his studies in the United States and introduced the game to his colleagues at the Japan national railways. In Japan, baseball was played predominately at the college level. Players were amateurs but trained with an intensive physical regimen. In 1905, the MLB in conjunction with Japanese baseball leaders organized a tour of Japanese players through the United States to play semi-pro and college teams. The group collaborated on these trans-Pacific exchanges until World War II. In 1934, Japan created its first professional baseball league, now known as the *Nippon Baseball League*.

Baseball has also been the place of some of the most important contract decisions in U.S. labor history. In 1969, Curtis Flood challenged his trade from the St. Louis Cardinals to the Philadelphia Phillies. The MLB had a reserve clause that forced a player to stay with his team throughout his career, and only the team's management could decide where a player could play. Flood's case went all the way to the Supreme Court where he lost. However, it shed light on the labor of baseball players who, through their union, won the right of free agency and the ability to leave a team at the end of their contracts.

Critical Thinking Questions

▶ What aspects of baseball have made it such a globally accepted game?

▶ How did the development of baseball reflect the contemporary attitudes about nationalism and racism?

Industrial Violence and the Rise of Unions

This cover from Frank Leslie's *Illustrated* in July 1892 depicted one of the nation's most violent strikes in Homestead, Pennsylvania, which pitted the Amalgamated Association of Iron and Steel workers against the Carnegie Steel Company.

What is happening in this image? Why are women and children so prominently displayed? Does the illustration side with the workers or the company? ▶

Library of Congress Prints and Photographs Division[LC-US262-75205]

FRANK LESLIE'S ILLUSTRATED WEEKLY

NEW YORK, JULY 16, 1892.

THE LABOR TROUBLES AT HOMESTEAD, PENNSYLVANIA—ATTACK OF THE STRIKERS AND THEIR SYMPATHIZERS ON THE SURRENDERED PINKERTON MEN.

---

craft unions Organization whose members have the same craft or trade and that did not believe in organizing all workers.

The Second Industrial Revolution that drew people from the countryside to rapidly expanding cities also transformed their workplaces and relations with their employers. A large urban industrial labor force emerged in which strangers from different ethnicities, races, and nationalities, speaking different languages, labored shoulder to shoulder. This new work environment was not just diverse; it was also communal. This was very different from farm work that was usually done alone or with just a few family members.

This gathering of workers in urban factories enabled them to find common causes against their employers. Companies were stubbornly resistant, sometimes violently, to workers' demands. Emerging labor unions struggled for legal recognition. The courts constantly ordered unions to stop organizing workers and cease disrupting their workplaces with strikes and other forms of protest. High rates of immigration, high unemployment, and the erratic economy during the depressions of 1873 and 1893 created a "reserve army of workers" of desperate people willing to work at almost any wage. Although the surplus hurt labor organization, advocates worked tirelessly on behalf of the nation's industrial workers, forming the basis for the dynamic growth of the U.S. labor movement.

☞ As you read, consider why creating a strong union movement in the United States was so difficult. What challenges did they face? What benefits were accrued?

16-4a Transformation of Work

Prior to the Civil War, **craft unions** or guilds were the predominant form of work-based organizations. Shoemakers, typesetters, and workers in many other crafts labored alone or in small workshops, providing goods and services to local communities. These

{ Labor shifts from small-scale craft work to large-scale industrialized work.

workers rarely considered the condition of those not in their professional guild. Master craftsmen trained young people in a particular craft during a long apprenticeship. Most major cities had more than fifty craft unions. The craft system of production, however, collapsed with industrialization, which transformed the way work was done. Unskilled workers who had no training in a particular craft performed simple, repetitive, mechanized jobs that required little training and no apprenticeship.

Unskilled work was demanding and remade the ways that men, women, and their families organized their lives. Men worked in the large factories that had emerged during the Second Industrial Revolution. Women, who had been the early industrial workforce in the United States, working in the antebellum textile industry, were also drawn into these new settings in the form of sewing shops and textile factories. Children also worked in the new factories, since high school was not mandatory and there were as yet no protective labor laws to prevent them from being exploited. Industrial labor was repetitive, often boring, and in many cases, dangerous. The workday was long, sometimes up to twelve hours, with few, if any, breaks. In most cases, workers had Sunday off, and sometimes their bosses closed shops early on Saturday, so that there would be time for doing errands, enjoying leisure, and taking rest. Workers had no safety net if they were fired, had their hours or pay reduced, or suffered injuries or extended illness. Employers could fire workers without hesitation and replace them from the reserve army of workers in the labor market.

Factory owners looked not only for low-wage workers but also for methods to boost their productivity, which was measured by the time it took to make goods at a set quality level. In the 1880s, Frederick Taylor decided not to attend Harvard College but to apprentice himself as a patternmaker. He observed his fellow laborers' work inefficiencies that cost the company both time and money. As Taylor worked his way up to become a foreman, he experimented with a wide variety of ways to increase laborers' productivity through a system that became known as **scientific management**, or Taylorism. His careful studies, the most famous of which broke down worker movements into discrete and timed tasks, became the basis of new work routines that greatly increased production across industries.

Although highly profitable for business owners, scientific management increased the pace of work and reduced any control that workers had over their labor. To raise profits, capitalists sought to keep wages low, the workday long, and the workplace devoid of expensive safety precautions. In the face of these working conditions, unions emerged in industrialized nations around the world. Treated like expendable cogs in the wheels of industrial profit, workers responded by turning to labor unions that negotiated for better wages, hours, and work conditions. Strikes, which were illegal at the time, were among the few tools that gave workers leverage against owners. U.S. labor leaders drew inspiration from British and European intellectuals and working-class reformers.

Three ideologies imported from across the Atlantic gained particular hold among U.S. workers. **Anarchism**, a broad set of radical ideas that pushed for a stateless society in which workers would govern themselves and not be subject to profit-seeking capitalists, appealed to the most radical workers. **Syndicalism**, which was associated with anarchism, advocated that workers organize themselves into small confederations and resist state power and the capitalist class. **Socialism**, in opposition to the other two ideologies, called for the state to cooperatively own industries and manage them collectively. First in Paris and then in London, the German émigré Karl Marx with Friedrich Engels developed widely influential theories about the role of economics and the class conflicts in world historical development. Engels published *Das Kapital, Volume II* espousing those theories. Many European immigrants were exposed to anarchist, syndicalist, and socialist ideas in their homelands and provided a key constituency for radical movements in the United States. With the exception of socialism, however, radical alternatives to capitalism did not win a mass following, and most Americans remained wedded to democratic and republican ideals.

16-4b Knights of Labor

The first nationwide confrontation between labor and capital came during the Great Railroad Strike of 1877. In the wake of the Panic of 1873 and the Hayes-Tilden contested presidential election of 1876, tensions ran high as Americans struggled financially and were uneasy about the partisan conflict that had wracked the Union. Since 1874, there had been strikes and labor violence throughout the country as the depression caused businesses to reduce workers' hours, cut wages, and ultimately lay off employees. At least eighteen thousand companies failed during the depression, including 89 percent of the nation's 364 railroad firms. In July 1877, workers at the Baltimore and Ohio (B&O) railroad in Martinsburg, West Virginia, went on strike spurred by the third in a series of pay cuts. B&O workers in Maryland stopped working and joined the West Virginians in the strike. The shipping of freight across the country came to a halt as newly elected President Rutherford B. Hayes called in the U.S. military to protect the nation from "insurrection." In Baltimore, federal troops fired on a crowd of protestors, killing eleven and leaving forty injured (see Map 16.3).

> The labor movement becomes a national economic and political force.

Hayes's heavy-handed response enraged workers and the public at large. Within weeks, the strike spread to railroad workers in Pennsylvania, Illinois, and Missouri. The peak of violence occurred in Pittsburgh where federal troops opened fire on strikers and their families, killing twenty people, including one woman and three small children. As news of the deaths spread through the town, Pittsburgh was thrown into turmoil. Striking workers set the Pennsylvania Railroad on fire. By morning, the roundhouse was burned to the ground, and twenty residents and five soldiers lay dead. In just over twenty-four hours, almost forty people had been killed in Pittsburgh.

After forty-five days, the Great Railroad Strike ended without any tangible gains for the workers. Yet it revealed the ability of unions to reach across local and state regions in their labor disputes. It also generated deep concerns about the threat of labor cooperation to the nation's economy among government officials and the U.S. public in general. Some worried that ideas from European labor movements, particularly the **Paris Commune of 1871**, a brief takeover of the French government by anarchists, would spread to the United States. Consequently, much of the nativist rhetoric against immigrants often focused on labor movements as conduits for the influx of radical ideas about politics and labor rights.

scientific management System driven by efficiency concerns intended to increase labor productivity.

anarchism Political theory that advocates a stateless society governed by independent and autonomous communities.

syndicalism Political theory associated with anarchism that advocated organizing governments around syndicates or confederations rather than a central government.

socialism Political theory that called for the state to cooperatively own the means of production and manage the economy for the benefit of all citizens.

Paris Commune of 1871 Revolutionary socialist action against the government in France whose success many Americans feared.

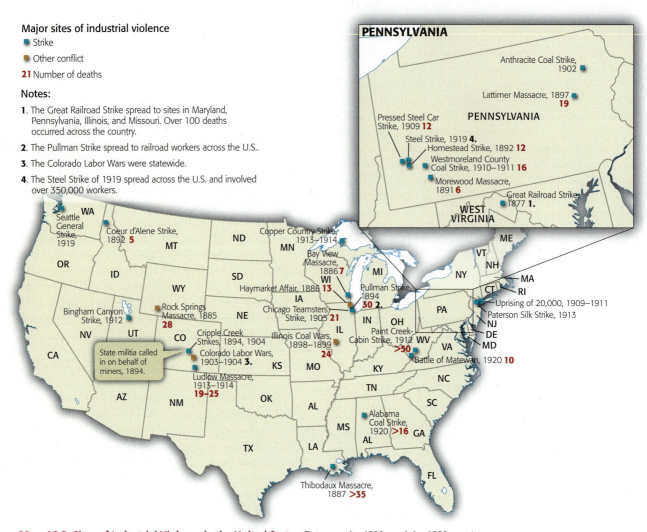

Major sites of industrial violence
- 🟦 Strike
- 🟫 Other conflict
- **21** Number of deaths

Notes:

1. The Great Railroad Strike spread to sites in Maryland, Pennsylvania, Illinois, and Missouri. Over 100 deaths occurred across the country.

2. The Pullman Strike spread to railroad workers across the U.S..

3. The Colorado Labor Wars were statewide.

4. The Steel Strike of 1919 spread across the U.S. and involved over 350,000 workers.

PENNSYLVANIA

Anthracite Coal Strike, 1902
Lattimer Massacre, 1897 **19**
Pressed Steel Car Strike, 1909 **12**
Steel Strike, 1919 **4.**
Homestead Strike, 1892 **12**
Westmoreland County Coal Strike, 1910–1911 **16**
Morewood Massacre, 1891 **6**
Great Railroad Strike 1877 **1.**
WEST VIRGINIA

Seattle General Strike, 1919
Coeur d'Alene Strike, 1892 **5**
Copper Country Strike, 1913–1914
Bay View Massacre, 1886 **7**
Haymarket Affair, 1886 **13**
Pullman Strike, 1894 **30 2.**
Bingham Canyon Strike, 1912
Rock Springs Massacre, 1885 **28**
Chicago Teamsters Strike, 1905 **21**
State militia called in on behalf of miners, 1894.
Cripple Creek Strikes, 1894, 1904
Colorado Labor Wars, 1903–1904 **3.**
Illinois Coal Wars, 1898–1899 **24**
Paint Creek-Cabin Strike, 1912 **>50**
Uprising of 20,000, 1909–1911
Paterson Silk Strike, 1913
Battle of Matewan, 1920 **10**
Ludlow Massacre, 1913–1914 **19–25**
Alabama Coal Strike, 1920 **>16**
Thibodaux Massacre, 1887 **>35**

Map 16.3 Sites of Industrial Violence in the United States Between the 1890s and the 1920s, major—and often violent—labor conflicts erupted throughout the United State's industrial centers. These strikes and uprisings attained only limited reforms. ▲

One of the most successful labor unions in the late nineteenth century was the Knights of Labor, first founded in Philadelphia in 1869. (It was also the first union that Mother Jones joined.) The Knights' power and membership increased significantly under the dynamic leadership of Terence V. Powderly, who became the union's grand master workman in 1879. Under Powderly, the union organized workers regardless of race, gender, nationality, occupation, or skill level, which was in direct contrast to craft unions. At the same time, the Knights were not beyond pushing Congress to exclude Italian, Hungarian, and especially Chinese immigrants.

The power and influence of the Knights continued through the early 1880s and peaked in 1886. That year, the union boasted almost a million workers as it advocated for better wages and safer working conditions. The Knights also joined the nationwide push to shorten the workday to eight hours, which would have given workers more rest and free time outside the rigidly controlled workplaces.

The union used the slogan "Eight Hours for What We Will." U.S. workers did not want to be "wage slaves" to capitalist employers.

The struggle over the eight-hour day came to a peak in Chicago in May 1886. On May 1, Albert Parsons, a leading labor and anarchist thinker, and his wife Lucy Parsons led a group of eighty thousand marchers through the streets of Chicago demanding the eight-hour workday. The demonstration was without incident. But two days later, when the protesters gathered in Haymarket Square outside the McCormick Reaper Works, violence broke out when police beat workers and fatally shot two men. Protesting the killings, Albert Spies, editor of a local working-class newspaper, called for a gathering on Haymarket Square the following night. The crowd was relatively small, but as people were leaving, a bomb exploded, killing seven policeman and four civilians. In the violence that ensued, dozens were injured.

In the aftermath of the Haymarket bombings, the police arrested eight anarchists including Spies and

Battle after the Explosion of a Bomb at Haymarket Square, Chicago, May 4, 1886 This image appeared in a Chicago newspaper just days after the violence in Haymarket Square. Note how the engraving conveys the sense of confusion and chaos. The Haymarket bombing was a turning point for labor organizing in the United States, as the Knights of Labor, although they had nothing to do with the bombing, came to be viewed by the American public as too radical. Not until the Industrial Workers of the World (IWW) emerged in 1905 was there such a broadly based union moement. ◄

Archive Photos/Getty Images

Parsons on charges of conspiracy to commit murder. After a trial in which no evidence was presented that linked the eight men to the actual bomb, they were all convicted and sentenced to death. Four of them, including Spies and Parsons, were hanged and one committed suicide. But, in 1893, the governor of Illinois pardoned the remaining three men.

Although there was significant doubt about the guilt of the accused Haymarket bombers, the damage had been done. The radical labor movement, symbolized by the Knights of Labor, became unpopular. Americans refused to embrace a labor movement that could turn violent and seemingly had ties to radical Communist, anarchist, and even socialist political views, all of which seemed foreign and un-American. The United States had little room for a union movement that was not enmeshed in the republican and democratic principles of the nation. Any hint of European radical influence doomed any labor organization.

Local, state, and federal government stepped up their efforts to suppress labor agitation by increasing local police forces, state militias, and national guard units. Business owners responded by opposing the eight-hour-a-day movement and hiring private police forces such as the **Pinkerton Detective Agency** to undermine labor organizing. Reaction to the Haymarket bombing resulted in antilabor, anti-immigrant, and anti-Communist rhetoric that was often associated with critiques of the working classes. Even though the Knights of Labor denounced the use of violence and disassociated themselves from Parsons and the others, the union suffered from anti-union efforts, and its numbers declined radically. By 1890, the Knights' membership had plummeted from almost 1 million in the 1870s to one hundred thousand.

16-4c Age of Strikes

Into the void left by the collapse of the Knights of Labor stepped the American Federation of Labor (AFL). Founded in 1886 by Samuel Gompers,

> Labor conflict continues and peaks through a series of new strikes.

an English-born cigar maker, it was the umbrella organization for numerous craft unions of skilled workers. Gompers distrusted government officials, who, he argued, served the interests of capitalists through legislation, tax breaks, the use of federal troops, and, most troublesome, court injunctions against strikes. A much more conservative union than the Knights, the AFL divided, rather than united, workers across trades, skill levels, and races. It excluded blacks, Chinese, and other nonwhite workers from its ranks and never organized women. The AFL was not interested in creating one big union to revolutionize society, choosing instead to advocate only for the "bread and butter" issues for the benefit of its own members. This type of conservative unionism was known as **business unionism**. The AFL was not opposed to going on strike and challenging the capitalist system to improve wages and work conditions, but it rejected radical ideas about overthrowing the capitalist system or establishing a worker's democracy that displaced business owners.

The true test of the AFL's power came in 1892 at Andrew Carnegie's Homestead Steel Works in Pittsburgh. The Amalgamated Association of Iron and Steel Workers (the Amalgamated) was a powerful union that three years earlier had secured wages that were one-third higher than the

Pinkerton Detective Agency Private agency hired by corporations to break strikes and intimidate workers.

business unionism A nonradical form of unionism that did not advocate socialist takeover but believed that unions should be run as business enterprises.

prevailing wages in the industry and increased the wages of nonunionized unskilled workers. From Amalgamated's perspective, the labor situation at Homestead was the best that workers could expect: work in a thriving industry, a fair and steady wage, and an owner who was known for his more enlightened ("Gospel of Wealth"), if paternalistic, thinking about giving workers opportunities to raise their standard of living. Despite this seemingly ideal situation, Carnegie and his associate Henry Clay Frick were not willing to share decision-making power with the Amalgamated by engaging in collective bargaining. In June 1892, as Carnegie headed to his summer estate in Scotland, he empowered Frick to break the union at Homestead.

Frick canceled contract renewal negotiations with the Amalgamated, declaring that he would negotiate only with individual workers. He then hired three hundred Pinkerton agents to patrol the mill's perimeter, which he had lined with three miles of twelve-foot steel fence topped with barbed wire. The workers labeled the mill Fort Frick. On July 2, Frick locked out the workers, closed the mill, and stated that he would reopen it with nonunionized labor. The Amalgamated, which was part of a tight-knit community in Pittsburgh, mobilized the entire town against Frick, barring strikebreakers and resources from entering or exiting the mill. Frick reacted by sending heavily armed Pinkertons who arrived on barges from the river to take over the mill. In the twelve-hour battle that ensued, nine strikers and three Pinkerton agents were killed. Scores more were injured when the strikers' families fought back against the Pinkertons, who eventually surrendered.

The win at Homestead was short lived because Frick, with the aid of the Pennsylvania militia, by November 1892 had secured the mill and resumed production without union labor. By Christmas of that year, the union had surrendered to the inevitable. Frick cabled Carnegie: "Our Victory is now complete and more gratifying. Do not think we will ever have any serious labor trouble again." The defeat was devastating to not only the Homestead community but also the national labor movement (see Table 16.2). What chance did other smaller, less-organized, and poorly funded unions have against corporations such as Carnegie Steel if Amalgamated could not stand up to them?

The American Railway Union (ARU) under the leadership of Eugene V. Debs built itself on the base of the Knights of Labor. In 1893, it was the fastest-growing union with increasing political power. The ARU's opportunity came when workers at the Pullman Palace Car Company struck. Pullman was well known for its **company town** just south of Chicago that housed its workers and their families in a controlled environment that included curfews and payment of goods from company-owned stores in company scrip, not cash. Although some people admired the high quality of housing and schooling for children, many workers resented the company's oversight on their lives. One worker complained, "We are

company town Community whose land and houses where workers lived as well as its businesses and roads were owned by a corporation that had workers under constant surveillance.

Table 16.2 Selected Unions Worldwide, to 1925

As indicated in this table, the drive to unionize workers was a global movement throughout the nineteenth and early twentieth centuries. Early unions, such as the Stonemasons in Australia and the guilds in the United States, organized according to the type of work. Later unions, beginning with the Knights of Labor and Great Britain's International Workingmen's Association, were organized regardless of type of work and coalesced around ideas of a laboring class that opposed the capitalist class and management. Leaders in labor unions across the globe were in contact and shared ideas and tactics about how to advance labor's cause.

Year	Country	Name
1855	Australia	Stonemasons Society
1864	Great Britain	International Workingmen's Association
1869	United States	Knights of Labor
1886	United States	American Federation of Labor
1890	United States	United Mine Workers of America
1892	Germany	Generalkommission der Gewerkschaften Deutschlands
1893	United States	American Railway Workers Union
1897	Japan	Metalworkers Union
1900	United States	International Ladies Garment Workers Union
1905	United States	International Workers of the World
1925	China	All-China Federation of Trade Unions

born in a Pullman house, fed from the Pullman shop, taught in the Pullman school, catechized in the Pullman church, and when we die we shall be buried in the Pullman cemetery and go to the Pullman hell." In April 1894, George Pullman, in response to global depression, laid off 33 percent of his workforce and reduced wages by 25 to 40 percent for those fortunate enough to retain their jobs. However, he did not reduce the rents or the prices charged at the company store. Workers responded by going on strike. They asked the ARU to support them and in response, its leader Debs asked that railway workers nationwide refuse to handle any trains that had Pullman cars. More than a quarter of a million workers across the nation complied and practically stopped train traffic.

The railroad companies responded by getting a federal court injunction against the ARU for impairing interstate delivery of mail, which effectively outlawed the strike. Debs went to jail for six months for ignoring the injunction, and the U.S. Supreme Court ruled in the 1895 case, *In re Debs*, that the federal government did indeed possess the power to regulate interstate commerce by ordering the ARU to call off the strike. Labor unionists then had a deep distrust of the federal government. It seemed to them that both the executive and judicial branches were willing to bend the law to destroy unions. By July, federal troops backed by U.S. marshals, state militias, and local governments began attacking the Pullman strikers. In mid-July, violence erupted in twenty-six states, practically making the strike a war between workers and capitalist interests. The Depression of 1893, combined with

The Kheel Center for Labor-Management Documentation and Archives int he ILR School at Cornell University

Global Americans In 1903, seventeen-year-old **Clara Lemlich** and her family fled a Ukrainian pogrom and immigrated to the United States. She grew up speaking Yiddish, a Germanic language written in Hebrew, but taught herself to read Russian and became well read in radical and revolutionary literature. By the time she immigrated to New York, she was a committed socialist. She eventually joined the U.S. Communist Party.

In New York, her family settled in the Lower East Side, and she quickly found work in one of the shirtwaist factories as a seamstress. She became involved in labor, joined the International Ladies Garment Workers Union (ILGWU), and was elected to its executive board. She was a vigorous and fearless leader. After a strike in 1909 when she had been beaten by police, suffering two broken ribs, she was arrested but returned the next day to the picket line.

In November 1909, thousands of shirtwaist workers and supporters gathered at The Cooper Union to discuss striking. After listening to the American Federation of Labor (AFL) leader speak, Lemlich was literally lifted to the stage and stated, "I have listened to all the speakers, and I have no further patience for talk. I am a working girl, one of those striking against intolerable conditions. I am tired of listening to speakers who talk in generalities. What we are here for is to decide whether or not to strike. I make a motion that we go out in a general strike." The crowd responded enthusiastically to call the strike, which became known as the Uprising of the Twenty Thousand.

changing technologies that allowed companies to reduce their labor force and the overwhelming tendency of state governments to side with businesses, hampered labor's ability to obtain reform.

By the turn of the century, as more women entered the workforce, they began to form their own unions and fight their own battles to secure safer conditions and higher wages. A coalition of women garment workers, most of whom were recent immigrants from southern Europe and Russia and many of whom were Jewish, founded the International Ladies Garment Workers Union (ILGWU) in 1900. All of these women, regardless of their background, worked in extremely difficult and unsafe conditions. They often brought their experiences with trade unionism and socialism from their home countries. In 1903, the Women's Trade Union League (WTUL), which had been founded in Great Britain thirty years earlier, was started in the United States as an affiliate of the AFL. The WTUL was often considered the more conservative of the two unions, but together they led the largest and most successful strikes.

The unions slowly gained membership but did not grow rapidly until 1909 when a general strike swept New York City. The workers were responding to protests by garment workers at the Triangle Shirtwaist Factory. A young Jewish activist, Clara Lemlich, spoke to a packed house at The Cooper Union and called for a general strike of garment workers. More than twenty thousand workers heeded her call and walked off their jobs for more than fourteen weeks. The long conflict was difficult because the police brutalized the strikers and arrested them. The brutality eased only when the **mink brigade**, a group of wealthy and middle-class women who included Anne Morgan, the daughter of banking magnate J.P. Morgan,

and Frances Perkins, joined the picket line. The strike resulted in a contract for the unionized workers. One of the few holdouts was the Triangle Shirtwaist Company, which refused to sign a union contract.

A little more than a year later, the Triangle Shirtwaist Company was again the center of labor agitation. On a beautiful spring afternoon, a fire broke out on the ninth floor of the building. The flames spread so rapidly that few of the women were able to escape. Dozens of them died when they jumped from the windows to the pavement as horrified onlookers watched, unable to help. Within an hour, 146 people died, 123 of whom were women. The youngest victims were fourteen years old. It became known later that the women had been locked into the shop, which was a common practice meant to keep workers from taking breaks. The next week, in one of the largest parades in the city's history, New Yorkers mourned the workers' deaths and agitated for reform. In response to the tragedy, New York City created a committee on public safety and passed laws to protect workers and improve building conditions.

mink brigade Upper-class New York women reformers who joined striking shirtwaist workers during the Uprising of the Twenty Thousand.

16-4d Labor Organization in the West

Organizing labor in the West had its own particular challenges and opportunities because of its geographical isolation and the lack of industrial development

Western labor unions concentrate on mining.

company unions Organization established by a company to represent workers in labor disputes and contract negotiations.

in mining. That business required a concentration of capital, which made attracting and keeping labor much more difficult than in the Northeast. Although labor radicalism was declining there and in the Midwest, it had a stronger following in the West where the IWW, led by Big Bill Haywood and Joe Hill, pushed the radical idea of creating "one big union" to represent all workers regardless of skill level, race, ethnicity, or gender. Although the IWW was considered the most radical of all unions, its message appealed to many of the rank and file workers in the western extractive industries. Unlike the AFL, the IWW and its less radical counterpart in the West, the United Mine Workers of America (UMWA), pushed for a broad coalition of workers that included African Americans in the South and Mexican Americans in the West.

The UMWA created a coalition of skilled and unskilled laborers from all over the world. By 1910, it had organized almost one-third of all miners across the United States, which had been a herculean task given the scope of workers involved. Tensions between mine owners and workers ran high throughout the turn of the century in places such as Bingham Canyon, Utah, and Cripple Creek, Colorado, but the conflict climaxed in Ludlow, Colorado, in 1913.

John D. Rockefeller's Colorado Fuel and Iron Company (CF&I) had resisted union organization throughout the early part of the twentieth century. Despite CF&I's best efforts, the UMWA under the leadership of John R. Lawson and Mother Jones launched a successful union organizational drive and called a strike against Rockefeller's network of coal mines throughout Colorado, New Mexico, and Wyoming. The UMWA also shut down his Minnequa Steel works in Pueblo, Colorado. In retaliation, Rockefeller's managers in Colorado evicted workers and their families from their homes in the middle of winter. The UMWA then leased a piece of land at Ludlow to set up a tent colony for the displaced workers, who continued the strike.

On a cold April morning in 1914, a coalition of company men, Pinkerton agents, and the Colorado national guard surrounded the tent encampment. An armed battle ensued throughout the day, and a fire swept through the worker's temporary homes. The fire killed eighteen women and children. The nation was outraged at the site of dead women and children who had been cowering in a dug-out cellar trying to escape the violence. CF&I and the Rockefeller family in particular were vilified, which prompted Congress to scrutinize the family and its labor practices. Although no major legislation came out of the tragedy, Rockefeller pushed fellow business leaders such as Henry Ford and E.I. DuPont to reconsider the relationship between labor and capital. They implemented **company unions** and reforms to improve working conditions for their employees and living conditions for their families while maintaining paternalist control and denying workers the right to engage in collective bargaining.

Summary

The late nineteenth and early twentieth centuries were transformative periods for U.S. workers and their families. Fueled by technological changes and unprecedented access to capital investment, the economy grew dramatically but did not favor everyone equally. Industrialization led to class divisions and inequality that were only exacerbated by the harsh global depressions in the 1870s and the 1890s during which millions lost their jobs.

All Americans felt the impact of economic growth, whether they stayed on farms and met increased demands for their products brought on by urbanization or moved to the cities. Meanwhile, tens of millions of immigrants from around the world chose the United States as their destination. Europeans, Latin Americans, and, to a lesser extent, Asians (whose journeys were cut short by race-based exclusionary laws) immigrated and made the nation's population one of the most diverse collections of peoples ever. The immigrants and internal migrants from the countryside met in urban neighborhoods, workplaces, and entertainment halls and—through their often unsettling and sometimes violent encounters—created a new idea of what it meant to be an American.

This comingling of people and ideas reordered individuals' relationships with their fellow workers, bosses, physical work, and home spaces. At the end of the nineteenth century, union activity increased, and some of the most violent strikes in U.S. history occurred but attained only limited reforms.

<Thinking Back, *Looking Forward* >

As you review this chapter, compare the nature and impact of the nation's Second Industrial Revolution with its first one in the nineteenth century. What new technologies emerged later in the century, and how did they transform the global economy and U.S. labor relations? Thinking back to Chapter 15, how did the development of the U.S. West impact the development of cities? How did industrialization create a common bond or experience across the nation, and how did it extend these bonds across the world? In the next chapter, look for ways in which progressive reformers sought to moderate the inequalities wrought by industrialization.

To make your study complete, review the timeline and reflect on the entries there. Think about their causes, consequences, and connections. How do they fit with global trends?

Additional Resources

Books

Andrews, Thomas G. *Killing for Coal: America's Deadliest Labor War*. Cambridge, MA: Harvard University Press, 2010. ▶ Environmental and labor history of the Colorado coal fields that culminated in the tragedy at Ludlow.

Beckert, Sven. *Monied Metropolis: New York City and the Consolidation of the American Bourgeoisie, 1850–1896*. New York: Cambridge Press, 2001. ▶ Analysis of the development of class divisions and status in New York.

Brands, H. W. *American Colossus: The Triumph of Capitalism, 1865–1900*. New York: Anchor Press, 2010. ▶ Popular narrative of the period with a gripping style that brings this period to life.

Gorn, Elliott J. *Mother Jones: The Most Dangerous Woman in America*. New York: Hill and Wang, 2001. ▶ Definitive biography of this labor activist whose career spanned decades.

Levy, Jonathan. *Freaks of Fortune: The Emerging World of Capitalism and Risk in America*. Cambridge, MA: Harvard University Press, 2012. ▶ A sweeping narrative about nineteenth-century capitalism and the development of the idea of risk and how to mitigate it.

Orleck, Annelise. *Common Sense and a Little Fire: Women and Working Class Politics in the United States*. Charlotte: University of North Carolina Press, 1995. ▶ Classic book about the power of women's political and labor organizing in this period.

Montgomery, David. *The Fall of the House of Labor: The Workplace, the State, and American Labor Activism, 1865–1925*. New Haven, CT: Yale Press, 1988. ▶ Still the definitive examination of the rise and fall of U.S. labor movements prior to the New Deal.

Peiss, Kathy. *Cheap Amusements: Working Women and Leisure in Turn-of-the-Century New York*. Philadelphia: Temple Press, 1986. ▶ Narrative about New York City leisure practices among the city's working classes.

Stilgoe, John R. *Borderland: Origins of the American Suburb, 1820–1939*. New Haven, CT: Yale University Press, 1989. ▶ Theoretical and historical look at how the earliest U.S. suburbs developed amid growing urbanization.

> Go to the MindTap® for **Global Americans** to access the full version of select books from this Additional Resources section.

Websites

Gilder Lehrman Institute of American History. https://www.gilderlehrman.org ▶ Excellent repository of documents and analytical essays about U.S. history.

Illinois Labor History Society. http://www.illinoislaborhistory.org/resources.html ▶ Exploration of Illinois' labor history.

Museum of Chinese in America. http://www.mocanyc.org/collections ▶ Comprehensive collection that covers the experiences of Chinese immigrants to the United States.

The Statue of Liberty—Ellis Island Foundation, Inc. http://www.libertyellisfoundation.org/passenger ▶ Exploration of more than 51 million passenger records of immigrants who passed through Ellis Island.

Continue exploring online through MindTap®, where you can:
- **Assess your knowledge with the Chapter Test**
- **Watch historical videos related to the chapter**
- **Further your understanding with interactive maps and timelines**

The Making of Industrial America

1869–1875

December 1869

Knights of Labor is founded.

March 1871

Paris Commune comes to power.

June 1871

Charles Darwin's *Descent of Man* is published.

October 1871

Great Chicago Fire destroys most of the city.

August 1875

Andrew Carnegie introduces Bessemer steel process in United States.

1876–1882

July 1877

Great Railway Strike begins.

November 1879

Thomas Edison is issued patent for incandescent bulb.

May 1882

Congress passes the Chinese Exclusion Act.

July 1882

Chinese Consolidated Benevolent Association is founded.

December 1882

First electrical plant in New York City opens.

1883–1884

May 1883

Brooklyn Bridge is completed.

October 1883

Metropolitan Opera House opens in New York City.

1885

February

Congress passes the Alien Contract Labor Law.

May

Friedrich Engels publishes *Das Kapital, Volume II* from Karl Marx's notes.

September

Anti-Chinese riot breaks out at Rock Springs, Wyoming.

First YMCA opens in New Jersey.

1886–1889

January 1886

Karl Benz patents first gasoline-powered automobile.

May 1886

Haymarket Riots erupt in Chicago.

American Federation of Labor is founded.

June 1889

Andrew Carnegie publishes "The Gospel of Wealth."

Britain
France
Germany
United States
China

1890–1892

July 1890
New Croton Aqueduct for New York City is completed.

October 1890
Louisiana state legislature passes Separate Car Act.

December 1890
First sewage system in United States opens in Worcester, Massachusetts.

January 1892
Ellis Island in New York harbor opens to immigrants.

May 1892
John Muir founds the Sierra Club in San Francisco.

June 1892
Workers strike against Carnegie at Homestead Steel Works.

1893–1896

May 1894
Railway workers nationwide begin Pullman Strike.

May 1895
Supreme Court issues decision for *In re Debs.*

May 1896
Supreme Court issues decision for *Plessy v. Ferguson.*

July 1896
Mercedes Benz begins production of its automobile.

1897–1900

September 1897
First subway in Boston opens for operation.

June 1900
International Ladies Garment Workers Union (ILGWU) founded in New York City.

November 1900
Paris World's Fair opens to an international crowd.

1901–1909

November 1903
Women's Trade Union League (WTUL) is founded.

August 1906
San Francisco earthquake sets off a massive fire.

November 1909
Twenty thousand shirtwaist workers strike in New York City in what becomes known as the Uprising.

1910–1914

January 1910
Angel Island opens as immigration processing center in San Francisco.

March 1911
Triangle Shirtwaist Factory fire occurs.

April 1914
Ludlow Massacre occurs at Rockefeller's coal mine in Colorado.

Go to MindTap® to engage with an interactive version of the timeline. Analyze events and themes with clickable content, view related videos, and respond to critical thinking questions.

17 Politics of Reform

1877–1917

After his wife Alice died in childbirth, Roosevelt headed to the American West to recover. His time in Dakota Territory transformed him, and throughout his life Roosevelt would turn to the wilderness for clarity and work for its preservation.

Theodore (Teddy) Roosevelt and his brother Elliott hung out the window that overlooked Union Square in New York City and watched the flag-draped casket of President Abraham Lincoln followed by the Invalid Brigade pass beneath their window. The Invalid Brigade, Civil War veterans who had been maimed in the war, particularly touched six-year-old Teddy. He revered those veterans with "the empty sleeve" who had given a part of themselves to save the Union. Teddy was a weak child who suffered from asthma; his mother remembered that he loved to dress up as a wounded soldier and play that he had lost his arm in glorious battle.

The Granger Collection, New York

After attending Harvard and marrying, Theodore Roosevelt was elected as the youngest member of the New York State Assembly and served three terms. He sponsored a bill, backed by the Cigar Makers Union, which regulated the manufacturing of cigars in homes because of the poor living conditions in tenements. The bill passed but was struck down by the New York courts. "It was this case which first waked me to [social] injustices," Roosevelt wrote, "and the Courts were not the best judges . . . they knew legalisms, but not life." From his early career, he pushed for reform.

While he was an assemblyman, however, tragedy struck. In the course of twenty-four hours, he became a new father, a widower, and an orphan. His wife Alice died in childbirth and his mother died of typhoid fever. Roosevelt sent his daughter to live with his sister, put the family house up for sale, and headed to the American West to recover. Throughout his life, the wilderness would be a space where he would find clarity, and its preservation became a top priority during his presidency. His experience in Dakota Territory transformed him. Returning east, he married again and began a long political career during which he spread his belief that an activist government should be a positive force in its citizens' lives.

Roosevelt's faith in an activist government entered mainstream U.S. political thought in the early years of the twentieth century. Decades earlier, European reformers and politicians had begun to use the power of government to address economic inequalities and dangerous working and living conditions wrought by industrial capitalism. Since the 1870s, cities such as London, Glasgow, and Berlin had used municipal government and scientific expertise to solve their infrastructure needs through sanitation, expansion of utilities, and centralized city planning. Roosevelt combined ideas about reform at home with a vision of America's place in the world. When he called the United States the "most belated of nations" in 1907 for not adopting European-style workers' compensation, he worried that Americans were falling behind in a world that was expanding government's role and adopting reforms to solve societal ills.

> Teddy Roosevelt believed that an activist government should be a positive force in its citizens' lives. How would these ideas, and the European models they were inspired by, come to transform political thought and actions at the turn of the century?
>
> Go to MindTap® to watch a video on Roosevelt and learn how his story relates to the themes of this chapter.

Germany had passed workmen's compensation laws in 1884, Austria in 1887, and Britain in 1897. Given the industrial violence and hardship that U.S. workers faced, looking to such nations for models of reform and humane alternatives to class warfare made sense.

17-1
Party System in an Industrial Age

This 1874 Thomas Nast illustration shows a braying ass (which represents the Democratic Party) in a lion's coat with a *New York Herald* collar frightening other animals in the forest. A giraffe (*New York Tribune*), a unicorn (*New York Times*), and an owl (*New York World*) represent other politically partisan newspapers. An elephant (which represents the Republican Party) stands near broken planks "Inflation" and "Reconstruction" over a pit labeled "Southern Claims. Chaos, Rum."

What does this cartoon suggest about the nature of partisan politics in the Reconstruction era? What was the role of newspapers, as suggested by Nast, in their political debates? ▶

Library of Congress Prints and Photographs Division [LC-DIG-ppmsca-15785]

During the late nineteenth century, politics and business were inextricably bound as government at all levels aided businessmen to secure financing (on railroads), suppress worker unrest (in Homestead and Ludlow), and pass business-friendly legislation. Many reformers and the general public complained about and worked to reform this cozy relationship at both the state and national levels. One of the most striking aspects of politics since the end of Reconstruction in 1877 had been how evenly balanced the two major parties were. The Republicans held the presidency for three terms and the Democrats for two. Presidents rarely had the luxury of their party having a majority in both the House and the Senate. The result was general stagnation in national governance, which provided an opening for reformers and third-party movements to push for changes.

☞ As you read, consider the sources of political stagnation. How did it affect different groups of Americans?

17-1a Big Business and Government

As a result of the government's laissez-faire economic policies and expanding global markets, business magnates gained tremendous wealth during this

{ Governments are unwilling to regulate businesses because of their close relationship to them.

period. A market that lacked oversight or regulation from local, state, or federal government agencies made this possible. Business leaders were eager to protect their gains and keep a cooperative government in place. Few government officials, and certainly no private citizens, had the power to curb the dominance over the consolidated corporations on the U.S. economy and political arena.

A wealthy class intent on preserving its own power dominated government at all levels. Businessmen made alliances with state and federal officials who could protect their interests and defend them against the rising tide of reform that began to sweep the nation in the 1890s. For example, John D. Rockefeller Jr., the heir to his father's vast fortune as the head of Standard Oil, married Abby Aldrich, the daughter of Senator Nelson Aldrich and sister to Congressman Richard Aldrich. Senator Aldrich and his cohort of Republicans were known for their ties to business and fierce protection of those interests. Businessmen such as J.P Morgan and Jay Gould were disappointed when Theodore Roosevelt turned out to be such a progressive reformer during his presidency. His background and political pedigree made businessmen believe that he would protect their interests. When he began prosecuting Rockefeller for violating antitrust laws, however, Henry Clay Frick, Andrew Carnegie's business partner, complained, "We bought the son-of-a-bitch and then he didn't stay bought." They saw his reforms as treachery to their common class interests.

Roosevelt represented a new constituency in U.S. politics: college-educated, middle-class professionals calling for government by impartial experts rather than party bosses or capitalists. Often trained in new social sciences such as statistics, the new constituency called for a larger government role in controlling industry and a smaller role for party politicians in controlling government. While the ideal of these professionals was government by public-spirited experts, they were suspicious of popular politics that emphasized popularity over expertise and civic virtue. These people pressed for reforms to protect vulnerable groups such as workers and women. Their brand of moralistic, nonpartisan, expertise-based government would come to be called *Progressivism*, and Teddy Roosevelt would be their champion.

17-1b Party Loyalty and Ideology

From the end of Reconstruction until the 1896 presidential election, U.S. political parties emphasized group loyalty over ideology. This is not to say that

> Voters tend to make decisions based on party loyalty, not beliefs or issues.

each did not have a coherent program. In general, Republicans continued to promote the commercial and industrial development of the nation through governmental support for railroads and corporations. They also worked to protect the morals and customs of native-born evangelical Protestants. Republicans favored a high tariff to protect domestic manufactured goods from foreign competition, and they sponsored laws to forbid state aid to church (primarily Catholic) schools, to require English to be the primary language of instruction in all schools, and to ban alcoholic beverages (temperance). Democrats, in contrast, favored a more laissez-faire agenda. They advocated low tariffs to reduce prices for consumers, supported states' rights, and opposed any governmental aid to corporations. Democrats denounced the Republican program of moral legislation, such as temperance as a paternalistic invasion in people's lives, which they believed was biased toward a New England Protestant sensibility.

These political agendas, however, were not the primary political drivers. Voters made **standing decisions** to favor a party based on their ethnic and religious backgrounds more than on their policy stances (see Table 17.1). Brand Whitlock, mayor of Toledo from 1906–1914, remembered that belonging to the Republican Party in his community in Ohio was "not a matter of intellectual choice, it was a matter of biological selection," an "elemental" fact of life. Native-born Protestants, especially those descended from New Englanders in the Northeast and upper Midwest, voted consistently for Republicans. Irish Catholics and other immigrant groups tended to favor the Democrats, a party that had long mobilized them.

The **Solid South** was made up of the sixteen southern states and the District of Columbia, which consistently

Table 17.1 U.S. Party Affiliation by Religion, Late Nineteenth Century

Religion and political affiliations often mapped onto one another, and politicians and political movements exploited those connections. Regional attachments and immigration status also influenced political affiliations.

Religion	Democrat (%)	Republican (%)
Immigrant		
Irish Catholic	80	20
Total Catholic	70	30
German Lutheran	65	35
Norwegian Lutheran	20	80
British Protestant	35	65
Northern Native Born		
Quaker	5	95
Congregational	25	75
Methodist	25	75
Baptist	35	65
Presbyterian	40	60
Episcopal	45	55
Southern Native Born		
Disciples of Christ	50	50
Presbyterian	70	30
Baptist	75	25
Methodist	90	10

Source: Paul Kleppner, *The Third Electoral System, 1853–1892* (1979).

voted for the Democratic candidate in presidential elections between Reconstruction and World War I. New York and Ohio were swing states that could tilt either way. Consequently, an inordinate number of presidential nominees came from Ohio as party leaders sought an advantage there in the general election. Republican politicians "waved the bloody shirt" by recalling the wounds inflicted on Union soldiers by the Democrat-led Confederacy. Southern Democrats responded by warning that Republicans would destroy white supremacy with "black rule" as they allegedly had done during Reconstruction. These raw Civil War memories led Thomas Nast, the New York cartoonist, to portray the Democrats as a stubbornly rebellious donkey and Republicans as an elephant who never forgets—symbols about past history and regional loyalties rather than particular policy positions.

Because of these strong feelings, voter turnout was extraordinarily high until the end of the century, routinely bringing out 80 to 90 percent of eligible voters, meaning males in the North and West and, increasingly, only white males in the South. Competition between the two parties was so fierce that between 1877 and 1897, each party won undivided control of the national government only for two years (the Republicans,

standing decisions Political choice made by voters based on their family history and background rather than issues.

Solid South Block of sixteen southern states and the District of Columbia that consistently voted Democrat in national elections.

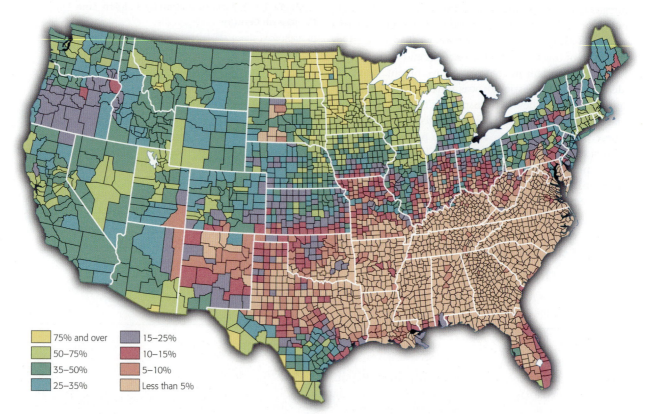

▢	75% and over	▢	15–25%
▢	50–75%	▢	10–15%
▢	35–50%	▢	5–10%
▢	25–35%	▢	Less than 5%

Map 17.1 Percentage of Foreign-Born People by County, 1910 Political parties paid close attention to the immigrant status of their constituencies and attempted to make political inroads with specific communities by meeting their particular political demands. Note the places where foreign-born people tended to concentrate. Obviously, cities like Los Angeles, Chicago, and Boston had high concentrations. However, rural areas such as the upper Midwest and the United States-Mexico borderland were also home to a majority of foreign-born populations. ▲

1889–1891 and the Democrats, 1891–1893). Between 1876 and 1892, no president received a majority of the popular vote. As a consequence, the entire executive branch tended to be weak and underfunded by Congress.

Voters' commitments to a party were not easily changed, so elections turned on mobilizing the party's supporters rather than changing undecided voters' minds. Parties relied heavily on professional organizers to whip up supporters' enthusiasm with spectacles such as torchlight parades, brass bands, bonfires, and campaign souvenirs, including clay pipes, ribbons, and matchboxes emblazoned with their candidate's image. Until the 1890s, there were no officially printed ballots, so voters simply filled out brightly colored ballots and handed them to party organizers at the polls, making it easy for party poll watchers to see how people had voted.

The organizational politics of parades and mass turnout cost time and money. Each party induced its supporters to contribute money and energy to campaigning with the lure

spoils system Political patronage system in which the winning party dismisses government workers and replaces them with its own loyal party members.

political machines Political organization, usually urban, that supports candidates who pushed its constituents' agenda.

of governmental jobs. Such "spoils" of electoral "war" required the winning party to fire thousands of incumbent civil servants and replace them with party loyalists. Under the **spoils system**, presidents spent much time handing out thousands of clerical jobs. Grover Cleveland and Benjamin Harrison each fired up to forty thousand post office employees, one of the few large organizations that the federal government operated, to make room for their own supporters. In return, the parties "assessed" jobholders a percentage, sometimes as much as 10 percent of their salaries, to hold their positions.

17-1c Voting and Disenfranchisement

For parties and politicians to protect their power, they had to control the electorate (see Map 17.1). In the growing northern industrial cities, **political machines** drew their power from appeals to recent immigrants, especially Catholics, whom

{ Political machines and discrimination limit democracy in the United States.

Protestant natives despised. Local ward bosses provided services to newly arrived immigrants, helping them to settle into their new lives. In return, they expected party loyalty and a high turnout on election day. William "Boss" Tweed's Tammany Hall in New York City was for a time the most successful political machine. Tweed was able to hand out patronage to loyal voters while making money for himself, actions satirized by cartoonists such as Thomas Nast, who looked for ways to curb the machines' influence.

In the rural South, disenfranchisement played a significant role in controlling the electorate. In the post-Reconstruction period in violation of the original intention of the Fifteenth Amendment, whites gradually stripped African American men of their right to vote by requiring measures such as paying a poll tax and meeting literacy requirements. Between 1890 and 1908, southern state legislatures passed new constitutions, amendments, and laws that made registration and voting more difficult for black citizens as well as many poor whites. In the U.S. West, Mexican Americans were also limited in participating in elections because of de facto practices and intimidation that kept them away from the polls.

At the federal level, Native Americans and Chinese immigrants were denied citizenship and therefore the right to vote. Because of the 1790 statute reserving citizenship to "free white persons," Chinese and other Asian immigrants could not become citizens and had no standing to vote regardless of how long they had lived in the United States. Numerous treaties and the Dawes Act had promised Native Americans a path toward citizenship once they had accommodated to U.S. culture, but enforcement was weak. The Fifteenth Amendment did not apply to Indians, and they were not granted citizenship until 1924. Even then, some states prohibited Indians from voting. By the end of the twentieth century, only white men had a secure constitutional right to exercise the vote and have a say in how the country was governed.

17-2

Early Reform Attempts

Members of a Woman's Christian Temperance Union branch that marched on Washington, D.C., pose in this 1909 image. Under the leadership of Frances Willard, the WCTU advocated for more than temperance extending its reform movement to include women's suffrage, labor unions, clean municipal government, and free education for children. Willard's motto was to "Do everything" (petition, protest, and lobby) possible to create real reform of U.S. society.

What do you notice about the class, gender, and race of the people in this photograph? What do you conclude from your observations? By reading their banners, can you tell what reforms they advocated? ▶

Topical Press Agency/Hulton Archive/Getty Images

Because the Democrats and Republicans did not sufficiently address issues of enfranchisement, corruption, and government regulation, there was an opening for challengers. Farmers, middle-class professional men and women, evangelical reformers (many of them women), and workers built social movements that defied party loyalty and instead pursued each group's particular area of concern. These groups believed they needed to work outside the party system in order to have government officials take up their cause. Although none succeeded in winning control of Congress or the presidency, all influenced public discourse—and ultimately the major political parties—to bring about reform at the national and local levels.

☞ As you read, consider how reform movements challenged the entrenched party system. What were their motives, and what was the nature of their challenges?

17-2a Farmers and Railroad Regulation

Because national parties focused primarily on party loyalty and patronage, they paid little attention to problems that plagued farmers

{ Farmers' organizations advocate and win regulations that bring railroads under public control.

and rural workers caused by competition from an expanding global market. Farmers organized to demand fair treatment against railroad and grain monopolies. They initially petitioned state governments but ultimately came to believe that only the federal government could exercise control over corporate monopolies. Farmers protested the railroads' practice of **pooling** and giving **rebates** to shippers who used a particular line exclusively. Farmers also objected to the lower rates that large enterprises received for sending goods long distances rather than the short hauls that farmers and small businesses used more frequently.

In the South, the Civil War had destroyed industrial infrastructure such as mines, machinery, railroads, and telegraphs. In the 1890s, most southern counties reported a per capita real estate value of between $100 and $200 in comparison to the $637 national average and $970 in New York City. After Reconstruction, southern Democratic state governments repudiated the debts incurred by their Republican predecessors, so northern banks were hesitant to lend further funds to rebuild the region. As a result, the South lagged far behind the rest of the country in economic development. Describing a southern farmer's funeral in the late 1880s, one observer bitterly noted that everything from the marble of the headstone to the nails in the coffin had been imported from the North: "The South didn't furnish a thing for that funeral but the corpse and the hole in the ground."

The Midwest and West had higher per capita investments in buildings, slaughterhouses, breweries, railroads, telegraphs, mines, and other industrial infrastructure, but capital was frequently owned by nonresident investors, many of them foreign. One-third of Minnesota's banks, for instance, were owned by nonresidents, compared with less than 10 percent of New England banks. The control over the economy exercised by eastern capitalists left Westerners feeling that they were an internal colony of eastern interests.

Organizations such as **The National Grange of the Order of Patrons of Husbandry** advocated for farmers. In the wake of the Panic of 1873, the Grange challenged the owners of railroads and grain elevators by starting **cooperatives**, which provided an alternative outlet for farmers' grain sales by pooling harvests and holding out for higher prices. Critics derided these "co-ops"

as socialism. Under pressure from local Granges, however, midwestern state legislatures passed laws that regulated railroads and grain elevators in an attempt to keep pricing fair. In 1876, the Supreme Court upheld these Granger Laws in *Munn v. Illinois*. The Court said that because Munn, a grain elevator owner, operated a business that was invested with a public interest, it could be regulated by state, as could railroads.

Farmers responded to corporate control and government collusion by forming economic and political coalitions that often resulted in **third-party** runs for state and national offices. In 1884, the Anti-Monopoly Party ran candidates in eleven midwestern and western states on a platform that included antitrust legislation, direct election of senators, and a graduated income tax. The party was short lived because it merged with the Greenback Party. Since the end of Reconstruction, the Greenbacks had been pressing the federal government to issue paper money that was not tied to the **gold standard**, which encouraged high inflation. An inflationary economy based on greenbacks benefited farmers who typically carried heavy debts (see Figure 17.1).

The strongest coalition emerged from the **Farmers Alliance**, which eventually supplanted the Grange as the most outspoken advocate for farmers. Local chapters created cooperatives that sold grain and purchased supplies in bulk to save money for their members. They also formed small banks to ensure farmers' control over their money. The Colored Farmer's Alliance, the Women's Alliance, and the Southern Alliance each catered to its members' particular concerns. Eventually, the coalition realized that it needed national laws to curb nationally

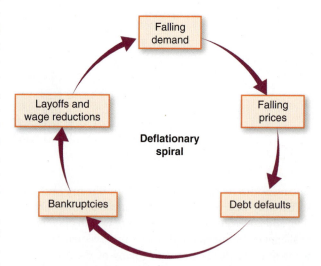

Figure 17.1 Deflationary Monetary Policy A debt-deflation cycle occurs when falling prices from a reduced money supply causes farmers and other producers to be unable to pay back their debts to the banks and other creditors. The resulting bankruptcies cause layoffs of workers and reduce purchasing power requiring yet lower rices, beginning the cycle anew. The period between 1873 and 1911 continuously struggled with deflationary cycles. Source: zerohedge.com ▲

pooling Practice used by railroads to minimize competition and set favorable rates among themselves.

rebates Money given back, in this case, to companies that shipped their goods on railroads exclusively, thus giving those companies a hidden discount and advantage.

The National Grange of the Order of Patrons of Husbandry Support group for farmers that focused on sociability and education, which eventually transformed into a political advocacy group.

cooperatives Group of individuals who come together to create a nonprofit entity to pool their resources to purchase goods in bulk and/or to create a sales outlet for their goods.

third-party Political party in the United States that challenged the Democrats and Republicans in a general election.

gold standard A monetary policy that ties the amount of currency in circulation directly to the amount of gold that a government holds in its treasury.

Farmers Alliance Outgrowth of the Grange made up of northern and southern branches that advocated for farmers at the national level.

scaled industries. In 1892, the alliances joined the Knights of Labor, and both eventually joined the People's and then the Populist parties.

When alliance members gained traction politically and were bolstered by the decision in the *Granger Cases*, businessmen lobbied recently elected President James A. Garfield to nominate an ally to the Supreme Court. In 1881, Garfield named Stanley Matthews, a probusiness Ohio senator. Aided by Matthews's vote, the Court in *Wabash v. Illinois* reversed its earlier decision in the *Granger Cases*, holding that state regulation of railroad traffic was unconstitutional because the Constitution granted exclusive jurisdiction over interstate commerce to Congress, not the states.

The *Wabash* decision placed 85 percent of railroad traffic beyond state control. Seeking federal regulation, a coalition of New York merchants, small oil producers in Pennsylvania, and farmers pressed for passage of the Interstate Commerce Act in 1887. Supporters argued that since railroads crossed state lines and were therefore engaged in interstate commerce, making them subject to the legal jurisdiction of Congress under the **Commerce Clause**. The Interstate Commerce Act's passage enabled the creation of the first-ever federal regulatory agency, the Interstate Commerce Commission, to enforce its provisions. The law's definition of illegal rate discrimination, however, was left deliberately vague until the 1906 Hepburn Act because of disagreements between shippers and railroads about what constituted a reasonable rate.

17-2b Urban Professionals and Civil Service Reform

A growing class of urban professionals—accountants, lawyers, middle managers, and engineers—claimed that the right to government jobs

> Progressive urban reformers take lessons from abroad to institute changes.

should be based on education and expertise, rather than the spoils system. These reformers contrasted their predicament with the British and German civil service systems, which hired educated professional experts from those nations' elite universities. In the United States, this professional class disproportionately came from Protestant New England families who were losing influence to newer ethnic groups through the political machines.

Many middle-class advocates of civil service reform were suspicious of universal suffrage, believing that elections dominated by Irish Catholic Democrats in northern cities and the newly enfranchised Republican-leaning freedmen in the South would result, in Charles Francis Adams's words, "government of ignorance and vice" controlled by "a . . . Celtic proletariat on the Atlantic coast; an African proletariat on the shores of the Gulf; and a Chinese proletariat on the Pacific." Finding common

cause with white Southerners seeking to disenfranchise the freedmen, these northern middle-class reformers also abandoned efforts to protect the black vote. The group opposed Massachusetts Senator Henry Cabot Lodge's 1890 Election Bill (which white Southerners derisively called the *Force Bill*) that would have protected southern blacks' voting rights with federal election monitors.

These reformers' nobler objective was transforming government administration along "scientific" lines with policy implemented by properly trained experts rather than party loyalists who pursued office for their own self-interest. Founded in 1881, the National Civil Service Reform League pressed for a law banning partisan hiring and firing of government workers. Both parties, however, ridiculed civil service reformers as ineffectual, elitists, even effeminate dreamers—"snivel service reformers"—who did not understand the organizational realities of mobilizing voters.

Despite this resistance, civil service reformers in the Republican Party succeeded in nominating the "good-government" congressman, James A. Garfield, in the 1880 presidential race. He won the election, but it was an assassin's bullet that pushed Congress to act. On July 2, 1881, as Garfield boarded a train in Washington, D.C., Charles Julius Guiteau, a mentally unstable man who believed that his earlier support for Garfield had earned him an ambassadorship, shot Garfield. He suffered from his wounds for more than two months before dying, making Vice President Chester Alan Arthur the next president.

The press proclaimed Garfield a martyr to civil service reform, and, in 1883, Congress passed the **Pendleton Civil Service Reform Act**. It established the Civil Service Commission to administer appointments to federal jobs based on merit. Modeled explicitly on the British system, the act required office seekers to demonstrate their qualifications by taking a written exam. In the beginning, the commission administered only about 10 percent of federal jobs. By the end of the nineteenth century, more than 50 percent of federal jobs had come under its jurisdiction. The system also created good-paying professional jobs for women. In the 1890s, almost half of the applicants who passed the exam were women.

The good government reformers shifted the tone of presidential politics. The 1884 Democratic presidential nominee, Grover Cleveland, was chosen because of his efforts to promote "educational" political campaigns as well as his hostility to government spending for partisan purposes. When Republicans nominated James Blaine, a **stalwart** supporter of the Republican party, which favored machine politics and

Commerce Clause Article 1, Section 8 of the U.S. Constitution gives Congress the right to regulate trade with foreign countries as well as between the states and Native Americans.

Pendleton Civil Service Reform Act Law that required federal jobs to be awarded on the basis of merit, not party loyalty, and instituted the Civil Service Exam.

stalwart Marked by loyalty, reliability, and hard work that describes the more conservative branch of the late nineteenth-century Republican Party, which favored machine politics rather than civil service reform.

Vintage Collection/The Granger Collection, New York

Frederic Howe (Center) Pictured with a Group of Hindu and Parsee Immigrants from India on Ellis Island, New York.

Global Americans The career trajectory of **Frederic Howe** was emblematic of the transatlantic world of Progressive reformers at the turn of the twentieth century. He lived at Toynbee Hall in England and studied in Germany with some of the leading urban reformers. He brought his knowledge to Cleveland, Ohio, where he became a leader in municipal reform as Cleveland successfully addressed the problems of rapid urban growth under the leadership of its mayor, Tom Johnson. Howe also shared his expertise with nationally known urban reformers. He was most concerned with the fairness of taxation and how to fund government infrastructure projects. He was one of the earliest proponents of tax reform and Henry George's single tax, which advocated taxing only undeveloped land rather than wages. Throughout his career, Howe traveled back and forth to Europe to meet with city managers and urban planners. Based on his meetings and observations with European municipal reformers, particularly in Denmark, Germany, and England, Howe published *The City: The Hope of Democracy* in 1905.

Howe's own political alliances as a progressive-minded reformer mirrored those of the time period. He began his career as a Republican but switched to the Democratic Party just as most Progressives shifted with the changes in the national parties. In 1914, President Wilson appointed Howe, who had since moved to New York, the Commissioner of Immigration of the Port of New York. He ended his career working for the New Deal in the Department of Agriculture.

patronage rather than civil service reform, many middle-class professionals left the Republican Party to support Cleveland.

17-2c Evangelicals Challenge Threats to the Home

Like farmers and middle-class professionals, evangelicals, particularly evangelical women, felt that the two major parties ignored their issues. **Evangelical Christians** believed that personal reformation and public advocacy should protect the home from what they regarded as destructive male behaviors—drinking alcohol, visiting prostitutes, gambling, and fighting. Evangelicals also built coalitions with other reform groups such as the farmer alliances and civil service reformers.

> Moral reformers push for temperance legislation in the name of preserving home and family.

Inspired by sermons denouncing alcoholic beverages, women in Ohio launched the **Woman's Crusade** in 1873. Their tactics included occupying saloons while singing hymns and praying to stop liquor sales. In smaller towns dominated by Yankee Protestants, these women were often successful. In cities with large immigrant-born communities, their campaigns stalled when urbanites resisted attacks on the saloons that were their social gathering places. The crusade, dominated by white middle-class women, denounced the sellers of alcohol in class-based terms. One temperance journalist was shocked that "the fine, old, respectable city of Chillicothe, Ohio" could "vomit forth such a crowd," a "masculine crowd" of "low-browed, stubby-haired sons of humanity," including one man with "a roaming red nose, pig eye, and soap-fat chin."

Inspired by the Woman's Crusade, Midwesterners formed the Woman's Christian Temperance Union (WCTU) in 1873 dedicated to protecting the home from male vices. The WCTU soon became an international organization with branches in Australia, England, Canada, and Japan. It joined forces with the Prohibition Party to push for legislation and to sponsor national candidates. Together they advocated a ban on the consumption and manufacture of alcoholic beverages. Led by Frances Willard, a charismatic evangelical woman who took control of the WCTU in 1881, the organization eventually moved beyond anti-alcohol measures to call for banning prostitution, "impure" (sexually explicit) literature, and child labor. The WCTU also lobbied for the eight-hour workday and suffrage for women and joined political coalitions to further their causes.

The common element in all of these reforms was the protection of the home as a safe haven from materialistic commercial values and male sinfulness. By focusing on maternal roles, WCTU activists could move from domestic settings to engage in public speaking, lobbying for legislation, and occupying demonstrations at taverns and saloons. As the WCTU broadened its agenda, however, its leadership in the anti-alcohol movement yielded to the Anti-Saloon League, which was dominated by male leaders.

Evangelical Christians Religious believers who stress that personal transformation accompanies conversion, offering a vision of individual self-respect.

Woman's Crusade Loose coalition of women's groups that protested the sale of liquor by picketing saloons and bars and was a precursor to the Women's Christian Temperance Union (WCTU).

New York Illustrated Times

Ann Lohman Arrested by Anthony Comstock, *New York Illustrated Times* Anthony Comstock, arrested Ann Trow Lohman, also known as Madame Restelle, on charges that she performed abortions, which were illegal in New York, and provided birth control to women through the mail. Comstock pursued women like Lohman, Margaret Sanger, Victoria Woodhull, and Emma Goldman who advocated for a woman's right to use birth control. He was derided by sexual progressives such as George Bernard Shaw who mocked his vigilance against sexuality and vice as "Comstockery." ▲

Alcohol and domestic abuse were only two aspects of urban life that motivated reformers. Another was vice. Anthony Comstock, a New York dry goods clerk affiliated with the YMCA, persuaded evangelically inclined wealthy merchants to create the **New York Society for the Suppression of Vice**. In 1876, prodded by Comstock's lobbying, Congress enacted the Comstock Act, banning from the mails not only "obscene, lewd, lascivious" materials but also information about contraception and related products. Comstock himself was appointed the postal service's special agent in charge of inspecting the mails for obscene materials. He brought hundreds of criminal cases against pornographers and reformers who mailed pamphlets advocating contraception or revision of marriage and divorce laws.

By the mid-1880s, some evangelical reformers expanded their political agenda to include attacks on economic inequality and poverty through what became known as the **Social Gospel**. Strong in midwestern centers of evangelical reform, the movement had its origins in the earlier abolitionist movement. Richard Ely, an American economist, argued that sinful behaviors such as drinking and visiting prostitutes were the direct result of industrial capitalism's mass unemployment, low wages, and poor working conditions. Blaming the corporate elite for un-Christian behavior toward workers, Ely argued that sin was social as well as individual, and that widespread economic well-being was a safeguard for Christian morality. The Social Gospel movement owed its intellectual origins to **Christian socialism**, a movement that made alliances with the secular Fabian Society in order to effect change in Great Britain. In Britain and in France and Germany, a coalition of socialists had influenced local and national governments to take direct action to alleviate poverty, improve housing, and create safe working conditions. U.S. reformers such as Frederic Howe and Frances Willard had direct and long-term interaction with their European counterparts to share ways to improve the quality of life for the masses.

New York Society for the Suppression of Vice Group founded to enforce laws that prohibited the sale and transport of lewd and obscene materials.

Social Gospel Christian principle focusing on the application of virtues, such as charity and forgiveness, to social problems such as poverty and vice.

Christian socialism Political ideology based on Christian belief that capitalism is rooted in greed, a mortal sin.

Toynbee Hall Toynbee Hall was England's first settlement house and was representative of the larger social reform movement. The same year, 1884, the Fabian Society was founded in London by a group of socialist reformers including Sidney and Beatrice Webb. Its logo was the tortoise, which reflected the reform movements' belief in slow and steady reform, rather than the revolutionary movements associated with Marxism and communism. The Fabian Society's and Toynbee Hall's influence extended internationally. Both European and U.S. reformers adopted their views and pushed for similar kinds of socialist agendas gained through moderate and slow reforms. ▶

Toynbee Hall, illustration from 'The Builder', February 14th, 1885 (litho), English School, (19th century)/Private Collection/The Bridgeman Art Library

17-2d Workers and Politics

Both political parties claimed to represent industrial workers, but the leaders of the most important labor unions refused to endorse either one.

> Workers challenge existing political parties.

Federal intervention on the side of corporations, such as during the Pullman and Homestead strikes, made workers distrustful of government. Samuel Gompers, head of the AFL, was reluctant to ask his members to back either party. He wanted the parties to pledge that government, especially the courts, would not interfere with unions' efforts to organize workers. Neither political party endorsed this principle, and consequently the labor movement looked elsewhere for a political home.

Thousands of workers worldwide were drawn to the concept of a **single tax** proposed by Henry George, a journalist who had published the phenomenally successful *Progress and Poverty* in 1879. According to George, economic injustice could be eliminated through a single tax imposed on land that was equal to its unimproved value. Such a tax would eliminate wealth not attributable to labor and encourage landowners to sell vacant land to those who could make productive use of it. Around the world, workingmen were attracted to George's message that wealth not based on labor was illegitimate. Groups fighting "landlordism" and clamoring for land redistribution in China, Australia, and Ireland warmed to George's single-tax remedy. He appealed directly to Irish immigrants in a pamphlet praising the Irish Land War, which was a popular movement to transfer land to tenant farmers from landlords, particularly absentee ones.

In 1886, George ran for mayor of New York City under the **United Labor Party**, declaring that "the use of the land belongs to the entire people," and "[e]veryone should be entitled to share in it." The Farmers Alliance and the liberal wing of the WCTU joined this third party. Frightened by George's mass appeal, business interests and Tammany Democrats united behind Abraham Hewitt, a wealthy owner of ironworks. Hewitt narrowly defeated George and a distant third-place finisher, Theodore Roosevelt. George's 1886 mayoral campaign marked the high tide of labor's influence for the next decade, and his ideas remained influential for the rest of the century, inspiring hundreds of single-tax clubs and proposals to nationalize railroads and utilities. A U.S. supporter, Elizabeth Magie, invented The Landlord's Game, a board game designed to demonstrate George's principles that over the decades evolved into Monopoly.

single tax Taxation system of mainly or exclusively one tax based only on unimproved land, not workers' wages that was popularized by Henry George in the United States.

United Labor Party Third party formed by a coalition of socialists, labor leaders, and single-tax advocates.

17-3

Economic Crisis and the Populist Party

This 1894 photo of Coxey's Army, also known as the *Army of the Commonwealth of Christ*, depicts the unemployed men who left their homes across the nation and marched to Washington, D.C. They demanded that the federal government spend more on relief efforts in the wake of the 1893 depression.

How would you describe the men in this photo? What do their dress and demeanor suggest to you? Why were they displaying two American flags? ▶

Picture History/Newscom

The political stalemate that characterized late nineteenth-century politics shifted dramatically in response to the largest economic crisis to hit the nation. The depression following the Panic of 1893 caused reformers to come together, and third-party coalitions rose to challenge the Democrats and Republicans to answer the needs of the U.S. electorate. The most successful was the Populist Party, which united the interests of farmers, evangelicals, and industrial workers for a short time. Although the Populists never won the presidency, they shifted the balance of political power to the Republican Party, which, along with the Democrats, ultimately co-opted some of their issues to broaden their bases.

☞ As you read, trace the rise and eventual decline of the Populist Party. Why did it fail to survive in the national political arena? Which of its ideas survived, and how?

17-3a Republican Coalition of Pensioners and Business

Republicans had a difficult time creating a winning coalition at both the national and state levels. Grover Cleveland's single-minded focus on

{ Republicans struggle to build a national coalition. }

lowering tariffs aroused fears in the industrial Northeast and cost him the election in 1888, although he won the popular vote. With dour Civil War general Benjamin Harrison in the presidency, Republicans initially pressed a program of Protestant piety. Following several Republican defeats in Midwest state elections in 1889, however, the national Republican leadership decided in 1890 to emphasize economic issues over the cultural issues favored by evangelical reformers.

Shepherded through Congress by Representative William McKinley of Ohio, the Tariff of 1890 imposed high tariffs on imported goods, winning support from some farmers as well as businesses and their employees who feared competition from cheap imports. But the tariff required importers to send scarce gold to the U.S. Treasury to pay the fees, creating a cash shortage. To win additional support and disburse the accumulated cash, Congress also enacted the Dependent and Disability Pension Act, which authorized pensions for disabled veterans and widows of

Union soldiers who had served at least 90 days during the Civil War. At its peak, the Pension Act disbursed more than $135 million annually for 970,000 veterans. The law ultimately cost $8 billion. By 1900, pensions consumed 40 percent of the federal budget.

The Republicans, in short, hoped to hold power with a coalition of business leaders and their employees, a few groups of farmers, and Union veterans. But the combined tariff-pension policy had the drawback of imposing extraordinarily high prices on consumers. Derided by Democrats as the **Billion-Dollar Congress**, Republicans chipped away at their probusiness image by enacting the Sherman Antitrust Act of 1890, which attempted to end monopolies but was ultimately judged as weak in its enforcement.

In an additional effort to win western farmers' support, the Republican-controlled Congress enacted the Sherman Silver Purchase Act, which required the federal government to purchase millions of ounces of silver from western mines and issue bonds repayable in either gold or silver coin. This took U.S. currency off the gold standard. By buying up virtually all the output of silver mines in Nevada, Colorado, and Montana, Republicans also hoped to win support from western silver producers.

17-3b Emergence of the Populists

Neither the Sherman Silver Purchase Act nor the Sherman Antitrust Act was sufficient to win agrarian or middle-class support for the Republican Party. The Anti-

{ Third-party Populists influence the tone and content of the national debate over monetary policy and government regulation. }

trust Act's language was so vague that in the first suit brought under it, *United States v. E.C. Knight Co.* (the Sugar Trust Case), the Supreme Court construed the Commerce Clause to apply only to the transportation of goods across state lines, not to manufacturing monopolies. The Silver Purchase Act permitted bondholders to be repaid in either gold or silver coin, and they predictably preferred the more valuable metal, reducing the U.S. Treasury's supply of gold currency to dangerously low levels. The tariff burdened farmers by increasing the costs of farming equipment and other manufactured goods.

In response, the Grange, Farmers Alliance, remnants of the Union Labor Party, and other agrarian organizations formed the People's or **Populist Party**, charging that both major parties ignored the interests of workers and farmers in favor of the "sham issue" of the tariff. Meeting in Omaha, Nebraska, on July 4, 1892, the new third party adopted a platform that outlined the reforms that

F. B. Opper/The Granger Collection, New York

"STEP UP TO THE CAPTAIN'S OFFICE AND SETTLE!"

Income Tax Cartoon, 1895 With few exceptions, American agricultural products did not compete with imports, giving farmers little benefit from high tariffs. This caused the economic burden of the tariff to fall on the farming regions. Wealthy individuals, in contrast, paid income taxes. In this cartoon, which appeared in *Puck*, Uncle Sam demands millionaire tax-dodgers to settle their outstanding tax bills to cover the U.S. Treasury deficits. ▲

Billion-Dollar Congress The fifty-first Congress, which was the first to pass a billion dollar budget, leading critics to deride it for what they saw as excessive spending.

Populist Party One of the most successful third parties in the history of the United States composed of a coalition of farmers and workers that the two parties ignored.

Finland was the first European nation to achieve women's suffrage, 1906.

Women related to WWI soldiers gained suffrage in Belgium, 1920.

AK 1913

2. CANADA

NORTH AMERICA

UNITED STATES

ATLANTIC OCEAN

see inset

EUROPE

ASIA

AFRICA

4.

PACIFIC OCEAN

PACIFIC OCEAN

SOUTH AMERICA

Pitcairn Is. (U.K.) 1838

INDIAN OCEAN

3.

1. AUSTRALIA
NT 1902   QLD 1905
WA 1899
SA 1894   NSW 1902
VIC 1908
TAS 1903

Inset (United States and Canada):

BC 1917   AB 1916   SK 1916   MB 1916   CANADA   NB 1919   NL 1925
WA 1910
OR 1912   ID 1896   MT 1914   ON 1917   QC 1940   PE 1922
NV 1914   WY 1869   SD 1918   NS 1918
CA 1911   UT 1896   CO 1893   KS 1912   MI 1918   NY 1917
AZ 1912   OK 1918   UNITED STATES

ATLANTIC OCEAN

US: States with women's suffrage prior to 1920 are labeled

PACIFIC OCEAN

Gulf of Mexico

Year women's suffrage gained

- Before 1930
- 1930–1950
- 1951–1994
- No women's suffrage
- International boundaries, 1994

Notes:

1. Australia: Non-aboriginal women gained suffrage, 1894–1908. Aboriginal women gained suffrage, 1962.

2. Canada: Non-aboriginal women gained suffrage, 1916–1940. Aboriginal women gained suffrage, 1960.

3. South Africa: White women gained suffrage, 1930; universal women's suffrage, 1994.

4. Spain: Women gained suffrage, 1931; rescinded, 1936; restored, 1976.

Suffrage Laws Globally 1838–1994 This map shows when women gained the right to vote across the world. The United States along with a handful of other countries were relatively early in granting suffrage to women. Note that in 1994 women in Saudi Arabia could not vote; they were finally granted the right in 2015. ▲

Feminism's origins date back centuries. In the seventeenth and eighteenth centuries, the "woman question" fueled public debate in Europe about the worth of women relative to that of men in terms of moral, spiritual, and intellectual capacity. In 1792, Englishwoman Mary Wollstonecraft made the case for men's and women's equality in the famous *A Vindication of the Rights of*

Women, and revolutionaries in France and the United States pushed for expanded female education. French suffragist Hubertine Auclert first used the word feminism or *feminisme* in the 1880s. By the first decade of the twentieth century, it was a concept celebrated in the United States as something new and modern: "All feminists are suffragists, but not all suffragists are feminists." Feminism, an

ideology far broader than the movement for voting rights, is based on three principles: First, women and men are fundamentally equal. Second, women's status is shaped by society, not determined by God or nature, and therefore is changeable. Finally, women and men who are feminists perceive themselves as part of a shared social grouping although there is lively debate over how much is shared.

Corbis

Seneca Falls This painting portrays Elizabeth Cady Stanton speaking during the first Woman's Rights Convention, held in the Wesleyan Methodist Chapel in Seneca Falls, New York. The very act of speaking in public in a mixed gender audience with men would have been, in and of itself, a radical act. Advocating for woman's equality even more so. ▲

Hulton Archive/Getty Images

Beatrice Webb Webb, a leader in the Fabian Society, was a historian, sociologist and economist. She is often credited with coining the term "collective bargaining," which is used to describe the negotiations that union leaders make on behalf of their members. Webb, along with her husband Sidney Webb, founded the London School of Economics. ▲

Educated free women in the early nineteenth century built a "woman movement" characterized by ideas of shared domesticity and motherhood, calling out the perils of bad marriages, alcoholism, and abuse by husbands. Even for reformers who focused on equality, the family was a major focus. Transatlantic socialist movements experimented with family arrangements based on equality, which, they claimed would elevate the position of women. Irish reformers William Thompson and Anna Wheeler wrote in 1825 that only when "women cease to be dependent on individual men for their daily support" could there be "perfect equality and entire reciprocity of happiness between women and men." Margaret Fuller, the first woman allowed to use Harvard's library, wrote "let them be sea-captains, if you will."

The revolution of 1848 in Europe raised questions of expanded political rights, fueling demands that women, should have the right to vote. In the United States, this demand was included in the 1848 Seneca Falls *Declaration of Sentiments*. Suffrage was a focus for the first international women's congress in Paris in 1878.

At the same time, the emergence of welfare states in Europe and the Progressive movement in the United States fostered maternalist movements claiming an expanded political role for women based in their roles as mothers. Urban reformers both in England and the United States such as Beatrice Webb and Jane Addams took these ideas and applied them to the settlement house movement, which provided not only services for immigrants and the poor but also careers for women to work outside the home and spread ideas about equality.

Several strands of feminism coalesced at the turn of the twentieth century around the New Woman who was educated, individualistic, and emancipated. Publications with *New Woman* in their titles emerged in Egypt, Japan, China, and Korea, promoting the idea that women had to be freed from a "savage" past that included practices like sati, veiling, polygamy, concubinage, harems, and foot binding. In Asian contexts, the New Woman was linked with the "modernizing" required to throw off imperialism.

Woman suffrage became the law in the United States in 1920, but feminism took divergent paths. In 1923, in

an attempt to write full equal rights for women into the Constitution, Alice Paul introduced the Equal Rights Amendment (ERA). In 1972, Congress finally passed the ERA with a resounding majority. Ratification, however, failed — just three states short of the 38 needed. Feminists worked for equal wages, access to birth control, prosecutions of rape, and Lesbian, Gay, Bisexual, Transgender (LGBT) rights.

☞ **Critical Thinking Questions**

▶ How and where has suffrage for women been granted around the world? Which countries were latecomers to granting suffrage? Which countries granted suffrage to women based on race?

▶ In the United States, what factors do you suppose contributed to women's suffrage being recognized earlier in the western states than in the eastern states?

Go to MindTap® to engage with an interactive version of **History without Borders: Feminism**. Learn from an interactive map, view related video, and respond to critical thinking questions.

free silver Economic policy that advocates basing currency on both gold and silver, thereby making more currency available for circulation in the economy.

fusion Synthesis; in this case, a coalition of a third party and a dominant political party to create a joint campaign or political ticket.

each group had been calling for since the early 1880s. To attract working-men, the Populist Party endorsed the eight-hour day for government work, restrictions on "undesirable immigration," and support for the Knights of Labor. Perhaps most controversially, Populists called for a more inflationary monetary policy known as **free silver**.

The Omaha Platform was one of the most strident attacks on the excesses of wealth and big business in U.S. history. The Populists' radicalism went beyond their platform. In Georgia, Populist Tom Watson tried to organize a biracial coalition of black and white farmers, declaring to racially mixed audiences that "[y]ou are made to hate each other because upon that hatred is rested the keystone of the arch of financial despotism which enslaves you both." Populists also endorsed feminism not only in the form of women's suffrage but also by sponsoring charismatic female orators such as Kansas lawyer and lecturer Mary Elizabeth Lease, who urged farmers to "raise less corn and more hell." The highly visible participation of female speakers in the Populist campaign attracted angry denunciations from conservatives shocked by women engaged in rough-and-tumble debate.

The Populist Party did surprisingly well in the 1892 elections, capturing eleven seats in Congress, several governorships, and the state legislatures of Kansas, Nebraska, and North Carolina. Their presidential candidate, James Weaver, a Civil War general and former Greenbacker, received more than a million popular votes and twenty-two electoral votes from four states, Colorado, Kansas, Idaho, and Nevada. This success was especially impressive because the major political parties used their influence over the electoral system to minimize Populist gains, especially in the South.

The Democratic Party avoided contentious issues such as monetary policy and government takeover of railroads and nominated former president Grover Cleveland. Campaigning almost solely against the McKinley tariff, Cleveland won a narrow victory over President Benjamin Harrison. The Democrats also made a special appeal to housewives, who were presumed to be "the most important factor" in the election because "in their shopping excursions. . . [they] found a rise in prices explained as due to the McKinley bill" and "went home and told their husbands."

17-3c Panic of 1893 and Its Political Aftermath

Cleveland's second presidency was doomed before it even began. Ten days before his inauguration, the Philadelphia & Reading Railroad

{ Economic upheaval sets the stage for changes within the two major parties.

declared bankruptcy, triggering the Panic of 1893, the nation's most severe depression until the Great Depression in 1929. In 1894, several "armies" of unemployed workers, such as Coxey's Army, left their homes to march on Washington, demanding that the federal government fund public works projects and hire workers to relieve unemployment. Labor unrest gripped the nation as workers headed the American Railway Union's call to honor the Pullman strike (see Chapter 16). Farm product prices plummeted, leading to a rash of farm foreclosures across the nation.

The Cleveland administration responded to these crises with probusiness policies. Convinced that the Silver Purchase Act had helped trigger the financial panic by depleting the gold supply, Cleveland called for its repeal and strenuously resisted any expansion of the money supply, including modest efforts to issue silver coin. Cleveland also was confronted by a rush of bondholders who wanted to redeem their notes for gold coin, an action that would threaten the U.S. government with the risk of defaulting on the bonds. To stave off such a disaster, Cleveland enlisted the financier J.P. Morgan to persuade fellow bankers to cease redeeming bonds for gold and to lend $65 million in gold coin to the federal government in exchange for federal bonds that promised to pay 4 percent interest. Although the effort staved off federal default, the deal (on which Morgan earned a handsome commission) also gave the impression that private bankers dictated federal monetary policy.

Voters blamed the Cleveland administration for the depression, and Democrats at the 1896 Chicago convention rejected its probusiness policies in favor of a less radical version of the Populist Party's agrarian program. William Jennings Bryan, a representative from Nebraska, delivered a fiery call for silver currency at the convention, declaring, "We shall answer their demands for a gold standard by saying to them: you shall not press down upon the brow of labor this crown of thorns. You shall not crucify mankind upon a cross of gold." The delegates enthusiastically nominated Bryan and called for unlimited coinage of silver. Eastern Democrats—including Cleveland Democrats who had embraced him as a symbol of middle-class professional reform—deserted the Democratic Party, disgusted by what they regarded as a demagogic appeal for inflation. Cleveland himself sat out the election, refusing to endorse Bryan, but Democrats won new support from the West and South when the Populist Party endorsed Bryan's **fusion** candidacy.

Republicans nominated William McKinley, who was backed by a coalition of wealthy businessmen. The most powerful of these was Mark Hanna from Ohio who spent much of his own money and raised large sums from wealthy supporters to ensure that the McKinley campaign was the best funded. The Republicans painted Bryan as a demagogic radical who would save debt-ridden farmers by inflicting an inflated currency on the nation. To counteract McKinley's campaign war chest, Bryan frenetically toured the nation in an effort to win support from eastern workers as well as western and southern farmers. In eastern cities, however, his appeal was limited because workers saw little to be gained from inflation, and Catholic and Jewish immigrants were suspicious of his evangelical style. In response to Bryan's calls for workers to make common cause with farmers, Samuel Gompers pointed out that farmers were also employers. McKinley defeated both Bryan and the idea of economic radicalism. For a generation, sectional distrust and economic prosperity buried the idea of a unified farmer-labor alliance of producers (farmers and workers) against capitalists.

McKinley's first term was as blessed by good fortune as Cleveland's had been cursed by depression. By the late 1890s, the depression of 1893 had begun to dissipate. As farm prices rose, agrarian discontent diminished. The 1898 war against Spain (see Chapter 18) contributed to a sense of national unity and pride that benefited the incumbent administration. In the 1900 campaign, McKinley again faced Bryan, but this time with Theodore Roosevelt running as McKinley's vice president to win middle-class reformers' support. Bryan supplemented his old message, denouncing monopolies with a new message attacking overseas expansion in the Philippines and the subsequent bloody struggle against Filipino guerillas as a brutal act of imperialism. But his anti-imperialist campaign was handily defeated by McKinley's slogan, "four more years of the full dinner pail," made credible by the return of economic prosperity.

The elections of 1896 and 1900 made it clear that no party could win national elections in an urbanizing and industrializing nation with the support of farmers alone. Winning the support of middle-class professionals, urban workers, and farmers was essential for national success, but assembling such a coalition proved to be elusive in a sectionally divided economy. Democratic efforts to woo the professional middle class alienated farmers. Bryan's appeal to farmers alienated the professional middle class. Workers refused to endorse either party. Bryan's failure to create a winning national coalition paved the way for Republican dominance, and, for the next sixteen years, Republicans held undivided control of the presidency and Congress. In 1901, Leon Czolgosz, an anarchist and unemployed factory worker, assassinated McKinley. As a result, Roosevelt, the man Mark Hanna had derided as "that cowboy," was president.

17-4

Limitations and Triumphs of Progressivism

This cartoon, which appeared in *Puck*, a New York humor magazine, portrays an infant President Roosevelt as the Greek hero, Hercules. He wrestles with the unwieldy serpents J.P. Morgan and John D. Rockefeller, the titans of U.S. finance and industry.

Why is Roosevelt portrayed as a baby Hercules? What was the cartoonist trying to convey by portraying Morgan and Rockefeller as serpents? ▶

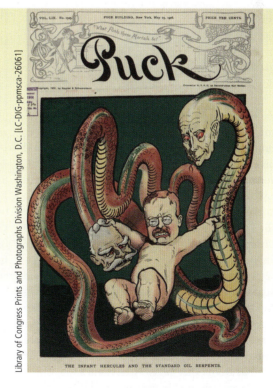

Library of Congress Prints and Photographs Division Washington, D.C. [LC-DIG-ppmsca-26061]

Go to MindTap® to practice history with the Chapter 17 **Primary Source Writing Activity: Brands of Progressivism.** Read and view primary sources and respond to a writing prompt.

Following McKinley's assassination, intense antiradical sentiment swept the nation because Czolgosz was linked to European anarchists. As radical political programs associated with anarchism, socialism, and communism became more popular in Europe, Americans became increasingly suspicious of immigrants, who might spread such ideas. Anti-immigrant legislation became a key Progressive reform. Theodore Roosevelt, however, also assured Americans that his solutions, adapted from European middle-class reformers, were meant to stop any potential socialist threat to the United States. In many western industrializing nations, new political coalitions wedged themselves between socialists on the left and the barons of land and industry on the right. Calling themselves New Liberals in Britain, radicals in France, social liberals in Chile, and Progressives in the United States, each group tried to steer government on a stable middle course that would avoid revolts by the poor or rule by the rich. Roosevelt practiced a top-down form of Progressive reform, aggressively asserting unilateral presidential power to control big business. At the same time, he exhibited little hostility toward either business or bigness. In contrast, grassroots-level reformers who continued to advocate for more sweeping reforms increasingly pressured lawmakers.

☞ As you read, try to understand the complexity of ideas that constituted Progressivism and why Roosevelt believed that his brand of it was the best one. What groups opposed Roosevelt's vision?

17-4a Progressive Era Anti-Immigrant Measures

Fear of immigrants had been a part of U.S. politics since the American Party's nativism against Irish and German immigrants during the 1850s.

> Progressive reformers embrace anti-immigrant legislation.

After the Civil War, however, anti-immigrant politics got a boost from pseudoscientific theories often linked to Darwin's theory of natural selection. Immigration controls became a popular means for protecting Americans from non-Anglo Saxon ethnic groups believed by many to be inferior. By 1905, anti-immigrant measures against new waves of immigrants from southern and eastern Europe became politically popular.

Formed in 1894, the Immigration Restriction League (IRL) argued that "Indians, Negroes, Chinese, Jews, and Americans cannot all be free in the same society." The IRL pressed for the exclusion of all immigrants who could not read twenty-five words of the U.S. Constitution—a test similar to the one used to bar blacks from voting in the South. The Democratic Party, however, had resisted such limits on immigration by styling itself as the champion of Irish Catholics and other immigrants. It won support by resisting evangelical efforts to ban saloons and giving aid to parochial schools and foreign language classes. During the 1890s, Democratic President Cleveland continued this pro-immigrant stance, vetoing the IRL's literacy test for immigrants and denouncing the "radical departure" from the generous and free-handed policy" of "welcom[ing] all who came to us from other lands." Cleveland's veto of the exclusion bill was bolstered by pro-immigrant Southerners, a key Democratic constituency, who wanted cheap labor to build up the South's new textile industry.

The debate against immigrants, however, began to change after 1905. Gompers of the AFL was persuaded that his membership's interest in higher wages required restricting competition from immigrant labor. Racial fears of Japanese were stoked both by a spike in Japanese immigration into California as well as the Japanese Navy's

decisive defeat of the Russian Empire in 1905, a victory that called into question the racial supremacy of white Europeans. Southerners increasingly saw the exclusion of migrants from southern and eastern Europe as part of their policy of white supremacy. Oscar Underwood, an Alabama senator, called for a literacy test for immigrants to protect "the great Celtic and Teutonic races" from immigration that would "contaminate our blood with an inferior race." Procedural maneuvering prevented the passage of the 1906 literacy test for immigrants.

In place of a literacy test, Congress created the Dillingham Commission, named for the anti-immigrant chair of the House Immigration Committee, to report on the peoples migrating to the United States. The Commission studied the British colonial settler nations of Australia, New Zealand, and Canada. Supporters and opponents of immigration testified before the Commission, often focusing on the supposed biological qualities of different ethnic groups. "The question before us is a race question," declared Robert deCourcy Ward of the IRL to the Dillingham Commission: "It is a question of what kind of babies shall be born." The Immigrant Protective League was formed by Chicago's Hull House to resist anti-immigrant measures and offer support

Library of Congress

Israel Zangwill, *The Melting Pot* Zangwill's 1908 play popularized the term *melting pot*. It told the story of a Russian-Jew who had fled the 1903 Kishinev pogrom in Russia. Wanting to make a new life in America, he composed *An American Symphony*, which praises the haven that the United States represents. At the climax of the play, the protagonist says, "What is the glory of Rome and Jerusalem where all nations and races come to worship and look back, compared with the glory of America, where all races and nations come to labour and look forward!" ▲

to recently arrived European immigrants. Grace Abbott, the League's chief, argued that industrial exploitation, not racial inferiority, caused broken families and crime among new immigrants. In 1910, the Dillingham Commission issued a forty-one-volume report laden with statistics and urging restrictions on immigrants that were eventually enacted in 1917 and 1924.

Fears about immigration also influenced Congress's domestic legislation. In 1910, Congress voted for the so-called White Slavery Act, prohibiting the transportation of women across state lines "for any immoral purpose." The law was passed in the wake of reports, often spurious, that brothels said to be owned by Chinese, Italians, and Jews, were kidnapping white women—"white slaves"—and forcing them into prostitution. "Shall we defend our American civilization . . . or lower our glorious flag to the most despicable foreigners—French, Irish, Italians, Jews, and Mongolians?" asked antiwhite slavery activist Ernest Bell. After Congress passed the White Slavery Act, its was often enforced against women themselves for entering into what federal prosecutors regarded as "immoral" relationships, such as interracial romance.

17-4b Roosevelt's Control over Monopolies

Theodore Roosevelt approached the problem of big business cautiously. As a reformer, he recognized that monopolies were unfair and

> The president's "gentlemen's agreements" with corporations begin to curb their excesses.

had to be controlled. The wave of mergers even disturbed conservative businessmen. When in 1901, J.P. Morgan organized the purchase of Andrew Carnegie's steel company and its merger with several other steel manufacturers to form U.S. Steel, he created the world's first billion-dollar firm and roused small businesses' fears that a tiny cabal of financial elites controlled industry. Fearing that they could not survive against such goliaths, these smaller businesses formed the **National Association of Manufacturers (NAM)** to lobby for more aggressive enforcement of the Sherman Antitrust Act to preserve competition. The NAM also opposed trade unions, calling them the "Labor Trust" on the grounds that unions operated like a monopoly in labor. Federal and local governments tended to agree with the NAM's characterization of unions.

Roosevelt did not, however, object to all large-scale businesses. For example, he endorsed the view that interstate railroads could not survive without pooling to control price wars. Instead of stopping all mergers, he believed that the federal government should closely supervise them. In 1902, Morgan attempted a second giant consolidation by negotiating with railroad titans J.J. Hill and E.H. Harriman to merge the Northern Pacific, the Great Northern, and the Chicago, Burlington, and Quincy railroads. Roosevelt instructed his attorney general to prosecute the company

for violation of the Sherman Antitrust Act. In *United States v. Northern Securities*, the Supreme Court upheld the prosecution, saying that the Commerce Clause could apply to railroad regulation. Roosevelt boasted that "the most powerful men in the country were held to accountability before the law."

Roosevelt used this accountability not to prohibit mergers but to ensure that they did not abuse consumers or competitors. He believed that mergers should be governed by informal meetings between titans of industry and titans of politics—that was, by himself. In 1903, Roosevelt secured congressional approval to create the Department of Commerce and Labor and, within it, the Bureau of Corporations. Under his plan, businesses seeking to consolidate would apply to the Bureau for preapproval of the deal. In return for assurances that the consolidated firm would act in a socially responsible manner, Roosevelt would give it immunity from antitrust prosecution. The leaders of U.S. Steel, Standard Oil, and International Harvester met with officials from Roosevelt's Departments of Justice and Commerce, opening their books to secure "gentlemen's agreements" that would relieve them from fear of antitrust prosecution.

17-4c Progressive Victories and Their Limits

With the nation prosperous and ascendant in world affairs, Roosevelt easily won a landslide victory in 1904, beating the Democratic

> The president and Congress pass a series of Progressive legislation.

nominee, Alton Parker, a New York judge who was honest but dull. The election's turnout was low and rhetoric was mild because the two main candidates were largely indistinguishable from each other. The two probusiness New Yorkers agreed on most issues, from colonizing the Philippines to their dislike of trade unions. The excitement in the election was that Eugene V. Debs, former head of the American Railway Union, who had been imprisoned for his labor activism, ran as the Socialist Party candidate, polling almost half a million votes.

Buoyed by his victory, Roosevelt was able to pass several important pieces of legislation through a Republican Congress despite the opposition of conservatives, who distrusted his excessive fondness for governmental intervention and regulation. The legislation shared a common feature: It delegated broad policy-making discretion to bureaucratic experts qualified not by their party loyalty but by special training.

For example, in 1905, Congress enacted the Forest Transfer Act, which gave the National Forest Service headed by Gifford Pinchot supervision over 150 million

National Association of Manufacturers (NAM) Coalition of small- and medium-sized companies that came together to lobby out because they feared major corporations.

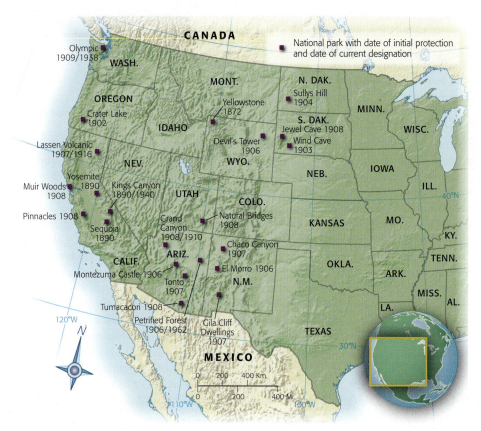

Map 17.2 Early National Park System Environmentalists such as John Muir, the founder of the modern conservation movement, opposed the policy of using natural resources for economic gain. He urged that wilderness areas be preserved in their natural state as game preserves and recreational areas. President Roosevelt added 150 million acres to the national forests, created fifty-one federal bird sanctuaries, four national game reserves, five national parks, and eighteen national monuments. ▲

acres of federal forest land formerly managed by the General Land Office (see Map 17.2). Pinchot, a pioneer in forestry, was a close personal friend of Roosevelt's. After studying at the French National Forestry School, he returned to the United States and established scientific stewardship of natural resources by government experts. Convinced that there would never be any constituency in favor of natural resource preservation unless it could be made to pay for itself, Pinchot urged that federal lands be opened for ranchers and timber companies to use so long as management practices guaranteed a "sustained yield."

In 1906, Congress enacted the Pure Food and Drug Act, which prohibited the interstate shipment or sale of polluted or mislabeled foods and drugs, and the Federal Meat Inspection Act, which ensured that meat was sanitarily processed. Support for the acts followed the publication of *The Jungle* by Upton Sinclair, a socialist tied to Progressive causes. Sinclair wrote an exposé about the miserable working conditions in Chicago's stockyards, but the public focused on the few pages that described in disgusting detail the

muckraking Investigating possible political, corporate, and social corruption used by journalists such as Ida B. Tarbell and Upton Sinclair who wrote exposés on corporations and politicians.

unsanitary conditions in which meat was processed. Sinclair mournfully noted, "I aimed at the public's heart, and by accident I hit it in the stomach." His story about a radical agenda watered down to create modest reform symbolized Progressivism's middle-class limitations. He and journalists such as Ida Tarbell practiced a new kind of investigative reporting termed **muckraking** that took aim at government and corporate corruption and unfair practices, but their efforts brought only modest reforms.

Urged by Roosevelt, Congress enacted the Hepburn Act (1906), which gave the Interstate Commerce Commission the power to set maximum railroad rates on interstate routes. The legislation pleased no one. Railroad owners darkly warned that rate setting by bureaucrats would drive railroads into bankruptcy. Farmers were disappointed by the complex, lengthy, and expensive proceedings the act required, preferring simpler rules such as uniform per mile prices or even outright government ownership. Nevertheless, the Supreme Court deferred to the Commission's experts and upheld the act.

During this period of rapid reform, labor policy remained an unresolved area of the law. In 1905, the U.S. Supreme Court decided in *Lochner v. New York* that the state had only limited power to regulate employees' work

Underwood & Underwood/Corbis

Global Americans **Florence Kelley** grew up in an abolitionist household in Philadelphia. Her father, William D. Kelley, was a U.S. congressman and had been one of the founders of the Republican Party. She graduated from Cornell University in 1882 and then left for Zurich, Switzerland, to join other Americans who were interested in learning from European social theorists. There she became friends with Friedrich Engels and worked on an English translation of his book, *The Condition of the Working Class in England*, which was published in the United States in 1887.

In Zurich, Kelley met and married Socialist Labor Party member Lazare Wischnewetzky with whom she had three children. They divorced, and she and the children moved to Chicago's Hull House. Kelley devoted her career to reforming labor conditions for U.S. workers and remained a committed socialist. She was appointed as Illinois's first inspector of factories and pushed through legislation that limited women and child labor to eight hours a day. In 1899, she formed the National Consumers League, an advocacy group that informed consumers about how goods were manufactured to enable them to make informed choices, and lobbied for fair labor standards. She worked closely with Louis Brandeis on his brief for *Muller v. Oregon*, supplying research. In keeping with her Quaker and abolitionist upbringing, Kelley was one of the founding members of the National Association for the Advancement of Colored People (NAACP).

hours. Lochner, a bakery owner, sued and asked for relief from the state law that mandated a ten-hour work day and a six-day workweek for bakers. The Court held that baking was not a dangerous job requiring such protections.

Three years later, however, the Court made an exception to this ruling. Influenced by a legal brief written by Louis Brandeis, the Court in *Muller v. Oregon* (1908) decided that a state did have an interest in regulating the work hours of women. The Court did not overturn *Lochner* but instead relied on the **Brandeis brief**, which distilled scientific and social scientific evidence about the ill effects on women's health and homes when they worked long hours. Some feminists, however, were dismayed by the assumption that women were weaker than men.

Despite the growth of its bureaucracy, the federal government still lacked a central bank. The system was vulnerable to panics and collapse. In 1906, the earthquake and fire that destroyed one-third of San Francisco forced insurance companies to ship millions of dollars to cover claims in the West. The resulting shortfall of money in the East produced a panic when a speculator attempting to corner the copper market could not repay his loans. Rumors of the default started a run on the banks as jittery citizens worried that withdrawals would cause the banks to fail. The run threatened even healthy banks, triggering a freeze on credit and a massive business slowdown known as the Panic of 1907.

As in 1894, Morgan stepped in to save the financial system. Gathering New York's most important bankers in his private library, he pressured them to pledge their deposits to rescue banks threatened by runs. Morgan personally pledged to buy $30 million of New York City's bonds to save the city, and he organized committees of bankers to urge the clergy and press to reassure citizens. Prodded by Morgan, the U.S. Treasury promised to use federal revenues to help avert panic.

To stave off the bankruptcy of an investment bank, Morgan asked Roosevelt to promise antitrust immunity if U.S. Steel purchased a company held by the bank, and the president agreed. Although a business slowdown followed the crisis, a massive recession was averted. But Morgan's general management of the crisis suggested how completely a tiny group of bankers controlled the economic life of the nation, and the private bargain between Roosevelt and Morgan later produced a major rift within the Republican Party.

Although Roosevelt and his administration pushed for reform on the national level and looked favorably on regulation and reform at the local and state levels, they were by no means radical in their ideas or deeds. Roosevelt and his wing of the Progressive movement wanted to regulate business but only within certain narrow limits that allowed businesses such as those held by Morgan to thrive.

Brandeis brief A statement of a client's case that in this case used research on topics such as history, sociology, and statistics rather than legal citations to convince a court to make a decision based on a particular opinion or version of a case.

17-4d Grassroots Progressive Movements

In opposition to the top-down views of national leaders, a series of reforms percolated from the bottom up, often initiated by those whose interests were not represented in national politics. Many of the reforms emerged from the activities of women, who were still denied the vote in most of the country but were determined to engage in the work of social and political reform.

After the Panic of 1893, Progressive reforms spread to all levels of society.

Although African American men had been granted the right to vote with the passage of the Fifteenth Amendment, all women were specifically excluded. The struggle to gain women's right to vote was a long one although women in many western states had been successful (see Chapter 15.) In 1890, the National American Woman Suffrage Association (NAWSA) elected Elizabeth Cady Stanton as its president. Lucy Stone was the head of its executive committee, but Susan B. Anthony was its most public face, eventually becoming president when Stanton stepped down. Their sole focus was the expansion of voting rights for women, and they pressed for the vote state-by-state while lobbying for a constitutional amendment to guarantee the right for women. Some of the group's younger and more radical members, such as Alice Paul, broke away to pursue additional causes, such as a more general equal rights amendment, that were deemed distracting to the NAWSA. Paul, who had spent time with the British suffrage movement, was considered too outspoken and radical for the NAWSA.

Progressives passed legislation to amend state constitutions to challenge the power of the two major parties and to attain direct democracy. Citing the precedent of Australia, they pushed for the **secret ballot** that would have the government print ballots with the names of all candidates on which voters could cast in secret at polling places. All states had adopted this practice by 1891. Some states, particularly western and southern ones, also instituted the initiative (right of voters to initiate legislative action), referendum (submission for popular vote of a measure passed or proposed by a legislative body), and recall (the right of citizens to vote to remove an official). These three direct democratic interventions were intended to make their elected representatives more directly answerable to their constituents. In 1913, the Progressives' scored their biggest victory for direct democracy with ratification of the Seventeenth Amendment, which moved the right to elect U.S. senators from state legislatures to individual voters.

African American Progressive reformers concerned themselves particularly with the elimination of segregation and discrimination. Booker T. Washington dominated the conservative end of the reform spectrum, advocating for occupational training for young African Americans. He built the Tuskegee Institute in Alabama, which he had helped found in 1881 with the labor of his students: They laid the bricks, glazed the windows, and painted the walls. Washington believed in the principle of equality for all but thought that campaigning for social equality was "extremist folly." Instead, he believed that if African Americans could prove themselves as worthy citizens through hard work, moral behavior, and economic uplift, white America would openly embrace, or at least not resist, some semblance of equality. In his speech at the 1895 Cotton States and International Exhibition, Washington called on white Southerners to "cast down your buckets where you are" and to hire blacks, rather than new immigrants, to work in their factories.

Other African American leaders such as Ida B. Wells and W.E.B. Du Bois criticized Washington's approach and instead advocated forcefully for total equality under the law. Du Bois also suggested that African Americans resist Washington's industrial education model, which emphasized technical skills for the trades. Instead, he advocated for the liberal education of the **talented tenth** of African Americans, whom he thought would be competitive and respected if given access to colleges and universities. From this group, leaders would emerge who could be effective spokespeople for African American rights. Dubois and Washington did not always agree or work together, but they were two sides of an effective reform movement that pushed forward on economic and social rights for blacks in America.

One of the most vocal groups of race reformers met in 1905 and formed the Niagara Movement. They directly repudiated Booker T. Washington's accommodationist approach, demanding instead equality under the law and full civil rights protections for African Americans. The Niagara Movement believed that only confrontational politics to force federal and state governments to implement the Fourteenth and Fifteenth amendments would truly secure African Americans' rights and economic advancement. As their influence grew, they sought white

Eartha M.M. White Collection, University of North Florida, Thomas G. Carpenter Library, Special Collections and Archives

National Association of Colored Women's Clubs In July 1896, a group of women including Harriet Tubman, Ida B. Wells-Barnett, and Mary Church Terrell founded the National Association of Colored Women's Clubs (NACWC). Adopting the motto, "Lifting as We Climb," they worked to end Jim Crow Laws, lynching, and also advocate for suffrage for all women, regardless of race. The national organization's many branches worked within local communities to provide social and educational services. By 1918, the organization had a membership of more than 300,000. ▲

secret ballot Practice of keeping a citizen's vote private, also known as the *Australian ballot*.

talented tenth Concept championed by W.E.B Dubois that emphasized the need for higher education in order to develop leadership capacity among the most able 10 percent of African Americans.

allies, including Jane Addams and Florence Kelley. In the wake of one of the worst race riots in Atlanta, a national meeting of race reformers met in New York City. They founded the **National Association for the Advancement of Colored People (NAACP)** in 1909. Hiring lawyers and using both the courts and legislative process, the NAACP pushed for voting rights, educational opportunities, and an end to Jim Crow laws. One of its major public protests came when *Birth of a Nation* was first screened in 1915. The movie, which depicted the rise of the Ku Klux Klan and racist depictions of blacks, was so popular that Woodrow Wilson held a public screening in the White House.

The problems that faced immigrants influenced young, unmarried, educated women to transplant the **settlement house movement** from England to the United States. These women, mostly college graduates, moved into urban homes in immigrant enclaves to work directly with newcomers to help them adjust to their new lives. The settlement movement had begun at Toynbee Hall, a pioneering social settlement in the East End of London founded in 1884, and was closely associated with English universities and the Christian socialism movement. Progressives from Gifford Pinchot to Lillian Wald and Frederic Howe visited and worked at Toynbee Hall. Jane Addams, after working with reformers there, returned to Chicago to open Hull House in 1889.

Settlement house staff and its backers across the United States, like Hull House, gave time and money to helping immigrants. Staff organized English language classes, intervened with exploitative landlords, provided public kitchens and baths and day care services for children, and homeless shelters for new immigrants. At the same time, they gathered data about the lives of the poor to be used in setting social policy. Settlement house workers, who were mostly women, became the first social workers who used their education to solve day-to-day problems associated with poverty and to push policy and legislative solutions. By the early 1920s, there were almost five hundred settlement homes across the country, serving mostly urban immigrant communities.

These Progressives battled against the anti-immigrant movement in U.S. politics. In 1894, a group of Boston intellectuals founded the Immigration Restriction League. These people believed that the New Immigrants were of moral, social, and biological inferior stock and threatened the supposed purity of Americans. At the same time, the **eugenics** movement was also gaining traction in the United States. Based on the theories of British biologist, Francis Galton, eugenicists believed that Americans could control their biological destiny through mate selection, anti-immigration measures, and antimiscegenation laws. Neither academics nor the public scorned their position.

National Association for the Advancement of Colored People (NAACP) Legal and social advocacy group that lobbies for advancing the rights of African Americans.

settlement house movement Reform based on improving the lives of urban immigrant families by working intimately with them, providing relief and practical education.

eugenics Field of scholarship seeking to identify and engineer the perfect blending of human genes in order to create healthy, intelligent, and internally compatible populations.

17-5

Progressivism and National Politics

This 1916 photo shows young workers advocating for the passage of legislation that would outlaw child labor. Notice the way that they are dressed.

Judging from the photo, would you surmise that this is an organized demonstration or a spontaneous one? If organized, which adults do you think organized them? Why would they wear their best clothes to a protest? ▶

Library of Congress

In the first two decades of the twentieth century, progressive ideas prevailed in reform movements and politics. The Democrats, Republicans, and a new third party, the Progressive Party, claimed to be progressive but had very different ideas about what that term meant. In the elections of 1912 and 1916, the parties battled over how to balance the needs of business, urban dwellers, educated professionals, workers, and farmers. Increasingly, the Democratic Party's vision of Progressivism prevailed, and Congress enacted protections for labor, an income tax, and lower tariffs during a productive legislative session before the turmoil that would engulf the nation in World War I.

☞ How did elements of Progressivism change as major political parties adopted them? What elements were left out?

17-5a Divisions in the Republican Party

In the wake of the 1907 panic and resulting business slowdown, Democrats saw an opportunity to retake the White House in the 1908 election. Running for a second time, William Jennings Bryan, a pioneer in modern political campaigning, had built a formidable political organization by then. Although probusiness Democrats such as the newspaper publisher Joseph Pulitzer tried to stop him, Bryan easily secured the Democratic nomination. Realizing that he could not win with farmer support alone, Bryan worked hard to win labor by courting Gompers and the AFL. The normally nonpartisan Gompers was brought over by the unusually prolabor Democratic platform of 1908, which called for an eight-hour day, a separate Department of Labor, an income tax to replace revenues from the tariff, and an end to federal court interference with strikes and boycotts.

> Issues of reform split the Republicans and create an opening for the Democrats.

Voters, however, did not embrace the Democrats' message of economic equality in 1908. As in 1896, Bryan lost eastern states soundly because Gompers could not deliver workers' votes. Bryan's evangelical style and support for prohibition alienated immigrant workers. Meanwhile, William Howard Taft, the Republican nominee, picked up support of middle-class professionals because he had Roosevelt's support. Despite that support, Taft rejected Roosevelt's advice on tariff reform, endorsing a probusiness platform with only vague promises for farmers. Taft's victory, however, seemed to confirm that support for business stability trumped social reform and equality in the majority of the voters.

Taft's handling of antitrust cases further alienated Roosevelt and Progressives. In 1911, Taft's attorney general charged U.S. Steel with violating antitrust laws despite the 1908 gentlemen's agreement between Morgan and Roosevelt. The case alleged that U.S. Steel officials had deceived Roosevelt. The insinuation that Roosevelt was unaware of his own administration's actions humiliated him. Vigorously denying this, Roosevelt accused Taft of deception and incompetence. What had begun as such a close political relationship was torn apart by Taft's very public rejection of Roosevelt and his brand of Progressivism.

The split between Taft and Roosevelt over the *U.S. Steel* case did not reflect disagreement about the substance of antitrust policy but about whether such policy should be carried out judicially or presidentially. Both Roosevelt and Taft supported a **rule of reason** in antitrust cases under which courts allowed businesses to engage in monopolistic operations out of economic necessity for the public benefit. In 1911, the U.S. Supreme Court adopted the rule of reason in *Standard Oil Co. of New Jersey v. United States* holding that only combinations and contracts that unreasonably restrained trade violated the Sherman Act, so monopolies were not inherently illegal. The rule of reason, however, further alienated farmers from the Republican Party because they regarded corporations as inherently undemocratic threats to their economic and political autonomy.

17-5b Progressive Party

Having lost Roosevelt's support, Taft faced new rules and familiar challengers when he decided to run for president again in 1912. He. As a result of Progressive lobbying, some states used direct primary elections to select delegates to presidential conventions rather than, for example, caucuses of state legislators. Taft was challenged for the nomination by the charismatic Roosevelt, who won nine primary victories by a landslide, and by Progressive Senator Robert LaFollette, who won the primaries in Wisconsin and Ohio, Taft's home state. Nevertheless, the Republican National Committee awarded enough contested delegates to Taft to secure his nomination.

> The Progressives create one of the most successful third-party movements in U.S. politics.

rule of reason Order based on a "gentlemen's agreement" between government and corporations as to who could form monopolies that benefit the consumer.

Campaign Flyer for the Progressive Party, 1912 The party nominated Hiram Johnson, governor of California, as Roosevelt's running mate. Johnson was one of the most progressive governors in the nation, and under his leadership, the state legislature passed laws that allowed for the direct election of senators and the initiative, referendum, and recall. The voting reforms gave California citizens unprecedented access to direct democracy. ▶

Corbis

Bain News Service, publisher

Global Americans
Born in 1877 to a Jewish family in Budapest, Hungary, **Rosika Schwimmer** began advocating for feminist causes at an early age. During the 1890s, she helped found the Hungarian Feminist Association, the Hungarian National Council of Women, and the Women's Trade Union. In 1913, she became the corresponding secretary for the International Woman Suffrage Association (IWSA). She became close friends with suffragists in the United States and toured with Carrie Chapman Catt through Europe and the United States, pushing for women's suffrage.

After the outbreak of World War I, Schwimmer could not return home to her war-torn nation. She helped form the Women's Peace Party in the United States and became a lifelong pacifist who lobbied President Wilson directly to establish an international peace commission to stop the war. Schwimmer worked with Henry Ford to fund the Peace Ship that sailed with relief workers and supplies to Stockholm. After the war, she became vice president of the International League for Peace and Freedom. In 1919, when the Communists briefly took over Hungary, Schwimmer fled and settled in Chicago, but she was denied U.S. citizenship because of her pacifist beliefs. Her case went to the Supreme Court in 1929. She told the Court: "My cosmic consciousness of belonging to the human family is shared by all those who believe that all human beings are the children of God." The U.S. government allowed her to stay in the country, but she died without citizenship in any country.

Roosevelt's followers angrily denounced Taft's nomination as brazen theft and bolted the convention to found the **Progressive Party**, which nominated Roosevelt for president and Governor Hiram W. Johnson of California for vice president. This third party had a base broad enough to threaten the two major parties because it had finally united middle-class and Social Gospel reformers in a reform tradition dating back to the abolitionist movement. The conservative (and Democratic) *New York Times* described the convention as "an assemblage of religious enthusiasts . . . a Methodist camp meeting." After singing "Onward Christian Soldiers!" the delegates were ecstatic when Roosevelt thundered, "We stand at Armageddon, and we battle for the Lord." Roosevelt electrified the convention with his appearance because he had just recently survived an attempt on his life. He declared at the convention that he was "as fit as a Bull Moose" to run for president. A new political mascot joined the donkey and elephant.

Democrats were also deeply divided between the pro-business and pro-immigrant East and the more evangelical and agrarian West and South. Leading the latter was the "Great Commoner," William Jennings Bryan. Having been defeated three times, however, he was an unlikely nominee for a party that could smell victory in Republican dissension. Instead, Champ Clark of Missouri assumed an early lead among the delegates. The eastern and conservative Democrats campaigned for Woodrow Wilson, the recently elected governor of New Jersey, former president of Princeton University, and a political newcomer.

The pious son of a Presbyterian minister, Wilson grew up in Virginia and Georgia and had strong southern sympathies. He was the first Southerner to run for and win the presidency since before the Civil War, marking a seeming reconciliation between North and South. He had spent most of his career as a professor of political science, first at Johns Hopkins and later at Princeton. In his writings, Wilson championed themes popular with middle-class reformers, advocating government by well-qualified experts and a professional civil service free from patronage politics. Wilson's antimachine stance had made him an ideal candidate for governor of New Jersey in 1910 when the Democratic Party was looking for someone to challenge the Republicans whose lax regulatory policies, which Lincoln Steffens, another muckraking journalist, had titled "traitor state." Wilson's victory in New Jersey gave him a national reputation without much political baggage. Bryan saw in him a possible unifier of the eastern and western wings of the party. Attracted both by Wilson's dislike of political machines and his Protestant piety, Bryan threw his support behind Wilson, who narrowly defeated Clark for the nomination.

Wilson had the Democratic nomination but not much of a program. His real opponent was not Taft—who had no chance of victory—but Roosevelt with his progressive track record. Wilson discovered a way to differentiate himself from Roosevelt and the Progressive Party by working with Louis Brandeis, a Boston labor lawyer (*Mueller v. Oregon*) and social reformer who became Wilson's most important campaign adviser. Brandeis advised Wilson to champion small businessmen and farmers in opposition to Roosevelt's "New Nationalism," supporting bureaucratically managed monopolies. Calling Wilson's program the "New Freedom," Brandeis helped him craft

Progressive Party Reform that would improve society by using the power of the federal government to distribute wealth and regulate businesses.

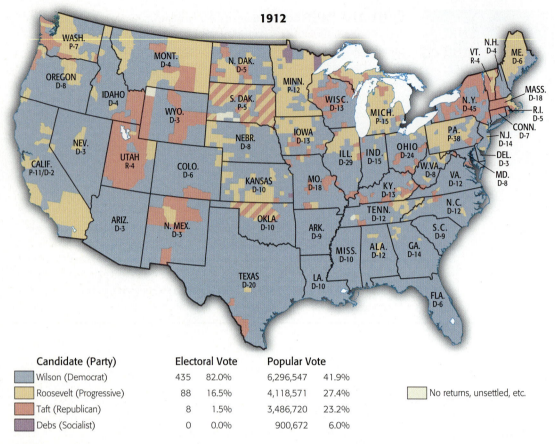

1912

Candidate (Party)	Electoral Vote		Popular Vote	
Wilson (Democrat)	435	82.0%	6,296,547	41.9%
Roosevelt (Progressive)	88	16.5%	4,118,571	27.4%
Taft (Republican)	8	1.5%	3,486,720	23.2%
Debs (Socialist)	0	0.0%	900,672	6.0%

No returns, unsettled, etc.

Map 17.3 Election of 1912 In this election, Wilson narrowly won a plurality of the popular vote with 42 percent against Roosevelt's 27 percent and Taft's 23 percent. Of electoral votes, Wilson had 435 against Roosevelt's 88 and Taft's meager 8. Eugene Debs, running on the Socialist ticket, took 6 percent of the popular vote. ▲

a policy of breaking up monopolies, creating a publicly accountable banking system, and regulating railroads for the benefit of farmers and small shippers. This policy was attuned to Bryan's agrarian ideology, but because it was championed by an Easterner with a southern background and sympathies, Wilson's program unified the party more than Bryan ever could. Wilson won the 1912 election (see Map 17.3).

17-5c Wilsonian Progressivism

In the election of 1912, the Democrats won control of the Senate and maintained their majority in the House of Representatives, so they had complete control over the federal government for the first time since 1894. With a mandate from the voters to control big business, Democrats used their new power to reduce tariffs, regulate banking, and impose new controls over monopolies (see Table 17.2).

> Wilson's presidency is bolstered by congressional Progressive legislation.

During the spring of 1912, Democrats in the House had set up a committee to investigate the "money trust." The Pujo Committee interrogated leading bankers, including the aging Morgan, and in early 1913 issued a report confirming that a small group of bankers linked to him controlled numerous manufacturing and transportation companies. Public outcry over such concentrated financial power demanded a major overhaul of the banking system, but the Democrats quickly divided over how much control the federal government should exercise. For populist agrarians like Bryan, then Wilson's secretary of state, it was essential that the government, not private bankers, control the money supply. Brandeis also urged the president to end private bankers' power over monetary policy.

The Federal Reserve Act created the seven-person Federal Reserve Board whose members the president would nominate and the Senate confirm as well as twelve private regional Federal Reserve banks, each with its own board of directors and branches. All nationally chartered banks were required to buy stock in and deposit reserves with their regional reserve bank in return for which that bank would give its member banks access to loans and dividends. By lending money to member banks according to the rules adopted by the Federal Reserve Board, the Federal Reserve banks could avert runs such as those that had occurred in all of the prior depressions.

Table 17.2 Legislation Passed during the Wilson Administration

Legislation passed during the Wilson administration was the culmination of Progressive reforms that had percolated at the local and state levels. Some regulated the economy and corporation, and others helped particular constituencies such as farmers, workers, and temperance advocates. This legislation revealed the Progressive belief that the federal government had an important and active role in regulating all aspects of society.

Date	Name	Description
1912	Federal Reserve Act	Created Federal Reserve Board and regulated monetary policy for the nation
March 1913	Webb-Kenyon Act	Prohibited interstate shipment or transportation of alcoholic beverages between states
October 1913	Revenue (Underwood) Act	Imposed an income tax and lowered tariff rates from 40% to 25%
October 1914	Federal Trade Commission Act	Regulated unfair trade practices and protected consumers as the result of the reforms begun with the Sherman Antitrust Act
	Clayton Antitrust Act	Regulated price discrimination, mergers, and acquisitions and prevented one person from being a director of two or more competing businesses
July 1916	Federal Farm Loan Act	Created a loan board and increased credit to rural families
July 1916	Federal Aid Road Act	Provided first federal highway funding
August 1916	National Park Service Organic Act	Created an agency to oversee and manage U.S. national parks and monuments
September 1916	Adamson Act	Established eight-hour day and overtime for interstate railroad workers
September 1917	Keating-Owen Child Labor Act	Prohibited the interstate sale of goods made by factories that employed children under 14 but was declared unconstitutional in 1918

In addition to creating the Federal Reserve system, Wilson signed legislation for other financial reforms. In 1913, Congress sent the Sixteenth Amendment, legalizing a federal income tax, to the states for ratification. Congress then passed the Revenue (Underwood) Act in 1913, which cut all tariffs substantially. To placate farmers who were skeptical about the centralized control of the Federal Reserve Act, Democrats enacted the Federal Farm Loan Act that allowed the federal government to loan funds secured by crops in warehouses to farmers. Congress also steeply increased the income tax rates on the highest incomes and created a workers' compensation program for federal employees.

The New Freedom had called for the breakup of corporate monopolies, but Wilson's antimonopoly laws were much less sweeping. At his urging, Congress passed the Federal Trade Commission Act and the Clayton Antitrust Act, which he signed in 1914. The first measure created the Federal Trade Commission, a regulatory agency charged with investigating unfair trade practices and mergers above a specified size as well as certain anticompetitive practices. The Clayton Act exempted union activities such as boycotts and strikes from injunctions by federal judges but did not overrule the Supreme Court's rule of reason, nor did it mandate the breakup of all monopolies. Samuel Gompers praised the measure as the "magna carta for labor."

Workers got part of what they wanted from the Wilson Administration and the Democratic Congress. Congress enacted the Keating-Owen Child Labor Act, which banned the interstate transportation of goods made with child labor. The measure was strongly backed by Social Gospel reformers and labor unions, hoping to prevent child exploitation. Labor unions wanted to eliminate competition by child laborers who worked for low wages. Faced with a national railroad strike, Congress also passed the Adamson Act, setting a maximum eight-hour day for railroad workers on interstate routes. In dealing with federal workers, Wilson took executive action and bowed to the wishes of his southern cabinet officials and instituted the segregation of the federal government. Most blacks who had the few federal government jobs available to them were fired and replaced with white workers. Women such as Mary Church Terrell and the NAACP voiced loud opposition but to no avail.

Because Wilson had won his first term as a result of the Republican split, many doubted whether he could win reelection against a united Republican Party. His legislative successes weakened the Progressive Party's appeal. Roosevelt declined to run again as a Progressive and instead sought the Republican Party nomination. Angered by his previous defection to the Progressives, however, Republican stalwarts instead chose Charles Evans Hughes, the former governor of New York and associate justice of the U.S. Supreme Court. Hughes's reputation as a strict regulator of business gave him sufficient credibility among Progressive Party members so that they endorsed the Republican ticket. Roosevelt fell in line and campaigned for Hughes.

In the 1916 presidential contest between Wilson and Hughes, two issues dominated the debate. First, the Democrats were firmly identified as the party of labor. Hughes attacked laws such as the Adamson Act and the Keating-Owen Act as detrimental to business. He also advocated something more akin to Roosevelt's New Nationalism as a means of regulating corporations as opposed to the more aggressive Wilsonian policies.

Second, the candidates also had to directly confront the Great War that had commenced in Europe in 1914 between France, England, and Russia on one side and Germany and Austria-Hungary on the other. Hughes accused Wilson of neglecting preparations for war in case the United States was dragged into the conflict. Germany's submarine strikes against neutral shipping and passenger liners made some Americans seek a more aggressive stand against Germany. Wilson, however, campaigned on the slogan, "He kept us out of war," a position popular with both Bryan's agrarian followers and voters of Irish and German descent who were hostile to England or sympathetic to Germany. Wilson's coalition of workers, farmers, and middle-class reformers was fragile, but it was enough for him to win reelection. This coalition and its progressive reform agenda, however, soon took a back seat as the war in Europe loomed menacingly over Americans' lives.

Summary

At the beginning of the Gilded Age, business and government interests were intricately and corruptly intertwined. Political parties were evenly matched, and consequently stagnation permeated national governance. Furthermore, a vast number of Americans, including all women as well as Asian, including the Oxford, African and Native Americans, were prevented from participating in democratic governance. Reform movements, however, emerged from a grassroots level as middle-class professionals, farmers, moral reformers, and workers sought the government's help in improving their lives.

Farmers organized against railroad monopolies, and urban workers formed unions and short-lived labor parties. Middle-class professionals sought to mitigate the worst effects of industrial capitalism and chaotic urban growth by promoting reform measures adopted from European precedents, ranging from civil service reform and city planning to unemployment insurance and workers' compensation. When small movements coalesced, national third-party organizations such as the Populists and the Progressives gained enough political strength to influence the Democrats and the Republicans.

Two strains of Progressivism, one touted as Roosevelt's New Nationalism and the other as Wilson's New Freedom, became integral to party politics. Progressivist management of government and social problems by educated experts combined with their desire to create better communities and uplift citizens became a hallmark of the Democratic Party. The legacy of these local grassroots movements, culminating in the Progressive movement, had long-term effects into the twentieth century.

<Thinking Back, *Looking Forward*>

As you review this chapter, think about how reform movements emerged in the United States in response to the vast changes brought by industrialization, immigration, and urbanization discussed in this and the two previous chapters. How did U.S. efforts compare to movements abroad? How did race and gender influence both the reform movements and those targeted for reform? In the next great era of reform—the 1930s—look, too, for the influence of race and gender. Identify which reforms came from the bottom up and which from the top down. How did Progressive ideas continue to shape reform including the New Deal and the Great Society into the twentieth century?

To make your study concrete, review the timeline and reflect on the entries there. Think about their causes, consequences, and connections. How do they fit with global trends?

Additional Resources

Books

Addams, Jane. *Twenty Years at Hull House.* **Urbana-Champaign: University of Illinois Press, 1990.** ▶ First-person, intimate account of life inside the settlement house movement; originally published in 1910.

Amar, Akhil Reed. *America's Constitution: A Biography.* **New York: Random House, 2005.** ▶ An overview of U.S. constitutional history that applies history, sociology, and legal reasoning to interpret each clause of the Constitution.

Bender, Thomas. *A Nation Among Nations: America's Place in World History.* **New York: Hill & Wang, 2006.** ▶ A study that makes the case for considering U.S. history in the context of global history by using the Progressive movement as a prime example.

DuBois, Ellen Carol. *Woman Suffrage & Women's Rights.* **New York: New York University Press, 1998.** ▶ A collection of essays that looks at the history of the suffrage movement and its complex legacy for other groups seeking the vote.

Edwards, Rebecca. *New Spirits, 1865–1905.* **New York: Oxford University Press, 2006.** ▶ A readable overview of the period with excellent examples and analyses of how corruption and reform were intimately tied.

Hahn, Steven. *A Nation Under Our Feet: Black Political Struggles in the Rural South from Slavery to the Great Migration.* **Cambridge, MA: Harvard University Press, 2004.** ▶ Pulitzer Prize-winning book that traces the way African Americans actively worked to preserve their rights during the Jim Crow era.

Rogers, Daniel. *Atlantic Crossings: Social Politics in a Progressive Era.* **Cambridge MA: Harvard University Press, 1998.** ▶ Presentation of the Progressive Era internationally with documents related to the transit of urban and social welfare reforms from Europe to the United States.

Sinclair, Upton. *The Jungle.* ▶ A 1906 novel that follows the lives of immigrant meat-packing workers and their families in the shadows of Chicago's stockyard.

Tyrrell, Ian. *Reforming the World: The Creation of America's Moral Empire.* **Princeton, NJ: Princeton University Press, 2010.** ▶ Review of the way the United States used cultural and military and economic influence globally to achieve its foreign policy goals.

> Go to the MindTap® for **Global Americans** to access the full version of select books from this Additional Resources section.

Websites

Documenting the South. http://docsouth.unc.edu/ ▶ University of North Carolina collection of primary sources that examine U.S. history from a southern perspective.

In Motion: The African American Migration Experience. http://www.inmotionaame.org/home.cfm;jsessionid=f83 0478521449987328734?bhcp=1 ▶ Schomburg Center overview of the major African American migrations with primary and secondary sources.

Oyez IIT Chicago-Kent College of Law. https://www.oyez .org/ ▶ Multimedia archive that explores the history of the Supreme Court of the United States.

Continue exploring online through MindTap®**, where you can:**
- **Assess your knowledge with the Chapter Test**
- **Watch historical videos related to the chapter**
- **Further your understanding with interactive maps and timelines**

Politics of Reform

1873–1877	1878–1881	1882–1884	1885–1889	1890
October 1873 President Grant signs the Comstock Act.	**May 1879** Henry George publishes *Progress and Poverty*.	**January 1883** Arthur signs the Pendleton Civil Service Act.	**October 1886** U.S. Supreme Court decides *Wabash v. Illinois*.	**June** Harrison signs the Dependent and Disability Pension Act.
December 1873 Woman's Christian Temperance Union is founded in Ohio.	**November 1880** James A. Garfield is elected president.	**May 1884** Anti-Monopoly Party is founded and nominates Benjamin Butler for president.	**February 1887** Cleveland signs the Interstate Commerce Act.	**July** Harrison signs the Sherman Antitrust Act.
		November 1884 Grover Cleveland is elected president.	**November 1888** Benjamin Harrison becomes president.	**October** Harrison signs the Sherman Silver Purchase Act.
March 1876 U.S. Supreme Court upholds *Munn v. Illinois*.	**August 1881** National Civil Service Reform League is founded.	**December 1884** Toynbee Hall is founded in London, England.	**September 1889** Hull House opens in Chicago.	Harrisons signs the McKinley Tariff.
January 1877 United Labor Party is formed.	**September 1881** Chester Alan Arthur becomes president after Garfield is assassinated.	Germany adopts workmen's compensation laws.		

Canada

United States

England   Germany

Spain

Mexico   Caribbean

The Pacif

New Z

1891–1893

July 1892
Populist Party adopts the Omaha Platform.

February 1893
Panic of 1893 begins.

September 1893
New Zealand becomes the first country in which women have the right to vote.

1894–1900

April 1894
Coxey's Army reaches Washington, D.C.

January 1895
U.S. Supreme Court decides *U.S. vs. E.C. Knight, Co.*

November 1896
William McKinley is elected president.

April 1898
U.S. declares war on Spain in the Spanish-American War, with battles fought in the Caribbean and in the Pacific.

1901–1904

April 1901
J.P. Morgan creates U.S. Steel.

September 1901
Leon Czolgosz assassinates McKinley, and Roosevelt becomes president.

February 1903
Department of Commerce and Labor is created.

March 1904
U.S. Supreme Court *decides U.S. v. Northern Securities.*

November 1904
Roosevelt wins reelection.

1905–1908

April 1905
U.S. Supreme Court decides *Lochner v. U.S.*

July 1905
Niagara Movement is founded.

February 1906
Upton Sinclair publishes *The Jungle.*

February 1908
U.S. Supreme Court decides *Muller v. Oregon.*

November 1908
William Howard Taft elected president.

1909–1914

February 1909
National Association for the Advancement of Colored People is founded.

November 1910
Mexican Revolution begins.

May 1911
U.S. Supreme Court decides *Standard Oil Co. of New Jersey v. United States* case.

May 1912
Congress forms the Pujo Committee.

November 1912
Woodrow Wilson is elected president.

February 1913
Sixteenth Amendment, instituting an income tax, goes into effect.

May 1913
Seventeenth Amendment allowing direct election of senators goes into effect.

18 Projecting Power

1875–1920

In 1900, W.E.B. Du Bois joined black leaders and intellectuals from Britain, the West Indies, and Africa, at the Pan-African Congress in London, where he delivered an "Address to the Nations of the World" on the dangers of racism to the ideals of justice and freedom.

In July 1900, W.E.B. Du Bois, thirty-two-year-old African American professor of history and economics at Atlanta University, traveled to London to attend the first Pan-African Congress. He joined black leaders and intellectuals from Britain, the West Indies, and Africa with a shared commitment to improving the status of African people around the world. Slavery in the United States had ended only thirty-five years before, and thus far Du Bois's academic study had focused on the history of African Americans and the economic and social conditions in which they lived. At the Congress, he had an opportunity to place African Americans into an international context. At the closing session of the Congress, he delivered the "Address to the Nations of the World" in which he declared: "The problem of the twentieth century is the problem of the color line, the question of how far differences of race . . . will hereafter be made the basis of denying to over half the world the right of sharing to their utmost ability the opportunities and privileges of modern civilization." He also predicted that the continued mistreatment of people of color would imperil "the high ideals of justice, freedom, and culture" enshrined in European civilization. Over the next sixty years, Du Bois would become a persistent critic of racism. A renowned intellectual, he understood that U.S. race relations were not simply a domestic social problem but a manifestation of deep-seated racial attitudes whereby white people justified the exploitation of peoples of color.

Scurlock Studio Records, ca. 1905–1994, Archives Center, National Museum of American History

In the late nineteenth century, European powers had divided Africa among themselves and consolidated their holdings in Asia and the Pacific. By 1900, Belgium, France, Great Britain, Germany, Italy, the Netherlands, Portugal, and Spain were extracting the African continent's raw materials—gold, diamonds, copper, rubber, ivory, and palm oil, as well as cocoa transplanted from Latin America—for the benefit of European consumers. But those who mined, cultivated, and prepared these resources were Africans working in conditions resembling slavery. Only two African nations remained independent—Abyssinia (Ethiopia), which had recently beaten back Italian aggressors, and Liberia, founded in 1821 by Americans as a haven for former slaves. In Asia, Europeans ruled or dominated India, Burma, Singapore, Malaya, Indochina (Vietnam, Laos, and Cambodia), the East Indies, the Pacific islands, Australia, and New Zealand. The Philippines, formerly a Spanish colony, had just come under U.S. control. China—the age-old empire that had long controlled the region—was severely weakened by European trade policies and territorial concessions.

Du Bois criticized the intersection of racism and capitalism—the need for raw materials as nations industrialized and competed for markets and profits—that drove European domination and exposed tensions in his own nation's rise to global prominence. Some Americans admired the colonial empires that European nations had built in Africa and Asia

> W.E.B. Du Bois understood that race relations were a manifestation of deep-seated racial attitudes whereby white people justified the exploitation of peoples of color. How do Du Bois's views on the dangers of racism to the ideals of freedom relate to the growing economic imperialism of the U.S. and Europe?
>
> Go to MindTap® to watch a video on Du Bois and learn how his story relates to the themes of this chapter.

and believed that the United States needed its own foreign territories to guard its economic and strategic interests and to export its products as well as its political and cultural ideals. Others pointed to the ironies of a democratic nation imposing U.S. rule on people in faraway lands. Still others feared that colonialism might encourage the immigration of people of color who were perceived as racially inferior. Between 1875 and 1920, America's projection of international power—economic, military, and political—generated tremendous economic growth and national pride, but it also sparked wars in Cuba and the Philippines, interventions in Central America and Mexico, and entry into a European war with profound global ramifications.

18-1

Roots of the U.S. Empire

Drawn in 1888, this U.S. cartoon depicts the British Empire. By the late nineteenth century, the British had colonial possessions in Africa, the Asian subcontinent, and the Far East. To protect their vast territorial holdings from competing colonial powers like France and Germany, they built the world's largest navy. Aided by an extensive network of civil servants and soldiers, the British maintained a firm grip on the diverse foreign peoples under their rule.

Does this image portray British colonialism positively or negatively? What does this image's appearance in a American publication suggest about U.S. attitudes toward imperial expansion in the late nineteenth century? ▶

Go to MindTap® to practice history with the Chapter 18 **Primary Source Writing Activity: Roots of the U.S. Empire**. Read and view primary sources and respond to a writing prompt.

The Granger Collection, New York

Although the United States lacked formal overseas colonies before 1898, it had become a continental empire long before. Through purchase, war, and treaty settlements, the U.S. government had extended the nation's boundaries. Americans and new immigrants moved west to settle new lands and pursue commercial opportunities. They embraced the idea of Manifest Destiny, a belief first articulated in the 1840s that U.S. territorial expansion across North America was inevitable and justified.

Almost since the beginning of the republic, U.S. leaders had sought to develop the country's economy without becoming embroiled in foreign wars and political controversies. In his 1796 farewell address, President George

Washington asserted, "The great rule of conduct for us in regard to foreign nations is in extending our commercial relations, to have with them as little political connection as possible." Although the U.S. government did not hesitate to wield its power in negotiating commercial treaties or defending its international economic interests, it did not join Europeans in occupying foreign territories.

Americans had an uncomfortable relationship with the concept of empire. From its founding, they had distinguished their country from nations driven by greed and the desire to subjugate foreign peoples. Although they recoiled at the violence and domination displayed in the European scramble for territory in Africa and Asia,

Americans also acquired land and displaced other peoples. Fusing economic, political, religious, and racial motives, white Americans conquered much of North America and began to project U.S. power globally. Although its path to empire differed from those of its European counterparts, the United States became an empire nonetheless.

☞ As you read, consider how and why the United States began to engage the wider world more extensively in the late nineteenth century. What were some of the most important domestic and international factors that drove the United States to expand its power internationally?

18-1a Commerce and National Pride

As the United States rapidly industrialized, its policy makers worried that their failure to challenge European **imperialism**—the cultural, political, and economic domination of foreign peoples—would have serious economic consequences. By the 1870s, despite a rapidly growing population, the United States was producing more foodstuffs and manufactured goods than its domestic markets could absorb. Without additional consumers abroad, U.S. leaders worried that markets would remain glutted, prices would plummet, and labor unrest would intensify. Such concerns became particularly strong during the economic depressions that rocked the United States during the Panics of 1873 and 1893. Eager to find a safety valve to defuse domestic tensions,

> Economic, political, religious, and racial factors propel an increased international role for the United States.

government officials, farmers, and businessmen began vigorously pursuing foreign markets. U.S. exports increased from $526 million in 1876 to more than $1 billion a year by the late 1890s.

As the United States became a dominant force in global trade, Europeans invested heavily in the nation's industries and railroads (see Chapter 15). American entrepreneurs borrowed extensively from British bankers. The financial risks paid off spectacularly and U.S. economic growth soared. On the eve of World War I, the United States generated nearly 20 percent of the world's economic output (see Figure 18.1).

This stunning economic success triggered European anxieties about a possible "Americanization" of the world. In 1902, when the British Empire encompassed one-fifth of the globe and one-quarter of its population, English writer F.A. McKenzie worried about the cultural impact of U.S. commercial power. In *The American Invaders*, McKenzie decried the proliferation of U.S. products in British daily life: "The average citizen wakes in the morning at the sound of an American alarm clock; rises from his New England sheets, and shaves with his New York soap, and a Yankee safety razor. He pulls on a pair of Boston boots over his socks from West Carolina, fastens his Connecticut braces, slips his Waterbury watch into his pocket, and sits down to breakfast. . . . [He] eats bread made from prairie flour, tinned oysters from Baltimore, and a little Kansas City bacon." Although foreign consumers eagerly purchased U.S. goods, many remained wary of U.S. influence and of Americans themselves.

imperialism Policy or practice of controlling a foreign territory or people through territorial acquisition or political, economic, or cultural domination.

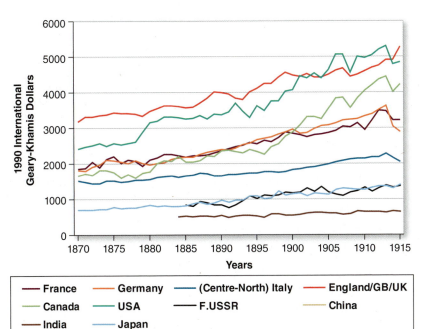

Figure 18.1 Gross Domestic Product of Major Economies, 1870–1915 Measuring the total value of all the goods produced and services provided in a single year, gross domestic product (GDP) is an important indicator of a nation's economic performance. This chart documents the spectacular economic growth the United States experienced from 1870–1915. The Geary–Khamis dollar (more commonly known as the *international dollar*) is a benchmark used to estimate the purchasing power of the U.S. dollar at different points in time. ◄

Sources: https://en.wikipedia.org/wiki/US-GNP-per-capita-1869–1918.png; Angus Maddison, The University of Groningen, Netherlands, 2006, http://www.ggdc.net/maddison/Historical_Statistics/horizontal-file_02–2010.xlsmethodology

Legend:
— France — Germany — (Centre-North) Italy — England/GB/UK
— Canada — USA — F.USSR — China
— India — Japan

NOTE: Precise economic statistics are not available for the eras of Indian, Chinese, and Russian history where data is not listed.

Americans were also conflicted about their nation's growing interconnections to the wider world. The telephone, telegraph, and transatlantic cable made them more aware of international politics, culture, and wars. As Americans imported millions of foreign goods, their homes and clothes became more cosmopolitan. But however much they may have enjoyed Japanese art or French fashion, most Americans did not view foreigners as equals. They expected millions of immigrants moving to the United States to assimilate and resented competing with them for jobs in the industrializing U.S. workforce. As the United States expanded its involvements abroad, many Americans believed that exposure to U.S. institutions of government, manufactured goods, and culture would elevate underdeveloped societies. They adopted transatlantic philosophies and pseudoscientific theories justifying the domination of the world's supposedly weaker races by peoples defined as "white."

Josiah Strong was an avid proponent of these ideas. As a Congregationalist minister, he traveled through the West working for the Home Missionary Society. His experiences inspired him to write *Our Country: Its Possible Future and Its Present Crisis*. Published in 1885, *Our Country* called for the expansion of U.S. power and trade. Led by missionaries working abroad to spread Protestant Christianity and consumerism, white Americans could uplift foreign peoples and prevail in a "final competition of races" that would "move down upon Mexico, down upon Central and South America, out upon the islands of the sea, over upon Africa and beyond." Voicing many of the attitudes fueling popular support for an increased international role for the United States, Strong became a national celebrity.

As the United States became more globally prominent, Americans left their imprint on many foreign societies, and foreigners shaped U.S. attitudes and daily life. Businesspeople pursued international markets for U.S. goods and overseas resources critical to the industrializing U.S. economy. Financiers from the United States orchestrated loans and banking practices that fueled spectacular economic growth, sometimes at the expense of other nations' autonomy. Missionaries and moral reformers dedicated themselves to converting foreigners to Christianity and ending prostitution, alcoholism, and opium use in their nations. Wealthy U.S. tourists traveled abroad. Flush with new money but rejected by local high society, a number of American heiresses married foreign nobles. Through exposure to college anthropology courses and exhibits at World's Fairs, Americans both celebrated and degraded non-European peoples. Published by a society of scientists and explorers founded in Washington, D.C., in 1888, *National Geographic* magazine also reflected these tensions. Its vibrant photographs presented indigenous peoples authentically, but images of bare-breasted native women both intrigued and scandalized readers in an age of taboos against nudity. As U.S. military, economic, and cultural power grew, so did the complexities and contradictions of American imperialism.

18-1b Protectorate over Latin America

In the aftermath of the Civil War, U.S. policy makers took tentative steps away from policies opposing foreign entanglements. In response to a rapidly changing global landscape, the United States acquired its first offshore territories and searched for ways to protect its unique qualities while increasing its political, economic, and cultural influence internationally. Although domestic opposition to direct colonialism constrained these efforts, the United States began more aggressively challenging its European rivals.

> For ideological and economic reasons, U.S. officials expand their involvement in Latin America.

Both idealism and prejudice shaped U.S. anti-imperialism. Many Americans took pride in their country's tradition of government with the consent of the governed and thought colonialism violated that principle. Some objected to the large navy and high costs that overseas territorial acquisition required. Others perceived the United States as a white, Protestant nation and opposed adding colonies with large nonwhite populations who did not share America's dominant religious faith. These views transcended party lines, and members of the same party often strongly disagreed on overseas expansion and its possible impact on issues like tariffs, immigration, and currency reform.

These limitations did not prevent Secretary of State James G. Blaine in the Garfield administration from significantly increasing U.S. involvement in Latin America. A firm believer in the Monroe Doctrine—James Monroe's 1823 message proclaiming the Western Hemisphere essential to U.S. security and warning European nations not to colonize the region—Blaine advocated the use of trade agreements and **arbitration**—third-party mediation of disputes—to undercut the nation's European commercial and political rivals. At the time, a growing transnational community of lawyers was playing a greater role in resolving disputes between states. Delegates frequently gathered to formulate and sign **multilateral conventions** outlining rules of international conduct in areas such as war, health, communication, and transportation. When the assassination of James Garfield forced Blaine to leave office in December 1880, the next Secretary of State Frederick Frelinghuysen continued Blaine's policies. He signed **reciprocity treaties**—pacts ensuring that benefits or penalties granted by one country to another are returned in kind—with Mexico, Cuba, Puerto Rico, the British West Indies, Colombia, and Santo Domingo.

arbitration Resolution of disputes through third-party legal negotiations.

multilateral convention Also called *multilateral treaty,* legal agreement binding three or more sovereign states to identical regulations and terms.

reciprocity treaties Agreement between two nations providing equal benefits and mutually binding rules and obligations.

In 1889, Blaine began a second term as secretary of state under new president Benjamin Harrison. Still determined to cultivate closer ties between the Americas, Blaine organized the first Inter-American Conference. In early 1890, representatives from nineteen nations negotiated several trade pacts. Hoping to strengthen cultural and scientific exchanges throughout the region, the delegates established the International Bureau of the American Republics, later renamed the Pan-American Union. But the spirit of cooperation evident in the meeting proved short lived.

18-1c West across the Pacific

Throughout this era, as the United States secured trade concessions in the Pacific and continued attempts to broaden access to overseas markets in

{ *Americans debate acquisition of Pacific territories and modernize their navy to protect trade.*

China, foreign peoples sometimes resisted these endeavors. In 1887, wealthy U.S. landowners in Hawai'i forced King Kalakaua to sign the so-called Bayonet Constitution, which stripped the Hawaiian monarchy of its authority and bestowed suffrage rights not only on naturalized citizens but also on foreign resident aliens. Hawaiian, American, and European men who met property and literacy requirements were permitted to vote, but Asians' voting rights were abolished.

In the early 1890s, a number of events triggered a U.S. attempt to annex Hawai'i. In 1890, the McKinley Tariff ended the special status given to Hawaiian sugar and enabled U.S. domestic sugar producers to sell at prices lower than their foreign competitors. The decision devastated the Hawaiian sugar industry. In 1891, after the ineffective King Kalakaua died, his sister Lili'uokalani assumed the Hawaiian throne. Fiercely nationalistic, the new queen instituted a new constitution restoring political power to the indigenous majority. In early 1893, disgruntled white elites assisted by U.S. Minister to Hawai'i John L. Stevens and 162 marines overthrew Queen Lili'uokalani. U.S. officials and the newly created provisional government signed an agreement annexing Hawai'i to the United States, thus ensuring that Hawaiian sugar would be classified as domestic rather than imported. With only two weeks remaining in his term, President Benjamin Harrison presented the treaty to the U.S. Senate.

But Grover Cleveland, Harrison's successor, withdrew the treaty only five days after taking office. A probusiness Democrat, Cleveland supported commercial expansion but believed that the annexation and administration of underdeveloped tropical areas would necessitate a large federal bureaucracy and jeopardize U.S. ideals of self-governance. After investigators concluded that the United States had acted illegally in

Hawai'i, Cleveland demanded that Queen Lili'uokalani be reinstated. The provisional government refused and instead created the Republic of Hawai'i. Outmaneuvered, Cleveland reluctantly recognized Hawai'i as an independent nation. The contentious issue of whether Hawai'i should be annexed to the United States remained unresolved for the time being.

In other areas in the world, the United States began clashing with European powers. In 1878, the country extended its range into the Pacific from Hawai'i and Midway Island by acquiring a coaling station on a group of fourteen volcanic islands called Samoa. Rivalry for control over it soon arose. Germany and the United States were on the brink of war until a typhoon scuttled the fleets of both nations. At the Berlin Conference of 1889, Britain, the United States, and Germany split Samoa into a tripartite protectorate. A decade later, the United States and Germany officially divided Samoa into colonies and compensated Britain with other Pacific territories.

Alarmed by the growing sea power of its commercial rivals, the United States began modernizing and expanding its naval capabilities. In *The Influence of Sea Power upon History* (1890), Alfred Thayer Mahan, a lecturer at the Naval War College, argued that a nation's greatness was inextricably connected to its naval strength. Because industrialization generated vast surpluses of manufactured and agricultural goods, foreign markets for the excesses were essential. Protecting those markets necessitated a large merchant marine to carry the goods and long-range steel battleships that could be deployed all over the globe. Such a force required a network of colonies to be used for coaling, making repairs, and obtaining raw materials. In addition to this string of strategic bases, Mahan called for the construction of a canal bisecting Central America and linking the Atlantic and Pacific Oceans. Mahan's ideas greatly influenced policy makers in the United States and several other countries, including fast-militarizing Japan. U.S. Secretary of the Navy Benjamin F. Tracy significantly expanded the U.S. battleship fleet and by 1900, the U.S. Navy ranked second in the world behind Great Britain. The Imperial Japanese Navy began challenging Russian naval expansion in the Far East.

In 1899, after thousands of private citizens urged their governments to address the escalating arms race, delegates from twenty-six countries gathered in The Hague, Netherlands, for an historic peace conference on disarmament and rules of war. Although the representatives did not agree to arms limitations, they adopted multilateral treaties on wartime conduct, ground and naval combat, and the use of certain weapons. The delegates' acceptance of a convention creating the Permanent Court of Arbitration set an important precedent for the League of Nations created after World War I.

War, Insurrection, and the Challenges of Empire

The "White man's burden," a phrase coined by British poet Rudyard Kipling, referred to the duty of the white race to uplift and Christianize peoples perceived as primitive and inferior. Such attitudes played a key role in justifying the acquisition of foreign territories in the late nineteenth and early twentieth centuries. This 1899 cartoon from the U.S. satire magazine *Judge* depicts Uncle Sam and John Bull as symbols of American and British colonization.

In this cartoon, what do the concepts etched into the rocks on the upward climb to "civilization" and the images of the Egyptian, Sudanese, Chinese, Indian, and Zulu in John Bull's basket and the Cuban, Hawaiian, Filipino, Puerto Rican, and Samoan in Uncle Sam's basket suggest about the artist's attitudes toward foreign peoples and his views of British and U.S. annexations of foreign territories? ▶

"The White Man's Burden (Apologies to Rudyard Kipling)." Victor Gillam, *Judge*, April 1, 1899.

---

reconcentration policy
Relocation of native rural populations to enclosed compounds in urban areas, often instituted as a means of undercutting popular support for insurgents.

yellow journalism Term originating in the 1890s to describe a style of news reporting emphasizing sensationalism and exaggeration over objective fact.

In the late 1890s, following decades of resistance to an overseas empire, the United States catapulted into the ranks of formal colonial powers after defeating Spain in a brief war. Sympathetic to Cubans seeking independence from Spanish rule and determined to guard American interests on the island, U.S. officials demanded that Spain accord Cuba more autonomy. Struggling to retain the remnants of its once-great empire, Spain resisted and political tensions escalated. After the Spanish-American War erupted, the United States expanded its power in the Pacific and gained improved access to Asian markets by annexing Hawai'i and seizing the Spanish-controlled Philippine Islands. At the same time, U.S. ground troops captured Spain's territories in the Caribbean.

These events forced Americans to confront challenges and contradictions. At home, they debated the economic, political, and racial implications of the new U.S. empire. Abroad, U.S. officials and soldiers attempted to govern, manage, and defend foreign peoples with different cultures and often fierce determination to resist U.S. domination.

☞ As you read, pay close attention to the causes and consequences of the U.S. pursuit of overseas territories. How did Americans differ in their attitudes about governing foreign peoples? How and why did foreign peoples' responses to U.S. control vary?

18-2a War with Spain

From 1868 to 1878, U.S. officials keenly observed, but did not intervene in, the Ten Years War, a failed Cuban revolt against more than four centuries of Spanish imperialism and slavery. Although Spain abolished slavery in 1886, it did not institute economic or political reforms. U.S. capitalists heavily invested in the island's sugar, mining, and tobacco industries and persuaded many Cuban planters to exchange their lands for stock or jobs in U.S.-owned firms. In 1895, after a new U.S. tariff imposed duties on imported sugar and Spain retaliated by restricting Cuban sugar shipments to the United States, the Cuban economy crashed and the insurgents rose again. The rebels hoped to win American backing for their struggle against Spain but not at the price of U.S. annexation of Cuba.

> The United States intervenes in a Cuban revolt against Spanish rule.

Determined to crush the uprising, Spanish governor-general Valeriano y Nicolau Weyler instituted a ruthless **reconcentration policy** that divided Cuba into districts and forced five hundred thousand civilians into fortified compounds. Rancid food, overcrowding, and terrible sanitation led to the deaths of approximately two hundred thousand people. At the same time, Weyler's troops ravaged the countryside, targeting rebels and their supporters and destroying livestock, crops, and water supplies. Vying for readers, American tabloids printed sensationalized accounts of Spanish atrocities that sparked calls for U.S. intervention. But such **yellow journalism** failed to sway U.S. policy makers. They were unwilling to provoke a war with Spain that could jeopardize American economic interests in Cuba and did not believe that Cubans—whom they considered backward and racially inferior—could rule themselves. Rejecting calls to buy or annex Cuba, President Cleveland instead declared U.S. neutrality, a policy reaffirmed by his successor, William McKinley.

But when renewed unrest in Cuba threatened U.S. citizens and investments, McKinley deployed the battleship *Maine* to Havana Harbor. On February 15, 1898, it exploded and sank, killing 266 Americans. Most Americans immediately blamed the Spanish, but McKinley tried to defuse the crisis by ordering an investigation. Advocates of intervention accused McKinley of cowardice and a lack of manhood. Assistant Secretary of the Navy Theodore Roosevelt proclaimed that McKinley had "no more backbone than a chocolate éclair."

In late March, after investigators attributed the sinking of the *Maine* to an undersea mine of undetermined national origin (recent studies blame a spontaneous explosion of coal dust), pressure for war against Spain intensified. Deferring to the bellicose public mood, McKinley won congressional approval for $50 million in emergency defense expenditures and sent Spain his final terms. But the Spanish would not accept a U.S.-brokered peace process or Cuban independence. Dissatisfied, the president sent Congress a message asking for the authorization of U.S. military intervention to stop the Spanish-Cuban war and to protect U.S. property and trade. Convinced that the Cubans were not yet suited for self-government, McKinley did not request diplomatic recognition of the "so-called Cuban Republic."

On April 19, 1898, Congress issued a joint resolution authorizing the use of force and declaring Cuba independent (without recognizing the rebels). To emphasize their anti-imperialist intentions, Congress also passed the **Teller Amendment** stating that the United States did not intend to annex Cuba. On April 21, Spain severed diplomatic ties with the United States and the next day, the United States began blockading Cuba. By April 25, the two nations were officially at war.

McKinley then deployed U.S. forces to Cuba and to the Philippines, a chain of Pacific islands colonized by Spain since the late 1500s. On May 1, 1898, implementing pre-existing plans drafted by the Naval War College, Admiral George Dewey led his Asiatic Squadron to Manila Bay and crushed the Spanish fleet in a single day, losing only one U.S. sailor (who died of heatstroke). By late June, U.S. ground troops in Cuba were poised outside Santiago, a critical Spanish stronghold. On July 1, U.S. soldiers—including Teddy Roosevelt, who had resigned from the Navy Department to lead a volunteer regiment called the *Rough Riders*—joined Cuban rebels in a victorious assault on San Juan Hill and secured Santiago. Two days later, U.S. naval forces defeated the Spanish naval squadron when it made a desperate effort to escape Santiago Harbor and reach open waters. With its battle fleet in ruins, Spain surrendered. Capitalizing on Spain's weakness, U.S. forces quickly seized Spain's nearby colony, the island Puerto Rico.

By mid-August, Spain had capitulated in the Philippines. Attempting to salvage its pride after yet another loss, Spain surrendered only to the United States, not to the Filipino nationalists who had been fighting for independence since 1896. Americans rejoiced at their overwhelming victory. Although 5,463 U.S. troops perished during the four-month conflict, only 379 died in battle. The others died in accidents or from diseases such as yellow fever and malaria.

The brief war against Spain provided McKinley a pretext for acquiring Hawai'i. Asserting that the islands were vital to the U.S. naval effort in the Philippines, he urged the Senate to approve an annexation treaty he had negotiated with the white-dominated Hawaiian government months earlier. Circumventing the constitutional requirement of a two-thirds Senate vote approving treaty ratification, McKinley asked for a joint resolution requiring only a majority vote. On July 7, 1898, both houses of Congress voted in favor of U.S. annexation of Hawai'i.

18-2b Debates on Empire and Response to Insurgents

> U.S. occupation of the Philippines sparks intense domestic debates and a Filipino revolt.

In the 1898 **Treaty of Paris** that ended the war, Spain recognized Cuban independence, assumed Cuba's debts, and ceded Guam, Puerto Rico, and the Philippines to the United States in exchange for $20 million. Even before the president sent the treaty to the U.S. Senate for ratification, a heated political debate erupted. Although most Americans accepted overseas commercial expansion, many were horrified at the occupation of Cuba, Puerto Rico, and the Philippines by U.S. troops. In June 1898, prominent individuals including former Democratic president Cleveland, steel magnate Andrew Carnegie, pacifist Lucia True Ames Mead, union leader Samuel Gompers, reformer Jane Addams, and writer Mark Twain formed the **Anti-Imperialist League** to protest possible annexation of the Philippines. Their platform declared that "imperialism is hostile to liberty" and vowed to defend the ideals enshrined in the Declaration of Independence.

Despite their shared commitment to republicanism, members of this diverse coalition had varied reasons for opposing the annexation of the Philippines. Some sought to guard U.S. society from the immigration of peoples considered racially inferior. Opposing the subjugation of foreign people as a violation of cherished

Teller Amendment
Congressional resolution added to the U.S. declaration of war on Spain proclaiming that the United States would not permanently occupy or annex Cuba.

Treaty of Paris Agreement ending hostilities between Spain and the United States and granting the United States the former Spanish colonies of Cuba, Guam, and the Philippines.

Anti-Imperialist League Diverse coalition founded in opposition to the U.S. annexation of the Philippines.

American principles, U.S. Senator George Hoar, a Republican from Massachusetts, warned that the United States was about "to be transformed from a Republic . . . into a vulgar, commonplace empire, founded upon physical force." Labor leaders across the political spectrum voiced fears that workers imported from the Pacific would undercut U.S. wages. Participation in the anti-imperialist cause inspired thousands of American men and women to build a peace movement that shaped discourse on U.S. foreign policy for years afterward.

Linking notions of masculinity and militarism, the imperialists mocked their opponents as "unmanly aunties" (a pun on *antis*) and extolled the strategic and economic advantages of expanding U.S. territorial holdings. They argued that the United States had a duty to spread "civilization" and to uplift morally and racially inferior foreigners. Protestant missionaries wanted to convert non-Christians and to bring sanitation, education, and health care to "backward" regions. Rudyard Kipling exhorted the United States to join Great Britain in assuming the **"White man's burden"** of governing an empire and "new-caught, sullen peoples, half devil and half child." Senator Albert Beveridge, a Republican representing Indiana, proclaimed that God intended Americans to be the "master organizers of the world" who could transfuse "the blood of government" into the veins of the Filipinos.

Such triumphalist rhetoric rankled Emilio Aguinaldo, leader of the Filipino resistance movement. After Admiral Dewey dispatched a ship to retrieve Aguinaldo from exile in Hong Kong, he and his comrades joined the ongoing U.S. war against Spain. Proclaiming an independent Philippine Republic in June 1898, the Filipino insurgents soon controlled most towns and appointed officials to lead them. But U.S. officials ordered them out of Manila and insulted Filipinos with racial epithets like "*gu gu*" (the antecedent of "*gook*," a term later used by U.S soldiers in the Korean and Vietnam wars). Determined to govern themselves and unwilling to submit to U.S. authority, the Filipinos drafted a constitution in late January 1899. Shortly thereafter, the rebels attacked U.S. troops stationed on the islands.

News of the insurrection intensified continuing debates over the Treaty of Paris. Anti-imperialists published accounts of U.S. war atrocities committed against the Filipino nationalist forces, stimulating cries to reject the treaty. Senator Henry Cabot Lodge, a Republican from Massachusetts, warned that if they rejected the pact, Americans would be "branded as a people incapable of taking rank as one of the greatest of world powers." On February 6, 1899, after defeating an amendment granting the Filipinos independence once they established a stable government, the Senate narrowly ratified the Treaty of Paris. The United States now had a territorial empire but also faced another war.

The Philippine-American War proved more bloody and difficult than the preceding conflict in Cuba. With significant popular support, the Filipinos launched guerilla assaults and then hid in the jungles. U.S. soldiers retaliated by destroying villages deemed friendly to the insurgents. Echoing the brutal tactics used by General Weyler in Cuba, American forces rounded up civilians and herded them into prison camps, where tens of thousands soon died from malnutrition and disease. After Filipino soldiers cut off captives' ears and noses or buried them alive, U.S. troops subjected prisoners to the "water cure," a torture technique that simulated drowning. By the time the war ended in 1902, 126,000 U.S. troops had fought in the $160 million conflict and the death toll included 4,165 of them, sixteen thousand Filipino insurgents, and two hundred thousand Filipino civilians.

Following his reelection in 1900, McKinley dispatched a special commission headed by William Howard Taft to the Philippines. Over the next several months, the commissioners issued 499 laws and established a judicial system. In March 1901, after U.S. soldiers captured him, Aguinaldo signed a decree urging the rebels to surrender. Some refused and the fighting continued for another year. On July 4, 1901, Taft became the civil governor of the islands. While suppressing Philippine resistance through censorship and jailing dissidents, U.S. officials tried to win the loyalty of elite Filipinos by introducing programs for education, road and bridge construction, tax reforms, sanitation, and vaccinations. These officials also sent scores of Filipino students to the United States to pursue higher education. The new colonial leaders promoted exports of agricultural products and raw materials to the United States, a model of trade that made the Philippines depend heavily on U.S. capital and imports of finished goods for decades afterward.

American leaders took steps to ensure that their governance of the islands would be temporary and would not make Filipinos U.S. citizens. In 1902, Congress allowed the Filipinos to create a bicameral legislature under the supervision of the U.S. War Department. Fourteen years later, the Jones Act formally committed the United States to granting the Philippines independence once a stable government was established. In 1935, it became a self-governing **commonwealth**, but the Japanese occupation of the islands during World War II forced the Filipino regime into temporary exile in the United States. On July 4, 1946, eleven months after Japan surrendered, the Philippines finally became an independent nation.

18-2c Political Nuances and the Question of Citizenship

How would the United States govern these colonies? Would their inhabitants enjoy the same rights as U.S. citizens? Whereas some Americans

> The acquisition of foreign possessions forces U.S. policy makers to confront a number of difficult questions.

"White man's burden" Taken from the name of a poem by Rudyard Kipling, a description of the presumed moral duty of the white race to govern and educate nonwhite peoples.

commonwealth Nation with local governmental autonomy but voluntarily united to another country.

believed that "the Constitution follows the flag," others contended that people residing in overseas territories owned or controlled by the United States should not necessarily be accorded constitutional protections. Another group sought to extend citizenship and basic civil rights such as trial by jury and voting rights but to withhold special privileges such as using U.S. currency and running for president.

To resolve these complicated issues, Congress created new legal frameworks for U.S. foreign possessions and their inhabitants. In 1900, the lawmakers designated Hawai'i an **incorporated territory** and made all white and indigenous Hawaiians—but not Asian residents—U.S. citizens with a U.S.-appointed governor and an elected legislature. In 1912, Alaska became a territory with a similar structure. These moves put Hawai'i and Alaska on the path to eventual statehood followed in earlier U.S. land acquisitions on continental North America.

But U.S. officials instituted different policies for territories recently acquired from Spain. In 1900, the Foraker Act made Puerto Rico an **unincorporated territory** subject to U.S. laws. In a series of important decisions between 1901 and 1904 known as the **Insular Cases**, the U.S. Supreme Court ruled that residents of Guam, Puerto Rico, and the Philippines were not automatically entitled to all of the rights and protections guaranteed by the U.S. Constitution. Although residents of these unincorporated territories were subject to U.S. laws, they were not U.S. citizens, nor were they granted voting representation in Congress or the Electoral College. These political nuances allowed the United States to govern possessions it did not intend to make states.

While resolving these legal complexities, U.S. policy makers quickly organized their new empire but in contrast to European imperial powers did not create large colonial bureaucracies. Small teams of U.S. administrators—often in collaboration with local inhabitants—forged creative solutions to the problems they encountered abroad. These teams took inspiration from territorial management policies in North America and in British-held colonies like Burma and Egypt but also pioneered new practices in policing, public health, agriculture, environmental management, and drug control. Through education, they sought to promote the values of U.S. democracy and to persuade foreign peoples of the superiority of Anglo-American culture and the English language.

Reactions to U.S. control differed. Unlike the Filipinos, Puerto Ricans readily accepted American rule and McKinley quickly withdrew U.S. troops. In 1900, the United States established a civilian government in Puerto Rico without extending U.S. citizenship. In March 1917, the Jones-Shafroth Act granted the island's residents U.S. citizenship and the right to create a locally elected bicameral legislature. But Congress could block any law passed by the Puerto Rican lawmakers, and the U.S. government retained control over the island's economy, defenses, and other matters. When the United States entered World War I shortly thereafter, Puerto Ricans were subject to conscription.

Cuba presented a far more complex situation. Having vowed not to annex the island in the Teller Amendment, the United States had promised to rule Cuba only until its inhabitants could form a successful government of their own. In 1900, General Leonard Wood, commander of U.S. forces in Cuba, supervised a census and organized delegate elections for a constitutional convention. In exchange for a U.S. pledge to end its military occupation, Cuba amended the resulting constitution. The **Platt Amendment** made Cuba a U.S. protectorate; it restricted Cuba's ability

incorporated territory Land acquisition directly governed by the United States but that has lower political and legal status than states.

unincorporated territory Areas controlled by the U.S. government but accorded only limited constitutional rights and privileges and lacking statehood status.

Insular Cases Series of Supreme Court decisions declaring that areas under U.S. control are not automatically entitled to full constitutional rights.

Platt Amendment U.S. policy asserting the right to intervene in Cuba in defense of Cuban independence and to ensure "protection of life, property, and individual liberty."

Dalrymple, Louis, 1866–1905/Library of Congress Prints and Photographs Division[LC-USZC2-1025]

"School Begins," 1899
American racial views and previous experience with continental expansion shaped U.S. policies toward newly acquired foreign territories. Many Americans felt it was a moral duty to educate and uplift peoples perceived to be ignorant and inferior. This 1899 image links America's interactions with African Americans, Native Americans, and Chinese immigrants to its success in putting continental territories on the path to statehood and the belief that foreign peoples needed supervision and instruction before transitioning to self-government. ◄

History without Borders

The 1904 Louisiana Purchase Exposition

The colonial powers and their possessions

- Belgium
- Britain
- France
- Germany
- Italy
- Japan
- Netherlands
- Portugal
- Russia
- Spain
- United States

The 1904 St. Louis Exposition

CHINA Underline indicates a country that built a pavilion

■ Homeland of the peoples featured in the fair

Global Imperialism Driven by a combination of economic, political, and cultural motives, Belgium, Great Britain, France, Portugal, the United States, Spain, Japan, Germany, Italy, Netherlands, and Denmark maintained imperial control over foreign territories in 1900. Beginning with the Great Exhibition held in London in 1851, world's fairs and exhibitions became important venues for imperial powers to demonstrate their products, culture, and the diversity of the peoples living under their rule. ▲

On April 30, 1904, an international exposition commemorating the one hundredth anniversary of the Louisiana Purchase opened in St. Louis. Delayed by a year in order to allow participation from more nations, the exposition filled twelve hundred acres with fifteen hundred buildings connected by seventy-miles of roads and paths. Sixty-two countries and forty-three of the forty-five U.S. states highlighted their industrial, scientific, and cultural achievements. Over the next seven months, nearly 20 million people

streamed through the exhibits and amusements of the largest world's fair to date. Many got their first opportunity to try Dr. Pepper, peanut butter, cotton candy, and ice cream cones.

Held shortly after the U.S. victory in the Spanish-American War, the exposition celebrated America's continental empire and its recent acquisitions of Hawai'i, Guam, Cuba, Puerto Rico, and the Philippines. Organizers presented the Louisiana Purchase and overseas expansion as inevitable results of the nation's Manifest Destiny. Reflecting prevailing theories about race and "civilization,"

its creators pointed to the U.S. political system, economic success, and technological prowess as evidence of the inferiority of nonwhite, "barbarous" or "semi-barbarous" peoples.

Anthropological displays of more than two thousand indigenous peoples exemplified this fusion of imperialism and racism. Living ethnological exhibits featured Ainu aborigines from Japan, Patagonian giants from Argentina, and a Congolese *Mbuti* pygmy named Ota Benga. The exposition's most popular exhibit featured one thousand Filipinos re-enacting their daily lives on a

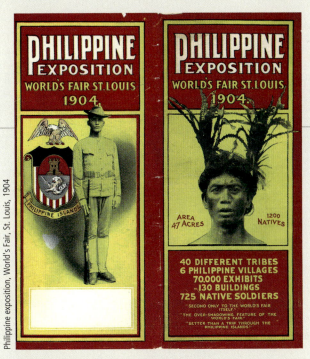

Philippine exposition, World's Fair, St. Louis, 1904

Poster Advertising the Philippine Exposition, The Louisiana Purchase Exposition, St. Louis, 1904 Organizers isolated the Philippine Exposition and further divided it to highlight different levels of societal advancement among the Filipinos as evidenced by the contrast between the constable and the Moro chief depicted here. ▲

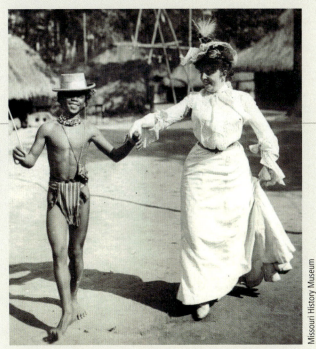

Missouri History Museum

A Filipino Boy and a Fairgoer, The Louisiana Purchase Exposition, St. Louis, 1904 A woman identified as "Mrs. Wilkins" teaches an "Igorot" boy the cakewalk, a dance first appearing among slaves in the plantation South. The photo reflects prevailing ideas about whites "civilizing" people of darker races but also hints at some of the erotic tensions created by the Filipinos' comfort in displaying the body and white Victorian taboos against nudity and sexuality. By dancing with this scantily clad boy, Mrs. Wilkins was exercising her white privilege but also challenging notions of appropriate behavior for upper-class white women. ▲

forty-seven acre site featuring mock villages, a man-made lake, a replica of the Walled City of Manila, and displays of traditional art, agricultural products, and weapons.

To simplify the complexities of Filipino society, organizers invented religious and racial groupings that did not exist and identified Igorot, Negrito, Moros, Bagobos, and Visayans "tribes." The Igorot Village housed one hunded twelve indigenous peoples from the Philippines and featured a stone fireplace in which the Igorot killed, roasted, and ate dogs as part of a ritual ceremony. Fairgoers erroneously assumed that the "savage" Igorot consumed dogs as part of their regular daily diet. Rumors of canines disappearing from St. Louis neighborhoods spread like wildfire, and derogatory characterizations of Filipinos as dog eaters persisted for decades. Afraid that the sight of Igorot in native breechcloths would offend delicate Victorian sensibilities, the Roosevelt administration demanded that they wear "brightcolored silk trousers" but withdrew the request after anthropologists complained that the directive would compromise the authenticity of the exhibit.

On "Receiving Day," the Igorot greeted American Indians including Chief Joseph, Geronimo, and Quanah Parker. Neither group knew that the two shared a common bond as peoples who had borne the sometimes devastating price of America's territorial conquests. U.S. policies had uprooted Native Americans from their tribal lands and had placed Filipino civilians in fortified reconcentration camps to prevent them from aiding armed rebels resisting U.S. occupation. Tens of thousands died from starvation and disease in these relocations. Such were tragic legacies of American imperialism that endured long after most of the buildings of the exposition were dismantled.

Critical Thinking Questions

▶ Why do you think that world's fairs and international exhibitions became so popular when nations were vying for global territories and markets?

▶ How do you think the experience of being a U.S. fairgoer compared to that of being one of the indigenous people on display at the 1904 St. Louis Exposition? What are some of the positive and negative ways these encounters might have shaped the fairgoers' views of foreign peoples and foreign peoples' views of Americans?

Go to MindTap® to engage with an interactive version of **History without Borders: The 1904 Louisiana Purchase Exposition.** Learn from an interactive map, view related video, and respond to critical thinking questions.

Hawai'i:
Overthrow of
monarchy, 1893;
annexed, 1898; U.S.
Incorporated
Territory, 1900

Cuba:
War with Spain, 1898;
U.S. protectorate, 1902

Philippines:
Acquired from
Spain, 1898

Puerto R
Acquired
Spain, 18
Incorpor
Territory,

Guam:
Acquired from
Spain, 1898

Samoa:
Potential naval conflict, 1889;
divided between Germany and
United States, 1899

Map 18.1 U.S. Overseas Expansion, 1893–1902 In the years following the Civil War, the United States began acquiring territories beyond continental North America in a quest to expand its military, economic, and cultural power. A series of federal acts and judicial rulings determined whether specific territories would become states and outlined the citizenship status, rights, and responsibilities of foreign peoples living under U.S. governance. ▲

to sign treaties or accrue debts, gave the United States the right to lease naval bases such as Guantánamo Bay, and permitted U.S. intervention if the Cuban government failed to protect "life, property, or individual liberty." Before departing in 1902, the U.S. military government rebuilt war-torn communities, constructed roads and bridges, and eradicated yellow fever. Cuba was superficially independent, but the United States dominated its economy and militarily intervened several times over the next two decades (see Map 18.1).

18-3

Economic Imperialism in the Pacific and in the Americas

In this drawing, Louis Dalrymple, a cartoonist renowned for his political satire, captures the blend of threats and mediation that punctuated President Theodore Roosevelt's interventionist approach to global affairs in the early twentieth century.

Why are Roosevelt's size and location in the cartoon important? What does the image suggest about the changing international role of the United States in the years immediately following the Spanish-American War? ▶

Cartoon of President Roosevelt portrayed as a giant policeman astride two continents/Private Collection/Bridgeman Images

From 1898 to 1914, as U.S. overseas investments increased from $445 million to $2.5 billion, U.S. policy makers defended, controlled, and expanded the country's new territorial and commercial empire. The United States clashed with other imperial nations and put down protests by peoples who resented American influence and power. In East Asia, U.S. officials pushed for expanded access to China and closely monitored Japan's rising military and economic capabilities. In Latin America, Roosevelt promised to "speak softly and carry a big stick" as he vigorously promoted U.S. interests in the region where its investments were sometimes so extensive and its corporations so powerful that they could undermine national autonomy. William Howard Taft, Roosevelt's successor to the presidency and a fellow Republican, adopted a less confrontational approach, using U.S. financial power to protect commerce and ensure national security. After winning the presidency in 1912, Woodrow Wilson, a Democrat, announced his intention to moderate the aggressive stance of his predecessors but then escalated their interventionist policies to protect U.S. lives, investments, and property.

☞ As you read, consider the tactics that U.S. policy makers used to defend, control, and expand the U.S. empire in this era. How and why did U.S. policies in the Western Hemisphere often differ from those pursued elsewhere in the world?

18-3a Protection of U.S. Interests in East Asia

The annexation of the Philippines deepened long-standing U.S. interest in China. Protestant missionaries hoped to spread Christianity there. Between 1890 and 1900, the number of U.S. missionaries in China doubled from 513 to more than 1,000. U.S. business leaders wanted to expand the nation's tiny share of the huge Chinese market, but Britain, Germany, Russia, and France had already divided China into **spheres of influence** with exclusive trading privileges. Following its quick victory in the Sino-Japanese War of 1895, Japan, too, had secured interests in China and established military control of the Korean peninsula that would lead to its annexation in 1910.

{ The United States competes with other imperialist powers in pursuit of greater engagement with China.

To avoid being blocked out of the China market, the McKinley administration had developed the **Open Door policy** calling for an end to foreign control of Chinese trade. In September 1899, Secretary of State John Hay sent diplomatic notes to Britain, Germany, Russia, France, Italy, and Japan requesting that they permit all nations to trade freely in their spheres of influence. Aware that the United States lacked the military or economic power to open international trade barriers, the six nations responded ambivalently. Nonetheless, in March 1900, Hay boldly announced that all the powers had accepted the principle of the Open Door.

But the eruption of a nationalistic revolt in China soon tested the policy. In June 1900, the Boxers, members of a secret society, demanded the expulsion of all foreigners and murdered hundreds of Christian missionaries and their Chinese converts. In Peking (now Beijing), terrified foreigners barricaded themselves in their respective diplomatic legations. Hoping to prevent a vindictive counterattack on the Chinese, McKinley, without congressional approval, redeployed 2,500 U.S. troops from the Philippines to China to join 15,500 from other countries in suppressing the **Boxer Rebellion**. On July 3, 1900, Hay issued another Open Door note proclaiming U.S. determination to guard the lives and property of its citizens, preserve Chinese sovereignty, and guarantee "equal and impartial trade." Nevertheless, the foreign powers that quelled the uprising forced the Chinese government to pay $300 million in damages. The United States used its portion to fund scholarships for Chinese students to attend American schools. The program became a model for the Fulbright international educational exchanges established after World War II.

In 1904, the United States again intervened in East Asia after Japan launched an attack on Russia over competing interests in Manchuria in northeast China. As Japan won a string of victories in the Russo-Japanese War and Russian authorities quashed protests in St. Petersburg that challenged the absolute rule of Tsar Nicholas II, Roosevelt sought to guard U.S. interests in the Pacific. In August 1905, he invited Russian and Japanese diplomats to Portsmouth, New Hampshire. After hammering out several territorial concessions, the delegates signed an armistice that won Roosevelt the Nobel Peace Prize. In Atlanta, W.E.B. Du Bois observed that Japan's triumph over Russia was proof that nonwhite people could successfully challenge white dominance of natural resources and political power.

Roosevelt understood that the victory made Japan the strongest force in East Asia. Although doing so violated the Open Door policy, the United States officially recognized Japan's colonization of Korea in exchange for the Japanese pledge not to invade the Philippines. Controversies generated by Japanese immigration to the United States proved more difficult to resolve. In 1907, after he failed to persuade the city of San Francisco not to segregate Japanese schoolchildren, Roosevelt brokered a **Gentlemen's Agreement** in which Japan voluntarily agreed to restrict emigration to the United States in return for U.S. elimination of anti-Japanese segregation. To ensure that Japan did not misinterpret his diplomacy as weakness, Roosevelt bolstered American defenses in the Pacific and expanded the navy. As a show of force,

spheres of influence Area outside a nation's territory but still under its control; in the case of empires, lands that conceded trading and other rights to imperial powers.

Open Door policy U.S. policy calling for an end to foreign control of Chinese trade and respect for Chinese territorial sovereignty.

Boxer Rebellion Anti-imperialist uprising led by nationalists attempting to expel Christian missionaries and all foreigners from China.

Gentlemen's Agreement 1907 pact under which Japan voluntarily restricted emigration to the United States in exchange for President Theodore Roosevelt's pledge to combat school segregation in San Francisco.

Source: Library of Congress (http://www.loc.gov/item/hec2008002821/)

Global Americans

William C. Gorgas (1854–1920) was a groundbreaker in the fields of public health and tropical medicine. His sanitation efforts were key elements of the U.S. occupation of Cuba and the successful completion of the Panama Canal. After graduating from medical school in 1879, Gorgas entered the U.S. Army Medical Corps. In July 1898, he became chief sanitary officer for U.S.-occupied Cuba. Inspired by Walter Reed's work in identifying mosquitos as carriers of disease, Gorgas implemented mosquito control efforts that eliminated yellow fever in the Havana area by late 1901. That same year, the U.S. government appointed him the sanitary expert on its new Panama Canal project. Initially, yellow fever outbreaks seriously hindered progress on the canal. But after winning cooperation from his superiors, canal employees, and Panamanians, Gorgas instituted measures that led to a steep decline in yellow fever cases. At the invitation of the Rockefeller Foundation, he later worked as an international public health consultant, first in Africa and then in Central and South America.

In January 1914, Gorgas was appointed U.S. Army surgeon general and promoted to major general soon after. When U.S. troops mobilized for World War I, he ensured that army camps had appropriate sanitation practices, and soldiers' deaths from disease significantly declined as compared to previous wars. After retiring from the army in October 1918, he spent two years investigating international outbreaks of yellow fever. He died of complications from a stroke in 1920.

---

dollar diplomacy Foreign policy promulgated by President William Howard Taft aimed at promoting financial stability in foreign countries deemed essential to U.S. commercial interests.

he sent sixteen new U.S. battleships—the "Great White Fleet"—around the world with a stop in Tokyo in October 1908. Shortly thereafter, the United States and Japan negotiated a pact promising to respect each other's Asiatic territories and reaffirming a commitment to the Open Door policy and Chinese independence.

The accord soon unraveled, and Japanese immigrants again faced racism in California when in 1913 the state restricted them from owning farmland (a law that was reinforced in 1920). Illustrating how U.S. commerce could be a tool of international power, a policy known as **dollar diplomacy**, President Taft encouraged private U.S. investments in the Manchurian railroad, infuriating Japan, Russia, and Britain. But the eruption of a revolution in China in May 1911 defused these tensions. Taft's successor Woodrow Wilson extricated the United States from the railroad deal and recognized the new Chinese Republic. Having reaffirmed the U.S. commitment to the political integrity of China, Wilson hoped to restore harmony in U.S.-Japanese relations.

18-3b Construction of the Panama Canal and Domination of Latin America

Determined to consolidate U.S. power in the Caribbean and Central America, Roosevelt pushed for the construction of a canal that would

{ The United States builds the Panama Canal and expands its interventions in the Western Hemisphere.

link the Atlantic and Pacific Oceans with obvious commercial advantages for trade with China and protection of U.S. interests in the Pacific. Europeans and Americans had long advocated such a waterway as a means of dramatically boosting America's global commerce and travel. In 1880, eleven years after successfully completing the Suez Canal in Egypt, the French started a canal project in Panama. But design flaws, epidemics, and financial mismanagement forced them to abandon it in 1893.

Roosevelt was determined to succeed where the French failed. Through the Hay-Pauncefote Treaty of 1901, the United States and Britain agreed to exclusive U.S. control over any Central American canal, voiding an earlier treaty that had promised shared access. After a site selection committee chose a fifty-mile route through Panama (then part of Colombia), Secretary of State Hay and Colombian chargé d'affaires Tomás Herrán signed an agreement granting the United States a ninety-nine-year lease on a six-mile wide canal zone in exchange for $10 million and a $250,000 annual leasing fee. But the Colombian Senate unanimously rejected the treaty, objecting to the loss of sovereignty over the zone and hoping for a higher payment. Incensed, Roosevelt considered ordering a U.S. invasion of Panama. Instead, he supported Panamanians in a revolt against Colombia and announced U.S. recognition of the Republic of Panama. Two weeks later, Panama and the United States signed the Hay-Bunau-Varilla Treaty granting U.S. control over a ten-mile wide canal zone. In exchange, the United States guaranteed Panamanian independence and paid the same fees originally offered to Colombia.

In August 1914 during Wilson's presidency, the first ship traveled through the new $375 million U.S. canal, a stunning feat of engineering enacted through the labors of tens of thousands of workers from Asia, Europe, Latin

Hulton Archive/Getty Images

Global Americans Born in 1845, **Elihu Root** became one of the most influential figures in the history of U.S. foreign relations. After a highly successful career in corporate law, he served as secretary of war from 1899 to 1904. Playing a major role in the administration of U.S. territories newly acquired from Spain, Root formulated plans for eventual self-governance in Cuba and the Philippines and abolished U.S. tariffs on goods imported from Puerto Rico. In 1905, at the invitation of President Roosevelt, Root became secretary of state. To curtail cronyism, he placed the consular service under the U.S. Civil Service. In 1907, he negotiated the Gentlemen's Agreement for restricting Japanese emigration to the United States.

After serving in the U.S. Senate from 1909 to 1915, Root remained active in global affairs well into his eighties, heading a special U.S. diplomatic mission to Russia in 1917 and helping to craft naval disarmament proposals at the Washington Naval Conference of 1921–1922.

Convinced that international law could be a tool for preserving world peace, Root was an impassioned advocate of arbitration. He was the leading architect of the Central American Court of Justice in 1907. In 1910, he became the first president of the Carnegie Endowment for International Peace and won the 1912 Nobel Peace Prize in recognition of his efforts to promote negotiation as an alternative to war. In 1920, he joined the League of Nations committee that established the Permanent Court of International Justice. Much to Root's disappointment, the United States opted not to join.

America, and primarily the West Indies. The workers battled torrential rains, venomous snakes, and segregation based on race and skill level. In 1922, the United States paid Colombia $25 million but did not apologize for seizing the canal. Many of the West Indians who worked on the canal later migrated to the United States, mostly to New York City.

As U.S. investments in the Caribbean and South America expanded, U.S. policy makers worried about Latin American countries defaulting on loans made by European governments and banks. In 1904, Roosevelt had become alarmed when the Dominican Republic veered near financial collapse and it appeared that Germany would invade to collect its debts. An economic powerhouse with one of the world's largest navies, Germany could easily threaten U.S. interests. On December 6, 1904, to warn Europe to stay out of the Western Hemisphere and to justify U.S. dominance of the region, Roosevelt issued a bold expansion of the Monroe Doctrine. The **Roosevelt Corollary** threatened U.S. intervention in Latin American nations that engaged in "chronic wrongdoing, or an impotence which results in a general loosening of the ties of civilized society . . . ." Convinced that the Dominicans lacked the ability or temperament to resolve their own affairs, U.S. officials seized control of the nation's customs collections. In 1912, after rebels from neighboring Haiti attacked customs houses, Taft sent a commission bolstered by seven hundred fifty marines to restore order. The commission redrew the border between Haiti and the Dominican Republic and forced out a corrupt Dominican president. Four years later, Wilson established a U.S. military occupation of the Dominican Republic that continued until 1922. Dominicans greatly resented these measures.

The United States played an equally intrusive role in Haiti. Although U.S. investment in the nation was minimal, French and German nationals controlled most of its

banks. When World War I erupted in Europe in 1914, U.S. policy makers worried that Germans would seize the port of Môle Saint Nicholas as a base for aggressive actions in the Caribbean. Accordingly, when Haitians began protesting their government the following year, Wilson sent two thousand marines to restore order. The U.S. occupation of the first independent black republic in the Western Hemisphere outraged activists such as Du Bois: "SHAME ON AMERICA!" he raged. The situation deteriorated as the United States took control of Haiti's finances and forced the election of a pro-U.S. president who instituted racial segregation, press censorship, and forced labor. In the 1920s, after a peasant revolt against these measures, U.S. officials began training Haitians to take control of their government but did not end the occupation until 1934.

Roosevelt Corollary Addition to the Monroe Doctrine asserting a U.S. right to intervene in Latin American nations at risk of European intervention or occupation.

18-3c Intervention in Mexico

Upon assuming office in 1913, Wilson declared, "The force of America is the force of moral principle." He intended to create a more humane, open, and peaceful world in the face of instability, militarism, and imperialism. Yet in most cases, Wilson pursued policies that differed little from those of his predecessors.

{ Revolution in Mexico creates unrest in the American Southwest and strains U.S.-Mexican relations.

Wilson's responses to the Mexican Revolution embodied these contradictions. In 1910, rebels in northern Mexico began violently resisting Porfirio Diaz, Mexico's dictatorial ruler for the previous thirty-four years. The upheaval troubled U.S. officials who feared the bloodshed might spread north to the borderlands where Mexicans and Mexican

Plan of San Diego
Anonymous manifesto circulated during the Mexican Revolution calling for nonwhite peoples to seize six U.S. states and create a new republic.

Americans far outnumbered Anglos and much of the local population supported the revolutionaries. After Diaz's ouster in 1911, Francisco I. Madero, a liberal reformer, took power but faced challenges to his authority from elite landowners, the Catholic Church, and the military. In 1913, troops led by General Victoriano Huerta imprisoned and then executed Madero. Denouncing Huerta's "government of butchers," Wilson withheld recognition of the rebels despite $1.5 billion in U.S. investments in Mexico. Strongly influenced by emerging doctrines of international law, Wilson explained that legitimate regimes must be "based upon law, not upon arbitrary or irregular force."

Such pious assertions did not, however, stop Wilson from orchestrating Huerta's overthrow. When diplomatic meddling did not work, Wilson sent U.S. ships to patrol Mexico's coastline. In 1914, after the brief detention of several U.S. sailors purchasing supplies in the port of Tampico, U.S.-Mexican tensions escalated. On April 20, Wilson discovered that a German arms shipment intended for Huerta was heading to Veracruz and asked Congress for authority to use force. Before receiving a response, Wilson ordered U.S. ships to bombard the harbor. The following day, eight hundred U.S. marines landed and captured the city despite ferocious resistance. Wilson did not withdraw the troops until November 23, 1914.

U.S. intervention did little to stop continuing unrest. After Huerta fled the country, a power struggle erupted between the forces of Venustiano Carranza and Pancho Villa. Civilians endured food shortages. Refugees flooded across the U.S. border into southwestern states. Mexican rebels in Texas drafted the **Plan of San Diego**, a manifesto calling for Mexican nationals, Mexican Americans, and African Americans to "free" Texas, New Mexico, Arizona, California, and Colorado from U.S. control. Although the proposed race war never materialized, it alarmed U.S. and Texas officials. Clashes between the Texas Rangers and Mexican raiders continued after Carranza supporters organized thirty guerilla raids in the lower Rio Grande Valley. Preoccupied with German U-boat attacks on neutral U.S. ships sailing the Atlantic Ocean, Wilson reluctantly acknowledged the Carranza regime's control of Mexico and blocked arms sales to opposing Mexican factions.

In retaliation, Pancho Villa led a March 1916 attack on Columbus, New Mexico, that left seventeen Americans and more than one hundred Mexicans dead. On Wilson's orders, General John J. Pershing and seven thousand U.S. troops quickly pushed three hundred fifty miles into Mexico in an unsuccessful hunt for Villa. The United States and Mexico teetered on the brink of war. In February 1917, in preparation for formal U.S. entry into World War I, Wilson abandoned the search and recalled Pershing and his troops (see Map 18.2).

Map 18.2 U.S. Interventions in Central America, 1898–1941 To guard its economic interests and expand its political power in the region, the United States intervened in Central America many times after entering the Spanish-American War in 1898. These interventions took numerous forms including business investments, financial oversight, construction projects, military occupations, and wars. ▼

Aultman, Otis A. [Mexican Revolution Refugees]. The Portal to Texas History. http://texashistory.unt.edu/ark:/67531/metapth63330/. Accessed December 23, 2015.

Arrival of Refugees of the Mexican Revolution at Fort Bliss, Texas Between 1910 and 1920, approximately 890,000 Mexicans legally entered the United States, most to escape the chaos and violence of the Mexican Revolution. Some continued to support different factions vying for power in their home country. Others permanently assimilated into extant Mexican American communities. Some returned to Mexico when peace was restored. ◄

18-4

The Great War

Throughout the Great War, later called World War I, the fusion of traditional combat tactics and modern military innovations like tanks, poison gas, and flamethrowers had horrific results. In this image, a U.S. Cavalry officer and his horse prepare for chemical warfare. An estimated 9 million soldiers and 8 million horses on all sides died during the war, the last conflict where mounted troops were used in battle on a wide scale.

What does this image suggest about the ways that this war marked a departure from earlier conflicts and how it affected those who fought it? ▶

Hirz/Getty Images

Beginning in June 1914, events across the Atlantic dwarfed the skirmishes on the U.S.–Mexican border. A four-year, worldwide conflict called the Great War (later World War I) toppled empires and killed millions. Although the assassination of the heir to the Austro-Hungarian throne by a Serbian nationalist was its immediate trigger, the war's root causes were much more complicated (see Table 18.1). Rivalries over colonies, raw materials, and markets had set the nations of Europe against each other and drawn them into local conflicts for half a century. Countries forged mutual defense alliances and militarized at a breathtaking pace. Nationalist Slavs, Hungarians, Poles, and other minorities agitated for independence from Austrian, Russian, and Ottoman rule. Once war began, each belligerent fielded huge armies—70 million soldiers in total—who faced carnage inflicted by new technologies of warfare, such as submachine guns, fragmentation shells, and

poison gas. They fought in Africa, where British and French troops seized German colonies. In East Asia, Japan seized German colonies too. In France, the armies soon barricaded themselves in trenches, where soldiers endured cold, mud, rats, lice, and the stench of dead comrades. Such realities shattered idealized notions of heroic warfare widely held prior to the conflict.

The most important question for the United States was whether to stay out of Europe's war and its entanglements. But the Wilson administration pursued policies that greatly favored Britain and France over Germany. German attacks on U.S. merchant ships and vessels bearing American passengers drew the United States into the conflict. After the United States formally declared war on Germany, U.S. troops played an important part in the Allies' final defeat of the Central Powers.

☞ As you read, consider the evolution of the U.S. response to the Great War and the impact of the conflict on those fighting against the Central Powers. How and why did Americans experience the Great War differently than their European allies did?

18-4a U.S. Neutrality

On July 28, 1914, in retaliation for a Serb nationalist's assassination of Archduke Franz Ferdinand the previous month, Austria-Hungary declared war on Serbia, setting in motion a series of actions based on defensive pacts and secret alliances. Germany backed Austria-Hungary. Russia, the protector of Slavic nations, mobilized to support Serbia. Germany then declared war on Russia and its ally France and

> When war engulfs Europe, the United States declares neutrality but favors the Allies.

Schlieffen Plan Formulated by General Count Alfred von Schlieffen, strategy for German forces invading and occupying France before Russia, France's ally, could mobilize its troops.

launched the **Schlieffen Plan**, a military strategy for the quick defeat of the French followed by a concentrated assault on the Russians. But on August 4, when the Germans invaded neutral Belgium on their way to Paris, Great Britain declared war on Germany, defying German assumptions that the British would not join a continental war. Within weeks, Japan joined the Allies, as Britain, France, and Russia were now designated, while the Ottoman Empire allied itself with the Central Powers led by Germany and Austria-Hungary. Italy reneged on its treaty with Germany and joined the Allies. Europe's alliances, intended to maintain a balance of power, had imploded.

When the war in Europe began, Wilson declared the United States neutral "in thought, as well as action." Because "the people of the United States are drawn from many nations, and chiefly from the nations now at war," he explained, fighting on either side would alienate millions of Americans. Wilson believed that the United States had a moral duty to remain the "one great nation at peace" and to mediate among the warring powers.

Most Americans supported Wilson's decision. Although some felt culturally and historically bound to the Allies, others had direct family ties to the Central Powers. Many Irish-Americans who opposed British control over Ireland and Jewish-Americans who had fled Russian religious persecution also sided with the Central Powers. Progressive reformers feared that U.S. involvement in the

Table 18.1 Origins of World War I

In July 1914, a combination of immediate and long-term causes contributed to the outbreak of a devastating global conflict. Mutual defense alliances, imperialism, militarism, nationalism, and the assassination of Archduke Franz Ferdinand of Austria-Hungary and his wife Sophie by a Serb nationalist were among them. The latter set off a chain of events that plunged Europe into a war that forever reshaped the continent and global politics.

Date	Event
June 28, 1914	Serbian nationalist Gavrilo Princep assassinates Franz Ferdinand, heir to the Austria-Hungarian throne, and his wife Sophie in Sarajevo
July 23, 1914	Austria-Hungary sends an ultimatum to Serbia, demands response in 48 hours
July 24, 1914	Germany declares its support for Austria-Hungary Serbia begins mobilizing for war Russia, a Serbian ally, masses troops along the Austrian border
July 28, 1914	Austria-Hungary declares war on Serbia
July 29, 1914	Great Britain warns Germany that it will not remain neutral in the burgeoning European conflict Germany prepares for war Great Britain asks France and Germany to pledge to support Belgian neutrality. France agrees, but Germany does not respond Germany asks France whether it will remain neutral in the event of war between Germany and Russia
July 30, 1914	Russia begins mobilizing for war
August 1, 1914	Germany declares war on Russia, and France begins mobilizing for war
August 2, 1914	Ottoman Empire (Turkey) and Germany forge a secret alliance
August 3, 1914	Germany declares war on France and invades Belgium. Britain begins mobilizing for war
August 4, 1914	Great Britain declares war on Germany
August 6, 1914	Russia and Austria-Hungary declare war
August 10, 1914	Austria-Hungary invades Russia
August 12, 1914	Great Britain declares war on Austria-Hungary

Sources: "How Did the First World War Start?" *The Week*, November 5, 2014, http://www.theweek.co.uk/world-news/first-world-war/59782/how-did-the-first-world-war-start; "Countdown to War: The Events That Triggered WWI," ITV *News*, July 21, 2014, http://www.itv.com/news/2014–07–21/countdown-to-war-the-events-that-triggered-ww1/

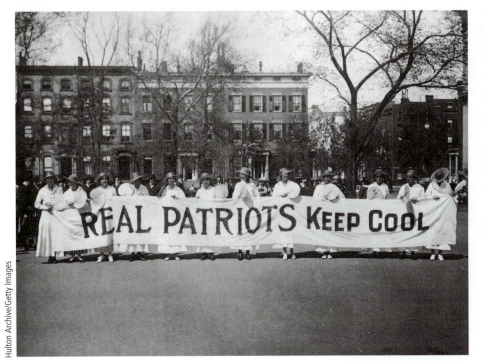

Hulton Archive/Getty Images

Women's Peace Parade, late 1910s In August 1914, more than fifteen hundred women marched down Fifth Avenue in New York City in a silent protest against the hostilities in Europe. The march inspired the creation of the Women's Peace Party (WPP) in January 1915. Under the leadership of Jane Addams, WPP played a major role in transnational women's peace activism. Critics found their public demonstrations unpatriotic and mocked the slogan "Real Patriots Keep Cool" by countering with "Real Patriots Fight Hard." ◀

European war would undermine their quest for improved working and living conditions at home.

Pacifists organized against the war. In April 1915, more than one thousand women from warring and neutral nations attended an International Congress of Women for Peace and Freedom in The Hague, Netherlands. With Jane Addams presiding, it adopted a proposal drafted by Rosika Schwimmer (see Chapter 17), a Hungarian feminist who called for belligerent nations to attend a mediation conference and formed a permanent committee. Later that year, Schwimmer persuaded automaker Henry Ford to send an antiwar delegation to Europe. On December 4, 1915, the Peace Ship sailed from Hoboken with one hundred forty activists and dozens of journalists aboard. After arriving in Norway, the delegates lobbied foreign diplomats in several countries but did not achieve their goal of arranging a cease-fire by Christmas.

Wilson discovered that maintaining strict neutrality was exceedingly difficult. Although international law decreed that neutral nations could trade nonmilitary goods with nations at war, Great Britain mined the North Sea and began stopping and searching neutral merchant vessels for contraband items useful to the enemy. Wilson repeatedly protested these violations of U.S. neutrality. The British, seeking to retain American goodwill, usually returned the goods or promised to compensate U.S. shippers after the war.

The balance of commerce further undermined American neutrality. U.S. factories and farms increased production to meet European needs, but they overwhelmingly sent war matériel, consumer products, and food to the Allies. After Wilson overrode Secretary of State William Jennings Bryan's opposition to private loans to belligerent nations, U.S. financiers also demonstrated bias toward the Allies, loaning them $2.3 billion while advancing the Central Powers only $27 million. After lending millions of dollars to European combatants, the United States shifted from debtor nation to creditor nation. In 1914, Americans owed foreigners $3 billion; by 1919, foreigners owed Americans $10 billion (see Figure 18.2).

In the face of British naval superiority and U.S. economic bias toward the Allies, Germany introduced the *Unterseeboot* (U-boat). International law dictated that any naval vessel firing on another must first warn its adversaries

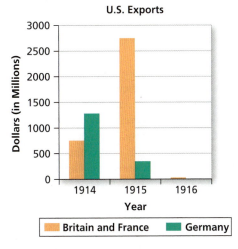

Figure 18.2 U.S. Trade with Europe, 1914–1916 Despite its proclamation of neutrality when war erupted in Europe in 1914, the United States adopted trade policies that greatly favored Britain and France over Germany—a trend that made the German government question U.S. impartiality. ▲ *Source:* Thomas G. Paterson et al. *American Foreign Relations,* vol. 2 (Boston: Wadsworth, 2010), p. 78.

Global Americans Born in 1860, **Jane Addams** was one of the most renowned women in the world in the early twentieth century. In 1887, while traveling in Europe with her friend Ellen G. Starr, she visited Toynbee Hall, a settlement house in London's East End. The visit inspired them to open a similar facility called Hull House in an impoverished part of Chicago. While raising funds and enlisting volunteers, they organized a kindergarten, classes, club meetings, a library, a public kitchen, and more. Hull House earned widespread acclaim and was emulated across the nation.

Ascribing to a world view interweaving social justice, democracy, and peace, Addams strongly supported women's suffrage and was very active in domestic and transnational peace movements. In 1898, she joined the Anti-Imperialist League, a coalition opposing U.S. annexation of the Philippines. In January 1915, following the outbreak of World War I in Europe, she became the national chair of the newly created Women's Peace Party (WPP). Three months later, she was elected president of the permanent committee created at the International Congress of Women in The Hague, which became the Women's International League for Peace and Freedom (WILPF) in 1919. Addams served as the organization's president for a decade. Many U.S. newspapers deemed her pacifist activities unpatriotic and the Daughters of the American Revolution expelled her. Undeterred, she worked as an assistant for Herbert Hoover's wartime relief efforts for women and children. In 1931, after becoming the first U.S. woman to win the Nobel Peace Prize, Addams donated the prize money to WILDF.

Library of Congress

and then allow all passengers and crew to evacuate prior to any attack. But submarines were small and vulnerable. British ships often rammed or fired on U-boats whose commanders tried to comply with the rules.

In February 1915, Germany struck back by announcing the creation of a war zone around Great Britain. The Germans warned neutral ships to stay out of the area to avoid being mistaken for enemy vessels and urged people not to travel on enemy passenger ships. When Bryan begged Wilson to bar Americans from entering the war zone, the president claimed that neutrality accorded Americans the right to travel wherever they wished. Although Great Britain was violating international law by arming merchant vessels obtaining supplies at neutral ports, Wilson excused Britain's actions while denouncing Germany's submarine warfare.

Wilson's response to Germany's sinking of the British liner *Lusitania* highlighted these contradictions. On May 1, 1915, the *Lusitania* departed New York with 1,257 travelers and a crew of seven hundred two. It also transported contraband including 4.2 million rounds of rifle ammunition and 1,250 cases of shrapnel shells. On May 7, a German U-boat torpedoed the ship, sinking it in only eighteen minutes: 1,198 passengers, 128 of whom were Americans, drowned.

Without holding Britain accountable for transporting war matériel, Wilson demanded that Germany stop attacking passenger ships and pay for U.S. losses. After the president rejected Bryan's calls for a simultaneous protest of British violation of rules regarding contraband, he resigned. Although the German government apologized for the deaths of Americans and offered compensation, it refused to modify its submarine strategy. Now convinced

that Germany posed a grave threat to global democracy, Wilson sent presidential adviser Colonel Edward House on several unsuccessful missions to negotiate a peace settlement among the warring European factions.

In March 1916, a German sub mistook the French steamer *Sussex* for a minesweeper and fired a torpedo, injuring several passengers including four Americans. Wilson warned Germany that if it failed to cease its attacks on passenger and cargo vessels, the United States would sever diplomatic relations. Reeling from the recent loss of five hundred thousand troops in the unsuccessful German assault on Verdun, Kaiser Wilhelm II decided not to risk war with the United States and agreed to Wilson's demands. His *Sussex* pledge temporarily eased tensions with the Wilson administration. Great Britain, meanwhile, was boycotting eighty U.S. companies that traded with the Central Powers.

18-4b America Enters the War

While trying to maintain U.S. neutrality, Woodrow Wilson confronted an American public bitterly divided about the war. Advocates like Roosevelt condemned Wilson's failure to bolster the nation's defenses. Pacifists decried any steps toward improving military readiness. When a popular antiwar song declared, "I Didn't Raise My Boy to Be a Soldier," their opponents retorted with the ditty "I Didn't Raise My Boy to Be a Slacker." Caught in the middle, Wilson embarked on a program of "moderate preparedness" and asked Congress for large increases in troops for the army and navy.

> The United States abandons neutrality and joins the war against the Central Powers.

Campaigning on the slogan "He kept us out of war," Wilson defeated Republican Charles Evans Hughes in the 1916 presidential election.

Having won a second term, Wilson renewed his efforts to negotiate peace. On the verge of defeating Russia on the Eastern Front and anticipating victory on the Western Front, the Germans expected to gain territories in eastern Europe, Africa, Belgium, and France—terms that the British, the French, and their allies would mightily resist. Certain that a punitive settlement would spark another catastrophic war, Wilson proposed a new vision of international relations. In an address to the U.S. Senate on January 22, 1917, he outlined a "peace without victory" based on "the equality of nations," consent of the governed, freedom of the seas, arms limitation, and a community of power. Such a peace would mark a stark departure from previous conflicts in which the victors humiliated their opponents by stripping them of territory and imposing harsh indemnities. Wilson's peace would replace fragile, secretive alliances and destructive arms races with a system in which all nations—whatever their size, strength, or wealth—worked collectively to maintain open trade and security.

Even as Wilson spoke, Germany was preparing to launch a major offensive to end the war before the United States could mobilize and send troops to Europe. On January 31, Germany announced that U-boats would attack *all* vessels—passenger or merchant, enemy or neutral—that entered waters near England or France. With the *Sussex* pledge now violated, Wilson severed diplomatic relations with Germany.

In late February, the exposure of a telegram from Arthur Zimmermann, the German foreign minister, pushed the United States closer to a declaration of war. Intercepted by British intelligence agents monitoring the transatlantic cable, the **Zimmermann telegram** asked Mexico to ally with Germany in case of war with the United States, promising financial assistance and help in regaining the former Mexican territories of Arizona, New Mexico, and Texas. Ironically, Wilson had withdrawn U.S. troops from Mexico and formally recognized the Carranza regime as Mexico's legal government less than a month earlier. When confronted with evidence of German plotting against the United States, Wilson asked Congress for the authority to arm merchant ships to thwart U-boat attacks. When the U.S. Senate filibustered his request, he issued an executive order arming the merchant vessels. But the measure did not prevent Germany from quickly sinking five U.S. ships. By late March, Wilson and his cabinet unanimously concluded the time for war had arrived.

On April 2, 1917, Wilson addressed a special joint session of Congress and asked for a declaration of war against Germany, arguing that the Germans' unrestricted submarine warfare and the Zimmermann telegram insulted America's national honor and imperiled U.S. economic interests. Hopeful that the Russians would adopt a democratic government similar to those of the other Allies, Wilson welcomed a partnership with the provisional regime that had recently deposed the autocratic Tsar Nicholas II. Insisting that the United States fought for principles like liberty, not for material gain, Wilson declared, "The world must be made safe for democracy." On April 4, the Senate voted 82 to 6 in favor of declaring war. Two days later, the House approved the measure 373 to 50. Representative Jeannette Rankin, a Montana Republican who was the first woman to serve in Congress and a pacifist, was among those voting "no."

Zimmermann telegram
German proposal urging Mexico to attack the United States in exchange for the return of territory lost during the Mexican-American War (1846–1848).

18-4c Combat in Europe

{ The U.S. mobilizes its troops, revolution rocks Russia, and the Allies force Germany to surrender.

When the United States declared war, the Allies were perilously close to defeat. Wilson selected John J. Pershing, leader of the recent U.S. incursion in Mexico, to command the American Expeditionary Force. With only one hundred thirty thousand active-duty troops (many of whom were poorly trained) and outdated equipment, the army was not ready for war in Europe. To build military strength as quickly as possible, Congress passed the Selective Service Act in May 1917. It required all men ages twenty-one to thirty (later expanded to eighteen to forty-five) to register for conscription. By the time the war ended in November 1918, more than 2.8 million conscripts of a pool exceeding 24 million had been inducted into the armed forces. Unwilling to place U.S. soldiers under the command of the European generals responsible for the slaughter of millions, Wilson and Pershing insisted that American units remain separate and independent. Desperate for reinforcements, the Allies acquiesced, and the first battalion of U.S. soldiers arrived in France on July 4, 1917.

While the United States mobilized for war, some troops contracted a virulent strain of influenza. U.S. soldiers first carried the disease from their home bases to Europe in the spring of 1918, but few victims died. When the disease resurfaced in the fall, it was deadly. Some victims died only hours after developing symptoms. Ravaging young and old alike, the virus soon infected one-fifth of the world's people. By the spring of 1919, an estimated 50 million people had died in the worst pandemic ever witnessed.

U.S. troops also carried American racism to Europe. Eager to demonstrate their patriotism, more than four hundred thousand African Americans enlisted in the army. W.E.B. Du Bois, then working in New York as editor of *The Crisis*, declared, "Let us, while this war lasts, forget our special grievances and close ranks." But the marines refused entirely to accept blacks, and the navy allowed them to serve only in menial capacities. Although the army did not technically bar African Americans from combat roles, most worked as laborers. The exclusion prompted

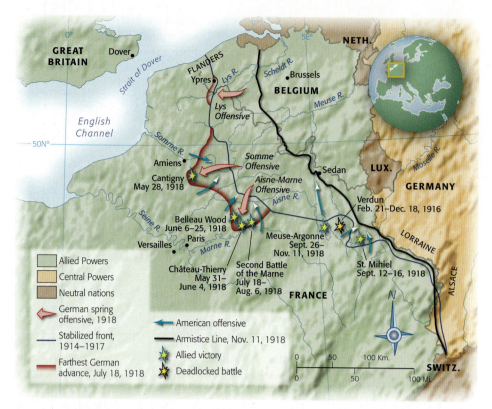

Map 18.3 The Western Front Throughout the fifty-one months of World War I, there was continuous action on the Western Front—a 435-mile line of trenches, shelters, and fields stretching from Switzerland to the North Sea. Most battles were fought in France and Belgium, and none occurred in Germany. Although France and Britain contributed the most soldiers and equipment of the more than twenty nations fighting for the Allies, the United States played a vital role in the conflict's last stages. ▲

genocide Deliberate and systematic destruction of all or part of an ethnic, religious, racial, or cultural group.

such an outcry from black communities that the War Department created two black combat units, the 92nd and 93rd Divisions, both sent into battle in France. Like the Buffalo Soldiers before them, these black soldiers rarely received equal treatment. In 1917, after a riot broke out on a military base near Houston leaving seventeen whites and two blacks dead, the army convicted one hundred ten black soldiers in the biggest court martial in U.S. history, but white soldiers and civilians escaped prosecution. The irony of fighting to make the world "safe for democracy" while facing discrimination at home did not escape African American soldiers.

Throughout 1917, political instability in Russia had profound ramifications on the Great War. In October 1917, the Bolsheviks, Communists committed to abolishing private property and imperialism, ousted the provisional government and honored their pledge to take Russia out of the conflict. In the Treaty of Brest-Litovsk, signed in March 1918, the Russians ceded one-quarter of their prewar population and arable land and half their coal fields and iron manufacturing to the Germans. After Russia's capitulation on the Eastern Front, Germany launched a major offensive in western Europe. By May, German

forces were encamped on the Marne River, only fifty miles outside Paris. U.S. troops saw their first action there. The following month, American forces stopped the Germans at Château-Thierry and in July, pushed them out of Belleau Wood.

After crushing a second German attempt to capture Paris, the Allies launched a counteroffensive. In late September 1918, more than 1 million U.S. troops joined French and British units in six weeks of fighting in the Meuse-Argonne (see Map 18.3). More than twenty-six thousand Americans died, and nearly ninety-six thousand sustained wounds. As the German army retreated, the Allies sank U-boats on the Atlantic, freeing supply lanes for the first time in months.

In early October, the German chancellor concluded the war was lost and asked Wilson for peace terms. Bulgaria, Turkey, and Austro-Hungary surrendered in quick succession. After forcing Kaiser Wilhelm II to abdicate, members of the new German government signed an armistice on November 11, 1918. The German, Austro-Hungarian, and Ottoman empires had collapsed, and 16 million people had died, including 6.8 million civilians and more than 1 million Armenian victims of a **genocide** orchestrated by Turks (see Figure 18.3).

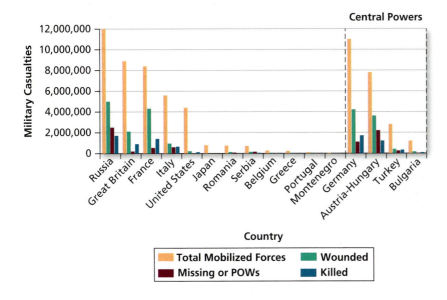

Figure 18.3 Estimated WWI Military Casualties A collision of nineteenth-century battlefield tactics with twentieth-century technologies contributed to high military casualties in World War I. Powerful, mobile artillery inflicted grave damage on enemy positions. Exploding shells and shrapnel were responsible for killing more soldiers than any other military innovation during the conflict. The continued use of infantry charges during trench warfare proved a particularly senseless tactic as waves of soldiers were often mowed down with modern weapons. ◀

Sources: WWI Casualty and Death Tables, http://www.pbs.org/greatwar/resources/casdeath_pop.html; Daily Chart, Remembrance, *The Economist*, November 11, 2013, http://www.economist.com/blogs/graphicdetail/2013/11/daily-chart-4

18-5

Home Front Mobilization for the War and the Peace Settlements

To mobilize Americans for war against the Central Powers, the Committee on Public Information produced thousands of propaganda posters like this one. Notice that "militarism" is inscribed on the ape's helmet and "kultur" is etched on his club as he steps on the shoreline identified as "America." Consider the possible symbolism of the woman the ape is carrying.

Why did U.S. officials portray their German foes in this manner, and how might such images have contributed to the deep divisions the war generated among Americans? ▶

U.S. entry into the Great War triggered great changes on the home front. Aided by a stronger and larger federal bureaucracy, business leaders and government officials worked closely to coordinate production. Workers seized new economic opportunities. Race riots, labor unrest, and political repression highlighted societal divisions. In the turmoil of wartime, Progressive reformers worked to advance causes such as racial equality, women's suffrage, and prohibition. European leaders' intransigence and domestic partisan politics derailed Wilson's ambitious plan to reshape foreign relations through open diplomacy, free trade, disarmament, and international cooperation. But the United States entered the 1920s as the world's leading economic, military, and cultural power.

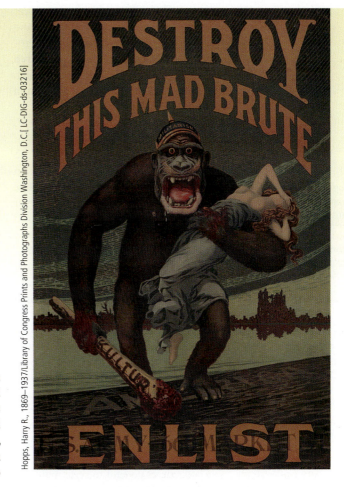

Hopps, Harry R., 1869–1937/Library of Congress Prints and Photographs Division Washington, D.C.[LC-DIG-ds-03216]

☞ As you read, consider how U.S. entry into World War I shaped life on the home front while President Wilson articulated a new framework for international relations. What were the key elements of Wilson's vision for the postwar world? Was he able to realize these aims at the Paris Peace Conference? Why or why not?

18-5a Government Expansion and Control

To mobilize for war, the Wilson administration greatly expanded the size and power of the U.S. government. Almost five thousand newly created federal agencies coordinated manufacturing, transportation, and agriculture. Increased cooperation between government and business tripled corporate profits and boosted U.S. industrial output 20 percent by 1919. The War Industries Board purchased war supplies, set production quotas, and allocated raw materials. The Food Administration, led by future president Herbert Hoover, ensured that U.S. troops had adequate diets. To encourage Americans to save vital supplies, Hoover instigated "meatless" and "wheatless" days and urged them to plant "victory gardens." Other agencies managed fuel, railroad traffic, shipping, and trade.

{ The U.S. government mobilizes for war, tries to build public support, and restricts civil liberties.

To maintain production and avoid strikes, the War Labor Board mediated disputes between employers and workers. The Wilson administration also supported Progressive reforms such as eight-hour workdays, improved wages and working conditions, and collective bargaining. Such policies strengthened organized labor, and union membership almost doubled during the war.

When the United States declared war in April 1917, Americans were still bitterly divided in their opinions of the Allies and the Central Powers. To generate popular support, Wilson created the **Committee on Public Information (CPI)**. Headed by former journalist George Creel, CPI used pamphlets, speeches, films, and advertising in dozens of different languages to shape public views of the war and to encourage patriotic sacrifice among America's varied ethnic populations.

Determined to curtail pro-German activity in the United States, Wilson persuaded Congress to pass the **Espionage Act of 1917**. It imposed penalties of up to $10,000 and twenty years in prison for anyone convicted of aiding the enemy, obstructing military recruitment, or encouraging disloyalty. The act also empowered the postmaster general to seize materials deemed treasonous. The following year, the **Sedition Act** expanded the law to encompass "disloyal, profane, scurrilous, or abusive language" about the U.S. government, the American flag, or the armed forces. More than fifteen hundred people

Committee on Public Information (CPI) U.S. propaganda agency created to generate public support for U.S. entry into World War I.

Espionage Act of 1917 U.S. federal law updating and expanding antispy statutes, criminalizing opposition to the draft, and giving postal officials authority to censor mail and newspapers.

Sedition Act Amendment to the Espionage Act outlawing criticism of the Constitution, the U.S. government, the U.S. armed forces, or the American flag in time of war.

Eighteenth Amendment Constitutional amendment prohibiting the manufacture, sale, and transportation of alcohol, later repealed by the Twenty-First Amendment in 1933.

Nineteenth Amendment Constitutional amendment signed into law on August 26, 1920, that prohibits denying a U.S. citizen the right to vote on the basis of sex.

were arrested for alleged violations of the laws. Acting on long-standing animosities toward immigrants and political radicals, law enforcement officials used the Espionage Act and the Sedition Act to arrest prominent leftists including journalist John Reed and Bill Haywood, leader of the Industrial Workers of the World (IWW). In June 1918, Socialist Party leader Eugene V. Debs was arrested for a second time, convicted of sedition, and sentenced to ten years after making an antiwar speech in Canton, Ohio.

18-5b Dissent and Resistance

CPI fueled a wave of intense anti-German sentiment. Publicizing German atrocities in Belgium, the committee depicted the Germans as "Huns, rapists, and pillagers." Schools stopped teaching German language courses and banned books by German authors such as the eighteenth-century writer and literary critic Johann Wolfgang von Goethe. Orchestras refused to play works by J.S. Bach, Ludwig van Beethoven, and Johannes Brahms. Restaurants renamed hamburgers "liberty sandwiches" and sauerkraut "liberty cabbage."

{ The war sparks political repression of some Americans while providing opportunities for others.

Exploiting the anti-German atmosphere, prohibition proponents emphasized the prominent role of German immigrants in operating breweries and saloons. Having succeeded in getting half of the states to ban alcohol prior to 1917, the Anti-Saloon League pushed for a constitutional amendment outlawing the manufacture, transportation, and sale of alcohol nationally. These xenophobic (antiforeigner) appeals combined with wartime demand for grains used in alcoholic beverages led to ratification of the **Eighteenth Amendment** in January 1919.

Despite the political discord it unleashed, the war also enabled some groups to make gains. Because Wilson opposed women's suffrage, Alice Paul and her fellow activists picketed outside the White House, emulating the confrontational tactics of the suffragists that Paul had witnessed in England. When the United States entered the war, some Americans considered the demonstrations unpatriotic and onlookers harassed and physically attacked the picketers. Police arrested the suffragists for obstructing traffic. While some women spent only a few days in jail, others were sentenced to seven-month terms. News of the protesters' mistreatment by prison officials outraged the public. Wilson used the incident to call for a federal women's suffrage amendment in recognition of women's vital contribution to the war effort. In June 1919, the Senate passed the measure by one vote and sent it to the states for ratification. On August 26, 1920, when Tennessee became the thirty-sixth state to adopt it, the **Nineteenth Amendment** went into effect.

After a labor shortage arose as men were drafted, employers began to hire women, African Americans, and Mexican Americans. Although the number of women working for wages did not significantly increase, some

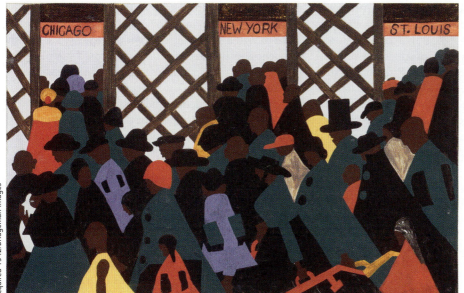

Lawrence, Jacob (1917-2000)/The Phillips Collection, Washington, D.C., USA/ Acquired 1942/Bridgeman Images

Jacob Lawrence, *Migration Series, Panel No. 1*, 1940–1941 By late 1919, with the influx of at least four hundred fifty thousand southern African Americans drawn by the prospect of better-paying wartime jobs, the black population of many major northern cities soared. Having moved to Harlem with his family in 1930 at age thirteen, Jacob Lawrence did not experience these events personally, but in 1940–1941, he depicted them in sixty paintings collectively entitled *Migration Series*. The series won national acclaim, and he became a celebrated artist. ◀

female workers moved into better-paying positions in defense plants. In most cases, however, women received less pay than their male coworkers.

African Americans also sought to take advantage of opportunities for industrial work. Starting in 1916, the exodus of southern blacks that began after Reconstruction spiked dramatically, and four hundred fifty thousand of them joined a **Great Migration** from the South to cities such as St. Louis, Chicago, and Detroit before the war's end. Many found better wages and living conditions, but tensions with whites often exploded. In mid-1917, a race riot erupted in East St. Louis, Illinois, that left nine whites and almost forty blacks dead. During the **Red Summer** of 1919, racial unrest swept more than three dozen U.S. cities including a thirteen-day riot in

Great Migration Movement of approximately 6 million African Americans from the rural South to northern urban areas beginning in 1916.

Red Summer Wave of intense racial unrest occurring across the United States from May to October 1919, the largest of which occurred in Chicago, Washington, D.C., and Elaine, Arkansas.

Will Brown, a Lynching Victim in Omaha, Nebraska, 1919 After World War I ended, racial hostilities escalated greatly and a wave of lynchings and race riots swept the country. In September 1919, more than ten thousand whites in Omaha, Nebraska, stormed and then burned the county courthouse, demanding the release of Will Brown, a black man accused of raping a white woman. After hanging Brown and burning his body, the mob destroyed more than $1 million of property before federal troops could restore order. ▼

Nebraska State Historical Society

Chicago. Between 1914 and 1920, 382 African Americans were lynched. Incensed by the violence, W.E.B. Du Bois and other activists called for a federal antilynching law and an end to segregation. Many African American veterans were embittered by the second-class treatment they received from the countrymen they had fought to defend.

Mexican Americans had similar experiences. Wartime labor shortages prompted some to move to cities for defense jobs. Many congregated in barrios similar to ethnic enclaves created by other minorities. After the Immigration Act of 1917 relaxed immigration restrictions on Mexico (while adding a literacy requirement for emigrants from other nations), more than one hundred thousand Mexicans eager to escape the upheavals of the Mexican Revolution and to pursue wartime economic opportunities migrated to the Southwest. Although racism was endemic, many built better lives in the United States.

18-5c Politics of Peacemaking

Even before the United States entered the war, Wilson envisioned a postwar world that transcended the imperialist rivalries, militarism, and destructive nationalism that triggered the conflict. In late 1917, after the Bolsheviks began publishing secret Allied agreements for dividing the Central Powers' colonies, Wilson and a group of experts drafted a proposal offering a global alternative to both imperialism and communism.

> Wilson's new framework for international relations meets Allied resistance and domestic political opposition.

On January 8, 1918, Wilson presented his **Fourteen Points** to Congress. The first five points called for open diplomacy, freedom of the seas, arms limitation, free trade, and "impartial adjustment of all colonial claims."

The next eight points proposed **self-determination** for national minorities in Europe. The final and most important point recommended the establishment of the **League of Nations**, an international organization that would mediate disputes peacefully and guarantee "political independence and territorial integrity to great and small states alike."

To promote the Fourteen Points, the CPI launched one of the world's first international advertising campaigns. Its representatives around the world received the message via radio and transatlantic cable and then disseminated posters and handbills promoting the information. In battle zones, artillery shells filled with leaflets were lobbed over enemy lines. Colonized peoples responded enthusiastically, but the Allies, eager to avenge the catastrophic losses they were suffering in the war, were skeptical. In October 1918, after Wilson threatened to sign a separate peace with Germany, the British, French, and Italians reluctantly accepted his plan. On November 11, all combatant nations signed an armistice ending the war.

In an unprecedented move, Wilson announced that he personally would represent the United States at the Paris Peace Conference. Energized after winning control of both houses of Congress in the recent midterm elections, Republicans attacked the president's refusal to rely on the diplomat corps who usually conducted U.S. foreign policy abroad and his failure to include any prominent Republicans in the American delegation. These decisions had grave domestic political consequences, but the cheering crowds that greeted Wilson when he arrived in Europe led him to believe he could dominate the peace process and gain universal acceptance of his Fourteen Points.

W.E.B. Du Bois was among the millions inspired by Wilson. He rushed to Paris and organized a **Pan-African Congress** to be held in conjunction with the peace negotiations. When the meeting began in February 1919, fifty-seven delegates from fifteen nations attended and immediately declared their support for global racial equality and anti-imperialism. The participants applauded the Japanese government's decision to share its concerns at the official proceedings of the Paris Peace Conference.

The meetings at the palace of Versailles got off to a rocky start. In the face of British and French resistance, Wilson repeatedly capitulated in order to save the League of Nations. Jettisoning his demands for open diplomacy and equality of nations, he agreed to conduct most of the talks in secret and to bar Germany and the Bolsheviks from the discussions. The United States, Great Britain, France, and Italy (The "Big Four") dictated terms presented to the other twenty-eight national delegations.

Transferring more than 1.1 million square miles of territory formerly controlled by Russia, Austro-Hungary, and Germany, delegates redrew the map of Europe. France regained Alsace-Lorraine, lost in the punitive settlement of the 1871 Franco-Prussian War. Italy annexed South Tyrol and Trieste. In an effort to grant self-determination to diverse peoples once under Austro-Hungarian rule, delegates made Austria, Hungary, Czechoslovakia, Romania, and Yugoslavia independent nations. Similarly, but also to intensify the political isolation of the Bolsheviks, the Allies recognized Poland, Finland, Estonia, Latvia, and Lithuania—all formerly parts of the Russian Empire—as independent states.

The delegates also addressed the issue of colonies. Long angered by white claims that nonwhites were inferior, the Japanese proposed a racial equality clause for the League of Nations Covenant. It would have guaranteed "equal and just treatment in every respect making no distinction, either in law or in fact, on account of their race or nationality." But representatives from Great Britain, South Africa, Australia, and New Zealand zealously opposed the proposal. So did Wilson.

Fourteen Points Proposal offered by President Woodrow Wilson that became a framework for peace negotiations following World War I.

self-determination Freedom of the people of a state or territory to choose their own government.

League of Nations International organization first proposed by Wilson in 1918 and founded in 1920 to promote global cooperation and to preserve peace, disbanded in 1946.

Pan-African Congress Originating in the mid-nineteenth century, an ideology and movement calling for all peoples of African descent to unite to further economic, political, and social aims.

The delegates' white supremacist views also shaped the **mandate system** created for governing colonies and regions previously controlled by the defeated German and Ottoman empires. "Peoples not yet able to stand by themselves under the strenuous conditions of the modern world," were placed under the "tutelage" of "advanced nations" in preparation for independence and economic self-sufficiency. In the Middle East, delegates created several new nations and mapped their boundaries. France was granted mandates for Syria and Lebanon, and Britain received Iraq, Trans-Jordan, and Palestine, where according to the **Balfour Declaration** (1917), a Jewish homeland was to be established—a **Zionist** goal not realized until Israel was founded in 1948. In the Pacific, the Japanese acquired mandates for some of Germany's islands as well as Shandong, a portion of China with 30 million inhabitants. In effect, the mandate system maintained colonialism.

These maneuvers outraged colonized people who had embraced the Fourteen Points' message of self-determination. Nationalist movements erupted in China, Tunisia, Indonesia, Egypt, India, and elsewhere. At the Paris Peace Conference, a Vietnamese who took the name Nguyen Ai Quoc (Nguyen the Patriot, later known as Ho Chi Minh) called for Indochina's independence from France and challenged Wilson to grant self-determination to all people, not just Europeans. Confident that the League of Nations would eventually resolve problems arising from imperialism, Wilson ignored such pleas.

Wilson's faith in the League also informed his decision to accept harsh peace terms against Germany. Britain and France pushed for high reparations and a "war guilt" clause that made Germany solely responsible for the conflict. Certain that the League would prevent excessive vengeance, Wilson agreed. It proved a major miscalculation. In 1921, an international commission presented Germany a $33 billion bill that had shattering economic and political consequences.

In February 1919, Wilson briefly returned to the United States to get feedback on a draft treaty that contained both the peace terms and the covenant creating the League of Nations. Polls indicated that most Americans supported the League, but Wilson encountered strong opposition from Congress, where leading senators such as Republican Henry Cabot Lodge feared the League would compromise U.S. sovereignty. To placate his critics, the president stormed back to Paris and secured Allied approval of amendments that safeguarded the Monroe Doctrine, removed the United States from the mandate system, prohibited League intervention in domestic disputes, and allowed nations to leave the League with two years' notice. On June 28, 1919, the Allies presented Germany the extremely vindictive **Versailles Treaty**.

In July, Wilson submitted the treaty to the U.S. Senate and expected quick ratification. Instead, the senators continued their barrage of criticisms. Many believed that **Article X**, the **collective security** provision of the League covenant obligating all members to come to the defense of a member facing external attack, would force U.S. troops to act as international police. Others claimed the treaty encroached on congressional warmaking powers.

mandate system Policy that granted authority to member states of the League of Nations to govern territories formerly under German or Ottoman rule.

Balfour Declaration British declaration of support for the establishment of a Jewish homeland in Palestine, later included in the League of Nations mandate for Palestine.

Zionist Political movement calling for the creation of a sovereign Jewish homeland in Israel, also called Palestine, Canaan, or the Holy Land.

Versailles Treaty Post-World War I agreement imposing extremely punitive Allied penalties on Germany including loss of colonies and territory, demilitarization, and payment of reparations.

Article X Provision in the Covenant of the League of Nations obligating members to defend a fellow member facing external aggression.

collective security Arrangement among nations under which an attack on one participating nation is met by all countries bound by the pact.

Library of Congress, Serials and Government Publications Division

"War of the Races—Men in the Great Conflict and Where They Come From," 1919 As shown in this map that originally appeared in the *New York Times*, soldiers of many races fought for both the Allies and the Central Powers. Colonized peoples and racial minorities hoped wartime sacrifices would be rewarded with independence and equality. While some European ethnic minorities were made part of newly created nation-states, many peoples living under imperial rule were bitterly disappointed by postwar negotiations and launched movements for self-determination. ◄

Unmoved, Wilson refused to alter any provisions of the treaty and embarked on a national tour during which he vigorously defended the League. A few days after giving an impassioned speech, he suffered a massive stroke that paralyzed his left side. In the following weeks, Edith Bolling Galt Wilson, the president's wife, handled her husband's political affairs and prevented his advisers from seeing him.

With Wilson incapacitated, the U.S. Senate resoundingly defeated the Versailles Treaty in two separate votes. In July 1921, Congress finally passed a joint resolution ending the war. The following month, the United States accepted the Versailles Treaty—but not the provisions on the League. In a tragic irony, the United States did not participate in the new international organization for which Wilson had fought so intensely.

Summary

In the years following Reconstruction, Americans expanded their continental empire abroad. A fusion of geostrategic, commercial, political, religious, and racial motives drove U.S. efforts to gain foreign territories. Although they claimed to reject the harsh methods of European imperialists, Americans engaged in brutal wars and economic exploitation while expanding their nation's international reach. From 1899 to 1902, U.S. troops battled nationalist insurgents in the Philippines, a first glimpse of the ferocious resistance that American interventionism sometimes provoked. At home, anti-imperialists alleged that imperialism endangered democracy, undercut U.S. workers, and jeopardized the white race. Imperialists countered by emphasizing the superiority of American political institutions and values and the economic necessity of securing markets and raw materials in an age of industrialization and international rivalries.

In the early twentieth century, the United States vigorously defended, controlled, and expanded its new empire. Despite their paternalism toward foreign peoples, U.S. officials, businessmen, missionaries, and moral reformers ushered in positive changes including public health initiatives, sanitation, road and bridge construction, and economic opportunities. U.S. policy makers instituted a variety of legal structures to govern new colonies. Through coercive policies such as the Platt Amendment and the Roosevelt Corollary, they subjugated Central Americans. Dollar diplomacy and the Open Door policy became additional tools for protecting U.S. commercial and security interests abroad. American interference in the Mexican Revolution brought the two nations to the brink of war.

Initially neutral when a world war began in 1914, the United States entered the conflict in April 1917. More than 2 million U.S. soldiers arrived in Europe before the armistice of November 1918. Although they played a critical role in the war's final stages, U.S. losses paled in comparison to those of other combatants. Determined to quash the Allies' desires for revenge against their German adversaries and eager to provide an alternative to worldwide Communist revolution, Woodrow Wilson put forward the Fourteen Points as a framework for a new era in international relations. Although he was able to win support for some of his aims at the Paris Peace Conference, he encountered intense political resistance at home. Congressional rejection of the Versailles Treaty ensured that the United States would not be a part of the League of Nations that Wilson believed would end destructive global conflicts.

The war triggered significant political and economic changes in the United States. Business and finance boomed. Workers won economic gains. Reformers advanced prohibition and women's suffrage. But the war also unleashed race riots, political repression, and labor unrest. Despite the tumult, the United States emerged from the war as the world's leading economic, political, and cultural power.

‹Thinking Back, *Looking Forward*›

As you review this chapter, consider the evolution of U.S. expansion beyond North America into foreign territories. How did U.S. acquisition of an overseas empire affect Americans and foreign peoples? Why did U.S. interactions with European imperialist powers change? How did the Great War shift global economic and political dynamics? In the next chapters, consider how World War I affected interaction among nations. What new institutions and treaties arose? How did the war impact American society and the postwar U.S. economy? What forces united Americans in the 1920s? What issues divided them?

To make your study concrete, review the timeline and reflect on the entries there. Think about their causes, consequences, and connections. How do they fit with global trends?

Additional Resources

Books

Hogansen, Kristen. *Fighting for American Manhood: How Gender Politics Provoked the Spanish-American and Philippine-American Wars.* **New Haven: Yale University Press, 2000.** ▶ Pioneering assessment of intersections of gender and imperialist politics.

Katz, Friederich, and Loren Goldner. *The Secret War in Mexico: Europe, the United States, and the Mexican Revolution.* **Chicago: University of Chicago Press, 1981.** ▶ Groundbreaking study placing the Mexican Revolution in international context.

Keegan, John. *The First World War.* **New York: Vintage, 2000.** ▶ Gripping account of the war's battles by a noted military historian.

Kennedy, David M. *Over Here: The First World War and American Society.* **New York: Oxford University Press, 1980.** ▶ Pulitzer Prize-winning account of the U.S. home front during the Great War.

Kramer, Paul A. *The Blood of Government: Race, Empire, the United States, and the Philippines.* **Chapel Hill: University of North Carolina Press, 2006.** ▶ Groundbreaking examination of the intersections of racial and imperial politics.

LaFeber, Walter. *The New Empire: An Interpretation of American Expansion, 1860–1898.* **Ithaca: Cornell University Press, 1963.** ▶ Classic text arguing that economic factors were the primary motivation for U.S. imperialism.

Manela, Erez. *The Wilsonian Moment: Self-Determination and the Origins of Anti-Colonial Nationalism.* **New York: Oxford University Press, 2009.** ▶ Exploration of the resonance of the anti-imperialist message of the Fourteen Points among colonized peoples worldwide.

McWhirter, Cameron. *Red Summer: The Summer of 1919 and the Awakening of Black America.* **New York: St. Martin's Griffin, 2012.** ▶ Narrative account of the wave of lynchings and race riots that engulfed the United States post-World War I.

Rydell, Robert W. *All the World's a Fair: Visions of Empire at American International Exhibitions, 1876–1916.* **Chicago: University of Chicago Press, 1987.** ▶ Examination of the racial and imperialistic dimensions of world's fairs by a noted expert.

Zahniser, J.D., and Amelia R. Fry. *Alice Paul: Claiming Power.* **New York: Oxford University Press, 2014.** ▶ Definitive biography of the acclaimed suffrage activist.

> Go to the MindTap® for **Global Americans** to access the full version of select books from this Additional Resources section.

Websites

The Great War and the Shaping of the 20th Century. (http://www.pbs.org/greatwar/). ▶ Multipart documentary accompanied by online videos, images, and oral histories.

In Motion: The African-American Migration Experience. (http://www.inmotionaame.org/migrations/landing.cfm;jsessionid=f830288482144013361 6962?migration=8&bhcp=1). ▶ Schomburg Museum's collection of texts, images, and maps on the Great Migration.

The National World War I Museum and Memorial. (https://theworldwar.org/). ▶ Global materials on the conflict that include a searchable database.

PBS American Experience: Woodrow Wilson. (http://www.pbs.org/wgbh/amex/wilson/). ▶ Collection of photos, primary sources, interviews, and teaching materials.

The World of 1898: The Spanish-American War. (http://www.loc.gov/rr/hispanic/1898/index.html). ▶ Collection offering interdisciplinary and multinational perspectives on the conflict.

MindTap®   Continue exploring online through MindTap®, where you can:
- **Assess your knowledge with the Chapter Test**
- **Watch historical videos related to the chapter**
- **Further your understanding with interactive maps and timelines**

Projecting Power

1878	1885	1887	1890	1893
U.S. acquires a coaling station on Samoa.	Josiah Strong publishes *Our Country: Its Possible Future and Its Present Crisis.*	**July** U.S. landowners in Hawai'i force King Kalākaua to sign the so-called Bayonet Constitution.	Alfred Thayer Mahan publishes *The Influence of Sea Power upon History.*	**January** U.S. forces help overthrow the Hawaiian monarchy.

January–April

First Inter-American Conference is held in Washington, D.C.

1898	1899–1905	1910–1915	1916–1918	1919–1920

1898

April

U.S. Congress adopts the Teller Amendment, pledging not to annex Cuba.

June

Anti-Imperialist League forms in opposition to U.S. annexation of the Philippines.

1899–1905

May-July 1899

Delegates from twenty-six nations convene in The Hague, Netherlands, to consider disarmament and rules of war.

1899–1901

Boxer Rebellion erupts in China and is suppressed by a multinational force.

1899–1902

Filipinos wage guerilla war against U.S. occupation.

July 1900

First Pan-African Congress meets in London.

Hawai'i becomes a U.S. territory.

August 1900

United States wins the Spanish-American War, gaining control of Puerto Rico, Cuba, and the Philippines.

March 1903

Platt Amendment makes Cuba a U.S. protectorate.

September 1905

Japan defeats Russia in the Russo-Japanese War.

1910–1915

November 1910

Mexican Revolution begins.

1911–1912

Revolution erupts in China, Chinese Republic established.

June 1914

Gavrilo Princep assassinates Archduke Franz Ferdinand of Austria.

August 1914

Panama Canal opens for shipping.

The Great War erupts in Europe, United States declares neutrality.

April 1915

International Congress of Women for Peace and Freedom convenes in The Hague.

May 1915

German submarine sinks the *R.M.S. Lusitania*, drowning 1,128 people.

July 1915

U.S. occupation of Haiti begins.

1916–1918

1916

Great Migration of southern blacks to northern U.S. cities begins.

March 1916

U.S. forces invade Mexico in pursuit of Pancho Villa.

May 1916

U.S. occupation of the Dominican Republic begins.

November 1916

Wilson wins reelection.

April 1917

United States enters World War I.

June 1917

Congress passes the Espionage Act.

October 1917

Bolshevik Revolution begins in Russia.

1918

Spanish flu pandemic begins, killing 50 million people.

January 1918

Wilson proposes the Fourteen Points.

November 1918

Armistice ending World War I is signed.

1919–1920

January 1919

Delegates convene at Paris Peace Conference.

February 1919

Pan-African Congress convenes in Paris amid peace conference ending World War I.

May-October 1919

Red Summer wave of racial violence sweeps the United States.

June 1919

Treaty of Versailles imposes severe punishments on Germany and redraws European borders.

August 1920

Nineteenth Amendment granting women the right to vote is ratified.

September 1920

Mohandas Gandhi launches noncooperation movement in India.

19 Managing Modernity

1919–1929

Charles Lindbergh's 1927 solo nonstop flight from New York to Paris made him the most famous person in the world. He became an instant symbol of the triumph of modern technology, a hero in an era of mass consumption that seems to have invented the very idea of "celebrity."

19-1
Aftermath of World War I

19-1a Communism and the Red Scare
19-1b "Normalcy" at Home and Abroad
19-1c Women's Activism
19-1d Prohibition

19-2
Economic Boom

19-2a Nation's Business
19-2b Fordism and Labor
19-2c Mass Consumption

19-3
Market Expansion

19-3a Infrastructure for Wires and Roads
19-3b Leisure and Popular Culture
19-3c Credit and Crisis

19-4
Americanization

19-4a Immigration Restriction
19-4b Ku Klux Klan and Conservative Politics
19-4c Secularization and Fundamentalist Christianity

19-5
Cultural Pluralism

19-5a Internal Migrations and the Multiracial City
19-5b New Negro and Harlem Renaissance
19-5c Jazz Age Liberation
19-5d Immigrant Generations and the Election of 1928

1898

April

U.S. Congress adopts the Teller Amendment, pledging not to annex Cuba.

June

Anti-Imperialist League forms in opposition to U.S. annexation of the Philippines.

1899–1905

May-July 1899

Delegates from twenty-six nations convene in The Hague, Netherlands, to consider disarmament and rules of war.

1899–1901

Boxer Rebellion erupts in China and is suppressed by a multinational force.

1899–1902

Filipinos wage guerilla war against U.S. occupation.

July 1900

First Pan-African Congress meets in London.

Hawai'i becomes a U.S. territory.

August 1900

United States wins the Spanish-American War, gaining control of Puerto Rico, Cuba, and the Philippines.

March 1903

Platt Amendment makes Cuba a U.S. protectorate.

September 1905

Japan defeats Russia in the Russo-Japanese War.

1910–1915

November 1910

Mexican Revolution begins.

1911–1912

Revolution erupts in China, Chinese Republic established.

June 1914

Gavrilo Princep assassinates Archduke Franz Ferdinand of Austria.

August 1914

Panama Canal opens for shipping.

The Great War erupts in Europe, United States declares neutrality.

April 1915

International Congress of Women for Peace and Freedom convenes in The Hague.

May 1915

German submarine sinks the *R.M.S. Lusitania*, drowning 1,128 people.

July 1915

U.S. occupation of Haiti begins.

1916–1918

1916

Great Migration of southern blacks to northern U.S. cities begins.

March 1916

U.S. forces invade Mexico in pursuit of Pancho Villa.

May 1916

U.S. occupation of the Dominican Republic begins.

November 1916

Wilson wins reelection.

April 1917

United States enters World War I.

June 1917

Congress passes the Espionage Act.

October 1917

Bolshevik Revolution begins in Russia.

1918

Spanish flu pandemic begins, killing 50 million people.

January 1918

Wilson proposes the Fourteen Points.

November 1918

Armistice ending World War I is signed.

1919–1920

January 1919

Delegates convene at Paris Peace Conference.

February 1919

Pan-African Congress convenes in Paris amid peace conference ending World War I.

May-October 1919

Red Summer wave of racial violence sweeps the United States.

June 1919

Treaty of Versailles imposes severe punishments on Germany and redraws European borders.

August 1920

Nineteenth Amendment granting women the right to vote is ratified.

September 1920

Mohandas Gandhi launches noncooperation movement in India.

19 Managing Modernity

1919–1929

Charles Lindbergh's 1927 solo nonstop flight from New York to Paris made him the most famous person in the world. He became an instant symbol of the triumph of modern technology, a hero in an era of mass consumption that seems to have invented the very idea of "celebrity."

NY Daily News Archive/Getty Images

Early on the morning of May 20, 1927, a 25-year-old pilot from Minnesota pushed the throttle of his tiny single-engine plane and took off toward New York's Long Island Sound. *The Spirit of St. Louis* was so heavy with fuel that it barely cleared the telephone wires at the end of the muddy runway. Charles Lindbergh was trying to do what more than a dozen aviators had failed to do—fly nonstop, solo, from New York to Paris. If he succeeded, he would win $25,000, but more acclaimed flyers had crashed, been injured, and died.

Lindbergh flew northeast toward Nova Scotia. As he headed out over the open ocean, darkness fell, and fog so thick enveloped the plane that he was forced to skim just ten feet above the waves. "Which way is Ireland?" he shouted to a fishing boat when the fog cleared in the morning. As darkness fell a second time, he was over the coast of France. At 10:00 P.M. Paris time, he first saw the city's lights, and he circled the Eiffel Tower. Twenty minutes later, he landed to the cheers of wildly enthusiastic fans who lifted him to their shoulders and shouted "Vive!" Radio transmitted the news, and at that moment, Charles Lindbergh, the "Lone Eagle," was the most famous person on Earth. Millions turned out to see him in England and Canada as he made his way back to a hero's homecoming in the United States. New York City officials closed public schools and shuttered the Wall Street stock exchange to stage the city's largest ever ticker tape parade for "Lindbergh Day." President Calvin Coolidge presented Lindbergh the Distinguished Flying Cross, and in 1928 *Time* magazine named him its first ever "Man of the Year."

Lindbergh was beloved, an instant symbol of the triumph of modern technology, a hero in an era of mass consumption that seemed to have invented the very idea of celebrity. Yet he was uncomfortable with much about contemporary society. His rugged individualism, as well as his racism against immigrants and non-whites, seemed to fit the nineteenth century better than the twentieth. Change was happening too fast. He was not alone in worrying about the downside to modernity—crowded, crime-ridden, and vice-ridden cities filled with immigrants and racial minorities that seemed to have no place for tradition and morality. The Great War had made the United States the world's leading economic, military, and cultural power; like many Americans, however, Lindbergh recoiled from global responsibility. When facing another emerging world war, he opposed U.S. involvement and sympathized with racist Nazi leaders in Germany.

The Great Aviator's perplexities reflected the contradictions that shaped the United States in the 1920s. How did a decade marked by modern developments in technology, economic activity, urban life, and global power give rise to a national mood seemingly opposed to the very concept of change? Since the middle of the nineteenth century, the word *modernity* had captured the welcoming embrace of new social, economic, cultural, and political trends that distinguished the present from past traditions and looked forward to the future. Most Americans, like Lindbergh, did not reject modernity so much as to seek to tame or manage its excesses. They yearned for social cohesion, law

Charles Lindbergh was a symbol of the triumph of modern technology, yet he was apprehensive of contemporary society. How do these perplexities reflect the contradictions that shaped the United States in the 1920s?

Go to MindTap® to watch a video on Lindbergh and learn how his story relates to the themes of this chapter.

and order, and a perfection of the social and political reforms of the Progressive Era. If they participated in global affairs, they wanted to do so on their own terms. While most of Europe was in turmoil, struggling to recover from the Great War and to stem the spread of Communist revolution, the United States experienced remarkable prosperity and social stability. Yet Americans were uneasy about their place in the world.

Nor was the U.S. economy so stable as it seemed. Farmers faced declining crop prices, wages remained stagnant, and many families took on debt to purchase the automobiles, radios, and new household appliances that now seemed to be necessities. Advertisers pushed consumer goods, which were produced in great volume by new efficiencies in management and production and made available through credit, another innovation of the 1920s. Overproduction in the domestic market and economic insecurities overseas were bad omens for the global economy that relied disproportionately on U.S. output and loans.

The rejection of Europe and its problems exemplified in 1919 by the refusal of Congress to join the League of Nations extended into the 1920s when there emerged a widespread rejection of foreigners. New laws severely limited the number of immigrants admitted each year, and some groups were excluded altogether. Many Americans associated immigrants with radicalism and with racial and religious minorities who were unwelcome in a republic that the majority defined as white, Protestant, and English or at least northern European in character. Intolerance and cultural conformity marked the decade. At the same time, however, diverse peoples pushed back, aligning themselves with a more inclusive vision of citizenship. Popular culture promised liberation and free expression, and consumer products offered a taste of the good life to a broad sweep of Americans.

19-1
Aftermath of World War I

This 1919 British graphic depicts the League of Nations as a flower blossoming from the graves of World War I, representing the massive human cost of the war. The dark sky at top, depicting the world's uncertain future, stands in contrast to the League of Nation's angelic white figure who appears to float upward toward a Christian notion of heaven.

How might have persons in the United States, disillusioned by the war and wanting to retreat from the problems of Europe, responded to this image? ▶

The Star/Associated Newspapers Ltd./Solo Syndication/British Cartoon Archive

The carnage and destruction of World War I was so great that for at least a decade after it ended, preventing another global bloodletting was high on the world's agenda. Reaching this goal was the main purpose of the League of Nations, which the United States did not join. But it did participate in major arms control agreements and joint international efforts to topple the newly founded Soviet Union and thwart its mission to foment a world Communist revolution. Fears of Communist takeover in Italy, Germany, and Spain fed an aggressive militarism in those countries, posing a threat to global peace. In the United States, a burst of labor and radical protests inspired in part by the Soviet mission provoked government crackdowns on radical activists and their organizations. The horrors of the Great War followed by the threat of class warfare pushed the majority of Americans to favor homespun Americanism rooted in small-town values, Protestantism, law and order, and racial and cultural homogeneity. This "return to normalcy" was evident in the fulfillment of Progressive Era reform movements for women's suffrage and temperance. At the same time, federal interventions on behalf of labor and the working classes ceased as the economy turned prosperous.

☞ As you read, consider the impact of World War I and its aftermath on U.S. politics and international relations. In what ways did it curb U.S. global intervention? In what ways did it compel it?

19-1a Communism and the Red Scare

Russian Communists started on the wrong foot vis-à-vis the United States and other leading capitalist nations. After coming to power during the Great War, Communist revolutionaries led by Vladimir Lenin fought and won a difficult civil war. Twelve nations, including the United States, Britain, and Japan, sent aid to anti-Communist forces and dispatched their own troops to defeat the revolutionaries (see Map 19.1). In 1922, Lenin founded the Soviet Union, a federation of Russian, Transcaucasian, Ukrainian, and Byelorussian republics. Beginning in 1925, Lenin's successor, Joseph Stalin, engaged in a series of political purges that sought to cleanse the new nation of supposed political enemies through execution or removal to forced labor camps.

Stalin, who remained in power for nearly three decades, never forgot the Allied "imperialist invasion" during his country's civil war. Equally antagonistic, the Allies withheld diplomatic recognition of the Soviet Union and did not invite the new country to join the League of Nations for some years. The Soviets responded by hosting a series of congresses known as the **Communist International (Comintern)** attended by people from around the world (including the United States) to create revolutionary parties answering to Moscow. Although there were no sustained Soviet-inspired revolutions during the 1920s, Communists rose up in Germany and Hungary in the immediate aftermath of World War I, and the Communist Party modeled after Lenin's movement flourished in China, where the Chinese Communist Party was founded in 1921.

In Italy, postwar Communist and socialist labor strikes gave strongman Benito Mussolini and his right-wing paramilitary units the chance to seize power. Mussolini, known as Il Duce (The Leader), became prime minister in 1922 and promised stability through **fascism**. This political and economic system was characterized by dictatorial leadership, economic regimentation, and restrictions on civil liberties. Mussolini ruthlessly suppressed opponents, dismantled labor unions, instituted a one-party rule, and mandated state control of business and banking. A dramatic, even bombastic speaker, he vowed to make Italy "great, respected, and feared." In 1923, he bombed and occupied the Greek island of Corfu and in so doing revealed the weakness of the League of Nations in protecting its weak members such as Greece.

In the United States, fears of revolutionary disruptions grew out of widespread labor unrest occurring during the nation's postwar economic slump. Triggering fear were acts of terror committed by anarchists seeking to undermine the capitalist order. In April 1919, thirty-six mail bombs were sent to state officials responsible for cracking-down on political dissent through policies such as the Espionage Act, Sedition Act, and the Immigration Act of 1917. Two months later, much larger bombs were delivered to eight different targets, including U.S. attorney general A. Mitchell Palmer, who escaped harm. The terrorist attacks culminated on September 16, 1920, with the explosion of bombs at the heart of New York's financial district on Wall Street, killing thirty-eight persons and seriously injuring more than one hundred forty.

Fears of labor and radical agitation erupted into what was later called the **Red Scare**. From late 1919 to mid-1920, Palmer orchestrated raids in twenty-three states, arresting more than eight thousand suspected radicals. Many were subjected to illegal searches and imprisoned without being formally charged. The United States deported approximately five hundred "alien enemies" (mainly Russian and Jewish immigrants), including the anarchist Emma Goldman, well known for her antidraft activities during the war and who fled to the Soviet Union, and socialist labor organizer Eugene V. Debs (see Chapter 18). The actions damaged the Industrial Workers of the World (IWW), one of the nation's most radical and violent labor unions that sought to unite all workers regardless of skill, industry, race, or gender.

In response to Red Scare persecutions, Roger Nash Baldwin, a conscientious objector who went to prison during the Great War, settlement house leader Jane Addams, and Helen Keller, the well-known advocate for the deaf and blind, joined in founding the American Civil Liberties Union (ACLU) to provide legal aid to radicals persecuted during the Red Scare and safeguard constitutional protections. The ACLU championed Debs's release as did many cities across the nation where amnesty zones for free speech were established. The organization also provided defense counsel to Nicola Sacco and Bartolomeo Vanzetti, Italian immigrant anarchists

> The Communist revolution in Russia intensifies class conflict at home and around the world.

Communist International (Comintern) Gathering of socialists from across the world organized by the Soviet Union in 1919 to oppose capitalism and install Soviet-style rule.

fascism Authoritarian and ultra-nationalist system of government led right-wing conservatives.

Red Scare Fear of communism and anarchism that gripped the United States, manifest in domestic terrorism, government suppression, and violations of civil liberties.

JAPANESE INTERVENTION IN SIBERIA, 1918–1922

British
French
Canadians
Italians
Serbs

Canadians
Americans

Barents
Sea

Murmansk

Archangel

MONGOLIA

Lake
Baikal

Irkutsk

Amur R.

Vladivostok

CHINA

Sea of
Japan
(East Sea)

KOREA
(Japan)

JAPAN

PACIFIC
OCEAN

0   300   600 Km.
0   300   600 Mi.

NORWAY

SWEDEN

FINLAND
(Independent
1917)

Helsinki
British
Kronstadt
Petrograd
(St. Petersburg)

ESTONIA

Pskok
Riga
Lativians
Lithuanians

LATVIA

LITHUANIA

Baltic Sea

Czechs

Perm

BOLSHEVIK
RUSSIA

Nizhniy
Novgorod

Kazan

Volga R.

Finns

Danzig
GERMANY
E. PRUSSIA

GERMANY

Minsk
Mogilev
Poles

Moscow

Smolensk

Kaluga

Penza

Samara

Ural R.

Orenburg

50°N

Vistula R.

Warsaw
Brest-
Litovsk
Poles

POLAND

Gomel

Orel

Tambov

Saratov

CZECHOSLOVAKIA

Zhitomir
Kiev

UKRAINE

Dniester R.

Dnieper R.

Poltava

Yekaterinoslav

Voronezh

Kharkov

Don R.

Tsaritsyn
(Stalingrad)

Volga R.

HUNGARY

Romanians

BESSARABIA

Odessa

Rostov-on-
Don

Novocherkassak

Astrakhan

Caspian Sea

YUGOSLAVIA

Danube R.

ROMANIA

French

French

Simferopol

British

Novorossiysk

British

Black Sea

Batum
Kars

Tiflis

GEORGIA

Baku
Krasnovodsk

British

British

ALBANIA

BULGARIA

TURKEY

Boundaries of Russian Empire 1914
Area controlled by the Bolsheviks, August 1918
Treaty of Brest-Litovsk
Non-Russian anti-Bolshevik forces
Territory lost to Russia, 1914–1921
Soviet territory, 1922
Boundaries, 1922

0   200   400 Km.
0   200   400 Mi.

SYRIA

Tabriz

PERSIA

Map 19.1 Foreign Intervention in Russian Civil War Communist control over Russia, beginning in 1917, was not secure until 1922 when the Bolsheviks won a brutal civil war. Foreign countries, including the United States, Great Britain, France, and Japan, sent troops in a failed attempt to oust the Communists. The seventy thousand Japanese troops who entered Russia through Vladivostok (see map insert) were the largest foreign contingent. The Bolsheviks remained wary and suspicious of these "foreign imperialist" nations long after the civil war ended. ▲

arrested outside Boston in May 1920 for allegedly murdering two men as part of an armed robbery. The stolen money, it was said during trial, had contributed to the Wall Street bombing that had occurred later that year. Sacco and Vanzetti were convicted of murder and received the death sentence. Their case elicited strong opposition from radicals and others who believed that the court's view of the two men had been biased by the climate of nativism and the Red Scare. Their execution in August 1927 provoked domestic unrest and anti-American protests around the world.

19-1b "Normalcy" at Home and Abroad

{ The search for domestic stability leads to the promotion of international peace. }

The 1920 presidential election—the first in which women could vote—marked a moment of reflection for Americans after a global war, a controversial peace treaty, and a tumultuous postwar period marked by labor unrest, recession, and the Red Scare. What the country most wanted, said the Republican candidate Warren G. Harding, was to close the chapter on the World War I era: "America's present need is not heroics, but healing; not nostrums, but normalcy, not revolution, but restoration." Harding won the election over fellow Ohioan, Democrat James M. Cox, by a record margin, receiving more than 60 percent of the popular vote and more than 76 percent of the electoral vote. Debs, the Socialist Party candidate, garnered 1 million votes despite being in prison.

The Harding administration ended debate about whether the United States should join the League of Nations and set the federal government on a course featuring sharp reductions in spending, increased cooperation with private business, and tax relief for the wealthy. Despite opposing Woodrow Wilson's internationalism, state-sponsored social reform, and organized labor, Harding was more forward looking than he seemed. The new president put an end to the raids by Attorney General Palmer, eased Federal Bureau of Investigation surveillance of radicals, oversaw the repeal of the Sedition Act, and commuted the sentences of Debs and other political prisoners. The British author H. G. Wells praised Debs's release as an indication the nation had realized that "the attempt to shout down and suppress unpopular opinions and to create panics of hostility against minority views is unworthy of the general greatness of American life."

The Harding administration also made historic inroads to securing international peace. His opposition to joining the League of Nations did not make him an **isolationist** in terms of global efforts to prevent war. He did urge the nation to join the Permanent Court of International Justice, which beginning in 1921 operated as the World Court for the League of Nations. Harding's efforts, however, were blocked by the "irreconcilable" senators who opposed joining the League of Nations. They saw World Court membership as a backdoor into the League. He had more luck in convening the **Washington Naval Conference** (1921–1922) to avoid the arms race that had preceded World War I. The conference produced the Five-Power Naval Limitation Treaty that restricted warship tonnage by means of a ratio (5:3:1.75) that allowed the United States and Britain (which maintained both Atlantic and Pacific fleets) the highest tonnage, Japan the next highest, and France and Italy the lowest. The five powers also agreed to a ten-year "naval holiday" during which there would be no construction of new battleships and aircraft carriers. Meeting the treaty requirements, said Secretary of State Charles Evans Hughes, meant scrapping 1.8 million tons of naval vessels. One newspaper proclaimed that "Hughes sank in thirty-five minutes more ships than all the admirals of the world have sunk in a cycle of centuries."

The success of the Washington Conference was not repeated. Further attempts to control arms in Geneva (1927) and London (1930) failed to ease the global arms race in submarines, destroyers, and cruisers, vessels that were not included in the Washington treaties. The United States (and Japan) refused to sign an international agreement banning poison gases, deeply disappointing Jane Addams and other members of the Women's International League for Peace and Freedom, which had advocated strongly for the agreement. The ultimate futility of U.S., attempts to build on the success of the Washington treaties was evident in the U.S.,-backed Kellogg-Briand Pact (1928), a much celebrated although unenforceable global renunciation of war.

A final international challenge stemmed from the increasing discontent of colonized and subordinated peoples around the world, who had been encouraged by the message of self-determination in President Wilson's Fourteen Points. These peoples were subsequently disappointed that neither the Versailles Treaty nor the League of Nations opposed empire building or white supremacy. The League established a *mandate* system that transferred colonies from the defeated powers of Germany and the Ottoman Empire to mainly England and France. Japan received German possessions in the Pacific, but it was more concerned with its existing colony in Korea when in March 1919 as many as 2 million Koreans demanded liberation from Japanese rule. Although the uprising failed—hundreds of protesters were killed and tens of thousands imprisoned—it galvanized support for Korean independence, especially from Korean immigrants in the United States and Hawai'i. A month earlier in February 1919, Du Bois reenergized the Pan-African Congress, which proceeded to meet three more times in a span of eight years after the Great War. Pan-Africanism sought the liberation of Africa and African peoples around the world as part of a global movement against racism and colonialism.

isolationist Term for a person who opposed allowing the United States to join the League of Nations.

Washington Naval Conference International gathering in Washington, D.C., in which the world's major powers agreed to a naval tonnage limitation.

History without Borders

International Organizations and the Construction of a Global Community

League of Nations
- ■ Founding members
- ■ Colonial possessions of founding members
- ■ Mandates
- ■ Non-members
- ■ Colonial possessions of non-members

League of Nations Founding Members, 1920 The nations that founded the League of Nations and their colonies and mandates covered most of the world in 1920. The number of member nations would grow for many years. ▲

During the 1920s, a significant expansion of international organizations raised awareness of global problems without being obligated to the interests of any one nation-state. The two types of these organizations were intergovernmental organizations (IGOs), such as the League of Nations, which functioned through collective actions among nation-states, and nongovernmental organizations (NGOs), such as the International Red Cross, which relied on support from groups and individuals who did not represent governments. Both types continued a process begun in the nineteenth century to build a global community.

The League of Nations was a foundational step toward global intergovernmental cooperation. Headquartered in Geneva, Switzerland, it had three main branches. The Executive Council included the leading powers and assumed the major responsibility for preventing war. Council measures needed majority consent from the Assembly, the second branch of League governance, in which each member nation-state had one vote. Once approved by the Council and Assembly, the League Secretariat, the body's third branch, administered and implemented its policies. The Secretariat consisted of more than six hundred officials who engaged in peacekeeping

and a wide variety of League programs. Affiliated with the League was the Permanent Court of International Justice, which opened in 1922 in The Hague, Netherlands. Popularly known as the *World Court*, its purpose was to adjudicate disputes between League member nations.

As important as the League was for advancing intergovernmental cooperation, it had even a greater impact by encouraging the the proliferation of NGOs. Ninety percent of the 478 international organizations listed by the League of Nations in 1929 were NGOs. They included various bodies to establish international regulations for air traffic,

Corbis

League of Nations Members Discuss Disarmament, 1924 The League of Nations created protocols to prevent war by seeking to enforce collective security and mandatory arbitration of international disputes. Even though the United States did not join the League, this intergovernmental organization was the most important of its kind during the 1920s, spawning the rapid proliferation of a global community through both intergovernmental and nongovernmental organizations. Americans played an active role in the latter, and the United States sent representatives to observe the League's proceedings. ◀

Archive Photos/Getty Images

Ambulance Driving Class for the American Red Cross, 1920 The Red Cross pioneered and epitomized the humanitarian spirit of nongovernmental organizations that enabled many concerned peoples, including Americans, to participate in ameliorating a wide variety of global challenges. In this case, trainees in Washington, D.C., were being taught about an ambulance motor. ◀

undersea cable communications, audio technology, and others to promote friendship among students worldwide and the international preservation of birds.

Two NGOs embodied the creation of a truly global community that extended beyond the Euro-American orbit to include areas in Asia-Pacific, Africa, and the Middle East. The Institute of Pacific Relations (IPR) was established in 1925 to establish representative bodies from every nation in the Pacific including the Soviet Union and colonies such as Korea and the Philippines. Begun in Hawai'i under the auspices of the YMCA, the IPR brought people from the vast and increasingly important Pacific region together to engage in joint research projects on problems threatening peace and on advancing international and cross-cultural understanding. The International Alliance of Women, created before World War I, mainly comprised European and North American members seeking to broaden women's suffrage in their nations. During the 1920s the Alliance greatly expanded its global campaign to include women from Argentina, Brazil, Egypt, India, Jamaica, Japan, Syria, and Turkey.

Critical Thinking Questions

▶ The growth of international organizations in the 1920s coincided with the intensification of nationalism in the United States, Germany, Italy, Japan, and elsewhere. How was it possible for internationalism and nationalism to coexist at this time? In what ways did the love of country conflict with the love for humanity?

▶ Today there are roughly forty thousand international NGOs around the world. Name the ones you know about. What do they do? To what extent were their general goals anticipated by international organizations during the 1920s? Explain.

From the perspective of many whites, colonial empires and racial hierarchies were bedrocks of Western civilization. In a widely regarded book, Lothrop Stoddard warned about *The Rising Tide of Color Against White World Supremacy* (1920). The Harvard-educated scholar claimed that the Great War was actually a terrible civil war among the ruling white races that damaged their power to control the "lesser" peoples of the world, particularly the Japanese, who seemingly posed the most significant threat to the United States. Stoddard's views resonated with many white Americans who blamed urgent social problems on the immigrant masses and the war on changing racial demographics through which Anglo-Saxons—the supposed makers of Western civilization—were being displaced by lesser peoples. In contrast, the well-known young writer F. Scott Fitzgerald parodied Stoddard's racial alarmism as that of an older, self-satisfied generation more interested in preserving the status quo than in embracing the modern world.

19-1c Women's Activism

In August 1920, the ratification of the Nineteenth Amendment granted American women the right to vote, fulfilling the aims of the suffrage movement. Many women in the U.S. West already had the right to vote in state and local elections as did women in the Soviet Union and in industrialized democracies such as the United Kingdom, Germany, New Zealand, Australia, and Canada. Six months before the amendment's ratification, Carrie Chapman Catt's National American Woman Suffrage Association established the **League of Women Voters**, a nonpartisan organization designed to encourage newly enfranchised women to assume a greater role in civic affairs. The 1920 presidential election was the first federal election in which all qualified adult U.S. citizens could vote. To the surprise of some activists in the League of Women Voters, the amendment did not result in a political revolution. Women went to the polls in far fewer numbers than men and when they did were not united as women. Women's reform issues did not make an impact except where they melded with the nation's general desire to eradicate crime, corruption, and immorality in American life and politics. Activists such as labor radical Mary Harris "Mother" Jones opposed women's suffrage because they saw it as a cause for privileged women and that a public role for women put in jeopardy vital child-raising responsibilities. Jones said, "You don't need the vote to raise hell!"

> Women' political influence increases, although suffrage fails to bring equal rights.

League of Women Voters
Nonpartisan organization that arose in 1920 with the granting of women's suffrage to advance the political interests of women as a group.

equal rights amendment
Failed effort by women's activists in the 1920s to embed equal treatment of women and men into the Constitution.

Prohibition U.S. public policy that banned the manufacturing, sale, and interstate transportation of alcoholic beverages.

Although the Nineteenth Amendment did not produce a national revolution in politics, it did expose other gender-based inequalities. Alice Paul's National Woman's Party sought to use it as a step for achieving an **equal rights amendment** that would guarantee women equal rights, much as the Fourteenth Amendment had been designed to guarantee equal treatment under the law for all individuals regardless of race. Congress did not consider the amendment. In 1922, Congress did approve the Cable Act, which eliminated nativist immigration laws that caused American women to lose their own citizenship upon marrying a foreigner. The new law, however, bowed to pressure from western states to make an exception for marrying Asians. Until the law was changed in 1931, U.S. citizens marrying Asian immigrant men lost their citizenship. Meanwhile, southern African American women mobilized successful voter registration drives through networks of churches, fraternal societies, women's clubs, and voluntary associations, but despite success in the 1920 elections, they were disenfranchised by whites who quickly closed loopholes for women under Jim Crow segregation.

Activists for women's rights, or "feminists" as they were called, were more successful at lobbying for issues supported by the increasing number of working women who typically opposed the equal rights amendment because it would have overturned special labor protections for women secured by the *Muller* decision in 1908. Working-class advocates, such as Jane Addams, Florence Kelley, and Margaret Sanger, and labor activists in the Women's Trade Union League focused on women's rights in the workplace and to birth control. A victory for these labor feminists came in 1921 when Congress provided modest funding for nurse training programs to improve care for infants and pregnant mothers in the Sheppard-Towner Act. The act's supporters pointed with alarm to a 1917 U.S. Children's Bureau study ranking the nation seventeenth of twenty nations in maternal morality and eleventh in infant mortality. The American Medical Association, in contrast, opposed Sheppard-Towner as a Communist plan in which the state reached into private business; by 1929, the association convinced Congress to stop funding the program, but it was later restored.

19-1d Prohibition

Women had long played a leading role in the temperance movement, which since the nineteenth century had sought to end urban crime and family instability by outlawing alcohol. The social experiment of **Prohibition** was not entirely new. Thirty-four states (almost entirely in the South and West) already had laws that either banned or severely regulated the sale of alcohol. Prohibition was not limited to the United States. Finland, which long had

> State authority over alcohol consumption expands greatly even though it is undermined by a sharp rise in criminal activity.

Global Americans The daughter of immigrant parents, **Margaret Sanger** grew up in a large Irish Roman Catholic family. Her mother endured eighteen pregnancies (eleven of which led to live births) in twenty-two years before dying at age forty-nine. As an adult, Sanger studied nursing and became involved in free-thinking socialist politics. She saw enough crude abortions and suffering among poor women to be convinced that contraception was essential for women's health. In the early twentieth century, however, contraceptives and abortion were illegal in the United States and most developed nations. Inspired by the radical Emma Goldman, Sanger began to publish writings that challenged the laws preventing the distribution of information about contraceptives. She popularized the term *birth control*, opened the first U.S. birth control clinic, and argued that in minimizing the possibility of getting pregnant, liberated women could enjoy the pleasures of sexual intercourse.

After the Great War and Red Scare, Sanger's influence peaked as she moved away from left-wing organizations to gain support from the mainstream eugenics movement whose goal was to reduce the birthrate of persons deemed inferior. In 1921, she established the American Birth Control League. By this time, the Soviet Union had become the first nation to legalize abortion and endorse birth control. Germany and Great Britain sanctioned birth control as a means of aiding poor families. During the 1920s, Sanger spread the birth control movement to China, Korea, and Japan. ◀ Library of Congress Prints and Photographs Division [LC-USZ62–29808]

been influenced by the U.S. temperance movement, followed suit.

Prohibition reduced alcohol consumption among Americans by one-third, and medical statistics from the 1920s reveal that this decline had positive health effects. In Massachusetts, the admission rate for patients with alcohol-related illnesses fell from 14.6 per one hundred thousand in 1910 to 7.7 in 1929. In New York, the rate was cut nearly in half, falling from 11.5 in 1910 to 6.5 in 1931. Nationwide, the death rate from alcohol-related illness, such as cirrhosis of the liver, dropped from 14.8 per one hundred thousand in 1907 to no more than 7.5 for every year in the 1920s.

Yet more apparent at the time was Prohibition's negative impact on law and order. The experiment initiated the largest expansion in federal authority since Reconstruction, continuing state interventions in the economy and society from the Progressive Era, and even so it was nearly impossible to enforce. The modest allocation of federal agents was not enough to secure the nation's wide-open borders, shutter illicit **speakeasy** bars, and otherwise win the war against alcohol. The journalist Herbert Asbury noted that those who expected Prohibition to create a more perfect U.S. society "were met by a horde of bootleggers, moonshiners, rumrunners, hijackers, gangsters, racketeers, trigger men, venal judges, corrupt police, crooked politicians, and speakeasy operators, all bearing the twin symbols of the Eighteenth Amendment—the tommy gun and the poisoned cup." Prohibition's enforcement difficulties put the great experiment in jeopardy. It gave rise to organized crime syndicates led by infamous gangsters such as Al Capone, and it diminished respect for governmental authority because millions of otherwise law-abiding Americans regularly violated that amendment.

speakeasy Illegal establishment where alcoholic beverages were sold and consumed during Prohibition.

Economic Boom

Photographed in 1927, Ford Motor Company's massive River Rouge plant in Dearborn, Michigan, was more than a mile long and a mile and one-half wide. Henry Ford took automobile manufacturing to a new level of self-sufficiency. He owned and controlled all stages of production from the raw materials and their transportation to the manufacture of automobile parts and their assembly. The plant also produced its own electricity.

Notice the river running through the plant. What advantages were gained by locating an automobile manufacturing plant on a river? ▶

Library of Congress Prints and Photographs Division [LC-D414-K3461]

After World War I, the United States was the leading global economic power. The nation's rise had occurred during the war when it served as the Allies' main source of food, munitions, and manufactured goods and provided much needed loans to them to pay for these items. The end of the war did not alter U.S. leadership while Britain, France, and Germany struggled to revive their economies. Already blessed with an abundance of raw materials and a huge consumer market, U.S. firms during the 1920s intensified labor management and innovated marketing strategies that together gave a tremendous boost to both production and sales. The automobile industry led the way, powering much of the nation's prosperity and global economic success. For the first time, automobiles and other large consumer products such as washing machines, refrigerators, and radios became widely available, and their production propelled the nation's economy. Improvements in the nation's infrastructure—roads, electricity, and communication networks—spread access to goods. A new emphasis on marketing increased sales at home and abroad. Hopeful that U.S. business innovations and success would produce lasting prosperity, the nation's political leaders unleashed big corporations from the trust busting and regulations they had faced during the Progressive Era. The "roaring twenties" was a time when business reigned supreme in U.S. politics and culture.

☞ As you read, look for the ways that World War I and its aftermath stimulated business and consumer trends that boosted the national economy. In what ways did the economy grow and transform?

19-2a Nation's Business

Harding's close relationship with big businesses, his critics charged, spawned political corruption. Starting in 1922 and continuing well after his death

{ The federal government prioritizes economic growth.

in office the following year, congressional investigators uncovered scandals involving the administration's issuance of oil contracts in Elk Hills, California, and Tea Pot Dome in Wyoming. Calvin Coolidge, the man elevated to the presidency after Harding's death, continued the former president's business relationships. Although as governor of Massachusetts, Coolidge had supported labor protections and other state interventions in the economy, he and Secretary of Commerce Herbert Hoover were adamant that such regulations were beyond the powers of the federal government. Contrary to social reformers, Coolidge followed a laissez-faire view of government that trusted rather than criticized private corporations. Banker Andrew Mellon, one of the richest men in the United States, served as his secretary of the treasury. "The chief business of the U.S. people is business," Coolidge said. "They are profoundly concerned with producing, buying, selling, investing and prospering in the world."

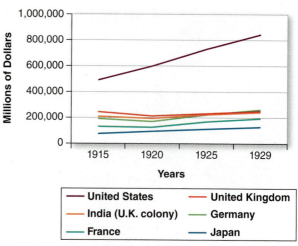

NOTE: Figures represent millions in 1990 dollars.

Figure 19.1 GDP by Nation, 1915–1929 America's gross domestic product (GDP) led the world in 1915 and had nearly doubled by 1929. Although the GDP of the United Kingdom remained far behind that of the United States, the significant GDP of India, its colony, provides a sense of the might of the British empire—and why the British strongly resisted Indian independence. ▲ Source: Maddison Project. (www.ggdc.net/maddison/Historical_Statistics/horizontal-file_02–2010.xls).

With the federal government's support, the nation's businesses built upon the gains made during World War I. Although leading the world in gross domestic product (GDP) before World War I, the United States far surpassed all nations after the war (see Figure 19.1). Central to this postwar economic boon in the United States was the automobile, which during the 1920s changed from an extravagance for wealthy persons to a necessity for masses of people. By the 1930s, the automobile industry was the nation's third largest employer and highest in average pay, a great rise from 1917 when it ranked fifteenth and seventh, respectively. Car and truck sales tripled during the 1920s, and by 1929, the United States produced nearly 90 percent of the world's automobiles.

The automobile bonanza reshaped much of the U.S. economy. It led to new and thriving industries for automobile parts and service as well as the tourist business. Gasoline production moved to the center of the U.S. oil industry, and mammoth orders for tires and windshields boosted rubber and glass manufacturing. The automobile industry increased overall manufacturing output in the United States by 50 percent during the 1920s. In 1929, the nation produced 40 percent of the world's coal, 70 percent of its gasoline, and 50 percent of its steel.

19-2b Fordism and Labor

What enabled the explosive increase in automobiles in the United States was Henry Ford's innovations in mass production that generated

{ New efficiencies of production developed by Ford transform the nature of work.

Global Americans Born of immigrant parents in 1863, **Henry Ford**, like most Americans of his day, was not a major world traveler. Yet by the 1920s, his automobiles were being shipped to six continents, and he had established assembly plants in Britain, Canada, France, Germany, Australia, and India. Ford's columns for his newspaper, *The Dearborn Independent*, drew praise in Germany from Adolf Hitler for exposing the supposed Jewish conspiracy for global domination. Hitler idolized Ford, who was the only American named in the German's autobiographical manifesto, *Mein Kampf* (*My Struggle*). Hitler singled him out for maintaining independence from the Jewish-led "controlling masters of the producers in a nation of one hundred and twenty millions."

Another example of Ford's global reach was Fordlandia, the company's massive rubber plantation the size of Connecticut. Started in 1928, the project that cut supplies from Brazil's Amazon rainforest was intended to supply the only major element missing from Ford's vertically integrated production process. Fordlandia was also a great experiment in welfare capitalism. The plantation resembled a U.S. company town where Brazilian workers were required to adopt not just Ford's work routines but also his standards of living, dress, diet, leisure, and social relations. The experiment failed. Workers resisted the imposition of U.S. culture, the Amazonia environment—particularly rubber plant pests—proved too much to manage, and synthetic rubber replaced the need for natural stocks. The plantation later closed before it could supply the rubber for even one automobile tire.

high-quality goods on a larger scale and at a lower cost than ever before. The genius of **Fordism**, a term of the time, was that it applied the mid-nineteenth century

Assembly Line, 1927 Workers in New York City operate a machine that filled bottles with salad dressing. "Mass production," said Henry Ford, "lightens work, but increases its repetitive quality." To its critics, Fordism stripped workers of their skills and creativity by turning them into human machines who had to keep pace with the moving assembly line. Doing the same small task again and again, hour after hour, brought no pride or satisfaction. Like parts, workers, too, were interchangeable. ▲

factory system of production (interchangeable parts and deskilling of labor) to automaking and with the application of electricity to industry greatly increased the scale of production. In 1914, Ford shocked his competitors by more than doubling the lowest worker's wage from $2.34 to $5.00 while shortening the workday from nine hours to eight. By 1923, he estimated that nearly 80 percent of manufacturing jobs in his company required no more than one week to learn. The compensation Ford offered for the **deskilling** of labor was higher pay and shorter hours. In 1926, he eliminated Saturday from the workweek by adopting the five-day, forty-hour standard that is still in effect today. Ford Motor Company paid African Americans and women equal pay to that of their white male counterparts, although African American men worked on more dangerous jobs. In the end, most workers had little choice but to accept the bargain of high wages for repetitive work because the spread of Fordism to other industries meant the decline of skilled jobs everywhere. To manufacturers, the **wage bargain** was a win–win proposition. The higher wages and shorter hours appeased labor demands while enabling workers to buy the products they made.

In seeking to ensure peaceful labor relations, Ford and fellow business leaders such as John D. Rockefeller offered workers benefits including sick leave, pensions, stock ownership, employee representation in management decisions, personnel services, and recreation programs. Advocates of these changes described

Fordism Streamlined and profitable manufacturing process based on Ford's development of fast assembly of parts leading to repetitive work that did not require skilled labor.

deskilling Process in which the skills once needed to perform work were rendered obsolete by either machines or new work routines.

wage bargain Trade-off experienced by workers in which higher wages (welcomed by workers) came with less pride and ownership of labor (which was not).

such worker benefits as **welfare capitalism**, and saw them as a sign of corporate social conscience. Yet such programs were not available to the vast majority of workers in private industry. Few companies, for example, offered pension plans, and those that did had only a fraction of workers who met the requirements needed to collect benefits. Critics charged that welfare capitalism in the long run hurt workers by forestalling unionism and efforts for a fairer and more reliable system of government-sponsored welfare.

The spread of Fordism led to the addition of white-collar managers, designers, researchers, and clerical staff to companies. Ford explained that in his system of production, the "mental load is shifted from men in production to men in designing." During the 1920s, the number of managers in the United States increased at a rate (29 percent) twice that of manual workers (14 percent). Universities created programs to meet the growing need for managers, and companies established their own research facilities, such as AT&T's Bell Labs, which opened in 1925. The number of research professionals nationwide increased nearly fourfold, from 2,775 in 1921 to 10,927 in 1933. Clerical work also expanded with the new emphasis on white-collar jobs and was redefined as a job for women rather than men. By 1920, more than 90 percent of stenographers who used a stenograph machine to take shorthand notes were women.

Another sign of the modern consumer age was the use of **marketing** by U.S. firms. Although production involved making products, marketing addressed the best ways to inform consumers about them and to distribute them. Marketing experts relied on product differentiation, pricing, distribution, and, especially, advertising to make their products attractive and desirable. Marketing bolstered the demand for products to keep pace with the increasing supply. Ford learned about the importance of marketing the hard way. In the 1920s, rival General Motors surpassed Ford Motor Company in sales by offering a variety of car colors and appealing to different income levels through its five brands. In 1938, *Fortune* magazine described these as "Chevrolet for *hoi polloi*,. . . Pontiac for the poor but proud, Oldsmobile for the comfortable but discreet, Buick for the striving, Cadillac for the rich." Although the original Model-T had come in various colors, Ford limited it to black from 1914 until the end of its production in 1927 to speed production.

The beverage company Coca-Cola, which dominated the U.S. soft drink market by the 1920s, also attested to the importance of marketing. Unlike Ford, Coca-Cola had no production advantages over its competitors because many companies produced good-tasting cola drinks. What distinguished its product was marketing. The company sent an army of sales agents throughout the country to lock the

19-2c Mass Consumption

The driving force for prosperity stemmed as much from mass consumption as it did from mass production. The wage bargain propelled consumer spending by putting more money into the pockets of workers. Sociologists Robert and Helen Lynd published a study depicting how consumption had become a universal fact of life in the "typical" U.S. city of Muncie, Indiana. Ball Corporation, a leading manufacturer of glass jars for canning, was located there. In the 1890s, Muncie residents had grown their own food, sewed their own clothing, and pumped water from their own wells. They moved about by horse, and because only 1 percent of homes had electrical service, their light came from candles and kerosene lamps. In the 1920s, when Ball was making not only canning jars but also glass insulators for electrical wiring and automobile engines, workers purchased groceries, ready-made clothing, and automobiles. At that time, 95 percent of homes had electrical service, and residents bought both electricity and water from the city. The Lynds documented a clear example of the spread of modernity.

> Increased production expands a culture of consumption.

Coca-Cola Advertisement Testifying to the power of marketing is the fact that Coca-Cola and other leading brands of the 1920s remain widely recognized today, including Kellogg breakfast cereals, Del Monte canned fruit, Wrigley chewing gum, Gold Medal flour, Life Saver candies, Gillette razors, Crisco shortening, Ivory soap, Campbell soups, Lipton tea, Goodyear tires, and Colgate toothpaste. ▼
Archive Photos/Getty Images

welfare capitalism Alternative to labor unions whereby businesses took responsibility for the well-being of workers, including their wages, safety, health, housing, and general happiness.

marketing Business strategies including product differentiation, pricing, distribution, and advertising designed to increase the sales of goods and services.

nation's bottling manufactures and retail soda fountains in exclusive contracts preventing them from working for competitors or supplying their products. In addition to this massive distribution system, Coca-Cola engaged in intensive and costly advertising that gave its drink brand recognition by displaying the company symbol on lighted signs, billboards, bottle openers, clocks, and many other everyday objects.

Many national brands became internationally recognized during the 1920s through increasing exports, especially of automobiles. By 1928, more than 70 percent of all cars and trucks exported worldwide were made in the United States. Japan at that time bought almost all of its automobiles from the United States, and the Soviets invested heavily in Ford tractors. Meanwhile, U.S. news services, the Associated Press (AP) and United Press International (UPI), expanded their global reach, and U.S. films surpassed European ones in international popularity. U.S. films constituted 95 percent of those shown in Britain, 70 percent in France, and 80 percent in Latin America. These films, like the globalization of U.S. products, spread the nation's culture and lifestyles around the world.

19-3

Market Expansion

Among the many fads sweeping the United States during the 1920s was mahjong, a Chinese board game similar to the card game gin-rummy but with a more elaborate set of rules.

What does this photograph of the women playing mahjong suggest about international linkages at this time? What does it reveal about the expanding popularity of leisure activities? ▶

Library of Congress Prints and Photographs Division Washington, D.C. 20540 USA

Emergence of new forms of mass production and consumption made far-reaching changes in the nation's electrical and transportation networks, leisure culture, and business of loans and credit. The increase in consumer products, especially automobiles, undergirded the transformation of each area. New electrical power plants made it possible for more Americans, especially those outside cities, to enjoy vacuum cleaners and washing machines. Highway construction changed transportation by automobile. The expansion of leisure activities—such as organized sports and movies—and the increase of credit resulted from the efforts of businesses to create new domestic and global markets for their products.

☞ As you read, identify the impact of economic innovations and prosperity on U.S. society and culture. What types of products and leisure activities became popular? How did people get access to credit?

19-3a Infrastructure for Wires and Roads

Major improvements in the nation's infrastructure fueled consumerism. Breakthroughs in electrical technology expanded the capacity of

{ Infrastructure improvements raise living standards and enable consumption.

central power stations to provide universal service to entire cities. Combined with the growth of indoor plumbing, electricity brought millions of new customers into the market for electrical appliances such as washing machines and refrigerators. Technological improvements in communication infrastructure also generated a robust market for radios and telephones, and the construction of gasoline pipelines hundreds of miles long ensured that automobile drivers would have a steady and inexpensive supply of fuel.

The nation's investment in highway construction literally paved the way for the expansion of automobile ownership. In 1916, 1921, and 1925, Congress increased funding for road improvement and created the numbered national highway system using the symbol of the shield. Federal involvement doubled the amount of paved highways from 257,291 miles in 1914 to 521,915 miles in 1926. Paved roads encouraged the growth of the trucking industry, which for the first time could compete for business with railroads. Farmers, who had long suffered under monopolistic railroad rates, were the first to rely extensively on trucking. Many other businesses used trucks and the highway system to grow from local to regional and even national companies. Milk sellers (dairies), for example, used refrigerated trucks and good roads to greatly expand their customer base by providing home deliveries.

The national highway system also made it easier and faster for people to move around the country, especially to the sparsely populated regions of the U.S. West opened by U.S. **Route 66**. Known as the "mother road," this highway began in Chicago where it connected hundreds of rural farm communities to the metropolis. It then followed an almost entirely paved "all-weather" road through the Great Plains and Southwest to end on the Pacific Ocean near Los Angeles, California. The new highway fed the population explosion in Los Angeles. The city doubled in size between 1920 and 1930, moving from tenth place to fifth on the list of the largest U.S. urban centers. Another major city that expanded with the automobile and highways was Houston, Texas. It more than doubled in size in the 1920s, moving from forty-fifth to twenty-sixth of the nation's largest cities. The expansion was caused by the many oil companies based in Houston, including what would become Texaco, Gulf, and Exxon, that supplied the increased consumer demand for gasoline.

Eastern cities, designed for getting around by foot and streetcar, had to adjust to new modes of transportation. Massive road construction linked them to each other and to surrounding communities. Cities such as New York City and Boston transformed the look and function of their streets by constructing wide boulevards and thoroughfares to accommodate automobile traffic.

19-3b Leisure and Popular Culture

The forty-hour workweek created the "weekend," a two-day break that gave workers time to engage in leisure activities previously reserved for wealthy individuals. In the late 1920s, a government committee led by Secretary of Commerce Herbert Hoover investigated the nation's recent social trends and found that Americans spent almost $10.25 billion per year on "leisure and recreation," equal to roughly 13 percent of the nation's total budget. The Hoover committee noted that in the 1920s, "the conception of leisure as 'consumable' began to be realized upon in business in a practical way and on a broad scale," which meant that fun, entertainment, and play had become a major market.

> Businesses capitalize on the shorter workweek to expand commercialized culture and recreation.

Expanding leisure time boosted urban entertainment in places such as bars, restaurants, nightclubs, and dance halls that catered to the increasing number of office workers, both men and women, who had more time for social activities. Unlike the utilitarian working-class saloons in the nineteenth century, these up-scale establishments were places where dress, manners, and dancing skills mattered. A population going out Friday night needed department stores, dance studios, and beauty parlors to get them ready, generating an extensive leisure economy.

Technological innovations and advertising built the radio and motion picture industries. The nation's radio infrastructure mushroomed virtually overnight from one station in 1920 to 623 at the decade's end. By 1929, 12 million Americans could tune in to music, sports, sermons, children's shows, and political speeches sponsored by advertisers eager to promote new products with this modern tool. Wireless radio was a marvel of technology that dramatically reduced distances and isolation among people in the United States and around the world.

At the same time, the audience for films more than doubled. In 1930, movie houses welcomed over 100 million patrons each week, out of a total U.S. population of only 123 million. As in the case of automobiles, Americans transformed films from artifacts of elite European culture to products of mass production and consumption. Silent films captivated audiences and established the first cohort of international movie stars including Charlie Chaplin,

Movie Poster of *The Jazz Singer* (1927) The allure of movies took on an added dimension in 1927 when the combination of sound recordings and moving images created the first "talkie," *The Jazz Singer*, which starred Jewish American Al Jolson in a dramatic musical about the breakdown of religious traditions in a contemporary Orthodox Jewish immigrant family. The film's content, which included Jolson in "blackface," embodied the racial mores of the day. ▼

GAB Archive/Redferns/Getty Images

Route 66 Transnational highway from Chicago to Los Angeles that boosted migration to urban centers and other parts of the West.

Mary Pickford, Douglas Fairbanks, Rudolf Valentino, and Sessue Hayakawa. The U.S. film industry was centered in the Los Angeles suburb of **Hollywood** where land was affordable, and the sunny climate made filming outdoors all year long possible.

Public money in the form of massive investments in popular recreation joined private money in expanding popular culture. The total acreage of city parks more than tripled during the first decades of the twentieth century, much of the growth occurring in the 1920s. During this decade, the number of golf courses and tennis courts tripled, and manufacturers of sporting goods experienced explosive success. The Rawlings Company reaped huge rewards when it had major league pitcher Bill Doak design the modern baseball glove by separating the thumb and forefinger with a few strands of rawhide leather. A rival company, Wilson, also innovated baseball equipment but became better known for creating the modern, double-stitched, valve-inflated leather football with the help of legendary Notre Dame University football coach Knute Rockne.

The use of celebrity advisers such as Rockne and Doak indicated the growing popularity of college and professional sports. During the 1920s, the audiences for and revenue from college football outpaced those of professional baseball. Celebrity players such as home-run hitter Babe Ruth led major league baseball to reach a new level of national interest. Radio broadcasts of baseball games created the new profession of sports reporting, and reporters and fans alike created a new language of statistics such as batting averages, pitcher's earned run average, and records for home runs in a season. Radio broadcasts and sports marketing developed further with the birth of the American Professional Football Association in 1920, which became the National Football League two years later.

In the late nineteenth century, wealthy Americans had toured the nation by rail, but the automobile revolution coupled with the expansion of leisure time transformed tourism into a mass phenomenon. Tourism often cultivated nostalgia for the past. Urbanites traveled to national and state parks to experience the great outdoors they had known on farms in their youth. With increased automobile access, attendance rates at national and state parks more than tripled. Hoover's committee on social trends calculated that nearly one-fourth of automobile use was for recreational purposes, leading to the emergence of road maps, guidebooks, roadside curio shops, diners, and motels. Curiosity about the past fueled a burst of museum building and historical projects such as the full-scale restoration of Virginia's Colonial Williamsburg started in 1926. In cities, ethnic enclaves such as Chinatowns, Little Tokyos, and Mexican barrios reinvented themselves as tourist markets, allowing white Americans to experience cultures that seemed frozen in time—pristine and untouched by the corrupting influence of modern, industrial society.

19-3c Credit and Crisis

> The excess purchases of consumer goods leads to a revolution in the credit system.

Personal loans made possible the explosion of consumption during the 1920s. Banks had always loaned money to wealthy clients, and they began to do so to working-class people during this time. But when a worker was sick, injured, unemployed, or faced a family or household emergency, the only source of money was a pawnbroker or **loan shark**, who might charge 10 percent interest a month (185 percent per year) although the practice was illegal. To counteract loan sharking, twenty-five states, encouraged by social reformers, had passed consumer loan protection laws by 1928. Under these laws, interest was limited to 3.5 percent per month on loans under $300 and was charged only on the loan's unpaid balance. New retail loan businesses capitalized on the proliferation of automobile sales to expand their customer base beyond emergency payday lending. The stunning profits made in car loans enticed automobile makers and even conservative banks to follow suit. By 1927, more than 60 percent of automobiles had been bought on **installment plans**, as opposed to almost no such purchases in 1919. The extension of credit spread to many consumer goods from furniture to radios to washing machines. The expansion transformed the idea of personal debt for many Americans from a mark of immorality to a way to equalize class differences. As one truck driver put it, "with his radio receiving set the workman can now listen to grand opera singers whose voices formerly were heard only by the socially elect."

The democratization of credit also allowed more Americans, although rarely the working classes, to invest in the stock market. The center of global finance shifted after World War I from London to New York City. Soaring stock prices for U.S. firms attracted increasing numbers of investors, including banks, corporations, affluent people, and middle-class individuals who engaged in **buying on the margin**. They paid as little as 20 percent down and borrowed the rest from a broker. One historian calls the stock boom of the 1920s "massive, exhilarating, and foolish." Both investors and brokers made money as long as the market was up, but when stock prices dropped, those who had bought on margin lost their down payment and still owed interest and transaction fees.

The sector of the U.S. economy that suffered the most from credit problems during the 1920s was agriculture. Skyrocketing crop prices during World War I had pushed farmers

Hollywood Suburb of Los Angeles where movie studios began to concentrate in the early twentieth century.

loan shark Person loaning money at exceedingly high (and often illegal) interest rates and who took advantage of the most desperate classes.

installment plans Type of loan that boosted consumption by allowing a buyer to pay for products purchased over a given period of time.

buying on the margin Purchasing stock market securities by paying a fraction of the price and borrowing the rest from a stock broker.

to buy land to increase production, amassing debts. When agricultural prices fell sharply after the war—by 1921, the prices of wheat, corn, and hogs had fallen to less than half of their value in 1918—a farm crisis ensued (see Figure 19.2). Farmers' share of national income dropped from 16 percent in 1919 to less than 9 percent in 1929. Congress sought to resolve the farm crisis by approving the McNary-Haugen relief bill, which provided price supports for farm commodities. But price supports were controversial, and in 1927 and 1928, Coolidge vetoed the measure as violating the principles of laissez-faire. Farmers also failed to receive the same level of tariff protection from foreign imports given to manufacturers under the Fordney-McCumber tariff of 1922.

Despite agricultural depression, the outlook for the U.S. economy was bright in the 1920s compared to that for Europe. In Germany, war reparations contributed to hyperinflation that erased personal savings by reducing the value of the country's currency to virtually zero. This led sociologist Robert Lynd to lament the middle-class men and women in Berlin he saw lining up for free meals at soup kitchens. Large U.S. banks led by Morgan and Company supplied billion-dollar loans to Germany under the 1924 Dawes Plan and 1929 Young Plan that enabled Germany to pay its debts. In the late 1920s, U.S. loans and investments in Europe totaled more than $10.3 billion per year, contributing to the

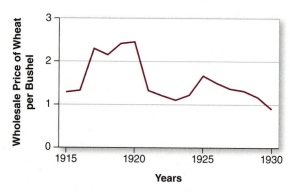

Figure 19.2 U.S. Wheat and Stock Prices, 1915–1930
The precipitous fall in wheat prices after World War I and throughout most of the 1920s created instability in U.S. agriculture. To compensate for the collapse in prices, farmers planted more crops, plowing up native prairie grasses and exposing the thin topsoil of the Great Plains to the ever-present wind. This created an environmental disaster in the making, especially in a season of drought. ▲ Source: U.S. Bureau of the Census. *Historical Statistics of the United States, Colonial Times to 1957.* Washington, D.C., 1960, 122–123.

Americanization of European cities where U.S. consumer goods, foods, and fashions were widely advertised and in abundance. "Paris," reported the historian Charles Beard, "was plastered with American signs."

19-4

Americanization

This cartoon, entitled "The Only Way to Handle It," appeared in the *Providence Journal* in 1921 when Congress considered restricting immigration by means of a quota system. What does the funnel represent? Recall the immigration flows into the United States in the late nineteenth century and the means by which progressives had attempted to deal with these newcomers.

Why were immigrants considered a problem that had to be "handled," and by what means did the United States erect a "gate" to limit them? ▶

In addition to rejecting the League of Nations and radicalism, the majority of Americans sought to remove foreign influence by painting the United States as a white, Anglo-Saxon Protestant nation. Major targets of this Americanization movement were new immigrants who were seen as inclined to radicalism, given to practicing strange religions, and spoke foreign tongues. Congress rejected the notion of the United States as a melting pot for the world's peoples, and for the first time limited European immigrants by national origin while excluding Asians completely. The restrictionist policies fit with a groundswell of conservative reform movements defending Prohibition, opposing ethnic and racial minorities, and promoting what were known as "traditional" values associated with small towns, white skin, Anglo-Saxon ancestry, and the Protestant faith. The rise of Fundamentalist Christianity and resurgence

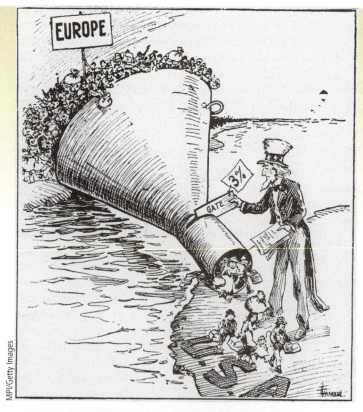

of the Ku Klux Klan were the more visible aspects of intolerance and cultural conformity that attracted many who were disillusioned by war, afraid of radicalism, and threatened by the dramatically increased numbers of African Americans and foreigners in U.S. cities.

19-4a Immigration Restriction

Evident during World War I, the momentum for immigration restriction gained strength after the peace. The causes were the Red Scare and fears that war-torn Europe would send boatloads of refugees and displaced persons to the United States. For the first time, immigrants were required to pass a literacy test. Southern and eastern Europeans and especially Asians were considered difficult, if not impossible, to Americanize, supposedly the result of immutable racial traits. Many of these immigrants were Jews and Catholics deemed incompatible with U.S. institutions and culture. In this context, restrictionists cast off the notion of America as a melting pot where peoples from all over the world were transformed into a common type and gradually made one community. On the one hand, Americans had been exposed to popular scientific theories in eugenics that seemed to prove that immigrants could degrade the U.S. racial stock (see Chapter 17). Eugenicists argued that in mixing with the older Anglo-Saxon stock of Americans, new immigrants had **mongrelized** the nation by lowering the quality of the intelligence, health, and propensity

> The nation ends unrestricted European immigration.

for democracy of its people. On the other hand, restrictionists condemned new immigrants not because they melted down, or assimilated, with Americans, but because they retained their foreign languages, cultures, and religions. Thus, immigrants were damned for contradictory reasons: because they blended in and because they did not.

During the postwar economic slump in 1921, Congress passed the Emergency Quota Act, which temporarily imposed the nation's first limit on total immigration, set at three hundred fifty thousand people per year, or about half the number of arrivals in that year. To restrict immigration from southern and eastern Europe even further, the act established a 3 percent quota for each nationality resident in the United States in 1910. Three years later, Congress replaced the temporary restrictions with the more severe **Immigration Act of 1924**, which reduced the annual limit by more than half to one hundred fifty thousand and further lowered the proportion of southern and eastern Europeans by setting national origins quotas to 2 percent of the nationalities resident in 1890, which was before the great surge of immigrants from those regions. The act also ended the Gentlemen's Agreement by disallowing, with minor exceptions, Japanese and any other "aliens ineligible to citizenship" from entering the United States (see Table 19.1). National origins quotas given to all nations

mongrelized Process that would result in a negative outcome if the introduction of "inferior" elements into a melting pot lowers the quality of a population.

Immigration Act of 1924 Legislation decreasing immigration to the United States that discriminated against southern and eastern Europeans as well as Asians.

Table 19.1 U.S. Immigration Restrictions, 1875–1924

Although the restriction of immigrants beginning in 1917 applied broadly to many groups based on literacy or national origins, most of the nation's restrictionist policies (including the 1917 and 1924 immigration acts) targeted Asian immigrants and other unwanted groups such as contract laborers, criminals, and persons likely to become a public charge.

Date	Law	Provisions
1875	Page Act	Prohibits immigration of Asian laborers forced into service, prostitutes, and convicts
1882	Chinese Exclusion Act	Prohibits immigration of Chinese laborers for a period of 10 years; renewed in 1892 and 1902, and made permanent in 1904
1882	Immigration Act	Imposes a head tax of 50¢; excludes "convicts, lunatics, idiots, or any person unable to take care of himself or herself without becoming a public charge"
1885	Alien Contract Labor Act	Prohibits importation of contract laborers but exempts professionals and skilled and domestic laborers
1907–1908	Gentlemen's Agreement	Ends immigration of Japanese laborers by agreement between President Roosevelt and Japanese officials
1917	Immigration Act	Establishes a literacy test requiring those over age 16 required to read 30–40 words in English or a language or dialect of their choosing, including Hebrew and Yiddish; 1 Asian exclusion by establishing an Asiatic Barred Zone (Japan exempted); expands excluded "undesirables" to include anarchists, epileptics, alcoholics, those with tuberculosis and other contagious diseases, polygamists, and prostitutes
1921	Emergency Quota Act	Sets quota[a] of 357,000 immigrants per year and limits numbers of each nationality to 3 percent of the number of that nationality in the census of 1910
1924	Immigration Act	Cuts quota[a] by more than half to 164,447, and recalculates numbers of each nationality to 2 percent of that nationality represented in the census of 1890. After July 1, 1927, quota[a] is 150,000 to be divided between countries in proportion to population in the census of 1920; Japanese immigrants excluded

[a]Quota laws do not apply to immigrants from Canada or Latin America.

and approved in 1929 favored those in western and northern Europe (see Map 19.2). The **National Origins System** required a new, complex immigration bureaucracy to track quota levels and waiting lists and to grant entrance visas to qualified applicants. To ease the overseas screenings, U.S. consular staff merged with the nation's diplomatic corps to form the modern Foreign Service. This change had a negative impact on black migration from English-speaking Caribbean islands (West Indies), which had flowed through a pipeline to New York City after the completion of the Panama Canal in 1914, enabling West Indian workers to follow their bosses back to the United States. Even though the national origins system did not restrict West Indians, U.S. officials in the Caribbean all but ended their migration by refusing to grant visas to non-whites. As with Prohibition, immigration restriction was a conservative reform that greatly expanded the size and responsibilities of the federal government.

So-called backdoor migration from within the Americas remained unrestricted. As had been true in the past, the largest number of these migrants came from Canada, and Mexicans joined the influx to U.S.

cities, many as refugees fleeing the nation's prolonged civil war. Mexican immigrants went where work was available—to the steel mills of Pennsylvania and Indiana, the meatpacking houses of the Midwest, cement plants, railroad lines, and sugar beet farms in Colorado, Nebraska, and Michigan. Most ended up in the Southwest, where they had already worked as seasonal agricultural laborers in newly irrigated regions of Texas, Arizona, and southern California. In addition, Mexican immigrants became a major source of labor in the Texas cotton belt as landowners shifted from tenant sharecropping to temporary migrant labor. Filipino immigrants, whose status as U.S. colonial subjects allowed them to enter, unlike other Asians, came through a backdoor to fill Western farmers' labor shortages.

Native Americans, who had a much longer and more complicated history of being "wards of the state" than did Filipinos, received U.S. citizenship in 1924 as a reward for their service during the Great War and to encourage their assimilation to the U.S. culture and protection of tribal lands. Although some indigenous people already had received citizenship through the Dawes Act or by joining the U.S. military or marrying white U.S. men, the Indian Citizenship Act gave citizenship to three hundred

National Origins System
Arrangement that established discriminatory quotas determining the number of immigrations per year for all nations and excluding all Asians.

Map 19.2 U.S. Immigration Quotas by World Areas, 1929 The racial basis of U.S. immigration policy was evident according to which countries had an immigration quota, and of those that did, which had the highest quotas. The largest were given to Great Britain and Northern Ireland. Southern and eastern Europe received much lower quotas than northern and western Europe, and all of Asia, with the exception of the U.S. colony of the Philippines, was excluded. Blacks from the West Indies faced informal exclusion. Independent nations and League of Nations mandates were eligible for quotas, but not colonies. ▼

Klan Marching in Washington, D.C., 1925 The rebirth of the Ku Klux Klan drew inspiration from Hollywood's first feature-length film, *Birth of a Nation* (1915). President Wilson had given his approval to this film adaptation of a novel and play, *The Clansman*, that portrayed Reconstruction as a criminal mistake and the KKK as the savior of both southern civilization and national reconciliation. The new Klan enjoyed major political success outside the South before it declined after 1925. ▲

thousand more individuals. But not all wanted to become American if this put in question their tribal sovereignty and citizenship.

19-4b Ku Klux Klan and Conservative Politics

Immigration restriction, business-friendly politics, and Prohibition were emblematic of a broad-based populism that galvanized white Protestant unity across sectional, class, and partisan divisions. Unlike the radical agrarianism of the late-nineteenth century Populist Party, this movement was concerned about cultural rather than economic displacement. Its leading symbol was the rebirth of the Ku Klux Klan during the late 1910s and early 1920s. Joined by as many as 5 million men and women, the **second Ku Klux Klan** spread beyond the South to the Midwest and was especially strong in Indiana. Klan members defended Prohibition and immigration restriction as the

{ Rural and small-town white Protestants fear displacement by foreigners and racial minorities.

way to take back the country from "wets," foreigners, radicals, Catholics, and Jews.

The Klan continued to use violence and terror, especially in the South. It also became a mainstream political force because a wide array of middle-class reformers, intellectuals, and elected officials who were not Klan members shared its brand of nativist conservatism. For example, U.S. icons such as Henry Ford and Charles Lindbergh also wished for a homogeneous white, Protestant nation and advocated theories of engineering a superior race of Anglo-Saxons. After the kidnapping and murder of his oldest child, Lindbergh fled his homeland to live in voluntary exile abroad, where his ambivalence about the modern United States became manifest as criticism of its low morals, high crime rates, drunkenness, and sexual impropriety.

Similar to the nativist Know-Nothings in the mid-nineteenth century, the second Klan suddenly burst on to the national political stage in the early 1920s to control state governments in Indiana, Colorado, Oregon, Oklahoma, and Alabama; and it also quickly collapsed. The momentum of the Klan declined after 1925 when its

Ku Klux Klan (second) Revival of racist domestic terror organization that grew outside the South and gained national recognition as a force in mainstream politics.

leader in Indiana was convicted of murder. Also, its members became disappointed when scandals involving the organization's public officials showed that Klan members were no more moral than Republicans or Democrats. Klan politicians in Indiana faced stiff opposition from powerful Republican business interests and throughout the country from increasingly influential organizations and voting blocs of immigrant and ethnic voters.

Internationally, the Klan's sudden popularity resonated with the rise of fascism in Italy. As one Klan member put it, the organization was "the Mussolini of America," as the result of the "vast volume of discontent in this country with things as they are." In both Italy and the United States, the growth of labor radicalism and the Communist Party stimulated the rise of conservative nationalism. Similarly, in postwar Germany, a small, right-wing fringe group, the **National Socialist German Workers' Party**, sought in 1923 to seize power in the German city of Munich. Led by the spellbinding orator Adolf Hitler, the Nazis, as they were called, sought to repair Germany's troubled economy and restore its national pride by reclaiming the nation from Communists, Jews, and liberals.

19-4c Secularization and Fundamentalist Christianity

Transformation of America's religious environment was another factor in the conservative groundswell. The horror of World War I had disillusioned many to the seemingly naïve message of universal brotherhood. The explosion of business and consumer cultures accentuated pleasure and materialism to an extent that was inconsistent with most Protestant practices. The nation's **secularization** was evident in the huge decrease in volunteers to serve as foreign missionaries (from twenty-seven hundred in 1920 to just two hundred twenty-five in eight years). The study of Muncie by the Lynds found that Methodists, Baptists, Congregationalists, Presbyterians, and other mainline faiths maintained a hold, especially on the working class, but church attendance (in general, 11 percent for men and 18 percent for women) was low. The Lynds placed part of the blame on leisure activities that took time away from church. In Muncie, the middle classes ranked the social status of

> Americans respond in different ways to the modernization of Protestantism.

ministers below that of the business and professional class.

Protestants responded to challenges of secularization. Mainline churches loosened theological strictures and sectarian differences and transformed ministers into helpful counselors rather than stern moralists. Advertising executive Bruce Barton published the best-selling book, *The Man Nobody Knew*, noting the humanity of Jesus Christ as the "founder of modern business" who created and marketed one of the biggest organizations of all time. Henry Emerson Fosdick, a leading Protestant modernizer, looked beyond sectarian differences in stressing the need to make Christianity relevant to the times by emphasizing the Social Gospel movement. Fosdick ascended the pulpit of New York City's mammoth Riverside Church, an **interdenominational** bastion of liberal Christianity, when it opened through the financial graces of John D. Rockefeller Jr.

Opposing the liberals was a wide variety of conservative evangelical Protestants emphasizing the literal interpretation of the Bible and the second coming of Christ. Catering especially to the white and black working classes, the evangelicals flourished in the 1920s with the spread of Pentecostal and **fundamentalist churches**—many operating from homes and storefronts. In Los Angeles, evangelical faith healer Aimee Semple McPherson enjoyed a huge following including Hollywood celebrities who enjoyed her elaborate "illustrated sermons" complete with professionally designed sets, actors, and musicians. Church records claimed that 40 million visitors came to her Angelus Temple within seven years of its founding in 1923, and even larger audiences listened to her radio broadcasts.

Fundamentalists rejected modern science, specifically Charles Darwin's theory of evolution, which contradicted the Bible's version of human creation, and they succeeded in banning the teaching of evolution in public schools in Oklahoma, Florida, and Tennessee. In 1925, schoolteacher John Scopes became the center of a widely followed trial for teaching Darwin's theory in Dayton, Tennessee. William Jennings Bryan, former secretary of state and populist legend, was the prosecutor in the **Scopes trial**. Defending Scopes was renowned lawyer and avowed agnostic Clarence Darrow, who was assisted by the American Civil Liberties Union. Although Scopes was convicted and had to pay a $100 fine, the main attention focused on Darrow's questioning of Bryan's faith in the veracity of Biblical miracles. The U.S. and international press mocked Bryan's literal interpretation of the Bible, and the famed orator's death shortly thereafter seemed to his opponents to confirm the weakness of his claims. Yet the law against teaching evolution remained in Tennessee for more than forty more years.

National Socialist German Workers' Party German political party whose eventual leader, Adolf Hitler, promoted fascism as an alternative to communism.

secularization Process of decreasing the influence of religion and religious institutions in society.

fundamentalist churches Religious movement focusing on the literal meaning of the Bible and the second coming of Jesus Christ.

interdenominational Relating to more blurring lines between religious sects or denominations, such as between Methodists and Baptists.

Scopes trial Legal proceeding that found high school teacher John Scopes guilty of violating the Tennessee state law against teaching Darwinian evolution.

19-5
Cultural Pluralism

Archibald Motley's *Octoroon Girl* portrays a beautiful, well-dressed woman in an elegant setting. Notice the leather gloves she is holding and the way she looks confidently at the viewer with calm grace. The only evidence of blackness is in the title of the painting: *Octoroon* denotes a person with one-eighth African ancestry.

Why do you think the artist choose the title *Octoroon Girl*? How did his choice embody his view of racism as well as the importance of combating class and gender stereotyping? ▶

Go to MindTap® to practice history with the Chapter 19 **Primary Source Writing Activity: Cultural Pluralism.** Read and view primary sources and respond to a writing prompt.

Michael Rosenfeld Gallery

Americanism was a conservative reaction to the nation's growing religious, cultural, and racial diversity that, in turn, prompted many Americans to reject intolerance and cultural conformity. According to the opponents of Americanism, the United States was like a jazz ensemble that emphasized spontaneity and freedom of expression in music rather than a marching band moving in lockstep to the same musical score. Novelist F. Scott Fitzgerald saw the impulse to reject old traditions and embrace new freedoms in the 1920s as indicative of what he called the **Jazz Age.** A generation of creative artists, urbanites, and youth embraced the 1920s as the time when the distance between strangers shrank and moral strictures relaxed. The "cultural pluralists" welcomed the continuation of migrations from the South that established the modern multiracial city with large populations of blacks, whites, and immigrants. Such urban centers gave rise to immigrant rights organizations and expressions such as *New Negro* and *New Woman* that sought liberation from the racial, sexual, and nativist policies perpetrated by conservatives. Thus, the opposition to conservative Americanization embraced a vision of the nation as a mosaic consisting of many peoples who would not and should not be melted down into one national culture.

☞ As you read, think about the concept of cultural pluralism. Who thought it was a positive attribute, and why?

19-5a Internal Migrations and the Multiracial City

By cutting off immigration, the Great War and its subsequent restrictive legislation stimulated internal migration.

Continued southern migrations generate new racial demographics in the nation's cities.

During the war, northern industries sent labor recruiters south to fill jobs formerly taken by immigrants. Although jobs were plentiful in the North, Southerners also were pushed to migrate because of shaky cotton prices and a boll weevil infestation that threatened the crop's future. In 1920, the census recorded that for the first time, the majority of Americans lived in cities with a population of at least twenty-five hundred. More proof of a great urban migration came a decade later when it was revealed that one-tenth of all farmers (a total of 1 million people) had moved to town (see Figure 19.3).

African American migrants especially wanted to escape Jim Crow segregation. By 1930, more than 1 million of them had arrived in northern industrial cities, the continuation of the Great Migration begun during World War I (see Map 19.3). In that year, 21 percent of African Americans, including the writer Richard Wright, lived in the North, double the percentage in 1910. Wright had left Mississippi for Chicago in 1927 to be free of the religious strictures of his grandmother and the racism that dogged him at school and work. He recalled in his autobiography, "My sustained expectation of violence had exhausted me. My preoccupation with curbing my impulses, my speech, my movements, my manner, my expressions had increased my anxiety. . . . I could not make subservience an automatic part of my behavior."

African Americans from the South as well as immigrants from the Caribbean, Mexico, and Asia laid the foundations for the multiracial

Jazz Age Period characterized by the social and cultural freedoms epitomized by young adult Americans during the 1920s.

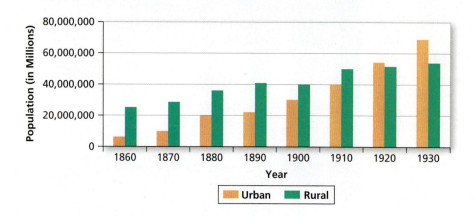

Figure 19.3 U.S. Urban and Rural Population, 1860–1930 This graph reveals the urbanization of the United States, showing that by 1920, the urban population had surpassed that of the rural population—and the disparity continued to increase during the 1920s. ◄

Source: U.S. Census

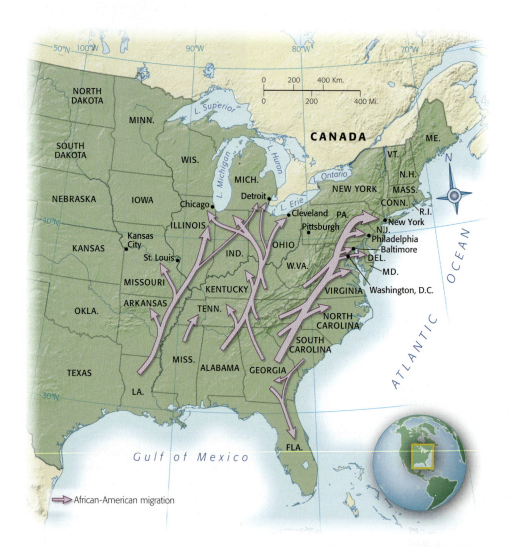

Map 19.3 Great Migration Migration pipelines channeled African Americans largely from the South to the North during and after World War I. To recruit blacks, a Cleveland factory official assured them that they would not be relegated to unskilled positions: "We have [black] molders, core makers, chippers, fitters, locomotive crane operators, melting furnace operators, general foremen, foremen, assistant foremen, clerks, timekeepers[;] in fact, there is no work in our shop that [you] cannot do and do well, if properly supervised." ▲

Keystone-France/Getty Images

Global Americans Born in St. Louis, Missouri, in 1906, **Josephine Baker** was raised in poverty by a single mother struggling to make a living in show business. By age thirteen, the young Baker dropped out of school and lived on the streets, scavenging for food in the garbage. Two years later, she was discovered dancing on street corners and became a performer in a stage show. From there, Baker went to New York City, where the Harlem Renaissance generated opportunities for her to perform in popular Broadway revues featuring all-African American casts, such as *Chocolate Dandies* in 1924. The next year she traveled to Paris to join a similar all-black revue. She was an immediate hit and became celebrated for her erotic style of dancing. Her breakout performance featured her dancing topless, clad only in a string of fake bananas dangling from her waist. A crucial part of Baker's persona embodied "primitive" African themes, which fit the modernist artistic movement that valued the supposed purity of nonwestern peoples unspoiled by capitalism and the modern world. She frequently danced on stage with her pet cheetah and could be seen walking it down the fashionable Champs-Elysee. Baker became the most popular American performer in Paris and a source of inspiration for the Lost Generation of expatriates. Ernest Hemingway called her "the most sensational woman anyone ever saw."

city. For the first time, nonwhite migrants rather than European immigrants became a growing and dynamic force in U.S. cities. But migrants of color were not always welcomed as the race riots of the Red Summer had attested. On the West Coast, immigrants from India and the Philippines endured forms of racist violence similar to those that African Americans suffered in the urban North, particularly concerning issues of housing. White residents relied on home owners' associations, real estate developers, bank lending policies, and urban planning to restrict nonwhite populations to the least desirable parts of a city. **Racial covenants**—private agreements that prevented owners from selling their homes to specific groups— also made moving into white neighborhoods difficult for racial minorities. The result was a concentration of ethnic groups in distinctive neighborhoods that developed unique subcultures.

The U.S. territory of Hawai'i had a different multiracial population: a small white planter oligarchy that ruled a labor force consisting of workers from Japan, the Philippines, Korea, China, Portugal, and Puerto Rico and oversaw an indigenous population of Hawaiians. In campaigning to make Hawai'i a state, planters sought to persuade a skeptical nation that the territory was a racial melting pot and members of its majority Asian population were capable of becoming good Americans. Congress, however, remained unconvinced. The workers on the islands took issue with the planter description of Hawai'i's "racial paradise" and accused the planters of pitting Japanese and Filipino workers against each other. In 1920, these groups overcame their antagonism to unite in the Great Hawai'i Sugar Strike that eventually led to increased wages and better labor conditions. Economic cooperation in this case proved stronger than racial division.

19-5b New Negro and Harlem Renaissance

The epicenter of urban black Americans became Harlem in New York City. It was not merely a large residential community for black migrants from the

> African Americans assert race consciousness in cultural expression, economic endeavors, and politics.

South and Caribbean but also a home to an ethnic infrastructure that included black-owned newspapers, local businesses and professional services, religious institutions, and various types of political organizations. Harlem advanced an assertive, unapologetic black identity that in 1925 Howard University philosopher Alain Locke dubbed the **New Negro**. In Harlem, as well as in Chicago's Bronzeville and many other black enclaves, New Negroes put a racial twist on mass consumption by buying and selling products, such as Madame C. J. Walker's hair-straightening agents, that reinforced race pride and solidarity. Black music, film productions, professional baseball leagues, and famous athletes such as world heavyweight boxing champion Jack Johnson were in their own ways expressions of the New Negro in a black world that provided its own identity, aesthetic, cultural symbols, and leisure activities.

In addition to being a center for jazz music, Harlem was home to an explosion of black expression in literature, the arts, dance, and scholarship. Culture makers of the

racial covenants Clause in property purchase agreements that maintained racial segregation by preventing the owner from selling the home to nonwhite racial groups.

New Negro African American identity during the Harlem Renaissance featuring the assertion of racial pride and the celebration of black history, culture, diaspora, and political power.

Harlem Renaissance addressed what it meant to be both American and black by engaging with what National Association for the Advancement of Colored People (NAACP) leader W.E.B. Du Bois called "two-ness": "two souls, two thoughts, two unreconciled strivings; two warring ideals in one dark body, whose dogged strength alone keeps it from being torn asunder." Writers, poets, and painters explored southern folk culture, the history of racism and its resistance, and persistent connections with Africa. Performers such as Josephine Baker took the New Negro identity to Paris, and her risqué cabaret act made her one of the most popular black stars overseas.

Du Bois and the NAACP focused on the natural leadership of the "talented tenth" of middle-class, educated African Americans in their push for civil rights reforms. In contrast, A. Philip Randolph, a black socialist and union leader, focused on the black working class. He organized black railroad porters into the Brotherhood of Sleeping Car Porters, a union that gained the favor of the Communist and Socialist Parties for its stand against exploitation that demanded "Fight or be Slaves." Nor did some artists, writers, and scholars of the Harlem Renaissance, including highly regarded jazz poet Langston Hughes, always agree with Du Bois. Although much of his poetry appeared in the NAACP's news organ, *The Crisis*, Hughes rejected the talented tenth strategy by appreciating the black "lowlife," including agricultural and industrial workers as well as their folk traditions. Hughes exposed what he perceived as a longing for whiteness among middle class blacks: "And so the word white comes to be unconsciously a symbol of all virtues. It holds for the children beauty, morality, and money. The whisper of 'I want to be white' runs silently through their minds."

Adored by millions during the 1920s, the most popular black leader was Marcus Garvey, a racial nationalist whose United Negro Improvement Association (headquartered in Harlem) advanced black economic empowerment. One of its ventures, the Black Star shipping line, offered African Americans transportation "back to Africa." Known for his **black nationalism**, the philosophy that saw blacks (not whites) as the global standard for civilization, Garvey proclaimed: "When Europe was inhabited by a race of cannibals, a race of savages, naked men, heathens and pagans, Africa was peopled with a race of cultured black men, who were masters in art, science, literature; men who were cultured and refined; men, who, it was said, were like gods." In truth, Garvey, the "black Moses," did not expect to lead a massive exodus of blacks from the United States, but his organization's promotion of black self-confidence and pride drew 4 million members worldwide.

Du Bois and Randolph criticized Garvey's Afrocentrism, deeming that the advocacy of black separatism was at odds with their aims of civil and

Marcus Garvey Delivers "Constitution for Negro Rights," 1920 A migrant from Jamaica, Garvey preached that the highest achievement of black pride and culture was for African Americans to go back to Africa not figuratively through literature and art but by actually leaving the United States and establishing a new nation in Africa. He developed a huge following by catering to the often unschooled and unskilled masses whereas leaders such as W.E.B. Du Bois focused on the black elite and A. Philip Randolph on organized workers. ▲

Library of Congress Prints and Photographs Division

economic rights. They were furious when Garvey met with Klan leaders to ask their support. Du Bois, Randolph, and other black leaders pushed Attorney General Palmer to expedite existing charges accusing Garvey of mail fraud related to his shipping line. In 1923, a federal court found him guilty and sentenced him to five years in jail. A year before he was to be released, President Coolidge commuted his sentence upon which Garvey was deported back to Jamaica. Although his back-to-Africa plans did not materialize, his Afrocentrism and racial separatism left a deep imprint in black America.

19-5c Jazz Age Liberation

Jazz, an entirely new type of popular music, emerged in the 1920s from a blending of African American musical traditions—West African call-and-response patterns, slave spirituals, gospel, blues, and ragtime—with Western classical music and marching band arrangements. More than just music, jazz was notorious

> New musical styles reject cultural traditions.

Harlem Renaissance
Explosion of African American creative expression centered in Harlem (New York City), Chicago's "black belt," and other urban centers.

black nationalism Expression of African American identity and pride that in extreme forms took precedence over U.S. nationalism.

Races Mix at Nightclub in Harlem, 1929 Nightclubs in urban centers such as New York City became places of interracial mingling during the 1920s. White youth flocked to Harlem and other black communities to hear live jazz music performed by African American musicians. ▲

Corbis

for its sensuality and racial impropriety as a form of "black music" that delighted white audiences. No one embodied the spirit of jazz more than Louis "Satchmo" Armstrong. Born poor and fatherless in 1901, he possessed natural musical gifts that developed as he sang for money on the streets of New Orleans, played gigs in the city's red-light district, and received music lessons at a home for black juvenile delinquents. By the early 1920s, Armstrong came under the tutelage of Joe "King" Oliver, then one of the best musicians in New Orleans who would be drawn to the emerging jazz mecca of Chicago. Armstrong followed and soon shuttled back and forth between Chicago and New York City playing and recording with the leading jazz bands and singers. His own gravelly voice and virtuoso trumpet playing became widely recognized. In 1929, his rendition of the popular song "Ain't Misbehaving" proved a crossover hit that helped to catapult jazz into the orbit of mainstream music.

A younger generation of white Americans—writers, artists, and musicians—were drawn to the rhythms and culture of jazz. During the Jazz Age, a younger generation of writers, including F. Scott Fitzgerald and Ernest Hemingway, fled to Paris, where they gathered with other American expatriates and drew inspiration from modern European writers, artists, and intellectuals. Hemingway, who had volunteered as an ambulance driver for the Red Cross during World War I, typified the "lost generation" that he portrayed in *The Sun Also Rises* (1926). Once attracted by the notion of heroism, these young people were disillusioned by the reality of war. Scarred, even disfigured, they struggled to find meaning to their lives outside the United States.

Other members of the postwar generation sought the cultural liberation that cities offered. The New Woman embraced independence and individual freedom, exemplified in the extreme by the **flapper**, a middle-class, often college-educated woman who dressed daringly, cut her hair short, listened to jazz, smoked, drank alcohol, and claimed sexual autonomy and pleasure. Fitzgerald depicted flappers as rebels who refused to be domesticated wives and mothers. The author's wife and muse, Zelda Sayre Fitzgerald, was a prominent flapper, as were screen stars Louise Brooks and Clara Bow and poet Edna St. Vincent Millay, each of whom was known for flaunting sexual norms. More generally, the decade celebrated a youth culture. Since the beginning of the twentieth century, the nation's birth rate had declined steadily, and with fewer youth under pressure to enter the job market, the period of adolescence expanded. New compulsory education laws kept young people in school through high school, increasing enrollments by 650 percent between 1900 and 1930, with most of the growth coming during the 1920s. For the first time, the vast majority of American teenagers went to school, and an increasing percentage of them continued on to college. In their study of Muncie, Indiana, the Lynds found that public schools, most of which were coeducational and had a wide

flapper Cultural rebel during the 1920s who opposed feminine conventions and expectations through dress, speech, writing, personal style, interracial relations, and sexuality.

Ernest Hemingway and Sylvia Beach infront of the 'Shakespeare and Company' bookshop, Paris, 1928 (b/w photo)/ Bridgeman Images

Lost Generation in Paris A young generation of U.S. artists and writers including F. Scott Fitzgerald and Ernest Hemingway gathered in Paris and other places outside the United States during the 1920s to partake in artistic, ideological, and racial freedoms not possible at home. In this 1928 photo Hemingway (far right) appears with Sylvia Beach (second from right) and others outside of Beach's Shakespeare and Company bookstore in Paris. ▲

range of socioeconomic classes, had become the central meeting places for young men and women, who engaged in new rituals such as going on "dates," "petting," seeing movies, and taking drives in automobiles. Yet premarital sexual intercourse remained taboo.

So too did same-sex erotic relations, which were banned by sodomy laws throughout the states. The term *homosexual* had been coined in the late nineteenth century by a German psychologist, and during this time some doctors sought to "cure" people of same-sex desires. Jazz Age freedoms extended as well to sexual minorities, who mixed freely within the heterosexual spaces of Harlem and other sites of social experimentation. The concentration of bars, restaurants, and dance clubs that drew gay, lesbian, transgendered, and bisexual clientele amounted to **"gay ghettos"** in New York City's Times Square and Greenwich Village, Chicago's Southside, and San Francisco's North Beach neighborhoods. To find these communities, one often needed a special guidebook, or word of mouth, and in this way, they thrived in the semisecretive world of the speakeasy where people defied Prohibition by drinking alcoholic beverages.

gay ghettos Hidden bars, restaurants, nightclubs, or speakeasies in which gay men, lesbians, and other sexual minorities gathered and socialized.

19-5d Immigrant Generations and the Election of 1928

Like Protestants, Catholics faced a growing division between new and older immigration groups as Church leadership—which was dominated by the Irish, Germans, and other older immigrant groups—responded to World War I by embracing Americanization and seeking to homogenize ethnic differences among congregations. In contrast, new Catholic immigrants, including Italians, Poles, Slovaks, and Mexicans, sought to maintain their own religious traditions. Jewish temples faced a similar division as the older and more established wave of German Jews pushed a liberal Reform faith against the wishes of the more Orthodox new immigrants from eastern Europe. These newcomers whose Yiddish language, working-class identity, and tendency toward labor radicalism exacerbated the theological conflict. Jews were also split by differences over Zionism, the quest for a Jewish homeland. In addition, both Catholics and Jews experienced a generational split as the sons and daughters of immigrants sought independence from their homeland traditions.

> Catholics and Jews promote cultural pluralism.

The Ku Klux Klan targeted new immigrants as much as blacks, a fact that gave Jews and Catholics cause to organize their own efforts on behalf of ethnic identity, pride, and self-defense. Harvard-trained philosopher Horace Kallen provided an overarching rationale for these new immigrants' resistance to Americanization. A German Jewish immigrant himself, Kallen advanced the notion that democracy in the United States did not require a melting pot in which everyone shared one culture. He argued instead that "in society each ethnic group is the natural instrument, its spirit and culture are its theme and melody, and the harmony and dissonances and discords of them all make the symphony of civilization." Amid the controversy over immigration in 1924, Kallen called the democratic harmonizing of differences "cultural pluralism."

Campaigns for immigration restriction also united Catholics and Jews. Established in 1919, the National Catholic Welfare Council brought various ethnic churches together to oppose Prohibition, immigration restriction, and education laws that disadvantaged parochial schools. New Jewish immigrants formed the American Jewish Congress in 1918 to compete with the older German Jewish-led American Jewish Committee. But both organizations,

as well as a third, B'nai B'rith's Anti-Defamation League, opposed the Klan's anti-Semitism and eugenic preference for white Nordic peoples. The organizations opposed Henry Ford's weekly newspaper, the *Dearborn Independent*, for the same reason. Speakers at a New York Jewish forum in 1924 denounced "Fordism, Nordism, and Klanism."

The clash between white Anglo-Saxon Protestant (WASP) conformity and cultural pluralism came to a head in the presidential election of 1928, which pitted Herbert Hoover, Coolidge's secretary of commerce, against the Democrat Al Smith. The first Catholic presidential candidate to be nominated by a major political party, Smith campaigned against Prohibition and for progressive social reforms that he, as New York's long-standing governor, had championed. Republicans countered by underscoring the nation's booming economy and benefited from popular fears that if elected, Smith would take his orders from the Pope. In the end, Hoover won by a landslide with more than 58 percent of the popular vote and more than 83 percent of the electoral vote. The Republicans, for the first time, made inroads into the solidly Democratic South. One reporter noted that Smith was defeated by the three Ps: "Prohibition, Prejudice, and Prosperity."

Summary

The United States in the 1920s was marked by Fordism, Nordism, and Klanism as well as the rise of the New Woman, New Negro, and new consumer culture, the latter of which built domestic and global markets for consumer goods and credit. Although each of these developments including that of the League of Nations had important roots in the years before World War I, they blossomed in the decade after the Treaty of Versailles. The horrors of the Great War caused Americans to retreat from the wartime vow to "make the world safe for democracy." Although the United States became a leader in international arms control and in economic and financial global integration, the nation turned inward, first to manage threats from radicalism and then to install a conservative, probusiness ethic that countered Communist calls for social equality with the realities of prosperity and

consumer freedoms. Republican presidents Harding and Coolidge celebrated mass production and consumption that were epitomized by the popularity and profitability of the automobile.

The nation also managed modernity by advancing Progressive causes such as Prohibition and immigration restrictions that were designed to suppress the nation's ethnic, cultural, and religious diversity. The influx of black and white Southerners to northern and western cities and migrations of Mexicans, West Indians, and Asians created multiracial demographics that induced a conservative popular movement in which millions joined the new Ku Klux Klan to assert the primacy of white Protestant power. Charles Lindbergh went into exile disgusted by what he considered to be the dangerous mix of radicals, criminals, and anti-Prohibition "wets". Many

free-thinking artists and writers disillusioned by the Great War also left the United States because it was too conservative, not too chaotic.

Meanwhile, an array of groups championed a new assertiveness and pride for women as well as ethnic, racial, religious, and sexual minorities. The Harlem Renaissance and flappers were expressions promoting cultural liberation from racist and Victorian traditions. Jim Crow segregation, immigration restriction, and Prohibition were contested by a variety of ethnic and religious organizations including the NAACP, Garvey's United Negro Improvement Association, the National Catholic Welfare Council, and the Anti-Defamation League. But the election of the Republican Herbert Hoover as president in 1928 revealed the continued strength of conservatism in the midst of rising demands for cultural pluralism.

<Thinking Back, *Looking Forward*>

As you review this chapter, trace the roots of U.S. economic, political, and international developments during the 1920s to the widespread impact of industrialization during the late nineteenth and early twentieth centuries. How were the 1920s influenced by U.S. businesses, labor relations, immigration, and progressive attempts to humanize the excesses of industrialization? In the next chapters, pay attention to how the developments of the 1920s were responsible for the origins of economic catastrophe and another world war.

To make your study concrete, review the timeline and reflect on the entries there. Think about their causes, consequences, and connections. How do they fit with global trends?

Additional Resources

Books

Baldwin, Davarian L. *Chicago's New Negroes: Modernity, the Great Migration, and Black Urban Life.* **Chapel Hill: University of North Carolina Press, 2007.** ▶ Studies black consumption, entrepreneurship, and celebrities in 1920s Chicago.

Dumenil, Lynn. *The Modern Temper: American Culture and Society in the 1920s.* **New York: Hill and Wang, 1995.** ▶ Classic account covering the major topics of the decade.

Grandin, Greg. *Fordlandia: The Rise and Fall of Henry Ford's Forgotten Jungle City.* **New York: Metropolitan Books, 2009.** ▶ A journalist's examination of an intriguing, though failed, attempt to spread Fordism to the Brazilian rainforest.

Gregory, James N. *The Southern Diaspora: How the Great Migrations of Black and White Southerners Transformed America.* **Chapel Hill: University of North Carolina Press, 2005.** ▶ Original analysis of the major demographic shifts during the 1920s.

Hyman, Louis. *Debtor Nation: The History of America in Red Ink.* **Princton, NJ: Princeton University Press, 2011.** ▶ Book that explains the origins of the widespread emergence of credit during the 1920s.

Iriye, Akira. *Global Community: The Role of International Organizations in the Making of the Contemporary World.* **Berkeley: University of California Press, 2004.** ▶ Discussion by a prominent international historian of the origins of today's global community.

Lauren, Paul Gordon. *Power and Prejudice: The Politics and Diplomacy of Racial Discrimination,* **2nd ed. Boulder, CO: Westview, 1996.** ▶ Broad global history that examines racial politics in the League of Nations and other institutional bodies during the 1920s.

Lynd, Robert Staughton, and Helen Merrell Lynd. *Middletown: A Study of American Culture.* **New York: Harcourt Brace, 1929.** ▶ Classic study of life in the average U.S. town of Muncie, Indiana.

MacLean, Nancy. *Behind the Mask of Chivalry: The Making of the Second Ku Klux Klan.* **New York: Oxford University Press, 1995.** ▶ Analysis of the rise of the Klan in the 1920s with some comparisons of movements in Europe.

Ngai, Mae M. *Impossible Subjects: Illegal Aliens and the Making of Modern America.* **Princeton, NJ: Princeton University Press, 2004.** ▶ Important study of U.S. immigration law and politics that starts with the Immigration Act of 1924.

Rosenberg, Emily. *Spreading the American Dream: American Economic and Cultural Expansion, 1890–1945.* **New York: Hill and Wang, 1982.** ▶ Time-tested account of expanding U.S. consumer and cultural influence around the world between the world wars.

Go to the MindTap® for **Global Americans** to access the full version of select books from this Additional Resources section.

Websites

The Great Gatsby at New Student Reading Project, Cornell University. (http://reading.cornell.edu/reading_project_06/gatsby/jazz_age.htm). ▶ Collection of many resources regarding the famous book, its author, and the period.

Harlem Renaissance at the Library of Congress. (http://www.loc.gov/teachers/classroommaterials/primarysourcesets/harlem-renaissance/). ▶ Outstanding collection of primary sources including songs, literary works, and images.

League of Nations Photo Archive. (http://www.indiana.edu/~librcsd/nt/db.cgi?db=ig&do=search_results&mh=12&sb=Notes&Cat=Secretariat). ▶ Information and photographs about this important organization.

Monkey Trial at PBS. (http://www.pbs.org/wgbh/amex/monkeytrial/index.html). ▶ Website for film devoted to the Scopes trial with primary sources, songs, and an opinion poll about teaching evolution in public schools.

The Roaring Twenties at the Gilder Lehrman Institute of American History. (https://www.gilderlehrman.org/history-by-era/progressive-era-new-era-1900–1929/roaring-twenties). ▶ Primary sources and essays about the era written by prominent historians.

Continue exploring online through MindTap®**, where you can:**
- **Assess your knowledge with the Chapter Test**
- **Watch historical videos related to the chapter**
- **Further your understanding with interactive maps and timelines**

Managing Modernity

1919

January
Eighteenth Amendment is ratified, beginning Prohibition.

February
Pan-African Congress meets in Paris amidst peace conference ending World War I.

March
Communist International is established to counter capitalism around the world.

June
League of Nations is established.

Marcus Garvey's organization establishes Black Star shipping line to return American blacks to Africa.

November
U.S. Attorney General A. Mitchell Palmer begins three-month crackdown on suspected domestic terrorists.

1920

January
Japanese, Filipino, and other workers unite in the Great Hawai'i Sugar Strike.

August
Nineteenth Amendment is ratified, giving women the right to vote.

September
Anarchists explode bomb on Wall Street, killing thirty-eight.

November
Harding (Republican) wins presidential election, and socialist Eugene V. Debs garners more than 1 million votes.

1921

May
Emergency Quota Act imposes first limit to immigration to the United States, enacting restrictions based on national origin.

July
Chinese Communist Party founded in Shanghai, China.

November
Harding signs Sheppard-Towner Act funding maternity and health care services.

1922

Louis Armstrong moves from New Orleans to Chicago to play in a popular jazz band.

February
Five-Power Naval Limitation Treaty agreement is reached during Washington Naval Conference.

September
Fordney-McCumber tariff increases U.S. protectionism against foreign competition in farm and industrial products.

October
Benito Mussolini becomes prime minister of Italy.

December
Soviet Union is founded with Vladimir Lenin as head of state.

1923

January
Angelus Temple opens, housing Aimee Semple McPherson's exciting brand of international Christian evangelism.

July
Federal court imposes five-year sentence on black leader Garvey for mail fraud.

August
Coolidge (Republican) becomes president after Harding's death.

August–September
Italy bombs Greek island of Corfu.

1924

Ford Model-T automobile sells for lowered price of $290.

January
Joseph Stalin becomes leader of the Soviet Union.

April
Fitzgerald and his wife Zelda Sayre Fitzgerald become part of the "Lost Generation" in Paris.

May
Immigration Act further reduces immigration by lowering annual quotas. Japanese immigrants excluded.

November
Ku Klux Klan wins control of state governments in Indiana and Colorado.

1925

Alain Locke declares the "New Negro."

Archibald Motely unveils *Octoroon Girl* exposing injustice of antiblack prejudice.

July
John Scopes is tried for teaching Darwinian evolution, and is found guilty after a dramatic defense.

1926

Ford Motor Company cuts workweek to five days.

November
U.S. Route 66 becomes one of the first roads within the U.S. highway system.

1927–1928

The Jazz Singer, starring Al Jolson, becomes the first feature-length "talkie" film.

May 1927
Charles Lindbergh is the first to fly solo across the Atlantic.

August 1927
Execution of convicted murders Nicola Sacco and Bartolomeo Vanzetti provokes anti-American protests around the world.

August 1928
Germany, France, and the United States sign toothless Kellogg-Briand treaty.

November 1928
Hoover (Republican) defeats Al Smith (Democratic) in presidential election.

1929

U.S. proportion of global production is coal (40%), steel (50%), gasoline (70%), and automobiles (90%).

July
Armstrong records popular cross-over hit "Ain't Misbehaving."

Go to MindTap® to engage with an interactive version of the timeline. Analyze events and themes with clickable content, view related videos, and respond to critical thinking questions.

20 Great Depression, New Deal, and Impending War

1929–1939

As a federal relief worker, Fabiola Cabeza de Baca crossed many social and cultural borders and drove thousands of miles, all within Santa Fe County.

When thirty-five-year-old Fabiola Cabeza de Baca began her job as a home demonstration agent in 1929, she set out on the great adventure of her life. Her job was to aid New Mexico farmers and their families, but she could not have known how impoverished they would be as the world plunged into the most severe economic depression of all time. Through the food she cooked and garden clubs she organized, she taught white, Hispano, and Pueblo farm women how to stretch their meager resources—the pickings from a garden, the last sheep for butchering, a bolt of cloth for winter clothes. She promoted good home management, helped women obtain canning equipment and sewing machines, and found a way for women's traditional weaving and needlework to reach a growing tourist market.

Traveling alone, she drove thousands of miles across mountains and deserts that lacked modern roads. The job and its demands were immense. "A home demonstration agent," she later recalled, "started her day no later than six o'clock in the morning and returning home as late as midnight at times." When she was at her busiest in 1932, she was in an accident. Her car stalled on a railroad track where it was hit by a train, severing her leg and leaving her face permanently disfigured. But by 1934, she was driving again and back at work.

In these years, Cabeza de Baca crossed social and cultural borders, all within Santa Fe County. Her work bridged the divide between white governmental reformers from the East and the world of rural New Mexicans. She wrote weekly newspaper columns in Spanish and spoke the native languages when she visited Pueblo homes. She brought modernity to a society still deeply rooted in historic practices. The encounter was sometimes difficult, because her clients did not always want to be Americanized or to accept modern ways of cooking and housekeeping. At the same time, the government bureaucracies, both state and federal, had no means of accommodating the complexity of Hispano and Indian cultures. Cabeza de Baca tried to bridge the two worlds. In her later life, she wrote cookbooks with recipes that used the traditional ingredients and practices she had observed in her home demonstration work but also incorporated the use of modern kitchen technology such as pressure cookers to save time and preserve food.

For Cabeza de Baca and those who worked for or benefited from state and federal relief agencies during the Great Depression, the experience transformed their lives. Many were absolutely destitute. Following the stock market crash in 1929, U.S. financial institutions and industries collapsed. Millions lost their jobs, savings, farms, and homes—literally everything they had. Private charities could not cope with the crisis, and the federal government, through programs established under President Franklin D. Roosevelt, took on the well-being of citizens as a federal responsibility. For the first time, the federal government played a major role in the economic, social, and cultural lives of ordinary Americans. Following a rush of legislation to stop the economy's downward spiral, Roosevelt implemented structural reforms

Fabiola Cabeza de Baca, Gilbert Photograph Collection, Center for the Southwest Research, University of New Mexico

Fabiola Cabeza de Baca in Front of a
New Mexican Schoolhouse, circa 1920s ▲

How does Fabiola Cabeza de Baca's service during the Great Depression reflect a shift in the role the federal government played in the lives of ordinary Americans?
Go to MindTap® to watch a video on Cabeza de Baca and learn how her story relates to the themes of this chapter.

in the nation's labor relations and welfare system to ensure stability. Government intervention in the economy regulated markets and created jobs but did not end the Depression. Toward the end of the decade, however, national attention was increasingly diverted by conflicts in Europe and Asia.

The United States was not the only nation in crisis in the 1930s. The severe downturn caused European economies to collapse, and many of the fragile new democracies established after World War I did not survive. Dictators took over—most notably in Italy, Germany, and Spain—reshaping national economies to militaristic purposes. Their societies under total government control were not unlike that of the Soviet Union, where another dictator under the banner of communism also directed the economy and subordinated the rights of citizens to the needs of the state. In Asia, the rising power of Japan led by a military faction similarly threatened the nations of East Asia. By 1939, aggression in Europe and Asia had engulfed much of the world—but not yet the Western Hemisphere—in war.

20-1
Enduring Economic Collapse

In the early 1930s, bread lines formed in cities and small towns, wherever private charities offered free food. This one is in Manhattan, New York, under the Brooklyn Bridge.

What events compelled these people to join the line? How did receiving aid influence people's ideas about self-reliance? ▶

Go to MindTap® to practice history with the Chapter 20 **Primary Source Writing Activity: Experiences of the Depression.** Read and view primary sources and respond to a writing prompt.

The Granger Collection, New York

In 1929, the U.S. economy collapsed, sending the nation into a deep economic depression from which it would not recover for more than a decade. From rural hamlets to urban centers, Americans suffered a loss of jobs, income, and wealth. The Depression quickly spread through Europe, Asia, and Latin America, which were linked to the United States by trade and finance. The Hoover administration took steps to cushion the impact of the economic downturn, but they were not enough. The Depression grew worse. In 1932, voters were ready for new leadership and elected Franklin Delano Roosevelt, a Democrat to the presidency. He promised bold programs to boost the economy into recovery and pledged "a new deal for the American people."

☞ As you read, assess the relationship between the U.S. and global economies. Why and how and did the Great Depression engulf so many nations around the world?

20-1a Stock Market Crash and Its Impact

Although the 1920s seemed prosperous, in reality wealth was unequally distributed, stocks were overvalued, and the global economy as a whole

{ Americans feel the first effects of the economic downturn.

was unstable. Farmers both at home and abroad who had overproduced during World War I and its aftermath faced declining demand and agricultural prices. They could not meet their increasing debts and began to default on loans and leave their farms. Production of consumer goods soared during the 1920s, but the wages of the workers who produced them did not. Few could buy what they made. As consumer goods were stockpiled and demand dropped, the economy softened. Farmers and most workers did not realize the gains of the roaring twenties. The gap between the rich and the poor increased. As the national and global economies began to teeter at the end of the decade, Americans were the first to feel the impact.

Then, on October 24, 1929, Black Thursday, a massive stock sell-off began at the New York Stock Exchange. Brokers sold millions of shares. At the end of the day, twenty-five Wall Street brokerage houses issued a statement saying that the "worst has passed" in an attempt to calm the market. But the next day, the sell-off continued. Investors panicked and dumped their stocks for any price. Those who had bought on the margins—that is, borrowed money to purchase stocks—frantically sold to pay their creditors. Five days later, on Tuesday, October 29, the bubble burst for good when 3 million shares were sold in the first thirty minutes of trading. More than 16 million shares changed hands that day, a volume that would not be reached again for almost forty years. Since early September, the value of the leading industrial stocks had declined by almost 40 percent. Stock losses for just the month of October 1929 totaled some $50 billion, an amount exceeding what the United States had spent in waging World War I.

The **stock market crash** did not cause the **Great Depression**. In fact, only about half a million people owned stocks. For almost a year after the crash, few Americans felt its direct impact or understand its implications. But by 1932, every American was painfully aware of the magnitude of the downward spiral. Its effects were felt across the country in every sector of the economy at every level of society.

As the value of stocks plummeted, businesses began to fail, companies laid off workers, and workers cut back on purchasing. Reduced demand for consumer goods caused more businesses to fail and more workers to lose their jobs. By the early 1930s, some 14 million Americans—one-quarter of the workforce—were out of work and another 40 million in a population of 123 million did not have sufficient income to meet their obligations. Between 1929 and 1932, families lost more than 30 percent of their income. For the nation's minorities, the situation was worse. A survey of one hundred six cities reported that half of African Americans were jobless.

The falling value of stocks also meant that banks called in their loans. As homeowners and farmers fell behind in mortgage payments, foreclosures hit an all-time high. In the South, shrinking cotton and tobacco markets squeezed sharecropping families. One Texas cotton picker explained: "I picked all week and made 85 cents. I can starve sitting down a lot easier than I can picking cotton." Although the economy had endured cycles of boom and bust for more than a century, this depression was unprecedented in its severity.

20-1b Global Economic Crisis

Because U.S. and European financial markets were interconnected, the U.S. economic crisis quickly spread to Europe. For the first time in its history, the United States was a creditor nation. U.S. banks and financiers had loaned European allies $10 billion during and after World War I and since the mid-1920s had been sending loans to Germany so it could make its reparations payments. This flow of money had helped to stabilize European economies **(see Figure 20.1)**. But when U.S. banks demanded repayment of loans to cover stock market losses, Europe, too, suffered a wave of bank failures. The most devastating was that of Austria's Kreditanstalt in 1931.

> As the depression spreads, people all over the world feel the effects.

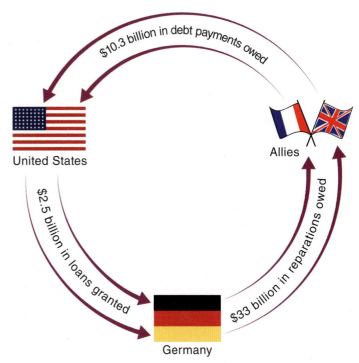

Figure 20.1 International Financial System between the End of World War I and the Great Depression After World War I, world financial markets became deeply intertwined by loans and debt. In 1924, after Germany ceased reparations payments to the Allies, former U.S. budget director Charles G. Dawes developed a payment plan that included U.S. loans to Germany. Dawes won the Nobel Peace Prize for his efforts, but the plan ultimately failed, and in 1932, Germany stopped reparations payments altogether. Allied war loan repayments to the United States had also ceased; only Finland paid its debt promptly. In 2010, Germany made the last of its reparations and debt payments under the Dawes Plan. ▲ Source: Leonard Gomes, *German Reparations, 1919–1932: A Historical Survey*. New York: Palgrave Macmillan, 2010.

Foreign investment in European industry also plummeted, and by 1931, the level of U.S. investment in Europe was zero. The withdrawal of U.S. money from European markets produced a shock, because throughout the 1920s, the United States had played a major role in European finance. As banks and factories closed in Europe, unemployment also soared, to 22 percent in Britain and more than 30 percent in Germany.

With credit cut off and the European economy crashing downward, the value of U.S. exports also declined from $5.4 billion in 1929 to $2.1 billion in 1933. To protect U.S. manufacturers from foreign competition, Congress passed the **Hawley-Smoot Tariff** in 1930, which taxed imported goods at the highest rates in U.S. history. Other industrialized counties retaliated with their own protectionist tariffs. Germany, for example, imposed a 50 percent tariff on all entering goods. As trade barriers went up, global trade slowed, declining by a

stock market crash Sudden plunge in stock prices that is made worse by panic and more selling. The crash of 1929 signaled the onset of the Great Depression.

Great Depression Deep and decade-long economic collapse, beginning with the U.S. stock market crash in 1929, which soon engulfed nations throughout the world.

Hawley-Smoot Tariff Tariff law passed in 1930 that raised import taxes to their highest levels ever. By suppressing trade, it heightened the impact of the Great Depression globally.

Image of postcard. Courtesy of Cathleen Cahill. Trieste, Italy.

Global Americans

In 1931, an aspiring singer from Oklahoma arrived in Berlin to study opera. **Tessie "Lushanya" Mobley** had been born in 1906 to a white father and a mother of Chickasaw descent. Her studies in Berlin coincided with the rise of Adolf Hitler and the Nazi Party, and her journals are rich with first-person accounts of the experience. She described the National Day of Boycott against Jewish businesses, April 1, 1933, shortly after Hitler assumed dictatorial powers; she recorded the dismissal of her Jewish professors and reflected on a close friend's decision to leave school to join the Nazi Party. Her April 28, 1933, entry concludes, "I believe that always the majority people will be victims or scapegoats of those who lead. . . . I am wondering what this next year will bring." Despite her isolation and fear, Mobley never hid her Chickasaw heritage, and the next years brought her international recognition as the "Songbird of the Chickasaws." In 1937, when she made her operatic debut at Trieste, Italy, she answered three hours of curtain calls before falling down in exhaustion. Her starring role in *Aida* (shown in this postcard) made her famous, and she repeated her success at La Scala in Milan. This image suggests that although Mobley was a renowned singer, she was often cast in ethnic roles that reflected her indigenous background. For example, at the Royal Albert Hall in London, she played Minnehaha in *Hiawatha*. Her career spanned decades, and while she often lived in Paris, she always maintained close family and tribal ties.

staggering 62 percent, from $3 billion to $1 billion. Japan's exports dropped by 50 percent. Britain's weekly newspaper *The Economist* blamed the Hawley-Smoot Tariff for turning "a stock market collapse into a crippling, decade-long Depression" (see Map. 20.1).

The repercussions were worldwide. When U.S. automakers stopped importing rubber for ties, the rubber industry in Malaya, Indochina, and the Dutch East Indies fell apart. Japan, devastated by the collapse of the silk trade, prohibited the importation of rice. Latin American exports of sugar, coffee, wool, copper, tin, silver, and petroleum almost ceased. Furthermore, as U.S. banks went into crisis, they stopped financing the Latin American projects that U.S. companies such as Ford and United Fruit had undertaken. No country escaped the impact of the Great Depression, and as each country walled off imports and tried to solve its own financial problems, international tensions increased.

Efforts at international cooperation faltered. In June 1931, President Hoover proposed a one-year **moratorium** on German reparations and on Allied war debt payments to the United States. But when the moratorium ended, all debtor nations except Finland defaulted. Germany stopped paying reparations altogether. In 1933, sixty-six nations, including the United States, came together at the **London Economic Conference** to find a way to revive international trade and stabilize international currencies. Although the participants agreed on the devastating effects of the Depression, none could agree on how to end it. With this failure,

moratorium Authorized delay in debt payment. In 1931, Hoover proposed a one-year moratorium for war debts and reparations.

London Economic Conference International meeting in 1933 that tried but failed to coordinate efforts to ease the global depression and stabilize national currencies.

totalitarianism Single-party political system in which the state has almost complete control over all aspects of civil society. An example is Nazi Germany.

nations turned inward, seeking individual, often nationalistic solutions rather than collaborative efforts that they feared would embroil them in their neighbors' economic problems.

20-1c International Responses to Global Depression

> National solutions involve varying degrees of government intervention.

For many, the unprecedented economic crisis seemed to signal that capitalism had failed. In some European parliamentary democracies, disagreements between the left and right wings of the socialist parties actually paralyzed governments and made them unable to enact programs of social welfare. Socialist leaders influenced by Marxist theories were reluctant to embrace any reforms short of total nationalization of industry. On the other hand, middle-class reform parties fearful of Communist revolution refused to form coalitions with socialists. As a result, elected leaders could not maintain stable governments. In France, for example, between 1931 and 1936, ten different premiers formed twelve different governments, one lasting only a week.

It is not surprising that some European nations turned to authoritarian solutions. One model for a new type of economy came from Italy, where since the 1920s, Benito Mussolini's fascism had protected capitalists from strikes and revolution through total state power over the economy. In 1933, Germany turned to a similar solution when Adolf Hitler's Nazi Party took control of the economy and subordinated the individual to the state by glorifying militarism and nationalism. Hitler's **totalitarian** dictatorship was also overtly racist. He pledged to rid the country of Jews, Communists, homosexuals, and others

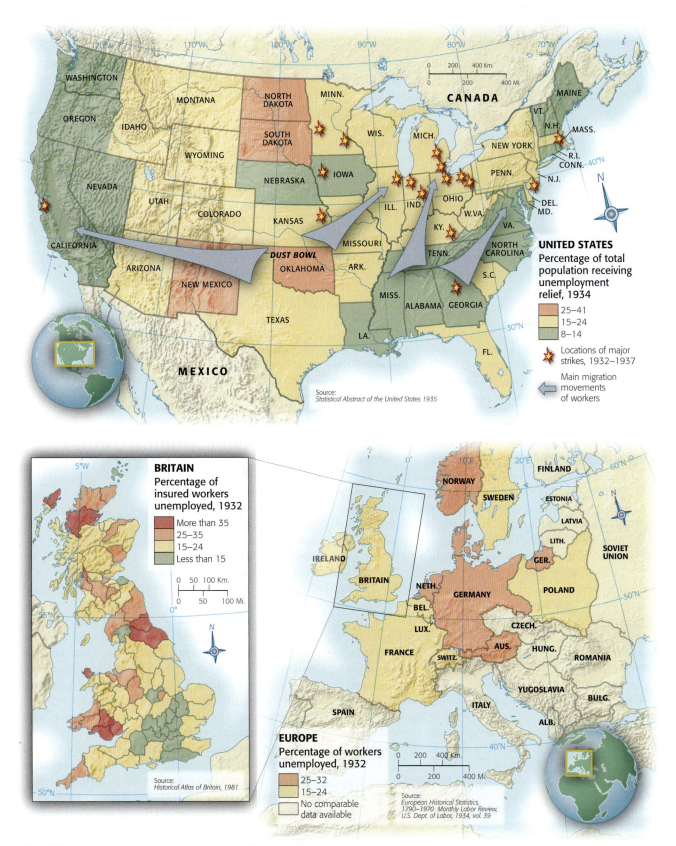

Map 20.1 The Great Depression at Home and Abroad, 1932–1934 The global depression threw millions of people across the United States and Europe out of work. At the height of the Depression, countries faced high unemployment rates, labor strikes, and, in the United States, mass migration. Under Hitler's command economy, Germany recovered the fastest. By 1939, all these countries were emerging from the economic downturn. ▲

AP Images

Global Americans As a young man, **Herbert Hoover** pursued a career and humanitarian work that took him around the world. Raised as a Quaker and orphaned at an early age, he entered Stanford University's first class in 1891 and graduated as a mining engineer. He developed mining companies in Australia, South Africa, and China, earning a reputation as a problem solver. When he and his wife, Lou, also a Stanford graduate, were trapped in Tianjin during China's Boxer Rebellion, his fluent Chinese helped U.S. troops evacuate foreigners. By the time World War I broke out in Europe, Hoover had lived abroad most of his adult life and amassed a fortune of $4 million. The war prompted him to turn from business enterprise to public service, and he worked tirelessly to provide humanitarian aid to the people of Belgium. At the height of the war, his Commission for Belgian Relief and American Relief Association supplied food to 10.5 million people every day. After the United States entered the war, he ran the U.S. Food Administration. During the Harding and Coolidge administrations, Hoover was secretary of commerce, overseeing programs that promoted open trade agreements and U.S. businesses abroad. When he was elected president in 1928, Americans were confident that his background as a successful businessman and a humanitarian with a reputation for efficiency had prepared him to lead the nation. "I have no fear for the future of our country," Hoover said at his inauguration. "It is bright with hope."

deemed unfit or incompatible. Political prisoners were sent to **concentration camps** such as Dachau, which was established shortly after the Nazis took power. But after the Nuremberg Laws stripped Jews of their civil rights in 1935, these camps filled with those accused of being enemies of the state for racial, moral, and religious reasons.

On the other side of the globe, imperial Japan was increasingly coming under the influence of military extremists bent on expansion. Desperate in 1931 for access to raw materials because of high protective tariffs, Japan invaded and occupied Manchuria, a region of China with 30 million inhabitants and rich supplies of coal, iron, timber, and soybeans. China, torn apart by a civil war between Nationalists led by Jiang Jieshi (Chiang Kai-shek) and Communists led by Mao Tse-tung (Mao Zedong), was unable to resist the takeover but did ask for help from the League of Nations. When the League ordered Japan to withdraw, it instead withdrew from the League. Renaming the former Chinese province Manchukuo, Japan incorporated it into its expanding Asian empire.

In the 1920s, the Soviet Union had stabilized under Communist Party control, and Joseph Stalin took command after Vladimir Lenin's death. Under Stalin, the party began a program of rapid industrialization and state-run agriculture that met production goals at a terrible human cost. In the winter of 1932–1933, an estimated 7 million peasants starved to death in the Ukraine, and later in the decade, Stalin's purges of state enemies and the Red Army officer corps killed millions.

concentration camp Isolated and enclosed location where political and/or ethnic undesirables were relocated to separate them from civil society.

command economy State-run economy with little or no participation from private firms or free competition.

volunteerism Practice of relying on charitable agencies and private sector cooperation rather than government action to provide relief.

Reconstruction Finance Corporation (RFC) Independent agency established in 1932 that distributed billions in loans to banks and railroads to stabilize the economy.

Yet **command economies**, in which the state controlled and directed all aspects of production, seemed to many to be more likely to withstand the economic crisis of the 1930s than the **free-market** economies of the Western democracies.

20-1d Hoover Administration Responses

After the stock market crash, President Hoover at first remained optimistic, predicting recovery in just sixty days. New York Governor Franklin Roosevelt agreed. But by the end of 1929, it was clear to state and local leaders such as Roosevelt that this depression was far worse than the post-World War I downturn. State and local governments were completely unprepared to deal with joblessness and hunger, and private charities and religious organizations could not keep up with the demands. There were no federal relief programs.

> Hoover's reforms and aid prove inadequate.

Yet Hoover remained committed to staying within the confines of what the federal government had always done—manipulate the tariff. He continued to call for private and local, not a national, response to the crisis. Steeped in the earlier Progressive movement, he believed in the power of the free market to reverse the downturn and advocated **volunteerism** rather than government aid. He personally donated generously to relief efforts and worked tirelessly to persuade others, such as the popular cowboy comedian Will Rogers, to promote charitable giving. Yet while giving was at an all-time high, it was not enough.

By January 1932, as banks failed, industries closed, and unemployment soared, Hoover realized that government action was needed. He asked Congress to create the **Reconstruction Finance Corporation (RFC)**, which

Sueddeutsche Zeitung Photo/Alamy Stock Photo

Bonus Marchers at the Capitol, Summer 1932 World War I veterans and their supporters traveled across the United States to pressure Congress to require immediate payment of the bonuses by passing the Bonus Bill. Proponents believed this would help alleviate the economic hardship of the global depression. Despite political pressure, the bill was defeated. Peaceful demonstrations, like the one depicted here, turned violent when the U.S. Army and local police dispersed the veterans' encampments. ▲

In Congress, the bonus bill was defeated, and most veterans left. Washington police sought to evict those remaining, and when violence erupted, Hoover called in federal troops under General Douglas MacArthur to restore order. In a display of force, MacArthur sent tanks and soldiers with drawn bayonets to remove the veterans and to burn the camp. During these attacks on the Bonus Army, two veterans were killed, two infants died from asphyxiation, and more than a thousand people were exposed to tear gas. The spectacle of MacArthur's troops attacking unarmed veterans and their families shocked Americans and led them to oppose a president who seemed incapable of dealing with the crisis.

Nevertheless, the Republicans nominated Hoover for a second term. The Democrats had no clear front-runner although Governor Roosevelt was attracting attention. Republicans and more conservative Democrats feared he would take the country in the direction of European democratic socialism. Others saw him as shallow. "An amiable boy scout," quipped journalist Walter Lippmann. The Democratic convention was a free-for-all as candidates jockeyed for the nomination, but after four ballots, Roosevelt won. As he campaigned, he promised Americans a **New Deal** to end the Depression but did not outline specific policies. Yet he won the general election with 57 percent of the popular vote to Hoover's 40 percent.

Adolf Hitler and Franklin Roosevelt assumed the leadership of their countries within one month of each other in early 1933. Both Germans and Americans were looking for a forceful leader who could provide a clear path for economic recovery. Although Hitler and Roosevelt each provided charismatic leadership, they took radically different approaches. Hitler, following a fascist model, became a dictator who suppressed his critics and initiated a military buildup as a means of strengthening the economy. Roosevelt, in contrast, had to fend off doubts about his leadership sown during the election as well as critics from both the left and the right. Nevertheless, the democratic solution to economic crisis that he pursued endured, and, as the rise of militarist regimes in Asia and Europe portended global conflict, Roosevelt sought to insulate the United States from international tensions.

made loans to banks, railroads, and insurance companies to keep them afloat. In July, with the crisis deepening, the Emergency Relief and Reconstruction Act authorized the RFC to make loans directly to farmers, states, and public works projects. Yet Hoover insisted on a very conservative set of guidelines. RFC loans carried high interest rates (to avoid competing with private lenders) and collateral requirements. Nevertheless, the loans totaled almost $2 billion in the RFC's first year, enough to delay a banking catastrophe but not enough to inspire an upturn.

To those who were suffering, Hoover seemed harsh and uncaring. Mocking him, homeless people forced to live under bridges and in tents and shacks called their new communities Hoovervilles. His reaction to the poverty-stricken veterans who straggled into Washington in the summer of 1932 branded him as uncaring. In 1924, Congress had granted a bonus to those who had served in World War I to be paid in 1945 as an insurance policy or pension. But the hardships of the Depression caused veterans to ask Congress for the bonus early. Starting in Oregon in the spring of 1932, they marched east, and by the time they arrived in Washington, they were known as the **Bonus Army**. More than 20,000 veterans and their families set up camp on Anacostia Flats, near the U.S. Capitol.

Bonus Army World War I veterans who marched on Washington in 1932 to demand that promised cash bonuses be paid immediately but were refused.

New Deal Roosevelt's program for providing relief during the Great Depression and reforming the nation's economy and financial institutions.

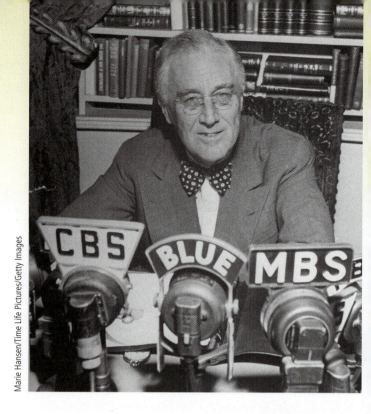

Marie Hansen/Time Life Pictures/Getty Images

20-2

The New Deal

Roosevelt was the first president to speak regularly to Americans by radio. His broadcasts masterfully allayed fears and rallied Americans to face and endure the difficulties of both the Great Depression and international conflicts.

How did regular radio broadcasts from the president change the relationship between the federal government and Americans? ▶

Although Roosevelt entered office in March 1933, determined to bring relief to Americans, the only consistent theme of his administration's first days was frenetic activity. Roosevelt himself lacked a unified philosophy of government, and his advisers sometimes gave conflicting advice about how to handle the crisis. He knew only that he needed to experiment constantly until the Depression ended. Some policies worked, but others did not. Although the Supreme Court overturned much of what Roosevelt set in motion in those first heady months of his presidency, he persisted with major reforms in labor legislation and in social welfare that restructured the U.S. economy.

☞ As you read, think about the goals of the New Deal. What impeded its success?

20-2a A Modern Presidency

Franklin Delano Roosevelt grew up wealthy and protected on his family's Hyde Park estate in New York. At the age of 14, he was sent to Groton,
an elite boarding school in New England. He then entered Harvard, where he was a class officer and editor of the Harvard *Crimson*. During this time, he dated his distant cousin Eleanor Roosevelt, the niece of President Theodore Roosevelt. Both were devoted to reform and public service, and they can be considered the first modern political couple. Roosevelt was assistant secretary of the navy under President Wilson and the Democratic Party vice presidential nominee in 1920. The Democrats lost to Republican Harding, and the next year, Franklin contracted polio, which left him paralyzed from the waist down. He was determined not to be an invalid. Both he and Eleanor believed that he should re-enter public life. Despite her personal shyness, Mrs. Roosevelt promoted her husband's place in New York and national politics.

> Franklin and Eleanor Roosevelt transform the American presidency.

Brains Trust Term used to describe Roosevelt's policy advisers, chosen for their expertise rather than their personal association with the president.

fireside chats Roosevelt's radio addresses to Americans in which he explained in clear language how his administration was addressing pressing issues.

Increasingly, she spent less time as his nursemaid and more time tending to his political fortunes in the public spotlight. This was an arrangement that would serve the couple throughout his governorship and presidency.

Following his election to the presidency in 1932, Roosevelt assembled what came to be known as the **Brains Trust**. These advisers were known for their policy specialties rather than their personal friendship with the president and shared his belief that an active government could solve the nation's economic problems. Deeply influenced by the Progressive movement, they envisioned the New Deal as the legacy of President Theodore Roosevelt's New Nationalism and President Wilson's New Freedom. Roosevelt saw his role as picking and choosing from among the policies his advisers presented even if the result lacked a coherent ideology. "Take a method and try it," Roosevelt said. "If it fails, admit it frankly, and try another. But above all, try something." Roosevelt's willingness to take action reassured Americans during the first months of his presidency. As his presidency proceeded, he enacted relief, reform and recovery programs that would have a lasting impact on the nation.

Both Franklin and Eleanor reached out to Americans in a way that personalized the presidency. Just eight days after his inauguration, Roosevelt went on the radio to explain in everyday language what his administration was doing to end the banking crisis. These radio messages came to be called **fireside chats**. Frances Perkins, secretary of labor and the first woman ever to serve in the cabinet, remembered that when the president began speaking into the radio microphone "his face would smile and light up as though he were actually sitting on the front porch or in the parlor with them. People felt this, and it bound them to him in affection." Eleanor Roosevelt also made a personal connection to Americans through her daily newspaper column, **"My Day."** One Nebraska woman said she had come to think of Eleanor Roosevelt as a personal friend because she knew so much about her from the columns.

20-2b First Hundred Days

The pressing crisis that Roosevelt faced immediately upon his inauguration was the failure of hundreds of banks. As panicked depositors with-

> Roosevelt administration takes decisive action to improve the economy.

drew their savings and some hoarded cash, banks without adequate reserves called in outstanding loans and foreclosed on farms and homes, evicting many from their property. When banks still could not keep pace with withdrawals, they defaulted, and depositors lost all their money. Although a few states suspended bank operations to stem the crisis, there had been no coordinated, federal response by the Hoover administration.

Roosevelt's first act in office was to declare a **Bank Holiday**. He closed all banks for four days (later extended to eight days), and no withdrawals were allowed. Under the Emergency Banking Act, passed on March 9, banks that were solvent reopened while the federal government guided those that were in trouble toward solvency. This action gave people confidence and ended the panicked withdrawals. The Bank Holiday was followed by the Glass-Steagall Act, which provided a long-term solution to bank failures. It created the Federal Deposit Insurance Corporation (FDIC), which insured individual deposits up to $2,500. It also prohibited banks from dealing in stocks and thus ended practices that put depositors' savings at risk.

Other financial reforms quickly followed. To stabilize the stock market, the Securities Act required sellers to disclose to investors information about the value of the stock. Taking the United States off of the **gold standard**, Roosevelt instructed the Treasury to print more money than was backed up by actual gold reserves held by the government. This move provided extra cash that could be directed to relief and jobs programs. The Roosevelt administration thus engaged in **deficit spending**, an approach recommended by the British economist John Maynard Keynes. **Keynesian economic theory** advocated centralized economic planning and government spending on public works to stimulate the economy, ideas that would eventually guide Roosevelt's program of economic recovery.

To stimulate production and trade, Roosevelt supported repeal of prohibition, which was accomplished by constitutional amendment in 1933. He also recognized the Soviet Union and signed a trade agreement designed to increase U.S. exports. Ford sold tractors to Soviet collective farms, and skilled U.S. workers went

MPI/Stringer/Archive Photos/Getty Images

NRA Cartoon, "In It Together," July 1933 This cartoon depicts Uncle Sam as a coalition builder between employers and their employees to bolster the sagging economy. Hugh Johnson, Administrator of the NRA, was sympathetic to Mussolini's ideology of corporatism, which meant that the government would broker and enforce a consensus between labor and management about how to make industry work for both sides. Corporatism, as embodied in Johnson's NRA, promised no more strikes and fair working conditions. ▲

to the Soviet Union to help build new factories and train technicians.

In addition to alleviating the financial crisis, the Roosevelt administration provided direct relief to individuals and families. The new Home Owners' Loan Corporation helped those who had defaulted on mortgages to keep their family homes. To get money into the hands of consumers so they could spend it, Roosevelt created the Federal Emergency Relief Agency (FERA), which provided work programs and direct cash payments to those with no other means of support. FERA was only a temporary measure, however, because both Roosevelt and Harry Hopkins, secretary of commerce, preferred to stimulate the economy by providing incentives for creating jobs rather than direct aid.

Two programs—the National Industrial Recovery Act (NIRA) and the Agricultural Adjustment Act (AAA)—best represent the approach Roosevelt took early in his administration. The NIRA established the National Recovery Administration (NRA), which negotiated with both

"My Day" Newspaper column written by Eleanor Roosevelt that ran six days a week between 1935 and 1962, describing her thoughts on events and issues.

Bank Holiday Roosevelt's first act in office, closing banks for four (later eight) days to prevent panic withdrawals and ensure that banks had adequate funds to cover deposits.

gold standard Monetary system in which the government can print and circulate only the amount of paper money backed by actual gold held in government vaults.

deficit spending Government policy of spending more on services than it collects in tax revenues and other income. This policy creates national debt.

Keynesian economic theory Economic policy advocated by British economist John Maynard Keynes in which monetary inputs by government keep the economy in balance.

business and labor to regulate wages, production quotas, and ceilings and floors on prices for consumer goods. Theoretically, it had the power to enforce these regulations but preferred voluntary compliance. Businesses had an incentive to agree to the NRA's codes because compliance exempted them from antitrust laws. Labor was granted the first federal protection for unions and the right of **collective bargaining** for wages and working conditions. Roosevelt's choice to head the NRA, Hugh Johnson, led a national campaign urging businesses to "do their part." Those that complied could display the Blue Eagle, the symbol of the NRA, as a way to attract clients and customers. New York City's largest parade in history was held to promote the Blue Eagle.

The NIRA also established the Public Works Administration (PWA). Under the direction of Secretary of the Interior Harold Ickes, the PWA implemented Keynesian ideas about "priming the pump" of the U.S. economy. The PWA was initially authorized to spend up to $3.3 billion on large infrastructure projects such as dams, schools, hospitals, airports, roads, and sidewalks. For every person the PWA employed directly, two additional workers were hired by private companies. Again, the idea was to provide jobs, not aid.

The Tennessee Valley Authority (TVA) undertook a massive infrastructure program to bring electricity, flood control, and land restoration to one of the poorest regions in the nation. Throughout the country, the government put unemployed young men to work in the newly created Civilian Conservation Corps (CCC), which engaged in reforestation projects, dam construction, and infrastructure improvements in national parks.

The AAA did for agriculture what the NIRA did for industry. It encouraged voluntary cooperation in ending overproduction—a major cause of the global depression—by paying farmers subsidies in return for letting their land lie fallow or slaughtering their animals. Although Americans suffering from want were shocked to see farmers killing piglets and dumping thousands of gallons of milk onto the ground, farm prices and farm income did stabilize and begin to rise. Meanwhile, the Farm Credit Administration worked to prevent foreclosures and increased the availability of credit.

During Roosevelt's first months in office—what came to be called the **Hundred Days**—a wide range of New Deal programs sought to address the nation's economic crisis (see Table 20.1). Some were successful, some not, and most had to be bolstered with additional legislation. But together they announced that the government was taking a new and active role in the economy by using public works to stimulate job creation and encouraging cooperation from business, workers, and farmers in nationwide economic planning. These steps were unprecedented in the United States, but they fell far short of the command economies implemented by force in the Soviet Union, Italy, and Germany, where Hitler's programs reduced unemployment by almost half in 1934. Although none of the New Deal programs brought an immediate end to the Depression, they did alleviate suffering, and they laid the foundation for a modern federal bureaucracy that addresses the well-being of people directly.

But not all Americans benefited equally. In southern states, the prevailing system of Jim Crow meant that African Americans hired for federal work programs were systematically placed in lower status jobs and paid less than white workers. By the second year of the NRA, not one African American held the rank of clerk or its equivalent, and the black press asserted that the NRA really stood for "Negro Removal Act." The farm subsidies, meant to be passed down from independent farmers to tenants and sharecroppers, never made it into the hands of those who needed the money most.

20-2c Limits and Critics

By early 1935, Roosevelt's New Deal confronted its limitations and vocal criticism from both the left and the right. Despite some success, the NIRA had become unpopular in some circles, and Congress was reluctant to renew it. On one hand, small businesses complained that the codes of competition favored big corporations, and a review board set up by Roosevelt denounced the legislation for promoting monopolies. On the other hand, consumers and workers thought it did not do enough to protect them from low wages and high prices, and unions protested that the Roosevelt administration had been too cooperative with business interests.

{ The New Deal faces many critics and crucial setbacks.

Critics charged that the New Deal did not go far enough to relieve the crisis. In 1934, Senator Huey Long, former governor of Louisiana, launched **Share Our Wealth**, a program that proposed to liquidate the wealth of every American who held more than $1 million in assets and distribute this money to the poor so that every family could purchase a home, a car, and a radio. The elderly would receive pensions, workers would earn a minimum wage, and deserving young men would be sent to college for free. From Royal Oak, Michigan, Father Charles Coughlin used his weekly radio show to attack Roosevelt's friendly dealings with banking and financial establishments in language that scarcely disguised his anti-Semitism. A third challenge came from Dr. Francis Townsend of Long Beach, California, who advocated a plan to secure the welfare of the country's senior citizens by taxing business transactions to fund pensions. These critics drew many vocal followers. Together, they signaled a trend toward experimentation with radical political ideologies that rejected capitalism.

collective bargaining Right of workers represented by a union to negotiate wage and workplace issues with management, first recognized by law during the New Deal.

Hundred Days Term for Roosevelt's first three months in office during which Congress passed fifteen major laws addressing relief and economic recovery.

Share Our Wealth Huey Long's program for redistributing wealth more equally among the American people.

Table 20.1 New Deal Agencies, Laws, and Programs

During the first two terms of the Roosevelt administration, Congress passed a series of laws meant to regulate the economy, stimulate economic growth, and provide both short-term aid and long-term entitlements to U.S. citizens.

Year	Legislation	Description
1933	Emergency Banking Act	Closed most U.S. banks to prevent further panic, allowed the Federal Reserve to direct cash to stable banks, and provided federal insurance to depositors
1933	Home Owners Loan Corporation (HOLC)	Provided refinancing assistance to those homeowners who had defaulted on their mortgages
1933	Banking Act (Glass-Steagall Act)	Created the Federal Deposit Insurance Corporation (FDIC) to insure individual bank deposits and limited banks' ability to engage in securities trading
1933	Farm Credit Act	Created the Farm Credit Administration (FCA) to make credit more available for agricultural production and help farmers refinance farm mortgages
1933	Securities Act	Superseded state laws and required disclosure to investors
1933	Federal Emergency Relief Act (FERA)	Gave federal grants to states for relief efforts but was later replaced by the Works Progress Administration (WPA)
1933	National Industrial Recovery Act (NIRA)	Established the National Recovery Administration, which regulated businesses in an effort to stabilize the economy and the Public Works Administration (PWA), which the Supreme Court overturned in 1935
1933	Agricultural Adjustment Act (AAA)	Created to limit agricultural products in order to raise prices and pay farmers subsidies not to grow crops but was overturned by the Supreme Court in 1936
1933	Tennessee Valley Authority (TVA)	Created as a regional economic development agency to provide aid and jobs by using centralized planning to prevent river flooding, generate electricity, manufacture fertilizer, and sponsor social programs
1933	Civilian Conservation Corp (CCC)	Assigned young men between the ages of 18 and 25 to public works projects, providing wages that most workers sent home to their families
1934	Securities and Exchange Act	Created the Securities and Exchange Commission, which regulated the trading of stocks and bonds
1934	National Housing Act (NHA)	Created the Federal Housing Authority (FHA), which insured loans made by banks or private lenders
1934	Indian Reorganization Act (IRA)	Reversed many provisions of the Dawes Act and gave Native Americans more control over their governance and assets, particularly land
1935	Works Progress Administration (WPA)	Provided work to millions of Americans through such programs as the National Youth Administration (NYA), the Farm Securities Administration (FSA), and the Federal Theatre Project
1935	National Labor Relations Act (Wagner Act)	Guaranteed workers the right to organize into trade unions freely and to engage in collective bargaining with their employers
1935	Social Security Act	Provided a social safety net for those most in need through such programs as Aid to Families with Dependent Children (AFDC) and the Old-Age Reserve Account, which provided a pension to elderly Americans
1938	Fair Labor Standards Act (Wages and Hours Bill)	Established the 44-hour work week and a national minimum wage and guaranteed "time-and-a-half" for overtime

History without Borders

International Communism in the 1930s

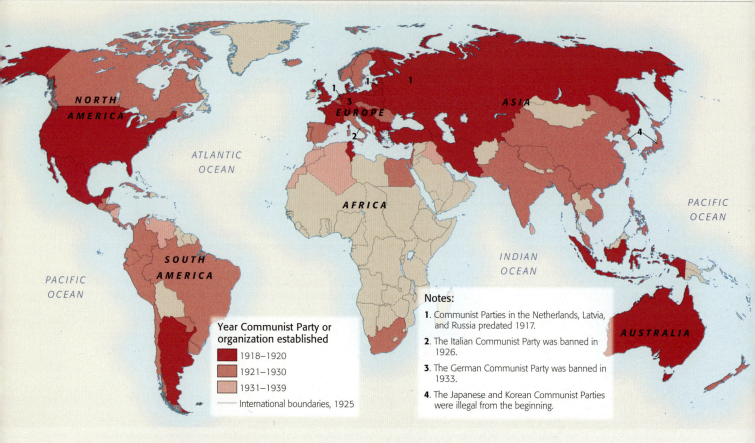

Year Communist Party or organization established

- 1918–1920
- 1921–1930
- 1931–1939
- International boundaries, 1925

Notes:

1. Communist Parties in the Netherlands, Latvia, and Russia predated 1917.

2. The Italian Communist Party was banned in 1926.

3. The German Communist Party was banned in 1933.

4. The Japanese and Korean Communist Parties were illegal from the beginning.

International Communism, 1905–1939 After the 1917 Russian revolution, Communist parties emerged rapidly in other nations. The Communist Party of the United States (CPUSA), established in 1919, was one of the earliest. By the height of the Depression, Communist parties were forceful political voices in suggesting ways to solve the economic downturn. Communism remained a strong political and economic ideology throughout the post–World War II period before declining in popularity. ▲

The global Great Depression gave Communists their best chance to win adherents worldwide since the Russian Revolution of 1917. As trade declined and factories closed, the Communist program of common ownership of production and the ideal of a classless society had a new, almost urgent appeal while capitalism seemed to be faltering. The Communist International (Comintern), a Soviet-led international organization, promoted communism throughout the Western world. In Britain, Communists made gains in trade unions and recruited spies at Cambridge University. In France, the Communist Party attracted workers, artists, and intellectuals.

In the United States, the Communist Party (CPUSA, founded in 1919), together with the Socialist and Socialist Labor parties, drew more than 1 million votes in the 1932 presidential election. The party's membership increased sevenfold from seven thousand five hundred in 1930 to fifty-five thousand in 1940 and, with its much larger following of "fellow travelers" and left-wing liberals, had significant influence in parts of the federal government, the labor movement, and Hollywood. Although the CPUSA gave up its fundamental opposition to capitalism, it continued to cooperate directly with the Soviet Union, and Soviet intelligence received secret reports from at least two hundred agents.

As the Depression deepened, the Communist Party stepped up its appeals to labor unions, university elites, and African Americans, whom the Comintern recognized as an oppressed national group. The party condemned the Scottsboro Trials as a sham and raised funds to appeal the convictions. It backed the Tenants Union, which organized white, African American, and Mexican American sharecroppers to protest the unfair terms and poor living conditions in the South.

But Communist activism also inspired a right-wing reaction. Benito Mussolini's fascist government suppressed Italian Communists, and German Chancellor Adolf Hitler used Communist conspiracies to claim the emergency powers that

May Day Rally in London, 1936 Socialists, Communists, and Popular Front organizations rallied together to show their support for labor rights, socialism, and other progressive issues. Students like those shown in this photo dressed in their finest clothes to publicly push the government to enact policies that would help end the Depression, equalize wealth, institute national health care, and give fair rights to workers. These were not fringe or radical organizations but groups that emerged from earlier progressive movements such as the Fabians. ◀

Female Communists Protest Germany in New York, 1938 Many Americans, particularly Communists, supported the Spanish Republicans, who fought to keep Francisco Franco's right-wing government from coming to power. Some, like these women carrying the Spanish flag in defiance of German intervention, publically protested. Others, like those who joined the Lincoln Brigade, went to fight alongside the Republicans, although the U.S. government prohibited it. These fighters thought of themselves as preserving a republican government against fascist aggression. ◀

made him dictator. By 1935 for capitalist democracies everywhere, fascist dictatorships seemed a more immediate threat than communism. The Communists recognized the threat as well, and the Comintern tempered its aims for world revolution to urge alliances with democratic parties called Popular Fronts. In France, the *Front Populaire* formed a liberal government that countered fascist factions. In China, the United Front joined nationalists and Communists to fight Japanese military aggression. In Spain, when fascist-backed forces attacked the *Frente Popular*, Communists from many countries joined international brigades to put down this right-wing revolt.

Most unexpected was the alliance between Western democracies and

the Communist Soviet Union, which was sealed with Hitler's invasion during World War II. But to Americans who had rallied to the Communist banner in the 1930s, including African Americans Langston Hughes, Richard Wright, and Paul Robeson, the postwar climate was chilling. In the context of Cold War hostility between the Soviet Union and the West, many who had fought against injustice at Scottsboro and against fascists in Spain were charged with "un-Americanism." In 1938, the House Un-American Activities Committee began holding hearings in an effort to find supposed Communist agitators. In 1954, Congress outlawed the CPUSA and made it a crime to be a member.

Critical Thinking Questions

▶ Why did the Soviet Union and the Comintern believe that they could gain adherents in capitalist democracies, such as the United States, during the 1930s?

▶ Why were Popular Front alliances among Communists, liberals, and "fellow travelers" so important to the fight against fascism?

Go to MindTap® to engage with an interactive version of **History without Borders: International Communism in the 1930s.** Learn from an interactive map, view related video, and respond to critical thinking questions.

Communist Party of the United States (CPUSA) Political party advocating centralized government control of the economy as opposed to capitalism.

House Un-American Activities Committee (HUAC) House of Representatives committee created in 1938 to investigate disloyalty and subversive organizations.

National Labor Relations Act (Wagner Act) Law passed in 1935 that protected American workers and allowed them to unionize freely.

Social Security Act New Deal legislation passed in 1935 that protected the elderly, disabled, widowed women, and orphaned children from economic insecurity.

unemployment insurance Payments made by the government to workers who have lost their jobs. The New Deal solidified this entitlement for American workers.

entitlements Government programs, enacted by legislation, that give a defined benefit to a specified group.

Some who challenged the New Deal joined the **Communist Party of the United States (CPUSA)**, which during the Great Depression became the leading leftist organization in the United States. The party courted African Americans with promises of social equality and unemployed workers with promises of economic equality. Unlike the domestic critics of the New Deal, the Communists had international ties. As global tensions mounted, those who sympathized with Communist ideology came under increasing suspicion. Later in the decade, some suspected Communists were called before an early incarnation of the **House Un-American Activities Committee (HUAC)**, where their loyalty to the United States was called into question.

But it was the Supreme Court—not Congress or Roosevelt's critics—who decided the fate of the NIRA and ultimately much of the early New Deal. In May 1935, the Court, in its unanimous decision in *Schechter Poultry v. U.S.*, struck down the NIRA as unconstitutional, citing its centralizing tendencies. Then in early 1936, in a six-to-three decision, the Court struck down the AAA as unconstitutional with much the same reasoning. The London *Daily Express* ran the headline: "America Stunned; Roosevelt's Two Years' Work Killed in Twenty Minutes."

20-2d Second New Deal

The London newspaper's view was an exaggeration. Despite the Supreme Court decisions invalidating sections of early New Deal legislation,

> The Roosevelt administration puts long-term reforms in place.

Roosevelt and Congress were working on even more radical legislation that the Supreme Court would ultimately uphold. Midterm elections in 1934 gave the Democrats control of Congress. Under pressure from his advisers and politicians in his own party, such as New York's senator Robert Wagner, Roosevelt made changes. He abandoned his attempts to cooperate with business and turned his attention to the plight of workers, the unemployed, and the poor. In his State of the Union address for 1935, he reiterated his commitment to placing "the security of the men, women and children of the Nation first." That spring, he used an executive order to create the Works Progress Administration (WPA), which put unemployed individuals to work in federally funded infrastructure,

social, and cultural projects. In summer, he kept Congress in session to pass two landmark laws, the **National Labor Relations Act (Wagner Act)** and the Social Security Act.

The NIRA had given the federal government the authority to regulate prices and wages and had recognized the right of unions to organize and engage in collective bargaining, but there had been no means of enforcement. The Wagner Act provided that means through the National Labor Relations Board, which was given the authority to supervise the election of union representatives and to force employers to bargain in good faith with them. It also outlawed unfair labor practices, among them the company-sponsored unions that industrialists such as John D. Rockefeller Jr. had used to suppress worker-organized unions. The act gave workers power against management and control over their working conditions. It also stimulated rapid growth in union organizing.

The **Social Security Act** sought to alleviate the hardships arising from unemployment, poverty, the death of the family breadwinner, and old age. It had taken shape under the guidance of the Committee on Economic Security chaired by Francis Perkins. Like the earlier Progressive reformers, New Dealers were open to learning from social welfare programs being tried in Europe. The committee spent the summer of 1934 researching European social insurance programs and listening to the ideas of Sir William Beveridge, a British economist who helped shape his nation's social insurance plan.

One provision of the new Social Security law helped fund state programs managing **unemployment insurance**, temporary cash payments to workers who lost their jobs through no fault of their own. Several states had already established these programs, funded largely by taxes on employers. By 1937, all states had similar **entitlement** programs. Another provision provided grants to states to assist blind individuals. The Aid to Dependent Children program was a similar state–federal partnership, providing $1 of federal money for every $2 of state money to help children who had lost one or both parents. The program was an outgrowth of earlier state programs that helped widowed mothers raise their children without having to enter the workforce full-time. On average, each recipient received $18 a month, but because states set benefit amounts, they varied considerably. Southern and western states paid the least. African American and Mexican American children who were concentrated in these regions received lower payments than white children on average.

The main provision of the Society Security Act was an arrangement under which payroll taxes, paid by employers and employees, funded an Old-Age Reserve Account that beginning in 1942 would pay benefits to workers over age 65 who no longer worked. When they began, payments averaged $33 a month although they varied according to how long a worker had been employed. Much to the chagrin of Perkins, the definition of *employment* excluded workers in agriculture, domestic service in a private home, and "casual labor," meaning day labor. Thus, like the Aid to Dependent Children program, Social Security operated in a way that at first largely excluded African Americans and Mexican Americans, who were more likely than white Americans to hold such jobs. It was also a **regressive tax** in that the proportion of wages to be paid into the system was highest for those who made the least.

The Roosevelt administration was careful to portray Social Security as a social insurance program. Although welfare programs in Britain and France were funded by general revenues, Social Security was funded entirely by employers and workers. The arrangement blunted criticism from conservatives that the New Deal was instituting a welfare state, and Social Security proved to be enormously popular. Townsend Plan supporters lobbied for its passage in the belief that Social Security would preserve people's dignity and save them from starvation and homelessness when they aged and left the workforce. The Social Security Act was watershed legislation, implementing a federal responsibility for the well-being of the nation's citizens (see Figure 20.2).

20-2e Election of 1936

As election year approached, a third-party challenge by followers of Roosevelt's critics Long, Coughlin, and Townsend largely disintegrated after Long was assassinated in September 1935 in the Louisiana state capitol. The Republicans nominated Alf Landon, a

{ Roosevelt solidifies his democratic base as he expands New Deal reforms.

candidate with $14 million in campaign funds but no clear program to challenge Roosevelt. In fact, Roosevelt was extraordinarily popular because most Americans felt they were better off than they had been in 1932. He won a landslide victory, capturing 60.8 percent of the popular vote and all but two states in the electoral vote.

The victory was also the result of Roosevelt's explicit bid to solidify his support among minorities and the working class. His reelection marked a political realignment that lasted for decades. Influenced by Mrs. Roosevelt and Ickes, Roosevelt placed African Americans in high-level posts. He named Mary McLeod Bethune, head of the National Council of Negro Women, director of Negro affairs for the WPA's National Youth Administration, which provided assistance and training for unemployed youth. Ickes created a new post, Director of Negro Economics, to help distribute New Deal aid among African American communities. Although they had long supported the party of Lincoln and Emancipation, African Americans shifted their allegiance to the Democrats. Labor leaders, who had worked closely with Labor Secretary Perkins and Senator Wagner to pass the Wagner Act, were also firmly behind Roosevelt. When United Mine Workers (UMW) leader John L. Lewis, a lifelong Republican, switched his allegiance to Roosevelt, he brought union votes with him. Roosevelt owed much of his success to this new coalition.

regressive tax Tax applied uniformly, like a sales tax, that disproportionately burdens the poor; also tax rate that decreases as the amount being taxed increases.

Figure 20.2 Public Expenditures on Social Welfare, 1890–1940 This graph shows how dramatically expenditures on social welfare programs increased both at the federal, state, and local levels. However, only in 1936 did the federal government spend more money than state and local governments combined. This was a trend that would last until 1967, when federal spending exceeded state and local expenditures. That pattern continued through the end of the twentieth century. ▼ Source: Carter, Susan B., Scott Sigmund Gartner, Michael R. Haines, Alan L. Olmstead, Richard Sutch, and Gavin Wright, eds. *Historical Statistics of the United States*, millennial ed. © Cambridge University Press, 2006.

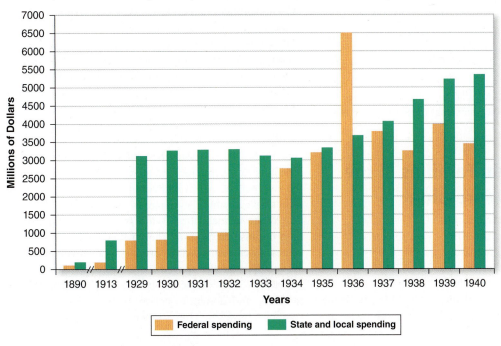

Good Neighbor Policy
Roosevelt's policy of
noninterference in Latin
American affairs to repair
relations and build hemispheric
solidarity.

The beginning of Roosevelt's second term marked the high point of the New Deal. The Democratic Party was united behind the president, whose bold spending and liberal policies appeared to be pulling the nation out of the Depression. In his second inaugural address, Roosevelt committed his administration to continuing its concern for those in need. "I see one-third of a nation," he stated, "ill-housed, ill-clad, and ill-nourished." He also affirmed the capacity of democratic government "to protect its people against disasters once considered inevitable, to solve problems once considered unsolvable."

Roosevelt also addressed growing concerns about international tensions and sought to shore up allies in the Western Hemisphere by his **Good Neighbor Policy**. In describing the United States as peaceful and "a good neighbor among the nations," he not only referred to his efforts in improving relations with Latin America but also implicitly contrasted U.S. democracy with aggressive military regimes in Europe and Asia. A government that does the will of the people, he affirmed, will be "strong among the nations in its example of the will to peace." Roosevelt's second administration would not match the lofty rhetoric of his inaugural address, but, in an increasingly threatening world, his first administration had proved that democracy could prevail.

20-3

Life in the 1930s

During the Great Depression, men who had formerly taken pride in their jobs and their families became tramps—hobos wandering on roads and "riding the rails" in search of work and a free meal. Severed from community and family, they concerned President Roosevelt and other reformers.

Study the man in the photograph. What narrative would you tell about him and how he found himself at this juncture in his life? ▶

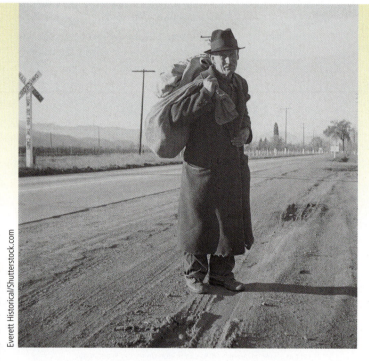

Everett Historical/Shutterstock.com

The economic crisis of the Great Depression caused social and cultural upheaval throughout the nation. Families were torn apart by economic hardship and, in some cases, government policies that failed to help them stay together in their homes and on their farms. Although the Wagner and Social Security acts began to bring some measure of stability to workers and families, labor organizing created conflict. Yet Americans were resilient, appreciating what they did have and enjoying new forms of popular entertainment such as movies and radio.

☞ As you read, consider the ways in which Americans were both displaced and drawn together in the 1930s. What programs brought stability, and what movements and events created strife?

20-3a American Families in the Great Depression

The Depression took a heavy toll on family life. Men thrown out of work often had to leave their families in search of work elsewhere, and some simply walked out on their responsibilities. The Majewski family in Chicago is one example. After Mr. Majewski abandoned

{ Families face overwhelming challenges.

his wife and five children, Mrs. Majewski scrubbed floors. She lost her job, and when she found another, it paid half her former wages. One daughter went to work as a domestic servant. By 1931, the family was making do on their wages and $5 of aid a week from a local private charity. Like many families in the Great Depression, they endured separation. Tensions in families also occurred when extended families had to move in together to save on rent and avoid eviction. Birth rates dropped. Suicide rates rose (see Figure 20.3). Louis Banks, who had moved from Arkansas to Detroit, remembered, "I'd see 'em floatin' on the river where they would commit suicide because they didn't have anything. White guys and colored."

White women often found getting work easier than men because employers believed they could pay women wages lower than what a "primary" breadwinner would accept. Women also moved more easily into poorly paid jobs traditionally defined as female work, such as clerical positions and domestic service. In taking domestic service jobs, however, white women often displaced African

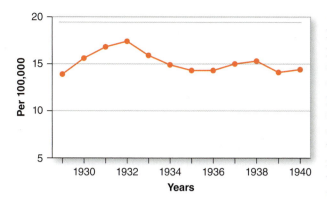

Figure 20.3 Suicides in the Great Depression, 1929–1940
In 1932, at the peak of the Great Depression, the suicide rate in the United States climbed to the highest point (17.4 per 100,000) that it ever had been or would be in the nation's history. In 2013 the suicide rate in the United States was 12.6 per 100,000, having climbed a bit since the recent low in 2000, when it was 10.4 per 100,000. ▲ Source: Carter, Susan B., Scott Sigmund Gartner, Michael R. Haines, Alan L. Olmstead, Richard Sutch, and Gavin Wright, eds. *Historical Statistics of the United States*, millennial ed. © Cambridge University Press, 2006.

American women, who could rarely get any work. Yet for both African American and white families, females were often the sole breadwinner, supporting not only young children but also older relatives. Most elderly people lived in poverty. For those who suffered most in the Great Depression, the New Deal programs that offered relief and jobs, such as Social Security, the CCC, WPA, and NYA, saved and changed lives. They also created new connections between government and the people that gave the most vulnerable, such as the rural New Mexicans whom Cabeza de Baca instructed, a means for sustaining their homes and families.

20-3b Dislocations and Racial Tensions

In March 1931, African American and white teenage boys were "riding the rails" together in a boxcar in Alabama when a fistfight broke out. The white youngsters jumped off the train and complained that a black gang had attacked them. At the next stop, two white women who had also been on the train accused the black teenagers of rape. Nine black teens were arrested and jailed. A mob formed, and only the bravery of the local sheriff kept them from being lynched. The prisoners were moved to the nearby town of Scottsboro for the first of a series of trials that would capture national and international attention.

In the first of the **Scottsboro Trials**, all but one (a thirteen-year-old) were convicted of rape and sentenced to death. Although the NAACP and ACLU denounced the hasty trial, the Communist Party took the case as its own and, through its legal arm, the International Labor Defense

> Extreme economic hardship pushes people from their homes and into conflict.

(ILD), appealed the verdicts and publicized the cases internationally. The party also used the Scottsboro Trials as a way to appeal to African Americans who were sympathetic to its support for workers, antiracist stance, and strong defense of the young men. Two cases went to the Supreme Court, which ruled that the defendants had not received fair trials because effective legal defense had not been provided and because African Americans were routinely excluded from juries. Ultimately, four were acquitted, but five served various prison terms. The racism of the U.S. legal system had been exposed to worldwide condemnation.

Scarcity increased racial tensions not only in the South but everywhere. In the cities of the Northeast, Puerto Ricans faced discrimination in the distribution of relief, and between 1929 and 1934, more than ten thousand of them returned to the island in search of work and aid. Although the federal government had created relief and reconstruction administrations for Puerto Rico, their programs were underfunded and could not meet the overwhelming needs of the island's population.

In southern California during the 1930s, the presence of the many Mexican Americans on relief rolls created tensions. Although most were citizens, Los Angeles officials proposed their **repatriation** across the border to

Scottsboro Trials Series of trials in Alabama from 1931 to 1937 in which nine black youths were unjustly convicted of rape. The trials drew worldwide condemnation of racial injustice.

repatriation Process of returning people to their home country. In the 1930s, Mexican Americans were forcibly repatriated to reduce relief rolls in the Southwest.

Mexican Family on the Road, 1936 This photo by Dorothea Lange shows Mexican American family members with a broken-down car as they look for work picking peas in California. Mexican American families faced not only the threat of deportation or removal across the border but also discrimination, which often prevented them from attaining the few jobs available during the Depression. Like the Okies fleeing the Dust Bowl, Mexican American families were forced onto the road to look for work. ▲ Library of Congress Prints and Photographs Division [LC-USZ62-131733].

Dust Bowl Severe dust storms on the Great Plains in the 1930s caused by drought and harmful farming practices. Thousands lost their farms and homes.

general strike Work stoppage in one union or industry that workers in other industries join in sympathy.

Mexico. In the beginning, the city offered free train tickets or cash to those families willing to move. When this policy proved ineffective, local law enforcement agencies with the help of Anglo vigilantes began forcible roundups. In one incident, local police and federal agents closed off a park that had drawn many Mexican American families to its green spaces and then asked each person for proof of citizenship. Of the four hundred people in the park that day, more than a dozen were deported to Mexico. Well-publicized incidents such as this had a chilling effect on all Mexican Americans, who wondered if they would be next. Between 1929 and 1945, more than half a million people, including many U.S. citizens, were moved across the border to Mexico.

Tensions over relief to people in California were further complicated by the mass migration of farmer families from the Great Plains, driven from their homes by drought and dust storms. The drought was most severe in the region that came to be known as the **Dust Bowl** (see Map 20.2). Starting in 1930, the rain stopped, crops dried up, and livestock and people baked and died. In 1936, a year in which *Newsweek* described the country as "a vast simmering cauldron," more than forty-five hundred people died from heat and dehydration. Financial losses associated with the drought in 1934 alone amounted to half of what the nation had spent on World War I. In 1936, the drought was costing farmers $25 million a day, and 2 million farm families were on relief.

Compounding the impact of the drought were strong winds that swept the desiccated soil up into the jet stream and transported it as far away as the North Atlantic. The dust storms lasted from 1931 until 1937, but the worst ones came in 1935. Black Sunday, April 14, 1935, started out as a clear spring Sunday morning, but by afternoon a monstrous dark blizzard appeared on the northern horizon. The dust storm trapped people in their cars, in stranger's homes, and in any makeshift shelter they could find.

Unable to farm or even to stay in their homes, families took to the road, creating one of the largest internal migrations in U.S. history. Some moved as individuals, some as families, and sometimes whole communities picked up and resettled as did five hundred families from the eastern plains of Colorado. The most desperate and adventurous set out for California, moving along Route 66 toward what they hoped would be paradise. In one year, more than eighty-six thousand people resettled in California, more than had arrived in the two years after the gold rush of 1849. But even in California, there were no jobs and no relief monies for them. Like Mexican Americans and other minorities, these "Okies" and "Arkies" from Oklahoma and Arkansas were despised and feared.

20-3c Industrial Conflict

The Wagner Act gave laboring men and women protections they had never had, and probably had been passed just in time to stave off both labor violence and the appeal of communism. Although trade unions in Europe had at times been powerful enough to call **general strikes**, involving workers in many industries

> Workers are emboldened by New Deal reforms to push for better conditions and higher pay.

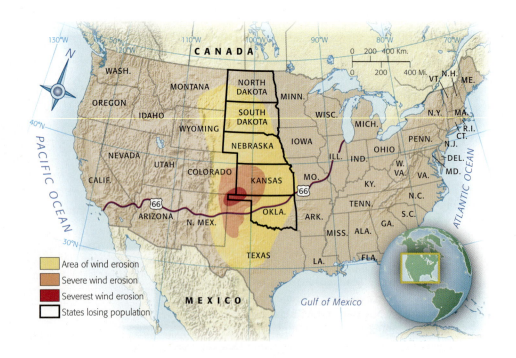

Map 20.2 The Dust Bowl, 1934–1940 While most of the country suffered from drought, these twelve midwestern states experienced the lowest precipitation on record. With the drought came intense heat with temperatures above 110 degrees. Accompanying dust storms wiped out almost 5 million acres of wheat: half of the crop in Kansas, one-quarter in Oklahoma, and all in Nebraska. These storms blew away twice as much earth as had been removed to create the Panama Canal. ▶

Flint Sit-Down Strike, 1936 These men, members of the United Auto Workers (UAW), went out on strike during the 1936 Christmas season. By refusing to work or to physically leave the Fisher Body Plant Number 1, which contained the dyes for GM's 1937 models, this small group of workers almost completely halted GM production. News of this successful strike spread through the auto industry and ushered in a new era of powerful unions. ▲

Rapport Press/Newscom

that shut down regions or even a nation, labor in the United States had not been so well organized. During the first years of the Depression, most workers had endured layoffs and firings without protest. But in 1934, West Coast longshoremen turned militant under the leadership of Harry Bridges, an Australian unionist with ties to the Communist Party. They went out on strike on May 9, 1934, blockading the transport of goods from the docks by rail. When in July the Industrial Association, a coalition of business owners, sought to break the strike by moving goods by truck, violence erupted; dozens were severely wounded and two men killed. The Teamsters and other powerful unions in the Bay Area then joined the longshoremen in a general strike that shut down commerce in San Francisco for four days before both sides agreed to arbitration.

Following passage of the Wagner Act, unions renewed their organizing efforts. The increase in union membership and power was dramatic. Soon Lewis's UMW made sure that more than 90 percent of the nation's coal was mined under union contracts. He also took the lead in founding the **Congress of Industrial Organizations (CIO)**, which challenged the American Federation of Labor (AFL) by organizing workers by industry instead of by trade and opening its ranks to women and ethnic minorities. The increasing power of industrial labor was dramatically symbolized in a fistfight at an AFL convention,

when Lewis punched the leader of the carpenters' union and sent him writhing on the floor.

The CIO rapidly unionized workers in the steel and automobile industries and began to organize transnationally into Latin America, particularly Mexico. In Flint, Michigan, a city dominated by General Motors, the local United Auto Workers (UAW) counted only one hundred twenty-two members when it launched a **sit-down strike** in December 1936. Instead of calling on the National Guard to break the strike, as happened so often in the nineteenth century, Michigan's governor called out the National Guard to protect the striking workers. In February 1937, GM agreed to negotiate with the workers, and Chrysler soon followed. Within a few months, the UAW's membership grew from 98,000 to 400,000 workers. The success of the strike showed reluctant workers the immense power of unions, which could win higher wages and better working conditions for them. At no other time in U.S. history were workers as free to organize unions as they were then, protected by federal legislation that allowed them to bargain fairly with their employers. Nevertheless, the Roosevelt administration remained cool to the pressures of the CIO, which it regarded as potentially threatening to the New Deal's more moderate agenda for labor. In the 1940 election, Lewis publically withdrew his support from Roosevelt.

20-3d A New Deal for Indians

Indians in general, and in particular the groups that Cabeza de Baca served, had been in a precarious economic situation since the end of the nineteenth century. Long before the Depression began, they suffered the highest poverty level, the worst health, and the highest unemployment of any Americans. Although they had made significant population gains since their nadir in 1891, when the federal government had removed most of them to reservations, they had the highest infant mortality rate and suffered from tuberculosis, whooping cough, and other communicable diseases at proportions far above the national average. Almost one-third of Indians lived in poverty in 1930, with no means of support.

> Reforms benefit Indian communities.

New Deal policies regarding Indians highlighted arguments that had been raging among Washington bureaucrats as well as among Indians themselves about how they should be incorporated into the modern world. Since the 1887 Dawes Act, Indians had struggled to find a way to modernize while maintaining their ties to tradition. Meanwhile, the federal policy of assimilation, including the Indian Citizenship Act of 1924, had forced many onto reservations and small parcels of land so they

Congress of Industrial Organizations (CIO) Umbrella organization of unions founded in 1935 representing workers, often unskilled, by industry rather than by trade.

sit-down strike Work stoppage in which workers stay at their work stations but refuse to work until their demands are met, preventing management from hiring strikebreakers.

could be farmers. The New Deal for Indians reversed this decades-long policy. Under the Indian Reorganization Act of 1934 (IRA), allotment, boarding schools, and assimilation as a goal were replaced by a program that fostered local control, encouraged the scientific management of land and water resources, and put governance in the hands of tribal councils, although many decisions were still subject to approval by the Department of the Interior. By the end of the New Deal, one hundred seventy-four tribes (about one hundred thirty-two thousand people) had passed referendums voting for reorganization and created constitutions to govern themselves.

John Collier, Roosevelt's choice to head the Bureau of Indian Affairs, spearheaded the legislation and took funds from existing New Deal programs to cobble together the Indian New Deal. Collier had been advocating on behalf of Native Americans for a decade before his appointment, and the IRA was his way of bringing those progressive changes to completion. He redirected more than $5 million from the CCC budget to provide for infrastructure projects on reservations that employed young Indian men. States also allocated monies for cooperative extension programs that directed aid to Native American communities, such as the one for which Cabeza de Baca worked in New Mexico. The seventy-three tribes (about seventy-eight thousand people) that rejected the IRA continued to operate under the federal government's previous terms.

20-3e Public Works and Popular Culture

With the Wagner and Social Security acts, the federal government touched the lives of ordinary Americans as never before. So did a series of projects that dammed and transformed America's rivers, created reservoirs, brought electricity to rural Americans, and changed agriculture through irrigation. Through monies that came from Hoover's RFC, the PWA, the TVA, and later New Deal legislation, the federal government spearheaded the largest public works projects in the nation's history, building sewers, bridges, schools, airports, and highways and making improvements in national parks.

> The New Deal encourages the creation of public goods that all Americans can enjoy.

With RFC funding, Boulder (later renamed Hoover) Dam, whose construction had begun under the Hoover administration, best exemplifies the planning, labor practices, consolidation of capital, and government intervention that marked these dam-building projects in the West. Costing $114 million and employing more than five thousand people over the course of the project, the fifty-story-high structure managed the Colorado River's erratic flow and generated four times the hydroelectric power of Niagara Falls. A group of ambitious businessmen, the Six Companies, won the bid for the project, and although none had ever managed such a large endeavor, they finished the dam in 1936, two years ahead of schedule and under budget, epitomizing the benefits of massive centralized government investment.

Perhaps no area was transformed as much as the South following the establishment of the TVA in May 1933 (see section 20-2b). It was part of a regional planning project that combined water resource management through dams with rural electrification, fertilizer production, and, reforestation, and aid for the rural poor. Before the TVA, less than 5 percent of farms in the region had electricity, but eventually, more than 90 percent had it. Families also had access to educational programs similar to those Cabeza de Baca offered in New Mexico. Men found work on the major dam projects and in facilities producing nitrate fertilizers at Muscle Shoals, Alabama. New Dealers saw projects such as the TVA, the Columbia Basin River project, and the dams along the Missouri River in the upper Midwest as a way to bring prosperity and comforts to farmers and rural Americans.

In the course of their work, many WPA writers and artists critiqued both the capitalist system that had allowed the Depression to occur and the federal government's response to the crisis. For example, filmmaker Pare Lorentz's visually stunning short film, *The Plow That Broke the Plains*, held capitalism, global demand for wheat, and overuse of the land responsible for the Dust Bowl. Dorothea Lange, one of the most prolific photographers employed by the Farm Security Administration, produced thousands of images depicting a cross-section of Americans. Whether it was a photograph of a Mexican American family being repatriated or a defeated migrant mother nursing her child in a labor camp, Lange put a real face on poverty in the United States. She wanted people to see themselves in these haunting images, and the Roosevelt administration used them to rally support for the New Deal's more liberal and redistributive aspects.

Art commissioned for private collectors sometimes had a different fate. A mural created by the Mexican artist Diego Rivera for New York City's Rockefeller Center was covered and then destroyed when Nelson Rockefeller objected to the Communist themes and the likeness of Lenin. Rivera returned to Mexico to create a smaller version of the mural, *Man at the Crossroads* with its praise for labor and Communist ideas. His mural for the Detroit Institute of Arts was also an ode to America's multiracial workforce. Edsel Ford, whose family had funded the institute and the mural, defended Rivera's work.

While artists such as Lange and Rivera critiqued capitalism, most Americans found comfort in popular culture. They flocked to movie theaters to see Hollywood films that, for a few hours, allowed them to escape the difficulties in their own lives. Charlie Chaplin and the Marx

Alfred Eisenstaedt/The Life Picture Collection/Getty Images

Global Americans **Paul Robeson**, son of an escaped slave, football All-American at Rutgers University, Phi Beta Kappa, and class valedictorian, seemed destined for success. He gravitated to the theater and, during the heyday of the Harlem Renaissance, became famous as an actor and singer known for his gift for oration and his resonating voice. At a time when few serious roles were open to African Americans, he starred in Eugene O'Neill's *Emperor Jones* and sang "Ol' Man River" in the musical *Showboat,* both later made into popular movies. During the 1920s and 1930s, Robeson often lived and performed in London, where he starred in *Othello,* a role he could not have performed in the United States. In London, he associated with leftist radicals, became interested in Africa, and was drawn to anticolonialism and communism. Visiting the Soviet Union in 1934, he extolled the lack of racial bias. "Here I am not a Negro but a human being," he remarked. "Here, for the first time in my life I walk in full human dignity." But in the United States, Robeson's Communist ties made him suspect. In the 1940s, he was investigated by the Federal Bureau of Investigation and the House Un-American Activities Committee and was blacklisted in Hollywood. In the 1950s, the State Department refused to renew his passport, thus preventing him from touring internationally. Although these restraints were later lifted, Robeson's career seemed tarnished in the United States even as he was welcomed abroad.

Brothers emerged from the silent era, and new stars such as Claudette Colbert and a young Katherine Hepburn introduced the age of romantic comedies. Americans also listened to the radio. The soap opera emerged in this era, taking its name from sponsors selling soaps, such as Palmolive and Procter & Gamble. First broadcast in 1937, *The Guiding Light* became a staple for millions of American women who turned on the radio. When it moved to television in 1956, its audience seamlessly followed the Spaulding and Bauer families in the fictional town of Springfield. Through movies, radio, and best-selling novels, such as *Gone with the Wind*, Americans across the country began to share a common culture that crossed class and racial boundaries.

Diego Rivera, *Man, Controller of the Universe*, Mexico 1934 This is a re-creation of Rivera's mural at Rockefeller Center in New York City. Abby Aldrich Rockefeller was an admirer of Rivera, one of the most famous artists of his time. However, Rivera's depiction of Vladimir Lenin and other anticapitalist imagery in the mural proved controversial. Amid protests, the mural was destroyed and replaced by *American Progress*, a mural featuring Abraham Lincoln. ▼

Artepics/Alamy Stock Photo

20-4

End of the New Deal and the Approach of War

In this cartoon titled "Isn't This What We Really Want?" the editorial cartoonist known as Herblock humorously depicts the debate over U.S. neutrality as world conflict increases. He suggested that the Roosevelt administration was attempting to solve all kinds of problems and to appease people both domestically and abroad.

What does the image suggest about the complexities and contradictions of U.S. neutrality policies in this era? ▶

Isn't This What We Really Want?

A NEUTRALITY ACT THAT WILL KEEP US OUT OF ANY WAR,

WILL INSURE THE CONTINUITY OF AMERICAN COMMERCE,

WILL ACT TO CURB THE POWER OF THE DICTATORSHIPS,

AND WILL SCRUB FLOORS AND DO THE DISHES IN ITS SPARE TIME.

Library of Congress Prints and Photographs Division[LC-DIG-ppmsc-03387]

After the landslide victory in 1936, the Roosevelt administration appeared to have unlimited power to push more programs for recovery. Moreover, Roosevelt and his advisers believed that because the economy was on the upturn, they could attempt to balance the budget and reduce their reliance on deficit spending, which the president had never liked or intended as a long-term solution to the economic crisis. They misjudged, however, and the administration made a number of strategic mistakes that put presidential authority and the economy in jeopardy. Moreover, as hostilities engulfed both Europe and Asia, the Roosevelt administration and Americans in general had to confront the prospect of war.

☞ As you read, consider the national and international concerns that Roosevelt faced in his second term. How did the economic turmoil of the 1930s contribute to the rising conflict in Europe and Asia?

20-4a Setbacks to the New Deal

Roosevelt worried most about what he called his "Court problem"—the Supreme Court rulings that had invalidated much of the early New Deal legislation. He wanted more influence, if not control, over future Court decisions to ensure the permanence of his legislative agenda. Less than two weeks after his 1937 inauguration, he shocked Congress and the public with a proposal for reorganizing the judicial branch of government, citing the need for efficiency and the principle of mandatory retirement. He proposed that the president appoint a new justice when one who had served for ten years did not retire within six months of turning seventy. This would also apply to judges of lower federal courts. Under this plan, Roosevelt would have been able to appoint six new justices to the Supreme Court immediately.

{ Roosevelt makes missteps as he seeks to increase his presidential powers.

Court-packing plan
Roosevelt's 1937 attempt to reorganize the judicial branch so that the constitutionality of New Deal laws would be decided by a more favorable set of judges.

It was not only the content of the bill that angered its opponents but also the imperious way in which Roosevelt presented it, without consultation. Opponents, many of them Democrats, saw what they called his **Court-packing plan** as an attack on the judicial branch that overstepped the constitutional boundaries of the presidency. Chief Justice Charles Evans Hughes composed a scathing letter to Roosevelt detailing the working of his court and revealing Roosevelt's "efficiency" argument as a sham.

The legislation lagged in Congress, and, in the meantime, the Court made some adjustments of its own. In a series of five-to-four decisions in the spring of 1937, the Court began to validate key pieces of New Deal legislation, such as the Wagner Act. Then on May 18, Justice Willis Van Devanter announced his retirement, and Roosevelt nominated Hugo Black to the bench. Eventually, retirements enabled Roosevelt to appoint five justices during his second term, and the plan for judicial reorganization died, but the New Deal coalition that had emerged during the 1936 presidential election had been damaged. Subsequently, the Democrats found it difficult to pass liberal reform legislation. They abandoned a plan to take up universal health care in 1937, although they did pass the Fair Labor Standards Act in 1938 that established a minimum wage and maximum number of work hours.

In the midst of the political crisis over the Court-packing plan, the nation experienced another economic downturn in the fall of 1937. Earlier that year, the economy had pulled above 1929 levels of output, and, as complete recovery seemed imminent, Roosevelt began to cut funding to balance the federal budget. He slashed

Paul G. Hallett Looking for Work, 1937 The plight of men such as that of Mr. Hallett during the Roosevelt Recession unnerved Americans who worried about both the sagging economy and tensions abroad. The renewed depression was caused by the federal government's attempts to balance the budget by cutting back spending programs. The growth in the global economy caused by the buildup to war, however, stimulated growth both at home and abroad as companies sought to meet the emerging wartime demands. ▲

the budget of the WPA and eliminated whole programs. Quite suddenly, the economy sank. Because the $2 billion collected in taxes for the new Social Security program was also withdrawn from the economy, one critic noted, "Not only is the government not priming the economic pump, they are taking some water out of the spout." This so-called **Roosevelt Recession** was not as severe as the 1929 downturn, but it unnerved Americans.

In 1938, 19 percent of Americans were out of work, 5 percent higher than in 1936. Between October 1937 and the spring of 1938, applications for WPA jobs soared 194 percent in Toledo and 434 percent in Detroit. In Cleveland, sixty-five thousand people were on the relief roles, unable to find food or housing. Children rummaged through garbage cans looking for spoiled produce. Many compared Roosevelt to Hoover, offering little more than a calculated and conservative response to an immense crisis.

The combination of the Court-packing plan and the recession left Roosevelt unable to work with Congress because Democrats distanced themselves from him. For the next three years, federal action on the economy stalled, and some suggested that having 5–9 million people out of work might be the new "normal" economy. In the end, however, the Depression ended not so much because of government intervention but by events in Europe and Asia that stimulated a massive military buildup.

20-4b Global Dangers

Centralized economic planning had pulled Germany out of depression by the mid-1930s, aided by increased military spending following Hitler's renunciation of the

{ *Threats from militarist regimes worry Americans and the Roosevelt administration.*

Treaty of Versailles's disarmament clauses in May 1935. The next year, his troops marched into the Rhineland in defiance of the treaty, which had established that region between Germany and France as a demilitarized zone. In October 1935, Mussolini's Italian troops invaded Ethiopia, the East African nation that had resisted an Italian takeover in 1896. This time, with superior weapons and planes that sprayed outlawed poison gas on civilians, the Italians easily overpowered the Ethiopians. It was clear to Roosevelt that the fascist dictatorships were embarking on dangerous military aggressions (see Map 20.3), especially after Italy and Germany signed a treaty of friendship in 1936 that Mussolini called the Rome-Berlin Axis. In 1937, Mussolini withdrew Italy from the League of Nations as Germany and Japan had already done (see Table 21.1).

The League was clearly weakened by such defections, and its response to Italy's takeover of Ethiopia only highlighted its lack of power. Although it briefly imposed economic sanctions on Italy, it did not provide collective security for Ethiopia. In May 1936, Haile Selassie, emperor of Ethiopia, fled the country. A month later, he implored the League to denounce the Italian invasion of his country: "It is us today. It will be you tomorrow." But the plea was ignored, and when Mussolini made Ethiopia an Italian colony, only six nations, including the United States and China, refused to recognize its status.

Then in July 1936, Spain plunged into a civil war that further aggravated the growing hostilities in Europe. The Nationalists—a coalition of conservative Catholics, landowners, soldiers, and businessmen—rebelled against the leftist Republican government and sought to institute a fascist state. They received troops and military equipment from Germany and Italy as in order to expand fascism and intimidate Britain and France. The Soviet Union and Mexico sent military assistance to the Republicans. In April 1939, the Nationalists prevailed, and General Francisco Franco established a long-lasting right-wing dictatorship.

Roosevelt Recession
Economic downturn of 1937–1938 believed to have been caused by government's pullback on deficit spending and the implementation of Social Security.

Map 20.3 Axis Aggression in Europe, 1933–1939 In the midst of the global depression, the militarized regimes of Benito Mussolini in Italy and Adolf Hitler in Germany pushed aggressively to acquire more territory. During this time period, Mussolini seized Ethiopia and Albania and Hitler annexed Austria and Czechoslovakia. Both supported the establishment of a fascist regime in Spain. This military expansion went unanswered by Britain and France until Hitler menaced Poland. His invasion there brought declarations of war from the Western democracies and began World War II. ▲

In July 1937, the Japanese launched an undeclared war on China, capturing Shanghai, Peking (now Beijing), and Nanjing before the end of the year. In Nanjing, obeying orders to "kill all captives," Japanese soldiers massacred more than three hundred thousand civilians and raped eighty thousand women. By the end of 1938, the Japanese held most of China's seaports and seemed intent on regional domination (see Map 20.4).

U.S. policy makers responded cautiously to the crisis in China. With ongoing global economic instability, Roosevelt did not want to jeopardize U.S. trade with either China or Japan. In an October 1937 speech, he had called for a "quarantine" of aggressor states. He was privately considering economic sanctions against Japan but took no further action and accepted a Japanese apology for bombing the U.S. gunboat *Panay* on the Yangtze River while it was evacuating Americans from Nanjing. Despite the massacre of Chinese civilians, Roosevelt was certain the Americans would not support going to war against Japan at this time. While helping the Chinese Nationalists buy U.S. military equipment to use against both the Communists and the Japanese, U.S. officials continued supplying Japan with nearly half of its imports, including oil, cars, iron, and steel. This delicate balance of political interests and economic imperatives proved impossible to sustain.

20-4c U.S. Neutrality

Recognizing the volatile international situation and convinced the United States would need more allies in the event of war, Roosevelt had already sought to improve U.S.–Latin American relations and promote hemispheric solidarity through the Good Neighbor Policy. This arrangement renounced the military interventionism that had punctuated U.S. actions in the region for decades. In 1934, U.S. officials had repealed the Platt Amendment, which had authorized U.S. meddling in Cuban affairs since 1901. By 1936, all U.S. troops had been removed from the Caribbean, although U.S. officials retained control over customs collections and some military bases. U.S. companies still dominated local production of sugar, cotton, coffee, and bananas. To improve trade, Secretary of State Cordell Hull launched the Export-Import Bank to extend credit for foreign purchases of American products. In 1938, when the Mexican government confiscated the properties of foreign oil companies, Roosevelt overruled calls for U.S. intervention in favor of a negotiated settlement. These changes proved economically beneficial. From 1933 to 1938, the value of U.S. exports to Latin America increased from $244 million to $642 million.

Although most Americans supported close ties with Latin America, they also opposed engagement in overseas conflicts, remembering the sacrifices of the Great War. Influenced by the best seller, *Merchants of Death* (1934), many people interpreted U.S. participation in that war as manipulated by the industrialists and bankers who profited from it. Congressional hearings led by Republican

> As world conflict intensifies, most Americans want to remain neutral.

senator Gerald Nye of North Dakota called on the financier J. P. Morgan Jr. and the industrialist Pierre du Pont to account for their roles as businessmen in World War I. With little evidence to substantiate its allegations, the Nye Committee concluded that U.S. bankers and munitions makers had dragged the United States into war in pursuit of profit. Already disdainful of business leaders because of the economic crisis, most Americans accepted these accusations, reinforcing the general isolationist sentiment, strong since the 1920s.

Determined not to replicate the same errors that had entangled the United States in World War I, Nye introduced a bill outlawing arms sales to nations at war and warning Americans traveling on combatants' ships that they did so at their own risk. In August 1935, Congress passed his **Neutrality Acts** and extended it in February 1936, adding a ban on loans and credits to belligerents. In May 1937, Congress made the first two acts permanent, expanding them to cover civil wars and prohibiting U.S. ships from transporting passengers or cargo to combatant states. Private U.S. citizens were also forbidden to travel on belligerent ships.

Roosevelt signed the Neutrality Acts and invoked them to prevent arms and ammunition shipments to either side during the Ethiopian crisis and the Spanish Civil War. But U.S. neutrality also drew criticism from constituencies sympathetic to belligerents in both conflicts. In 1935, W.E.B. Du Bois described Italy's seizure of Ethiopia as one more instance of white imperialism and aggression against "the dark peoples." He also warned that Japan "is regarded by all colored peoples as their logical leader, the one non-white nation that has escaped forever the dominance and exploitation of the white world." Leftist supporters of Spain's Republican government also charged that Roosevelt had betrayed democracy, and some three thousand Americans volunteered to fight for Spain's defense. Vocal congressional leaders, on the other hand, were outraged when Roosevelt did not invoke the Neutrality Acts in Japan's war against China but continued to trade with both belligerents.

Whereas economic and geopolitical imperatives shaped Roosevelt's approach to neutrality, he privately wanted to aid Britain and France should war break out in Europe. With the long view in mind and on the advice of Bernard Baruch, in 1937 he convinced Congress to amend the Neutrality Acts to include a two-year "cash-and-carry" provision that permitted the sale of nonmilitary items to combatants as long as they paid cash for the items and transported them. It was clearly intended to benefit Britain and France, which could meet these terms, over Germany, which could not. In 1939, the act was made permanent.

Neutrality Acts Series of laws passed in the late 1930s to prevent direct U.S. involvement in international conflicts.

Map 20.4 Japanese Invasion of China, 1934–1938 The militarist regime in Japan seized Manchuria from China in 1931 and in 1937 launched a full-scale attack on China. Japan's expansionist program aimed to secure natural resources and dominate East Asia. During their occupation of China, the Japanese set up large farming and industrial operations and forced millions of Chinese to work in these enterprises. The Chinese people suffered harsh treatment and brutal conditions, and hundreds of thousands were massacred at Nanjing. ▲

Jewish Refugees Disembarking from the *SS St. Louis*, Belgium, 1939 Two weeks earlier, these passengers had been turned away from Cuba as they sought to escape the Nazis. Most possessed visas, but Cuba had changed its laws while the boat was at sea. Captain Gustav Schroeder negotiated with both the Cuban and U.S. governments to allow the ship to discharge its passengers. The boat sailed along the Florida coast but was not allowed to dock and returned to Europe. Historians estimate that about 250 of the 937 passengers died in the Holocaust. ◄

20-4d Europe in Crisis

In the late 1930s, Hitler intensified his campaign to rid Germany of Jews. Yet Jews who were desperate to leave Germany and Austria found that few nations would receive them. Unwilling to accept immigrants who might be an additional burden on the already fragile economy, U.S. officials did not adjust the 1924 immigration quotas to permit entrance of these refugees. These quotas, combined with pervasive anti-Semitism in the State Department, made it difficult for Jews to obtain U.S. visas. In July 1938, Roosevelt convened (but did not attend) a conference to address the growing Jewish refugee crisis. Delegates from thirty-two nations met at Évian-les-Bains, France, but most of the represented countries refused to accept large numbers of refugees.

> Nazi Germany persecutes Jews and embarks on conquest.

In September, after a young Jewish refugee murdered a German diplomat in Paris, the Nazis escalated their attacks. On November 9–10, later known as *Kristallnacht* (Night of Broken Glass), they destroyed Jewish property throughout Germany and Austria, fined Jews $400 million for the damage, and sent thirty thousand Jews to concentration camps at Buchenwald and Dachau. News of the violence and detentions swept the world, but Western nations were still reluctant to take more Jewish émigrés.

Emboldened by the lack of a concerted global response to his remilitarization efforts and his intervention in Spain, Hitler launched an ambitious plan to conquer Europe. Seeking first to absorb nations with large populations of ethnic Germans, he had seized neighboring Austria in 1938. He then demanded to annex the Sudetenland, a province of Czechoslovakia with 3 million people of German descent. Meeting in Munich in September 1938, British and French leaders acceded to this demand in exchange for a promise that Hitler would not annex any more Czech territory. The Czech government was not invited to the proceedings.

Upon returning to England, British prime minister Neville Chamberlain announced that the Munich agreement ensured "peace in our time." But the strategy of what came to be known as **appeasement** backfired when just six months later, Hitler seized the rest of Czechoslovakia. In April 1939, Mussolini invaded Albania. The following month Germany and Italy—the **Axis Powers**—formalized their military alliance. A new crisis in Poland soon erupted when Hitler demanded Danzig, a free city under the protection of the League of Nations. Determined not to surrender their access to the Baltic Sea, the Polish government resisted Hitler's desire to control the port. The British and French, recognizing that appeasement had failed, vowed to support Poland.

Fearing German expansionism and dismayed when the British and French rebuffed his attempts to form alliances, Soviet premier Stalin directed his foreign minister to get guarantees from Germany. Despite their diametrically opposed political ideologies, the two nations signed a non-aggression pact on August 23, 1939. It included secret protocols that divided Romania, Poland, Lithuania, Latvia, Estonia, and Finland into German and Soviet spheres of influence. On September 1, German troops invaded Poland. Two days later, Britain and France declared war on Germany. On September 17, Soviet troops invaded Poland from the east. World War II was under way, and the U.S. commitment to neutrality was to be severely tested.

appeasement Diplomatic policy that makes concessions to an aggressive foreign power in order to avoid military conflict.

Axis Powers Alliance of Germany, Italy, and Japan that fought in World War II against the Allied nations of the United States, Britain, France, Poland, and later the Soviet Union.

Summary

Although the crash of the U.S. stock market in October 1929 was the most dramatic signal of a global depression, it was only one aspect of the worldwide economic downturn. Americans, as well as Europeans, Asians, and Latin Americans, faced the loss of jobs, homes, and lifetime savings as industrial production and trade declined and nations turned inward in search of security.

In the United States, families suffered from the Depression in differing degrees, based on whether they lived in cities or in rural areas, were old or young, were male or female, or were white or people of color. Although the New Deal never met the expectations of the liberal reformers who wanted a complete restructuring of the economy and a redistribution of wealth, it was not the radical overhaul that conservatives feared.

In the end, the New Deal was a set of moderate reforms that provided relief, shored up the economy, and kept Americans from turning to more radical solutions that were evident elsewhere, such as national socialism in Germany, communism in the Soviet Union, and militarism in Japan. The New Deal also put in place a set of programs such as Social Security, protections for workers and unions, farm supports and subsidies, and infrastructure projects that would have a long-term impact on the economy and individual lives. These pieces of New Deal legislation were the foundation for the modern welfare state, entitlements for individuals, and government contracts that would come to dominate twentieth-century American life.

The end of the Second New Deal and the Roosevelt Recession of 1937 raised questions about the effectiveness of New Deal reforms. At the same time, overseas conflicts strengthened Congress's resolve that the United States should remain neutral. Roosevelt cautiously tried to preserve U.S. neutrality even as German, Italian, and Japanese aggression made another world war seem inevitable.

‹Thinking Back, *Looking Forward*›

As you review this chapter, think about the role of the federal government in bringing about reforms that regulated markets and aided struggling Americans. What made the New Deal so different from earlier attempts at reform, such as those in the Progressive era? Why did the New Deal mark a turning point in how Americans viewed their relationship with the federal government? Keep New Deal reforms in mind when you study the Great Society reforms of the 1960s in later chapters. How was the New Deal different from economic programs to end the Depression in other parts of the world?

To make your study concrete, review the timeline and reflect on the entries there. Think about their causes, consequences, and connections. How do they fit with global trends?

Additional Resources

Books

Brinkley, Alan. *Voices of Protest: Huey Long, Father Coughlin, and the Great Depression.* New York: Vintage Press, 1982. ▶ Award-winning book examining the opposition to Roosevelt's New Deal.

Cohen, Lizabeth. *Making a New Deal: Industrial Workers in Chicago, 1919–1939.* New York: Cambridge University Press, 1991. ▶ Engaging study about the families who struggled during both the "roaring twenties" and the Great Depression.

Gilmore, Glenda Elizabeth. *Defying Dixie: The Radical Roots of the Civil Rights Movement, 1919–1950.* New York: Norton, 2008. ▶ Compelling stories of those who worked within radical organizations such as the CPUSA to push for civil rights.

Gordon, Linda. *Dorothea Lange: A Life Beyond Limits.* New York: Norton Press, 2009. ▶ Award-winning biography of perhaps the greatest U.S. photographer and the historical context in which she worked.

Katznelson, Ira. *Fear Itself: The New Deal and the Origins of Our Time.* New York: Norton, 2013. ▶ Argument that the New Deal was based on a general sense of fear in order to pull the nation through the Great Depression and World War II.

Kelly, Robin D. G. *Hammer and Hoe: Alabama Communists during the Great Depression.* Chapel Hill: University of North Carolina Press, 1990. ▶ Argument that the CPUSA was the most effective agent for social change in the U.S. South.

Kennedy, David. *Freedom from Fear: The American People in War and Depression, 1929–1945.* New York: Oxford University Press, 1999. ▶ Pulitzer-Prize-winning book that gives a clear and general overview of the period.

O'Neill, Colleen. *Working the Navajo Way: Labor and Culture in the Twentieth Century.* Lawrence: University of Kansas Press, 2005. ▶ Compelling narrative about how the Navajos adapted to the changes brought on by the Depression and New Deal policies.

Sanchez, George. *Becoming Mexican-American: Ethnicity, Culture and Identity in Chicano Los Angeles, 1900–1945.* New York: Oxford University Press, 1993. ▶ Consideration of how both long-time residents and recent immigrants to Los Angeles found work, created families, and endured through the Great Depression

Worster, Donald. *The Dust Bowl: The Southern Plains in the 1930s.* 25th anniv. ed. New York: Oxford University Press, 2004. ▶ Most comprehensive and gripping narrative about the Dust Bowl and its impact.

> Go to the MindTap® for **Global Americans** to access the full version of select books from this Additional Resources section.

Websites

American Life Histories: Manuscripts from the Federal Writers Project, 1936–1940. (http://www.loc.gov/collection/federal-writers-project/about-this-collection/) ▶ Almost three thousand stories of people collected from twenty-four states during the late 1930s.

Franklin Delano Roosevelt Presidential Library and Museum. (http://www.fdrlibrary.marist.edu/library/) ▶ Repository of the personal papers of Franklin and Eleanor Roosevelt's as well as those of many of their colleagues and friends.

Museum of Modern Art (MOMA): Dorothea Lange Collection. (http://www.moma.org/collection/artist.php?artist_id=3373) ▶ Collection of thirty-five images Lange produced for the Farm Security Administration.

New Deal Network. (http://newdeal.feri.org/) ▶ Database of more than two hundred thousand primary sources including newspapers, letters, and advertisements.

Slave Narratives from the Federal Writers Project: American Memory (http://memory.loc.gov/ammem/snhtml/snhome.html). ▶ Most comprehensive repository of oral history testimonies from former slaves.

MindTap®

Continue exploring online through MindTap®, **where you can:**
- **Assess your knowledge with the Chapter Test**
- **Watch historical videos related to the chapter**
- **Further your understanding with interactive maps and timelines**

Great Depression, New Deal, and Impending War

1929

October

Stock market crashes, indicating a global economic crisis.

1930

June

Hawley-Smoot protective tariff suppresses global trade.

1931

March

Scottsboro trials of black youths draw international condemnation.

June

Hoover proposes moratorium on reparations and war debt payments.

September

Japan seizes Manchuria from China.

1933

January

Adolf Hitler becomes chancellor of Germany and shortly assumes dictatorial powers.

March

Roosevelt is inaugurated president.

June

London Economic Conference fails to revitalize international trade.

December

Twenty-First Amendment is ratified, ending Prohibition.

Good Neighbor Policy seeks to improve U.S. relations with Latin America.

1934

April

Nye Committee hearings on munitions profits in World War I heightens skepticism.

July

Longshoremen launch a general strike in San Francisco.

Soviet Union
Britain
Germany
Spain
Italy
United States
China
Japan
Ethiopia

1935

April
Dust Bowl storms destroy crops, leave thousands homeless.

May
Hitler renounces disarmament clauses of the Treaty of Versailles.

Supreme Court strikes down much of the Hundred Days legislation.

July
Wagner Act gives protections to labor.

August
Social Security Act provides for the unemployed, poor, and elderly.

Neutrality Acts begin to define U.S. neutrality as international tensions rise.

September
Nuremberg Laws deprive German Jews of civil rights.

October
Italy invades and shortly conquers Ethiopia.

1936

July
Spanish Civil War begins.

September
Hoover Dam is completed, controlling water flow and generating electricity.

November
Benito Mussolini announces the Rome-Berlin treaty between Axis powers.

Roosevelt wins second term in landslide.

December
Flint sit-down strike begins.

1937

February
Roosevelt's Court-Packing Plan proves unpopular.

July
Japan launches attack on China.

October
During Roosevelt Recession, profits and production decline and unemployment rises.

November
Japan occupies Nanjing and begins massacre of civilians.

1938

March
Germany annexes Austria.

June
Fair Labor Standards Act establishes minimum wages and maximum hours.

September
Germany negotiates agreement to annex Czechoslovakia's Sudetenland.

November
During anti-Jewish riots called *Kristallnacht*, Nazis destroy Jewish property.

1939

March
Germany seizes the rest of Czechoslovakia.

April
Italy invades Albania.

May
Germany and Italy form a military alliance.

August
Germany and the Soviet Union sign a nonaggression pact.

September
Germany invades Poland, World War II begins, and the Soviet Union invades Poland.

21

The World at War
1939–1945

Albert Einstein left Hitler's Germany in 1933 and settled in Princeton, New Jersey, becoming a U.S. citizen in 1940.

I n 1940, Albert Einstein became a U.S. citizen. Having witnessed firsthand the rise of fascism and anti-Semitism in Europe, he celebrated the freedoms found in the United States. America, he explained, protected the "right of individuals to say and think what they pleased" and fostered creativity and upward mobility.

Einstein was the most famous physicist in the world, and his renunciation of German citizenship was Germany's loss. In 1905, his so-called miracle year, he had published four internationally renowned papers on the photoelectric effect, Brownian motion, special relativity, and the equivalence of matter and energy (expressed in the equation $E = mc^2$). During World War I, while a research professor at Humboldt University in Berlin, he revolutionized physics with his theory of general relativity.

After the war, the intensification of German anti-Semitism caused Einstein to embrace his Jewish identity, though he had been raised as

Library of Congress Prints and Photographs Division [LC-DIG-ppmsca-05649]

Albert Einstein accepts his U.S. citizenship certificate from Judge Philip Forman on October 1, 1940.

a non-observant Jew. He did not join or worship at a synagogue, but he supported Zionism, the movement for the establishment of Jewish settlements in Palestine. In June 1922, Einstein was devastated when far-right extremists assassinated his close friend Walter Rathenau, a wealthy Jew who was serving as Germany's foreign minister. Although threatened by members of the fledgling National Socialist (Nazi) Party because of his Jewish identity, Einstein remained in Germany until 1933 when Adolf Hitler became the German chancellor. Moderating his strict pacifist views, he urged Western nations to prepare for war. After the Nazis barred Jews from holding any official positions, Einstein emigrated to America and accepted an appointment at the Institute for Advanced Study in Princeton, New Jersey. In January 1936, he filed his Declaration of Intention to become a U.S. citizen. Reflecting the racialized thinking that permeated Western democracies as well as authoritarian governments at the time, the form required Einstein to identify his color (white), complexion (fair), race (Hebrew), and nationality (German). Under Nazi policies, Einstein's racial identification disqualified him from participation in civic life. In the United States, his color did not, but wartime social change accelerated movements for equality that would challenge discrimination against those whose color identification was not white.

Throughout the 1930s, Einstein communicated with other physicists who had emigrated to the United States to escape Nazi persecution. In the summer of 1939, just weeks before World War II began in Europe, Leo Szilard, a refugee nuclear physicist from Hungary, alerted Einstein to the potential military uses of chain reactions triggered by the fission of uranium. Together, they wrote a letter to President Franklin Roosevelt warning that German scientists might develop an atomic weapon and encouraging the president to launch a U.S. program of atomic research. Roosevelt acted on their recommendation, and the program he established produced the world's first atomic bombs with the help of other refugees from Nazi persecution and scientists from Canada and Great Britain.

How do the circumstances of Einstein's emigration to America and his support of atomic bomb research and development reflect the grave threats posed by totalitarianism and racial ideologies?

Go to MindTap® to watch a video on Einstein and learn how his story relates to the themes of this chapter.

Einstein was only one of millions of people whose lives were irreparably changed by history's most destructive conflict. After Germany invaded Poland on September 1, 1939, democratic nations could no longer ignore the grave threats posed by potential Nazi domination of western Europe, Japanese aggression in Asia, and Italian incursions in Africa and Albania. Fusions of totalitarianism and racial ideology imperiled the political freedoms and economic viability of the democratic capitalist world. At the same time, they highlighted the contradictions posed by the colonialism and segregation practiced by nations ostensibly committed to freedom. By August 1945, when the six-year worldwide conflagration ended, more than 60 million people had died—an average of twenty-seven thousand deaths per day. The conflict transformed warfare, displaced millions, sparked anti-imperialist and civil rights movements, and left most of Europe and much of Asia in ruins.

Although fighting a war on two fronts, the United States was spared this destruction and chaos. In fact, the war catapulted the country out of the Great Depression and ushered in a period of economic growth that continued until the late 1960s. As the nation mobilized, economic opportunities for American workers abounded. Cities swelled as people migrated from rural areas in pursuit of defense jobs. Altogether 16 million U.S. men and women served in the armed forces over the course of the war. Traditionally underrepresented groups enjoyed new visibility and opportunities. When the conflict concluded, the United States was indisputably the world's strongest military and economic power.

21-1
From Neutral to Belligerent

This 1939 editorial cartoon titled, "The Only Way We Can Save Her," reflects popular and congressional debates over how the United States should respond to the outbreak of war in Europe.

What is the core message of this cartoon? Does it advocate intervention or neutrality? How might someone with an opposing view have challenged the cartoon's claims? ▶

" STAY OUT! STAY OUT FOR MY SAKE, AS WELL AS YOUR OWN!"

WAR MAD EUROPE

DEMOCRACY

AMERICA, THE LAST REFUGE OF DEMOCRACY

The Granger Collection, New York

The September 1, 1939, German invasion of Poland shattered the illusion that Adolf Hitler was a leader who could be restrained through appeasement and triggered a six-year global war. Intent on building a German empire (the Third Reich) based on ideas about the racial superiority of the Germanic peoples, Hitler believed that because Britain and France had acquiesced to his recent seizure of Czechoslovakia, neither nation would honor its agreements to defend Poland. To his surprise, Britain and France declared war on Germany on September 3. Undaunted, German troops plunged onward toward Warsaw, and on September 17, their Soviet allies attacked Poland from the east, following the plan of the nonaggression pact signed the month before.

Throughout much of the 1930s, international tensions had run high (see Table 21.1), and the outbreak of war in Europe created serious political challenges for President Roosevelt. Although constrained by the Neutrality Acts passed by Congress to keep the United States out of another European war, he took steps to guard U.S. security and to aid the British and French. These

actions sparked intense public debates. At the same time, U.S.–Japanese relations collapsed after negotiations and economic sanctions failed to resolve a diplomatic crisis in Asia. After the Japanese launched a surprise attack on Pearl Harbor, a U.S. naval base in Hawai'i, the United States finally joined the battle against the Axis Powers.

☞ As you read, pay attention to how the changing international situation affected U.S. policies. Why and how did the Roosevelt administration begin moving away from neutrality once war erupted in Europe?

Table 21.1 The Rise of Militarist Regimes and the Coming of World War II

During the 1930s, repressive regimes in Italy, Germany, Japan, and the Soviet Union began to rise. While Soviet leaders brutally suppressed internal political enemies, Italian, German, and Japanese leaders militarized and embraced expansionism as a means of realizing nationalistic, economic, and racial aims. In 1939, despite their diametrically opposed political philosophies, the Soviets and Germans forged an alliance and attacked Poland, triggering World War II.

Year	Italy	Germany	Japan	Soviet Union
1922	Fascists march on Rome			Union of Soviet Socialist Republics (Soviet Union) is established
1923	Benito Mussolini establishes a fascist state	Adolf Hitler tries to overthrow Bavarian government but fails and is imprisoned		
1924				Vladimir Lenin dies; Joseph Stalin becomes Communist Party leader
1925		In *Mein Kampf,* Hitler outlines his plans for the future of Germany		
1928				Stalin's first Five-Year Plan calls for rapid industrialization and the collectivization of agriculture
1931			Japanese forces seize Manchuria from China, set up puppet government Japan withdraws from the League of Nations	
1932				Failure of collectivization results in two-year famine in Ukraine, 7 million people die
1933		Hitler becomes chancellor of Germany and soon assumes dictatorial powers Nazis begin imprisoning political enemies in concentration camps Nazis eliminate opposition parties Germany withdraws from the League of Nations		
1935	Italy invades Ethiopia, and the next year makes it an Italian colony	Hitler begins rearming Germany, reintroduces conscription Nazis announce Nuremberg Laws that restrict the civil rights of Jews		
1936	Italy supports military uprising against the Spanish Republic Italy signs Rome-Berlin Axis Treaty with Germany	Germany supports military uprising against the Spanish Republic Germany signs Rome-Berlin Axis Treaty with Italy Germany signs Anti-Comintern Pact with Japan	Military faction comes to power Japan signs Anti-Comintern Pact with Germany	Show trials of individuals deemed to be state enemies begin in Moscow, and defendants found guilty are sent to labor camps or executed Soviet Union sends aid to Spanish Republic
1937	Italy withdraws from the League of Nations		Japan launches all-out assault on China, captures Peking (now Beijing) and Shanghai At Nanjing, Japanese troops kill 300,000 civilians	Stalinist purge of the leadership of the Red Army and Military Maritime Fleet begins

(continued)

Table 21.1 The Rise of Militarist Regimes and the Coming of World War II *(continued)*

Year	Italy	Germany	Japan	Soviet Union
1938	Manifesto of Race declares Italians to be descendants of the Aryan (Germanic) race Italian racial laws restrict the civil rights of Jews, and laws target Africans in Italian colonies	Germany invades and annexes Austria Germany annexes Czechoslovakia's Sudetenland In anti-Jewish riot called *Kristallnacht*, Nazis kill and destroy property	Japan issues plan to dominate East Asia	After an estimated 1.5 million detentions and nearly 700,000 executions, the Great Purge ends
1939		Germany annexes the rest of Czechoslovakia Germany signs a nonaggression pact with the Soviet Union Germany invades Poland		Soviet Union signs a nonaggression pact with Germany Soviet Union invades Poland Soviet Union attacks Finland

21-1a War in Europe

Fiercely nationalistic, the Poles tried to stop the onslaught of the **Wehrmacht**, Germany's combined ground, naval, and air forces. Using the tactic *blitzkrieg* (lightning war), the Nazis aimed to create disarray among enemy troops and to score a quick victory with minimal loss of life and equipment. Although Poland had the fourth largest army in Europe, its outdated equipment and airplanes were no match for the *Wehrmacht*, and its allies Britain and France—unwilling to send ill-prepared troops into battle—never contributed to Poland's defense. After the Soviets invaded from the east, Poland succumbed, and on October 6, following the secret protocols of the nonaggression pact they had concluded, Germany and the Soviet Union divided the country between them.

In the months to come, the Soviets arrested and held captive approximately 1.5 million Poles. Of these, three hundred fifty thousand eventually died, including twenty-five thousand murdered by the Soviet secret police (the NKVD) and buried in mass graves in the forests near Katyn and other sites. Some seven hundred thousand Polish solders were taken as German prisoners of war (POWs). Compared to other European countries later occupied by

> The Axis Powers and the Soviet Union initially score victories in Europe and Africa.

Germany, there was little collaboration between the Poles and the Nazis. Approximately one hundred fifty thousand Poles fled westward, the largest exodus of all of the nations that fell under German domination. Some Polish soldiers and pilots eventually fought with the **Allies**, as the nations fighting the Axis Powers came to be called. Polish refugees in London established an unelected Polish government in exile to which hundreds of thousands Poles pledged their loyalty as they waged an armed struggle against their German and Soviet occupiers. It became the largest underground resistance movement in Europe.

Deeply alarmed by these events, President Roosevelt feared that the Germans would now conquer Europe, isolate the United States politically and economically, and then launch military strikes in the Western Hemisphere. Accordingly, he adopted cautious—and sometimes duplicitous—methods to circumvent the Neutrality Acts and aid the Allies. On September 21, 1939, three weeks after Germany invaded Poland, he asked Congress to lift the arms embargo as a means of keeping the United States out of the European conflict. Allowing the British and French to buy U.S. weapons and war matériel on a "cash-and-carry" basis would also safeguard against the tensions created by U.S. loans and supply shipments to both sides during World War I. In early November, Congress approved the president's proposal. Eager to avoid being drawn into another world war and sympathetic to the Allies, most Americans supported these measures.

Roosevelt also took steps to ensure security in the Western Hemisphere. In the fall of 1939, the United States and several Latin American nations signed the Declaration of Panama, proclaiming their neutrality and establishing a coastal security zone closed to belligerent navies.

Wehrmacht Unified armed forces of Germany from 1935 to 1945, consisting of the *Heer* (army), the *Kriegsmarine* (navy), and the *Luftwaffe* (air force).

blitzkrieg German for lightning war, a method of warfare in which highly mobile, mechanized infantry supported with air forces use short, rapid maneuvers to destabilize the enemy.

Allies Countries that opposed the Axis Powers during World War II; sought to stop German, Japanese, and Italian aggression.

U.S. officials convinced Latin American colleagues to limit or end their trade with Germany and its ally Italy. The following year, Roosevelt established an Office of Inter-American Affairs headed by Nelson Rockefeller. Through radio programs, publications, and Hollywood films such as *The Three Caballeros* (1944), the office sought to improve hemispheric relations. Despite persistent anxieties about U.S. imperialism in the region, all Latin American countries eventually joined the Allies, although Chile and Argentina waited until the conflict's final weeks to do so.

While U.S. policy makers fostered hemispheric unity, the Allies anxiously awaited the Nazis' next move. Following Poland's quick collapse, many in Britain and France concluded that their governments had committed them to waging an unwinnable war, and some politicians called for a negotiated settlement with Hitler. Neither nation had ground or air forces capable of defeating the *Wehrmacht.* Hoping to buy enough time to rearm and mobilize, the Allies bolstered defenses on France's eastern border while imposing a naval blockade off the German coast.

With the Allies' attention focused on Germany, Stalin grabbed more territory. In October 1939, Soviet troops invaded Finland and met ferocious resistance. On March 12, 1940, with their supplies depleted and no significant military assistance from Britain or France forthcoming, the Finns signed an armistice ceding 10 percent of their land. Determined to regroup after losing more than one hundred twenty-five thousand soldiers, Stalin allowed the Finns to retain their independence and turned his energies toward modernizing the Red Army and rebuilding an officer corps weakened by the political purges of the late 1930s.

In April 1940, the Nazis launched another *blitzkrieg*, and waves of German soldiers supported by tanks, artillery, and bombers seized Norway and Denmark. After the British military failed in an attempt to assist the Norwegians, Prime Minister Neville Chamberlain lost the support of many fellow Conservatives and resigned. Winston Churchill, a more bellicose leader with a gift for inspiring the masses, became his successor. At the same time, the Nazis began marching westward. They quickly captured Holland, Luxembourg, and Belgium and advanced on France. As French defenses collapsed, 8 million people fled their homes, the largest mass migration in western European history. German troops sped toward Paris, and to rescue British, French, Dutch, and Belgian troops trapped behind their lines at Dunkirk, the British sent almost nine hundred civilian and military vessels across the English Channel. In nine days, they evacuated nearly three hundred forty thousand men but abandoned huge stores of ammunition, weapons, and military vehicles that took months to replace.

On June 14, the Germans marched into Paris, and on June 22, France signed an armistice with Germany. The newly formed **Vichy French** state collaborated with the Nazis in exchange for a pledge that France and its colonies would not be divided among the Axis Powers. Although many French citizens supported the Vichy regime's efforts to maintain French territorial sovereignty, others resisted the German occupiers and backed the **Free French** movement led by General Charles de Gaulle, then exiled in London.

Meanwhile, the Soviets seized Bessarabia and the Baltic States of Latvia, Estonia, and Lithuania. Unwilling to miss out on the spoils from an Axis victory, Benito Mussolini brought Italy into the war, and Italian troops soon invaded France, Sudan, Kenya, British Somaliland, and Egypt. Reactions in Africa were mixed. Some Africans hoped that the fascists would liberate them from decades of British and French colonial rule whereas others fought for the British but were disillusioned by salaries and conditions inferior to those of their white comrades in arms.

Great Britain was now the only major European democracy not under German occupation. To weaken it in preparation for a land invasion, the **Luftwaffe** began bombing British cities, soon with nightly raids known as the *blitz*. Contrary to Hitler's expectations, the bombings only stiffened British resolve, and German pilots met intense resistance from the Royal Air Force (RAF) in battles over the English Channel.

21-1b U.S. Support for the Allies

As German victories mount, Roosevelt leads the United States toward intervention.

Certain that a Nazi-dominated Europe would imperil U.S. economic and political interests, Roosevelt vowed to help the British and started preparing the nation for war. He persuaded Congress to increase the defense budget from $2 billion to $10 billion. In September 1940, he transferred fifty World War I–era destroyers to England in exchange for rights to build or lease bases on eight British territories in the Western Hemisphere. He also signed the Selective Service Act requiring all men between the ages of twenty-one and forty-five to register for conscription, the first peacetime draft in U.S. history.

These measures outraged advocates for neutrality. Organized as the America First Committee, they denied that Hitler posed a threat to the United States and warned that participating in Europe's war would permanently militarize U.S. life. At its peak, the committee had more than eight hundred thousand members. In response, interventionists formed the Committee to Defend America by Aiding the Allies. Rejecting claims that the war in Europe did not endanger the United States, the group defended Roosevelt's policies and advocated all measures to help the Allies short of direct U.S. participation in the war.

At the same time, the war escalated. On September 27, Germany, Italy, and Japan—hoping to dissuade the United States from entering the war on the side of the Allies—signed the **Tripartite Pact**, an agreement in

Vichy France Authoritarian regime that governed France and collaborated with the Axis after the Axis took control of the country in July 1940 to the Allied liberation in August 1944.

Free French Individuals and military units that joined the resistance founded by Charles de Gaulle from exile in London to fight Axis and Vichy troops.

Luftwaffe Aerial warfare branch of the *Wehrmacht* from 1935 to 1945.

Tripartite Pact Treaty signed by Nazi Germany, fascist Italy, and imperial Japan in Berlin on September 27, 1940, established the Axis Powers.

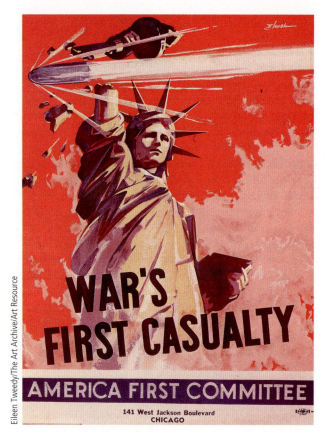

Eileen Tweedy/The Art Archive/Art Resource

WAR'S FIRST CASUALTY

AMERICA FIRST COMMITTEE

141 West Jackson Boulevard
CHICAGO

America First Poster, circa 1940 The views of Americans were quite divided on the appropriate U.S. response to war in Europe. This poster was used by the America First Committee, the largest noninterventionist group. At its peak, the organization's eight hundred thousand members included film producer Walt Disney, aviator Charles Lindbergh, and future U.S. president Gerald Ford. While Lindbergh openly declared Nazi sympathies, other members claimed that intervention would permanently militarize daily life and undermine civil liberties. ▲

Four Freedoms Liberties that President Roosevelt argued "everyone in the world" ought to have: freedom of speech, freedom of religion, freedom from want, and freedom from fear.

Lend-Lease U.S. program that supplied Allied nations with $50.1 billion of weapons and supplies during World War II.

Atlantic Charter Statement of postwar aims drafted by Roosevelt and Churchill in August 1941.

which they pledged to defend one another from attack by any nation not already involved in the European conflict or the ongoing war between China and Japan. In October, Italy invaded Greece.

After carefully avoiding additional steps toward war while campaigning in the 1940 presidential race, Roosevelt won an unprecedented third term and resumed his efforts to assist the British and their allies. In a fireside chat, he called for the United States to become "the great arsenal of democracy." To prevent German world domination, he announced his intention to manufacture and supply the Allies with "the implements of war, the planes, the tanks, the guns, and the freighters that will enable them to fight for their liberty and for our security."

In his State of the Union address on January 6, 1941, Roosevelt built on these themes and recommended that the United States loan or rent supplies to the Allied nations whose war efforts were depleting their national treasuries. Without such measures, he argued, the world risked losing **Four Freedoms** essential to humanity: freedom of speech, freedom of religious worship, freedom from want, and freedom from fear. Over the next two months, he urged Americans to support **Lend-Lease** as a means of protecting the democracy they cherished and keeping the United States out of the conflict. In March 1941, after a heated political battle, Congress approved the bill authorizing the president to "sell . . . exchange, lease, lend, or otherwise dispose of" war matériel "to any country whose defense the President deems vital to the defense of the United States." Starting with an initial $7 billion appropriation, the United States eventually provided more than $50 billion in interest-free Lend-Lease aid. Britain alone received more than $31 billion.

Although the legislation provided critically needed financial aid to the British, it did nothing to guard their vessels from German submarines (U-boats) that were sinking Allied and U.S. merchant ships carrying five hundred thousand tons of cargo per month. Determined to help, Roosevelt ordered the U.S. Navy to patrol the North Atlantic. U.S. troops occupied Greenland as part of the president's expanded defense of the Western Hemisphere.

In June 1941, after months of Allied–Axis battles confined to the Balkans and Africa, World War II took a dramatic turn when the Germans invaded the Soviet Union, thus violating the nonaggression pact. This action catapulted the Soviet Union—Germany's ally in the division of Poland—into the Allied camp. Setting aside Americans' traditional antipathy toward communism (and hoping that the Soviets would weaken the German war machine), Roosevelt began sending Lend-Lease aid to the Soviet Union. Nothing could stop the *Wehrmacht*, however, which quickly overran Belorussia and the Ukraine and was soon besieging Leningrad and Moscow.

Convinced that it was only a matter of time before the United States would join the battle against the Axis Powers, President Roosevelt and Prime Minister Churchill met to outline postwar aims. Aboard a ship off the coast of Newfoundland, U.S. and British teams spent four days drafting a statement of goals. They renounced territorial aggrandizement and called for the self-determination of nations, free trade, global cooperation, disarmament, and a peace that allowed people everywhere to "live out their lives in freedom from fear and want." Formally issued on August 14, the **Atlantic Charter** echoed Roosevelt's Four Freedoms as well as Woodrow Wilson's Fourteen Points.

To persuade a still wavering public of the need for direct intervention, Roosevelt allowed the U.S. Navy to take steps certain to provoke German retaliation that would, he anticipated, outrage Americans. On September 4, after a German submarine fired two torpedoes that narrowly missed the U.S. destroyer *Greer*, the president revealed in a fireside chat that he had ordered U.S.

naval commanders to shoot German submarines on sight and authorized naval convoys to go as far as Iceland. His description of the attack on the *Greer* as unprovoked omitted the fact that the *Greer* had tracked the German submarine for more than three hours. In two incidents in October, German submarines sank U.S. ships—the *Kearney* and the *Reuben James*—killing more than one hundred U.S. sailors. In November, Roosevelt asked for repeal of the sections of the Neutrality Act that prohibited the arming of merchant vessels and barred such ships from war zones. Congress agreed, acknowledging the public's shift toward intervention. Roosevelt's strategy had worked, and the United States was inching closer to war.

21-1c Path to Pearl Harbor

Ironically, events in Asia, not Europe, triggered the U.S. entry into the war against the Axis Powers. While still fighting in China, the militant Japanese government sought to capture Indochina and the Dutch East Indies, the Asian colonies of recently defeated France and the Netherlands. In a radio broadcast on June 29, 1940, the Japanese regime called for the creation of a Greater East Asia Co-Prosperity Sphere, an economically self-sufficient "bloc of Asian nations led by the Japanese and free of Western powers." A few weeks later, the Vichy French allowed the Japanese to seize northern Indochina. The recently formed Viet Minh (Vietnamese nationalists), later backed by China and the United States, ferociously opposed their Vichy and Japanese occupiers.

> Japan attacks Pearl Harbor and captures territories throughout Asia and the Pacific.

Elsewhere, Japanese propagandists used slogans like "Asia for the Asiatics!" and disseminated pamphlets celebrating pan-Asian unity. In actuality, the Japanese militarists held racially supremacist views similar to those of the Nazis and secretly planned to dominate their Asian neighbors. Although some Asians initially welcomed Japanese troops who drove out their European rulers, the subsequent brutality of the Japanese military and the sexual enslavement of so-called **comfort women** forced to serve as prostitutes for the Japanese Army persuaded many that Japanese colonialism was even worse than Western imperialism.

Confronted with a global totalitarian threat, Roosevelt attempted to deter Japanese aggression by increasing aid to Nationalist China and using economic sanctions against Japan. The United States halted sales of aviation fuel, scrap metal, and steel but initially continued oil sales for fear that a petroleum embargo would trigger a war. But after Japan and the Soviet Union signed a neutrality agreement and Japanese troops marched into southern Indochina, Roosevelt halted all trade, including the sale of American oil, and froze Japanese assets held in U.S. banks. The Dutch government, then in exile in London, took similar actions.

U.S. and Japanese diplomats attempted to defuse the crisis. On November 20, the Japanese offered to withdraw from Indochina if the British, Dutch, and Americans stopped aiding the Chinese and lifted their economic sanctions. Six days later, U.S. officials rejected the proposal and insisted that Japan withdraw from China without conditions—a demand that was unacceptable to Prime Minister Hideki Tojo and the militarists dominating the Japanese government. Facing serious shortages as a result of the U.S. embargo and convinced that further talks would be futile, Japan decided to attack the United States. Because U.S. cryptographers had broken the Japanese diplomatic code, the Roosevelt administration knew that a Japanese attack on U.S. forces in the Pacific was being planned but not exactly where or when.

On December 7, 1941, Japanese planes launched from six aircraft carriers struck the U.S. naval base at Pearl Harbor, Hawai'i. In this surprise attack, 2,403 Americans died, eight U.S. battleships were sunk or damaged, and 188 planes destroyed, most while still on the ground. Axis leaders rejoiced at news of the attacks on the United States, a nation they viewed as degenerate and described by Mussolini as "a country of Negroes and Jews."

The following day, Roosevelt appeared before Congress. "Yesterday, December 7, 1941—a date that will live in infamy"—he announced, the United States "was suddenly and deliberately" attacked by Japan, and he asked for a declaration of war. The vote was nearly unanimous. Only Congresswoman Jeannette Rankin of Montana, a pacifist who had also voted against U.S. entry into World War I, voted no. Three days later, Germany and Italy honored the Tripartite Pact and declared war on the United States.

During his speech to Congress, Roosevelt also announced that the Japanese had invaded the Philippines. Because of damages to U.S. air forces stationed in Hawai'i, U.S. naval forces had lacked aerial protection and retreated. In March 1942, Douglas MacArthur, commander of the U.S. Army forces in the Far East, fled to Australia, vowing "I shall return." A month later, seventy-six thousand U.S. and Filipino defenders on Bataan surrendered, including seventy-eight army and navy nurses, the largest group of American women ever captured by an enemy. The Japanese forced the male POWs to walk eighty miles, and thousands perished on what came to be known as the "Death March," a notorious atrocity that exemplified the Japanese government's official policy of showing no mercy to its enemies. During the ensuing three-year Japanese occupation, Filipino guerillas, supplied and reinforced by MacArthur's troops, maintained control of 60 percent of the islands. Motivated by U.S. guarantees of independence and outraged by the Japanese use of their fellow citizens as forced laborers and sexual slaves, most Filipinos remained loyal to the United States.

Within weeks of striking Pearl Harbor, Japan also captured the oil-rich Dutch East Indies and Britain's colonies Malaya, Burma, Hong Kong,

comfort women Women and girls forced to serve as prostitutes for the Japanese Imperial Army during World War II.

Mohandas K. Gandhi and Jawaharlal Nehru Discuss Indian Concerns During World War II, many Indians, Arabs, and Africans protested the disjuncture between the Allied governments' democratic ideals and the injustices of life under British and French imperial rule. ▲

Underwood Archives/Getty Images

colonies because the fleeing British generals and colonial administrators did not orchestrate a general evacuation—a betrayal of the imperial ideal that colonial masters protected their subjects. In Burma, as Japanese troops swept across the country to close off the Burma Road—the Allied supply route to China—fifty thousand Indians who worked for the British died of exposure, disease, and starvation. In India, Jawaharlal Nehru and Mohandas Gandhi pointed to the British failure to provide humanitarian aid as another justification for their **Quit India movement**, a nonviolent campaign calling for the orderly withdrawal of the British from their nation. To quash the independence movement, the British government imprisoned Gandhi, Nehru, and more than thirty thousand Quit India supporters until 1945. In 1942, Britain had more troops maintaining internal control of India than it had fighting the Japanese. In a harbinger of the decolonization and civil rights movements that swept the postwar era, Gandhi warned Roosevelt that any Allied proclamation about "fighting to make the world safe for freedom of the individual and for democracy sounds hollow, so long as India and, for that matter, Africa are exploited by Great Britain, and America has the Negro problem in her own home."

While Japan won a string of victories in Asia and occupied islands throughout the Central Pacific, Germany scored gains elsewhere. By the spring of 1942, German troops had penetrated far into Soviet territory, holding all or part of nine Soviet Republics, and were poised to capture valuable oil fields in the Caucasus Mountains. In North Africa, German forces threatened the Suez Canal, a waterway critical to maintaining Allied supply lines. To many, a total Axis victory seemed imminent.

Quit India movement
Nonviolent resistance campaign launched in India in August 1942 that called for an end to British rule.

and Singapore. As their defenses in Southeast Asia collapsed, the British concentrated their forces in the Middle East where the Nazis had support among many Arab nationalists who shared their anti-Zionist views and wished to free themselves from British and French imperialism. This decision had terrible consequences for the people in Britain's Asian

21-2
First Challenges to Axis Power

This poster, created in 1942 by the U.S. Office of Facts and Figures, includes the flags of the twenty-six nations opposing the Axis Powers. Other countries later joined the coalition.

What is the core message of this propaganda poster? Why would U.S. officials consider it important to impart such a message to Americans? ▶

War posters/Alamy Stock Photo

The Japanese government hoped that Americans would be so demoralized by the Pearl Harbor attacks that they would elect not to go to war and acquiesce to Japanese expansionism in Southeast Asia. This proved a grave miscalculation. The raids outraged Americans and obliterated any significant isolationist sentiment. Determined to defeat the Axis Powers and to protect their nation,

Americans mobilized for war and U.S. leaders coordinated political aims and military strategies with the Allies. By mid-1942, the Allies began winning critical battles that turned the tide of the war in Europe and the Pacific. Although not always in agreement on proposed tactics or plans for the postwar world, the Allies put their enemies on the defensive.

☞ As you read, set aside your knowledge of the outcome of World War II and consider the formidable obstacles the Allies had to surmount to defeat the Axis. What challenges did the United States and its allies face in the early stages of the war? In what ways did the Allied coalition both help and complicate the war effort against the Axis Powers?

21-2a Allies and Adversaries

On January 1, 1942, twenty-six countries signed the **Declaration by the United Nations** calling for "complete victory" over the "savage and brutal forces seeking to subjugate the world." The United Nations, commonly called the Allies, agreed that the defeat of the authoritarian powers ruling Germany, Italy, and Japan was essential to the preservation of human rights and pledged to uphold the Atlantic Charter. By the end of the war, several additional countries had endorsed these principles and joined the coalition. This unity of purpose gave the Allies a significant advantage over their enemies. Whereas the Allies coordinated their strategies and diplomatic objectives, Germany and Japan—the major Axis Powers—did not jointly plan their military operations or political aims.

> The Allies formulate strategies for defeating the Axis and try to reconcile differing views on tactics and war aims.

The United States and Great Britain formed the closest Allied partnership. Roosevelt and Churchill spoke or wrote virtually every day until Roosevelt's death in 1945. In late December 1941, top U.S. and British military leaders agreed that Germany posed a greater global threat than Japan and that victory in the European theater must therefore be first priority.

But Allied relations were sometimes difficult. Roosevelt and Churchill disagreed over the future of Britain's colonies. Roosevelt argued that colonized peoples have the right to govern themselves, but Churchill resisted the idea of dismantling the British Empire. China, at war with Japan since 1937, was displeased by the "Europe First" strategy. Although the Nationalists hoarded supplies instead of fighting their Japanese occupiers, the Roosevelt administration was eager to make China one of the world's "Four Policemen." The United States continued to prop up the government of Chinese Nationalist leader Jiang Jieshi (Chiang Kai-shek) in anticipation of resuming the suspended civil war against the Communists led by Mao Tse-tung (Mao Zedong). At the same time, U.S. cooperation with the Vichy French rankled Charles de Gaulle, leader of the Free French government-in-exile.

Relations among the British, Americans, and the Soviets—**The Big Three**—were the most contentious. With his forces singlehandedly fighting more than two hundred divisions of the *Wehrmacht* and sustaining enormous losses, Stalin wanted the Allies to open a second front in western Europe that would force the Germans to split their armed forces. Although Roosevelt tried to placate him with personal flattery and a stream of Lend-Lease aid ($11 billion total), Stalin believed—with much justification—that the Americans and British were intentionally allowing the Soviets to bear the largest burden in fighting Germany. Roosevelt and Churchill's delays saved U.S. and British soldiers' lives but created distrust that had long-term ramifications for relations with the Soviet Union.

21-2b End of the German Offensive

Conquest of the lands around the Mediterranean was not part of Hitler's initial strategy, but his maladroit Italian allies forced him to change course. Mussolini invaded the Balkans and North Africa in the hope of securing territorial gains in the soon-expected Axis victory, but British, Australian, New Zealander, and Indian troops defeated Italian forces in East Africa, Egypt, and Libya. To prevent more Italian losses, the Germans sent troops into North Africa and won victories in Yugoslavia, Greece, and Crete.

> After critical victories, the Allies prepare to invade France and envision the postwar world.

But the tide began turning against the Axis when U.S. and British forces landed in Algeria and Morocco in November 1942 and began to push back German gains. To assuage Stalin's anxieties about the delayed opening of the second front, Roosevelt and Churchill met in Casablanca in January 1943 and committed to a policy of unconditional surrender, rejecting the possibility of making a separate peace with any of Germany's allies. But with German submarines still inflicting losses on Allied vessels in the Atlantic, they continued to delay plans for an invasion of northwestern France until the United States could reach maximum troop levels and war production. Instead, they opted to try to push Italy out of the war and force the Germans to divert troops from the Soviet Union to Italy.

On July 9, 1943, British, American, and Canadian amphibious forces landed on Sicily. Two weeks later, Benito Mussolini—discredited by his

Declaration by the United Nations Document signed by twenty-six Allied nations January 1, 1942; term "United Nations" became a synonym for the Allies.

The Big Three Colloquial term describing the three most prominent Allied leaders: U.S. President Franklin Roosevelt, British Prime Minister Winston Churchill, and Soviet Premier Joseph Stalin.

Map 21.1 Axis and Allied Military Actions in Europe, North Africa, and the Soviet Union, 1941–1945 Early in the war, the Germans occupied many western and eastern European nations and made great gains in North Africa and the Soviet Union. But in 1942, the tide turned. After the D-Day landings in June 1944, the Allies retook France and began pushing German forces back into Germany while Soviet troops pushed at them from the east. In May 1945, Germany surrendered. ▲

disastrous military campaigns—was ousted and imprisoned by a new Italian government. Although German special forces soon broke him out of prison, Mussolini did not escape the wrath of his countrymen. In April 1945, he was captured and executed by Italian partisans. The new Italian government soon surrendered to the Allies, but German troops and Italians who remained loyal to the Axis fought with fierce determination to slow the Allied advance north from Naples to Rome toward the Alps. Fighting in Italy continued even after the fall of Berlin in May 1945. In the interim, the task of caring for Italy's devastated civilian population fell to the Allies (see Map 21.1).

By the time the Allies invaded Sicily, the tide had turned against the

Battle of Stalingrad Pivotal Soviet victory over German troops following a protracted siege from August 23, 1942, to February 2, 1943; the turning point of World War II.

Axis in the east as well. At the **Battle of Stalingrad**, where nearly 2 million people died in a protracted siege, the German Sixth Army was forced to surrender when the Red Army encircled it. This loss forced the Germans to withdraw from the east and put them on the defensive for the remainder of the war. But the German invasion had decimated the Soviet Union: 1,700 cities and towns, more than 70,000 villages, and 31,000 factories had been demolished. Millions of acres of croplands and tens of millions of farm animals were destroyed. This devastation combined with memories of Russia's catastrophic losses in World War I and suspicions left by the failed Allied intervention in the Russian Civil War intensified Stalin's determination to protect his nation from another invasion. Accordingly, as the Red Army marched west into eastern Europe, he vowed to hold power in the

The Battle of Stalingrad, 1942–1943 After losing the protracted siege at Stalingrad, German forces withdrew and never regained the offensive on the vast Russian front. A major strategic miscalculation, the German invasion of the Soviet Union left more than 10 million Soviet soldiers, 2 million German soldiers, and 17 million civilians dead as a result of battles, atrocities, mistreatment of POWs, food and medicine shortages, and the mutual use of scorched earth tactics that left millions homeless and starving. ◀

Interfoto/Alamy Stock Photo

region, to expand Soviet borders to encompass the Baltic States and eastern Poland, to ensure pro-Communist governments ruled in key eastern European states, and to punish Germany through demilitarization, deindustrialization, and high reparations.

In October 1943, American, British, and Soviet diplomats gathered in Moscow to plan the next phase of the war. They created a council to coordinate Allied policy in Italy and a European Advisory Commission to formulate recommendations for peace agreements. In a significant departure from the U.S. rejection of collective security in the aftermath of World War I, Secretary of State Cordell Hull persuaded the delegates to commit to a postwar replacement for the defunct League of Nations.

A few weeks later, Roosevelt, Churchill, and Stalin met in Tehran. Emphatically rejecting a British proposal for an amphibious landing in the Balkans, Stalin demanded a firm commitment on the long-delayed invasion of France. He also proposed territorial adjustments after the war that would guarantee Soviet security by creating a protective buffer against Germany, but Roosevelt rejected Stalin's contention that the Baltic States were now Soviet Republics. Although Stalin reaffirmed his pledge to enter the war against Japan after Germany surrendered, the meeting highlighted the Allies' differences over territorial concessions, an issue hotly contested after the war.

21-2c End of the Japanese Offensive

The Allies faced a daunting task in defeating the Japanese across the vast Pacific theater. While implementing their

{ Allied forces begin advancing on Japan.

"Europe First" strategy in the early stages of the war, they sought to prevent Japan from seizing additional territories. Before attacking Japan itself, the Allies planned to recapture Japanese-held islands in the Pacific (a strategy called *island-hopping*) and Japan-occupied Southeast Asia.

In June 1942, U.S. forces stopped the Japanese advance at Midway, an island northwest of Hawai'i held by the United States since 1867. A turning point, the victory put the Japanese navy on the defensive for the remainder of the war. Thereafter, Allied forces under MacArthur's command won back the Solomon Islands, Guadalcanal, and New Guinea. In Burma, 450,000 mostly Indian troops under British command held the line against 300,000 Japanese soldiers. By early 1943, American, Australian, and New Zealander troops were moving northward in preparation for a strike on the Philippines (see Map 21.2).

While Allied forces took the offensive throughout Southeast Asia, the Japanese still occupied much of China. U.S. officials in China complained about the corruption and incompetence of Jiang Jeishi and his generals, but the Roosevelt administration continued to support the Nationalists in hope that China would someday become the leading capitalist democracy in Asia. At a November 1943 conference in Cairo, Roosevelt and Churchill met with Jiang and pledged that the Chinese territories "stolen by Japan" would be restored after the war. The following month, as a gesture of respect to China, Congress repealed the Chinese Exclusion Act, which had barred Chinese laborers from the United States since 1882. The repeal allowed only one hundred five Chinese to emigrate, but it also enabled Chinese already in the United States to become U.S. citizens. In 1946, in a similar overture to India and the Philippines, Congress ended the exclusion of these peoples and allowed them to naturalize.

Map 21.2 Major Military Engagements in the Pacific Theater, 1941–1945 By early 1942, Japanese forces had control of the Central Pacific and the Philippines, Burma, Singapore, the Dutch East Indies, and parts of the Solomon Islands, the Gilbert Islands, and New Guinea. At the Battle of Midway in June 1942, the Allies stopped the Japanese advance and began winning back Japanese strongholds. In August 1945, after the atomic bombings of Hiroshima and Nagasaki, the Japanese surrendered. ▲

21-3
On the Home Front

In this March 1942 photograph by Dorothea Lange, a Japanese American store owner in Oakland, California, demonstrates his patriotism in the aftermath of the Pearl Harbor attacks. He was soon forced to abandon his business and sent to an internment camp after Roosevelt mandated the relocation of one hundred ten thousand Japanese Americans living along the West Coast.

How does this photograph reflect some contradictions in U.S. democracy that were highlighted during the war? What were some of these injustices, and how did different groups attempt to combat them? ▶

Library of Congress Prints and Photographs Division[LC-USZ62-23602]

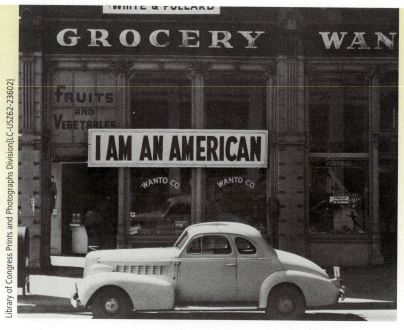

While combat and occupation devastated much of Europe and Asia, the war affected the United States differently. Wartime production ended the Great Depression as factories retooled and increased hiring to meet the nation's defense needs. Farmers increased their yields and sold crops at a profit. Many Americans earned good incomes, and historically underemployed groups entered the paid workforce in record numbers. The war sparked mass migration as men and women who joined the armed forces moved to military bases and families left rural communities for urban defense jobs. At the same time, the war against fascism abroad forced Americans to confront racism at home.

☞ As you read, consider ways the United States changed during World War II. How did the government mobilize the nation for war? What opportunities and challenges did the war create?

21-3a Mobilization for War

Upon entering World War II, the United States had to build its armed forces, jump-start a stalled economy, and win a two-front war. To expedite

> Mobilization alters the U.S. economy, the federal bureaucracy, and the civilian workforce.

the process of U.S. military expansion begun in 1940, Roosevelt set staggering war production goals. Draftees were required to serve for the duration of the war instead of the previous twelve-month obligation. Throughout 1942, the army increased from 1.5 million to 5.4 million soldiers. By 1945, the United States had more than 8 million men and women in uniform, more than half the number who served in the wartime armed forces (see Figures 21.1 and 21.2).

Figure 21.1 Estimated Number of Combatants per Nation, 1939–1945 This figure illustrates the populations of several major combatant nations in 1939 and the number of citizens who served in each country's armed forces over the course of the war. Consider how the numbers of combatants compare to the overall national populations. How and why do the percentages of combatants differ?

▶ Sources: World War II Casualties, http://en.wikipedia.org/wiki/World_War_II_casualties; Historical Statistics for the World Economy, 1–2003 AD, www.ggdc.net/maddison/historical_statistics/horizontal-file_03–2007.xls

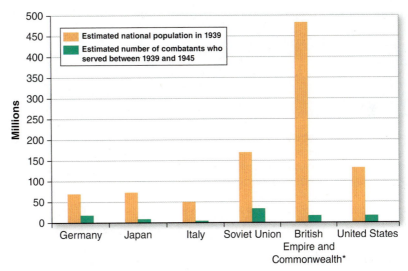

*British Empire and Commonwealth includes United Kingdom, Canada, Australia, New Zealand, South Africa, India, Singapore, Malta, Malaya, and Burma.

Figure 21.2 Strength of the Armed Forces, 1939–1944 As the war progressed, the major combatant nations mobilized their armed forces to the maximum level their populations and economies could support. What might account for different force sizes at different points of the war? ▶ Sources: Dear, I. C. B., and M. R. D. Foot, *The Oxford Companion to World War II* (Oxford, 2003), 2014 online ed., http://www.oxfordreference.com/view/10.1093/acref/9780198604464.001.0001/acref-9780198604464-e-1566?p=emailAWogkKzU5LJo2&d=/10.1093/acref/9780198604464.001.0001/acref-9780198604464-e-1566

Galerie Bilderwelt/Getty Images

When you ride ALONE you ride with Hitler!

Join a Car-Sharing Club TODAY!

Office of Price Administration Poster, 1943 Throughout the war, the U.S. government relied on Americans' patriotism and voluntarism in enforcing rationing of supplies vital to the war effort. Americans were urged to "Use it up, wear it out, make it do, or do without." This poster aims to help citizens understand the necessity of sharing rides because of the three-gallon-per-week gasoline ration. ▲

Mooziic/Alamy Stock Photo

MATERIAL CONSERVATION

"JAP TRAP"

U.S. Information Service Propaganda Poster, 1941–1945 Aware that many Americans held racist views of the Japanese and wanted to avenge the Pearl Harbor attacks and the Bataan Death March, the U.S. government played on these sentiments in propaganda posters designed to motivate defense workers and soldiers. Such materials may have contributed to the savagery of the Pacific theater where U.S. soldiers frequently retaliated for enemy atrocities by mutilating the corpses of Japanese troops. ▲

To meet production needs, the nation needed big business, a target of frequent criticism during the Great Depression. Motivated by patriotism and generous economic incentives, industrialists accepted federal defense contracts. Thousands became "dollar-a-year men," serving on government commissions and agencies for $1 a year, often while retaining their private sector salaries. Businessmen and bureaucrats retooled the nation for war production. In Detroit, auto factories retooled to make tanks and airplanes. Ford Motor Company completed a B-24 bomber every sixty-three minutes. In California, huge new shipyards reduced the time needed to build a merchant ship from one hundred four to fourteen days. By war's end, U.S. industries had produced 1,500 ships, 88,000 tanks, almost 300,000 airplanes, more than 2 million trucks, 6.5 million rifles, and 40 million bullets. The United States had become "the great arsenal of democracy" Roosevelt had envisioned.

War Production Board (WPB) U.S. government agency established in 1942 and charged with supervising production of materials and supplies for the war effort.

Office of Price Administration (OPA) U.S. government agency that instituted rent and price controls and rationed items essential to the war effort.

Office of War Information (OWI) U.S. government agency whose domestic and overseas branches delivered propaganda though radio broadcasts, publications, posters, films, and other media.

The war elevated the prestige of corporate America and further expanded the size and power of the federal government. In January 1942, the new **War Production Board (WPB)** began to regulate production and allocate materials. To prevent shortages of vital military materials and to control inflation, the **Office of Price Administration (OPA)** set prices on most retail goods and rationed scarce supplies such as tires, automobiles, shoes, nylon, sugar, gasoline, coffee, and meats.

To shape public attitudes, the Roosevelt administration created the **Office of War Information (OWI)**. Its domestic branch coordinated the release of war news and used posters and radio broadcasts to encourage Americans to support the war effort, join the armed forces, and guard against espionage and sabotage. Overseas, OWI disseminated information about the Allies' war aims and propaganda about the Axis Powers. The Nazis were usually depicted as caricatures of Hitler, while the Japanese were portrayed as superhuman killing machines or as myopic, buck-toothed rats or monkeys. Echoed throughout

Global Americans Born in Vienna in 1914, Hedy Keisler was an intellectually curious girl, and her father taught her about the mechanics of machinery. She became an actress and married Friedrich Mandl, a half-Jewish munitions manufacturer with close ties to the fascist governments of Italy and Germany. When they entertained, her husband and his associates discussed secret military technologies, assuming beautiful Hedy could not understand. Mocking such sexism years later, she declared, "Any girl can be glamourous. All you have to do is stand still and look stupid." Escaping her controlling husband, Hedy fled to Paris and then to Los Angeles, where she began making films under the name **Hedy Lamarr**. Bored by Hollywood socializing, she took up inventing as a hobby, setting up a bench and drafting tools in a corner of her drawing room. In 1940, when German submarines attacked British ships evacuating children to Canada to escape Nazi bombing raids, she decided to use her technical skills to help her adopted nation (though she was still an enemy alien who did not become a naturalized U.S. citizen until 1953). In 1941, Lamarr and composer George Antheil developed frequency-hopping technology that prevented jamming of radio signals used to control torpedoes. U.S. officials kept the innovation top-secret and did not use it until 1962. Because their patent expired, Lamarr and Antheil earned no royalties, but they are now recognized for essential contributions to the development of Wi-Fi, Bluetooth, and other elements of the wireless communication revolution.

American public culture, these deeply entrenched racial stereotypes may have contributed to the decision to intern Japanese Americans and to use atomic weapons on Japan.

Hollywood worked closely with the government in promoting war aims and raising morale. Studios made films featuring ethnically diverse soldiers with shared devotion to democracy. Cartoons showed beloved characters like Bugs Bunny and Daffy Duck doing their part to support the war effort. Not wishing to highlight contradictions in U.S. democracy or to undermine Allied unity, government censors ensured that films sent abroad did not depict the nation's racial segregation, suggest that the United States was solely responsible for victories, or present U.S. allies as imperialists.

Government-sponsored research became a major new industry during the war. To counter Germany's scientific and technological superiority, Roosevelt created the Office of Scientific Research and Development. Its most ambitious undertaking was the $2 billion **Manhattan Project**, the top-secret venture to build an atomic bomb. Federal funds also supported the development of napalm (jellied gasoline), flame throwers, and rockets. The government financed medical research that produced penicillin and plasma, both of which contributed to a 50 percent decrease in the death rate of wounded soldiers compared with that of World War I. New pesticides and antimalarial drugs protected soldiers in tropical environments from insect-borne diseases.

The huge increase in federal spending—from $9 billion in 1940 to $98 billion in 1944—had a ripple effect throughout society. The United States reached full employment, and the standard of living rose. Despite high income taxes on the wealthy (up to 90 percent) and new income taxes on the middle and lower classes, U.S. workers' average annual per capita income increased from $373 in 1940 to $1,074 in 1945. The war created

17 million new civilian jobs. As millions of married women entered the paid workforce, many families had two incomes for the first time. Traditionally underemployed groups such as racial minorities, teenagers, senior citizens, and disabled people found work. Although federal wage controls limited salary increases, many factory workers doubled or even tripled their paychecks with overtime pay. Because consumer goods such as radios and toasters were in short supply, most Americans saved rather than spent.

Despite a thriving economy, many Americans resisted increased government intervention. Manufacturers and farmers disliked price controls. Labor leaders criticized wage freezes. Although unions pledged not to strike during the war, inflation and wage restrictions triggered unauthorized "wildcat" strikes. Although most strikes ended quickly and did not undermine wartime production, some Americans viewed them as unpatriotic. In 1943, Congress overrode Roosevelt's veto to pass the Smith-Connally Act, which banned strikes in defense industries, granted the president the right to seize plants critical to the war effort, and limited unions' political activity. These provisions represented a bipartisan backlash against New Deal liberalism.

Although the Democrats maintained a narrow majority in Congress after the 1942 midterm elections, Republicans believed that they could win the 1944 presidential election. They nominated New York governor Thomas Dewey, who supported Roosevelt's direction of the war effort but opposed additional expansion of federal programs. Despite his failing health, Roosevelt waged a vigorous campaign that was boosted by his proposal for veterans' benefits. The Servicemen's Readjustment Act, better known as the **G.I. Bill of Rights**, offered every man

Manhattan Project U.S. government-sponsored research collaboration that produced the first atomic bombs.

G.I. Bill of Rights U.S. law passed in 1944 granting returning veterans benefits for home ownership, business start-ups, and education.

and woman who served honorably in the armed forces access to low-cost mortgages, business loans, educational assistance, and unemployment compensation. Mindful of the mistreatment of U.S. veterans in the Bonus Army during the Great Depression, Congress unanimously passed the bill in March 1944, and the promises it held helped Roosevelt win an unprecedented fourth term.

21-3b Migration and Social Changes

Over the course of World War II, one in every five Americans moved to a different county. Military volunteers and recruits left their homes for training camps and overseas deployments. Heading mostly south and west, rural families moved in pursuit of jobs at defense plants and shipyards, signaling a geographic shift in the U.S. population that would continue after the war (see Map 21.3).

{ Women and minorities challenge the United States to fulfill its democratic ideals.

New migrants created housing shortages and over-burdened schools, social service agencies, and recreational facilities. Racial tensions increased as urban whites (many themselves emigrants from rural areas) resisted sharing spaces and jobs with newly arrived African Americans. In June 1943, a three-day race riot in Detroit left twenty-five blacks and nine whites dead and caused $2 million in property damage. Similar racial violence occurred among U.S. troops in England. Clashes between black and white soldiers at Bamber Bridge, Launceston, and Leicester resulted in deaths, injuries, and courts-martial.

In addition to new migration patterns, the war years sparked social changes. Marriage and birth rates rebounded after hitting all-time lows during the Great Depression. Before men left for war, many couples conceived "good-bye babies" born nine months later. As wartime separations and experiences tested marriages, divorce rates also increased.

On the home front, the war greatly affected women's lives. Many volunteered at Red Cross chapters or entertained troops at United Service Organizations (USO) clubs. Many more entered the paid workforce, replacing men who were serving in the military. The number of women with paid jobs rose by 57 percent from 12 million in 1940 to 20 million by 1945. For the first time in U.S. history, a majority of married women worked outside the home. Although more than one-third of American women

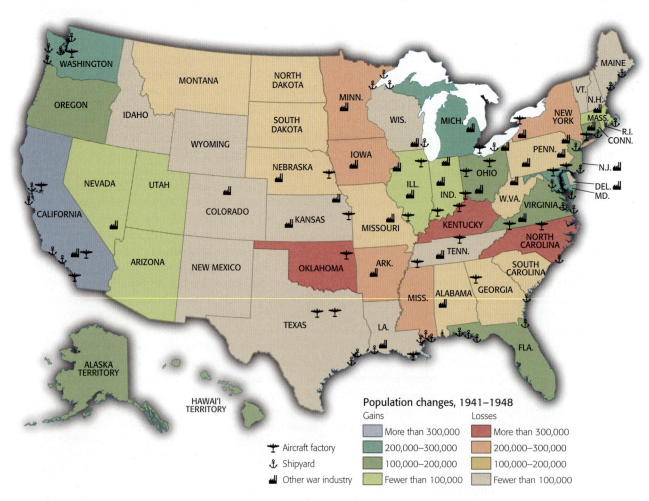

Map 21.3 Wartime Migration Patterns Defense industry jobs played a key role in shaping wartime migration patterns in the United States. ▲

Library of Congress Prints and Photographs Division [LC-USZC4-1334]

Pvt. Joe Louis says...

"We're going to do our part ...and we'll win because we're on God's side"

Global Americans

The son of Alabama sharecroppers, the great-grandson of a slave, and the great-great-grandson of a white slave owner, **Joe Louis** attained fame and wealth unprecedented for African Americans of his era. While he held the heavyweight boxing championship from 1937 to 1949 (a record that still stands), two of his fights had particular resonance at a time of rising international tensions. In June 1935, many, especially African Americans, cheered Louis's victory over Italian Primo Carnera while Mussolini's armies invaded Ethiopia. A year later, the Nazis touted Max Schmeling's victory over Louis as proof of Germanic superiority. But in the rematch in June 1938, Louis knocked out Schmeling in the first round as nearly 100 million people worldwide listened on the radio. Louis became an international inspiration for those who opposed fascism, and Americans of all races embraced him as a symbol of democratic values and racial unity. He enlisted in the army right after Pearl Harbor, and rather than sending him into combat, the army used him for morale-boosting boxing exhibitions and recruitment campaigns aimed at African Americans. He donated tens of thousands of dollars from his matches to war relief efforts. At one exhibition, Louis declared, "We're going to do our part and we'll win 'cause we're on God's side," a phrase that U.S. propagandists quickly used in their campaigns. Privately, Louis challenged the military's racist practices. After the war, he struggled financially due to back taxes and unscrupulous managers. When he died broke in 1981, Schmeling, Louis's friend and former adversary, paid part of his funeral costs.

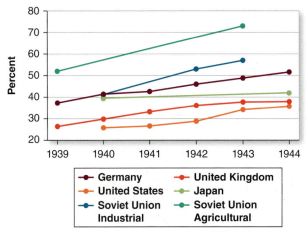

NOTE: No data available for United States, 1939; Soviet Union Industrial, 1939, 1941, 1944; Japan, 1939, 1941–1943; Soviet Union Agricultural, 1940–942, 1944.

Figure 21.3 Women Workers as a Percentage of the Civilian Workforce, 1939–1944 More than one-third of American women joined the civilian workforce during World War II, but this proportion was smaller than that of their British and Soviet counterparts, some of whom were involuntarily conscripted. Although the Nazis placed special emphasis on women's roles as wives and mothers, hundreds of thousands of German women served in auxiliaries of the armed forces and worked in hospitals, offices, and factories. Despite patriarchal cultural norms, Japanese women played vital roles in war production and agriculture. ▲ Source: Dear, I. C. B., and M. R. D. Foot, *The Oxford Companion to World War II* (Oxford, 2003), 2014 online ed, http://www.oxfordreference.com/view/10.1093/acref/9780198604464.001.0001/acref-9780198604464-e-1566?p=emailAWogkKzU5LJo2&d=/10.1093/acref/9780198604464.001.0001/acref-9780198604464-e-1566

worked for wages for all or part of the war, higher percentages of German, Japanese, British, and Soviet women were part of the wartime workforce (see Figure 21.3).

Some American women took traditionally "male" jobs such as welding. **Rosie the Riveter** became a patriotic symbol of women working in defense industries, although few women were actually trained as riveters. But women

sometimes paid a price for their new economic independence. Many struggled to find adequate child care. Recruiters stressed that female employees were needed "only for the duration."

U.S. women also joined the armed forces. Each branch of the military organized women's auxiliary units with special uniforms, officers, and pay equal to that of male soldiers. By 1945, more than 350,000 women had joined the Women's Army Corps (WACs), the U.S. Navy's Women Accepted for Volunteer Emergency Service (WAVES), the Women's Auxiliary Service Pilots (WASPs), the Army and Navy Nurses Corps, the Coast Guard (SPARs), and the Marines.

World War II was a transformative era for African Americans. Continuing the Great Migration that had begun in the early twentieth century, 700,000 additional southern blacks moved north during the war. More than 2 million worked in defense jobs, but ongoing wage and housing discrimination limited their wartime gains. To call attention to these problems, in the spring of 1941, labor leader A. Philip Randolph and the National Association for the Advancement of Colored People (NAACP) threatened to stage a march on Washington, D.C., protesting discrimination at defense plants and in federal employment and calling for the integration of the armed services. Worried about the implications of such a demonstration, Roosevelt made a deal. In exchange for the organizers' canceling the march and dropping their demand for integration in the military, the president issued an executive order banning discrimination in defense industries and establishing the Fair Employment Practices Committee (FEPC). By the end of the war, the number of African American federal employees had risen from 60,000 in 1941 to 200,000. Although the understaffed and poorly funded FEPC was less successful in striking down inequities in the private sector, FDR's actions were a historic step toward racial equality.

Rosie the Riveter Cultural icon representing American women who worked in factories during World War II, many in defense industries.

The nearly 1 million African Americans in the military served in segregated units that were mostly relegated to noncombat assignments. For most of the war, the marines excluded blacks entirely and the navy accepted them only for kitchen duties. The army created separate black regiments commanded by mostly white officers. The Red Cross even segregated its blood supply.

These injustices prompted tremendous growth in civil rights activities during the war. Black organizations embraced the **Double V Campaign**, calling for victory over fascism abroad and over segregation and discrimination at home. Membership in the NAACP rose from 18,000 to almost 500,000. In May 1942, the Fellowship of Reconciliation organized one of the nation's earliest sit-ins to protest a Chicago diner's refusal to serve blacks. Other African Americans joined the newly established Congress of Racial Equality (CORE). At a 1944 CORE demonstration in Washington, D.C., participants challenged segregation and carried signs asking, "Are You for Hitler's Way or the American Way?"

Mexican Americans also benefited from the booming wartime economy, and many found industrial work that offered an escape from migrant farm work. Patriotism temporarily overrode cultural mores that discouraged Mexican American women from working outside the home, and they took jobs in offices, hospitals, and defense plants. When the demand for manual labor exceeded the available domestic workforce, the federal government established the *bracero* **program** allowing Mexicans to enter the United States as guest agricultural or railroad workers.

Almost 400,000 Latinos served in the U.S. armed forces, the highest proportional representation of any ethnic group in the United States. Hundreds of Latinas joined the WACs, WAVES, and other women's military auxiliary branches. Puerto Rican soldiers guarded the Panama Canal and the Caribbean. More than 9,000 Latinos died in combat.

Although Mexican Americans were categorized by the U.S. government as white and served in integrated military units, they still experienced discrimination. In the summer of 1943, white sailors stationed in the Los Angeles area clashed with Latino youths wearing zoot suits, colorful and loose garments worn with long key chains and pork-pie hats. The suits violated WPB regulations limiting the amount of fabric that could be used in clothing, but a network of bootleg tailors continued to produce them. Racism combined with anger about the youths' flouting of federal rationing rules triggered the **Zoot Suit riots**, a series of episodes in which sailors physically assaulted Mexican American youths, stripped them, burned their clothing, and cut their ducktail-styled hair. Ordered not to arrest any of the servicemen, police arrested more than five hundred Latinos. The episodes triggered similar attacks on Latinos in Beaumont, Chicago, New York, San Diego, and Philadelphia.

World War II had a mixed effect on Native Americans, bringing some into contact with whites, often for the first time. Approximately twenty-five thousand Native Americans served in the military. A select group of soldiers, mostly Navajos, worked as "code talkers," soldiers who used their native languages in military communications. Enemy forces were unable to break those codes, and they proved invaluable in operations in the Pacific theater. For Native Americans who stayed on reservations, the war years were difficult. There were few defense jobs nearby, and government subsidies dwindled as federal funds were diverted to the war effort.

Asian Americans were especially attentive to the Pacific theater of the war because Chinese, Korean, and Filipino immigrants sent money and supplies to their homelands to defeat the Japanese. Many members of these ethnic groups enlisted in the U.S. military, seeing action in both Europe and the Pacific. Those who remained in the United States benefited from nondiscriminatory policies in U.S. war industries.

Although few Americans noticed at the time, World War II was a crucial turning point in the formation of gay communities nationwide. The mobility of the war years created many venues where gay men and women could find others like themselves. As they moved from small towns to gay subcultures in places such as New York, San Francisco, and Los Angeles, many experienced personal liberation. With so many men overseas, lesbians could travel or go out together without attracting much notice. Driven by the same patriotism as their straight counterparts, thousands of gay men and women joined the armed services. Some men did so in order to disprove stereotypes linking homosexuality and effeminacy. Most easily passed the psychological tests the Pentagon had instituted to identify gays prior to enlistment. Although military regulations outlawed sodomy, many commanders refused to report gays who served their units well. Expulsion from the armed services could have grave consequences. A dishonorable discharge not only disqualified one from receiving G.I. Bill benefits but also contained a code alerting potential employers to the reason for dismissal. At a time when homosexuality was illegal in all fifty states and considered a mental illness by the medical profession, many companies refused to knowingly hire gay people.

21-3c Civil Liberties

Whereas World War I had divided Americans and triggered severe repressions of civil liberties such as the 1918 Sedition Act, World War II had broad-based popular support and did not spark repressive laws. The 1940 Alien Registration Act (better known as the *Smith Act*), which criminalized speech advocating the overthrow of the U.S. government, was not frequently applied during the war, although it was later

> The war triggers opposition to as well as demands for incarceration of those perceived to be disloyal.

Double V Campaign Launched by the *Pittsburgh Courier*, a black newspaper, demanded that African Americans fighting abroad be granted full citizenship rights at home.

bracero **program** Spanish for "one who uses his arms"; agreement that allowed for the temporary importation of contract workers from Mexico into the United States.

Zoot Suit riots Series of clashes between Mexican American youth and white sailors in Los Angeles in 1943; police response triggered outrage among Latinos.

used to prosecute U.S. Communists. When FBI director J. Edgar Hoover concluded that Albert Einstein's lifelong associations with pacifist and socialist organizations violated the Smith Act and recommended deportation, the State Department overruled him. Einstein quickly became a U.S. citizen, and as a gesture of loyalty to his newly adopted country, he donated a handwritten copy of his 1905 paper on special relativity to be auctioned at a war bond drive. It sold for $6.5 million.

With German Americans constituting nearly one-quarter of the U.S. population by 1940, the OWI carefully avoided the tactics of World War I's Committee on Public Information, which demonized anything or anyone German. In that era, Socialist Party leaders had gone to jail for denouncing the 1917 conscription law, but in 1941, after Germany attacked the Soviet Union, the Communist Party of the United States backed the campaign to defeat Nazism and fascism. U.S. Communists enlisted in the armed forces, sold war bonds, collected burn dressings, and enforced blackouts.

The war effort united Americans across religious lines, transcending long-standing divisions among Catholics, Jews, and Protestants. Almost everyone viewed the war against fascism as a "just war," a conflict that is morally necessary to defeat a larger evil. Many soldiers found prayer essential to surviving the horrors of combat and forged close bonds with comrades of different faiths. Soldiers' increasing religiosity contributed to a great rise in church attendance and overseas missionary work in the postwar era.

There were, however, Americans who opposed World War II on ethical and religious grounds. Nation of Islam leader Elijah Muhammad, a black separatist, advised his followers to resist the draft and was subsequently jailed for violating the Selective Service Act. Quakers and Mennonites were among those who refused to violate peace traditions of their churches. World War II marked the first time that Congress legally recognized **conscientious objector (CO)** status. Under the law, objectors could fulfill their military obligation by accepting noncombat roles in the armed forces or civilian jobs with "national importance." Many pacifists served as military ambulance drivers or medics. Others volunteered as smoke jumpers fighting forest fires or as guinea pigs in dangerous medical experiments. But 6,000 of the 72,345 Americans who applied for CO status refused to support the war in any way and went to prison. They were often derided as unpatriotic and cowardly.

Although government authorities arrested 14,000 Italian and German potential security risks living in North and South America during the war, only 5,000 Italian and German enemy aliens and U.S. citizens were held in detention camps. Japanese immigrants and Japanese Americans faced far greater curtailment of civil liberties. Following the Pearl Harbor attacks, Hawai'i—then a U.S. territory—instituted martial law, and military police arrested several hundred suspected Japanese spies and saboteurs. None was found to have committed an offense. Military officials considered but decided against interning the island's 100,000 residents of Japanese descent because they constituted almost half of Hawai'i's population and played a critical role in the local economy.

People of Japanese descent on the mainland were treated much more harshly. A tiny percentage of the U.S. population and socially isolated, people of Japanese descent drew the ire of Americans long hostile to Asian immigrants and eager to avenge the Pearl Harbor attacks. Although the U.S. government arrested approximately 2,000 potential subversives with Japanese ancestry, it found none guilty of crimes. In February 1942, Roosevelt nonetheless issued Executive Order 9066, establishing a defense zone along the entire West Coast. More than 110,000 Japanese Americans were evacuated to makeshift "assembly centers," at least two-thirds of them **Nisei**, native-born U.S. citizens of Japanese extraction. From the assembly centers, Japanese Americans were sent to ten **internment camps** in remote parts of the West and South (see Map 21.4). Living conditions and medical care were basic at best. Armed guards patrolled the fortified compounds.

About thirty-five thousand detainees found ways to leave the camps after they pledged loyalty to the United States and promised to obey a law prohibiting return to their homes within the West Coast defense zone. Some accepted jobs in labor-deprived industries or received college scholarships provided by churches and philanthropies. Around 1,300 Nisei men, about 5 percent of the draft-eligible individuals in the internment camps, volunteered for the all-Nisei 442 Combat Team, which consisted primarily of Japanese Americans from Hawai'i. This unit won more than 1,000 citations for bravery and lost more than 500 men in battle, one of the army's highest casualty rates. Despite an edict from Emperor Hirohito declaring them traitors who should be executed upon capture, a small contingent of Nisei from the internment camps volunteered to serve as military translators in the Pacific.

The Supreme Court confirmed the constitutionality of the Japanese American internment in two decisions handed down in December 1944. Both **Korematsu v. United States** and **Endo, Ex Parte** upheld the federal government's right to detain Japanese residents on the West Coast as a means of ensuring national security. But the *Endo* decision ruled that the War Relocation Authority had not proven the disloyalty of a Nisei internee named Mitsuye Endo and therefore ordered that she be released and allowed to return to the West Coast. Anticipating the ruling, military authorities proclaimed one day before it was announced that it was

conscientious objector (CO) Individual who refuses military service on the basis of religious or ethical beliefs.

Nisei Japanese term used to describe second-generation children born to immigrants in a new country, as opposed to the first-generation immigrants called *Issei*.

internment camps Ten camps in isolated locations in seven U.S. states used as prisons to which more than one hundred ten thousand Japanese and Japanese Americans were relocated from the Pacific Coast.

Korematsu v. United States U.S. Supreme Court ruling in 1944 upholding the constitutionality of the internment of Japanese Americans during World War II, regardless of citizenship.

Endo, Ex Parte Unanimous 1944 U.S. Supreme Court decision that led to the reopening of the West Coast for resettlement by Japanese American citizens following their internment.

Map 21.4 Internment Camps for Japanese Americans, 1942–1945

Under the internment policy imposed in 1942, the U.S. government gave one hundred ten thousand Japanese Americans living along the West Coast seventy-two hours to close their businesses, find custodians for their farms and pets, and vacate their houses prior to their evacuation to ten isolated compounds scattered across seven states. Most were forced to surrender their property permanently. Others returned months later to homes that had been burglarized or destroyed. ▶

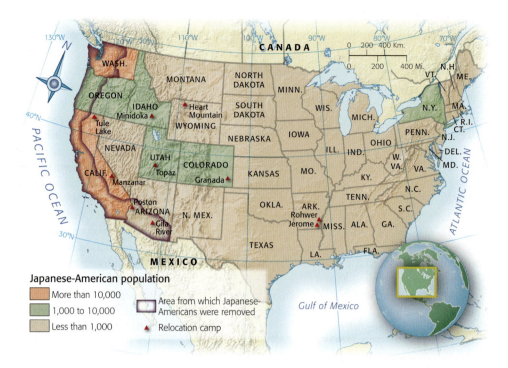

Japanese-American population
- More than 10,000
- 1,000 to 10,000
- Less than 1,000
- Area from which Japanese-Americans were removed
- ▲ Relocation camp

no longer necessary to detain the West Coast Japanese and ordered the release of approved internees starting January 2, 1945.

The internment disillusioned many detainees. After the war, 5,000 renounced their U.S. citizenship and moved to Japan. Although the evacuations had cost those Japanese affected an estimated $400 million in lost property, Congress provided only $37 million in reparations in 1948. Forty years later, federal lawmakers officially apologized for its wartime violation of Japanese American civil liberties and voted to give each of the 60,000 surviving detainees a $20,000 indemnity.

21-4
Road to Victory

On August 14, 1945, the Japanese surrendered. In this U.S. Army photograph taken the following day, American servicemen and women gathered in front of the "Rainbow Corner" Red Cross club in Paris to celebrate the end of World War II.

Examine the faces of the American men and women in this photograph, and imagine how members of the armed forces in Allied and Axis nations might have responded to the end of the war. How had race and gender shaped wartime experiences? ▶

> Go to MindTap® to practice history with the Chapter 21 **Primary Source Writing Activity: The Road to Victory.** Read and view primary sources and respond to a writing prompt.

McNulty/American Military Activity/National Archives

After gaining the offensive in 1943, the Allies implemented a two-stage strategy to defeat the Axis. After first defeating the Germans in the European theater, the Allies turned to defeating the Japanese in the Pacific theater. The war's latter months witnessed brutal battles, revealed the horrors of the Holocaust, and marked the beginning of the atomic age. Determined not to repeat the punitive treaties that ended World War I, American, Soviet, and British policy makers planned for peace. They were unable, however, to resolve some issues which had serious ramifications in the postwar era. Inspired by Atlantic Charter objectives, racial minorities and colonized peoples were ready to fight for inclusion and independence.

☞ As you read, compare and contrast the final stages of combat in the European and Pacific theaters. Explain why American, Soviet, and British policy makers differed in their respective peace aims.

21-4a Defeat of Nazi Germany

On June 6, 1944—known as **D-Day**—the Allies under the command of U.S. general Dwight D. Eisenhower opened the long-delayed second front

{ Following the opening of a second front in France, Allied and Soviet forces push into Germany.

in northwestern France. Facing minimal threat from the *Luftwaffe*, which had been weakened by severe losses in air battles and Allied bombings of defense plants, a vast flotilla of 160,000 (ultimately 3 million) troops crossed the English Channel in the first wave. A few hours earlier, paratroopers had dropped behind German lines. At dawn, British, American, and Canadian troops had made amphibious landings at six different points on the coast of Normandy. After meeting strong resistance and incurring heavy casualties, the troops secured the beachhead and began pushing the German defense back. A month later, certain that defeat was imminent, several German military commanders tried to assassinate Hitler to secure peace terms that would spare Germany from invasion, but their plot failed. Hitler retaliated by having 4,000 people executed.

On July 25, after a devastating aerial and artillery assault, the Allies opened a path for their armies to pursue the Germans across France. By August 25, U.S. and Free French troops had liberated Paris. After their successful eastward push through France, the Allies' front lines stretched from the Netherlands in the north to Switzerland in the south.

Aiming to recapture the valuable port at Antwerp before the Allies could resupply and use their superior airpower, Hitler ordered a risky counteroffensive in Belgium. In mid-December, mechanized German divisions broke through weak Allied lines in the Ardennes Forest and then struck Bastogne, a small town where seven major roads converged. But a much smaller U.S. force managed to defend the vital crossroads in a week-long siege. After reinforcements arrived and the weather improved, the Allies defeated the Germans in the **Battle of the Bulge**. Having used most of their reserves and left the western part of Germany vulnerable, the Germans knew that their last gamble had failed.

Within weeks, the Allies crossed into Germany itself. In mid-January 1945, Soviet troops advanced westward across the Oder River and headed toward Berlin. In March, American forces crossed the Rhine River and secured the industrial Ruhr region. In late April, U.S. and Soviet troops met at the Elbe River. On April 30, as the Red Army neared the outskirts of Berlin, Hitler committed suicide by taking a cyanide capsule and then shooting himself in the head. On May 7, his successor unconditionally surrendered to General Eisenhower, and on May 8 people all over the world participated in Victory in Europe Day—**V-E Day**—celebrations.

21-4b The Holocaust

As U.S. and Soviet troops advanced through Germany in 1945, they liberated concentration camps and found

{ U.S. and Allied leaders struggle to comprehend and confront reports of unprecedented Nazi genocide.

incontrovertible evidence of the Nazis' atrocities against Jews, political dissidents, the Roma, Soviet POWs, and others. As many as 500,000 Nazis and Nazi collaborators had identified, deported, enslaved, and killed more than 11 million people at approximately 42,000 facilities in Germany and German-occupied territories. But the Allies had been slow to respond to the **Final Solution**, the Nazis' secret plan to exterminate all of the Jews in Europe formalized in January 1942. During the war, escapees from the camps had informed U.S. and British officials and the Polish government in exile of the mass executions and the Nazis' use of poison gas and crematoria. However, Allied officials had difficulty grasping the enormity of the genocide. In December 1942, the United Nations issued a joint declaration denouncing the Nazis' "bestial policy of cold-blooded extermination" and vowing that war criminals would be prosecuted after the war. The Allies could do little else during the war because the Germans occupied most of Europe.

D-Day June 6, 1944, the day of Allied landings on the Normandy coast, in which the first wave of 160,000 Allied troops challenged heavily fortified German forces along fifty miles of coastline.

Battle of the Bulge Failed German offensive in December 1944 in the Ardennes region, costliest battle of the war in terms of U.S. casualties.

V-E Day (Victory in Europe Day) Public holiday celebrated on May 8, 1945, to mark the Allies' formal acceptance of Nazi Germany's unconditional surrender.

Final Solution Nazi plan formulated in January 1942 following years of severe Nazi discrimination against Jews to systematically exterminate the Jewish people in Nazi-occupied Europe.

AP Images/Dpa/picture-alliance

The Liberation of Concentration Camps In November 1944, American troops rescue the emaciated and exhausted survivors of the concentration camp Woebbelin. Like all who liberated the camps, they were horrified by the magnitude of Nazi atrocities. Images of mass graves, gas chambers, and ovens used as killing machines and the emaciated, haunted survivors shocked the world and convinced millions of the evil nature of Nazism and the need for global action to prevent the recurrence of such human rights abuses forever. ▲

History without Borders

Eugenics

Nations and States with Sterilization Laws, 1907–1940 Eight nations, provinces and states in Canada and Mexico, and thirty-one U.S. states adopted laws permitting or mandating the sterilization of people found to be "mentally deficient" by authorities. Although some jurisdictions required the voluntary consent of those being sterilized, such consent was sometimes obtained through coercive means. In many places, state-sanctioned sterilizations were not discontinued until the mid-1970s. ▲

The Nazis' glorification of a white, blond, blue-eyed "master race" and persecution of Jews and others deemed genetically inferior were grounded in a transnational movement called *eugenics*. Some of the most prominent social scientists in the West contributed to its development, including Thomas Malthus, Herbert Spencer, Charles Darwin, and Gregor Mendel. Sir Francis Galton, a British intellectual, built on their ideas of human population,

natural selection, and inherited characteristics to begin the modern field of eugenics in the 1880s. He argued that the human race could be improved by selective breeding amplifying physical health, intelligence, and high moral character. Thus, he advocated early marriage for the production of children among genetically superior people, whom he equated with the British upper classes, an approach known as *positive eugenics*. In the United States, scientists

such as the zoologist Charles Davenport flipped Galton's ideas to promote *negative eugenics*. To suppress disease, imbecility, and criminality, Davenport advocated limiting the fertility of those deemed genetically inferior through marriage prohibitions, involuntary sterilization, and even euthanasia.

Backed by Carnegie Institution and the Rockefeller Foundation, Davenport and his researchers collected hereditary data and tried to identify the genetically

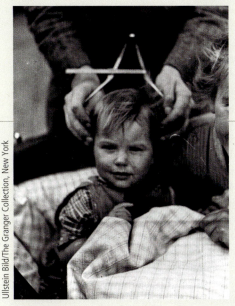

A University of Kiel Researcher Measures the Skull of a Child in a German Village, 1932 Developed by German physician Franz Joseph Gall in 1796, phrenology extrapolated personality traits from measurements of the human skull. Although the principles behind phrenology had been largely debunked by the end of the nineteenth century, the pseudoscience was adopted by eugenicists, notably the Nazis, in attempts to provide scientific evidence of Aryan superiority. ▲

Ullstein Bild/The Granger Collection, New York

CBW/Alamy Stock Photo

Nazi Propaganda Poster, 1938 This 1938 poster promoting Nazi Germany's Aktion T4, a Nazi program of forced euthanasia, reads: "This person suffering from hereditary defects costs the community 60,000 Reichsmark during his lifetime. Fellow German, that is your money, too." ▲

desirable and undesirable. Prominent scientists, reformers, and social workers embraced eugenics as a humane and progressive means of addressing social ills.

In the early twentieth century, more than thirty states enacted statutes prohibiting the mentally ill from marrying and requiring their sterilization, a practice upheld by the Supreme Court in *Buck v. Bell* (1927). Between 1907 and 1964, approximately 64,000 Americans were sterilized, primarily in prisons and state-run insane asylums. In 1924, eugenics policy informed the Immigration Act that placed strict quotas on the number of immigrants from eastern and southern Europe, believed to be of racial stock genetically inferior to that of northern Europeans.

U.S. eugenics inspired similar movements throughout Europe, Latin America, and Asia. From 1934 to 1975, Sweden forcibly sterilized more than 62,000 people. In Brazil, the government backed efforts to increase the white population while reducing the fertility of descendants of African slaves and Asian immigrants. Canadian officials legalized the forcible sterilization of

First Nation peoples. Australia adopted policies removing mixed-race Aboriginal children from their parents. Japan's National Eugenic Law (1940) authorized the sterilization of criminals and those with genetic diseases such as color-blindness, hemophilia, albinism, mental illness, or epilepsy.

Eugenics fed notions of race purity and Aryan superiority. Adolf Hitler studied American eugenics, using it to justify his call to rid Germany of the polluting influence of Jews. After taking power in 1933, Nazi officials hand selected victims for sterilization and euthanasia. By 1937, they had forcibly sterilized 400,000 people and killed thousands of the institutionalized disabled through programs like Aktion T4. After the war began, gassing victims proved more efficient than lethal injections, a lesson applied to the creation of gas chambers for the mass exterminations of the Holocaust. The Nazis also instituted positive eugenics programs that rewarded Aryan women who gave birth to several children and that placed "racially valuable" children from Nazi-occupied countries with German families.

In the Nazi racial program, eugenics pushed to its extreme in genocide provoked global revulsion. The trajectory of race science changed course from creating categories and hierarchies to rejecting them. Eugenics was renamed *genetics*, a field that now concentrates on the mechanism of heredity, not its social or political application.

Critical Thinking Questions

▶ What factors do you think explain why eugenics became a transnational movement in the early twentieth century? How did Nazi Germany's application of eugenics differ from that of other nations?

▶ What long-range ramifications did eugenics have? How do contemporary ideas about genetics differ from those common in the early twentieth century?

War Refugee Board (WRB)
U.S. government agency, established in January 1944, charged with rescuing European Jews and other victims of Nazi persecution.

Bretton Woods economic system First-ever negotiated monetary order governing currency relations among sovereign states; created in 1944 and operated until the early 1970s.

World Bank UN international financial institution founded in 1944 that provides loans and technical assistance to developing nations; aims to reduce global poverty.

International Monetary Fund (IMF) International organization created in 1944 that promotes global monetary and exchange stability and the expansion of world trade.

developing nations Countries seeking to foster economic growth, diversification, and industrialization, often heavily reliant on the export of a few agricultural crops.

United Nations (UN) International organization that promotes global peace and human rights, established on October 24, 1945, as a replacement for the League of Nations.

Yalta Conference Meeting in February 1945 in the Crimea during which Roosevelt, Stalin, and Churchill planned the next phase of the war and discussed the postwar world.

Jewish leaders in the United States, such as Rabbi Stephen Wise, implored President Roosevelt to stop the mass murders. Despite his deep sympathies for the Jews and victims of Axis-sponsored terror, the president was constrained by anti-Semitic and xenophobic sentiments in Congress and among the American public. Many found it difficult to believe that the Nazis were capable of committing the heinous crimes being described by eyewitnesses. In April 1943, U.S. and British officials met in Bermuda to discuss possible solutions, but after the British refused to allow Jewish refugees to emigrate to Palestine, the delegates concluded that the best way to help the refugees was to end the war as quickly as possible. Some Zionists in Palestine and the United States feared helping Jews escape from Nazi Germany would undermine political support for the postwar creation of a Jewish state.

Secretary of the Treasury Henry Morgenthau, the only Jew in Roosevelt's cabinet, disagreed. After an aide submitted *Report to the Secretary on the Acquiescence of This Government in the Murder of the Jews*, a scathing indictment of the U.S. State Department's obstruction of rescue efforts for European Jews, Morgenthau used the report to persuade Roosevelt to create the **War Refugee Board (WRB)**. Established in January 1944, the board enlisted foreign governments and nongovernmental organizations (NGOs) to provide for the evacuation and relief of refugees. But U.S. military commanders, unwilling to divert American planes from key Allied military operations and still unsure that reports of the mass executions were accurate, rejected the WRB's calls to bomb the notorious Auschwitz death camp and its feeder rail lines. By the end of the war, the WRB had rescued approximately 200,000 Jews and 20,000 non-Jews.

21-4c **Plans for Postwar Peace**

In late 1943, as they went on the military offensive in Europe, the Allies accelerated their planning for the postwar era. In contrast to Wilson's rigidity and obsession with the League of Nations, Roosevelt was an adept compromiser who supported the creation

> Allied policy makers establish institutions to secure economic and political stability in the postwar world.

of several new international organizations that would reshape postwar politics and economics.

In July 1944, representatives from forty-four countries convened in Bretton Woods, New Hampshire, to establish regulations on global monetary policy, later known as the **Bretton Woods economic system**. Seeking to avoid the economic protectionism of the interwar period, the delegates committed their nations to free trade and open borders. To promote economic stability and growth, they created the International Bank for Reconstruction and Development, known as the **World Bank**, and the **International Monetary Fund (IMF)** to issue short- and long-term loans to **developing nations** to promote their stability and growth. Providing over one-third of $9 billion of original capital and holding one-third of each board's votes, the United States dominated the institutions. The use of the U.S. dollar as the benchmark for the new international currency valuation system became an especially potent illustration of U.S. economic power. Unwilling to surrender its state-centered economic system or give capitalist countries access to its finances, the Soviet Union refused to join either the World Bank or IMF, a decision reflecting growing tensions among the Big Three.

From August to October 1944, U.S., British, Soviet, and Chinese officials met in Washington, D.C., to draft a charter for the **United Nations (UN)**. Renouncing the ideologies of the Axis Powers, the charter's preamble decried "the scourge of war" and reaffirmed "faith in fundamental human rights, in the dignity and worth of the human person, in the equal rights of men and women and of nations large and small." It pledged to uphold international law and "to promote social progress and better standards of life in larger freedom."

The UN delegates created a Security Council comprised of five permanent members (the United States, the Soviet Union, Great Britain, China, and France) and a much larger General Assembly. To address the failings of the League of Nations, the Security Council was charged with maintaining international peace and security through peacekeeping operations, sanctions, and military intervention. Each permanent member of the Security Council could veto any proposed action. In April 1945, two hundred eighty-two UN delegates from fifty countries convened for the first time in San Francisco. On July 28, in a significant contrast to its refusal to join the League of Nations after World War I, the U.S. Senate voted 89-2 to ratify the UN charter. In the postwar era, the United States strongly embraced the principles of collective security that it had previously rejected, and the United Nations built its headquarters in New York City on land donated by the Rockefeller family.

In February 1945, Winston Churchill, Franklin Roosevelt, and Joseph Stalin met for the last time at **Yalta**, a resort town on the Crimean Sea. In ten days of hard bargaining, the Big Three decided to include France in postwar governance of Germany and to require Germany to pay reparations, the amount to be determined later. The question of how to deal with the defeated or liberated nations of Eastern Europe★ dominated the conference. With the Red Army already entrenched in much of the region and acutely aware of the Soviets' disproportionate military sacrifices, Churchill and Roosevelt were reconciled to a temporary Soviet sphere of influence there. Accordingly, they accepted Stalin's demands regarding the location of Poland's borders in exchange for a guarantee of free elections. But they hoped that Stalin would make future concessions in exchange for U.S. aid in rebuilding his shattered country.

There was some reason for optimism. The Big Three issued a Declaration on Liberated Europe calling for democratic elections in Eastern Europe. Stalin also promised that the Soviet Union would enter the war against Japan three months after Germany surrendered. In exchange, Roosevelt and Churchill granted the Soviets concessions in Manchuria and Sakhalin Island, thus restoring territories lost in the 1905 Russo-Japanese War. Stalin then pledged to support Jiang Jieshi and the Chinese Nationalists, not their Communist opponents led by Tse-tung (Mao Zedong). Although the delegates were confident that they had made good compromises based on political and military realities, the ambiguity of several agreements made at Yalta later sparked heated debates.

But Roosevelt would not live long enough to defend those decisions or to resolve the issues left unaddressed. On April 12, during a trip to Warm Springs, Georgia, where he had established a polio treatment center, he had a fatal stroke. Vice President Harry S. Truman, a former senator from Missouri with little foreign policy expertise, would now have to lead the United States to victory over Germany and Japan and deal with Soviet demands for the peace.

Joe Rosenthal, *Raising the Flag on Iwo Jima on Mount Suribachi,* **March 1945** This photograph is one of the war's most iconic images. Marines Harlon Block, Franklin Sousley, and Michael Strank were killed in action soon after the photo was taken. The three surviving flag raisers, Marines Rene Gagnon and Ira Hayes (a Pima Indian) and sailor John Bradley were celebrated as national heroes and helped sell billions of dollars of war bonds. Each, however, was deeply scarred by his wartime experiences and conflicted about participating in the photograph. ▲

21-4d Defeat of Imperial Japan

In late 1944, the Allies launched their Pacific offensive and quickly won a series of battles. By February 1945, they had control of the Gilbert, Marshall, and Caroline Islands as well as New Guinea and the Philippines. In October 1944, the U.S. Navy defeated the Japanese at Leyte Gulf, the largest naval battle in history. Japanese human wave assaults called *Banzai* charges, civilian suicides at Saipan, and *kamikaze* attacks in which pilots deliberately crashed themselves and their planes into American battleships at Leyte, intensified U.S. soldiers' and sailors' hatred for an enemy whose culture they found difficult to understand. On January 20, 1945, Emperor Hirohito approved *Ketsu-Go,* a plan calling for the Japanese soldiers and civilians to fight to the death if the Americans invaded Japan.

On February 19, 1945, U.S. marines landed on Iwo Jima, an island six hundred fifty nautical miles south of the Japanese mainland. Although they outnumbered the Japanese almost four to one, they met ferocious resistance from 22,060 Japanese troops, only 216 of whom survived

> Fierce fighting in the Pacific ends with the first combat uses of atomic weapons.

the thirty-five-day battle. Meanwhile, a campaign of intensive bombing began. On March 9, three hundred B-29s flying at low attitude dropped enough incendiary bombs and napalm to destroy sixteen square miles of Tokyo, killing approximately 83,000 people in less than three hours and leaving 1 million homeless. The previous month, the Allies had carried out a similar fire-bombing of the German city of Dresden. Both attacks exemplified the ways that World War II had shattered distinctions between combatants and noncombatants. This was a **total war** in which millions of people—soldiers and civilians alike—were war targets and war casualties.

Such brutality was evident in the Battle of Okinawa. After Allied troops landed on the island on April 1, they fought Japanese forces holed up in caves. At the same time, Japanese *kamikaze* pilots struck the U.S. Fifth Fleet off the coast of Okinawa, and the Japanese navy sent the battleship *Yamato* on a suicide mission. U.S. naval and air forces sank it, killing 3,000 Japanese sailors. On Okinawa, more than 95,000 Japanese and 12,000 Allied soldiers died in the eighty-four-day battle, the bloodiest of the Pacific theater. Tens of thousands of Okinawan civilians were also killed, wounded, or took their own lives.

Banzai Shortened form of Japanese exclamation "Tenno Heika Banzai" ("Long live the Emperor"), and Allied term for the Japanese infantry's human wave attacks in the Pacific.

kamikaze Japanese for "spirit wind," suicide attacks made by Japanese aviators on Allied naval vessels in the last stages of World War II.

total war Warfare in which every human and material resource is used for defense or targeted offensively.

Everett Collection Inc/Alamy Stock Photo

★ NOTE: When capitalized, Eastern and Western Europe indicate the post–World War II political division of Europe. When not capitalized, eastern and western Europe indicate geographical regions.

Everett Collection Inc/Alamy Stock Photo

Global Americans

Ernie Pyle was an American journalist best known for his columns about World War II. In 1940, after spending seven years traveling the United States writing newspaper stories, Pyle journeyed to England to report on the Battle of Britain. In 1942, he began covering America's involvement in the war, reporting on Allied operations in North Africa, Sicily, Italy, and France. Instead of recounting battlefield maneuvers or actions of heroic generals, Pyle usually wrote from the perspective of the common soldier, an approach that won him great popularity and the Pulitzer Prize for journalism. "I love the infantry because they are the underdogs," he wrote. "They are the mud-rain-frost-and-wind boys. They have no comforts, and they even learn to live without the necessities. And in the end they are the guys that wars can't be won without." In 1944, in response to one of Pyle's columns, Congress authorized $10 a month "fight pay" (a 50 percent salary increase) for combat infantrymen similar to the "flight pay" given to airmen. On April 18, 1945, while covering the invasion of Okinawa, Pyle was killed in a Japanese machine gun attack on the island Iejima (formerly Ie Shima). He was among the few U.S. civilians killed during the war to be awarded the Purple Heart, and a monument in his honor stands on Okinawa. Pyle's columns remain a valuable source on the combat experience in World War II. He is also the subject of *The Story of G.I. Joe*, a feature film released shortly after his death.

The plan for the invasion of the Japanese main islands called for an attack on Kyushu in November 1945 and on Honshu in March 1946. American commanders expected to incur hundreds of thousands of U.S. casualties. But these plans did not take into account the tremendous power of the new atomic bomb. On July 16, while attending a diplomatic meeting of the Big Three in **Potsdam**, Germany, Truman received word that the first test of the atomic bomb in Alamogordo, New Mexico, had been successful. Bolstered by the news and eager to demonstrate his strength to his Soviet counterpart, the president told Stalin that the United States had developed a weapon of "unusual destructive force." Having already received reports from Soviet spies who had infiltrated the Manhattan Project, Stalin showed no special interest. But neither leader fully trusted the other.

Nevertheless, over the next two weeks, the American, British, and Soviet delegations attempted to resolve several lingering disputes. They agreed on new borders for Germany and Poland. Rejecting earlier calls to weaken Germany permanently through high reparations and territorial divisions, they called for four zones of occupation and economic rehabilitation. Each of the four occupying powers (the Soviet Union, the United States, Great Britain, and France) could extract reparations only from its zone. The delegates agreed to prosecute Nazi war criminals. They also established a Council of Foreign Ministers that would address unresolved issues such as the withdrawal of Allied troops from Iran and the fate of Italian colonies. In a declaration issued on July 26, 1945, the United States and Great Britain (the Soviet Union was not yet at war with the Japanese) demanded Japan's unconditional surrender and threatened its "prompt and utter destruction" if it did not comply.

Japan's failure to respond had immediate consequences. Determined to end the war quickly to save American lives and prevent possible gains by the Soviet Union in an attack on the Japanese in Manchuria, the Truman administration commenced with its plans. On August 6, an American B-29 bomber dropped an atomic bomb on the midsized industrial city of Hiroshima. The bomb obliterated six square miles and instantly killed more than 60,000 people. Approximately 75,000 perished later as the result of the effects of radiation. On August 8, Stalin, worried that the United States would renege on the Asian territorial concessions promised at Yalta, ordered 1.5 million Soviet troops into Manchuria and quickly captured it. The following day, hoping to make the Japanese capitulate before the Soviets made additional gains in Asia, the United States used a second, larger atomic bomb on Nagasaki, killing 40,000 people and destroying one-third of the city. On August 14, with Japan reeling from two atomic attacks and the Soviet Union's entry into the Pacific war, Emperor Hirohito defied Allied expectations and persuaded his deadlocked cabinet to accept an unconditional surrender. Victory over Japan—**V-J Day**—celebrations erupted all over the world. On September 2, the Japanese formally capitulated in a ceremony held aboard the USS *Missouri*.

After six years, the most devastating war in history was over. Approximately 65 million people had died—nearly 27 million in the Soviet Union alone; 6 million in both Poland and Germany; at least 15 million in China; 3.1 million in Japan; and millions more in Yugoslavia, Indonesia, Vietnam, and elsewhere (see Table 21.2). Approximately 11 million people died as a result of Nazi atrocities, including 6 million Jews. Although the United States lost more than 407,000 soldiers in the war, its physical landscape was virtually untouched by the conflict, and its economy was booming. By contrast, much of Europe and Asia lay in ruins and economic desolation. With the United States unquestionably the world's strongest power, an unprecedented global reconstruction effort and a major reordering of world politics lay ahead.

Potsdam Meeting in July 1945 at which British, American, and Soviet officials discussed punishment for Germany, strategies for defeating Japan, and plans for the postwar era.

V-J Day (Victory over Japan Day) Public holiday marking Japan's unconditional surrender to the Allies on August 14, 1945.

Table 21.2 Estimated Military and Civilian Casualties of World War II (in Thousands)

More people died in World War II than in any other military conflict. Although it is impossible to have precise numbers because of the challenges of record keeping in time of war, historians estimate that between 50 and 80 million soldiers and civilians died worldwide from battlefield injuries, strategic bombings, accidents, starvation, war crimes, disease, and poor treatment during captivity.

AXIS Powers	Military Deaths	Civilian Deaths	Total Deaths
Germany	4,400	1,400–2,400	5,800–6,800
Japan	2,120	1,000	3,120
Romania	300	160	460
Hungary	300	280	580
Italy	301.4	153.2	454.6
Austria (German controlled)	260	120	380
Finland	95	2	97
AXIS Totals	**7,776.4**	**3,115.2–4,115.2**	**10,891.6–11,891.6**

Allied Powers	Military Deaths	Civilian Deaths	Total Deaths
Albania	30	2	32
Australia	39.7	12	51.7
Belgium	12	76	88
Brazil	1	1	2
Bulgaria	22	3	25
Burma (British colony)	22	250	272
Canada	45.4		45.4
China	3,000–4,000	12,000–16,000	15,000–20,000
Cuba		0.1	0.1
Czechoslovakia	25	300	325
Denmark	2.1	1.1	3.2
Dutch East Indies		3,000–4,000	3,000–4,000
Ethiopia	5	95	100
France	200	350	550
French Indochina		1,000–2,000	1,000–2,000
Greece	20–35.1	300–600	320–635.1
Guam	1–2		1–2
Iceland		0.2	0.2
India (British colony)	87	1,500–2,500	1,587–2,587
Iran	0.2		0.2
Iraq	0.5		0.5
Luxembourg	2		2
Malaya (British colony)		100	100

(continued)

Table 21.2 Estimated Military and Civilian Casualties of World War II (in Thousands) *(continued)*

Allied Powers	Military Deaths	Civilian Deaths	Total Deaths
Malta (British colony)		1.5	1.5
Mexico		100	100
Netherlands	17	284	301
New Zealand	11.9	2	13.9
Norway	6.4	6.5	12.9
Philippines (U.S. territory)	57	500–900	557–957
Poland	240	5,800	6,040
Singapore (British colony)		50	50
South Africa	11.9		11.9
Soviet Union	8,700–13,850	13,000–18,000	21,800–28,000
United Kingdom (England, Scotland, Wales, and Nortern Ireland)	383.8	67.1	450.9
United States	407	12	419
Yugoslavia	300–446	1,400	1,700–1,846
Allied Totals	**13,649.9**	**40,113.6**	**53,763.5**
Overall Totals	**21,426.3**	**43,228.8–44,228.8**	**64,655.1–65,655.1**

Sources: For examples of how estimates of World War II deaths vary, see World War II Casualties, http://en.wikipedia.org/wiki/World_War_II_casualties; By the Numbers, World War II Deaths, http://www.nationalww2museum.org/learn/education/for-students/ww2-history/ww2-by-the-numbers/world-wide-deaths.html; and Estimated War Dead World War II, http://warchronicle.com/numbers/WWII/deaths.htm

Summary

After war erupted in Europe in 1939, Roosevelt tried to bolster the Allies in resisting German aggression without eroding his domestic political support or impeding America's economic recovery. His decisions positioned the United States for a leading role in international political, economic, and military affairs for decades afterward. Yet, domestically, those decisions generated an intense political debate among Americans who were reluctant to become involved in Europe's wars again. But after the Japanese attacked Pearl Harbor in December 1941, Americans were united in going to war against the Axis Powers. The postwar world envisioned by Roosevelt and Churchill earlier that year aimed for stability and security,

self-government, and an end to the use of force. But the possibility of such a world receded as the Axis Powers conquered much of Europe and Asia, enslaving and exterminating captured peoples. By mid-1942, however, the Allies had seized the offensive, and their policy makers met repeatedly to coordinate military strategies. At times, they struggled to reconcile differing objectives and to face the contradictions of their own colonialism, racial discrimination, and political repression.

With the devastation of the war confined largely to Europe and Asia, the United States prospered throughout the conflict. The federal government pumped billions of dollars into war production and instituted strict

controls on goods, wages, and prices. Business owners and workers alike benefited from a thriving economy. Traditionally underemployed groups seized unprecedented job opportunities. Millions of Americans left their communities as a result of military enlistments or in pursuit of economic advancement. Women and minorities demonstrated their patriotism and sought expanded civil rights. Marriage and birth rates rebounded from the historic lows of the Great Depression. As communities struggled to deal with burgeoning new populations, racial and class tensions sometimes exploded. More than one hundred ten thousand Japanese Americans were forced into internment camps.

Brutal battles were waged in the Atlantic and Pacific theaters during the war's final two years. As German strongholds collapsed, the Allies became aware of the full magnitude of Nazi atrocities against Jews, political dissidents, and others. After defeating Germany in May 1945, the Allies prepared for a long campaign to defeat the Japanese. But in August 1945, the use of the world's first atomic bombs brought World War II to a close, forever changing international relations and the nature of warfare.

<Thinking Back, *Looking Forward*>

As you review this chapter, consider how legacies of World War I contributed to a second global conflict. How did economic weaknesses and national grievances generate the rise of military dictatorships and ideologies that boasted of racial superiority? As the world went to war again, how did the changing nature of warfare strengthen international support for self-government, world cooperation, and human rights? In coming chapters, look for new international organizations and laws that sought to promote justice and preserve peace. What issues rooted in World War II contributed to the subsequent Cold War and to anti-imperialist upheavals in Europe's colonies and civil rights movements in the United States?

To make your study concrete, review the timeline and reflect on the entries there. Think about their causes, consequences, and connections. How do they fit with global trends?

Additional Resources

Books

Adams, Michael C. C. *The Best War Ever: America and World War II*, 2nd ed. Baltimore, MD: Johns Hopkins Press, 2015. ▶ Synthesis that demythologizes the war and describes its impact on soldiers and civilians.

Alvarez, Luis. *The Power of the Zoot: Youth Culture and Resistance in World War II*. Berkeley: University of California Press, 2009. ▶ Exploration of Zoot Suit culture among racial minorities nationwide.

Bérubé, Allan. *Coming Out Under Fire: The History of Gay Men and Women in World War Two*. New York: Free Press, 1990. ▶ Path-breaking study of gay Americans in the armed forces and on the home front.

Breitman, Richard. *FDR and the Jews*. Cambridge, MA: Harvard University Press, 2013. ▶ Balanced account of the constraints that limited Roosevelt's ability to aid victims of Nazism.

Dear, I. C. B., and M. R. B. Foot, eds. *The Oxford Companion to World War II*. Oxford University Press, 2001 print, 2003 online. ▶ Single-volume reference work commemorating the fiftieth anniversary of the war.

Dower, John. *War without Mercy: Race and Power in the Pacific War*. New York: Pantheon, 1987. ▶ Award-winning examination of racism in the war between Japan and the United States.

Frank, Richard B. *Downfall: The End of the Imperial Japanese Empire*. New York: Penguin, 2001. ▶ Exhaustive analysis of Japanese resistance in the last stages of the war.

Hastings, Max. *Inferno: The World at War, 1939–1945*. New York: Knopf, 2011. ▶ Highly readable narrative of the global war and its participants.

Reeves, Richard. *Infamy: The Shocking Story of the Japanese American Internment in World War II*. New York: Henry Holt, 2015. ▶ Best-selling author's account of the origins and impact of the internment.

Walker, J. Samuel. *Prompt and Utter Destruction: Truman and the Use of Atomic Bombs against Japan*, rev. ed. Chapel Hill: University of North Carolina Press, 2005. ▶ Brief overview of U.S. motives for using atomic weapons on Japan.

> Go to the MindTap® for **Global Americans** to access the full version of select books from this Additional Resources section.

Websites

The Institute on World War II and the Human Experience. (http://ww2.fsu.edu/) ▶ Repository of more than six thousand collections from U.S. and non-U.S. participants in the war.

The National World War II Museum. (http://nationalww2museum.org/) ▶ Collection of many learning resources and artifacts.

Researching World War II Records. (http://www.archives.gov/research/military/ww2/) ▶ Comprehensive overview of extensive collection of textual, audiovisual, and photographic records held at the National Archives.

United States Holocaust Memorial Museum. (http://www.ushmm.org/) ▶ Collection of many resources for academic researchers and educators.

World War II Documents. (http://avalon.law.yale.edu/subject_menus/wwii.asp) ▶ Multinational primary source collection created by the Avalon Project at Yale University.

Continue exploring online through MindTap®, **where you can:**
- **Assess your knowledge with the Chapter Test**
- **Watch historical videos related to the chapter**
- **Further your understanding with interactive maps and timelines**

The World at War

1939

November

Congress approves "cash and carry" plan to assist Britain.

1940

April

Germany seizes Norway and Denmark.

May–June

British evacuate Allied forces from Dunkirk.

June

Germany defeats France.

Japan calls for the creation of a Greater East Asia Co-Prosperity Sphere.

1940

September

Germany begins bombing British cities.

Roosevelt arranges destroyer deal to aid Britain.

Germany, Italy, and Japan sign Tripartite Pact.

U.S. stops sales of scrap metal and steel to Japan.

November

Roosevelt wins unprecedented third term as president.

1941

March

Congress approves Lend-Lease to aid Britain.

"STAY OUT! STAY OUT FOR MY SAKE, AS WELL AS YOUR OWN!"

DEMOCRACY

AMERICA THE LAST REFUGE OF DEMOCRACY

April

Japan and the Soviet Union sign a neutrality pact.

June

Germany invades the Soviet Union, violating the Nonaggression Pact.

1941

July

Japan invades Indochina.

U.S. halts trade with Japan and freezes Japanese assets.

August

Winston Churchill and Roosevelt issue the Atlantic Charter, stating peace goals.

December

Japan attacks Pearl Harbor and the Philippines.

U.S. declares war on Japan.

Germany declares war on the United States.

THE UNITED NATIONS FIGHT FOR FREEDOM

Britain

Germany

France

Italy

Soviet Union

United States

Japan

1942

January

Nazis formalize the Final Solution.

January

Roosevelt issues an executive order relocating Japanese Americans on the West Coast to internment camps.

April

Japan conquers the Philippines; U.S. and Filipino POWs die on forced Death March.

June

U.S. naval and air forces defeat the Japanese fleet in the Battle of Midway.

1943

January

In Casablanca, Roosevelt and Churchill announce policy of unconditional surrender.

February

Soviets defeat German forces at the Battle of Stalingrad.

June

Three-day race riot erupts in Detroit.

July

Allied invasion of Sicily begins, and Benito Mussolini is captured.

December

Congress repeals the Chinese Exclusion Act.

1944

March

Congress unanimously passes the G.I. Bill of Rights.

June

Allies launch D-Day landings at Normandy.

July

Allied nations meet in Bretton Woods to craft a new global monetary system.

August

U.S. and Free French troops liberate Paris.

November

Roosevelt wins fourth term as president.

December

Allies prevail against German counteroffensive in the Battle of the Bulge.

1945

February

Roosevelt, Churchill, and Joseph Stalin meet at Yalta to plan the postwar world.

March

U.S. marines defeat the Japanese at the Battle of Iwo Jima.

April

Roosevelt dies, and Truman becomes president.

Delegates from fifty Allied nations convene in San Francisco to establish the United Nations.

Mussolini is executed.

Hitler commits suicide.

1945

May

Germany surrenders.

July

American, British, and Soviet policy makers meet at Potsdam.

August

U.S. drops atomic bombs on Hiroshima and Nagasaki.

Japan surrenders.

Go to MindTap® to engage with an interactive version of the timeline. Analyze events and themes with clickable content, view related videos, and respond to critical thinking questions.

22 The Cold War

1945–1965

Although based in Washington, D.C., Willis Conover was familiar to millions in the Soviet Bloc thanks to his Voice of America radio shows.

I n 1959, a crowd of curious Soviet citizens gathered on the streets of Moscow to ask visiting Americans about life in the United States. One wanted to know the price of U.S. automobiles, another about the nation's unemployment rate, and a third wondered what Americans thought of Willis Conover. This final question stumped the visitor—Harvard University's head reference librarian. He had never heard of Willis Conover, and he was not alone.

Few Americans knew about Conover because the source of his popularity, a Voice of America (VOA) radio show with 30 million listeners in more than eighty nations, was not broadcast in the United States.

Willis Conover Hosting the Radio Show "Jazz Hour," 1959. Conover was an international celebrity whom few Americans knew. ▲

Begun during World War II, the VOA was—and continues to be—the federal government's direct channel of communication to the world. After the great jazz musician Duke Ellington completed a successful tour of the Soviet Union in 1954, the VOA hired Conover, a Washington, D.C., disc jockey, to create and host a jazz show. An army brat and veteran, Conover proved to be a valuable cultural soldier. "People in other countries love jazz because they love freedom," he explained, making a connection between jazz—the United States' contribution to great music—and American democracy. Conover's show, as the Harvard librarian discovered, was surprisingly popular in the Soviet Union and other Communist countries that had banned jazz because it was seen as typifying capitalist decadence and corruption.

Conover's effort to subvert the jazz ban was one tiny element of the titanic global conflict between the United States and Soviet Union known as the *Cold War*. Although not inevitable, this conflict stemmed from core ideological differences that had begun after the Russian Revolution in 1917. It pitted the U.S. mission to spread democracy and free-market capitalism (an "empire of liberty") against the Soviet Union's mission to spread socialist revolution and broad-based economic equality (an "empire of justice"). The conflict erupting after World War II was "cold" because their mutual hostility and suspicion, although intense, stopped short of a "hot" military showdown between the two rivals. Instead, it produced a massive nuclear weapons buildup and arms race, an unprecedented division of the world into two camps, ferocious propaganda attacks and ideological repression, and military actions in Korea, Vietnam, and other places that took the lives of at least 4.5 million people. The total financial costs of the Cold War are not known, but for nuclear weapons alone, the United States spent $1 trillion to build 37,737 devices between 1951 and 1965, according to one estimate.

The Cold War lasted more than forty years, but it formed over three phases in the two decades covered in this chapter. Allies during World War II, U.S. and Soviet officials prepared for postwar conflict soon after the United States revealed its superior military technology in dropping atomic bombs on Japan. The alliance crumbled as the two powers clashed

What does the surprising popularity of Willis Conover's show in the Soviet Union and other Communist countries reveal about U.S.-Soviet relations during the Cold War era?

Go to MindTap® to watch a video on Conover and learn how his story relates to the themes of this chapter.

over rebuilding war-torn Europe and controlling the eastern Mediterranean. Ideological conflict, especially in Europe, highlighted the first phase of the Cold War and proved a mainstay of U.S.–Soviet relations. The Cold War's second phase, begun in 1949, became increasingly focused on the military as the Soviets produced their own atomic bomb and the United States countered by rapidly upgrading its nuclear arsenal. At the same time, the conflict intensified in East Asia with the Communist Revolution in China and the Korean War between Communist North Korea and UN-backed South Korea. The militarization of the Cold War generated a culture and politics of military preparedness. In the United States, a pervasive fear of Communists promoted political repression, cultural conformity, and the search for spies, especially in the federal government and labor organizations. In the Soviet Union, military preparedness prolonged war-era economic sacrifices and justified the continued persecution of ideological enemies.

The death of Soviet leader Joseph Stalin in 1953 marked the beginning of the Cold War's third phase as U.S.–Soviet relations reached the brink of war in Cuba and then modestly improved. The return of dialogue between the two nations emboldened peace groups to press for arms control and enabled cultural exchanges, including Willis Conover's radio show. But even as Americans and Soviets found common ground, the Cold War raged in Asia, Africa, the Middle East, and the Caribbean, where scores of economically underdeveloped and newly independent nations proved testing grounds for the U.S.–Soviet conflict. Both sides competed to gain a footing in poor and unstable developing nations that played one superpower off against the other.

22-1

From Allies to Enemies

In this cartoon, published in France in 1949, Uncle Sam and Soviet Premier Stalin stare warily at each other across a pair of conjoined twins. The French caption, which has not been printed here, reads: "My Dear, your sister has some strange friends."

Why is there tension between the two national figures, and what do the conjoined twins represent? ▶

World War II marked the height of cooperation between the United States and the Soviet Union. The Allies down-played ideological differences and conflict over military strategy to be unified in fighting the Axis Powers and to plan a postwar world in which each nation received a sphere of influence. But, at the end of the war, dis-trust deepened over U.S. possession of atomic weapons, which, to the Soviets, created a dangerous imbalance of military might. Exacerbating the tension was the U.S. booming wartime economy, which as the war ended gave the United States both economic and military suprem-acy over the Soviet Union where cities and factories lay in ruin. Stalin used the Red Army's occupation of east-ern Germany to rebuild the Soviet economy and protect the nation from future attack. Problems arose when U.S. officials sought to counter Soviet influence in Europe by advocating democratic governments and free markets whereas Stalin insisted on protecting Soviet borders by controlling neighboring countries.

The Granger Collection, New York

📖 As you read, focus on the way the U.S.–Soviet alliance, forged during World War II, dissolved into an intense international rivalry. What soured U.S.-Soviet relations, and what were the major effects of this conflict?

22-1a Legacies of War

Both Americans and Soviets hoped to continue their functioning partnership after the war. Despite persistent disagreement as allies, especially

{ The outcome of World War II transforms the global order and puts the United States and the Soviet Union on a collision course.

over the opening of a second front in Western Europe, the two powers negotiated agreements for the postwar world at the Yalta and Potsdam conferences. The establishment of the United Nations, in which both the United States and Soviet Union played a crucial role, was another basis for prolonged cooperation.

But within less than two years of V-J Day, U.S.–Soviet cooperation unraveled, devolving into an intense, if not entirely new, ideological struggle that marked the first phase of the **Cold War**. The two powers had clashed since the 1917 Communist Revolution in Russia despite a shared antipathy to European power politics and the nineteenth-century imperial order. While the Soviets saw America's faith in free-market capitalism as producing global inequality and perpetuating poverty, Americans considered the Soviets' command economy, single-party system, and suppression of personal freedoms as a violation of basic human rights. Added to these core differences were unrealistic fears on both sides that each was bent on destroying the other.

Another reason for the collapse of the wartime alliance went beyond ideology. For the first time, the United States had become actively involved in the internal affairs of European nations during peacetime. There were three reasons for this reversal of U.S. foreign policy principles in place since the Monroe Doctrine of 1823. First, the development of long-range bombers (and later missiles) shattered forever the protection provided by the Atlantic and Pacific Oceans. Second, because U.S. officials believed that the origins of World War II lay in the worldwide depression in the 1930s, they pushed to rebuild war-torn Europe to prevent another economic collapse. Third, the war taught U.S. officials about the need to stand up early and forcefully to aggressive expansionists such as Adolf Hitler. In 1945, for example, Secretary of the Navy James Forrestal warned that Stalin's desire to control Eastern Europe should not be appeased. "We tried that once with Hitler," he said. "There are no returns on appeasement."

The sustained U.S. involvement in European affairs, something that Stalin did not expect, set it on a collision course with the Soviet Union. An important source of U.S.–Soviet conflict involved the reconstruction of the world's economy under the Bretton Woods economic system, which was designed to ensure open borders and free trade. The Americans welcomed these arrangements that aligned with the nation's manufacturing preeminence, but the Soviets refused to place the free market above the socialist goal of economic equality. The Soviets also recognized that their nascent industrial economy could not withstand free competition with U.S. manufacturers.

Another source of U.S.–Soviet friction involved nuclear weapons. Although Stalin had expressed little interest in the new weapon that President Harry Truman had revealed to him at Potsdam, Soviet officials reacted with alarm at the prospect of a U.S. monopoly on atomic weapons. They feared that it could be used as blackmail to threaten their nation with nuclear destruction. U.S. officials, in turn, faced pressures from within and outside the nation to prevent the further development of nuclear technology by turning over its atomic weapons and technology to the newly established UN Atomic Energy Commission, which sought to safeguard atomic energy development and use. Yet Truman, along with Secretary of State James Byrnes, made the fateful decision to oppose sharing atomic secrets or relinquishing control over the U.S. nuclear arsenal.

The main U.S.–Soviet conflict in the months after World War II involved the political status of Eastern Europe and occupied Germany. Although agreements reached at Yalta required free elections in Soviet-occupied Eastern Europe, Stalin had never intended to give up control. Having been invaded by Germany twice in the twentieth century, he sought a protective buffer that would guarantee Soviet security. In addition, Stalin sought compensation for what World War II had cost the Soviet people: nearly 27 million soldiers and civilians dead, more than 10 percent of the nation's total population. For every two Americans killed in the war, the Soviets lost one hundred. Moreover, Stalin's firm grip on Eastern Europe was immensely popular with the Soviet people, who revered him as the champion of what they called the *Great Patriotic War* and who blamed the United States for compromising the nation's hard-won security.

22-1b Reconstruction of Europe

The impasse over Eastern Europe set the stage for a shift in U.S. policy toward the Soviet Union that came to be called **containment**. In February 1946, George F. Kennan, a leading U.S. diplomat in Moscow and a historian of Russia, sent a secret "long telegram" to the secretary of state reporting that U.S.–Soviet cooperation was not possible. Instead, he recommended a strategy focusing on rebuilding the industrial centers of Western Europe and Japan and doing everything short of war to restrain Soviet designs on promoting a world Communist revolution. The next month, Winston Churchill described an "**iron curtain**" descending across the continent of Europe, "from Stettin in the Baltic to Trieste in the Adriatic," behind which the nations of Eastern

{ The first phase of the Cold War centers on competing U.S. and Soviet visions of postwar Germany and Eastern Europe.

Cold War Major U.S.–Soviet Union diplomatic and ideological conflict producing massive arms buildup and regional wars but no direct military conflict between the two powers.

containment U.S. national security strategy emerging with the Cold War designed to thwart the spread of real or perceived Soviet-sponsored communism around the world.

iron curtain Churchill's metaphor, first expressed in March 1946, characterizing a Europe divided between the West and Soviet-controlled Eastern European nations.

Europe were subject to "control from Moscow." This warning was intended for President Truman, who had invited Churchill to speak at Westminster College in his home state of Missouri and was in the audience.

Europe was not the only region in which U.S. and Soviet plans for the future clashed. In Iran, which was divided into British and Soviet occupation zones, Stalin sought to retain control of the country's northern oil fields and to keep the British and Americans away from his nation's southern border. But Britain, the United States, and the United Nations pressured him to remove Soviet troops from the country. Stalin sought to gain access to the Mediterranean through Turkey's Sea of Marmara, an ambition that reached back to Czarist Russia, but here, too, he met stiff U.S. opposition. Greece was a different matter because Stalin relied on Yugoslavian Communists to foment socialist revolution in its southern neighbor.

Truman knew that Communist victories in Greece and Turkey would destabilize the oil-rich Middle East, home to two-thirds of the world's reserves. Whoever held the eastern Mediterranean, he worried, could cut off the vital oil supply to Western Europe and Japan. Formerly, the British had controlled vast regions of the Middle East as well as the Suez Canal, but after World War II, they could no longer afford to sustain their empire and stopped supplying anti-Communist forces in Greece and Turkey. Truman committed the United States to assuming Britain's burden.

In March 1947, the president addressed a joint session of Congress to articulate a sweeping vision of a bipolar world in which those who favored freedom and democracy stood against the supporters of totalitarian repression (he concealed concerns about Middle Eastern oil). Although not naming the Soviet Union, Truman warned that without U.S. aid, Communist victory was assured in Greece, and "like apples in a barrel infected by one rotten one, the corruption of Greece would infect Iran and all to the east." This was an early version of the **domino theory**, an explanation for how a Communist revolution in one nation sets up a chain reaction that spreads, toppling one regime after another. To prevent this from happening, the president asked for and received $400 million from Congress to provide economic and military aid to the governments of Greece and Turkey. In what came to be known as the **Truman Doctrine**, he committed the nation to "support free peoples who are resisting attempted subjugation by armed minorities or by outside pressures." This was the hard-line stance against the spread of Soviet influence that Churchill, Kennan, and others had been advocating.

The soft side of U.S. Cold War policy came in the form of massive economic aid that reasserted the Four Freedoms by combatting "freedom from want." Also in 1947, Truman's secretary of state, General George C. Marshall, called on the United States to take a bold step to fight "not against any country or doctrine but against hunger, poverty, desperation, and chaos" in postwar Europe. Reconstructing European economies, Marshall claimed, was necessary to diminish the appeal of communism, especially in France and Italy, by permitting "the emergence of political and social conditions in which free institutions can exist." The **Marshall Plan's** aid of more than $13 billion ($103 billion in 2014 dollars) from 1948 to 1952 required a degree of economic integration that laid the foundation for the European Common Market (established in 1958), and it carried the bonus of benefiting U.S. manufacturers by enabling European nations to purchase goods from the United States.

The Marshall Plan drove a final wedge between the Americans and Soviets, dividing Europe into eastern and western spheres of influence known as "blocs." Although the Soviets desperately needed American money to recover from the war, U.S. planners did not expect Stalin to agree to the free-trade principles of Bretton Woods, a requirement for receiving aid. Stalin indeed rejected aid and forbade Eastern European nations from accepting much-needed reconstruction funds. Instead, he launched the Council for Mutual Economic Assistance (COMECON) in 1949 as an eastern bloc alternative to the Marshall Plan. More importantly, the prospect of massive U.S. aid pushed Stalin to take bolder, more overt measures to shore up the Soviet sphere, including an overthrow of Czechoslovakia's elected government in February 1948 and the installation of a Communist regime. Stalin also took a hard line in Germany.

22-1c Occupation of Germany

Occupied Germany was the epicenter of Cold War Europe. The defeated nation was divided into four zones, controlled by the Soviet Union, United States, Great Britain, and France. All agreed that although Germany should eventually be reunited, it must first be stripped of Nazi influence and held responsible for its actions. The process of de-Nazification included trials of suspected war criminals that took place in Nuremberg, Germany, from 1945 to 1949. The Allies had a much harder time agreeing about the future of Germany's political and economic systems. Stalin sought heavy war reparations from Germany and relocated much of its industrial capacity from the Soviet zone to the Soviet Union. Truman, in contrast, sought to restore Germany's economy and bring it squarely within the orbit of the Western democracies. By 1948, the British, Americans, and French had combined

> The reconstruction of Germany brings the United States and Soviet Union into direct conflict.

domino theory U.S. Cold War assumption that if one country became Communist, others in the region would "fall" like dominoes to communism.

Truman Doctrine Foreign policy strategy in March 1947 promising economic and financial aid to "free peoples" fighting communism anywhere, specifically in Greece and Turkey.

Marshall Plan Massive economic aid to rebuild war-torn Europe, remove trade barriers, and blunt the appeal of communism by restoring Europe to prosperity.

their zones, making it three against one. Berlin, Germany's former capital, was likewise divided into two occupation zones, although it sat like an international island one hundred miles inside Germany's Soviet zone, accessible to the West only through designated roads, rail lines, canals, and air corridors.

In June 1948, seeking to push the Western nations out of Berlin altogether as a precondition for German reunification, Stalin cut off Western road, rail, and canal access to the city. The blockade was provocative, but he did not want war. Truman, although giving serious thought to resolving the Berlin crisis with atomic weapons, also wanted to avoid military conflict. Instead, he opted for a massive airlift that for one year flew thirteen thousand tons of supplies per day to West Berlin. Stalin did not challenge the **Berlin airlift** and ended the blockade in May 1949.

The blockade and airlift made the division of Germany inevitable because the occupation zones hardened into separate countries. The Federal Republic of Germany (West Germany) was established in September 1949 as a capitalist democracy. The Soviet zone became the German Democratic Republic (East Germany), a socialist state in the Soviet bloc. Berlin and Germany remained divided for the next forty-one years, a constant source of U.S.–Soviet friction. East Germany suffered under heavy Soviet war reparations and restrictions while West Germany, the beneficiary of Marshall Plan aid, became the economic powerhouse of Europe.

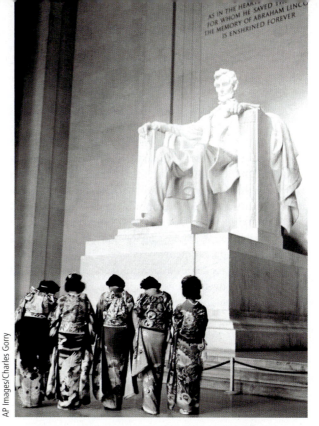

AP Images/Charles Gorry

Japanese Women Visiting Lincoln Memorial, 1951
The U.S. occupation of Japan resolved wartime conflict with Japan serving as the junior partner to the victorious Americans. The women in this photograph are advertising the first Hollywood film, *Tokyo File 212*, set in postwar Japan. Approved by SCAP leader General MacArthur, the plot reflects the fear of losing Japan to communism. ▲

22-1d U.S. Occupation of Japan

Unlike Germany, the United States took sole possession of Japan. The Soviet Union had joined the war against Japan right after the atomic destruction of Hiroshima, but against the spirit of the Potsdam declaration, the United States excluded the Soviets from the occupation, although it allowed them to reclaim territories in Manchuria and Sakhalin Island. The future of Japan thus served as an early pivot toward the Cold War. The massive economic aid the United States gave Japan to reconstruct its economy and reintegrate it into the global economy was similar to what would come later with the Marshall Plan. U.S. officials saw a stable and prosperous Japan as an essential counterbalance to Soviet, and later Chinese, expansionism in East Asia.

> Massive U.S. aid ensures Japan's stability and pro-Western stance.

General Douglas MacArthur was named Supreme Commander of the Allied Powers (SCAP). He and several hundred U.S. civil servants and three hundred fifty thousand troops, governed Japan, in the words of one

AP Images/dpa DENA

Styling Hair during Power Cut Because of Berlin Blockade, 1948 Stalin's blockade of West Berlin set back the city's postwar recovery and threatened military conflict between the Soviet Union and the United States. To conserve resources, power in West Berlin operated for only two hours in the morning and two hours at night. ▲

Berlin airlift U.S. military operation, June 1948–May 1949, to bypass Soviet blockade of West Berlin by using a convoy of airplanes.

reverse course Policy change, beginning in 1947 for the U.S. occupation of Japan, from purging wartime leaders and business conglomerations to restoring them as a bulwark against communism.

historian, "as neocolonial overlords, beyond challenge or criticism, as inviolate as the emperor and his officials had ever been." MacArthur's orders to "demilitarize and democratize" Japan had been spelled out at Potsdam. As in occupied Germany, the Americans established a military tribunal for prosecuting suspected war criminals, including Prime Minister Hideki Tojo and those responsible for the Nanjing massacre in 1937. MacArthur spared Emperor Hirohito from trial against the protests of Japan's victims because the revered leader's cooperation was crucial to winning the hearts and minds of the Japanese people.

SCAP initiated a revolution from above that included breaking up concentrations of big businesses, such as the Mitsubishi conglomerate, maker of the well-known Zero fighter plane. The transformation also included democratizing land ownership, severing ties between religion and the state, ensuring women's rights, and writing a new constitution that prevented Japan's ability to make war. But MacArthur could not always control the reform process. Faced with rampant inflation, unemployment, and no legitimate market economy, the public sought alternatives to capitalism and increasingly flocked to Japan's newly legalized Communist Party. As U.S.–Soviet relations dissolved, the new U.S. objective for Japan, like the Marshall Plan for Western Europe, was to combat "freedom from want" by quickly rebuilding the nation's considerable industrial capacity. Beginning in the winter of 1947, SCAP initiated a **reverse course**, removing labor advocates, Communists, and other leftists from official positions while relying on right-wing business and political leaders who had supported the old imperial regime. The right-wingers, in turn, worked with SCAP to generate stability and prosperity through a conservative, U.S.-backed political order. Thus, the foundation was laid for Japan's postwar "economic miracle" that propelled it, along with West Germany, to become one of the world's leading economic powers.

22-2
Militarization of the U.S.–Soviet Conflict

Two middle school girls commemorate the death of General MacArthur in April 1964 by placing a wreath with the name of their school written in Chinese characters at his statue in Jayu (Freedom) Park in South Korea. Since it was erected in 1957, the statue has been a popular sightseeing destination in the city of Incheon, where it marks the site of a historic offensive during the Korean War.

Consider why people in other countries would build statues to Americans. How is this monument to a U.S general connected to "freedom"? ▶

AP Images/Kim Chon-Kil

At the onset of the Cold War, the United States held distinct military advantages over the Soviet Union. Despite Stalin's planned industrialization, his nation remained largely agricultural, relying on government control of the economy to turn its abundant natural and human resources into military might. This plan was almost entirely land based, for the Soviets had yet to develop commanding air and sea power. The United States, by contrast, possessed the world's leading navy and air force, sustained by the most productive and technologically advanced economy in human history—advantages that helped break the Soviet blockade in Berlin and rebuild Western Europe and Japan. Moreover, the United States had the atomic bomb and did not hesitate to remind the Soviets about this "winning weapon" to gain diplomatic advantage. In 1949, however, U.S. fortunes changed as the Soviets developed their own atomic bomb, and China, the world's most populous nation and a crucial U.S. ally, became Communist. In addition to these "twin shocks" came the outbreak of a civil war in Korea that quickly drew Chinese and U.S. troops into combat.

☞ As you read, focus on the factors that pushed the Cold War beyond its first phase of ideological antagonism. How and why did the Cold War become more dangerous? What were the characteristics of its second, military, phase?

the U.S. nuclear arsenal and the creation of much more powerful "thermonuclear" or **hydrogen bombs**. The Soviet threat was then seen as mainly military—not just ideological—and events in China and Korea brought that threat home to the American public.

22-2a Nuclear Arms Race

U.S. possession of atomic weapons spurred the Soviets to build their own atomic bomb. Like those of the Americans, Soviet efforts relied in part on German scientists who in this case served as captured labor. In addition, the Soviet team had the advantage of being second by using a vast spy network able to steal secrets from the Americans. Klaus Fuchs, a German physicist who defected to Britain and was assigned to the Manhattan Project, gave Soviet intelligence thousands of pages of documents, including a detailed picture with measurements of the atom bomb dropped on Nagasaki. A longtime Communist, Fuchs was convinced that the Soviet Union was the world's best hope for resisting antidemocratic regimes and improving the plight of the poor and working classes.

> The stockpiling of nuclear weapons begins the second phase of the Cold War as military strategy and conflict move to the forefront.

The successful test of a Soviet atomic bomb in August 1949 came ten years earlier than U.S. officials had predicted. Now there were two **superpowers**, each possessing military power far greater than all other nations. The United States lost its atomic monopoly in the same year that Germany became partitioned. The heightened Communist challenge was countered by a new U.S. defense strategy based on military alliance with Britain and European partners. The **North Atlantic Treaty Organization (NATO)**, signed in April 1949, was based on the principle that an attack against any member nation was tantamount to an attack on all and would be retaliated. NATO reversed the long U.S. tradition of avoiding "entangling alliances." Whereas U.S. allies gained protection from the perceived Soviet threat, the United States gained the chance to build up Western Europe's military defenses, access to strategic locations from which to strike the Soviet Union, and the flexibility of not having to rely on the UN Security Council to check Soviet expansionism. The Soviets responded to NATO in May 1955 by combining eight Communist states in Eastern and Central Europe then firmly under Soviet control into the **Warsaw Pact** (see Map 22.1).

The stockpiling of atomic weapons in Europe signaled the militarization of U.S. Cold War policy and a more aggressive anti-Communist stance. Epitomized by an April 1950 secret National Security Council Study known as **NSC 68**, this new strategy continued the policy of containment but placed more emphasis on building up military defenses and weaponry, including

22-2b Communist China

Civil war in China resumed at the end of World War II as the shaky wartime alliance between Jiang Jieshi's Nationalist government and Mao Zedong's Communist Party fell apart. The United States provided $2.5 billion in aid, mostly military, to bolster Jiang's regime even as Truman sent General Marshall to bring the Nationalists and Communists together. Although there was mixed opinion among America's China experts regarding the outcome of the civil war, Truman sided with Jiang because it was difficult to walk away from the tremendous investment already made in his regime. Containment policy also made it almost impossible to see Mao as anything other than a Stalin ally antagonistic to U.S. interests. As it turned out, the United States backed the losing side in the **Chinese Communist Revolution**. Jiang's army disintegrated as Mao's forces, which had gained the support of millions of peasants, marched to Beijing and in October 1949 declared the People's Republic of China (PRC). The Soviet Union was the first to recognize the PRC, and in the subsequent Sino-Soviet pact, Stalin sent $300 million in aid to the new nation. China became the top recipient of Soviet foreign aid, receiving 7 percent of the Soviet Union's national income for much of the 1950s until the two Communist powers split and became bitter rivals. The United States had little choice but to continue supporting Jiang, who fled with his army and 1.3 million civilian supporters to the island of Taiwan off China's southeastern coast. Truman immediately recognized Jiang's regime as China's only legitimate government and made sure it retained China's seat in the UN Security Council. Taiwan relied on the U.S. Seventh Fleet for protection from Mao's threatened invasion.

> The Chinese Communist Revolution intensifies U.S.–Soviet conflict in East Asia.

superpower A nation possessing supreme power and influence, referring especially to the United States and the Soviet Union during the Cold War.

North Atlantic Treaty Organization (NATO) U.S.-led military alliance established in 1949 to provide collective security to nations in Western and Central Europe in opposition to Soviet power.

Warsaw Pact Soviet-led military alliance established in 1955 that countered NATO by providing collective security for Soviet satellite states in Eastern Europe.

NSC 68 A hardening of the Truman Doctrine, national security policy advancing permanent military strategy to thwart communism anywhere in the world.

hydrogen bomb Nuclear weapon, first tested by the United States in 1952 and the Soviet Union in 1953 with far greater destructive capacity than atomic bombs.

Chinese Communist Revolution Overthrow of Nationalist regime in October 1949 by the Chinese Communist Party led by Mao Zedong.

Map 22.1 Divided Europe, 1946–1965 The Cold War divided Europe by an "iron curtain" into eastern and western blocs. United by the Warsaw Pact and Council for Mutual Economic Assistance (COMECON), the East was held together by socialist ideology and, at times, Soviet force. Socialist Yugoslavia, led by Josip Broz Tito, would prove an exception. The West countered with NATO and the beginnings of the European Common Market undergirded by massive U.S. economic aid via the Marshall Plan. ▲

---

land redistribution State-led transfer of agricultural estates from landowners to landless peasants.

Mao's success in China compelled the United States to place even more significance on Japan as the bulwark against the spread of communism throughout Asia. The "reverse course" that MacArthur's occupation forces had begun following the Truman Doctrine accelerated as the United States rebuilt Japan's industrial capacity and supplied it with billions of orders for goods. The U.S. occupation of Japan ended in 1952 with the understanding, confirmed in the U.S.–Japan Security Treaty in 1960, that U.S. protection of Japan required a vast network of permanent military bases on its soil.

22-2c Partition of Korea and Outbreak of Civil War

Unlike Japan's four main islands, which were under sole U.S. occupation, Korea became subject to Soviet as well as U.S. influence when the two powers hastily and arbitrarily divided the country along the 38th parallel. North of the dividing line, the Soviets encouraged the growth of socialism through **land redistribution**, which appropriated large estates from the wealthy and gave them to landless peasants.

> Civil war in Korea becomes the Cold War's first military conflict.

Myron Davis/The LIFE Picture Collection/Getty Images

Global Americans Born Yi Su·ng-man in 1875, **Syngman Rhee** was raised in a Christian mission school in Korea, and he converted to Methodism while imprisoned for reform activities forbidden by the autocratic kingdom of Korea. Upon release from jail in 1904, he came to the United States to advocate for Korea's sovereignty and to study, eventually earning a Ph.D. from Princeton University. In 1910, Rhee returned home to head the Seoul YMCA but within two years fled back across the Pacific after Japan formally annexed Korea. For nearly four decades, Rhee lived in the United States where he mobilized Korean immigrants and pressed Western nations to support Korea's independence. In 1933, Rhee lobbied in Geneva for the League of Nations. Rhee married Austrian immigrant Francesca Donner. After World War II, U.S. officials returned him to Seoul as the president of the Korean government in exile, and in October 1950, he became the first president of South Korea, serving until 1960. Some people revere Rhee as a George Washington figure liberating his people from Japanese and then North Korean tyranny. Others revile him as an iron-fisted dictator whose anti-Communist purges made McCarthyism seem benign. Yet most overlook the fact that Rhee was also a U.S. immigrant who spent almost half of his life outside of his homeland. His final days were spent in Hawai'i, where he died in 1965. His many transpacific migrations revealed the confluence of exile, immigration, and international relations.

In the South, the United States imposed an authoritarian regime that opposed land distribution in order to protect private property. Koreans on both sides of the divide hoped for a quick reunification of their country, but the ideological differences imposed by the two occupying powers became fixed in 1948. The country became two sovereign nations, the Democratic People's Republic of Korea (North Korea) and the Republic of Korea (South Korea). Syngman Rhee, long-standing Korean exile in the United States, became the first president of South Korea, and war hero Kim Il Sung became the North's champion.

After repeated cross-border conflicts between the two Koreas, the North launched a major offensive in June 1950 to reunite the Korean people. Mao and Stalin approved the attack, although Stalin did not pledge troops. Kim planned to defeat the South in a matter of days, hoping the United States would not actively intervene as it had not during the Chinese Revolution. He badly miscalculated. After losing its atomic monopoly to the Soviets and China to Mao's Communists, Truman refused to accept another global embarrassment. Wary of opposition in Congress to U.S. involvement in foreign wars he took his case to the UN Security Council, which—unlike the League of Nations—enforced its collective security commitment by sending troops to defend South Korea against the North's aggression. The expected Soviet veto did not happen because Stalin was boycotting the Security Council to protest its refusal to seat the PRC instead of Jiang's regime. Truman appointed General MacArthur to lead a UN force composed of troops from sixteen nations, including

akg-images

U.S. Soldiers Marching into Battle, South Korean Refugees Fleeing the Other Way, 1950 Before MacArthur's successful landing at Incheon in September 1950, North Korean troops were on the verge of victory, having gained control of almost all of the South and sending millions of civilians fleeing for safety as is shown in this photograph. The Americans were instrumental in reclaiming the South, but civilian security remained uncertain on both sides of the Korean divide until 1953. ▲

many NATO members and allies in Asia, Africa, and South America, but most troops were South Korean and American.

In the first stage of the **Korean War**, the North Koreans wiped out half of the South's army and pinned the remainder, as well as tens of thousands of UN troops, far down the Korean peninsula at the southern port of Pusan. In a stroke of tactical brilliance, MacArthur launched an assault behind enemy lines at

Korean War Civil war between North and South Korea, 1950–1953, in which UN troops led by the United States fought with the South and Chinese forces supported the North.

limited war Warfare in which a party cannot use every weapon available in its military arsenal; during the Cold War this meant fighting without the use of nuclear weapons.

Incheon and proceeded to reclaim the nearby capital of Seoul. With his troops sandwiched and cut off from supplies, Kim retreated far to the north near the Chinese border. In September 1950, Americans were elated with victory.

But the United States was next to blunder. Truman ordered MacArthur to invade North Korea, arguing that the South's ultimate security required the elimination of communism on the Korean peninsula. UN forces quickly occupied North Korea's capital of Pyongyang and pressed beyond to finish off Kim's army. With their supply lines stretched thin, MacArthur's troops marched into a trap as hundreds of thousands of fresh Chinese soldiers crossed the Yalu River and quickly pushed U.S. forces back across the 38th parallel. The Chinese then crossed into South Korea and occupied Seoul. Secretary of State Dean Acheson called this "the worst defeat of U.S. forces since Bull Run" during the Civil War. UN forces regrouped, however, and were able to recapture Seoul and push the Sino-Korean forces back across the 38th parallel.

The United States was then in an undeclared war with China, a rising military power with a massive army. After the Chinese offensive began, President Truman noted, "I've worked for peace for five years and six months and it looks like World War III is here. I hope not—but we must meet whatever comes—and we will." It was in this context that U.S. officials relied on superior air power to lay waste to every major military installation, factory, city, and village in North Korea. Truman and his officers considered using more lethal chemical and nuclear weapons but in the end did not (see Map 22.2).

Meanwhile, MacArthur became convinced that a complete victory demanded a naval blockade of Chinese ports and the bombing of China's industrial capacity. Truman strongly opposed these actions, fearing a Soviet declaration of war. In April 1951, he relieved the hero of the Philippines and Korea of his command, but, when MacArthur returned to the United States to much adulation, it seemed that the public supported the push for total victory in Korea. The idea of a **limited war** in which the military could not use every weapon in its arsenal and the goal was something short of total victory was a new and strange concept. But it was an inescapable reality for both the United States and the Soviet Union in the age of nuclear weapons. Although the Korean War had reached an effective stalemate by the time of MacArthur's departure, it took two more years to reach a ceasefire in July 1953. By that time, at least 2.2 million North and South Koreans, 600,000 Chinese, and 36,500 Americans had been killed. North and South Korea remained divided at the 38th parallel by a 160-mile long and 2.5-mile wide demilitarized zone, a

Map 22.2 Korean War, 1950–1953 The North Korean army controlled almost the entire Korean peninsula by the end of summer 1950, but MacArthur's September landing at Incheon gave UN and South Korean troops the upper hand until the Chinese entered the war in October. North Koreans and the Chinese pushed back into the South. The 1953 armistice restored the status quo boundary line at the 38th parallel. ▲

heavily fortified buffer between the two nations. The end of the Korean War did not bring peaceful relations. Both Koreas stood prepared to resume the fight at a moment's notice for the next sixty years while the hostility between the superpowers intensified.

Cold War at Home

Films such as *I Married a Communist* released in 1949 reflected Americans' fear that Soviet spies had infiltrated the United States, and no one—not even family members—could be trusted. In this movie, the threat comes from a seductive woman involved in labor organizing whose "one mission is to destroy."

What gender and sexual stereotypes does this film poster draw on to portray fears about communism? ▶

Moviestore Collection Ltd/Alamy Stock Photo

The combination of the Soviet atomic bomb, Chinese Communist Revolution, and the Korean War unleashed a wave of fear about national security *within* the United States. It targeted not only members of the Communist Party but also a wide variety of political dissidents and cultural outcasts. The threat of nuclear devastation and the consequent emphasis on national security and military buildup forever changed the U.S. economy and society, whereas survival strategies and new genres of entertainment contributed to anxiety about the future.

☞ As you read, pay attention to efforts made to protect Americans from Communist threats. What did the government do? What roles did the movie studios and other branches of entertainment have? What impact did these actions have on the lives of ordinary Americans?

22-3a Spies and Scares

Fear of communism unleashed a **Second Red Scare** more pervasive than the one following World War I. The Communist Party of the United States (CPUSA) was founded in 1919. As a branch of Vladimir Lenin's movement for socialist world revolution, it had been the leading leftist organization in the United States during the 1930s and found a new legitimacy during the wartime U.S.–Soviet alliance. But it operated more like a secret society than a political party. It is known that some two hundred party members passed U.S. military secrets to Moscow.

Nevertheless, the party's actual influence became greatly exaggerated by J. Edgar Hoover, the director of the Federal Bureau of Investigation (FBI). He committed his powerful agency to an obsessive anti-Communist campaign. Motivating the FBI was the shocking exposure in September 1945 that a network of more than eighty Communist spies had infiltrated the federal government. The most important was Alger Hiss, a rising star in the State Department who had

> The shocking discovery of Soviet spies induces a wave of anti-Communist fear that targets dissident or vulnerable social groups.

served as an assistant to Roosevelt at Yalta and participated in the creation of the United Nations. Because the FBI had no hard evidence against the left-leaning Hiss, the burden was put upon the House Un-American Activities Committee (HUAC) to establish a case. Led by freshman representative Richard Nixon, HUAC in August 1948 produced Whittaker Chambers, a former Communist Party member, who accused Hiss of being a Soviet operative and produced incriminating evidence to back up his claim (which decoded Soviet intelligence documents later confirmed). In January 1950, a federal jury convicted Hiss of perjury for falsely claiming that he did not know Chambers, but he escaped the charge of espionage because the statute of limitations had expired on acts allegedly committed in the late 1930s.

A second spy case that riveted the nation involved a network of Soviet agents working on the Manhattan Project. The 1948 arrest of Klaus Fuchs, the Manhattan Project scientist who had turned secret documents over to the Soviets, led the FBI to a cadre of Communist engineers in New York City. The agency charged the leader of the group, Julius Rosenberg, with passing crude sketches of atomic technology to Soviet intelligence (a crime also subsequently confirmed by decoded Soviet cables). Unlike Fuchs, Rosenberg refused to confess to being either a spy or a Communist. The FBI sought to coax cooperation from him by arresting his wife Ethel on charges of espionage (which have yet to be confirmed). Both husband and wife were tried, convicted, and sentenced to death. They were executed in June 1953 despite worldwide protests.

Pressured by the Republican congressional victory in 1946 and repeated charges by political rivals that he was "soft on communism," Truman in March 1947 instituted a **Loyalty Program**, subjecting federal

Second Red Scare Fear of Communist infiltration that in the 1950s led to widespread, publically sanctioned, and often unjustified violations of civil liberties.

Loyalty Program First extensive security screening by the U.S. government, subjecting federal employees to investigations for suspicious activities ranging from spying to Communist Party membership.

employees to loyalty oaths and background checks that over nine years resulted in two thousand seven hundred dismissals. Even more Americans were subjected to loyalty tests implemented by state and local governments, universities, school districts, and private companies. Congress updated sedition legislation and placed restrictions on Communist-led labor unions, and immigration officials arrested and deported two hundred fifty foreign-born Communists and ex-Communists for violating immigration statues. Meanwhile, in October 1949, a federal criminal court convicted eleven Communist Party leaders for violating the 1940 Smith Act, which banned speech that advocated the violent overthrow of the U.S. government.

In this climate of fear, the undistinguished junior senator from Wisconsin, Joseph McCarthy, shocked the nation by declaring that he had a list of two hundred five Communist agents working in the State Department. In retrospect, McCarthy's claims were groundless, but at the time, many found him credible. He charged that Secretary of State Dean Acheson and other "striped pants diplomats" were susceptible to communism because they had been made effeminate by the genteel world of wealth and privilege. To the Wisconsin senator, effeminacy was a sign of homosexuality, and homosexuality in turn made a person even more susceptible to communism. Real men, he argued, worked their way up in society from the bottom rather than "being born with a silver spoon in their mouths." Ironically, McCarthy himself fell victim to the taint of homosexuality when the media latched on to the suspicion that two of his closest aides were gay men. The senator's charade came to an end in 1954 following televised hearings in which he was humiliated. With President Dwight D. Eisenhower's support, the Senate censured McCarthy, mainly for ethics violations by a vote of sixty-seven to twenty-two. McCarthy lost his audience and three years later died from complications due to heavy drinking.

Yet McCarthy was not alone in connecting gay bashing and anti-communism. The Second Red Scare relied on stereotypes of gender and sexuality to create a profile of disloyalty. Although anti-Red crusaders after World War I had identified dangerous radicals by their ethnicity (often Jewish or Italian), their post–World War II counterparts used homosexuality as a telling mark of disloyalty. Gays and lesbians were seen as emotionally susceptible to communism. Disguising their sexuality could make them vulnerable to blackmail by Communist agents seeking secret information.

In this way, the Second Red Scare generated a moral panic. Under Eisenhower in 1953, the State Department legitimized what has been subsequently called a **Lavender Scare** by increasing the dismissal of its gay and lesbian employees. By the 1960s, it had purged one thousand employees because of suspected homosexuality. A formal Senate investigation and subsequent security programs under Eisenhower expanded the persecution of gays and lesbians to all branches of the federal bureaucracy. Such measures netted far more homosexuals than Communists and roused calls for gay and lesbian civil rights that were amplified in the late 1960s.

22-3b National Security State

It is easy to dismiss the Red and Lavender Scares as the work of demagogues such as McCarthy, but doing so risks failing to grasp the major

{ The Cold War boosts defense spending and programs to a degree unprecedented during peacetime.

challenges to U.S. national security that policy makers faced after World War II. Advances in weapons technology coupled with the Soviet threat made clear that the United States needed to strengthen its defense. One element was the reorganization of foreign policy decision making to include the military, the principal goal of the **National Security Act of 1947**. This act also created the **Central Intelligence Agency (CIA)**, the permanent version of a temporary World War II intelligence bureau, to gather information on which government officials based their recommendations for national security. To address

Lavender Scare Part of the Second Red Scare targeting sexual minorities as particularly vulnerable to Communist influence, resulting in widespread violations of civil liberties.

National Security Act of 1947 Law that reorganized federal agencies to increase U.S. capacity to make and prepare for war.

Central Intelligence Agency (CIA) Federal agency responsible for gathering secret information about foreign threats to the United States.

Bettmann/Corbis

Elvis Presley Getting a Haircut on His First Day in the U.S. Army In contrast to the period before World War II, Americans during the early Cold War were more likely to support foreign wars, military expenditures, overseas alliances, and sacrifices to civil liberties due to national security concerns. Military conscription, though unusual during peacetime, became a normal part of American youth during the 1950s. ▲

AP Images/Denis Paquin

Global Americans **Wilma L. Vaught** grew up in a small, midwestern farming town and earned a bachelor of science degree from the University of Illinois in 1952. After graduation, she joined the corporate world only to realize that there were no opportunities for women to rise into management positions. But the newly created U.S. Air Force was different. "I'd always wanted a job that would let me be in charge," she told an interviewer, "so as soon as I found out I could get a direct commission as a second lieutenant, I chose to join." As it turned out, the air force even allowed women to serve with men in integrated noncombat units. Despite the persistence of gender stereotypes and discrimination, Vaught became one of a handful of women who were able to climb the military chain of command. Like millions of other Americans with military careers, Vaught benefited from the unprecedented growth in the nation's armed forces, and she served in Spain, Guam, and Vietnam. U.S. global influence spread through an expanding web of military bases and alliances as well as covert and overt operations. In this way, the Cold War provided women in the United States such as Vaught increasingly equal opportunities.

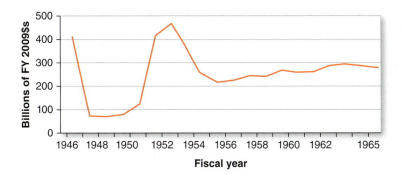

Figure 22.1 **U.S. Military Budget, 1949–1965** The U.S. military budget reflects the emphasis on military preparedness that dominated the Cold War. After a huge decline following World War II, spending shot up during the Korean War and remained at 6 percent to 11 percent of GDP, which at least doubled the 1 percent to 3 percent rate before World War II. An average of 2.3 million Americans served in the military between 1946 and 1957; this was eight times the figure from the 1920-1940 period. ◄ Source: Center for Strategic and Budgetary Administration, March 2008. Based on Office of Management and Budget and Department of Defense data.

the new nature of warfare, the act elevated the air force, formerly under the direction of the army, to a third military branch and combined it with the army and navy in the newly created Department of Defense (replacing the Department of War).

The National Security Act also established the National Security Council (NSC), the president's main advisory team whose NSC 68 policy in 1950 permanently militarized U.S. Cold War strategy. Although the Truman Doctrine had recognized the Soviet sphere of influence and tolerated setbacks in less industrialized parts of the world, the new policy painted the Communist threat in even bolder terms. Now armed with the atomic bomb, the Soviet threat, said NSC 68, posed a military challenge everywhere in the world.

The sudden rise of the Cold War also pushed Congress to restore the military draft just one year after it had been suspended. The 1948 Selective Service Act—the second peacetime draft in U.S. history—required every male turning eighteen to register with a local draft board. Even celebrities such as rock star Elvis Presley and baseball great Willie Mays were inducted into the army. The draft increased the armed forces from 1.5 million troops in 1950 to more than 3.6 million in 1952. The number declined after the Korean War, but the nation's troop level remained unusually high until it increased again in 1965 with the Vietnam War.

Military spending was also high (see Figure 22.1), and the most concerning aspect of the national security state was the increasingly close, and thus potentially corrupt, relationship between the federal government and private weapons manufacturers. In his farewell address in 1961, Eisenhower labeled this relationship the **military-industrial complex** and warned that the "conjunction of an immense military establishment and a large arms industry is new in the American experience. The total influence—economic, political, even spiritual—is felt in every city, every statehouse, every office of the federal government."

The reach of the national security state extended into schools and private life through the Federal Civil Defense Administration, which, starting in 1950, mapped evacuation routes and sponsored campaigns to inform Americans about how to protect themselves in the event of a nuclear attack. At school, children practiced "duck and cover" drills, quickly crawling under desks and covering their eyes lest they be melted away during a nuclear blast. Families built backyard bomb shelters stocked with canned food, water, and supplies so they could stay underground until radiation levels had dropped. In this way, fears about the nation's defense touched the daily lives of millions of students, families, and communities: No one seemed to be safe.

military-industrial complex Eisenhower's name for conjoining military and private business interests that he warned in 1961 threatened democratic institutions.

22-3c Cold War Culture

The climate of fear created by the threat of Communists and nuclear annihilation was evident in culture and entertainment, and HUAC investigated

> Entertainment industries fuel anti-Communist fears.

Hollywood, concerned that Communists were spreading their ideology through films. The committee found no Communist plot, but in November 1947, it cited ten people—the Hollywood Ten—for refusing to testify about their past and present connection to the Communist Party. HUAC's investigation benefited from friendly witnesses such as actor and Screen Actors Guild president Ronald Reagan. To remove even the hint of impropriety, film studios created a **blacklist** of suspected Communists who were banned from employment in Hollywood, including actor and singer Paul Robeson. The studios also began producing movies that portrayed communism as a dangerous menace. Starting in 1953, the British writer Ian Fleming began a celebrated series of books featuring the anti-Communist secret agent James Bond. In addition, films such as *I Was a Communist for the FBI* (1951) and *Big Jim McClain*

blacklist List of persons not charged with a crime but who were not to be employed by the entertainment industry because of their radical beliefs—usually associated with communism and labor organizing.

(1952) celebrated the U.S. agents who exposed traitorous spy rings, while others such as *I Married a Communist* (1949), *The Fearmakers* (1958), and the television show *I Led Three Lives* (1953–1956) warned that even trusted loved ones could actually be Communists in disguise.

During this time, the genre of science fiction was directly related to the fear of Communist infiltration and threat of nuclear holocaust. Films such as *It Came from Outer Space* (1953) and especially *Invasion of the Body Snatchers* (1956) used space creatures invading Earth as a metaphor for a Communist plot to conquer the United States. In *Body Snatchers*, Americans in a small town are killed and replaced by a species of "pod people" who look exactly like them but lack emotions and the ability to think for themselves. The novel *1984* (1949) by British author George Orwell achieved great popularity in the United States for its critique of communism by imagining a future Soviet-style society in which the state (Big Brother) keeps track of an individual's every move or thought. In contrast, the Academy-Award-nominated *Dr. Strangelove* (1964) satirized Cold War fears through black comedy. About an insane U.S. general who orders a nuclear attack on the Soviet Union, the film's subtitle captured the general's dangerously absurd point of view: "How I Learned to Stop Worrying and Love the Bomb."

22-4

Superpower Crisis and Diplomacy

This political cartoon, published in *The Washington Post* in November 1962, shows Soviet Premier Nikita Khrushchev and President John F. Kennedy trying desperately to "lock" away the beast of nuclear war. Their worried looks as well as the unclosed lid revealed the difficulty of achieving this goal.

Compare this cartoon to the one depicting Stalin and Uncle Sam in Section 22-1. How has the Cold War become more dangerous? What is at stake? ▶

> Go to MindTap® to practice history with the Chapter 22 **Primary Source Writing Activity: Cold War Prospectives.** Read and view primary sources and respond to a writing prompt.

Stalin's death in 1953 initiated the third phase of the Cold War in which the two foes resumed dialogue and eventually signed arms control agreements but not before pushing the world to the brink of nuclear destruction. Even as they engaged in a nuclear arms race, Soviet and U.S. leaders encouraged opportunities for their peoples to understand each other's culture and society. The relatively improved atmosphere drew strong support from American peace advocates, who since the end of World War II had promoted nuclear arms control.

☞ As you read, pay attention to efforts made to de-escalate the Cold War. What did U.S. and Soviet leaders do to create a more solid foundation for U.S.–Soviet diplomacy? What were the outcomes of these efforts?

"Let's Get A Lock For This Thing"

NUCLEAR WAR

HERBLOCK ©1962 THE WASHINGTON POST CO.

Library of Congress Prints and Photographs Division Washington, D.C.[LC-DIG-ppmsca-19978]

22-4a Eisenhower and the Arms Race

Dwight D. Eisenhower, the supreme allied commander of World War II, was elected president in 1952 in part because of his pledge that "I will go to Korea" to end what

{ U.S.–Soviet competition intensifies with new military strategies and more dangerous weaponry.

had become an unpopular war in the United States. The Korean War ceasefire and Stalin's death the next year presented Eisenhower dramatically altered circumstances that enabled the old wartime allies to come together at a **summit meeting** in Geneva, Switzerland, in 1955, the first time leaders of the two nations had met since Potsdam a decade earlier. That Eisenhower and the two new leaders of the Soviet Union, Nikolai Bulganin and Nikita Khrushchev, met at all was cause for hope, but the only real agreement reached was to engage in cultural exchanges. Eisenhower dismissed Soviet calls to end NATO, remove U.S. troops from Europe, and ban the production and use of nuclear weapons, whereas the Soviet leaders ignored his request for free elections in East Germany and arms reduction. The world delighted in the peaceful "spirit of Geneva," but U.S.–Soviet relations continued along the dangerous path of militarization.

Despite his friendly face and big smile, Eisenhower was an ardent cold warrior, who along with Secretary of State John Foster Dulles, believed that Soviet expansionism could be held in check by the threat of massive U.S. bombing of Soviet targets from military bases in Europe. The plan of **massive retaliation** was at the heart of the president's military strategy and led to the stockpiling of nuclear weapons and an emphasis on air supremacy over the use of ground troops. Khrushchev, who took sole control of the Soviet Union, also had two faces: one calling for liberalizing Soviet control over Eastern Europe and another crushing Hungary's attempt to break free from Soviet control in 1956. Khrushchev called Stalin's purges "vile" and "monstrous" and instituted "de-Stalinization" to provide more freedoms for his people, but he had no inclination and was in no position as a new premier to retreat from the nation's revolutionary ideology. Under Eisenhower and Khrushchev, the Cold War generated an arms race spiraling out of control in which the superpowers sought to outdo each other in increasing the production and strategic placement of nuclear weapons. The United States put missiles aimed at the Soviet Union in Turkey, which had joined the NATO alliance in 1952, as had Greece, both recipients of Truman Doctrine aid and firmly in the West's camp.

The successful launch of the Soviet satellite **Sputnik** October 1957 opened outer space to superpower conflict. It was the first human-made satellite to orbit the Earth, a historic achievement revealing Soviet superiority in missile and space technology. In response, Eisenhower

U.S. Nike Anti-aircraft Missiles Protect Washington, D.C., 1954 The development of threats from the air removed U.S. natural ocean protections and generated a greater need for missile defense. This photograph shows one of seventeen missile defense sites surrounding the nation's capital. The United States also deployed offensive missiles in Turkey and other sites to threaten the Soviet Union. ▲

established the National Aeronautics and Space Administration (NASA), which quickly launched America's own orbiting satellite and under President John F. Kennedy, NASA set sights on the moon. More pragmatically, space flight gave birth to intercontinental ballistic missiles (ICBMs), which each superpower armed with hydrogen bombs and pointed at each other's major cities.

As Americans were recovering from the Sputnik shock amid fears that the United States had fallen behind in missile technology, Khrushchev maneuvered to take control of West Berlin in part to stem defections—3 million since 1949—from impoverished and politically repressive East Berlin. As with the Berlin airlift, the United States in 1958 stood united with its Western European allies in refusing to give up the western half of the city, and Khrushchev temporarily backed off.

For his part, Eisenhower sought to defuse the second Berlin crisis by inviting Khrushchev to the United States. During the visit, Eisenhower proposed a number of arms control agreements, but only one, a multilateral agreement banning nuclear weapons testing in the Antarctic, reached fruition. Khrushchev's famous temper was on display when he was told he could not visit Disneyland and when he banged his shoe on the podium at the UN General Assembly, denouncing a representative from the Philippines as a "toadie of American imperialism." The Soviet leader's lack of subtlety and tact contributed to the fear that his foreign policy was overly aggressive, even reckless.

summit meeting Talks between two or more superpowers designed to improve relations and reduce conflict or the threat of war.

massive retaliation U.S. national security strategy under Eisenhower to deter enemy attack by amassing enough weapons to ensure "mutually assured destruction" in an immediate counterattack.

Sputnik First of its kind, Earth-orbiting satellite made and launched by the Soviet Union.

22-4b Cultural Diplomacy

Khrushchev's outbursts aside, superpower tension seemed to relax, most notably through **cultural diplomacy** in which each side engaged in wide-scale public relations to promote its interests. The State Department encouraged scholarly exchanges and established U.S. centers around the world that offered English lessons and books and magazines about the way of life in the United States. The Voice of America broadcast news, music, and other programs in nearly every language, including twenty spoken in the Soviet Union. Disc jockey Willis Conover built a following for U.S. jazz, and jazz greats Louis Armstrong, Duke Ellington, and Dizzy Gillespie toured Europe and Africa as cultural ambassadors for the United States. The Soviets sought to counter the popularity of U.S. cultural diplomacy by sending their best orchestras, ballet troupes, and folk dancers for exhibitions in the United States.

{ Cultural exchanges between the United States and the Soviet Union open new chances for cooperation. }

The most celebrated U.S.–Soviet cultural exchange was the 1959 U.S. exposition in Moscow. The event featured displays of U.S. automobiles, cosmetics, and sporting goods, as well as free samples of Pepsi-Cola, which Khrushchev liked so much that he allowed it to be bottled and sold in the Soviet Union. A special highlight was a full-scale suburban ranch-style home complete with a washing machine, dishwasher,

cultural diplomacy Foreign relations strategy of building goodwill among people in rival or neutral states by exchanging ideas and programs in art, music, sports, literature, and other fields.

and other modern labor-saving devices. Escorting the Soviet premier through the display, Vice President Richard Nixon engaged Khrushchev in what became known as the "kitchen debate." "We don't have one decision made at the top by one government official," said Nixon. "We have many different manufacturers and many different kinds of washing machines so that the housewives have a choice." Khrushchev did not deny the superiority of American technology and consumer goods but praised his nation's ability to "overtake our American partners in peaceful economic competition."

Soviet citizens may have flocked to see American consumer goods, but their suspicions of the United States were reinforced in 1960 when a U.S. spy plane over Soviet territory crashed. Eisenhower claimed it was conducting weather research. He did not know at the time that the Soviets had recovered the plane with its cameras and photographs of secret Soviet military installations and that the pilot, who survived, had confessed to being a CIA agent. Caught in a major cover-up, Eisenhower made a historic address to Americans in which he admitted to U.S. espionage regarding the Soviet Union. The incident ruined a long-planned Paris summit meeting, and whatever good cultural diplomacy the two nations had generated seemed to be lost.

22-4c Kennedy and the Cuban Missile Crisis

In the 1960 presidential election, the Democratic candidate John F. Kennedy, a handsome war hero, won a narrow victory over Richard Nixon by blaming Republicans for not keeping pace with Soviet advances, citing the Sputnik shock and the much-feared "missile gap." The youngest president elected to office, Kennedy brought a fresh optimism to U.S. foreign policy. Although every bit as much a cold warrior as his predecessor, he distinguished himself from Eisenhower by criticizing the strategy of massive retaliation for posing an unnecessary risk of nuclear destruction. Kennedy's plan was to provide the United States with "flexible options" enabling it to defeat the Soviets using either conventional or nuclear weapons. Yet, ironically, the new president soon confronted a series of crises that pushed the world to the brink of nuclear war.

{ Pushed to the brink of war over Cuba, the United States and the Soviet Union begin to emphasize cooperation. }

Kennedy inherited an Eisenhower plan for overthrowing the new Communist regime in Cuba. As in much of Latin America, the United States regularly supported military dictators capable of suppressing communism, but in 1959, Fidel Castro, a young lawyer advocating land redistribution, led a revolution that

Nixon and Khrushchev Hold "Kitchen Debate" in Moscow, 1959
Nixon, a hard-charging anti-Communist, became Eisenhower's vice president as the result of recognition he won as a leader of the House Un-American Activities Committee. Khrushchev, a Stalinist stalwart with only four years of formal education, climbed the ranks of the Communist Party to become Soviet premier. Their "debate" about the merits of consumer capitalism was a historic meeting even though neither changed the other's mind. ▲

Sovfoto/Getty Images

ousted dictator Fulgencio Batista, a U.S. ally, and seized $1 billion worth of property belonging to U.S. corporations. Although not a Communist at first, Castro quickly gravitated toward the Soviet Union, proclaiming Cuba to be part of the worldwide Communist revolution and pledging to paint Latin America red. In April 1961, Kennedy implemented Eisenhower's plan for a secret CIA expedition that would land at the Bay of Pigs and ignite an uprising of the Cuban people. The expedition landed, but the uprising did not happen. It was only the first of the **covert operations** aiming to unsettle Cuba's Communist regime and assassinate Castro, but it was a great embarrassment for the new president and placed him in a weak position going into the next crisis over Berlin.

In 1958, Khrushchev had backed down from his threat to go to war over West Berlin, but in June 1961, he repeated it, hoping to bully the shaken president into giving up control over the western half of the city. Kennedy stood firm, however, and the Soviets then built a concrete wall that sealed off the border between East and West Berlin to halt defections altogether. The **Berlin Wall** became an enduring symbol of the Cold War.

Berlin and the divided Germanys remained a superpower standoff, but the next crisis was closer to the United States and the closest that Americans and Soviets ever came to nuclear war—the **Cuban Missile Crisis**. In 1962, Castro agreed to install Soviet missiles in Cuba that would be aimed at the United States and just eight minutes from launch to the White House. For Khrushchev, the missiles offset the U.S. atomic weapon advantage (seventeen to one) and checkmated the U.S. missiles installed in Turkey. When aerial photographs by CIA spy planes confirmed the construction of launch sites, Kennedy went on nationwide TV to declare a U.S. naval blockade of Cuba to prevent the delivery of nuclear warheads. On October 24, the world held its breath as twelve Soviet ships approached the islands, only to make a U-turn at the last moment. After four uncertain days, the world finally exhaled as Khrushchev agreed to remove the missiles from Cuba and Kennedy promised to cease menacing the Castro regime and, more important though not publicized, to remove U.S. missiles in Turkey.

The missile crisis proved an embarrassment for the Soviet Union, toppling Khrushchev and necessitating a huge rearmament campaign to close the nuclear weapons gap with the United States. The arms race continued for nearly two more decades, but what was called **brinkmanship** between the two superpowers subsided. Both agreed to be connected by a private teletype "hotline" to improve communication and prevent future nuclear conflict. Moreover, the near miss pushed them to agree in 1963 to the **Limited Test Ban Treaty**, which prohibited nuclear weapons tests in the atmosphere, outer space, and underwater—all of which could be easily monitored by the more than one hundred signatory nations. Although the treaty did not cover underground tests, a major shortcoming, it paved the way for more extensive arms control agreements between the superpowers in the late 1960s and early 1970s.

22-4d Peace Movements

Superpower conflict and crises with the threat of nuclear war revived the U.S. peace movement, which had declined during World War II despite the presence of conscientious objectors. In the aftermath of Hiroshima and Nagasaki, scientists became the most conspicuous group to join traditional pacifists and religious leaders in speaking out against the use of atomic weapons. Albert Einstein was among them, observing that if World War III were waged with nuclear weapons, World War IV would be fought "with sticks." Einstein helped found the Federation of Atomic Scientists, which lobbied the government for peace and the safeguarding of nuclear weapons. Its bestseller *One World or None* (1948) described what would happen if an atomic bomb were dropped on New York City, and its *Bulletin of the Atomic Scientists* still features a Doomsday Clock with hands indicating how many minutes to midnight—the end of the world. After the signing of the Limited Test Ban Treaty, the clock was moved back, to 23:48, and Americans gained confidence that superpower diplomacy was reducing the threat of nuclear holocaust. A 1959 poll had suggested that 64 percent of Americans considered nuclear war the nation's most urgent problem, but by 1964, that figure had fallen to 16 percent.

National and international movements continued to warn of the dangers of nuclear war and the health and environmental hazards of nuclear testing. The logo for Britain's Campaign for Nuclear Disarmament became the international symbol for peace, and in the United States, the National Committee for a Sane Nuclear Policy (SANE) founded in 1957 garnered celebrity endorsements for its lobbying and educational campaigns. The activist Women Strike for Peace, founded in 1961, engaged white middle-class mothers in street demonstrations that called out "End the Arms Race—Not the Human Race."

> Nuclear threats reinvigorate international peace activism.

covert operations Secret, state-sponsored tactics used in a foreign country, usually to prop up an existing government or to promote regime change that the CIA had routinely used since 1947.

Berlin Wall Highly militarized and patrolled cement wall erected by Soviets in 1961 to prevent an embarrassing stream of defections from East Berlin.

Cuban Missile Crisis U.S.–Soviet showdown in 1962 over the placement of Soviet missiles in Cuba that was resolved but pushed the world to the brink of nuclear war.

brinkmanship Security strategy used during Cold War to win a global dispute by pushing the stakes to the brink of nuclear destruction.

Limited Test Ban Treaty Global agreement signed by the United States, the Soviet Union, and other nations, which provided the first limitation on nuclear testing.

History without Borders

Nuclear Testing

Ninety-one tests were conducted above the Arctic Circle on Novaya Zemlya, detonating material equivalent to 239 megatons of TNT.

At least 151 nuclear tests were conducted in the Pacific with total detonations equivalent to 171 megatons of TNT.

Atmospheric nuclear tests, 1949–1980

Nation	Test site
Soviet Union	
United States	
United Kingdom	
France	
China	

—— International boundaries, 1950

Number

Soviet Union	219 tests, 1949–1962	247.30 megatons
United States	194 tests, 1951–1963	153.74 megatons
United Kingdom	21 tests, 1952–1958	8.05 megatons
France	45 tests, 1960–1974	10.20 megatons
China	22 tests, 1964–1980	20.72 megatons

Major Test Sites for Atmospheric Nuclear Weapons, 1949–1980

The twenty test sites on this map spanned the globe with only South America and Antarctica excluded. No spot on Earth was spared nuclear fallout because ever more powerful tests spewed radioactive material into the stratosphere where it could remain for several years and disperse globally. ▲ Sources: Steven L. Simon, André Bouville, and Charles E. Land. "Fallout from Nuclear Weapon Tests and Cancer Risks: Exposures 50 Years Ago Still Have Health Implications Today That Will Continue into the Future." *American Scientist*, (January–February 2006), p. 50. United Nations Scientific Committee on the Effects of Atomic Radiation, *UNSCEAR 2000 REPORT Vol. I: SOURCES AND EFFECTS OF IONIZING RADIATION*, "Annex C: Exposures from man-made sources of radiation."

On March 1, 1954, twenty-three Japanese fishermen on the *Diago Fukuryu Maru* (*Lucky Dragon*), some eighty-five miles from the Bikini atoll in the South Pacific, were stunned by a brilliant flash of light, thunder claps, and then a ball of fire that lit up the sky. Two hours later, a shower of white ashes rained down, and soon every one of them was ill from acute radiation poisoning. That day, the United States exploded a hydrogen bomb at Bikini

Atoll that was 750 times more powerful than the one that destroyed Hiroshima. Later, one member of the *Lucky Dragon's* crew died. The ship's entire haul of fish was contaminated with nuclear fallout.

The *Lucky Dragon* was not the only Japanese fishing boat to suffer from nuclear testing. The nuclear arms race between the Soviets and Americans led to repeated tests of newer and more explosive weapons that posed health risks to life forms across the planet. By

December 1954, more than eight hundred other Japanese fishermen had been exposed to radioactive fallout, leading to the destruction of 490 tons of "A-bomb tuna" caught by these fishermen. A "radiation scare" swept Japan, the only nation to have suffered a nuclear attack. Japanese scientists found radioactive material in the smallest sea creatures around Bikini, raising fears that nuclear fallout was being passed on through the food chain. The public, including

Japanese Fishing Boat *Daigo Fukuryu Maru*
(*Lucky Dragon*), 1954 From 1946 to 1958, the
United States detonated twenty-three nuclear devices
at the Bikini Atoll in the central Pacific. Hundreds of
residents were relocated. In addition to contaminating
their home environment with radioactivity, the tests'
fallout irradiated the *Lucky Dragon* (and other fishing
boats) eighty-five miles away. The poisonous effects of
radiation have remained despite the return of residents
to Bikini. ◄

AP Images

Still from *Godzilla, King of the Monsters*,
1954 Wakened by nuclear tests, Japan's cinematic
monster Godzilla embodied global nuclear fears in
the wake of the *Lucky Dragon* incident. The aquatic
dinosaur-like monster was cast as a metaphor of nuclear
destruction with "atomic breath" that destroys cities
and rough, scaly skin resembling the scars seen on
survivors of the Hiroshima and Nagasaki blasts. ◄

Andrea Ferrari/Photoshot

the Japanese emperor, stopped eating
fish, and fish markets across the country
closed. The Japanese were also concerned
about fallout from Soviet nuclear tests
in Siberia, and the government warned
housewives to wash vegetables in case
they contained radioactive residue.

In response to the *Lucky Dragon*
incident, the United States paid
$2 million as compensation for the
medical expenses of the irradiated
fishermen, but neither Eisenhower nor
the U.S. press gave credence to the
widespread radiation scare in Japan. No
one seemed concerned about dangers
from radioactive fallout from Soviet
nuclear tests near the Arctic Circle
or U.S. tests in Nevada. The head of
the U.S. Atomic Energy Commission
contradicted the findings of Japanese

scientists, proclaiming that fallout from
nuclear tests had a negligible effect on
sea life. But movements for arms control
beginning in Japan and spreading to
many nations indicated the depth of
ordinary people's concern.

One of the most unusual expressions
of the arms control spirit was the
release of *Godzilla, King of the Monsters*
in late 1954, the first in a series of more
than twenty films made in Japan featuring
the mutant, fire-breathing creature. The
Lucky Dragon influence was apparent
from the start of the film when an atomic
test sinks a number of Japanese fishing
boats and awakens Godzilla from his
prehistoric sleep to embark on a path of
destruction leading to Tokyo. Publicizing
the negative impact of nuclear testing
through Godzilla movies enabled the

Japanese to get around their government's
policy of remaining silent on this issue.

Critical Thinking Questions

▶ What factors encouraged the United States,
the Soviet Union, and other nuclear powers to
test hundreds of nuclear weapons above ground
during the Cold War?

▶ Why was convincing authorities of the dangers
of nuclear fallout difficult?

Go to MindTap® to engage with an
interactive version of **History without
Borders: Nuclear Testing.** Learn from an
interactive map, view related video, and
respond to critical thinking questions.

Cold War in the Third World

Prime Minister Kwame Nkrumah (center) waves to the cheering crowd as newly independent Ghana replaced the British colony known as Gold Coast. In attendance were Vice President Richard Nixon and a host of prominent African Americans, including Martin Luther King, Jr., A. Philip Randolph, and Ralph Bunche.

What interests might the United States have had in Ghana? Why did African Americans in particular embrace the country? What is the political implication of Prime Minister Nkrumah wearing African dress instead of a conventional coat and tie? ▶

Bettmann/Corbis

decolonization Process through which colonies gain political, economic, cultural, and psychological independence and autonomy from colonial rulers.

nonaligned movement Alternative to taking sides during Cold War advanced by newly independent nations, especially in Asia and Africa.

Third World Cold War era classification given to developing nations, largely in Africa and Asia, that were not firmly aligned with U.S.-influenced developed nations (First World) or Soviet-influenced nations (Second World).

As superpower relations stabilized, Cold War tensions erupted in former colonies around the world that were gaining independence. With 70 percent of the world's population in 1950, these emerging nations taken together posed a significant alternative to the U.S. and Soviet spheres of influence. Many pledged to stay out of the Cold War and to advance their own collective interests instead. But they also approached one or both of the superpowers when they needed economic and military aid, sometimes playing the Americans and Soviets against each other. To stop what was believed to be the spread of communism, the United States intervened in the internal affairs of nations in the Middle East, Africa, and Southeast Asia as well as the traditional U.S. sphere of influence in Latin America.

☞ As you read, focus on how the Cold War in its third phase spread to the developing world. How did fears about a worldwide Communist revolution influence U.S. responses to the emergence of newly independent nations?

22-5a Newly Independent Nations and Foreign Aid

Within two decades after World War II, the vast majority of colonies achieved independence, a global process known as **decolonization** (see Map 22.3). The age of imperialism with few exceptions had ended as European empires could no longer afford

{ Independence for former colonies brings new players into world politics.

to maintain colonies, especially in the context of Soviet and Chinese support for independence movements. The largest number of the newly independent nations was in Africa, and in 1960, seventeen of them joined the United Nations. Others of these countries were in Asia and the Middle East. The largest new nations—India, Egypt, and Indonesia (with China's support)—led an international movement to establish an alternative to the bipolar politics of the Cold War. Meeting at Bandung, Indonesia, in 1955, the **nonaligned movement** articulated a third way to engage global affairs that addressed the largest but least powerful populations in what came to be known as the **Third World**. Although the United States and its NATO and Pacific allies represented the First World and the Soviet Union and its Warsaw Pact allies constituted the Second World, the Third World encompassed the remaining nations that were typically less economically and militarily developed.

Despite the spirit of the Bandung Conference, the political and economic realities of decolonization worked against the nonaligned movement. The leaders of newly independent nations often found it easier to claim freedom than to manage a country, and some were military dictators who squashed hopes for democracy and provoked a cycle of armed response and regime change. The Cold War further inflamed conflicts internal to these nations as the Soviets and Chinese actively nurtured Communist revolution within them and the Americans sought to counter Communist moves by backing undemocratic regimes, sowing discord, and staging coups.

Applying the model used in the reconstruction of Japan and the Marshall Plan, U.S. officials spurred the

Map 22.3 Decolonization, 1932–1977 Independence from colonial rule accelerated greatly after World War II. This trend applied to all of Africa, with the exception of Egypt, and much of Asia and the Middle East. However, independence did not always mean freedom from influence by the superpowers and former colonial rulers in the form of foreign and military aid and covert operations. ◀

1960 Year independence achieved

Former ruler

Great Britain	Belgium	Portugal
France	United States	Other
Netherlands	Italy	

ATLANTIC OCEAN

PACIFIC OCEAN

INDIAN OCEAN

Arabian Sea

Bay of Bengal

Caspian Sea

Black Sea

Mediterranean Sea

GREAT BRITAIN
FRANCE
NETHERLANDS
BELGIUM
ITALY
SPAIN
PORTUGAL
JAPAN

NORTH KOREA 1948
SOUTH KOREA 1948 (From Japan)
PHILIPPINES 1946
NORTH VIETNAM 1954 (Unified 1975)
SOUTH VIETNAM 1954
CAMBODIA 1953
MALAYSIA 1963
SINGAPORE 1965 (From Malaysia)
BRUNEI 1984 (From Gr. Br.)
INDONESIA 1949
TIMOR-LESTE 1999 (From Indonesia)
PAPUA NEW GUINEA 1975 (From Australia)
LAOS 1949
MYANMAR (BURMA) 1947
PAKISTAN 1947, BANGLADESH 1973
SRI LANKA (CEYLON) 1948
MALDIVES 1975 (From Gr. Br.)
INDIA 1947
PAKISTAN 1947
P.D.R. OF YEMEN 1967 (Unified 1990)
YEMEN
OMAN 1971
UNITED ARAB EMIRATES 1971
QATAR 1971
BAHRAIN 1971
KUWAIT 1961
IRAQ 1932
JORDAN 1946
SYRIA 1944
LEBANON 1944
ISRAEL 1948
CYPRUS 1960
MALTA 1964 (From Gr. Br.)
TUNISIA 1957
LIBYA 1951
EGYPT 1922
ERITREA 1993 (From Ethiopia)
SUDAN 1956
DJIBOUTI 1977
ETHIOPIA
SOMALIA 1960
SEYCHELLES 1976 (From Gr. Br.)
COMOROS 1975 (From France)
MADAGASCAR 1960
MAURITIUS 1968 (From Gr. Br.)
KENYA 1963
UGANDA 1962
TANZANIA 1964
RWANDA 1962
BURUNDI 1962
DEM. REP. OF CONGO 1960
CENTRAL AFRICAN REPUBLIC 1960
CHAD 1960
CAMEROON 1960
GABON 1960
REPUBLIC OF CONGO 1960
ANGOLA 1975
ZAMBIA 1964
MALAWI 1964
MOZAMBIQUE 1974
ZIMBABWE 1980
BOTSWANA 1966
NAMIBIA 1990 (From South Africa)
SOUTH AFRICA (Republic 1961)
SWAZILAND 1968
LESOTHO 1966
MOROCCO 1956
WESTERN SAHARA 1975 (From Spain)
MAURITANIA 1960
ALGERIA 1962
MALI 1960
NIGER 1960
BENIN 1960
NIGERIA 1960
SENEGAL 1960
GAMBIA 1965
GUINEA-BISSAU 1974
GUINEA 1958
SIERRA LEONE 1961
LIBERIA 1820s
CÔTE D'IVOIRE 1960
BURKINA FASO 1960
GHANA 1957
TOGO 1960
EQUATORIAL GUINEA 1968 (From Spain)
SÃO TOMÉ AND PRÍNCIPE 1975 (From Port.)
CAPE VERDE 1975 (From Port.)

Equator 0°
Tropic of Cancer
Tropic of Capricorn

2,000 Mi.
2,000 Km.

N

Global Americans Born of humble origins in Detroit, **Ralph Bunche** arrived in Los Angeles with his grandmother in 1918. He attended high school and then UCLA, where he excelled at debating, starred on the basketball team, and was valedictorian when he graduated in 1927. He went on to get a Ph.D. at Harvard University and to teach political science at Howard University, a historically black university in Washington, D.C. Bunche was a critic of colonialism and imperialism, which he attributed to capitalism. During World War II, he served as an Africa expert in the Office of Strategic Services. After the war, the United Nations became his passion. He was a member of the U.S. delegation at the San Francisco Conference that drafted its charter, and he assisted in the development of its Universal Declaration of Human Rights. In the late 1940s, he was a UN peace negotiator in Africa and the Middle East, and he earned the Nobel Peace Prize for brokering the end of the Arab–Israeli War in 1949. During the Suez Crisis in 1956, Bunche established the first UN peacekeeping force and later supervised subsequent forces in Lebanon, Cyprus, and the Congo. Committed to civil rights and nonviolent protest, he marched with Martin Luther King Jr., and in 1965 contributed to the success of the Voting Rights Act. Bunche's life's work embodied the connection between civil rights struggles in the United States and global efforts for human rights and international peace.

Keystone-France/Getty Images

economic development of Third World nations to create conditions favorable to the growth of free-market capitalism and to winning the hearts and minds of Third World peoples. In some cases, this process was dictated by U.S. business interests, but most aid from the United States had more to do with political control than economic markets. **Developmentalism** is an economic theory associated with these ideological aims that prioritized a nation's economic and political stability as well as its participation in the Bretton Woods economic system above that country's democratic rule and social equality. Critics see developmentalism as a disguised form of colonialism in which the recipients of foreign aid are "client states" or "puppet regimes" controlled by the United States, but the defenders of foreign aid underscore its humanitarian motivations and faith in free markets.

Kennedy was even more interested than Eisenhower in using foreign aid and cultural diplomacy to spread the American way of life around the world. The program that came to symbolize these goals was the **Peace Corps**, a volunteer service organization established in 1961 that, like missionary work, sent idealistic, mostly young Americans to live and work in developing nations "to promote world peace and friendship." Kennedy's inaugural address had issued a call for public service. "Ask not what your country can do for you," he declared, "ask what you can do for your country." And he told those "citizens of the world" listening on VOA radio to "ask not what America will do for you, but what together we can do for the freedom of man."

Developmentalism Theory applied to the Third World that emphasizes the significance of free-market economic development and participation in the global capitalist system.

Peace Corps U.S. international social service organization established to fight poverty and aid in the economic development of less-advantaged nations and to counter Communist influence.

22-5b Middle East and Africa

Complicating efforts by both the United States and the Soviet Union to win allies in the Middle East was the issue of Israel, a long-promised homeland for Jews, especially for survivors of the Holocaust. A UN resolution in 1947 recommended the establishment of separate Jewish and Arab states with control over the contested city of Jerusalem placed under international trusteeship. Jewish representatives in Palestine accepted the partition plan, but their Arab counterparts did not. When Britain relinquished control over its Palestine mandate in 1948 and the independent State of Israel was proclaimed, eight neighboring Arab nations sent troops to aid the Palestinian Arabs in an attack that sought to reclaim the land they believed was theirs. The ensuing Arab–Israeli War lasted a year before a UN cease-fire agreement enlarged the boundaries of Israel but permitted Jordan to annex the West Bank, including East Jerusalem, and Egypt to take the Gaza Strip.

> The United States succeeds European nations as the key Western power in these regions.

Neither the United States nor the Soviet Union sent troops to the Arab–Israeli War because each recognized the State of Israel and supported UN partition for its own reasons. Stalin sought to divert attention from his anti-Semitic policies and to use the thorn of Israel to galvanize Arab opposition to Western imperialists. Truman expressed sympathy for Holocaust survivors, believed that the transplanted European Jews brought stability and civilization to the Middle East, and, to a lesser extent, sought Jewish American votes. Yet his support for Israel cost him a chance to bring Arab nations into a NATO-like alliance against the Soviet Union.

Superpower tensions were more evident in Iran, where they had already clashed in 1946. In 1951, parliament forced the pro-U.S. Shah Muhammad Reza Pahlavi to accept the new prime minister Mohammed Mossadeq and his intention to nationalize Iran's oil fields. U.S. officials suspected Soviet intervention, and two years later Eisenhower authorized CIA-led covert operations that ousted the nation's democratically elected government, leaving the nation's oil in the hands of British and increasingly U.S. companies.

Cold War tensions also influenced relations with Egypt, a former British colony and the most populous Arab nation. To gain Egypt's favor, U.S. and British officials agreed to work with the World Bank to build the Aswan High Dam, a flood-control and electric power project that the country's socialist leader Gamal Abdel Nasser deemed essential for his nation's economic development. Yet Eisenhower withdrew from the project to punish Nasser for maintaining ties with the Soviets. In response, Nasser in 1956 seized the Suez Canal from Britain only to have British, French, and Israeli forces take it back. In a surprising turn of events, the United States and Soviet Union joined to pressure the invading nations to withdraw. Egypt suffered huge war losses but won a diplomatic victory over the West and convinced the Soviet Union to fund the Aswan High Dam to its completion in 1971.

Following this Suez Crisis, in 1957 Eisenhower vowed to increase the U.S. military role in the Middle East through the **Eisenhower Doctrine**, which announced a commitment to defend the region from "any nation controlled by International Communism." It rested on domino theory fears about the importance of stopping communism and led to interventions in the internal affairs of Jordan, Syria, and especially Lebanon, to which Eisenhower sent fifteen thousand U.S. troops in 1958 to calm political unrest.

U.S. strategy in Africa varied by country but generally involved the combination of economic incentives, covert operations, and foreign aid. The inaugural group of Kennedy's Peace Corps volunteers went to Ghana, the first black African nation to proclaim independence, led by the visionary pan-African organizer Kwame Nkrumah. He had studied in the United States at Lincoln University in Pennsylvania, where he developed close relations with socialists and African American activists such as W.E.B. Du Bois, who spent his final days in Ghana and died there. As the new nation's first prime minister, Nkrumah focused on the development and liberation of Africa rather than taking sides in the Cold War. Like Nasser, he came under suspicion by U.S. officials, who distrusted his nonaligned position and were concerned about socialist connections from his college days. In 1966, while Nkrumah was visiting North Vietnam and China, the CIA arranged a coup that toppled him from power and forced his exile.

Another U.S. covert operation occurred in central Africa where in 1960, Patrice Lumumba, a labor organizer and independence leader, won election as the first prime minister of the newly independent Republic of Congo. During the struggle to free the central African colony from Belgium, Lumumba had articulated a vision of independence for his people: "We are going to institute social justice together and ensure everyone just remuneration for his labor. We are going to show the world what the black man can do when he works in freedom, and we are going to make the Congo the focal point for the development of all of Africa." As prime minister, Lumumba appealed to the Soviet Union for help in resolving a bitter civil war within the Congo but made it clear that he did so as an African nationalist who was not aligned with either side in the Cold War. This stance proved dangerous, because U.S. officials, who often equated nationalism with communism, did not trust Lumumba and in 1960 worked with Belgian operatives to arrange his murder. The new Congolese president, Joseph Mobutu, was a staunch U.S. ally who received millions in U.S. aid, military equipment, and, at his own request, parachute training in the United States at Fort Benning and at the Special Warfare School at Fort Bragg.

22-5c Latin America

Latin America was more important to U.S. officials than Africa because of its proximity to the United States and the long-standing practice of U.S. intervention throughout the region. By the 1950s, U.S. officials sought to keep Latin American nations' dependence on the United States. An example was Nicaragua, whose exports of sugar, cocoa, and coffee to the United States were so critical to the Nicaraguan economy that one local official could claim his nation "served the dessert at the imperialist dining table."

> The United States struggles to maintain control over the Western Hemisphere amid Communist-influenced democratic movements.

U.S. economic domination, however, was serious business. In 1954, when Guatemala sought to nationalize the huge landholdings of U.S. firm United Fruit Company, Eisenhower had the CIA overthrow the democratically elected government of Jacobo Árbenz Guzmán in the name of anticommunism. The coup ignored the support of the Guatemalan people for land redistribution and the fact that Guzmán was tied neither to communism nor to the Soviet Union. The new military government, a U.S. ally, reclaimed United Fruit Company's banana plantations and ruled the nation for the next three decades.

The result of U.S. dominance was the **underdevelopment** of Latin American economies, a see-saw process in which rising profits for U.S. firms (and low food costs for American consumers) led directly to the declining economic independence of Latin American nations. Although U.S. influence made the

Eisenhower Doctrine Foreign policy under which the United States supports Middle East nations in resisting Soviet and Communist influence.

underdevelopment Process through which the rising economic fortunes of wealthy nations or classes contributes directly and indirectly to the declining economic fortunes of poorer nations or classes.

nations in the Western Hemisphere far more economically and politically stable than newly independent nations in Africa, this stability reinforced a huge gap between rich and poor that pushed millions to migrate to the United States.

Stability most often meant dictatorial rule, and the United States supported military regimes in Argentina (1946–1955), Venezuela (1952–1958), Chile (1973–1989), Nicaragua (1937–1956), the Dominican Republic (1930–1961), Brazil (1964–1985), and Cuba until Castro's revolution of 1959. The contradiction between U.S. Cold War rhetoric about freedom and democracy and its support of military dictators angered those who suffered under repressive rule. In 1958 on an official visit to Venezuela, Vice President Nixon and his wife narrowly escaped harm. In 1961, Kennedy sought to counter anti-Americanism—and isolate Communist Cuba—by creating the **Alliance for Progress**, a program of $20 billion in aid. The money did not usually reach the region's poor, however, because the military regimes diverted it and were forbidden to use it for land redistribution or other programs the State Department considered Communistic.

22-5d Southeast Asia

The region that drew increasing attention from the United States was Southeast Asia, which had been divided since the nineteenth century into

> The United States struggles to prevent Communist victory in Vietnam.

French, British, and Dutch colonies. Japan seized the region during World War II, and after the war, Britain and the Netherlands granted their colonies independence. But the French chose to hold onto Indochina—Vietnam, Cambodia, and Laos—for its resources of rubber, tungsten, and rice. Yet they could not suppress Vietnamese independence fighters who rose to power under the leadership of Ho Chi Minh ("the enlightened one"). Ho exemplified the complicated blending of communism and nationalism exhibited by Mao, Kim Il Sung, Castro, Nkrumah, and Lumumba. The revered freedom fighter was first and foremost a Vietnamese patriot who, as a young man, tried to convince President Wilson at the Paris Peace Conference in 1919 that Vietnam deserved self-determination. Failing this, Ho turned to communism as the vehicle for national liberation. In August 1945, he proclaimed the establishment of the Democratic Republic of Vietnam (DRV) to cheering crowds in the capital city of Hanoi. But the French did not accede.

The war between the French and the DRV that began the next year was embroiled in the emerging Cold War conflict (see Map 22.4). The Soviets supported Hanoi with China also contributing after Mao came to power. The United States backed the French, paying for 80 percent of war expenses in 1950 but not sending troops. Following a disastrous French defeat at Dien Bien Phu in 1954, a Geneva peace treaty recognized the DRV victory and called for the withdrawal of French troops. The treaty granted independence to the neighboring colonies of Cambodia and Laos but partitioned Vietnam at the 17th parallel, postponing the question of reunification for two years when popular elections were to be held. Hanoi retained control over northern and central Vietnam, and the French-backed emperor Bao Dai was reinstalled in the South.

The agreed-upon elections never took place. Even before the peace treaty was signed, U.S. officials moved to establish a permanent anti-Communist regime in South Vietnam that could resist a North Vietnamese takeover. The U.S. choice to head this new regime was the Vietnamese nationalist Ngo Dinh Diem, who had the support of Vietnam's Catholic, land-holding elite and the nearly 1 million people pushed out of the north by land redistribution and crackdowns on dissent. Within a year, Diem deposed the emperor and became head of the newly established Republic of Vietnam whose capital was Saigon. To protect Diem's regime, U.S. officials in 1954 formed the **Southeast Asia Treaty Organization (SEATO)**, a collective security alliance including the United States, Britain, France, Australia, New Zealand, Pakistan, Thailand, and the Philippines.

The emergence of South Vietnam had profound political repercussions in Hanoi. By 1960, Vietnamese Worker's Party head Le Duan and his right-hand man Le Duc Tho had taken control, and they shamed Ho and his supporters into submission for agreeing to the North–South partition and for failing in land redistribution. Ho followed a "North-first" strategy to advance socialist revolution, whereas Le Duan changed to a "South-first" plan seeking military conquest through the combination of a general offensive (GO) from the North and general uprising (GU) within the South. The **GO-GU plan** relied on the emergence of the National Liberation Front, which served as Hanoi's covert military arm in the South.

The execution of Hanoi's GO-GU plan in the early 1960s propelled Kennedy to rapidly increase the number of military advisers sent to South Vietnam. In June 1963, Buddhist monks and nuns began to set themselves on fire to protest the Diem regime's religious intolerance. The world gasped in horror upon seeing photographs of their burning bodies. The self-immolations convinced Kennedy that Diem had become a liability, and so in August 1963, the president authorized the CIA to dispose of him. Three months later, South Vietnamese military officers toppled Diem's government and murdered its leader. Not long after this, Kennedy himself was assassinated, and the direction of the U.S. involvement in Vietnam fell to a new president, Lyndon Johnson.

Alliance for Progress Program of U.S. economic aid to Latin America to ward off Cuba's Communist influence.

Southeast Asia Treaty Organization (SEATO) U.S.-led military alliance established to counter Communist influence in the region.

GO-GU plan North Vietnamese military strategy that combined a general offensive (GO) against South Vietnam and a general uprising (GU) of insurgents in South Vietnam.

Map 22.4 Cold War Confrontations and Military Presence, 1945–1992
Conflict between the United States and the Soviet Union played out around the world in episodes of conflict and vast networks of military installations, which were far greater in number considering cooperative agreements providing superpower access to allied facilities (not shown on map). Also not shown on the map was the extensive global reach of intelligence gathering by the CIA and its Soviet counterpart, the KGB. ▲

Legend:
- NATO nations
- Warsaw Pact nations
- Soviet military base
- U.S. military base
- U.S. Strategic Air Command base
- U.S. Intercontinental Ballistic Missile base
- U.S. naval fleet
- Cold War point of conflict

Conflict points labeled:
- SOUTH KOREA 1950–1953
- FORMOSA (TAIWAN) 1958
- LAOS 1960–1975
- SOUTH VIETNAM 1945–1954, 1957–1975
- CAMBODIA 1969–1975
- PHILIPPINES
- THAILAND
- INDONESIA 1965
- AFGHANISTAN 1979
- PAKISTAN
- IRAN 1945–1946, 1951–1953
- IRAQ 1958
- TURKEY 1945–1947
- LEBANON 1958
- GREECE 1946–1949
- EGYPT 1956, 1967, 1973
- SAUDI ARABIA
- SOMALIA 1970s–1980s
- ETHIOPIA 1975–1991
- DEMOCRATIC REPUBLIC OF THE CONGO 1961–1965
- ANGOLA 1976–1992
- GUATEMALA 1954
- EL SALVADOR 1979–1992
- NICARAGUA 1981–1990
- PANAMA
- CUBA 1961–1962
- DOMINICAN REPUBLIC 1965–1966
- GRENADA 1983
- CZECHOSLOVAKIA 1948,1968
- EAST GERMANY 1948–1949, 1953, 1958–1962
- POLAND 1956
- YUGOSLAVIA 1948–1953
- HUNGARY 1956

675

Summary

Following the end of World War II, the United States and the Soviet Union became bitter rivals. Beginning as a struggle to gain ideological control in Europe, this rivalry intensified through the formation of security alliances and the emergence of a nuclear arms race. Although the United States and the Soviet Union avoided direct military conflict, Americans fought in Korea against Communist forces that included hundreds of thousands of Chinese troops. The two superpowers also engaged in proxy wars in the Middle East, Africa, Latin America, and Southeast Asia. Each superpower channeled aid and military support to opposite sides of internal conflicts within newly independent states. In the unstable politics of Third World nations, U.S. officials often confused the nationalism and nonalignment of Third World leaders with support for a world Communist revolution. Thus, the ideological conflict that began the first phase of the Cold War added a military dimension in the second phase and then in the third phase spread to the Third World.

The Cold War crisis on the U.S. home front produced the Second Red Scare and for the first time transformed sexual orientation into a major issue of national security. The impact was the persecution of thousands of U.S. citizens on the basis of their ideological beliefs or sexual orientation. Although high-level policy makers and military leaders played the key roles in shaping the overall patterns of the Cold War, peace activists, novelists, and the entertainment industry influenced how Americans understood these patterns in seeking to avert the potential nightmare of nuclear war. The fear of a nuclear attack combined with the nation's worst era of political repression ended, for the time being, U.S. interest in socialism and communism that began during the Great Depression.

<Thinking Back, *Looking Forward*>

As you review this chapter, think about the causes and the legacy of the Cold War. Why did anti-Communist fears explode in the United States at this time, and how did the Second Red Scare compare to the Red Scare that followed World War I? In the coming chapters, look for the Cold War's impact on the U.S. economy, civil rights, and subsequent war in Vietnam. Did the Cold War ultimately suppress progressive reforms as Americans looked for security in materialism, conformity, God, family, and the flag, or did the Cold War generate a new political activism advocating equality, dissent, and the power of popular participation?

To make your study concrete, review the timeline and reflect on the entries there. Think about their causes, consequences, and connections. How do they fit with global trends?

Additional Resources

Books

Boyer, Paul. *By the Bomb's Early Light: American Thought and Culture at the Dawn of the Atomic Age.* Chapel Hill: University of North Carolina Press, 1994. ▶ Original account of the response to nuclear weapons in U.S. culture.

Craig, Campbell, and Fredrik Logevall. *America's Cold War: The Politics of Insecurity.* Cambridge, MA: Harvard University Press, 2009. ▶ Good overview focusing on domestic politics in the United States that influenced the Cold War.

Cumings, Bruce. *The Korean War: A History.* New York: Modern Library, 2011. ▶ Insight into North Korean regime and U.S. atrocities by a recognized expert on Korean history.

Dower, John W. *Embracing Defeat: Japan in the Wake of World War II.* New York: Norton, 1999. ▶ Extensive examination of the U.S. occupation of Japan.

Gaines, Kevin K. *American Africans in Ghana: Black Expatriates and the Civil Rights Era.* Chapel Hill: University of North Carolina Press, 2006. ▶ Pioneering analysis of the role played by African Americans in African decolonization.

Pells, Richard. *Not Like Us: How Europeans Have Loved, Hated, and Transformed American Culture since World War II*. New York: Basic Books, 1997. ▶ Path-breaking study of the Americanization of Europe during the Cold War.

Schrecker, Ellen. *The Age of McCarthyism: A Brief History with Documents*, 2nd ed. New York: Palgrave, 2002. ▶ Updated classic overview of the Second Red Scare.

Von Eschen, Penny M. *Satchmo Blows Up the World: Jazz Ambassadors Play the Cold War*. Cambridge, MA: Harvard University Press, 2006. ▶ Study of U.S. cultural diplomacy during the Cold War.

Westad, Odd Arne. *The Global Cold War: Third World Interventions and the Making of Our Times*. Cambridge, UK: Cambridge University Press, 2007. ▶ Important study of the significance of the developing world to the Cold War.

Zubok, Vladislav M. *A Failed Empire: The Soviet Union in the Cold War from Stalin to Gorbachev*. Chapel Hill: University of North Carolina Press, 2007. ▶ Insightful analysis from the Soviet perspective based on recently opened Soviet archives.

Go to the MindTap® for **Global Americans** to access the full version of select books from this Additional Resources section.

Websites

Cold War International History Project at Woodrow Wilson Center. (http://www.wilsoncenter.org/program/cold-war-international-history-project) ▶ Excellent compilation of international historical documents and resources related to the Cold War.

Foreign Relations of the United States at the U.S. Department of State. (https://history.state.gov/historicaldocuments) ▶ Official historical records of U.S. foreign policy decision making since World War II arranged by presidential administration.

Hibakusha: Atomic Bomb Survivors at UN Office for Disarmament Affairs. (http://www.un.org/disarmament/content/slideshow/hibakusha) ▶ Repository of links to Websites, videos, and testimonials related to the experience of atomic bomb survivors and their struggle for nuclear disarmament.

The National Security Archive. (http://nsarchive.gwu.edu/) ▶ Nongovernmental repository for declassified documents including those addressing CIA involvement in Europe, Asia, and the developing world.

Preparatory Commission for the Comprehensive Nuclear-Test-Ban Treaty Organization. (http://www.ctbto.org) ▶ Good historical information and video about international efforts since World War II to ban nuclear weapons tests, by the UN treaty organization.

Continue exploring online through MindTap®, where you can:
- **Assess your knowledge with the Chapter Test**
- **Watch historical videos related to the chapter**
- **Further your understanding with interactive maps and timelines**

The Cold War

1946

February
United States formulates policy of containment to counter Soviet threat.

March
Churchill describes Soviet sphere as an "iron curtain" dividing Europe.

May
Soviets seek to control Iran's oil fields, provoking U.S. opposition.

August
Soviet ambitions in the eastern Mediterranean push Turkey into U.S. sphere.

1947

March
Truman Doctrine commits United States to containing communism.

Truman initiates loyalty tests to remove Communists from federal government.

September
National Security Act lays foundation for national security state.

November
Congress investigates Communists in entertainment industry.

Winter
U.S. reconstruction of Japan reverses course to fight communism.

1948

February
Soviets overthrow Czechoslovakian government.

April
Marshall Plan aid begins to reconstruct European economy.

May
State of Israel is established, Arab–Israeli War begins.

June
Soviets blockade West Berlin, United States begins airlifting supplies.

August
Hiss trial enhances fears of Communist spies in U.S. government.

1949

April
NATO reverses longtime U.S. policy of avoiding overseas alliances.

August
Soviets' successful test of atomic bomb changes U.S. diplomatic strategies.

October
Success of Chinese Communist Revolution transforms Cold War in East Asia.

1950

February
Joseph McCarthy's claim of Communists in the State Department intensifies climate of fear and repression.

HER BEAUTY served a mob of terror whose one mission is to destroy!

I MARRIED a Communist

April
NSC 68 initiates an increasingly militaristic stance toward the Soviet Union.

June
Korean War begins; the first U.S. combat against Communist forces during Cold War.

Soviet Union

United States

Cuba

Israel

Egypt

Iran

China

Korea

Japan

Vietnam

Indonesia

1952–1953	1954–1955	1956–1959	1960–1962	1963
November 1952 Eisenhower is elected president, promising to end the Korean War.	**May 1954** French lose to Vietnamese independence fighters and withdraw from Indochina.	**July 1956** Gamal Abdel Nasser's nationalization of Suez Canal shows rising significance of developing world.	Seventeen African nations join the UN.	**July** Limited Test Ban Treaty reduces superpower tension.
April 1953 State Department legitimizes Lavender Scare by dismissing homosexual employees.	CIA deposes Guatemala's president to prevent land redistribution from U.S. companies to peasants.	**October 1957** Success of Soviet *Sputnik* evokes great fear in United States over "missile gap."	**January 1960** U.S.–Japan Security Treaty guarantees U.S. military force in East Asia.	**November** Kennedy is assassinated, and Johnson becomes president.
March 1953 Joseph Stalin dies, creating new opportunities for superpower dialogue.	**April 1955** Asian–African Conference at Bandung reveals nonalignment option during Cold War.	**July 1959** "Kitchen debate" between Nixon and Khrushchev reveals ideological importance of consumer products.	**November 1960** Kennedy is elected president, promising tough Cold War stance.	
June 1953 Julius and Ethel Rosenberg are executed for spying despite international protests.	**May 1955** Soviets establish Warsaw Pact to counter NATO.		**March 1961** Kennedy establishes Peace Corps, increases aid to developing nations.	
July 1953 Korean War ends in stalemate with a ceasefire but no official treaty.			**October 1962** Cuban Missile Crisis pushes United States and Soviet Union to the brink of nuclear war.	
August 1953 CIA deposes Iran's prime minister to prevent nationalization of its oil fields.				

23 Prosperity and the Cold War Economy

1945–1965

In 1957, Los Angeles Mayor Norris Poulson engineered the relocation of the Brooklyn Dodgers from their original, legendary home at Ebbets Field. When the new Dodger Stadium opened in Los Angeles in 1962, one sportswriter called it the "most modern baseball temple in the world."

When Mayor Norris Poulson welcomed Soviet Premier Nikita Khrushchev to Los Angeles in September 1959, he had a strong message for the Russian. "You shall not bury us and we shall not bury you." He was referring to a widely circulated remark Khrushchev had made in 1956 directed to the United States, "We will bury you." Khrushchev explained to Paulson that he had not meant nuclear war but the inevitable victory of communism over capitalism. The mayor, however, was determined to demonstrate capitalism's achievements.

There was no better showcase of capitalism in the United States than Los Angeles. The production of the city's aircraft, auto, and defense industries that had spurred growth during World War II had increased afterward, fueling a population boom, sprawling suburban development, and hundreds of miles of new freeways. As mayor, Poulson, a great city promoter, oversaw the expansion of Los Angeles Harbor, the construction of Los Angeles International Airport, and, dearest to his heart, the building of Dodger Stadium.

The LIFE Picture Collection/Getty Images

Dodger Stadium in Los Angeles, 1962, a ballpark for the automobile and suburban age.

In 1957, Poulson had engineered the relocation of the Brooklyn Dodgers, the legendary baseball team based in Brooklyn, New York that played in Ebbets Field, a state-of-the-art stadium when it opened on a streetcar line in 1913. The name "Dodgers" derived from the streetcars that locals were skilled at dodging. But by the 1950s, Ebbets Field was obsolete, and many of its fans had left the gritty streets of Brooklyn for the green suburbs of Long Island. So when Los Angeles offered to build the team a dream ballpark, owner Walter O'Malley agreed. The Dodgers' move to Los Angeles was unprecedented, but then cross-town rival New York Giants relocated to San Francisco.

Dodger Stadium opened in April 1962 with space for twenty thousand more fans, convenient freeway access, abundant parking, and picturesque views of the downtown skyline. One sportswriter called it the "most modern baseball temple in the world." The new stadium catered to middle-class suburbanites whose love of professional sports was matched only by their enchantment with Hollywood (which Khrushchev visited) and Disneyland (which he did not because of safety precautions).

The Soviet premier's famous temper flared in being denied a visit to Disneyland. "Is there an epidemic of cholera there or something?" he blasted, or "have gangsters taken hold of the place that can destroy me?" A few months earlier during the kitchen debate at the U.S. Moscow exhibition, Khrushchev had boasted to Vice President Richard Nixon that his country would soon build better consumer products than the Americans. But he was being excluded from seeing the ultimate display of modern American lifestyles and consumer ingenuity. Such was the United States' mid-century allure; a nation whose wealth, prosperity, and innovations attracted even the leader of the Communist

> How does the relocation of the Dodgers from Brooklyn to Los Angeles reflect the major transformations in the U.S. economy and society in the mid-twentieth century?
>
> Go to MindTap® to watch a video on Los Angeles Mayor Norris Poulson and learn how this story relates to the themes of this chapter.

world—to say nothing of millions around the world who also longed to experience Disneyland and the nation's abundant consumer pleasures. Although the Soviets rivaled U.S. military might, no country at that time came close to matching its productive capacity and the social and cultural influence associated with unrivaled economic power. This was the apex of American global influence.

The relocation of professional baseball teams reflected a major transformation in the nation's economy and society that was moving the center of production away from manufacturing and historic urban centers, toward service and information industries as well as newer urban and suburban locales, largely in the South and West. Massive Cold War spending and assiduous preparedness plans propelled these economic and social trends and underwrote the longest era of prosperity in U.S. history. The good times shaped a new version of the American Dream: a home in the suburbs, a college education, and a professional job. Federal dollars supported home ownership, too, and higher education for the children of prosperity. But not everyone was prosperous. As obsolete factories closed and old manufacturing jobs disappeared, unemployment and poverty marked declining central cities, and the poor were disproportionally people of color. In Los Angeles, many lived in three Mexican American communities where the city went back on its promise to build affordable public housing, and instead displaced residents and destroyed their homes as part of the deal to attract the Dodgers. Those residents who struggled with police before bulldozers razed their homes were branded socialists. Others still remember: "What they did to me . . . was the biggest and worst thing of all."

23-1
Government and Prosperity

This photograph depicts a North Carolina State University classroom in 1954 after the federal government extended educational benefits to veterans of the Korean War. Many of the students here were able to go to college as the result of a government program for veterans.

What do you notice about the students and how they are dressed? What factors could explain the gender and racial makeup of the class? ▶

Special Collections Research Center, North Carolina State University Library

Although adjusting from World War II was not easy, the nation's economy eventually righted itself and entered a period of prosperity, consumer spending, and high employment that Americans had not experienced since before the Great Depression. The global context favored the United States because of the war's devastating impact on the world's leading economic powers including Great Britain, Germany, France, and Japan. Americans also benefited from new technology developed during the war that afterward contributed to the growth of airlines, pharmaceuticals, and a host of innovations in industrial research sparking an explosion of new commercial products and services. The federal government played a major role in facilitating this consumer revolution by actively boosting home ownership through low-interest loans to veterans. In this way, the Korean War, which required a high level of military personnel, continued the nation's historic expansion of the middle class.

☞ As you read, focus on economic recovery of the United States as well as the rise of new industries and types of work. What impact did the nation's involvement in World War II, and the Cold War especially, have on these economic trends?

23-1a Transition from Total War

Following the attack on Pearl Harbor in December 1941, U.S. war production went into overdrive, so the sudden shift into peacetime, a process known as **reconversion**, was destined to be bumpy. Consumers got a taste of hard times when the cost of living skyrocketed after President Harry Truman abruptly halted wartime rationing and price controls. Inflation in meat prices at the end of summer 1946 prompted the *New York Daily News* to declare: "PRICES SOAR, BUYERS SORE—STEERS JUMP OVER THE MOON." The shortage of housing was even more desperate. After a boom in home construction in the 1920s, the real estate industry dried up for sixteen years through depression and war. Although housing was scarce during the war, the shortage reached crisis level with the demobilization of troops. In 1947, 6 million Americans doubled up with relatives or friends, and half a million lived in converted army barracks and other forms of temporary housing. Playing on an old campaign slogan, the *Kansas City Star* described the situation as "Two Families in Every Garage."

The demobilization of nearly 11 million U.S. troops within two years of the war's end also exacerbated labor relations as veterans re-entered a job market that was already adjusting to reconversion. Organized labor emerged from the war stronger than ever. Both union membership rates (15 million nationwide, or one-third of all nonfarm labor) and the range of unionized industries were at record highs. A remarkable 70 percent of all workers in manufacturing were covered by collective bargaining arrangements with prospects for union expansion into the growing white-collar professional and service sectors (see Figure 23.1). Yet the end of the war brought new tensions between workers and management. Businesses cut hours, wages, and overtime pay with the drastic drop in defense spending. Workers suffered further because inflation diminished their real earnings; they responded by going on strike. The climax of the strike wave came in May 1946 when railroad

> The nation's economic recovery from World War II is difficult for consumers and workers.

workers brought the nation's rail system to a standstill for two days before Truman was able to settle the strike. All told, 5 million workers marched on picket lines in 1946, more than any year during the peak of labor protest in the 1930s.

But absent from labor protests were most of the 4.7 million women who had taken jobs outside the home during World War II. Many "Rosie the riveters" happily handed over their hard hats to returning veterans, but those who were the main wage earners in their families and others who had enjoyed being in the workforce did so with great reluctance. Congress provided no unemployment assistance to working women and ignored pleas to ensure gender equality in the workplace. Those fortunate to keep their jobs during reconversion saw their wages almost cut in half, from 90 to 50 cents per hour.

23-1b Commercial Innovation

Surprisingly, the U.S. economy recovered quickly from its postwar readjustment because of domestic supply and demand. The supply grew out of a remarkable degree of commercial innovation. World War II had induced more scientific breakthroughs than had any previous U.S. military conflict, and many of these innovations stimulated the subsequent growth of commercial products. The most immediate impact was on the production of airplanes, pharmaceuticals, plastics, and other industrial chemicals. The war almost overnight had established the modern U.S. aircraft industry as the nation's production of airplanes rose sixteen times from 5,865 units in 1939 to 95,672 by 1944. At the same time, jet engines made the leap in 1958 from military to commercial use. The extensive use of large jet airliners such as the Boeing 707 enabled the commercial airline industry, which had begun in the 1930s, literally to take off in

> The rise of new or formerly marginal industries spurs economic recovery.

reconversion Transition from special economic circumstances under total war to a peacetime economy in which governments remove controls on businesses and millions serving in the military return to the civilian labor force.

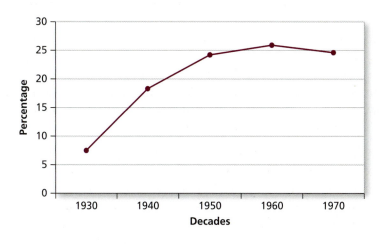

Figure 23.1 Percentage of Union Membership among Employed Workers in the United States, 1930–1970 Labor union membership grew rapidly in the United States after having won collective bargaining rights during the Great Depression and continued to grow through World War II and into the postwar era. ◀ Source: Meyer, Gerald, *Union Membership Trends in the United States*. Washington, DC: Congressional Research Service, 2004, http://digitalcommons.ilr.cornell.edu

History without Borders

Norin 10 and the Worldwide Green Revolution

Increase in yield of cereal crops

143% —Percent gain
1980
1961
1,000 lbs/acre

Major beneficiary of the Green Revolution

International boundaries, 1980

Major Beneficiaries of the Green Revolution, 1961–1980 New technologies in fertilizers and strains of wheat and other cereal grains produced robust increases in the production of agricultural staples, which especially influenced the developing world. This map shows the nations that benefited the most from the Green Revolution during the 1960s and 1970s. ▲

Although new technologies bolstered prosperity in the United States after World War II, their role in promoting a worldwide *Green Revolution* proved even more historically significant. *Green Revolution* is a term that describes the modernization of agriculture, promoted largely by the United States, enabling many developing nations to dramatically increase their production of staple crops such as wheat, corn, and rice. This rapid growth of food supply in poor countries was seen as a key to ending world hunger and promoting Third World economic development.

Another important factor for the Green Revolution was artificially created nitrogen, a chemical that when mixed with natural manure became a cheaply produced but potent fertilizer. Scientists in Japan were among the first to experiment with a shorter variety of wheat that would respond well to large doses of nitrogen fertilizer. In 1946, a U.S. adviser in Japan noticed unusual "semi-dwarf" wheat and sent a sample to the United States to be studied. Agricultural scientists in Pullman, Washington, combined one of them, known as *Norin 10*, with native strains of wheat to produce a significantly higher-yielding grain used

with spectacular results by farmers in the Pacific Northwest.

In 1953, a Pullman scientist passed samples of the new grain to Norman Borlaug, an American conducting research for the Rockefeller Foundation on increasing wheat production and fighting hunger in Mexico. Borlaug crossed the Washington varieties of Norin 10 with Mexican grains and within two years developed a winning combination of the two. When used with high amounts of nitrogen fertilizer, the hybrid produced at least 50 percent more wheat per hectare of land. The Mexican government quickly adopted

Art Rickerby/Time Life Pictures/Getty Images

Norman Borlaug in the Field Norman Borlaug, a U.S. scientist whose research was instrumental in generating the Green Revolution, is shown here holding stalks of wheat designed to be disease resistant and to produce maximum yields. ◄

Gamma-Rapho/Getty Images

Rice Fields By 1980, when women in this photograph worked rice fields in West Bengal, India, the country's total yield of cereal grains had increased by 42 percent since 1961. ◄

the high-yielding grain, and within a decade, Mexico no longer confronted shortages of wheat. Instead, its farmers generated a surplus that was exported abroad.

In 1963, scientists in India, aware of Borlaug's success in Mexico, asked him to study the prospects for Norin 10 there. He then sent samples of the Mexican varieties to India, which were well received by the Indian officials. In 1966 with funding from the Rockefeller Foundation, the Indian government imported a large amount of Mexican wheat seeds. The subsequent increase in Indian wheat production played a major role in enabling India to become self-sufficient in food production. Indian varieties of Norin 10 went on to boost wheat production in Pakistan, Afghanistan, Turkey, and other developing countries. For his crucial role in greatly expanding the world's food supply, Borlaug received the Nobel Peace Prize.

The effects of the Green Revolution, however, were not uniformly positive. The huge rise in wheat production in Mexico by medium and larger farms wiped out the livelihood of millions of small farmers, forcing them to relocate to the cities. There they provided the cheap labor needed for the industrial revolution in Mexico. In addition, the dependence on chemical supplements hindered poor developing nations when the price of nitrogen fertilizers dramatically increased in the early 1970s. Another problem was the reliance on artificially produced pesticides to keep insects from destroying crops. Such chemicals were linked to health problems in field-workers and a host of environmental ills. Finally, solving food supply shortages did not end world hunger. Starvation and malnutrition exist because people are too poor to afford a good diet, even in wealthy countries. Thus, the increased production of crops

around the world did not mean that nations were able to distribute the resulting food to the people in need or that those in need were able to purchase it.

Critical Thinking Questions

▶ In what ways did the Green Revolution reveal the importance of international cooperation in the production of staple crops?

▶ Why was the Green Revolution unable to end starvation around the world?

Go to MindTap® to engage with an interactive version of **History without Borders: Norin 10 and the Worldwide Green Revolution.** Learn from an interactive map, view related video, and respond to critical thinking questions.

Levittown, New York, 1955 A new method for building houses after World War II mirrored the approach of the assembly line for automobiles. By 1950, Levitt and Sons had manufactured a four-room house every sixteen minutes for a fraction of the cost of custom-built homes. The average price for a two-story home ($7,900) was often more affordable than renting an apartment in the city. ▶

Hulton Archive/Archive Photos/Getty Images

the 1950s. The number of air passengers doubled during that decade with more Americans traveling by air than railroad.

The emergence of the modern pharmaceutical industry was as impressive as the rise of large-scale air travel. The federal government's investment in the production of antibiotics such as sulfa and penicillin during the war was a huge boon to the commercial drug industry. After the war, Merck, Pfizer, Squibb, and other large drug companies introduced a wide range of antibiotics, antihistamines, steroids, and other pharmaceuticals based on their experience producing drugs for the military. The new drugs, which were much more complex than previous ones, stimulated the emergence of the modern pharmaceutical industry. It no longer simply mixed and mass-produced over-the-counter remedies but engaged in expensive, cutting-edge scientific research. Such innovation resulted in the ability to cure or manage tuberculosis (TB), pneumonia, malaria, and other diseases. The postwar explosion of drug and medical treatments formed the basis of what has been called the **therapeutic revolution**.

The production of these new drugs was part of large breakthroughs in the field of industrial chemistry that had developed significantly from the shortage of natural rubber supplies during the war. The military's need for artificially created, or synthetic, rubber opened the door to a wave of chemically fabricated materials that produced substitutes for metal, wood, paper, and almost every other type of commonly used industrial material. Neoprene, for example, substituted for rubber, nylon for silk, and Plexiglas for natural glass.

A leading postwar scientist was the African American chemist Percy Julian, whose research with soybeans paved the way for water-based (latex) paint, linoleum, plywood glue, and other products that would become household staples. His work with artificial sex hormones (namely progesterone, testosterone, and cortisone) created breakthroughs in the field of steroid medicine that garnered him both scientific fame and material fortune. The revolution in industrial chemicals also had agricultural applications with the development of more effective fertilizers and pesticides that expanded the world's food supply, contributing to the **Green Revolution** that dramatically increased the production of staple crops such as wheat, corn, and rice.

23-1c Consumer Revolution

The most important factor for America's postwar prosperity was the rapid and sustained growth of consumer spending. The combination of high household savings, renewed availability of consumer products, and pent-up demand for these goods after doing without them during the Depression and the war fueled the dramatic rise in consumption. The federal government, which had urged citizens to save money during the war, encouraged them to spend to stimulate the economy. Walt Disney animators supported government efforts. Although Mickey Mouse had symbolized the nation's fighting spirit, a cartoon character named Scrooge McDuck, introduced in 1947, embodied the noble pursuit of wealth and its consumer rewards.

> Consumers and the expansion of mass consumption undergird sustained economic growth.

The demand for automobiles, radios, washing machines, and other household goods boomed after the war. But real estate proved the most important single force for postwar recovery. Given the nation's severe housing shortage, William Levitt, a builder of barracks and war workers' housing, innovated home construction by abandoning the standard practice of constructing houses one

therapeutic revolution Explosion of new drug research and treatments that produced cures for polio, whooping cough, diphtheria, and other devastating illnesses.

Green Revolution Major increase in food production, most noticeably in poor countries, as the result of the application of agricultural and chemical research in the 1950s to produce high-yield grains.

at a time. Instead, he proved that it was more efficient and profitable to mass-produce an entire community or tract of homes. Between 1947 and 1951, Levitt and Sons transformed four thousand acres of farmland on New York's Long Island into a planned community of curved streets and 17,450 look-alike homes. Furthermore, the developer racially segregated **Levittown**, another selling point for whites disgruntled with the increasing presence of racial minorities in the central city. Levittown's success paved the way for a revolution in U.S. home ownership because real estate developers across the country joined the tract housing revolution. By 1960, one of every four homes standing in the United States had been built in the 1950s. As a result of the affordability and supply of new houses, 62 percent of white Americans were home owners in 1960, compared to 44 percent in 1940—the largest increase recorded in the nation's history. This is when home ownership became an essential element of the American Dream.

The federal government contributed to the home owner revolution by providing a home loan benefit to World War II veterans in the G.I. Bill passed in 1944. Congress extended this benefit to Korean War veterans in 1952. The G.I. Bill included low-cost home and business loans, three years of free college tuition or vocational training with paid living expenses, lifetime medical coverage, and preferential treatment when applying for federal government jobs. The $14.5 billion spent on veterans' benefits during the G.I. Bill's first decade was part of the federal government's commitment to boost consumption by expanding access to credit, a process initiated by automobile loans during the 1920s. The federal government through the Veterans Administration (VA) provided home loans to one-fifth of the nation's single-family households between 1945 and 1966, half of whom lived in California and other states in the fast-growing Southwest. These VA loans coincided with Federal Housing Administration (FHA) programs designed to transform the private home loan industry from an exclusive boutique for the well-to-do to a supermarket for common folk. The FHA democratized credit in three ways: It encouraged private banks to lend money to middle- and low-income applicants by ensuring that the government would pay defaulted loans. It also made the cost of home loans more affordable by lowering the minimum required down payment from 30 to less than 10 percent of the house price ($50,000 savings on a typical house today) and by increasing the payment period from ten to thirty years ($15,000 savings per year on a typical house today). Together, the FHA and VA provided crucial access to credit enabling the huge expansion of home ownership in the United States.

The G.I. Bill was a milestone in the postwar expansion of the U.S. middle class. Its package of economic and educational benefits for veterans was so popular that its support programs quickly moved beyond the realm of partisan politics to become an untouchable political issue, much like Social Security today. In this way, the measure was an extension of the New Deal state. But the G.I. Bill also continued the New Deal's discrimination against women and racial minorities. Former soldiers got preference for jobs and college admission over nonveterans, most of whom were women. Married female veterans did not receive unemployment benefits and had their educational stipends reduced unless they could prove they were the main breadwinner in their household. Finally, racist policies at universities, banks, and new housing tracts like Levittown prevented a large number of veterans of color from using their G.I. Bill benefits. A black veteran in Corpus Christi, Texas, noted that "all the districts that we [Negro veterans] may choose to live have been ruled out" and in this situation, "NO NEGRO VETERAN is eligible for a loan."

Levittown First mass-produced residential community featuring quickly produced and affordable tract housing.

23-2
Cold War Economic Growth

The construction in 1965 of the Vehicle Assembly Building at NASA's Kennedy Space Center was a major achievement in U.S. space exploration. This building, the tallest in Florida at the time, was used to assemble and launch rockets into space.

Why would the United States invest in space flight technology during the Cold War? ▶

Steven Siceloff/NASA

Taft-Hartley Act Also known as the *Labor Management Relations Act*, Republican-sponsored legislation that limited the rights of labor unions and discriminated against Communists and other radicals.

right to work laws State measures that prevented organized labor from requiring workers to join a union, which would have increased unions' power against management.

In the late 1940s, no one could have imagined that postwar prosperity would continue for two decades, the longest period of high-level economic growth in U.S. history. During this extended prosperity, the United States for the first time became a largely middle-class nation, propelled by billions of dollars of Cold War defense-related spending. The federal government cooperated closely with big industrialists as if the country were in a permanent state of war. The Cold War economy contributed to the development of information and service industries that became increasingly important even as industrial manufacturing remained a vital economic sector. At the same time, U.S. businesses faced little competition from foreign competitors in Europe and Japan who were preoccupied with postwar recovery. The United States dominated global markets.

☞ As you read, pay attention to how and why the U.S. economy continued to grow and information and service industries continued to rise. How did Cold War developments further these economic trends?

23-2a Politics and the Middle-Class Nation

U.S. politics after World War II embarked on a new type of business–government cooperation rooted in the goals of sustaining economic growth and individual social mobility. To meet these ends, the Employment Act of 1946, a compromise measure between Democrats and Republicans, established the federal government as the nation's main vehicle for economic planning including stabilizing inflation and unemployment. Postwar politics also embodied the assumption that private industry—not only government—could be relied on to take care of the working classes in a reprise of welfare capitalism from the 1920s.

{ Truman sustains labor rights, welfare legislation, and the New Deal coalition.

Nowhere was the idea of corporate caretaking more evident than in the Labor Management Relations Act approved in June 1947. Better known as the **Taft-Hartley Act**, this legislation rolled back important gains that unions had made since the 1930s and encouraged the widespread fear that Communists had hijacked the labor movement. This legislation allowed states to pass **right to work laws** outlawing the closed shop that required workers to join the local union. In response to the national railway strike in 1946, the act also empowered the president to prohibit strikes deemed against the national interest and to order strikers back to work during labor negotiations. Reflecting Cold War fears, Taft-Hartley excluded Communist-led unions, largely the Congress of Industrial Organizations (CIO), from National Labor Relations Board protections and required union officials to sign affidavits forswearing allegiance to the Communist Party or another "subversive" group. Although the unions vigorously opposed Taft-Hartley as a "slave labor bill," leading labor organizations such as the American Federation of Labor (AFL) accepted the exclusion of Communist unions and jettisoned grand visions of workers' authority over management in order to survive, and even thrive, during the Cold War. The AFL and the now non-Communist CIO merged in 1955 as labor unions centralized and became legitimate power brokers in U.S. politics. As such, they were able to raise the level of real wages more in one postwar decade than during the previous half century. The strength of organized labor in the United States, however, paled in comparison to some other developed countries (see Figure 23.2).

Like mainstream labor unions, Truman was more interested in sustaining prosperity than in elevating worker authority over management. To him, economic growth was necessary in order for the government to expand social support programs. This thinking opened the doors of his administration to conservative, probusiness groups such as the National Association of Manufactures (NAM). Another pressure on Truman was the resurgence of the Republican Party. Taft-Hartley never would have passed if the Republicans had not reclaimed both houses of Congress in the 1946 midterm elections, the first time they had been in power since the Hoover administration. The act's major sponsor, Senator Robert Taft, was an outspoken critic of the New Deal and subsequent social programs.

Figure 23.2 Percentage of Worldwide Union Membership for Wage and Salary Workers, 1960 U.S. labor union membership increased significantly from the Depression to the postwar era and commanded about the same percentage of workers as many other developed countries. However, it did not match the number of unions in the United Kingdom, Australia, Norway, and other nations where unionized workers represented between 40 to 60 percent of the workforce. ▲ Source: Visser, Jelle. Data Base on Institutional Characteristics of Trade Unions, Wage Setting, State Intervention and Social Pacts, 1960–2011 (ICTWSS), vers 4.0. April 2013.

The LIFE Picture Collection/Getty Images

Walter Reuther Testifies at Senate Committee Hearing, 1958 A left-wing labor organizer during the 1930s, Reuther, as head of the United Automobile Workers, proved instrumental after World War II in removing Communists from the CIO. He became the first president of the merged AFL-CIO in 1955. ◀

Son of President William Howard Taft, the Ohio senator led the Republican revival asserting, "We have got to break with the corrupting idea that we can legislate prosperity, legislate equality, legislate opportunity."

But as much as Taft and the Republicans sought to eradicate the New Deal, they simply could not. Instead of dismantling it, they had to settle for shifting the burden of social welfare from government to private businesses. The dramatic presidential race in 1948 in which Truman stumbled but ultimately defeated the Republican candidate Thomas Dewey indicated that whereas Republicans had gained political clout in the postwar era, the New Deal state was there to stay. In the end, the coalition of Democratic voters who had backed FDR stayed with Truman and in the election virtually ignored the more radical platform of longtime New Dealer Henry Wallace who ran on the Progressive Party ticket and the segregationist campaign of southerner Strom Thurmond.

23-2b **Education and Defense Spending**

While commercial innovation and consumer demand continued to fuel prosperity, massive Cold War defense spending also sustained the nation's economic growth. It was no coincidence that the long and unprecedented period of economic growth in the United States corresponded to an equally long and unprecedented period of war production. Following a sharp decline after V-J Day, the nation's defense budget spiked during the Korean War and afterward remained unusually high for peacetime. The bulk of money went

> The federal government responds to the Cold War by fueling explosive growth in higher education and defense industries.

to private corporations engaged in military research and development. Consequently, **defense-contracting firms** swelled with profit and power as their business interests became intertwined with winning the Cold War. Although extensive public–private collaboration had occurred during both world wars, it did not become a permanent feature of politics in Washington, D.C., until after World War II. At that time, a triumvirate among military officials, Congress, and large defense firms emerged—which Eisenhower had dubbed the *military-industrial complex.*

American universities benefited tremendously from the prolonged military buildup. During its peak usage in 1947, the G.I. Bill funded half of the nation's 2 million college students. In 1930, less than 8 percent of college-age people were enrolled in higher education, whereas in 1965, the figure had more than tripled to nearly 30 percent (see Figure 23.3). The Soviet launch of Sputnik in 1957 pushed the federal government to expand its support for higher education. **The National Defense Education Act**, approved in September 1958, established programs for low-interest student loans (later known by the name *Perkins*) and direct assistance for instruction in the sciences, mathematics, foreign languages (especially but not limited to Russian), and other areas that could benefit national security. At the same time, the government increased research funding through federal agencies such as the National Science Foundation (NSF), the Atomic Energy Commission (AEC), the Office of Naval Research (ONR), and the National Institutes of Health (NIH). The budgets of many universities in the United States came to rely on these agencies. Starting in 1945, 80 percent of all federally funded industrial research involved military applications. When the

defense-contracting firms Private businesses, usually large corporations, whose primary customer is the Department of Defense or other military-related parts of the federal government.

The National Defense Education Act Legislation that dramatically increased the federal government's financial assistance and commitment to making higher education affordable.

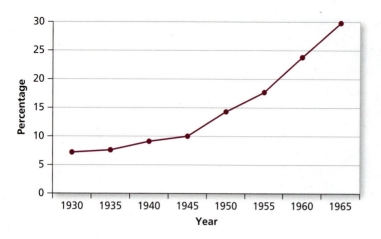

Figure 23.3 Percent of Americans Ages Eighteen to Twenty-Four Enrolled in Higher Education by Year, from 1930–1965 To increase production, expand the nation's middle class, and win the Cold War with new high-tech weaponry, the U.S. expanded its commitment to higher education. It offered research funds to colleges and universities and grants and loans to students. The result was explosive growth in the nation's colleges and universities that allowed more Americans than ever to take advantage of higher education. ◀

Source: Snyder, Thomas D., ed. *120 Years of American Education: A Statistical Portrait.* Washington, DC: National Center of Education Statistics, U.S. Department of Education, January 1993.

Korean War erupted in 1950, there were fifteen thousand of these military research projects. A decade later, the number had increase more than five times to eighty thousand.

23-2c United States and the World Market

The United States was the only industrial powerhouse left standing after World War II. Europeans and the Japanese relied on massive U.S. funds and U.S. manufacturers to rebuild their economies, which took about a decade to complete. One sign that the global economy was ready to take off again was the creation in March 1957 of the **European Economic Community (EEC or common market)**, to promote ease of investment and trade among six western European nations including West Germany and France. A series of **General Agreement on Tariffs and Trade (GATT)** rounds followed the creation of the EEC to ease trade barriers around the world, not just in Europe. Another sign that the global economy had recovered was that by December 1958, most European currencies had returned to convertibility, meaning they were freely bought and sold on the world market. The combination of trade agreements and unrestricted currency exchange marked the full-fledged functioning of the Bretton Woods system.

U.S. corporations were poised to take full advantage of new global opportunities given their technological

> U.S. businesses take advantage of favorable international circumstances to dominate global manufacturing and trade.

European Economic Community (EEC or common market) Agreement among European nations to form an economic alliance that would prevent the protectionist policies that had contributed to the Great Depression and would enable European businesses to better compete with large nations such as the United States.

General Agreement on Tariffs and Trade (GATT) International accord resulting from UN negotiations to lower tariffs and boost trade around the world.

advantages, managerial efficiencies, and high worker productivity. The world demand for U.S. products from sewing machines to automobiles to soft drinks was so great that the United States enjoyed a highly favorable balance of trade for more than two decades after World War II. In the mid-1950s, the United States, a nation consisting of 6 percent of the world population, produced 50 percent of the world's manufactured goods, including 75 percent of automobiles, 60 percent of telephones, and 30 percent of radios and televisions. At the same time, the emergence of the common market encouraged Americans to set up overseas offices and manufacturing plants to reap the benefits of doing business within the walls of this economic pact. The number of U.S.-based multinational corporations dramatically increased as direct investment in Europe became more important than capturing a global market share.

The influx of U.S. businesses and products generated mixed reactions abroad. For the first time, Europeans embraced mass consumption in clamoring for U.S. fashions such as blue jeans and leather jackets, tastes such as Coca-Cola, and household appliances such as washing machines. After a 1960 visit to Stockholm, Sweden, African American writer James Baldwin noted that he had seen ubiquitous posters of a movie idol from the United States seated on a motorcycle accompanied by a "masochistic girlfriend." At the same time, critics in Europe warned about the shallowness of U.S. culture and consumerism and the threat that U.S. economic power posed to traditional European businesses, products, and lifestyles. Protests in 1949 by beverage companies and the Communist Party in France pushed the government to ban Coca-Cola in part because it was said to be addictive and rot children's teeth. The beverage was also seen as a threat to the local wine industry. Although Coke prevailed, in no small part because of U.S. State Department influence to keep France's market opened to Americans, European businesses learned to adapt to the new consumer market, enabling them to better compete with Coke and other U.S. goods.

Library of Congress Prints and Photographs Division[LC-USZ62-42481]

Global Americans After emerging as a promising young African American writer, **James Baldwin** moved in 1948 to France, where his writing flourished in a cultural atmosphere far removed from the conformity, racism, and homophobia of Cold War America. "Once I found myself on the other side of the ocean," Baldwin told *The New York Times*, "I could see where I came from very clearly, and I could see that I carried myself, which is my home, with me. You can never escape that. I am the grandson of a slave, and I am a writer. I must deal with both." Among American expatriates in Paris, he was free to explore the ghosts of his own African American past and to reveal himself as a gay man. His published literary criticism and his first novel, *Go Tell It on the Mountain* (1953), established Baldwin as a major literary talent, innovator of gay fiction, and keen observer of U.S. race relations. Largely autobiographical, the book centers on the struggles of a young black man who comes to challenge his stepfather's dictatorial authority and in the process explores his own budding sexuality. Baldwin's expatriation to Europe reveals the obstacles faced by racial and sexual minorities in the United States. He returned to the United States in 1957 and became a participant and shrewd observer of the nation's struggles over civil rights and racial equality.

23-3
Social and Cultural Trends

This photograph taken on July 17, 1955, provides an aerial view of the entrance to Disneyland flanked by a massive parking lot. The theme park was erected close to a major interstate freeway to provide access for automobiles. Building Disneyland required removing groves of orange trees, the remainder of which can be seen beyond the park, in the photograph's upper right corner.

Why was freeway access and automobile parking considered important to the success of Disneyland? How did Disneyland compare to Dodger Stadium in these ways? ▶

Go to MindTap® to practice history with the Chapter 23 **Primary Source Writing Activity: Changes in Work, Society, and Culture.** Read and view primary sources and respond to a writing prompt.

AP Images

Prosperity and the upturn of the Cold War economy resulted in major changes in the nature of work, society, and culture. The United States witnessed a rapid increase in professional careers and white-collar jobs in office and service work. The historic expansion of white-collar jobs coincided with the greatest movement of Americans across city and state lines in U.S. history. Like the Brooklyn Dodgers, people and businesses left cities in the nation's historic urban centers and migrated either to nearby suburbs or across country to newly developed areas in the South and West that had largely been designed for middle-class white Americans. The migrants were seeking cheaper, safer, less crowded, and often more racially homogeneous places where a modern, automobile-based society that was heralded as a welcome step beyond the traditional city emerged.

The suburban ideal begun in the United States at this time was celebrated in the new medium of television as well as in other forms of popular entertainment and leisure culture such as Disneyland. The movement to the suburbs also influenced a revival among the major religions in the United States as centers of worship provided important sources of community that reflected the overall interest in wholesome, middle-class values throughout the postwar era.

☞ As you read, pay attention to the increase in white-collar work and suburban communities. What factors caused this growth? How did both of these trends influence new forms of consumption, developments in entertainment, leisure culture, and religious life? How did they perpetuate and create new forms of racial inequality?

23-3a White-Collar Work

The two postwar decades continued a fundamental shift in the nation's economy beginning in the 1920s with a steep rise in the **information and service economy** that contained a wide range of white-collar jobs from secretaries to engineers to high-level managers. Federal and state governments played a key role in furthering this economic transformation. Blue-collar industrial jobs in the United States began to lose ground to clerical, intellectual, and managerial work in corporations and fast-expanding government bureaucracies. A white-collar society emerged fully blown by 1970 when nearly half of all U.S. jobs were in this category (a growth of more than 65 percent since 1930), whereas blue-collar jobs constituted 37 percent (a slight decline from 40 percent in 1930). The most striking decline was in the agricultural sector, falling from more than 21 percent of jobs in 1930 to just over 3 percent in 1970.

Whereas before World War II most American men hoped to obtain a secure factory job, after the war, they set their sights on white-collar work.

> New economic conditions stimulate expansion of office and professional employment.

information and service economy The result of a shift from an industrialized economy based in manufacturing to one based in information technology and services.

pink ghettos Environment that offered low-paying office work limited to women.

Instead of performing manual labor in factories, millions of men earned college degrees and became mid-level managers in corporations and government bureaucracies. The predominance of managerial work required them to pay attention to the supposed "feminine" virtues of appearance, manners, communication skills, and social graces. Women, in turn, became more "manly" by leaving the home and filling positions at the bottom of the corporate ladder. Just as during World War II, labor shortages and restricted immigration created a huge demand for both single and married women in the workplace. The result was the growing trend of middle-class mothers who engaged in part-time work, usually in low-paid work in the growing **pink ghettos** of office labor. Yet being in the working world gave women an independence from the home that went beyond their domestic role.

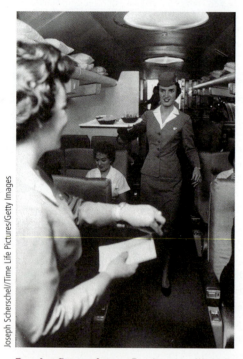

Pan Am Stewardesses Pan American World Airways was the first airline to replace male stewards with beautiful stewardesses to attract customers in the increasingly competitive commercial airline industry. Pan Am provided women with corporate prestige and a rare opportunity to see the world. However, many stewardesses also experienced sex and racial discrimination, harassment, and exploitation. ▲

Joseph Scherschel/Time Life Pictures/Getty Images

23-3b Migration, Population Shifts, and New Highways

In the two decades after World War II, a major demographic shift occurred. The nation's population dispersed from the Northeast and Midwest to the South and West (see Map 23.1). A look at the nation's one hundred largest cities in 1940 and 1960 reveals the rapid population growth in California and Texas especially. During this period, Los Angeles moved from being the fifth largest U.S. city to the third, and San Diego jumped from the forty-third to eighteenth. Houston broke into the top ten, and Dallas moved from thirty-first to fourteenth. Phoenix, Arizona, which was not counted in 1940, leaped to twenty-ninth. As the population shifted to the South and West, so too did Major League baseball teams such as the Dodgers. Before 1950, there were no teams west of St. Louis or south of Washington, D.C.; by 1965, there were six (and in 2008, there would be fourteen).

> Extensive highway construction promotes migration to the West and South.

The shift to the warm climates of the **Sunbelt** corridor stretching from California to Florida had much to do with the widespread use of central air conditioning in business and home construction starting in the 1950s. But if technology made it comfortable to live and work in the Sunbelt, the federal government provided the infrastructure for moving there by constructing a comprehensive national highway system. Franklin Roosevelt had sought to create such a system in the 1930s to spur the Depression-era economy, and Congress had passed a number of highway proposals in the late 1940s and early 1950s. But it took Eisenhower's leadership and concerns about troop movements and evacuations of cities in the event of a nuclear attack to pass the **Interstate Highway Act** in June 1956. Hailed as one of the greatest public works projects in U.S. history, this act allocated $31 billion also to improve the safety and efficiency of automobile travel. The system linked all cities with a population of more than fifty

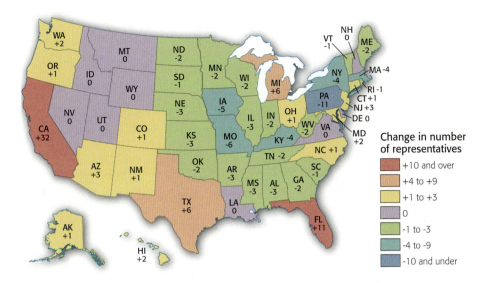

Map 23.1 House of Representatives Reapportionment, 1920–1970 The number of seats apportioned to each state in the House of Representatives represents the sweeping shift of the U.S. population from the Northeast and Midwest to the South and West. The share of seats in the West more than doubled whereas the slight decline in the South did not reflect the growth in Florida, which more than tripled. The Northeast and Midwest experienced the sharpest declines. ▲

thousand in a network of "interstate and defense" highways that stretched for more than forty-two hundred miles (see Map 23.2). These highways enabled the trucking industry to surpass railroads as the nation's predominant means for hauling goods, and businesses catering to the needs to domestic travelers flourished. Consequently, the United States led the world in automobile ownership. In 1960, Los Angeles County alone had more cars than in all of South America or Asia.

23-3c Growth of Suburbs

The Highway Act also was a boon to **suburbanization** because freeway construction between cities and suburbs constituted the bulk of its total expenditures. The suburban population swelled as millions of Americans fled central cities and businesses followed them to take advantage of lower taxes, cheaper land, and a skilled and educated workforce that resulted from the white middle classes that had left the central cities. Between 1947 and 1960, the number of suburbanites increased 100 percent, and by 1960, one-third of the nation's population was living in suburbia (see Figure 23.4). Ten years later, the number of suburban dwellers would surpass those living in the central city. Consequently, the nation's population fanned out over huge conglomerations of urban and suburban areas that linked large parts of the nation into an endless series of **strip cities**. The U.S. census counted thirteen of these areas in 1960, including the

> The Cold War economy and highway system enable suburban communities to flourish.

corridors connecting San Francisco with San Diego, linking Boston, New York, and Washington, D.C., and joining Dallas, Fort Worth, San Antonio, and Houston.

The federal government further accelerated internal migration and suburbanization through Cold War militarization. The major share of defense spending went to California and Texas, but every western state benefited disproportionately including Alaska and Hawai'i, both of which joined the union in 1959. One study estimated that more than half of California's economic growth from 1947 to 1957 was due to the defense industry and that without this support, its migration would have been cut in half. Cold War funds created a synergy between military bases and defense contracting firms that boosted suburban growth. For example, military air stations in California's Orange County attracted a host of defense contractors that, in turn, produced astronomical suburban growth for twenty years starting in 1950: Fullerton's population rose fivefold, from 13,958 to 85,826, and its neighbor Anaheim (home to Disneyland) grew more than ten times, from 14,556 to 166,701. In 1960, two of every three manufacturing jobs in Orange County were tied to military contracts. This same pattern of military-driven economic and suburban development occurred in the San Francisco Bay Area

Sunbelt Area with warm climate in southern and western regions of the United States that had large population growth and economic development in the second half of the twentieth century.

Interstate Highway Act Legislation that dramatically expanded the system of highways in the United States.

suburbanization Process in which population shifts from central cities to nearby suburbs, that are connected by highways.

strip cities Combinations of urban and suburban communities that form a large, continuous mass of development.

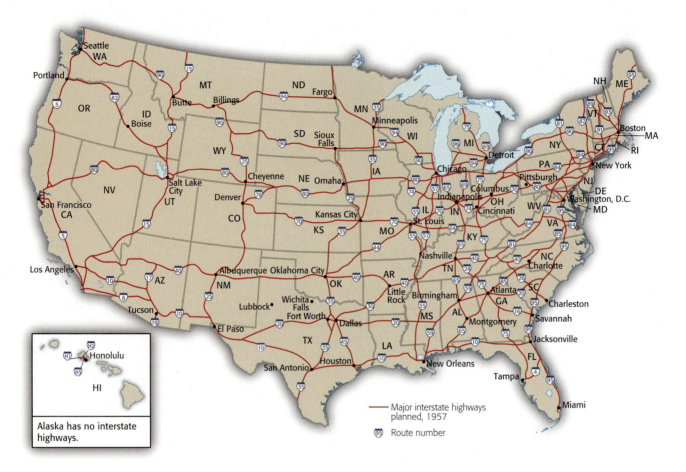

Map 23.2 Major Interstate Highways Planned, 1957 Designed in part for defense reasons under Eisenhower, this highway plan greatly expanded the ability for sales agents, truck drivers, suburban commuters, and tourists to get where they needed to go without using railroads or public transportation. The red, white, and blue numbered signs marking interstate highways came to stand for the world's most modern and extensive highway infrastructure. ▲

triple melting pot Fusion among the nation's three great religious faiths.

with Moffitt Field; in Tucson, Arizona, with the Davis-Monthan Air Force base as the hub; and in Colorado Springs with the combination of Fort Carson Air Force Base, the Air Force Academy, and North American Aerospace Defense Command (NORAD) headquarters.

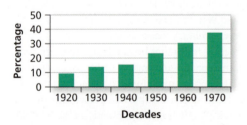

Figure 23.4 Suburban Population, 1920–1970
Highway expansion and the movement of industries and other businesses to the suburbs enabled the dramatic rise in suburban dwellers who often migrated from central cities. ▲ Source: Decennial Census of Population, 1920–1970. Washington, DC: U.S. Census Bureau, 1920–1970.

23-3d Suburbia, Central Cities, and Segregation

> Suburbs accept ethnic, cultural, and religious differences but contribute to racial segregation.

Many ethnic and cultural strains from the great influx of European immigrants during the late nineteenth and early twentieth centuries had come together in a middle-class melting pot. Suburbanization also induced assimilation as revealed by the breakdown of once forbidding religious barriers. After World War II, adherents of the nation's three largest religions, Protestantism, Catholicism, and Judaism, were increasingly intermarrying in what one scholar called the **triple melting pot**. Despite continuing religious bigotry, there was a growing and historic level of tolerance among these faiths. Catholics reached a new level of mainstream acceptance with John F. Kennedy's presidency, and Jews achieved something similar through the nation's support for Israel. Protestant evangelicals achieved the same kind of recognition through the rising celebrity of Billy Graham, the radio preacher who became a welcomed guest in the White House for every president beginning with Harry Truman.

An overall surge in the nation's religious attendance resulted to some extent from the mainstreaming of Catholicism, Judaism, and Protestantism. Although 43 percent of Americans had attended a place of worship before World War II, nearly 70 percent did so by the late 1950s. Compared to the economic hard times during the Great Depression, the prosperity of the postwar era boosted the size of congregations, leading to the construction of a historic number of churches, temples, and other religious institutions across the country. Most of this new construction was in suburbs, where religion was stripped of its connection to "old-world" traditions and infused with the sensibilities of middle-class American life. Suburban religious institutions became important centers of community formation for people uprooted from family and ethnic ties.

Meanwhile, the central cities increasingly were composed of racial minorities as whites fled to suburbs that, like Levittown, made racial segregation a major part of their appeal. The use of nefarious tactics, such as charging higher housing costs, discouraged racial minorities from moving into the suburbs. Most damaging to racial minorities, including those seeking to use G.I. Bill benefits, was the practice of **redlining**, which became another way to perpetuate racial segregation. Using this practice, banks drew a red line around minority neighborhoods identified on city maps to designate places where they would not offer home or business loans, ostensibly because of the financial risk involved. Such practices did not technically discriminate on the basis of race but limited equal opportunities to much-needed credit for African Americans and other racial minorities.

23-3e Suburban Culture and the Rise of Television

The growth of suburban communities generated new ways of living such as the "drive-in" society that developed with the extensive use

> New forms of leisure and entertainment emerge that maintain old notions about race.

of the automobile. In August 1952, the owners of Holiday Inn opened the first of many clean, inexpensive, and respectable motels convenient to highways. Theater chains catered to this new culture by creating drive-in theaters where customers remained in their automobiles, attached a speaker to their car window, and watched movies on a towering outdoor screen. The proliferation of "fast-food" restaurants was another characteristic of suburbia. The iconic story here concerned two brothers, Maurice and Richard McDonald, who in 1948 sought to perfect the fast and efficient assembly of hamburgers in their southern California restaurant. Their business model took off under the control of Ray, Kroc who obtained the rights

to establish McDonalds franchises across the country from the brothers. In 1955, Kroc opened the first of these restaurants in Des Plaines, Illinois, and by 1965, he had bought out the McDonald brothers and built their brand into the nation's leading fast-food chain, which was listed on the New York Stock Exchange. Although the McDonald brothers had been uncertain whether fast-food would catch on with the American public, Kroc knew that it fit well with the changing lifestyles and tastes generated in the suburbs.

Disneyland, the famously successful amusement park that opened in July 1955 in southern California, also embodied the growing significance of suburban culture. Built in the suburb of Anaheim, Disneyland also celebrated lifestyles built around the automobile. To the park's visionary Walt Disney, automobiles were a marvel of modern transportation that made it possible to live a more peaceful life in the suburbs outside of crowded, dirty, and hostile cities. This explains why Disneyland's Autopia, the park's major ride featuring automobiles, could be found in the futuristic part of the park known as Tomorrowland. Beyond his faith in technology and urban planning, Disney's overall vision for the amusement park was to underscore the importance of capitalism and democracy for creating orderly, middle-class environments conducive to the animator's brand of creativity and imagination.

Walt Disney also became part of the television medium that embraced suburban middle-class culture and promised a more wholesome and efficient lifestyle. Delayed because of World War II, television technology became standardized in the late 1940s and by the 1950s, it had begun to replace radio as the nation's primary form of entertainment. Sales of television sets skyrocketed from 16,000 in 1947 to 11 million in 1959. Nearly every home had at least one set by the late fifties. Disney created a series of television programs, such as *Wonderful World of Color*, that presented wholesome entertainment reinforcing the values and attractions of his amusement park. The most popular programs were situation comedies (sitcoms) that addressed the lives of white middle-class suburbanites such as the Nelsons of *The Adventures of Ozzie and Harriet*, the Andersons of *Father Knows Best*, and the Cleavers of *Leave It to Beaver*. The most successful sitcom was *I Love Lucy*, starring Lucille Ball and Desi Arnez. Married in real life, they played a middle-class housewife and Cuban band leader who lived in a New York City apartment, slept in separate beds, and eventually moved to a bucolic suburban home. A January 1953 episode in which Lucy had a baby drew 44 million viewers, twice the number that had watched President Eisenhower's inauguration that same month.

Although racial minorities were scarce on television, *Amos 'n' Andy*, a popular radio show featuring heavily

redlining Practice of designating areas of the city (usually racial minority areas) where banks would not provide home and business loans.

I Love Lucy Popular television comedy that revealed and enacted middle-class lifestyles and gender roles in the middle of the twentieth century.

stereotyped African American characters, made the transition to television in 1951, revealing the connection of early sitcoms to black-faced minstrelsy. Even though *Amos 'n' Andy* showcased an all-black cast, its reputation prompted African American protests leading to its prime-time cancellation, but this did not halt its syndication. Reruns aired on twice as many television stations in 1954. The show's boycott, ironically, also made television producers and sponsors wary of hiring black actors until the mid-1960s.

23-4
Family-Centered Culture in an Uncertain World

This photograph of the cast of *Father Knows Best,* a popular television comedy series from 1954 to 1967, epitomizes the wholesome entertainment that celebrated modern, white middle-class families amid Cold War fears. Despite the show's title, the wife and children typically undermined the father's traditional male authority.

How does the photo represent the typical American family in terms of race and gender roles? How does their clothing reinforce gender and cultural norms? ▶

NBC Television/Courtesy of Getty Images

The rise of the Cold War economy produced new forms of family-centered culture. More than at any time in the twentieth century, Americans celebrated the institution of family, not merely as an economic unit but as source of ultimate happiness and refuge from fears of communism and nuclear destruction. In this way, the American Dream, as expressed by Nixon in his kitchen debate with Khrushchev and by U.S. cultural propaganda spread throughout the world, came to center on the suburban home as a cure for individual, national, and global problems. Many Americans in the suburbs believed that they could achieve a modern type of family in which husbands did not dominate but shared responsibilities with their wives and parents worked together to create an educationally stimulating and psychologically fulfilling environment for their children. Although some celebrated the mutual sexual fulfillment of married couples, they condemned sex between unmarried partners and examined the diversity of human sexual behavior.

As you read, note changes in the American family after World War II. How did these reflect new trends in gender relations and sexuality emerging at mid-century?

23-4a Baby Boom and the Nuclear Family

After World War II, the birthrate in the United States rose sharply during a twenty-year **baby boom**.

{ The sudden increase in the nation's birthrate generates attention to family life.

Newly married couples and those who had postponed having children during the Depression and the war, had a record number of children. By 1957, the U.S. birthrate had reached its twentieth-century highpoint of 3.7 babies per woman, double the rate from the 1930s and higher than the vast majority of high-income countries in Europe and Asia, although Canada's birthrate was slightly higher than that of the United States. Like postwar economists, demographers could not have predicted that unprecedented prosperity would change the Depression-era pattern in which Americans had postponed marriage and limited family size (see Table 23.1).

The baby boom was part of a larger cultural shift in which families were seen as the main source of happiness and fulfillment. The sudden change from Depression and wartime uncertainties to the postwar faith in unlimited economic growth encouraged Americans to seek fulfillment in marriage and large families. The availability of good-paying jobs and affordable housing after the war enabled women to marry at younger ages (the average was 20 years). These factors also enabled couples to live separately from parents and relatives, causing a decline in the number of extended family households. The independent, self-contained **nuclear family** living in a suburban home came to symbolize mid-century American culture. The immediate family, moreover, served as a sanctuary in a world riddled with Cold War anxieties about atomic destruction.

Table 23.1 Global Birthrates, 1950–1970

Although an expanding population was the normal pattern in low-income countries, Britain and most other high-income nations experienced only a slight increase in births. Canada was one of the few other industrialized nations that experienced a baby boom on par with that in the United States. In Japan, however, the rate sharply declined.

	1950–1955	1955–1960	1960–1965	1965–1970
High-income countries	3.0	3.0	3.0	2.6
Low-income countries	6.4	6.5	6.5	6.6
United States	3.3	3.7	3.4	2.6
Canada	3.7	3.9	3.7	2.6
United Kingdom	2.2	2.5	2.9	2.6
France	2.8	2.7	2.8	2.6
Soviet Union	2.9	2.8	2.6	2.0
Germany	2.1	2.3	2.5	2.4
Japan	3.0	2.2	2.0	2.0

Source: United Nations

Estimated total fertility (children per woman).

23-4b Companionate Household

At the center of the family culture was a more equal partnership between husbands and wives. Middle-class men who held the white-collar managerial values of cooperation and consensus carried them home, and the entrance of their wives into the permanent workforce made it increasingly difficult for them to perform their "womanly" duties. As a result, the postwar generation embraced the theory of **companionate marriage**, which, according to *Reader's Digest*, meant that the "dominating husband and submissive wife are things of the past." In the modern postwar marriage, husbands and wives shared decision making. According to a 1959 study by the U.S. Department of Labor, marketers had become aware that husbands and wives were shopping together, and, as a result, advertisers began to target men for food, household goods, and other products that had been bought primarily by women. The image of the softer, family-oriented man appeared regularly in television comedies. Shows such as *Leave It to Beaver*, *Father Knows Best*, and *The Adventures of Ozzie and Harriet* regularly poked fun at notion of the domineering men as king of the family. In one *Ozzie and Harriet* episode, Ozzie, the husband, grew a mustache to symbolize his manly authority. But his sons pretended to be intimidated by the mustache, and his wife Harriet cut off half the mustache while he slept because she worried that his new manliness would attract other women. In the end, Ozzie learned that maintaining a harmonious household is more important than clinging to traditional notions of masculine appearance.

The ideal of companionate marriage, however, did not mean that men and women shared an equal burden of childrearing and household duties. After all, 70 percent

> Changes in gender relations increase women's authority in the family and their domestic responsibilities.

of all households in 1960 were nuclear families with a stay-at-home mother (this percentage varied for racial minorities). Some women, such as Congresswoman Coya Knutson, who worked outside the home confronted heavy pressure to make their husbands and children their primary focus. Knutson's political career as Minnesota's first female representative, was cut short in the 1958 congressional election by a vicious campaign in which her estranged husband accused her of neglecting her "womanly" duties as wife and mother. The publication of a letter in which her husband pleaded, "Coya, Come Home" was a large part of her loss.

Another problem for women was not necessarily being homemakers but managing homes. Postwar housewives faced new challenges related to their **domesticity**. The combination of the baby boom and the rise of the nuclear family meant that women had more children to raise with less help from grandparents and other family members who earlier might have lived in the home. Despite the promises of "labor-saving" appliances, such as washing machines, housewives also spent more time than ever doing domestic chores.

baby boom Period of significant increases in birthrates.

nuclear family Common and desirable family structure focused on immediate family members (the nucleus) of a single household, usually in the suburbs.

companionate marriage Union characterized by increased equality between husbands and wives and lesser roles for the autocratic males.

domesticity Having to do with home or family, which can include housework and child care.

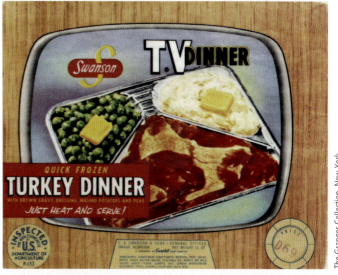

The Granger Collection, New York

TV Dinner, 1954 As more married women entered the labor market during the 1950s, C. A. Swanson & Sons created the frozen dinner as a quick and easy substitute for preparing a full-course meal. The company sold 10 million of these heat-and-eat frozen foods in their first year on the market ▲.

Global Americans The most popular toy in the United States after its introduction in 1959 was **Barbie**, the first adult-looking doll mass-marketed to children. Before the Mattel Corporation created Barbie, dolls were mainly toy babies that girls took care of as mothers in training. Barbie, however, was more babe than baby. Modeled after Lilli, a sexy adult doll popular among German bachelors, she appealed to the grown-up aspirations of teenage girls interested in dating, having a career, and, above all else, shopping for clothes, accessories, and even a dream house. The original Barbie featured a pony-tail hairstyle, black and white zebra-striped bathing suit, sunglasses, and earrings. Buyers for toy stores were not interested in the doll at first, fearing that parents would look askance at her sex appeal and curvaceous body. But they were wrong, and soon enough Barbie was flying off the shelves across the country. Mattel sold three hundred fifty-one thousand dolls in the first year of production, and soon Barbie became the most popular and profitable doll ever sold in the United States. The Barbie franchise adapted with the times, introducing her boyfriend Ken in 1961 and her sister Skipper four years later. A sexy doll for girls that encouraged fantasies of not just marriage and children but career and personal growth, Barbie influenced and was influenced by the youth-centered focus of parenting and consumer culture that arose amid the postwar baby boom.

Original Barbie Doll

New technology had raised the bar of expectations that encouraged homemakers, like industrial managers, to seek higher levels of efficiency and productivity that meant more, not less, work. Finally, the role of women in the household expanded to providing full-time counseling services for all family members, not only caring for the family's basic needs (food, clothing, and shelter). Postwar psychologists replaced the Freudian assumption that a person's personality was set in stone in early childhood with the idea that an individual develops in stages throughout that person's entire life. For housewives, this meant facing the never-ending challenge of creating a fulfilling, educational, emotionally satisfying home environment that catered to the life stage needs for each family member.

23-4c **Children of Plenty**

At no time before were Americans more optimistic about their children's future. A great deal of this optimism stemmed from medical break-throughs that conquered devastating childhood diseases such as polio, whooping cough, and diphtheria. The first polio vaccine, developed by Jonas Salk in April 1952, was a stunning achievement because this paralyzing childhood disease had reached epidemic proportions after World War II. The future looked bright for a generation that was immune to polio. In addition, parents had growing confidence that experts such as pediatrician Benjamin Spock better understood the keys to children's emotional development than the previous generation of experts. Spock's famous child-raising manual, *The Common Sense Book of Baby and Child Care* (1946), emphasized the need for parents to listen to their children and to discipline them with flexible rather than strict rules. Armed with the latest psychological theories, American parents were excited at the

> Children and youth receive new attention and have influence in the expanded consumer society.

prospect of creating a perfect generation of children. Given the nation's overall prosperity, baby boomers were assumed to exceed their parents' remarkable social mobility, pushing the nation to greater heights of achievement and power.

These rosy expectations coupled with prosperity fueled the development of a commercial culture centered on the health and happiness of children. Nowhere was this trend more evident than in the skyrocketing sales of toys: The $84 million spent in 1940 had increased to $1.25 billion by 1960. Popular culture, too, came to center increasingly around baby boomer consumption. The boomers were the first generation to grow up with television, and in many ways TV proved a powerful engine for youth spending. The news spread about the latest "must-have" toy from television commercials during *Howdy Doody*, the *Mickey Mouse Club*, and other popular children's shows. Print media also tapped into the youth market through the expanded production of educational books, such as Dr. Seuss's *Cat in the Hat* series, and periodicals, including the irreverent and satirical *Mad Magazine*.

The creation of a thriving youth market meant that marketers had a vested interest in accelerating the maturity of young consumers. The suburban context also encouraged youth to grow up faster by placing them in adult situations much earlier in life. A community of single-family homes provided youth with more privacy than had living with one's relatives in homes and central city apartments in previous generations. The proliferation of automobiles gave young people more chances to get away from adult authority. As a result of their newfound independence, the baby boomers pushed beyond the traditional boundaries of youth, generating national conversations about problems of juvenile delinquency, gang fighting, drag racing, violent comic books, and teenage sex.

In the 1950s, Hollywood glamorized anxieties about the nation's youth through the emergence of teen-oriented cinema such as *The Wild Ones* (1953), *Teenage Rebel* (1956), *Untamed Youth* (1957), *Reform School Girl* (1957), and *Riot in Juvenile Prison* (1959). The most legendary film was *Rebel without a Cause*, starring the young, enigmatic actor James Dean. The 1955 film featured three white, suburban middle-class teenagers who "tick . . . like a bomb" because of childhoods riddled with misunderstanding, loneliness, parental abandonment, overprotection, and divorce. In the film, Dean's character survives a "manly" car race that kills his high school rival. But tragically and ironically, Dean died in real life while speeding his roadster on a California highway before the movie made him an international symbol of youth rebellion.

The media that became most closely tied to youth culture was commercial radio. The hottest genre of popular music, **rock 'n' roll**, originated in the U.S. South where in the early 1950s, a critical mass of radio disc jockeys and record producers began to experiment with mixing together African American blues and gospel music with white country and folk music. One of the most celebrated of these early pioneers was Sam Phillips, owner of Sun Records in Memphis, Tennessee. An avid lover of black music, he searched for ways to share it with a broad white audience. The discovery of young Elvis Presley in 1954 gave him a golden opportunity to blend his favorite types of music. According to Phillips, Elvis "sings Negro songs with a white voice which borrows in mood and emphasis from the country style, modified by popular music." The young man jetted to popular music stardom, becoming the center of a youth craze for the combined black-white musical styles of rock 'n' roll. Elvis's appearance on the Ed Sullivan Show in 1956 became the most watched moment in TV history up to that time. The performer's bodily gyrations earned him the nickname Elvis "the pelvis," and his brazen sexuality stirred protests against the "devil's music." Alarmed by Elvis's pelvic thrusts, network censors permitted the Ed Sullivan Show to film the singer only from the waist-up.

Although Elvis almost never performed outside North America, his music spread around the world. Most famously, four youths in Liverpool, United Kingdom, grew up idolizing the king of rock 'n' roll, one of them (John Lennon) stating, "Before Elvis, there was nothing." In August 1965, on their second U.S. tour as the Beatles rock band, they finally met their idol in his Hollywood home, which in retrospect was the passage of the old guard to a new generation of rockers fueled to a great extent by the British and other foreigners.

23-4d Beginnings of the Sexual Revolution

A point of contention within the family-centered culture was the assertion that the United States was no longer a place for "real men." Although television characters such as

{ Men and women embrace the new freedom of sexual expression, but the results are not necessarily liberating.

Ozzie Nelson adapted to the new "feminized" nature of work and family life, cultural critics extolled the virtues of rugged individualism and resistance to authority and rejected the ideal of companionate marriage. One critic was Hugh Hefner, a midwesterner from a conservative family who began a men's magazine that cast bachelorhood, not family life, as the pinnacle of male fulfillment. Begun in December 1953, *Playboy* magazine took the daring step of featuring nude photographs of attractive women. The magazine sold out its entire first print run of 70,000 copies showcasing the Hollywood sex symbol Marilyn Monroe. According to one sociologist, the main target of Hefner's rebellion was not conservative sexuality but the institution of marriage itself. "From the beginning," she wrote, "*Playboy* loved women—large-breasted, long-legged, young women . . . —and hated wives." The magazine said that marriage for men was "the biggest mistake of their lives" because it tied them down to one woman and prevented them from exercising their sexual freedom.

The **sexual revolution** made possible the popularity of *Playboy*, diminishing social pressures to form traditional families and interrupting polite silences about human sexuality. Alfred Kinsey's *Sexual Behavior in the Human Male* (1948) paved the way for this revolution and made a believer of Hugh Hefner. In a neutral, scientific voice, Kinsey revealed that 37 percent of men in his study had experienced orgasm with another man. He also noted that 15 percent of the time, married men, reached orgasm with women other than their wives and men and through masturbation and nocturnal emissions. Kinsey's book (followed in 1953 by a companion study on American women) became one of the rare scientific studies to become a best seller.

Kinsey's nonjudgmental approach to human sexuality and separation of morality from normal behavior assisted in removing the stigmas against prolonged bachelorhood. Traditional family values viewed men who did not become husbands, fathers, and breadwinners as failures. One psychoanalyst who studied homosexuality created an equation conveying the logical connections associated with these "failed" men: *I am a failure = I am castrated = I am not a man = I am a woman = I am a homosexual*. This was a shorthand description of the heterosexual ideal that justified discrimination against women, gays and lesbians, and "feminized" men. As with *Playboy*, the Kinsey findings were a factor in the sexual revolution that undermined the traditional ideal for heterosexual men by giving them options to marriage and family life.

A major breakthrough in birth control enabled millions of women to join in the sexual revolution by freeing themselves from the connection between sex and procreation. As in

rock 'n' roll Popular American musical form emerging from the mixture of Southern country music with African American blues and gospel that would spread rapidly around the world and evolve as foreigners (especially the British) innovated new styles.

sexual revolution Rebellion having to do with human sexuality and its popular expression as normal and healthy, not sinful and immoral.

birth control pill Innovation in medical technology that enabled women to prevent pregnancy by taking a simple and effective tablet.

the early days of the birth control movement, the impetus came from social activist Margaret Sanger. By the 1940s, medical doctors were increasingly embracing her efforts to prevent women from becoming pregnant, and the law tolerated them. In 1942, Planned Parenthood, a new organization emerged to lead the U.S. birth control movement and four years later encouraged the establishment of an international organization with the same name. Sanger headed both organizations, arguing that birth control was necessary because babies were

healthier when planned by the mother and conceived in love. More controversially, Sanger turned to theories of eugenics in supporting the sterilization of those with severe learning disabilities. She also prodded researchers and philanthropists to create the first **birth control pill**, which, after its approval by the Food and Drug Administration (FDA) in May 1960, soon became the most popular form of contraceptive in the United States. In the 1965 *Griswold v. Connecticut* decision, the Supreme Court upheld the legality of birth control clinics in introducing and distributing the pills and other contraceptive devices.

23-5
New Social Divisions

This photograph, taken in 1951, shows children playing in a muddy Chicago alley on the city's south side. This part of the city experienced tremendous redevelopment and the closure of major factories, such as those dedicated to meatpacking, during the two decades after 1945.

How does this photograph square with the rapid expansion of wealth taking place throughout the United States? What historical factors can explain the conditions depicted in the photograph? ▶

Archive Photos/Getty Images

affluence Possession of great wealth that in the 1950s some critics saw as a great weakness for the United States.

Not everyone embraced—or was embraced by—the prosperity and opportunities created by the new economy. Prominent intellectuals, artists, and youth railed against the materialism, conformity, and alienation accompanying the new suburban American dream. Meanwhile, certain industries that had been top performers in the U.S. economy before World War II were becoming obsolete as the result of overseas competition and the depletion of once abundant domestic natural resources. These collapses led to increased unemployment that hurt the most vulnerable classes of industrial workers who were left few opportunities in the Cold War economy. Most of these workers were racial minorities who during and after World War II had migrated to northern industrial cities. Their persistent unemployment became part of a cycle of poverty that generated a growing sense of urban crisis. Nor did rural communities share equally in U.S. prosperity, and labor shortages in agriculture resulted in an immigration conflict between Mexico and the United States.

☞ As you read, focus on the social and economic costs of the nation's postwar prosperity. Why did some Americans question the impact of prosperity? How and why did information and service industries disadvantage certain social groups?

23-5a Critics of Prosperity

Not everyone celebrated technological progress and prosperity as unambiguous achievements. Scientists issued dire warnings about possible consequences of nuclear technology, and social scientists began to uncover problems related to economic developments. John Kenneth Galbraith, one of the nation's most respected economists, argued that the economic goal of maximum production was no longer relevant and the resulting **affluence** actually was hurting U.S. society. His best-seller *The Affluent Society* (1958) targeted the advertising industry for creating unnecessary consumer desires. To Galbraith, prosperity would be better spent on public services that improved everyone's quality of life. Other critics, such as sociological thinkers David Reisman and William H. Whyte, turned a discerning eye toward white-collar work and the suburbs. Riesman's best-selling *The Lonely Crowd: A Study of the Changing American Culture* (1950) distinguished between

> Scholars, artists, and activists warn Americans about the downside to economic growth.

the self-reliant "inner-directed" personality of the nineteenth century and the conformist "other-directed" type that was characteristic of postwar Americans. Whyte's best seller, *The Organization Man* (1956), bemoaned the managerial revolution in the U.S. corporate world that had replaced the values of ambition and inventiveness with a new emphasis on teamwork, obedience, and loyalty to the firm. Conformity, to him, had replaced the self-reliance that Ralph Waldo Emerson and other nineteenth-century American philosophers had idealized.

Creative artists joined the revolt against the dispiriting influences of postwar prosperity. Some of the best-known nonconformists of the 1950s were the **Beat poets** Allen Ginsburg and Jack Kerouac who raged against materialism, pioneering what was later called "new-age" spirituality in search for deeper inspirations through Buddhism and other non-Western religions. The men stood at the forefront of a movement of young, urban, and mostly white bohemians gathering in New York City's Greenwich Village and San Francisco's North Beach neighborhoods. In its art and lifestyle, the Beat movement also absorbed "hipster" language, sexual freedom, and the drug and alcohol lifestyle of jazz culture. The stereotypical "beatnik" called men "daddy-o," women "chicks," and uttered words such as "far-out" and "groovy." Males wore untrimmed

goatees, sandals, turtlenecks, and jeans, and females donned black leotards, short skirts, black eye shadow, and black tights.

In 1959, *Life* magazine negatively characterized the Beats as unwashed, uneducated, unmotivated, and unprincipled. But the same could not be said of the white middle-class college students who revived folk music of the Great Depression era. They, too, rejected the values of the suburbs in searching for more authentic expressions of the American spirit. Young folk musicians rediscovered the protest songs of Popular Front singers such as Woody Guthrie, Huddie "Leadbelly" Leadbetter, and Pete Seeger, all of whom were closely identified with the political left. In a stark contrast to rock 'n' roll, folk music rejected commercialism, favoring the unpretentious over the faddish and the intellect over bodily passions. The launch of the Newport Folk Festival in July 1959 gave shape to the folk music revival, introducing Joan Baez, Woody Guthrie's son Arlo, and the incomparable Bob Dylan. Born Robert Zimmerman to middle-class Jewish American parents, Dylan dropped out of the University of Minnesota to learn and perform folk music. A self-declared "Woody Guthrie jukebox," he more than anyone else was able to translate

Beat poets Cultural nonconformists in the 1950s who wrote poetry, gathered in urban neighborhoods, and assumed the characteristics of jazz musicians, Asian religions, and other alternative groups.

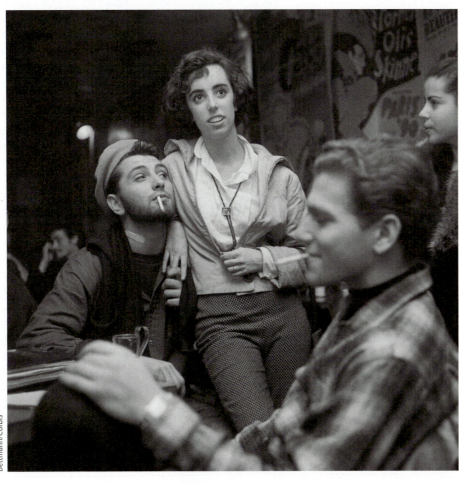

Bettmann/Corbis

Beatniks in Greenwich Village, New York City, 1959 One of the prominent forms of youth rebellion during the 1950s was the Beatnik who embraced Beat poetry that adopted idioms of jazz culture and the spirituality of Eastern religions and pushed the boundaries of sexual freedom. ◀

the protest spirit of Depression-era folk music into political anthems for the baby boom generation. By 1964, Dylan reigned as king of the international folk music movement, galvanizing a generation with the antiwar sensation "Blowing in the Wind" and the youth manifesto "The Times They Are a-Changin'."

23-5b Costs of Suburban Development

Suburbanization and the rise of the Sunbelt carried immediate and long-term costs for central cities as corporations moved manufacturing plants to new locations, decreasing much-needed city tax revenues. U.S. automobile makers led the way as they cut high-paid union wages by downsizing and closing old factories and building new ones in states (almost always outside the central cities) that had lower-cost labor because they constrained labor union organizing through right to work laws made possible by the Taft-Hartley Act. Another problem for unions was **automation**, a process by which firms reduced labor costs by replacing workers with machines (see Chapter 19). Between 1947 and 1958, the big three automakers (General Motors, Ford, and Chrysler) built twenty-five new plants in Detroit, all of them in the suburbs. The corporations leapt at the opportunity to build larger single-story factories in the suburbs, and cost-saving labor concerns influenced decisions to downsize or close central city plants. During the same time period, Detroit lost more than one hundred twenty thousand manufacturing jobs. This especially hurt African Americans and young people who were often last hired and first fired because of their lack of seniority. Deindustrialization in the 1950s and 1960s began to affect other industries and spread throughout the urban Midwest from Milwaukee to Chicago, Detroit, Cleveland, Pittsburgh, and other cities that came to be known as the **rust belt** because of these economic trends.

America's central cities not only faced alarming levels of unemployment but had a vast and growing population of racial minorities who were often unable to find jobs or housing in the suburbs. Southern migrations beginning during World War I had continued during the 1940s and

> Suburban migration exacts heavy costs on urban communities.

1950s when more than 2.5 million African Americans left the rural South to live in urban communities, often New York, Chicago, and Los Angeles. Michael Harrington, a socialist writer, revealed many of the problems that the African American migrants faced in his best-selling exposé of the nation's poverty, *The Other America*, published in 1962. He revealed the disturbing fact that one of every five Americans (40 million) was poor. This high rate of poverty was puzzling: Why was there extensive poverty amid a historic period of prosperity? The cause, argued Harrington, was that the new economy obliterated the economic usefulness of large sectors of American workers, often replacing them with machines. Suburbanization made matters worse by isolating the middle classes from the problems of poverty, leaving them blissfully ignorant of the crises that raged in rural America and African American urban communities. In short, Harrington maintained that key engines that had powered postwar prosperity (the Cold War economy and suburbanization) also had produced racial segregation and poverty.

The relationship between suburban prosperity and central city poverty also resulted from the good intentions of government officials and social reformers involved in **urban redevelopment**. The process began in July 1949 with the federal **Housing Act**, which authorized the demolition of slums to make way for eight hundred thousand new housing units throughout the nation. The goal was to help the increasing number of African American central city residents by replacing old and substandard housing. Problems, however, occurred when local governments that had accepted $13 billion in federal funds for urban redevelopment handed over cleared slum land to private real estate developers. With few incentives or requirements to supply housing for the poor, the developers instead built more profitable commercial projects and middle-class housing. In the case of Dodger Stadium, the city of Los Angeles gave three Mexican American communities to a privately owned baseball team instead of fulfilling its plan to build new public housing units. Most cities across the nation also chose to use slum-clearance funds for commercial purposes that would bring tax revenues rather than construct housing for low-income residents. Between 1949 and 1968, only one of every three housing units destroyed through redevelopment was replaced. As a result, the majority of affected residents did not receive new housing but were relocated to nearby and growing slums.

Moreover, cities often used federal highway construction funds to remove central city residents in order to build freeways and interchanges. With commercial and highway construction and middle-class housing taking up most of the cleared land downtown, **public housing** often took the form of hastily planned high-rise complexes packing as many as twelve thousand residents into small urban spaces. The largest concentration of these communities was on a four-mile corridor of sixteen-story identical buildings on the south side of Chicago. Known as the "projects," these

---

automation Business process that seeks to save money, streamline production, or subvert labor unions by using machines to do the work of people.

rust belt Former industrial heartland, centered in the urban upper Midwest but including other areas, suffering from postwar flights of industrial production to other regions and countries.

urban redevelopment Process of transforming central city neighborhoods ostensibly to remove blight and slum conditions that often displaced and disadvantaged working-class people and communities while benefiting city governments, private businesses, and the middle classes.

Housing Act Legislative support for widespread urban redevelopment and creation of new public housing.

public housing Government-subsidized housing designed to benefit poor and working-class people but often were incubators of crime, disorder, and poverty.

AP Images

Housing Projects in Chicago before 1965 Housing projects, like this one on the south side of Chicago, stemmed from egalitarian impulses to ensure decent housing for everyone. But soon living in "the projects" became synonymous with seemingly permanent class and racial inequality that became an endemic part of the new economy. ▲

forms of public housing that segregated the poor from mainstream society quickly became centers of vandalism, drug use, and violent crime.

The origin of urban problems in postwar Oakland, California, represents the process of central city decay. Like nearly all West Coast cities, this port city across the bay from San Francisco experienced a major boom in industry and population during World War II. But in the two following decades, Oakland lost both as nearby suburban cities such as San Leandro, Hayward, and Fremont raided its industrial base and drew away its white residents. As was the case in Levittown, the G.I. Bill and federal highway funds laid the groundwork for much of the white flight. What was left in Oakland was an expanding working-class black population competing for a diminishing number of industrial jobs and even for low-paying, dead-end jobs in the service sector, such as maintenance and garbage collection. In addition, federally backed redevelopment (slum-clearance) programs as well as the construction of the Nimitz freeway and Bay Area Rapid Transit (BART) destroyed established African American neighborhoods, uprooting hundreds of families and businesses, usually without transplanting them elsewhere. The new transit network created a pipeline between Eastbay suburbs and the city of San Francisco that enriched these two ends but enabled only modest construction of high-rise office buildings in downtown Oakland.

If San Francisco and the Eastbay suburbs benefited from a concerted process of urban and suburban

development, the plight of Oakland can be said to have resulted from a related process of **underdevelopment**. This can be seen as the dark side of postwar prosperity through which stable central city communities such as Oakland turned into poverty-ridden ghettos. For nearly a week in August 1965, a local conflict between African American residents in the south-central Los Angeles community of Watts and local police erupted into a devastating conflagration of destruction, violence, and street protest. During what were known as the **Watts riots**, clashes between ten thousand residents and more than thirteen thousand California guardsmen left thirty-four (mostly African Americans) dead, more than four thousand arrested, and six hundred buildings destroyed or damaged. The Watts riots were the first in a series of urban protests that would rock the nation and increase the pressure for racial and class reform if not a social revolution. The riots accelerated suburban migration by pushing whites in the central cities to sell their homes and flee to the presumed safety and racial homogeneity of the suburbs. Enhancing this **white flight** were unscrupulous real estate agents and hustlers who promoted fears of black invasion in order to profit from panicky whites selling their homes. In this way, the division between white suburbia and black and brown central cities hardened as the latest white suburban migrants divested themselves of inner city communities.

underdevelopment Side effect or unintended consequence of economic development in which poor and working class people are often disadvantaged by the types of development that benefit the middle and upper classes.

Watts riots Violent uprisings of urban African Americans in Los Angeles County triggered by police harassment and prolonged and systemic poverty.

white flight Process of whites leaving central cities and moving to the suburbs as the result of a combination of incentives for suburban living, such as affordable and spacious housing, and disincentives for urban living, such as crowds, noise, crime, and large populations of racial minorities.

23-5c Agricultural Labor and Mexican Migration

The steady stream of rural migration to the cities led to shortages of agricultural labor, particularly for crops that were not easily mecha-

{ Growers push the federal government to import foreign workers during an age of immigration restriction.

nized, such as cotton and fruits. During World War II, U.S. growers had resorted to the long-standing practice of using low-cost foreign workers by pressuring the federal government to form an agreement with Mexico to bring two hundred thousand bracero guest workers into the country. Conflict erupted after the war when Mexican officials pushed for higher wages and better living conditions for the braceros but their U.S. counterparts responded by opening the nation's border, allowing growers to avoid braceros altogether and hire cheaper undocumented workers who were also from Mexico. After the two nations solved their differences and renewed the

Global Americans A married couple, **Ezekiel** and **Rosaura Perez** were born and raised in an area of Jalisco, Mexico, that traditionally sent migrants to the United States. Both their fathers had come in the late 1920s. Ezekiel came in 1947, six years after he married Rosaura and they had three children. From his perspective, he was fortunate to enter as a bracero guest worker in a program operated by the U.S. government. He picked sugar beets and harvested wheat and beans for ten months in Billings, Montana. Not long after returning to Mexico, Ezekiel tried four times to cross into the United States without formal papers. He was caught each time and sent back. But on his fifth try, he and seventeen others led by a paid guide were successful. Ezekiel worked for three years throughout California picking various crops and in a restaurant. He gradually began to shake the constant fear of being caught and deported. But then loneliness for family and home overcame the excitement of being in a new and wealthy country. Meanwhile, Rosaura was making do back home, thankful that her husband, unlike others who went north, was consistently sending money to her. When he returned for good, they had enough money to purchase parcels of land and send their then seven children to school. The experience of this family reveals both the challenges and benefits of migration to the United States for peoples from less wealthy countries.

Registering Braceros at Labor Center in Hidalgo, Texas, 1959

Bettmann/Corbis

Operation Wetback Federal government program to halt the migration of undocumented workers who often were responding to inefficiencies in U.S. guest worker programs.

agribusinesses Large, often multinational, corporations in agricultural industries whose economies of scale often doomed family farming.

guest worker program in 1954, the U.S. border patrol implemented **Operation Wetback**, a campaign that detained and deported at least fifty-seven thousand undocumented Mexicans from California alone. This resulted in huge drops in the number of undocumented immigrants in the United States while raising concerns about the fairness of the nation's immigration policies.

In theory, the bracero program was designed to benefit both Mexico and the United States, but in reality, most of the benefits remained north of the border. A survey of more than six thousand returning guest workers in the Mexican state of Jalisco revealed that the program had utterly failed to achieve its stated goals of teaching the workers new skills in the United States and paying them enough to uplift their rural economies. These failures had a devastating impact, especially on the humble Mexican families who had borrowed money to pay for bracero expenses and went into further debt when the main bread-winner was picking crops across the border. To make ends meet, the wives and children of braceros worked long hours in Mexico. When they still could not earn enough, they scattered throughout the country, taking low-paying, exploitative work. Families were torn apart with little prospect for improving their lot. In addition, thousands of men who did not meet the bracero program's strict requirements crossed the border illegally to fill the huge demand for low-paid migrant labor. Nine of ten males in one Jalisco rural town ended up migrating one way or another to the United States.

23-5d Rural Transformations

The bracero experience reflected the broader transformation of rural U.S. areas where large agricultural corporations made earning a decent living difficult for everyday people. As had industrial factories, corporate **agribusinesses** took advantage of their size by investing in new labor-saving technologies enabling them to produce more and better products at faster and cheaper rates. In addition, a number of federal government assistance programs, such as agricultural subsidies, favored big farms because policy makers were more interested in protecting the nation's food supply than the tradition of family-owned farms. The result was a long-term migration of rural families, including Native Americans, to the cities beginning in the 1920s, increasing with the Dust Bowl in the 1930s, and continuing through the height of agribusiness consolidation after World War II. By 1960, the soaring costs of farming, as the result of the scale required to make a profit, had nearly eliminated Native American agriculture. Between 1945 and 1960, these farmers declined from 45 to 10 percent of the total tribal population in the United States. As a consequence, Indian reservations experienced some of the worst poverty rates in rural America.

The depletion of the nation's once abundant natural resources resulting from World War II needs and the extended postwar economic boom also had a negative impact on jobs in rural America. By 1949, the United States was importing more oil from abroad (particularly

> Prosperity covers up long-term reductions in family farming and major unemployment in mining.

AP Images

Native American Poverty on the Reservation, before 1965 Native Americans did not share equally in the benefits of the Cold War economy either as migrants to central cities or, as in this photo, residents of a reservation. This photo shows a dwelling on the Havasupi reservation near the south rim of the Grand Canyon in Arizona. ◄

the Middle East) than it generated domestically. The country's supply of timber declined as forests were cut down at a faster rate than they could be replenished to meet the insatiable demands for lumber from the housing boom. The nation's depletion of its mineral resources was especially acute. Its reliance on foreign cooper and bauxite (for making aluminum) increased significantly over the next twenty years. Corporations were able to offset the loss of native mineral deposits by using inexpensive foreign imports—but workers suffered widespread unemployment. The area hardest hit was Appalachia, a nine-state mountainous region stretching from eastern Pennsylvania to Alabama. The area suffered when the coal industry drastically reduced its labor force by downsizing and automation. Another devastated region was the Mesabi iron range, spanning the northern parts of Minnesota and Wisconsin and upper Michigan. This area once contained the nation's largest deposits of iron ore used for making steel. The depletion of its high-quality ore by the early 1960s caused massive unemployment as mining companies closed, downsized, and retooled to compete against foreign competition.

Summary

Two decades of tense U.S.–Soviet relations after World War II transformed the U.S. economy as well as the nation's military, government, society, and culture. Information and service industries had a powerful and far-reaching impact on American life during the early stages of the Cold War. The transformation did not happen overnight but emerged through five simultaneous and interconnected developments so that by 1970 white-collar jobs represented almost half of all jobs in the nation, far surpassing the number of blue-collar jobs. One reason is that federal policies advanced consumer spending, which in concert with Cold War spending sustained overall prosperity. Another is that through highway construction and labor union limitations, the federal government enabled the nation's manufacturing base to relocate away from central cities. A third reason is that suburbanization and internal migration to the South and West affected the nature of work, community life, and urban development. Also, changing gender roles resulting from the increase of white-collar work and women's employment affected all family members. Finally, the Cold War economy had negative consequences for central cities, racial minorities, and the most vulnerable classes of industrial and agricultural workers. The emergence of the information and services economy created an urban crisis that deepened as deindustrialization accelerated after 1965. Thus, the historic prosperity generated by the U.S. Cold War economy did not become a golden age. Instead it became a transitional era in which the nation and its culture began to emerge from a system of manufacturing rooted in the urban Northeast and upper Midwest. The postindustrial information and service industries housed outside the urban centers of the old economy characterized the nation's economy in the late twentieth century

<Thinking Back, *Looking Forward*>

As you review the Cold War economy, recall the superpower conflict with the Soviet Union as well as global crises occurring in places such as Berlin, China, and Egypt. Decisions made by U.S. officials expanded the U.S. economy and encouraged the growth of suburbs, service and information industries, and higher education. In the coming chapters, look for the impact of the Cold War on movements for civil rights and the U.S. war in Vietnam.

To make your study concrete, review the timeline and reflect on the entries there. Think about their causes, consequences, and connections. How do they fit with global trends?

Additional Resources

Books

Avila, Eric. *Popular Culture in the Age of White Flight: Fear and Fantasy in Suburban Los Angeles.* **Berkeley: University of California Press, 2004.** ▶ Examination of the postwar transformation of a prominent western city with attention to Hollywood, Disneyland, and the building of Dodger Stadium.

Cobble, Dorothy Sue. *The Other Women's Movement: Workplace Justice and Social Rights in Modern America.* **Princeton, NJ: Princeton University Press, 2004.** ▶ Penetrating analysis of the history of working women and their struggles for social justice during the twentieth century.

Cohen, Lizabeth. *A Consumers' Republic: The Politics of Mass Consumption in Postwar America.* **New York: Vintage Books, 2003.** ▶ Path-breaking study of the nation's explosion in consumer spending and its ironic consequences for social inequality.

Gilbert, James. *Men in the Middle: Searching for Masculinity in the 1950s.* **Chicago, IL: University of Chicago Press, 2005.** ▶ Original study of changing roles for men in the emerging postindustrial economy.

Gillett, Charlie. *The Sound of the City: The Rise of Rock and Roll.* **1970. Reprint, New York: De Capo Press, 1996.** ▶ One of the best examinations of the early history of rock music.

Harrington, Michael. *The Other America: Poverty in the United States.* **1962. Reprint, New York: Touchstone, 1997.** ▶ Analysis of the problems that the War on Poverty sought to resolve.

Katznelson, Ira. *When Affirmative Action Was White: An Untold History of Racial Inequality in Twentieth-Century America.* **New York: Norton, 2005.** ▶ Innovative rethinking of affirmative action policies, such as the G.I. Bill, that targeted white people.

May, Elaine Tyler. *Homeward Bound: American Families in the Cold War Era.* **New York: Basic Books, 1988.** ▶ Classic account of changing gender roles after World War II.

Ngai, Mae M. *Impossible Subjects: Illegal Aliens and the Making of Modern America.* **Princeton, NJ: Princeton University Press, 2004.** ▶ Important historical analysis of U.S. immigration law and politics that address postwar policies including the bracero program.

Segrue, Thomas J. *The Origins of the Urban Crisis: Race and Inequality in Postwar Detroit.* **Princeton, NJ: Princeton University Press, 1996.** ▶ Award-winning study of the historical factors contributing to the degeneration of a major American city.

> Go to the MindTap® for **Global Americans** to access the full version of select books from this Additional Resources section.

Websites

A Guide to Beat Poets. (https://www.poets.org/poetsorg/text/brief-guide-beat-poets). ▶ Selection of poems, videos of poets reading their work, and biographies of key poets in the Beat movement.

America on the Move: City and Suburb. (http://amhistory.si.edu/onthemove/exhibition/exhibition_15_1.html). ▶ Online interactive exhibit with images, text, and videos about American suburban life in the 1950s.

America on the Move: On the Interstate, 1956–1990. (http://amhistory.si.edu/onthemove/exhibition/exhibition_16_1.html). ▶ Online interactive exhibit with images, text, and videos about highway construction along Interstate 10 spanning the Southwest from California to Texas to Florida.

Bittersweet Harvest: The Bracero Program 1942–1964. (http://americanhistory.si.edu/bracero/introduction). ▶ Extensive coverage of the bracero guest worker program with images and firsthand perspectives from migrants.

The Pan-Am Historical Foundation. (http://www.panam.org/enter). ▶ Video, audio, and textual sources related to a U.S. airline that became an icon of global air travel.

Continue exploring online through MindTap®**, where you can:**

- **Assess your knowledge with the Chapter Test**
- **Watch historical videos related to the chapter**
- **Further your understanding with interactive maps and timelines**

Prosperity and the Cold War Economy

1946

Benjamin Spock publishes *The Common Sense Book of Baby and Child Care*.

May

Railroad strike shuts down major U.S. transportation system.

November

Republicans claim both houses of Congress for first time since 1932.

1947

G.I. Bill funds half of all college students in its peak year.

March

Levittown tract home community opens in New York.

Truman Doctrine commits United States to containing communism.

June

Congress enacts Taft-Hartley Act.

1948–1949

1948

Alfred Kinsey publishes *Sexual Behavior in the Human Male*.

November 1948

Truman wins second term as president.

1949

U.S. oil imports begin to exceed domestic production.

Protests erupt against Coca-Cola in France.

July 1949

Housing Act authorizes widespread slum clearance.

August 1949

Soviet Union conducts successful test of atomic bomb.

1950–1953

April 1950

NSC 68 initiates an increasingly militaristic stance toward the Soviet Union.

August 1952

Holiday Inn opens first highway convenience hotel.

January 1953

Record 44 million television viewers watch episode of *I Love Lucy*.

December 1953

Playboy magazine begins.

1954–1955

1954

Operation Wetback begins to detain and deport undocumented Mexicans.

1955

Rebel Without a Cause makes James Dean a global symbol of youth rebellion.

April 1955

McDonald's restaurant chain opens in Chicago suburb.

May 1955

Soviets establish Warsaw Pact to counter NATO.

July 1955

Disneyland opens on converted farmland in Anaheim, California.

Soviet Union

Canada

England

France

United States

Cuba

1956–1957

June 1956

Congress passes Interstate Highway Act.

September 1956

Program featuring Elvis Presley has largest television audience.

1957

U.S. baby boom reaches twentieth-century high point (3.7 babies per woman).

Brooklyn Dodgers move to Los Angeles.

Beat poet Jack Kerouac publishes *On the Road*.

October 1957

Success of Soviet Sputnik evokes great fear in United States over "missile gap."

1958

Pan American World Airlines flies first fleet of commercial jet airplanes.

Bretton Woods global economic system becomes fully operational.

John Kenneth Galbraith publishes *The Affluent Society*.

July

United States establishes NASA to compete with Soviet space missions.

September

Congress approves National Defense Education Act.

1959–1960

July 1959

Bob Dylan performs at first Newport Folk Festival.

September 1959

Nikita Khrushchev visits the United States.

1960

U.S. Census counts thirteen "strip cities."

U.S. suburban population doubles from that in 1947.

May 1960

U.S. government approves first birth control pill.

1961–1962

1961

Canada's baby boom peaks at nearly four babies per woman.

January 1961

Eisenhower warns about "military-industrial complex."

Michael Harrington publishes *The Other America*.

April 1962

Dodger Stadium opens in Los Angeles, California.

October 1962

Cuban Missile Crisis pushes United States and Soviet Union to the brink of nuclear war.

1963–1965

February 1964

The Beatles embark on first tour of the United States.

August 1965

Racial uprising erupts in Watts, California.

24 Civil Rights and Human Rights

1945–1965

Rejected from the University of North Carolina and Harvard University because of her race and gender respectively, Pauli Murray nevertheless racked up achievements—such as being the first African American deputy attorney general of California—thanks to her indomitable spirit. She was a committed political activist whose legal contributions led the way to decisions like *Brown v. Board of Education*.

In 1938, Pauli Murray, a twenty-eight-year-old Hunter College graduate who had been raised in rural North Carolina, applied to law school at the University of North Carolina and was rejected—on account of her race. Murray was African American—or at least she identified as African American, though with Swedish, French, Irish, and Native American ancestors, she once described her family as a "United Nations in miniature." She subsequently enrolled in the law school at the historically black Howard University, where the faculty included lawyers in the forefront of the National Association for the Advancement of Colored People's (NAACP) legal challenges against racial segregation. Graduating first in her class, she applied to a master's program at Harvard University and was rejected—on account of her gender.

AP Images/Frank C. Curtin

Murray then moved to California and earned a master's degree in law from the University of California, Berkeley. The next year she became the first African American deputy attorney general of California. The National Council of Negro Women and *Mademoiselle* magazine recognized this achievement by naming her Woman of the Year. Such honors, which Murray garnered throughout her life, testified to her talents, and indomitable spirit as well as to the enormous obstacles she confronted as a black female in the United States.

A committed political activist familiar with the passive resistance tactics of India's Mohandas Gandhi, Murray helped stage sit-ins at restaurants in Washington, D.C. In 1940, she and a girlfriend were arrested in Petersburg, Virginia, for sitting in the white section of a segregated bus. Murray began a lifelong correspondence with First Lady Eleanor Roosevelt while leading an unsuccessful campaign to free Odell Waller, a black sharecropper in Virginia accused of killing his white landlord. Her *States' Laws on Race and Color* (1950) became the "bible" for NAACP lawyers who advanced legal challenges culminating in *Brown v. Board of Education*, a landmark U.S. Supreme Court ruling in May 1954 that outlawed racial segregation in public schools.

The *Brown* decision established a crucial legal standard for the postwar "rights revolution." It coincided with a profound and growing revulsion, felt across the United States and around the world, against the Holocaust and other racist acts committed during World War II. The newly established United Nations (UN) put pressure on the United States and other nations to end all forms of discrimination based on race, sex, and religion. More important was the fact that racism in the United States was tarnishing the country's image as the leader of the "free world" in the Cold War fight against communism. To counter Soviet criticism, the U.S. government—for the first time since Reconstruction when the Thirteenth, Fourteenth, and Fifteenth Amendments established the legal basis for nondiscrimination—took a bold step to guarantee the equal treatment of all Americans, thus providing a key element to the civil rights revolution.

> How do the many honors that Pauli Murray garnered in her work as a political activist testify to her indomitable spirit—as well as to the obstacles she confronted as a black woman in the United States?
>
> Go to MindTap® to watch a video on Murray and learn how her story relates to the themes of this chapter.

At the same time, a mass movement opposing racial segregation emerged that included visionary leader Martin Luther King Jr., a host of activist organizations with varying strategies and tactics, and an army of everyday people—white and black, male and female. The movement came together to fight against Jim Crow at the ballot box and segregation in public conveyances, restaurants, and the nation's commercial transactions. The Civil Rights Movement, by exposing southern racism to a watchful nation and world community, inspired federal policies and court decisions that dismantled the legal infrastructure of racial discrimination. Murray's career was dedicated to abolishing Jim Crow, but she made sure that the rights revolution also challenged gender discrimination, which she called *Jane Crow*. A founding member of the National Organization for Women, she helped develop the legal arguments for Supreme Court decisions in favor of gender equality.

Yet the new laws and protections were not enough to rectify years of white rule and institutional racism, nor did they relieve the poverty that plagued blacks in the South as well as in the nation's cities. President Lyndon Johnson responded to the crisis of economic inequality by generating the largest expansion of the welfare state since the New Deal. As Murray's critique of Jane Crow attested, civil rights struggles also stimulated the movement for women's rights that pushed for employment equality with men and a critique of the postwar ideal of the happy suburban mother and housewife.

24-1

International Context for Civil and Human Rights

The newly founded UN reacted to the Holocaust and postwar global circumstances by advocating for human rights, a broad notion of universal and inalienable natural rights to nondiscrimination for all peoples and in all places. Here former First Lady Eleanor Roosevelt in 1948 holds up the UN Universal Declaration of Human Rights, which she played a key role in crafting.

Why do you think the UN made human rights one of its first major initiatives? How did World War II change the global demand for protections against vulnerable groups? From what you know of Roosevelt and women's rights activism, can you suggest why she played a key role in promoting human rights? ▶

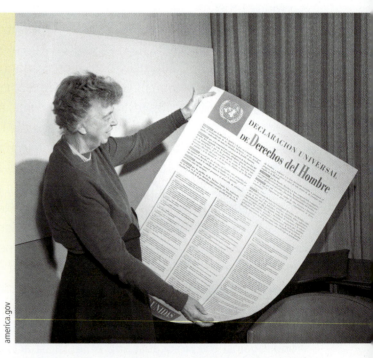

america.gov

The revolution against white supremacy, evident in global efforts for human rights, was made possible by a sea change in racial beliefs that emerged during and after World War II. Although racial segregation and discrimination remained entrenched in political, economic, and everyday life throughout the United States, war atrocities fostered the spirit of racial equality. The creation of the United Nations boosted racial egalitarianism and marked an important step in the U.S. campaign for civil rights. Although similar to human rights, civil rights in the United States were based not only in a UN treaty but also in U.S. law, particularly the Thirteenth and Fourteenth Amendments. In 1948, President Harry Truman took a major step for civil rights by desegregating the federal government and military personnel. The rise of the Cold War strengthened the momentum for civil rights because Soviet criticism of inequality in U.S. society compelled the leader of the free world to address its racism at home.

☞ As you read, pay attention to the struggle against racial prejudice that emerged in full force after World War II. What domestic and global circumstances enhanced this struggle? Which ones impeded it?

24-1a Legacies of a Race War

From the beginning, the United Nations exceeded the support for **human rights** contained in the Atlantic Charter and UN preparations

{ The UN influences civil rights reforms in the United States.

at Dumbarton Oaks, and proved a vast improvement from the League of Nations, which had rejected a racial equality clause at its founding in 1919. The UN charter's first article addressed the goal of promoting human rights and fundamental freedoms "for all without distinction to race, sex, language, or religion." Moreover, the first session of the UN's General Assembly approved a resolution opposing the systematic racism faced by Indians in South Africa, thus continuing the struggle for civil rights in that country that Mohandas Gandhi led in the late nineteenth and early twentieth centuries (see Chapter 21). But the United States, Britain, and white British Commonwealth nations (South Africa, Canada, and New Zealand) constituted a visible minority who voted against the resolution. South Africa's UN representative Jan Smuts complained bitterly that the organization had been taken over by "colored peoples" of the world.

The UN in December 1948 confirmed and elaborated its purpose by crafting the **Universal Declaration of Human Rights**, which Eleanor Roosevelt, who chaired the committee that wrote the document, called an "international Magna Carta of all men everywhere." Roosevelt, the former first lady, had been called by the NAACP's Walter White one of only two white American women who understood the experience of black Americans—the other

was Pearl S. Buck, a Nobel Prize-winning American writer and avid social justice activist. In the same month as the Universal Declaration of Human Rights was unveiled, the General Assembly voted to make genocide a crime of international law, whether perpetrated during wartime or not. At the same time, however, UN member nations balked at the petition sent by W.E.B. Du Bois and the NAACP proclaiming that racism against African Americans placed the United States in violation of international standards for human rights. Even in defeat, Du Bois revealed that the UN could provide a forum for advancing U.S. civil rights (Table 24.1).

24-1b U.S. Military and Racial Equality

The NAACP's Double-V campaign had asked racial minorities who had served in World War II to fight for victory over enemies abroad

{ U.S. veterans face discrimination that provokes racial reform.

and against racism at home. Upon their return to the United States, veterans of color realized that the racial battle at home was far from over. White veterans in Hood River, Oregon, removed the names of sixteen Japanese American servicemen from an American

human rights Universal and inalienable natural rights to life, liberty, pursuit of happiness, and nondiscrimination; codified in UN international treaties (unlike civil rights, which have a basis in the U.S. Constitution).

Universal Declaration of Human Rights Statement by the United Nations, approved in 1948, inspiring the proliferation of the principle of nondiscrimination in domestic and international laws around the world.

Table 24.1 UN Actions Promoting Human Rights, 1945–1965

When the fifty-one nations met in San Francisco to establish the United Nations, they made human rights a core reason and purpose for the newly established international body. The following are UN actions concerning human rights, many of which the United States initially did not support.

Year	Action
1945	UN Charter addresses human rights in six different articles
1946	Resolution opposing Discrimination of Indians in South Africa
1946	Commission on Human Rights established to set standards for human rights
1947	Sub-Commission on Prevention of Discrimination and Protection of Minorities established
1948	Universal Declaration of Human Rights
1948	Convention on the Prevention and Punishment of the Crime of Genocide
1956	Supplementary Convention on the Abolition of Slavery, the Slave Trade, and Institutions and Practices Similar to Slavery
1958	Convention Concerning Discrimination in Respect to Employment and Occupation
1960	Resolution opposing colonialism as a violation of human rights and supporting the granting of independence to colonized peoples
1961	Special UN committee to implement the resolution against colonialism
1962	Convention against Discrimination in Education
1965	International Convention on the Elimination of All Forms of Racial Discrimination
1966	International Covenant on Civil and Political Rights

Source: Lauren, Paul Gordon, *Power and Prejudice,* 2nd ed. Boulder, CO: Westview, 1996.

President's Committee on Civil Rights Including members from private industry, labor, and nongovernmental organizations this committee, established in October 1947, recommended sweeping reforms to provide equal opportunity to all races.

Legion honor roll for fallen soldiers, and only restored them in April 1945 after succumbing to intense pressure from Japanese American veterans, military officials, and the national media.

The burial of Felix Longoria, a Mexican American soldier who died in the Philippines, sparked another link between World War II veterans and civil rights activism. In January 1949, the army returned Longoria's body to his hometown of Three Rivers, Texas, where his widow asked the only funeral home in the city to hold a wake for her deceased husband. She was turned away because Longoria was not white. After protests from Mexican Americans, the national press responded by condemning the funeral home's actions as an affront to U.S. patriotism. Although the State Department concurred and privately encouraged the Longoria family to seek redress, the newly elected U.S. senator from Texas, Lyndon Baines Johnson, arranged to have Felix Longoria given a hero's burial at the nation's most hallowed grounds for fallen soldiers, Arlington National Cemetery.

The most consequential racist act targeting a veteran of color involved Isaac Woodard, who in February 1946 got into an argument with a white bus driver after Woodard returned late from a rest stop break. The driver called the South Carolina police and at the next bus stop the officers pulled Woodard off the bus and beat him, leaving the veteran, who was dressed in uniform, permanently blinded. A national outcry encouraged President Truman to order a federal investigation into the incident, which resulted in the indictment of several police officers who were later absolved of all charges by an all-white jury. Deeply upset, Truman established a special commission to investigate the nation's racial problems. The **President's Committee on Civil Rights** in October 1947 published *To Secure These Rights*, a 178-page report declaring that the "separate but equal doctrine is inconsistent with the fundamental equalitarianism of the U.S. way of life in that it marks groups with the brand of inferior status." Based on this report, Truman called on Congress to make lynching a federal crime and to prevent job discrimination, racial segregation, and voting rights infringements. When Congress failed to consider such legislation, the president used an executive order to desegregate the nation's armed forces and to outlaw racial discrimination in both federal employment and all private firms doing business with the government, which composed one-fifth of the U.S. economy by 1952. Although motivated by personal convictions, Truman was also concerned about Soviet criticism of U.S. race relations and winning the northern black vote in the 1948 election.

24-1c Signs of Immigration Reform

New international responsibilities initially made Congress more responsive to reforming immigration policy than to civil rights. The plight of

{ Racial reform also influences U.S. immigration policies.

Felix Longoria Funeral at Arlington, 1949 The racist treatment of veterans of color exposed the contradictions of U.S. ideals in fighting World War II to defeat Nazi and Japanese racism. This photo shows the burial of Felix Longoria, a Mexican American killed in the war, who was interred at Arlington Cemetery because his body would not be handled by a segregated Texas mortuary. ◄

MUTO; AL/Corbis

Everett Collection Historical/Alamy Stock Photo

Global Americans Born and raised in China, as the daughter of American missionary parents, **Pearl Sydenstricker Buck** was fluent in Chinese and, although a U.S. citizen, she identified with her birth country throughout her life. She is best known for being the third American to win the Nobel Prize for Literature, which was primarily a testament to her best-selling novel set in China, *The Good Earth* (1931). Buck's acceptance speech as a Nobel Laureate focused on the subject of the Chinese novel, explaining that "I am an American by birth and by ancestry," but "my earliest knowledge of story, of how to tell and write stories, came to me in China." In addition to her fiction, Buck also published extensively on current events, especially to correct misunderstandings of Asia and the developing world in general, as well as racial minorities in the United States. NAACP leader Walter White considered her, along with Eleanor Roosevelt, to be a white woman who understood African Americans. In 1949, Pearl Buck established Welcome House Adoption Program to cater to abandoned biracial children who were often the "most cruelly treated child" around the world. Welcome House initially focused on mixed race Asians, who Buck called *Amerasians*, the often unwanted consequence of U.S. military occupations Japan and Korean after World War II and the Korean War. Buck's efforts countered prejudice against mixed-race peoples and established the field of transpacific adoption.

displaced persons after World War II softened the nation's opposition to further immigration. Despite entrenched anti-Semitism in Congress, it would have damaged the nation's international reputation to turn away victims of Nazi persecution and others who had lost everything in the war. U.S. officials also sought to score points against the Soviets by granting asylum to the growing number of anti-Communist refugees fleeing Soviet-controlled Eastern Europe. Congress passed the Displaced Persons Act in June 1948 and a number of subsequent policies that circumvented the nation's restrictive immigration quotas. As a result, more than a million displaced persons and refugees came into the United States between 1945 and 1960.

Although most of the newcomers admitted were European, a smaller number of migrants from Asia reflected a significant transformation in the nation's long-standing policy of Asian exclusion. As an anti-Communist measure, Congress permitted refugees from the People's Republic of China and North Korea to enter the country. Moreover, by granting Japan an immigration quota in 1952 and enabling those immigrants to become U.S. citizens, it continued a trend, started during World War II, of dismantling the systematic discrimination of Asian Americans. Small influxes of Asian immigrants transformed Chinatowns and Filipino communities from bachelor societies to family-based communities, as wives were now able to join overseas husbands. Some of these women were war brides from Japan and Korea married to white U.S. military personnel. Their mixed marriages were a subject of curiosity in all-white communities even though many states, including California and others in the West that had long discriminated against Asian Americans, overturned laws banning miscegenation. These same states, in part due to the influence of the UN Declaration of Human Rights,

also repealed discriminatory laws discouraging Asian immigrants from owning or leasing agricultural land. A final telling sign of the abrupt change in attitude toward Asians was the first contingent of "Hiroshima maidens" who came to New York in May 1955 seeking plastic surgery to repair injuries and scars from the atomic bomb. The *Dayton News* revealed the nation's global caretaking role by expressing sympathy toward the bomb survivors: "We're sorry it had to be you—and we want to help you!"

24-1d Anticommunism and Black Loyalty

A crucial moment in the postwar decline of racial discrimination came in 1947 when Jackie Robinson and Larry Doby broke the barrier against black players in major league baseball. Both players were former American GIs and were chosen because of their baseball talent as well as ability to weather racist taunts and actions on the field. Robinson won Rookie of the Year honors for the Brooklyn Dodgers and within two seasons became the league's Most Valuable Player. Within a couple of years, most major league teams integrated their clubs, although the Boston Red Sox held out until 1959 (see Figure 24.1).

{ Racial reforms become decidedly anti-Communist.

Robinson, it turned out, was perfectly suited to become a symbol for postwar antiracism. In addition to being a four-sport star at UCLA, he had vocally opposed racial segregation and while serving in the military was court-martialed (later rescinded) for refusing to move from the white-only section of an army bus near the base

Jackie Robinson and Larry Doby, 1947 Jackie Robinson receives most of the accolades for breaking the color barrier in major league baseball in 1947. Less remembered is that Larry Doby broke the barrier in the same year and became an all-star for the Cleveland Indians. The next year he and former Negro professional league star pitcher Satchel Paige helped the team win the World Series. ▲

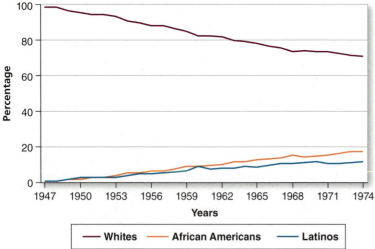

Figure 24.1 Race in Major League Baseball, 1947–1975 When the last Major League team was integrated in 1959, African Americans comprised nearly 9 percent of all rosters, which was almost the same as the proportion of blacks in the United States (10 percent). In the same year, Latino players comprised more than 6 percent of rosters. Such integration put a severe strain on Negro professional baseball, whose national league folded in 1948 while its American league held on for another decade. ▲
Source: Society for American Baseball Research. http://sabr.org/bioproj/topic/baseball-demographics–1947–2012, accessed January 22, 2016.

where he was stationed in Fort Hood, Texas. During the height of Cold War fears, Robinson's anticommunism was also crucial to his becoming an international icon for racial reform. In July 1949, he was called to testify at the HUAC investigation of Paul Robeson, the well-known African American singer and actor who made headlines by saying that blacks would not fight against the Soviet Union because of that nation's opposition to racism (see Global Americans, Chapter 20).

Robeson, like many racial minorities and nationalists in colonized countries in the 1920s and 1930s, had been drawn to the Communist Party's commitment to racial equality. The younger Robinson respected Robeson's many talents, but did not support his views of the Soviet Union. "We [African Americans] can win our fight without the Communists," he told HUAC, "and we don't want their help." At the same hearing, the NAACP's Walter White stressed that the vast majority of African Americans did not share Robeson's views and were solidly anti-Communist. In the end, the Red crusade against Robeson ruined his concert career and caused him in 1958 to flee with his family to Europe, where he was warmly received in the Soviet Union and other Eastern bloc. Robeson preceded his friend W.E.B. Du Bois in escaping political persecution by relocating overseas. His difficulties in the United States reflected the larger McCarthy era purge of leftists in the Communist Party, labor movement, and Hollywood.

24-1e School Desegregation and the Supreme Court

While major league baseball was being integrated, civil rights lawyers kept chipping away at Jim Crow in

{ Breakthroughs for racial reform emerge via public education.

the nation's public schools by adhering to the **NAACP's legal strategy** worked out in the 1930s by Charles Hamilton Houston, dean of Howard University's law school. Houston was one of the reasons why Pauli Murray and other civil rights activists came to study at Howard. He, along with his protégé Thurgood Marshall and a team of other black attorneys, used the courts to require states and school districts to live up to the letter of the *Plessy* decision (1896) by providing fully equal schools for blacks. They believed such a requirement would lead to integration as the cheaper and more expedient option. In 1950, the NAACP team won the *Sweatt v. Painter* case in which the U.S. Supreme Court required integration of the University of Texas law school because the state could not provide an equal education for black students. A year later, the Court handed down a similar ruling with respect to university education in Oklahoma.

Another challenge came with *Mendez v. Westminster*. Gonzalo Mendez, a Mexican American tenant farmer, worked with the **League of United Latin American Citizens (LULAC)**, a Mexican American civil rights organization, to take the school district of Orange Country, California, to federal court so that his children could attend the city of Westminster's all-white schools. The U.S. Court of Appeals for the Ninth Circuit affirmed the lower court ruling upholding Mendez's right to send his daughter to the white school. The California legislature quickly followed the verdict with legislation outlawing the state's segregated schools. California's governor Earl Warren, who approved of this desegregation and signed it into law, would later become chief justice of the U.S. Supreme Court presiding over the landmark **Brown v. Board of Education of Topeka, Kansas** (1954), which overturned the long-standing *Plessy decision* (1896) that had sanctioned racial segregation.

Brown originated in 1951 when Oliver L. Brown, an African American welder and assistant pastor at a local church, worked with the NAACP to allow his daughter Linda to attend a white elementary school in Topeka. Unlike earlier test cases, *Brown* directly challenged the constitutionality of *Plessy*'s separate-but-equal doctrine. By 1954, the case, along with four others of its kind, made its way to the Supreme Court, where Chief Justice Warren presided over a unanimous 9-0 decision finding that "Separate education facilities are inherently unequal." In making his decision, Warren was aware of Cold War pressures to improve race relations that the Justice Department emphasized in its friend of the court brief for the Brown case, which included a quote from Secretary of State Dean Acheson lamenting mounting criticism in the foreign press concerning racism within the United States. More explicitly, Warren's decision relied upon studies of racism by social scientists including the psychologists Kenneth and Maime Clark, who showed that racial segregation ruined self-esteem in black children.

The *Brown* decision disappointed President Eisenhower, who supported gradual, not immediate, civil rights. He had nominated Earl Warren as chief justice of the Supreme Court based on the Californian's reputation for law and order that included, when he was the state's attorney general, a racist campaign that advanced Japanese American internment.

When Warren came out as the architect of the *Brown* decision, Eisenhower said that nominating him for chief justice was the "biggest damned-fool mistake I ever made."

A year after the *Brown* decision, the Supreme Court moderated its position. It responded to school board requests for relief from the burdens of immediate integration by issuing an ambiguous decision for desegregation to proceed "with all deliberate speed." Known as *Brown II*, this ruling gave school districts the option to initiate a gradual rather than immediate end to segregation. Consequently, many white Southerners were encouraged to slow down the implementation of the *Brown* decision, if not ignore it altogether.

NAACP's legal strategy Approach to fight racial discrimination primarily through the courts.

League of United Latin American Citizens (LULAC) Civil rights organization started in 1929 by Mexican American veterans whose aim was to end the discrimination of Latinos.

Brown v. Board of Education of Topeka, Kansas Landmark U.S. Supreme Court ruling in 1954 overturning the legal precedent for racial segregation in public schools.

The LIFE Picture Collection/Getty Images

Dwight D. Eisenhower Speaks with Earl Warren In talking with Chief Justice Warren (right in photo) as the Supreme Court was considering the *Brown* case, President Eisenhower told him that white segregationists were "not bad people" and that all "they are concerned about is to see that their sweet little girls are not required to sit alongside some big overgrown Negroes." Hoping for a gradual solution, Eisenhower was unhappy with the Court's verdict to end racial segregation in public schools with all deliberate speed. ▲

Civil Rights Movement and Southern Race Relations

This statue honoring the "A&T Four"—Franklin McCain, Ezell Blair Jr. (later known as Jibreel Khazan), Joseph McNeil, and David Richmond—stands on the campus of North Carolina A&T in Greensboro, North Carolina. As college freshmen in February 1960, these young men protested against racial segregation at a local Woolworth's store lunch counter.

Why do you think these men have been commemorated? What might explain the way in which they are positioned, standing erect and looking straight ahead with arms hanging down on both sides? What does their appearance and dress suggest about the nature of their protest? ▶

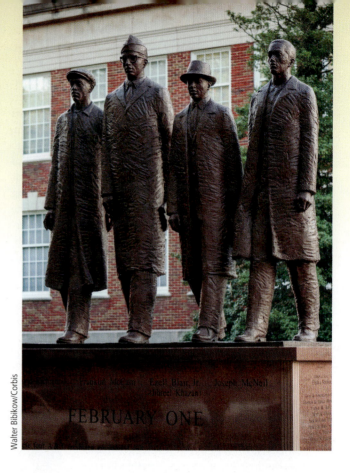

Walter Bibikow/Corbis

Highlander Folk School
Founded in 1932 by labor organizers, the school trained Martin Luther King Jr., Rosa Parks, and other civil rights leaders in tactics of civil disobedience.

Although civil rights activists, along with the UN, and the U.S. federal government made important progress in countering racial segregation and discrimination after World War II, the pace of change was not fast enough for African Americans who lived with Jim Crow's everyday indignities. Galvanized by the brutal lynching of fourteen-year-old Emmett Till, ordinary people formed the backbone of the Civil Rights Movement that received national attention in 1955 when a prolonged dispute over segregated bus seating in Montgomery, Alabama sparked grassroots protests led by a twenty-six-year-old Baptist minister named Martin Luther King Jr. The movement spread throughout the South requiring federal troops to ensure the integration of an Arkansas high school as well as restaurants, starting in Greensboro, North Carolina. These local struggles awakened the nation and world to the problem of southern race relations, setting in motion a pattern of black protest, white resistance, and federal intervention that would have an impact far beyond the South.

☞ As you read, focus on how the Civil Rights Movement developed over time. What were its key turning points, and why and how did they occur? How did white Southerners and the federal government respond to the Civil Rights Movement? How did their responses shape the course of the movement?

24-2a Emmett Till and the Montgomery Bus Boycott

In August 1955, two boys fishing in the Tallahatchie River in Mississippi discovered fourteen-year-old Emmett

{ The vicious murder of a black youth inspires protests that fuel the Civil Rights Movement.

Till's decomposed body. Three days before, Till, who had been visiting from Chicago, was abducted at gunpoint from his uncle's house by two white men who vowed to get even with the black teenager for allegedly whistling suggestively at the wife of one of the men. Although the idea of sexual relations between black men and white women always had been charged in the South, Till's murder shocked both white and black Southerners. After Till's mother, Mamie Till Bradley, insisted on an open casket funeral, photographs of the boy's bloated and mangled body triggered widespread revulsion. The Soviets, whose crackdown on protests in support of Hungary's independence the U.S. had criticized, used the occasion to denounce the United States as hypocritical. "These accusations ring particularly false," reported *Pravda*, the official Soviet news agency, in referring to the Till case, "because the United States does not protect the elementary rights of man." The outrage over Till's murder reached fever pitch when the accused murderers were acquitted by an all-white jury. Once the two suspects could no longer be tried for the crime, they admitted to killing Till. Jury members said they knew as much, but had acquitted the men to send a message against "sassy niggers making passes at white women."

The racism and miscarriage of justice involving Emmett Till intensified African Americans' demands for an immediate end to white supremacy. Turning her horror at Till's death into action, Rosa Parks, a black seamstress and hospital worker in Montgomery, Alabama, was arrested for refusing to give up her seat on the bus to a white man. An NAACP organizer who had learned Gandhian passive

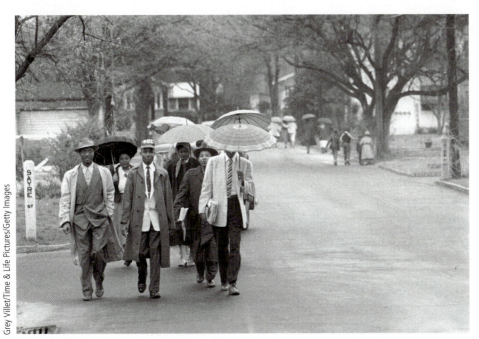

African American Commuters Walk to Work, Montgomery, 1956 As president of the organization behind the Montgomery Bus Boycott, Martin Luther King Jr. backed a federal lawsuit designed to desegregate Montgomery buses and supported a car-pooling system that enabled the boycott to continue throughout the year. Many boycotters also choose to walk instead of ride the bus. ◄

Montgomery Improvement Association Organized by Montgomery's black community leaders and out-of-town black ministers in the wake of Rosa Parks's arrest in December 1955, this association led the famous boycott protesting racial segregation of city buses in Montgomery, Alabama.

White Citizens' Council Network of organizations concentrated in the South prompted by the Brown decision to protest against desegregation mainly in public schools.

Montgomery bus boycott Protest against racial segregation on Montgomery, Alabama, buses and the mistreatment of African American riders.

Southern Christian Leadership Council (SCLC) Organization of African American church leaders, including King, providing provided crucial leadership for the Civil Rights Movement; founded in January 1957.

resistance techniques at the **Highlander Folk School**, Parks was aware of the momentum for desegregation stimulated by the *Brown* decision. But her main motive for getting arrested had to do with the daily indignities that blacks suffered on public transportation. Like Pauli Murray and Jackie Robinson before her, Parks took a stand against this type of abuse: "People always say that I didn't give up my seat because I was tired, but that isn't true. I was not tired physically, or no more tired than I usually was at the end of a working day. . . . No, the only tired I was, was tired of giving in."

After Parks's arrest on December 1, 1955, the Women's Political Council (a leading group of Montgomery's black women), the local NAACP, and prominent out-of-town Christian ministers organized the **Montgomery Improvement Association**, which conducted a massive boycott of city buses, calling for the hiring of African American bus drivers and restraints against the brutal enforcement of racial segregation on public transportation. The association chose as its president Reverend Martin Luther King Jr., the pastor of Dexter Avenue Baptist Church in Atlanta. The city's patience wore thin with the boycott in January as the mayor and city commissioners joined the **White Citizens' Council** of Mississippi, a popular segregationist organization prompted by the *Brown* decision. Soon the police arrested King, and a bomb exploded at his house while he and his family were away. The bombing generated great sympathy and financial contributions from white liberals and cemented King's image as the spokesperson for a broad-based movement for civil rights.

The **Montgomery bus boycott** continued for over a year, ending in December 1956, a month after the U.S. Supreme Court upheld a lower court ruling that declared bus segregation in Alabama violated the Fourteenth Amendment's equal protection clause. The civil rights activists had won an important victory that heightened King's popularity and influence. In January 1957, the Montgomery Improvement Association helped launch the **Southern Christian Leadership Council (SCLC)**, a newly established civil rights organization led by black ministers practicing nonviolent means to end all forms of racial segregation. King served as the organization's first president.

24-2b Little Rock and Greensboro

The Civil Rights Movement spread to Little Rock, Arkansas, in 1957 when the **Little Rock Nine,** African American teenagers carefully selected by the NAACP, sought to attend a white high school following the *Brown* decision. Arkansas governor Orval Faubus called on the state's National Guard to block the black students from entering Central High School. The move provoked a constitutional crisis that ended in September 1957 when President Eisenhower sent one thousand federal troops to Little Rock to ensure that African Americans could attend the school unharmed. Meanwhile, the president took control of the Arkansas National Guard from Faubus, and for the

{ The Civil Rights Movement focuses on implementing desegregation decisions.

Grey Villet/Time & Life Pictures/Getty Images

History without Borders

Racial, Ethnic, and Caste Discrimination

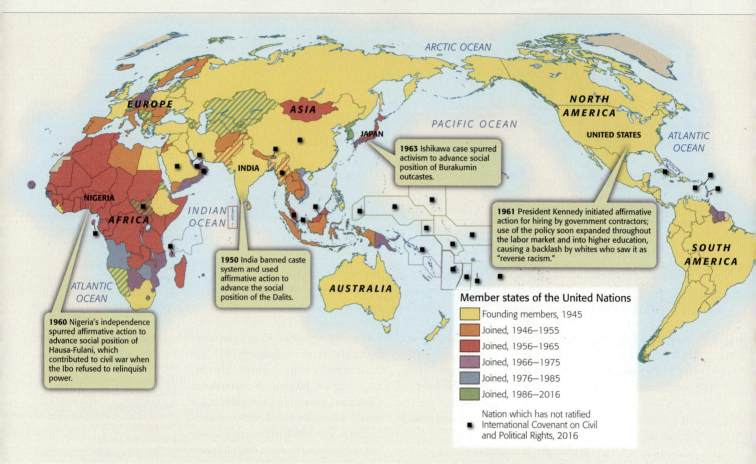

1963 Ishikawa case spurred activism to advance social position of Burakumin outcastes.

1961 President Kennedy initiated affirmative action for hiring by government contractors; use of the policy soon expanded throughout the labor market and into higher education, causing a backlash by whites who saw it as "reverse racism."

1950 India banned caste system and used affirmative action to advance the social position of the Dalits.

1960 Nigeria's independence spurred affirmative action to advance social position of Hausa-Fulani, which contributed to civil war when the Ibo refused to relinquish power.

Member states of the United Nations

- Founding members, 1945
- Joined, 1946–1955
- Joined, 1956–1965
- Joined, 1966–1975
- Joined, 1976–1985
- Joined, 1986–2016
- ■ Nation which has not ratified International Covenant on Civil and Political Rights, 2016

United Nations Member States, 1945-2016 Based on affirmative action programs practiced in India, Japan, Nigeria, and the United States, the United Nations Committee on Human Rights in 1969 announced that the overwhelming number of nations that had (or would) ratify the International Covenant on Civil and Political Rights must redress various forms of discrimination through special action, such as preferential treatment accorded to underprivileged group. ▲

The shocking murder of the young Emmett Till and other racist crimes committed against African Americans returned global attention to the horror of white supremacy that had killed millions of European Jews and other supposedly inferior racial groups during World War II. Asians and Africans also perpetrated crimes against groups of people based upon inherited ancestry. No country or people in the postwar world held a monopoly on this kind of discrimination.

India, the newly independent nation that impressed the world with its nonviolent revolution, was one of the worst offenders of human rights due to its ancient social hierarchy based on divisions known as "castes." While complex and unique unto itself, the four-tiered caste system in India was similar to the Jim Crow South discrimination in terms of its rigid and inherited ranking of groups, as well as its culturally accepted discrimination and violence perpetrated against the lowest people in the social order. In India these were the Dalits (the oppressed), who did not even have a position in the caste hierarchy—which made them "outcaste" peoples. Mohandas Gandhi bucked tradition in calling them *Harijans* (children of God), and in 1950, India outlawed the caste system and was the first country to use affirmation action policies—in this case to advance Dalit education and social

mobility. But as in the United States, change came slowly and with great resistance.

Postwar Japan also made concerted efforts to rectify centuries of discrimination against its own outcastes, known as Burakumin (people of rural hamlets). Although the nation's caste system was abandoned in 1871 with Japan's modernization, and social equality was expanded in the postwar constitution, de jure Burakumin discrimination continued, especially in terms of housing, employment, and marriage. After World War II, the Buraku Liberation League emerged to raise awareness of these problems and fight, along with Japan's Socialist and Communist Parties, for the

Dinodia Photos/Alamy Stock Photo

Gandhi at Bhangi Untouchables Colony, Delhi, India, 1946 Mohandas Gandhi went on hunger strikes to protest the segregation of Indian untouchable castes (Dalit). His activism also involved changing the name of this group to "Harijan," or children of God. Yet Dalits themselves did not always welcome Gandhi's actions on their behalf, with some dubious as to the intentions of the privileged castes. Could a social revolution really come from above, or did it need to be generated from the Dalits themselves? ◄

AP Images/Koichiro Morita

Tokyo Demonstrators Scuffle with Riot Police, Tokyo, 1974 The Kazuo Ishikawa case sparked ongoing protests in Japan when in 1964 he was sentenced to death for the rape and murder of a sixteen-year-old girl. Activists claimed his arrest and conviction were the result of discrimination against his outcaste class, the burakumin. ◄

group's civil rights. One of the major cases centered on the 1963 arrest of Kazuo Ishikawa, a resident of a Burakumin community in Sayama City, who was accused of and sentenced to death for the rape and murder of a high school girl. Activists proclaimed the Ishikawa case was a miscarriage of justice and that he was falsely accused because of his social group status. Ishikawa's sentence was subsequently reduced to life imprisonment, and Japan too went on to enact affirmative action measures designed to promote speedy integration.

When Nigeria became independent in 1960, it too confronted the problem of social hierarchy based on inherited difference. In this case it centered on rival groups of black Africans, especially the Ibos, who descended from the country's southeast, and the Hausa-Fulani, who were based in the north. British colonialism had elevated the Ibos to become an educated, Christianized class who taught school and managed much of the empire's bureaucracy in West Africa, including in northern regions. The Hausa-Fulani, followers of Islam

who resisted British missionary education, played little, if any, role in colonial administration. In 1951, only one person out of a northern population of 16 million had a university degree. When independence came, the Hausa-Fulani used affirmative action to advance their uneducated brethren into political positions in the north, while expelling the more qualified Ibo and others. Such ethnic conflict proliferated throughout Nigeria leading to an Ibo-led military coup in which the president, a northerner, was assassinated. Bloody riots erupted against the Ibo in the north that led southerners to secede from the nation, which, in turn, provoked civil war.

To compare struggles against Jim Crow in the U.S. South to simultaneous conflicts over racial, ethnic, and caste discrimination in India, Japan, and Nigeria is in no way to diminish the hateful and unique forms of racism that African Americans experienced. But such a comparison reveals global parallels to U.S. race relations in three ways. First, like the United States, India, Japan, and Nigeria possessed entrenched and rigidly

enforced systems of social hierarchy based on inherited characteristics like race, ethnicity, or caste. Second, in the United States, India, Japan, and Nigeria, laws banning discrimination, while symbolically important, were not enough to create equality. Finally, eventually all of these countries used affirmative action programs in order to address past discrimination, and in each case the results were mixed at best.

Critical Thinking Questions

▶ How did race relations in the American South after World War II compare to social divisions in India, Japan, and Nigeria?

▶ What solutions did each country try for resolving entrenched discrimination, and what limited their success?

Go to MindTap® to engage with an interactive version of **History without Borders: Racial, Ethnic, and Caste Discrimination.** Learn from an interactive map, view related video, and respond to critical thinking questions.

Bettmann/Corbis

Global Americans

Thurgood Marshall studied at Lincoln University, a historically black college in Pennsylvania, with the Harlem Renaissance poet Langston Hughes and the Cotton Club musician Cab Calloway. (Ghana's first president Kwame Nkrumah graduated from Lincoln nine years after Marshall.) After graduation, Marshall attended Howard University, where he fell under the influence of its dean, Charles Hamilton Houston, and graduated first in his class in 1933. Marshall went on to join the NAACP and lead its legal strategy to overthrow racial segregation, which included the victory in *Brown v. Board of Education* (1954). In 1967, he was the first African American appointed to the U.S. Supreme Court. Before this, Marshall was invited to newly independent Kenya in 1960 to participate in writing the nation's Bill of Rights. Drawing on the UN Declaration for Human Rights as well as the constitutions of newly independent Nigeria and Malaya, his efforts centered on the legal principle that "All persons are equal before the law and are entitled without discrimination or distinction of any kind . . . to equal protection of the law." As it turned out Kenyans did not follow Marshall's recommendation and did not accord equal protections either to the minority of white settlers who comprised the former colonial ruling class, or long-standing residents from India. Nevertheless, his involvement showed how ideas of American civil rights spread around the world and were adapted, or not, to differing societies and circumstances.

Little Rock Nine African American students enrolled at Little Rock's Central High School whose testing of desegregation orders in 1957 set off a storm of white protests.

remaining eight months of the school year, federal troops protected the Little Rock Nine. Not since Reconstruction had the federal government asserted its constitutional power to enforce civil rights against calls for states' rights.

Eisenhower's intervention in Little Rock stemmed not only from his defense of federal authority over the states, but also from Cold War concerns. He was aware that massive resistance to civil rights was damaging America's global image as a beacon of democracy. The Soviets highlighted U.S. civil rights violations as the sign of a white supremacist society that was ill equipped for world

leadership. In a televised address to the nation during the Little Rock crisis, Eisenhower squarely addressed the international implications of American racism in saying, "Our enemies are gloating over this incident and using it everywhere to misrepresent our whole nation. We are portrayed as a violator of those standards of conduct which the peoples of the world united to proclaim in the Charter of the United Nations."

In February 1960, the Civil Rights Movement entered a new phase when four freshmen at North Carolina Agricultural and Technical (A&T) State University in Greensboro, North Carolina, directly confronted racial segregation by sitting down at a lunch counter in a store where they were allowed to buy school supplies but not to

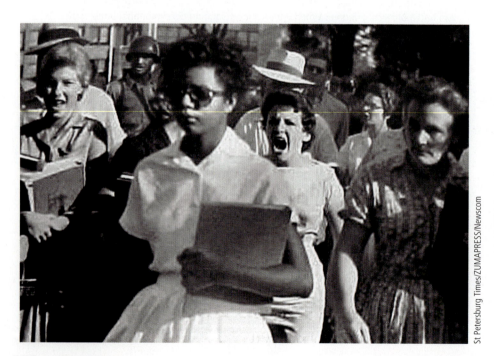

St Petersburg Times/ZUMAPRESS/Newscom

Angry White Mob Protests Little Rock Nine at Central High, 1957 After a three-week standoff with President Eisenhower in September 1957, Arkansas governor Orval Faubus removed the state guardsmen from Little Rock's Central High, allowing an angry mob of white parents and supporters to chase off the black students while beating up seven journalists (three white, four black). This "Black Monday" forced Eisenhower to send in federal troops to thwart massive resistance and allow the Little Rock Nine to attend school. ◄

eat. Their sit-in protest electrified students at black colleges throughout the South. Within two weeks, the lunch-counter struggle had spread to fifteen cities in five states, thus politicizing a new generation of African Americans who were impatient waiting for court victories against segregation to become everyday reality. By August 1960, King and Ella Baker of SCLC worked with young activists to found the **Student Nonviolent Coordinating Committee (SNCC)**, which joined with the Congress of Racial Equality (CORE) to take civil rights struggles in a bolder, more assertive direction.

Established in Chicago in 1942, CORE grew out of the largely white pacifist Fellowship of Reconciliation, which supported conscientious objectors during World War II. One of these was James L. Farmer, an African American who came to embrace nonviolent resistance while studying at Howard University in the late 1930s, just before Pauli Murray entered its law school. A founder of CORE, Farmer and other CORE members took part in some of the first organized sit-in protests when they had successfully integrated Chicago restaurants during World War II. After working for America's Socialist Party, Farmer in the late 1950s returned to civil rights struggles, first with the NAACP and then back at CORE. In 1961, he led an interracial group on a **"freedom ride"** during which they sat in sections reserved for whites while traveling on buses throughout the South. A white mob in Alabama attacked and beat the "freedom riders" while also setting their Greyhound bus ablaze. Freedom riders actually sought to provoke this kind of violence in order to highlight to growing audiences outside the South the failure of southern states to observe Supreme Court rulings, which banned Jim Crow on interstate transportation, bus stops, and train stations, such as the one ending the Montgomery bus boycott.

The youthful SNCC members expanded the freedom ride campaign while at the same time launching a grass roots strategy of empowering rural people to lead their own struggles, rather than simply following the NAACP or King and the SCLC. This "bottom-up" strategy transformed the Civil Rights Movement from a drive for legal and political reform to a call for social revolution.

24-2c Perspectives of Movement Activists

Since the Montgomery bus boycott, Martin Luther King Jr. remained the movement's most recognized figure. Charismatic and a spell-binding orator, King became celebrated across the nation mainly because his vision of interracial democracy was consistent with postwar sensibilities. Like Walter White and Jackie Robinson, he asserted the loyalty of black Americans and warned that civil rights struggles needed to be ever vigilant against "exploitation by Communist forces."

{ Civil Rights Movement activists express varying positions on strategy, tactics, and leadership.

And like Pauli Murray and James L. Farmer, he assured that racial reform was best achieved through nonviolent means. Known as the "American Gandhi," King, along with Rosa Parks and labor activists, had been taught tactics of civil disobedience at the Highlander Folk School. Owing to his Christianity, anticommunism, and nonviolence, King attracted widespread national and global support for the Civil Rights Movement, including sizable financial contributions.

But King was more than just a symbol of the nation's best intentions. Despite his rejection of communism as giving too much power to the state, he did not embrace U.S. capitalism. Privately, he chose the path of democratic socialism that combined the country's commitment to political freedoms with the emphasis on the government's responsibility to respect workers' and poor people's economic rights. His model for democratic socialism was Sweden, not the autocratic socialism of the Soviet Union. King appreciated Gandhi not only for his nonviolent tactics, but also for his rejection of material possessions and identification with outcaste peoples. The preacher's concerns about economic justice also drew him to the black labor organizer A. Philip Randolph, who since the 1920s was a major figure in linking the struggle for civil rights with the U.S. labor movement. Finally, King's interest in socialism put him in good stead with Third World leaders such as Ghana's Kwame Nkrumah and India's first prime minister, Jawaharal Nehru, both of whom advocated nonalignment, refusing to ally with either the Soviet Union or United States in the Cold War. Thus, there were two sides to King: the crusader working to desegregate the South and the radical seeking to transform the entire country into a model of democratic socialism.

King's complex motivations reflected those of the Civil Rights Movement as a whole. The African Americans who risked their lives and livelihoods for the movement were not necessarily in it for the same reasons. King himself recognized differences between middle-class blacks like himself and the working-class blacks who constituted the bulk of the Montgomery boycotters. To the middle class, the boycott was a sign that blacks would no longer tolerate demeaning segregation, while to the workers, it was a way to expose an economic system that exploited black labor. While the middle-class wanted equal respect, the working class wanted equal pay.

The nature of leadership proved another division within the movement. Whereas organizations such as NAACP and SCLC relied on the "talented tenth" of blacks to lead the black masses, SNCC wanted to help them to articulate and advance their own struggles. The talents of someone like King proved crucial for soliciting valuable support from outside the South and inspiring a mass movement. But longtime female

Student Nonviolent Coordinating Committee (SNCC) Founded in August 1960, the committee introduced to the Civil Rights Movement new and more provocative tactics, like sit-in protests.

"freedom ride" Tactic of riding in the whites-only section of segregated interstate buses to provoke violent responses; used effectively by Congress of Racial Equality (CORE) starting in 1961.

activists like Septima Clark and Ella Baker encouraged him to promote a bottom-up approach. Clark asked King "not to lead all the marches himself, but instead to develop leaders who could lead their own marches." Baker pushed him to reach out to rural blacks whom the movement all but ignored. Although neither were able to change SCLC's top-down leadership style, Baker was able to ensure that the young SNCC activists took on the bottom-up priorities that she championed.

Confronting a virtually all-male leadership, Clark and Baker also opposed sexism within the movement. Although King and other civil rights leaders knew that black women were invaluable soldiers for the struggle, they discounted their leadership potential. This was a classic form of male chauvinism, but for black men who had been stripped of their manhood by white racism, it took on special significance. Much of the motivation for the civil rights struggles came from the desire by both men and women to give black men decent jobs so that they could provide for their families. For many black women, an economically stable, male-oriented household, common in white suburbs at the time, would be a welcome step-up on the social ladder. In this way, Murray's criticism of **Jane Crow** did not possess a large appeal in the black community until after the proliferation of feminism in the 1970s.

24-2d Perspectives of White Resisters

As with black civil rights activists, the perspectives of white resisters were not all the same. Their response to the movement can be divided into two groups: those who actively resisted integration and those who accepted the inevitability of integration but sought to limit it to superficial levels.

> Resistance to civil rights reforms reflects growing diversity in the white South.

The first group engaged in **massive resistance** to civil rights reforms, and consisted largely of white Southerners. Its leaders included governors such as Alabama's George Wallace and Arkansas's Orval Faubus, and other high-ranking politicians whose electoral base was in rural counties. Immediately after the *Brown* decision, one hundred and one members of Congress signed a **southern manifesto** to "resist forced integration by any lawful means." The resistance coalesced in White Citizens' Councils that with more than two hundred fifty thousand members held significant clout in state and local governments. In addition, at least ten southern states passed **interposition**

laws that declared the *Brown* decision unconstitutional in order to prevent racial integration. Schools closed rather than integrate and public funds went to various "academies" that excluded blacks. In addition, the resistance garnered support from the business community, which during the Montgomery bus boycott, for example, put pressure on white employers to fire civil rights activists from their jobs and to cut off supplies and loans to black farmers and businesses that supported the movement. Finally, white resisters did not limit themselves to political and economic tactics, but engaged in repeated and systematic violence, including murder, designed to intimidate civil rights workers. The notoriously racist and nativist Ku Klux Klan, that garnered national attention during Reconstruction as well as during the 1920s, rose again as a vehicle of resistance and terror.

Yet there was another white South that embraced the nation's new postwar economy rather than looking back to the region's segregationist past. Five southern states (Texas, Tennessee, Florida, Maryland, and North Carolina) rejected massive resistance and implemented the *Brown* decision without major incident. Even within those states engaging in massive resistance, some county and city governments, as well as newspapers, adopted a gradual, rather than hostile, approach to integration. In this way, both Little Rock's mayor and its leading newspaper opposed Governor Faubus's showdown at Central High, pleading with Eisenhower to send federal troops.

Southern acceptance of civil rights stemmed from the wave of postwar prosperity that benefited the South and the rest of the nation. Prosperity expanded the South's higher education institutions, white-collar professions, high-tech industries, and suburban neighborhoods. The average Southerner's income rose from 50 percent of the national average in 1940 to 77 percent in 1960. The region's economy attracted waves of northern professionals while the mechanization of the cotton industry and switch to less labor-intensive crops such as soybeans and peanuts sent an equal number of black and white agricultural workers away from the South. Southern suburbanites were most receptive to limited racial reform.

A revealing expression of the post-World War II South was the open-school movement that occurred in Atlanta, Georgia. The struggle pitted white, upper-middle class women against the state's segregationist governor, Ernest Vandiver. Shocked at the resistance to integration in Little Rock, the women established Help Our Public Education (HOPE) and campaigned against Vandiver's reelection in the name of integrating Atlanta schools so that the city would be in compliance with the *Brown* decision. The women framed the issue as in the best interest of white children and the city's overall commerce and industry. In so doing, HOPE gave little, if any, credence to the perspectives of black activists or the social justice reasons for civil rights. HOPE won huge support in urban and suburban Atlanta, forcing Vandiver to give up massive

Jane Crow System of gender and sex segregation in which women suffer discrimination.

massive resistance Fierce public opposition to civil rights struggles and laws by a vocal and active portion of white Southerners.

southern manifesto Document signed by one hundred one members of the U.S. Congress, nearly all from the South, opposing Supreme Court orders to desegregate public places.

interposition Legal theory, often seen as synonymous with nullification, through which a state or group of states has the right to oppose federal rulings.

resistance. But the floodgates to integration did not open; instead, local school boards used a host of mechanisms to severely limit the number of African Americans in formerly all-white schools. This pattern of resistance through tokenization would become the norm throughout the nation as suburbanites in all regions would come to see meaningful racial integration as a threat to property values and the quality of neighborhood schools.

24-3

Enactment of Rights-Based Liberalism

King highlighted the March on Washington in August 1963 with his stirring "I Have a Dream" speech that envisioned an America where persons "will not be judged by the color of their skin but by the content of their character." The signs held by activists in this photograph reveal the breadth of issues subsumed under the rubric of civil rights.

Why do you think that voting rights, jobs, and decent housing were important to civil rights activists? ▶

Go to MindTap® to practice history with the Chapter 24 **Primary Source Writing Activity: Peak of the Civil Rights Movement.** Read and view primary sources and respond to a writing prompt.

Historical/Corbis

The peak of the Civil Rights Movement occurred during the early 1960s when conflict over civil rights at home as well as condemnation of racism around the world pressured Presidents Kennedy and Johnson to ensure the enactment of major civil and voting rights legislation. These were the goals that movement activists had been working toward. Yet because winning political rights did little to help millions of poor, unemployed black Americans within and outside the South, attention turned to securing economic rights. President Johnson urged Congress to enact a historic package of legislation that provided historic social welfare rights, liberalized immigration policy, and offered new federal support for the aged, the natural environment, consumers, and those lacking health care insurance.

☞ As you read, pay attention to the main components of the U.S. "rights-based liberalism." What problems did these rights intend to resolve?

24-3a New Frontiers for Civil Rights

The first televised presidential debate in 1960 presented a visual contrast between the youthful good looks of the Democrat candidate John

{ The Civil Rights Movement employs new tactics to encourage major legislation.

F. Kennedy and the staid and somewhat uneasy appearance of the Republican Richard Nixon. The reality was that both men were ardent cold warriors with weak records on civil rights. Kennedy, who barely won the election, owed his victory to support from crucial southern states that disenfranchised black voters. Because his chances for reelection depended upon votes from white southern Democrats, the new president did not act quickly to fulfill campaign promises he had made to black voters.

Yet mounting international pressure against racial segregation in the United States forced the president's hand. Acknowledging such pressure, Secretary of State Dean Rusk admitted, "The biggest single burden that we carry on our backs in our foreign relations in the 1960s is the problem of racial discrimination." Meanwhile, UN representatives from newly independent African and Asian nations pressured the General Assembly to adopt the Declaration of the Granting of Independence to Colonial Countries and Peoples, which condemned colonialism as a violation of the UN Charter and Declaration of Human Rights, and a threat to world peace. Another sign of the growing power of Afro-Asian nations was the election of U Thant as UN Secretary-General in 1961. Thant, the first nonwhite leader of a major organization of international governance, was a civil servant in Burma's colonial government and major player in the Bandung conference in 1955 that galvanized the nonalignment movement among newly independent nations (such as his own country of

Burma), who chose to ally with neither the United States nor the Soviet Union.

At this moment, many civil rights activists in the United States found common cause with independence movements in Africa and Asia. While most activists, such as King, continued to embrace the example of India's nonviolent revolution, a growing number, given the intransigence of American racism and violent resistance to civil rights, began to embrace more militant models of anticolonial revolution. One such model was Frantz Fanon's *The Wretched of the Earth*, a manifesto for Third World revolutionaries published in 1961 that posed a stunning critique of white racism and its impact on black African colonial subjects. Younger activists in particular were drawn to radical intellectuals such as Fanon, who fought for Algerian independence from French rule, and Ernesto "Che" Guevara, the Latin American revolutionary instrumental in Castro's victory in Cuba. For similar reasons, civil rights activists were drawn to Malcolm X, spokesman for the Nation of Islam, a black Muslim organization in the United States. Rooted in the tradition of Marcus Garvey's "back to Africa movement" of the 1920s, the Nation of Islam saw white racism to be an insurmountable barrier to racial equality in the United States. As a result, they called for blacks to separate from the degrading influence of white America and to develop all-black communities that nurtured and sustained black identity.

By the early 1960s, the national media portrayed Malcolm X as a hate-monger whose racial separatism and condoning of black self-defense "by any means necessary" was in dangerous opposition to King's nonviolent civil disobedience. The reality was more complicated. Like King, Malcolm changed his views over time and in March 1964, Malcolm left the Nation of Islam due to conflict with its leader, Elijah Muhammad, and began to forge ties with whites as well as civil rights organizations such as SNCC. At the time of his assassination in February 1965, Malcolm had been speaking out against the Nation of Islam.

In addition to increasing pressure from abroad and the radicalization of the Civil Rights Movement at home, President Kennedy also faced his own brother, Attorney General Robert Kennedy, who urged him to take progressive action for civil rights. Meanwhile, confrontations in the South grew more violent. Like the freedom rides, James Meredith's attempt to enroll at the all-white University of Mississippi ignited a showdown between Kennedy and white supremacists. The crisis began in September 1962 when the Mississippi governor, backed by an angry mob of white students, defied a federal court order by literally blocking the African American veteran from campus registration. Kennedy responded by sending five hundred federal marshals to protect Meredith in his multiple attempts to enroll, but this was not enough to prevent a violent campus riot that left two persons dead and a large number of the marshals wounded. The president then deployed five thousand army troops to disperse the mob and gain control of the campus. Although order was restored, Meredith required armed guards at Ole Miss until he graduated in August 1963.

A second showdown in Birmingham, Alabama, pushed Kennedy solidly into the civil rights camp. King chose to provoke a confrontation in this large industrial city because it was a bastion of violent racial oppression— the press nicknamed it "Bombingham" because since 1947 the city's civil rights workers had been victimized by fifty "unsolved" bombings. The white segregationist Eugene "Bull" Connor, Birmingham's powerful police chief, turned the Ku Klux Klan loose on freedom riders

Archive Photos/Pictorial Parade/Getty Images

Malcolm X Meets with Saudi Arabian Prince (later King) Faisal al-Saud in Mecca, Saudi Arabia, 1964 Malcolm Little joined the Nation of Islam when he was in prison and after being paroled in 1952, he revealed his devotion to black nationalism by replacing his surname with the letter X, which stood for the African name that had been taken from his ancestors. In 1964, he traveled to the Middle East on a holy pilgrimage and received invitations from pan-African leaders to serve in the governments in Egypt, Ghana, and Algeria. ◄

and closed all of the city's parks, playgrounds, and golf courses when a court ordered their integration. From January to May 1963, SCLC and local civil rights activists engaged in nonviolent resistance, including the acceptance of police brutality and mass incarceration, in order to gain sympathy from a watchful national and world audience. For the first time, the activists deployed a **children's movement** in which hundreds of children and youth marched into the center of the conflict, a deliberate strategy to increase emotional appeal.

Connor arrested hundreds of civil rights protesters including King, who then wrote **Letter from a Birmingham Jail,** an eloquent and widely circulated statement about the necessity to break morally unjust laws. More important, television and still cameras captured images of defenseless movement activists (some of whom were children) being assaulted by high-pressure water cannons and vicious police dogs. This violence, and the international condemnation that the United States received from it, compelled Kennedy to act. In a televised address to the nation, he asked "are we to say to the world, and, much more importantly, for each other, that this is a land of the free except for the Negroes; that we have no second-class citizens except Negroes; that we have no class or caste system, no ghettos, no master race, except with respect to Negroes?"

After the Birmingham crisis, Kennedy promised to push Congress to pass major civil rights legislation to enforce court-ordered integration. King and the labor leader A. Philip Randolph organized a **March on Washington for Jobs and Freedom** in August 1963 to make sure the president lived up to his word. More than one-quarter of a million people rallied at the Lincoln Memorial, including all major civil rights groups (NAACP, SCLC, CORE, and SNCC) together with leading labor unions, and white liberal organizations. The folk singer Joan Baez led the hand-holding crowd in a memorable rendition of "We Shall Overcome," the movement's unofficial theme song. The climax of the day was King's "I Have a Dream" speech in which he shared a vision of a harmonious, interracial United States that would inspire not only Americans but also generations of downtrodden people around the world seeking to become "Free at last!"

Kennedy did not live to see his civil rights bill become law; he was assassinated in November 1963 by Lee Harvey Oswald, a former Marine and outspoken Communist. As the nation mourned, Lyndon Johnson took over as president and forced the bill successfully through Congress as a tribute to Kennedy. The resulting **Civil Rights Act**, signed into law on July 2, 1964, outlawed segregation and discrimination in all businesses involved in interstate commerce. Another part of the act responded to sit-in protests and freedom rides by forbidding racial discrimination in restaurants, hotels, theaters, and other forms of "public accommodation." (An exception, which would later prove important, was made for religious institutions.) The new law also backed the *Brown* decision by disallowing discrimination in any organization that received federal funds, which by the mid-1960s included almost all public school districts. The act's most important protection involved employment discrimination, and the **Equal Employment Opportunity Commission,** a federal investigatory agency, was established to monitor employment practices. Overlooked by many lawmakers who debated it, the Civil Rights Act also included women as a protected class, which meant that for the first time in U.S. history, it was unlawful to discriminate on the basis of sex in public accommodations, federal funded organizations, or any type of employment.

children's movement Civil rights strategy used in Birmingham, Alabama, that gained worldwide sympathy to the cause in Birmingham 1963 by subjecting school children to arrest and violent counter protests.

Letter from a Birmingham Jail Written statement made by Dr. Martin Luther King Jr. in April 1963 about the purpose and necessity of nonviolence resistance.

24-3b Johnson and the Election of 1964

Although the Civil Rights Act was the most comprehensive civil rights legislation since Reconstruction, movement activists found it difficult to

{ Johnson is elected despite infringements on black voting rights in the South.

celebrate when the vast majority of southern blacks could not vote (in many states the figure was as low as 23 percent of the eligible black electorate). SNCC and other civil rights workers understood this through their work in rural Mississippi and in the summer of 1964, when nine hundred volunteers, mostly white college students, sought to counteract blacks' disenfranchisement. At the start of the **Mississippi Freedom Summer** program, two white volunteers and one black SNCC activist were killed, drawing international attention to the cause. After they were prevented from registering blacks to vote, the activists organized an alternative "freedom ballot" that elected a slate of almost all African American delegates to the Democratic National Convention held that summer in Atlantic City, New Jersey. These delegates from the **Mississippi Freedom Democratic Party** sought unsuccessfully to replace those from the state's white-only Democratic Party. Johnson, seeking to avoid controversy, brokered a deal in which only two of the Freedom delegates would be seated at the convention. Disillusioned by Johnson, the black activists denounced him and white liberals in general. Fanny Lou Hamer, a cotton

March on Washington for Jobs and Freedom Massive Washington, D.C., civil rights demonstration in 1963 featuring King's famous "I Have a Dream" speech.

Civil Rights Act Landmark legislation approved in July 1964 outlawing a wide range of discrimination on the basis of race, sex, color, religion, and other forms of prejudice.

Equal Employment Opportunity Commission, Federal body established in 1965 to enforce Civil Rights Act's protections against workplace discrimination regarding race, sex, color, religion, and other forms of prejudice.

Mississippi Freedom Summer SNCC program in the summer of 1964 that recruited white college students from the North to promote black voting in Mississippi.

Mississippi Freedom Democratic Party Alternative Democratic Party in Mississippi whose challenge to the state's white-only Democratic Party created a showdown at the Democratic National Convention in August 1964.

Voting Rights Act Landmark legislation approved in August 1965 guaranteeing the nonrestriction of voting rights based on race, gender, color, and other forms of prejudice.

International Convention on the Elimination of All Forms of Racial Discrimination U.N. treaty approved in 1965 that contributed to the lessening of formal discrimination in the vast majority of nations that signed it.

sharecropper who testified on television about the troubles she faced in trying to register to vote, proclaimed, "We didn't come all this way for no two seats, 'cause all of us is tired."

Johnson, even without the support of either the white or black Mississippi delegates, went on to win the Democratic nomination. The Republican candidate was Arizona senator Barry Goldwater, who strongly opposed the Social Security Act along with other parts of the New Deal welfare state. Goldwater also took a hard-line position against communism, telling a reporter that he would drop a "low-yield atomic bomb" to fight Communists in Vietnam. Goldwater's election slogans tried to appeal to the nation's core anti-Communist sentiment by saying: "In your heart, you know he's right." The Johnson campaign portrayed Goldwater as a dangerous extremist who would start a nuclear war by ignoring the internationalist precedents and organizations established by Truman, Eisenhower, and Kennedy. The Democrats parodied Goldwater's slogan by saying: "In your heart, you know he might."

Johnson won in a landslide, capturing 16 million more votes than Goldwater and winning every state but Arizona and five in the South. In addition, he carried thirty-seven new Democrats to the House of Representatives and two to the Senate, giving the party solid control in both houses. The stage was set for Johnson to forge his own liberal domestic agenda that would exceed Kennedy's and arguably match that of Roosevelt's New Deal.

24-3c Voting Rights

In 1965, King and the SCLC initiated another confrontation when they came to Selma, Alabama, and marched to Governor George Wallace's office in Montgomery to deliver a list of grievances that called particular attention to voting rights. The Selma march provoked an attack by the local authorities and pressured President Johnson to call for stronger legislation to protect black voters. Raised in segregated Texas, Johnson was personally familiar with the problem of black and Mexican American disenfranchisement. In August 1965, he signed into law the **Voting Rights Act,** another legislative landmark that overruled a jumble of state and local policies preventing southern blacks from voting and, more important, provided federal

> Johnson secures voting rights for southern blacks, but the United States balks at helping the United Nations to secure broad-based human rights.

oversight for voter registration and elections. The act's impact was immediate and striking. Within four years, black voter registration in Mississippi shot up from 7 to 59 percent and in Alabama increased from 23 to 59 percent (Map 24.1).

Not long after the Voting Rights Act, the United Nations, led by the Afro-Asian contingent, also stepped up its opposition to racism by approving the **International Convention on the Elimination of All Forms of Racial Discrimination**. For the first time in history, nations of the world bound themselves by treaty "to adopt all necessary measures for speedily eliminating racial discrimination in all its forms and manifestations, and to prevent and combat racist doctrines and practices in order to promote understanding between races and to build an international community free from all forms of racial segregation and racial discrimination." A handful of countries rejected the convention, including Israel and South Africa, which by this time had implemented a full-scale separation of the races (apartheid). Despite the U.S. government's support for civil and voting rights at home, the Senate did not ratify the UN convention until 1994 due to the nation's reliance on South Africa and its equally white supremacist neighbor Rhodesia for rare raw materials crucial for military weaponry. Until the late 1970s, U.S. Cold War strategy prevented the nation from opposing apartheid and other forms of racism abroad.

It could also be said that Americans were halfhearted in their attempts to eliminate all forms of racism, given the deep structural racism in the United States that was not remedied by civil and voting rights legislation. As the critic Michael Harrington argued in *The Other America* (1962), poverty and racial inequality were built in to the U.S. economy and therefore could not be easily eliminated (see Chapter 23). Women and racial minorities still faced economic, social, and political disadvantages in a society that had been designed to ensure the liberties and social mobility of white men. Massive resistance in the South and racial inequality in the nation's central cities called for a comprehensive government response to rectify decades of structural inequality.

24-3d Great Society Welfare State

As with the Civil Rights Act, Johnson followed Kennedy's initial response to the nation's economic and social crises. A New Deal administrator who had grown up poor, Johnson was already sensitive to the disadvantages of poverty well before Harrington's book influenced a national conversation about it. Johnson closely identified with Franklin Roosevelt. On becoming president, Johnson's

> Johnson initiates the most expansive social and economic welfare and environmental protections since the New Deal.

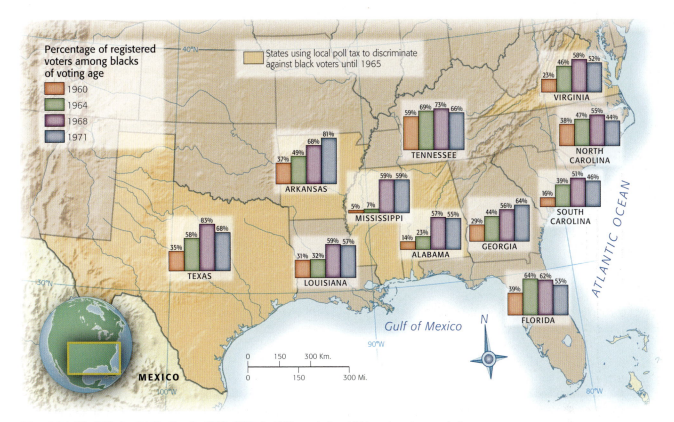

Map 24.1 **Black Voting in the South, 1960–1971** In 1960 a majority of African Americans voted in only one (Tennessee) out of eleven states in the South. By 1968, due to compliance with the Voting Rights Act, this was true in all eleven states. ▲

leadership led Congress to pass a wealth of social welfare programs known collectively as the **Great Society**. The centerpiece was the Economic Opportunity Act of 1964, which established the Office of Economic Opportunity (OEO) to oversee the administration's self-declared **War on Poverty**. A major part of OEO's efforts was to increase Social Security benefits for the aged and restore Depression-era programs providing job training, food stamps, and housing assistance. The biggest increase in spending went to Aid to Families with Dependent Children (AFDC), a New Deal welfare program that during the 1960s doubled in size, expanding coverage from 3.1 million to 6.1 million children. Although Johnson was not able to end poverty, his programs helped to cut in half the number of poor people between 1960 and 1970, to just over 10 percent of the nation's population, the lowest level in the twentieth century.

Johnson also spurred Congress to offer federally backed health care to nonveterans for the first time in U.S. history. **Medicare and Medicaid** covered millions of uninsured aged and poor citizens respectively, prompting a historic expansion of the health care industry. The Great Society also provided the first major federal aid for elementary and secondary education in the United States. These funds were given to states based upon their number

of poor students, and in order to receive them school districts had to comply with all federal civil rights statutes. As a former teacher, Johnson had an expansive view of educational support that included programs for preschoolers, increased loans for college students, funds for the arts and humanities, and the establishment of the Corporation for Public Broadcasting, which sponsored noncommercial television channels that gave birth to educational programs like kid-favorite *Sesame Street*.

Civil rights leaders compelled Johnson to commit the nation to India's idea of atoning for past inequalities by giving special aid to aggrieved groups. In the United States this **affirmative action** meant that any group either doing business with the federal government or receiving funds from it must have programs giving women and racial minorities an advantage over their competition. The classic case was an elite university that

Great Society Legislation passed under President Johnson expanding and initiating social welfare programs as well as environmental and consumer protections.

War on Poverty An early and crucial part of President Johnson's Great Society addressing widespread poverty through the newly created Office of Economic Opportunity (OEO).

Medicare and Medicaid Federal social insurance programs, established in 1965 as part of the Great Society program, guaranteeing access to health care for the elderly and disadvantaged.

affirmative action Policies that take into account race, sex, class, and other bases of disadvantage as a remedy for racial discrimination and inequality.

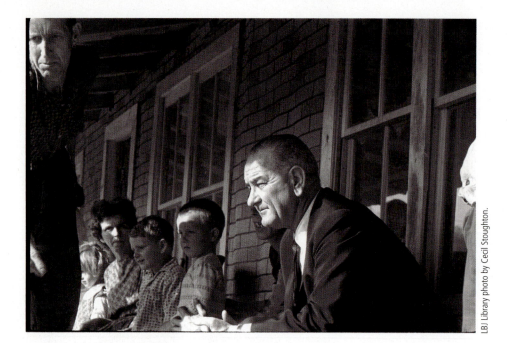

LBJ Library photo by Cecil Stoughton.

President Johnson on a Tour of Poverty in Appalachia, 1964 In a commencement address given at the University of Michigan in May 1965, Johnson unveiled his vision of the United States as a "great society" that was not just rich and powerful but that "demands an end to poverty and injustice." Postwar prosperity made him far more confident than Franklin Roosevelt that the nation could provide all citizens with a decent standard of living. ◄

had discriminated against women and racial minorities for decades, changing its admissions standards in order to give preference to applicants based on their race or gender. In an effort to remedy hard-hit central cities, Johnson created Veterans Health Information Systems and Technology Architecture (a VISTA), a domestic equivalent to the Peace Corps that encouraged American youth to devote themselves to their fellow citizens in need. More controversial was the OEO's Community Action Program (CAP). The philosophy behind these programs borrowed from SNCC's goal in the rural South: to help disadvantaged communities by empowering residents to lead themselves. Many young activists from the Civil Rights Movement found their way to one of the one thousand CAP programs around the country. And like SNCC, CAP's bottom-up perspective provoked hostility from competing groups seeking to impose top-down solutions. City officials were the most distrustful of CAP programs, and in one case, the mayor of Los Angeles blamed CAP workers for the violence in the city's Watts neighborhood.

Consumer and environmental crises also encouraged Johnson to expand federal regulations in new directions. Great Society legislation regarding truth in advertising forced cigarette manufacturers to print warnings on their packages about the health risks associated with smoking. He also responded favorably to activist Ralph Nader's campaigns for safer automobiles and children's products by increasing the reach of federal consumer protections. Finally, environmentalists were pleased when the president set aside millions of acres of wilderness from economic development and when his wife Lady Bird Johnson led efforts to clean up and control advertising on federal highways. Younger environmentalists pressured the president to establish clean air and water standards and enforcement

agencies that would hold businesses responsible for toxic waste and other dangers to the public's health and the natural environment (see Table 24.2).

The hidden costs of postwar economic development involved environmental and consumer problems that affected rich and poor alike. While Michael Harrington made middle-class Americans feel guilty about their suburban comforts, Rachel Carson's *Silent Spring* (1962) aroused fears that capitalism threatened their health. A biologist who worked for the U.S. Fish and Wildlife Service, Carson targeted agribusinesses and the chemical industry for introducing pesticides and herbicides that were harmful to humans. The title *Silent Spring* referred to a nightmare scenario in which the antimosquito pesticide DDT had the unintended effect of destroying an area's entire bird life and even worse, working its way up the food chain from insects, to fish, birds, other animals, and humans. Carson added that the chemical revolution in agriculture was destroying the beauty of the natural environment by encouraging the development of pesticide-resistant strains of insects and opportunistic weeds. She raised the nation's awareness about the negative effects that came with seemingly benevolent industrial chemicals and brought increased attention to other ways that pollution compromised the nation's health and natural beauty.

The Great Society's gains were real but limited. The nation's income gap did not close as the richest fifth of the population continued to receive 44 percent of total income while the poorest fifth claimed 4 percent. The results regarding race relations were also mixed. Although civil rights protections and affirmative action preferences helped to expand the middle-class in black, Mexican American, and other racial minority communities, these

Table 24.2 Great Society Agencies, Laws, and Programs

If the New Deal built the foundation for U.S. welfare policies, then the Great Society added on to this foundation by eliminating racial discrimination, expanding social and economic rights for the nation's most vulnerable groups, and increasing medical, environmental, educational, and cultural benefits for all Americans.

Year	Legislation	Description
1963	Clean Air Act	Initiated federal attempt to control air pollution
1964	Civil Rights Act	Outlawed discrimination based on race, color, religion, sex, or national origin and established the Equal Employment Opportunity Commission (EEOC) to ensure implementation
1964	Office of Economic Opportunity (OEO)	Implemented and oversaw War on Poverty programs including increases in Social Security benefits, job training, food stamps, assistance for rural families, VISTA, and community action programs (CAP)
1965	Voting Rights Act	Prohibited racial discrimination in voting
1965	Social Security Act	Authorized Medicare and provided federal funding for older people's health care.
1965	Immigration Act	Reformed unequal and discriminatory immigration policy by establishing equal and expanded quotas for all nations outside the Western Hemisphere and for the first time limited immigration from countries there
1965	Elementary and Secondary Education Act	Provided federal funding to public schools, particularly in low-income areas and established a program to prepare low-income children for kindergarten (Head Start)
1965	Higher Education Act	Increased federal funding for enabling low-income persons to enroll in postsecondary and higher education
1965	National Foundation on the Arts and Humanities Act	Established the channels for federal funding of the arts and humanities through the National Endowment for the Arts and National Endowment for the Humanities
1965	Water Quality Act	Required states to set standards for water quality on interstate rivers and other bodies of water
1965	Housing and Urban Development Act	Provided rent subsidies and home ownership aid for low-income Americans
1965	Highway Beautification Act	Limited billboards and other types of advertisements, as well as junkyards, and abandoned vehicles on interstate highways
1966	Highway Safety Act	Established bureau that would become the National Highway Traffic Safety Administration (NHTSA) to reduce highway fatalities and promote safe automobiles
1967	Public Broadcasting Act	Chartered the Corporation for Public Broadcasting as a private, non-profit organization receiving federal funds to promote television programs catering to the public interest.
1968	Fair Housing Act	Banned racial discrimination in housing and provided federal assistance to the rehabilitation of low-income housing

breakthroughs did little to alter persistent structures of disadvantage that plagued the urban and rural poor. For most of those at the bottom of the economic ladder, Great Society programs failed to overcome the inexorable forces of the Cold War economy, which expanded and made more permanent the divide between white suburbs and nonwhite central cities.

24-3e Immigration Reform and Criminalization

A final element of the Great Society was comprehensive immigration reform. Although reforms had begun to take

> Although imperfect, immigration reform removes the legacy of racial and national discrimination.

Immigration Act of 1965 Policy shift that proved an unexpected boon to immigration by ending discriminatory national origins quotas and setting preferences for family reunification, job skills, and refugees.

place under Truman, the discriminatory national origins quotas remained in place. Like civil rights legislation, immigration reform reflected the larger rejection of racism operating throughout the world. Canada took the lead in 1962 by removing its own race-based immigration preferences (known as the *"White Canada policy"*) in order to operate more effectively in the United Nations. (Australia all but removed its race-based *"White Australia"* policies in 1966). Immigration reform in the United States, was held up in Congress until the Johnson administration in October 1965 facilitated passage of the **Immigration Act of 1965**. The 1965 act nearly doubled the annual cap on immigration from 155,000 to 290,000. It also eliminated the bias against immigrants from Asia and Eastern and Southern Europe by giving the same yearly quota of twenty thousand immigrants for every nation outside the Western Hemisphere. This was intended to be what one historian calls a "cautious reform." Doubling the annual ceiling on immigration to two hundred ninety thousand still amounted to just one-sixth of 1 percent of the nation's population, a miniscule fraction compared to the more than 10 percent figures for incoming European immigrants in the nineteenth and early twentieth centuries. The Japanese American Citizens League, a prominent Asian American civil rights organization, while accepting the act, criticized its design to preserve the numerical dominance of whites in the United States. And yet, unforeseen by its sponsors, the Immigration Act actually greatly boosted the number of Asian and especially Latino immigrants, which soon became the nation's top two sources of newcomers. The reasons for this unexpected outcome are complicated, but they centered on the preferences established by the Immigration Act, which privileged family reunification, needed workers, and refugees from Communist countries. In

gaining access to the United States through one of these preferences, immigrants were able to bring their parents, children, siblings, and other relatives through a process of "chain migration" in which the coming of one led to that of many others.

For Latino immigrants and other peoples in the Western Hemisphere, the Immigration Act was not a cautious reform but a clear setback. When the United States began to protect its borders after World War I, immigrants from North and South America had been exempt from the 155,000 annual ceiling. The 1965 act cancelled this exemption. It limited the number of immigrants from the Americas to no more than 120,000 out of the 290,000 total annual cap. The 120,000 figure represented a 40 percent decline in the pre-1965 level of Western Hemisphere migration. Liberal congressmen expressed equity concerns in seeking to bring in line the nation's two different policies for the Eastern and Western Hemispheres. Was it fair, they asked, for Mexicans (and Canadians) to enjoy unlimited migration while the European nations were limited to 20,000? Conservatives warned about the dramatic increase in Mexican immigrants—a "brown peril" replacing the early twentieth century fear of being flooded by "yellow hordes" from Asia. They also pointed to a rapid population increase throughout Latin America and predicted that the Latino population in the United States would triple in forty-five years (see Figure 24.2).

Mexican immigrants suffered the most from the new limitation. By 1965 with Asian immigration cut off for decades and increasing numbers of whites and blacks heading to cities, Mexicans became the main source of migrant farm labor throughout the Southwest. No immigration policy could stop the demand for Mexican labor. From World War II until 1964, U.S. immigration officials sought to regulate the northward flow of Mexican workers (sometimes for their own good) through *bracero* guest worker programs. But in the end, U.S. farmers kept hiring cheaper and easier to obtain undocumented workers

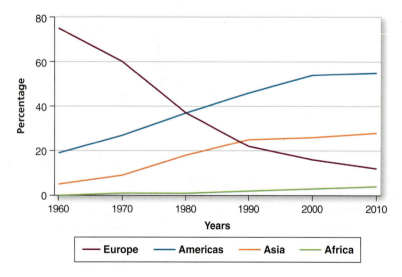

Figure 24.2 U.S. Immigrant Population by World Region, 1960–2010 Even before the Immigration Act of 1965, immigration from Europe was declining while that from the Americas (mainly Mexico) and Asia was rising. The result, as shown here, is that number of immigrants in the United States from these regions dramatically increased as more entered while the older generation of European immigrants passed away. ◀ Source: Migration Policy Institute tabulation of data from the U.S. Census Bureau, including the U.S. Census Bureau's 2006 to 2013 American Community Survey and 2000 Decennial Census. Data for 1960 to 1990 were from Campbell J. Gibson and Emily Lennon, "Historical Census Statistics on the Foreign-born Population of the United States: 1850-1990," U.S. Census Bureau, Population Division, Working Paper No. 29, February 1999.

AP Images/David Kennedy

Global Americans Born in Brownsville, Texas, on the U.S.–Mexico border in 1915, **Américo Paredes** grew up familiar with life in the borderlands between two nations, saluting the American flag in public school during the day, and at night listening to Mexican ballads (*corridos*) and folk tales. While facing discrimination as a Mexican American (his high school counselor assumed that he would not go to college), Paredes found an escape through poetry, which he wrote and published while studying for his degree at junior college. In 1944, he served as an infantryman in the U.S. Army, and after World War II was assigned to the army publication *Stars and Stripes* to cover war crimes trials in Tokyo. Paredes returned to Texas in 1950 after living for five years in East Asia and had a new appreciation for the cultural blending and conflicts that comprised his life experiences on the U.S.–Mexico border. Like the African American writer James Baldwin, his time abroad enabled him to better understand himself, his borderland community, and the peculiarities of racial experience in the United States. A sign of Paredes's connection between Asians and Latinos was his wife Amelia Nagamine, a half-Japanese, half-Uruguayan women he had met while in Japan. Paredes's experience in Japan informed his novels and pioneering research, as a professor at the University of Texas–Austin, on trans-border corridos. His writing and research, especially on the legendary Gregorio Cortez and his heroic victories against U.S. law enforcement (Texas Rangers), revealed how global experiences had reshaped his understanding of local environments.

who crossed the border illegally. The Immigration Act's Western Hemisphere limit added another obstacle preventing Mexicans from working on U.S. farms that led increasing numbers of them to cross the border illegally.

In this way, the act (as well as the 1976 imposition of a 20,000 quota for Western Hemisphere nations) criminalized workers for doing what previously had been tolerated if not encouraged.

24-4
Expanded Struggle for Equality

In this photograph, Cesar Chavez (second in line, holding flag) marches in 1965 supporting a strike, or *huelga*, by a union of agricultural workers sponsored by the AFL-CIO. The flags contain the symbol of Chavez's National Farmworkers Association, an eagle whose wings outline steps on a pyramid. The eagle and pyramid harken back to the Meso-American civilizations and are key icons of Mexican history.

Why do you think the farmworkers' protest used the Spanish language and Mexican historical symbols? What advantages and disadvantages might this have in the United States? ▶

1976 George Ballis/Take Stock/The Image Works

Although President Johnson's Great Society took action against racial discrimination, poverty, and a host of other social and environmental problems, it could not anticipate the rise of women's activism and youth protests on college campuses that were beginning to develop at the same time as the Civil Rights Movement. Assumptions about women and their position in the workplace were particularly in flux, and a re-invigorated women's movement pressured the federal government to dismantle the legal structure of gender bias. At the same time, the farmworkers' movement and protests on college and university campuses brought new actors into the civil rights coalition as they used strategies and tactics, as well as the vision of racial and economic justice, learned from black struggles in the South and across the nation.

☞ As you read, consider the Civil Rights Movement's influence on other struggles for social and economic justice. Why did these new movements emerge?

24-4a Postwar Status of Women

The return of women workers to the labor market because of labor shortages in the booming postwar economy revived the momentum for women's rights. Officials in the federal government's Women's Bureau suggested that employers pay women the same wages for doing work comparable to what men did. The legal concept of **comparable worth** made possible a liberal interpretation of the dollar value of women's work that did not require women to perform the exact same tasks as male coworkers. In this way, a female secretary might get paid the same wages as a male clerk even though they performed different duties.

{ After World War II, women continue to seek legal protections and economic equality.

Although dormant during the Eisenhower administration, equal pay bills in Congress gained new support under Kennedy because of the Democrats' close ties to organized labor. Esther Peterson, a trade unionist and new head of the Women's Bureau, was able to get Congress to consider equal pay legislation. Conservatives managed to water down the bill by, among other things, replacing the concept of comparable worth with a strict definition of equal work that made it much easier for employers to dismiss women's claims to wage equality with men. Even so, the passage of the Equal Pay Act in 1963 was an important step forward for women's rights.

Other moves toward gender equality resulted from Kennedy's December 1961 establishment of the **President's Commission on the Status of Women,** a move reminiscent of Truman's creation of the President's Commission on Civil Rights. Eleanor Roosevelt, who no longer chaired the UN Committee on Human Rights, headed the Kennedy commission and made sure to include her fellow gender activist Pauli Murray as a member. The commission drew attention to the ill effects that women suffered from gender inequality in employment, as well as in civil rights, voting, and property rights; labor legislation; and social insurance and tax laws. But it stopped short of recommending the elimination of legislation designed to protect female workers.

comparable worth Idea that women and men should receive equal pay for jobs at similar skill levels and of similar worth to employers.

President's Commission on the Status of Women Established by President Kennedy in December 1961, the commission highlighted ill effects that women suffered from gender inequality.

feminine mystique Notion originating from Betty Friedan's *The Feminine Mystique* (1963) that being womanly or performing supposed female duties is a noble achievement for women rather than a myth tied to their subordination to men; the concept originated method of subjugation.

Such protective labor laws, considered major victories against the exploitation of women during the Progressive era, required shorter workdays, lighter responsibilities, and other forms of gender difference that prevented working women from earning the same pay as men.

24-4b Resurgent Feminism

Although the Kennedy commission and the Equal Pay Act were early signs of the feminist revival, neither had the force of Betty Friedan's best-selling exposé of U.S. gender norms: *The Feminine Mystique* (1963). Neither the presidential commission nor the Equal Pay Act challenged the traditional and pervasive assumption that women's "maternal functions" made them fundamentally different from men. Friedan, on the other hand, objected to the notion that women's primary function and source of fulfillment was as mothers, wives, and homemakers. Following the French philosopher Simone de Beauvoir's path-breaking analysis of women's subordination, *The Second Sex* (1949), Freidan argued that the idea of the "happy housewife" was a smokescreen or **feminine mystique** that covered up the discrimination and subordination faced by the female half of the population. Friedan concluded that educated, middle-class women were unhappy because their identity was defined by marriage, childrearing, and household management, while their education and aspirations were broader. In addition to being a housewife, Friedan was a left-wing activist who attended the same Highlander Folk School in Tennessee that had served as a catalyst for labor and civil rights leaders including CIO activists, King, and Parks. For nearly a decade after college, Friedan worked as a journalist for a left-wing news service and wrote articles that supported labor unions and civil rights, activities that she kept concealed well beyond the Second Red Scare. The hidden origins of *The Feminine Mystique* revealed the linkage between the labor movement, civil rights activism, and postwar feminism.

{ New ideas of women's equality and the way to obtain it emerge.

Feminist political activism escalated quickly after the publication of Freidan's book. A key achievement was the inclusion of a gender equality clause in the Civil Rights Act of 1964. The clause (which fell under Title VII of the act) was introduced by a segregationist Virginia congressman who hoped to derail the bill by adding sex to its protected categories. But committed feminists such as Murray lobbied vigorously for the bill. "The Negro woman," she wrote, "can no longer postpone or subordinate the fight against discrimination because of sex to the civil rights struggle but must carry on both fights simultaneously." As the Civil Rights Act was being debated, Murray sent a memorandum around Capitol Hill arguing that unless women were included as a protected category, "the civil rights bill would be including only one half of the Negroes." With solid backing from a

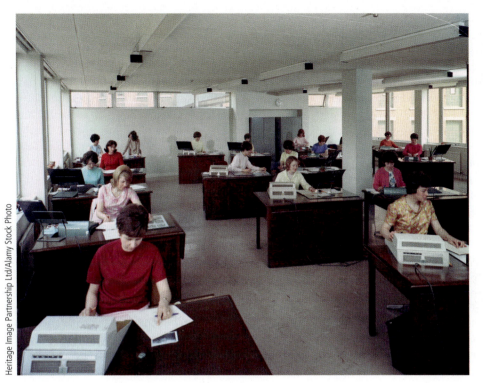

Heritage Image Partnership Ltd/Alamy Stock Photo

Women Office Workers, 1968 Most Americans in the 1950s and 1960s did not see a problem with a workplace segregated by sex. Even Martin Luther King Jr. was typical of movement activists in seeing civil rights as key to restoring black men to their "proper" role as breadwinners. ◄

handful of congresswomen, the Senate and House bills were approved with overwhelming support.

The implementation and enforcement of Title VII was left to the Equal Employment Opportunity Commission (EEOC), but this did not mean that the federal government would automatically become a vehicle to advance feminism. Murray and other feminists faced tremendous opposition from the EEOC and the broader civil rights community because gender equality was never their major goal. These activists, like most Americans, had no problem with the segregation of men and women into different jobs, duties, and responsibilities.

24-4c Beginnings of Campus Unrest

During the early 1960s, radicalism grew on college campuses as an increasing number of white students took on the cause of civil

{ Civil rights struggles spark early student protests.

rights, and like their SNCC peers, became impatient with the pace of achieving racial equality. In 1962, **Students for a Democratic Society (SDS)** emerged as the organizing force behind the revival of left-wing, socialist politics on U.S. college campuses. Unlike youth activism of the 1930s, SDS was not closely aligned with the Communist Party or the Soviet Union; and it was not rooted solely in labor and working-class struggles. Indeed, the beginning of the organization's founding manifesto, the **Port Huron Statement,** focused on the era of postwar

prosperity: "We are people of this generation, bred in at least modest comfort, housed now in universities, looking uncomfortably to the world we inherit." Like Betty Friedan, the SDS members highlighted negative effects of prosperity and mass society. But instead of focusing on the plight of middle-class mothers, the young radicals were drawn toward struggles for African American freedom, socialism, and nuclear disarmament. One of their main goals was to transform the U.S. government into a "participatory democracy" in which blacks, workers, peace advocates, youth, and other aggrieved groups gained increased power over political and economic decision making.

While SDSers pointed out the differences between their New Left and the Depression-era radicals they called the Old Left, there was one important connection between the two generations of activists. Approximately one-third of the one hundred thousand New Left radicals were "red diaper babies," the children of Popular Front-era socialists and Communists. And as was common in the 1930s, almost two-thirds (60 percent) of New Left activists came for Jewish backgrounds and, although there were exceptions, a much smaller percentage came from Catholic homes.

New Left activism spiked at the University of California–Berkeley in the fall 1964 when the school administration prevented students from promoting civil rights causes on campus. In the eyes of student activists, the administration's actions not only

Students for a Democratic Society (SDS) Organization, established in 1962, by a new generation of radical students, advancing youth protests for civil rights and against the Vietnam War.

Port Huron Statement SDS manifesto promoting "participatory democracy" to increase control over political, economic, and social institutions by everyday people.

Free Speech Movement (FSM) Student activism, inspired by the Civil Rights Movement and beginning at the University of California, Berkeley, in fall 1964, revealing a growing interest on campuses for more student autonomy vis-á-vis the school administrations.

opposed the Civil Rights Movement, but also violated their constitutional right to gather and express opinions. The suspension and arrest of a handful of students who continued campus activism provoked a large student uprising at Berkeley. What started as a campaign to support African American struggles turned into the **Free Speech Movement (FSM)** in which even conservative students stood up for their rights against the university administration. FSM activists such as Mario Savio, who had recently returned from SNCC's Mississippi Freedom Summer, used civil disobedience tactics in taking over the school's main administration building, and, like civil rights activists, allowed themselves to be arrested for the cause. In the end, the administration gave in to FSM demands for greater political expression on campus but not before a good portion of students became politicized about social injustice within and outside their campus, and from there, became involved in movements for peace and the liberation of women and racial minorities.

24-4d Stirrings on the Farms

Another group inspired by labor and civil rights activism was agricultural workers, who as a rule were excluded from the collective bargaining agreements won by industrial labor as well as from most federal protections. Adding to their troubles, many were *braceros* or undocumented workers lacking the

> Farmworkers adapt strategies, tactics, and aims of the Civil Rights Movement to fight labor exploitation.

rights and protections of U.S. citizenship. Cesar Chavez and Dolores Huerta spoke up for agricultural workers in leading strikes, boycotts, and other forms of protest in Delano, California, part of the extensive grape-growing region in the state's Central Valley. Born in Arizona, Chavez spent much of his youth with his family as migrant farmworkers in California, which prevented him from going to school beyond the eighth grade. After two years in the U.S. Navy, he spent ten years in San Jose, California, learning how to advance progressive social change through community organizing. During this time, he became inspired by Gandhi's writings on nonviolent protest and those by Saint Francis of Assisi on serving the poor.

In 1962, Chavez moved with his wife and children to Delano and immediately organized the National Farm Worker's Association (NFWA), adopting the distinctive flag bearing the Mexican-inspired eagle with the outline of ancient Meso-American pyramids. Despite this symbol and the organization's decidedly Mexican American leadership, Chavez opposed ethnic chauvinism, seeking actively to include African Americans, who composed the bulk of his staff and volunteers. Chavez also relied on support from white students in frequent trips to college campuses to raise awareness of the farmworker struggle. Finally, he and the NFWA made the fateful decision in September 1965 to join Filipino farmworkers in a strike against grape growers. By this time the fledgling organization had only 1,700 members distributed over fifty local bodies. They launched a protracted struggle that, like the Montgomery Bus Boycott, would catapult into the nation's spotlight a charismatic new leader for social justice.

Summary

The March on Washington for Jobs and Freedom in 1963 was a powerful example of Americans— "black men and white men, Jews and Gentiles, Protestants and Catholics"— coming together in a way that signaled the dawn of a historic era of the struggle for inclusiveness. In the three decades after World War II, persistent social divisions of race, ethnicity, religion, and sex had softened and the restrictions on black voting and the legal interpretation of civil rights collapsed. The change resulted from two interrelated sources: long-standing domestic protests by the NAACP and other civil rights groups that exploded into mass protests during the age of human rights; and from international pressures against racism in the United States that the U.S. in its drive to win the Cold War was compelled to oblige.

During this period, more Americans than ever achieved newfound rights as racial minorities, women, workers, consumers, voters, and students. At the same time, the nation ended long-standing discriminatory immigration policies. But the surge in freedoms did not make up for decades, and in many instances centuries, of mistreatment and inequality suffered by racial minorities, women, agricultural workers, and the poor. Real social equality, for most disadvantaged Americans, would come gradually, if at all. Although groups and individuals committed to the status quo slowed and stalled expansions of freedoms, the underdevelopment of America's decaying cities created class barriers to social mobility that trapped millions of racial minorities in persistent poverty. For many Americans the revolution in rights and freedoms could not compensate for the economic losses suffered from the wrenching transformation from industrial to postindustrial capitalism.

‹Thinking Back, *Looking Forward*›

As you review, consider how and why the civil rights won by African Americans after the Civil War were taken away from them, and how the civil rights struggles addressed in this chapter were part of a long movement since the end of Reconstruction to get them back. How did World War II and especially the Cold War contribute to civil rights achievements? In the next chapters, pay attention to further expansions of the rights revolution and the negative reaction to them. To make your study concrete, review the time line and reflect on the entries there. Think about their causes, consequences, and connections. How do they fit with global trends?

Additional Resources

Books

Branch, Taylor. *Parting the Waters: America in the King Years 1954–63*. New York: Simon and Schuster, 1988. ► Comprehensive history of the Civil Rights Movement that has become a classic.

Brooks, Charlotte. *Alien Neighbors, Foreign Friends: Asian Americans, Housing, and the Transformation of Urban California*. Chicago, IL: University of Chicago Press, 2009. ► Incisive examination tracing the impact of international pressures on the repeal of anti-Asian policies related to housing.

Dudziak, Mary L. *Cold War Civil Rights: Race and the Image of American Democracy*. Princeton, NJ: Princeton University Press, 2000. ► Pioneering study connecting America's Cold War imperatives to its civil rights revolution.

Gaines, Kevin K. *American Africans in Ghana: Black Expatriates and the Civil Rights Era*. Chapel Hill: University of North Carolina Press, 2006. ► Fascinating social history of black migration to Africa after World War II.

Gutiérrez, David G. *Walls and Mirrors: Mexican Americans, Mexican Immigrants, and the Politics of Ethnicity*. Berkeley: University of California Press, 1995. ► Examination of how Mexican immigration has shaped politics in the Southwest for more than a century.

Harrington, Michael. *The Other America: Poverty in the United States*. 1962. Reprint, New York: Touchstone, 1997. ► Study of poverty that shocked the nation in 1962 and sparked the War on Poverty.

Isserman, Maurice, and Michael Kazin. *America Divided: The Civil War of the 1960s*, 3rd ed. New York: Oxford University Press, 2007. ► Inclusive reader of primary sources on the United States during the 1960s that pays particular attention to race, gender, and civil rights.

Lewis, David Levering. *King: A Biography*, 3rd ed. Urbana: University of Illinois Press, 2013. ► Major biography of the civil rights leader.

MacLean, Nancy. *Freedom Is Not Enough: The Opening of the American Workplace*. Cambridge, MA: Harvard University Press, 2008. ► Innovative analysis of civil rights and workplace issues that conjoins racial and gender movements and issues.

Ngai, Mae M. *Impossible Subjects: Illegal Aliens and the Making of Modern America*. Princeton, NJ: Princeton University Press, 2004. ► Path-breaking study that addresses the politics of the 1965 Immigration Act and the criminalization of undocumented workers in the United States.

> Go to the MindTap® for **Global Americans** to access the full version of select books from this Additional Resources section.

Websites

Changing America: The Emancipation Proclamation, 1863, and the March on Washington, 1963. (http://americanhistory.si.edu/changing-america-emancipation-proclamation-1863-and-march-washington-1963) ► Smithsonian online exhibit with explanatory text and images of historical artifacts regarding the Emancipation Proclamation and March on Washington.

Civil Rights History Project at the Library of Congress. (http://www.loc.gov/collections/civil-rights-history-project/) ► Rich collection of essays and oral history videos about the Civil Rights Movement.

Free Speech Movement Digital Archives. (http://bancroft.berkeley.edu/FSM/) ► Collection of primary sources, images, and oral history transcripts with key players in the Berkeley struggles.

History of the United Nations. (http://www.un.org/en/sections/history/history-united-nations/index.html) ► Text and some audio/visual materials related to the background and beginning of the United Nations.

The Universal Declaration of Human Rights. (http://www.un.org/en/documents/udhr/index.shtml) ► UN Website devoted to the declaration and its history with a page of Web-based resources.

MindTap®

Continue exploring online through MindTap®, where you can:
- **Assess your knowledge with the Chapter Test**
- **Watch historical videos related to the chapter**
- **Further your understanding with interactive maps and timelines**

Civil Rights and Human Rights

1945–1946

October 1945

United Nations is established.

February 1946

Discharged soldier Isaac Woodard is blinded by police in South Carolina.

1947–1948

1947

Jackie Robinson and Larry Doby break the colorline by playing in Major League Baseball.

March 1947

Truman Doctrine commits United States to containing communism.

October 1947

President's Committee on Civil Rights publishes *To Secure These Rights*, recommending elimination of racial discrimination.

December 1948

UN approves Universal Declaration of Human Rights.

1949–1952

1949

French intellectual Simone de Beauvoir publishes *The Second Sex*—kicks off postwar feminism.

January 1949

Funeral home in Texas refuses to bury deceased Mexican American veteran Felix Longoria.

1950

Pauli Murray publishes *States' Laws on Race and Color*, the "bible" for NAACP civil rights lawyers.

India outlaws centuries-old caste system.

June 1950

Korean War begins.

1952

Malcolm Little is paroled from jail, changes name to Malcolm X.

June 1952

Congress ends exclusion of all Asian immigrants and permits their naturalization.

1954–1955

May 1954

U.S. Supreme Court hands down decision in *Brown v. Board of Education*, which overturns the *Plessy* era of segregation.

May 1955

Soviets establish Warsaw Pact to counter NATO.

August 1955

Emmett Till murdered in Mississippi.

December 1955

Montgomery bus boycott erupts in Alabama when Rosa Parks refuses to comply with racial segregation; boycott propels Martin Luther King Jr. into leadership of Civil Rights Movement.

1957–1959

January 1957

Southern Christian Leadership Council (SCLC) is established with Martin Luther King Jr. as president.

March 1957

Ghana becomes independent.

September 1957

President Eisenhower sends troops to Little Rock, Arkansas, to integrate Central High School.

Soviet Union

France

United States

Korea

India

Ghana

738

1960

February

Four Greensboro college students spark sit-in protests at lunch counters throughout the South.

August

Student Nonviolent Coordinating Committee (SNCC) is established, bringing new tactics and youth into the civil rights struggle.

September

Richard Nixon and John F. Kennedy engage in first televised political debate.

1961–1962

1961

Frantz Fanon publishes *The Wretched on the Earth.*

James L. Farmer and CORE start "freedom rides" to integrate public transportation in South.

African and Asian nations comprise majority in UN General Assembly.

President Kennedy enters the White House, establishes the President's Commission on the Status of Women; Freedom rides used to integrate inter-state buses and trains.

1962

Rachel Carson's *Silent Spring* generates broad environmental awareness.

Students for a Democratic Society (SDS) is established in Ann Arbor, Michigan.

October 1962

Kennedy sends troops to allow James Meredith to integrate University of Mississippi.

1963

Betty Friedan publishes *The Feminine Mystique*, stimulates new wave of women's activism.

January–May

King and SCLC provoke violent confrontation in Birmingham, Alabama.

King writes "Letter from a Birmingham Jail."

August

March on Washington for Jobs and Freedom assembles massive civil rights demonstration; King delivers "I Have a Dream" speech.

November

Kennedy is assassinated, Lyndon Johnson becomes president.

1964

January

President Johnson declares "War on Poverty" to greatly expand welfare programs.

July

Civil Rights Act is passed.

Summer: Mississippi Freedom Summer strives to re-enfranchise blacks.

August

Congress authorizes greatly increasing U.S. troops in Vietnam.

October–December

Free Speech Movement protests erupt at the University of California, Berkeley.

November

Johnson is elected president to serve first full term in office.

1965

March

King leads marches for voting rights in Selma, Alabama.

July

Equal Employment Opportunity Commission (EEOC) opens for business as federal government agency devoted to upholding Civil Rights Act.

August

Congress passes Voting Rights Act.

Racial uprising erupts in Watts, California.

September

Cesar Chavez and National Farm Workers Association join grape strike in Delano, California.

October

Johnson signs Immigration Act.

December

UN approves the International Convention on the Elimination of All Forms of Racial Discrimination.

25

The Vietnam War Era

1965–1975

After fleeing Cambodia on foot to the Thai border, Dith Pran came to the United States, with the help of friend Sydney Schanberg, to be reunited with his family.

In April 1975, Cambodian journalist Dith Pran chose to remain in his war-torn country while his wife and children fled to safety in the United States. He stayed to document the end of the bloody Cambodian civil war as the Communist Khmer Rouge defeated the regime of U.S.-backed dictator Lon Nol. This victory came after the United States had withdrawn its troops and military support from Vietnam and neighboring Cambodia and Laos. Without the world's greatest superpower to oppose them, Communist parties seized power throughout Indochina.

Jerry Soloway/Corbis

Dith was relieved that the fighting was over and, like his friend and fellow journalist *New York Times* foreign correspondent Sydney Schanberg, was optimistic about Cambodia's future. The victorious Khmer Rouge, however, dashed their hopes. In the name of overthrowing the remnants of capitalism and Western imperialism, the new regime turned on its own people, slaughtering innocent civilians. In reporting on the casualties, Dith and Schanberg rushed to a local hospital, where they were captured by Khmer Rouge soldiers, who, if not for Dith's heroic pleading, would have executed them. Once released, the two found their way to the French embassy, where they created a fake passport so that Dith could flee the country. The scheme failed, forcing Schanberg to return to the United States without his dear friend.

Because the Khmer Rouge sought to "cleanse" the nation of "intellectuals," "foreigners," and Western influences, Dith disguised himself as a peasant taxi driver, threw away his money and material possessions, and concealed the signs of his French education and English-language skills. He ended up in a labor camp where city folk like him were forced to work in rice fields while receiving political indoctrination. Khmer Rouge cruelty seemed to have no bounds as they let "lucky" ones like Dith starve, while butchering 1.5 to 2 million people in what became known as the "killing fields."

After more than three years, Dith was liberated when Vietnam invaded and overthrew the Khmer Rouge regime. But he still was not safe given his earlier connection to the United States, so he fled Cambodia on foot via a harrowing sixty-mile jungle trek to the Thai border. Upon hearing that Dith had made it to freedom, Schanberg, who refused to believe rumors that his friend was dead, immediately flew to Thailand and then brought Dith to the United States where he was reunited with his wife and children, and became a U.S. citizen.

Dith's ordeal had a fortunate ending, but the military conflicts throughout Indochina did not. These wars came at great costs for all parties involved. The Khmer Rouge committed gruesome atrocities in Cambodia. The U.S. withdrawal from the region also sealed the fate of U.S.-backed regimes in South Vietnam and Laos, whose collapse displaced millions of people and subjected those who could not escape to vicious victor's justice. Although North Vietnam effectively won the war against the U.S. enemy and achieved the long- sought

How does Dith Pran's harrowing experience in Cambodia during the Khmer Rouge regime and Vietnam's invasion reflect the tragedies and costs of the region's military conflicts?

Go to MindTap® to watch a video on Dith and learn how his story relates to the themes of this chapter.

goal of reuniting the country, these victories came at the cost of millions of lives, millions of acres of defoliated countryside, and other tragedies that destroyed the promise of Ho Chi Minh's socialist revolution. Fallout from the U.S. war also embroiled Vietnam in further military conflicts against former Cambodian and Chinese allies. The fighting, deaths, and destruction continued in Indochina for almost fifteen years after the Americans left. The region had experienced nearly half a century of continuous warfare.

For the United States, its withdrawal constituted the nation's worst military defeat. More than fifty thousand Americans died, and billions of dollars were spent on a lost cause in which the United States sacrificed much of its prestige as the leader of the "free world." The war also took its toll on two U.S. presidents: Johnson ended his reelection campaign because of military setbacks and domestic opposition, and Nixon was forced to resign from office due to spying on political enemies opposed to the war. Intense antiwar protests revealed how the conflict polarized the nation, as Americans were torn between their sense of patriotism and their own moral conscience. The Vietnam question, furthermore, exacerbated deep race and gender divisions related to the nation's unfinished civil rights agenda, as well as cultural conflicts brought on by the coming-of-age of the baby boomer generation. The violence in Indochina seemed to beget violent conflicts at home.

25-1
U.S. Escalates War in Vietnam

This photograph depicts the reconnaissance in February 1965 of a bridge in North Vietnam destroyed by a U.S bomber. The United States' Operation Rolling Thunder counted on U.S. air supremacy to destroy Hanoi and targets throughout North Vietnam.

How does this image convey a sense of U.S. advantages during the Vietnam War? What other advantages do you think the United States had that are not revealed by this photo? What advantages do you think the North Vietnamese had? ▶

akg-images/Newscom

Vietnam was one of many sites of Cold War conflict in the Third World in which the United States and Soviet Union, as well as China, clashed. America's involvement in Vietnam began during the French war (1950–1954) in which the United States backed and paid for 80 percent of France's war to reclaim its former colony from the newly declared Democratic Republic of Vietnam (North Vietnam) led by the Communist revolutionary Ho Chi Minh. The United States took over from the French after 1954 as the main Western force in Indochina (Vietnam, Cambodia, and Laos), and ensured the establishment of the Republic of Vietnam (South Vietnam) with its capital in Saigon. President Eisenhower sent military advisers and aid to prop up the anti-Communist regime in Saigon. President Kennedy stepped up this support as South Vietnam faced increased threats of invasion from North Vietnam as well as a homegrown insurgency (for U.S. involvement in Vietnam before 1964, see chapter 22). His successor, Lyndon B. Johnson launched an all out war, albeit one that was undeclared.

With air superiority and the world's largest and most sophisticated stockpile of weapons, the United States was poised to overwhelm its smaller and weaker opponents in Vietnam. President Johnson relied on massive aerial bombing to get them to sue for peace, but despite air raids that destroyed Hanoi and killed countless North Vietnamese troops and civilians, the United States was still unable to defeat its opponent. Hanoi's Le Duan, like Johnson, was also seeking total victory. He attacked the Americans and their South Vietnam allies by launching an offensive meant to provoke a popular uprising in the south. But these efforts failed to subdue his enemies. In the first three years of the war, neither side gained a clear advantage.

☞ As you read, pay attention to military conflict in Vietnam. What was the military strategy on both sides of the conflict? Explain why or why not it was effective in the early years of the war?

25-1a Washington's War

Responding to Hanoi's General Offensive-General Uprising (GO-GU) surge in 1964, President Johnson realized that the twenty-three thousand U.S. military advisers and troops in the South were not enough to overcome 170,000 Communist guerillas. When a U.S. naval destroyer clashed with North Vietnamese torpedo boats in August of that year, the president portrayed this skirmish in which both sides were at fault as a call to arms to for the United States to greatly expand its troop strength in Vietnam. Congress obliged with the nearly unanimous **Gulf of Tonkin Resolution**, permitting the president "to take all necessary steps, including the use of armed force, to assist any member or protocol state of the Southeast Asia Collective Defense Treaty requesting assistance in defense of its freedom." Thus began the U.S phase of North Vietnam's war for independence as the number of American troops rose dramatically (see Figure 25.1).

> U.S. conventional tactics flounder in Vietnam.

Scholars have debated Johnson's motivations regarding Vietnam, but it is clear that his escalation of the war was in step with the policy goals inherited from the two preceding administrations. In fact, Johnson retained many of Kennedy's military advisers, including Secretary of Defense Robert McNamara. Whereas Kennedy had rejected McNamara's requests to engage in overt warfare, Johnson, once empowered by the Gulf of Tonkin Resolution, approved bombing raids in North Vietnam and the deployment of U.S. ground troops to South Vietnam. The defense secretary and General William C. Westmoreland did not seek to defeat the enemy as much as bring them to the negotiating table. Johnson and his advisers believed that overwhelming U.S. firepower would eventually break the North Vietnamese resolve. They paid close attention to enemy "body counts" on the assumption that a higher death rate would produce a lower motivation to fight.

Johnson's major air offensive, Operation Rolling Thunder, began in March 1965 with assaults designed to destroy Hanoi's supply lines to **National Liberation Front (NLF)** insurgents based in South Vietnam, derisively labeled *Vietcong* (Vietnamese Communists) by their enemies. What started out as targeted bombing of minor sites far from Hanoi, gradually developed into the kind of massive urban bombing campaigns such as those that had leveled Dresden, Tokyo, and Pyongyang during earlier wars. Hanoi was flattened. In addition, the U.S. Air Force defoliated hundreds of square miles of jungles in attempting to interdict what Americans called the **Ho Chi Minh trail**, a number of clandestine transportation routes that snaked through Laos and Cambodia by which North Vietnam sent troops and supplies south to NLF insurgents.

By spring 1967, McNamara knew the U.S. war plan was not working. There were not as many targets to bomb in Hanoi because the government had evacuated most of the population and relocated key industries underground or to nearby caves. Organized teams of North Vietnamese civilians quickly rebuilt roads, bridges, and the crucial Ho Chi Minh trail. Moreover, Soviet-supplied fighter planes and surface-to-air missiles enabled the North Vietnamese air force to scuttle numerous bombing raids, preventing total U.S. domination of the skies. While President Johnson kept telling the American public that their country was winning the war, the reality in Vietnam was far from Johnson's claims.

Meanwhile, U.S. ground troops faced a very different challenge than in the Korean War or World War II. The closest precedent was the U.S. repression of Philippine independence after the Spanish–American War. As in the Philippines, U.S. soldiers confronted an enemy of

Gulf of Tonkin Resolution Congressional authorization giving the president power to send combat troops to fight Communist forces in Vietnam.

National Liberation Front (NLF) Hidden military force within South Vietnam struggling to overthrow the Saigon regime through an alliance with its North Vietnamese enemies.

Ho Chi Minh trail Path of clandestine routes snaking through neighboring Laos and Cambodia over which North Vietnam supplied NLF insurgents in the south.

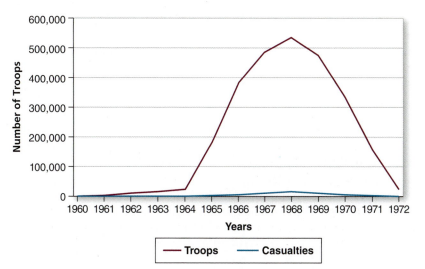

Figure 25.1 Number of U.S. troops in Vietnam and U.S. casualties, by year Following the Gulf of Tonkin Resolution, the presence of U.S. soldiers in South Vietnam increased more than sevenfold in one year to 184,000. By 1968 (the peak of the troop buildup), that figure had nearly tripled, rising to 536,000. The apex of troop numbers corresponded with the peak of U.S. casualties. ◄ Sources: U.S. Census (for data regarding total U.S. troops); National Archives (for data regarding U.S. casualties)

LBJ Library photo by Yoichi Okamoto

President Lyndon B. Johnson with Defense Secretary Robert McNamara, 1967 Using the same type of sophisticated statistical analysis that made his reputation as a corporate "whiz kid," Secretary McNamara calculated precisely how much death and destruction the United States needed to inflict before Hanoi would abandon the war as unwinnable. It turned out that his calculations were wrong and that the U.S. war plan had misjudged the enemy's capacity and resolve. ◄

guerilla fighters who blended into and were supported by local populations. U.S. soldiers implemented pacification strategies seeking to root out insurgent strongholds among South Vietnam's vast rural peasantry while at the same time winning their "hearts and minds" through aid and development programs. At the same time, U.S. troops sprayed 19 million gallons of toxic herbicides, most notably **Agent Orange**, defoliating more than 4 million acres of forest to uncover insurgent hideouts. The chemicals had a devastating human cost as over time both Vietnamese and U.S. veterans suffered elevated cases of cancer, miscarriages, birth defects, and type-2 diabetes.

Soldiers implementing the pacification program pointed out the difficulty in distinguishing friend from foe when securing rural villages from insurgents. They dehumanized the Vietnamese enemy by referring to them as *gooks*, a racialized term derived from earlier U.S. wars in the Philippines and Korea that could stand for any or all Asians (even South Vietnamese allies). The confusion and blind hatred of the enemy that sometimes resulted from pacification campaigns were evident in March 1968 in **My Lai**, a section of the Son My village where "Charlie Company," a one hundred twenty-man U.S. army unit, entered on a mission to root out and destroy insurgents who were planting land mines and stealthily murdering U.S. troops. Unaware that their intended target was actually nowhere nearby and eager to avenge recent combat losses, the soldiers massacred more than five hundred unarmed women, children, and elderly persons. Horrified by the episode, U.S. Army officials attempted to cover it up. But months later, journalists exposed the killings and in a subsequent investigation, the army found that about thirty soldiers had participated in the massacre, while the vast majority watched until U.S. helicopter pilot

Agent Orange Poisonous chemical used by the U.S. military in Vietnam to defoliate jungles in order to expose NLF insurgents.

My Lai Site in central Vietnam of a massacre in March 1968 perpetrated by U.S. troops that when exposed the next year, became a symbol of an immoral war.

Hugh Thompson Jr. stopped the rampage by landing his craft between the attackers and victims. My Lai became a powerful symbol of a war that had gone terribly wrong. Although a court-martial court charged fourteen officers as being responsible for the massacre or its cover up, almost all of these cases were dropped, and the one that went to trial was acquitted. William Calley was the only enlisted man, out of twenty-six charged, who was convicted. He received a life sentence for the premeditated murder of no less than twenty persons, but he served only three and a one-half years of house arrest for his crimes. In 1998, thirty years later, Thompson and his crew received the Soldier's Medal for bravery.

25-1b Hanoi's War

The North Vietnamese had learned from the French War that the longer their troops held out, the more public opinion abroad would sour on the war. As it turned out, their forces could hang on much longer than McNamara's statistical analyses had predicted. The men and women loyal to Hanoi not only knew the territory in this guerilla war, they were charged by the passion for freedom. They characterized the Americans as imperialists who were propping up an illegitimate puppet regime in the South that had refused to honor the 1954 peace treaty by preventing elections for national reunification. South Vietnamese officials, and their U.S. advisers, had known that such elections, if held, would end in Communist victory.

Despite their desire for independence, North Vietnamese officials were of different minds regarding war strategy. Le Duan, along with his chief assistant Le Duc Tho, took control of the nation in 1960 and pursued the GO-GU strategy that had initially prompted U.S. escalation. Le Duan's plan failed to topple South

> North Vietnam overestimates its strengths against the Americans.

Map 25.1 The U.S. War in Vietnam and Indochina Compelled by the French surrender in 1954, U.S. military involvement in Vietnam escalated greatly a decade later with congressional backing in the form of the Gulf of Tonkin Resolution. U.S. attempts to interdict the movement of enemy troops and supplies from north to south via the Ho Chi Minh trail expanded the war to neighboring Laos and Cambodia. ▲

Vietnam, which not only triggered the massive U.S. response, but also failed to incite a general uprising among the South Vietnamese. As a result, Le Duan's critics, including Ho Chi Minh, did not want to rely exclusively on the GO-GU plan, proposing, instead, prolonged **guerilla warfare** to wear the enemy down (see Map 25.1).

guerilla warfare Military strategy that employs small-scale surprise attacks rather than large-scale direct combat; it is often used by weaker powers to gain an advantage over strong ones and to prolong conflict.

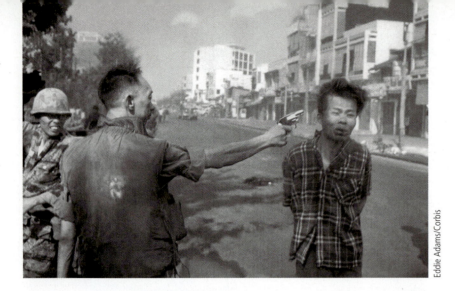

South Vietnamese Shooting NLF Insurgent at Close Range, 1968 This is a Pulitzer Prize–winning photograph of South Vietnamese police chief General Nguyen Ngoc Loan executing an NLF insurgent during the Tet Offensive. General Loan had witnessed the insurgent kill one of his fellow officers along with the officer's wife and three children. Taken out of context, the photograph was seen as an example of South Vietnamese cold-hearted brutality, and fueled global antiwar protests. ◄

Eddie Adams/Corbis

Tet Offensive Major offensive launched by North Vietnam in tandem with insurgents in South Vietnam who were defeated but caused the U.S. public's faith in their leaders and the overall war effort to falter.

Le Duan, in turn, silenced his critics to pave the way for an even larger GO-GU attack. He secured his power by purging North Vietnam of political dissent, causing Ho Chi Minh to flee to China, ostensibly for health reasons. But Le Duan, the leader of the Vietnamese Worker's Party, still had to contend with his allies, who also opposed the GO-GU strategy. The Soviets, fearful that U.S. involvement would lead to nuclear warfare, were pushing Hanoi to come to terms with the United States. The Chinese, on the other hand, supported Ho Chi Minh's idea of extending the war indefinitely through the use of guerilla warfare. In response, Le Duan brilliantly exploited Soviet–Chinese tensions to his advantage by securing continued military aid and support from both by threatening to side with one Communist superpower over the other. This kept the Soviets and Chinese in check because neither wanted to be shut out from the biggest showdown of the Cold War.

The road was clear for Le Duan to implement a second GO-GU plan in January 1968 during Tet, Vietnam's lunar New Year holidays. The **Tet Offensive**, the largest of the war to that point, sent eighty thousand troops in three different waves to attack the U.S.-backed Saigon regime in South Vietnam. But, again, the plan failed to provoke a general uprising and proved a military setback for both North Vietnam and the NLF insurgency. Tet's main damage was psychological; U.S. citizens, who had been repeatedly told their country was winning the war, were shocked to see television coverage of NLF insurgents invading the U.S. embassy in Saigon.

The world's first televised war, the Vietnam conflict drew more staff from the major U.S. networks than any place outside of New York City and Washington, D.C. After the Tet Offensive, respected news anchor Walter Cronkite came to see the war as unwinnable, reporting to millions of viewers that he was "disappointed by the optimism of the U.S. leaders, both in Vietnam and Washington, to have faith any longer in the silver linings they find in the darkest clouds." But the impact of television on the war can be exaggerated. Although news accounts focused on U.S. soldiers, they rarely showed their deaths and suffering at close range. Moreover, public support for the war had been dropping even before the Tet Offensive. Fall 1967 polls revealed that a majority of Americans saw the Vietnam War as a "mistake."

25-2
Fighting for Peace and Freedom

The escalation of U.S. troop numbers in Vietnam provoked antiwar protests at home, beginning on college campuses but eventually including politicians, religious leaders, homemakers, and even Vietnam War veterans. In this photograph, taken in August 1968, a young, unarmed woman, holding a flower and sign reading "Stop the War," confronts a guardsman wearing a helmet and a gas-mask who is pointing a bayonet at her.

How does this photo reveal the tension between the state (police) and antiwar protesters? ▶

Paul Sequeira/Getty Images

An antiwar movement in the United States gained momentum in 1968 after the Tet Offensive, as doubts about the war pushed the nation to a crisis point in that year's presidential election. The negative public reaction to Tet ruined President Johnson's reelection campaign, and he refused to seek a second term. Although both Democratic and Republican candidates called for peace in Vietnam, many young antiwar protesters supported neither party and sought instead to stop the war through civil disobedience, draft resistance, and even violence. Such protests meshed with increasingly radical calls for equal rights for African Americans and other racial minorities, women of all races, the New Left, and sexual minorities. The increased radicalism sparked a conservative resurgence that enabled Republican Richard Nixon to win the White House. Nixon, along with National Security Adviser Henry Kissinger, transformed the war strategy in Vietnam by seeking total victory in renewing attacks in Laos and broadening the conflict to Cambodia.

☞ As you read, focus on the impact that the Vietnam War had on the U.S. home front. How did various Americans respond to the war? How did the issues raised by this response change U.S. political culture?

25-2a War at Home

The conflict in Vietnam ignited the largest groundswell of antiwar sentiment in U.S. history. Longtime peace activists such as Quakers and the Women's International League for Peace and Freedom joined with newer ones such as the Committee for a SANE Nuclear Policy and Women Strike for Peace in opposition to the Vietnam War. The Civil Rights Movement also brought forth new voices, rationales, and tactics to peace activism. But the main catalysts of the antiwar movement were America's youth, especially college students. Many of them had already been active in politics through campus protests and civil rights organizing. Young people were at the forefront of a mass movement for peace, as many men who deferred military conscription by pursuing undergraduate or graduate degrees joined the antiwar cause. Major centers of peace activism included the University of California–Berkeley, University of Wisconsin–Madison, Harvard University, and Columbia University.

> The peace movement combines with the youth movement during the Vietnam War.

No youth group was more active in the antiwar struggle than Students for a Democratic Society (SDS), which in May 1965 joined ten thousand antiwar protesters at a demonstration in Washington, D.C. The organization's three hundred fifty chapters called for the withdrawal of U.S. troops, protested against military conscription and recruitment, and demanded that universities sever ties to the military by ending ROTC programs and weapons research. By the fall of 1967, students engaged in

seventy-one antiwar demonstrations on sixty-two campuses across the nation. Following the Tet offensive in the winter of 1968, these figures rose to two hundred twenty-one demonstrations on one hundred one campuses.

The antiwar message also spread through the **counterculture**, a youthful alternative to mainstream authority and respectability emerging from centers in New York City and San Francisco but arising at the same time throughout the U.S., Canada, Great Britain, Western Europe, Japan, Australia, and New Zealand. The counterculture was a global transformation of social values and lifestyles that pitted baby boomers against their parents' generation. The icon of the counterculture was the "hippie," a young man or woman dressed in faded blue jeans, tie-dyed T-shirt, beaded necklaces, and long natural hair. Hippies experimented with LSD, marijuana, peyote, and other mind-altering substances; they embraced the sexual revolution, collective living and ownership of property, Eastern religions and spirituality, and a new form of rock 'n' roll music rooted in radical politics and psychedelic states of consciousness. One of the legendary hippie experiences was the Woodstock Festival where for three days in August 1969 four hundred thousand youths descended on a dairy farm in upstate New York to hear the leading acts of psychedelic and folk rock.

counterculture Reaction to and rejection of the normative culture that embodies a wide range of alternative cultural forms and lifestyles through music, art, literature, film, collective housing, communities, and use of hallucinogenic drugs.

Despite the counterculture's popularity and attention-getting tactics, slogans, and demonstrations, a large percentage of young people continued to support the war in Vietnam. The majority of Americans who served overseas, after all, volunteered for duty. Although many did so for practical reasons, such as to gain preferential placement in military units, most of them, especially early in the war, believed wholeheartedly in the U.S. government's anti-Communist campaign and the virtues of military honor and sacrifice. Others serving in Vietnam were drafted. These included men who were at least age eighteen and were not married with children or enrolled in higher education or technical training programs. U.S. enlisted men were disproportionately from poor and lower income backgrounds because these groups were least likely to qualify for a college deferment from the draft.

25-2b Transition from Civil Rights to Black Nationalism

In April 1967, Martin Luther King Jr. paused from domestic causes to speak out against the U.S. war in Vietnam: "I knew that I could never again raise my voice against the violence

> The Civil Rights Movement adopts antiwar protests and divides over black nationalism and the use of violent tactics.

History without Borders

Asian Religions, the Beatles, and Kung Fu

1950 Japanese priest Daisetz Teitaro (D. T.) Suzuki, a major influence in spreading Zen Buddhism in the West, was invited by the Rockefeller Foundation to lecture across the U.S. He wasa visiting professor at Columbia University from 1952–1958, and was nominated for the Nobel Peace Prize in 1963.

1950s Beat poets, including Allan Ginsberg and Jack Kerouac, studied Buddhism with Japanese Americans in the San Francisco Bay Area. Kerouac's *Dharma Bums* (1958) exemplified his engagement with Buddhism.

1966 The Hindu-derived International Society for Krishna Consciousness, popularly known as the Hare Krishna movement, was founded in New York City by A. C. Bhaktivedanta Swami Prabhupada, and gained followers throughout the U.S., England, and Europe.

1968 Members of The Beatles traveled to Rishikesh, India to learn from their "spiritual advisor" Maharishi Mahesh, who popularized Transcendental Meditation (or TM), a method to attain higher consciousness. That year, Mahesh established the global headquarters for TM in Seelisberg, Switzerland, as adherents joined the practice worldwide.

1969 Thich Nhat Hanh established the United Buddhist Church in France and in 1975 founded Plum Village, its spiritual center, near Bordeaux.

1962 San Francisco Zen Center founded, with Shunryu Suzuki (no relation to D. T. Suzuki) spreading Buddhism to white converts. Meanwhile, over 125 Pure Land Buddhist temples served Asian Americans in Hawai'i, North America, and South America.

1966 Vietnamese exiled Buddhist monk Thich Nhat Hanh met with Dr. Martin Luther King, Jr., urging him to denounce the Vietnam War. The following year King nominated Nhat Hanh for the Nobel Peace Prize.

International boundaries, 1975

The Spread of Eastern Religions, 1950-1975 The U.S. attraction to Eastern religions reflected larger religious trends. Always a multireligious nation, the United States, according to Gallup polling, experienced a dramatic rise in non-Christian religions (including atheists who did not claim any religion) during the half century from 1958 to 2008, a period in which the proportion of Protestants declined from 92 to 77 percent. ▲

The Vietnam War, more than any previous event, raised awareness of Buddhism and other Asian religions little-known to Western audiences. While self-immolating Buddhists protesting religious persecution in South Vietnam had left a lasting impression on world opinion, Martin Luther King Jr. came to appreciate the prospects for world peace through discussions with Thich Nhat Hanh, an exiled scholar and peace activist whom the civil rights leader called a "gentle Buddhist monk from Vietnam." In 1967, King used his privilege as a Nobel Peace Prize winner to nominate Thich Nhat Hanh for the award. "Here is an apostle for peace and non-violence," King wrote, "cruelly separated from his own people while they are oppressed by a vicious war which has grown to threaten the sanity and security of the entire world." Although no award was given that year (King had violated Nobel protocol in making his nomination public), Thich Nhat Hanh's following in the West grew. As a formal representative to the Paris peace talks, he supported neither side in the war. But still North Vietnam, after it won the war in 1975, permanently exiled him, causing the monk to establish headquarters for a global peace movement in France.

Meanwhile, one of the first Buddhist training monasteries outside of Asia was being established in San Francisco, where Japanese Zen Buddhist priest Shunryu Suzuki developed an enthusiastic following consisting of Beat poet Allan Ginsberg and counterculture youth looking to get beyond conventional Christianity. Zen Center, founded in San Francisco's youth-oriented Haight-Ashbury district in 1969, spawned a growing interest in Buddhism

Hulton Archive/Getty Images

Dave Pickoff/AP Images

Beatles in India with Maharishi Mahesh, 1968 Maharishi Mahesh, guru to the world's most popular rock band, the Beatles, embodied the kind of non-Western religions that had a long history in the United States, Great Britain, and Western Europe, but reached its zenith of popularity as a result of the age of experimentation during the 1960s. Thus was born the "new age" spirituality and healing. Mahesh (center back) is seated behind Paul McCartney (left) and George Harrison (right). ▲

Thich Nhat Hanh Calls for Peace in Vietnam, 1966 Thich Nhat Hanh spoke at a press conference in New York City upon returning to the United States, where he earlier had studied at Princeton University. By this time, the Vietnamese monk had been exiled from South Vietnam for leading a peace movement among his students to stop the Vietnam War. ▲

throughout the nation, especially among intellectuals and artists.

Other Asian religions also gained an audience in the West, including Hinduism, Sufism, Islam, and various sects of Buddhism from Tibet, Thailand, Nepal, and other places. Hinduism was one of the most popular Asian religions in the West due to the influence of celebrities like the Beatles who turned for inspiration to Indian guru Maharishi Mahesh. In 1966, Beatle George Harrison said "he believed much more in the religions of India than anything he ever learned in Christianity." By the mid-1970s, Maharishi Mahesh, whom *The New York Times* called "chief guru to the Western world," had founded a university in

Iowa and three hundred seventy centers around the United States for teaching transcendental meditation designed to relieve stress while promoting health and peaceful well-being.

The fascination with Asian spirituality overlapped with the rising interest in Asian martial arts. Many Westerners attributed North Vietnam's ability to withstand U.S. superior firepower not only to the tactics of guerilla warfare, but mysterious Asian fighting techniques. Outside of Asian immigrant communities, Americans knew little about such skills until Bruce Lee, a Chinese American martial arts champion and actor from Hong Kong, launched the genre of Kung Fu films. The success

of Lee's Hollywood premiere, *Enter the Dragon* (1973), inspired the proliferation of Kung Fu–themed movies and television shows, from Chuck Norris adventures to the family favorite *Karate Kid*, that inspired a generation of Americans to embrace Asian martial arts.

Critical Thinking Questions

▶ What factors influenced the spread of Asian religions and martial arts in the West?

▶ What impact do you think they have on U.S. views of Asia and Asian peoples?

of the oppressed in the ghettos without having first spoken clearly to the greatest purveyor of violence in the world today: my own government." According to King, Johnson's war was wrong on two counts: It opposed the legitimate national liberation of the Vietnamese people, and, by overwhelming the U.S. budget, prevented the full implementation of the president's War on Poverty. Here King expanded his focus on civil and voting rights for African Americans in seeking to resolve problems of economic inequality for all races. Like socialist critic Michael Harrington, King called on the federal government to radically transform the economic and social conditions that made it nearly impossible for poor people to achieve the American Dream. To this end, he criticized institutional racism, police brutality, and the undemocratic power of corporations. He also promoted affirmative action, full-employment policies, and raising the minimum wage as a means to ending the cycle of poverty that offered little hope of escape.

Seeking economic justice, King went to Memphis, Tennessee, in April 1968 to support striking African American sanitation workers. It was there that white segregationist James Earl Ray shot and killed the civil rights leader. King's assassination sparked another wave of urban unrest as blacks in more than one hundred cities rose up against the kind of economic and racial injustice that King had been opposing in Memphis and throughout the nation. Race riots the year before had spurred President Johnson to appoint the **Kerner Commission** to investigate the nation's racial problems. In February 1968, the commission produced a widely circulated report warning "our nation is moving toward two societies, one black, one white—separate and unequal."

King sought solutions to poverty through a racially inclusive poor people's movement, but others advocated empowering African Americans through the radical strategies of black nationalism. In 1966, SNCC adopted the practice of racial separatism by having its chapters sever ties with white liberal organizations. In a speech at Greenwood, Mississippi, SNCC leader Stokely Carmichael defended Malcolm X and the Nation of Islam, dismissing the image perpetuated by the mainstream media of them as antiwhite racists who threatened to destroy the nation's interracial goodwill. The only way for blacks to make it in America, Carmichael maintained, was to come together as a newly independent nation-within-a-nation with its own identity, culture, and economic self-sufficiency. Carmichael called this kind of racial nationalism **black power**. The phrase stuck and became a rallying cry for racial minorities who began to see integration as a dead end. King's assassination by a white man seemed to prove to many activists and disgruntled ghetto dwellers that the United States was still not ready for interracial democracy. A year later, Carmichael expatriated to Guinea and eventually changed his name to Kwame Ture in honor of pan-African leaders Kwame Nkrumah (Ghana) and Ahmed Sekou Toure (Guinea). The activist then traveled to North Vietnam, China, Cuba, and throughout Africa preaching revolution against racist imperialism.

At the same time, Muhammad Ali, the world's heavyweight boxing champion, refused to be inducted when drafted into the U.S. Army. A follower of the Nation of Islam, Ali, like other black Muslims, declared conscientious objector status and refused to fight because of his faith and his racial solidarity with the nonwhite enemy, saying "no Vietcong ever called me nigger." As a result, he was arrested, found guilty of draft evasion, and stripped of his boxing titles. It took four years for the champ to clear his name in a 1971 Supreme Court decision that allowed him to resume his legendary boxing career.

The African American organization most identified with radicalism was the **Black Panther Party**. The first chapter began in New York City in 1965, but it was the second chapter—established the next year in Oakland, California, by Huey Newton and Bobby Seale—that garnered national attention for its use of guns and violence in the name of black self-defense and the struggle to overthrow American capitalism. In this sense, Newton and Seale combined the racial separatism of Malcolm X with the revolutionary socialism of Karl Marx, Vladimir Lenin, and Mao Zedong. Like Ali, the Panthers opposed the Vietnam War as an act of imperialist aggression in which Americans of color fought and died in disproportionate numbers.

While the Panthers pushed black power to revolutionary extremes, African Americans also revealed a willingness to work within the political system toward black nationalist ends. In 1967 the New York City Board of Education experimented with an alternative to school integration that enabled a version of black power to influence the curriculum of public schools in Brooklyn's Ocean Hill and Brownsville neighborhoods. With support from the New York City mayor and funds provided by the Ford Foundation, the people in these largely black neighborhoods were able to control local schools by electing their own school officials. The new black-run school board fired several unionized Jewish American teachers, provoking a series of teachers' strikes against the Ocean Hill and Brownsville schools that doomed the short-lived experiment in "community control." The conflict revealed the limits of civil rights reforms and strained the black-Jewish coalition that had collaborated in earlier civil rights struggles.

Kerner Commission
Presidential committee whose report warned about the nation's growing racial schism that pitted poor blacks against affluent whites.

black power Slogan used by African American social activists based on the strategy of racial separatism and total liberation from white racism and its legacy.

Black Panther Party Radical organization begun in 1965 that used humanitarian and violent means to liberate African Americans from poverty and racial discrimination.

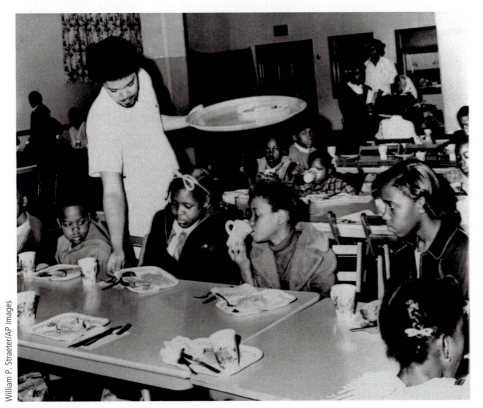

William P. Straeter/AP Images

Black Panthers' Free Breakfast Program, 1969 In addition to its militant black nationalism and opposition to the Vietnam War, the Black Panthers provided free meals and other services to the black poor, and they worked to forge a broad-based revolutionary movement that reached out to a wide variety of radical groups within and outside the United States. ▲

25-2c 1968

The simultaneous rise of black nationalism, race riots, and antiwar protests reached a crisis point in the presidential election of 1968. In November 1967, Eugene McCarthy entered the presidential race as an antiwar candidate seeking to unseat the incumbent Johnson as the Democratic Party nominee. McCarthy (not to be confused with the anti-Communist crusader Joseph McCarthy) was a U.S. senator from Minnesota with a long history of supporting liberal domestic and international causes, and his candidacy became a barometer measuring the nation's response to Johnson's Vietnam War. In March 1968, after McCarthy defeated Johnson in the New Hampshire primary, Senator Robert Kennedy, President John Kennedy's brother, also entered the race as an antiwar Democrat challenging Johnson. With mounting political opposition and serious health problems, the president announced that he would not run for reelection and would begin peace talks with the North Vietnamese. McCarthy and Kennedy then battled for the Democratic nomination as Vice President Hubert Humphrey also announced his candidacy. In June, after winning the California primary, Kennedy was assassinated by a Christian Palestinian who was upset about the candidate's support for Israel. But this did not clear the way for McCarthy. After the Republicans

> Domestic upheavals in 1968 enable the Republicans to gain the White House.

nominated Richard Nixon as their candidate, Humphrey beat out McCarthy at the Democratic National Convention in Chicago in August 1968.

The Chicago convention proved to be a turning point for the Democratic Party and the antiwar movement. Thousands of activists from the New Left, counterculture, and black power movement came to the city to oppose Humphrey's nomination. They organized large demonstrations before and during the DNC convention. Humphrey had the support of the party's old guard, especially labor unions and big-city bosses such as Chicago mayor Richard Daley, who comprised the heart of the New Deal coalition. While the convention was deciding on the nominee, Mayor Daley's police cracked down on antiwar protests to prevent them from disrupting the proceedings. Dressed in riot gear, the police used tear gas and billy clubs against the demonstrators, some who returned fire by throwing rocks, bottles, and broken glass. As millions of Americans viewed the clashes on television, the youth chanted the "the whole world is watching."

The win by Humphrey, who had supported Johnson's war as his vice president, was a bitter pill for antiwar activists to swallow. The antiwar movement responded to the "days of rage" in Chicago by increasing the volume and volatility of their protests. Students at the University of Akron, for example, shouted down Richard Nixon in a campus election speech, yelling "Ho, Ho, Ho Chi Minh, Ho Chi Minh is gonna win" (they did not know that the legendary Vietnamese leader was but a figurehead at this point). A number of Vietnam veterans began to openly oppose the war and spoke out about the atrocities they saw and even committed in the defense of "freedom." Even more dramatic was the surge in student protests around the world. Antiwar sentiment in France spawned popular student strikes in Paris that generated violent clashes with police. West German students called for its government to take full responsibility for the Holocaust and to stop another genocide in Vietnam. Antiwar demonstrations in Japan combined with student strikes and radical opposition to the nation's security alliance with the United States. At the same time, students propelled revolutionary impulses in Eastern bloc countries such as Czechoslovakia in which leader Alexander Dubcek responded to university strikes by experimenting with a less repressive form of communism dubbed "socialism with a human face." This **Prague Spring** lasted seven months until Soviet leaders stopped the experiment by invading Czechoslovakia. Violent government crackdowns also produced misery for Mexican university students who opposed the 1968 Olympic Games to be held in Mexico City, chanting "No queremos Olimpiadas, queremos revolución" ("We do not want Olympic Games, we want revolution").

Back in the United States, Nixon, the Republican presidential candidate, emphasized the importance of law and order and appealed to what he called the **silent majority** of loyal, law-abiding Americans. Nixon also distanced himself from the third-party candidacy of segregationist George Wallace, the Alabama governor who engaged in massive resistance to civil and voting rights reforms. Instead of attacking such reforms, Nixon, following a script from Barry Goldwater, the 1964 Republican presidential candidate, deployed a **southern strategy** that emphasized the importance of states rights in order to woo southern whites to his campaign. The strategy worked, and Nixon defeated Humphrey by a large number of electoral votes but only a fraction of the popular vote to become the thirty-seventh president (see Map 25.2).

25-2d Nixon and Kissinger's War

Nixon came to the presidency with a mandate to bring U.S. troops home from Vietnam and spoke publicly about achieving "peace with honor." Together with his trusted

{ Nixon expands the Vietnam war into Laos and Cambodia.

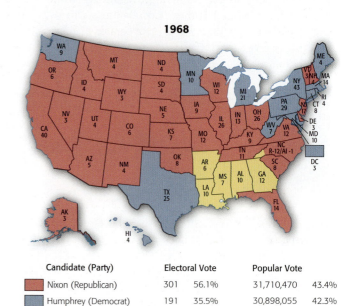

1968

Candidate (Party)	Electoral Vote		Popular Vote	
Nixon (Republican)	301	56.1%	31,710,470	43.4%
Humphrey (Democrat)	191	35.5%	30,898,055	42.3%
Wallace (American Independent)	46	8.4%	9,446,167	12.9%

Map 25.2 Presidential Election of 1968 The solid Democratic South was no more in 1968 as only Texas voted for Hubert Humphrey, while the rest of the states split between Nixon and Wallace. Although Wallace won electoral votes from five southern states (an impressive showing for a third-party candidate), Nixon's southern strategy also netted him five states in the South, continuing Republican inroads into this heavily Democratic region and revealing the weakening of the New Deal coalition. ▲

military adviser Henry Kissinger, he developed a four-pronged strategy for ending the war. First was to use North Vietnam's superpower allies, the Soviets and Chinese, to pressure Le Duan to reach a negotiated settlement. Second was to reduce the number of U.S. troops by empowering the South Vietnamese military to fight the southern insurgency on its own—what Nixon called **Vietnamization**. Third was to engage in formal peace negotiations that would build on Johnson's 1968 agreement reached with North Vietnam to stop U.S. bombings. Nixon's Vietnamization and peace negotiations represented a new kind of thinking that appealed to the war-weary American public. But like Johnson, who did not want to be the first president to lose a foreign war, the new president was seeking a total victory that would give the United States the upper hand at the bargaining table. This led to the secret implementation of the fourth part of his war strategy. In March 1969, while Americans were being told that the war was winding down, Nixon ordered airstrikes against Communist strongholds in ostensibly neutral Laos and Cambodia in order to interdict troop movement and destroy the Ho Chi Minh trail.

The Geneva Accords in 1954 granted Laos independence, and the United States supported the anti-Communist Laotian government while North Vietnam-backed Pathet Lao revolutionaries who controlled the mountain regions that contained and concealed the supply lines feeding NLF insurgents from North Vietnam. Beginning in the early 1960s, the Central Intelligence Agency (CIA) recruited a secret army of mountain peoples known as the Hmong to help defeat North Vietnam and their Pathet Lao allies. The forty-five thousand Hmong fighters represented roughly 10 percent of the total population of this minority group in Laos. The majority, who had earlier fought with the Viet Minh against the French, sided with North Vietnam.

Like Laos, Cambodia had received independence after the French left Indochina in 1954. The widely popular Prince Norodom Sihanouk took over as head of state and steered the small nation on the difficult path of non-alliance, seeking to protect his country from being overpowered by neighboring Thailand, as well as by North and South Vietnam. In 1965, the prince broke off diplomatic relations with the United States because of its support for South Vietnam. At the same time, he reached secret agreements allowing Chinese war supplies to be shipped to North Vietnam and NLF insurgents via Cambodian ports and the "Sihanouk trail" into South Vietnam. When Nixon learned about such shipments, he expanded the war into Cambodia and ordered massive bombings to interdict the Sihanouk trail in successive attacks—Operations Breakfast, Lunch, Snack, Supper, Dessert—that became known collectively as *Operation Menu*. In 1970, a U.S.-backed coup forced Sihanouk into exile and ushered in the aggressively anti-Communist regime of Lon Nol, who purged Cambodia of Communists and consented to a U.S. ground invasion of his country.

Nixon's bombings in Laos and Cambodia confirmed Le Duan's fear that the U.S. would remain committed to total victory in Vietnam. In Nixon and Kissinger, Le Duan and Le Duc Tho now had counterparts who were equally adept at silencing dissent within their governments, while stubbornly waiting for an opportunity to land a knock-out punch to end the war. Ho Chi Minh's death in 1969 added to Le Duan's concerns about the war by casting a pall across North Vietnam even though the beloved revolutionary leader had long been a mere figurehead. The failure of the Tet invasion combined with the rejuvenation of U.S. war effort under Nixon pushed Le Duan to change his war strategy from toppling the Saigon regime to obtaining favorable peace terms that would require the United States to leave Indochina.

Nixon's new strategy in Indochina also had an impact at home. In May 1970, when the news media reported that U.S. soldiers had invaded Cambodia, antiwar activists across the United States protested Nixon's widening of the war. Amidst angry clashes at Kent State University in Ohio and the historically black Jackson State College in Mississippi, six students were shot and killed by law enforcement officers. In 1971, Nixon received another blow when former defense analyst Daniel Ellsberg leaked the Pentagon Papers, a top-secret Defense Department study revealing that previous administrations had misled the nation about the government's involvement in Vietnam. In the *Sullivan* decision, the Supreme Court overruled Nixon's attempts to prevent *The New York Times* and other major newspapers from publishing the documents. It was a landmark decision affirming the freedom of the press. Illegal actions taken by Nixon aides attempting to discredit Ellsberg became part of the major scandal that later doomed Nixon's presidency.

Bettmann/CORBIS

Henry Kissinger and Le Duc Tho at Paris Peace Talks for War in Vietnam, 1972 The United States and North Vietnam entered into peace talks in May 1968 with neither side ready to give up the war effort. In addition to the four-party peace talks occurring in Paris between representatives from the United States, North Vietnam, South Vietnam, and the southern (NLF) insurgents, Henry Kissinger (left) and Le Duc Tho (right) held secret two-party talks starting in August 1969 in order to get around the interests of South Vietnam, which opposed peace on any terms. ◄

AP Images/Dang Ngoc Khoa

Global Americans In 1970, **Le Ly Hayslip** married a U.S. civilian worker in Vietnam and eventually left her country to join him in starting a new life with her two sons in San Diego, California. She was twelve when the war came to her village of Ky La in central Vietnam. Both sides of the conflict recruited children to serve as spies and saboteurs; Hayslip fell in with NLF insurgents. Within two years, she was caught for holding "revolutionary sympathies" and tortured at a South Vietnamese prison. After being released, she was then accused by NLF insurgents of being a traitor, raped, and sentenced to death. Although members of Hayslip's family fought on both sides of the conflict, she was more concerned about surviving the war than taking sides. She managed to evade the NLF death sentence and flee to Saigon where she became a housekeeper for a wealthy Vietnamese family. She was fired after becoming pregnant by her employer. After working in the black market as a drug courier and prostitute, Hayslip met and married Ed Munro, the American who would bring her and her children (one of them his) to San Diego. A year after Munro died in 1973, Le Ly Hayship married Dennis Hayslip and bore a third son. The marriage, however, ended in divorce as she charged her husband with domestic abuse. Le Ly Hayslip would eventually write two books that documented her ability to survive horrifying challenges in Vietnam and the United States. Such suffering, she wrote in her memoir *When Heaven and Earth Changed Places*, taught her "how to be strong while we are weak, how to be brave when we are afraid, how to be wise in the midst of confusion, and how to let go of that which we can no longer hold. In this way, anger can teach us forgiveness, hate can teach us love, and war can teach us peace."

25-3

Rights Revolution

The push to legalize abortion was part of the expansion of rights that many activists called for during the turbulent Vietnam War era. In this photograph, demonstrators marched to the U.S. Capitol in Washington, D.C. where they met a counterprotest by anti-abortion forces.

Why was the right to abortion considered an important part of the movement for women's equality? Why would groups oppose the right to abortion? ▶

Go to MindTap® to practice history with the Chapter 25 **Primary Source Writing Activity: Protest Movements.** Read and view primary sources and respond to a writing prompt.

AP Images

The proliferation of antiwar and black power protests inspired a wide array of activists to assert their own causes and claims on the state. While many had already been working to expose and eliminate discrimination against women, young people, African Americans, Latinos, Asian Americans, Native Americans, and sexual minorities, the "war at home" provided an opportunity to broaden support for their causes by joining together with antiwar and black power activists to create a broad coalition for political and social change. The coalition included both liberal reformers and radical extremists who criticized the status quo but often disagreed over strategies, tactics, and goals. President Nixon and most conservatives were especially alarmed by leftist extremists, who proclaimed violence to be a legitimate means of protest. As a result, the FBI closely monitored dissent and cracked down on those deemed most threatening.

☞ As you read, notice the differences between liberal and radical views about society and its problems. How and why were these expressed within the antiwar movement as well as struggles seeking social justice for women, racial minorities, and sexual minorities?

25-3a Third World Movements in the United States

Black power thrived on many college and university campuses, and given the prominence of youth radicalism in the San Francisco Bay Area,

> Black nationalism influences other racial minorities.

it was not surprising that the agitation for black nationalist university courses and service programs began there. In winter 1968, racial minority students at San Francisco State College and the University of California–Berkeley waged general strikes that pressured these schools to establish departments of black studies along with programs run by Native Americans, Mexican Americans, and Asian Americans. **Ethnic studies** departments created classes to counteract what they viewed as the damaging psychological effects of living in a fundamentally racist society that devalued the experiences and contributions of nonwhites. The idea of ethnic studies quickly spread and inspired cultural heritage movements that included the invention of Kwanza, a seven-day holiday offering a noncommercial alternative to Christmas drawing on African traditions to build black unity, pride, and economic and cultural self-sufficiency.

As the strikes for ethnic studies revealed, the notion of black power resonated with other racial minority groups. Native Americans faced the same urban ghetto conditions as blacks as a result of federal Indian relocation programs that encouraged them to leave reservations. In the late 1960s, nearly one in three Indian youths in Minneapolis dropped out of school, and while Native Americans made up only 10 percent of the city's population, they comprised 70 percent of its prison inmates. The **American Indian Movement (AIM)**, a national struggle to advance Native American economic and cultural autonomy, grew out of these dire conditions. To draw attention to their cause, AIM occupied Alcatraz Island, protested at historic sites such as Mount Rushmore and a replica of the *Mayflower* ship, and took over the headquarters of Bureau of Indian Affairs in Washington, D.C. In 1973, these protests culminated in the occupation of Wounded Knee, the historic site on the Pine Ridge Indian reservation in South Dakota where the U.S. military had massacred families of Lakota Siouxs in 1890.

Mexican Americans also embraced the spirit of racial nationalism. While older civil rights organizations such as the League of United Latin American Citizens (LULAC) and the G.I. Forum relied on the courts to fight discrimination, radical Chicanos such as the paramilitary Brown Berets took the Black Panthers' revolutionary stance. This was not surprising given that Mexican American communities experienced many of the same urban problems as African Americans and Native Americans. The **Chicano movement** emerged within rapidly growing Mexican American urban ghettos, or *barrios*. The Brown Berets sought to provide "self-defense" against police brutality, protested against the disproportionate death rate of Latino soldiers in the Vietnam War, and encouraged "blowouts" in which thousands of high school students, starting in March 1968, walked out of public schools in the East Los Angeles area to protest poor educational conditions. Meanwhile, activists in Texas sought to improve *barrio* conditions by running candidates for public office from

ethnic studies Academic interdisciplinary study of race and ethnicity that emerged from racial protest movements inspired by black power and antiwar protest.

American Indian Movement (AIM) Social movement to liberate and empower Native Americans catalyzed by black power and antiwar movements.

Chicano movement Social movement to liberate and empower Mexican Americans inspired by black power and antiwar movements.

JIM MONE/AP Images

Resolution of the Siege at Wounded Knee, 1973 This photograph captures a peace-pipe ceremony between leaders of the American Indian Movement (AIM) and a representative from the U.S. government (seated at right). The ceremony marked the end of AIM's ten-week seizure of the town of Wounded Knee. The takeover was part of a militant struggle by Native American activists to reclaim land, independence, and dignity that was the birthright of their ancestors. ◄

Global Americans In the fall of 1972, **Stanley Ann Dunham** enrolled in a master's of arts program at the University of Hawai'i's East-West Center, a magnet for international students, as well as Americans like Dunham who were drawn toward cross-cultural relations. Her two husbands had each come to the center from newly independent Third World countries—the first from Kenya, and the second from Indonesia. Dunham herself was transplanted to Honolulu, having moved there with her parents after living in Kansas, California, Oklahoma, Texas, and Washington state. As a result of her marriages and birth of her two biracial children, she embodied the kind of open-minded race and culture mixing upon which the center, and Hawai'i as a whole, had built its reputation. Dunham also stood out for academic reasons. Having lived and taught in Indonesia for eleven years and being fluent in the language and folk arts, she was seen as a promising scholar of development programs in that country. Her research and activities were supported by the UN's International Labour Organization, the United States Agency for International Development (USAID), the Ford Foundation, the World Bank, and the Indonesian government. But while she would become a respected anthropologist, it was through her son, President Barack Obama, that the world would come to know about her—a white, single mother from Kansas whose internationalism epitomized the growing significance of the Asia-Pacific region during America's Vietnam War era.

Obama Presidential Campaign/AP Images

United Farm Workers Labor union for agricultural workers in California led by Cesar Chavez and Dolores Huerta.

Asian American movement Social operation to liberate and empower Asian Americans spurred by black power and antiwar movements.

the *La Raza Unida* (the unified race) political party. On college and university campuses, student groups such as *Movimiento Estudiantil Chicano de Aztlan* (MEChA) established Chicano and Chicana feminist studies to foster a separatist identity rooted in a sense of Mexican peoplehood.

The most widely known Latino protests were Cesar Chavez's efforts on behalf of agricultural workers in California. Together with Dolores Huerta and Filipino farmworkers like Philip Vera Cruz, Chavez led a successful boycott of California table grapes in 1966 leading to America's first collective bargaining agreement in agriculture later that year. The charismatic, Gandhi-like Chavez garnered widespread notoriety for engaging in marches and hunger strikes to provide the civil and economic rights for one of the most aggrieved groups of workers in U.S. society. His **United Farm Workers'** (UFW) union expanded the California cause throughout the nation and enabled millions of migrant laborers for the first time to receive the job protections and security of a union contract.

The Filipino Americans who helped found the UFW revealed that Asian Americans, who comprised less than one percent of the U.S. population in 1970, were also swept up in the activist spirit. Yet the **Asian American movement** derived from the growing Chinese and Japanese American middle classes. "Yellow power" activists established social service programs in Chinatowns, Little Tokyos, and Little Manilas that drew inspiration from both the Black Panthers' free breakfast programs and Mao Zedong's mandate to "serve the people." The movement's antiwar protests emphasized U.S. racism against the Vietnamese and even

against Asian American soldiers whose own U.S. officers and unit-mates sometimes confused as enemy "gooks." Asian American studies programs emerged on college and university campuses to counteract the ignorance and invisibility of Asians within the mainstream curriculum. Of all the struggles, the most well-known was the demand for redress for the internment of Japanese Americans during World War II. Movement activists pushed the community's established civil rights organization, the Japanese American Citizens League, to raise awareness about the injustice of internment, and began the campaign that culminated in 1988 with Congress issuing an official apology, along with awarding each living survivor of the forced relocation $20,000.

25-3b **Women's Rights**

The women's movement, like other protest movements during the Vietnam Era, experienced divisions between radical separatists and liberal reformists. Liberals were represented by Betty Friedan and other feminists who joined the National Organization of Women (NOW) and worked to gain equal rights through the courts and the federal government's Equal Employment Opportunity Commission (EEOC). By 1968, the EEOC began to back away from its position of treating male and female workers differently in order to protect women from doing "men's work." NOW feminists saw such protection as gender discrimination that prevented women from working the same hours as men. Wracked by indecisiveness, the EEOC referred many of these cases to the courts, and in the *Weeks* decision in

> A new generation of feminists win economic and reproductive rights.

Table 25.1 Equal Employment Opportunity Commission (EEOC) Milestones, 1964–1973

One of the main achievements of the Civil Rights Movement, the EEOC began its mission with a decided focus on racial discrimination and only a token interest in gender equality. But it became a major player in creating new economic opportunities for both women and racial minorities.

Year	Milestone
1964	Civil Rights Act (Title VII) establishes the EEOC to eliminate unlawful employment discrimination.
1965	EEOC begins with a budget of $2.25 million and 100 employees to investigate charges of unlawful employment practices and if found to be true, to try to reach a voluntary agreement to rectify the problem. The EEOC cannot bring its own lawsuits, but it can support individuals who sue.
1965	EEOC maintains that businesses cannot fire female employees when they marry.
1966	EEOC gets 111 businesses, mostly in the South, to desegregate employee facilities such as cafeterias, restrooms, and showers and locker rooms.
1966	EEOC requires 50 percent of the nation's private employers to report on their workers and work conditions regarding women and racial minorities.
1966	EEOC issues its guidelines on employment testing procedures used for hiring purposes, which can intentionally or unintentionally discriminate against women and racial minorities.
1966	EEOC issues guidelines on discrimination because of religion.
1967	EEOC holds public hearings about employment discrimination in the textile industry, the largest of complaints.
1968	EEOC has a budget of approximately $6.5 million and 380 employees to investigate a record 15,058 complaints filed that year.
1968	EEOC issues revised guidelines on sex discrimination to ban widespread help-wanted advertisements that use "*male*" and "*female*" column headings.
1968	EEOC decides that policies designed to protect women workers in 43 states constituted unlawful sex discrimination.
1968	EEOC holds public hearings on employment discrimination in white-collar employment.
1969	EEOC holds public hearings on employment discrimination in the aerospace, motion picture, radio, television, and financial services industries.
1970	EEOC issues guidelines on discrimination because of language or national origin.
1972	Congress amends Title VII allowing the EEOC to bring a lawsuit against nongovernment employers.
1972	EEOC issues revised guidelines on sex discrimination to prohibit employers from requiring pregnant employees from taking a mandatory leave of absence or firing them because of their pregnancy.
1973	EEOC joins with the Department of Labor, Department of Justice to require that AT&T, the nation's largest private employer, eliminate discriminatory recruiting, hiring, and promotion practices against women and racial minorities. The company agrees to provide $15 million in back-pay to 13,000 women and 2,000 men of color, and $30 million in immediate pay raises to 36,000 employees.
1973	EEOC has a $43 million budget, 2,000 employees, and a backlog of 80,000 cases awaiting investigation.

Source: Milestones in the History of the U.S. Equal Employment Opportunity Commission, http://www.eeoc.gov/eeoc/history/35th/milestones/index.html.

1969, the Supreme Court overturned protective labor legislation, which allowed women to work at jobs that had been reserved for men, such as those requiring the lifting of heavy objects. By the late 1960s, feminists had succeeded in getting the EEOC to collaborate openly with NOW in challenging sex segregation in the workplace. They pushed to make child care an essential right for working women, but the campaign for a national policy fell short, leaving it to businesses to develop child care programs on their own accord. Feminists also sought to define sexual harassment as workplace discrimination. In June 1972, they welcomed passage of **Title IX**, an amendment to the Education Act that barred gender discrimination in all federally funded school programs and activities. As a result, collegiate women's athletics blossomed as colleges and universities were required to provide equal opportunities and financial support for female student athletes (see Table 25.1).

Title IX Amendment to Education Act requiring gender equity in all schools that receive federal funding.

reproductive rights Legal empowerment of women to have ultimate control over whether to become pregnant or to abort a pregnancy.

Roe v. Wade Landmark U.S. Supreme Court decision legalizing abortion and establishing guidelines for when and under what conditions it can be performed.

sexist Term used by the women's liberation movement to characterize gender bias and discrimination, as in "sexist pig."

male chauvinism Term used especially by the women's liberation movement for biased and discriminatory views about women that men held.

homophile Term connoting a positive view of homosexuality that gay and lesbian activists in the United States commonly used during the 1950s and 1960s.

Not all women benefited equally from obtaining economic rights. As was the case for racial minorities, affirmative action for jobs and college admissions offered the greatest benefits to those with the most educational and class privileges. Moreover, the elimination of protective labor legislation, which viewed women as equal to men, did unexpected damage to women who relied on welfare programs. In 1967, Congress revised the Social Security Act to reflect the new view of women as independent workers rather than dependent on a male breadwinner. This revision required mothers receiving Aid to Families with Dependent Children (AFDC) to get a job rather than receive benefits for staying at home with their children. Although appreciating being treated as independent women, many preferred the older protections that did not require them to leave the home for work.

Feminism at this time also concerned **reproductive rights**. During the 1950s and early 1960s, practicing birth control became legal in most states, which the Supreme Court confirmed in the landmark *Griswold v. Connecticut* case (1965) upholding the right to privacy of married couples to obtain birth control counseling and prescriptions from a Planned Parenthood clinic in New Haven, Connecticut. The decision struck down the last remaining state laws against birth control, and in 1972, the Court found that unmarried couples too could practice birth control.

The next step for reproductive rights advocates was to challenge laws that banned abortion in forty-six states and Washington, D.C. In 1970, Norma McCovey provided two young lawyers, Sara Weddington and Linda Coffee, with a test case for challenging the constitutionality of the Texas ban on abortion, which only exempted cases when it was necessary to preserve a mother's life. McCovey had been unable to obtain an abortion in Texas, and subsequently asked Weddington and Coffee to represent her in challenging the law. The case made its way to the Supreme Court, which in January 1973 ruled in favor of McCovey (named as plaintiff under the pseudonym "Jane Roe") and other defendants added to the case as part of a class action suit. The ***Roe v. Wade*** decision, as did *Griswold*, turned on the right to privacy, which in the former decision was counterbalanced by the state's concerns about a woman's health and the potential for human life.

Roe v. Wade divided the term of pregnancy into three parts (trimesters) and held that preventing abortion during the first trimester violated a woman's right to privacy between her and the attending physician—a point that abortion opponents insisted disregarded Christian principles for the "right to life." Though weakened and under continuous threat of being overturned, *Roe v. Wade* continues to stand as a hallmark to postwar feminism.

25-3c Radical Feminism and Gay Liberation

{ Protests push for radical understanding of gender and sexual equality.

While feminists worked to gain equal rights through the courts and the EEOC, a younger generation, inspired by antiwar and black power struggles, lost hope in the nation's ability to reform itself through the regular political process. These radical feminists separated themselves from male activists in order to better empower women. Such an approach saw **sexist** laws, **male chauvinism**, and gender-biased hiring practices as merely symptoms of more fundamental social, cultural, and psychological problems relating to women's oppression. Radical organizations such as Redstockings, Cell 16, The Feminists, and New York Radical Feminists forced liberal organizations such as NOW to move farther to the left. Betty Friedan herself called on NOW to form political alliances with the younger activists to stage a national women's strike that called for twenty-four-hour child care centers, unlimited access to abortion, and equal employment and educational opportunities for women.

But both radical and liberal feminists in many cases balked at the place of sexual minorities within the movement. Friedan called lesbians a "lavender menace" that threatened to damage the reputation of the feminist movement by associating it with a stigmatized sexuality. Others dismissed lesbians as re-enacting, and thus supporting, male power dynamics through their relations with other women. Lesbian activists countered these claims by asserting themselves as the true feminists because they, unlike others who dated and married men, identified exclusively with women. Despite these pleas, the feminist movement in the early 1970s was not able yet to accept homosexuality as readily as it did youth radicalism.

The marginalization of sexual minorities from activist organizations, combined with their stigmatization throughout U.S. society, laid the foundation for the gay liberation movement. Beginning in 1950, **homophile** organizations including Mattachine and the Daughters of Bilitis had mobilized to resist the inequities of the McCarthy-era lavender scare largely through education campaigns. But in the late 1960s, a new generation of radical activists rejected the reformist strategies of the homophile groups. The spark for gay liberation ignited in June 1969 at the Stonewall Inn in New York City, where a routine police raid of the unlicensed bar induced a riot by its gay, lesbian, transvestite, and transsexual patrons. Influenced by black power, a crowd of roughly four hundred resisted police

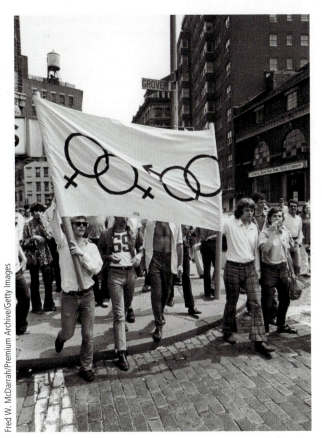

Fred W. McDarrah/Premium Archive/Getty Images

Gay Pride March, 1969 One month after the Stonewall Rebellion, gay rights activists marched in New York City. By 1973 almost eight hundred lesbian, gay, bisexual, and transgender (LGBT) organizations had been established, and LGBT bars, restaurants, churches, synagogues, health clinics, community centers, and other businesses and nonprofits had opened across the country. Gay pride marches began in a number of cities to commemorate the Stonewall Rebellion as a new beginning for gay liberation. ◀

arrest, shouting chants of "gay power." A larger mob returned the next night, engaging in another round of clashes with the police that would be known as the **Stonewall Rebellion**. The rioters paid a high price as those arrested had their names printed in newspapers and many lost their jobs during a time when homosexuality was criminalized in most states and people could be involuntarily hospitalized on the mere suspicion of same-sex attraction. After the Stonewall Rebellion, calls significantly increased to bring the lesbian, gay, bisexual, and transgender (LGBT) community "out of the closet" and into the plain sight of mainstream America.

25-3d Extremism and Government Repression

In December 1969, the most extreme members of SDS dissolved the organization and advocated the use of violence to promote a revolution in the United States that would eliminate race, sex, and economic inequality, as well as end "imperialist" wars in Vietnam and around the world. They were known as the *Weathermen*, a name taken from lyrics of a popular Bob Dylan song. The group later changed its name to the gender-neutral

> Political conflicts become violent when some radicals become armed revolutionaries, and the U.S. government counterattacks them.

Weather Underground, reflecting its fugitive status as well as commitment to women's empowerment. Group members were largely white leftist revolutionaries from middle-class backgrounds who became utterly disillusioned with the status quo while at the same time convinced that their violent acts would incite a general uprising among the country's poor to overthrow the government. They were wrong. From 1969, when they blew up a statue paying tribute to Chicago police, until the mid-1970s, when most of its founding members were arrested, the group engaged in seventeen acts of domestic terrorism, mostly bombing government buildings such as the Senate wing of the U.S. Capitol and the ROTC building at the University of Washington. They identified with revolutionaries in Japan, France, Mexico, Algeria, Germany, and other nations.

Meanwhile, the FBI was engaged in covert operations to counteract extremist organizations on the left and right, including the Black Panthers, AIM, the Ku Klux Klan, and antiwar protesters. The plan began in 1956 as a counterintelligence program known by its acronym, **COINTELPRO**, to spy on the Communist Party and later expanded to include civil rights groups like SCLC, SNCC, and the NAACP. By December 1969, the program had engaged in secret acts of violent repression, including the murder of Chicago Black Panther leader Fred Hampton and the sowing of internal discord within the Panthers and between its members and rival black militants and street gangs. In this way, the FBI played a key role in the decline of the Panthers. One of the last gasps of left extremism was the Symbionese Liberation Army (SLA), a revolutionary terrorist group headed by an escaped convict who identified with the violent wing of the black power movement. SLA members, most of whom were white, murdered two people, engaged in bank robberies, and, most famously, kidnapped Patty Hearst —the heiress to the Hearst newspaper fortune—and coerced her to join their acts of urban guerilla warfare. SLA terrorism ended in 1975 with the killing of many group leaders in a police shootout in southern California and the subsequent capture and arrest of Hearst and other SLA members.

Stonewall Rebellion June 1969 riot at a New York City gay bar kicking off the movement for gay liberation.

Weather Underground Revolutionary organization that splintered off from SDS and used violence, such as bombing government buildings, as a means of protest.

COINTELPRO Counterintelligence program through which the U.S. government repressed radical protest groups such as the Black Panthers.

25-4

Nixon Triumphs and Then Resigns

President Nixon and First Lady Pat Nixon toured the Great Wall of China in February 1972, as Nixon and Mao Zedong re-established relations between their countries. Nixon sought to create a friendship between the two superpowers in part to compel China to stop supporting North Vietnam.

Can you identify the Americans in this photo by their clothing? What do the differences in dress reveal about the differences between China and the United states at that time? ▶

Fotosearch/Getty Images

desegregation busing
Program backed by the federal government that uses buses to bring racial minorities to all-white schools.

Swann v. Charlotte-Mecklenburg Board of Education U.S. Supreme Court ruling that upheld the constitutionality of school busing for purposes of desegregation.

Nixon's reelection by a landslide in 1972 revealed the continuing rise of a new brand of conservatism that stood for law and order at the time of increasingly violent political protest. Nixon transformed the nation's Cold War stance by thawing relations with the Soviets through arms control agreements and with the Chinese by re-establishing diplomatic relations. These international breakthroughs were part of the president's successful strategy to pressure North Vietnam to negotiate an end of the Vietnam War. In 1973, both combatants reached a peace agreement that ended the war and brought U.S. troops home. Their withdrawal spelled doom for South Vietnam and pro-American regimes in Cambodia and Laos. Meanwhile, at home, Nixon confronted his own crisis involving unlawful wiretaps of his political enemies that became a major scandal, ultimately forcing him to resign from office, which in turn created a historic loss of faith in U.S. public officials. The simultaneous collapse of the nation's global economic supremacy gave the public a rather glum outlook on the future.

☞ As you read, focus on Nixon's second term as president. What were his successes? What were his failures? How did his failures contribute to a pessimistic outlook for the nation as a whole?

25-4a Republicans and the New Conservatives

The nation's growing antiwar sentiment had little impact on Nixon's bid for reelection in 1972. The incumbent routed

{ Nixon advances civil rights reforms within limits.

George McGovern, the Democratic challenger, to keep the Republican momentum going strong. The party's success was driven by the transformation of American conservatives who, after Barry Goldwater's trouncing in the 1964 presidential election, softened their Cold Warrior stance on foreign policy while moving away from the white supremacist stance of segregationist George Wallace. Nixon came to epitomize conservatives' openness to cautious racial reform in advancing desegregation; on his watch, the overwhelming number of school districts in the South turned away from Jim Crow. The Nixon administration also was the first to sanction the use of racial quotas to promote affirmative action in the workplace.

But the president drew the line at **desegregation busing** programs designed to transport racial minorities out of poor, inner-city neighborhoods to predominantly white suburban schools. Soon after the Civil Rights Act (1964), many cities such as New York and Boston relied upon school busing to quickly integrate public schools. Such programs met stiff resistance from white parents who not only held racial stereotypes about nonwhites but also were convinced that integration devalued their children's education and their property values. Nixon sided with the white parents in opposing the U.S. Supreme Court's decision in ***Swann v. Charlotte-Mecklenburg Board of Education*** (1970). Rooted in the same desegregationist logic of the original Brown decision, the *Swann* ruling ordered the North Carolina school district involved to use busing as a weapon against the legacy of Jim Crow, paving the way for similar programs in Los Angeles, Boston, Cleveland, and Indianapolis. In 1972, a public opinion poll revealed that 70 percent of Americans opposed race-based school busing, and a later poll found that the nation was more concerned about busing than abortion. One victory for the antibusing proponents was the Supreme Court's decision in *Milliken v. Bradley* (1974) to prevent school busing programs in Michigan that crossed from one school district to another.

Opponents of desegregation busing found ingenious ways to delay or defeat racial integration. In 1969, after courts ordered school districts to speed up the pace of desegregation, many whites removed their children from public schools and enrolled them in private schools that were beyond the purview of the government's orders. The stunning increase in private school enrollment was revealed in the huge growth of non-Catholic private schools in Mississippi: from seventeen schools with a combined total of 2,362 students in 1964 to one hundred fifty-five schools enrolling 42,000 students in 1970. The "white flight" from public schools was in no way limited to the South as parents in all parts of the country got around court-ordered busing. By the 1970s, few Americans championed the racism of segregationists such as George Wallace, let alone extremist organizations including the KKK. Instead, these Americans resisted desegregation busing by arguing, in ostensibly nonracial terms, that the federal government had overstepped its authority and interfered with the right of their children to a good education. In this way, racial segregation lived on even after the passage of civil rights laws.

25-4b Grand Strategy for U.S. Foreign Policy

Despite the war in Vietnam, the Cold War competition with the Soviet Union continued to preoccupy U.S. officials. In 1969, Nixon had enjoyed a welcome victory in the race to land on the moon. In 1961, Soviet cosmonaut Yuri Gargarin was the first human to orbit the Earth, but eight years later, Americans Neil Armstrong and Buzz Aldrin were the first to walk on the moon as part of NASA's successful **Apollo program** that fulfilled President Kennedy's goal.

> Nixon and Kissinger relax tensions with China and the Soviet Union.

From the start of the Nixon administration, the president and Kissinger adopted a realist approach to foreign policy that emphasized pragmatism over ideology. In an effort to ease international tensions, they crafted a grand strategy called **détente**, a French term for the relaxation of a drawn bow and arrow. Their first efforts at détente involved the People's Republic of China (PRC). Although the United States had yet to establish formal diplomatic relations with the PRC, a country founded in 1949, the vehemently anti-Communist Nixon believed that he could approach China without his political rivals accusing him of being soft on communism. The Chinese government, reeling from the internal tumult unleashed by the Cultural Revolution (1966–1976) and unsettled by recent military clashes along its 4,150-mile border with the Soviets, proved receptive to Nixon and Kissinger's overtures.

A major breakthrough occurred in April 1971, after Chinese Premier Zhou Enlai directed the Chinese national table tennis team to invite its U.S. counterpart to play a series of matches in Beijing. In February 1972, Nixon and Kissinger (along with First Lady Pat Nixon) traveled to China. The men met privately with Mao and Zhou. Although they failed to resolve differences over Taiwan, both sides agreed that no nation should seek to establish hegemony over the Asian Pacific region. After the historic exchange, the Chinese gave the First Lady a pair of panda bears as a symbol of friendship (President Nixon reciprocated with a gift of two musk oxen).

Improving relations with the Soviet Union was the second component of Nixon and Kissinger's détente. After the 1962 Cuban Missile Crisis, the Soviets had made a concerted effort to match U.S. nuclear capabilities. By 1970, they had achieved a 1,140 to 1,054 advantage over the United States in intercontinental ballistic missiles (ICBMs), but the huge arms buildup was severely straining the Soviet economy. The Soviets also had feared that their deteriorating relationship with the PRC could trigger a war. The two behemoths had long vied for leadership of the Communist world and the loyalty of nations recently liberated from colonialism. To capitalize on the Sino-Soviet split, Nixon and Kissinger pursued a triangular diplomacy that used a combination of incentives and penalties to play the Chinese and Soviets off against the other.

The strategy worked. After Nixon's trip to China, the Soviets—troubled at the prospect of a Sino–American partnership—made concessions in long-stalled **Strategic Arms Limitation Talks (SALT)**. During a May 1972 visit to Moscow, Nixon and General Secretary Leonid Brezhnev signed two SALT agreements, one restricting each superpower to two hundred antiballistic missiles (ABMs) and the other freezing the development of offensive missiles for a five-year period. In addition to the SALT pacts, Brezhnev and Nixon agreed to avoid direct military confrontations and to prevent nuclear war. Although ambiguous and unenforceable, this code of conduct reflected a new spirit of optimism in Soviet–U.S. relations.

25-4c U.S. Withdraws from Indochina

Despite historic breakthroughs with China and the Soviet Union, Nixon's quest for total victory in Vietnam by stepping up bombings in Laos and Cambodia failed to induce Le Duan to give up the strategy of "talking while fighting." In fact, the North's victory over South Vietnamese forces in Laos gave Le

> The U.S. and North Vietnam sign a peace agreement after each fails to achieve total victory.

Apollo program NASA space flight project committed to having an American be the first human to land on the moon.

détente Foreign policy strategy designed to advance the interests of a state through de-escalating conflict with among major superpowers.

Strategic Arms Limitation Talks (SALT) Breakthrough arms control agreement between the United States and Soviet Union signed in May 1972.

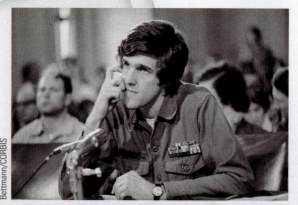

Global Americans In 1966, during his last year at Yale University, **John Kerry** both enlisted in the U.S. Navy and criticized America's war in Vietnam as a speaker for his class graduation. After completing officer training, he volunteered to serve on a patrol boat in Vietnam, thinking that it would keep him away from military action. As it turned out, he was assigned to a region in the Mekong Delta that was in the thick of conflict. Within two years of service, Kerry was wounded three times in battle, receiving three Purple Hearts along with Silver and Bronze star medals. In spring 1969, he returned to the United States where he joined nearly a thousand Vietnam veterans in discarding their service medals on the steps of the U.S. Capitol. Kerry also testified against the war before the Senate Foreign Relations Committee, where he was asked the now memorable question: "How do you ask a man to be the last man to die for a mistake?" In 1972, Kerry lost an election to serve as a representative to U.S. Congress from Massachusetts. Twelve years later he would arrive on Capitol Hill as a U.S. senator. In 2004, he lost the presidential election as the Democratic candidate. In 2009 he then served as secretary of state.

Easter Offensive Last failed attempt by North Vietnam at the GO-GU plan in March 1972 that caused Le Duan to make a serious push for a peace settlement.

Operation Linebacker One of the last attempts by the United States to gain a total victory in Vietnam whose failure, as well as the failure of a second attempt (Operation Linebacker II), pushed Nixon to accept a negotiated peace settlement.

Duan a boost of confidence that encouraged him to give the GO-GU strategy another try. Worried that Nixon and Kissinger's grand strategy would convince the Soviets and Chinese to end their support of the war in Vietnam, North Vietnamese leaders launched a new attack on South Vietnam in March 1972. But the **Easter Offensive** failed; for the third time, the North Vietnamese were repelled and no general uprising emerged. In addition, China and the Soviet Union, neither of whom supported the offensive, began limiting military support to North Vietnam.

Nixon responded to the Easter Offensive by waging **Operation Linebacker**, which for the first time since Johnson's no-bombing agreement in 1968, engaged in a barrage of aerial assaults on Hanoi and other northern cities. At this point, Le Duan admitted the failure of the GO-GU plan and had no choice but to take the ongoing peace talks seriously. Still hopeful for total victory, Nixon launched Operation Linebacker II during Christmas 1972. But this attempt failed again to bring Hanoi to its knees and, in the end, stirred up world opinion against the United States to a fever pitch. This proved to be Nixon's breaking point, as he too was now prepared for a negotiated peace.

On January 27, 1973, the United States, North Vietnam, South Vietnam, and the provisional government representing NLF insurgents signed a peace treaty in Paris that officially ended the war. The Paris Peace Treaty called for the withdrawal of American troops, the end of U.S. bombings, dismantling of mines in North Vietnamese waters, a cease-fire between the insurgents and South Vietnam military, and the return of prisoners of war. The

United States, after blocking democratic elections in Vietnam since 1954, consented to holding elections regarding the reunification of North and South Vietnam. The long-term dream of a united and independent Vietnam was finally possible, while South Vietnam's fear of being abandoned by the United States was realized.

By April 1975, with U.S. troops gone, North Vietnam toppled the South Vietnamese government, and Saigon was renamed Ho Chi Minh City. Lacking both U.S. and South Vietnamese support, the anti-Communist regimes in Cambodia and Laos fell to the Khmer Rouge and Pathet Lao, respectively. In this sense, domino theory predictions were correct that a Communist victory in Vietnam would cause other Indochinese nations to follow suit, but the chain reaction did not spread beyond Laos and Cambodia. If anything, the removal of the U.S. threat in Indochina also revealed deep conflicts among the Communist regimes. The reunified Vietnam soon clashed with China, resuming a long-standing enmity that had been papered over by their alliance against the United States. Vietnam also invaded Cambodia in part because of the Khmer Rouge's close ties to the Chinese. In return, China invaded Vietnam in February 1979 and engaged in three weeks of hostilities before withdrawing.

In the end, the U.S. war in Indochina proved to be the nation's longest military endeavor and its worst defeat. Over 50,000 Americans had died trying to prevent the reunification of Vietnam under Communist rule. The overall death rate for Vietnamese civilians and troops (both North and South) has been variously reported from 800,000 to more than 3 million. The Laotian war dead numbered about 60,000. The death toll in Cambodia is estimated to have been around 250,000, not including the 1.7 million victims of the Khmer Rouge genocide. In proportion to the country's overall population, the Cambodian genocide was more devastating than the mass murders and starvation committed under Hitler, Stalin, or Mao.

After U.S. troops went home leaving behind thousands missing in action, the 5 million veterans of the former South Vietnamese military suffered at the hands of their former enemies. They represented half of the 1 million people forced to leave Saigon to work on rural land development projects. Many other veterans were among the 300,000 "enemies of the people" sent to re-education camps. The fortunate few former South Vietnamese military were among the 125,000 South Vietnamese refugees who were airlifted out of Saigon before reunification. Thousands of other refugees fled Cambodia and Laos.

Later on, a second and larger wave of refugees began to flee Vietnam through perilous journeys by sea on makeshift boats. These so-called **boat people** joined hundreds of thousands of "land people" fleeing persecution in Cambodia and Laos to create a humanitarian crisis throughout the region. Refugee camps in Thailand, Malaysia, Singapore, Hong Kong, and the Philippines overflowed with occupants, some of whom were forced to return to their home countries. The United States responded to the crisis by taking in an additional 400,000 refugees from Indochina. Although this figure was more than half of the total number of refugees, smaller nations such as Canada, Australia, France, and Germany stepped up by accepting as many or even more refugees than the United States in per capita terms. In addition, China gave asylum to 265,000 ethnic Chinese from Vietnam.

25-4d Watergate

Before entering the White House, Richard Nixon had a reputation for being a no-holds barred political fighter; to him, politics was war. After winning the presidency in 1968, Nixon was planning for reelection by using the power of his administration, as well as the CIA, FBI, Internal Revenue Service (IRS), and other federal agencies to discredit two hundred political opponents, including another Kennedy younger brother, Massachusetts congressman Edward M. "Ted" Kennedy. Added to this "enemies list" was Daniel Ellsberg, the defense department official who in 1971 had leaked the Pentagon Papers that aided the antiwar movement. Nixon authorized a team of special agents to discredit the whistle-blower by breaking into his psychiatrist's office to obtain personal records. White House tape recordings later revealed that the president justified the illegal actions by saying, "We're up against an enemy conspiracy. They're using any means. We're going to use any means."

The "dirty tricks" used to attack Nixon's political opponents included accusations of sexual improprieties, financial misconduct, and the falsification of State Department records. But the most notorious campaigns came from Nixon's own Committee to Reelect the President (CRP). Known as CREEP by its opponents, this fund-raising organization run by high-level White House officials waged a covert offensive against the Democratic Party and the campaign of its 1972 presidential candidate George McGovern. In the early morning of May 28, 1972, covert operatives connected to the White House including former CIA agent E. Howard Hunt and former New York district attorney G. Gordon Liddy, broke into the headquarters of the Democratic National Committee at the **Watergate**, an office complex in Washington, D.C., to wiretap phones, photograph documents, and plant listening devices. Some of the burglars—known as "plumbers" because of their role in closing leaks to the media of confidential information damaging to Nixon—returned on June 17 to fix an improperly planted bug and were caught by a security guard. One of the men arrested carried a phone number that was traced back to the White House.

Nixon's staff promptly denied that he or his administration had any connection to what the president's press secretary dismissed as a "third-rate burglary attempt." Meanwhile, *Washington Post* reporters Bob Woodward and Carl Bernstein began to uncover the relationship between the arrested plumbers and Nixon's reelection committee. The reporters received tips from the FBI's number two officer W. Mark Felt, known only as "Deep Throat" at the time and for thirty years after the Watergate scandal broke. Felt passed on top-secret information to the reporters because he worried that the FBI was becoming the personal spy agency for the White House.

In January 1973, after Nixon was reelected, the arrested plumbers went on trial and, when faced with harsh prison sentences, began to reveal their ties to the White House. The Senate then launched a formal investigation into the Watergate scandal and aired its hearings on live television with damaging results for the Nixon administration. The president, then, faced his toughest challenge when Archibald Cox, the independent prosecutor looking into the scandal, discovered that Nixon had installed a system that generated audio recordings of all phone calls and conversations in the Oval Office. Both Cox and the Senate investigating committee pressed hard to gain access to the recordings that could link Nixon to the Watergate break-ins and their cover-up.

In October 1973, Nixon responded to Cox's demands for the White House tapes by having him fired. The move revealed the withering of support for Nixon as both the president's attorney general and his assistant resigned in protest over Cox's removal. By July 1974, Nixon's refusal to turn over the Oval Office recordings set up a constitutional showdown between the president and Congress. Nixon claimed that it was his executive privilege to withhold evidence, and Congress charged him with obstruction

> A major scandal forces Nixon to resign the presidency and diminishes U.S. citizens' faith in their government.

boat people Refugees fleeing Southeast Asia after the end of the Vietnam War who did not have the means or connections to leave by airplane or automobile. Instead they left by boat.

Watergate Washington, D.C., hotel and office complex where covert operatives sent by the White House broke into the headquarters of the Democratic National Committee, the crime whose subsequent exposure led to the Watergate scandal that eventually forced Nixon to resign from office.

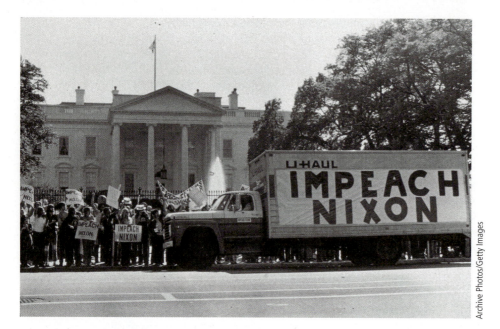

Impeach Nixon Protest in Front of White House Protests to impeach President Nixon, such as this one in front of the White House in 1974, revealed a deep disillusionment among Americans about the nature of their government. It would take more than the pardon of Nixon for Americans to recover from the shock of Watergate. America's faith in their public officials, already battered and bruised by the Vietnam War, had been reduced to a new low in U.S. history. ◄

Archive Photos/Getty Images

War Powers Act
Congressional act passed in November 1973 that made it illegal after forty-eight days for a president to engage in an undeclared war.

of justice. The conflict was settled by the U.S. Supreme Court, which required Nixon to turn over the Oval Office tapes to the new independent prosecutor, Leon Jaworski.

Next, the House of Representatives voted to impeach Nixon on three counts: obstruction of justice, contempt of Congress, and abuse of power (charges of tax evasion and concealment from Congress of the secret war in Cambodia were not approved). Nixon, however, resigned from office on August 8, 1974, before he could be impeached; he was the only president to do so. Gerald R. Ford, Nixon's vice president, took over as president. Two years earlier, Ford, a House representative from Michigan, had been appointed vice president, replacing Spiro Agnew who had resigned from office due to a tax evasion scandal. Ford was the only person to serve as president and vice president without being elected by the electoral college. His first action in the White House was to pardon Nixon of all crimes related to the Watergate scandal and to put to rest the nation's "long national nightmare" (see Table 25.2).

During the Watergate scandal, Congress pushed to reassert the authority of the legislative branch by limiting the president's authority to conduct foreign affairs. The **War Powers Act**, passed over Nixon's veto in November 1973, sought to prevent another Vietnam fiasco by making it illegal for the president to carry on an undeclared war for more than forty-eight days and giving to Congress the power to shut down the president's military engagement if it is not adequately apprised on the situation. In addition, Congress strengthened the Freedom of Information Act (1974), guaranteeing citizens' access to federal records. The Ethics in Government Act (1978) sought to clean up corruption by requiring public officials to disclose their

financial information, and in response to Nixon's firing of special investigator Archibald Cox, Congress established the Office of Independent Counsel. Finally, the Foreign Intelligence Surveillance Act (1978) made it unlawful for federal officials to engage in domestic wiretapping without a warrant.

Despite these protections against government intrusion, the fallout from Watergate and the Vietnam War lived on in the disillusionment experienced by many Americans who no longer assumed the U.S. government to be a force of good at home and in the world. Nixon retired to California, and although he enjoyed moments of renewed appreciation, his misdeeds were forever etched into U.S. consciousness by the naming of any scandal in government, business, and even entertainment and sports with the suffix *gate* as in Iran-Contragate or Deflategate.

25-4e Collapse of Postwar Prosperity

The shock of Watergate and the embarrassment of Vietnam occurred at the same time as United States dominance in the global economy ceased. While the U.S. in 1964 enjoyed a trade surplus of 6.8 billion dollars with the rest of the world, this declined by 1971 to a trade deficit, and for the first time in the twentieth century, U.S. merchandise imports exceeded exports. The transition resulted mainly from foreign competition in the steel, textiles, transportation equipment, and electronics industries. Yet U.S. officials also were convinced that the rapid swing in world trade reflected a disadvantage in the Bretton-Woods monetary system that

> The end of two decades of continuous economic growth reveals major shortcomings of the U.S. economy.

Table 25.2 Watergate-Related Chronology

November 1968	Nation elects Richard Nixon president.
June 1971	*New York Times* and *Washington Post* begin publishing Pentagon Papers, a Defense Department secret history of the Vietnam War smuggled by former defense analyst Daniel Ellsworth.
September 1971	White House "plumbers" break into psychiatrist's office searching for files on Ellsworth.
May 1972	Plumbers break into Democratic National Committee headquarters, at Watergate hotel and office complex.
June 1972	Arrests made in second Watergate break-in to fix listening device; one plumber is tied to White House; Nixon denies any connection to plumber.
October 1972	*Washington Post* reports from secret information gained from the FBI that the Watergate break-in was part of orchestrated campaign of spying and sabotage by Nixon reelection committee.
November 1972	Nixon is reelected as president in a landslide.
January 1973	Five of the plumbers plead guilty to Watergate break-in; the two who refused to do so were convicted of conspiracy, burglary, and wiretapping.
April 1973	Nixon issues statement saying that he had no prior knowledge of Watergate break-in.
May 1973	Senate Committee begins televised hearings on the Watergate affair.
May 1973	Justice Department appoints Archibald Cox as special investigator for Watergate scandal.
June 1973	Former White House Counsel John Dean testifies to the Senate Committee that Nixon was involved in the cover-up of the Watergate break-in.
July 1973	Senate Committee and Archibald Cox demand that Nixon hand over tape recordings of Oval Office conversations; Nixon refuses, setting up a constitutional showdown.
October 1973	Vice President Spiro Agnew resigns amid a scandal involving tax evasion; Gerald Ford appointed in his place.
October 1973	Nixon orders Attorney General Elliot Richardson to fire special investigator Archibald Cox; Richardson resigns in protest and new attorney general fires Cox.
November 1973	Leon Jaworski becomes Justice Department's new special investigator.
April 1974	Jaworski subpoenas Nixon to surrender 64 White House tapes; Nixon refuses but provides edited transcripts of them.
May 1974	Impeachment hearings begin in House Judiciary Committee.
July 1974	Supreme Court issues order for Nixon to surrender White House tapes.
July 1974	House Judiciary Committee adopts three articles to impeach Nixon.
August 1974	Nixon releases transcripts of tapes that prove he was involved in Watergate cover-up; Nixon resigns from office and Gerald Ford becomes president.
September 1974	Ford pardons Nixon.

allowed every nation except the United States to devalue their currency. A strong U.S. dollar meant that it was cheaper for Americans to buy foreign goods while more difficult to sell U.S. products abroad. In 1971, attempting to prop up U.S. exports, President Nixon surprised the world by abolishing the global system of exchange rates to allow the dollar to weaken in order to boost U.S. exports. Since then, there have been no stable exchange rates as all currencies, including the U.S. dollar, have been allowed to fluctuate.

Floating exchange rates, however, did little (if anything) to prop up the U.S. economy. The problems went deeper. The productive capacity of workers in both Germany and Japan had more than tripled the U.S. rate from 1950–1973. On top of this, U.S. companies paid much higher salaries and benefits to workers than their foreign counterparts. Thus, while the U.S. economy grew "fat and content," the foreign competition became "leaner and meaner" by investing in new, more efficient technologies and keeping labor costs low (see Figure 25.2).

In addition, the nation's depletion of natural resources, especially oil, ensured that it would remain a debtor nation for all but two years from 1973 to 2010. From 1890 to 1940, America's natural resources abundance made it the world's largest exporter of minerals. But this changed as lead, zinc, and copper imports climbed in the late 1940s, and iron ore deposits dwindled in the 1950s. By the 1980s, the U.S. imported most minerals from abroad. The same

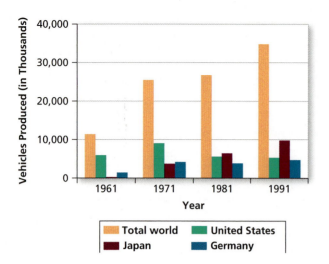

Vehicles Produced (in Thousands)

Figure 25.2 Global Automobile Production, 1961–1991
Foreign economic competition began to catch up to the U.S. manufacturers by the 1970s. This emerged most strikingly in the tremendous increase in Japanese and German automobile production. In 1950, U.S. firms produced 85 percent of the world's automobiles, but two decades later the Germans and Japanese were catching up, and by 1981, the Japanese overtook the Americans to become the world's largest car manufacturer. ◀ Source: U.S. Department of Transportation, http://www.rita.dot.gov/bts/sites/rita.dot.gov.bts/files/publications/national_transportation_statistics/html/table_01_23.html_mfd.

Organization of Petroleum Exporting Countries (OPEC) A group of oil-producing nations, mainly in the Middle East, agreeing to collude on the price and supply of oil in order to gain control over the global petroleum market.

trend of declining supplies was true for the nation's oil reserves. This contrasted with the abundant and cheap supplies of oil in the Persian Gulf. In 1960, this region surpassed the United States as the world's leader in oil production.

To offset this disadvantage, U.S. officials and oil executives, beginning in the 1940s, brokered deals with Middle Eastern nations that put much of the region's oil fields under U.S. control. In 1959, Congress imposed a limit on the importation of foreign oil in order to forestall the inevitable dominance of the Middle East. A year later, in an effort to obtain more control and profit from their oil supplies, Saudi Arabia, Iran, Iraq, Kuwait, Venezuela,

and other oil-rich nations came together to form the **Organization of Petroleum Exporting Countries (OPEC)**. The first sign of OPEC's influence came in June 1967 with the return of Arab–Israeli warfare. In June, conflicts between Israel and its neighbors erupted into the Six Day War in which the Jewish state quickly defeated combined Arab nations to claim the Gaza Strip and Sinai Peninsula from Egypt, the West Bank and East Jerusalem from Jordan, and the Golan Heights from Syria. OPEC's Arab nations responded by cutting off the supply of oil to Israel and its U.S. ally. The oil embargo, however, failed as non-Arab nations including Indonesia and Venezuela stepped up production.

By 1973, increasing global demand for oil strengthened the position of the Persian Gulf nations. The price of oil tripled to $10 per barrel between 1970 and 1974, and

Long Lines for Gasoline, OPEC Embargo, 1973 Many of the iconic images of the 1970s were of gasoline stations feeling the ill-effects of an OPEC embargo, which twice during the decade caused consumers to suffer bouts of high prices, long lines, and short supplies. Pain at the gas pumps, however, did not reveal the whole economic picture, as the United States suffered an overall loss of competitiveness in the global economy.

AP Images

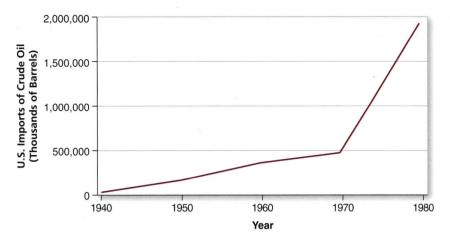

Figure 25.3 Oil Imports in U.S., 1940–1980
The spike in oil imports to the United States reflected the huge rise in worldwide demand for oil. Between 1948 and 1972, U.S. consumption of oil tripled, Western Europe's increased sixteen times, and Japan's skyrocketed one hundred thirty-seven times. Most of this growth came from the proliferation of automobiles, increasing more than eight times worldwide during the postwar era. Another reason for U.S. dependency on foreign oil was the discovery of abundant oil reserves in the Persian Gulf region.

◄ Source: U.S. Energy Information Administration

during this time the United States—which consumed an astonishing 40 percent of world petroleum—ended its restrictive quota on foreign oil imports. Within a few months, U.S. purchases of foreign oil doubled. Oil-rich Middle Eastern nations finally became cash rich and enjoyed the market power that their natural abundance all but guaranteed. They renegotiated unfavorable deals with U.S. and European oil companies to gain nearly total control of their own oil fields and, just as important, OPEC won the right to set the price of oil. OPEC's newfound power became apparent when the return of Arab-Israeli warfare in October 1973 pushed it to declare a second oil embargo on nations friendly to the Jewish state. In one fell swoop, OPEC raised the price of a barrel of oil by 70 percent and removed 14 percent of the world's oil production.

Given the heightened global demand for oil, the **OPEC oil embargo** this time had a devastating impact on world economies. A third embargo after the Iranian Revolution in 1979 had an even more powerful impact. Consequently, OPEC had become a political as well as economic powerhouse (see Figure 25.3).

The new competitiveness of Germany and Japan combined with dependence on Middle Eastern oil sent the U.S. economy into a tailspin for most of the 1970s. The U.S. economy, which had been growing at an annual rate of 3 percent since World War II, slowed to 1.6 percent for nearly two decades after 1973.

OPEC oil embargo Ceasing of oil exports by OPEC nations in 1967, 1973, and 1979 as a result of Middle Eastern affairs that produced energy crises in the United States and around the world.

Summary

The Vietnam War was a watershed in U.S. history. The nation's most devastating military defeat significantly lowered America's reputation around the world. At home, the conflict provoked the country's largest antiwar protests, while heightening the militancy of black power, as well as social movements by feminists; Native, Latino, and Asian Americans; and sexual minorities. At the same time, the war exposed the secretive and deceptive ways that the president and military leaders manipulated Congress as well as

the public to gain consent for their policies and practices. The Pentagon Papers and Watergate scandal were the two most obvious examples of how the public lost respect for President Nixon and public officials in general. The simultaneous collapse of the U.S. postwar economic supremacy added energy, trade, and financial crises to an already bleak political and social environment.

The Vietnam War was also a watershed for Southeast Asian and world history. Its scale of death and destruction was unprecedented in

Indochina, delaying postcolonial economic development and sacrificing the promise of North Vietnam's social revolution. The region's numerous wars also meant decades of political repression, civil wars, and regional instability. Yet for the world as a whole, the war influenced a positive transformation in superpower relations when the United States engaged in détente with both the Soviet Union and China. Although the Cold War continued, the odds of global nuclear destruction lessened considerably.

<Thinking Back, *Looking Forward*>

As you review the Vietnam War era, think about how World War I, World War II, and then the Cold War gave hope for national independence to the Vietnamese and other colonized peoples. Also consider how civil rights reforms, and the U.S. urban crisis, encouraged the demand for even more radical social equality within the United States. In the coming chapters, look for the consequences of the Vietnam War for U.S. politics, society, and international relations. How did the war's legacy continue to influence Americans for decades after the conflict ended?

To make your study concrete, review the timeline and reflect on the entries there. Think about their causes, consequences, and connections. How do they fit with global trends?

Additional Resources

Books

Bloom, Joshua, and Waldo Martin. *Black against Empire: The History and Politics of the Black Panther Party.* **Berkeley: University of California Press, 2013.** ▶ Definitive study of this influential black nationalist organization.

Borstelmann, Thomas. *The 1970s: A New Global History from Civil Rights to Economic Inequality.* **Princeton, NJ: Princeton University Press, 2012.** ▶ Far-reaching study of this understudied but crucial decade.

Echols, Alice. *Daring to Be Bad: Radical Feminism in America 1967–1975.* **Minneapolis: University of Minnesota Press, 1989.** ▶ Important study of the radicalization of the women's rights movement.

Karnow, Stanley. *Vietnam: A History.* **1983. Reprint, New York: Penguin, 1997.** ▶ Widely regarded history of the war that served as the foundation for the thirteen-hour, award-winning PBS video series on the subject.

Kutler, Stanley I. *Wars of Watergate: The Last Crisis of Richard Nixon.* **New York: W. W. Norton, 1992.** ▶ One of the major studies of the subject by a historian who has contributed to public release of Nixon's White House tapes.

Maeda, Daryl J. *Chains of Babylon: The Rise of Asian America.* **New Brunswick, NJ: Rutgers University Press, 2009.** ▶ Study of political, social, and cultural activism of the Asian American movement.

Means, Russell. *Where White Men Fear to Tread: The Autobiography of Russell Means.* **New York: St. Martins Press, 1995.** ▶ Autobiography of one of the American Indian Movement's leading figures involved in the siege at Wounded Knee.

Muñoz, Carlos. *Youth, Identity, Power: The Chicano Movement.* **1989. Reprint, New York: Verso, 2007.** ▶ Classic account that has been updated and expanded.

Nguyen, Lien-Hang T. *Hanoi's War: An International History of the War for Peace in Vietnam.* **Chapel Hill: University of North Carolina Press, 2012.** ▶ Important rethinking of the war based on North Vietnamese documents and perspectives.

Ung, Loung. *First They Killed My Father: A Daughter of Cambodia Remembers.* **New York: Harper Perennial, 2006.** ▶ Powerful first-hand account of the genocide in Cambodia.

Go to the MindTap® for **Global Americans** to access the full version of select books from this Additional Resources section.

Websites

Cambodian Genocide Project at Yale University. (http://www.yale.edu/cgp/index.html) ▶ Descriptions, photos, maps, chronology, resources, and searchable database of information regarding the genocide and subsequent war crimes tribunal.

Experiencing War: Vietnam War Looking Back, part 1. (http://www.loc.gov/vets/stories/ex-war-vietnam50.html) ▶ Part of Library of Congress project collection of texts, photos, and oral interviews with U.S. veterans (parts 2–4 of same series on Vietnam War veterans).

FBI Records: The Vault (https://vault.fbi.gov/) ▶ A library of sixty-seven thousand primary sources gained through the Freedom of Information Act related to FBI activity concerning many radical organizations and individuals including Malcolm X, Stokely Carmichael, Abbie Hoffman, the Black Panther Party, and the Weather Underground.

Fiftieth Anniversary of the Equal Opportunity Employment Commission (EEOC). (http://www.eeoc.gov/eeoc/history/50th/) ▶ In-depth chronology of EEOC milestones, text of laws and executive orders related to employment discrimination, and a twenty-four-minute video regarding EEOC history.

The Price of Freedom: Americans at War. (http://amhistory.si.edu/militaryhistory/printable/section.asp?id=12&sub=1) ▶ Smithsonian exhibition with many exceptional photographs of the Vietnam War.

Continue exploring online through MindTap®, **where you can:**
- **Assess your knowledge with the Chapter Test**
- **Watch historical videos related to the chapter**
- **Further your understanding with interactive maps and timelines**

The Vietnam War Era

1964–1965

August 1964
Congress approves Gulf of Tonkin Resolution.

1965
United States has 184,000 U.S. troops deployed fighting in Vietnam.

February 1965
President Johnson approves Operation Rolling Thunder.

March 1965
President Johnson escalates U.S. aerial assaults on enemy targets in Vietnam.

1966

SNCC practices racial separatism and proclaims "black power."

Cesar Chavez and farm workers' union strike expands to boycott grapes.

October
Black Panther Party for Self Defense is established in Oakland, CA.

1967

April
Martin Luther King Jr. opposes Vietnam War.

June
Arab members of OPEC cut off supply of oil to U.S. in protest of its position on Six Day War between Israel and the neighboring states of Egypt, Jordan, and Syria.

1968

January
Prague Spring begins amid liberalization in Czechoslovakia.

United States has 543,000 troops deployed in Vietnam.

North Vietnam and NLF insurgents launch Tet Offensive.

March
President Johnson announces that he will not seek second term.

Mexican American youth in Los Angeles walk out of classes to protest substandard schooling.

1968

April
King is assassinated in Memphis.

May
North Vietnam and United States begin peace talks in Paris.

June
Robert Kennedy is assassinated in Los Angeles.

August
Protests erupt into riots against police during the Democratic National convention in Chicago.

October
Mexican students clash with organizers of Olympic Games held in Mexico City.

1969

January

Nixon becomes president and promises to end the war in Vietnam while renewing bombing in Laos and expanding war to Cambodia.

March

Weeks decision removes sexual discrimination in employment.

June

Stonewall Rebellion sparks gay liberation movement.

November

Public learns of U.S. massacre at My Lai.

December

FBI murders Black Panther Fred Hampton.

Weather Underground is formed; SDS dissolves.

1970–1971

May 1970

Ohio National Guard shoots antiwar protesters at Kent State University.

1971

U.S. has trade deficit for first time in twentieth century.

June 1971

Excerpts of Pentagon Papers are published in *The New York Times*.

1972

February

Nixon and First Lady visit China.

May

U.S. and Soviet Union sign SALT arms reduction agreement.

Five men are caught breaking into DNC headquarters at the Watergate hotel.

1973

U.S. trade deficit is $6 billion.

January

Nixon begins second term as president.

Peace treaty ends Vietnam War, U.S. withdraws from Vietnam, Cambodia, and Laos.

Roe v. Wade decision legalizes abortion.

February–May

American Indian Movement occupies Wounded Knee historical site.

October

OPEC implements second OPEC oil embargo against the U.S. to protest its position on another Arab–Israeli war between Israel and a coalition of Arab states led by Syria and Egypt.

1974–1975

August 1974

Nixon resigns from presidency; Gerald Ford takes over.

April 1975

North Vietnamese troops and NLF insurgents topple Saigon regime, and Vietnam is reunited.

Khmer Rouge topples Lon Nol regime in Cambodia and starts genocide.

May 1975

Pathet Lao comes to power in Laos.

Go to MindTap® to engage with an interactive version of the timeline. Analyze events and themes with clickable content, view related videos, and respond to critical thinking questions.

26 The Global Conservative Shift

1975–1988

Fifty years after having immigrated to Detroit to pursue her American Dream, Lily Chin returned to her homeland of China, her faith in the U.S. justice system destroyed.

Lily Chin's American Dream imploded on June 23, 1982, the day her son Vincent died. A Chinese American, he had been assaulted by two men who mistook him for Japanese and blamed him for the depressed state of the U.S. auto industry. Her story intersects the economic struggles and racial divisions in American society in the late 1970s and 1980s.

Lily was an unlikely public figure. She was born Lilly Yee in 1920 in Canton, China, the only child of a successful merchant. Her youth was scarred by the Sino-Japanese War and World War II. In 1947, friends told her about David Bing Hing Chin, the son of her grandmother's neighbor who

Lily Chin leaving the courthouse after hearing the verdict in the trial of the two men who beat her son to death. ▲

emigrated to the United States twenty-five years earlier. The next year, despite only knowing David from a photograph, Lily moved to Detroit and married him.

Lily's father was displeased by the union and worried for his daughter because his grandfather, who had temporarily worked in the United States building rail lines, had told stories of American racism and discrimination against the Chinese. Lily tried to calm her father's fears and promised she would return home to visit. But after the Communists won control of China in 1949, she was unable to see her family for decades.

The Chins worked hard to build a life in Detroit, despite the racial tensions that escalated as U.S. auto manufacturing declined and thousands were out of work. They took jobs in laundries, restaurants, and factories. Unable to have children of their own, they adopted Vincent from a Chinese orphanage when he was six years old. After completing his education, Vincent worked full-time as a draftsman and part-time as a waiter to help his mother, recently widowed, and to save money for his coming wedding.

On June 19, 1982, three of Vincent's friends took him to a Detroit strip club to celebrate his bachelor party. Ronald Ebens, a plant supervisor at Chrysler, and his stepson Michael Nitz, an unemployed autoworker, sat nearby. Soon they started muttering racial epithets, engaging in the Japan-bashing that was common in Detroit where laid-off workers blamed Japanese automakers for their lost jobs and homes. A scuffle ensued, and Vincent and his friends left the bar, but Ebens and Nitz followed. In a McDonald's parking lot, Nitz pinned Vincent down while Ebens beat him with a baseball bat. Vincent died four days later. He was twenty-seven years old. The case drew little attention until Judge Charles Kaufman sentenced Ebens and Nitz on March 18, 1983. Having pled guilty to killing Vincent, the pair each received three years of probation and $3,780 in fines and court costs. "These are not the kind of men you send to jail," Kaufman explained. "You fit the punishment to the criminal, not the crime."

Vincent Chin's murder catapulted Asian Americans into political action. Joining across ethnic lines, they held rallies across the nation protesting Kaufman's lenient sentence and accusing him of racial bias in the case.

How does the Vincent Chin case reflect the deep divisions among Americans in the post–Vietnam War Era?
Go to MindTap® to watch a video on Lily Chin and learn how her story relates to the themes of this chapter.

773

Although she spoke little English, Lily also demanded justice for her son. These efforts resulted in federal charges against Ebens and Nitz for criminal violations of Vincent Chin's civil rights, the first such case involving an individual of Asian descent. The June 1984 trial drew international attention and sparked bitter debates over whether Asian Americans faced racial discrimination equivalent to that experienced by other minorities. Although Nitz was acquitted and Ebens's twenty-five year sentence was overturned on appeal in May 1987, the Vincent Chin case was a critical turning point in the Asian American civil rights movement. In September 1987, Lily Chin won a $1.5 million civil judgment against Ebens, but he made few payments and then disappeared without a trace. Her faith in the U.S. justice system destroyed, Lily returned to China after spending fifty years in the United States.

The Vincent Chin case reflected the deep divisions among Americans in the post-Vietnam War era. Politicians battled over taxes and the proper role of government. Economic changes triggered by structural shifts in the U.S. economy, increased foreign competition, and free market reforms created both opportunity and hardship. Women and lesbian, gay, bisexual, and transgender (LGBT) people pushed for inclusion and equal treatment while political conservatives and religious fundamentalists mobilized in defense of more traditional notions of family and morality. Confronted with a wave of immigration that included people from many nations traditionally underrepresented in the United States, Americans both embraced and resisted their country's increasing diversity.

Throughout the era, Americans contended with shifting dynamics of international relations and the resurgence of religious fundamentalism. In the United States and many other nations, conservatives gained political power. New nonstate actors pushed governments to protect human rights. In the late 1970s, upheavals in the developing world and the escalating nuclear arms race unraveled détente, and Cold War tensions escalated. By the early 1980s, millions feared that a superpower confrontation would spark a nuclear holocaust. But the convergence of a new Soviet leader intent on reforming his ailing nation and a president willing to alter his assumptions about his adversary soon transformed Soviet–American relations and set the stage for the Cold War's end.

26-1
Shifts in Global Dynamics

After a revolution deposed the Shah of Iran, Mohammad Reza Pahlavi, protestors stormed the U.S. Embassy in Tehran and seized dozens of American hostages on November 4, 1979. Images of the blindfolded captives being paraded before crowds of angry Iranians stunned millions in the United States.

Why do you think that images like this shocked Americans? How had the U.S. been involved in establishing the Shah's regime in 1953? What are some of the reasons that anti-American protestors might target a U.S. Embassy? ▶

AP Images

In the aftermath of the Vietnam War, U.S. global power declined, and the superpowers' attempts in the third phase of the Cold War to create a more stable and cooperative relationship collapsed. In the final phase of this global struggle, Cold War competition intensified, especially in the volatile developing world. Millions of people were uprooted by wars and political upheavals, and many fled their homelands. At the same time, heightened concerns about human rights violations inspired transnational activism and policy change.

Throughout his successful 1976 presidential campaign against incumbent Gerald Ford, Democrat Jimmy Carter capitalized on the Republicans' damaged reputation in the wake of Watergate. He promised to make significant changes to U.S. foreign policy and to stop supporting foreign leaders who violated human rights. He vowed to reduce military spending, U.S. foreign arms sales, and nuclear proliferation. He hoped to prioritize global economic inequities over traditional Cold War concerns.

But as president, Carter's actions were riddled with contradictions. He cut U.S. aid to some foreign dictators but continued to support others. Rather than slash defense spending and arms sales abroad, he increased both significantly. Although Carter enjoyed some diplomatic successes in the Middle East and Central America, the Iranian Revolution and the Soviet invasion of Afghanistan forced him to confront new threats posed by radical Islamists and renewed Cold War tensions. His critics charged that rather than restoring America's international status and confidence in the post-Vietnam War era, Carter only further weakened the U.S. position in the world.

☞ As you read, pay attention to the ways in which Carter attempted to modify U.S. foreign relations. What were his major aims? What were his major successes and failures?

26-1a Latin America and the Middle East

A man whose deep religious convictions and integrity had helped him win the presidency, Carter pursued an active agenda in Latin America to improve U.S. relations with countries there. In Panama, he opted to end U.S. control over the ten-mile-wide Canal Zone, which it had held since 1903. The Canal Zone bisected Panama, and under U.S. jurisdiction, Panamanians within it could be jailed under U.S. laws by U.S. courts using English, a language few natives understood. Most Panamanians had low-paying, unskilled jobs. None had high-level jobs operating the locks or piloting ships through the canal. In 1977, Carter negotiated two treaties with Panama. The first increased the share of canal revenue Panamanians received, voided the 1903 agreement granting the United States legal jurisdiction, and ceded U.S. operation of

{ Carter tries to lessen anti-Americanism in Latin America and to facilitate peace in the Middle East.

the canal to Panama effective December 31, 1999. The second extended indefinitely the U.S. right to keep the canal neutral. Carter won praise for his efforts to generate goodwill in the Western Hemisphere, but critics who viewed the Panama Canal as U.S. property denounced the treaties. In 1978, after a protracted debate, the Senate voted sixty-eight to thirty-two to approve both treaties—only one vote more than the minimum required for ratification.

Carter's diplomatic overtures elsewhere in the region had mixed results. He suspended U.S. military aid to Guatemala and Bolivia because of human rights violations and persuaded right-wing dictatorships in Haiti, Argentina, and the Dominican Republic to free political prisoners. But talks aimed at normalizing U.S.–Cuban relations failed because of Cuba's support for leftist rebels in Angola and Ethiopia. In April 1980, after ten thousand Cubans seeking asylum flooded the Peruvian Embassy in Havana, Fidel Castro announced that anyone who wished to leave Cuba could do so, and a mass exodus from the port of Mariel ensued. By late October, one hundred twenty-five thousand Cuban refugees in seventeen hundred vessels of varying seaworthiness had landed on U.S. shores. The "freedom flotillas" sometimes overwhelmed the U.S. Coast Guard, and twenty-seven migrants died en route.

Upon their arrival, the **Marielitos** were placed in crowded camps and stadiums until they could be processed. U.S. officials were dismayed to discover that as many as forty thousand of the migrants were criminals and mental patients whom Castro had released to purge his nation of "undesirables." Although fewer than twenty-eight hundred refugees were denied U.S. citizenship because they were classified as violent criminals, negative stereotypes of the Marielitos persisted.

Carter's efforts to mediate the Arab–Israeli conflict were more successful. When Egyptian–Israeli diplomatic talks to resolve disputes stemming from the Six Day War stalled, Carter tried to re-ignite the process by inviting Egypt's Anwar el-Sadat and Israel's Menachem Begin to the presidential retreat in Camp David, Maryland, in September 1978. For two weeks, the president brokered discussions, which eventually resulted in two significant agreements. The first called for negotiations concerning self-government for Palestinians living in the West Bank and Gaza. In the second, Israel vowed to withdraw its troops from the Sinai Peninsula in exchange for Egyptian recognition of Israel as a sovereign nation. After Israel and Egypt formalized these agreements in a March 1979 treaty, the signatories were surprised when no other Arab nation—not even Jordan and Saudi Arabia, both U.S. allies—joined the peace process. Instead, many Arabs denounced the treaty for its failure to grant autonomy to the Palestinians. Syrian-backed troops of the **Palestinian Liberation Organization (PLO)**—then a paramilitary organization fighting for the

Marielitos Cuban immigrants who departed from the port of Mariel in a mass exodus to the United States in 1980.

Palestinian Liberation Organization (PLO)
Established in 1964, uses a variety of tactics to defend Palestinian nationalism. Defined by the United States and Israel as a terrorist group until 1991.

creation of a Palestinian homeland—began attacking Israeli forces based in Lebanon. Other Arab states ostracized Egypt where serious internal tensions arose. The conflicts did not bode well for a sustainable peace in the volatile region.

26-1b Iranian Revolution and Hostage Crisis

Carter's most vexing foreign policy problems arose in Iran. Placed in power by U.S. and British intelligence operatives during a 1953 coup, Shah Mohammed Reza Pahlavi was

{ U.S. policy makers confront anti-Americanism, an Islamic revolution, and a hostage situation in Iran.

a loyal ally who allowed the United States to use his nation as a base for electronic surveillance of the Soviet Union. He also continued U.S. oil sales when all other OPEC nations imposed a 1973 embargo. But the 1970s petroleum boom triggered high inflation and exacerbated the economic gap between Iran's rich and poor. The Shah and his family kept billions of dollars in national oil revenues for themselves. Oil companies imported tens of thousands of foreign skilled workers instead of employing Iranians. Rather than address unemployment, housing shortages, and poverty, the Shah spent $19 billion on U.S. weapons and military equipment between 1973 and 1978.

The Shah's extravagance and efforts to westernize and secularize Iran outraged Muslim clerics, students, merchants, and workers. These disparate groups began protesting the Shah's rule and his close ties to the United States. In response, SAVAK, the Iranian secret police, brutally suppressed demonstrations and arrested thousands. By 1977, Amnesty International, a nongovernmental organization focused on human rights, estimated that SAVAK had incarcerated as many as fifty thousand political dissidents.

Despite this repression and his own professed commitment to human rights, Carter supported the Shah. In a 1977 visit to Tehran, Carter praised him for creating "an island of stability in one of the most troubled areas of the world." Although the Shah ordered the release of some dissidents and permitted the Red Cross to treat prisoners, he did not institute political or economic reforms. After his diagnosis with inoperable cancer, he became even less attuned to the simmering discontent in his country.

Throughout 1978, massive demonstrations and riots rocked Iran. After the Shah declared martial law in September, his security forces shot and killed dozens of protestors. In October, a general strike paralyzed the entire country. Ayatollah Ruhollah

Khomeini, an eighty-year-old **Shi'ite** cleric leading the Iranian revolution from France after the Shah exiled him, called for the Shah's removal and the establishment of an Islamic **theocracy**. For months, U.S. officials vacillated between supporting the Shah and urging him to resign so Iran's autocratic monarchy could be replaced with a civilian government.

On January 16, 1979, after naming a prime minister, the Shah and his wife fled to Egypt. Two weeks later, Ayatollah Khomeini returned to Iran. He rejected the new regime and appointed his own competing government. Denouncing the Shah and characterizing the United States as the **"Great Satan,"** Khomeini tried to capitalize on anti-Americanism and to undermine moderates battling Islamists for control over the government. At the same time, the deposed Shah moved from Egypt to Morocco, to the Bahamas, to Mexico in an unsuccessful quest for asylum. In late October 1979, Carter reluctantly permitted him to come to New York for cancer treatment.

The move triggered enormous demonstrations in Iran. On November 1, three million people protested outside the U.S. Embassy in Tehran. Three days later, hundreds of militants stormed the compound and seized sixty-nine Americans. Although they released sixteen hostages, the captors proclaimed they would not release the other fifty-three until the Shah returned to Iran for trial. In the United States, television viewers were stunned by images of the blindfolded captives being paraded through the streets in front of hostile crowds. Each evening, a U.S. news program called *America Held Hostage* (later renamed *Nightline*) provided updates on the crisis. Millions of Americans tied yellow ribbons around trees in a gesture of support for the hostages' safe return.

Carter quickly froze $8 billion of Iranian assets held in U.S. banks and asked the Shah to leave the United States. But as the hostage crisis dragged on, it consumed Carter's presidency. On April 7, 1980, after several failed secret overtures, the United States severed diplomatic relations with Iran. Carter then approved a covert rescue mission that failed after a helicopter and a C-130 military transport aircraft collided during a heavy dust storm in the staging area outside Tehran. Eight U.S. servicemen died. The Iranian captors then scattered the fifty-three hostages, making another rescue attempt impossible. Iran did, however, release one of the hostages after he became seriously ill with multiple sclerosis.

But subsequent events resolved the hostage crisis. In late July 1980, the Shah died in Egypt. Shortly thereafter, the Islamic clerics consolidated their control over the Iranian parliament and decided that the hostages no longer had political value. In September, after Iraq's Saddam Hussein attacked Iranian oil fields and threatened the Khomeini regime, Iran redirected its energies toward marshaling allies and funding for war against the Iraqis that ultimately lasted for eight years. Two months later, Ronald Reagan defeated Carter in the 1980 presidential election. In the final weeks of his term, Carter negotiated

Shi'ite Also called *Shi'a*, the second-largest branch of Islam whose adherents believe that the Prophet Muhammad's proper successor was his son-in-law and cousin Ali ibri Abi Talib.

theocracy System of government that places supreme civil authority in a religious deity and whose officials are regarded as agents of that deity.

"Great Satan" Derogatory term used by some Iranians to describe the United States that first came to prominence during the Iranian Revolution in the late 1970s.

the hostages' release in exchange for unfreezing Iranian assets. On January 20, 1981, in a final insult to Carter, the Iranians waited until after Reagan had been sworn in before allowing the Americans to leave Iranian airspace. After a four hundred forty-four-day ordeal, the hostages joyfully returned to the United States.

26-1c End of Détente

Throughout the mid-1970s, détente—the de-escalation of superpower tensions initiated by Nixon and Secretary of State Henry Kissinger— had mixed results. In Africa, leftist rebels backed by the Soviet Union or Cuba battled U.S.-sponsored forces in Angola, Ethiopia, and Somalia. In Europe, under a variant of détente called **Ostpolitik** (German for "new eastern policy"), East Germany and West Germany expanded trade and travel between the two nations. In July 1975, representatives from thirty-five countries gathered in Helsinki, Finland, and signed an agreement recognizing existing European boundaries, accepting territorial adjustments in Germany and Eastern Europe that had been made in the late 1940s. The conferees pledged to uphold détente and to support human rights. As newly created Helsinki Watch groups monitored the compliance of all signatories, organizations like Czechoslovakia's Charter 77 and Poland's Solidarity pushed for political and civil rights behind the Iron Curtain. Such dissidents later played a critical role in bringing down Communist regimes in 1989.

> Détente helps de-escalate Cold War tensions in Europe but unravels in the developing world.

But détente generated passionate criticism in the United States. Conservatives remained suspicious of Soviet intentions and argued that maintaining nuclear superiority was essential to U.S. security. Liberals condemned increases in U.S. arms sales abroad and continued U.S. support for regimes that violated human rights. In 1976, attacks on détente grew so intense that Ford barred his aides from using the term.

Carter's contradictory policies toward the Soviet Union further eroded détente. Sensitive to any perceived insult to their superpower status, the Soviets objected when Carter attempted to modify previously agreed-upon arms limitations. The aging Kremlin leadership seemed blind to how provocative U.S. policy makers found Soviet actions in the Middle East, Africa, and Asia. To put the Soviets on the defensive, Carter formally recognized China on January 1, 1979, thereby completing the reconciliation begun by Nixon and Mao.

Despite the tense atmosphere, the Soviet Union and the United States signed the SALT II agreement in June 1979. The pact limited nuclear warheads and granted each side the right to verify the other's compliance. When Carter submitted the treaty to the Senate for ratification, critics of détente led by Democrat Henry "Scoop" Jackson of Washington vociferously opposed it. They argued that any nuclear arms agreement should be contingent on

Soviets' respect for human rights and abandonment of their support for Communist revolutionaries in the developing world. Carter tried to mollify his critics by approving the installation of five hundred seventy-two Pershing-II missiles in Western Europe to counter recently deployed Soviet SS-20 missiles.

Attacks on détente intensified after Cuba and the Soviet Union began backing leftist uprisings in Central America. Cognizant of the region's severe economic inequality and political repression, U.S. policy makers were forced to balance human rights concerns and fears that communism would spread in a region deemed vital to national security. In 1979, after a junta seized power in El Salvador, U.S. officials provided military aid for its internal war against leftist insurgents.

In Nicaragua, Carter took the opposite approach and supported the leftist **Sandinistas** when they overthrew dictator Anastasio Somoza Debayle in July 1979. After decades of his family's corrupt and brutal rule, Somoza fled the country, but Sandinista assassins killed him in Paraguay a year later. Despite Republican charges that he was abetting the spread of communism in Central America, Carter continued economic aid to Nicaragua, a practice Reagan stopped when he became president.

The Soviet invasion of Afghanistan ended any pretense of a Soviet–U.S. détente. In December 1979, fifty thousand Soviet troops crossed into Afghanistan to prop up a faltering Marxist regime and to stem the spread of Islamic fundamentalism in Central Asia. Carter portrayed the Soviet invasion as the first step of a master plan to dominate oil supplies. He withdrew the SALT II treaty from Senate consideration, halted U.S. grain and technology sales to the Soviet Union, and removed the United States from the 1980 Summer Olympics to be held in Moscow. He also called for a massive $1.2 trillion expansion in defense spending over the next five years and ordered the reinstitution of draft registration. Privately, he directed the CIA to increase its covert aid to the Afghan Islamist resistance. On January 24, 1980, the president announced that the United States would protect its "vital interests" against any "outside force" attempting to gain control over the Persian Gulf region. The **Carter Doctrine** sent a strong warning to the Soviets that reflected escalating Cold War tensions.

Carter's tough stance did little to improve his standing at home and abroad. His critics saw Communist gains in Latin America, the Iranian hostage crisis, and the Soviet invasion of Afghanistan as proof that the international reputation of the United States was declining. Carter's own inconsistencies worsened his political problems. His diplomatic successes in the Egyptian–Israeli peace process, Panama, and China were not enough to convince voters to support him for a second term.

Ostpolitik Instigated by West German politician Willy Brant in the late 1960s, policy aimed at improving diplomatic and trade relations with the Communist nations of Eastern Europe.

Sandinistas Members of the Sandinista National Liberation Front, a left-wing Nicaraguan political group that overthrew the long-time dictatorship of the Somoza family in 1979.

Carter Doctrine Policy issued in 1980 warning that foreign incursions in the Persian Gulf region threatened U.S. national security and would be repelled.

26-1d Political Upheaval and Immigration

Cold War politics and global conflicts shaped U.S. immigration policies. Under the Immigration Act of 1965, less than 10 percent of visas had been reserved for refugees. As a result of this cap, many families displaced by wars languished in refugee camps, sometimes for years, awaiting sponsorship from relatives, churches, or humanitarian organizations. In 1975, when Congress refused to provide additional visas for those displaced by the wars in Indochina, President Ford used his executive parole powers to admit more refugees. But many

> Global conflicts contribute to changes in U.S. immigration laws.

others were fleeing political upheavals in the Middle East, Central America, and Africa.

In response, Congress passed the Refugee Act of 1980, a law that systemized procedures for resettling refugees and raising annual refugee admissions from seventeen thousand four hundred to fifty thousand. Once in the United States, many refugees gravitated to immigrant enclaves such as those formed by Somalis and Hmong in Minneapolis and Arabs in Detroit. Not all prospered in the United States. Many struggled with the English language and languished in poverty. Vietnamese American fishermen clashed with local residents in coastal communities in Texas and Louisiana. Many Americans welcomed refugees, but others viewed them as another strain on a weak economy that Carter had done little to fix.

26-2 Economic Transformations

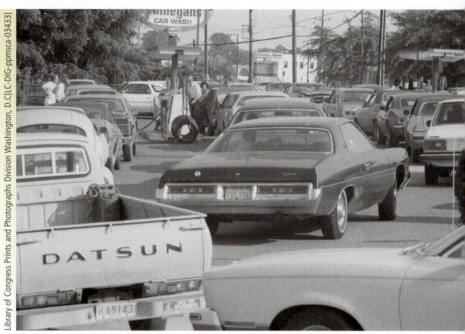

Drivers in Maryland wait to purchase gas during the 1979 oil shock. High gasoline prices prompted many Americans to purchase more fuel-efficient vehicles such as the Datsun (later renamed Nissan) truck shown. Rising sales of Japanese cars contributed to a major downturn in the U.S. automobile industry that had devastating economic consequences for many communities. As the U.S. manufacturing sector declined, unions struggled to protect wages and benefits and battled conservatives intent on weakening organized labor.

How do you think that gas lines like this affected Americans' attitudes toward the U.S. economy and their political leaders? ▶

Library of Congress Prints and Photographs Division Washington, D.C[LC-DIG-ppmsca-03433]

The onset of a global recession in 1973 had ended nearly three decades of unprecedented prosperity and growth of the middle class in the United States. Energy crises, foreign competition, and high inflation severely strained the U.S. economy. As the manufacturing sector of the economy declined, American workers moved to new service-oriented jobs, many of which paid far less than positions in heavy industry. Influenced by an international network of economic theorists, the federal government reduced its regulation of private business. The resulting free market reforms generated unprecedented wealth and economic growth but also undermined organized labor and exacerbated the income gap between the rich and poor. At the same time, a transnational environmental movement pushed for population control and more cautious stewardship of natural resources.

☞ As you read, pay attention to the factors that created the economic downturn of the 1970s. What were some of the reasons that the United States lost its global economic dominance in the 1970s? What were some of the ways that people attempted to restore prosperity?

26-2a Energy Shocks and Economic Stagnation

The shock of the 1973 OPEC oil embargo was only the beginning of the struggle over energy consumption that created political and economic vulnerabilities for the nation. Although the United States contained only 6 percent of the world's population, it used

> Dependency on oil imports, increased foreign competition, and inflation impede the U.S. economy.

40 percent of the world's petroleum. Cheap energy had been a vital component of the abundance and prosperity most Americans had enjoyed after World War II. In the course of the 1970s, a sixfold increase in petroleum prices imperiled U.S. standards of living built on inexpensive gasoline, heating, and air conditioning.

The 1973 oil shock had global ramifications. Many nations were even more oil dependent than the United States. In 1970, Europe had derived 60 percent of its energy from imported foreign petroleum. In response to the 1973 OPEC embargo and rising international prices, some countries expanded their domestic oil production and exploration. In 1977, the United States greatly increased its domestic production as oil began flowing from the northern slopes of Alaska through a 789-mile pipeline to the ice-free port at Valdez. Meanwhile, the Soviet Union drilled additional wells in Siberia. After the discovery in 1969 of large oil fields under the North Sea, a part of the Atlantic Ocean linking Britain, Western Europe, and Scandinavia, oil companies built offshore drilling platforms and a European oil and natural gas boom ensued despite the hazards of oil extraction in such a harsh environment.

But the energy crisis was only one of the economic challenges facing the United States in the 1970s. As the costs of defense and social welfare programs expanded, the federal budget shifted from a $3.2 budget surplus in 1969 to annual deficits as high as $73.7 billion over the next decade. Global food shortages triggered by world population increases and poor harvests led to rising food prices. Health care and housing costs were increasing. Buffeted by high unemployment and inflation combined with a stalled economy (a phenomenon termed **stagflation** by economists), the typical U.S. family income rose only $36 from 1973 to the late 1970s. At the same time, ninety-eight nations had higher rates of economic growth than the United States.

Presidents Gerald Ford and Jimmy Carter attempted to redress the nation's economic travails. In 1975, Ford persuaded Congress to pass a $23 billion federal tax reduction in order to stimulate the economy, but the recession continued into Carter's presidency. In 1979, the situation worsened when the Iranian Revolution led to a second, deeper oil shock. When Iran's oil production plummeted by 90 percent, the price of crude oil doubled from $18 to $36 per barrel. U.S. gasoline prices spiked to more than $1 per gallon, triple the 1973 average cost. Having quintupled its petroleum imports since 1970, the United States felt the effects of restricted international oil production almost immediately. More than 50 percent of U.S. gas stations temporarily closed because supplies were limited.

Continued inflation also hindered economic recovery. After annual price increases averaging 2.5 percent throughout the 1960s, U.S. prices rose an average of 6.6 percent each year from 1973 to 1980 when inflation peaked at 13.5 percent. Britain's inflation rate was even worse, averaging 15.6 percent over the same period. Facing the biggest economic crisis since the Great Depression, U.S. and British policy makers concluded that Keynesian economic policies no longer seemed to increase standards of living and reduce rates of inequality. Seeking alternatives, officials began adopting ideas espoused by a transatlantic network of **neoliberal** economists, journalists, think tanks, and politicians calling for less intervention in the economy.

In August 1979, Carter appointed Paul Volcker to chair the Federal Reserve Board. A **monetarist**, Volcker abandoned the long-held practice of supporting a specific interest rate through the purchase and sale of government securities. Instead, he set strict new targets to control the amount of currency in circulation and allowed interest rates to fluctuate. But Volcker's tight money policies did not immediately stop the recession. As unemployment and interest rates rose, voters blamed Carter for the nation's deepening economic travails.

26-2b Challenges and Opportunities for U.S. Business, Industry, and Labor

Throughout the 1970s, foreign competition seriously eroded the global economic supremacy that the United States had enjoyed since World War II. In the mid-1950s, U.S. manufacturers produced half of the world's goods, including 75 percent of all automobiles and more than 50 percent of global steel supplies. But over time, foreign countries began to dominate highly profitable, technologically advanced fields such as aerospace, consumer electronics, and machine tools. In addition, American and even Japanese companies shifted low-skill production work to such places as South Korea, Taiwan, Hong Kong, Singapore, and Indonesia where goods could be produced more cheaply because of lower wage scales and limited worker protections. As many as 30 million U.S. jobs—most of them in manufacturing—disappeared as a result of such **outsourcing**. If U.S. displaced workers found new jobs, they often had to accept lower-paying positions. The growth of the postindustrial service economy ballooned, and by 1980, 70 percent of Americans

> Economic changes result in job losses and lower wages but also prompt innovation and migration.

stagflation Term coined in the 1970s to describe a combination of rising prices, high unemployment, and slow economic growth.

neoliberal Calls for smaller government and expansion of the private sector through deficit reduction, tax reforms, fluctuating exchange rates, privatization of public enterprises, free trade, and deregulation.

monetarism Developed by Milton Friedman, economic theory that argues that overproduction of money leads to increased inflation. Calls for close government oversight over cash supply.

outsourcing Assigning core functions of a company to a contractor or subcontractor or obtaining goods or services from an outside vendor as a cost-saving strategy.

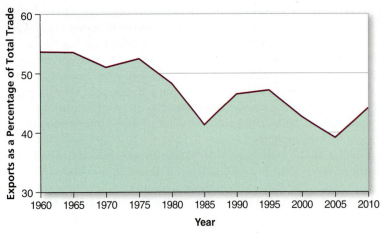

Figure 26.1 U.S. Trade Balance, 1960–2003

In the late 1960s, foreign competition began to erode U.S. economic dominance. Manufacturing declined in the United States, and consumers began importing many products such as cars and electronics. By the early 1970s, the United States had developed a trade deficit, importing more than it exported—a trend that has continued at differing levels ever since. ◀ Source: U.S. Census Bureau, Economic Indicator Division, https://www.census.gov/foreign-trade/statistics/historical/gands.pdf.

Note: Less than 50 percent indicates an export deficit and above 50 percent indicates an export surplus.

worked in the **service sector**. Rather than producing tangible goods, such workers provided a wide array of services including sales, housekeeping, health care, education, and financial consulting.

These trends had a devastating impact on the U.S. automobile industry. As oil prices increased, so had U.S. consumer demand for more fuel-efficient vehicles. German and Japanese automakers captured one-fifth of the U.S. market by 1977. Already struggling to meet new federal safety and emissions guidelines, U.S. companies including Ford and General Motors raced to retool production facilities to build smaller cars with higher gas mileage. In September 1979, Congress approved a $1.5 billion loan that enabled the Chrysler Corporation to avert bankruptcy (see Figure 26.1).

The shift toward a service economy dramatically affected organized labor in the United States. After impressive wages and benefits from their employers in the 1950s, unions in manufacturing industries like steel and automobiles lost membership as foreign competition rose. Public sector employees fared better. In 1962, John F. Kennedy issued an executive order allowing federal employees to bargain collectively and public unions grew as the Great Society programs of the Johnson administration led to expansion of government, social welfare, and teaching jobs. But total U.S. union membership fell from 1970 to 1981, dropping from 25 percent to 16 percent of the civilian workforce.

In the face of these trends, many workers wondered whether the American Dream was slipping away. Popular culture of the era reflected these fears in songs like Johnny Paycheck's "Take This Job and Shove It" (1977) and Bruce Springsteen's "The River" (1980). The film *Saturday Night Fever* (1977) popularized disco but also told the story of

a white working-class man's efforts to escape a life of dead-end, low-wage work.

Despite (or sometimes because of) the sluggish economy of the 1970s, entrepreneurship flourished in the era. Facing rising overhead and increased competition, investors were willing to back innovators offering cost- and time-saving efficiencies. After making Wal-Mart a publicly traded company in 1970, Sam Walton built a nationwide chain of "big-box" stores promising "the lowest prices, anytime, anywhere" and used computers to track sales and inventory—a practice then rare in the retail industry. The computing industry also transformed as small desktop or personal computers joined (and in many cases replaced) large mainframe computers that had descended from the army's ENIAC (1946). Bill Gates and Paul Allen started the company Micro-Soft in April 1975 and soon created MS-DOS, a computer operating system that required users to type in specific command codes. In 1976, Steve Jobs and Steve Wozniak formed Apple Computer to market the Apple II, widely considered the first personal computer suited for business tasks. In 1984, Apple revolutionized desktop computing by creating the Macintosh computer which allowed users to make commands by pointing and clicking on the screen through the combination of a graphical user interface and a "mouse." A year later, Gates's company, now known as Microsoft, came out with its own operating system (Windows) also based on the use of a mouse interface.

The wave of technological advances accelerated the demographic shift in the United States toward the Sunbelt. Many technology start-up companies were located near universities in California, North Carolina, and Texas. Other corporations were drawn to the South and the West by the regions' right-to-work laws, weak unions, warm climates, and skilled workforces. As workers fled the urban decay and unemployment of northern and midwestern rust-belt industrial cities, the Sunbelt prospered (see Map 26.1).

service sector Portion of economy that produces intangible goods such as investment management, retail, food service, scientific and technological expertise, health care, housekeeping, and entertainment.

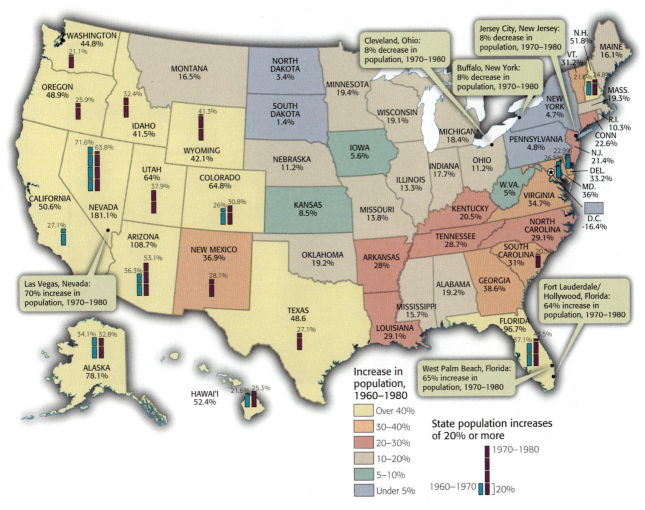

Map 26.1 Relocation in the Sunbelt Since the 1960s, the Sunbelt has witnessed a surge in its population fueled by people seeking warmer climates, comfortable retirement communities, and well-paying jobs in the defense, aerospace, and petroleum industries. Tourism and agriculture also contributed to the economic success of the region. While the Sunbelt boomed, many urban areas of the northern United States experienced economic decline and population loss. ▲

26-2c Resurgent Environmentalism

Throughout the 1970s, many nations began trying to find the best ways to control pollution and to safeguard natural resources and wildlife without restricting economic growth. Developing nations ("the South") pushed wealthier, industrialized countries ("the North") to increase their foreign assistance programs, cut their tariffs, and share power in international organizations like the World Bank. In many areas of the developing world, droughts, pollution, and shortages of land and fertilizer resulted in mass hunger. Rising birth rates and falling death rates

> A burgeoning global population, economic challenges, and limited natural resources fuel a transnational environmental movement.

intensified the scramble for natural resources. In 1975, after the global population reached 4 billion, the United States and other developed nations expanded their international family planning, nutrition, and health initiatives. In 1979, following a twelve-year global campaign, the World Health Organization (WHO) announced that smallpox, one of the world's deadly diseases, had been completely eradicated.

The economic challenges of the 1970s provided new incentives for Americans to adopt more environmentally conscious practices and policies. In 1975, Congress instituted the first federal fuel-efficiency standards and fines for auto manufacturers that failed to meet them. Between 1974 and 1989, the average mileage per gallon of gasoline rose from 13.8 to 27.5. As the price of oil rose, many drivers stopped buying gas-guzzling cars, a trend that later reversed when fuel prices declined in the mid-1980s

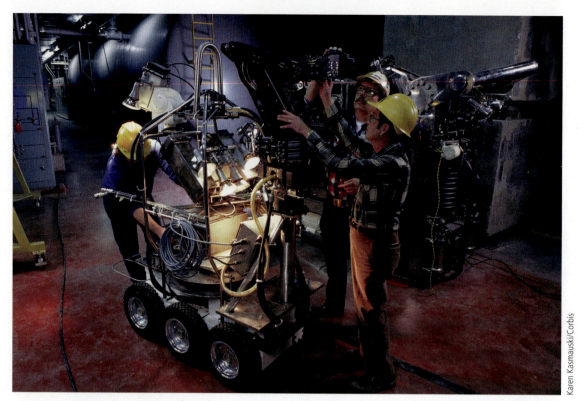

Cleanup at Three Mile Island, 1979 In October 1979, a crew cleans up radioactive contamination at the Three Mile Island nuclear plant. Although Three Mile Island's containment building remained intact and its small radioactive releases had no detectable health impacts on plant workers or nearby residents, the accident prompted sweeping changes to commercial nuclear emergency response planning, training, and federal oversight. ▲

Three Mile Island A nuclear reactor near Middletown, Pennsylvania, that experienced a partial meltdown in March 1979, the worst nuclear accident in U.S. history.

Chernobyl Soviet-run nuclear power plant in the Ukraine, site of the world's worst nuclear accident in April 1986.

deregulation Removal or reduction of government oversight over an industry, usually aimed at fostering economic competition.

when the popularity of large vehicles including SUVs and trucks soared. Communities instituted recycling programs. Design changes made homes and appliances more energy-efficient. Environmentalists advocated alternative sources of energy such as solar, wind, and hydroelectric power.

The era also witnessed renewed discussions about nuclear energy. Nuclear power plants did not release carbon or other "greenhouse" gases into the atmosphere, by-products scientists later linked to increases in global warming. But nuclear reactors produced waste that remained radioactive for hundreds of years, prompting fierce debates over how and where to store such materials. Popular anxieties about nuclear energy skyrocketed in March 1979 after a cooling system malfunction and human errors triggered the partial meltdown of a nuclear reactor at the **Three Mile Island** plant outside Harrisburg, Pennsylvania. In 1986, an even more devastating nuclear accident at the **Chernobyl** plant in the Soviet Union forced the permanent evacuation of three hundred thousand people. Although antinuclear protests led to the premature closure of some facilities and

cancellation of dozens of plant construction projects, the U.S. government tightened safety guidelines, and the production of nuclear-generated electricity more than tripled over the next three decades.

26-2d Rise of the Free Market Economy

The 1970s marked the beginning of a major shift toward a free market economy (see **free enterprise**). Influenced by economists like Friedrich von Hayek and Milton Friedman, advocates of free-market doctrines believed that economic regulations limited innovation and wealth creation. They strongly opposed socialist or Communist command economies in which the state controlled production, wages, and prices. Such collective decision making, they argued, violated individual freedoms. Instead, they called for a system of economics that minimized (or outright abolished) taxes, subsidies, and regulations, thus allowing unrestricted competition among private businesses to determine wages and prices. As bipartisan support for **deregulation** increased, the

> Advocates of free market doctrines deregulate private industries, lower taxes, and cut government spending.

Keystone/Hulton Archive/Getty Images

Global Americans Milton Friedman (1912–2006) was an economist

renowned for his theories on monetary policy. After completing a doctorate at Columbia University in 1946, he accepted a professorship at the University of Chicago and became part of a transatlantic network of experts challenging the prevailing macroeconomic theories of John Maynard Keynes. Since the 1930s, Keynesians had argued that government spending provided a corrective to economic downturns. Friedman's monetarist theories rejected the Keynesians' reliance on government spending and instead advocated controlling the amount of money in circulation to combat inflation and ensure economic stability. His ideas gained worldwide exposure though his prolific publications. In 1976, the same year he retired from the University of Chicago, Friedman was awarded the Nobel Prize in Economics. In the late 1970s, President Jimmy Carter, influenced by Friedman's views, began deregulating banking and transportation and appointed Paul Volcker, a monetarist, to chair the Federal Reserve. British prime ministers Harold Wilson and James Callaghan also embraced some of Friedman's ideas and made deep cuts in government spending to control inflation.

A key adviser to Reagan and British Prime Minister Thatcher, Friedman called for a free market with minimal government intervention. His ideas on taxation, deregulation, and privatization shaped government policies around the world. Near the end of his life, Friedman advocated the legalization of drugs, prostitution, and same-sex marriage—positions consistent with his lifelong belief in limiting the role of government to protect individual freedoms. He is widely considered one of history's most influential economists.

federal government shifted from interventionist policies instituted in the Progressive era and by the New Deal and the Great Society.

To foster competitive pricing in transportation, both Ford and Carter decreased the power of the Interstate Commerce Commission. Private railroad and trucking companies were granted more control over rates and routes, a move especially valuable to firms using **containerization** to ship standardized containers of goods across land and sea. In 1978, Congress passed legislation disbanding the Civil Aeronautics Board and permitting airlines more autonomy in setting prices. The move generated intense competition among carriers and resulted in more passengers flying at much lower fares.

Deregulation swept other industries too. Looser federal rules on telecommunications led to increased competition and significantly lower rates on telephone calls. Relaxed regulation of the New York Stock Exchange sparked more competitive stock prices and much higher trade volume. New banking rules enabled small investors to put their money in Treasury bills and mutual funds, financial instruments with higher yields than traditional savings accounts. In 1978, the Supreme Court ruled that credit card companies could base themselves in states with low interest rates and continue to market their products nationwide. The decision made credit cards more accessible to U.S. consumers than ever before. As the free market took hold worldwide, its supporters lauded the rapid growth of individual and corporate wealth that it created. Critics, however, blamed the introduction of less restricted forms of capitalism for a deepening of global income inequality and erosion of worker protections in the years that followed.

The United States was not alone in implementing free market reforms in the 1970s. Troubled by rising unemployment and declining economic growth, many Western Europeans challenged their governments to cut generous social welfare benefits such as pensions and health care. Great Britain made a significant political shift to the right after Margaret Thatcher, leader of the Conservative Party, won the general election in May 1979. As prime minister, she advocated deregulation, restricting trade unions, privatizing state-owned companies, reducing taxes, and cutting government spending on social services such as housing and education.

Even some Communist nations instituted free market reforms. In 1979, a new Chinese regime led by Deng Xiaoping introduced limited forms of capitalism in order to rebuild a society shattered by the Cultural Revolution. "Poverty is not socialism," Deng declared. "To get rich is glorious." While still defining itself as Communist or socialist, the government opened China to foreign trade, dismantled the commune system, and allowed some private ownership and market competition. In coming years, China had one of the fastest growing economies in world history, and hundreds of millions of Chinese were lifted out of poverty. In the mid-1980s, both Vietnam and the Soviet Union emulated China's attempt to blend Communist and free market principles.

containerization Shipping method that uses standardized freight containers that do not have to be unloaded and are transferred with cranes from one means of transport to another.

26-3
Private Lives and Public Debates

This 1976 *Time Magazine* cover reflects some of the ways that changes in women's lives had great ripple effects through American society and culture in the post-Vietnam era.

What do these images suggest about the changing professional and personal lives of women in the 1970s? Why was it significant for *Time* to devote this issue to "Women of the Year?" ▶

Go to MindTap® to practice history with the Chapter 26 **Primary Source Writing Activity: Private Lives and Public Debates**. Read and view primary sources and respond to a writing prompt.

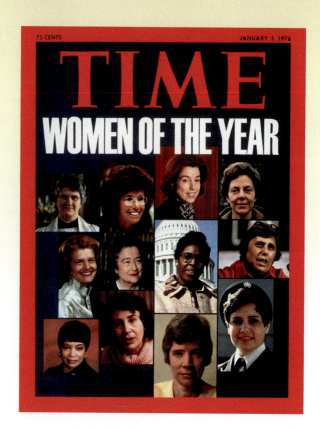

In the 1970s, economic imperatives, social movements, and individual decisions contributed to significant changes in the private lives of most Americans. As more women joined the workforce, more families became two-income households. Divorce rates soared. Unmarried couples cohabited. Men and women alike pursued sexual liberation. Lesbian, gay, bisexual, and transgender (LGBT) Americans shattered stereotypes and demanded equal rights. At the same time, a multifaceted religious revival swept the United States and other nations. Echoing earlier responses to modernity in the 1920s, many Americans embraced faith as a source of stability and community in an age of rapidly changing social mores and rising individualism. In some nations, religious fervor fueled political activism and catapulted religious figures into political power. Newly politicized American social conservatives defended their ideals of family, gender, and sexuality and helped reshape the Republican Party.

☞ As you read, think about the roots and impact of shifting family dynamics and views of morality on American society as a whole. What were the major changes in individuals' lives during this era? How and why did they become politically and socially divisive?

26-3a Changes for Families and Women

Family life changed dramatically in the 1970s. Inspired by economic imperatives and broader acceptance of white women employed outside the home, more married women with children under eighteen joined the workforce, and the number of two-income households increased. With rising rates of divorce, unmarried cohabitation, and single

> Family structures change as women's economic status increases and rates of divorce and single parenthood climb.

parenthood, fewer and fewer U.S. families resembled the nuclear family ideal.

Divorces climbed sharply from the late 1960s through the 1970s. Following California's adoption of the nation's first "no-fault" divorce law, forty-six states adopted similar statutes allowing spouses to dissolve their legal unions on the basis of incompatibility instead of the previously required charges of spousal neglect, cruelty, or disloyalty. More than 1 million couples divorced in 1975 alone. In the early 1980s, the divorce rate leveled at about 50 percent of all marriages, but an increasing number of people waited longer to get married or chose not to at all (see Figure 26.2).

As women's economic status rose, U.S. birth patterns also shifted. After the postwar baby boom ended in the mid-1960s, fertility rates dropped during the 1970s from 2.5 to 1.7 per woman of childbearing age, levels comparable to the pre-World War II era. Simultaneously, more women over the age of thirty began having children, and an increasing number of single women became mothers.

Other nations experienced similar shifts. In 1980, unmarried women in Sweden accounted for almost 40 percent of all live births—more than double the rate in the United States. But Western Europe, Canada, and Japan had far fewer single-parent households than the 1980 U.S. rate of nearly 20 percent. In the 1970s, many Roman Catholic nations in Europe including Spain, Portugal, and Italy legalized divorce. Echoing trends in the United States, the divorce rate in many industrialized nations rose as more women secured economic autonomy, families had fewer children, and divorce became more readily available and socially acceptable.

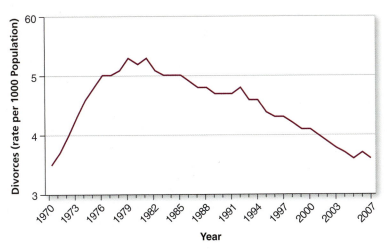

Figure 26.2 U.S. Divorce Rates, 1970–2007

Divorce rates in the United States escalated in the 1970s, peaking at nearly 50 percent, or half of all marriages. Divorce rates are inexact, however, because they are based on the number of people marrying every year, and some states stopped gathering divorce statistics in the 1980s. It is also difficult to discern how rates of divorce differ among different racial and cultural groups, ages, and educational and income levels. ▶ Source: U.S. National Center for Health Statistics, Vital Statistics of the United States, National Vital Statistics Reports (NVSR), http://www.cdc.gov/nchs/nvss.htm.

Note: Includes reported annulments and some estimated state figures for all years.

During the same years, dramatic changes in the lives of American women occurred. Inspired by feminism, economic needs, or individual aspirations, women continued to rapidly enter the workforce. Female employees secured more than 60 percent of the 19 million jobs created during the decade, most of which were low-paying, entry-level positions. Even with two incomes, many families struggled to make ends meet because of high inflation and economic stagnation.

But women also made important breakthroughs. Centuries-old employment barriers fell, and women became corporate executives, small business owners, law enforcement officers, firefighters, and construction workers. In 1976, the nation's military academies became coed. The numbers of women attending medical and law schools rose significantly. In 1981, Sandra Day O'Connor won confirmation as the first female justice to sit on the Supreme Court.

Some obstacles proved more difficult to surmount. Many working women remained in traditional **"pink-collar" jobs** such as nursing, office administration, and teaching— positions with little chance of upward mobility. Despite civil rights protections backed by the Equal Opportunity Employment Commission (EEOC), women who entered better-paying corporate or professional jobs often hit the **glass ceiling**, discriminatory barriers that prevented women and nonwhite men from reaching the highest levels of compensation and responsibility. A **wage gap** between the sexes also persisted. After hovering at about 60 percent since the mid-1950s, the ratio of women's to men's median pay for full-time employment began to rise in the late 1970s and reached about 70 percent by 1990. Despite this gain, the gender disparities in pay and rising divorce rates that often removed the male breadwinner from the family economy helped to explain the disproportionate percentage of women among America's poor, a trend described as the **feminization of poverty**. Burdened by racial and language barriers in addition to gender-based obstacles, African American and Latina single mothers experienced the highest rates of poverty.

26-3b Lesbian, Gay, Bisexual, and Transgender Rights Movement

In the years following the June 1969 Stonewall Riots, the lesbian, gay, bisexual, and transgender (LGBT) rights movement made impressive gains. Police harassment of LGBT establishments declined. Half of the states repealed their **sodomy laws**. In 1974, the American Psychiatric Association removed homosexuality from its list of mental disorders, and the following year, the U.S. Civil Service Commission lifted its ban on the employment of gay men and lesbians by the federal government. Several dozen cities, including Detroit, Boston, Los Angeles, San Francisco, and Houston, incorporated sexual orientation into their municipal nondiscrimination protections in housing, public accommodations, and employment. Across the country, openly gay candidates ran for public office and heterosexual candidates sought political support from the LGBT community. In 1980, the Democratic Party included a gay rights plank in its national platform for the first time.

Such advances were echoed in many nations. In the 1970s, Austria, Costa Rica, Finland, Norway, Malta, Cuba, and Spain decriminalized homosexuality. In 1977, Quebec became the world's first jurisdiction larger than a municipality to outlaw discrimination based on sexual orientation. In 1978, the International Lesbian

> The LGBT rights movement becomes more visible and pushes for civil rights.

"pink-collar" jobs Positions traditionally held by women such as secretary, nurse, or telephone operator, juxtaposed to blue-collar jobs involving manual labor and "white-collar" jobs in management.

glass ceiling Perceived or actual barrier that prevents women and minorities from obtaining the best-paying, highest-ranking jobs in a specific industry or company.

wage gap Statistical indicator of women's average yearly pay expressed as a percentage of men's average annual earnings.

feminization of poverty Disproportionate representation of women among the world's poor as a result of low average annual incomes and gender biases.

sodomy laws Statutes defining certain sexual acts as criminal that were found to be unconstitutional in *Lawrence v. Texas* (2003).

Bowers v. Hardwick U.S. Supreme Court five-to-four ruling upholding a Georgia law barring private, consensual oral or anal sex between men.

and Gay Association, an advocacy organization aimed at securing LGBT rights worldwide, was formed.

But these changes triggered fierce opposition. In 1977, after Dade County, Florida, outlawed discrimination on the basis of sexual orientation, Anita Bryant—best-known as a beauty pageant queen, singer, and spokesperson for the Florida Citrus Commission—led a coalition called Save Our Children that successfully pushed for the repeal of the ordinance. The campaign drew on fundamentalist Christian doctrine that equated homosexuality with sin and claimed that homosexuals "recruited" and molested children. It proved instrumental in persuading the Florida legislature to prohibit gays from adopting children, a ban that was not lifted until 2008. Following her victories in Florida, Bryant led successful efforts to repeal gay rights ordinances in Eugene, Oregon, and Wichita, Kansas. But her supporters failed to win passage of the Briggs Initiative (Proposition 6), a California ballot measure that would have barred LGBT teachers or anyone who supported LGBT equality from working for the state's public schools. Harvey Milk, an openly gay man elected to the San Francisco Board of Supervisors in 1977 and later assassinated by a colleague, played a leading role in the initiative's defeat.

Bryant was a polarizing national figure. Some Americans praised her work, but others declared her a dangerous extremist. Many of her detractors boycotted orange juice, and gay bars across North America swapped orange juice and vodka "screwdriver" cocktails with "Anita Bryants" made of vodka and apple juice. In 1979, stung by the national boycott of orange juice, the Florida Citrus Commission allowed its contract with the controversial Bryant to expire. Although Bryant faded from public life, organized efforts to block gay rights continued for decades.

With the onset of the AIDS (Acquired Immune Deficiency Syndrome) epidemic in 1981, many gay men encountered harsh discrimination from people who erroneously believed it was a "gay disease." As the epidemic cut a devastating path through the country, gay men and lesbians joined forces to care for the ill, promote safer sexual practices, and demand more public funding for research and prevention. In **Bowers v. Hardwick** (1986), the Supreme Court handed gays a major setback by upholding sodomy laws barring consensual sex between homosexuals in private. Already reeling from the impact of AIDS on their community, gays escalated their efforts to secure civil rights.

26-3c Religious Revivalism

As in the 1920s and the 1950s, a strong wave of religious revivalism occurred during the 1970s. While most worshippers embraced monotheistic

> A multifaceted religious revival has great social and political effects.

faiths such as Christianity, Judaism, and Islam, alternative spiritual practices including Buddhism, Native American traditions, and New Age also gained adherents. Some of the religious enthusiasm found expression in cults and pseudofaiths like the Church of Scientology (founded by science fiction writer L. Ron Hubbard in 1952), Reverend Sun Myung Moon's Unification Church (whose followers were sometimes called "Moonies"), and Reverend Jim Jones's People's Temple. In the summer of 1977, Jones abruptly moved his congregation from San Francisco to a compound named *Jonestown* in the jungles of Guyana. In November 1978, his guards shot and killed Congressman Leo Ryan and four others engaged in a fact-finding mission to investigate allegations of human rights abuses at Jonestown. Jones then ordered his followers to drink cyanide-laced grape drink. Nine hundred and nine people, including more than three hundred children, died in the mass suicide. The phrase "drinking the Kool-Aid" became a synonym for blind devotion to a destructive cause or leader.

Fundamentalism and evangelicalism were much more common expressions of the wave of religiosity. Fundamentalists strictly adhere to religious orthodoxy and rigorously defend their view of religious truth against secularism. Protestant fundamentalism in the United States arose in the late nineteenth century and is characterized by beliefs in the inerrancy of the Bible and in the possibility of personal atonement through acceptance of Jesus Christ. Many fundamentalist Christians reject the scientific doctrine of evolution and instead embrace the biblical story of Creation. Fundamentalists are part of a larger group of evangelicals who share

Pat Benic/Upi/Newscom

U.S. Postal Service Commemorates Harvey Milk, 2014 This U.S. postage stamp honors Harvey Milk, one of the nation's first openly gay elected officials. While serving on the San Francisco Board of Supervisors, he played critical roles in the passage of a nondiscrimination ordinance and in the successful campaign to defeat a statewide ballot initiative that sought to bar LGBT teachers from California's public schools. Following his death by assassination in 1978, Milk became a worldwide symbol of LGBT equality. ▲

AP Images/Carl R. Battreall

Global Americans **Bill Bright** (right) was an American evangelical and founder of Campus Crusade for Christ. Born in Oklahoma in 1921, he graduated from Northeastern State University and moved to California. After becoming an evangelical Christian in 1944, he attended Princeton and Fuller Theological Seminaries but did not graduate from either. In 1951, he and his wife Vonette founded Campus Crusade for Christ (now known as *Cru* in the United States) to preach to students at UCLA. Over the next five decades, it went on to become the biggest Christian ministry in the world with over 27,000 staff members and 225,000 volunteers working in 190 countries.

In 1956, Bright published "The Four Spiritual Laws," a pamphlet offering guidance on how to establish a personal connection to Jesus Christ. It is perhaps the most widely distributed religious publication in history, with 2.5 billion copies disseminated in two hundred languages. Building a global network worth more than $500 million, Bright wrote more than 100 publications and reached hundreds of millions through radio broadcasts, television, films, billboards, the Internet, and training conferences. In 1994, he co-founded Alliance Defending Freedom, a conservative Christian nonprofit organization supporting litigation aimed at protecting the religious provisions of the First Amendment. Two years later, Bright won the $1.1 million Templeton Prize for Progress in Religion, donating the proceeds to publicizing the spiritual value of prayer and fasting. Although unfamiliar to many Americans, Bright was an essential figure in the expansion of American evangelicalism's influence on U.S. politics, business, and culture in the post–World War II era.

a belief in individual conversion through a direct relationship with God but who interpret the Bible less literally and are more willing to associate with people who have different religious faiths in the greater cause of bringing people to Christ.

Fundamentalists and evangelicals both played important roles in a broad movement of conservatives that dramatically changed modern U.S. politics. As the booming post-1945 economy lifted many evangelicals into the middle-class, some abandoned their traditional detachment from politics. Evangelicals joined anti-Communist organizations that criticized the official atheism and repressive practices of the Soviet Union. Others became politically engaged after the U.S. Supreme Court declared mandatory school prayers and school-sanctioned Bible readings unconstitutional.

By the mid-1970s, more than 70 million Americans described themselves as "born-again" Christians who had established a direct personal relationship with Jesus. Christian evangelicals owned their own businesses and operated their own schools and universities including Oral Roberts University in Tulsa, Oklahoma, and Liberty Baptist College (later renamed Liberty University) in Lynchburg, Virginia. Televangelists including Pat Robertson, Jimmy Swaggert, and Jim and Tammy Faye Bakker built huge domestic and international audiences for their television and radio ministries.

Jimmy Carter, a southern Baptist and self-described "born-again" Christian, won the presidency in 1976 with the support of many evangelical voters. His public discussion of his faith was unusual among public officials of the era and garnered widespread media attention. But Carter's liberal views on women's liberation, abortion, and other social issues alienated more conservative evangelicals. So did a 1978 ruling by the Internal Revenue Service stripping racially segregated Christian academies of their tax-exempt status. Distressed by a culture they perceived as increasingly immoral and godless, the **Christian Right** began mobilizing politically.

Jerry Falwell, a fundamentalist minister in Virginia, launched the **Moral Majority**. Founded in 1979, the organization paired support for free market capitalism and a strong U.S. presence in global affairs with opposition to abortion, divorce, feminism, and homosexuality. It intentionally adopted a platform that would draw conservatives from many faiths including evangelical Protestants, Catholics, Jews, and Mormons. Moral Majority chapters around the nation registered millions of voters and urged them to support like-minded political candidates running for local, state, and federal offices. These voters played a significant role in Reagan's 1980 presidential victory.

Conservative people of faith were also instrumental in the defeat of the Equal Rights Amendment (ERA). First introduced in Congress in 1923, the proposed amendment read, "Equality of rights under the law shall not be denied or abridged by the United States or by any state on account of sex." Support for it had languished for many years, but the revitalization of the women's movement prompted the House of Representatives to pass it by a vote of three hundred fifty-four to twenty-three in October 1971. Five months later, the Senate approved the ERA by a vote of eighty-four to eight, and the process of ratification began. Within a year, twenty-two of the required thirty-eight states ratified the amendment. With prominent supporters including Nixon and his successors Ford and Carter (and their wives Betty and Rosalyn, respectively) and celebrities such as Alan Alda, Phil Donahue, and Valerie Harper, passage of the ERA within the allotted seven-year period seemed assured.

But the ERA soon met passionate opposition. Led by long-time conservative activist Phyllis Schlafly, the STOP

Christian Right Social conservatives of several faiths that mobilized politically in the late 1970s.

Moral Majority Founded in 1979 by Reverend Jerry Falwell, political organization that mobilized social conservatives. Major influence on the Republican Party throughout the 1980s.

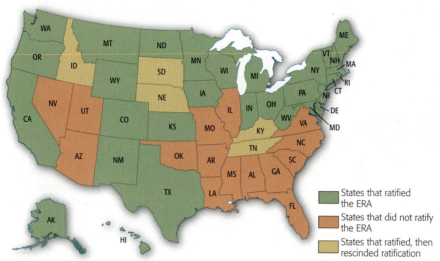

Map 26.2 Struggle for the Equal Rights Amendment First introduced in 1923, the Equal Rights Amendment (ERA) passed Congress in 1972. While 22 of the necessary 38 states quickly ratified the amendment, progress stalled as ERA opponents mobilized. Pro-ERA forces, despite massive lobbying and public education campaigns, proved unable to secure enough popular support to win ratification before the extended ratification deadline of June 30, 1982. Since then, pro-ERA advocates have adopted different strategies for securing ratification, but none has succeeded so far. ◄

States that ratified the ERA

States that did not ratify the ERA

States that ratified, then rescinded ratification

ERA campaign rapidly gained supporters who viewed the amendment as an assault on traditional womanhood. They claimed that the ERA would lead to the legalization of same-sex marriage, the conscription of women into the armed forces, and the establishment of mandatory unisex restrooms and taxpayer-funded abortions. They feared that the ERA would free men from their legal and financial responsibilities as husbands and fathers. As popular backing for the ERA began to erode, Congress extended the ratification deadline by three years. Nonetheless, in 1982, the ERA fell three states short of ratification after failing to win support in much of the South (see Map 26.2).

26-3d Global Fundamentalism

Throughout the era, religious conservatives were also gaining power internationally. In 1978, traditional Catholics welcomed the election of Archbishop Karol Wojtyla of Cracow, Poland, to the papacy. The first non-Italian Pope in four hundred fifty-five years, he adopted the name John Paul II and energetically promoted Catholicism around the world. He improved the Church's relations with Jews, Muslims, and Anglicans. He strongly defended the all-male, celibate priesthood and condemned artificial contraception and abortion. He attacked the godlessness and human rights abuses of Communist regimes.

> In an age of great flux, religious belief gives millions refuge but also generates conflict.

A new generation of Israeli Jews vigorously defended their faith too. Shaken by Israel's near defeat in the October War of 1973, a radical right-wing movement called the *Gush Emunim* (or *Bloc of the Faithful*) arose. Its supporters—to the dismay of Israeli authorities—established Jewish settlements in the West Bank, the Gaza Strip, and the Golan Heights, all then occupied by Palestinian Arabs.

Islamism Muslim revivalist movement that seeks to reorder government and society to support moral conservatism and a literal interpretation of the Koran.

Gush Emunim believed that, according to the Torah, God had granted Jews these lands. In 1977, such views gained more influence when the religiously conservative Likud party defeated the long-ruling Labor Party. Although Gush Emunim's influence declined, its aggressive Zionism and claims to the Occupied Territories affected Israeli politics for decades.

Because Judaism, Christianity, and Islam traced their origins to the "Holy Land," religion as well as geopolitics shaped connections between the United States and Israel. As the Soviets forged alliances with Arab states including Iraq and Syria, U.S. officials drew closer to the anti-Communist, democratic Israelis. Abandoning their historic anti-Semitism, fundamentalist Christian Americans embraced Israel as the site of the Battle of Armageddon described in the Book of Revelation, the conflict in which God defeats the Antichrist and Satan prior to the Second Coming of Christ. Jewish American support for Israel also intensified.

The 1970s Muslim fundamentalism also surged around the globe. One variant stemmed from the teachings of Hasan al-Banna, an Egyptian who began calling for renewed dedication to the Koran as a means of reinvigorating Muslim communities undermined by Western colonialism and cultural domination. In 1928, al-Banna established the Muslim Brotherhood, an educational organization dedicated to these principles. In subsequent decades, it clashed violently with secular rulers promoting socialism and modernization.

But the Egyptian government's harsh repression of the Muslim Brotherhood did little to stop the spread of Islamic fundamentalism throughout the Middle East. Demoralized by the Israeli victory over Syria, Egypt, and Jordan in the Six-Day War (1967) and frustrated by the limited economic opportunities under authoritarian, secular governments, many educated young people gravitated toward religious critics of these repressive regimes. Some embraced **Islamism**, a political ideology calling for the creation of governments based on Sharia (Islamic law).

In the late 1970s, Islamism gained momentum in Afghanistan. Electrified by the Iranian Revolution, Islamist rebels called the *mujahidin* (soldiers of God) won U.S. backing in their war against the Communist regime that took power in Afghanistan in late 1978. At the time, America's Cold War rivalry with the Soviet Union obscured the possible ramifications of arming Islamic militants with deep contempt for Western values.

26-4
Triumph and Travail on the Right

Reagan's presentation of proposed tax reduction legislation was televised in July 1981.

How would you describe Reagan's presentation and demeanor in this photograph? Why do you think his advisers thought it was important for him to have a chart? ▶

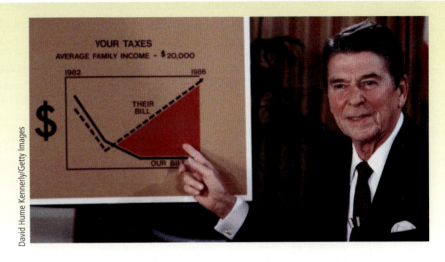

David Hume Kennerly/Getty Images

In the late 1970s, a powerful alliance of social and fiscal conservatives reshaped the Republican Party and propelled Ronald Reagan to victory in the presidential election of 1980. Dismayed by the weak economy and a growing federal bureaucracy, he slashed government programs, cut taxes, and instituted market-based reforms that empowered the private sector. To some Americans, he was a hero who reinvigorated a nation demoralized by war, social upheaval, and economic stagnation. To others, he was a reckless ideologue who amassed huge budget deficits and harmed the poor and disfranchised.

To combat Communist gains in the developing world, Reagan adopted strongly anti-Communist rhetoric and embarked on a major defense buildup. He hoped to pressure the Soviets into making concessions and cutting nuclear arsenals, but the deaths of a succession of Soviet leaders undermined his attempts at negotiations, and an enormous antinuclear movement mobilized worldwide. U.S.–Soviet relations were fraught with distrust. At the same time, the rise of Islamist militancy exacerbated tensions in the already volatile Middle East and presented U.S. policy makers with escalating dangers of global terrorism.

Although dogged by scandal during his second term, Reagan simultaneously responded to changes in the Soviet Union that dramatically affected the Cold War. In March 1985, the Soviets selected Mikhail Gorbachev as general secretary of the Communist Party. He and Reagan forged a partnership that produced historic arms control agreements. Gorbachev's internal reforms and Reagan's openness to them ushered in the Cold War's mostly peaceful end.

☞ **As you read, consider how and why conservatives in the 1980s influenced U.S. domestic and foreign policies. What were Reagan's major initiatives? Were they successful? Explain why or why not.**

26-4a Mobilization on the Right

In the 1970s, a diverse coalition of conservatives arose and quickly gained momentum. The **New Right** included businesspeople, white Southerners, evangelical Christians, Catholics, and others who supported a smaller federal government, greater economic competition, and traditional morality. The movement originated in the early 1960s when grassroots conservatives backed Arizona Senator Barry Goldwater. Goldwater called for cuts in social welfare spending and claimed that big government threatened individual liberties and inhibited economic growth. Undeterred by Goldwater's loss in the 1964 presidential race, conservatives positioned themselves for future electoral victories. Through innovative use of direct mail, the New Right developed strong communications and fund-raising networks. They established conservative think tanks and lobbying firms. They cultivated leaders who supported a strong national defense, traditional values, and limited government.

{ Fiscal and social conservatives join forces and transform U.S. politics.

Reagan exemplified the new conservative ideal. Once a New Deal Democrat, he switched parties as the Cold War arose in the late 1940s. A popular actor, Reagan became a spokesman for the General Electric Company, touring the nation making speeches extolling **free enterprise** and attacking communism. After winning acclaim for a speech he made at the 1964 Republican convention, Reagan successfully ran for governor of California two years later and easily won reelection to a second term. In 1976, he nearly defeated Ford in the Republican presidential primaries. A moderate, Ford

New Right Diverse coalition of fiscal and social conservatives that arose in the late 1970s and played a major role in defining the modern Republican Party.

free enterprise Economic system permitting private businesses to compete with little or no government intervention.

Proposition 13 Ballot initiative approved by California voters in 1978 that lowered property taxes significantly and helped make tax reduction a key element of modern U.S. conservatism.

supply-side economics Theory that lower taxes inspire corporate investment, higher production, and lower prices, thus elevating the economy as a whole.

had alienated his party's growing right wing by continuing the Nixon administration's détente policy. Once he secured the nomination, Ford placated conservatives by dropping liberal Nelson Rockefeller as his running mate and supporting a platform mostly written by North Carolina senator Jesse Helms, a Reagan ally and the leading social conservative in Congress. Ford's subsequent loss to Carter catapulted Reagan to Republican front-runner status for the 1980 election.

A revolt against high tax rates also fueled the New Right. In 1978, California voters approved **Proposition 13**, a referendum that lowered property taxes statewide. Conservative activists realized that tapping into popular resentment of paying taxes provided a way to win support for reducing the size of government without targeting individual programs that had vocal constituencies. The anti-taxation message became an effective political tool for conservatives across the country.

All of these factors converged in Reagan's victory in the 1980 presidential race. His optimism contrasted sharply with Carter's focus on "a crisis of confidence" plaguing the nation. Although Reagan was not a particularly religious man, he convinced evangelical voters to abandon Carter, a devout Christian. Despite his close ties to the wealthy, he appealed to working-class people. Some "Reagan Democrats" even crossed party lines to vote for him.

Howard Jarvis Campaigns for Proposition 13, 1978 This 1978 photograph from the *Los Angeles Times* shows tax cut advocate Howard Jarvis promoting Proposition 13. ▲

AP Images/FILE

Reagan capitalized on the fact that many Americans blamed Carter for a decline in U.S. international prestige and an economy hobbled by high interest rates, unemployment, and inflation. When Reagan asked potential voters "Are you better off than you were four years ago?" few could answer affirmatively. The Iranians' seizure and long captivity of fifty-two U.S. hostages and the recent Soviet invasion of Afghanistan provided fodder for Reagan's attacks on Carter's foreign policy. Winning forty-four states (but only 51 percent of the popular vote), Reagan trounced Carter and helped Republicans gain control of the Senate for the first time since 1954.

26-4b The Reagan Revolution

On taking office in January 1981, Reagan promised Americans the most sweeping changes in the federal government since the New Deal. "In this present crisis, government is not the solution to our problem," Reagan declared; "government is the problem." Fueled by the president's charisma and communications skills, the "Reagan Revolution" fell short of its most grandiose aims but profoundly altered the U.S. economic and political landscape.

> U.S. conservatives and their counterparts abroad limit the role of government and adopt free market policies.

Building on the neoliberal reforms launched by Carter, the Reagan administration instituted a vigorous economic agenda built on belief in the supremacy of the free market. Government officials expanded Carter's deregulation initiatives, opened public lands to private development, and adopted looser interpretations of federal environmental protections. At Reagan's urging, Congress passed several bills reducing taxes, closing tax loopholes, and eliminating many tax deductions. By 1987, the highest income tax rate was capped at 28 percent, down from 70 percent in 1980. Reagan's advisers argued that their **supply-side economics** (or "Reaganomics") would result in increased investment by wealthier people, creating more jobs. The resulting prosperity would then "trickle-down" to people lower on the income scale.

In August 1981, Reagan's response to a strike by federal air traffic controllers had long-term ramifications for workers in the United States and abroad. Formerly president of the Screen Actors' Guild, Reagan supported federal employees' right to bargain collectively for improved pay and benefits. But after negotiations with the Federal Aviation Administration stalled, about sixteen thousand members of the Professional Air Traffic Controllers Organization (PATCO) went on strike. Two days later, calling the work stoppage a violation of federal law, Reagan fired nearly all of the PATCO strikers. His unprecedented dismissal of skilled laborers encouraged private employers to hire replacement workers rather than bargain with strikers and later inspired calls for dismantling public employee unions—a position that Reagan himself never adopted (see Figures 26.3 and 26.4).

Figure 26.3 U.S. and Global Union Membership Although the decline of U.S. manufacturing and the passage of state right-to-work laws have contributed to a decrease in unionization among private sector employees, protections for collective bargaining by federal workers and an expansion of government programs have stablized rates among public employees including civil servants and teachers. Overall union membership, however, has trended downward for decades. ▼

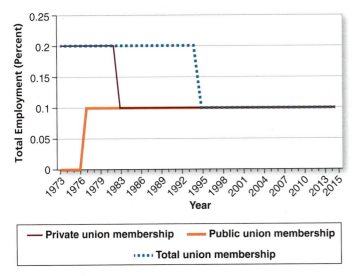

Figure 26.3(a) U.S. Union Membership, 1973–2015

Sources: For the years 1973–1981, the May Current Population (CPS), and for the years 1983–2015, the CPS Outgoing Rotation Group (ORG) Earnings Files, http://www.unionstats.com/. © 2016 by Barry T. Hirsch and David A. Macpherson.

Notes: No union questions were in the 1982 CPS. The definition of union membership was expanded in 1977 to include "employee associations similar to a union."

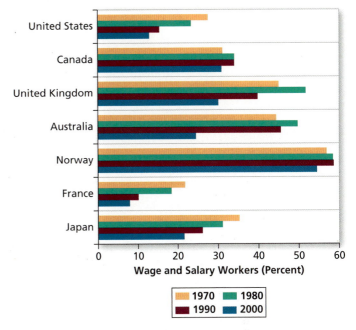

Figure 26.3(b) Union Membership Worldwide, 1970–2000

Source: Visser, Jelle. Data Base on Institutional Characteristics of Trade Unions, Wage Setting, State Intervention and Social Pacts, 1960–2011 (ICTWSS), vers 4.0, April 2013.

Reagan's supply-side policies were echoed in several other nations. Australia's economic rationalists and proponents of New Zealand's Rogernomics also favored deregulation, privatization of state-owned industries, reduction of the welfare state, and lower direct taxes. Inspired by Reagan's firing of the PATCO strikers, British prime minister Thatcher vigorously assaulted trade unions and launched more free market reforms. Thatcher's supporters credited her policies with transforming Britain's stagnant economy and re-establishing the nation as a world power, but critics blamed her for increasing social unrest, poverty, and unemployment.

Reductions in the size of the federal bureaucracy and cuts in many federal programs were core elements of Reagan's economic plans. Claiming that welfare created dependency and eroded individual initiative, the administration reduced spending on child care subsidies for low-income families, food stamps, child nutrition initiatives, job training, child abuse prevention programs, and mental health services. It also slashed funding for consumer protections, workplace safety, housing assistance, and agricultural subsidies. At the same time, Reagan argued that détente had weakened the United States internationally and pushed for a huge expansion of the defense

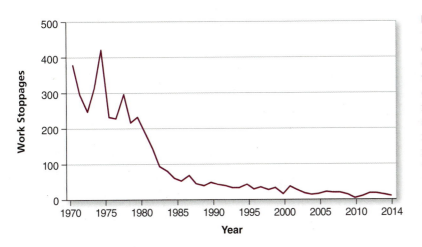

Figure 26.4 U.S. Work Stoppages, 1970–2014 Although strikes by public employees including teachers, police officers, and firefighters spiked in the 1970s, the number of work stoppages markedly declined after the early 1980s. In the aftermath of Reagan's dismissal of thirteen thousand striking federal air traffic controllers, a number of private employers began hiring replacement workers rather than negotiating with unionized workers who went on strike.
◄ Source: U.S. Bureau of Labor Statistics, http://www.bls.gov/news.release/wkstp.t01.htm.

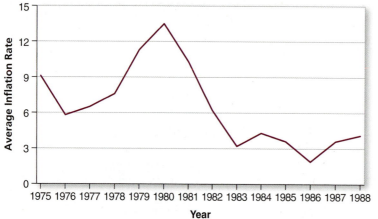

Figure 26.5 U.S. Inflation Rates, 1975–1988
U.S. inflation rates demonstrated a great deal of volatility in the Carter and Reagan years. In 1979, Federal Reserve Chairman Volcker instituted strict monetarist policies designed to lower inflation. Within three years, inflation rates had fallen from their 13.5 percent peak in 1980 to an annual average of about 4 percent. Economists' views on whether monetarist policies were responsible for the decline differ. ◄ Source: U.S. Inflation Calculator, U.S. Historical Inflation Rates, 1914–2015, http://www.usinflationcalculator.com/inflation/historical-inflation-rates/.

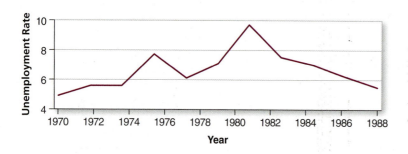

Figure 26.6 U.S. Unemployment Rate, 1970–1988 Energy shocks, foreign competition, outsourcing, and economic stagnation led to a marked increase in unemployment rates in the late 1970s, peaking at 10.8 percent in November 1982, the highest level of unemployment in the United States since 1940. ◄ Source: U.S. Department of Labor, Bureau of Labor Statistics, stats.bls.gov.

budget. U.S. military spending rose from $153.8 billion to $281.8 billion (22.69 percent and 26.48 percent of annual public expenditures, respectively).

Reaganomics did not have an immediate impact, and the recession deepened through 1982. Interest rates hit 20 percent. In November 1982, unemployment reached 10.8 percent, its highest level since 1940. In early 1983, Reagan's approval ratings plummeted to 35 percent and his chances of reelection seemed slim.

But as a combination of loosening the money supply, tax cuts, and defense spending stimulated the economy, the recession gradually ended. Inflation fell from 10 percent in 1981 to an annual average of less than 4 percent in 1983. Unemployment fell to 7.25 percent. Declaring it "morning in America" thanks to the reinvigorated national economy, Reagan crushed Democrat Walter Mondale in the 1984 presidential race (see Figures 26.5 and 26.6).

26-4c Divisions Deepen

Critics claimed that Reagan's policies created only the illusion of recovery. Because large tax cuts and defense expenditures were not offset by commensurate spending cuts, the national debt rose from $900 billion in 1981 to $2.8 trillion in 1988. Cuts to farm subsidies and high mortgage interest rates contributed to a wave of family farm foreclosures. Rising housing prices, cuts in federal welfare spending and housing assistance, the de-institutionalization of the mentally ill, and the decline of well-paying unskilled jobs led to a rapid spike in homelessness in the nation's cities (see Figure 26.7).

The federal "war on drugs" also reflected growing social divides. In the early 1980s, a cartel in Medellin,

> Debt, class and racial tensions, and inner city turmoil spark criticisms of Reagan's policies.

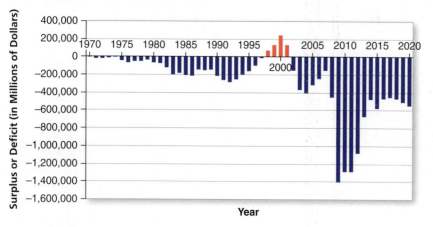

Figure 26.7 Federal Budget Deficits, Historic and Projected, 1970–2022 A federal budget deficit occurs when government spending exceeds tax revenues. The federal government then borrows money to offset the shortfall, thus increasing the national debt. This chart shows the long-range trend of deficit spending since 1970 and projections. ◄ Source: Office of Management and Budget, *Budget of the U.S. Government, FY 2013; Historical Tables,* Table 1.1, February 2012, https://www.whitehouse.gov/omb/budget/Historicals/.

"STRANGE HOW SOME CHOOSE TO LIVE LIKE THAT INSTEAD OF CHOOSING TO BE RICH LIKE US"

Library of Congress, Prints & Photographs Division, [reproduction number, LC-DIG-hlb-10762]

Herblock Parodies Reagan Economic Policies, 1984
This February 1984 political cartoon by Herbert Block (Herblock) reflects some of the criticisms aimed at the Reagan administration's supply-side economic policies. ▲

Colombia, began shipping cocaine into the United States first via Panama and Miami and later through Mexico. Americans created "crack," an inexpensive, cooked form of powder cocaine, a drug formerly accessible only to the wealthy, which reached the masses, leaving a trail of broken families and drug-related violence in its wake.

In response, Reagan signed the Anti-Drug Abuse Act of 1986. The bill appropriated $1.7 billion for interdiction. Under the law's new sentencing guidelines for selling or possessing narcotics, a conviction for possession of twenty-eight grams of crack or five hundred grams of powder cocaine received the same mandatory five-year penalty—a policy that disproportionately affected the poor, blacks, Latinos, and women. Between 1986 and 2000, the U.S. prison population rose from 300,000 to 2 million—an incarceration rate second only to Russia on a global per capita basis.

The era's uneasy political climate intensified debates about immigration. Experts disagreed on whether the costs of social services used by immigrants such as education, welfare, and health care exceeded the taxes they contributed to the U.S. economy. Although numerous businesses such as meatpacking, construction, and agriculture heavily depended on Latino immigrant labor, some economists

claimed that these immigrants displaced U.S. workers, depressed wage scales, and lacked the education and job skills necessary for upward mobility. Latinos made educational and economic gains in the 1980s, but fewer than one-half graduated from high school (the highest dropout rate among U.S. minorities), and many remained mired in low-paying jobs.

In 1986, concerns over undocumented Mexican immigrants prompted Reagan to sign the Immigration Reform and Control Act. The law criminalized knowingly recruiting or hiring undocumented workers for the first time in U.S. history. It introduced the **I-9 form** requiring job applicants to provide proof of their eligibility for legal employment and the **H1B visa**, allowing U.S. companies to temporarily employ foreign workers in specialized professions. The law also granted amnesty to immigrants who illegally entered the country before January 1, 1982, and had continuously resided there for at least five years if they admitted their guilt, paid a fine and back taxes, had no criminal record, and possessed basic knowledge of U.S. history and government and the English language. Approximately 3 million undocumented immigrants secured legal status under this policy. But weak employer penalties, poor enforcement, and the ease of obtaining fraudulent documents for the I-9 verification undermined the reform effort, and the number of people immigrating illegally, particularly from Mexico and Central America, continued to rise.

The era's popular culture reflected the nation's increasing polarization. Originating in the South Bronx, hip-hop blended innovative musical techniques with spoken word rhymes. Songs like Grandmaster Flash's "The Message" (1982) offered searing commentary about urban crime, drugs, and poverty and reached both radio and television audiences, thanks to MTV, a cable network devoted to music videos launched in 1981. While television programs *Dynasty* and *Dallas* celebrated the lifestyles of the rich, Oliver Stone's film *Wall Street* (1986) and Tom Wolfe's novel *The Bonfire of the Vanities* (1987) offered more cautionary tales about corruption and excess.

As probusiness books like Donald Trump's *The Art of the Deal* (1987) topped the best-selling lists, the rise of the low-grade, risky "junk bond" market and an unprecedented wave of mergers and acquisitions made Wall Street speculators and "corporate raiders" folk heroes to millions. But after the New York Stock Exchange's Dow Jones industrial average plummeted five hundred eight points on October 19, 1987 (a 22.6 percent decline in stock values), several Wall Street firms laid off employees. Although the market recovered quickly, the 1987 crash and the prosecution of once-venerated financial figures like Michael Milken and Ivan Boesky for illegal trading practices tarnished Wall Street's reputation.

I-9 form Federal document used by employers to verify employees' eligibility to work in the United States.

H1B visa Allows foreigners with certain professional skills to work in the United States for a maximum of six years.

AP Images/Carlos Rene Perez

Global Americans On a November evening in 1982, Samantha Smith, a ten-year-old girl from Manchester, Maine (population two thousand), wrote a letter to the new Soviet general secretary Yuri Andropov. She inquired whether he was planning to launch a nuclear attack on the United States. If that was not his intention, Samantha asked, "How you are going to help to not have a war?"

In April 1983, a time of heightened Soviet–U.S. tensions, Andropov wrote Samantha and assured her of the Soviets' peaceful intentions. Eager to score a propaganda victory in the Cold War, he invited Samantha and her parents to visit his nation. At the time, most tourists were only able to enter the Soviet Union with visas and itineraries provided by the state travel agency.

That July, the Smiths visited the Soviet Union for two weeks. Their hosts carefully shielded them from evidence of the country's chronic shortages of food and consumer products. Although illness forced Andropov to cancel his meeting with Samantha, she nonetheless told reporters "not a single Soviet person, neither old, nor young, wants war." After returning to the United States, the Smiths admitted that both U.S. and Soviet intelligence operatives had monitored their trip and acknowledged they had not been shown the worst aspects of the Soviet Union. But they defended Samantha's "propaganda mission" for "peace and kindness." In 1985, she and her father co-authored *Journey to the Soviet Union*, a nonfiction account of their visit. Later that year, they both died in a plane crash, but their story illustrates the important role of U.S.–Soviet cultural exchanges during the Cold War.

26-4d Confrontations with Communism and Terrorism

Intent on restoring U.S. power and prestige throughout the world, Reagan adopted harsh anti-Communist rhetoric and demonized the Soviet Union. In his first press conference, the president accused the Soviets of using détente as a means of promoting "world revolution." Soviet leaders, Reagan alleged, "reserve to themselves the right to commit any crime, to lie, to cheat…." In a 1983 speech, he evocatively described the Soviet Union as "the focus of evil in the modern world."

> Tensions with the Soviet Union escalate, and the threat of terrorism intensifies.

At the same time, the United States embarked on the biggest peacetime defense buildup in its history. Adding another $400 billion to the $1.2 trillion military expansion begun by Carter, Reagan supported the development of new weapons including the B-2 (Stealth) bomber and the MX missile and called for the extension of the U.S. fleet from four hundred fifty-six to six hundred vessels. After Congress authorized Reagan's plans, military appropriations increased by 50 percent, hitting $294.7 billion by 1985—an average of $28 million per hour.

Reagan vowed that he would not negotiate with the Soviets until the United States had overwhelmingly superiority in conventional and nuclear arms, an approach he described as "peace through strength." His tough stance alarmed Soviet leaders who believed that the United States was preparing to launch a preemptive nuclear strike on the Soviet Union. Their anxieties deepened in March 1983 when Reagan announced plans to develop the **Strategic Defense Initiative (SDI)**, an atmosphere-based defensive shield that could intercept and destroy nuclear missiles before they struck U.S. soil. Although few experts thought that SDI was technologically feasible, Reagan's statement nonetheless exacerbated Soviet fears.

Superpower relations deteriorated even further in late 1983. In September, a Soviet pilot shot down a South Korean civilian airliner that had inadvertently strayed into Soviet airspace. All two hundred sixty-nine passengers, including sixty-one Americans, died. Reagan denounced the incident as "an act of barbarism." The Soviets' failure to demonstrate much remorse and unsubstantiated claims that the airliner had been engaged in espionage heightened tensions. In December, the Soviets withdrew from arms control negotiations in protest of the recent NATO deployment of Pershing II and Cruise missiles in Western Europe. For the first time since 1972, U.S. and Soviet officials were not engaged in any diplomatic talks.

The collapse of détente and the escalation of the nuclear arms race inspired a resurgence of transnational antinuclear activism. Throughout the early 1980s, millions of Europeans and Americans participated in massive antinuclear rallies. Scientists including Carl Sagan predicted that the debris thrown into the atmosphere by a nuclear conflict would cause temperatures to plummet, creating a **nuclear winter** that would destroy all life on Earth. Although severe restrictions on freedom of speech limited antinuclear protests behind the Iron Curtain, isolated dissidents such as Soviet physicist Andrei Sakharov spoke out against nuclear proliferation.

Strategic Defense Initiative (SDI) Antiballistic missile system proposed by Reagan in 1983 to guard the United States from nuclear missile attacks. Never implemented.

nuclear winter Scientific theory positing that a nuclear war would have devastating environmental consequences that would imperil most of the living creatures on Earth.

At first dismissive of calls for a **nuclear freeze**, Reagan realized that intensifying popular opposition to his military policies might jeopardize his reelection. Accordingly, he softened his position and introduced a new framework for nuclear disarmament talks with the Soviets. He also carefully avoided direct U.S. military confrontation with Communist states. One exception occurred in October 1983 when he authorized the U.S. invasion of Grenada after a Communist regime took power on the tiny Caribbean island. After six thousand marines quickly defeated Grenada's six hundred-man army and ousted the Marxist leader, Americans cheered a decisive victory in an era of so much international uncertainty.

The 1985 **Reagan Doctrine** more closely resembled the president's preferred approach to combatting international communism. Under this policy, the United States provided financial support and military equipment to anti-Communist insurgents resisting Soviet-supported regimes throughout the world. With congressional approval, the CIA engaged in covert operations aiding anti-Communist rebels in Angola, Cambodia, Afghanistan, and Ethiopia. In Nicaragua, U.S.-backed **contras**—whom Reagan described as "freedom fighters . . . the moral equal of the Founding Fathers"—began mining harbors, sabotaging crops and infrastructure, and raiding Sandinista strongholds. In October 1984, disturbed by the contras' brutality toward civilians and wary of another entanglement resembling the Vietnam War, Congress passed the **Boland Amendment** barring any U.S. government agency from providing financial assistance to the Nicaraguan rebels. Undeterred, presidential aides continued supporting the contras—a decision that had serious consequences during Reagan's second term (see Map 26.3).

Tumult in the Middle East tested U.S. policy makers throughout Reagan's presidency. They closely monitored the implementation of the 1979 Israeli–Egyptian treaty negotiated by Carter. At first, implementation of the agreement appeared to be proceeding smoothly. In April 1982, Israel withdrew its troops from the Sinai Peninsula. But Arabs and Jews continued to differ on the question of a Palestinian homeland. Israel expanded settlements on the West Bank, an area long claimed by Palestinians. In protest, PLO forces based in southern Lebanon launched raids against Israel. On June 6, 1982, Israel retaliated by attacking PLO camps in Lebanon.

To quell the violence, the United States joined a multinational peacekeeping force to oversee the evacuation of the PLO to Tunisia and the withdrawal of Israeli troops.

nuclear freeze A transnational movement that arose in the 1980s calling for the United States and the Soviet Union to stop testing and producing nuclear weapons.

Reagan Doctrine Proclamation pledging U.S. overt and covert support for rebels resisting Communist tyranny around the world.

contras Nicaraguan counterrevolutionaries who opposed the left-wing Sandinistas in a civil war from 1979 to 1990, received U.S. covert aid.

Boland Amendment Three legislative addenda passed from 1982 to 1984 prohibiting U.S. support to contra forces seeking to overthrow the Sandinista government in Nicaragua.

Map 26.3 United States in the Caribbean and Central America Determined to quash the leftist insurgencies that swept the Caribbean and Central America as the détente policy collapsed and Cold War tensions intensified, the Reagan administration extensively intervened in the region, using a combination of overt and covert financial, military, and political tactics.▼

History without Borders

The Global Anti-Apartheid Movement

United States, 1977: "Sullivan Principles" demanded equal rights for employees regardless of race. By the 1980s they were adopted by 125 U.S. corporations who did business in South Africa, and at least 100 had withdrawn completely.

United Kingdom, 1988: The UK did its utmost to block the passage of the 1988 Commonwealth of Nations act, consistent with its behavior during this time period.

Sweden and Norway, 1987: Ended all trade with South Africa.

Iran, 1973: Broke with OPEC and supplied oil to South Africa; after its Islamic Revolution of 1979, it joined the oil embargo.

Japan, 1986: Adopted very limited trade boycotts against South Africa.

India, 1946: Enacted a trade embargo and cut off relations in protest of treatment of Indian community in South Africa.

Major trading partners of South Africa that applied sanctions by 1989

International boundaries, 1989

1962
Nonbinding call by the **General Assembly of the United Nations** for member nations to sever trade and transportation links, and to enact an oil embargo.

1963
The Organization for African Unity called for a total economic boycott.

1964–1988
The International Olympic Committee barred South Africa from competing in the Olympic Games.

1973
The Organization of Petroleum Exporting Countries (OPEC) imposed an oil embargo.

1977
The U.N. Security Council enacted an arms embargo, making the resolution of 1962 mandatory.

1986
The European Community banned all exports of oil, arms, and sensitive equipment, and ended imports of South African iron and steel.

1988
The Commonwealth of Nations imposed trade sanctions on certain imports. Exports of arms, nuclear material, and petroleum were banned. New loans and investments were prohibited.

Economic Sanctions on South Africa in the late 1980s While activists within South Africa risked their lives in anti-apartheid protests, foreigners organized economic sanctions and boycotts against the South African government. In the late 1980s, the white regime brutally repressed anti-apartheid activities, but the move backfired and inspired even more stringent sanctions imposed by the United States and the European community. In 1989, facing severe economic problems and isolation from the international community, South African president F.W. de Klerk began negotiations to end apartheid.

While the Cold War raged, a multinational movement pushed for the end of apartheid in South Africa. Instituted by the National Party in 1948, apartheid was a system of racial segregation similar to the Jim Crow laws in the United States and the caste system in India. Under apartheid, the Afrikaner white minority severely restricted the legal rights of the black majority. By 1970, the government had stripped nonwhites of their citizenship and had segregated the nation's education,

health care, beaches, transportation, and other public services and venues. In June 1976, after the government mandated that all educational instruction be conducted in Afrikaans (the language of the white minority), students in Soweto demonstrated. In response, police opened fire and killed up to seven hundred people.

At the same time, a global anti-apartheid movement grew in scope and intensity. Transnational networks of churches and faith-based groups, students, and labor unions protested.

Athletic associations and the International Olympic Committee barred South African teams from global competitions. Artists, writers, and actors campaigned for cultural boycotts. Divestment activists successfully persuaded colleges, universities, and local and state governments to sell their holdings in companies that traded with or had operations in South Africa. Others boycotted companies conducting business with the apartheid regime. By the late 1980s, the United States and twenty-four other nations had imposed

AP Images/Catharine Krueger

Anti-apartheid Protest at the University of California, Berkeley, March 1986
U.S. college students played an important role in the global movement against apartheid. In 1977, students at Haverford College persuaded administrators to sell the school's stock in companies that did business with the South African regime. Similar calls quickly arose on other campuses and by 1988, one hundred fifty-five universities had at least partially divested. President Barack Obama later called his participation in an anti-apartheid rally while attending California's Occidental College his "very first political action." ▲

AP Images/Ron Edmonds

Singer Stevie Wonder Arrested in an Anti-apartheid Demonstration at the South African Embassy in Washington, D.C., February 1985 In 1965, after the South African government prohibited multiracial performances, the United Nations Special Committee against Apartheid recommended a cultural boycott, a plea subsequently honored by many governments, organizations, and individuals. Alarmed by its increasing isolation, the South African government relaxed some rules and offered entertainers generous financial incentives. But many performers escalated their anti-apartheid protests. In early 1985, upon winning the Academy Award for Best Song, Stevie Wonder dedicated the prize to Nelson Mandela. ▲

trade sanctions on South Africa, resulting in approximately $35 billion in lost revenue from 1986 to 1989.

In the mid-1980s, massive demonstrations and political violence in South Africa escalated. The government issued state of emergency decrees giving the president, the police, and the military sweeping powers. Media outlets were heavily censored, and thousands of anti-apartheid protestors were arrested. After government agents tortured and killed suspected members of the African National Congress (ANC) and Pan Africanist Congress (PAC) both at home and abroad, the organizations retaliated by bombing restaurants, stores, and public buildings.

In February 1990, with South Africa's international reputation and economy in tatters and its domestic politics in chaos, President F.W. de Klerk announced that he would repeal

racially discriminatory laws and lift the thirty-year ban on anti-apartheid groups including the ANC and PAC. He offered to work with black leaders to devise a new constitution under which all races would share power. On February 11, 1990, ANC leader Nelson Mandela was freed after more than twenty-seven years of imprisonment. In 1993, de Klerk and Mandela jointly won the Nobel Peace Prize for moving South Africa toward democracy. On April 27, 1994, 20 million South Africans voted in the nation's first racially inclusive elections and elected Mandela the nation's first black president. His government adopted a new constitution and established a Truth and Reconciliation Commission to address the crimes and heal the wounds of the apartheid era. With the repeal of economic sanctions, companies that had divested returned to South Africa. The efforts of activists

both within South Africa and all over the globe had succeeded in ending one of the most repressive forms of institutionalized racism ever created. Divestment remains a powerful tool for prodemocracy, workers' rights, and environmental activists.

Critical Thinking Questions

▶ What do you think motivated people around the world to join forces to oppose apartheid? What do you believe were the most effective strategies these activists used to pressure the South African government?

▶ Why do you believe that the South African government finally abandoned apartheid?

terrorism Use of coercion and violence as a means of advancing political goals.

Hezbollah Literally "Party of God," a radical Shi'ite Muslim organization that arose in Lebanon in 1982. Took responsibility for several terrorist incidents in the 1980s.

Iran-Contra affair Elaborate scheme orchestrated by members of the Reagan administration in which funds raised by illicit arms sales to Iran were channeled illegally to Nicaraguan counterrevolutionaries.

But the decision embroiled U.S. troops in the bloody civil war between the Christian-dominated Lebanese government and Muslims who opposed the regime's pro-Western policies. After erroneously concluding that the neutral U.S. Marines were aligned with the Christian government, Muslim troops began firing on American soldiers. When members of Congress urged Reagan to withdraw the vulnerable U.S. peacekeepers, he claimed the troops were necessary to protect Lebanon from an attack by Soviet-backed Syria.

The decision had deadly ramifications as a wave of terrorism engulfed the region. Used by a variety of states and groups across the political spectrum, **terrorism** usually involves violent acts that are perpetrated for a religious, political, or ideological goal and often intentionally aimed at noncombatants to maximize their emotional impact. In 1982, **Hezbollah**, a Shi'a Islamic militant group, began kidnapping Westerners in protest of U.S. involvement in Lebanon, seizing approximately 96 people from 21 nations over the next decade. In April 1983, 63 people died in a bombing of the U.S. Embassy in Beirut. Then, on October 23,

1983, two truck bombs struck barracks housing American and French troops, killing 241 U.S. and 57 French servicemen. Although Reagan withdrew U.S. forces in February 1984, Islamist militants continued targeting Westerners.

The Reagan administration blamed the incidents on Libya's Muammar el-Qaddafi. A radical Islamist who seized power in a 1969 coup, Qaddafi financed terrorist activities around the world. In response, U.S. officials severed diplomatic ties with Libya and imposed a trade embargo. In April 1986, in retaliation for Libyan-backed bombings of European airports and a Berlin nightclub, U.S. planes bombed Qaddafi's residence and air bases. Although the raids failed to kill Qaddafi, dozens died, and the Libyan air force was destroyed. But terrorist incidents escalated in the years to come.

26-4e Cold War's Final Phase

During Reagan's second term, his controversial policies in Nicaragua and the Middle East became intertwined and resulted in the

> President Reagan and Soviet Premier Gorbachev dramatically change the nature of the Cold War.

Iran-Contra affair, the biggest scandal of his presidency. In 1985, National Security Advisor Robert McFarlane secretly approached the Iranians with a bold proposal: If Iran would persuade terrorists thought to be sympathetic to Ayatollah Khomeini to release six U.S. hostages being held in Lebanon, the United States would sell Iran antitank missiles, which it desperately needed in its war against Iraq. McFarlane directed Lt. Col. Oliver North, an aide at the National Security Council, to work with CIA director William Casey in implementing the arms-for-hostages plan. Casey convinced Reagan to approve the missile shipments to Iran despite the fact that the United States had severed its diplomatic ties to Iran in 1978 amid the Iranian Revolution and the fleeing of the Shah. Violating the Boland Amendment and the Constitution's separation of powers, North helped Israeli and private arms merchants ship hundreds of missiles and aircraft parts to Iran. He then directed the money from the arms sales to the contras in Nicaragua.

After the media broke the story of the arms-for-hostage deal, a congressional commission investigated the Iran-Contra affair. It could not determine whether Reagan had authorized the illegal diversion of funds to the contras, but it faulted him for not being more aware of the activities of his subordinates. Several top administration officials, including North and John Poindexter (who succeeded McFarlane as national security adviser), were indicted or convicted of illegalities. A federal appeals court later overturned the convictions of North and Poindexter because they had been granted immunity in exchange for testifying before Congress.

The fallout from the Iran-Contra affair, the biggest government scandal since Watergate, did not preclude Reagan from making historic changes in the U.S. relationship with the Soviet Union. After Leonid Brezhnev died

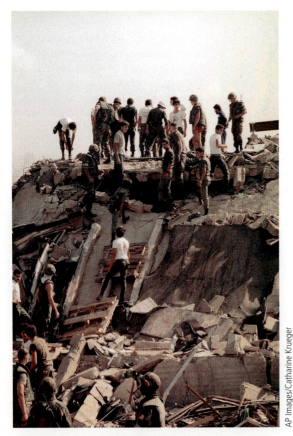

Aftermath of Suicide Bombing in Beirut, 1983 U.S. marines and local Beirut residents search for survivors of a terrorist bombing of a barracks in October 1983. ▲

AP Images/Catharine Krueger

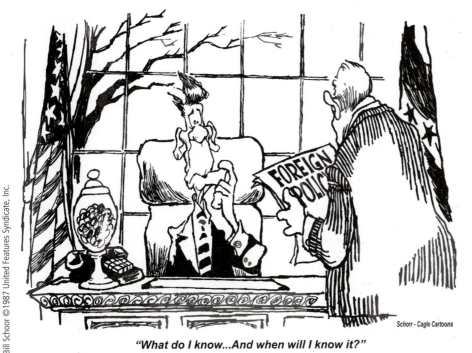

Bill Schoor ©1987 United Features Syndicate, Inc.

Schorr - Cagle Cartoons

"What do I know...And when will I know it?"

Political Cartoon on the Iran-Contra Affair As depicted in this political cartoon, the Iran-Contra affair harmed Reagan's reputation. The final report of the committee that investigated the scandal did not find conclusive proof that Reagan had ordered his subordinates to violate the law, but it criticized his lack of awareness of actions that others were committing in the name of his administration. ◄

Perestroika Russian for "restructuring," policy implemented by Mikhail Gorbachev aimed at reforming the Soviet political and economic systems.

Glasnost Russian for "openness," policy instituted by Mikhail Gorbachev loosening Soviet restrictions on political speech and the press.

in 1982, the deaths of his successors, Yuri Andropov and Konstantin Chernenko, quickly followed. But in 1985, Gorbachev, a fifty-four-year-old reformer, became general secretary. Tackling the economic stagnation and social apathy plaguing his nation, Gorbachev instituted two major initiatives, perestroika (restructuring) and glasnost (openness). **Perestroika** introduced some aspects of capitalism into the Soviet economy. **Glasnost** loosened state restrictions on freedom of speech and of the press. To ease the crushing economic burden created by the nuclear arms race, Gorbachev also sought to improve relations with the West in order to free resources for his proposed domestic reforms.

A staunch anti-Communist, Reagan was at first wary of Gorbachev but later embraced him. After a contentious first meeting in Geneva in November 1985, the two men met again the following October in Reykjavik. They came incredibly close to agreeing to abolish their respective nuclear stockpiles, but Reagan's refusal to abandon SDI scuttled the deal. Nonetheless, superpower relations continued to improve. Gorbachev dropped his insistence that the United States abandon SDI as a prerequisite for any arms reductions. In December 1987, Reagan and Gorbachev signed the Intermediate Nuclear Forces (INF) Treaty, a landmark agreement that abolished an entire class of nuclear weapons. The U.S Senate quickly ratified the pact, which led to the destruction of eighteen hundred forty-six Soviet and eight hundred forty-six U.S. nuclear weapons over a three-year period and granted each side unprecedented inspection of the other's missile sites.

Cold War tensions continued to dissipate in 1988, Reagan's final year in office. Gorbachev began withdrawing Soviet troops from the costly and inconclusive war in Afghanistan and pressured his Cuban allies into withdrawing from Angola. In August, U.S. and Soviet diplomats jointly persuaded Iran and Iran to agree to a cease-fire after an eight-year war. Just months later, as a result of events unleashed by Gorbachev and Reagan, the decades-long Cold War would also reach its end.

Soviet Leader Mikhail Gorbachev and President Ronald Reagan Meet in Moscow, 1988 Gorbachev and Reagan in Red Square during Reagan's May 1988 visit to Moscow. At first wary of one another, the men developed a warm friendship as they forged agreements that led to the end of the Cold War. ▲

AP Images/Ira Schwartz

Summary

Over the course of the 1970s, Americans struggled with a loss of faith in government following Watergate and the Vietnam War and the collapse of the economic supremacy that the United States had enjoyed since World War II. Fluctuations in the international price per barrel of petroleum made the highly oil-dependent U.S. economy quite unstable. High inflation constricted families' earning power. Rising foreign competition undercut U.S. manufacturing. Organized labor lost power. Activists and public officials raised awareness about the planet's finite resources. Despite these obstacles, entrepreneurship thrived as new business opportunities created by technological innovations and increasing global interconnectedness emerged. To stimulate economic growth, advocates of free market doctrines pushed for tax cuts, privatization, deregulation, and cuts in public spending.

In the late 1970s, détente unraveled and superpower dynamics shifted. The Carter administration's efforts to promote human rights collided with difficult political realities and anti-Americanism in the developing world. A revolution in Iran had ripple effects throughout the Middle East. The Soviet invasion of Afghanistan re-ignited Cold War tensions. Determined to restore U.S. stature in the world and to put the Soviets on the defensive, the Reagan administration dramatically increased military spending. An intensification of superpower rivalries in the early 1980s generated mass anxieties about nuclear war, and emerging threats posed by terrorism and religious radicalism signaled new dangers that would punctuate the post-Cold War era.

American society changed significantly. The number of two-income households rose. Increasing rates of unmarried cohabitation, single parenthood, and divorce reshaped norms of family life. Some women remained mired in poverty, but others broke gender barriers and enjoyed great professional and economic success. LGBT people became more open and made political gains, sparking intense opposition from those who believed that homosexuality was immoral.

An international wave of religious revivalism arose. Some worshippers gravitated to mainstream faiths such as Christianity, Islam, and Judaism. Others adopted alternative spiritualities. A resurgence of fundamentalism had enormous political and societal ramifications in the United States, Iran, and other nations. Governments responded to powerful blocs demanding the preservation of traditional gender roles and strict adherence to religious doctrines.

The same years witnessed the rise of political conservatives who celebrated a free market economy and who sought to dismantle the social welfare programs of the New Deal and the Great Society. As the U.S. government curtailed its regulation of the private sector and slashed spending, some Americans amassed unprecedented wealth while others languished in poverty. Conservatives in other nations adopted similar agendas.

Although the Iran-Contra affair overshadowed much of his second term, Ronald Reagan forged a remarkable partnership with Soviet Premier Mikhail Gorbachev. As Gorbachev tried to reform an economically stagnant and politically repressive Soviet Union, Reagan moved from initial skepticism about his Communist rival's professed desire to de-escalate U.S.–Soviet tensions toward negotiating agreements that helped end the Cold War entirely.

<Thinking Back, *Looking Forward*>

As you review this chapter, contemplate how the legacies of the Vietnam War, Watergate, and the social movements of 1960s shaped the post-1975 era. How did free market reforms affect workers in capitalist and Communist nations? How and why did the United States and the Soviet Union evolve from the mid-1970s to the late 1980s? What roles did nonstate actors play in drawing attention to human rights and global concerns? What triggered the resurgence of religious fundamentalism and conservatism in the United States and elsewhere? In future chapters, assess how and why global dynamics shifted in the aftermath of the Cold War.

To make your study concrete, review the chapter timeline and reflect on the entries there. Think about their causes, consequences, and connections. How do they fit with global trends?

Additional Resources

Books

Borstelmann, Thomas. *The 1970s: A New Global History from Civil Rights to Economic Inequality.* **Princeton, NJ: Princeton University Press, 2012.** ▶ Synthesis of the 1970s placing the United States in transnational context.

Brands, H.W. *Reagan: The Life.* **New York: Doubleday, 2015. Engaging and exhaustive biography written by a celebrated historian.**

Chang, Jeff. *Can't Stop Won't Stop: A History of the Hip-Hop Generationz.* **New York: Picador, 2005.** ▶ Journalist's account of origins and impact of hip-hop on U.S. history and culture.

Cowie, Jefferson. *Stayin' Alive: The 1970s and the Last Days of the Working Class.* **New York: The New Press, 2010.** ▶ Examination of how political and economic changes during the 1970s affected working-class Americans.

Farber, David. *Taken Hostage: The Iran Hostage Crisis and America's First Encounter with Radical Islam.* **Princeton, NJ: Princeton University Press, 2004.** ▶ Gripping history of the hostage crisis and its connection to the current war on terrorism.

Iriye, Akira, Petra Goedde, and William I. Hitchcock, eds. *The Human Rights Revolution: An International History.* **New York: Oxford University Press, 2012.** ▶ Collection of essays on human rights activism from 1945 to the present.

Jones, Daniel Steadman. *Masters of the Universe: Hayek, Friedman, and the Birth of Neoliberal Politics.* **Princeton, NJ: Princeton University Press, 2012.** ▶ Brilliant analysis of the origins and impact of transatlantic neoliberalism.

Moreton, Bethany. *To Serve God and Wal-Mart: The Making of Christian Free Enterprise.* **Cambridge, MA: Harvard University Press, 2009.** ▶ Fascinating history of Wal-Mart's interconnections between evangelicalism and capitalism.

Rossinow, Doug. *The Reagan Era: A History of the 1980s.* **New York: Columbia University Press, 2015.** ▶ Synthesis of the political, cultural, economic, and international dimensions of the 1980s.

Wilson, James Graham. *The Triumph of Improvisation: Gorbachev's Adaptability, Reagan's Engagement, and the End of the Cold War.* **Ithaca, NY: Cornell University Press, 2014.** ▶ Study of leadership and decision making based on newly declassified materials.

> Go to the MindTap® for **Global Americans** to access the full version of select books from this Additional Resources section.

Websites

Cold War International History Project. https://www.wilsoncenter.org/program/cold-war-international-history-project ▶ Rich array of multinational publications and primary sources related to the Cold War.

Jimmy Carter Presidential Museum and Library. http://www.jimmycarterlibrary.gov/ ▶ Research and teaching sources on Jimmy Carter's presidency and postpresidential activities.

Like Totally 80s. http://www.liketotally80s.com/ ▶ Fun, exhaustive collection of blog posts and news stories on the history of 1980s popular culture.

PBS *American Experience:* **"The Presidents." http://www.pbs.org/wgbh/americanexperience/collections/presidents/** ▶ Excellent primary sources and film documentaries on Jimmy Carter and Ronald Reagan.

Ronald Reagan Presidential Library and Museum. http://www.reagan.utexas.edu/ ▶ Collection of textual, audiovisual, and photographic sources on the Reagan presidency.

Continue exploring online through MindTap®**, where you can:**
- **Assess your knowledge with the Chapter Test**
- **Watch historical videos related to the chapter**
- **Further your understanding with interactive maps and timelines**

The Global Conservative Shift

1975–1976

April 1975
Gates founds software company Micro-Soft.

July 1975
Delegates from thirty-five nations sign the Helsinki Accords.

July 1976
Bicentennial celebrations in the United States.

November 1976
Carter defeats Ford in presidential race.

1978

Deng Xiaoping launches economic reforms in China.

June
California voters approve Proposition 13, a statewide ballot initiative slashing property taxes.

September
Carter brokers the Camp David Accords between Israel and Egypt.

November
Nine hundred members of the People's Temple commit mass suicide in Jonestown, Guyana.

San Francisco supervisor Harvey Milk and mayor George Moscone are assassinated by their colleague Dan White.

1979

March
Partial nuclear meltdown occurs at Three Mile Island in Pennsylvania.

May
Thatcher is elected Britain's first woman prime minister.

August
Carter appoints Volcker to chair the Federal Reserve Board.

November
Islamic radicals in Tehran seize Americans

U.S. gas prices exceed $1 per gallon for the first time.

December
Soviet forces invade Afghanistan to bolster a faltering Communist regime.

1980

January
United States imposes grain and technology embargo on Soviet Union in retaliation for Soviet invasion of Afghanistan.

March
Carter signs Refugee Act, permits immigration of refugees for humanitarian purposes.

April
U.S. effort to rescue fifty-three Americans being held hostage in Tehran fails.

U.S. Olympic Committee votes to boycott 1980 Summer Olympics in Moscow.

November
Reagan defeats Carter by a landslide in presidential race.

1981

January
Reagan inaugurated.

U.S. hostages in Iran freed.

March
Reagan shot in an assassination attempt, recovers.

August
Reagan fires striking air traffic controllers.

September
Sandra Day O'Connor sworn in as first female U.S. Supreme Court justice.

October
Egyptian president Anwar el-Sadat assassinated by Islamic extremists in Cairo.

1983	1984	1985	1986	1987
March Reagan gives fiercely anti-Soviet "evil empire" speech before the National Association of Evangelicals.	**October** Congress passes the Boland Amendment.	**March** Gorbachev becomes leader of the Soviet Union.	**April** In retaliation for sponsoring terrorism, United States launches air raids on Libya.	**February** Tower Commission condemns Ronald Reagan for failing to monitor subordinates' activities in the Iran-Contra affair.
April U.S. Embassy in Beirut bombed.	**November** Reagan defeats Mondale, wins second term.	**November** Reagan and Gorbachev meet in Geneva, and agree to resume arms reduction talks.	World's worst nuclear accident occurs at Soviet Chernobyl plant, and radioactive contamination spreads to Western Europe.	**June** Reagan speaks in West Berlin, challenges the Soviets to destroy the Berlin Wall.
September Soviets shoot down Korean civilian airliner, killing two hundred sixty-nine passengers and crew.			**October** Reagan signs Anti-Drug Abuse Act imposing mandatory minimum sentences for drug possession and selling narcotics.	**December** Intermediate Nuclear Forces Treaty signed in Moscow.
October U.S. Marines and French paratroopers die in suicide bombing of a barracks in Beirut, Lebanon.			**November** Lebanese magazines reveal U.S. weapons-for-hostages deal, Iran-Contra affair begins.	
U.S. forces invade Grenada to oust a Marxist regime.				

Go to MindTap® to engage with an interactive version of the timeline. Analyze events and themes with clickable content, view related videos, and respond to critical thinking questions.

27

Closer Together, Further Apart

1988–2000

In 1976, Linda Alvarado launched Alvarado Construction. She initially submitted bids signed only with her initials in order to conceal her gender from potentially sexist readers.

In 1992, Linda Alvarado became the first Latina and only the second woman—the first was Cincinnati Reds owner Marge Schott—to buy a stake in a major league sports team, the Colorado Rockies. Part of a wave of entrepreneurs who capitalized on opportunities created by the economic shifts of the 1970s and the women's and civil rights movements, Alvarado reached the highest echelons of American business. Her career is a microcosm of the great demographic and economic changes characterizing U.S. society in the 1980s and 1990s.

Denver Post/Getty Images

Born in Albuquerque in 1952, Alvarado was the only daughter in a family of eight. She and her brothers lived with their parents in a three-room adobe house without indoor heating or plumbing. Undaunted by their difficult living conditions, the Alvarado children embraced their mother's optimistic worldview—*empieza pequeña, pero piensa muy grande* ("start small, but think big"). In 1969, Alvarado accepted an academic scholarship to Pomona College. To help pay expenses, she applied for a part-time job on an all-male landscaping crew. When the supervisor asked, "What are you doing here? Don't you understand that all the girls work in food service?" she refused to leave until he hired her.

After graduating with an economics degree, she became a contract administrator on a construction site. Despite harassment from some of her male coworkers, she learned the estimating, blueprinting, and computer scheduling techniques that were transforming the construction industry. Deciding to launch her own company, she drew up a business plan and sought financing from six banks, but none was willing to issue a loan to a Latina in a male-dominated business. Her parents took out a $2,500 mortgage on their home that she combined with aid from the Small Business Administration to launch Alvarado Construction in 1976. To conceal her gender from potentially sexist readers, she initially submitted bids signed only with her initials. After proving its skills on small structures like bus shelters, the firm won contracts for shopping centers, hotels, sports facilities, and other multimillion-dollar projects in the United States and several foreign countries. In the early 1980s, Alvarado founded Palo Alto, Inc., a fast-food franchise company. By 2002, it operated more than one hundred fifty Taco Bell, Kentucky Fried Chicken, and Pizza Hut restaurants. She serves as president, and her husband Robert is CEO.

Alvarado has spent many years working as a mentor for women, minorities, and youth. She has received many awards. She plays an active role in the United States Hispanic Chamber of Commerce and travels the world giving lectures about leadership. She has served on the boards of several multinational corporations including 3M Company and Pepsi Bottling Company. A mother of three, she lauds her husband's vital role in helping her balance professional and family responsibilities. When she

Linda Alvarado embraced her mother's world view "start small, but think big," and reached the highest echelons of business. In what ways does her career trajectory illustrate the transformations in American society during the 1980s and 1990s?

Go to MindTap® to watch a video on Alvarado and learn how her story relates to the themes of this chapter.

attended Career Day at her son Rob's kindergarten, his teacher asked him, "Don't you want to be a contractor like your mother . . . and build high-rises, schools, and sports facilities?" He replied, "No. That's women's work." His nonchalant answer spoke volumes about how much pathbreakers like his mother had helped transform daily life in the United States.

As Alvarado built her business career, U.S. society became more inclusive and diverse. But the transition was not an easy one, and Americans often intensely battled matters of identity, politics, and culture. New campaign techniques and ideologically charged media outlets amplified these debates. A new wave of immigrants, largely from Asia and Latin America, shifted the demographics of the U.S. population. The Cold War's end added both hope and uncertainty to international relations. Although President George H.W. Bush won praise for his foreign policy acumen, more conservative Republicans criticized his moderate positions on social and fiscal issues. Victory in the Persian Gulf War sent Bush's approval ratings to record highs, but an economic recession helped Democrat Bill Clinton prevail in the 1992 presidential race.

As Clinton attempted to implement centrist policies, a polarized political system complicated efforts to redress economic inequities and social problems. Yet the era also witnessed a communications revolution triggered by the Internet, fostering greater interconnectivity among the world's peoples. Fueled by technological innovations, the U.S. economy experienced its most vigorous growth since the 1960s. But in spectacularly dramatic fashion, the election of 2000 demonstrated the depth of American political divides at the beginning of the twenty-first century.

27-1

Victories Abroad and Challenges at Home

The 1988 presidential race pitted Vice President George H.W. Bush against Massachusetts governor Michael Dukakis and witnessed an intensification of the media's scrutiny of political candidates. In October 1987, the same week that Bush announced his candidacy, *Newsweek* ran a cover story called "The Wimp Factor." To offset the damage, Bush's team highlighted his participation in traditionally masculine pursuits (see top photo). In September 1988, during a campaign stop at a defense contractor, Dukakis donned a helmet while riding in an M1A1 Abrams tank (see bottom photo). This photo sparked widespread ridicule. Even today, many political candidates refuse to wear headgear in public because of it.

What messages about themselves do you think that George H.W. Bush and Michael Dukakis hoped these photographs would convey? Why do you think each succeeded or failed? How does media coverage of politics shape our views of those seeking or holding public office? ▶

AP Images/Eric Gay

AP Images/Michael E. Samojeden

After prevailing in one of the most negative political campaigns in U.S. history, George H.W. Bush faced an increasingly polarized electorate and large federal budget deficits from the Reagan era that forced him to break a no-tax pledge. Although he scored domestic policy victories with passage of a landmark disability rights law and new environmental protections, he clashed with more conservative members of his own party. As the Cold War ended and a regional conflict arose in the Persian Gulf, Bush confronted complicated global dynamics and won praise for his foreign policy acumen. But when the nation experienced an economic downturn, he discovered that his international accomplishments were not enough to guarantee reelection.

☞ As you read, contemplate why and how the end of the Cold War changed international relations. Do you think that President Bush was right to respond cautiously to the rapidly changing events in Eastern Europe and the Soviet Union? Explain your answer. Why was success in foreign policy not enough to win him a second term?

27-1a Polarization of Politics

In 1988, both parties hoped to prevail in an electoral contest marked by increasing reliance on political consultants, "sound bites," and "photo ops." George H.W. Bush entered the presidential race as the Republican frontrunner. A former World War II aviator and Texas oilman, Bush had been a successful congressman, U.S. ambassador to the United Nations, director of the Central Intelligence Agency, and Ronald Reagan's vice president. Despite this distinguished record, some observers characterized Bush as a "wimp" and believed that his privileged background (son of a U.S. senator from Connecticut) would not resonate with voters. After several leading Democrats either declined to run or dropped out of the primaries, little-known Massachusetts governor Michael Dukakis secured enough delegates to capture the Democratic nomination. Civil rights leader Jesse Jackson won the second-highest delegate count, becoming the nation's most successful African American presidential candidate to date. Attempting to mobilize a **Rainbow Coalition** of racial minorities, farmers, gays, working-class, and poor people, Jackson had campaigned on a very liberal platform that aimed to unite an increasingly diverse society and to mitigate racial and economic disparities that had deepened during the Reagan years.

> The 1988 presidential race ushers in an era of negative campaigning and increasing political divisions.

Upon discovering that Dukakis had an unexpected seventeen-point lead, the Bush campaign defied conventional wisdom and focused on defining Dukakis rather than trumpeting Bush's achievements. "You gotta go negative. You just gotta," explained political strategist Lee Atwater. Although Bush had promised a "kinder, gentler America," he ran one of the nastiest campaigns in U.S. history, reshaping politics for years afterward. Bush supporters produced an ad attacking Dukakis's record on crime by featuring Willie Horton, an African American man who raped a white woman during a prison furlough in Massachusetts. Critics blasted the commercial's racist overtones and its failure to mention that Dukakis had not created the

prison furlough program. Simultaneously, Bush operatives made *liberal* an epithet by assaulting Dukakis's membership in the American Civil Liberties Union (ACLU), a political organization committed to defending the Bill of Rights. Refusing to engage in reciprocal mudslinging, Dukakis ran an uninspired campaign. In November, Bush carried 53 percent of the popular vote and won forty states.

The race coincided with a seismic shift in the media landscape. In 1987, the Federal Communications Commission repealed the **Fairness Doctrine**, a policy it had introduced in 1949 mandating that broadcast licensees cover both sides of controversial issues in an honest, balanced way. The decision opened the airwaves to much more ideologically charged programming, and stations could now align themselves with one political perspective or another. Conservatives, long convinced of liberal media bias, pounced at the chance to promote their views. In August 1988, Rush Limbaugh launched a nationally syndicated talk radio program just weeks before the Republican National Convention. He quickly became the nation's most popular talk radio host and his audience—composed mainly of white men like Limbaugh—delighted in his withering, often humorous, jibes at liberals. He and other conservative radio commentators soon wielded great influence in Republican politics.

27-1b End of the Cold War

Bush's foreign policy expertise served him well as a series of momentous events ended the Cold War and China transformed its economy. In December 1988, Soviet general secretary Mikhail Gorbachev traveled to Washington for a final meeting with Reagan and President-Elect Bush. During this trip, Gorbachev appeared before the United Nations and announced that he was cutting 500,000 troops from the Soviet armed forces and removing and disbanding six tank divisions from East Germany, Czechoslovakia, and Hungary. Because of the growing trust between the superpowers, Gorbachev asserted, the entire world could "breathe a sigh of relief."

> Communism collapses in Eastern Europe and the Soviet Union but endures in China.

Gorbachev's glasnost policy removed restrictions on the press and freedom of speech in the Soviet Union and Eastern Europe, but the Communist government of the Peoples Republic of China (PRC) was more cautious in embracing reforms. Following the chaotic and economically disastrous Cultural Revolution (1966–1971) and especially the death of Mao Zedong in 1976, the PRC under Mao's revolutionary comrade Deng Xiaoping began liberalizing the state-controlled economy by including key elements of a capitalist free market such as foreign

Rainbow Coalition Nonprofit political alliance of minorities and groups who are disadvantaged founded by Jesse Jackson in 1984.

Fairness Doctrine Introduced in 1949, policy of the Federal Communications Commission requiring publicly licensed broadcasters to devote equal time to both sides of controversial issues.

The Fall of the Berlin Wall, 1989 On November 9, 1989, after hearing the announcement that citizens of the GDR were free to cross the country's borders, hundreds of thousands of East and West Berliners flocked to the Berlin Wall, launching what one journalist called "the greatest street party in the history of the world." Between 1961 and 1989, armed East German guards killed at least one hundred seventy-one people trying to cross the Wall, but more than five thousand managed to reach the West. ▶

Patrick PIEL/Getty images

investment, competition, and a global business outlook. But China's second generation of Communist leaders stopped short of removing restrictions on the press despite the pleas of the liberal general secretary of the Communist Party Hu Yaobang. After Hu was deposed and executed in April 1989, thousands of university students and other prodemocracy activists occupied Beijing's Tiananmen Square and demanded more political openness, freedom of expression, and better economic opportunities for highly educated citizens. The activists constructed a Goddess of Democracy statute loosely modeled on the Statue of Liberty. With millions of people watching the protests on the Cable News Network (CNN), the aging Chinese rulers decided that the peaceful demonstrations presented an unacceptable challenge to their authority. On the night of June 3, Deng Xiaoping deployed soldiers and tanks to crush the protests. By the next morning, hundreds of demonstrators lay dead and thousands were arrested.

Although the brutal crackdown sparked international outrage, President Bush rejected calls for sanctions against the PRC. Convinced that severing U.S.–Chinese ties would be detrimental to global security, he maintained China's most-favored nation trade status while privately pressuring the Chinese to improve their record on human rights. The Chinese government continued to oppose political reforms, but country's economy grew at the astonishing rate of 10 percent per year, and its exports to the United States soared. In years to come, it became increasingly difficult for U.S. policy makers to balance America's economic reliance on China with their desire to promote a more democratic Chinese society.

Throughout 1989, a series of independence movements swept Eastern Europe. Gorbachev refused to use military force to stop them in stark contrast to his predecessors' responses to the 1956 Hungarian Revolution and the 1968 Prague Spring. By 1990, Poland, Hungary,

Czechoslovakia, Bulgaria, Romania, East Germany, Yugoslavia, and Albania overthrew or transformed their Communist governments. All regained their national sovereignty, established democracies, and adopted capitalism.

Nothing exemplified the stunning shift more than the opening of the Berlin Wall on November 9, 1989. A huge global audience watched television coverage of East and West Germans celebrating the collapse of the twenty-eight-mile long concrete barrier that was both a literal and figurative reflection of Cold War divides. In October 1990, the Communist German Democratic Republic (GDR) ceased to exist, and Germany became a unified nation for the first time since 1945.

The political earthquake soon reverberated in the Soviet Union. By July 1990, the Soviet republics of Lithuania, Estonia, Latvia, and Ukraine declared independence. By the end of 1991, following the failure of a coup that sought to reverse Gorbachev's policies, the Soviet Union had disintegrated into fifteen separate nations, and the Soviet Communist Party disbanded (see Map 27.1). Russia, the largest of the former Soviet republics, declared its independence and formed a new government led by Boris Yeltsin. On December 25, 1991, the Soviet Union formally ceased to exist. Gorbachev, having unwittingly unleashed forces that destroyed the Soviet empire, resigned. The Cold War came to an abrupt, mostly peaceful, end. For the first time in nearly five decades, the world was not split along capitalist and Communist lines.

27-1c Rise of Regional Conflicts

While some observers viewed the collapse of communism as the inevitable triumph of liberal democracy and free market capitalism,

> A multinational coalition forces Iraq to withdraw from Kuwait.

Map 27.1 Map of Europe at the End of the Cold War Between 1989 and 1993, the end of the Cold War transformed the map of Europe as nations formerly part of the Eastern bloc regained their independence and transformed their governments and economies. The Soviet Union's dissolution into separate countries changed the geographic landscape even more. Most nations transitioned from communism relatively peacefully, but Yugoslavia fragmented into four different states and degenerated into civil war. ▲

others predicted that a "clash of civilizations" between different cultural and religious groups would arise in the post-Cold War era. Although few Americans advocated a complete U.S. retreat from global affairs, many hoped that the United States would slash military spending and use the resulting "peace dividend" to address pressing domestic issues. But a series of regional conflicts signaling new dangers in an unstable, multipolar world soon consumed the attention and resources of U.S. policy makers.

Ignoring calls to celebrate the U.S. victory in the Cold War, President Bush responded cautiously to the rapidly changing political events in the Soviet Union and Eastern Europe. At a summit in Washington in June 1990, Bush and Gorbachev signed two treaties significantly reducing their respective nuclear arsenals. Bush encouraged the International Monetary Fund (IMF) and private investors to support Russia's difficult transition to a free market economy. He was also instrumental in gaining Soviet support for the inclusion of a reunified Germany in the NATO alliance.

In some places, ethnic and religious tensions that had been suppressed under communism exploded. Czechoslovakia split into separate Czech and Slovak republics. After Yugoslavia fragmented into four different republics, a civil war ensued in which Serbian soldiers killed as many as twenty thousand, mostly Muslim, civilians in Bosnia and Herzegovina. While urging European nations to send humanitarian aid to Sarajevo, the capital of Bosnia-Herzegovina, the Bush administration refused to intervene militarily in the Balkan conflict.

The end of the Cold War prompted a reassessment of U.S. policies throughout the Western Hemisphere. In Nicaragua, Bush ended U.S. support for the contras after the Sandinistas agreed to free elections. U.S. officials worked closely with the IMF to cut Latin American debt. To curb the illegal drug trade (and aware that voracious U.S. demand helped fuel it), U.S. policy makers aided regional counternarcotic operations. The booming drug trade also played a role in a December 1989 U.S. invasion of Panama to capture dictator Manuel Noriega. After his extradition to the United States, Noriega was convicted on

Wayne Scarberry/Getty Images

Global Americans Urvashi Vaid has committed her life to working for social justice. Born in 1958 in New Delhi, India, she was eight when her family moved to the United States after her father accepted a position at the State University of New York in Potsdam. Within three years, she was protesting against the Vietnam War. After graduating from Vassar College and Northeastern University School of Law, she worked as a staff attorney for the American Civil Liberties Union's National Prisons Project.

In 1989, she became executive director of the National Gay and Lesbian Task Force (NGLTF). In keeping with her belief that LGBT rights are interwoven with other human rights struggles, she spoke out for reproductive justice and strongly opposed the Persian Gulf War. She amplified her views on the interconnections between the LGBT movement and larger familial and social institutions in her book *Virtual Equality: The Mainstreaming of Gay and Lesbian Liberation* (1995).

After leaving NGLTF in 2001, Vaid worked for the Ford Foundation and spent five years as executive director of the Arcus Foundation. In 2012, she founded the nation's first lesbian political action committee, LPAC. She also launched The Vaid Group, a social justice-oriented consulting firm.

Vaid has won several awards for her writing and activism. She continues to advocate a more inclusive society that values all people equally, regardless of race, class, sexual orientation, physical ability, or age. Her multifaceted identity is emblematic of the increasing diversity of the United States.

eight counts of drug trafficking, racketeering, and money laundering and sentenced to thirty years in federal prison.

In the Middle East, after Iraq invaded its oil-rich neighbor Kuwait on August 2, 1990, Bush took immediate steps to stand up to Iraqi aggression. To avoid repeating mistakes of the Vietnam War, the Bush administration embraced the **Powell Doctrine,** a policy articulated by chairman of the Joint Chiefs of Staff Colin Powell that called for the use of overwhelming force and a clear exit strategy to ensure that regional conflicts were brief and decisive. After Bush won support for stationing U.S. troops in Saudi Arabia, Osama Bin Laden, a thirty-three-year-old Islamic fundamentalist who had fought against the Soviets in Afghanistan, accused the Saudi government of desecrating Muslim holy sites, and its regime imprisoned him.

On August 7, two hundred thousand U.S. troops began arriving in Saudi Arabia to guard petroleum supplies from potential Iraqi attack. Two months later, the U.S. force exceeded more than 500,000. By that time, the United Nations Security Council had imposed harsh economic sanctions and passed twelve resolutions demanding that the Iraqis withdraw from Kuwait by January 15, 1991.

Powell Doctrine Named after General Colin Powell, policy calling for U.S. military intervention only after all nonviolent strategies have failed and there are clear and attainable goals.

Operation Desert Storm
Code name for the combat phase of the U.S.-led United Nations mission to liberate Kuwait after its occupation by Iraq.

Through adroit diplomacy, Bush built a multinational coalition of 700,000 troops from thirty countries. Many Arab nations and even the Soviet Union, Iraq's long-time military sponsor, joined the partnership.

The global outrage surprised Saddam Hussein, Iraq's president since 1979. He viewed the dispute with Kuwait as a local affair. Because the United States had provided intelligence and helped to broker secret and

illegal loans to Iraq during its 1980–1988 war against Iran, Saddam found the U.S. response baffling. The loans had enabled him to purchase $2 billion in equipment for his nuclear, biological, and chemical weapons programs and to support more than 1 million Iraqi troops. By 1990, Iraq had built the world's fourth largest army.

Whatever their previous relationship with Saddam, U.S. officials were not willing to imperil the Persian Gulf's oil supplies. After diplomacy failed to resolve the crisis, Bush asked for congressional authorization to use military force under the terms of the UN Security Council's resolutions. Despite large antiwar demonstrations held across the country, the war resolution won majority support in both houses.

On January 16, 1991, eighteen hours after the passage of the UN deadline, coalition troops began **Operation Desert Storm** and unleashed an aerial assault on Iraq and Kuwait (see Map 27.2). Millions watched CNN's live coverage of "smart bomb" raids, but Pentagon officials, cognizant of the negative impact of news coverage of the Vietnam War, carefully controlled images of the death and destruction. On February 23, coalition ground forces entered Kuwait and eastern Iraq, meeting virtually no resistance. Four days later, Bush announced that the coalition had achieved its aims of liberating Kuwait and compelling Iraq to accept a cease-fire.

Rather than risk a bloody and long U.S. occupation of Baghdad, Bush allowed Saddam to remain in power. Within days after the cease-fire, the Iraqi Republican Guard crushed rebellions among Shi'a in the south and Kurds in the north. Although Bush had encouraged Iraqis to rise up against Saddam during the war, he denied that insurgents were promised U.S. aid. Subsequently, critics attacked Bush's decision not to oust Saddam. Bush and his aides remained unrepentant, insisting that their decision

AP Images/Peter DeJong

The Persian Gulf War, Saudi Arabia, January 31, 1991. A U.S. Marine Corps Cobra helicopter flies over Iraqi and coalition ground forces approaching the Saudi-Kuwait border during the battle for Khaf ji. ◀

saved U.S. lives and a weakened Iraq could have been captured by neighboring Iran. In the aftermath of the war, Osama Bin Laden fled to Sudan, vowing to exact revenge on the United States for defiling sacred Muslim land.

The Persian Gulf conflict left at least 20,000 Iraqi troops and 2,300 civilians dead and much of Iraq in ruins. Despite predictions of high casualties, only 303 U.S. soldiers died. But approximately 250,000 of the 697,000 Gulf War veterans later developed **Gulf War Syndrome**, a chronic medical condition linked to exposure to toxic nerve agents such as sarin gas. Coalition partners provided more than $35 billion to reimburse the United States for its costs in the war.

Gulf War Syndrome Medical condition found among veterans of 1991 Gulf War. Symptoms include chronic fatigue, migraine, and respiratory problems. Possible origins in anthrax vaccines or chemical exposure.

Map 27.2 Gulf War This map shows the progression of major Allied military operations during the Gulf War as well as the location of Allied military forces and Iraqi missile targets. The path of Kurds seeking refuge from the conflict is also shown. ▼

Allied troop build-up, Aug. 1990–Feb. 1991
Kurdish region
Major oil field
Allied advances in ground war
Main allied air base
Allied naval forces
Primary Scud missile target

7 Kurdish refugees flee Iraq toward Turkey and Iran, March–April.

6 Kuwaiti forces enter capital city as Iraqi troops flee, Feb. 27.

5 Allied ground assault begins, Feb. 23.

4 U.S. Navy and Marine units fake amphibious landings outside Kuwait City to divert Iraqi troops, prior to ground assault.

3 Saudi and Qatari troops, supported by U.S. Marines and aircraft, repulse Iraqi attack into Saudi Arabia, Jan. 30–31.

2 Iraqi Scud missile launchers attack civilian areas in Israel and Saudi Arabia, Jan. 17–Feb. 16.

1 U.S. and allied air forces attack Baghdad and Kuwait, Jan. 16–Feb. 26.

Allied Central Command

History without Borders

HIV/AIDS

The AIDS Memorial Quilt, begun in 1987 by The Names Project, served to humanize victims of AIDS in the **United States.** The last time it was displayed in its entirety, in 1996, it covered the entire National Mall in Washington, D.C.

A large outbreak of HIV infection among injecting drug users in Moscow resulted in over three times as many new cases reported in 1999 as in all previous years. In **Russia,** approximately 90% of all HIV infections in 1998–1999 were in injecting drug users.

With an infection rate of only 0.07% in 1999 of its population of over 1.2 billion people, **China** has mounted a strong national response to HIV/AIDS, including participating in drug trials for vaccines.

NORTH AMERICA
900,000
0.58%

UNITED STATES

WESTERN EUROPE
520,000
0.23%

RUSSIA

EASTERN EUROPE AND CENTRAL ASIA
420,000
0.21%

CHINA

ATLANTIC OCEAN

NORTH AFRICA AND MIDDLE EAST
220,000
0.12%

EAST ASIA AND PACIFIC
530,000
0.06%

PACIFIC OCEAN

CARIBBEAN
360,000
2.11%

SUB-SAHARAN AFRICA
24,500,000
8.57%

SOUTH AND SOUTHEAST ASIA
5,600,000
0.54%

CAMBODIA

LATIN AMERICA
1,300,000
0.49%

BRAZIL

UGANDA

INDIAN OCEAN

PACIFIC OCEAN

Brazil offered universal access to antiretroviral drugs to all identified infected people, and mortality was cut in half from 1996 to 1999. To reduce costs, some drugs were imported in bulk, and those that were not patent-protected were manufactured locally.

Uganda has the highest number of "AIDS orphans"—children under 15 who have lost both parents or their mother—per population in the world, at 1.7 million children in 1999. The NGO Uganda Women's Effort to Save Orphans provides support for the children by helping with their education and training.

In **Cambodia's** port city of Sihanouk, a "100% condom use" campaign was launched in 1998. By the next year, condom use had increased in many vulnerable populations; for brothel-based sex workers, it had doubled from 40% in 1997 to almost 80% in 1999.

AUSTRALIA AND NEW ZEALAND
15,000
0.13%

15,000 Total number of people living with HIV/AIDS

0.13% Rate of infection in adults

People Living with HIV/AIDS Worldwide, 2000 By 2000, 18.8 million people around the world had died from AIDS-related complications. Nearly twice that many—34.3 million—were living with HIV, the virus that causes AIDS. A few sub-Saharan African nations successfully stabilized their HIV infection rates, but most did not. Efforts to control the global AIDS epidemic were complicated by the difficulty of persuading people to modify risky personal behaviors and the economic and logistical obstacles to providing antiretroviral drugs. ▲

Human immunodeficiency virus infection/acquired immunodeficiency syndrome (HIV/AIDS) is a disease of the immune system triggered by infection with the human immunodeficiency virus (HIV). While the disease itself is not fatal, it makes people much more susceptible to certain types of cancers and opportunistic infections that can be deadly. HIV is transmitted primarily through unprotected sex or contaminated syringes, but it can also be transmitted from mother to child in pregnancy, delivery, and by breastfeeding.

Although experts disagree on the origins of HIV, the spread of the virus unquestionably increased with globalization. Some medical researchers think the disease originated in central Africa in the early twentieth century when a virus affecting wild chimpanzees passed to humans engaged in hunting and eating these creatures. The researchers believe that the virus mutated into HIV and then spread as colonialism and the growth

of large African cities increased sexual promiscuity and prostitution. Another theory posits that unsafe medical practices used in post-World War II vaccination campaigns exposed the general population to HIV.

Although isolated cases of what was later confirmed to be HIV/AIDS appeared as early as 1959, it did not reach epidemic proportions until the 1980s. In early 1981, the Centers for Disease Control (CDC) noted an unusually high number of cases of Pneumocystis carinii

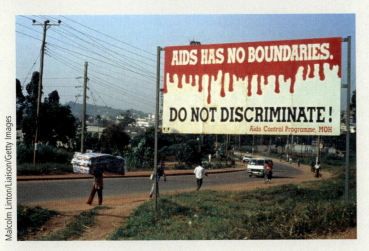

The Advertising Archives/Alamy Stock Photo

Malcolm Linton/Liaison/Getty Images

David Kirby, AIDS Patient, 1990 In May 1990, graduate student and hospice volunteer Therese Frare took a black and white photograph of David Kirby surrounded by his family shortly before he died of AIDS-related complications at age thirty-two. In November 1990, *Life* magazine published the image, and it later appeared in hundreds of newspapers, magazines, and televised stories around the world. In 1992, with the permission of Kirby's family, the clothier Benetton launched a controversial advertising campaign using a colorized version of the photo to generate awareness of the disease. ◀

Billboard for HIV/AIDS Educational Campaign, Kampala, Uganda, February 1, 1997 At a time when many African leaders refused to speak publicly about HIV/AIDS, Ugandan president Yoweri Museveni earned worldwide acclaim for his response to the disease. Shortly after taking office in 1986, he launched a three-pronged AIDS prevention campaign calling for abstinence from premarital sexual activity, monogamy within marriage, and condom use as a last resort (shorthanded as "ABC"). HIV infection rates dropped from about 15 percent in 1991 to approximately 6 percent in 2007. ◀

pneumonia (PCP) and Kaposi's sarcoma (KS) among gay men in New York and Los Angeles. Doctors also reported cases among heterosexual drug users, hemophiliacs, and Haitian refugees. At the same time, African physicians noted striking medical parallels between the U.S. cases and nondrug-using, heterosexual patients in Zaire. Despite the obviously diverse group of people contracting the strange ailments, the CDC called the disease *gay-related immune disorder* (GRID) until August 1982 when the agency quietly adopted the new name AIDS—Acquired Immune Deficiency Syndrome. Throughout this period, scientific and health communities worked with no knowledge of the disease's origins or means of transmission. They had no idea how many people were infected. They only knew the disease was lethal.

By 1983, with more than one thousand cases in the United States alone, it was no longer possible to ignore the possible worldwide impact of AIDS. Much of the international scientific community refused to accept claims that HIV could be contracted heterosexually even as the World Health Organization estimated that approximately six hundred twenty thousand Africans had been infected between 1980 and 1997, and

a total social breakdown consumed sub-Saharan Africa.

The politics of the Reagan administration exacerbated this already grave situation. Because the disease initially struck marginalized populations like gay men and drug users, officials were reluctant to provide research funding or public information. Erroneous reports that AIDS could be spread through casual contact generated widespread panic. In 1984, French and U.S. doctors identified HIV, the virus that causes AIDS and is passed through blood, saliva, and semen. But the discovery did little to mitigate the stigma and discrimination people with HIV and AIDS faced.

Enraged by the government's indifference to the devastating impact of AIDS on their community, gay men and lesbians began raising public awareness about the disease and providing services for people with AIDS. In 1987, the playwright Larry Kramer and others founded AIDS Coalition to Unleash Power (ACT UP), a direct action group whose confrontational tactics and motto ("Silence = Death") inspired the opening of chapters around the world.

Advocacy and education helped foster greater compassion toward people living with HIV/AIDS, but the disease reached pandemic proportions as it

spread quickly and globally. In 1995, the introduction of antiretroviral therapy was a major medical breakthrough that enabled people to live with HIV/AIDS for years. But the expense and complexity of the treatment made it inaccessible to many in the developing world. In December 2000, UNAIDS estimated that 36.1 million people were living with HIV/AIDS worldwide and that approximately 21.8 million people had died of AIDS since the epidemic began.

Critical Thinking Questions

▶ Why do you think this photograph of David Kirby had such a powerful effect on people's attitudes toward those with HIV/AIDS? Why was the use of the image in an advertising campaign so provocative?

▶ What were some of the factors that made combatting HIV/AIDS particularly difficult in the early stages of the epidemic? Why does globalization both complicate and help the world community's ability to respond to public health emergencies?

Go to MindTap® to engage with an interactive version of **History without Borders: HIV/AIDS**. Learn from an interactive map, view related video, and respond to critical thinking questions.

27-1d Domestic Struggles

Although Bush's approval ratings reached 90 percent in the days following the Gulf War, a troubled economy soon diminished his popularity. On accepting the Republican presidential nomination in 1988, Bush—eager to win backing from conservatives wary of his moderate views—invoked a Clint Eastwood movie and declared: "The Congress will push me to raise taxes, and I'll say no . . . and they'll push again, and I'll say to them, 'Read my lips, no new taxes." The pledge came back to haunt Bush when he began focusing on serious economic problems created in the Reagan years. These issues included a crisis spawned by deregulation of savings and loan institutions and a federal budget deficit that had tripled to $220 billion since 1980.

{ Bush addresses difficult economic problems while trying to advance a multifaceted domestic policy agenda.

Aware of the possible political consequences, Bush supported what became a $500 billion federal bailout of the savings and loan industry and worked with the Democrat-controlled Congress on a budget deal that would have combined tax increases and spending cuts to slash the deficit by one-half trillion dollars over a six-year period. When his Republican colleagues balked at his violation of his no-tax pledge and killed the deal, Bush was forced to accept a Democratic counterproposal that included even higher taxes and spending *increases*. The deficit rose to $269 billion in 1991 and to $290 billion the following year. Bush never regained the trust of conservative Republicans, but supporters praised his courage in adopting policies that saved Reagan's political legacy and set the stage for booming economic growth for much of the 1990s.

While fending off criticisms from the right wing of his party, Bush increased federal spending on education, highway improvements, and technological research. He signed the Radiation Exposure Compensation Act providing monetary assistance to those suffering health problems resulting from exposure to irradiated materials during nuclear tests or uranium mining. In 1990, Bush signed the **Americans with Disabilities Act (ADA),** a landmark bill that expanded accessibility requirements and civil rights protections for disabled persons and those debilitated by HIV/AIDS. It culminated decades of work by people with disabilities and their allies who had challenged discrimination in employment, housing, education, transportation, and public spaces. Responding to the environmental damage caused when the tanker *Exxon Valdez* ran aground and spilled millions of gallons of oil on the Alaskan coast, warnings about climate change, and increased rates of air pollution, Bush backed the Federal Clean Air Act, a law originally passed in 1970, but was allowed to lapse under the Reagan administration.

Americans with Disabilities Act (ADA) 1990 federal civil rights law outlawing discrimination in employment, transportation, public spaces, and housing.

Hill–Thomas hearings October 1991 hearings before the Senate Judiciary Committee in which law professor Anita Hill accused Supreme Court justice nominee Clarence Thomas of sexual harassment.

A controversy over Bush's choice to fill a vacancy on the Supreme Court reflected the deepening fissures in American political culture over race and sex. In the fall of 1991, Bush nominated federal appeals judge Clarence Thomas to succeed Thurgood Marshall on the U.S. Supreme Court. Thomas's confirmation seemed assured until Anita Hill, a University of Oklahoma law professor who had worked with Thomas at the U.S. Department of Education and the Equal Employment Opportunity Commission (EEOC), accused him of sexual harassment. Because sexual harassment had been recognized as a violation of Title VII of the 1964 Civil Rights Act following a ruling in *Meritor Savings Bank v. Vinson* (1986), Hill's allegations enraged civil rights and feminist groups who were already lobbying against Thomas's confirmation because of his opposition to affirmative action. In three days of televised testimony, Hill, Thomas, and several witnesses addressed Hill's claims. Members of the all-white male Judiciary Committee grilled Hill, an African American woman, while Thomas, an African American man, denounced the proceedings as "a high-tech lynching." The hearings became a lightning rod for national attitudes about racism and sexism. On October 15, the Senate confirmed Thomas with a 52-48 vote. In the aftermath of the **Hill–Thomas hearings,** employers across the nation implemented antiharassment codes and diversity training. Hill's harsh treatment by the all-male Judiciary Committee inspired dozens of women to run for public office, and a record twenty-nine women were elected to Congress in 1992.

Earlier that year, Bush's reelection seemed assured. His approval ratings remained high. Interest and inflation rates were low. But by mid-year, the outsourcing of jobs overseas, the savings and loan bailout, the Gulf War, and rising health care costs contributed to a recession. Retail and housing sales nose-dived, and unemployment reached 7.4 percent. States cut social welfare spending in response to budget shortfalls.

When Bush refused to extend unemployment benefits for fear of increasing the budget deficit, many voters found him out of touch with their financial realities. While fellow Republican and conservative pundit Pat Buchanan attacked Bush for raising taxes, Democratic nominee Bill Clinton, the five-term governor of Arkansas, adopted the informal slogan "It's the economy, stupid" and put forth a program of economic growth and job creation that attracted some voters even as revelations of his draft evasion, marijuana use, and adultery repelled others.

The late entry of H. Ross Perot added drama to the race. A billionaire businessman with no previous political experience, Perot spoke directly to potential voters and announced on CNN's *Larry King Show* that he would run for president if supporters got him added to the ballot in all fifty states. Rejecting the tactics and fund-raising of both mainstream parties, Perot ran as an independent and self-financed 90 percent of his campaign. Instead of the usual political ads, he bought thirty-minute blocs of television time and used charts, an easel, and a pointer to illustrate his protectionist and isolationist views. His ideas and unconventional style resonated with voters frustrated with mainstream politics and the sputtering economy. Although many polls showed him leading Bush and Clinton, Perot unexpectedly dropped out of the race in July, only to re-enter it in October.

The following month, Clinton won with 43 percent of the popular vote to Bush's 38 percent. Perot won 19 percent of the vote, the highest showing by a third-party candidate since Teddy Roosevelt ran as a Progressive in 1912 (see Map 27.3). Clinton's victory also helped the Democrats regain control of both houses of Congress for the first time since Jimmy Carter was in the White House. Like the

previous three presidential races, the 1992 elections reflected a gender gap in which a higher percentage of women than men preferred the Democratic candidate, a political trend that continues to the present day (see Table 27.1).

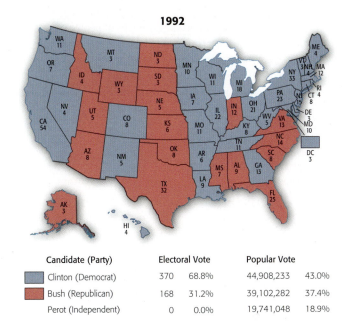

1992

Candidate (Party)		Electoral Vote		Popular Vote	
	Clinton (Democrat)	370	68.8%	44,908,233	43.0%
	Bush (Republican)	168	31.2%	39,102,282	37.4%
	Perot (Independent)	0	0.0%	19,741,048	18.9%

Map 27.3 Election of 1992 Ross Perot's unexpectedly strong third-party run, a stream of damaging revelations about Bill Clinton, and an electorate frustrated by an economic recession made the 1992 presidential race especially unpredictable. Although commentators such as Rush Limbaugh allege that Ross Perot cost George H.W. Bush a second term, political experts refute those claims, pointing to data showing that Perot drew voters away from both Bush and Clinton and that Bush lagged behind Clinton throughout the entire race. ▶

Table 27.1 Gender Gap and Presidential Elections, 1980–2012

Since the 1980 presidential race, political experts have noted differences in the political views and voting choices of women and men. In general, women tend to support a more activist government, federal social welfare programs such as Medicaid, and gun control—a trend that has favored Democratic candidates.

Year	Presidential Candidates	Women Voters (percentage)	Men Voters (percentage)	Gender Gap (percentage points)	Information Source
2012	Barack Obama (D)	55%	45%	10	Edison Research
	Mitt Romney (R)	44%	52%		
2008	Barack Obama (D)	56%	49%	7	Edison Media Research and Mitofsky International
	John McCain (R)	43%	48%		
2004	George W. Bush (R)	48%	55%	7	Edison Media Research and Mitofsky International
	John Kerry (D)	51%	41%		
2000	George W. Bush (R)	43%	53%	10	Voter News Service
	Al Gore (D)	54%	42%		
	Ralph Nader (Green)	2%	3%		
1996	Bill Clinton (D)	54%	43%	11	Voter News Service
	Bob Dole (R)	38%	44%		
	Ross Perot (Reform)	7%	10%		
1992	Bill Clinton (D)	45%	41%	4	Voter News Service
	George H.W. Bush (R)	37%	38%		
	Ross Perot (Reform)	17%	21%		
1988	George H.W. Bush (R)	50%	57%	7	CBS News/New York Times
	Michael Dukakis (D)	49%	41%		
1984	Ronald Reagan (R)	56%	62%	6	CBS News/New York Times
	Walter Mondale (D)	44%	37%		
1980	Ronald Reagan (R)	46%	54%	8	CBS News/New York Times
	Jimmy Carter (D)	45%	37%		
	John Anderson (I)	7%	7%		

Source: Center for the American Woman and Politics, Fact Sheet on The Gender Gap: Voting Choices in Presidential Elections, http://www.cawp.rutgers.edu/sites/default/files/resources/ggpresvote.pdf.

A Changing Population

Since the mid-1970s, changes in immigration trends, birth rates, and life expectancy have transformed the U.S. population. In November 1993, Ted Thai morphed photographs of people of different racial and ethnic backgrounds to create this computer-generated image for a special issue of *Time Magazine*. Some readers believed that the photo echoed demeaning presentations of people of color found in late nineteenth-century publications and world's fairs, but others saw it as a beautiful reflection of American multiculturalism.

How does this image reflect some of the ways that U.S. society has changed over the last few decades? Why do you think that readers had such diverging responses to this image of "the new face of America"? ▶

The LIFE Picture Collection/Getty Images

multiculturalism Coexistence of differing races, ethnicities, cultures, and religion in a single society.

English-only laws Statutes mandating the use of the English language in government documents and interactions with public officials.

In the late twentieth century, the United States became a larger, older, and more racially and ethnically diverse nation. The Immigration Act of 1965 had ended the discriminatory national origin quota system by raising the annual quota of immigrants legally permitted to enter the United States and admitting those from Africa, the Middle East, and Asia in equal proportion to those from Europe. Medical advances enabled people to live longer, and the nation's median age began to rise. A wave of births beginning in the early 1980s produced the nation's second-largest generation ever. Many nations experienced similar trends, and concerns about the economic and environmental implications of the globe's burgeoning population fueled international population control efforts.

☞ As you read, closely note changing demographics of the United States. What factors increased the diversification of the nation's population?

27-2a Debating Multiculturalism

In the late twentieth century, the United States became more diverse as immigration surged and the number of nonwhite Americans

{ The first large wave of immigrants since the early twentieth century transforms U.S. society.

increased. Although rates of immigration had declined during the economic downturn of the 1970s, more than 7 million immigrants arrived in the 1980s and another 9 million came in the 1990s. Between 1970 and 1990, the percentage of whites in the U.S. population dropped from 87.6 percent to 83.9 percent. By 2000, 31.1 million

Americans—11.1 percent of the total U.S. population of 281.4 million—were foreign born.

These trends ignited debates over **multiculturalism.** For reasons that varied from nation to nation, Canada, Australia, and several European countries made the recognition of cultural and racial diversity an official government policy. For example, Canada adopted the Canadian Multiculturalism Act (1988) to ensure mutual respect among the nation's different ethnic, religious, and linguistic subgroups. The United States—a multicultural society from its inception—did not adopt similar laws. But racial minorities successfully pushed for the inclusion of nonwhite and non-European perspectives in school curricula and programming. In the 1980s, critics attacked these initiatives as "political correctness" and claimed that multicultural education would erode America's cohesive civic identity. Several states passed **English-only laws** requiring the use of the English language in all government operations and publications.

These tensions coexisted with a shortage of skilled U.S. workers that prompted Congress to pass the Immigration Act of 1990 (see Table 27.2). The law increased annual caps on immigrants and simplified requirements for proving English competency and establishing permanent residency. It provided legal sanctuary for those fleeing violence and war and expanded the number of H1B visas available to skilled workers seeking permanent residence in the United States from fifty thousand to one hundred forty thousand per year. To obtain such visas, U.S. employers

Keith Birmingham/ZUMA Press/Newscom

Global American In December 1978, **David Tran**, a former major in the South Vietnamese army, joined more than thirty-three hundred refugees fleeing Vietnam on a Taiwanese freighter. One of thousands of boat people displaced by the Vietnam War, he eventually came to Los Angeles. To support himself, he began making Sriracha, a hot sauce blended from serrano peppers (later switched to red jalapeños), vinegar, garlic, and salt. Naming his business Huy Fong Foods after the ship that took him out of Southeast Asia, he packaged his Sriracha in green-topped clear plastic bottles marked with a rooster, the Vietnamese zodiac sign for the year of his birth, 1945. Text in five languages (Vietnamese, English, Chinese, French, and Spanish) identifies the sauce's contents. By 1987, sales were so good that the company moved to a 68,000 square-foot facility in Rosemead, California.

Although the company has never advertised its products, Sriracha has become a culinary phenomenon. After *Bon Appétit* magazine chose Sriracha as its Ingredient of the Year for 2010, the company sold 20 million bottles. By 2012, annual sales were more than $60 million. The subject of documentaries, festivals, and cookbooks, Sriracha is now found in hamburgers, potato chips, popcorn, candy, ice cream, vodka, and beer. Tran trademarked his distinctive rooster logo and bottle but not his hot sauce. He insists he does not mind that it has inspired countless imitators, and he does not charge royalty fees for those who legitimately license products using Sriracha. He has not only succeeded in his adopted country but also added to its diet.

had to attest that no Americans with comparable skills were available to fill specific positions. The Immigration Act helped professionals including doctors, scientists, educators, and athletes move to the United States permanently. But as non-English speaking, nonskilled workers exploited loopholes in the law, controversies over border control and deportation continued.

Debates about undocumented immigrants often obscured the fact that the majority of immigrants came to the United States legally. During the 1980s, the rate of Asian immigrants from China, South Korea, Vietnam, the Philippines, and India rose dramatically. Sometimes called "model minorities," many Asian Americans excelled academically and economically. They completed high school and college and earned professional degrees in the highest percentages of any minority, and their national income was 20 percent above the national average in 2004. Yet many Southeast Asian refugees (especially rural groups

Table 27.2 Major U.S. Immigration Laws, 1965–1990

Year	Legislation	Description
1965	Immigration and Nationality Act (Hart-Cellar Act)	Abolishes national origin quota system and replaces it with a system admitted immigrants based on relationships with a U.S. citizen, employer, or legal resident. Sets annual caps on total number of immigrants permitted with the exception of "immediate relatives" (spouses, parents, or minor children).
1975	Indochina Migration and Refugee Assistance Act	Expands the legal category of *refugee* to include those fleeing violence and persecution in Cambodia and Vietnam.
1980	Refugee Act	Creates a new system for processing and admitting refugees and asylum seekers. Legally defines *a refugee* as someone unable or unwilling to return to his or her country of origin because of maltreatment or possible persecution on the basis of race, religion, social group, or political opinion.
1986	Immigration Reform and Control Act (IRCA)	Increases number of border patrol agents by 50 percent. Penalizes employers who knowingly hire or recruit undocumented workers. Provides a path to legal citizenship for unauthorized immigrants who entered the United States prior to 1982. Allows unauthorized immigrants in certain agricultural jobs to apply for permanent resident status.
1988	Anti-Drug Abuse Act (ADAA)	Allows the deportation of resident aliens found guilty of murder or trafficking drugs or weapons.
1990	Immigration Act	Increases number of legal immigrants permitted by 50 percent, loosens regulations on temporary foreign workers, and expands grounds for deportation for immigrants committing aggravated felonies.

Source: Migration Policy Institute, Fact Sheet, http://www.migrationpolicy.org/research/timeline-1790.

deindustrialization Economic and social changes resulting from the removal or decline of well-paying factory jobs.

Los Angeles riots. Three days of destruction, looting, and arson following the April 1992 acquittal of four white police officers in a highly publicized police brutality case.

al-Qaeda Founded by Osama bin Laden in 1998, militantly anti-Western radical Sunni Muslim organization responsible for numerous terrorist incidents around the world.

such as the Hmong) struggled with poverty, welfare dependency, cultural alienation, and the persistent effects of war trauma. Some youth joined urban street gangs and became embroiled in the competition and violence of the drug trade.

At the same time, socioeconomic stratification divided the African American community. The number of black women graduating from college steadily increased throughout the 1980s while the number of men declined. The number of black-owned businesses rose, and African Americans broke into the ranks of corporate executives as celebrities like singer Michael Jackson and talk show host Oprah Winfrey amassed fortunes worth hundreds of millions of dollars. But the black community was also hit hard by changes in the U.S. economy.

The continuing crisis in America's central cities, descending back to the Watts Riots in 1965, decimated black working-class communities, and now included a large and fast-growing population of Latinos. **Deindustrialization** resulted in the loss of millions of well-paying industrial and manufacturing jobs in urban areas with high black populations. Faced with declining tax revenue, many cities reduced spending on education and public services at the same time that the Reagan administration cut budgets for federal job training and urban development programs. In some inner-city neighborhoods, African American unemployment rates exceeded 40 percent and poverty, addiction, and violence tore formerly tight-knit communities apart. Arrest rates soared as police cracked down on drug trafficking. By 2000, half of the nation's 2 million prisoners were African American, and one-third of all black men in their twenties were incarcerated, on parole or probation, or awaiting criminal sentencing.

Such harsh realities inspired a subgenre of hip-hop music called *gangsta rap*. Emerging in Los Angeles, gangsta rap lyrics were often violent, misogynistic, and profane, but also vividly reflected inner-city life. N.W.A.'s "F— tha Police" (1988) and "Cop Killer" (1990), penned by Body Count lead vocalist Ice-T, offered scathing critiques of police brutality—a phenomenon that gripped the world's attention after four white Los Angeles police officers arrested Rodney King, an African American man, for reckless driving on March 3, 1991. Pulling King from his vehicle, the officers forced him to the ground and beat him fifty-six times with their batons. A bystander filmed the episode on a video camera and released the footage to the media (a rare occurrence in an age before smart phones), sparking outrage in the black and Latino communities of Los Angeles over long-standing patterns of excessive force and racial profiling by local law enforcement.

In April 1992, after the four police officers were acquitted, racial tensions exploded during the **Los Angeles riots.** Unleashing rage at deepening economic disparities and a criminal justice system perceived to be biased, African Americans and Latinos destroyed property and looted stores, most owned by whites and Asian Americans. The three-day disturbance left fifty-five people dead and $1 billion in property damage. Law enforcement advocates and politicians suggested that gangsta rap encouraged urban violence but proved less able to redress inner city economic and racial inequalities.

Terrorism highlighted other divisions in American society. In February 1993, after Islamic radicals linked to **al-Qaeda** bombed the World Trade Center in New York City, killing six people and wounding more than one thousand, many U.S. citizens' suspicions of Arab Americans and Islam intensified, complicating some Arab Americans' pursuit of a better life in the United States.

Armed Volunteers at a Korean American–Owned Market, Los Angeles, May 1992 In South Central Los Angeles, Korean Americans call the May Los Angeles riots "Sa-I-Gu" (Korean for "four-two-nine," the date the unrest began). During the disturbance, more than twenty-two hundred Korean American-owned stores were burned or looted by largely African American and Latino rioters, resulting in more than $400 million in damage. Korean immigrants, many of them armed, tried to protect Koreatown, their ethnic enclave. Since the riots, the Korean American community in Los Angeles has become more visible and politically powerful. ▶

AP Images/JOHN GAPS III

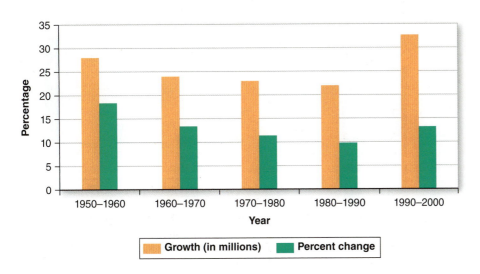

Figure 27.1 U.S. Population Growth, 1950–2000 Fueled by the birth of the so-called Millennial generation, the U.S. population increased 13.2 percent between 1990 to 2000, from 248.7 million to 281.4 million—the largest census increase in U.S. history. Thanks to the post-1965 wave of immigration, the Millennials were more ethnically diverse than the Baby Boomers. Nearly 20 percent were of Hispanic origin, almost double the proportion among the Boomers. Source: U.S. Census Bureau, *Census 2000 Brief*, https://www.census.gov/prod/2001pubs/c2kbr01-2.pdf. ◄

27-2b Demographic Trends

During the twentieth century, the U.S. population changed dramatically. From 1900 to 2000, it almost quadrupled, increasing from 76 million in 1900 to 200 million in 1968 to 281.4 million in 2000 (see Figure 27.1). The population concentrated in urban areas and by 1990, 78 percent of Americans lived in cities. As the shift westward and southward continued, California and Texas became the two most populous U.S. states. From 1982 to 2003, 80 million so-called Millennials were born, making them a generation as proportionally large as the Baby Boomers.

{ The U.S. population grows as the birth rate spikes and people live longer.

Fueled by post-1965 immigration trends and the Millennial generation, the United States was becoming more racially diverse. In 2000, whites composed 69.1 percent of total U.S. population, but rising numbers of Asian and Latino Americans signaled that nonwhites would become the majority as early as 2043 (see Figure 27.2). More Americans also began to identify as multiracial. In 1997, after becoming the youngest and first person of color to win the prestigious Masters golf tournament, Tiger Woods—who is half-Asian (Thai, Chinese), one-quarter African American, one-eighth Native American, and one-eighth Dutch—described himself as "Cablinasian" as a way of honoring all the elements of his racial and cultural heritage. To acknowledge Americans with such complex identities, Congress passed the "Tiger Woods bill" adding a multiracial option on the U.S. census effective in the year 2000.

At the same time, medical advances increased the percentage of the U.S. population over age sixty-five. In the first half of the twentieth century, immigration, relatively high fertility rates, and declining infant mortality gave the

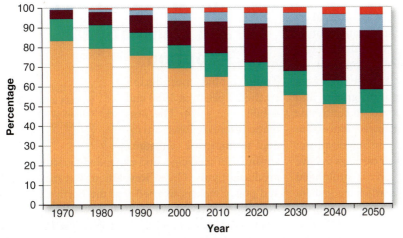

Other and multiracial
Latino or Hispanic (of any race)
Non-Hispanic White
Asian American and/or Asian Pacific Islander
Black or African American

Figure 27.2 Racial and Ethnic Composition of the United States, 1970–2050 Racial and ethnic demographics of the United States have changed a great deal since 1970 and are projected to shift dramatically by 2050. Because the U.S. Census Bureau has used different racial categories over time, some changes are difficult to trace. In 2000, for example, the categories "Native Hawaiian or Other Pacific Islander" and "Two or More Races" were used for the first time, enabling people to self-identify differently than they might have previously. Sources: Data for 1970 and 1980 from Statistical Abstract of the United States. Data for 1990, 2000, and 2010 from the U.S. Census Bureau. Data for 2020 through 2050 from the U.S. Census Bureau Population Projections by Race and Ethnicity (2008). ◄

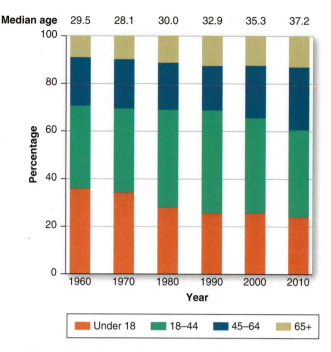

Figure 27.3 U.S. Age Distribution and Median Age, 1960–2010 Thanks to improvements in medical care and pharmaceuticals, Americans are living longer than in previous times. With longer average survival rates than men, women over age eighty composed 4.3 percent of the total U.S. population in 2000 compared to only 2.2 percent of men. Some experts predict that by 2050, people over age eighty will be the nation's largest age group. Source: United States Census Bureau, "Age and Sex Composition: *2010,*" *2010 Census Briefs,* http://www.census.gov/prod/cen2010/briefs/c2010br-03.pdf. ▲

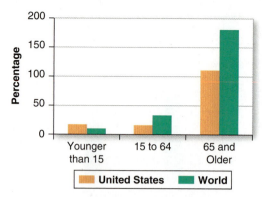

Figure 27.4 U.S. and Global Population by Age, 2010–2050 Demographers predict that the number of people over age sixty-five worldwide will triple by 2050, a trend particularly strong in developed nations like the United States, Japan, South Korea, and Germany. Younger workers in these countries may have to support older family members in addition to their own children. As a consequence of falling birth rates, the global population of people under age fifteen is projected to increase by only 10 percent over the same period. Source: United Nations, Department of Economic and Social Affairs, World Population Prospects: 2012 Revision, June 2013, http://esa.un.org/unpd/wpp/index/htm. ▲

United States an overall young population. But as Americans lived longer, the median age rose from 29.5 in 1960 to 35.3 in 2000 (see Figure 27.3). These trends were even more pronounced in Japan, South Korea, and Germany. Demographers predict that the global population of people over sixty-five will reach 1.5 billion in 2050, almost triple the 531 million in 2010 (see Figure 27.4).

Like their counterparts abroad, U.S. policy makers wrestled with the possible economic implications of an aging population. With the Internal Revenue Service's approval of **401(k) plans** in 1978, more employers curtailed pension programs and encouraged employees to contribute to the new tax-deferred retirement savings plans. But few Americans put aside enough of their earnings to have income security over a prolonged postretirement life, which made them rely more on the publicly funded Social Security system. Poor health or disability could also exacerbate the financial precariousness of older Americans' lives. An increasing number of American families began taking care of elderly parents or struggling to

401(k) plans Established by the Internal Revenue Service in 1978, defined contribution pension plan in which an employee applies a portion of salary toward retirement savings.

Gray Panthers Social justice organization founded in 1970 by Maggie Kuhn in response to her forced retirement at age sixty-five.

American Association of Retired Persons (AARP) Founded in 1958, leading U.S. lobbying and educational organization working on behalf of people age fifty and older.

absorb often exorbitant costs of placing a parent in a long-term care facility. Hamstrung by a gridlocked political system, politicians proved unwilling to confront the challenge of adjusting Social Security or Medicare to meet the needs of a population with a higher proportion of senior citizens, many of whom lived longer than people in previous generations. Advocacy organizations like the **Gray Panthers** and the **American Association of Retired Persons (AARP)** pushed for public policies that protected senior citizens, and older voters tended to be much more politically engaged than their younger counterparts.

27-2c Global Population Control and Transnational Adoption

Total global population reached 3 billion in 1960 and 4 billion in 1974. The dramatic increase was attributed to improved sanitation,

> Fears that the Earth will not sustain a rapidly growing population prompt international action.

advances in medicine, and expanded agricultural yields produced by the Green Revolution. But many scholars and policy makers worried that the Earth's energy and food supplies could not withstand such continued rates of growth. Paul Ehrlich's *The Population Bomb* (1968) heightened such anxieties. A demographer and ecologist, he warned that overpopulation would trigger famines, epidemics, and social chaos. To prevent such tragedies, he called for governments to institute population control programs.

Although few of Ehrlich's most dire predictions came to pass, his views influenced population control initiatives in many nations. In 1970, Congress enacted **Title X of the Public Health Service Act,** a measure providing birth control counseling and supplies to people with low incomes. Title X became a vital source of funding for reproductive health clinics across the United States and made contraception accessible for millions of Americans.

But some countries resorted to more coercive methods. In April 1976, India adopted a forced sterilization policy that used propaganda and financial incentives to persuade people to undergo vasectomies or tubal ligations. The program generated an intense backlash against family planning with aftereffects enduring for decades. In 1979, China instituted a policy permitting most Chinese couples to have only one child. Although the **one-child policy** prevented at least 250 million births over the next thirty years, local officials also invasively tracked women's fertility, forcing abortions and compulsory sterilizations on those who failed to comply. Because of the cultural value placed on boys, many families elected to terminate pregnancies if tests indicated that a fetus was female. Girl babies were abandoned and even murdered. Although the government banned prenatal sex screening in 1994, a striking gender imbalance emerged among those under age twenty with boys outnumbering girls by as many as 32 million. Fearful that there would not be enough young people to care for the elderly or to resolve China's labor shortage, government officials abolished the one-child policy in 2015.

International population control efforts met opposition. The Roman Catholic Church protested the promotion of birth control and condemned sterilizations and abortion. At the 1984 United Nations International Conference on Population in Mexico City, Ronald Reagan announced that the U.S. Agency for International Development would not fund non-governmental organizations (NGOs) that promoted or performed abortions "as a method of family planning" anywhere in the world. The **Mexico City policy** became a political football in years to come as Democratic presidents rescinded it and Republican presidents reinstituted it. Critics charged that the policy limited the ability to dispense birth control and accurate medical information. Supporters viewed it as a vital component of the transnational pro-life movement.

This era also witnessed an increase in the number of transnational adoptions by which an individual or couple from one nation adopts a child or children from a different country. Between 1982 and 2004, annual international adoptions to the United States nearly quadrupled from 5,749 to 22,991. Most of these children originated from China (overwhelmingly girls abandoned as a result of the one-child policy), Ethiopia, Russia, South Korea, and Guatemala (see Figure 27.5). In 1993, The Hague Adoption Convention (1993) protected children from traffickers and promoted transparency and legal documentation of the adoption process. In 2000, Congress passed the Child Citizenship Act, automatically granting U.S. citizenships to foreign-born children when at least one adoptive parent is a U.S. citizen.

Title X of the Public Health Service Act Established in 1970, federal grant program for comprehensive family planning and reproductive health services.

one-child policy Enacted in the late 1970s, official Chinese policy of permitting families to have only one child. Abolished in 2015.

Mexico City policy Intermittent U.S. policy of barring NGOs that perform abortions or provide abortion counseling from receiving federal funds that Republican administrations upheld and Democratic ones repealed.

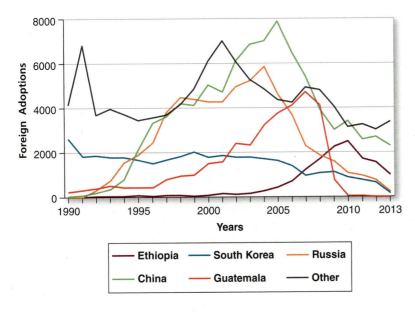

Figure 27.5 International Adoption in the United States by Selected Countries, 1990–2013 After peaking in 2004, the number of foreign-born children adopted by U.S. citizens began to decline. The U.S. government halted adoptions from Cambodia and Guatemala and restricted adoptions from Nepal in response to kidnapping and baby selling. China, once the largest source of transnationally adopted children, instituted strict qualifications for foreign parents seeking to adopt. In 2013, after a U.S. couple returned their adopted Russian child, the Russian government outlawed adoptions to the United States. Source: Johnston's Archive, http://www.johnstonsarchive.net/policy/adoption-statsintl.html. ◀

The Clinton Years

Editorial cartoonist Mike Luckovich speculates on how the Clinton presidency might be remembered.

Why is it significant that this cartoon includes Bill Clinton among the presidents etched on Mt. Rushmore? Which of the images of President Clinton, the "statesman" or the "frat boy," do you think will prove the more enduring? Why? ▶

Mike Luckovich/Atlanta Journal-Constitution/Creators Syndicate

---

Family Medical Leave Act
Legislation that permits workers up to twelve weeks of unpaid leave after the birth of a child or to care for a sick family member.

RU-486 Trademark name for mifepristone, a drug that can terminate a pregnancy of less than seven weeks.

New Democrat Centrist faction of the Democratic Party that emerged after Michael Dukakis lost the 1988 presidential race.

Third Way Centrist political philosophy attempting to fuse right-wing economic ideas and left-wing social policies.

Clinton was undoubtedly among the most colorful presidents in U.S. history. An extraordinarily gifted politician though a rather careless individual, Clinton energized—and polarized—the country. When he took office in 1993, he proposed the most ambitious legislative agenda since the Great Society. Clinton wanted to focus on economic recovery and health care reform, but missteps and scandals jeopardized his political goals. Repeatedly outmaneuvering his political rivals and surviving a failed effort to impeach him, Clinton remained popular, and his presidency ended with a booming economy and federal budget surpluses. But the 2000 presidential election revealed continuing deep divisions among Americans.

Contrary to initial predictions, the end of the Cold War did not usher in an age of peace and stability. Instead, it highlighted ongoing struggles in the developing world and exposed bitter ethnic and nationalist tensions that sometimes erupted into violence. Such a tense international landscape, the nation's policy makers concluded, demanded active and engaged U.S. leadership. Both triumph and tragedy would punctuate the new U.S. role as the world's only remaining superpower.

☞ As you read, consider the domestic politics of the Clinton era. How and why did politics become more polarized? How did this polarization affect the Clinton presidency?

27-3a Ambitious Agenda

After being shut out of the White House since 1980, liberals had high hopes for Clinton. He appointed more African Americans, Latinos, and women to the Cabinet than any previous president. He signed the **Family Medical Leave Act**, a law granting workers up to twelve weeks of unpaid leave to tend a newborn or adopted child or to care for an ailing relative. Although 35 million Americans took advantage of the new law by 2001, the United States was one of the only industrialized nations in the world where such leave was not paid. Through executive orders, Clinton lifted Reagan- and Bush-era restrictions on abortion. He revoked a "gag rule" that prevented clinics that received federal aid for serving low-income patients from providing abortion counseling. He struck down a ban on the importation of **RU-486,** a drug that terminates early pregnancy by preventing a fertilized egg from attaching to the uterine wall. Clinton also ended restrictions prohibiting the use of federal funds for research using fetal tissue, a move praised by scientists seeking new treatments for neurological diseases, leukemia, and diabetes.

A **New Democrat,** Clinton pushed a **Third Way** agenda that moved away from the Keynesianism of the New Deal and the Great Society. To jump-start the nation's stalled economy, he called for tax increases on the wealthy, spending cuts, deficit reduction, and investment in education and technology. On the advice of his economic advisers, Clinton dropped a campaign promise to cut taxes for the middle class. After intense debate, his budget plan very narrowly passed Congress—significantly without a single

> Clinton tries to advance policy goals despite missteps and political opposition.

Republican vote. The Deficit Reduction Act of 1993 raised taxes on the wealthiest 1.2 percent of taxpayers while expanding the **Earned Income Tax Credit** for 15 million Americans and reducing taxes for 90 percent of small businesses. Through spending cuts and tax increases, it slashed the budget deficit by $496 billion over five years. The act put the nation on course for debt reduction and budget surpluses, but the Democrats would pay a high political price for increasing taxes.

Clinton's efforts to honor a campaign pledge to allow gays and lesbians to serve openly in the U.S. armed forces met a fusillade of opposition from military leaders and conservatives. In June 1993, he struck a compromise that barred the military from inquiring about soldiers' sexual orientation and prevented soldiers from disclosing their sexual orientation. The "don't ask, don't tell" policy (DADT) resulted in the involuntary discharges of more than thirteen thousand troops before Congress repealed the policy in December 2010. Although many LGBT Americans lambasted the DADT compromise, they applauded President Clinton for making the first-ever appointments of openly gay people to administrative positions, expanding federal funding for the treatment and prevention of HIV/AIDS, and issuing an executive order allowing qualified LGBT people to receive federal security clearances—a move that ended a policy enacted at the height of the Lavender Scare in the early 1950s.

When Clinton introduced a sweeping proposal for national health insurance in response to skyrocketing health care costs and rising number of uninsured Americans, his decision to make Hillary Clinton its point person riled critics who thought such a high-profile public policy role was inappropriate for a first lady. A graduate of Wellesley and Yale Law School, Mrs. Clinton impressed supporters with her mastery of the thirteen hundred-page plan's intricacies. But the proposal drew widespread criticism. Conservatives objected to its expansion of the role of government and restriction of patient options. The health insurance industry launched ads criticizing its highly bureaucratized structure. In September 1994, after a year of contentious debate and the Clintons' refusal to accept alternatives, the Democratic-controlled Congress abandoned the complicated legislation.

President Clinton also launched major initiatives aimed at reducing crime and improving education. Gun control advocates cheered his signing of the **Brady Bill,** a federal law mandating a five-day waiting period and criminal background checks for handgun purchases, and a federal ban on assault weapons. In 1994, Congress approved his $30.2 billion plan expanding community policing and crime prevention programs. While experts differed in their views on what caused the trend, the overall national crime rate soon dropped to its lowest level since 1973. Clinton expanded federal funding for **Head Start** and K-12 education. To expand access to higher education and foster civic engagement, Clinton established **AmeriCorps,** a program in which people work as community service volunteers to earn college aid. Within five years, almost 200,000 young Americans were enrolled. He increased **Pell Grants** for low-income college students and supported the **Federal Direct Loan Program** that made student loans more accessible and affordable.

Earned Income Tax Credit Federal tax credit benefiting low-to-moderate income families, especially those with children.

Brady Bill Named after former Reagan press secretary and gun control advocate James Brady, 1993 federal law instituting background checks on those who buy firearms.

Head Start Federal program founded in 1965 that provides early childhood education and health and nutrition programs to low-income children and their families.

AmeriCorps Created by the Clinton administration in 1993, the federal community service program fostering volunteerism and viewed as the domestic counterpart of the Peace Corps.

Pell Grants Need-based federal aid to low-income college students that does not have to be repaid.

Federal Direct Loan Program National program that simplified student loans and removed private intermediaries to save money for both students and the federal government.

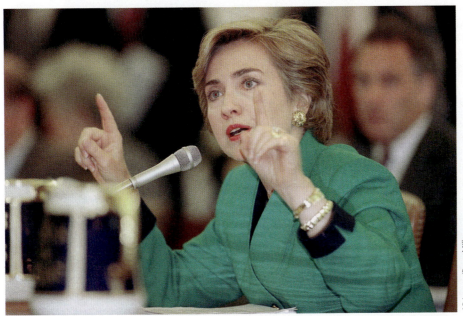

AP Images/Doug Mills

Hillary Clinton Testifying to Congress on Health Care Reform, 1993 While heading the Task Force on National Health Care Reform, Clinton drew criticism for the secrecy of the committee's proceedings but won praise for her ability to explain the administration's complex proposals. Although that initiative failed, she continued her health care advocacy, promoting a program that raised childhood immunization rates to 90 percent and working to secure passage of the State Children's Health Insurance Program providing federally funded health care to 6 million children. ◄

27-3b Partisan Backlash

The Clinton administration drew passionate detractors. On April 19, 1993, after a fifty-one-day standoff, federal agents used tear gas to expel members of the Branch Davidians, a religious group, from their compound in Waco, Texas. A fire erupted, and eighty-six people perished. Many Americans criticized the use of military force on civilians, and the incident fueled antigovernment extremism. In May 1994, the president's troubles mounted when Paula Jones, a former Arkansas state employee, filed a sexual harassment lawsuit against him. A few weeks later, Congress held hearings on Whitewater, a failed Arkansas real estate development project in which both Clintons had invested.

Republicans won a landslide victory in the 1994 midterm elections that was enabled by Clinton's legal challenges and mixed domestic record. For the first time in forty years, the GOP controlled both houses of Congress. Newt Gingrich (Republican from Georgia) became Speaker of the House and vowed to enact the **Contract with America,** a conservative plan for balancing the federal budget, reforming the welfare system, reducing government regulations, and cutting taxes. With notable discipline, House Republicans passed most of the Contract's agenda but it met staunch opposition in the Senate. Rather than be cowed by the Gingrich juggernaut, Clinton stuck to his Third Way principles and moved to the right as the political center shifted. In late 1995, after Clinton and the House reached an impasse over Republican proposals to cut taxes on the wealthy and to slash federal spending on education and health care, the federal government shut down twice. Voters blamed Gingrich, and the Speaker's popularity tumbled.

Clinton and the Republicans found common ground in responding to terrorism. In April 1995, on the second anniversary of the Waco incident, Timothy McVeigh detonated a truck filled with five thousand pounds of ammonium nitrate and racing fuel in front of the Alfred P. Murrah Federal Building in Oklahoma City. One hundred sixty-eight people, including nineteen children, died

> Republicans capitalize on opposition to Clinton's policies and win historic electoral gains.

Contract with America
Blueprint for Republican legislative agenda once the party gained control of Congress and signed on the Capitol steps in September 1994.

Murrah Federal Building after the Oklahoma City Bombing, 1995 Motivated by their hatred of the U.S. government, Timothy McVeigh and Terry Nichols orchestrated the bombing of a federal building in Oklahoma City. The huge explosion killed one hundred sixty-eight people and damaged or destroyed more than three hundred nearby structures. The community's immediate and overwhelming humanitarian response set what became known as "the Oklahoma standard" for dealing with disaster. McVeigh was sentenced to death and executed in 2001. Nichols is serving a life sentence without the possibility of parole. ▼

AP Images

in the massive explosion, the worst act of domestic terrorism in U.S. history. Some initial media reports speculated that Islamic radicals were responsible for the Oklahoma City bombing, but upon arrest, McVeigh, a U.S. citizen and Army veteran, stated that his actions were motivated by hatred of the federal government. In April 1996, Clinton signed a $1 billion antiterrorism bill permitting deportation of noncitizens suspected of terrorism and barring fundraising by terrorist groups.

Clinton deprived the Republicans of a powerful campaign issue by keeping his promise to "end welfare as we know it." In August 1996, he signed legislation overhauling welfare policies enacted during the New Deal that had guaranteed federal support for families with dependent children. The new law required welfare recipients to find work within two years and placed a five-year cap on total lifetime benefits. By 2001, the number of federal welfare recipients had dropped by 50 percent and most of those on public assistance had found jobs.

In September 1996, Clinton dealt LGBT Americans a major blow when he supported the **Defense of Marriage Act (DOMA).** The bill was introduced after a Hawai'i Supreme Court ruling sparked fears that the state might legalize same-sex marriages and that the **full faith and credit clause** of the U.S. Constitution would require other states to recognize them. To prevent such a scenario, Republicans introduced legislation defining marriage as a union of one man and one woman and barring married same-sex couples from receiving federal benefits (although no state legalized same-sex marriage until Massachusetts did so in 2004). Just weeks before the 1996 presidential elections, the legislation sped through Congress and passed both chambers with veto-proof majorities. Clinton called the legislation "divisive and unnecessary" but signed it into law, enraging many of his LGBT supporters.

A strategy of maintaining control of the political center enabled Clinton to win reelection in 1996. He faced Senator Robert Dole, Republican from Kansas, who ran on a platform combining supply-side economics with social conservatism. While deflecting charges of fundraising improprieties, Clinton emphasized the nation's booming economy. On Election Day, Clinton won with 49 percent of the popular vote to Dole's 41 percent. Ross Perot, who mobilized his 1992 supporters in the new Reform Party, won 8 percent. In his January 1997 State of the Union address, Clinton proclaimed "the era of big government is over." Four months later, Tony Blair, a New Labour politician who also ascribed to the Third Way, became Britain's prime minister after a landslide victory. Inspired by Clinton's centrism, Blair introduced market-based reforms in education and health care, revamped the welfare system, and advocated tough antiterrorism legislation.

Clinton pursued a modest second-term agenda aimed at helping the middle class. In 1997, he signed legislation to balance the federal budget and implement $152 billion in tax cuts by 2002. The bill also instituted new tax credits for child care and college expenses. In 1998, he announced that the United States had a budget surplus for the first time since 1969, and his next three budgets also ran surpluses, all used to pay $452 billion in public debt. Persuaded by neoliberal arguments that additional banking deregulation would help U.S. financial institutions compete with their European counterparts, Clinton in 1998 supported the repeal of the Glass-Steagall Act, a 1933 law mandating the separation of commercial and investment banking.

The Clinton years coincided with the longest period of economic expansion in U.S. history. More than 22.5 million jobs were created. Unemployment fell from 6.9 percent in 1993 to 4.0 percent in 2001, and inflation dropped from 4.7 to 2.5 percent, the lowest rates since the 1960s. Over the same period, poverty rates declined significantly, and home ownership rates exceeded 67 percent, the highest rate in U.S. history. But critics noted that rising levels of employment coexisted with dramatically increasing levels of corporate executive pay and that 16 million Americans had lost their jobs when companies downsized their workforces. Although many found new employment, they often earned lower wages, one of many factors exacerbating income inequality in the 1990s.

27-3c Confronting the Post-Cold War World

In his January 1993 inaugural address, Clinton declared, "There is no longer a clear division between what is foreign and what is domestic. The world economy, the world environment, the world AIDS crisis, the world arms race: they affect us all." With the Cold War's end, Clinton warned, "The new world is more free, but less stable." As commerce and technology increasingly interconnected the global population, U.S. officials set new priorities and met new adversaries.

After the Cold War ends, U.S. policy makers foster free trade and encounter new global challenges.

Clinton made free trade an integral element of his global policy. Although some Americans feared that easier access to cheaper foreign products would result in the loss of U.S. jobs, Clinton saw free trade as a means of increasing American exports and compelling antidemocratic nations to embrace human rights and economic reforms. Eager to compete with the **European Union**— a partnership of European states established in 1993 that were linked by a common currency called the

Defense of Marriage Act (DOMA) Federal law defining marriage as between one man and one woman and granting states permission not to recognize same-sex marriages performed in other jurisdictions.

full faith and credit clause Provision outlined in Article IV of the U.S. Constitution mandating that states recognize the acts, records, and legal proceedings of other states.

European Union Established in 1993, grouping of European countries operating as a single economic unit.

euro—and to decrease the $150 billion U.S. trade deficit, he won bipartisan support for the **North American Free Trade Agreement (NAFTA),** a pact in which the United States, Mexico, and Canada created a trade bloc. In 1994, the Senate ratified a modification of the **General Agreement on Tariffs and Trade (GATT),** approving the most significant restructuring of international trade regulations since the 1944 Bretton Woods Agreement. Designed to gradually eliminate obstacles to global free trade, the revised GATT established the **World Trade Organization (WTO)** to enforce its provisions. In 1999, Clinton brokered a landmark trade deal with China. The following year, despite concerns about China's human rights record and the possible implications of expanding Chinese imports to the United States, Congress ratified the agreement, thus paving the way for China's acceptance in the WTO. While many Americans enjoyed the lower prices and increased product selection these trade agreements facilitated, others linked free trade to worker exploitation, environmental degradation, and political repression.

Trade played an important role in the re-establishment of U.S.–Vietnamese relations. In February 1994, after the Vietnamese government provided photographs and data that accounted for the last two thousand two hundred sixty-five U.S. soldiers still listed as missing in action in the Vietnam War, Clinton lifted the trade embargo that the United States had placed on Vietnam in 1975. Eager to compete with foreign rivals in the thriving Vietnamese market, U.S. companies such as PepsiCo, General Electric, and Mobil began operating in the Socialist Republic of Vietnam (SRV). In July 1995, Clinton formally recognized the SRV and appointed Pete Peterson as U.S. ambassador, a Vietnam veteran and former Air Force pilot who spent more than six years in a North Vietnamese prison after his plane was shot down.

At the same time, economic issues strained U.S.–Japanese relations. By 1990, Japanese investors owned almost half of downtown Los Angeles, and Sony's acquisitions of CBS Records and Columbia Pictures made it a powerhouse in the U.S. entertainment industry. A wave of Japan-bashing like the one in which Vincent Chin was murdered in 1982 (see Chapter 26) began as Americans worried about Japanese economic and cultural domination. Such fears subsided in the 1990s, however, when Japan experienced a prolonged recession triggered by financial and ethical scandals that paralyzed its huge conglomerates and its business culture struggled to adapt to the rapidly globalizing economy. Although the Japanese maintained large trade surpluses in the United States, Tokyo's stock exchange, the Nikkei, lagged far behind the New York Stock Exchange. In 1997 and 1998, Japanese banks were hit hard when a financial crisis swept much of Asia. Despite their sometimes contentious economic relations, the United States and Japan remained close military allies who shared the costs of supporting tens of thousands of U.S. troops stationed in Japan and worked cooperatively to check North Korean nuclear ambitions and Chinese threats to Taiwan.

In the aftermath of the Cold War, many U.S. leaders hoped to help war-torn and underdeveloped societies, but their experiences in Somalia revealed that **nation-building** activities could have unanticipated consequences. A vital U.S. ally in battles against communism on the Horn of Africa during the late 1970s, Somalia degenerated into famine and civil war after the overthrow of its long-time dictator in 1991. In December 1992, George H.W. Bush sent more than twenty-eight thousand U.S. troops to Somalia to aid **Operation Restore Hope,** a UN coalition mission that rebuilt roads and bridges and protected relief workers.

Foreign intervention triggered the ire of a local warlord, and his soldiers killed several UN peacekeepers. After efforts to apprehend the warlord failed, Clinton deployed four hundred elite Army Rangers and Delta Force operatives to Somalia. In early October 1993, these soldiers and accompanying UN troops encountered fierce resistance in Mogadishu. After armed Somalis shot down two U.S. Black Hawk helicopters, soldiers sent to rescue the crews got locked in an overnight firefight that left eighteen U.S. troops dead and seventy-four wounded. Up to two thousand Somalis, mostly civilians, were also killed and injured. Television footage of cheering Somalis dragging the corpse of a U.S. soldier through the streets outraged Americans. Stung by the failure of the mission, Clinton announced that all U.S. combat troops would be withdrawn from Somalia by April 1994 and issued strict new guidelines on U.S. participation in future peacekeeping operations. The UN mission ended in defeat, and Somalia remained mired in violence and poverty for years afterward.

The debacle in Somalia shaped the global response to an outbreak of horrific violence that engulfed the east African nation of Rwanda. In April 1994, the deaths of the presidents of Rwanda and Burundi—both members of the Hutu majority—in a suspicious plane crash sparked mass killings of members of the Tutsi minority. Up to 1 million people were murdered over an eighty-nine-day period—the fastest pace of genocide in world history.

Reluctant to enter the fray of another complicated African conflict, the UN Security Council directed UN peacekeepers in Rwanda to evacuate foreign nationals and to begin withdrawing. Clinton rejected calls for U.S. intervention. Fearful of Tutsi retribution, about 2 million Hutus fled the country and poured into neighboring countries. In

North American Free Trade Agreement (NAFTA) Implemented in 1994, free trade agreement abolishing most tariffs between the United States, Mexico, and Canada.

General Agreement on Tariffs and Trade (GATT) 1948 international law aimed at fostering free trade in the aftermath of World War II replaced by the World Trade Organization in 1995.

World Trade Organization (WTO) Created in 1995, the only international organization that regulates trade between nations, tries to foster trade stability and openness. Target of antiglobalization protests.

nation-building Umbrella term for policies designed to make citizens embrace a commonality of interests, goals, and identities with their compatriots.

Operation Restore Hope Code name for a UN humanitarian relief operation in Somalia led by the United States from December 1992 to May 1993.

July, after the violence ended, the United States sent troops to Rwanda on a three-month mission to help with the refugee crisis. On a 1998 trip to Rwanda, Clinton apologized for failing to do "as much as we could have and should have done" to limit what U.S. officials had earlier refused to label as genocide.

Ethnic violence also consumed Yugoslavia. Although most of the former Soviet satellite states had transitioned to non-Communist governments peacefully, Yugoslavia disintegrated into the most devastating conflict in Europe since 1945. Serbs took up arms against their Muslim neighbors in campaigns of "ethnic cleansing" marked by murder, atrocities, detentions, and mass rapes. In 1995, after Clinton had hesitated for months to get involved in what he called "a problem from hell," U.S. diplomats helped broker accords ending the Serbs' campaign against the Croats and Bosnians. The United States contributed twenty thousand troops to a NATO contingent charged with implementing the agreement, providing humanitarian aid, and disposing of weapons and unexploded ordinance. More than 200,000 people were killed during the war, and 1.8 million became refugees.

In 1999, another Balkan crisis erupted after the Serbs launched a campaign of genocide against ethnic Albanians living in Kosovo. When the Serbs ignored calls for withdrawal, U.S. and NATO forces commenced seventy-eight days of bombing raids throughout Yugoslavia. A monstrous refugee crisis ensued as 800,000 people fled Kosovo for neighboring Albania and Macedonia. In June 1999, the Serbs agreed to remove their troops from Kosovo and to accept the terms of a cease-fire. Several top Serbian leaders were charged with crimes against humanity and extradited to stand trial at The Hague, the headquarters of United Nations International Court of Justice located in a coastal city in the western Netherlands.

Throughout the 1990s, the Clinton administration dealt with ramifications of the Persian Gulf War. Left in control of Iraq, Saddam continued to bedevil U.S. policy makers. Although UN economic sanctions created mass suffering among the Iraqi populace, Saddam repeatedly obstructed UN weapons inspectors searching for hidden stores of chemical and biological weapons. In 1996, Clinton ordered missile strikes on Iraq in retaliation for Saddam's attacks on Kurds. Two years later, a joint U.S.–British force bombed suspected Iraqi military sites. But Clinton rejected calls to overthrow Saddam.

International terrorism also escalated. In June 1996, members of Hezbollah, a Shi'a Islamist militant group financed by Iran, killed nineteen U.S. airmen and wounded hundreds more in a truck bombing at Khobar Towers, a U.S. military housing complex in Dharan, Saudi Arabia. In August 1998, Osama bin Laden's terrorist group Al-Qaeda launched simultaneous truck bombings at the U.S. embassies in Nairobi, Kenya, and Dar es Salaam, Tanzania, that left two hundred people dead and wounded more than four thousand. In retaliation, Clinton ordered air strikes on sites in Sudan and Afghanistan allegedly linked to al-Qaeda. In October 2000, an al-Qaeda suicide attack on the *U.S.S. Cole* killed seventeen sailors in the port of Aden in Yemen. The bombings signaled escalating dangers to national security posed by terrorist networks that were extremely difficult to track and combat.

27-3d Scandal, Impeachment, and the Election of 2000

Allegations of sexual impropriety overshadowed much of Clinton's second term. In January 1998, attorneys representing Paula Jones announced plans to depose Monica Lewinsky, a twenty-four-year-old former White House intern, about an alleged affair with the president. Although a judge dismissed Jones's lawsuit three months later, Kenneth Starr, the independent counsel whom Congress had appointed to examine the Whitewater real estate scandal, broadened his inquiry and convinced former White House staff member Linda Tripp to secretly record her conversations with Lewinsky. As a result of Starr's investigation, eleven people were convicted of fraud and other crimes related to Whitewater. Critics blasted Starr's tactics and close ties to the Republican Party.

> Surviving a failed impeachment, Clinton leaves office with high approval ratings and a flourishing economy.

In January 1998, news of Clinton's alleged affair with Lewinsky became public. He denied the claim, memorably declaring, "I did not have sexual relations with that woman." In August 1998, after Clinton was forced to testify to a grand jury, he gave a nationally televised speech admitting having had a sexual relationship with Lewinsky. While the legal proceedings unfolded, Lewinsky became the subject of intense media scrutiny and ridicule on the Internet. In September, Starr submitted a four hundred forty-five-page report to Congress offering salacious details about Clinton and Lewinsky's sexual encounters and accusing Clinton of perjury, obstruction of justice, witness tampering, and abuse of power. On October 8, 1998, the Republican-controlled House of Representatives voted two hundred fifty-eight to one hundred seventy-six to conduct impeachment hearings. Two months later, the House approved two articles of impeachment for perjury and obstruction of justice. In February 1999, the Senate acquitted Clinton. In September 2000, Robert Ray, Starr's successor as independent counsel, closed the $50 million Whitewater investigation after finding insufficient evidence to merit criminal charges against the president or the first lady.

Although the Lewinsky scandal markedly harmed Clinton's reputation, it also hurt the Republicans. In the 1998 elections, the Democrats gained five congressional seats—a testament to voters' satisfaction with a thriving economy and disdain for the partisanship driving the impeachment process. Ironically, two Republicans, not Clinton, were pushed from office. First, Newt Gingrich

red states and blue states Term taken from the color code on television news maps indicating which states vote Republican or Democratic and used to describe prevailing political and cultural views.

resigned as Speaker of the House after the disappointing election returns and allegations of fund-raising improprieties. Then Bob Livingston, a Republican from Mississippi who was Gingrich's designated successor, resigned when reporters exposed his own marital infidelity. Clinton, meanwhile, retained a 59 percent approval rating.

The changing nature of the media helped to fuel partisanship. In October 1996, Australian media mogul Rupert Murdoch hired former NBC executive and Republican operative Roger Ailes as CEO of Fox News, a twenty-four-hour cable news channel. By 2000, Fox was reaching 56 million homes nationwide, experiencing a 440 percent increase in viewers, and becoming a highly influential platform for conservative politics. So did the *Drudge Report*, a Web-based news aggregator that gained nationwide attention for breaking the story of the Lewinsky scandal in 1998.

Despite the increasingly partisan political culture, no one could have predicted the drama of the 2000 presidential elections. With a booming economy, the Democrats expected their nominee, Vice President Al Gore, to win election easily. The Republicans picked George W. Bush, two-term governor of Texas and son of former president George H.W. Bush. Both Gore and Bush ran as centrists but differed in their views on the best uses for projected federal budget surpluses and the proper role of the federal government. Bush advocated large tax cuts, partial privatization of Social Security, and government-funded vouchers for private education. Gore supported putting the surpluses into Social Security and Medicare. Bush was pro-life; Gore was pro-choice. Although Pat Buchanan ran as the Reform Party nominee and Ralph Nader represented the Green Party, neither won significant national support.

The election itself was a forty-two-day roller coaster ride. Senate elections resulted in a fifty-fifty Democratic-Republican split. Early on election night, commentators declared Gore winner of Florida. Later, they claimed Bush had won. Then they said that the race was too close to call. Returns from the rest of the nation gave Gore a 337,000 lead in the popular vote and two hundred sixty-seven electoral votes. Carrying the South and much of the Midwest, Bush had two hundred forty-six electoral votes. Because neither had the two hundred seventy electoral votes needed to win, the outcome of the election hinged on Florida's twenty-five electoral votes. Television commentators used map graphics highlighting states that Bush won in red and those voting for in Al Gore in blue. **Red states and blue states** quickly became a shorthand way to describe the partisan and cultural differences among Americans.

In Florida, mandatory recounts began. Voters protested unclear "butterfly ballots," "under votes," antiquated

voting machines, and unhelpful poll officials. With the nation's attention riveted on his state, Governor Jeb Bush, brother of George W. Bush, tried to keep order as his state's voting irregularities were exposed. Baffled officials tried to interpret ballots with pregnant, dimpled, and hanging "chads," the cardboard removed when punching a ballot. On November 27, Florida secretary of state Katherine Harris, a leader in the state Bush campaign organization, ended the recounts and certified Bush the winner by five hundred thirty-seven votes. After Gore won an appeal to the Florida Supreme Court demanding a statewide hand recount, the Bush campaign appealed to the U.S. Supreme Court, insisting that the recounts be stopped. On the evening of December 12, the U.S. Supreme Court issued a 5-4 decision ordering the completion of all recounts by December 13—a deadline that was obviously impossible to meet. The four opposing justices issued blistering dissents to the *Bush v. Gore* ruling. Despite winning the popular vote by a 540,000 margin, Gore lost the electoral vote, two hundred sixty-seven to two hundred seventy-one. Bush became the nation's forty-third president (see Map 27.4). While some Americans cheered the end of the political chaos and welcomed Bush's victory, others were dismayed by the politicization of the Supreme Court. One protestor held a poster that read, "The people have spoken—all five of them." It was only one sign of the many ways that Americans had grown more politically divided during the Clinton years.

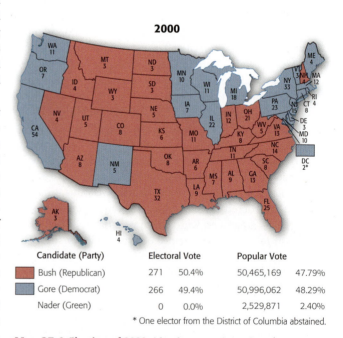

2000

Candidate (Party)	Electoral Vote		Popular Vote	
Bush (Republican)	271	50.4%	50,465,169	47.79%
Gore (Democrat)	266	49.4%	50,996,062	48.29%
Nader (Green)	0	0.0%	2,529,871	2.40%

* One elector from the District of Columbia abstained.

Map 27.4 Election of 2000 After forty-two days of recounts, legal challenges, and a Supreme Court ruling, George W. Bush was declared the winner of the 2000 presidential race, winning 271–261 in the electoral vote but trailing Democratic challenger Al Gore by 540,000 votes in the popular vote. ▲

27-4
Global Village

In the late twentieth century, globalization generated anxieties about U.S. cultural domination.

What does this cartoon suggest about the artist's views about globalization and the United States? Why do you think he used imagery evoking the D-Day invasion of World War II? ▶

Go to MindTap® to practice history with the Chapter 27 **Primary Source Writing Activity: The Americanization of Global Culture**. Read and view primary sources and respond to a writing prompt.

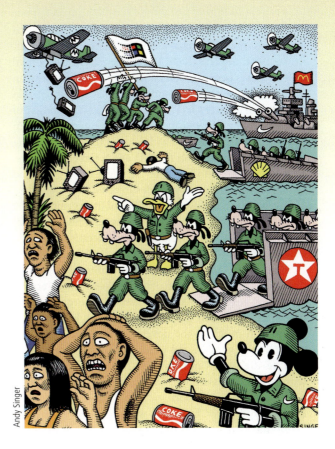

Andy Singer

The post-1975 era witnessed remarkable transformations in the ways people across the globe communicated, learned, shopped, worked, and played. Intergovernmental and nongovernmental organizations proliferated. Corporations expanded their operations across national borders. The Internet, facsimile (fax) machines, and mobile phones made keeping in touch with transnational friends, family, and business associates much easier. Technological innovations drove an economic boom and created a new class of billionaire entrepreneurs.

But the revolution created new challenges as well. Some foreign audiences objected to the ubiquity of U.S. products and culture. Technology changed the nature of personal relationships and notions of privacy. As the amount of readily available information exploded, distinguishing legitimate facts from satire or misinformation became more difficult. Criminals found new tactics for victimizing others and disseminating illegal goods and services. Multinational corporations could locate their operations in nations that did not guard the rights of workers or protect the environment. Although the overall effects of these trends were disputed, there was no denying that the pace and scope of change was profound.

☞ As you read, evaluate the impacts of globalization. How and why was the world more interconnected in 2000 than it was in 1975? What do you think are the most positive and negative aspects of globalization?

27-4a Proliferation of Intergovernmental and Nongovernmental Organizations

In the late twentieth century, **globalization**, the process of integrating people culturally, politically, and economically across national lines, expanded

> Nonstate actors play an increasing role in addressing global problems.

dramatically. The increasing number of nonstate actors engaging international issues illustrated this trend. In the 1970s, as détente eased superpower tensions and economic stagnation and public distrust limited governmental power, intergovernmental (IGOs) and nongovernmental organizations (NGOs) tackled problems that states were either unable or unwilling to address. Others worked together to challenge sovereign countries to improve how they treated their own citizens or addressed societal and economic problems. The number of **intergovernmental organizations** (groups, such as the UN, that were comprised of member states) grew from 280 in 1972 to 1,530 by 1984. Over the same period, the number of NGOs increased from 2,795 to 12,686. They took on a wide array of causes including human rights, humanitarian relief, disarmament, and environmental protection.

A flurry of organizers championed women's rights. In 1975, the UN General Assembly launched the International Decade of Women that began with an international congress of women in Mexico City. It inspired transnational campaigns aimed at improving women's status throughout the world. In 1979, one hundred eighty-seven nations signed a UN convention outlawing discrimination against women, but only twenty countries ratified the treaty, and it was hampered by differing interpretations of its provisions and weak enforcement mechanisms.

globalization International interconnectedness created by the global exchange of ideas, products, services, and culture.

intergovernmental organizations Body composed of at least two separate nations.

Transnational organizations also increased global awareness of crimes against women and gender inequality. In 1994, the U.S. State Department's annual human rights reports began documenting crimes against women including forced abortions and involuntary sterilizations in China, sexual slavery in Thailand, and "dowry killings" of women in India. In 1996, the United States granted asylum to Fauziya Kassindja, who had escaped from Togo fleeing female genital mutilation (FGM) and a forced marriage. The ruling helped to highlight the plight of an estimated 2 million women worldwide still subjected to ancient rituals involving the removal of portions of their genitalia as a means of ensuring chastity or marking adulthood, a practice that can have serious health consequences.

At the Fourth World Conference on Women held in Beijing in 1995, First Lady Hillary Clinton proclaimed "women's rights are human rights"—a call to action echoed by governments and transnational organizations that intensified their efforts to combat global women's poverty. In much of the developing world, social and cultural taboos restricted women's labor opportunities outside the home and limited their economic power within their households. Illiteracy; lack of access to health care, land, inheritance, and credit; and inadequate supplies of food and water created additional economic and physical hardships for many of these women. In 2000, the United Nations estimated that the majority of the 1.5 billion people in the world living on less than $1 a day were female. Worldwide, women's incomes averaged about half those of men. The provision of small loans—sometimes called **microcredit**—has proved a particularly successful strategy for eradicating women's poverty.

NGOs played a vital role in responding to famines, epidemics, natural disasters, and civil strife. One of the most influential was Doctors without Borders (Médecins Sans Frontières) founded in France in 1971. Its medical professionals helped refugees displaced by the Indochina wars and conflicts in Africa and aided victims of earthquakes and floods. In war zones such as Somalia and the Balkans, relief workers sometimes became targets of violence.

Other transnational activists worked to protect endangered species and the environment. NGOs such as the World Wildlife Fund and Friends of the Earth mobilized campaigns to safeguard whales, elephants, and other animals. In 1989, eighty-six nations pledged to phase out the use of chlorofluorocarbons (CFCs) that were damaging the ozone layer. In 1997, the United States and one hundred ninety other nations signed the **Kyoto Protocol** requiring industrialized countries to lower their production of greenhouse gases linked to global warming. But the United States rejected other environmental initiatives. Although it joined one hundred sixty-seven nations in signing a 1992 convention on biological diversity, the U.S. Senate refused to ratify the treaty.

27-4b The Digital Revolution and Its Critics

In the late twentieth century, digital computing and communications technology changed daily life in much of the world. Developed in the 1940s, computers were originally large machines using vacuum tubes, relays, and large bundles of wires. Within twenty years, the federal government, businesses, and universities were using more than thirty thousand mainframe computers. In 1971, Intel's introduction of the microprocessor greatly expanded the possible applications of computers. Six years later, Steven Jobs and Stephen Wozniak released the Apple II, the first personal computer (PC). In 1981, International Business Machines (IBM) released its own PC. Between 1989 and 2000, the number of U.S. households that owned at least one PC rose from 15 percent to 51 percent. Computers and digital technologies transformed banking, publishing, medicine, and many other industries.

The digital revolution fueled the development of the Internet, a worldwide system of interconnected computer networks. In the 1960s, the U.S. Department of Defense established Arpanet, a network linking computers at federally funded research facilities. Information-sharing applications for the system such as electronic mail (e-mail) and file transfer protocol (FTP) soon emerged. Packet-switching technology enabled computers that were not directly wired together to exchange large amounts of information. Centralized communications circuits routed messages to individual computers. In the early 1980s, as the number of computers linked by Arpanet grew, the Department of Defense withdrew from the project because of security concerns, and Arpanet was renamed the Internet. As private companies and government agencies poured resources into the Internet, it expanded rapidly. In 1989, Tim Berners-Lee and his colleagues in Geneva developed the World Wide Web (WWW), a system that allowed users to access the vast amount of documents on the Internet by means of electronic tags called *hyperlinks*. In 1993, Marc Andreessen and others at the University of Illinois released Mosaic (later called *Netscape*), the first widely used Web browser that greatly simplified the retrieval, transfer, and display of Internet files. The same year, the federal government approved the use of the Internet by commercial e-mail services. President Clinton directed all federal agencies to use information technologies to make the U.S. government more accessible to its citizens and launched an educational technology initiative that significantly

> Digital technologies spark a communications revolution that changes personal interactions, business practices, and consumerism.

microcredit Small, low-interest loans made to help people, especially women, in developing nations establish businesses and become economically self-sufficient.

Kyoto Protocol International agreement brokered by the United Nations to address global climate change by reducing carbon emissions around the world.

expanded Internet access at schools and libraries. Between 1984 and 1994, the number of computers linked to the Internet rose from less than 1,000 to 6 million. In 2001, the total reached 400 million, including 130 million in the United States.

Digital technology spawned thousands of new businesses and products. In the 1970s, the success of Atari's *Pong*, a simulated table tennis game, inspired a thriving video gaming industry. Hit arcade games such as *Space Invaders* (1978) and *Pac-Man* (1980) were adapted for home computers and helped drive PC sales. Nintendo's Entertainment System (1987), Sony's PlayStation (1994), and Microsoft's X-Box (2001) made video gaming a multibillion-dollar, transnational industry drawing people together in both the real and virtual worlds.

The music industry changed dramatically in this era too. In the 1980s, digital compact discs (CDs) supplanted analog vinyl records and cassettes. At the same time, foreign-owned media conglomerates bought most U.S. record companies and began to dominate the production and distribution of music. To recoup the costs of mergers and acquisitions, these companies privileged homogenized, marketable music and artists often found that concert tours were their only means of earning money. In the 1990s, computer-formatted MP3 files that compress sound (primarily music) for digital transmission and storage began supplanting CD. In 1999, Shawn Fanning launched Napster, a peer-to-peer file-sharing program that allowed individuals to swap selections from their personal digital music collections. As Napster became the fastest-growing application in Internet history, the music industry sued Fanning for copyright infringement and forced the site's closure in 2001.

The digital revolution also transformed the film, television, camera, and telecommunications industries. With the introduction of the digital video disc (DVD) in 1997, sales of analog videocassettes and players began to decline. In 1990, the first digital cameras were marketed in the United States and led to major changes in how people took, processed, and shared photographs. The following year, the first digital cellular phones were sold commercially, and the number of cell phone subscribers increased from 12.4 million in 1990 to 1.2 billion in 2002, nearly 20 percent of the world's population.

The digital revolution contributed to tremendous growth in the U.S. economy for much of the 1990s. Corporations maximized profits through mergers, reduction of labor costs, and restructuring. The "New Economy" created thousands of jobs. Many entrepreneurs gravitated to the Internet, and national interest in "dot-coms" and "e-commerce" appeared boundless. Enthusiasm for technology stocks lifted the Dow Jones Industrial Average over eleven thousand, its highest rate ever, and spawned the NASDAQ, a stock exchange exclusively for technology shares. Productivity and incomes soared as unemployment and inflation remained low. But in March 2000, the dot-com bubble burst as investors began rejecting overvalued technology stocks. By October 2002, technology companies had lost $5 trillion in market value and many "dot-bombs" had failed, but many Internet-based businesses regrouped and became highly profitable.

The digital revolution had both positive and negative aspects. It became harder for totalitarian regimes to suppress information. Small businesses could reach huge markets. People had access to an astonishing array of entertainment, news, products, and services. Individuals and organizations could create and share information with a global audience at a negligible cost. But the sheer amount of information could be overwhelming, and the Internet created new ways for predators to find victims. Spreading

Seattle Police Pepper Spray Antiglobalization Protestors, 1999 In November 1999, during the World Trade Organization's ministerial conference in Seattle, Washington, approximately forty thousand antiglobalization protestors demonstrated in the streets. The participants included NGOs and local activists from a variety of political perspectives and causes. Some used nonviolent techniques to protest specific WTO policies or to advocate more broadly for labor rights or environmental protections. Others, many of them anarchists, tried to disrupt the meetings by blocking roads, disrupting proceedings, and destroying property. ▶

Christopher J. Morris/Corbis

cyber-espionage Use of computer networks to gain access to confidential information held by governments or corporations.

inaccurate or libelous material and entrapping people in financial scams became much easier, and digital communication could exacerbate social isolation. Fears arose about possible misuse of the vast amount of personal data being collected by governments and businesses. Businesses faced new threats of piracy, copyright infringement, hacking, and **cyber-espionage.** In 2000, a single computer virus resulted in $15 billion in damage in the United States alone after Filipino hackers released ILOVEYOU, a computer worm that infected more than 45 million Windows-based computers in only ten days. To protect their systems, the Pentagon, the CIA, the British Parliament, and most major corporations temporarily disabled their e-mail systems.

As the digital revolution transformed economic and cultural interactions, criticisms of the labor and environmental aspects of globalization intensified. In November 1999, antiglobalization protests at the WTO meeting in Seattle, Washington, drew international attention. Ironically, many of those demonstrators had used the Internet, itself a tool of globalization, to mobilize supporters. Approximately forty thousand people gathered in Seattle to stage a variety of mostly peaceful protests accusing the WTO of displacing local cultures, exploiting workers, and undermining environmental protection. But violent factions clashed with police who responded with tear gas and rubber bullets. By the time the WTO meeting had ended, Seattle had sustained more than $3 million in property damage. Similar demonstrations engulfed meetings of the World Bank and IMF held in Washington, D.C., and Genoa, Italy. To avoid more protests, IMF and World Bank delegates met in more isolated locations.

27-4c Americanization of Global Culture

> U.S. culture and products are welcomed, re-interpreted, and rejected abroad.

Globalization renewed debates over the "Americanization" of the world first voiced by the British journalist William Stead in 1901. But Stead, who died in the sinking of the *Titanic* in 1912, never lived to see how air travel, multinational corporations, and technology expanded the international reach of U.S. cultural power. Nor could he have predicted how foreign audiences would embrace, reject, and transform the avalanche of U.S. products and ideas they encountered.

Film and television became major vehicles for exposing foreign audiences to U.S. clothing, interior design, and verbal expressions. Hollywood films became hugely popular overseas and earned most of their profits in foreign markets. International broadcasts and distribution made U.S. television shows, such as *Baywatch* and *The Simpsons*, global hits. Foreign listeners bought millions of albums from American musicians including Michael Jackson and Madonna, and global tours by U.S. bands became commonplace. U.S.-based multinational companies such as Coca-Cola, McDonald's, Starbucks, and Apple opened outlets around the world.

Yet the increased visibility and presence of American cultural exports and businesses abroad did not equate to total U.S. control of global culture and commerce. In the 1970s, European and Japanese investments in the United States expanded and continued to rise. Two decades later, China began buying U.S. Treasury bonds and eventually became the world's largest holder of U.S. debt. In the 1990s, U.S. companies including Wal-Mart increased

McDonald's in Seoul, South Korea

In 1967, McDonald's opened its first two international franchises in British Columbia and Costa Rica. By 1996, when it opened a location in Belarus, it had expanded into one hundred countries. As a reflection of McDonald's international scope, *The Economist* magazine publishes an annual "Big Mac index" using the price of the famous hamburger as a light-hearted way to gauge the comparative purchasing power of global currencies. ▶

Chung Sung-Jun/Getty Images

Manny Millan/Getty Images

Global Americans **Michael Jordan** dominated the National Basketball Association (NBA) from the mid-1980s to the late 1990s. After three years playing for the University of North Carolina, he left school and was drafted by the Chicago Bulls. Jordan led them to six national championships, earning the NBA Most Valuable Player Award five times. In 1984 and 1992, he played on gold medal–winning U.S. Olympic basketball teams. In 1996, Jordan starred in *Space Jam*, a mixed live action and animation film that paired him with legendary cartoon characters Bugs Bunny and Daffy Duck.

Although basketball is not played in much of the world, Jordan's endorsements for Nike made him internationally famous. In 1984, the company offered him a five-year contract worth $500,000 annually plus royalties, an astonishing sum at the time. Largely because of sales of its Air Jordans—basketball shoes emblazoned with an iconic image of Jordan dunking a basketball—Nike's sales hit nearly $10 billion in the mid-1990s. Even though Jordan had retired from the NBA a decade earlier, the 2013 Air Jordan 10 Powder Blue retro sneaker generated $2.25 billion in U.S. sales alone, earning Jordan $90 million.

In the late 1990s, however, Nike and Jordan came under fire when activists exposed child labor, $2 daily wages, and physical abuse of workers among Nike's subcontractors in Asia. Facing boycotts and eager to protect its brand, Nike took steps to ensure more equitable conditions at its production facilities abroad. The same forces of globalization that made Nike and Jordan millions also created tools for activists to expose injustice.

importation of products from China. Companies like Nike and General Motors displaced U.S. workers by outsourcing production to subcontractors in Indonesia, Vietnam, and Mexico. India's Bollywood produced more films than Hollywood. Even in markets saturated with U.S. television programs and music, foreign audiences continued to watch locally produced shows and to support their own artists. Foreign opponents of Americanization objected when U.S. restaurants and advertising appeared in historic neighborhoods. In August 1999, a French sheep farmer became a folk hero when he bulldozed a McDonald's in protest of its "McDomination" of small agricultural producers and regionally distinctive cuisines.

Rather than unilaterally impose their goods and practices on foreign markets, U.S. companies adjusted to local mores, tastes, competition, and criticism. McDonald's, for example, modified its menu for specific countries. In Germany, its restaurants sell beer. In Japan, it offers a shrimp burger. In predominately Hindu India, it does not serve beef. As digital technologies transformed the media, U.S. news outlets faced new competitors such as Al Jareeza, an Arabic current affairs satellite network launched in Qatar in 1996. In the late 1990s, under fierce international criticism for the working conditions and low pay at facilities of its foreign subcontractors, Nike created the Fair Labor Association, an international collaboration of corporations and human rights activists devoted to ensuring safe working conditions and equitable pay for laborers around the world. Some observers claim that the United States is uniquely suited to tailor its products, services, and entertainment to diverse audiences because of its own multicultural society. "In the end, American mass culture has not transformed the world into a replica of the United States," notes cultural historian Richard Pells, "Instead, America's dependence on foreign cultures has made the United States a replica of the world."

Summary

The election of 1988 signaled the rise of a more negative style of political campaigning. The victorious candidate, George H.W. Bush made tough, politically costly fiscal choices. While trying to advance civil rights and environmental protections at home, he responded cautiously to a tense international landscape. But Bush failed to translate his foreign policy achievements into a successful 1992 reelection bid.

Changes in immigration law and birth patterns made the United States a more populated and ethnically diverse nation. As medical advances prolonged life, people over age sixty-five composed an increasing percentage of the total population. The rapidly rising global population generated concerns about the limits of natural resources and governments' ability to meet basic needs for burgeoning and diversifying populaces.

Although Clinton helped to usher in one of the greatest periods of economic growth in U.S. history, his efforts to institute national health insurance triggered a conservative backlash that enabled the Republicans to win control of Congress. Clinton outmaneuvered his rivals by adopting more moderate positions on issues such as welfare reform, but scandal and a failed impeachment attempt plagued his second term. At the same time, U.S. policy makers adjusted to the complexities of an increasingly unstable global environment. The presidential elections of 2000 highlighted how polarized Americans had become.

Technological and communications innovations significantly increased the ways that people could connect across national boundaries. Nonstate actors played a larger role in humanitarian relief, human rights, disarmament, and environmental protection. Multinational corporations maximized profits by expanding their operations into countries with lower labor and production costs but met controversy when such efforts displaced U.S. workers, exploited foreign workers, or harmed the environment.

The digital revolution transformed daily life. People could create and share information globally, a trend that frightened totalitarian governments, aided social justice advocates, and greatly altered journalism and entertainment. The rise of the Internet not only generated astounding opportunities for business innovation but also created new opportunities for criminals to find victims and for governments and corporations to intrude on private lives.

Globalization compounded and complicated long-standing fears about the ubiquity of American culture and products abroad. Although foreigners undoubtedly embraced U.S. goods, services, and entertainment, they did not reject their local cultures and proved that not even a country as diverse as the United States could supplant individuals' cultural and national identities.

<Thinking Back, *Looking Forward*>

As you review this chapter, compare post-1965 migration patterns to previous waves of immigration in U.S. history. How and why did the composition of the U.S. population change, and what were the political consequences? How did globalization and technology affect communications, commerce, and culture? In the last chapter, pay attention to how globalization and technology have influenced and accelerated developments with deep historical roots: terrorism and income inequality.

To make your study concrete, review the timeline and reflect on the entries there. Think about their causes, consequences, and connections. How do they fit with global trends?

Additional Resources

Books

Boys, James D. *Clinton's Grand Strategy: US Foreign Policy in a Post-Cold War World.* **London, U.K.: Bloomsbury Academic, 2015.** ▶ Assessment of key ideas, individuals, and events shaping U.S. strategies.

Briggs, Laura. *Somebody's Children: The Politics of Transracial and Transnational Adoption.* **Durham, NC: Duke University Press, 2012.** ▶ Examination of transnational adoption in the United States since 1945.

Connelly, Matthew. *Fatal Misconception: The Struggle to Control World Population.* **Cambridge, MA: Belknap Press, 2008.** ▶ Multinational, archival history of population control programs.

Harris, John F. *The Survivor: Bill Clinton in the White House.* **New York: Random House, 2006.** ▶ Political reporter's account of the Clinton presidency.

Harrison, Colin. *American Culture in the 1990s.* **Edinburgh, UK: Edinburgh University Press, 2010.** ▶ Synthesis that places major cultural trends of the decade into historical context.

Iriye, Akira. *Global Interdependence: The World after 1945.* **Cambridge, MA: Belknap Press, 2014.** ▶ Massive collection on international, environmental, cultural, political, and economic trends.

Isaacson, Walter. *The Innovators: How a Group of Hackers, Geniuses, and Geeks Created the Digital Revolution.* New York: Simon and Schuster, 2014. ► Bestselling author traces the evolution of computers and the Internet.

Meacham, Jon. *Destiny and Power: The American Odyssey of George Herbert Walker Bush.* New York: Random House, 2015. ► Pulitzer Prize–winning author's biography based on extensive interviews and archival sources.

Pells, Richard. *Not Like Us: How Europeans Have Loved, Hated, and Transformed American Culture since World War II.* New York: Basic Books, 1997. ► Entertaining and persuasive history of U.S. cultural transmission and reception.

Thompson, Graham. *American Culture in the 1980s.* Edinburgh, UK: Edinburgh University Press, 2007. ► Overview of the decade's films, television programs, art, music, and literature.

Go to the MindTap® for **Global Americans** to access the full version of select books from this Additional Resources section.

Websites

Computer History Museum. http://www .computerhistory.org/ ► Exhibits, archival materials, and teaching resources on the history of computing and the Digital Revolution.

George Bush Presidential Library and Museum. http:// bush41.org/ ► Extensive collection of teaching resources and textual, audio, video, and photographic primary sources related to George H.W. Bush.

PBS *American Experience*: "The Presidents." http:// www.pbs.org/wgbh/americanexperience/collections/ presidents/ ► Excellent documentaries on George H.W. Bush and Bill Clinton plus teaching resources.

PBS *Frontline:* "The Gulf War." http://www.pbs.org/ wgbh/pages/frontline/gulf/ ► Collection of oral histories, video clips, and teaching resources.

William J. Clinton Presidential Library and Museum. http://www.clintonlibrary.gov/ ► Research and teaching materials on Clinton's presidency and postpresidential activities.

Continue exploring online through MindTap®**, where you can:**
- **Assess your knowledge with the Chapter Test**
- **Watch historical videos related to the chapter**
- **Further your understanding with interactive maps and timelines**

Closer Together, Further Apart

1989

January
George H.W. Bush is inaugurated as president.

March
Exxon Valdez oil spill occurs in Prince William Sound, Alaska.

June
Chinese authorities crush pro-democracy protests in Beijing.

December
The Simpsons debuts on FOX television.

Romanian dictator Nicolae Ceausescu and his wife are executed.

1990

February
Sandinistas lose free elections in Nicaragua, coalition government takes power.

May
Latvia declares independence from the Soviet Union.

June
President Bush accepts tax increases in budget deficit reduction plan.

August
Iraq invades Kuwait.

October
Germany reunites.

1991

February
UN coalition forces oust Iraq from Kuwait.

August
World Wide Web is publicly launched.

October
Clarence Thomas wins confirmation as Supreme Court justice.

December
Soviet Union dissolves, Cold War ends.

1992

April–May
Riots in Los Angeles result in more than fifty deaths.

November
Bill Clinton wins 1992 presidential race.

1993

February
Terrorist bombing at the World Trade Center kills six, injures thousands.

April
Stand-off ends between federal agents and Branch Davidians in Waco, Texas, and eighty-six people perish.

June
Clinton accepts "Don't ask, don't tell" compromise.

1994	1995	1998	1999	2000
January North American Free Trade Agreement goes into effect.	**March** Religious terrorists launch sarin attacks on Tokyo railway.	**January** Hillary Clinton denounces "vast right-wing conspiracy" against her husband.	**February** Clinton is acquitted in impeachment proceedings.	**May** ILOVEYOU virus causes Internet havoc, costing millions to repair.

1994

January

North American Free Trade Agreement goes into effect.

April

Nelson Mandela is elected president of South Africa.

April–July

Genocide occurs in Rwanda.

November

Republicans win control of both chambers of Congress.

1995

March

Religious terrorists launch sarin attacks on Tokyo railway.

April

Terrorist bombing of federal building in Oklahoma City kills one hundred sixty-eight people.

July

Bosnian Serbs massacre 8,000 Muslim men and boys in Srebrenica.

September

Online auction site eBay is launched.

October

Former NFL star O.J. Simpson is acquitted of murder, millions watch verdict.

December

Dayton Agreement ends more than three years of war in Bosnia.

1998

January

Hillary Clinton denounces "vast right-wing conspiracy" against her husband.

July

In Rome, 120 countries vote to create permanent International Criminal Court.

August

Al-Qaeda operatives bomb U.S. embassies in Kenya and Tanzania.

September

Larry Page and Sergey Brin, Stanford PhD students, found Google.

September

Kenneth Starr issues his report.

October

Gay college student Matthew Shepard is tortured and killed near Laramie, Wyoming.

1999

February

Clinton is acquitted in impeachment proceedings.

October

World population reaches 6 billion, up from 4 billion in 1974.

2000

May

ILOVEYOU virus causes Internet havoc, costing millions to repair.

October

U.S.S. Cole is bombed while in port in Yemen.

December

George W. Bush is declared winner of disputed U.S. presidential election.

28

Global Americans Today

2000–2016

Young religious seeker John Walker Lindh left home to become an Islamic scholar, and in the fall of 2000 made the fateful decision to venture into Afghanistan to join the Taliban.

I n December 2001, John Walker Lindh returned to the United States, the country where he was born and held citizenship but no longer considered home. The American public received the twenty-one-year-old with scorn and disbelief: How could a young, white man from an affluent suburb take up arms against U.S.-backed allies in Afghanistan? Pundits condemned his supposedly overly permissive "hippie" parents for encouraging their son's journey into the Islamic faith, which led him to study Arabic in Yemen and to fight for the Taliban in Afghanistan. Upon closer look, however, Lindh's route to becoming the "American Taliban" was more complex than it seemed.

AP Images

A brainy and sickly kid who repeatedly changed schools and eventually studied at home with a tutor, he had a difficult childhood and adolescence. After seeing a popular feature film about the radical black nationalist Malcolm X, he began to study Muslim websites and converted to Islam at age sixteen. His newfound spirituality pleased his parents because, in their eyes, he had finally found a community where he belonged—and a wholesome one with strictures against alcohol and drugs. After Lindh completed high school, he studied in Yemen, fulfilling his dream of becoming an Islamic scholar.

The young religious seeker, however, grew frustrated with education in Yemen, where classes welcomed women and classmates repeatedly violated Islamic protocols. He kept searching for more orthodox religious training, a quest that brought him to a village in Pakistan where he memorized one-third of the Muslim holy book, the Koran. In the fall of 2000, Lindh made the fateful decision to venture into nearby Afghanistan to join its government (the Taliban) in fighting against an internal rebellion by the Northern Alliance. In November 2001, U.S. forces seeking revenge on the Taliban for sheltering the terrorists responsible for the September 11, 2001 attacks, captured Lindh. Filthy and wounded, Lindh insisted he had joined the Taliban for religious reasons, not to harm Americans, a fact that later made it possible for him to avoid conviction for treason. He accepted a plea bargain in which the U.S. government charged him with the lesser offense of "supplying services to the Taliban." In exchange, Lindh dropped charges that he had been tortured while in U.S. custody. He was sentenced to twenty years in prison and remains a devout Muslim.

His odyssey from suburban misfit to "American Taliban" revealed the changing historical circumstances that empowered and confounded Americans in the early twenty-first century. With the Cold War's end, the United States and its allies confronted religious and ethnic tensions, economic shifts, and environmental challenges. On September 11, 2001, al-Qaeda

> How does John Walker Lindh's odyssey from suburban misfit to "American Taliban" reveal the changing historical circumstances that empowered and confounded Americans in the early twenty-first century?
> Go to MindTap® to watch a video on Lindh and learn how his story relates to the themes of this chapter.

attacked the United States, killing over three thousand people and demonstrating the threat to global security posed by radical Islamic terrorism. The attack shocked the entire world and transformed the presidency of newly elected George W. Bush, son of former President George H.W. Bush.

The 9/11 attacks and the aftermath occurred in an era of broad economic and technological changes that enabled Lindh, an isolated young man, to join a virtual community sharing his religious views. With unprecedented speed, the Internet became the greatest connector of, and resource for, humans around the world. It was the centerpiece of an information and communication revolution that altered the structure of the global economy, which had expanded to include 30 million people in China, India, Russia, and other nations formerly closed to trade during the Cold War. More people than ever were linked in a single global trading network, but not everyone benefited equally. As with the industrial revolution in the late nineteenth century and the postindustrial revolution after World War II, the new global economy exacerbated social divisions between rich and poor. The rapid industrialization of China and other developing countries due to globalization also contributed to climate changes with the potential to wreak worldwide environmental and human destruction.

With the expansion of the global economy came an accompanying economic downturn in 2007. The United States and the world plunged into recession, the deepest since the Great Depression of the 1930s. Risky financial products and practices, deregulation, and a collapse of the housing market threw both the U.S. and global economies into turmoil. During this crisis, Barack Obama was elected as the first African American president in an era of highly polarized domestic politics. In the early twenty-first century, the United States was more connected to the world than ever but also an extremely divided society.

28-1
National Security and the Global Order

On the first anniversary of 9/11, David Horsey, an editorial cartoonist for the *Seattle Post-Intelligencer*, portrays the impact of the terrorist attacks on Americans.

How does the cartoonist contrast U.S. society before and after the 9/11 attacks? What are some of the ways he suggests that the United States changed in the year following the assaults? ▶

Go to MindTap® to practice history with the Chapter 28 **Primary Source Writing Activity: War on Terrorism**. Read and view primary sources and respond to a writing prompt.

Seattle Post Intelligencer

After his contested victory in the 2000 presidential election, George W. Bush took office intending to focus on domestic affairs. But after over three thousand people died in orchestrated terrorist attacks on the United States on September 11, 2001, Bush shifted his attention to foreign policy and built a multinational coalition to wage what he dubbed the "War on Terror." In the fall of 2001, U.S. and British forces invaded Afghanistan in pursuit of the Islamic radicals responsible for the 9/11 attacks. In March 2003, the Bush administration mobilized international support for a controversial invasion of Iraq followed by a protracted process of pacification and reconstruction.

Upon winning the presidency in 2008, Obama vowed to withdraw U.S. troops from the unpopular war in Iraq, to expand military operations in Afghanistan, and to continue the global war on terrorism. When a wave of mass protests swept much of the Arab world in early 2011, it appeared that democracy might supplant authoritarianism there. But devastating civil wars in Libya and Syria and a powerful new radical Islamic insurgency soon dimmed those hopes.

☞ As you read, consider how and why the 9/11 attacks changed U.S. foreign policy and American daily life. Has the United States prevailed in the fight against terrorism? Explain your answers.

28-1a 9/11 and War on Terrorism

After his inauguration in January 2001, President Bush began limiting U.S. commitments abroad. At the UN, he refused to grant the International Criminal Court jurisdiction over U.S. soldiers accused of violating international law while participating in multinational peacekeeping operations. Most controversially, Bush abandoned ratification of the Kyoto Protocol, an international treaty signed by one hundred eighty nations to reduce global warming by setting limits on industrial emissions. Accustomed to a more collaborative approach to international affairs, such moves alarmed domestic critics and foreign allies.

> The 9/11 attacks on the United States reorder global diplomatic relations.

September 11, 2001 changed the global landscape. That morning, four commercial jets departed from East Coast cities. Shortly after each reached cruising altitude, hijackers killed or disabled the pilots and steered the planes toward their intended targets. At 8:48 a.m., the first— American Airlines flight 11 from Boston— hit the North Tower of New York's World Trade Center. At 9:03 a.m., United flight 175, which also departed from Boston, struck the South Tower. Less than two hours later, both one hundred ten-story buildings collapsed. At 9:37 a.m., American 77, scheduled to travel from Dulles International Airport to Los Angeles, collided into the south wall of the Pentagon. At 10:03 a.m., passengers aboard United flight 93, who had received word of the other three hijackings shortly after taking off from Newark, almost overpowered their attackers before the hijackers crashed the plane in a field outside Shanksville, Pennsylvania, thwarting another planned assault on the nation's capital. All 246 people aboard the planes perished. Another 2,753 died at the World Trade Center, including 343 firefighters and 72 law enforcement officers among the first responders to the attacks. Another 184 died at the Pentagon. Citizens of more than eighty nations were among the casualties of 9/11.

Globally, millions watched these events unfold on live television. For weeks afterward, news stations repeatedly

Sergey Komarov-Kohl/Alamy Stock Photo

Thomas Franklin, *Flag-Raising at Ground Zero*, September 11, 2001 Thomas Franklin's photograph of firefighters Dan McWilliams, George Johnson, and Billy Eisengrein raising the U.S. flag over the rubble of the World Trade Towers became a symbol of hope and heroism on a day of horrific violence. First responders and cleanup crews worked at the site for five months following the 9/11 attacks. Many later experienced serious health complications as a result of exposure to highly toxic dust. ▲

showed footage of the explosions, people jumping to their deaths to escape flames and smoke, and the Towers' collapse. Commentators interviewed anguished family members seeking answers about the fate of their loved ones and hailed the courage of police officers and firefighters helping with rescue efforts. Swept up in a wave of patriotism, Americans rushed to buy flags, give blood, enlist in the armed forces, and volunteer for relief organizations. U.S. charities received $1 billion in donations. Vigils for the victims were held all over the world.

Within days, the nineteen Saudi hijackers were identified and linked to Osama bin Laden, the fundamentalist Muslim leader of the al-Qaeda terrorist network. Many of the hijackers had lived and worked in the United States for years, blending in inconspicuously while awaiting directives from al-Qaeda. A few took flying lessons from U.S. schools, requesting instruction on flying large planes but expressing no interest in mastering takeoffs or landings—demands their teachers found puzzling. Al-Qaeda chose its targets precisely, aiming for maximum symbolism and physical damage to centers of U.S. finance, militarism, and politics. In the weeks immediately preceding 9/11, CIA director George Tenet and other counterterrorism experts presented evidence of an al-Qaeda plot to use commercial aircraft as missiles, but neither President Bush nor National Security

Richard Drew, *The Falling Man*, September 11, 2011
At 9:41 a.m. on 9/11, Associated Press photographer Richard Drew took twelve shots of a man falling from the North Tower of the World Trade Center, one of an estimated two hundred people who either fell or jumped from the upper floors to escape smoke and flames. When Drew's image appeared in newspapers around the world, it prompted a huge outcry and was pulled from circulation. The falling man's identity has never been confirmed. ▲

Taliban Political movement in Afghanistan based in Islamic fundamentalism and a strict obedience to Islamic law (*Sharia*) that is particularly restrictive for women and girls.

drone attacks Missile strikes by unmanned, remote controlled aircraft used in risky areas of combat for surveillance and attack.

enemy combatants Detainees, mainly from al-Qaeda or the Taliban held by the United States who were not subject to international rules governing prisoners of war.

USA Patriot Act U.S. counterterrorism legislation enhancing government surveillance, antimoney-laundering policies, border security, and information sharing among federal agencies and between the United States and other nations.

Advisor Condoleezza Rice gave the briefings much credence.

But after the attacks, the Bush administration reacted decisively. The president vowed to capture bin Laden "dead or alive" and warned nations of dire consequences if they assisted terrorists. To explain what motivated the attackers, Bush posed the question "Why do they hate us?" and answered "They hate our freedoms: our freedom of religion, our freedom of speech, our freedom to vote and assemble and disagree with each other." The president described Islam as a peaceful religion that forbids the killing of innocents and condemns suicide, but some Americans found it difficult to distinguish nonviolent Muslims from Islamic radicals who called for a holy war, *jihad*, against the United States. Although critics called the president's rhetoric jingoistic, his popular approval ratings soared to 90 percent.

Bush demanded that the **Taliban**, the Islamist regime ruling Afghanistan, surrender bin Laden, who ran al-Qaeda training camps there. In October 2001, after the Taliban refused to comply, U.S. and U.K. pilots began bombing Afghanistan. With the assistance of anti-Taliban forces, U.S. ground troops gained control of Afghan cities and captured John Walker Lindh, an American fighting with the Taliban. In early December, the Taliban collapsed, but bin Laden, likely with the aid of allies in Pakistani intelligence, escaped. In 2003, a coalition force representing forty-seven nations began battling a Taliban insurgency. Although vastly outnumbered and outgunned, the Taliban fought back to regain influence in rural areas. Fighting soon spilled over into neighboring Pakistan where the Pakistani Army clashed with local tribes who aided Taliban and al-Qaeda rebels. In response, the United States launched unmanned **drone attacks** on enemies in Pakistan. Afghani civilians struggled as reconstruction efforts faltered.

While waging war in Afghanistan, U.S. soldiers and intelligence operatives backed by a multinational coalition pursued al-Qaeda across the globe. By 2003, more than 2,700 suspected terrorists in 98 countries had been abducted or killed. Because captives were not seized during an officially declared war against any nation's armed forces, the Bush administration made the controversial decision to characterize them as **enemy combatants** who were not protected by either the U.S. Constitution or the Geneva Conventions. Seven hundred and seventy-five alleged terrorists, 420 of whom were eventually released without charge, were sent to a newly created U.S. prison camp at Guantánamo Bay, Cuba. Bin Laden, however, remained at large.

At home, the war on terror produced tremendous changes (see Table 28.1). Expanded security procedures transformed air travel and the postal service. Enacted in October 2001, the **USA Patriot Act** granted law enforcement officials sweeping new powers to detain and deport suspected terrorists, to use wiretapping and other surveillance tools on U.S. citizens, and to conduct searches without warrants. In November 2002, Congress approved the **Department of Homeland Security**, a consolidation of twenty-two federal agencies charged with responding to terrorism, man-made accidents, and natural disasters.

28-1b War in Iraq

In the aftermath of 9/11, the Bush administration reshaped U.S. foreign policy. Abandoning Cold War-era policies of collective security and deterrence, President Bush and his aides developed a doctrine of preemptive self-defense in which the United States used overwhelming military superiority to defend itself against emerging as well as imminent threats. In place of permanent regional alliances, the **Bush Doctrine** called for

> The Bush administration launches a controversial war in Iraq.

Table 28.1 Selected Global Terrorist Attacks, 1972–2015

Originating in the term *terrorisme* used to describe violence practiced by the French government during the 1793–1794 Reign of Terror, *terrorism* refers to acts perpetrated by states or nonstate groups that harm and frighten civilians or non-combatants in order to further ideological, racial, ethnic, religious, political, or nationalistic goals. This chart documents many of the varied terrorist acts that have occurred globally since 1972.

Date	Location	Description
July 1972	Belfast, Ireland	Irish Republican Army attacked British government and citizens, killing 11 and injuring 130 on "Bloody Friday"
September 1972	Munich, Germany	12 Israeli athletes killed by Black September (Palestinian group) at the Olympic Games
April 1983	Beirut, Lebanon	Islamic Jihad bombed U.S. embassy, killing 63 and injuring 120
October 1983	Beirut, Lebanon	Islamic Jihad attacked French and U.S. embassies, killing 301 and injuring 161
December 1988	Lockerbie, Scotland	Libyan government agents bombed, in mid-air, Pam-Am flight, killing 270 and injuring 12
February 1993	New York, NY	Islamic terror cell used truck bomb to attack World Trade Center, killing 6 and injuring 1,040
March 1993	Mumbai (Bombay), India	Dawood Ibrahim implemented 15 simultaneous bombings, killing 317 and injuring 1,400
March 1995	Tokyo, Japan	Aum Shinrikyo attacked subway with sarin nerve gas, killing 12 and injuring 5,511
April 1995	Oklahoma City, OK	Timothy McVeigh bombed a federal building, killing 169 and injuring 675
June 1996	Dhahran, Saudi Arabia	Hezbollah bombed U.S. military base, killing 18 and injuring 515
August 1998	Nairobi, Kenya and Dar es Salaam, Tanzania	Al-Qaeda bombed U.S embassies, killing 244 and injuring 4,877
September 2001	Washington, DC; New York, NY; Shanksville, PA	Al-Qaeda attacked U.S., killing 2,993 and injuring 8,900
October 2002	Moscow, Russia	Chechen separatists attack and take hostages, killing 170 and injuring 656
March 2004	Madrid, Spain	Al-Qaeda bombs 4 trains, killing 191 and injuring 1,876
September 2004	Beslan, Russia	Chechen separatists attack and take hostages at a school, killing 372 and injuring 747
July 2005	London, England	Islamic extremists bomb 3 subways and a bus, killing 56 and inuring 784
July 2006	Mumbai (Bombay), India	Lashkar-e-Taiba bombs 7 commuter trains, killing 209 and injuring 714
January 2012	Kano, Nigeria	Boko Haram attacks multiple sites, killing 178 and injuring 50
April 2015	Garissa, Kenya	Al-Shabaab attacks college campus, killing 152 and injuring 79

Sources: http://fas.org/irp/threat/terror_chron.html; http://www.johnstonsarchive.net/terrorism/wrjp255i.html

selective cooperation with foreign allies while emphasizing U.S. willingness to act unilaterally to build democratic states. In January 2002, Bush reiterated his intention to punish nations who sponsored terrorism, singling out Iran, Iraq, and North Korea as an "axis of evil, arming to threaten the peace of the world. " Many people around the world who had expressed solidarity with the United States on 9/11 now criticized Bush's unapologetic embrace of unilateral action.

Iraq soon became the test case for the new doctrine. Accusing Iraqi dictator Saddam Hussein of secretly possessing **weapons of mass destruction (WMD)** and having ties to al-Qaeda, Bush called for "regime change" and demanded that Iraq allow UN weapons inspections for the first time since 1998. While fending off more hawkish members of the Bush administration calling for a U.S. invasion of Iraq, Secretary of State Colin Powell tried to build a UN coalition. In October 2002, persuaded by Bush's claims that Saddam was attempting to acquire fissile materials to build nuclear weapons, the

Department of Homeland Security Executive department resulting from the merger of twenty-two federal agencies to better coordinate the U.S. government's counterterrorism programs.

Bush Doctrine Foreign policy paradigm calling for the United States to act alone (unilaterally) in striking against threats outside its borders.

weapons of mass destruction (WMD) Nuclear, chemical, biological, or other type of weapons that can kill or bring great harm to a large number of human beings.

Operation Iraqi Freedom Name given by George H. Bush to U.S. war in Iraq to remove Saddam Hussein from power and to capture his reported arsenal of weapons of mass destruction.

Republican-led House voted two hundred ninety-six to one hundred thirty-three, and the Democrat-led Senate voted seventy-seven to twenty-three to grant Bush authorization to use force in Iraq. British Prime Minister Tony Blair, alone among America's closest allies, endorsed Bush's call for Saddam's ouster. Although the UN redeployed inspectors to Iraq, they failed to find stores of biological, chemical, or nuclear weapons. At Bush's insistence, Powell—despite his reservations about the intelligence being used to justify U.S. intervention—then made the case for war at the Security Council. On February 15, 2003, more than 10 million people participated in antiwar demonstrations in six hundred cities around the world, the largest peace demonstrations ever. Later that month, the UN defeated the war resolution by a large margin. Undaunted, Bush prepared to attack Iraq.

On March 20, 2003, **Operation Iraqi Freedom** began with U.S. airstrikes on Baghdad, and two hundred forty thousand U.S. and U.K. ground troops invading Iraq (see Map 28.1). Within five weeks, the Saddam regime collapsed and coalition forces controlled Iraq. Saddam himself eluded capture until December, when U.S. commandos

President George W. Bush on the U.S.S. *Abraham Lincoln*, May 1, 2003 On May 1, 2003, Bush, a former pilot in the Air National Guard, landed a fighter on the aircraft carrier USS *Abraham Lincoln*. Standing before a banner reading "Mission Accomplished," Bush announced that major combat operations in Iraq were over and vowed to continue the search for banned weapons there. To critics of the war, the banner later symbolized the flawed assumptions the Bush administration made about Iraq before the invasion and during the occupation. ▲

STEPHEN JAFFE/AFP/Getty Images

Map 28.1 Iraq in Transition, 2003–2008 This map details the trajectory of the initial U.S.-led invasion of Iraq and sites of subsequent battles between U.S. forces and Iraqi insurgents. Ethnic and religious factionalism greatly complicated U.S. efforts to unite and rebuild Iraq. ◄

AP Images/Tulsa World

Global Americans Born near Miami, Oklahoma, in 1970, **Fern Holland** graduated from the University of Oklahoma and then volunteered in children's hospitals in South Africa and Russia. In 1999, three years after finishing law school at the University of Tulsa, she left her law practice and joined the Peace Corps to work in Namibia as an HIV/AIDS educator. Returning to the United States after 9/11, she entered the LLM program at Georgetown Law Center and developed a program to train journalists, lawyers, and judges in Africa. But she interrupted her studies to aid victims of sexual exploitation in Guinea.

In July 2003, Holland was hired by the U.S. Agency for International Development (USAID) to investigate human rights abuses under the Saddam Hussein regime. She then joined the Coalition Provisional Authority to help Iraqis establish democracy. Determined to help women in a society that had rendered them powerless, Holland instituted centers where Iraqi women learned about representative government, drafted portions of the Iraqi interim constitution that protected women's rights, and demanded that women hold one-quarter of the seats in the National Assembly.

On March 9, 2004, on the road between Karbala and Al Hillah, Holland, her Iraqi counterpart, Salwa Ali Oushami, and CPA press liaison Robert Zangas were assassinated by insurgents. Holland and Zangas were the first U.S. civilians to die in the Iraq War. She exemplified the millions of aid workers and ordinary citizens who believe that democracy can supplant autocracy in the Middle East.

captured him. Three years later, he was executed after an Iraqi tribunal found him guilty of crimes against humanity.

The process of democratizing and rebuilding a shattered Iraq proved challenging and costly. Contrary to Vice President Richard "Dick" Cheney's assertion that U.S. forces would be "greeted as liberators," many Iraqis harbored great bitterness about prior U.S. support of Saddam's dictatorial regime. Jettisoning plans for a brief occupation and quick transfer of power to a provisional government led by Iraqi exiles, Bush created the U.S-led Coalition Provisional Authority (CPA). In the United States, many Americans remained skeptical about Bush's rationale for intervention, and support for the war in the world community eroded as investigators found no evidence that Iraq possessed WMD, had attempted to acquire unenriched uranium to build nuclear weapons, or collaborated with the 9/11 attackers.

The situation in Iraq deteriorated. U.S. soldiers faced suicide bombers and **improvised explosive devices (IEDs)**. Many troops, including those in the Reserves and National Guard, endured multiple tours of duty and mounting casualties. Repeated deployments added hardships for military families separated for months at a time and increased the likelihood of soldiers experiencing post-traumatic stress disorder (PTSD).

By 2007, almost 2 million Iraqis were displaced by violence and became refugees. Sabotage, unemployment, corruption, and outdated infrastructure undermined efforts to jump-start the Iraqi economy. Factionalism between Shi'ite (Shi'a) and **Sunni** Muslims and Kurdish demands for independence complicated efforts to create a stable Iraqi government.

In April 2004, tensions in Iraq heightened after CBS News broadcast graphic photographs of U.S. soldiers abusing Iraqis held in **Abu Ghraib** prison, sparking widespread condemnation of some of the Bush administration's policies in the war on terror. The International Red Cross and Amnesty International challenged U.S. officials' claims that the incidents at Abu Ghraib were an aberration and pointed to a broader pattern of brutality at U.S. overseas detention centers in Iraq, Afghanistan, and Guantánamo Bay. In late 2004, after the release of memos detailing the administration's approval of "enhanced interrogation techniques" like prolonged sleep deprivation, restraining prisoners in positions that maximized physical discomfort, and using waterboarding to simulate drowning, a debate over the efficacy and morality of such tactics arose. These discussions intensified when the media reported on secret CIA prisons and the agency's use of **extraordinary renditions** where "high-value detainees" were shipped to nations that subjected them to torture, a practice intended to distance the Bush administration from human rights abuses. In *Hamdan v. Rumsfeld* (2006) and other cases, the U.S. Supreme Court rejected the administration's characterization of the prisoners at Guantánamo as enemy combatants and ruled that the detainees there were fully protected by the Constitution and the Geneva Conventions. While critics claimed that the U.S. tactics in the war on terrorism were exacerbating anti-Americanism and Islamist radicalism, supporters argued that extreme measures were

improvised explosive devices (IEDs) Bombs made and deployed in nonstandard ways for military combat, linked to over 50 percent of deaths among U.S. and allied forces during the Iraq War.

Sunni Largest of two major branches of Islam, Sunnis contend that the Muslim community was to select the Prophet's successor (caliph), whereas Shi'a believe the Prophet chose his his son-in-law, Ali, as his successor.

Abu Ghraib Jail located west of Baghdad used by U.S. forces and their allies during the Iraq War to hold military captives and political enemies.

extraordinary renditions Covert abduction of persons for the purpose of torture that is conducted in countries that permit such human rights abuse.

Courtesy Wikipedia/ZUMA Press/Newscom

Prisoner at Abu Ghraib, 2003 A hooded prisoner at Abu Ghraib stands on a box with electrical wires used to shock him attached to his hands. Investigations revealed widespread human rights violations including physical and sexual abuse, torture, rape, sodomy, and murder. Eleven U.S. soldiers were court-martialed and dishonorably discharged for dereliction of duty, mistreatment, and aggravated assault and battery. Specialists Charles Graner and Lynndie England were sentenced to imprisonment for ten and three years, respectively. ▲

merited in obtaining information about those who engaged in terrorist activities.

Despite these controversies, Bush narrowly defeated Democratic nominee John Kerry in the 2004 presidential election, and democratization efforts in Iraq continued. In January 2005, six months after the CPA ended its formal occupation, Iraq had its first free elections in fifty years and voters adopted a new constitution soon after. But the elections did not stem the insurgency, which grew increasingly sectarian during 2005 and witnessed Sunni insurgents targeting Shi'ite and Kurdish civilians in suicide bombings. One hundred thirty thousand U.S. troops remained in Iraq, and costs of the war soared to $5 billion per month. In November 2006, with Bush's approval ratings below 40 percent, the Democrats regained control of both houses of Congress.

In January 2007, responding to mounting criticism of the war effort and the fragile Iraqi political situation, Bush announced a new multinational "surge" of thirty thousand additional advisers and trainers to help the Iraqis. In December 2008, Bush and Iraqi prime minister Nouri al-Maliki agreed on a December 31, 2011, deadline for the complete withdrawal of U.S. combat forces.

The war in Iraq was only part of the expansion of U.S. defense and intelligence capabilities. To confront global terrorists and the regimes that supported them, the Pentagon constructed a string of new military facilities in the Middle East, Central Asia, and Africa. U.S. defense spending rose from $304 billion in 2001 to $696 billion in 2008—far more than any other nation in the world. As it had done since initiating the Marshall Plan, the United States promoted economic development and political stability by expanding the U.S. foreign aid budget from $13 billion in 2000 to $34 billion in 2008. In 2003, similar motives inspired Bush to create the President's Emergency Plan for AIDS Relief (PEPFAR), a $15 billion campaign to combat HIV/AIDS in selected developing nations, the largest commitment ever by a nation to fight a single disease.

28-1c U.S. Troops Leave Iraq and Afghanistan

After defeating Senator John McCain in the 2008 presidential election, Obama, a biracial American and self-described "citizen of the world" with a Kenyan father and a white American mother, promised a less confrontational approach to international affairs. In June 2009, Obama gave a speech in Cairo calling for "a new beginning between the United States and Muslims around the world, one based upon mutual interest and mutual respect."

> The Obama administration withdraws U.S. forces from Iraq and Afghanistan but continues war on terrorism.

The Obama administration used a mix of military power and diplomacy. He pursued nuclear nonproliferation agreements with Iran and North Korea. In 2010, he signed a major nuclear arms reduction treaty with Russia, but U.S.–Russian relations soon deteriorated over crises in Georgia and Ukraine. In pursuit of al-Qaeda and its affiliates, Obama increased counterinsurgency aid to the Pakistani government and escalated the use of drones in Pakistan, Yemen, and Somalia. From 2009 to 2015, an estimated 2,464 people, including more than 300 noncombatants and four American aid workers, were killed in U.S. drone strikes, more than nine times the drone casualties of the Bush era.

Facing an intensifying insurgency in Afghanistan, Obama escalated the war (see Map 28.2). Bolstered by a "surge" of thirty thousand additional U.S. troops, coalition forces captured and killed hundreds of Taliban. In May 2011, Obama scored a political and military victory when U.S. Navy SEALs found Osama bin Laden in a compound in Abbottabad, Pakistan. The result of months of careful intelligence analysis and planning, the raid resulted in bin Laden's death and seizure of valuable al-Qaeda materials. In June 2013, the United States and Afghanistan signed a bilateral security agreement, and

Map 28.2 War in Afghanistan, 2001–2014 After U.S. and British troops invaded Afghanistan in October 2001 to punish the Taliban for harboring terrorists and to capture those responsible for 9/11, they ousted the Taliban quickly. But it proved quite difficult to stabilize and reconstruct Afghanistan. Multinational forces battled a Taliban insurgency that soon spread into neighboring Pakistan. After U.S. commandos killed Osama bin Laden in May 2011, the United States and NATO began a gradual withdrawal from Afghanistan. ◄

U.S. conducts bombing campaign in support of anti-Taliban forces, 2001. As Taliban regain strength, the Obama administration intensifies combat operations, 2009. U.S. and NATO operations end, although close to 10,000 U.S. soldiers remain for non-combat operations, 2014.

U.S. Navy SEALs find and kill al-Qaeda founder Osama bin Laden, 2011.

Taliban retreat from Afghanistan to border areas in Pakistan, 2003. As Taliban expand influence, Pakistan's military pushes back, 2009.

• Suspected terrorist and fighter training camp

U.S. military leaders began transferring combat operations to their Afghani counterparts. U.S. and NATO combat operations ended in late 2014, but ninety-eight hundred U.S. soldiers remained behind to conduct military training and counterinsurgency operations.

In Iraq, Obama reaffirmed the December 31, 2011, troop withdrawal deadline agreed upon by the Bush administration and the Iraqi government. Obama and al-Maliki outlined plans for postwar cooperation on trade, energy, economic development, and security. The United States maintained its embassy in Baghdad and consulates in Basra, Mosul, and Kirkuk. On December 15, 2011, the United States formally ended its mission in Iraq and withdrew its last five hundred troops.

U.S. intervention in Iraq and Afghanistan had high human and financial costs. Two thousand three hundred and fifty seven U.S. troops died in Afghanistan and another 4,489 died in Iraq (see Table 28.2). The United States spent $1.65 trillion on the Afghan conflict and another $1.71 trillion on the Iraq war. Experts predicted that care for U.S. veterans of both wars could cost as much as $4.3 trillion by 2054. More than fifty thousand U.S. soldiers were wounded in the two conflicts. But not all injuries were immediately apparent or occurred on the battlefield. By 2015, the Veterans Administration (VA) had approved more than six hundred seventy-five thousand disability claims for conditions such as physical trauma, brain injury, and post-traumatic stress disorder (PTSD). High rates of suicides among veterans and sexual assaults of female soldiers by male comrades sparked calls for improved mental health services and policy reforms to help the nation's warriors.

Throughout his presidency, civil liberties groups assailed Obama's continuation of government surveillance programs established in the aftermath of 9/11. Beginning in 2011, the website WikiLeaks began to release, amid the protests of the U.S. government, hundreds of thousands of classified State Department documents. In June 2013, Edward Snowden, a contractor for the National Security Agency, leaked a huge cache of classified materials about the agency's worldwide collection of electronic data to reporters. The scope and targets of the program outraged Americans and foreigners alike. To avoid prosecution for violating the Espionage Act, Snowden fled first to Hong Kong then to Russia and began seeking permanent asylum in nations without extradition treaties with the United States. A polarizing figure, Snowden was seen by some as a patriotic whistleblower who exposed a dangerous expansion of government intrusion into private lives. Others saw him as a traitor who gravely damaged intelligence-gathering capabilities. In June 2015, as a result of Snowden's revelations and federal cases challenging the constitutionality of the bulk collection of Americans' phone records, Congress added new limits on electronic surveillance of U.S. citizens when it reauthorized several provisions of the Patriot Act.

Obama defended the National Security Agency's (NSA's) data-gathering practices and made little progress in reigning in the excesses of the war on terror. Although the administration announced that it would no longer define detainees at Guantánamo Bay as enemy combatants, its efforts to close the prison and to prosecute suspect terrorists in civil courts instead of military tribunals ran

Table 28.2 Casualties in Iraq and Afghanistan, 2001–2015

The Pentagon has carefully tracked U.S. military deaths in the wars in Iraq and Afghanistan, but private contractors (many of whom were not U.S. citizens) and soldiers fighting on behalf of international coalition partners and the Afghan and Iraqi security forces (military and police) have also perished. These casualty figures do not include soldiers and contractors who died as a result of suicide or risky behaviors associated with PTSD after completing their military tours.

Iraq

Affiliation	Description	Deaths
Nonaffiliated	Iraqi civilians	137,000–165,000[a]
Opposition	Opposition combatants	36,400[a]
Allied armed forces	U.S. armed forces	4,424[b]
Allied armed forces	Iraqi national military and police	12,000[a]
Allied armed forces	Other (non-U.S.) armed forces	319
Allied civilians	U.S. contractors	3,481
Allied civilians	Journalists	221
Allied civilians	Humanitarian and NGO workers	62

Afghanistan

Affiliation	Description	Deaths
Nonaffiliated	Afghani civilians	26,000[a]
Opposition	Opposition combatants	35,000[a]
Allied armed forces	U.S. armed forces	2,215[c]
Allied armed forces	Afghani national military and police	23,470
Allied armed forces	Other (non-U.S.) armed forces	1,114
Allied civilians	U.S. contractors	3,401
Allied civilians	Journalists	25
Allied civilians	Humanitarian and NGO workers	331

[a] Indicates rounded figures.

[b] Includes 14 Department of Defense civilian employees.

[c] Includes 4 Department of Defense civilian employees.

Sources: http://www.defense.gov/casualty.pdf; http://watson.brown.edu/costsofwar/files/cow/imce/figures/2015/SUMMARY%20CHART%20-%20Direct%20War%20Death%20Toll%20to%20April%202015.pdf; https://www.iraqbodycount.org/database/.

into congressional opposition. By 2011, the global war on terrorism had resulted in 119,044 arrests and 35,117 convictions in sixty-six countries.

28-1d Revolutions and Negotiations

{ U.S. officials confront insurgencies in the Arab world and reach out to old adversaries.

In late 2010, popular revolutions erupted throughout the Arab world, inspiring hopes that democracy could prevail over Islamic radicalism and authoritarianism. After the government in Tunisia was overthrown in January 2011, demonstrations arose in Oman, Yemen, Syria, and Morocco. In Cairo, thousands of protestors gathered in Tahrir Square to demand the resignation of Egyptian president Hosni Mubarak. On February 11, with his international

Arab Spring Wave of revolutionary protests throughout the Arab world from December 2010 to mid-2012 that pushed rulers out of power in Tunisia, Egypt, Libya, and Yemen.

and domestic support collapsing, Mubarak stepped down. Four days later, demonstrations against Muammar Qaddafi erupted in Libya. Throughout the **Arab Spring**, prodemocracy activists spread their calls for freedom around the world via YouTube videos, tweets, and Facebook posts—a potent illustration of the political power of the Internet, mobile technology, and smart phones.

In March 2011, after Qaddafi used violence to crush a burgeoning civil war in Libya, the UN Security Council voted to establish an arms embargo, a no-fly zone, and a naval blockade to protect civilians. While the Obama administration refused to provide ground troops to the NATO-led coalition that enforced the UN sanctions, the United States provided air and naval support. In August, after rebel forces seized Tripoli, Qaddafi was ousted from power. On October 23, three days after rebels captured and killed Qaddafi, their governing committee declared an end to the Libyan civil war.

But democracy and peace in the region proved short lived. In July 2013, after months of increasing popular unrest, Mohammed Morsi, Egypt's recently elected president, was ousted in a military coup. Syrian president Bashar al-Assad unleashed a violent crackdown and used chemical weapons on rebel forces. In August 2013, a multinational coalition prepared to intervene militarily but cancelled operations after Russia persuaded the Syrian government to destroy its chemical weapons. A horrific civil war nonetheless ensued. More than two hundred thousand Syrians died, and a refugee crisis spilled into neighboring nations. On September 11, 2012, Islamic militants in Libya attacked the U.S. Consulate in Benghazi and killed U.S. ambassador Christopher Stevens and three other Americans. The Obama administration's shifting explanations of the attackers' motives and security lapses at the compound prompted a series of congressional investigations. In 2014, tensions between rival military and Islamist factions plunged Libya back into civil war.

Nothing better exemplified the ongoing challenges of the global war on terrorism than the rise of the **Islamic State (IS)**. In 2014, the Sunni militants started capturing territory in Iraq and Syria. Through social media and propaganda, they publicized their destruction of cultural antiquities and beheadings of aid workers, soldiers, and journalists. Muslim clerics around the world condemned these actions and more than sixty nations declared IS terrorists. A U.S.-led coalition began launching manned and unmanned attacks against IS strongholds in Iraq and Syria.

While confronting new adversaries like IS, Obama normalized U.S. relations with former Cold War adversary Cuba. In July 2015, Cuba and the United States restored full diplomatic relations, severed since 1961. Some issues remained unresolved, such as whether the U.S. would lift its fifty-three-year trade embargo on Cuba and whether Cuba would agree to improve its human rights record.

Islamic State (IS) Offshoot of al-Qaeda also known as *ISIS, ISIL,* and *Daesh;* fundamentalist Islamist terrorist group that began capturing territory in Iraq and Syria in 2014.

28-2
Global Capitalism

In 2011, protesters dressed as corpses lie prone in front of a Hong Kong computer store dressed up as high tech workers. The skull and crossbones on a mock computer product represent dangerous working conditions at a U.S. supplier in China, while slogans and the face of Apple Computer head Steve Jobs hold the U.S. firm responsible.

Why did a U.S. company like Apple rely on workers in China to build its products, and how was this possible given the distance from its headquarters in California? ▶

AP Images/Kin Cheung

America's post-9/11 conflicts coexisted with a major economic transformation that began decades earlier. After World War II, developed nations like the United States grew increasingly multinational as companies reduced labor costs by relocating manufacturing operations to countries where wages were lower. The end of the Cold War greatly accelerated this process by enabling three of the world's largest nations—China, India, and Russia—to participate fully in the global economy. At the same time, technological breakthroughs, such as the Internet and wireless technology, further shrank the world by dramatically increasing the speed of global business transactions and, more importantly, empowering individuals to communicate with any person, government, business, or organization around the world. Like industrialization and postindustrialization, globalization also had a downside as nations struggled to maintain economic autonomy, and workers in the developed world fought to keep jobs while those in developing countries fought to improve pay and labor conditions. The interconnected global economy became vulnerable to local shocks anywhere in the world. Moreover, in many nations, the expansion of global capitalism did not reduce poverty or underdevelopment, and the increase in manufacturing and living standards in the developing world heightened global environmental hazards.

☞ As you read, pay attention to the conditions that gave rise to the spreading of global capitalism as well as its impact on U.S. economic and social trends. In what ways did the world become smaller? What impact did this have on consumers, workers, and businesses?

28-2a Economic Integration

Capitalism reached a new stage of development after World War II with the Bretton Woods economic system, which included the creation of the International Monetary Fund, World Bank, and General Agreements on Trade and Tariffs (GATT). The World Trade Organization (WTO), founded in 1995 by one hundred twenty-five nations that controlled 90 percent of world trade, grew by 2015 to include one hundred sixty-one nations, including free market Communist states like China and Vietnam. The WTO remains an engine of neoliberal economic theory that sees open borders to trade as the best possible opportunity for sustained global economic growth and development. A stunning example is China, home to the world's largest population (1.3 billion in 2013). Eight years after joining the WTO in 2001, China became the world's leading exporting nation, rising from .75 percent of global exports in 1978 to over 9 percent in 2009. At the same time, foreign investments exploded from $3 billion in 1983 to $94 billion in 2008. In 2010, China surpassed Japan to become the second largest economy in the world and in late 2014, according to the IMF, surpassed the U.S. to lead the world in gross domestic product (GDP). Given the nation's stunning growth rate of 10 percent per year since Deng Xiaoping's economic reforms took hold in the 1980s, there is little chance that the United States can reclaim the top spot even though China's growth slowed to 7 percent in 2014 (compared to the U.S. rate of 2.2 percent).

> The removal and lowering of trade barriers creates an expansive global economy.

India, the only nation with a population rivaling China's, also experienced swift economic ascent, and, according to the IMF, is the only nation that over the long-term can surpass China's GDP. After gaining independence in 1947, India had the most restricted economy in the non-Communist world. But in 1991, it began drastically reducing tariffs, deregulating businesses, and encouraging foreign investment. The effect was particularly pronounced in high-tech industries as Bangalore became India's Silicon Valley and Hyderabad turned into "Cyberbad." Between 1991 and 2001, sales in India's computer industry increased from $150 million to $9.6 billion. India also became a major hub for a wide range of global business services that operated over the telephone and Internet, including call centers and medical recordkeeping. In less than two decades, the rapid economic ascent of China and India revealed how much globalization had changed the world.

The development of China and India continued the economic ascendance of the Asia-Pacific region. The process began with Japan's economic takeoff and was followed by the rise of many other economies including South Korea, Singapore, Hong Kong, Taiwan, and then China and India (see Map 28.3). In October 2015, eleven nations, including the United States and Japan but excluding China, signed the Trans-Pacific Partnership (TPP), a historic agreement to lower or remove trade barriers for the Asia-Pacific region similar to the European Union and the smaller-scale North American Free Trade Agreement (NAFTA). Americans, however, were divided about whether the of elimination of tariffs on Asian imports (like Japanese automobiles) and U.S. exports to Asia like beef and rice benefits U.S. corporations more than consumers. Organized labor and many members of President Obama's own Democratic Party opposed the TPP that his administration spent seven years negotiating. The TPP was part of the economic side of Obama's "pivot to East Asia," a new foreign policy program designed to shift attention and U.S. military resources from Europe and the Middle East to Asia in order to offset China's growing military power and its impact throughout the Asia-Pacific region.

Call Center in Bangalore, India, 2012 Initially motivated mainly by low labor costs, many multinational companies began outsourcing call center jobs to India. But in response to customer complaints about Indians' English accents and idioms, some U.S. companies like J.P. Morgan Chase, AT&T, and Expedia moved their operations to the Philippines, now the world's biggest call center hub. Realizing cost savings was only part of successful globalization, employers were willing to pay higher wages in exchange for more Americanized workers. ◄

Money sharma/EPA/Newscom

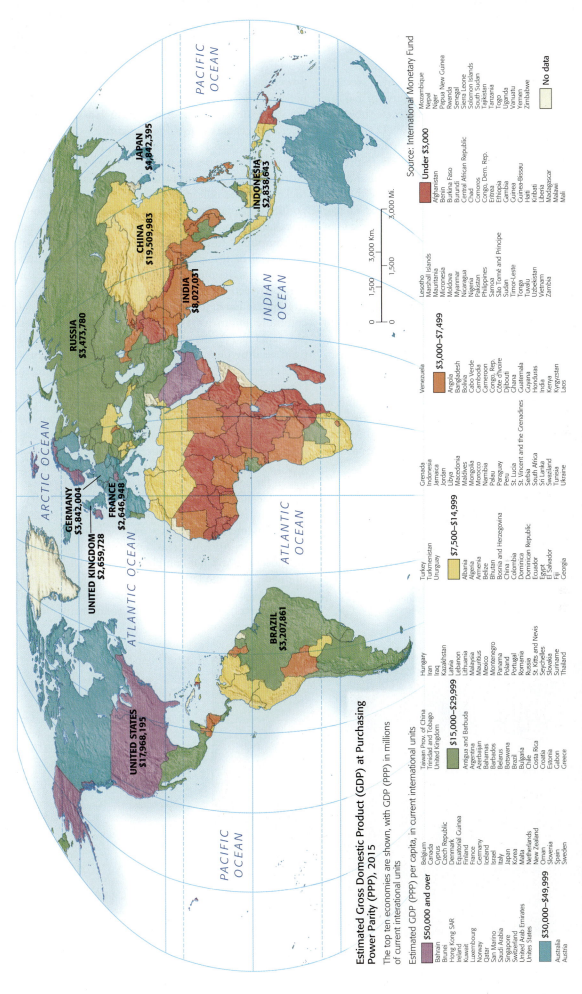

Estimated Gross Domestic Product (GDP) at Purchasing
Power Parity (PPP), 2015

The top ten economies are shown, with GDP (PPP) in millions
of current interational units

Estimated GDP (PPP) per capita, in current international units

$50,000 and over	Belgium	Taiwan Prov. of China
	Canada	Trinidad and Tobago
Bahrain	Cyprus	United Kingdom
Brunei	Czech Republic	
Hong Kong SAR	Denmark	**$15,000–$29,999**
Ireland	Equatorial Guinea	
Kuwait	Finland	Antigua and Barbuda
Luxembourg	France	Argentina
Norway	Germany	Azerbaijan
Qatar	Iceland	Bahamas
San Marino	Israel	Barbados
Saudi Arabia	Italy	Belarus
Singapore	Japan	Botswana
Switzerland	Korea	Brazil
United Arab Emirates	Malta	Bulgaria
Unites States	Netherlands	Chile
	New Zealand	Costa Rica
$30,000–$49,999	Slovenia	Croatia
	Spain	Estonia
Australia	Sweden	Gabon
Austria		Greece

Hungary	Turkey
Iran	Turkmenistan
Iraq	Uruguay
Kazakhstan	
Latvia	**$7,500–$14,999**
Lebanon	
Lithuania	Albania
Malaysia	Algeria
Mauritius	Armenia
Mexico	Belize
Montenegro	Bhutan
Panama	Bosnia and Herzegovina
Poland	China
Portugal	Colombia
Romania	Dominica
Russia	Dominican Republic
St. Kitts and Nevis	Ecuador
Seychelles	Egypt
Slovakia	El Salvador
Suriname	Fiji
Thailand	Georgia

Grenada	Venezuela
Indonesia	
Jamaica	**$3,000–$7,499**
Jordan	
Libya	Angola
Macedonia	Bangladesh
Maldives	Bolivia
Mongolia	Cabo Verde
Morocco	Cambodia
Namibia	Cameroon
Palau	Congo, Rep.
Paraguay	Côte d'Ivoire
Peru	Djibouti
St. Lucia	Ghana
St. Vincent and the Grenadines	Guatemala
Serbia	Guyana
South Africa	Honduras
Sri Lanka	India
Swaziland	Kenya
Tunisia	Kyrgyzstan
Ukraine	Laos

Lesotho	**Under $3,000**
Marshall Islands	
Mauritania	Afghanistan
Micronesia	Benin
Moldova	Burkina Faso
Myanmar	Burundi
Nicaragua	Central African Republic
Nigeria	Chad
Pakistan	Comoros
Philippines	Congo, Dem. Rep.
Samoa	Eritrea
São Tomé and Príncipe	Ethiopia
Sudan	Gambia
Timor-Leste	Guinea
Tonga	Guinea-Bissau
Tuvalu	Haiti
Uzbekistan	Kiribati
Vietnam	Liberia
Zambia	Madagascar
	Malawi
	Mali

Mozambique	
Nepal	
Niger	
Papua New Guinea	
Rwanda	
Senegal	
Sierra Leone	
Solomon Islands	
South Sudan	
Tajikistan	
Tanzania	
Togo	
Uganda	
Vanuatu	**No data**
Yemen	
Zimbabwe	

Source: International Monetary Fund

Map 28.3 Global Distribution of Wealth, 2004 Despite neoliberalism and globalization, a major division of wealth
between nations above (the Global North) and below the equator (the Global South) still exists. In 2004, one billion people
owned 80 percent of the world economy, while another billion earned merely one dollar per day. ▲

851

digital divide Division between peoples and countries who do and do not have reliable access to digital technologies linked to economic opportunities and improved quality of life.

While economic integration from the perspective of neoliberalism was supposed to be a boon for the entire global economy, it required diminishing sovereignty for nations as their economies became subject to standards set by the WTO and other international bodies. Proponents of neoliberalism worried that globalization made it nearly impossible to protect economies from external shocks—such as natural disasters, wars, and financial crises. A devastating earthquake and tsunami that hit Japan in March 2011 caused a major slowdown in the global production of automobiles. Globalization increased the risk of worldwide economic meltdown by making it possible for any economy, including weak and poorly managed ones, to start a calamitous chain reaction leading to depression.

Under globalization, poor nations feared rich nations as well. While China and India exemplified the benefits of neoliberalism, the majority of the developing world saw little or no improvement in economic standing under globalization. People in the Middle East, Northern Africa, and sub-Saharan Africa with few exceptions did not experience improvement in their standards of living, and in many cases, suffered a decline. Poorer nations decried that richer ones were using the WTO, IMF, and World Bank to bully them into opening up their economies while protecting their own from global competition.

28-2b Innovation and Infrastructure

Debates over inequality in the global economy occurred at the same time as new technologies were leveling the playing field for

> Technology accelerates global commerce and changes the nature of business.

nations, companies, and individuals to compete for its riches. The invention of the Internet browser made the World Wide Web an "information superhighway" that powered the expansion of global business. The Internet's potential to revolutionize global communication attracted substantial investments, such as transoceanic fiber optic cables that wired the entire world between 1995 and 2000. During this period the number of Internet users across the globe rose 2,000 percent from 20 to 400 million, and by 2012, that figure had skyrocketed to 2.4 billion, nearly one-third of the world's population (see Figure 28.1). The expanded ability of cellular phones and other mobile devices like tablet computers to access the Internet accounted for a great deal of this growth. Mobile technologies were especially welcomed in developing nations because they provided Internet and phone access via satellites circling the Earth to places otherwise lacking a reliable communications infrastructure. But many poor peoples remained on the opposite side of the **digital divide** from wealthy ones. Only 15 percent of Africans used the Internet in 2012 compared to 83 percent in the United States.

New technologies generated divisions within the United States. Older persons (age sixty-five and above) lagged behind younger age groups in Internet usage. Even though usage rate by senior citizens rose dramatically from only 14 percent in 2000 to 58 percent in 2015, they still lagged far behind the 96 percent of eighteen- to twenty-nine-year-olds who used the Internet. A digital divide also emerged between persons with differing levels of education. Internet usage rates for college graduates were 95 percent in 2015, whereas they were only 65 percent for those who did not complete high school. The digital divide, although less pronounced, also distinguished whites, Asian Americans, and urban dwellers (higher Internet users) from blacks, Latinos, and rural dwellers (lower Internet users).

JOHN STANMEYER/National Geographic Creative

John Stanmeyer, *Signals from Djibouti*, 2013 Mobile technologies have transformed global communications, making it possible to connect with people even from remote locations. This award-winning photograph shows Somali migrants living in Djibouti trying to catch an inexpensive cellular signal from their neighboring homeland. Each evening, people visit the beach, hoping to reconnect with their loved ones or to make business and financial transactions. ◄

Global Americans Born in Moscow in 1973, **Sergey Brin** was part of a stream of Jews fleeing the Soviet Union during the late twentieth century. Most went to Israel, but in 1979, at age six, he came with his parents and grandmother to the United States. Michael and Eugenia Brin both held degrees in mathematics from the prestigious Moscow State University and lived in relative comfort but bristled at anti-Semitic restrictions and sought a better life for Sergey. With the help of a former professor, Michael joined the mathematics faculty at the University of Maryland, and the family settled nearby with Eugenia finding employment at NASA as a research scientist.

Given his family's background and emphasis on academics, it was not surprising that Sergey breezed through the University of Maryland in three years as an award-winning honors student in math and computer science. He went on to study for a Ph.D. in computer science at Stanford University, where in 1998 he dropped out to start a company named Google (with Larry Page) that revolutionized search engines on the emerging World Wide Web. After Google's initial public offering of stock in 2004, Brin became one of the wealthiest and most powerful players in Silicon Valley. Ten years later, he was named the eighteenth richest person in the world, and Google was a titan of the global economy. Brin's story reveals how the "brain drain" from the Soviet Union (as well as China, India, and other nations) has powered the U.S. digital economy.

In the early years, the Internet retained an antimaterialist spirit that was evident through such practices as free "open-source" software but soon businesses exerted powerful control. In the wake of the **dot.com bust**, the technology-heavy NASDQ stock exchange lost 78 percent of its value from 2000 to 2002. But online retailers like Amazon.com and the auction site eBay rebounded and grew rapidly, raising the question of whether "brick-and-mortar" stores would become obsolete. At the same time, Internet service providers made huge profits, and free "social networking" websites like Facebook as well as the search engine Google became publicly traded corporations with revenues generated largely through advertising.

28-2c Production, Work, and Climate

U.S. consumers, including millions shopping on the Internet, were some of the biggest beneficiaries of globalization. *Newsweek* reported that between 1996 and 2005, the United States, which comprised 20 percent of the world's total economic worth, generated 45 percent of its growth in consumer spending. But because Americans spent much more for imports than they made on exports,

> The new economy creates a global marketplace that empowers individuals but exploits vulnerable workers.

more consumption increased the U.S. trade deficit from around $96 million in 1995 to almost $560 million in 2011 (see Figure 28.2).

One of the main reasons for cheaper products was the liberalization of rules regarding foreign investment that enabled U.S. manufacturers to use much cheaper labor in China, India, and other developing countries. As a result, more products than ever emerged from a "global assembly line." A Boeing 787 commercial airplane was produced from parts made across four different continents (see Figure 28.3). The three major parts composing the front, mid, and center fuselage alone originated from Kansas, Japan, and Italy, respectively. Improvements in technology and communication made this process much faster and more

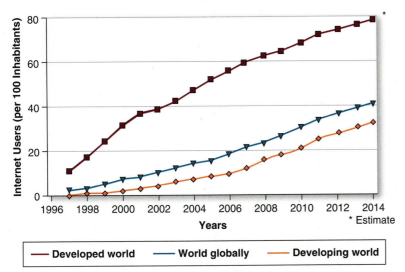

Figure 28.1 Global Internet Usage, 1996–2014 The blue line on this chart displays the growth of Internet users around in the world, which increased from an average of two to forty users per one hundred people from 1997 to 2014. In addition, comparing the purple and orange lines reveals the digital divide between the developed and developing world that was not lessened during the same seventeen-year period. ▲ Source: https://en.wikipedia.org/wiki/Internet_users_per_100_inhabitants_ITU.svg.

dot.com bust Major downturn in the formally skyrocketing stock prices of technology firms largely connected to the World Wide Web.

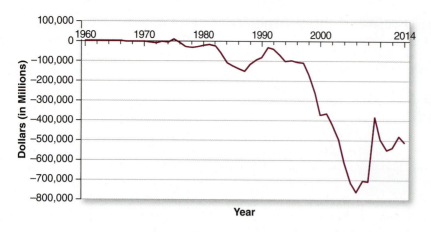

Figure 28.2 U.S. Trade Deficit Until the early 1980s, the U.S. maintained a balance between exports and imports, but since then imports have dominated and the balance, with some exceptional years, turned into deeper deficit. ◄ Source: Data presented on a balance of payment (BOP) basis. Information on data sources and methodology are available at United States Census, Foreign Trade Statistics, http://www.census.gov/foreign-trade/guide/sec2.html#bop

global supply chains High-tech system through which a product moves from manufacturing to consumer that balances supply and demand for a given product, benefiting consumers and businesses alike.

efficient so that major retailers like Walmart created a sophisticated system of **global supply chains** enabling its stores to calibrate stock to meet shifting consumer demand. A shortage of a particular item would immediately activate the entire global assembly line to produce more of it.

During the late twentieth and early twenty-first centuries, more companies switched from being

domestic firms with some international branches to transnational firms with multiple headquarters around the world and a vision of a single, global market. As a result, businesses required new types of managers who could communicate in more than one language, deal effectively with cultural diversity, and have a stateless view of the world. Following businesses, universities responded to globalization by integrating global perspectives and experiences by admitting increasing numbers of international students and building satellite campuses in China,

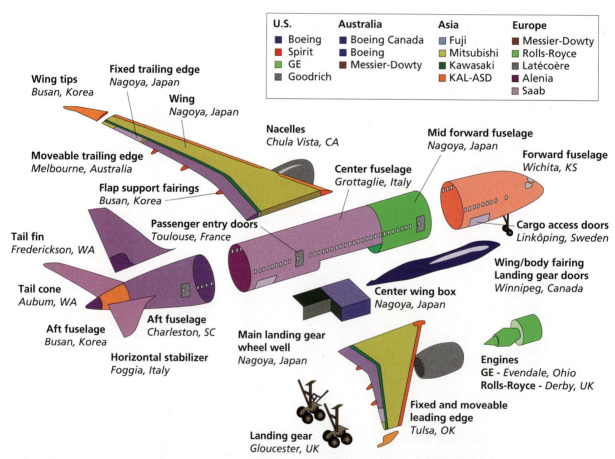

Figure 28.3 Global Supply Chain for the Boeing 787, 2012 The expansion of the global economy meant that manufacturing various parts for a product could be achieved in places around the world that produce high-quality items for the lowest cost. The Boeing airplane was produced from parts made across four different continents. ▲ Source: http://aerospacereview.ca/eic/site/060.nsf/eng/00040.html

the Middle East, and other fast-developing areas. The global economy generated millions of jobs in developing nations and in so doing expanded the middle class and increased consumer demand for services, information, and education.

In the United States and other developed countries, new job opportunities emerged in high-tech industries, especially in the areas of management, research, and design. High-tech companies like Apple and Google filled their ranks with recent university graduates. But manufacturing jobs in the United States suffered great insecurity as firms moved factories **offshore** to countries with cheaper labor, lower taxes, and less restrictive labor and environmental regulations. The relatively high cost of U.S. labor made it more attractive for businesses to relocate overseas.

In a neoliberal global economy that encouraged off-shoring and other means of sending work overseas, the power of U.S. labor unions fell to an all-time low since union membership peaked during the 1950s, when almost 30 percent of all employed Americans were union members. By 2003, this figure shrank to less than 7 percent. The decline of unions, which had been evident since President's Reagan's firing of striking federal air traffic controllers in 1981, corresponded with millions of U.S. workers being forced to accept less pay and benefits or risk losing their jobs. In 1998, the California Labor Commissioner said, "Global competition results in a feeding frenzy in which local producers compete against one another and against foreign factories in a brutal race to the bottom." One of the few signs of hope for labor unions came in Los Angeles in the mid-1990s with the organization of seventy-four thousand home care workers, mostly women of color, by the Service Employees International Union (SEIU). Since then, some of labor's biggest victories involved making union members out of immigrants and racial minorities who were previously deemed "unorganizable."

In global areas of manufacturing, labor problems were often more severe than in the United States. In places like Guangdong province in China, a manufacturing hub for both the nation and the world, workers had little power to demand better wages and working conditions. In 2009, an employee at Foxconn, a Taiwan-based firm that manufactured electronics such as Apple's iPhone, committed suicide in order to draw attention to exploitative labor practices at the company's plant. After more worker suicides followed, the company was forced to raise the monthly wage by 30 percent. While human rights activists had successfully pressured Nike to improve labor conditions for thousands of workers in the developing world making its shoes and apparel, most workers in developing nations were not fortunate enough to have their cause taken up by outside activists. Labor disputes spread to other manufacturers in China including Japanese automakers Honda and Toyota.

The transformation of work and production were part of a sea change in the global economy that had powerful implications for society. Many saw the wonders of instant communication and information accessed almost anywhere and at any time as the sign of progress in human civilization portending a bright future. Others were less certain and instead focused on the digital divide by which the poor and disadvantaged in the United States and around the world lacked access to new technology and economic opportunities. Such differences were part of the uneven experience of globalization.

offshore Relocation of a business process from one country to another to take advantage of more efficient production, lower labor costs, and less costly environmental restrictions.

MUNIR UZ ZAMAN/Stringer/AFP/Getty Images

Savar Building Collapse, Dhaka, Bangladesh, 2013 On April 24, 2013, an eight-story building containing a bank, shops, and a garment factory collapsed in Dhaka, killing one thousand one hundred twenty-nine people and leaving two thousand five hundred fifteen injured. The accident highlighted disjunctures in working conditions and safety standards across the supply chains used by multinational corporations. In June 2015, Bangladeshi police filed murder charges against forty-one people, including the building's owner and several government officials, for failing to close the plant despite warnings about its serious structural flaws. ◀

global warming Long-term transformation of the Earth's atmosphere generating a rise in temperatures, triggering severe droughts and hurricanes, a rise in oceans leading to flooding, and extinction of animal species.

The global economy had far-reaching environmental effects as well. The rapid industrialization in the developing world stimulated the growth of a new, global middle class that consumed goods and pursued lifestyles much like Americans had done during their country's middle-class expansion for two decades after World War II. From 1993 to 2011, automobile ownership increased almost ten times in three Chinese cities (Beijing, Shanghai, and Guangdong), adding more than 100 million new cars and trucks to cities that struggled to accommodate them. The growing global middle class also led to a construction boom that saw the building of millions of new homes in urban and suburban locations greatly increase demand for water and fossil fuels.

The population generated by globalization and the demands of the global middle class have had a negative impact on the Earth's climate, leading to **global warming**. The burning of fossil fuels (coal, natural gas, and oil) and automobile exhaust release carbon dioxide into the air, changing the Earth's upper atmosphere such that more heat is trapped, as in a greenhouse, thus warming up the planet's surface. This results in increasingly severe weather events like droughts and hurricanes. It also melts glaciers and sea ice leading to rising ocean levels and contributing to flooding. Global warming also changes habitats,

triggering the extinction of many animal species and new infestations of pests. Between 1970 and 2013, the United States was the world's leading producer of the "greenhouse gases" responsible for global warming, but China and India have now taken the lead and face pressure from the United States and other developed nations to reduce their emissions.

Scientists, government officials, and a wide range of advocates mobilized to educate the U.S. public about the pending disasters of climate change. President Obama made climate change a major part of his agenda and through executive action, enacted a host of measures designed to reduce the consumption of fossil fuels including tougher standards against carbon pollution, incentives to research and deploy environmentally friendly technologies (such as solar and wind energy), and the highest-ever fuel economy requirements for automobiles. Environmental advocates claimed that Obama's efforts fell well short of what was needed to reduce global warming. Yet some Americans who denied a causal link between human behavior and climate change attacked Obama's actions as expensive and unnecessary. In December 2015, one hundred eighty-eight nations, including the United States, agreed to an important UN treaty to prevent the worst possible scenarios due to climate change. This was a major step forward, but it is unclear whether the Republican-controlled U.S. Senate will ratify the accord.

28-3
Twenty-First Century America

In the early twenty-first century, a highly segmented news media and the Internet made it easier for people to ignore perspectives different from their own. National politicians, especially those on the far right, became less willing to compromise for fear of attacks from members of their own base, a trend that worsened legislative gridlock. In this April 2015 drawing, Pulitzer Prize–winning cartoonist Nick Anderson offers a liberal perspective on Republican responses to President Barack Obama.

What does this cartoonist suggest are the root causes of Republican opposition to Obama? Is the cartoon a fair reflection of U.S. partisan politics? Why or why not? ▶

Nick Anderson/Cartoonist Group

Despite the contested election of 2000, President George W. Bush pursued a vigorous agenda of tax cuts, educational reforms, and new drug benefits for older people. But spiraling costs of the wars in Afghanistan and Iraq

limited his legislative successes in his second term. Then a collapse of the nation's housing market combined with risky, unregulated practices in the financial sector triggered a banking crisis that imperiled the global economy.

Governments around the world tried to lessen the impact of the crisis on their economies, but it took years before most countries slowly emerged from the recession.

Americans reacted to the economic downturn in a variety of ways. Some benefited from the new economy while others languished. In 2008, the election of Obama as the nation's first African American president generated great optimism about a more unified populace. But those hopes quickly ebbed as a controversial plan to expand federal health coverage sparked intense conservative opposition. New grassroots movements appeared on both the right and the left, each with profoundly different views of the proper role of government. Americans also battled over changing social mores and race relations. By 2016, the United States found itself a very divided nation.

☞ As you read this section think about the kinds of issues that divided Americans. What were the major reasons that Americans were so polarized in the early twentieth-first century? Can you imagine a way in which these issues could be resolved and consensus developed?

28-3a Divided Government

Upon taking office in 2001, George W. Bush embarked on an ambitious domestic agenda. Avidly pro-life, he emulated Ronald Reagan and George H.W. Bush in blocking federal financing of international family planning programs that provided abortions or abortion counseling. George W. Bush also limited federally funded stem cell research to extant cell lines already extracted from human embryos and signed legislation banning late-term abortions, the first federal law to ban an abortion procedure since *Roe v. Wade* (1973). An

{ George W. Bush wins policy victories in his first term but meets resistance after reelection.

evangelical Christian, Bush also created the new Office of Faith-Based and Community Initiatives that made it easier for religious organizations to secure federal funds for humanitarian work at home and abroad.

With the economy in recession because of the dot .com bust and a $237 billion federal budget surplus, Bush won congressional support for $1.35 trillion in tax cuts over the next eleven years, one of the largest tax reductions in U.S. history. In May 2003, backed by a Republican majority that defied historic trends and increased its margin in the House of Representatives and regained control of the Senate in the midterm elections, he won approval of a second $350 billion tax cut, although Congress slashed his original $674 billion proposal by almost one-half because of escalating costs of the wars in Afghanistan and Iraq.

Later that year, Bush signed into law a major Medicare reform that included a new $400 billion prescription drug provision. In 2002, although he had shifted the focus of his presidency to foreign affairs after 9/11, Bush signed the **No Child Left Behind Education Reform Act** instituting new performance and testing standards for public schools.

With rising poverty rates, a rapidly increasing national debt, and an erosion of public support for the war in Iraq, Bush enjoyed less legislative success in his second term. In 2005, after he proposed partially privatizing Social Security, he met intense political opposition from Democrats and advocates for senior citizens. In August, the administration drew widespread criticism for its response to massive destruction and flooding in New Orleans after Hurricane Katrina hit the southern coast. Scenes of poor, mostly African American residents of the city stranded atop their homes and in chaotic conditions at inadequately

No Child Left Behind Education Reform Act
Federal law intended to improve public education by requiring annual assessment tests in a wide variety of subjects, higher teaching qualifications, and school performance standards.

New Orleans Police Rescue Residents of the Lower Ninth Ward, New Orleans, August 29, 2005 Although Hurricane Katrina was only a Category 3, poorly engineered levees in New Orleans burst and 80 percent of the city flooded. One hundred twelve thousand of almost five hundred thousand residents had not evacuated because they did not have access to cars. The Federal Emergency Management Agency's delayed, disorganized response to the crisis left thousands without food, water, or medical attention for days. The storm killed nearly two thousand people and left over $100 million in damage in its wake ▶.

Marko Georgiev/Getty Images

subprime mortgage Variable-interest loan given to a person with poor credit history who normally would not be able to qualify for a mortgage.

underwater Condition when one's home loan is higher than the value of the property, making it impossible to repay the loan even upon selling the house.

prepared shelters highlighted deepening economic and racial disparities in the United States.

Bush's second term also witnessed intensifying political polarization. Bush's successful appointments of John Roberts and Samuel Alito to the Supreme Court shifted its ideological balance to the right. But in November 2006, Democrats recaptured control of both houses of Congress. When they attempted to expand the federal health care benefits to children of low-income families, Bush vetoed the legislation, deriding it as socialism.

28-3b Economic Reckoning

Throughout much of the early twenty-first century, recession hobbled the U.S. economy. The dot.com bust, 9/11, and a wave of corporate scandals impeded recovery. To stimulate growth and consumer spending, the Federal Reserve (the Fed) repeatedly lowered interest rates, eventually setting them at 1 percent in June 2003—the lowest rate since 1958. Capitalizing on easy credit, Americans racked up debt on cars and other major purchases. Many sold and bought homes, eager to take advantage of rapidly increasing housing values. The market boomed after President Bush, working with Congress, signed legislation that made homeownership available to a wider swath of Americans, much like Franklin Roosevelt's Federal Housing Administration and G.I. Bill initiatives had done.

The combination of low interest and federal incentives triggered a **subprime mortgage** frenzy where lenders approved even borrowers with no income, no job, and no assets (so-called NINJA loans). Investment banks in turn

> The collapse of the U.S. housing market triggers a devastating global economic crisis.

bundled these mortgages into complex stock instruments that were traded on financial markets. At the same time, the Securities and Exchange Commission allowed five major investment banks to lessen their capital reserve requirements, meaning the firms could leverage investments worth up to forty times more than their liquid assets. In 2004, after the Fed started raising interest rates and U.S. homeownership peaked at 70 percent, housing prices began to tumble. Unable to pay higher interest and often **underwater** on mortgages higher than the worth of the house, many subprime borrowers defaulted and a number of lenders filed bankruptcy (see Figure 28.4).

The housing collapse put severe stress on the nation's shadow banking system. Beginning in the late 1970s, as the U.S. government loosened banking regulations, investment banks and hedge funds began issuing credit but were not subject to federal disclosure rules. In 2007, with trillions of dollars invested in subprime loans that were failing, panic began to sweep Wall Street. By March 2008, crushed by billions of dollars of bad mortgages, investment bank Bear Stearns was perilously close to bankruptcy, creating great market volatility. In a stunning departure from the neoliberalism of the last three decades, Federal Reserve Chairman Ben Bernanke, a former Princeton University economist who was an expert on the Great Depression, orchestrated a deal in which the commercial bank JPMorgan acquired Bear Stearns and received $30 billion from the federal government to cover the firm's toxic assets. The move discomforted conservatives like Secretary of the Treasury Henry Paulson, a former Goldman Sachs executive, who feared government intervention in the free market would encourage firms to take on excessive financial risks for which someone else bore the burden. But on September 7, 2008, Paulson himself brokered a deal in which the federal government took over quasifederal mortgage giants Fannie Mae and Freddie Mac.

The move encouraged executives at Lehman Brothers, the nation's fourth largest investment bank, who were

Figure 28.4 U.S. Homeownership Rates by Race Home ownership rates follow the same course across different racial groups in the United States, steadily rising from the mid-1990s until 2004 when they start to decline. But the percentages for each race varies considerably with a roughly thirty percent advantage for non-Hispanic whites over African Americans and Latinos. ▶ Source: United States Census, http://www.census.gov/.

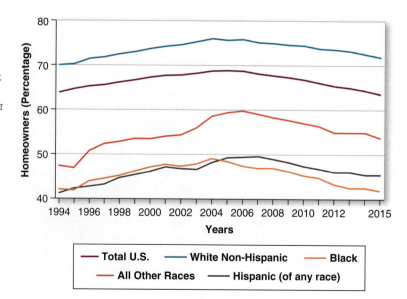

also on the brink of bankruptcy. The firm had leveraged its assets by borrowing more money than it had to back up the debt and then used the loans to overinvest in the subprime mortgage market. Opposed to more government bailouts, conservative Republican leaders urged Paulson to let Lehman Brothers fail. On September 15, after Paulson proved unable to persuade another bank to buy Lehman, the company filed the biggest bankruptcy in history. Its demise sent shockwaves throughout global financial markets. On October 2, persuading horrified lawmakers of the risk of a total economic meltdown, Bernanke and Paulson won congressional passage of the Emergency Economic Stabilization Act, creating a $700 billion **Troubled Asset Relief Program (TARP)** under which the federal government purchased distressed securities (most related to subprime mortgages). Nonetheless, by the end of October, the value of U.S. companies' stocks had fallen by an astonishing $10 trillion, 50 percent of the total worth. It was the worst recession since the Great Depression of the early 1930s.

The global downturn had a dramatic impact on the auto industry. Prior to the **Great Recession**, the U.S. "Big Three" automakers, Ford, General Motors, and Chrysler, were flailing as high fuel prices combined with their overproduction of fuel-guzzling models led to lower sales. The task of solving the crisis fell to President Obama after he took office. In early 2009, to prevent catastrophic U.S. job losses, he continued a process initiated by the Bush administration and worked with Congress on a $79.6 billion bailout of the auto industry to help it cover costs and avoid bankruptcy. Only Ford did not take the bailout money. Chrysler filed for bankruptcy protection. By late 2014, the industry had recovered and the automakers had repaid the government all but $9.3 billion of the total bailout costs, a far smaller loss than economists had predicted five years earlier.

The low point of the recession came in spring 2009, and it hit globally. The European Union economy shrank by 4 percent with unemployment reaching 10 percent on average with countries such as Greece, Ireland, Spain, Portugal, and Italy hit the hardest. Global trade decreased by 13 percent. Exports by the United States, Japan, China, and Germany each decreased by about 20 percent.

Globally, Keynesian economic principles were employed as governments pumped money into their economies to jump-start them, a dramatic shift from neoliberal policies that proliferated throughout the late twentieth and early twenty-first centuries. The United States spent $787 billion, the European Union $634 billion, China $586 billion, and Japan $486 billion in economic stimulus. In the United States, the money was used to help rebuild infrastructure. The Chinese Communist Party went much further and used its significant government resources to push the Chinese economy ahead of all other industrializing economies. In July 2010, Congress passed the **Dodd-Frank Act**, enacting regulatory reforms aimed at preventing a recurrence of a similar financial crisis.

28-3c Protesting Inequality

> Grassroots movements protest the widening global income gap and institutionalized racism.

The Great Recession hit average Americans hard. Between June 2007 and November 2008, they lost more than $6 trillion of their net worth as home equity values and retirement assets plummeted. At the peak of the crisis in 2010, almost 4 million homes were in foreclosure. Many owners just walked away from their homes and sent a "jingle mail" (mailed the keys) to the bank. Unemployment rose to 6.1 percent and was disproportionately higher among blacks and Hispanics. In some urban areas, African American unemployment peaked at almost 16 percent in the summer of 2010, a year after the recession had supposedly ended, and it remained that high nationwide through 2011. Many Americans felt great bitterness that they had lost homes and jobs while banks and businesses deemed by the government to be "too big to fail" received government bailouts.

The Bush tax cuts were set to expire in 2013 and became an important political issue during the 2012 presidential campaign as partisan conflict about growing income inequality intensified. But in January 2013, after Obama won reelection over Republican challenger Mitt Romney, he made a budget deal with the Republican-controlled Congress in which most of the tax cuts were made permanent with the American Taxpayer Relief Act of 2012.

The combination of the tax cuts, decreased spending on social services, and the Great Recession created an economy based on a record-high level of income inequality. In 2009, one in seven people were living below the poverty line. Young children were the hardest hit with nearly one in four children under the age of six classified as poor. Historically, racial and ethnic minority families have been more likely to be living in poverty than white non-Hispanic families, regardless of whether the economy was in an expansion or recession phase. During the Great Recession, these trends were particularly pronounced and roughly one in four Hispanics and African Americans were living in poverty (see Figure 28.5).

The issue of income equality was also a problem globally with the gap between rich and poor around the world increasing dramatically. In October 2013, the international bank, Crédit Suisse, reported that people with a net worth of more than $1 million represented just 0.7 percent of the global population but they held 41 percent of the world's wealth. Meanwhile, those with a net

Troubled Asset Relief Program (TARP) Authorized U.S. government purchase of bad assets from financial institutions in order to prevent bankruptcies that would ripple through the national and global economy.

Great Recession Major economic downturn in the global economy starting with the subprime mortgage crisis in December 2007 and continuing for almost two years until June 2009.

Dodd-Frank Act Most comprehensive regulation of financial markets since the Great Depression, increased transparency of financial products, ensured financial institutions could withstand market shocks, and strengthened consumer protections.

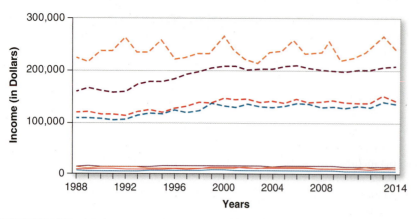

Figure 28.5 Income Inequality in the United States Differences between income in the U.S. have varied significantly by race judging by the highest twenty percent of earners. Asian Americans and whites have earned at least $50,000 more on average than African Americans and Latinos. But there is no income gap by race for the poorest twenty percent of these groups. ◄ Source: http://www.census.gov/hhes/www/income/data/historical/inequality/

White Non-Hispanic	Black	Asian	Hispanic
—— Lowest Fifth	—— Lowest Fifth	—— Lowest Fifth	—— Lowest Fifth
- - - Highest Fifth	- - - Highest Fifth	- - - Highest Fifth	- - - Highest Fifth

Occupy Movement Grassroots protests against economic inequality and undemocratic power of large corporations starting near Wall Street in New York City in September 2011 and spreading globally.

Millennials Generation of Americans born since the 1980s and raised during a period of more uneven economic growth than experienced by Generation X (1960s–1980s) or the Baby Boomers (1940s–1960s).

worth of less than $10,000 (far below the U.S. poverty line) represented 69 percent of the global population but held just 3 percent of global wealth. Economists, like Thomas Pikkety and Paul Krugman, pointed out that the income inequality was greater in the 2010s than it had been during the Gilded Age in the era of so-called Robber Barons.

Many people globally, particularly the younger generation, protested the negative impact of the recession, income inequality, and the globalization of capital. Inspired by the Arab Spring and antiausterity protests in Spain, the **Occupy Movement** launched into

the public view in September 2011, taking its first aim at Wall Street, where its members protested the government bailout of faltering banks as well as banks' unfair treatment of failing homeowners and students mired in debt. Occupy decried the fact that Wall Street bonuses in 2010 alone outstripped the wages of all minimum wage workers in the United States. Using the slogan "We are the 99%," in reference to the fact that 1 percent of the world's people held the majority of the wealth, the movement focused on income and wealth inequality and spread nationally and globally through the use of social media to organize protests in cities across the world.

The Occupy Movement tapped into unrest not only about income inequality but also about the place of the younger generation, the **Millennials**, in the global economy. Both this generation and their parents worried that as a

Occupy Wall Street Protest, New York City, New York, October 2011 In September 2011, a protest movement called Occupy Wall Street began in Zuccotti Park near New York City's Wall Street financial district. Adopting the slogan "We are the 99%" to emphasize disparities between the wealthiest 1 percent and the rest of the population, the movement spread rapidly across the United States. Although Occupy lost its momentum, it inspired campaigns for a $15 per hour minimum wage, divestment from private prisons, and student loan relief. ▶

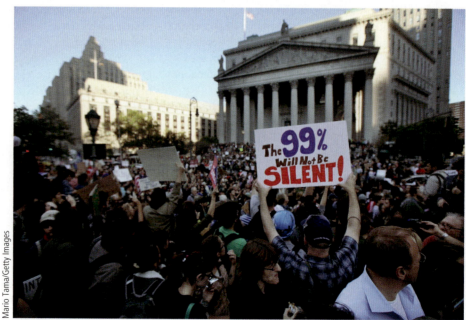

Mario Tama/Getty Images

class, this group would not have the same upward mobility as earlier generations had. The Occupy Movement tapped into the feelings of fatigue and disillusion that young Americans felt about the economy, the relentless war on terrorism, and political gridlock.

Anger at institutionalized racism and police brutality fueled another mass movement called **Black Lives Matter**. In July 2013, after the acquittal of George Zimmerman, a neighborhood watch coordinator who shot and killed Trayvon Martin, an unarmed African American teenager, protesters created the hashtag #BlackLivesMatter and inspired hundreds of protest rallies across the nation. In 2014, the movement gained momentum after the deaths of several African Americans at the hands of law enforcement officers under questionable circumstances. Black Lives Matter criticized the militarized police response to popular uprisings in Ferguson, Missouri, and Baltimore, Maryland. At the same time, other civil rights activists denounced new state laws requiring voter identification and restricting voting periods. After the Supreme Court's ruling in *Shelby County v. Holder* (2013) struck down portions of the Voting Rights Act of 1965, fears of minority voter suppression intensified.

28-3d Polarized Politics

In 2008, Obama ran on a platform that pushed for universal health care, immigration reform, and economic stimulus to boost the economy. John McCain, the Republican candidate, emphasized deficit reduction, free trade, and national security. In a surprise move, McCain chose Sarah Palin, a little-known, first-term governor from Alaska, as his running mate. Her rise in national politics during and after the 2008 election mirrored the shift to the right in Republican politics for the next eight years.

In January 2009, enormous, joyous crowds attended Obama's inauguration, but that buoyant optimism proved

> The election of Obama further divides Americans along partisan lines.

difficult to sustain as the president encountered intense personal and political opposition. Some Americans questioned Obama's U.S. citizenship, demanding that he release his long-form birth certificate. Others erroneously claimed he was a Muslim, although he attended a Christian church regularly.

But Obama's governing philosophy and legislative agenda drew the strongest criticism. In February 2009, with the nation still mired in the Great Recession, Obama signed a $787 billion economic stimulus bill that not a single Republican member of Congress supported. In March 2010, after months of lobbying efforts, Obama won congressional passage of the Patient Protection and Affordable Care Act (ACA), a sweeping national health insurance program soon known as *Obamacare*. While the Democratic majority hailed the law as a landmark achievement that had taken decades to bring to fruition, no Republican voted in favor of the bill.

Fueled by frustration about the health care law and skyrocketing national debt (see Figure 28.6), a grassroots movement on the right arose. On Tax Day (April 15) 2009, supporters of the **Tea ("Taxed Enough Already") Party** staged rallies all over the country. Groups tied to David and Charles Koch, billionaire co-owners of Koch Industries, the nation's second-largest privately held company, played a key role in the Tea Party. It opposed the bailout of banks and corporations as well as the economic stimulus package that the Obama administration adopted to address the Great Recession. Tea Party leaders, however, rarely said anything about the Bush administration's earlier relief package or the cost of the Iraq War, giving it a partisan slant that opposed the Democrats. The Tea Party aimed to tap into the anger that some Americans felt about the sinking economy and the liberal leanings of President Obama. They adopted their name to evoke the colonists'

Black Lives Matter Mass movement arising in 2013 to challenge police brutality, mass incarceration of African Americans, and institutionalized racism.

Tea ("Taxed Enough Already") Party Conservative political movement rising in 2009 to oppose Obama's economic and health care agenda and to advocate lower taxes and smaller government.

Figure 28.6 U.S. National Debt National debt measures the balance between the amount a government spends versus the amount it receives as revenue. Since the early 1980s, the United States has dramatically increased spending mainly for health care, social security, defense, and interest payments on treasury bonds. The increase was not offset by a corresponding rise in income taxes or social security payments, the main sources of revenue. ▶

Source: TreasuryDirect, http://www.treasurydirect.gov/govt/reports/pd/histdebt/histdebt.htm.

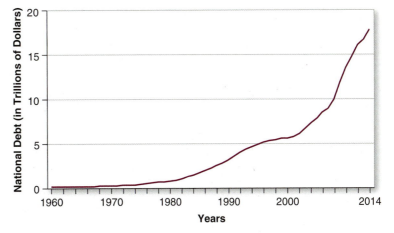

History *without* Borders

Same-Sex Marriage

Finland's legislation to legalize same-sex marriage will take effect in 2017; efforts are underway to rescind the law.

Russia's anti-gay legislation does not outlaw homosexual acts; it prohibits "propaganda of homosexuality."

Israel has recognized some same-sex marriages performed in other countries.

The death penalty as punishment for "carnal intercourse against the order of nature," will become law in **Brunei Darussalam** by the end of 2016.

Some states in **Mexico** have legalized same-sex marriages; all states recognize them.

In 2013, **Nigeria** passed the Same Sex Marriage (Prohibition) Act, which also prohibits all gay organizations.

Legalization of same-sex marriage achieved by:
- Referendum
- Legislation
- Court decision

Same-sex marriages recognized, or legalization pending

Same-sex relationships granted some rights of marriage

Countries with discriminatory laws
- Punishable by prison
- Punishable by death

Nations with Legalized Same-Sex Marriage, 2015 By late 2015, eighteen nations had legalized same-sex marriage. Several states in Mexico perform same-sex marriages that are recognized in all thirty-one states. Finland's same-sex marriage law goes into effect in 2017. ▲

Same-sex marriage moved swiftly to prominence in national and international politics, growing out of civil rights activism and changing ideas about the hierarchical nature of marriage itself. In the late twentieth century, a few nations began granting same-sex couples the rights accorded married opposite-sex couples in matters such as taxes, inheritance, and health care decisions. In 1989, Denmark became the first country to permit civil partnerships for same-sex couples. In 2001, the Netherlands went further, becoming the first nation to legalize same-sex marriages. As of late 2015,

eighteen countries recognize same-sex marriages.

Same-sex marriage has been legalized through a combination of legislative action, judicial rulings, and popular referenda. Each nation's experience differs. On July 20, 2005, Canada became the fourth country in the world and the first country in the Americas to legalize same-sex marriage after the Civil Marriage Act defined marriage in gender-neutral terms. In South Africa, after a Constitutional Court's ruling that existing marriage laws discriminated on the basis of sexual orientation, the National Assembly passed legislation

making South Africa the first and so far only African nation to legalize same-sex marriage. In July 2010, Argentina became the first Latin American country to legalize same-sex marriage.

In April 2013, the Socialist-led National Assembly and upper house of Parliament voted to legalize same-sex marriage in France. Opponents of same-sex marriage violently clashed with police in Paris and Lyon. After a failed legal challenge of the bill's constitutionality, President François Hollande signed it into law on May 18, 2013.

On May 22, 2015, after 62 percent of voters supported the measure,

AP Images/Thibault Camus

Same-Sex Marriage Opponents March, in Paris, March 2013
In early 2013, as the French National Assembly and Parliament prepared to vote on whether or not to legalize same-sex marriage, hundreds of thousands of French citizens rallied in opposition to allowing same-sex couples to wed or adopt children legally. ◄

AP Images/Pablo Martinez Monsivais

Supporters of Same-Sex Marriage Celebrate, Washington, D.C., June 2015 In June 2015, the U.S. Supreme Court ruled in *Obergefell v Hodges* that a state's failure to recognize the same-sex marriage of a couple in another state violated the Fourteenth Amendment's due process of law and equal protections clauses. Same-sex marriage thus became legal in all fifty states. Here, supporters of the ruling celebrate outside the Supreme Court. ◄

Ireland became the first country in the world to approve same-sex marriage in a nationwide referendum. A month later, the U.S. Supreme Court ruled 5-4 in *Obergefell v. Hodges* that states could not prohibit the issuing of marriage licenses to same-sex couples or deny recognition of lawfully performed out-of-state marriage licenses to same-sex couples, thus striking down same-sex marriage bans in thirteen states and certain U.S. territories.

With the exceptions of South Africa and Israel, no country in Africa or Asia currently recognizes same-sex marriage. While proponents see same-sex marriage as a civil right essential to the dignity and protection of gay and lesbian people and their families, opponents view such unions as an affront to their religious beliefs or cultural practices. There are seventy-six nations where homosexuality itself is criminalized. Several African and Eastern European nations and Russia have recently passed laws that impose severe penalties on same-sex relationships.

The world's largest religions vary widely in their views on same-sex marriage. The Roman Catholic Church officially opposes same-sex marriage, as do the Orthodox Church, a majority of Muslims, and Orthodox Jews. But many faith communities around the world support same-sex marriage or conduct religious ceremonies solemnizing same-sex marriage including U.S. Episcopalians, Presbyterians, Congregationalists, Native American religions with a two-spirit tradition, and Reform Jews, the United Protestant Church in Belgium, and the Protestant Church in the Netherlands.

Critical Thinking Questions

▶ How and where has same-sex marriage been legalized around the world?

▶ What societal factors do you think have contributed to legalization? Do you believe that same-sex marriage will be legalized worldwide? Why or why not?

revolt against British taxation in 1773 when they dumped British tea into Boston Harbor.

The Tea Party was not an organized third party, and some considered it to be a re-branding of the conservative wing of the Republican Party. Not only did leaders such as Sarah Palin oppose the Democratic policies such as extending social services, reforming immigration laws, and using Keynesian economic principles to stimulate the economy but they also usually stood in opposition to Republican moderates, leaving the GOP fragmented through much of the second decade of the twenty-first century. In 2010, successful Tea Party candidates helped the Republicans regain control of the House of Representatives in midterm elections, but they often challenged their party leadership and brought the legislative process to a standstill over formerly routine matters like raising the debt ceiling or approving the budget. They filed numerous legal challenges to the Affordable Care Act and repeatedly led unsuccessful attempts to repeal the law—an impossibility as long as Obama was in office and sure to veto any such measure. Critics accused Tea Party supporters of valuing ideology more than the best interests of the nation.

The rise of the Tea Party deepened long-standing partisan differences on the issue of immigration reform with immigration from Mexico and Central America a particular flashpoint. In the summer of 2001, Mexican President Vicente Fox and President Bush were set to negotiate major immigration reform that would have allowed for a path to citizenship for undocumented immigrants already in the United States, a guest worker program, as well as tightened security along the U.S.–Mexican border to stem the drug trade. As governor of Texas, George W. Bush had been a proponent of immigration and free trade between his state and Mexico. But after the attacks on 9/11, the opportunity for immigration reform was lost as most Americans were unwilling to consider the possibilities of more open borders.

In 2005 and 2006, each house of Congress passed an immigration bill, but no law resulted as the two bills could not be reconciled and the parties could not agree on a compromise package that balanced secure borders with fair treatment of undocumented immigrants who had been working as law-abiding guests in the United States. The Great Recession exacerbated these tensions as many Americans accused immigrants of taking jobs away from U.S. citizens.

Secure Fence Act Policy approved in 2006 to strengthen the U.S.–Mexico border by building seven hundred miles of secure fencing to keep out drug traffickers, security threats, and illegal immigrants.

One of the most potent reflections of the debate over border control was the building of a security fence between the United States and Mexico. In 2006, the **Secure Fence Act** appropriated monies to better secure the border. More than $1 billion dollars was set aside to build an actual wall. While there is not and probably never will be a wall extending along the one thousand nine hundred fifty-one-mile-long border between the United States and Mexico, by 2010, the Department of Homeland Security estimated that it had more than six hundred miles of fence in place along the highest trafficked areas. The wall, better security technology, and efforts by citizen vigilante groups like the Minutemen Project shut off what had been a regular ebb and flow of immigrants across the border. The result was that many immigrants who otherwise would have returned home instead stayed in the United States for fear of being unable to return or having to pay a prohibitively higher fee to coyotes who brought them across the border. The fence also made the crossings more perilous as immigrants had to choose paths that went through dangerous deserts in order to evade the increased border security.

In 2009, the Obama administration called on Congress to pass legislation that included better border and interior enforcement of laws, more flexible allocation of visas to adjust with the changing economic climate, and a path to U.S. citizenship for those who had been living as law-abiding but undocumented persons. Congress was unable to enact any legislation because of partisan gridlock. Some states reacted to the Obama administration's perceived leniency toward immigrants. In 2009, the Arizona state legislature passed SB 1070. It allowed state and local police to stop anyone who had a reasonable suspicion of being an illegal immigrant. Critics charged that this amounted to racial profiling or "Driving while Brown." A national boycott of the state ensued and eventually the state legislature amended the bill to tone down its language. Nevertheless, across the country, anti-immigrant, and what many perceived as anti-Latino, sentiment was on the rise.

In 2012, with the failure of Congress to pass any legislation and state initiatives to block any reform, the Obama administration put in place the Deferred Action for Childhood Arrivals (DACA or Dreamers) policy. This allowed children under the age of sixteen whose parents had brought them into the United States illegally to remain in the country and to apply for citizenship. Subsequent expansions of DACA, however, led to political pushback from Congress as well as injunctions from the federal courts. In 2013, a bipartisan group of senators, who became known as the *Gang of Eight*, passed an immigration bill that was widely viewed as promising. The bill, however, languished in the House of Representatives. The politically polarizing issue of immigration further solidified the Latino vote for Democrats while the Republicans continued to use anti-immigrant rhetoric.

In November 2012, Obama defeated Mitt Romney and was re-elected president. He continued to lead a nation beset by stark contrasts in Americans' views on

Brad Barket/Getty Images

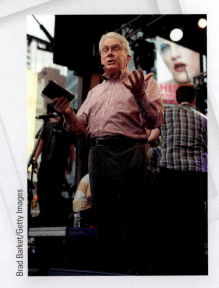

Global Americans The nature of Christianity among American Latinos has changed dramatically in the last half century as they shift from Catholicism to Evangelicalism. Much of that change is due to ministers such as **Luis Palau**, who was born in Argentina. Palau migrated to the United States as a young man after hearing Billy Graham, the American evangelist, give a sermon broadcast over the radio to his hometown. Palau moved to Oregon, earned a degree in Biblical Studies, and began working for Billy Graham as a translator. With both mentoring and financial aid from Graham, Palau launched his own ministry, which has grown exponentially as he aims his ministry to draw in younger people.

Palau spread his teachings through old-fashioned tent revivals that drew thousands of worshippers, and in his hometown of Portland, Oregon, which is not known for its ties to religion, he drew one hundred forty thousand people for a weekend event. His popularity and appealing message of service and hope were so striking that George W. Bush asked Palau to accompany him on his visit to China where he and Bush visited one of the few Christian churches in Beijing, and Palau preached. In an interview Palau gave in 2007, he claimed to have reached over 25 million people globally with his message of service to others, particularly the homeless and addicted.

Today, Palau draws thousands to his tent revivals from Central Park in New York City to the cornfields of Nebraska and can be heard on twenty-six hundred radio stations across forty-two countries in both English and Spanish.

race relations, income inequality, reproductive justice, climate change, same-sex marriage, and immigration. This divide was quite apparent in how different groups of Americans got their information and news. The advent of the Internet and the domination of cable news opened the door to partisan news reporting such as *The Drudge Report* and *The Huffington Post* as well as FOX News and MSNBC. While younger Americans relied more on the Internet to obtain news, older Americans still relied largely on televised newscasts. The biggest demographic shift in news culture came with the rise of news parody programs such as *The Daily Show with Jon Stewart* and *The Colbert Report*, popular among young viewers. Critics worried that the polarization of media outlets combined with the comedic news contributed to cynicism and apathy among young voters.

But other forces united Americans with fellow citizens and foreigners. One of the major social and political phenomena to coalesce in the early twenty-first century was the place of Protestant evangelicalism in both U.S. and global society. Between one-quarter and one-third of all Americans identified themselves as Protestant evangelicals. They found their religious homes in small congregations as well as in the growing megachurches, defined as churches that have more than two thousand attendees in any given week and generate more than $25,000 in television revenue for their congregations. The largest

megachurch in the United States is Lakewood Church in Houston, Texas, which boasts a congregation of more than forty thousand. However, only one of the ten largest megachurches in the world is located in the United States. Five are in South Korea and the rest are in Africa, Latin America, and one in India. Some U.S.-based megachurches, like Rick Warren's Saddleback Churches, have international branches in Argentina, South Korea, and Hong Kong. The Republican Party has capitalized on these organizations to make them the core of their political base since the late 1970s.

By the middle of the second decade, mass mobilization campaigns on both sides of the political spectrum combined with the expansion of political action committees (PACs) who financed campaigns behind a veil of secrecy significantly shifted the nature of U.S. politics. In 2010, the U.S. Supreme Court held in *Citizens United v. FEC* that corporations, like individuals, could assert First Amendment rights of free speech. This opened the door for unlimited funds to be spent on campaigns without any restrictions. Although Democrats and Republicans called for campaign finance reform, none came about, and the costs of political campaigns and ballot initiatives skyrocketed and led to further polarization.

Citizens United v. FEC U.S. Supreme Court decision ruling that the federal government cannot limit campaign spending by organizations, upholding the influence of big money on elections.

Summary

The 9/11 terrorist attacks fundamentally reshaped U.S. foreign policy and society. The United States built a multinational coalition to wage a global "War on Terror" and adopted controversial tactics against suspected terrorists. New security procedures affected Americans' daily lives and the government expanded its surveillance operations. In October 2001, U.S. and allied forces invaded Afghanistan to punish the regime that harbored those responsible for 9/11. In March 2003, driven by a new doctrine of preemption, the Bush administration launched a controversial and costly war in Iraq.

In early 2011, popular protests in the Arab world generated optimism that democracy would supplant dictatorships there, but such hopes quickly unraveled as civil wars and Islamic radicalism engulfed the region.

Furthermore, the globalization of the world's economy created vast amounts of wealth for some in the United States and around the world while impoverishing and limiting the economic chances of many others who remained on the poor side of the global economy and the digital divide. Meanwhile the entire planet felt the negative effects of global warming as many parts of the Earth experienced their hottest-ever recorded temperatures. Climate change demanded responses that twenty-first century governments seemed disinclined or unable to provide.

The cost of war combined with the Great Recession created the conditions for a political and cultural polarization as red states and blue states squared off on taxes, government spending, health care, labor unions, and abortion. These issues combined with increasingly vitriolic responses to immigration polarized the nation's politics as other Americans sought other venues for compromise and protest.

Thinking Back

As you review this chapter, think about the collapse of the Cold War global order in the face of a world economy in which the former Communist enemies (Russia and China) of the United States were fundamental players. Also consider the new challenges faced by the United States in a world in which it existed as the main military and economic power. How did nonstate actors confront U.S. power? What did the United States do to thwart such confrontations? Finally, consider how the post-9/11 global role of the United States and the new global economy affected its society.

What were the forces and issues that united and divided Americans?

To make your study concrete, review the timeline and reflect on the entries there. Think about their causes, consequences, and connections. How do they fit with global trends?

Additional Resources

Books

Alexander, Michelle. *The New Jim Crow: Mass Incarceration in the Age of Colorblindness*. New York: The New Press, 2010. ▶ Civil rights advocate's provocative depiction of the War on Drugs as systematized racial subjugation.

Bravin, Jess. *The Terror Courts: Rough Justice at Guantánamo Bay*. New Haven, NJ: Yale University Press, 2014. ▶ Legal reporter's narrative of war on terror's military tribunals.

Chandrasekaran, Rajiv. *Imperial Life in the Emerald City: Inside Iraq's Green Zone*. New York: Knopf, 2006. ▶ Journalist's account of the U.S. administration of postwar Iraq.

Finkel, David. *The Good Soldiers*. New York: Sarah Crichton Books, 2009. ▶ Award-winning recounting of a Ranger battalion during a fifteen-month deployment in Iraq.

Jones, Seth G. *In the Graveyard of Empires: America's War in Afghanistan*. New York: W.W. Norton, 2009. ▶ A military policy analyst's assessment of the U.S. war against the Taliban.

Lewis, Michael. *The Big Short: Inside the Doomsday Machine*. New York: W.W. Norton & Company, 2010. ▶ Gripping account of the housing and credit bubble in the 2000s.

Packer, George. *The Assassins' Gate: America in Iraq*. New York: Farrar, Straus and Giroux, 2005. ▶ Nonfiction book detailing the U.S. invasion of Iraq and its aftermath.

> Go to the MindTap® for **Global Americans** to access the full version of select books from this Additional Resources section.

Websites

National September 11 Memorial & Museum. (http://www.911memorial.org/museum) ▶ Collection of exhibits, photographs, and primary sources on 9/11 and its aftermath.

Costs of War Project. (http://watson.brown.edu/costsofwar/) ▶ Human, economic, and political costs of the post-9/11 wars in Afghanistan, Iraq, and Pakistan.

PBS *Frontline*: "Inside the Meltdown." (http://www.pbs.org/wgbh/pages/frontline/meltdown/) ▶ Documentary, interviews, timeline, and teacher's guide on the global financial crisis that began in 2007.

Occupy Archive. (http://occupyarchive.org/) ▶ Repository of first-hand accounts, photographs, and videos of Occupy protests.

The State of Working America. (http://stateofworkingamerica.org/about/) ▶ Published by the Economic Policy Institute, a nonpartisan think take that collects statistics about workers in the United States.

Continue exploring online through MindTap®, where you can:

- **Assess your knowledge with the Chapter Test**
- **Watch historical videos related to the chapter**
- **Further your understanding with interactive maps and timelines**

Global Americans Today

2000–2001

December 2000
George W. Bush is declared winner over Al Gore in contested presidential election.

March 2001
Bush abandons ratification of the Kyoto Protocols aimed at reducing global warming.

June 2001
Bush signs $1.35 trillion tax cut into law.

September 2001
Nineteen Saudi hijackers linked to al-Qaeda attack the World Trade Center and the Pentagon.

October 2001
In pursuit of Osama bin Laden and al Qaeda, U.S. and U.K. forces attack Afghanistan.

USA Patriot Act becomes law.

2002–2003

January 2002
Bush signs the No Child Left Behind Act, a major education reform.

March 2003
U.S. and U.K. troops invade Iraq.

April 2003
Saddam regime collapses, coalition forces capture Iraq.

October 2003
Chief U.S. weapons inspector reports his team's failure to find chemical, biological, or nuclear weapons in Iraq.

2004

April
CBS News releases photographs of U.S. soldiers abusing prisoners at Abu Ghraib.

May
Massachusetts becomes first U.S. state to legalize same-sex marriage.

June
U.S. ends formal occupation of Iraq and grants interim Iraqi government sovereignty.

November
Bush defeats Kerry and wins second term as president.

2005–2006

August 2005
Hurricane Katrina strikes the Gulf Coast, New Orleans floods.

2006
U.S. trade deficit hits all-time high of $761 billion.

October 2006
To deter illegal immigration, Bush signs legislation approving construction of a seven hundred-mile fence along the U.S.-Mexican border.

November 2006
Democrats recapture control of both houses of Congress in midterm elections.

December 2006
After being found guilty of crimes against humanity by an Iraqi tribunal, Saddam Hussein is hanged.

2007–2008

January 2007
Vietnam joins the WTO.

December 2007
Great Recession begins.

October 2008
Bush signs Troubled Assets Relief Program (TARP).

November 2008
Barack Obama defeats John McCain in 2008 presidential election.

WTO's Doha Round of talks breaks down.

2009–2010

April 2009
Tea Party emerges as a viable political force.

March 2010
Obama signs Patient Protection and Affordable Care Act into law. No Republican member of Congress votes for the bill.

November 2010
Republicans regain control of the U.S. House of Representatives in midterm elections.

December 2010
Arab Spring begins with revolution in Tunisia.

2011

May
U.S. special forces assassinate Osama bin Laden in Pakistan.

September
Occupy Movement begins in New York City.

2012–2013

2012
One-third of world's population (2.4 billion people) use the Internet.

November 2012
Defeating Mitt Romney, Obama wins reelection as president.

August 2013
Google stock trades above $870 per share, a 900 percent rise from its initial offering price ($85) in 2004.

2014

September
Multinational coalition launches air strikes in Syria.

October
IMF reports that China has the world's largest economy, surpassing the United States.

November
In midterm election, Republicans win the Senate and control of both houses of Congress.

2015

May
Walmart owns more stores abroad (6,283) than it does in the U.S. (5,212).

July
Countries using the euro, for the third time, bail out Greece, preventing it from going bankrupt and leaving the Eurozone.

U.S. and Iranian negotiators announce nuclear deal.

United States and Cuba resume diplomatic relations for the first time since 1961.

Go to MindTap® to engage with an interactive version of the timeline. Analyze events and themes with clickable content, view related videos, and respond to critical thinking questions.

Appendix

The Declaration of Independence

In Congress, July 4, 1776

The Unanimous Declaration of the Thirteen United States of America

When in the Course of human events it becomes necessary for one people to dissolve the political bands which have connected them with another, and to assume among the Powers of the earth, the separate and equal station to which the Laws of Nature and of Nature's God entitle them, a decent respect to the opinions of mankind requires that they should declare the causes which impel them to the separation.

We hold these truths to be self-evident, that all men are created equal, that they are endowed by their Creator with certain unalienable Rights, that among these are Life, Liberty and the pursuit of Happiness. That to secure these rights, Governments are instituted among Men, deriving their just Powers from the consent of the governed. That whenever any Form of Government becomes destructive of these ends, it is the Right of the People to alter or to abolish it, and to institute new Government, laying its foundation on such principles and organizing its Powers in such form, as to them shall seem most likely to effect their Safety and Happiness. Prudence, indeed, will dictate that Governments long established should not be changed for light and transient causes; and accordingly all experience hath shewn, that mankind are more disposed to suffer, while evils are sufferable, than to right themselves by abolishing the forms to which they are accustomed. But when a long train of abuses and usurpations, pursuing invariably the same Object evinces a design to reduce them under absolute Despotism, it is their right, it is their duty, to throw off such Government, and to provide new Guards for their future security. Such has been the patient sufferance of these Colonies; and such is now the necessity which constrains them to alter their former Systems of Government. The history of the present King of Great Britain is a history of repeated injuries and usurpations, all having in direct object the establishment of an absolute Tyranny over these States. To prove this, let Facts be submitted to a candid world.

He has refused his Assent to Laws, the most wholesome and necessary for the public good.

He has forbidden his Governors to pass Laws of immediate and pressing importance, unless suspended in their operation till his Assent should be obtained; and when so suspended, he has utterly neglected to attend to them.

He has refused to pass other Laws for the accommodation of large districts of people, unless those people would relinquish the right of Representation in the Legislature, a right inestimable to them and formidable to tyrants only.

He has called together legislative bodies at places unusual, uncomfortable, and distant from the depository of their Public Records, for the sole Purpose of fatiguing them into compliance with his measures.

Text is reprinted from the facsimile of the engrossed copy in the National Archives. The original spelling, capitalization, and punctuation have been retained. Paragraphing has been added.

He has dissolved Representative Houses repeatedly, for opposing with manly firmness his invasions on the rights of the People.

He has refused for a long time, after such dissolutions, to cause others to be elected; whereby the Legislative Powers, incapable of Annihilation, have returned to the People at large for their exercise; the State remaining in the mean time exposed to all the dangers of invasion from without, and convulsions within.

He has endeavoured to prevent the Population of these States; for that purpose obstructing the Laws for Naturalization of Foreigners; refusing to pass others to encourage their migrations hither, and raising the conditions of new Appropriations of Lands.

He has obstructed the Administration of Justice, by refusing his Assent to Laws for establishing Judiciary Powers.

He has made Judges dependent on his Will alone, for the tenure of their offices, and the amount and payment of their salaries.

He has erected a multitude of New Offices, and sent hither swarms of Officers to harass our People, and eat out their substance.

He has kept among us, in times of peace, Standing Armies without the Consent of our legislatures.

He has affected to render the Military independent of and superior to the Civil Power.

He has combined with others to subject us to a jurisdiction foreign to our constitution, and unacknowledged by our laws; giving his Assent to their Acts of pretended Legislation: For Quartering large bodies of armed troops among us: For protecting them, by a mock Trial, from Punishment for any Murders which they should commit on the Inhabitants of these States: For cutting off our Trade with all parts of the world: For imposing Taxes on us without our Consent: For depriving us in many cases, of the benefits of Trial by Jury: For transporting us beyond Seas to be tried for pretended offences: For abolishing the free System of English Laws in a neighbouring Province, establishing therein an Arbitrary government, and enlarging its Boundaries so as to render it at once an example and fit instrument for introducing the same absolute rule into these Colonies: For taking away our Charters, abolishing our most valuable Laws, and altering fundamentally the Forms of our Governments: For suspending our own Legislatures, and declaring themselves invested with Power to legislate for us in all cases whatsoever.

He has abdicated Government here, by declaring us out of his Protection, and waging War against us.

He has plundered our seas, ravaged our Coasts, burnt our towns, and destroyed the lives of our people.

He is at this time transporting large Armies of foreign Mercenaries to compleat the works of death, desolation and tyranny, already begun with circumstances of Cruelty and perfidy scarcely paralleled in the most barbarous ages, and totally unworthy the Head of a civilized nation.

He has constrained our fellow Citizens taken Captive on the high Seas to bear Arms against their Country, to become the executioners of their friends and Brethren, or to fall themselves by their Hands.

He has excited domestic insurrections amongst us, and has endeavoured to bring on the inhabitants of our frontiers, the merciless Indian Savages, whose known rule of warfare, is an undistinguished destruction of all ages, sexes and conditions.

In every stage of these Oppressions We have Petitioned for Redress in the most humble terms: Our repeated Petitions have been answered only by repeated injury. A Prince, whose character is thus marked by every act which may define a Tyrant, is unfit to be the ruler of a free People.

Nor have We been wanting in attentions to our British brethren. We have warned them from time to time of attempts by their legislature to extend an unwarrantable jurisdiction over us. We have reminded them of the circumstances of our emigration and settlement here. We have appealed to their native justice and magnanimity, and we have conjured them by the ties of our common kindred to disavow these usurpations, which, would inevitably interrupt our connections and correspondence. They too have been deaf to the voice of justice and of consanguinity. We must, therefore, acquiesce in the necessity, which denounces our Separation, and hold them, as we hold the rest of mankind, Enemies in War, in Peace Friends.

We, therefore, the Representatives of the United States of America, in General Congress, Assembled, appealing to the Supreme Judge of the world for the rectitude of our intentions, do, in the Name, and by Authority of the good People of these Colonies, solemnly publish and declare, That these United Colonies are, and of Right ought to be Free and Independent States; that they are Absolved from all Allegiance to the British Crown, and that all political connection between them and the State of Great Britain, is and ought to be totally dissolved; and that, as Free and Independent States, they have full Power to levy War, conclude Peace, contract Alliances, establish Commerce, and to do all other Acts and Things which Independent States may of right do. And for the support of this Declaration, with a firm reliance on the protection of divine Providence, we mutually pledge to each other our Lives, our Fortunes and our sacred Honor.

The Constitution of the United States of America

We the People of the United States, in Order to form a more perfect Union, establish Justice, insure domestic Tranquility, provide for the common defence, promote the general Welfare, and secure the Blessings of Liberty to ourselves and our Posterity, do ordain and establish this Constitution for the United States of America.

Article I

SECTION 1. All legislative Powers herein granted shall be vested in a Congress of the United States, which shall consist of a Senate and House of Representatives.

SECTION 2. The House of Representatives shall be composed of Members chosen every second Year by the People of the several States, and the Electors in each State shall have the Qualifications requisite for Electors of the most numerous Branch of the State Legislature.

No Person shall be a Representative who shall not have attained to the Age of twenty five Years, and been seven Years a Citizen of the United States, and who shall not, when elected, be an Inhabitant of that State in which he shall be chosen.

Representatives and direct Taxes[1] shall be apportioned among the several States which may be included within this Union, according to their respective Numbers, which shall be determined by adding to the whole Number of free Persons, including those bound to Service for a Term of Years, and excluding Indians not taxed, three fifths of all other Persons.[2]

The actual Enumeration shall be made within three Years after the first Meeting of the Congress of the United States, and within every subsequent Term of ten Years, in such Manner as they shall by Law direct. The Number of Representatives shall not exceed one for every thirty Thousand, but each State shall have at Least one Representative; and until such enumeration shall be made, the State of New Hampshire shall be entitled to chuse three; Massachusetts eight; Rhode Island and Providence Plantations one; Connecticut five; New York six; New Jersey four; Pennsylvania eight; Delaware one; Maryland six; Virginia ten; North Carolina five; South Carolina five; and Georgia three.

When vacancies happen in the Representation from any State, the Executive Authority thereof shall issue Writs of Election to fill such Vacancies.

The House of Representatives shall chuse their Speaker and other Officers; and shall have the sole Power of Impeachment.

SECTION 3. The Senate of the United States shall be composed of two Senators from each State, chosen by the Legislature thereof, for six Years; and each Senator shall have one Vote.[3]

Immediately after they shall be assembled in Consequence of the first Election, they shall be divided as equally as may be into three Classes. The Seats of the Senators of the first Class shall be vacated at the Expiration of the second Year, of the second Class at the Expiration of the fourth Year, and of the third Class at the Expiration of the sixth Year, so that one third may be chosen every second Year; and if Vacancies happen by Resignation, or otherwise, during the

---

Text is from the engrossed copy in the National Archives. Original spelling, capitalization, and punctuation have been retained.

[1] Modified by the Sixteenth Amendment.

[2] Replaced by the Fourteenth Amendment.

[3] Superseded by the Seventeenth Amendment.

Recess of the Legislature of any State, the Executive thereof may make temporary Appointments until the next Meeting of the Legislature, which shall then fill such Vacancies.[4]

No Person shall be a Senator who shall not have attained to the Age of thirty Years, and been nine Years a Citizen of the United States, and who shall not, when elected, be an Inhabitant of that State for which he shall be chosen.

The Vice President of the United States shall be President of the Senate, but shall have no Vote, unless they be equally divided.

The Senate shall chuse their other Officers, and also a President pro tempore, in the Absence of the Vice President, or when he shall exercise the Office of President of the United States.

The Senate shall have the sole Power to try all Impeachments. When sitting for that Purpose, they shall be on Oath or Affirmation. When the President of the United States is tried, the Chief Justice shall preside: And no Person shall be convicted without the Concurrence of two thirds of the Members present.

Judgment in Cases of Impeachment shall not extend further than to removal from Office, and disqualification to hold and enjoy any Office of honor, Trust or Profit under the United States: but the Party convicted shall nevertheless be liable and subject to Indictment, Trial, Judgment and Punishment, according to Law.

SECTION 4. The Times, Places and Manner of holding Elections for Senators and Representatives, shall be prescribed in each State by the Legislature thereof, but the Congress may at any time by Law make or alter such Regulation, except as to the Places of chusing Senators.

The Congress shall assemble at least once in every Year, and such Meeting shall be on the first Monday in December, unless they shall by Law appoint a different Day.[5]

SECTION 5. Each House shall be the Judge of the Elections, Returns and Qualifications of its own Members, and a Majority of each shall constitute a Quorum to do Business; but a smaller Number may adjourn from day to day, and may be authorized to compel the Attendance of absent Members, in such Manner, and under such Penalties as each House may provide.

Each House may determine the Rules of its Proceedings, punish its Members for disorderly Behaviour, and, with the Concurrence of two thirds, expel a Member.

Each House shall keep a Journal of its Proceedings, and from time to time publish the same, excepting such Parts as may in their Judgment require Secrecy; and the Yeas and Nays of the Members of either House on any question shall, at the Desire of one fifth of those Present, be entered on the Journal.

Neither House, during the Session of Congress, shall, without the Consent of the other, adjourn for more than three days, nor to any other Place than that in which the two Houses shall be sitting.

SECTION 6. The Senators and Representatives shall receive a Compensation for their Services, to be ascertained by Law, and paid out of the Treasury of the United States. They shall in all Cases, except Treason, Felony and Breach of the Peace, be privileged from Arrest during their Attendance at the Session of their respective Houses, and in going to and returning from the same; and for any Speech or Debate in either House, they shall not be questioned in any other Place.

No Senator or Representative shall, during the Time for which he was elected, be appointed to any civil Office under the Authority of the United States, which shall have been created, or the Emoluments whereof shall have been encreased during such time; and no Person holding any Office under the United States, shall be a Member of either House during his Continuance in Office.

---

[4] Modified by the Seventeenth Amendment.
[5] Superseded by the Twentieth Amendment.

SECTION 7. All Bills for raising Revenue shall originate in the House of Representatives; but the Senate may propose or concur with Amendments as on other Bills.

Every Bill which shall have passed the House of Representatives and the Senate shall, before it become a Law, be presented to the President of the United States; If he approve he shall sign it, but if not he shall return it, with his Objections to that House in which it shall have originated, who shall enter the Objections at large on their Journal, and proceed to reconsider it. If after such Reconsideration two thirds of that House shall agree to pass the Bill, it shall be sent, together with the Objections, to the other House, by which it shall likewise be reconsidered, and if approved by two thirds of that House, it shall become a Law. But in all such Cases the Votes of both Houses shall be determined by yeas and Nays, and the Names of the Persons voting for and against the Bill shall be entered on the Journal of each House respectively. If any Bill shall not be returned by the President within ten Days (Sundays excepted) after it shall have been presented to him, the Same shall be a Law, in like Manner as if he had signed it, unless the Congress by their Adjournment prevent its Return, in which Case it shall not be a Law.

Every Order, Resolution, or Vote to which the Concurrence of the Senate and House of Representatives may be necessary (except on a question of Adjournment) shall be presented to the President of the United States; and before the Same shall take Effect, shall be approved by him, or being disapproved by him shall be repassed by two thirds of the Senate and House of Representatives, according to the Rules and Limitations prescribed in the Case of a Bill.

SECTION 8. The Congress shall have power To lay and collect Taxes, Duties, Imposts and Excises, to pay the Debts and provide for the common Defence and general Welfare of the United States; but all Duties, Imposts and Excises shall be uniform throughout the United States; To borrow Money on the credit of the United States; To regulate Commerce with foreign Nations, and among the several States, and with the Indian Tribes; To establish an uniform Rule of Naturalization, and uniform Laws on the subject of Bankruptcies throughout the United States; To coin Money, regulate the Value thereof, and of foreign Coin, and fix the Standard of Weights and Measures; To provide for the Punishment of counterfeiting the Securities and current Coin of the United States; To establish Post Offices and post Roads; To promote the Progress of Science and useful Arts, by securing for limited Times to Authors and Inventors the exclusive Right to their respective Writings and Discoveries; To constitute Tribunals inferior to the supreme Court; To define and punish Piracies and Felonies committed on the high Seas, and Offences against the Law of Nations;

To declare War, grant Letters of Marque and Reprisal, and make Rules concerning Captures on Land and Water; To raise and support Armies, but no Appropriation of Money to that Use shall be for a longer Term than two Years; To provide and maintain a Navy; To make Rules for the Government and Regulation of the land and naval Forces; To provide for calling forth the Militia to execute the Laws of the Union, suppress Insurrections and repel Invasions; To provide for organizing, arming, and disciplining, the Militia, and for governing such Part of them as may be employed in the Service of the United States, reserving to the States respectively, the Appointment of the Officers, and the Authority of training the Militia according to the discipline prescribed by Congress; To exercise exclusive Legislation in all Cases whatsoever, over such District (not exceeding ten Miles square) as may, by Cession of particular States, and the Acceptance of Congress, become the Seat of the Government of the United States, and to exercise like Authority over all Places purchased by the Consent of the Legislature of the State in which the Same shall be, for the Erection of Forts, Magazines, Arsenals, dock-Yards, and other needful Buildings;— And To make all Laws which shall be necessary and proper for carrying into Execution the foregoing Powers, and all other Powers vested by this Constitution in the Government of the United States, or in any Department or Officer thereof.

SECTION 9. The Migration or Importation of such Persons as any of the States now existing shall think proper to admit, shall not be prohibited by the Congress prior to the Year one thousand eight hundred and eight, but a Tax or duty may be imposed on such Importation, not exceeding ten dollars for each Person.

The Privilege of the Writ of Habeas Corpus shall not be suspended, unless when in Cases of Rebellion or Invasion the public Safety may require it.

No Bill of Attainder or ex post facto Law shall be passed.

No Capitation, or other direct, Tax shall be laid, unless in Proportion to the Census or Enumeration herein before directed to be taken.

No Tax or Duty shall be laid on Articles exported from any State.

No Preference shall be given by any Regulation of Commerce or Revenue to the Ports of one State over those of another: nor shall Vessels bound to, or from, one State, be obliged to enter, clear, or pay Duties in another.

No Money shall be drawn from the Treasury, but in Consequence of Appropriations made by Law, and a regular Statement and Account of the Receipts and Expenditures of all public Money shall be published from time to time.

No Title of Nobility shall be granted by the United States: And no Person holding any Office of Profit or Trust under them, shall, without the Consent of the Congress, accept of any present, Emolument, Office, or Title, of any kind whatever, from any King, Prince, or foreign State.

SECTION 10. No State shall enter into any Treaty, Alliance, or Confederation; grant Letters of Marque and Reprisal; coin Money; emit Bills of Credit; make any Thing but gold and silver Coin a Tender in Payment of Debts; pass any Bill of Attainder, ex post facto Law, or Law impairing the Obligation of Contracts, or grant any Title of Nobility.

No State shall, without the Consent of the Congress, lay any Imposts or Duties on Imports or Exports, except what may be absolutely necessary for executing its inspection Laws: and the net Produce of all Duties and Imposts, laid by any State on Imports or Exports, shall be for the Use of the Treasury of the United States; and all such Laws shall be subject to the Revision and Controul of the Congress.

No State shall, without the Consent of Congress, lay any Duty of Tonnage, keep Troops, or Ships of War in time of Peace, enter into any Agreement or Compact with another State, or with a foreign Power, or engage in War, unless actually invaded, or in such imminent Danger as will not admit of delay.

Article II

SECTION 1. The executive Power shall be vested in a President of the United States of America. He shall hold his Office during the Term of four Years, and, together with the Vice President, chosen for the same Term, be elected, as follows: Each State shall appoint, in such Manner as the Legislature thereof may direct, a Number of Electors, equal to the whole Number of Senators and Representatives to which the State may be entitled in the Congress: but no Senator or Representative, or Person holding an Office of Trust or Profit under the United States, shall be appointed an Elector.

The Electors shall meet in their respective States, and vote by Ballot for two Persons, of whom one at least shall not be an Inhabitant of the same State with themselves. And they shall make a List of all the Persons voted for, and of the Number of Votes for each; which List they shall sign and certify, and transmit sealed to the Seat of the Government of the United States, directed to the President of the Senate. The President of the Senate shall, in the Presence of the Senate and House of Representatives, open all the Certificates, and the Votes shall then be counted. The Person having the greatest Number of Votes shall be the President, if such Number be a Majority of the whole Number of Electors appointed; and if there be more than one who have such Majority, and have an equal Number of Votes, then the House of Representatives shall immediately chuse by Ballot one of them for President; and if no Person have a Majority, then from the five highest on the List the said House shall in like Manner chuse the President. But in chusing the President, the Votes shall be taken by States, the Representation from each State having one Vote; A quorum for this Purpose shall consist of a Member or Members from two thirds of the States, and a Majority of all the States shall be necessary to a Choice. In every Case, after the Choice of the

President, the Person having the greatest Number of Votes of the Electors shall be the Vice President. But if there should remain two or more who have equal Votes, the Senate shall chuse from them by Ballot the Vice President.[6]

The Congress may determine the Time of chusing the Electors, and the Day on which they shall give their Votes; which Day shall be the same throughout the United States.

No Person except a natural born Citizen, or a Citizen of the United States, at the time of the Adoption of this Constitution, shall be eligible to the Office of President, neither shall any Person be eligible to that Office who shall not have attained to the Age of thirty five Years, and been fourteen Years a Resident within the United States.

In Case of the Removal of the President from Office, or of his Death, Resignation, or Inability to discharge the Powers and Duties of the said Office, the Same shall devolve on the Vice President, and the Congress may by Law provide for the Case of Removal, Death, Resignation or Inability, both of the President and Vice President, declaring what Officer shall then act as President, and such Officer shall act accordingly, until the Disability be removed, or a President shall be elected.[7]

The President shall, at stated Times, receive for his Services, a Compensation, which shall neither be encreased nor diminished during the Period for which he shall have been elected, and he shall not receive within that Period any other Emolument from the United States, or any of them.

Before he enter on the Execution of his Office, he shall take the following Oath or Affirmation:—"I do solemnly swear (or affirm) that I will faithfully execute the Office of President of the United States, and will to the best of my Ability, preserve, protect and defend the Constitution of the United States."

SECTION 2. The President shall be Commander in Chief of the Army and Navy of the United States, and of the Militia of the several States, when called into the actual Service of the United States; he may require the Opinion, in writing, of the principal Officer in each of the executive Departments, upon any Subject relating to the Duties of their respective Offices, and he shall have Power to grant Reprieves and Pardons for Offences against the United States, except in Cases of Impeachment.

He shall have Power, by and with the Advice and Consent of the Senate, to make Treaties, provided two thirds of the Senators present concur; and he shall nominate, and by and with the Advice and Consent of the Senate, shall appoint Ambassadors, other public Ministers and Consuls, Judges of the supreme Court, and all other Officers of the United States, whose Appointments are not herein otherwise provided for, and which shall be established by Law; but the Congress may by Law vest the Appointment of such inferior Officers, as they think proper, in the President alone, in the Courts of Law, or in the Heads of Departments.

The President shall have Power to fill up all Vacancies that may happen during the Recess of the Senate, by granting Commissions which shall expire at the End of their next Session.

SECTION 3. He shall from time to time give the Congress Information of the State of the Union, and recommend to their Consideration such Measures as he shall judge necessary and expedient; he may, on extraordinary Occasions, convene both Houses, or either of them, and in Case of Disagreement between them, with Respect to the Time of Adjournment, he may adjourn them to such Time as he shall think proper; he shall receive Ambassadors and other public Ministers; he shall take Care that the Laws be faithfully executed, and shall Commission all the Officers of the United States.

SECTION 4. The President, Vice President and all civil Officers of the United States, shall be removed from Office on Impeachment for, and Conviction of, Treason, Bribery, or other high Crimes and Misdemeanors.

---

[6] Superseded by the Twelfth Amendment.

[7] Modified by the Twenty-fifth Amendment.

Article III

SECTION 1. The judicial Power of the United States, shall be vested in one supreme Court, and in such inferior Courts as the Congress may from time to time ordain and establish.

The Judges, both of the supreme and inferior Courts, shall hold their Offices during good Behaviour, and shall, at stated Times, receive for their Services, a Compensation, which shall not be diminished during their Continuance in Office.

SECTION 2. The judicial Power shall extend to all Cases, in Law and Equity, arising under this Constitution, the Laws of the United States, and Treaties made, or which shall be made, under their Authority;—to all Cases affecting Ambassadors, other public Ministers and Consuls;—to all Cases of admiralty and maritime Jurisdiction;—to Controversies to which the United States shall be a Party;—to Controversies between two or more States;—between a State and Citizens of another State;[8]—between Citizens of different States,—between Citizens of the same State claiming Lands under Grants of different States, and between a State, or the Citizens thereof, and foreign States, Citizens or Subjects.

In all Cases affecting Ambassadors, other public Ministers and Consuls, and those in which a State shall be Party, the supreme Court shall have original Jurisdiction. In all the other Cases beforementioned, the supreme Court shall have appellate Jurisdiction, both as to Law and Fact, with such Exceptions, and under such Regulations as the Congress shall make.

The Trial of all Crimes, except in Cases of Impeachment, shall be by Jury; and such Trial shall be held in the State where the said Crimes shall have been committed; but when not committed within any State, the Trial shall be at such Place or Places as the Congress may by Law have directed.

SECTION 3. Treason against the United States, shall consist only in levying War against them, or in adhering to their Enemies, giving them Aid and Comfort. No Person shall be convicted of Treason unless on the Testimony of two Witnesses to the same overt Act, or on Confession in open Court.

The Congress shall have Power to declare the Punishment of Treason, but no Attainder of Treason shall work Corruption of Blood, or Forfeiture except during the Life of the Person attainted.

Article IV

SECTION 1. Full Faith and Credit shall be given in each State to the public Acts, Records, and judicial Proceedings of every other State. And the Congress may by general Laws prescribe the Manner in which such Acts, Records and Proceedings shall be proved, and the Effect thereof.

SECTION 2. The Citizens of each State shall be entitled to all Privileges and Immunities of Citizens in the several States.

A Person charged in any State with Treason, Felony, or other Crime, who shall flee from Justice, and be found in another State, shall on Demand of the executive Authority of the State from which he fled, be delivered up, to be removed to the State having Jurisdiction of the Crime.

No Person held to Service or Labour in one State, under the Laws thereof, escaping into another, shall, in Consequence of any Law or Regulation therein, be discharged from such Service or Labour, but shall be delivered up on Claim of the Party to whom such Service or Labour may be due.

SECTION 3. New States may be admitted by the Congress into this Union; but no new State shall be formed or erected within the Jurisdiction of any other State, nor any State be formed by the Junction of two or more States, or Parts of States, without the Consent of the Legislatures of the States concerned as well as of the Congress.

---

[8] Modified by the Eleventh Amendment.

The Congress shall have Power to dispose of and make all needful Rules and Regulations respecting the Territory or other Property belonging to the United States; and nothing in this Constitution shall be so construed as to Prejudice any Claims of the United States, or of any particular State.

SECTION 4. The United States shall guarantee to every State in this Union a Republican Form of Government, and shall protect each of them against Invasion; and on Application of the Legislature, or of the Executive (when the Legislature cannot be convened) against domestic Violence.

Article V

The Congress, whenever two thirds of both Houses shall deem it necessary, shall propose Amendments to this Constitution, or, on the Application of the Legislatures of two thirds of the several States, shall call a Convention for proposing Amendments, which, in either Case, shall be valid to all Intents and Purposes, as Part of this Constitution, when ratified by the Legislatures of three fourths of the several States, or by Conventions in three fourths thereof, as the one or the other Mode of Ratification may be proposed by the Congress; Provided that no Amendment which may be made prior to the Year One thousand eight hundred and eight shall in any Manner affect the first and fourth Clauses in the Ninth Section of the first Article; and that no State, without its Consent, shall be deprived of its equal Suffrage in the Senate.

Article VI

All Debts contracted and Engagements entered into, before the Adoption of this Constitution, shall be as valid against the United States under this Constitution, as under the Confederation.

This Constitution, and the Laws of the United States which shall be made in Pursuance thereof; and all Treaties made, or which shall be made, under the Authority of the United States, shall be the supreme Law of the Land; and the Judges in every State shall be bound thereby, any Thing in the Constitution or Laws of any State to the Contrary notwithstanding.

The Senators and Representatives before mentioned, and the Members of the several State Legislatures, and all executive and judicial Officers, both of the United States and of the several States, shall be bound by Oath or Affirmation, to support this Constitution; but no religious Test shall ever be required as a Qualification to any Office or public Trust under the United States.

Article VII

The Ratification of the Conventions of nine States, shall be sufficient for the Establishment of this Constitution between the States so ratifying the Same.

Done in Convention by the Unanimous Consent of the States present the Seventeenth Day of September in the Year of our Lord one thousand seven hundred and Eighty seven and of the Independence of the United States of America the Twelfth. In witness whereof We have hereunto subscribed our Names,

Articles in Addition to, and Amendment of, the Constitution of the United States of America, Proposed by Congress, and Ratified by the Legislatures of the Several States, Pursuant to the Fifth Article of the Original Constitution.

Amendment I[9]

Congress shall make no law respecting an establishment of religion, or prohibiting the free exercise thereof; or abridging the freedom of speech, or of the press; or the right of the people peaceably to assemble, and to petition the Government for a redress of grievances.

---

[9] The first ten amendments were passed by Congress September 25, 1789. They were ratified by three-fourths of the states December 15, 1791.

Amendment II

A well regulated Militia, being necessary to the security of a free State, the right of the people to keep and bear Arms shall not be infringed.

Amendment III

No Soldier shall, in time of peace, be quartered in any house, without the consent of the Owner, nor in time of war, but in a manner to be prescribed by law.

Amendment IV

The right of the people to be secure in their persons, houses, papers, and effects, against unreasonable searches and seizures, shall not be violated, and no Warrants shall issue, but upon probable cause, supported by Oath or affirmation, and particularly describing the place to be searched, and the persons or things to be seized.

Amendment V

No person shall be held to answer for a capital or otherwise infamous crime, unless on a presentment or indictment of a Grand Jury, except in cases arising in the land or naval forces, or in the Militia, when in actual service in time of War or public danger; nor shall any person be subject for the same offence to be twice put in jeopardy of life or limb; nor shall be compelled in any criminal case to be a witness against himself, nor be deprived of life, liberty, or property, without due process of law; nor shall private property be taken for public use, without just compensation.

Amendment VI

In all criminal prosecutions, the accused shall enjoy the right to a speedy and public trial, by an impartial jury of the State and district wherein the crime shall have been committed, which district shall have been previously ascertained by law, and to be informed of the nature and cause of the accusation; to be confronted with the witnesses against him; to have compulsory process for obtaining witnesses in his favor, and to have the Assistance of Counsel for his defence.

Amendment VII

In suits at common law, where the value in controversy shall exceed twenty dollars, the right of trial by jury shall be preserved, and no fact tried by a jury, shall be otherwise reexamined in any Court of the United States, than according to the rules of the common law.

Amendment VIII

Excessive bail shall not be required, nor excessive fines imposed, nor cruel and unusual punishments inflicted.

Amendment IX

The enumeration in the Constitution, of certain rights, shall not be construed to deny or disparage others retained by the people.

Amendment X

The powers not delegated to the United States by the Constitution; nor prohibited by it to the States, are reserved to the States respectively, or to the people.

Amendment XI[10]

The Judicial power of the United States shall not be construed to extend to any suit in law or equity, commenced or prosecuted against one of the United States by Citizens of another State, or by Citizens or Subjects of any Foreign State.

Amendment XII[11]

The Electors shall meet in their respective States and vote by ballot for President and Vice-President, one of whom, at least, shall not be an inhabitant of the same State with themselves; they shall name in their ballots the person voted for as President, and in distinct ballots the person voted for as Vice-President, and they shall make distinct lists of all persons voted for as President, and of all persons voted for as Vice-President, and of the number of votes for each, which lists they shall sign and certify, and transmit sealed to the seat of the government of the United States, directed to the President of the Senate;—The President of the Senate shall, in the presence of the Senate and House of Representatives, open all the certificates and the votes shall then be counted;—The person having the greatest number of votes for President, shall be the President, if such number be a majority of the whole number of Electors appointed; and if no person have such majority, then from the persons having the highest numbers not exceeding three on the list of those voted for as President, the House of Representatives shall choose immediately, by ballot, the President.

But in choosing the President, the votes shall be taken by states, the representation from each state having one vote; a quorum for this purpose shall consist of a member or members from two-thirds of the states, and a majority of all the states shall be necessary to a choice. And if the House of Representatives shall not choose a President whenever the right of choice shall devolve upon them, before the fourth day of March next following, then the Vice-President shall act as President, as in the case of the death or other constitutional disability of the President.—The person having the greatest number of votes as Vice-President, shall be the Vice-President, if such number be a majority of the whole number of Electors appointed, and if no person have a majority, then from the two highest numbers on the list, the Senate shall choose the Vice-President; a quorum for the purpose shall consist of two-thirds of the whole number of Senators, and a majority of the whole number shall be necessary to a choice. But no person constitutionally ineligible to the office of President shall be eligible to that of Vice-President of the United States.

Amendment XIII[12]

SECTION 1. Neither slavery nor involuntary servitude, except as a punishment for crime whereof the party shall have been duly convicted, shall exist within the United States, or any place subject to their jurisdiction.

SECTION 2. Congress shall have power to enforce this article by appropriate legislation.

Amendment XIV[13]

SECTION 1. All persons born or naturalized in the United States, and subject to the jurisdiction thereof, are citizens of the United States and of the State wherein they reside. No State shall make or enforce any law which shall abridge the privileges or immunities of citizens of the United States; nor shall any State deprive any person of life, liberty, or property, without due process of law; nor deny to any person within its jurisdiction the equal protection of the laws.

---

[10] Passed March 4, 1794. Ratified January 23, 1795.
[11] Passed December 9, 1803. Ratified June 15, 1804.
[12] Passed January 31, 1865. Ratified December 6, 1865.
[13] Passed June 13, 1866. Ratified July 9, 1868.

SECTION 2. Representatives shall be apportioned among the several States according to their respective numbers, counting the whole number of persons in each State, excluding Indians not taxed. But when the right to vote at any election for the choice of electors for President and Vice-President of the United States, Representatives in Congress, the Executive and Judicial officers of a State, or the members of the Legislature thereof, is denied to any of the male inhabitants of such State, being twenty-one years of age, and citizens of the United States, or in any way abridged, except for participation in rebellion, or other crime, the basis of representation therein shall be reduced in the proportion which the number of such male citizens shall bear to the whole number of male citizens twenty-one years of age in such State.

SECTION 3. No person shall be a Senator or Representative in Congress, or elector of President and Vice-President, or hold any office, civil or military, under the United States, or under any State, who, having previously taken an oath, as a member of Congress, or as an officer of the United States, or as a member of any State legislature, or as an executive or judicial officer of any State, to support the Constitution of the United States, shall have engaged in insurrection or rebellion against the same, or given aid or comfort to the enemies thereof. But Congress may by a vote of two-thirds of each House, remove such disability.

SECTION 4. The validity of the public debt of the United States, authorized by law, including debts incurred for payment of pensions and bounties for services in suppressing insurrection or rebellion, shall not be questioned. But neither the United States nor any State shall assume or pay any debt or obligation incurred in aid of insurrection or rebellion against the United States, or any claim for the loss or emancipation of any slave; but all such debts, obligations, and claims shall be held illegal and void.

SECTION 5. The Congress shall have the power to enforce, by appropriate legislation, the provisions of this article.

Amendment XV[14]

SECTION 1. The right of citizens of the United States to vote shall not be denied or abridged by the United States or by any State on account of race, color, or previous conditions of servitude—

SECTION 2. The Congress shall have power to enforce this article by appropriate legislation.

Amendment XVI[15]

The Congress shall have power to lay and collect taxes on incomes, from whatever source derived, without apportionment among the several States, and without regard to any census or enumeration.

Amendment XVII[16]

The Senate of the United States shall be composed of two Senators from each State, elected by the people thereof, for six years; and each Senator shall have one vote. The electors in each State shall have the qualifications requisite for electors of the most numerous branch of the State legislatures.

When vacancies happen in the representation of any State in the Senate, the executive authority of such State shall issue writs of election to fill such vacancies: Provided, That the legislature of any State may empower the executive thereof to make temporary appointments until the people fill the vacancies by election as the legislature may direct.

---

[14] Passed February 26, 1869. Ratified February 2, 1870.

[15] Passed July 12, 1909. Ratified February 3, 1913.

[16] Passed May 13, 1912. Ratified April 8, 1913.

This amendment shall not be so construed as to affect the election or term of any Senator chosen before it becomes valid as part of the Constitution.

Amendment XVIII[17]

SECTION 1. After one year from the ratification of this article the manufacture, sale, or transportation of intoxicating liquors within, the importation thereof into, or the exportation thereof from the United States and all territory subject to the jurisdiction thereof for beverage purposes is hereby prohibited.

SECTION 2. The Congress and the several States shall have concurrent power to enforce this article by appropriate legislation.

SECTION 3. This article shall be inoperative unless it shall have been ratified as an amendment to the Constitution by the legislatures of the several States, as provided in the Constitution, within seven years from the date of the submission hereof to the States by the Congress.

Amendment XIX[18]

The right of citizens of the United States to vote shall not be denied or abridged by the United States or by any State on account of sex.

Congress shall have power to enforce this article by appropriate legislation.

Amendment XX[19]

SECTION 1. The terms of the President and Vice-President shall end at noon on the 20th day of January, and the terms of Senators and Representatives at noon on the 3d day of January, of the years in which such terms would have ended if this article had not been ratified; and the terms of their successors shall then begin.

SECTION 2. The Congress shall assemble at least once in every year, and such meeting shall begin at noon on the 3d day of January, unless they shall by law appoint a different day.

SECTION 3. If, at the time fixed for the beginning of the term of the President, the President elect shall have died, the Vice-President elect shall become President. If a President shall not have been chosen before the time fixed for the beginning of his term, or if the President elect shall have failed to qualify, then the Vice-President elect shall act as President until a President shall have qualified; and the Congress may by law provide for the case wherein neither a President elect nor a Vice-President elect shall have qualified, declaring who shall then act as President, or the manner in which one who is to act shall be selected, and such person shall act accordingly until a President or Vice-President shall have qualified.

SECTION 4. The Congress may by law provide for the case of the death of any of the persons from whom the House of Representatives may choose a President whenever the right of choice shall have devolved upon them, and for the case of the death of any of the persons from whom the Senate may choose a Vice-President whenever the right of choice shall have devolved upon them.

SECTION 5. Sections 1 and 2 shall take effect on the 15th day of October following the ratification of this article.

SECTION 6. This article shall be inoperative unless it shall have been ratified as an amendment to the Constitution by the legislatures of three-fourths of the several States within seven years from the date of its submission.

[17] Passed December 18, 1917. Ratified January 16, 1919.
[18] Passed June 4, 1919. Ratified August 18, 1920.
[19] Passed March 2, 1932. Ratified January 23, 1933.

Amendment XXI[20]

SECTION 1. The eighteenth article of amendment to the Constitution of the United States is hereby repealed.

SECTION 2. The transportation or importation into any State, Territory, or possession of the United States for delivery or use therein of intoxicating liquors, in violation of the laws thereof, is hereby prohibited.

SECTION 3. This article shall be inoperative unless it shall have been ratified as an amendment to the Constitution by conventions in the several States, as provided in the Constitution, within seven years from the date of the submission hereof to the States by the Congress.

Amendment XXII[21]

No person shall be elected to the office of the President more than twice, and no person who has held the office of President, or acted as President, for more than two years of a term to which some other person was elected President shall be elected to the office of the President more than once.

But this Article shall not apply to any person holding the office of President when this Article was proposed by the Congress, and shall not prevent any person who may be holding the office of President, or acting as President, during the term within which this Article becomes operative from holding the office of President or acting as President during the remainder of such term.

Amendment XXIII[22]

SECTION 1. The District constituting the seat of Government of the United States shall appoint in such manner as the Congress may direct: A number of electors of President and Vice President equal to the whole number of Senators and Representatives in Congress to which the District would be entitled if it were a State, but in no event more than the least populous State; they shall be in addition to those appointed by the States, but they shall be considered, for the purposes of the election of President and Vice President, to be electors appointed by the State; and they shall meet in the District and perform such duties as provided by the twelfth article of amendment.

SECTION 2. The Congress shall have power to enforce this article by appropriate legislation.

Amendment XXIV[23]

SECTION 1. The right of citizens of the United States to vote in any primary or other election for President or Vice President, or for Senator or Representative in Congress, shall not be denied or abridged by the United States or any State by reason of failure to pay any poll tax or other tax.

SECTION 2. The Congress shall have power to enforce this article by appropriate legislation.

Amendment XXV[24]

SECTION 1. In case of the removal of the President from office or of his death or resignation, the Vice President shall become President.

SECTION 2. Whenever there is a vacancy in the office of the Vice President, the President shall nominate a Vice President who shall take office upon confirmation by a majority vote of both Houses of Congress.

---

[20] Passed February 20, 1933. Ratified December 5, 1933.

[21] Passed March 12, 1947. Ratified March 1, 1951.

[22] Passed June 16, 1960. Ratified April 3, 1961.

[23] Passed August 27, 1962. Ratified January 23, 1964.

[24] Passed July 6, 1965. Ratified February 11, 1967.

SECTION 3. Whenever the President transmits to the President pro tempore of the Senate and the Speaker of the House of Representatives his written declaration that he is unable to discharge the powers and duties of his office, and until he transmits them a written declaration to the contrary, such powers and duties shall be discharged by the Vice President as Acting President.

SECTION 4. Whenever the Vice President and a majority of either the principal officers of the executive department or of such other body as Congress may by law provide, transmit to the President pro tempore of the Senate and the Speaker of the House of Representatives their written declaration that the President is unable to discharge the powers and duties of his office, the Vice President shall immediately assume the powers and duties of the office of Acting President.

Thereafter, when the President transmits to the President pro tempore of the Senate and the Speaker of the House of Representatives his written declaration that no inability exists, he shall resume the powers and duties of his office unless the Vice President and a majority of either the principal officers of the executive department or of such other body as Congress may by law provide, transmit within four days to the President pro tempore of the Senate and the Speaker of the House of Representatives their written declaration that the President is unable to discharge the powers and duties of his office. Thereupon Congress shall decide the issue, assembling within forty-eight hours for that purpose if not in session. If the Congress, within twenty-one days after receipt of the latter written declaration, or, if Congress is not in session, within twenty-one days after Congress is required to assemble, determines by two-thirds vote of both Houses that the President is unable to discharge the powers and duties of his office, the Vice President shall continue to discharge the same as Acting President; otherwise, the President shall resume the powers and duties of his office.

Amendment XXVI[25]

SECTION 1 The right of citizens of the United States, who are eighteen years of age or older, to vote shall not be denied or abridged by the United States or by any State on account of age.

SECTION 2. The Congress shall have power to enforce this article by appropriate legislation.

Amendment XXVII[26]

No law, varying the compensation for the service of the Senators and Representatives, shall take effect, until an election of Representatives shall have intervened.

---

[25] Passed March 23, 1971. Ratified July 5, 1971.

[26] Passed September 25, 1789. Ratified May 7, 1992.

Admission of States

Order of admission	State	Date of admission	Order of admission	State	Date of admission
1	Delaware	December 7, 1787	26	Michigan	January 26, 1837
2	Pennsylvania	December 12, 1787	27	Florida	March 3, 1845
3	New Jersey	December 18, 1787	28	Texas	December 29, 1845
4	Georgia	January 2, 1788	29	Iowa	December 28, 1846
5	Connecticut	January 9, 1788	30	Wisconsin	May 29, 1848
6	Massachusetts	February 6, 1788	31	California	September 9, 1850
7	Maryland	April 28, 1788	32	Minnesota	May 11, 1858
8	South Carolina	May 23, 1788	33	Oregon	February 14, 1859
9	New Hampshire	June 21, 1788	34	Kansas	January 29, 1861
10	Virginia	June 25, 1788	35	West Virginia	June 20, 1863
11	New York	July 26, 1788	36	Nevada	October 31, 1864
12	North Carolina	November 21, 1789	37	Nebraska	March 1, 1867
13	Rhode Island	May 29, 1790	38	Colorado	August 1, 1876
14	Vermont	March 4, 1791	39	North Dakota	November 2, 1889
15	Kentucky	June 1, 1792	40	South Dakota	November 2, 1889
16	Tennessee	June 1, 1796	41	Montana	November 8, 1889
17	Ohio	March 1, 1803	42	Washington	November 11, 1889
18	Louisiana	April 30, 1812	43	Idaho	July 3, 1890
19	Indiana	December 11, 1816	44	Wyoming	July 10, 1890
20	Mississippi	December 10, 1817	45	Utah	January 4, 1896
21	Illinois	December 3, 1818	46	Oklahoma	November 16, 1907
22	Alabama	December 14, 1819	47	New Mexico	January 6, 1912
23	Maine	March 15, 1820	48	Arizona	February 14, 1912
24	Missouri	August 10, 1821	49	Alaska	January 3, 1959
25	Arkansas	June 15, 1836	50	Hawai'i	August 21, 1959

Population of the United States

Year	Total population	Number per square mile	Year	Total population	Number per square mile	Year	Total population	Number per square mile
1790	3,929	4.5	1828	12,237		1866	36,538	
1791	4,056		1829	12,565		1867	37,376	
1792	4,194		1830	12,901	7.4	1868	38,213	
1793	4,332		1831	13,321		1869	39,051	
1794	4,469		1832	13,742		1870	39,905	13.4
1795	4,607		1833	14,162		1871	40,938	
1796	4,745		1834	14,582		1872	41,972	
1797	4,883		1835	15,003		1873	43,006	
1798	5,021		1836	15,423		1874	44,040	
1799	5,159		1837	15,843		1875	45,073	
1800	5,297	6.1	1838	16,264		1876	46,107	
1801	5,486		1839	16,684		1877	47,141	
1802	5,679		1840	17,120	9.8	1878	48,174	
1803	5,872		1841	17,733		1879	49,208	
1804	5,065		1842	18,345		1880	50,262	16.9
1805	6,258		1843	18,957		1881	51,542	
1806	6,451		1844	19,569		1882	52,821	
1807	6,644		1845	20,182		1883	54,100	
1808	6,838		1846	20,794		1884	55,379	
1809	7,031		1847	21,406		1885	56,658	
1810	7,224	4.3	1848	22,018		1886	57,938	
1811	7,460		1849	22,631		1887	59,217	
1812	7,700		1850	23,261	7.9	1888	60,496	
1813	7,939		1851	24,086		1889	61,775	
1814	8,179		1852	24,911		1890[1]	63,056	21.2
1815	8,419		1853	25,736		1891	64,361	
1816	8,659		1854	26,561		1892	65,666	
1817	8,899		1855	27,386		1893	66,970	
1818	9,139		1856	28,212		1894	68,275	
1819	9,379		1857	29,037		1895	69,580	
1820	9,618	5.6	1858	29,862		1896	70,885	
1821	9,939		1859	30,687		1897	72,189	
1822	10,268		1860	31,513	10.6	1898	73,494	
1823	10,596		1861	32,351		1899	74,799	
1824	10,924		1862	33,188		1900	76,094	25.6
1825	11,252		1863	34,026		1901	77,585	
1826	11,580		1864	34,863		1902	79,160	
1827	11,909		1865	35,701		1903	80,632	

Figures are from *Historical Statistics of the United States, Colonial Times to 1957* (1961), pp. 7, 8; *Statistical Abstract of the United States: 1974*, p. 5, Census Bureau for 1974 and 1975; and *Statistical Abstract of the United States: 1988*, p. 7.

Note: Population figures are in thousands. Density figures are for land area of continental United States.

[1] Indians living in Indian Territory or on reservations were not included in the population count until 1890.

Year	Total population	Number per square mile	Year	Total population[1]	Number per square mile	Year	Total population[1]	Number per square mile
1904	82,165		1941	133,894		1978	218,717	
1905	83,820		1942	135,361		1979	220,584	
1906	85,437		1943	137,250		1980	226,546	64.0
1907	87,000		1944	138,916		1981	230,138	
1908	88,709		1945	140,468		1982	232,520	
1909	90,492		1946	141,936		1983	234,799	
1910	92,407	31.0	1947	144,698		1984	237,001	
1911	93,868		1948	147,208		1985	239,283	
1912	95,331		1949	149,767		1986	241,596	
1913	97,227		1950	150,697[1]	50.7	1987	234,773	
1914	99,118		1951	154,878		1988	245,051	
1915	100,549		1952	157,553		1989	247,350	
1916	101,966		1953	160,184		1990	250,122	70.3
1917	103,414		1954	163,026		1991	254,521	
1918	104,550		1955	165,931		1992	245,908	
1919	105,063		1956	168,903		1993	257,908	
1920	106,466	35.6	1957	171,984		1994	261,875	
1921	108,541		1958	174,882		1995	263,434	
1922	110,055		1959	177,830		1996	266,096	
1923	111,950		1960	178,464	60.1	1997	267,901	
1924	114,113		1961	183,642		1998	269,501	
1925	115,832		1962	186,504		1999	272,700	
1926	117,399		1963	189,197		2000	282,172	80.0
1927	119,038		1964	191,833		2001	285,082	
1928	120,501		1965	194,237		2002	287,804	
1929	121,700		1966	196,485		2003	290,326	
1930	122,775	41.2	1967	198,629		2004	293,046	
1931	124,040		1968	200,619		2005	295,753	
1932	124,840		1969	202,599		2006	298,593	
1933	125,579		1970	203,875	57.5[2]	2007	301,580	
1934	126,374		1971	207,045		2008	304,375	
1935	127,250		1972	208,842		2009	307,007	
1936	128,053		1973	210,396		2010	308,746	87.4
1937	128,825		1974	211,894		2011	311,588	
1938	129,825		1975	213,631		2012	313,914	
1939	130,880		1976	215,152		2013	316,439	
1940	131,669	44.2	1977	216,880				

[1] Figures after 1940 represent total population including armed forces abroad, except in official census years.

[2] Figure includes Alaska and Hawai'i, were territories through 1950, and were first included in the United States in the 1960 census.

Presidential Elections

Year	Number of states	Candidates[1]	Parties	Popular vote	Electoral vote	Percentage of popular vote[2]
1789	11	**George Washington**	No party designations		69	
		John Adams			34	
		Minor Candidates			35	
1792	15	**George Washington**	No party designations		132	
		John Adams			77	
		George Clinton			50	
		Minor Candidates			5	
1796	16	**John Adams**	Federalist		71	
		Thomas Jefferson	Democratic-Republican		68	
		Thomas Pinckney	Federalist		59	
		Aaron Burr	Democratic-Republican		30	
		Minor Candidates			48	
1800	16	**Thomas Jefferson**	Democratic-Republican		73	
		Aaron Burr	Democratic-Republican		73	
		John Adams	Federalist		65	
		Charles C. Pinckney	Federalist		64	
		John Jay	Federalist		1	
1804	17	**Thomas Jefferson**	Democratic-Republican		162	
		Charles C. Pinckney	Federalist		14	
1808	17	**James Madison**	Democratic-Republican		122	
		Charles C. Pinckney	Federalist		47	
		George Clinton	Democratic-Republican		6	
1812	18	**James Madison**	Democratic-Republican		128	
		DeWitt Clinton	Federalist		89	
1816	19	**James Monroe**	Democratic-Republican		183	
		Rufus King	Federalist		34	
1820	24	**James Monroe**	Democratic-Republican		231	
		John Quincy Adams	Independent Republican		1	
1824	24	**John Quincy Adams**	Democratic-Republican	108,740	84	30.5
		Andrew Jackson	Democratic-Republican	153,544	99	43.1
		William H. Crawford	Democratic-Republican	46,618	41	13.1
		Henry Clay	Democratic-Republican	47,136	37	13.2
1828	24	**Andrew Jackson**	Democratic	647,286	178	56.0
		John Quincy Adams	National Republican	508,064	83	44.0

[1]Before the passage of the Twelfth Amendment in 1804, the Electoral College voted for two presidential candidates; the runner-up became vice president. Figures are from *Historical Statistics of the United States, Colonial Times to 1957* (1961), pp. 682–83; and the U.S. Department of Justice.

[2]Candidates receiving less than 1 percent of the popular vote have been omitted. For that reason the percentage of popular vote given for any election year may not total 100 percent.

Year	Number of states	Candidates	Parties	Popular vote	Electoral vote	Percentage of popular vote[1]
1832	24	**Andrew Jackson**	Democratic	687,502	219	55.0
		Henry Clay	National Republican	530,189	49	42.4
		William Wirt	Anti-Masonic		7	
		John Floyd	National Republican	33,108	11	2.6
1836	26	**Martin Van Buren**	Democratic	765,483	170	50.9
		William H. Harrison	Whig		73	
		Hugh L. White	Whig	739,795	26	
		Daniel Webster	Whig		14	
		W. P. Mangum	Whig		11	
1840	26	**William H. Harrison**	Whig	1,274,624	234	53.1
		Martin Van Buren	Democratic	1,127,781	60	46.9
1844	26	**James K. Polk**	Democratic	1,338,464	170	49.6
		Henry Clay	Whig	1,300,097	105	48.1
		James G. Birney	Liberty	62,300		2.3
1848	30	**Zachary Taylor**	Whig	1,360,967	163	47.4
		Lewis Cass	Democratic	1,222,342	127	42.5
		Martin Van Buren	Free Soil	291,263		10.1
1852	31	**Franklin Pierce**	Democratic	1,601,117	254	50.9
		Winfield Scott	Whig	1,385,453	42	44.1
		John P. Hale	Free Soil	155,825		5.0
1856	31	**James Buchanan**	Democratic	1,832,955	174	45.3
		John C. Frémont	Republican	1,339,932	114	33.1
		Millard Fillmore	American	871,731	8	21.6
1860	33	**Abraham Lincoln**	Republican	1,865,593	180	39.8
		Stephen A. Douglas	Democratic	1,382,713	12	29.5
		John C. Breckinridge	Democratic	848,356	72	18.1
		John Bell	Constitutional Union	592,906	39	12.6
1864	36	**Abraham Lincoln**	Republican	2,206,938	212	55.0
		George B. McClellan	Democratic	1,803,787	21	45.0
1868	37	**Ulysses S. Grant**	Republican	3,013,421	214	52.7
		Horatio Seymour	Democratic	2,706,829	80	47.3
1872	37	**Ulysses S. Grant**	Republican	3,596,745	286	55.6
		Horace Greeley	Democratic	2,843,446	[2]	43.9
1876	38	**Rutherford B. Hayes**	Republican	4,036,572	185	48.0
		Samuel J. Tilden	Democratic	4,284,020	184	51.0

[1] Candidates receiving less than 1 percent of the popular vote have been omitted. For that reason the percentage of popular vote given for any election year may not total 100 percent.

Presidential Elections (continued)

Year	Number of states	Candidates	Parties	Popular vote	Electoral vote	Percentage of popular vote[1]
1880	38	**James A. Garfield**	Republican	4,453,295	214	48.5
		Winfield S. Hancock	Democratic	4,414,082	155	48.1
		James B. Weaver	Greenback-Labor	308,578		3.4
1884	38	**Grover Cleveland**	Democratic	4,879,507	219	48.5
		James G. Blaine	Republican	4,850,293	182	48.2
		Benjamin F. Butler	Greenback-Labor	175,370		1.8
		John P. St. John	Prohibition	150,369		1.5
1888	38	**Benjamin Harrison**	Republican	5,477,129	233	47.9
		Grover Cleveland	Democratic	5,537,857	168	48.6
		Clinton B. Fisk	Prohibition	249,506		2.2
		Anson J. Streeter	Union Labor	146,935		1.3
1892	44	**Grover Cleveland**	Democratic	5,555,426	277	46.1
		Benjamin Harrison	Republican	5,182,690	145	43.0
		James B. Weaver	People's	1,029,846	22	8.5
		John Bidwell	Prohibition	264,133		2.2
1896	45	**William McKinley**	Republican	7,102,246	271	51.1
		William J. Bryan	Democratic	6,492,559	176	47.7
1900	45	**William McKinley**	Republican	7,218,491	292	51.7
		William J. Bryan	Democratic; Populist	6,356,734	155	45.5
		John C. Wooley	Prohibition	208,914		1.5
1904	45	**Theodore Roosevelt**	Republican	7,628,461	336	57.4
		Alton B. Parker	Democratic	5,084,223	140	37.6
		Eugene V. Debs	Socialist	402,283		3.0
		Silas C. Swallow	Prohibition	258,536		1.9
1908	46	**William H. Taft**	Republican	7,675,320	321	51.6
		William J. Bryan	Democratic	6,412,294	162	43.1
		Eugene V. Debs	Socialist	420,793		2.8
		Eugene W. Chafin	Prohibition	253,840		1.7
1912	48	**Woodrow Wilson**	Democratic	6,296,547	435	41.9
		Theodore Roosevelt	Progressive	4,118,571	88	27.4
		William H. Taft	Republican	3,486,720	8	23.2
		Eugene V. Debs	Socialist	900,672		6.0
		Eugene W. Chafin	Prohibition	206,275		1.4
1916	48	**Woodrow Wilson**	Democratic	9,127,695	277	49.4
		Charles E. Hughes	Republican	8,533,507	254	46.2
		A. L. Benson	Socialist	585,113		3.2
		J. Frank Hanly	Prohibition	220,506		1.2

[1] Candidates receiving less than 1 percent of the popular vote have been omitted. For that reason the percentage of popular vote given for any election year may not total 100 percent.

[2] Greeley died shortly after the election; the electors supporting him then divided their votes among minor candidates.

Year	Number of states	Candidates	Parties	Popular vote	Electoral vote	Percentage of popular vote[1]
1920	48	**Warren G. Harding**	Republican	16,143,407	404	60.4
		James N. Cox	Democratic	9,130,328	127	34.2
		Eugene V. Debs	Socialist	919,799		3.4
		P. P. Christensen	Farmer-Labor	265,411		1.0
1924	48	**Calvin Coolidge**	Republican	15,718,211	382	54.0
		John W. Davis	Democratic	8,385,283	136	28.8
		Robert M. La Follette	Progressive	4,831,289	13	16.6
1928	48	**Herbert C. Hoover**	Republican	21,391,993	444	58.2
		Alfred E. Smith	Democratic	15,016,169	87	40.9
1932	48	**Franklin D. Roosevelt**	Democratic	22,809,638	472	57.4
		Herbert C. Hoover	Republican	15,758,901	59	39.7
		Norman Thomas	Socialist	881,951		2.2
1936	48	**Franklin D. Roosevelt**	Democratic	27,752,869	523	60.8
		Alfred M. Landon	Republican	16,674,665	8	36.5
		William Lemke	Union	882,479		1.9
1940	48	**Franklin D. Roosevelt**	Democratic	27,307,819	449	54.8
		Wendell L. Willkie	Republican	22,321,018	82	44.8
1944	48	**Franklin D. Roosevelt**	Democratic	25,606,585	432	53.5
		Thomas E. Dewey	Republican	22,014,745	99	46.0
1948	48	**Harry S. Truman**	Democratic	24,105,812	303	49.5
		Thomas E. Dewey	Republican	21,970,065	189	45.1
		J. Strom Thurmond	States' Rights	1,169,063	39	2.4
		Henry A. Wallace	Progressive	1,157,172		2.4
1952	48	**Dwight D. Eisenhower**	Republican	33,936,234	442	55.1
		Adlai E. Stevenson	Democratic	27,314,992	89	44.4
1956	48	**Dwight D. Eisenhower**	Republican	35,590,472	457	57.6
		Adlai E. Stevenson	Democratic	26,022,752	73	42.1
1960	50	**John F. Kennedy**	Democratic	34,227,096	303	49.9
		Richard M. Nixon	Republican	34,108,546	219	49.6
1964	50	**Lyndon B. Johnson**	Democratic	43,126,506	486	61.1
		Barry M. Goldwater	Republican	27,176,799	52	38.5
1968	50	**Richard M. Nixon**	Republican	31,785,480	301	43.4
		Hubert H. Humphrey	Democratic	31,275,165	191	42.7
		George C. Wallace	American Independent	9,906,473	46	13.5
1972	50	**Richard M. Nixon**	Republican	47,169,911	520	60.7
		George S. McGovern	Democratic	29,170,383	17	37.5
1976	50	**Jimmy Carter**	Democratic	40,827,394	297	50.0
		Gerald R. Ford	Republican	39,145,977	240	47.9

[1] Candidates receiving less than 1 percent of the popular vote have been omitted. For that reason the percentage of popular vote given for any election year may not total 100 percent.

Year	Number of states	Candidates	Parties	Popular vote	Electoral vote	Percentage of popular vote[1]
1980	50	**Ronald W. Reagan**	Republican	43,899,248	489	50.8
		Jimmy Carter	Democratic	35,481,435	49	41.0
		John B. Anderson	Independent	5,719,437		6.6
		Ed Clark	Libertarian	920,859		1.0
1984	50	**Ronald W. Reagan**	Republican	54,281,858	525	59.2
		Walter F. Mondale	Democratic	37,457,215	13	40.8
1988	50	**George H. Bush**	Republican	47,917,341	426	54
		Michael Dukakis	Democratic	41,013,030	112	46
1992	50	**William Clinton**	Democratic	44,908,254	370	43.0
		George H. Bush	Republican	39,102,343	168	37.4
		Ross Perot	Independent	19,741,065		18.9
1996	50	**William Clinton**	Democratic	45,628,667	379	49.2
		Robert Dole	Republican	37,869,435	159	40.8
		Ross Perot	Reform	7,874,283		8.5
2000	50	**George W. Bush**	Republican	50,456,062	271	47.9
		Albert Gore	Democratic	50,996,582	266	48.4
		Ralph Nader	Green	2,858,843		2.7
2004	50	**George W. Bush**	Republican	62,040,606	286	51
		John F. Kerry	Democratic	59,028,109	252	48
		Ralph Nader	Green/Independent	411,304		1
2008	50	**Barack Obama**	Democratic	66,882,230	365	53
		John McCain	Republican	58,343,671	173	46
2012	50	**Barack Obama**	Democratic	65,917,258	332	51
		Mitt Romney	Republican	60,932,235	206	47

[1]Candidates receiving less than 1 percent of the popular vote have been omitted. For that reason the percentage of popular vote given for any election year may not total 100 percent.

Presents and Vice Presidents

Term	President	Vice President	Term	President	Vice President
1789–1793	George Washington	John Adams	1901–1905	William McKinley (d. 1901) Theodore Roosevelt	Theodore Roosevelt
1793–1797	George Washington	John Adams			
1797–1801	John Adams	Thomas Jefferson	1905–1909	Theodore Roosevelt	Charles W. Fairbanks
1801–1805	Thomas Jefferson	Aaron Burr	1909–1913	William H. Taft	James S. Sherman (d.1912)
1805–1809	Thomas Jefferson	George Clinton			
1809–1813	James Madison	George Clinton (d. 1812)	1913–1917	Woodrow Wilson	Thomas R. Marshall
			1917–1921	Woodrow Wilson	Thomas R. Marshall
1813–1817	James Madison	Elbridge Gerry (d. 1814)	1921–1925	Warren G. Harding (d. 1923) Calvin Coolidge	Calvin Coolidge
1817–1821	James Monroe	Daniel D. Tompkins			
1821–1825	James Monroe	Daniel D. Tompkins	1925–1929	Calvin Coolidge	Charles G. Dawes
1825–1829	John Quincy Adams	John C. Calhoun	1929–1933	Herbert Hoover	Charles Curtis
1829–1833	Andrew Jackson	John C. Calhoun (resigned 1832)	1933–1937	Franklin D. Roosevelt	John N. Garner
1833–1837	Andrew Jackson	Martin Van Buren	1937–1941	Franklin D. Roosevelt	John N. Garner
1837–1841	Martin Van Buren	Richard M. Johnson	1941–1945	Franklin D. Roosevelt	Henry A. Wallace
1841–1845	William H. Harrison (d. 1841) John Tyler	John Tyler	1945–1949	Franklin D. Roosevelt (d. 1945) Harry S Truman	Harry S Truman
1845–1849	James K. Polk	George M. Dallas	1949–1953	Harry S Truman	Alben W. Barkley
1849–1853	Zachary Taylor (d. 1850) Millard Fillmore	Millard Fillmore	1953–1957	Dwight D. Eisenhower	Richard M. Nixon
1853–1857	Franklin Pierce	William R. D. King (d. 1853)	1957–1961	Dwight D. Eisenhower	Richard M. Nixon
1857–1861	James Buchanan	John C. Breckinridge	1961–1965	John F. Kennedy (d. 1963) Lyndon B. Johnson	Lyndon B. Johnson
1861–1865	Abraham Lincoln	Hannibal Hamlin			
1865–1869	Abraham Lincoln (d. 1865) Andrew Johnson	Andrew Johnson	1965–1969	Lyndon B. Johnson	Hubert H. Humphrey, Jr.
1869–1873	Ulysses S. Grant	Schuyler Colfax	1969–1974	Richard M. Nixon	Spiro T. Agnew (resigned 1973); Gerald R. Ford
1873–1877	Ulysses S. Grant	Henry Wilson (d. 1875)			
1877–1881	Rutherford B. Hayes	William A. Wheeler	1974–1977	Gerald R. Ford	Nelson A. Rockefeller
1881–1885	James A. Garfield (d. 1881) Chester A. Arthur	Chester A. Arthur	1977–1981	Jimmy Carter	Walter F. Mondale
			1981–1985	Ronald Reagan	George Bush
			1985–1989	Ronald Reagan	George Bush
1885–1889	Grover Cleveland	Thomas A. Hendricks (d. 1885)	1993–1993	George Bush	J. Danforth Quayle III
1889–1893	Benjamin Harrison	Levi P. Morton	1993–2001	William Clinton	Albert Gore, Jr.
1893–1897	Grover Cleveland	Adlai E. Stevenson	2001–2005	George W. Bush	Richard Cheney
1897–1901	William McKinley	Garret A. Hobart (d. 1899)	2005–2009	George W. Bush	Richard Cheney
			2009–	Barack Obama	Joseph Biden

Justices of the U.S. Supreme Court

Name	Term of service	Years of service	Appointed by	Name	Term of service	Years of service	Appointed by
John Jay	1789–1795	5	Washington	Robert C. Grier	1846–1870	23	Polk
John Rutledge	1789–1791	1	Washington	Benjamin R. Curtis	1851–1857	6	Fillmore
William Cushing	1789–1810	20	Washington	John A. Campbell	1853–1861	8	Pierce
James Wilson	1789–1798	8	Washington	Nathan Clifford	1858–1881	23	Buchanan
John Blair	1789–1796	6	Washington	Noah H. Swayne	1862–1881	18	Lincoln
Robert H. Harrison	1789–1790	—	Washington	Samuel F. Miller	1862–1890	28	Lincoln
James Iredell	1790–1799	9	Washington	David Davis	1862–1877	14	Lincoln
Thomas Johnson	1791–1793	1	Washington	Stephen J. Field	1863–1897	34	Lincoln
William Paterson	1793–1806	13	Washington	**Salmon P. Chase**	1864–1873	8	Lincoln
John Rutledge[1]	1795	—	Washington	William Strong	1870–1880	10	Grant
Samuel Chase	1796–1811	15	Washington	Joseph P. Bradley	1870–1892	22	Grant
Oliver Ellsworth	1796–1800	4	Washington	Ward Hunt	1873–1882	9	Grant
Bushrod Washington	1798–1829	31	J. Adams	**Morrison R. Waite**	1874–1888	14	Grant
Alfred Moore	1799–1804	4	J. Adams	John M. Harlan	1877–1911	34	Hayes
John Marshall	1801–1835	34	J. Adams	William B. Woods	1880–1887	7	Hayes
William Johnson	1804–1834	30	Jefferson	Stanley Matthews	1881–1889	7	Garfield
H. Brockholst Livingston	1806–1823	16	Jefferson	Horace Gray	1882–1902	20	Arthur
Thomas Todd	1807–1826	18	Jefferson	Samuel Blatchford	1882–1893	11	Arthur
Joseph Story	1811–1845	33	Madison	Lucius Q. C. Lamar	1888–1893	5	Cleveland
Gabriel Duval	1811–1835	24	Madison	**Melville W. Fuller**	1888–1910	21	Cleveland
Smith Thompson	1823–1843	20	Monroe	David J. Brewer	1890–1910	20	B. Harrison
Robert Trimble	1826–1828	2	J. Q. Adams	Henry B. Brown	1890–1906	16	B. Harrison
John McLean	1829–1861	32	Jackson	George Shiras, Jr.	1892–1903	10	B. Harrison
Henry Baldwin	1830–1844	14	Jackson	Howell E. Jackson	1893–1895	2	B. Harrison
James M. Wayne	1835–1867	32	Jackson	Edward D. White	1894–1910	16	Cleveland
Roger B. Taney	1836–1864	28	Jackson	Rufus W. Peckham	1895–1909	14	Cleveland
Philip P. Barbour	1836–1841	4	Jackson	Joseph McKenna	1898–1925	26	McKinley
John Catron	1837–1865	28	Van Buren	Oliver W. Holmes, Jr.	1902–1932	30	T. Roosevelt
John McKinley	1837–1852	15	Van Buren	William R. Day	1903–1922	19	T. Roosevelt
Peter V. Daniel	1841–1860	19	Van Buren	William H. Moody	1906–1910	3	T. Roosevelt
Samuel Nelson	1845–1872	27	Tyler	Horace H. Lurton	1910–1914	4	Taft
Levi Woodbury	1845–1851	5	Polk	Charles E. Hughes	1910–1916	5	Taft

[1] Acting chief justice; Senate refused to confirm appointment.

Note: Chief justices appear in bold type.

Name	Term of service	Years of service	Appointed by	Name	Term of service	Years of service	Appointed by
Willis Van Devanter	1911–1937	26	Taft	Sherman Minton	1949–1956	7	Truman
Joseph R. Lamar	1911–1916	5	Taft	**Earl Warren**	1953–1969	16	Eisenhower
Edward D. White	1910–1921	11	Taft	John Marshall Harlan	1955–1971	16	Eisenhower
Mahlon Pitney	1912–1922	10	Taft	William J. Brennan, Jr.	1956–1990	34	Eisenhower
James C. McReynolds	1914–1941	26	Wilson	Charles E. Whittaker	1957–1962	5	Eisenhower
Louis D. Brandeis	1916–1939	22	Wilson	Potter Stewart	1958–1981	23	Eisenhower
John H. Clarke	1916–1922	6	Wilson	Byron R. White	1962–1993	31	Kennedy
William H. Taft	1921–1930	8	Harding	Arthur J. Goldberg	1962–1965	3	Kennedy
George Sutherland	1922–1938	15	Harding	Abe Fortas	1965–1969	4	Johnson
Pierce Butler	1922–1939	16	Harding	Thurgood Marshall	1967–1994	24	Johnson
Edward T. Sanford	1923–1930	7	Harding	**Warren E. Burger**	1969–1986	18	Nixon
Harlan F. Stone	1925–1941	16	Coolidge	Harry A. Blackmun	1970–1994	24	Nixon
Charles E. Hughes	1930–1941	11	Hoover	Lewis F. Powell, Jr.	1971–1987	15	Nixon
Owen J. Roberts	1930–1945	15	Hoover	**William H. Rehnquist**	1971–2005	34	Nixon
Benjamin N. Cardozo	1932–1938	6	Hoover	John P. Stevens III	1975–2010	35	Ford
Hugo L. Black	1937–1971	34	F. Roosevelt	Sandra Day O'Connor	1981–2006	25	Reagan
Stanley F. Reed	1938–1957	19	F. Roosevelt	Antonin Scalia	1986–2016	30	Reagan
Felix Frankfurter	1939–1962	23	F. Roosevelt	Anthony M. Kennedy	1988–	—	Reagan
William O. Douglas	1939–1975	36	F. Roosevelt	David Souter	1990–2009	19	Bush
Frank Murphy	1940–1949	9	F. Roosevelt	Clarence Thomas	1991–	—	Bush
Harlan F. Stone	1941–1946	5	F. Roosevelt	Ruth Bader Ginsburg	1993–	—	Clinton
James F. Byrnes	1941–1942	1	F. Roosevelt	Stephen G. Breyer	1994–	—	Clinton
Robert H. Jackson	1941–1954	13	F. Roosevelt	**John G. Roberts, Jr.**	2005–	—	G. W. Bush
Wiley B. Rutledge	1943–1949	6	F. Roosevelt	Samuel Anthony Alito, Jr.	2006–	—	G. W. Bush
Harold H. Burton	1945–1958	13	Truman	Sonia Sotomayor	2009–	—	Obama
Fred M. Vinson	1946–1953	7	Truman	Elena Kagan	2010–	—	Obama
Tom C. Clark	1949–1967	18	Truman				

Note: Chief justices appear in bold type.

Index

Guerrillas, 375
Guerrilla warfare, 745
Guevara, Ernesto "Che," 726
The Guiding Light, 607
Guilford Court House, Battle of, 178
Guiteau, Charles Julius, 499
Gulf of Tonkin Resolution, 743
Gulf War Syndrome, 811
Gun control legislation, 823
Gush Emunim movement, 788
Gutenberg, Johannes, 40
Guthrie, Arlo, 701
Guthrie, Woody, 701
Guzmán, Jacobo Árbenz, 673

Habeas corpus, 375
Habitants, 69
Hague Adoption Convention, 821
Hague Regulations (1907), 397
Haile Selassie, 609
Haiti: Carter diplomacy, 775; U.S. expansionism and, 348; U.S. occupation of, 537
Haitian Embargo Act, 232
Haitian Revolution, 217–218, 217 (illus.), 223–225, 224 (tbl.), 232
Hakluyt Martyr map, 41 (illus.)
Hale, John P., 344
Hale, Sarah Josepha, 285 (illus.)
Half-Way Covenant, 113
Hallett, Paul G., 609 (photo)
Hamdan v. Rumsfeld, 845
Hamer, Fanny Lou, 727–728
Hamilton, Alexander: on citizen uprisings, 205; as Constitutional Convention delegate, 207–208; duel with Burr, 227; *Federalist Papers*, 210; in Washington administration, 219
Hamilton, Andrew, 144
Hammond, James Henry, 298, 356
Hampton, Fred, 759
Hampton Institute, 406
Handsome Lake (Seneca Indian), 234
Hanna, Mark, 506
Harding, Warren G., 559, 564
Harlan, John Marshall, 477
Harlem Renaissance, 577–578
Harmony School, 286 (tbl.)
Harper's Weekly, 371, 387 (illus.), 406 (illus.), 494 (illus.)
Harriman, E.H., 509
Harrington, Michael, 702, 728
Harris, Katherine, 828
Harrison, Benjamin, 496, 506, 527
Harrison, George, 749, 749 (photo)
Harrison, William Henry, 238, 321, 322, 449
Hart-Cellar Act (Immigration and Nationality Act, 1965), 731 (tbl.), 732, 817 (tbl.)
Harte, Bret, 455
Hartford Convention, 242
Harvey, William, 141
Hat Act (1732), 132
Haudenosaunee: British trade with, 155, 164; colonial expansion and, 104–105; formation of, 27; King William's War and, 117; Treaty of Fort Stanwix

(1784), 200–201, 201 (illus.). *See also* Six Nations
Hauling the Whole Week's Picking (Brown), 264 (illus.)
Hawai'i: American economic and political control of, 454–455; annexation failures, 347, 527; annexation of, 529; Bayonet Constitution, 527; Civil War impact on, 397; Great Hawai'i Sugar Strike, 577; multicultural population, 577; native peoples, 24; Reciprocity Treaty (1875), 440 (tbl.), 454; statehood, 693; territorial status, 531
Hawkins, Benjamin, 232, 233
Hawley-Smoot Tariff, 589–590
Hawthorne, Nathaniel, 345
Hay, John, 535, 536
Hay-Bunau-Varilla Treaty, 536
Hayden, Ferdinand V., 441, 456
Hayek, Friedrich von, 782
Hayes, Ira, 643 (photo)
Hayes, Rutherford B., 427, 483
Haymarket Square riot, 484–485, 485 (photo)
Hay-Pauncefote Treaty (1901), 536
Hayslip, Le Ly, 754, 754 (photo)
Haywood, William D. "Big Bill," 463, 488, 546
Headright system, 76
Head Start, 823
Health care: Affordable Care Act (Obamacare), 861, 864; Medicare and Medicaid, 729, 857; reform proposals, 823, 823 (photo), 858
Health issues: and agriculture development, 11; sanitation and waterworks, 473. *See also* Disease and epidemics
Healy, Michael, 415, 415 (photo)
Hearne, Thomas, 163
Hearst, Patty, 759
Hebrews, 36
Hecker, Friedrich, 347
Hefner, Hugh, 699
Helms, Jesse, 790
Help Our Public Education (HOPE), 724–725
Hemingway, Ernest, 577, 579, 580 (photo)
Henry, Patrick, 162, 210–211
Henry IV (King of France), 66
Henry VII (King of England), 38
Henry VIII (King of England), 40
Hepburn Act (1906), 499, 510
Herbivores, defined, 7
Herblock, 608 (illus.), 793 (illus.)
Herrán, Tomás, 536
Hessians, 172
Hetch Hetchy River, 473
Hewes, George, 166
Hewitt, Abraham, 502
Hezbollah, 798
Hiawatha, 28
Hibernian Society for the Relief of Immigrants, 282
Hicks, Edward, 93 (illus.)
Higher Education Act, 731 (tbl.)

Highlander Folk School, 718, 719, 723, 734
Highway Beautification Act, 730, 731 (tbl.)
Highway construction, 567–568, 692–693, 694 (map)
Highway Safety Act, 731 (tbl.)
Hill, Anita, 814
Hill, J.J., 437, 437 (photo), 509
Hill, Joe, 488
Hill–Thomas hearings, 814
Hinduism, 749
Hippies, 747
Hiraoka, Hiroshi, 481
Hirohito (Emperor of Japan), 643, 644, 656
Hiroshima bombing, 644
Hiroshima maidens, 715
Hispaniola, 43–44, 46–47
Hispanos, 329
Hiss, Alger, 661
Hitler, Adolf: assassination plot against, 639; Axis aggression by (1933–1939), 609, 610 (map), 613, 620; campaign against Jews, 590–592, 613; eugenics study, 641; leadership of, 574, 593; rise to power, 621–622 (tbl.); suicide, 639
HIV/AIDS, 786, 812–813, 812 (map), 813 (photo), 846
Hmong, 753
Hoar, George, 530
Hobkirk's Hill, Battle of, 178
Hobos, 602 (photo)
Hochelaga (present Montreal), 53
Ho Chi Minh, 171, 549, 674, 753
Ho Chi Minh trail, 743
Hohokam, 19, 20 (map)
Holding company, 467
Holland, Fern, 845, 845 (photo)
Hollywood, 569
Hollywood Ten, 664
Holt, Benjamin, 449
"Holy Experiment," 93
Holy Roman Empire, 176
Home ownership. *See* Housing and home ownership
Home Owners' Loan Corporation, 595, 597 (tbl.)
Homer, Winslow, 387, 407
Homespun, 163
Homestead Act, 391, 434, 440, 440 (tbl.)
Homestead certificate, 439 (illus.)
Homesteading, 440
Homestead Steel Works strike, 482 (illus.), 485–486
"Home! Sweet Home!" (Howard), 294
Homo erectus, 5
Homophile, 758
Homo sapiens, 5
Homo sapiens sapiens, 5
Homosexuality: in colonial America, 145–146; term coined, 580. *See also* LGBT
Hondius, Abraham, 81
Hone, Philip, 281
Hood, John B., 393
Hooker, Joseph, 384, 386
Hooker, Thomas, 82

Memphis race riot, 409 (illus.), 410

Mendel, Gregor, 640

Mendez, Gonzalo, 717

Mendez v. Westminster, 717

Menéndez de Avilés, Pedro, 53, 54

Mennonites, 637

Mental illness treatment reform, 302–303

Mercantilism: defined, 50; Dutch rejection of, 70; English, 132, 161; French, 100; Napoleonic Wars and, 237; Spanish, 50, 101. *See also* Navigation Acts

Mercenary, defined, 172

Merchants of Death, 611

Meredith, James, 726

Mergers. *See* Corporate mergers

Meritor Savings Bank v. Vinson, 814

Mesa Verde (Colorado), 20

Mesoamerica: agriculture development in, 11; chocolate production and trade, 56–57, 56 (map), 57 (illus.); cultural sites, 14 (map), 16 (map); defined, 9; Inca, 18, 48; Mayans, 13–15; Mexica (Aztecs), 15–18, 17 (illus.), 47, 58 (illus.)

Metacomet (King Philip of Wampanoag), 112 (illus.), 113–114

Methodist Episcopal Church, 289 (illus.), 291

Métis, 130, 283

Metropolitan Opera, 479

Mexica (Aztec) Empire, 14 (map), 15–18, 16 (map), 17 (illus.), 47, 58 (illus.)

Mexican Americans: Chicano movement, 755–756; in Cold War era, 682; in Great Depression, 603–604, 603 (photo); migration to U.S. cities, 548; in Texas Republic, 311; veteran discrimination, 714; westward expansion and, 335; WWII era, 636

Mexican War, 326–331, 326 (illus.), 327 (map), 328 (illus.)

Mexico: French intervention, 384, 395 (illus.), 397; immigrants from, 572, 636, 703–704, 704 (photo), 732; independence, 243; Mexican Revolution, 537–538; railroad boom, 436–437, 439; Reform War, 363; refugees from, 539 (photo), 548; secession in, 363; Second Mexican Empire, 384; slavery abolition, 303; Spanish conquest, 47; Texas independence, 319–321, 321 (illus.), 323; U.S. emigration to, 319; U.S. expansionism and, 348; U.S. intervention, 537–538

Mexico City policy, 821

Meynell, Francis, 109

Miami Indians, 220

Microcredit, 830

Microsoft Corporation, 780

Middle class: development of, 283, 284–285, 284 (map); G.I. Bill effect on, 687; global, 856; sentimentalism in, 294

Middle Colonies: economy, 128, 128 (map), 132; inequality in, 136; population, 124 (tbl.), 128–129, 128 (tbl.), 129 (tbl.). *See also specific colonies*

Middle East: Cold War in, 654, 672–673; decolonization, 670, 671 (map); overland trade networks, 35, 37 (map). *See also* Oil supply and reserves; *specific countries*

Middle Passage, 108–110, 224 (illus.), 225

Midway, Battle of, 629

Midway Islands, 414

Migrants and migration: African American Great Migration, 547, 575–577, 576 (map), 702; ancient Americans, 4–7, 6 (map), 8 (map); Dust Bowl, 604, 604 (map); German-speaking, 288 (illus.), 289; Mexican farm workers, 636, 703–704, 704 (photo), 732–733; Mormons, 318, 318 (illus.); post-revolutionary, 197–202, 199 (map); to suburbs, 693–694; to Sunbelt, 692, 693, 693 (map), 780, 781 (map); to U.S. cities, 280, 469–471, 470 (map), 471 (map), 548, 575–577, 576 (fig.), 576 (map); to U.S. West, 318, 323, 335, 438 (fig.), 448–449; WWII patterns, 634, 634 (map). *See also* Immigration

Migration Series (Lawrence), 547 (illus.)

Miles, Nelson, 445

Military. *See* Armed forces, U.S.; Draft

Military-industrial complex, 663, 689

Militias (colonial), 172 (illus.); composition of, 156–157; defined, 156; in early fighting against British, 167–169. *See also specific wars or battles*

Milk, Harvey, 786, 786 (photo)

Milken, Michael, 793

Mill, John Stuart, 414

Millay, Edna St. Vincent, 579

Millennialism, 291

Millennials, 819, 860–861

Milliken v. Bradley, 760

Minard, Charles Joseph, 375

Mines and mineral resources, 452 (map), 453–454, 453 (photo), 705. *See also* Gold discoveries

Minimum wage, 608

Mining Act (1872), 441

Mink brigade, 487

Minoans, 35

Minor, Virginia, 414

Minor v. Happersett, 414, 415

Minstrel shows, 296, 296 (illus.)

Missionaries: American, 291–292; disease and epidemics and, 68, 140, 292; Native Americans and, 67–68, 140, 291–292; New World, 50, 65, 67–68, 140; women's rights and, 304

Missions: California, 139–140; Florida, 65, 68; New Mexico, 68; Texas, 136 (illus.), 138

Mississippians, 25–27, 26 (map)

Mississippi Freedom Democratic Party, 727–728

Mississippi Freedom Summer, 727

Mississippi River: in Civil War, 377, 386; Spanish trade concession, 377

Mississippi statehood, 243

Missouri: in Civil War, 375; Harmony School, 286 (tbl.)

Missouri Compromise (1820), 266–267, 267 (map), 358

Mixed and balanced government, 143

Mixed-race communities, 283–286, 286 (illus.), 334

Mobley, C.C., 332

Mobley, Tessie "Lushanya," 590, 590 (photo)

Mobutu, Joseph, 673

Moctezuma (Aztec ruler), 47

Model minorities, 817

Modernity, 467, 555, 566

Mohawks, 101

Mohegans, 83

Molasses, 84, 85

Molasses Act (1733), 132

Moley, Archibald, 575

Mondale, Walter, 792

Monetarist theories, 779, 783

Monetary policy. *See* Currency and monetary policy

Mongol Empire, 35

Mongrelization, 571

Monitor (ship), 378

Monks Mound, 26

Monogenesis, 298

Monopolies, 66, 467, 503, 509, 514

Monopoly (board game), 502

Monotheism, 36

Monroe, James, 242, 268, 269

Monroe, Marilyn, 699

Monroe Doctrine, 268, 526, 537

Montcalm, Louis-Joseph de, 158

Monterey, California, 139–140, 331

Montesquieu, Charles, Baron de, 207

Montgomery, Richard, 168–169

Montgomery bus boycott, 718–719, 719 (photo)

Montgomery Improvement Association, 719

Montreal, in Seven Years' War, 158

Moon, Charlotte "Lottie," 424, 424 (photo)

Moral Majority, 787

Moran, Thomas, 455, 456

Morant Bay Rebellion, 411

Moratorium, 590

Moravians, 126

Morgan, Anne, 487

Morgan, J.P., 494, 506, 507 (illus.), 509, 511

Morgan, J.P., Jr., 611

Morgenthau, Henry, 642

Mormon Battalion, 318

Mormons, 293, 318, 318 (illus.), 357, 442

Mormon Trail, 318

Morrill Act, 391, 434, 437, 440 (tbl.)

Morris, Robert, 202, 350

Morsi, Mohammed, 848–849

Morton, Samuel George, 298–299

Mossadeq, Mohammed, 673

"Mother Jones" (Mary Harris Jones), 463–464, 463 (photo), 484, 488

Mott, Lucretia, 279, 304, 327

Moundville (Alabama), 27

Mourning culture, 294, 294 (illus.)

Movies. *See* Films and film industry

ALASKA
(U.S.)

CANADA

UNITED STATES

GREENLAND
(DENMARK)

80°N

ICELAND

60°N

IRELAND

40°N

PORTUGAL

Azores
(Port.)

Bermuda
(U.K.)

ATLANTIC OCEAN

MOR

WESTERN
SAHARA
(MOROCCO)

Midway Is.
(U.S.)

Hawaiian Is.
(U.S.)

MEXICO

BAHAMAS

DOMINICAN REP.
Virgin Is.
(U.S.)

CUBA

JAMAICA

HAITI

BELIZE

Puerto Rico
(U.S.)

HONDURAS

GUATEMALA
EL SALVADOR

NICARAGUA

ST. KITTS AND NEVIS
ANTIGUA AND BARBUDA
DOMINICA
BARBADOS
ST. LUCIA
GRENADA
ST. VINCENT AND
THE GRENADINES

20°N

MAURITAN

CAPE
VERDE

SENEGAL

GAMBIA

GUINEA-BISSAU

GUINEA

PACIFIC OCEAN

COSTA RICA

PANAMA

VENEZUELA

TRINIDAD AND TOBAGO

GUYANA

FR. GUIANA
(FRANCE)

SIERRA
LEONE

LIBERIA

IV
CC

G

COLOMBIA

SURINAM

ECUADOR

SÃO TOMÉ

EQU

Galapagos Is.
(Ecuador)

Equator

0°

SAMOA

PERU

BRAZIL

French Polynesia
(France)

BOLIVIA

TONGA

PARAGUAY

20°S

Easter Is.
(Chile)

CHILE

URUGUAY

ARGENTINA

0   1,000   2,000 Km.

0   1,000   2,000 Mi.

Falkland Is.
(U.K.)

40°S

160°W   140°W   120°W   100°W   80°W   60°W   40°W   20°W

60°S

80°S